Lecture Notes in Computer Science 10145

Commenced Publication in 1973
Founding and Former Series Editors:
Gerhard Goos, Juris Hartmanis, and Jan van Leeuwen

Advanced Research in Computing and Software Science
Subline of Lecture Notes in Computer Science

More information about this series at http://www.springer.com/series/7407

Ahmed Bouajjani · David Monniaux (Eds.)

Verification, Model Checking, and Abstract Interpretation

18th International Conference, VMCAI 2017
Paris, France, January 15–17, 2017
Proceedings

Editors
Ahmed Bouajjani
IRIF, Université Paris Diderot
Paris
France

David Monniaux
VERIMAG, CNRS & Université
  Grenoble Alpes
Grenoble
France

ISSN 0302-9743   ISSN 1611-3349 (electronic)
Lecture Notes in Computer Science
ISBN 978-3-319-52233-3   ISBN 978-3-319-52234-0 (eBook)
DOI 10.1007/978-3-319-52234-0

Library of Congress Control Number: 2016963156

LNCS Sublibrary: SL1 – Theoretical Computer Science and General Issues

Printed on acid-free paper

This Springer imprint is published by Springer Nature
The registered company is Springer International Publishing AG
The registered company address is: Gewerbestrasse 11, 6330 Cham, Switzerland

Preface

This volume contains the papers presented at VMCAI 2017, the 18th International Conference on Verification, Model Checking, and Abstract Interpretation, held during January 15–17, 2017, in Paris, France, co-located with POPL 2017 (the annual ACM SIGPLAN/SIGACT Symposium on Principles of Programming Languages). Previous meetings were held in Port Jefferson (1997), Pisa (1998), Venice (2002), New York (2003), Venice (2004), Paris (2005), Charleston (2006), Nice (2007), San Francisco (2008), Savannah (2009), Madrid (2010), Austin (2011), Philadelphia (2012), Rome (2013), San Diego (2014), Mumbai (2015), and St. Petersburg, Florida (2016).

VMCAI provides a forum for researchers from the communities of verification, model checking, and abstract interpretation, facilitating interaction, cross-fertilization, and advancement of hybrid methods that combine these and related areas. VMCAI topics include: program verification, model checking, abstract interpretation and abstract domains, program synthesis, static analysis, type systems, deductive methods, program certification, debugging techniques, program transformation, optimization, hybrid and cyber-physical systems.

This year the conference attracted 60 submissions. Each submission was reviewed by at least three Program Committee members. The committee decided to accept 27 papers. The principal selection criteria were relevance, quality, and originality. We are pleased to include in the proceedings the contributions of three invited keynote speakers: Ernie Cohen (Amazon Web Services), Pascal Cuoq (Trust in Soft), and Jasmin Fisher (Microsoft Research). We warmly thank them for their participation and for their contributions.

We would like also to thank the members of the Program Committee and the external reviewers for their excellent work. We also thanks the members of the Steering Committee, and in particular Andreas Podelski and Lenore Zuck, for their helpful advice, assistance, and support. We also thank Laure Gonnord for her invaluable help in all aspects related to the organization of the conference. We thank Annabel Satin for the help in coordinating the events co-located with POPL 2017, and we thank the POPL 2017 Organizing Committee for providing all the logistics for organizing VMCAI. We are also indebted to EasyChair for providing us with an excellent conference management system.

Finally, we would like to thank our generous sponsors: AdaCore, Amazon Web Services, Facebook, and Microsoft Research.

December 2016

Ahmed Bouajjani
David Monniaux

Organization

Program Committee

Erika Abraham	RWTH Aachen University, Germany
Mohamed Faouzi Atig	Uppsala University, Sweden
Roderick Bloem	Graz University of Technology, Austria
Ahmed Bouajjani	IRIF, Paris Diderot University, France
Wei-Ngan Chin	National University of Singapore, Singapore
Deepak D'Souza	Indian Institute of Science, Bangalore, India
Cezara Drăgoi	Inria, ENS, France
Roberto Giacobazzi	University of Verona, Italy
Laure Gonnord	University of Lyon/LIP, France
Orna Grumberg	Technion - Israel Institute of Technology, Israel
Dejan Jovanović	SRI International, USA
Konstantin Korovin	Manchester University, UK
Laura Kovacs	Vienna University of Technology, Austria
Shuvendu Lahiri	Microsoft Research, USA
Akash Lal	Microsoft Research, India
Rupak Majumdar	MPI-SWS, Germany
David Monniaux	VERIMAG, CNRS & Université Grenoble Alpes, France
Madhavan Mukund	Chennai Mathematical Institute, India
Corina Pasareanu	CMU/NASA Ames Research Center, USA
Andreas Podelski	University of Freiburg, Germany
Jean-Francois Raskin	Université Libre de Bruxelles, Belgium
Sriram Sankaranarayanan	University of Colorado, Boulder, USA
Armando Solar-Lezama	MIT, USA
Marielle Stoelinga	University of Twente, The Netherlands
Boris Yakobowski	CEA, LIST, France

Additional Reviewers

Basso-Blandin, Adrien	Costea, Andreea
Ben-Amram, Amir	Coti, Camille
Blom, Stefan	Darabi, Saeed
Bobot, François	Dehnert, Christian
Brain, Martin	Demange, Delphine
Braud-Santoni, Nicolas	Enea, Constantin
Cai, Zhouhong	Feret, Jerome
Castellan, Simon	Forget, Julien
Chakarov, Aleksandar	Frenkel, Hadar

Garg, Pranav
Ghilardi, Silvio
Girault, Alain
Gleiss, Bernhard
Habermehl, Peter
Hadarean, Liana
Halbwachs, Nicolas
He, Shaobo
Heußner, Alexander
Ho, Hsi-Ming
Iusupov, Rinat
Jansen, Nils
Jaroschek, Maximilian
Jecker, Ismaël
Khalimov, Ayrat
Koenighofer, Bettina
Konnov, Igor
Korovina, Margarita
Kremer, Gereon
Kretinsky, Jan
Lange, Tim
Le Roux, Stephane
Le, Quang Loc
Le, Ton Chanh
Lee, Benedict
Mastroeni, Isabella
Matteplackel, Raj Mohan

Merz, Stephan
Mukherjee, Suvam
Muoi, Tran Duc
Narayan Kumar, K.
Navas, Jorge A.
Ngo, Tuan Phong
Niksic, Filip
Petri, Gustavo
Rakamaric, Zvonimir
Rasin, Dan
Rensink, Arend
Rezine, Othmane
Rodriguez, Cesar
Roeck, Franz
Rothenberg, Bat-Chen
Sangnier, Arnaud
Scherer, Gabriel
Schilling, Christian
Shi, Jinghao
Sofronie-Stokkermans, Viorica
Suda, Martin
Tiwari, Ashish
Urban, Caterina
van Glabbeek, Rob
Vedrine, Franck
Verdoolaege, Sven
Widder, Josef

Abstracts of Invited Talks

Bringing LTL Model Checking to Biologists

Zara Ahmed[1], David Benque[2], Sergey Berezin[3],
Anna Caroline E. Dahl[4], Jasmin Fisher[1,5], Benjamin A. Hall[6],
Samin Ishtiaq[1], Jay Nanavati[1], Nir Piterman[7],
Maik Riechert[1], and Nikita Skoblov[3]

[1] Microsoft Research, Cambridge, UK
jasmin.fisher@microsoft.com
[2] Royal College of Art, London, UK
[3] Moscow State University, Moscow, Russia
[4] Center for Technology in Medicine and Health,
KTH Royal Institute of Technology, Huddinge, Sweden
[5] Department of Biochemistry, University of Cambridge, Cambridge, UK
[6] MRC Cancer Unit, University of Cambridge, Cambridge, UK
[7] University of Leicester, Leicester, UK

Abstract. The BioModelAnalyzer (BMA) is a web based tool for the development of discrete models of biological systems. Through a graphical user interface, it allows rapid development of complex models of gene and protein interaction networks and stability analysis without requiring users to be proficient computer programmers. Whilst stability is a useful specification for testing many systems, testing temporal specifications in BMA presently requires the user to perform simulations. Here we describe the LTL module, which includes a graphical and natural language interfaces to testing LTL queries. The graphical interface allows for graphical construction of the queries and presents results visually in keeping with the current style of BMA. The Natural language interface complements the graphical interface by allowing a gentler introduction to formal logic and exposing educational resources.

Verified Concurrent Code: Tricks of the Trade

Ernie Cohen

Amazon Web Services, Wyncote, USA
ecohen@amazon.com

Abstract. Modular code verification, suitably extended with shared atomic objects, supports a number of useful verification idioms and semantic models, without further logical extension.

Keywords: Real-time · Hybrid systems · Probability · Stopping failures · Weak memory · Cryptography · Ownership · Permissions · Simulation · Knowledge · Behavioral polymorphism · Device drivers · Concurrent data structures · Transactions · Linearizability · Deductive verification · VCC

Detecting Strict Aliasing Violations in the Wild

Pascal Cuoq[1], Loïc Runarvot[1], and Alexander Cherepanov[2,3]

[1] TrustInSoft, Paris, France
cuoq@trust-in-soft.com
[2] Openwall, Moscow, Russia
[3] National Research University Higher School of Economics,
Moscow, Russia

Abstract. Type-based alias analyses allow C compilers to infer that memory locations of distinct types do not alias. Idiomatic reliance on pointers on the one hand, and separate compilation on the other hand, together make it impossible to get this aliasing information any other way. As a consequence, most modern optimizing C compilers implement some sort of type-based alias analysis. Unfortunately, pointer conversions, another pervasive idiom to achieve code reuse in C, can interact badly with type-based alias analyses. This article investigate the fine line between the allowable uses of low-level constructs (pointer conversions, unions) that should never cause the predictions of a standard-compliant type-based alias analysis to be wrong, and the dangerous uses that can result in bugs in the generated binary. A sound and precise analyzer for strict aliasing violations is briefly described.

Detecting Sharp ... relations in the Wild

... and Alexander ...

...

Contents

Bringing LTL Model Checking to Biologists

Zara Ahmed[1], David Benque[2], Sergey Berezin[3], Anna Caroline E. Dahl[4],
Jasmin Fisher[1,5(✉)], Benjamin A. Hall[6], Samin Ishtiaq[1], Jay Nanavati[1],
Nir Piterman[7], Maik Riechert[1], and Nikita Skoblov[3]

[1] Microsoft Research, Cambridge, UK
jasmin.fisher@microsoft.com
[2] Royal College of Art, London, UK
[3] Moscow State University, Moscow, Russia
[4] Center for Technology in Medicine and Health,
KTH Royal Institute of Technology, Huddinge, Sweden
[5] Department of Biochemistry, University of Cambridge, Cambridge, UK
[6] MRC Cancer Unit, University of Cambridge, Cambridge, UK
[7] University of Leicester, Leicester, UK

Abstract. The BioModelAnalyzer (BMA) is a web based tool for the
development of discrete models of biological systems. Through a graphical user interface, it allows rapid development of complex models of gene
and protein interaction networks and stability analysis without requiring users to be proficient computer programmers. Whilst stability is a
useful specification for testing many systems, testing temporal specifications in BMA presently requires the user to perform simulations. Here
we describe the LTL module, which includes a graphical and natural language interfaces to testing LTL queries. The graphical interface allows
for graphical construction of the queries and presents results visually in
keeping with the current style of BMA. The Natural language interface
complements the graphical interface by allowing a gentler introduction
to formal logic and exposing educational resources.

1 Introduction

Formal verification techniques offer a powerful set of approaches for analysing
and understanding the behaviours of different systems. The advantages of such
approaches are well understood and widely applied in the development of hardware and software systems. Outside of computing the usage of such techniques
has been less widespread. Whilst standard techniques such as SAT solving and
BDDs have been highly successful in individual investigations (see [1–5] for some
recent examples), their broader utility has been limited by the fundamental
requirement for proficiency in computing.

To address this skills gap tools such as BioModelAnalyzer (BMA, [6]) and
GinSim [7] have been developed explicitly to better enable users to construct
and analyse biological models. BMA presently allows users to construct models,
perform simulations, and stability analysis. Stability analysis in BMA typifies
the opportunities for algorithm discovery in biology. Standard approaches are

© Springer International Publishing AG 2017
A. Bouajjani and D. Monniaux (Eds.): VMCAI 2017, LNCS 10145, pp. 1–13, 2017.
DOI: 10.1007/978-3-319-52234-0_1

insufficient in analysing many usefully large and complex biological models, so a bespoke algorithm [8] is used to analyse the models. Users do not need an in-depth knowledge of that algorithm to apply it, and BMA enables this, by effectively encapsulating the computer science. By making model development and checking simple, this has prompted further algorithm development as models can be constructed more quickly and easily by users with deep expertise in a variety of biological systems [9]. As such, tool development has supported both biologists who wish to use powerful but inaccessible technology and computer scientists interested in addressing novel challenges that can arise from under-explored interdisciplinary areas. However, many questions that biologists wish to address require more complex tools than stability analysis. Some may want to ensure a specific dynamic behavior is observed; others may wish to explore instability in more depth. The present release of BMA only allows for such questions to be answered using simulation based approaches. Claessen et al. recently reported an LTL (bounded) model checker for biological models [10] that adapts the stability proving algorithm of Cook et al. [8] to enable faster model checking than provided by naive SAT based approaches. This had, however, not been integrated into the tool's front-end and, as such, was not available to most users.

Supporting LTL for users who do not have experience with logic and programming, poses distinct problems relative to the stability analysis. In this paper we report on our solution to make LTL more accessible for biologists. We allow users two possible approaches for constructing LTL queries. First, we present a graphical interface that abstracts the nuances of LTL by providing users with a graphical language, making use of visual cues such as icons, shapes and colour to denote operators, formulas and results respectively. Users are then able to use graphical controls and intuitive gestures such as drag-and-drop to visually construct queries as well as evaluate results. Second, we present a natural language interface (NLI), which exposes query creation and testing through a text-based *chatbot* (an interactive virtual assistant). The conversational nature of the chatbot's interface provides users with a higher level of abstraction over LTL than the graphical interface as it functions by interpreting *intents* rather than requiring explicit instructions. This means that instead of learning how to encode their queries into semantically valid LTL formulas, biologists can perform analysis by using natural language to describe queries in terms of cell states over time.

We further discuss the engineering and design challenges identified in the construction of this module, and describe how it may be adapted in the future to provide biologists with more accessible as well as scalable ways to leverage formal methods in their analysis.

BioModelAnalyzer is available at http://biomodelanalyzer.org/.

2   BMA Basics

BMA and the motivations for developing such a dedicated tool for biologists has been described in depth previously (see, e.g., [6,7,11]). Briefly, users are able to develop models by "drawing" onto a blank canvas, in the same way that models of cell signaling are communicated in scientific literature. Variables representing molecules within a cell or its environment and their relationships are depicted, and the resultant directed graph is treated as a *qualitative network* (QN) [11]. A QN $Q(V, T, N)$, of granularity $N + 1$ consists of variables: $V = (v_1, v_2, \cdots, v_n)$. The state of the system is a map $s : V \rightarrow \{0, 1, \cdots N\}$. The set of initial states is the set of all states. Each variable $v_i \in V$ has a *target function* $T_i \in T$ associated with it: $T_i : \{0, 1, \cdots, N\}^n \rightarrow \{0, 1, \cdots N\}$, describing the relationship between the variable and its inputs.

Target functions in qualitative networks direct the execution of the network from state $s = (d_1, d_2, \cdots, d_n)$. Variables in the QN update synchronously, i.e., the system is deterministic. The *next state* $s' = (d'_1, d'_2, \cdots, d'_n)$ is computed by:

$$d'_v = \begin{cases} d_v + 1 & d_v < T_v(s) \text{ and } d_v < N, \\ d_v - 1 & d_v > T_v(s) \text{ and } d_v > 0, \\ d_v & \text{otherwise.} \end{cases} \qquad (1)$$

A target function of a variable v is an algebraic function over several variables $w_1, w_2, \cdots w_m$. Variables $w_1, w_2, \cdots, w_m$ are called *inputs* of v and v is an *output* of each one of $w_1, w_2, \cdots, w_m$.

3 Graphical User Interface (GUI)

LTL queries are substantially more complex than stability testing. Whereas the workflow of stability testing is simple, and common to every model (that is to say, attempt to prove stability, and then optionally search for counter examples), each step in performing an LTL query requires manual intervention. This cannot be avoided; each query represents a specification that will differ depending on the specific model being tested. In other biologist-targeted tools, this is achieved by exporting the model to SMV and expecting the user to independently use NuSMV or a similar tool [7,12]. One of the major design principles of BMA is to avoid the requirement for use of command-line and computing proficiency, so this is not appropriate here. However, the requirement to write LTL queries poses some unique challenges. We do not expect users to be comfortable with complex operator precedence issues and balancing parentheses. Furthermore, there are some specific challenges that relate to BMA and exploring biological systems; notably models are expected to have large numbers of variables, and endpoints are of particular interest due to their role in describing cell fate and other developmental processes.

Two Stage Workflow

Our graphical interface addresses these issues through a two stage workflow. We separate *states*, and a *temporal and logical* layer. States are defined as a conjunction of linear constraints on variable values. Constraints can be set up by either selecting variables through a drop down menu, similar to the menus found in file browsers, or by dragging variables from the canvas onto the drop down

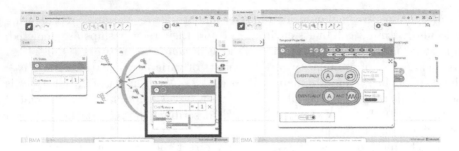

Fig. 1. The LTL state editor and the LTL query editor.

menu (Fig. 1). This makes adding linear constraints substantially less complex. LTL states also correspond closely to states that can be observed in simulations, and as such their construction and use is intuitive to non-experts (confirmed in user testing).

The second part of the workflow is to use the states within a temporal (and further logical layer) query (Fig. 1). This is achieved by making a new canvas available for users, onto which they can drop logical and temporal operators (rendered as bubbles with sockets) and states. Each operator contains the appropriate number of sockets that match its expected number of operands. Operands can be dragged and dropped into sockets. Operands can be states, or other formulas constructed in the same way. As such, complex queries are created by repeatedly nesting different operators. Operators and queries can also be dragged to a *copy zone* that effectively allows for rapid copy and pasting in situations where this is desirable. Operator precedence and parenthesis checking is effectively enforced by the nested bubbles and missing elements are highlighted if the user should try to check an incomplete query. The final stage is the testing of the query, which requires the user to define the length of paths (relating to bounded model checking).

Default States

In addition to user defined states, we also include default states that can be used. We include the nullary (state) operators True, self-loop, and oscillation. The self-loop and oscillation describe states that, respectively, lie on a self loop or within a (strictly) larger loop. The description of these states through other operators would be extremely cumbersome. For example, a self loop state is characterised by the formula $\bigwedge_{v \in V} v = Xv$.[1] Self-loop and oscillation are important features in biological models, as developmental processes where end results are known require reasoning about the values of such end results.

---

[1] To the best of our knowledge, most LTL tools do not support such a direct comparison between the value of a variable and its value in the next state.

Non-standard Temporal Operators

User testing revealed that the operators *until* and *weak until* are very confusing in that they allow their first operand not to hold at all. We have supplemented these operators with the operator *Upto*, which carries similar meaning in English but can be assigned the stricter semantics without confusing users who are familiar with LTL.

Result Visualisation

Finally, in response to running a query users are presented with three possible outcomes (Fig. 2). The query is determined to be true for all traces, some traces or no traces. These results are determined by performing both the query as stated and the negation of the query on the back-end. Examples of traces that satisfy or fail to satisfy the query are made available, and can be visualised as graphs using the existing simulation visualisation tools. In the LTL tool, these traces are further annotated with the states that are satisfied at each time point, to aid analysis and interpretation of the results.

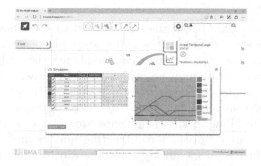

Fig. 2. An example trace from an LTL query.

4   Natural Language Interface (NLI)

While the GUI makes syntactic aspects of LTL more accessible by handling operator precedence and formula parenthesisation, biologists are still required to have an understanding of LTL semantics in order to express biological concepts in the context of formal logic. Furthermore, the subtle differences between temporal operators as well as the discrete notion of time in LTL adds complexity, as biologists have to learn how to reason about biological processes (which are often stochastic and concurrent) in terms of discrete time-steps. By design, these issues cannot be addressed directly through the GUI and yet they contribute towards raising the barrier to entry to LTL-based analysis for users that have little to no experience with formal logic. In some cases, advanced users might appreciate the use of a simple text interface and prefer it to the GUI. For example, complicated

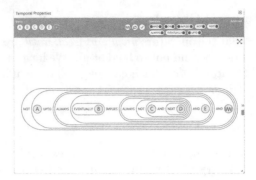

Fig. 3. An example of a complex LTL query in the GUI

and large queries may become unclear in the GUI, c.f., Fig. 3. At the same time, writing manually the Boolean part describing a "state" comprised of a large number of variables could be an issue with the NLI.

Knowledge Base

In order to help users learn about the semantics of LTL, we developed a knowledge base that consists of definitions as well as example usages of LTL operators and developmental end states. The user can simply ask the NLI questions about a given operator in natural language, which the NLI answers using the knowledge base. The NLI supports simple questions such as: *"what is the meaning of until?"* and *"can you show me an example of always operator?"*. We believe this is an effective way of filling in knowledge gaps around the semantics of LTL on the fly. That is, the user can start constructing queries and cross check their understanding of the operators quickly along the way, reinforcing their learning at the same time.

Step-by-Step Tutorials

The NLI also supports step-by-step tutorials, which guide users through an example LTL querying exercise using a pre-built BMA model. At each step the NLI generates intermediate BMA model files as well as screenshots so the users can verify that they are following the tutorial correctly. The user can access these tutorials by asking questions such as: *"show me the LTL tutorials"* and selecting the complexity of the tutorial they would like to follow. This functionality is useful as it shows LTL querying in action, helping the user understand how LTL can be applied in the context of realistic biological models as well as making them familiar with LTL querying using the GUI at the same time.

Natural Language Understanding

In addition to understanding basic questions about LTL operators, the NLI can also interpret LTL queries from natural language. The aim of this feature is to let biologists conceptualise their analysis as if they were discussing it with a colleague, rather than inputting instructions to a simulator in a different language.

To that end, the NLI supports questions such as: *"I'd like to see a simulation where ras is 1 to begin with and sometime later proliferation is true"* or *"show me a simulation where if notch is greater than 5 then the process always results in an oscillation"*.

The queries mentioned above also show how the user can use natural language to perform inferential cell fate analysis by asking for simulations of the form *"if ϕ then ψ"*. This is effective as it provides users with a more intuitive way of expressing inferential relationships between cell states than the *implies* operator in LTL.

Finally, the NLI is able to interpret conversational temporal phrases such as: *"later"*, *"sometime later"*, *"in the future"* and *"never"* that are likely to be used by biologists when conceptualising their analysis but can be hard to encode using LTL, as multiple temporal modalities are involved. This is beneficial as it handles very subtle semantical differences that can be overlooked by users who are less familiar with LTL. An example of this is where a user might not realise that the *eventually* operator tests the current state as well as future next states and that the *next* operator is required to omit testing the current state, something that is expressed implicitly in natural language when phrases such as *sometime later* are used.

The chatbot can be effective especially when working with multiple operators where subtle differences in operator ordering can result in formulas that are semantically inconsistent with the user's intention. For example, a query that tests if a cell is *never* in the state ϕ can easily be encoded wrongly in LTL as $\neg\Box\phi$ instead of $\Box\neg\phi$, where the former actually means *"ϕ is eventually false"*. This results in a query that is inconsistent with the original intention as it will evaluate to true for traces that contain evaluations of ϕ as true, as long as ϕ evaluates to false at some time step. The same query can be performed more easily using the chatbot by describing the core intention, for example, as *"show me a simulation where it is never the case that ϕ is true"*.

Formula History

A history of user-entered formulas is maintained throughout the session to let users construct complex formulas by combining simple formulas easily. Each formula is assigned a "formula pointer", which is a generated name that the user can change to signify domain specific meaning. Users are able to access the formula list by instructing the NLI by writing phrases such as: *"show me the formula list"*. Similarly, existing formulas can be deleted and renamed. This addresses the GUI related issues identified by experienced users, who prefer a command line like interface that eliminates overheads such as scrolling and drag drop when working with complex formulas.

In-line Execution

The bot can also execute queries from within the context of a conversation and provide a textual summary of the results. This makes the NLI fit for exploratory research as users can leverage formula pointers to rapidly construct very complex queries and test them in place. For the full results the NLI refers the users back to the GUI.

5   System Overview

The general architecture of the LTL moduele of BMA is presented in Fig. 4. The *evaluation* of queries is performed in an F# back-end, which is exposed using a service-orientated architecture (SOA) through a set of REST endpoints. Taking an SOA approach allows the interfaces to be decoupled from the back-end, making the architecture more suitable for future expansion of additional back-end features.

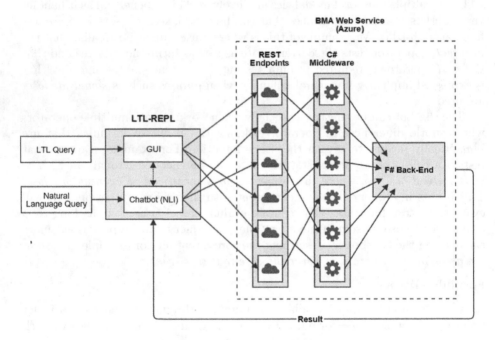

Fig. 4. High level system architecture

The REST endpoints represent a Web API. This is reflected in several stages all the way to the back-end, in a traditional ASP.NET Web API 2 stack. Starting from the outside, a C# controller implements each API function. For instance, the api/Analyze API is implemented using an AnalyzeController class, and the Post method of this class takes exactly the arguments (typed—by this time—from the untyped JSON representation sent over the wire) that the front-end passes as the payload when it makes a POST call to the *api/Analyze* REST endpoint. The second stage is between this thin C# controller implementation and the core back-end functionality. This is mediated by a C# interface that is essentially the set of functions (checkStability, findCExBifurcates, checkLTL, simulateTick, etc.) that can be called in an atomic/synchronous way; the result returned immediately to the front-end. The interface has no state, and uses types that are shared between C# and F#.

The back-end runs on the Windows Azure cloud platform. LTL queries put a significant load on the back-end and we use several approaches to ensure BMA remains responsive. Firstly, front-end requests and back-end analysis run in two separate Azure roles (akin to processes in the cloud). This enables us to support interface updates instantaneously even when the system is busy. Secondly, Azure's autoscale feature automatically spawns new instances of servers if the average CPU usage increases above a given threshold. Finally, long queries are terminated after a time out period, and the user is notified.

GUI Implementation

The GUI is developed as an HTML5 front-end, written in TypeScript using the Model-View-Presenter (MVP) architectural pattern: the Model stores the objects (biological models, proof results, simulation graphs) of the current session; the View implements the graphics the user sees and interacts with. The implementation uses and extends JQueryUI HTML5 controls; the Presenter is the "middle man", which understands and performs all the logic of the front-end. The Presenter passes actions undertaken in the View by the user to the Model for the latter's state to be updated, and similarly passes updates from the Model back to the View for the canvas to be updated.

As seen in Fig. 5, we take a Pub/Sub (publish-subscribe) approach to handle View-Presenter communication, decoupling the View logic from the Presenter

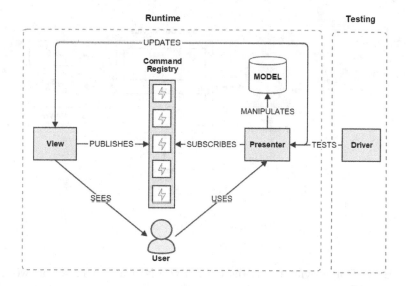

Fig. 5. MVP implementation in the GUI

logic. The Viewer publishes a set of events to a Command Registry, which the Presenter subscribes to. As the user interacts with the View, events are asynchronously fired and handled by the Presenter. This adds scalability to the GUI as additional Presenters can be added easily to handle multiple view events concurrently, to support more complex GUIs in the future. The Pub/Sub mechanism also allows us to perform functional unit testing of the Presenter logic independently of the View. We do this by using the Jasmine testing library to "mock" the View logic through a Driver object and invoke the event handlers in the Presenter directly.

The MVP implementation is a light-weight, custom-built one, not relying on any existing JavaScript frameworks. The whole implementation is bundled and minified, and then deployed on to the server.

NLI Implementation

The NLI is developed as an independent Node.js application and written in TypeScript. It uses technologies such as the Microsoft Bot Framework [13], Microsoft Cognitive Services [14] and Chevrotain [15]. As seen in Fig. 6, the Bot Framework is used to expose the NLI's functionality as a chatbot. The Bot Framework is a software development kit (SDK) that allows cross platform conversational agents (i.e., chatbots) to be developed easily. We use this framework to handle the boilerplate aspects of a conversational agent. For example, client connectivity, session management and file import/export. While we currently only support the Skype chat client, the Bot Framework can allow us to support other chat clients such as Facebook messenger, Telegram and Slack easily in the future thanks to its homogeneous REST interface, which we have implemented in the BMA Bot Service.

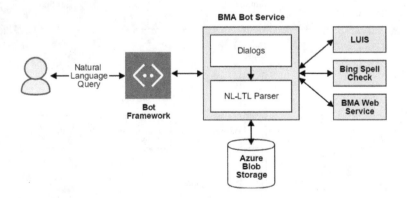

Fig. 6. NLI architecture

The BMA Bot Service forms the core of the NLI and consists of two main components: Dialogs and NL-LTL Parser. The NLI generates BMA model files whenever a user requests an LTL query to be executed. This model can be automatically opened in BMA by following a URL sent in the conversation. This feature relies on Azure blob storage and saves the user the need to download files from Skype and upload them to BMA.

We used Microsoft's Language Understanding Intelligent Service (LUIS) to solve the problem of handling a range of query types through a single interface. That is, from simple questions about LTL operators to LTL formulas described in natural language. LUIS is a web service that allows language understanding models to be built from sample utterances, which can classify natural language queries based on their underlying *intent*. In order to build a LUIS model fit for our problem domain, we worked with biologists to identify the kind of phrases that they may utter when interacting with the NLI. We used this information to build a hierarchy of intents (Fig. 7) that covered all query types supported by the NLI and used it to train our LUIS model.

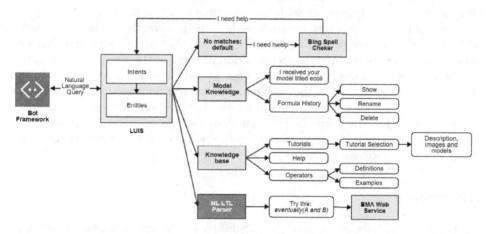

Fig. 7. NLI natural language processing infrastructure

As seen in Fig. 7, valid queries can be classified as belonging to either the Model Knowledge, Knowledge Base or NL-LTL Parser intent categories. Queries that cannot be assigned an intent category are passed through the Bing spell checker web service once and fed into the system as a new user input, given spelling errors were corrected in the original query. The Model Knowledge intent category captures queries that either change the state of the current BMA model. For example, uploading of a new model or contain references to aspects relating to an existing model such as formula pointers. Queries that require the NLI to use its Knowledge Base in order to provide definitions or example usage of LTL operators as well as run tutorials are labelled as having a Knowledge Base intent. Finally, queries relating to the construction and execution of LTL formulas are labelled with an NL-LTL Parser intent and are passed through the NL-LTL Parser pipeline, where a further set of NLP tasks are performed to infer logical structure from NL.

6 Conclusion and Future Work

Providing an extensive front-end for users to use LTL represents a major step forward in functionality in BMA. In addition to expanding the types of analysis that can be performed in the tool, the underlying changes, both in terms of the web app architecture and the visual technique for constructing formulas, will support the future development of new features. Future work will draw on these improvements to expand the range of analyses offered and refine existing features, such as the target function editor, by adapting the LTL query editor.

We are currently working on taking the insights from the graphical editor for LTL to offer an alternative approach to the construction of target functions. This will carry some of the advantages of the GUI editing, such as no need to consider operator precedence and parentheses balancing to another technical part of model construction. At the same time, we would like to offer an alternative textual editor interchangeably with both formula creation GUIs.

Some of our most advanced users have been using directly the back-end part of BMA to do thorough testing of their models. We are looking into better supporting these users through incorporation of some of their requirements into the NLI interface. Thus, an advanced user would be able to replace a script that automates some calls to the back-end with instructions to the NLI interface to do the same. Furthermore, expanding the natural language understanding capabilities of the NLI would increase the tool's effectiveness and improve user experience. For example, we could replace the reliance on a static dictionary by using word semantic similarity, as in [16,17].

References

1. Bonzanni, N., Garg, A., Feenstra, K.A., Schütte, J., Kinston, S., Miranda-Saavedra, D., Heringa, J., Xenarios, I., Göttgens, B.: Hard-wired heterogeneity in blood stem cells revealed using a dynamic regulatory network model. Bioinformatics **29**, i80–i88 (2013)
2. Chuang, R., Hall, B., Benque, D., Cook, B., Ishtiaq, S., Piterman, N., Taylor, A., Vardi, M., Koschmieder, S., Gottgens, B., Fisher, J.: Drug target optimization in chronic myeloid leukemia using innovative computational platform. Sci. Rep. **5**, 8190 (2015)
3. Moignard, V., Woodhouse, S., Haghverdi, L., Lilly, J., Tanaka, Y., Wilkinson, A., Buettner, F., Nishikawa, S., Piterman, N., Kouskoff, V., Theis, F., Fisher, J., Gottgens, B.: Decoding the regulatory network of early blood development from single cell gene expression measurements. Nat. Biotechnol. **33**, 269–276 (2015)
4. Remy, E., Rebouissou, S., Chaouiya, C., Zinovyev, A., Radvanyi, F., Calzone, L.: A modeling approach to explain mutually exclusive and co-occurring genetic alterations in bladder tumorigenesis. Cancer Res. **75**, 4042–4052 (2015)
5. Terfve, C.D.A., Wilkes, E.H., Casado, P., Cutillas, P.R., Saez-Rodriguez, J.: Large-scale models of signal propagation in human cells derived from discovery phospho-proteomic data. Nat. Commun. **6**, 8033 (2015)

6. Benque, D., et al.: BMA: visual tool for modeling and analyzing biological networks. In: Madhusudan, P., Seshia, S.A. (eds.) CAV 2012. LNCS, vol. 7358, pp. 686–692. Springer, Berlin (2012). doi:10.1007/978-3-642-31424-7_50
7. Naldi, A., Thieffry, D., Chaouiya, C.: Decision diagrams for the representation and analysis of logical models of genetic networks. In: Calder, M., Gilmore, S. (eds.) CMSB 2007. LNCS, vol. 4695, pp. 233–247. Springer, Berlin (2007). doi:10.1007/978-3-540-75140-3_16
8. Cook, B., Fisher, J., Krepska, E., Piterman, N.: Proving stabilization of biological systems. In: Jhala, R., Schmidt, D. (eds.) VMCAI 2011. LNCS, vol. 6538, pp. 134–149. Springer, Berlin (2011). doi:10.1007/978-3-642-18275-4_11
9. Cook, B., Fisher, J., Hall, B.A., Ishtiaq, S., Juniwal, G., Piterman, N.: Finding instability in biological models. In: Biere, A., Bloem, R. (eds.) CAV 2014. LNCS, vol. 8559, pp. 358–372. Springer, Cham (2014). doi:10.1007/978-3-319-08867-9_24
10. Claessen, K., Fisher, J., Ishtiaq, S., Piterman, N., Wang, Q.: Model-checking signal transduction networks through decreasing reachability sets. In: Sharygina, N., Veith, H. (eds.) CAV 2013. LNCS, vol. 8044, pp. 85–100. Springer, Berlin (2013). doi:10.1007/978-3-642-39799-8_5
11. Schaub, M., Henzinger, T., Fisher, J.: Qualitative networks: a symbolic approach to analyze biological signaling networks. BMC Syst. Biol. 1, 4 (2007)
12. Bean, D., Heimbach, J., Ficorella, L., Micklem, G., Oliver, S., Favrin, G.: esyN: Network building, sharing, and publishing. PLoS ONE 9, e106035 (2014)
13. Microsoft: Microsoft bot framework (2016). https://dev.botframework.com/
14. Microsoft: Microsoft cognitive services (2016). https://www.microsoft.com/cognitive-services/
15. SAP: Chevrotain a JavaScript parsing DSL (2014). https://github.com/SAP/chevrotain/
16. van der Plas, L., Tiedemann, J.: Finding synonyms using automatic word alignment and measures of distributional similarity. In: Proceedings of the COLING/ACL on Main Conference Poster Sessions. COLING-ACL 2006, Stroudsburg, PA, USA, pp. 866–873. Association for Computational Linguistics (2006)
17. Richardson, R., Smeaton, A., Murphy, J.: Using wordnet as a knowledge base for measuring semantic similarity between words (1994)

Detecting Strict Aliasing Violations in the Wild

Pascal Cuoq[1(✉)], Loïc Runarvot[1], and Alexander Cherepanov[2,3]

[1] TrustInSoft, Paris, France
cuoq@trust-in-soft.com
[2] Openwall, Moscow, Russia
[3] National Research University Higher School of Economics, Moscow, Russia

Abstract. Type-based alias analyses allow C compilers to infer that memory locations of distinct types do not alias. Idiomatic reliance on pointers on the one hand, and separate compilation on the other hand, together make it impossible to get this aliasing information any other way. As a consequence, most modern optimizing C compilers implement some sort of type-based alias analysis. Unfortunately, pointer conversions, another pervasive idiom to achieve code reuse in C, can interact badly with type-based alias analyses. This article investigate the fine line between the allowable uses of low-level constructs (pointer conversions, unions) that should never cause the predictions of a standard-compliant type-based alias analysis to be wrong, and the dangerous uses that can result in bugs in the generated binary. A sound and precise analyzer for "strict aliasing" violations is briefly described.

Keywords: Strict aliasing · Type-based alias analysis · C · Static analysis

1 Introduction

Until approximately 1999 [10,11], the static analysis literature tended towards ignoring low-level aspects of C programs completely. Sound analyzers (either actual prototypes or hypothetical implementations of the entirety of the analyzer described in an article) would not deal with low-level programming idioms that are, for better or for worse, present in C code as it exists and as it gets written. An example, seen in safety-critical embedded code, is to take the address of the first member of a struct that contains only floats, and proceed to initialize the struct via a loop, through pointer arithmetic, as if it were an array. Rejecting this construct outright means giving up on making the analyzer useful for this kind of code. Alternately, the analyzer might maintain soundness by becoming very imprecise in presence of such low-level constructs. This also makes the analyzer unusable in practice. As sound static analysis gained industrial adoption as a useful tool for the certification of safety-critical embedded software, the design choice of accepting the low-level construct and handling it precisely became more common [9].

© Springer International Publishing AG 2017
A. Bouajjani and D. Monniaux (Eds.): VMCAI 2017, LNCS 10145, pp. 14–33, 2017.
DOI: 10.1007/978-3-319-52234-0_2

Attempts to handle low-level constructs with precision in sound static analyzers sometimes works at cross-purposes with increasingly sophisticated optimizations, based on *undefined behavior*[1], in C compilers. In presence of constructs that invoke undefined behavior for some or all inputs, compilers are allowed to generate binary code:

- without any diagnostic at compile-time,
- that does not raise any exception at run-time,
- and only works as intended for inputs that do not invoke undefined behavior— this can be the empty set in the case of intentional reliance on undefined behavior by the developer.

Optimizations based on undefined behavior are useful[2]. But these optimizations can have the unfortunate effect of making static analyzers intended to be sound unsound in practice. To be fair, the problem, as long as one is aware of it, can easily be circumvented by disabling the optimization, aligning the semantics of the compiler and the analyzer. GCC understands -fwrapv for wrapping signed arithmetic overflows, and -fno-strict-aliasing for no type-based alias analysis. Awareness is the only difficulty in this plan. For instance, legacy C libraries that have worked well for 25 years and are now deployed everywhere may violate the rules in a way that new versions of C compilers written in 2017 suddenly become sophisticated enough to take advantage of.

This article is concerned with the optimization named -fstrict-aliasing in GCC and Clang, and with guaranteeing that programs do not invoke the kind of undefined behavior that allows this optimization to change the behavior of the program from what was intended by the developer. With funding from the Linux Foundation's Core Infrastructure Initiative, we are building a static analyzer to detect violations of strict aliasing, so that legacy C libraries at the heart of the Internet can be diagnosed with strict aliasing violations, and fixed before the problem becomes urgent. This is work in progress.

2   Strict Aliasing in the C Standards

When the C programming language was standardized in 1980 s the Committee considered the question whether an object may be accessed by an lvalue of a type different from the declared type of the object. This would hamper optimization and, thus, "[t]he Committee has decided that such dubious possibilities need not be allowed for"[3]. However, certain prevalent exceptions were recognized: types differently qualified and with different signedness may alias and any type may be accessed as a character type. Interaction between aggregates (and unions) and their members was also accounted for. The resulting rules were included in C89 and got known as "strict aliasing rules".

---

[1] See http://blog.regehr.org/archives/213.
[2] See https://gist.github.com/rygorous/e0f055bfb74e3d5f0af20690759de5a7.
[3] C89 Rationale, http://std.dkuug.dk/jtc1/sc22/wg14/docs/rationale/c89/rationale.ps.gz.

In 1997, it was pointed out[4] that the text in the C89 standard does not cover the case of allocated objects which do not have a declared type. The standard was corrected and the strict aliasing rules in C99 have the following form:

[C99, 6.5:6] The effective type of an object for an access to its stored value is the declared type of the object, if any.[75] If a value is stored into an object having no declared type through an lvalue having a type that is not a character type, then the type of the lvalue becomes the effective type of the object for that access and for subsequent accesses that do not modify the stored value. If a value is copied into an object having no declared type using memcpy or memmove, or is copied as an array of character type, then the effective type of the modified object for that access and for subsequent accesses that do not modify the value is the effective type of the object from which the value is copied, if it has one. For all other accesses to an object having no declared type, the effective type of the object is simply the type of the lvalue used for the access.

[C99, 6.5:7] An object shall have its stored value accessed only by an lvalue expression that has one of the following types:[76]
- a type compatible with the effective type of the object,
- a qualified version of a type compatible with the effective type of the object,
- a type that is the signed or unsigned type corresponding to the effective type of the object,
- a type that is the signed or unsigned type corresponding to a qualified version of the effective type of the object,
- an aggregate or union type that includes one of the aforementioned types among its members (including, recursively, a member of a sub-aggregate or contained union), or
- a character type.

75) Allocated objects have no declared type.
76) The intent of this list is to specify those circumstances in which an object may or may not be aliased.

There were no changes in the text in C11 except for renumbering footnotes.
The rules are symmetric with regard to signedness of types but not to qualified/unqualified versions.
The rules are quite clear for objects declared with one of the basic types. Everything more complex poses some kind of problems.
The natural aliasing between aggregates (and unions) and their members is permitted by the fifth item in C99, 6.5:7, but the formulation is quite sloppy. The problem was pointed out[5] at least in 1997, a later discussion can be found in

---

[4] http://open-std.org/jtc1/sc22/wg14/www/docs/n640.ps.
[5] http://open-std.org/jtc1/sc22/wg14/3406.

defect reports 1409[6] and 1520[7]. A shared understanding of the intended meaning seems to exist, although nobody has found yet a fixed wording.

Unions have members of different types which naturally alias each other. Possibility of uncontrolled access to these members would undermine the idea of strict aliasing. Thus, we have to conclude that strict aliasing rules govern the use of members of unions. But there is an exception—it's always permitted to read any member of a union by the . operator (and the -> operator). The relevant part of the C99 standard is:

[C99, 6.5.2.3:3] A postfix expression followed by the . operator and an identifier designates a member of a structure or union object. The value is that of the named member,[82)] and is an lvalue if the first expression is an lvalue.

82) If the member used to access["read" in C11] the contents of a union object is not the same as the member last used to store a value in the object, the appropriate part of the object representation of the value is reinterpreted as an object representation in the new type as described in 6.2.6 (a process sometimes called "type punning"). This might be a trap representation.

3   Examples

This section lists examples of simple functions where a memory access can be optimized, or not, depending on the interpretation of the strict aliasing rules. On the right-hand side of each example, the assembly code generated by an optimizing compiler is shown[8]. While reading the examples, bear in mind that in the x86-64 calling convention, %rax or its 32-bit subregister %eax is used for the return value when it is an integer or a pointer. %rdi or %edi holds the function's first integer/pointer argument, and %rsi or %esi holds the second one. The result, when a float, is instead placed in the floating-point register %xmm0, and %xmm0 also holds the function's first float argument if any.

```
int ex1(int *p, float *q) {        ex1:
    *p = 1;                          movl $1, (%rdi)
    *q = 2.0f;                       movl $1, %eax
    return *p;                       movl $0x40000000, (%rsi)
}                                    ret
```

---

[6] http://open-std.org/jtc1/sc22/wg14/www/docs/n1409.htm.
[7] http://open-std.org/jtc1/sc22/wg14/www/docs/n1520.htm.
[8] https://godbolt.org/g/ggZzQo.

```c
unsigned ui(unsigned *p, int *q) {
  *p = 1;
  *q = 2;
  return *p;
}
```

```
ui:
  movl $1, (%rdi)
  movl $2, (%rsi)
  movl (%rdi), %eax
  ret
```

```c
long lll(long *p, long long *q) {
  *p = 1;
  *q = 2;
  return *p;
}
```

```
lll:
  movq $1, (%rdi)
  movl $1, %eax
  movq $2, (%rsi)
  ret
```

```c
int x;
unsigned y;
int *pp(int **p, unsigned **q) {
  *p = &x;
  *q = &y;
  return *p;
}
```

```
pp:
  movq $x, (%rdi)
  movl $x, %eax
  movq $y, (%rsi)
  ret
```

```c
typedef int (*f1)(int);
typedef int (*f2)(float);
int foo(int);
int bar(float);
f1 pf(f1 *p, f2 *q) {
  *p = foo;
  *q = bar;
  return *p;
}
```

```
pf:
  movq $foo, (%rdi)
  movl $foo, %eax
  movq $bar, (%rsi)
  ret
```

```c
struct s { int a; };
struct t { int b; };
int st1(struct s *p, struct t *q) {
  p->a = 1;
  q->b = 2;
  return p->a;
}
```

```
st1:
  movl $1, (%rdi)
  movl $1, %eax
  movl $2, (%rsi)
  ret
```

```c
struct s { int a; };
struct t { int b; };
int st2(struct s *p, struct t *q) {
  int *pa = & (p->a);
  int *qb = & (q->b);
  *pa = 1;
  *qb = 2;
  return *pa;
}
```

```
st2:
  movl $1, (%rdi)
  movl $2, (%rsi)
  movl (%rdi), %eax
  ret
```

The assembly code shown was produced by GCC 6.2.0

For each of the example functions in this section, the question is whether it behaves the way a programmer with a naïve view of memory use in C would expect, when somehow invoked with aliasing pointers as arguments, regardless of how the aliasing has been created at the call-site. Reading the assembly generated for one example by a particular compiler is faster and less distracting that building a caller that creates the aliasing condition.

For the sake of completeness, here is what a problematic caller would look like for the first example ex1:

```
int main(int c, char *v[]) {
  static_assert(sizeof(int) == sizeof(float),
    "Only for 32-bit int and IEEE 754 binary32 float");
  void *p = malloc(sizeof(float));
  ex1((int *)p, (float *)p);
}
```

The main function here is creating the conditions for ex1 to misbehave, and, in a "code smell" sense, it can be said to be where the programmer's error lay. Experienced programmers familiar with strict aliasing rules in particular would worry about the conversions of the same p to two distinct pointer types. Regardless, it is the code inside function ex1 that, when invoked in this context, violates the rules. Any reasonably precise analyzer can only hope to diagnose the problem there. The two pointer conversions in the above main are not invalid, and would constitute a valid program if put together with a different implementation for the function ex1. We do not show additional examples of calling contexts precisely in order to avoid wrongly thinking of the calling context as the place where the strict aliasing issue is located. Warning about pointer conversions is, essentially, what GCC's -Wstrict-aliasing option does, and this is not satisfactory because, to be blunt, pointer conversion is the sole code reuse mechanism available in the C language, and as such it is used as much as necessary, both in patterns that ends up violating strict aliasing rules and in patterns that do not. This is especially true of legacy code written in the 1990s, a time at which C was used to program high-level concepts for which a high-level language would hopefully be the obvious choice for new implementations today.

The example ex1 shows the simplest, least controversial form of strict aliasing optimization. The only C developers who disagree with it reject the concept of type-based alias inference as a whole.

The example ui is not expected to be optimized, as C11 makes allowances for accessing an unsigned effective type with an int lvalue and vice-versa. In contrast, even when the standard integer types int and long (or respectively long and long long) happen to have the same width, compilers can assume that an lvalue of one type is not used to access an object with the other, as the standard allows them to—the types int and long are not compatible even when they have the same width.

In the example ppp, GCC 6.2.0 (but none of the Clang versions available at the time of this writing) correctly uses the fact that the types int* and unsigned* are not compatible with each other to optimize the returned value into &x. Similarly, in example pf, GCC version 6.2.0 takes advantage of the incompatibility of the types "pointer to function taking an int and returning an int" and "pointer to function taking a float and returning an int" to optimize the returned value to the address of foo.

An example similar to st1 was a crucial part of an internal committee discussion about the notion of type compatibility as early as 1995[9]. This example has popped again occasionally, for instance in GCC's mailing list in 2010[10] and later in Sect. 4.1.2 of "C memory object and value semantics: the space of de facto and ISO standards"[11]. GCC versions 4.4.7 and 4.5.3 optimize st2 identically to st1, but later GCC versions do not. It is not clear whether this change is incidental or results from a decision to limit the scope of strict aliasing optimizations: the reasoning that justifies the optimization of st1 in GCC justifies the optimization of st2, too. A consequence for any sound static detector of strict aliasing violations is that the information of "pointed struct member" must be propagated associated to pa and qb in order to detect that the harmless-looking assignments *pa = 1, *qb = 2 and retrieval return *pa; violate GCC's memory model because of previous statements.

```
int ar1(int (*p)[8], int (*q)[8]) {
  (*p)[3] = 1;
  (*q)[4] = 2;
  return (*p)[3];
}
```

```
ar1:
  movl $1, 12(%rdi)
  movl $1, %eax
  movl $2, 16(%rsi)
  ret
```

```
int ar2(int c, int (*p)[8],
        int (*q)[8]) {
  int z = 0;
  if (2 < c && c < 4) {
    (*p)[c+z] = 1;
    (*q)[4] = 2;
    return (*p)[c];
  }
  else
    return 0;
}
```

```
ar2:
  xorl %eax, %eax
  cmpl $3, %edi
  je .L
  rep ret
.L5:
  movl $1, 12(%rsi)
  movl $1, %eax
  movl $2, 16(%rdx)
  ret11
```

---

[9] Example y.c in http://std.dkuug.dk/jtc1/sc22/wg14/docs/c9x/misc/tag-compat. txt.gz.

[10] https://gcc.gnu.org/ml/gcc/2010-01/msg00013.html.

[11] https://www.cl.cam.ac.uk/~pes20/cerberus/notes30.pdf, Draft, Revision 1571, 2016-03-17.

```
int ar3(int (*p)[8], int (*q)[7]) {     ar3:
  (*p)[3] = 1;                             movl $1, 12(%rdi)
  (*q)[3] = 2;                             movl $2, 12(%rsi)
  return (*p)[3];                          movl 12(%rdi), %eax
}                                          ret
```

```
enum e1 { A = 0 };
enum e2 { B = 1 };
int ex1_enum(enum e1 *p, enum e2 *q)     ex1_enum:
{                                          movl $0, (%rdi)
  *p = A;                                  xorl %eax, %eax
  *q = B;                                  movl $1, (%rsi)
  return *p;                               ret
}
```

```
enum e1 { A };
unsigned ex2_enum(unsigned *p, enum e1 *q) ex2_enum:
{                                          movl $1, (%rdi)
  *p = 1;                                  movl $1, %eax
  *q = A;                                  movl $0, (%rsi)
  return *p;                               ret
}
```

The assembly code shown was produced by GCC 6.2.0

The same optimization that GCC exhibits when compiling the function st1, GCC 6.2.0 also applies to array types in example ar1, where index 3 of an array of 8 ints is assumed not to alias with index 4 of an array of 8 ints. Clang versions available as of this writing do not optimize ar1.

The example ar2 shows that there are no a priori bounds to the ingenuity of compiler in order to infer that the indexes being accessed are necessarily different. As a consequence, a sound and precise static analyzer cannot limit itself to constant array indexes.

The example ar3, where the array types pointed by the arguments differ in size, seems easier to optimize than ar1, but is surprisingly optimized by neither Clang nor GCC as of this writing. Optimizing ar1 already constrains the developer never to view a large array as a superposition of overlapping smaller arrays, so GCC could optimize ar3. Showing this example to GCC developers is taking them in the direction of not optimizing ar1 instead[12].

In C, enum types have an underlying integer type, chosen by the compiler according to the set of values to hold by the enum. GCC chooses unsigned int for an enum destined to contain only the values 0 and 1 or 0. Despite these two enum types being compatible with unsigned int, GCC 6.2.0 optimizes programs as if a memory location of effective type one such enum could not be modified by an access to unsigned int, or an access to another such enum. We think this is a bug[13], but meanwhile, it is possible to detect that a program might be

---

[12] https://gcc.gnu.org/ml/gcc/2016-11/msg00111.html.
[13] See https://gcc.gnu.org/bugzilla/show_bug.cgi?id=71598.

miscompiled by GCC 6.2.0 by treating in the analyzer an **enum** type based on **unsigned int** as if it were incompatible with **unsigned int** and other enum types based on **unsigned int**.

```
union u { int a; float b; };

int fr(float f) {
  union u t = { .b = f };
  return t.a;
}
/* q is really a pointer to a union u */
int u1(int *p, void *q) {
  *p = 1;
  *&((union u *)q)->b = 2;
  return *p;
}

int u2(int *p, union u *q) {
  *p = 1;
  q->b = 0.1;
  return *p;
}

void *mem(void);

int u3() {
  union u *p1 = mem();
  union u *p2 = mem();
  float *fp = &p2->b;
  p1->a = 1;
  *fp = 3.0;
  return p1->a;
}


int u4(void) {
  union u *p1 = mem();
  union u *p2 = mem();
  int* ip = &p1->a;
  *ip = 1;
  p2->b = 3.0;
  return *ip;
}
```

```
fr:
  movd %xmm0, %eax
  retq




u1:
  movl $1, (%rdi)
  movl $1073741824, (%rsi)
  movl $1, %eax
  retq



u2:
  movl $1, (%rdi)
  movl $1036831949, (%rsi)
  movl $1, %eax
  retq

u3:
  pushq %rbx
  callq mem
  movq %rax, %rbx
  callq mem
  movl $1, (%rbx)
  movl $1077936128, (%rax)
  movl $1, %eax
  popq %rbx
  retq

u4:
  pushq %rbx
  callq mem
  movq %rax, %rbx
  callq mem
  movl $1, (%rbx)
  movl $1077936128, (%rax)
  movl $1, %eax
  popq %rbx
  retq
```

```
int u5(void) {
  union u *p1 = mem();
  union u *p2 = mem();
  p1->a = 1;
  p2->b = 3.0;
  return p1->a;
}
```

```
u5:
  pushq %rbx
  callq mem
  movq %rax, %rbx
  callq mem
  movl $1, (%rbx)
  movl $1077936128, (%rax)
  movl $1, %eax
  popq %rbx
  retq
```

The assembly code shown was produced by Clang 3.9.0

The interactions of unions with type-punning and type-based alias analyses have caused enormous amounts of discussion, starting with a C99 standard that initially implied that reading from a union member other than the one used to setting the value of the union produced unspecified results (6.5.2.3:3) and a defect report about a regression of the type-punning powers of union with respect to C89[14]. Type-punning through unions remains ambiguously described in the C11 standard, and compilers that want to take advantage of type-based alias analyses for optimizations need to define their own rules[15], and convey them to the developer, which they do not always do clearly.

One extreme example of union use for type-punning is the function fr to convert a float to its representation as an int. This function is compiled to the intended binary code by all the compilers we tried. At the other end of the spectrum, the very function ex1 that we used as first example can be an example of type-punning through unions when it is invoked in the following context:

```
int main(int c, char *v[]) {
  union { float f; int i; } u;
  ex1(&u.i, &u.f);
}
```

Obviously, compilers do not want to compile the function ex1 cautiously just because any other compilation unit might invoke it with the addresses of distinct members of a same union. Between these two extremes exists a limit of what a compiler defines as reasonable use of a union for type-punning. Only programs within the limit are guaranteed to be translated to code that behaves as intended. All three of GCC, ICC and Clang fit in this general framework, but with different limits between reasonable and unreasonable uses of union for type-punning. GCC

---

[14] DR283, http://www.open-std.org/jtc1/sc22/wg14/www/docs/dr_283.htm.

[15] See for instance https://gcc.gnu.org/bugzilla/show_bug.cgi?id=65892#c9 or the words "GCC doesn't implement C99 aliasing as written in the standard regarding unions. We don't do so because we determined that this can't possibly have been the intent of the standard as it makes type-based aliasing relatively useless" in https://gcc.gnu.org/ml/gcc/2010-01/msg00263.html.

documents its expectations comparatively well[16], and sticks to what it documents: from the documentation, we expect functions u1 through u5 not to be optimized by GCC 6.2.0, and indeed, they are not. Clang does not document what usages of unions it deems acceptable that we could find. All the examples u1 through u5 are optimized, implying that perhaps the only acceptable use of a union for type-punning recognized by Clang is that of a variable accessed directly, without any pointer dereference being involved. ICC appears to adopt a middle-ground, by optimizing functions u3 and u4, but not u5.

4 Detecting Strict Aliasing Violations

In this section we sketch out the functioning principles of a static analyzer for detecting strict aliasing violations. The analyzer is a forward abstract interpreter [2] that assumes that the values of expressions are computed at the same time as the effective types, or have been computed and saved in a usable form [4]. The analyzer propagates "memory states", starting with the entry point of the program, until a fixpoint has been reached. In this case, a "memory state" assigns possible effective types to each bit of memory. The bit-level memory model is necessary in order to handle low-level constructs such as unions and pointer conversions, when they are used in accordance to strict aliasing rules.

The lattice used for each memory bit is the lattice of sets of effective types, ordered by inclusion (the power set lattice). The empty set of effective types is the least element. It would technically not be necessary to keep information about all the possible effective types an object can have during the analysis. As soon as two sufficiently distant effective types are possible effective types for an object, there exists no declared type, compatible with both, with which this object can be accessed without a warning. In other words, it would not lead to a loss of precision to simplify the abstract domain used by identifying with the greatest element all sets containing at least two incompatible effective types. Our implementation avoids making all these sets of distant types the same in order to improve the usefulness of warning messages. In particular, the attitude of the analyzer's user towards the message "there may be a violation here because this int lvalue is used to access some unknown effective type" may be "I see why the analyzer is imprecise here, this is a false positive". The same user, provided with the better warning message "there may be a violation here because this int lvalue is used to access effective types long and float" may be "I see that the analyzer is imprecise here when it predicts that a float can be accessed, this is a false positive; but accessing a long can happen and is a genuine strict aliasing bug".

4.1 Effective Types

We describe the grammar of effective types using an OCaml-like notation.

---

[16] Documentation at https://gcc.gnu.org/onlinedocs/gcc-6.2.0/gcc/Optimize-Options. html.

```
type ival = ...

type integer_type =
  | Bool
  | Char | SignedChar | UnsignedChar
  | Short | UnsignedShort
  | Int | UnsignedInt
  | Long | UnsignedLong
  | LongLong | UnsignedLongLong

type float_type = Float | Double | LongDouble

type function_type =
  { return_type : simple_type;
    formals : simple_type list }

type simple_type =
  | Structure of structure
  | StructureField of field * simple_type
  | Array of simple_type * expr (* size *)
  | ArrayElement of simple_type
    * expr (* declared size for array *)
    * ival (* set of actual values for the index *)
  | Union of union_t
  | Enum of enum_t
  | IntegerType of integer_type
  | FloatType of float_type
  | FunctionType of function_type
  | VariadicFunctionType of function_type
  | PointerType of simple_type
  | FirstAccessType
  | VoidType
  | MayAlias
```

Listing 1.1. Effective Types

The effective types used by the analyzer unsurprisingly resemble the static types familiar to the C programmer. Below are the most notable departures from the grammar of static types.

An effective type can be "member m of ...", (resp. "array element at index ...of array ..."). This is not the same effective type as the type of the struct member m (resp. the type of elements of the array). In order to handle example functions st1, st2, ar1, ..., all the available information about the location of the subobject inside its containing objects must be memorized in the effective type.

The FirstAccessType constructor indicates that the effective type will be that of the lvalue used for reading until some effective type is written, following C11 6.5:6. The effective type `FirstAccessType` is used for the contents of memory blocks allocated through `calloc`, as well as for contents written by `read`, `fread`, `memset`, ... This constructor is not necessary for the contents of a block allocated through `malloc`, because in this case the contents of the allocated block are uninitialized ("indeterminate" in C standard parlance). Reads of uninitialized dynamically allocated memory can be assumed not to happen in a defined execution, and any such reads that can happen in the conditions of the analysis should have been warned about by the companion value analysis. Since the value analysis already warns about such uses of dynamically allocated memory, the allocated block should rather be set to bottom (the empty set of effective types) for maximum accuracy.

The `MayAlias` constructor corresponds to the type attribute GCC[17] and Clang compilers to inform the optimizer that lvalues of a certain type are expected to be used to access memory of a different effective type.

The possibility that the types in stdint.h are mapped to "extended integer types" (in the sense of the C11 clause 6.2.5:4) can be taken into account by adding as many constructors as necessary to `integer_type`. This is particularly relevant for the types `int8_t` and `uint8_t` because a 8-bit extended integer type that these would have been defined as aliases of would not need to benefit from the exception for "character types" in 6.5:7[18].

Note that the effective types "member m of type int of ..." and "int" are unordered. It may initially seem that the latter should be included in the former, but not doing so allows to distinguish the case of a pointer that can only point to a certain `struct` member m of type `int` from the case of a pointer that may point to a `struct` member m of type `int` or to an `int` variable, say, depending on the execution path that has been followed.

4.2 Notable Analysis Rules and Checks

Compared to, say, a more traditional value analysis, the followed aspects of the strict aliasing violation analysis deserve mention:

- When an lvalue read access occurs in an expression being evaluated, the type of the lvalue is checked against the effective type contained by the memory model for the location being accessed. This is the check that detects a problem in the program `int x = 1; 0.0f + *(float*)&x;` and also in the program `void *p = malloc(4); *(int*)p = 1; 0.0f + *(float*)p;`
- Upon assignment to an lvalue, if the location designated by the lvalue being assigned is a variable or a subobject of a variable, then the static type of the lvalue is checked against the type of the variable. This is the check that detects a problem in the program `int x; *(float*)&x = 1.0f;`.
- Union types are handled specially only in the case of an assignment directly to or a read directly from a variable. Outside these cases, `union` types are

---

[17] https://gcc.gnu.org/onlinedocs/gcc-4.0.2/gcc/Type-Attributes.html.
[18] See discussion at https://gcc.gnu.org/bugzilla/show_bug.cgi?id=66110.

ignored: the effective types have to match as if there was no union. This is intended to catch the cases where Clang might optimize despite the union type.

4.3 A Short Example

```
int x;
FILE *stream = ...;
void *p = malloc(sizeof(int));
if (fread(p, sizeof(int), 1, stream) == 1)
  x = *(int *)p;
else
  /* ... */
```

After the third line of the example above, the allocated object pointed by p has no effective type. Assuming the call to fread succeeds, it sets the effective type of that memory zone to FirstAccessType. The pointed block having the effective type FirstAccessType results in the read access *(int *)p succeeding. Since the effective type of the memory zone pointed by p is FirstAccessType, the effective type of the expression *(int *)p is determined by the type of the lvalue, and thus automatically matches it: IntegerType(Int).

5 Analyzing Legacy C Libraries for Strict Aliasing Violations

The analysis summarized in Sect. 4 is implemented as a Frama-C plug-in [3]. It works best when applied on definite inputs. In these conditions, the value analysis plug-in [1] avoids false positives, and builds a result graph [4] that contains *all* the information that has been inferred about the execution of the program, so that the analyzers exploiting these results are not limited by any loss of information about the order in which program variables take their values.

Finally, the strict aliasing violation analysis is itself designed to assign exactly one effective type to each memory location, avoiding imprecisions and the resulting false positives, for programs applied to definite inputs resulting in bounded execution. "Subjective false positive" may exist, where compilers do not currently exploit a strict-aliasing-violating pattern, and it turns out to be impossible to convince the maintainer of the library that they are doing something wrong. As long as the C standard's definition of allowed memory accesses is as poorly formalized as it is, and as long as the standard's ambiguity is invoked as excuse for compilers to invent their own, undocumented, rules, these "subjective false positives" seem unavoidable.

5.1 Expat

We applied the strict aliasing analyzer described in this article to Expat, a widely-used C library for parsing XML. The first of several strict aliasing violation detected by our analyzer has been reported[19]. This violation is caused by uses of struct types with a common initial sequence as a poor man's subtyping, as is otherwise extremely common in object-oriented code written in C. In this case, the struct-with-common-initial-sequence pattern is used in an attempt at implementing a generic hash-table data structure.

```
typedef struct {
    char *name;
} NAMED;

typedef struct {
    char *name;
    char *rawName;
    /* [...] */
} TAG;

typedef struct {
    char *name;
    PREFIX *prefix;
    /* [...] */
} ELEMENT_TYPE;

typedef struct {
    NAMED **v;
    size_t size;
    /* [...] */
} HASH_TABLE
```

The two structs `TAG` and `ELEMENT_TYPE` have the same initial sequence as the struct the hashtable is nominally intended to store pointers to, `NAMED`. The `lookup` function retrieves an existing element, or, if none is found, allocates one of the size given as parameter. This new element's **name** member is initialized through the `NAMED` struct type:

```
static NAMED *
lookup(XML_Parser parser, HASH_TABLE *table, KEY name,
        size_t createSize)
{
    /* [...] find the element or resize the table */
    /* The element was not found into the table: create it. */
    table->v[i] = (NAMED *)table->mem->malloc_fcn(createSize);
    if (!table->v[i])
        return NULL;
    memset(table->v[i], 0, createSize);
    table->v[i]->name = name;
```

---

[19] https://sourceforge.net/p/expat/bugs/538/.

```
    (table->used)++;
    return table->v[i];
}
```

In the analysis described in Sect. 4, the assignment `table->v[i]->name = name` sets the effective type of the memory location being written to "member name of the struct `NAMED`". This means that subsequent read accesses to this part of memory must be made through a pointer to the struct `NAMED`. Reading the memory location through a pointer to another struct may interact badly with compiler optimizations, as shown in the example functions `st1` and `st2`.

```
static ELEMENT_TYPE *
getElementType(XML_Parser parser, const ENCODING *enc,
               const char *ptr, const char *end)
{
    DTD * const dtd = _dtd;
    const XML_Char *name = poolStoreString(&dtd->pool, enc,
                                           ptr, end);
    ELEMENT_TYPE *ret;

    if (!name)
        return NULL;
    ret = (ELEMENT_TYPE *) lookup(parser, &dtd->elementTypes,
                                  name, sizeof(ELEMENT_TYPE));
    if (!ret)
        return NULL;
    if (ret->name != name) {
        ...
    } else {
        ...
    }
}
```

The function `getElementType` exemplifies how the library Expat uses the value returned by `lookup`. The member `name` is read through a pointer to the structure `ELEMENT_TYPE`. This leads to a violation of strict aliasing as shown by the following warning:

```
expat/lib/xmlparse.c:6470:[sa] warning: Reading a cell with
 effective type (struct __anonstruct_NAMED_13).name[char *]
 through the lvalue ret->name of type
 (struct __anonstruct_ELEMENT_TYPE_22).name[char *].
 Callstack: getElementType :: expat/lib/xmlparse.c:4080 <-
            doProlog :: expat/lib/xmlparse.c:3801 <-
            prologProcessor :: expat/lib/xmlparse.c:3618 <-
            prologInitProcessor :: expat/lib/xmlparse.c:1693 <-
            XML_ParseBuffer :: expat/xmlwf/xmlfile.c:184 <-
```

```
processStream :: expat/xmlwf/xmlfile.c:243 <-
XML_ProcessFile :: expat/xmlwf/xmlwf.c:853 <-
main
```

As part of the code normalization in the analyzer's front-end, the anonymous structures receive names: in the example above, struct __anonstruct_ELEMENT_TYPE_22 is the name given to struct { char *name; PREFIX *prefix; ... }.

The resolution of this bug report was to add -fno-strict-aliasing, a perfectly reasonable solution for legacy C code

5.2   Zlib

We applied our strict aliasing analyzer to the general-purpose data compression library Zlib. One strict aliasing violation was found and reported, and appears as a comment in the source code[20]. The violation[21] is caused by accessing four unsigned char through a pointer to unsigned int:

```
#define DOLIT4 c ^= *buf4++; c = crc_table[3][c & 0xff] ^ \
            /* ... */
#define DOLIT32 DOLIT4; DOLIT4; DOLIT4; DOLIT4; DOLIT4;\
                DOLIT4; DOLIT4; DOLIT4

local unsigned long crc32_little(crc, buf, len)
    unsigned long crc;
    const unsigned char FAR *buf;
    unsigned len;
{
    register z_crc_t c;
    register const z_crc_t FAR *buf4;
    /* ... */
    buf4 = (const z_crc_t FAR *)(const void FAR *)buf;
    while (len >= 32) {
        DOLIT32;
        len -= 32;
    }
    while (len >= 4) {
        DOLIT4;
        len -= 4;
    }
    /* ... */
}
```

---

[20] https://github.com/madler/zlib/commit/e08118c401d5434b7b3a57039263f4fa9b1f-7d1a.

[21] https://github.com/pascal-cuoq/zlib-fork/commit/d7cde11e0b44f4e97cc1fd5250d8-26967841e614.

In the simplified pattern above, the type z_crc_t is defined as unsigned int. Our analyzer, when handling the statement buf4 = (const z_crc_t FAR *)(const void FAR *)buf, sets the effective type of the variable buf4 to "pointer to unsigned char" by ignoring the pointer conversions. Accessing to the object through the pointer buf4 is a violation of strict aliasing rules, as shown by the following warning of the analyzer:

```
zlib/crc32.c:267:[sa] warning: Reading a cell with effective type
  char through the lvalue *tmp_0(buf4) of type unsigned int.
  Callstack: crc32_little :: zlib/crc32.c:224 <-
             crc32 :: zlib/inflate.c:1182 <-
             inflate :: zlib/gzread.c:191 <-
             gz_decomp :: zlib/gzread.c:248 <-
             gz_fetch :: zlib/gzread.c:347 <-
             gzread :: zlib/test/minigzip.c:439 <-
             gz_uncompress :: zlib/test/minigzip.c:540 <-
             file_uncompress :: zlib/test/minigzip.c:629 <-
             main
```

In the warning, the temporary variable tmp_0, introduced by code normalization, corresponds to the variable buf4 at that point of the function crc32_little.

6 Related Work

The closest forms of analyses we are aware of are libcrunch [7] and SafeType [5]. The tool libcrunch takes a dynamic approach and instruments pointer casts for violations to be revealed when executing. Since our analyzer handles whole-programs only and can behave as a C interpreter when deterministic inputs are provided, it is the most directly comparable of the two. Safetype is a static analysis implemented inside a compiler, that is, a modular static analysis that does not have access to the whole program. This in itself is a source of both false positives and false negatives.

Each of libcrunch and SafeType warns at the level of the pointer conversion, for instance when the address of an int ends up being converted to a float*. SafeType can also warn about memory accesses with the wrong type. Our analysis warns at the level of forbidden memory access only.

7 Conclusion

We have provided a number of examples showing the difficulty of analyzing C programs precisely and soundly for strict aliasing violations. We think that working from examples is crucial in this endeavor because the description of the rules in the C standards are particularly open to interpretation by both C developers and compiler authors.

An analyzer for strict aliasing violations is being implemented. Our target is legacy C code. We think that this justifies our chosen, and as far as we know, original approach of warning only for actual strict aliasing violations, as opposed to warning for suspicious uses of pointers that may not technically break the rules. Legacy code should not be modified willy-nilly: billions of systems may rely on it, and at the same time, this software is not always maintained by the original developer, or even actively maintained at all. Contrary to first appearances, a simple makefile change to explicitly disable strict aliasing optimizations is an extremely satisfying outcome after successfully identifying an illegal pattern with our analyzer. The analyzer can also help to eliminate the bad patterns one by one, tweaking the code until the analyzer eventually remains silent, but such is the respect due to legacy code that we do not expect this usage to be very common.

Out of 18000 Debian packages indexed by Debian Code Search[22], 1001 packages contain the string `-fno-strict-aliasing`, and 131 contain the string `may_alias`, GCC's extension to get the benefits of the type-based alias analysis while informing the compiler that some specific memory accesses may be to a different effective type than expected. Our goal is to make every package that needs it use one of these two options. According to Debian Sources[23], 45 % of the lines of code in Debian are written in C, so a lot of work remains after the first two successful analyses of Expat and Zlib.

References

1. Canet, G., Cuoq, P., Monate, B.: A value analysis for C programs. In: Proceedings of the 2009 Ninth IEEE International Working Conference on Source Code Analysis and Manipulation, SCAM 2009, pp. 123–124. IEEE Computer Society, Washington, DC (2009). http://dx.doi.org/10.1109/SCAM.2009.22

2. Cousot, P., Cousot, R.: Abstract interpretation: A unified lattice model for static analysis of programs by construction or approximation of fixpoints. In: Proceedings of the 4th ACM SIGACT-SIGPLAN Symposium on Principles of Programming Languages, POPL 1977, pp. 238–252. ACM, New York (1977). http://doi.acm.org/10.1145/512950.512973

3. Cuoq, P., Kirchner, F., Kosmatov, N., Prevosto, V., Signoles, J., Yakobowski, B.: Frama-C. In: Eleftherakis, G., Hinchey, M., Holcombe, M. (eds.) SEFM 2012. LNCS, vol. 7504, pp. 233–247. Springer, Heidelberg (2012). doi:10.1007/978-3-642-33826-7_16

4. Cuoq, P., Rieu-Helft, R.: Result graphs for an abstract interpretation-based static analyzer. To appear

5. Ireland, I.: SafeType: Detecting type violations for type-based alias analysis of C. Ph.D. thesis, University of Alberta (2013)

6. ISO: ISO/IEC 9899:2011 Information technology – Programming languages – C, December 2011. http://www.iso.org/iso/iso_catalogue/catalogue_tc/catalogue_detail.htm?csnumber=57853

---

[22] https://codesearch.debian.net.
[23] https://sources.debian.net.

7. Kell, S.: Dynamically diagnosing type errors in unsafe code. In: Proceedings of the 2016 ACM SIGPLAN International Conference on Object-Oriented Programming, Systems, Languages, and Applications, OOPSLA 2016, pp. 800–819. ACM, New York (2016). http://doi.acm.org/10.1145/2983990.2983998
8. Krebbers, R.: The C standard formalized in Coq. Ph.D. thesis, Radboud University, December 2015
9. Miné, A.: Field-sensitive value analysis of embedded c programs with union types and pointer arithmetics. SIGPLAN Not. **41**(7), 54–63 (2006). http://doi.acm.org/10.1145/1159974.1134659
10. Siff, M., Chandra, S., Ball, T., Kunchithapadam, K., Reps, T.: Coping with type casts in C. In: Nierstrasz, O., Lemoine, M. (eds.) ESEC/SIGSOFT FSE - 1999. LNCS, vol. 1687, pp. 180–198. Springer, Berlin (1999). doi:10.1007/3-540-48166-4_12
11. Yong, S.H., Horwitz, S., Reps, T.: Pointer analysis for programs with structures and casting. SIGPLAN Not. **34**(5), 91–103 (1999). http://doi.acm.org/10.1145/301631.301647

Effective Bug Finding in C Programs
with Shape and Effect Abstractions

Iago Abal[✉], Claus Brabrand, and Andrzej Wąsowski

IT University of Copenhagen, Copenhagen, Denmark
{iago,brabrand,wasowski}@itu.dk

Abstract. Software tends to suffer from simple resource mis-manipulation bugs, such as double-locks. Code scanners are used extensively to remove these bugs from projects like the Linux kernel. Yet, these tools are not effective when the manipulation of resources spans multiple functions. We present a *shape-and-effect* analysis for C, that enables efficient and scalable inter-procedural reasoning about resource manipulation. This analysis builds a program abstraction based on the observable side-effects of functions. Bugs are found by model checking this abstraction, matching undesirable sequences of operations. We implement this approach in the EBA tool, and evaluate it on a collection of historical double-lock bugs from the Linux kernel. Our results show that our tool is more effective at finding bugs than similar code-scanning tools. EBA analyzes nine thousand Linux files in less than half an hour, and uncovers double-lock bugs in various drivers.

Keywords: Bug finding · Type and effects · Model checking · C · Linux · Double lock

1 Introduction

Today, the source code of the Linux kernel is continuously analyzed for bugs [12] using a handful of static code scanning tools (so-called *linters*). Code scanners find bugs by pattern matching against the structure and flow of the program. For instance, Linux commits ca9fe15[1] and 65582a7 fix locking bugs found by two of these tools. Linux-tailored linters like SMATCH[2] have seen adoption because they are easy to use, run fast, and are reasonably effective at finding certain classes of bugs. However, code scanners are commonly restricted to intra-procedural analysis of isolated functions; hence, they mostly find shallow bugs, and do not deal well with nested function calls.

Software bugs often cross the boundaries of a single function. The VBDb bug collection [2] documents 30 runtime bugs in Linux, 80% of which involve deeply nested function calls. Many of these bugs are conceptually simple, but will be missed by conventional linters. Examples include bugs fixed in commits: 1c17e4d (read of uninitialized data), 6252547 (null pointer dereference), 218ad12

---

[1] See https://github.com/torvalds/linux/commit/hash with *hash* replaced by the identifier.

[2] http://smatch.sf.net.

© Springer International Publishing AG 2017
A. Bouajjani and D. Monniaux (Eds.): VMCAI 2017, LNCS 10145, pp. 34–54, 2017.
DOI: 10.1007/978-3-319-52234-0_3

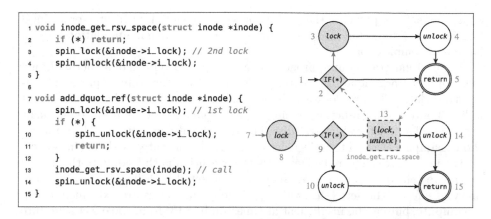

```
1 void inode_get_rsv_space(struct inode *inode) {
2     if (*) return;
3     spin_lock(&inode->i_lock);   // 2nd lock
4     spin_unlock(&inode->i_lock);
5 }
6
7 void add_dquot_ref(struct inode *inode) {
8     spin_lock(&inode->i_lock);   // 1st lock
9     if (*) {
10        spin_unlock(&inode->i_lock);
11        return;
12    }
13    inode_get_rsv_space(inode);   // call
14    spin_unlock(&inode->i_lock);
15 }
```

Fig. 1. An illustration of our bug-finding technique on a double-lock bug in Linux fixed by commit d7e9711. The *simplified* code is shown to the left. To the right, the associated CFG annotated with *lock* and *unlock* effects. The numbers next to the CFG nodes show corresponding line numbers. The red edges visualize the path (via the function call in line 13) to the double-lock (in line 3). (Color figure online)

(memory leak), and d7e9711 (double lock). Traditionally, static analysis of inter-procedural data-flow, or symbolic execution, could be used to find such bugs, but these analyses tend to be expensive, and have seen little adoption in practice. We argue that the above bugs can be handled by code scanners enriched with a minimal amount of semantic information.

We propose a bug-finding technique consisting in model-checking a light-weight program abstraction based on the notion of *side-effect* [34,37]. This abstraction is automatically inferred by a flow-insensitive shape-and-effect analysis, built on the work of Talpin and Jouvelot on polymorphic type-and-effect inference [47]. This analysis infers types that approximate the *shape* of data in memory—hence the term *shape*-and-effect analysis, and also computational *effects* that describe how data is manipulated by the program. The inferred effects reveal at which points the program performs operations like reading or writing variables, opening or closing files, acquiring or releasing locks, etc. The domain of effects is extensible. The inference algorithm is a small variation of the classic Damas-Milner's *Algorithm W* [18]. Since our goal is bug finding and not program optimization nor verification, we trade soundness for scalability [33].

The inferred shape-and-effect information is superimposed on the control-flow graph (CFG), obtaining what we call the *shape-and-effect abstraction* of the program. In this abstraction, each program expression and statement is described by a set of computational effects. The abstraction is built in a modular fashion, and each program function is given a polymorphic shape-and-effect signature, that summarizes its computational behavior. Bugs are found by matching temporal bug patterns on this abstraction, using a standard model checking algorithm. The search is inter-procedural *on demand*, and function calls can be inlined if they are of interest. Although, in practice, the majority of function calls are deemed irrelevant simply by examining their effect signature, and hence treated as opaque expressions. This prevents the path explosion associated with inter-procedural bug finding. This technique scales and finds deep resource manipulation bugs in large and complex software.

Figure 1 illustrates our approach using a simplified version of an actual Linux bug. Function add_dquot_ref enters a *deadlock* by recursively acquiring a non-reentrant lock. The first lock acquisition occurs in line 8, and the second occurs in line 3, after calling function inode_get_rsv_space in line 13; both conditionals (lines 2 and 9) must evaluate to *false* (i.e., take the *else* branch). To the right, we show a simplification of the effect-decorated CFG, annotated with locking effects on inode->i_lock. The red edges mark the execution path leading to the double lock. The call to inode_get_rsv_space is abstracted by a flow-insensitive summary of effects (the set: {*lock*, *unlock*}). These summaries are extremely cheap to compute, but can be insufficient at times. In line 13, from the effect signature of inode_get_rsv_space alone, it is unclear as to whether the acquisition of the lock happens *before* or *after* its release. Our bug finder needs to inline the call to inode_get_rsv_space, to find a path to the second lock in line 3, and finally confirm the double-lock bug. Note that if this function did not manipulate the lock at all, its effect signature would be the empty set, and the bug finder would have ignored it.

Our contributions are:

– An adaptation of Talpin-Jouvelot's [47] polymorphic type-and-effect inference system to the C language, that can be used to infer abstract discrete effects of computations, and shapes of structured values on the heap (Sect. 3). We use *shape inference and polymorphism* in order to add a degree of context sensitivity to our analysis, and to handle some common patterns to manipulate generic data in C.
– An inter-procedural bug-finding technique that combines shape-and-effect inference, to build lightweight *program abstractions*, with model-checking, to match *bug patterns* on those abstractions (Sect. 4). This technique finds several classes of bugs, even when these span multiple functions. We use function inlining as a sort of abstraction refinement, to disambiguate the ordering of operations when it is needed.
– An open-source proof-of-concept implementation of the shape-and-effect system, and the proposed bug-finding technique: EBA (Effect-Based Analyzer).[3] EBA can analyze individual Linux files for bugs in seconds and the entire x86 *allyesconfig* Linux kernel in less than an hour, and has uncovered about a dozen of previously unknown double-lock bugs in Linux 4.7–4.9 releases.
– An evaluation and comparison of our proposed analysis technique with two popular bug-finding tools within the Linux kernel community (Sect. 5): (1) on a collection of historical double-lock bugs in the Linux kernel, and (2) on the set of device drivers included in the 64-bit x86 *allyes* configuration of Linux 4.7.

---

[3] http://www.iagoabal.eu/eba/.

We proceed by discussing related work (Sect. 2) to contextualize our main contribution, the shape-and-effect system (Sect. 3). We then outline our bug-finding technique (Sect. 4), and evaluate it (Sect. 5). Finally, we present our conclusions (Sect. 6).

2   Related Work

Types and Effects. Side-effect analysis is used to compute which memory locations are accessed or updated by a function call [6,15,16]. Traditionally, this information is used by compilers to determine whether it is legal to perform certain code optimizations. Lucassen proposed a type-and-effect system [34] that, unlike previous analyses, correctly handles function pointers. Talpin and Jouvelot developed a complete type reconstruction algorithm for such a polymorphic type-and-effect system [47]. We extend their work to the C programming language. In order to accommodate the use of type casts in C, our system infers the shape of objects in memory, rather than standard C types. KOKA [32] is a functional programming language featuring an effect system based on row types [41]. This effect system is designed to be exposed to, and understood by the programmer. Our effect system is an internal program abstraction, thus we settled on Talpin-Jouvelot's system as a basis instead. Nielson and Nielson [37] survey the development of type-and-effect systems and their applications [35,49,50].

Pointer Analysis. Pointer analysis is used to approximate the values of pointer expressions at compile-time [43]. Side-effect analysis tracks operations on memory locations, hence it naturally embeds pointer analysis. Our shape-and-effect system implements context-sensitive alias analysis. Shapes are annotated with *regions* that abstract the locations where objects are stored in memory. Aliasing relations are recorded by unification during shape inference. This is similar to Steensgaard's points-to analysis [45], but it is significantly more precise thanks to shape and region polymorphism [20,22,26]. We prioritized a precise analysis of C structure types, as this is a well-known requirement to analyze real-world programs [44,52].

Type-safe Resource Management. These techniques impose stricter typing disciplines that guarantee safe manipulation of resources. They are valuable for languages with restricted aliasing, but often do not work well for C. Some of these disciplines are too strict to accommodate complex resource manipulation patterns, like those used in Linux. EBA is different in that it employs type inference to build abstractions, rather than to check specifications. We discuss the simplest flow-insensitive approaches first. Kyselyoiv and Shan rely on *monadic regions* to ensure the safe use of file handles [30]. Foster et al. implemented CQUAL, a constraint-based type checker that extends the C type system with user-defined type qualifiers [23]. CQUAL could be used to enforce the correct manipulation of user- and kernel-space pointers in Linux [27].

Strom and Yemini introduce the concept of *typestate* [46], a flow-sensitive abstraction of the state of an object, where operations specify *typestate transitions*—e.g. `fclose` will turn an open file into a closed file. In [24] Foster et al. extend [23] and introduce *flow-sensitive* type qualifiers. This is essentially the same concept of typestate, but they support subtyping and consider the problem of aliasing in C. This newer version of CQUAL can be used to find double-locks and similar bugs. However, using CQUAL requires code annotations and rewrites, and otherwise reports too many false positives. Using a similar analysis to that of [24], LOCKSMITH infers the set of locks that protect shared memory locations and detects data races [40]. LOCKSMITH uses an effect system to infer which locations are thread-shared.

Code Scanning. Static code scanners are mostly syntax-based bug finding tools. They are lightweight and know little about semantics: do no compute function summaries, ignore aliasing, and work intra-procedurally. Hence they are fast and scale well. For the same reasons, they are able to find relatively simple and shallow bugs. The degree of sophistication of these tools varies significantly. Some do not even fully parse the source code [10], whereas others check finite-state properties against the control-flow of programs [21]. One of the first tools of this class was LINT [19], a static checker for C created by Stephen Johnson at Bell Labs in 1970s. We discuss three tools that are used to analyze the Linux kernel source code for bugs [12], and have led to thousands of bug-fixing commits; these are SPARSE, COCCINELLE and SMATCH.

SPARSE exploits Linux-specific annotations to perform simple checks. However, some checks, like those related to locking, require too many annotations and are unpopular among developers. COCCINELLE is a program transformation tool [11], with an associated language (SmPL) to specify flow-based transformations. While originally conceived for managing collateral evolution of code [38], COCCINELLE can also encode bug-finding rules [31,39]. SMATCH realizes the idea of *meta-level compilation* proposed by Engler et al. [21], where bug checkers are scripts run by an intra-procedural data-flow analysis engine.

These tools cannot directly find interprocedural bugs such as that of Fig. 1. For SPARSE to find this bug, the functions involved need to be properly annotated with their locking behavior—they are not. COCCINELLE and SMATCH would have to rely on ad-hoc scripts to traverse the source code and collect all functions that may perform locking. Compared to an effect system, these scripts are more difficult to extend, do not track aliasing, nor handle function pointers appropriately. SMATCH ships with such an script which, in addition, only explores one level of function calls on each run. EBA works similarly to code scanners, but effectively supports inter-procedural bug finding.

Static Analysis & Software Model Checking. Static analyzers and software model checkers have a deep understanding of program semantics, and they quite precisely track the values of expressions, and the shape of the objects in the heap. These tools can find very complex and deep bugs, even when these involve non-trivial data dependencies. In order to scale, they rely heavily on *abstraction* [3,8,14,17] to model the program state. Maintaining such precise descriptions of the program state incurs in longer execution times and higher memory utilization. EBA offers a compromise solution between code scanners and these heavyweight tools, for bugs involving simple data dependencies.

ASTRÉE is a tool for analyzing safety-critical embedded C software based on abstract interpretation [17]. ASTRÉE can prove the absence of runtime errors, such as null-pointer dereferences, but only for a restricted subset of C. Reps, Horwitz and Sagiv show how an important class of inter-procedural data-flow analyses can be performed precisely and efficiently [42]. Their algorithm is popularly known as RHS. In [25] Hallem et al. extend *xgcc* [21] to perform inter-procedural analysis based on the RHS algorithm. The software model checkers BLAST [8] and SLAM [4,5] employ path-sensitive extensions of RHS. CBMC is a bounded model checker that reduces the verification of C programs into Boolean satisfiability problems [13]. These are whole-program analyses and do not scale to the extent of being adequate for regular use by developers.

INFER is a static analyzer based on symbolic execution and separation logic [7,9]. It is used by Facebook and others to find specific kinds of memory and resource manipulation errors in mobile apps. Similarly, SATURN is a SAT-based symbolic execution framework for checking temporal safety properties [51]. Both INFER and SATURN compute elaborated path-sensitive summaries for functions, and can model the runtime shape of complex data structures precisely. We do not model the heap as precisely as these two tools, and our function summaries are flow-insensitive; but we tackle the loss in precision by relying on heuristics and inlining, respectively. As a result, EBA is significantly simpler, and scales better.

3   The Shape-and-Effect System

At the core of EBA there is a new type-and-effect inference system for C in the style of Talpin and Jouvelot [29,47]. Because of unsafe casts, the standard C type system provides only a meager description of run-time objects. Thus, as known in pointer analysis [44,45], we describe objects by their memory shape. Our system is *polymorphic* in *shapes*, *regions*, and *effects*; and it supports *sub-effecting*. We use shape and region polymorphism to add context-sensitivity to our analysis, and to handle the most common pattern of use for unsafe casts: generic data structures in C. Effect polymorphism and sub-effecting allow handling function pointers.

EBA analyzes programs in CIL (<u>C</u> <u>I</u>ntermediate <u>L</u>anguage), an analysis-friendly intermediate representation of C [36]. CIL has a simpler syntax-directed type system than C, without implicit type conversions. Using CIL allows us to scaffold a tool prototype faster, while still being able to handle the entire C (via a C-to-CIL front-end). For space reasons, we present the shape-and-effect system declaratively and for a much smaller language than CIL. The declarative and algorithmic formulations for CIL [1], including support for structures, are available online.[4]

----

[4] http://dl.iagoabal.eu/eba/cil.pdf.

3.1   The Source Language

We assume that the analyzed programs are well-typed with respect to a C-like base type system. This is easily ensured using a compiler. We consider only the following types in the base type-system:

$$\textit{l-value types } T^L \;:\; \mathsf{ref}\, T^R \;\mid\; \mathsf{ref}\, (T_1^R \times \cdots \times T_n^R \rightarrow T_0^R)$$
$$\textit{r-value types } T^R \;:\; \mathsf{int} \mid \mathsf{ptr}\, T^L$$

We distinguish l-value (T^L) and r-value (T^R) types, corresponding to the *left* and *right* sides of assignments, respectively. Unlike in C, reference types are explicit. A reference object, of type $\mathsf{ref}\, T$, is a memory *cell* holding objects of type T. We distinguish between mutable references to r-values (data), and immutable references to function values (code). A pointer value, of type $\mathsf{ptr}\, \mathsf{ref}\, T$, is the *address* of a reference in memory. Like in C, functions are not first-class citizens, but function pointers are allowed. Expressions are also split into l-values (L) and r-values (E):

$$\textit{l-value expressions } L \;:\; x \;\mid\; f \;\mid\; *E$$
$$\textit{r-value expressions } E \;:\; n \;\mid\; E_1 + E_2 \;\mid\; \mathsf{if}\, (E_0)\; E_1 \,\mathsf{else}\, E_2 \;\mid\; (T)E$$
$$\mid\; \mathsf{new}\; x : T = E_1;\, E_2 \;\mid\; !L \;\mid\; \&L \;\mid\; L_1 := E_2;\, E_3$$
$$\mid\; \mathsf{fun}\; T\; f(T_1\; x_1, \cdots, T_n\; x_n) = E_1;\, E_2 \;\mid\; L_0(E_1, \cdots, E_n)$$

L-value expressions (L) designate memory locations and are always assigned reference types T^L. We distinguish between mutable variables x and immutable function variables f. Dereferencing a pointer, $*E$, looks up the corresponding reference cell in memory; e.g., $*\&x$ evaluates to x.

R-value expressions (E), or simply *expressions*, denote *data* values, i.e. integers and pointers. Basic integer expressions are constants (n) and additions. The language includes if conditional expressions. As in C, a type cast $(T)E$ converts the value of an expression E to type T. The expression $\mathsf{new}\; x : T = E_1;\, E_2$ introduces a new local variable x, initialized to E_1 and visible in E_2; x names a memory cell of type $\mathsf{ref}\, T$. (We assume that memory is automatically managed.) The bang operator, $!L$, reads an l-value. Pointer values are obtained from reference cells using the *address-of* operator $\&$. L-values can be assigned a new value before evaluating another expression, as in $x := E_1;\, E_2$. The expression $\mathsf{fun}\; T\; f(T_1\; x_1, \cdots, T_n\; x_n) = E_1;\, E_2$ introduces a function variable f visible in E_2; function f binds n arguments ($x_1, \ldots, x_n$) and evaluates E_1. Function variables name immutable reference cells holding function values. Functions may either be invoked, or passed as pointers (using $\&$). We assume that fetching of and assignment to function references is forbidden by the base type system.

For clarity, we omit loops and jumps, which do not present specific challenges for our flow-insensitive inference system. Yet, they are considered in our implementation.

3.2 The Shape and Effect Language

Effects. Types describe *what* expressions compute, whereas effects describe *how* expressions compute [28]. From the type perspective, the expression $y := 1 + !x;\ !y$ evaluates to an integer value. From the effect perspective, it reads from locations x and y, and writes to y. Effects are a framework to reason about such and similar aspects of computations. An example set of effects is $\varphi = \{read_x, read_y, write_y\}$, which records reading variables x and y, and writing y. A set of effects is a *flow-insensitive abstraction* of an execution. It specifies the effects that *may* result from evaluating an expression (or statement), disregarding the flow of control.

We assume a finite number of *effect constructors* of finite arity, including nullary. A constructor ε applied to a tuple[5] $\bar{\rho}$ of memory regions (see below) defines a discrete effect $\varepsilon_{\bar{\rho}}$. Built-in effects, inherent to the C language, include reading and writing of memory locations, recorded as $read_\rho$ and $write_\rho$; and calling to functions (e.g. through function pointers), recorded as $call_\rho$. Other effects can be introduced to capture new kinds of bugs. The example of Sect. 1 used effects $lock_\rho$ and $unlock_\rho$ to represent lock manipulation actions. Effects are combined into sets (φ), ordered by the usual set inclusion. We use effect variables (ξ) to stand for sets of effects, to achieve effect polymorphism.

Regions. In practice, it is not enough to track effects involving single variables. A variable is one of many possible names for a particular memory cell. Consider the C program int x; int *y = &x; S. Within S's scope, both x and $*y$ denote the same memory cell—they *alias*. To address aliasing, we track abstract sets of possibly-aliased memory references, *memory regions* (ρ).

The shape-and-effect system performs integrated flow-insensitive alias analysis, similar to Steengaards's points-to analysis [45] but polymorphic. The analysis assigns a memory region ρ to each reference. If during pointer manipulation two regions become indistinguishable for the analysis, they are unified into a single one. For instance, if reference x belongs to region ρ_1 and y belongs to ρ_2, the effect of evaluating $y := 1 + !x;\ !y$ is $\{read_{\rho_1}, read_{\rho_2}, write_{\rho_2}\}$. If the analysis determines that ρ_1 and ρ_2 may alias, they will be merged—as $\rho_{\{1,2\}}$, reducing the effect set to $\{read_{\rho_{\{1,2\}}}, write_{\rho_{\{1,2\}}}\}$.

Shapes. A *shape* approximates the memory representation of an object [44,45]. Whereas, in the base type system, an expression can be coerced to a different type, in this system, the shape of an expression is fixed and preserved across type casts (cf. Sect. 3.3). Shapes are annotated with regions, recording points-to relations between references. We use the following terms to represent shapes:

$$l\text{-value shapes}\quad Z^L \quad : \quad \mathsf{ref}_\rho\, Z^R \ \mid\ \mathsf{ref}_\rho\,(Z_1^L \times \cdots \times Z_n^L \xrightarrow{\varphi} Z_0^R)$$
$$r\text{-value shapes}\quad Z^R \quad : \quad \bot \ \mid\ \mathsf{ptr}\, Z^L \ \mid\ \zeta$$

---

[5] We use overline to denote tuples.

As for types, we split shapes into l-value (Z^L) and r-value (Z^R) shapes. The shape language resembles the type language, without integer type but with shape variables (ζ).

R-value shapes denote the shape of r-value objects. An *atomic* shape $\perp$ denotes objects that have no relevant structure, for instance integers, when these are not masquerading pointers to implement genericity (see below). Pointer expressions have pointer shapes, ptr Z^L, where Z^L is the shape of the target reference cell of the pointer. A pointer represents the *address* of a reference cell, and therefore a pointer shape necessarily encloses a reference shape. Pointers may be cast to integers to emulate generics; such integer values will thus have a pointer shape. *Shape variables* ζ are used to make shapes polymorphic, they stand for arbitrary r-value shapes. For instance, functions manipulating a generic linked list are shape polymorphic, since they abstract from the shape of objects stored in the list.

L-value shapes denote *references* to either data or functions. Data (r-value) references have shape $\mathsf{ref}_\rho\ Z^R$, where ρ is a memory region, and Z^R is the shape of the objects that it holds. If a reference ρ_1 holds a pointer to another reference ρ_2, as in $\mathsf{ref}_{\rho_1}\ \mathsf{ptr}\ \mathsf{ref}_{\rho_2}\ Z$, we say that ρ_1 *points to* ρ_2. Function references have shape $\mathsf{ref}_\rho\ (Z_1^L \times \cdots \times Z_n^L \xrightarrow{\varphi} Z_0^R)$. A function shape maps a tuple of reference shapes $(Z_1^L \times \cdots \times Z_n^L)$, corresponding to the formal parameters, to a value shape (Z_0^R), corresponding to the result. The shape-and-effect system describes function parameters as l-value shapes, since actual parameters are in fact stored in stack variables. The returned value is an r-value expression, hence Z^R. Function shapes carry a so-called *latent effect*, φ, which accounts for the actions that (depending on the flow of control) *may* be performed during execution of the function.

Figure 2 shows the shapes inferred for a small C program. We assign constant 42 the shape $\perp$ (Fig. 2(a)). Variable x holding the value 42 at location ρ, gets the shape $\mathsf{ref}_\rho\ \perp$ (Fig. 2(b)). Region ρ is an abstraction of the actual memory address, 0xCAFE.

Fig. 2. Shapes of expressions in the C program: int x = 42; int *p = &x; return p;

Figure 2(c) shows the shape of &x, which is ptr $\mathsf{ref}_\rho\ \perp$. Finally, Fig. 2(d) shows the shape of the pointer variable p, $\mathsf{ref}_{\rho'}\ \mathsf{ptr}\ \mathsf{ref}_\rho\ \perp$.

Shape-Type Compatibility. As mentioned in the shape description above, there is often correlation between types and shapes. The compatibility of a shape Z with a type T, written $Z \leq T$, is defined as follows:

$$[\text{INT}] \; \frac{}{Z^R \leq \text{int}} \qquad\qquad [\text{PTR}] \; \frac{Z \leq T}{\text{ptr } Z \leq \text{ptr } T} \qquad\qquad [\text{REF}] \; \frac{Z \leq T}{\text{ref}_\rho \, Z \leq \text{ref } T}$$

$$[\text{FUN}] \; \frac{Z_i \leq T_i \text{ for } i \in [0, n]}{\text{ref}_{\rho_1} \, Z_1 \times \cdots \times \text{ref}_{\rho_n} \, Z_n \xrightarrow{\xi} Z_0 \;\; \leq \;\; T_1 \times \cdots \times T_n \;\; \to \;\; T_0}$$

Intuitively, shape-type compatibility requires that the given shape and type are structurally equivalent (rules [PTR] and [REF]), with two exceptions. First, any r-value shape is compatible with the integer type. The relations $\bot \leq \text{int}$, $\text{ptr } Z \leq \text{int}$, and $\zeta \leq \text{int}$ are subsumed by rule [INT]. In other words, integer values can be used to encode arbitrary r-value objects at runtime, when they are used as pointers. Second, function shapes capture the storage location of function parameters, thus they are reference shapes, which is ignored by function types (rule [FUN]).

Environments and Shape Schemes. An environment Γ maps variables x to their reference shapes: $\Gamma(x) = \text{ref}_\rho \, Z$; and function variables f to *function shape schemes*:

$$\Gamma(f) = \forall \, \overline{v}. \; \text{ref}_{\rho_0} \, (Z_1^L \times \cdots \times Z_n^L \xrightarrow{\varphi} Z_0^R) \qquad \text{where } \rho_0 \notin \overline{v}$$

A function shape scheme is a function shape quantified over shape, region, and effect variables v for which the function poses no constraints. We say that the function is *polymorphic* on such variables, which should occur free in the function shape (i.e. they are mentioned in $Z_1^L \times \cdots \times Z_n^L \xrightarrow{\varphi} Z_0^R$). As such, these variables are parameters that can be appropriately instantiated at each call site. If φ is of the form $\varphi' \cup \xi_0$ where $\xi_0 \in \overline{\xi}$, we say that f is effect-polymorphic: the effect of f is extended by the instantiation of ξ_0. In general, it is unsound to generalize reference types [48], but we can safely generalize function references because they are immutable. The memory region ρ_0 identifies the function; it is used to track calls to it through function pointers, and it cannot be generalized (thus $\rho_0 \notin \overline{v}$).

3.3   Shape-and-Effect Inference

L-values. Judgment $\Gamma \vdash_L L : \text{ref}_\rho \, Z \; \& \; \varphi$ (Fig. 3a) specifies that, under environment Γ, the l-value expression L has shape $\text{ref}_\rho \, Z$, and evaluating it results in effects φ. The shape of a variable x is obtained directly from the environment (rule [VAR]). Pointer dereferencing proceeds by evaluating an expression E, obtaining a shape, from which we drop the pointer constructor obtaining a reference shape (rule [DEREF]). Dereferencing has no effects by itself, but transfers the effects φ from evaluating E. The shape of a function variable f is obtained by appropriately instantiating its shape scheme (rule [FUN]). This instance is generated by substituting quantified variables with concrete shapes, regions and effects. In a typing derivation, these will depend on the calling context: the actual parameters passed to the function, and the expected shape of the function's return value in that context.

(a) Inference rules for l-value expressions, $\vdash_L \subseteq$ ENV $\times$ L-VALUE $\times$ SHAPE $\times$ EFFECT.

$$[\text{VAR}] \frac{\Gamma(x) = \text{ref}_\rho \, Z}{\Gamma \vdash_L x : \text{ref}_\rho \, Z \,\&\, \emptyset} \qquad\qquad [\text{DEREF}] \frac{\Gamma \vdash_E E : \text{ptr ref}_\rho \, Z \,\&\, \varphi}{\Gamma \vdash_L *E : \text{ref}_\rho \, Z \,\&\, \varphi}$$

$$[\text{FUN}] \frac{\Gamma(f) = \forall \overline{\zeta} \, \overline{\rho} \, \overline{\xi}. \, \text{ref}_{\rho_0} \, Z \qquad Z = Z_1^L \times \cdots \times Z_n^L \xrightarrow{\varphi} Z_0^R}{\Gamma \vdash_L f : \text{ref}_{\rho_0} \, (Z[\zeta \mapsto Z'][\rho \mapsto \rho'][\xi \mapsto \varphi']) \,\&\, \emptyset}$$

(b) Inference rules for r-value expressions, $\vdash_E \subseteq$ ENV $\times$ EXP $\times$ SHAPE $\times$ EFFECT.

$$[\text{INT}] \frac{}{\Gamma \vdash_E n : Z \,\&\, \emptyset} \qquad\qquad [\text{ADD}] \frac{\Gamma \vdash_E E_1 : Z \,\&\, \varphi_1 \qquad \Gamma \vdash_E E_2 : Z \,\&\, \varphi_2}{\Gamma \vdash_E E_1 + E_2 : Z \,\&\, \varphi_1 \cup \varphi_2}$$

$$[\text{IF}] \frac{\Gamma \vdash_E E_0 : Z_0 \,\&\, \varphi_0 \qquad \Gamma \vdash_E E_1 : Z \,\&\, \varphi_1 \qquad \Gamma \vdash_E E_2 : Z \,\&\, \varphi_2}{\Gamma \vdash_E \text{ if } (E_0) \; E_1 \text{ else } E_2 : Z \,\&\, \varphi_0 \cup \varphi_1 \cup \varphi_2}$$

$$[\text{NEW}] \frac{\Gamma \vdash_E E_1 : Z_1 \,\&\, \varphi_1 \qquad Z_1 \leq T \qquad \Gamma, x : \text{ref}_\rho \, Z_1 \vdash_E E_2 : Z_2 \,\&\, \varphi_2}{\Gamma \vdash_E \text{ new } x \,:\, T = E_1; E_2 : Z_2 \,\&\, \varphi_1 \cup \{write_\rho\} \cup \varphi_2}$$

$$[\text{FETCH}] \frac{\Gamma \vdash_L L : \text{ref}_\rho \, Z \,\&\, \varphi}{\Gamma \vdash_E !L : Z \,\&\, \varphi \cup \{read_\rho\}} \qquad\qquad [\text{ADDR}] \frac{\Gamma \vdash_L L : \text{ref}_\rho \, Z \,\&\, \varphi}{\Gamma \vdash_E \&L : \text{ptr ref}_\rho \, Z \,\&\, \varphi}$$

$$[\text{ASSIGN}] \frac{\Gamma \vdash_L L : \text{ref}_\rho \, Z \,\&\, \varphi_1 \qquad \Gamma \vdash_E E_1 : Z \,\&\, \varphi_2 \qquad \Gamma \vdash_E E_2 : Z' \,\&\, \varphi_3}{\Gamma \vdash_E L := E_1; E_2 : Z' \,\&\, \varphi_1 \cup \varphi_2 \cup \{write_\rho\} \cup \varphi_3}$$

$$[\text{DEF}] \frac{\begin{array}{c} \Gamma; x_1 : \text{ref}_{\rho_1} \, Z_1; \cdots ; x_n : \text{ref}_{\rho_n} \, Z_n \vdash_E E_0 : Z_0 \,\&\, \varphi_0 \\ Z_f = \text{ref}_{\rho_1} \, Z_1 \times \cdots \times \text{ref}_{\rho_n} \, Z_n \xrightarrow{\varphi_0} Z_0 \qquad \overline{v} = \text{FreeVars}(Z_f) \setminus \text{FreeVars}(\Gamma) \\ \Gamma' = \Gamma; f : \forall \overline{v}. \, \text{ref}_{\rho_0} \, Z_f \qquad \Gamma' \vdash_E E' : Z' \,\&\, \varphi' \qquad Z_i \leq T_i / i \in [0, n] \end{array}}{\Gamma \vdash_E \text{ fun } T_0 \; f(T_1 \; x_1, \cdots, T_n \; x_n) = E_0; E' : Z' \,\&\, \varphi'}$$

$$[\text{CALL}] \frac{\begin{array}{c} \Gamma \vdash_L L_0 : \text{ref}_{\rho_0} \, (\text{ref}_{\rho_1} \, Z_1 \times \cdots \times \text{ref}_{\rho_n} \, Z_n \xrightarrow{\varphi'} Z_0) \,\&\, \varphi_0 \\ \Gamma \vdash_E E_i : Z_i \,\&\, \varphi_i / i \in [1, n] \end{array}}{\Gamma \vdash_E L_0(E_1, \cdots, E_n) : Z_0 \,\&\, \varphi_0 \cup (\bigcup_{i \in [1,n]} \varphi_i) \cup \{call_{\rho_0}\} \cup \varphi'}$$

$$[\text{SUB}] \frac{\Gamma \vdash_E E : Z \,\&\, \varphi' \qquad \varphi' \sqsubseteq \varphi}{\Gamma \vdash_E E : Z \,\&\, \varphi} \qquad\qquad [\text{CAST}] \frac{\Gamma \vdash_E E : Z \,\&\, \varphi \qquad Z \leq T}{\Gamma \vdash_E (T)E : Z \,\&\, \varphi}$$

Fig. 3. Shape-and-effect inference system.

R-values. The judgment $\Gamma \vdash_E E : Z \,\&\, \varphi$ (Fig. 3b) specifies that, under environment Γ, r-value expression E has shape Z, and side effects φ.

Scalars. A constant n is given an arbitrary shape Z (rule [INT]). Each use of a constant can receive a different shape depending on the surrounding context. The shape of an integer is unknown *a priori* and depends on how this integer value is used by the program. For instance, in a expression like `ptr + 1`, where `ptr` is a pointer variable, constant `1` would be given the same shape as `ptr`. The effect of scalar addition is the combined effect of evaluating its operands (rule [ADD]). Both operands must have the same shape. Arithmetic between pointers with incompatible shapes is disallowed.

Conditionals. Both alternatives of an *if* conditional contribute to the effect of the entire expression (rule [IF]). In a particular execution, either E_1 or E_2 will be evaluated, but not both. The union of all three effects is a flow-insensitive *over*-approximation. (Loops, which we have omitted in this presentation, are treated analogously.) Both branches shall have the same shape, which is also the shape of the overall expression.

References. The **new** operator allocates a reference cell in a region ρ (rule [NEW]). The shape of the initializer expression E_1 must be compatible with the type T of x. Fetching the value stored in a reference returns an object of the expected shape, and produces a read effect on the corresponding memory region (rule [FETCH]). Given a reference cell, the computation of the memory address of such cell is side-effect free (rule [ADDR]). Assignment writes the result of evaluating an expression E_1 into a memory location denoted by L (rule [ASSIGN]). This requires evaluating both expressions, which introduces effects φ_1 and φ_2. Left- and right-hand side must be of the same shape. Hence, given a pointer assignment like **ptr = &x;**, this system considers that ***ptr** and **x** alias. In addition, we record the effect of writing to memory region ρ.

Functions. When introducing a function definition (rule [DEF]) we analyze the body E_0 under a new environment, where each parameter x_i is given a shape $\mathsf{ref}_{\rho_i}\ Z_i$. This shape Z_i should be chosen according to the use of x_i in E_0, and must be compatible with its type, T_i. The shape (Z_0) and effects (φ_0) of evaluating E_0 constitute the result shape and latent effects of f, respectively. The shape of function f is generalized over $\overline{v}$ and added to the scope of E'. Variables $\overline{v}$ must be unique to f and hence cannot occur in Γ. The C(IL) version of this type system [1] handles recursive definitions through monomorphic recursion. Function application takes a function reference L_0 and a tuple of arguments of the right shape (rule [CALL]). Calls to functions are recorded with calling $call_{\rho_0}$ effects, where region ρ_0 identifies the callee. The latent effects φ' of the function are recorded as potential side-effects of the invocation. A particular application may perform only a subset of these effects, but cannot perform any effect outside φ'.

Subsumption. It is always safe to enlarge the set of effects inferred for an expression (rule [SUB]). Consider two function variables: f with shape $\mathsf{ref}_{\rho_0}\ (\langle\rangle \xrightarrow{read_{\rho_1}} \bot)$ and g with shape $\mathsf{ref}_{\rho_0}\ (\langle\rangle \xrightarrow{write_{\rho_1}} \bot)$, where $\langle\rangle$ is the empty tuple. Without subsumption we could not write a program like **if (*) &f else &g**. Functions f and g perform different kinds of effects (one reads from and the other writes to ρ_1) and hence their shapes are not equal, as required by rule [IF]. With subsumption, we can enlarge the latent effects of f with $write_{\rho_1}$ and the latent effects of g with $read_{\rho_1}$, so that their shapes match—now both having latent effects $\{read_{\rho_1}, write_{\rho_1}\}$.

Type Casts. In this system, type casts are reduced to shape-type compatibility checks (rule [CAST]). A type cast is allowed only if the shape Z of the expression is compatible with the target type T. Type casts between integer and compatible pointer types, often used to work around type genericity, are correctly handled by this system. Casts that are not generally sensible are rejected, for instance, casting between pointers to functions with different number of arguments.

Principality. We have not proven principality of the inference system. However the original work of Talpin-Jouvelot [47] does guarantee principality, and we have followed their method closely. We have no reason to believe that the same does not hold here.

Soundiness. Our inference system for C(IL) was deliberately made unsound, to gain in simplicity and in precision. This is a necessary trade-off for a bug finding technique [33]. For instance, analyzing the Linux kernel, we have found some complex pointer usage that leads to cycles in the inferred shapes, and also casts between incompatible structure types. We approximate cyclic shapes, and accept any type cast, at the cost of missing aliasing relations. We invite the reader to look at the CIL formulation of our inference system for more details [1]. In any case, our implementation produces an effect-based abstraction for any program that the compiler accepts.

4   Effect-Based Bug Finding

We propose the following bug-finding method based on the inference system presented in Sect. 3, which we have implemented in the EBA tool and evaluated in Sect. 5.

1. Specification of Effects for Basic Operations. We axiomatize the behavior of each relevant operation f with a signature of the form $\overline{Z_i^L} \xrightarrow{\varphi} Z_0$ (cf. Sect. 3.2). The axiom specifies shapes of the input arguments expected by the function (references $\overline{Z_i^L}$), the shape of the output produced by the function (Z_0), and the effects of executing the function (φ). For example, to find the double-lock bug of Fig. 1, we specify the operations spin_lock (effect $lock_\rho$) and spin_unlock (effect $unlock_\rho$) with the following:

$$\text{spin\_lock}: \qquad \text{ref}_{\rho_1} \text{ ptr ref}_{\rho_2} \zeta \xrightarrow{lock_{\rho_2}} \bot \tag{1}$$

$$\text{spin\_unlock}: \qquad \text{ref}_{\rho_1} \text{ ptr ref}_{\rho_2} \zeta \xrightarrow{unlock_{\rho_2}} \bot \tag{2}$$

These signatures specify that the functions spin_lock and spin_unlock receive a pointer as argument (stored as formal parameter in ρ_1) which points to some object stored in ρ_2; the effects above the function arrows indicate that the operations respectively *lock* and *unlock* the object in ρ_2. The shape of the object in question is not relevant and thus has been abstracted away by a shape variable ζ. Note that variables ρ_1, ρ_2, and ζ are local to each signature, and implicitly universally quantified.

2. Shape-and-effect Inference. Following Jouvelot and Talpin [29] we derived an inference algorithm from the declarative system of Sect. 3 (a classical example is the derivation of Damas-Milner's *Algorithm W* [18]). Essentially, we distributed the effect of the non syntax-directed rule [SUB], and replaced guesses with meta variables and constraints. We use the obtained algorithm to infer the memory shapes and aliasing relationships of all program variables, and the effects for all statements. Each function is assigned a shape-and-effect signature, which establishes aliasing relationships between inputs and outputs, and provides a flow-insensitive summary of its observable behavior.

3. Effect-CFG Abstraction. We construct the *Effect-based Control-Flow Graph* (φ-CFG) of the program as in Fig. 1. We begin with a standard CFG, where nodes represent program locations and edges specify the control-flow. We distinguish branching decisions (diamond nodes), atomic operations (circles), function calls (dotted squares), and *return* statements (double-circles). A φ-CFG is an effect-abstraction of a program obtained from the standard CFG by annotating variables with their memory shapes, and nodes with the effects inferred for the corresponding locations. Function call nodes hold a flow-insensitive over-approximation of the callee's behavior. This abstraction can be refined, if needed, by inlining the callee's φ-CFG into the caller's φ-CFG (cf. Fig. 1).

4. Specification of Bug Patterns. We express bug patterns using existential Computational Tree Logic (CTL) formulae with effects as atomic propositions. The formulae must describe incorrect execution paths. In our example, an execution containing a double-lock bug can be matched using the following CTL formula:

$$\top \; \mathsf{EU} \; (lock_\rho \; \wedge \; \mathsf{EX} \; (\neg unlock_\rho \; \mathsf{EU} \; lock_\rho)) \tag{3}$$

The region ρ works as a meta variable specifying that we are interested in finding a second lock on the *same* memory object, rather than two unrelated lock calls. As shown in Fig. 1, this formula reveals buggy execution paths of the form:

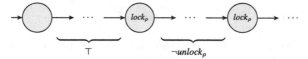

5. Model Checking. Matching execution patterns representing bugs can be reduced to the standard CTL model-checking problem for dual safety formulae over the φ-CFG graph. A φ-CFG is interpreted as a transition system where program statements act as states, and effects act as propositions. For instance, a proposition $lock_\rho$ holds in a state (statement) S_i iff the effects of S_i include $lock_\rho$. The dual property, testifying absence of double-locks, for the example above is AG $(lock_\rho \; \Rightarrow \; \mathsf{AX} \; (unlock_\rho \; \mathsf{AR} \; \neg lock_\rho))$.

We analyze each function's φ-CFG separately, in a modular fashion, relying on the effect-summaries of called functions. A *match* (a counterexample of the safety property) is a bug candidate represented by an *error trace*. If no counterexample is found, we may regard the function as "correct" only if no complex use of pointers is involved (e.g., the use of `container_of` macro in Linux). In general, some complex cases are handled unsoundly, and hence bugs may be missed. This is part of a necessary trade-off [33].

6. Abstraction Refinement. Our function summaries are flow-insensitive, so a match may be inconclusive. For instance, in Fig. 1 we first model-check `add_dquot_ref` independently of `inode_get_rsv_space` and obtain the following bug candidate:

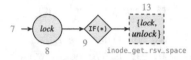

Yet, in this match, the second lock acquisition happens at node 13, which is a call to `inode_get_rsv_space`. As reflected in its signature, function `inode_get_rsv_space` both acquires and releases the lock, but the order of these operations is unknown when model-checking `add_dquot_ref`. In such a case, we *refine* the effect-abstraction of `add_dquot_ref` by inlining the call to `inode_get_rsv_space`. The model-checker resumes the search on the refined φ-CFG and a new match, this time conclusive, is found (cf. Fig. 1). This inlining strategy is a simple form of Counter Example Guided Abstraction Refinement (CEGAR) [14]. It allows us to support precise inter-procedural bug finding with a very simple effect language—which otherwise would have to capture ordering.

Other types of bugs. Notice that this technique is fairly general. It can be instructed to find other kinds of resource manipulation bugs using different bug patterns. For example:

$$\text{double free} \qquad \top \text{ EU } (\textit{free}_\rho \wedge \text{ EX } (\neg \textit{alloc}_\rho \text{ EU } \textit{free}_\rho)) \qquad (1)$$

$$\text{memory leak} \qquad \top \text{ EU } (\textit{alloc}_\rho \wedge \text{ EX EG } \neg \textit{free}_\rho) \qquad (2)$$

$$\text{use before initialization} \qquad \neg \textit{init}_\rho \text{ EU } \textit{use}_\rho \qquad (3)$$

5 Evaluation

Our objective is to assess the *effectiveness* and *scalability* of our bug-finding technique. For this purpose, we have implemented a prototype static analyzer, EBA, that realizes the bug-finding method described in Sect. 4.

Implementation. EBA is implemented in OCAML and built on top of the CIL [36] front-end infrastructure. We use CIL to generate the CFG of the program, and subsequently decorate it with the inferred shapes and effects. A custom reachability engine matches patterns, of the form P EU Q, against the decorated CFG of each function; a trace is returned upon a match. This engine can perform function inlining on demand. A *bug checker* is a small script that combines reachability queries to search for specific bug patterns. The source code of EBA is publicly available under an open-source license.[6]

---

[6] https://github.com/iagoabal/eba/.

Method. We measure the performance of EBA in terms of analysis time and bugs found. We compare EBA against similar bug-finding tools on (1) a benchmark of historical Linux bugs (Sect. 5.1) and (2) the set of device drivers shipped with Linux 4.7 (Sect. 5.2). For simplicity, we only target one type of bug: *double locks.* (Yet our technique is general and can find other types of bugs, see Sect. 4.) Locking bugs are a good representative of resource mis-manipulation, they are introduced regularly, and often have bad consequences for the user (e.g. a device driver hangs). Double-lock checkers are also part of many research tools that have used the Linux kernel for evaluation [24, 39, 51].

Subjects. We compare EBA against SMATCH and COCCINELLE, two tools that are popular within the Linux kernel community. SMATCH is developed and used at Oracle. COCCINELLE is a program matching and transformation tool, but it is also used as a bug finder [12] and a double-lock checker is shipped with the Linux distribution.[7]

We selected these two baseline tools for two reasons. First, they are able to run out-of-the-box on the source code of Linux, without major adaptation or further research. Second, there exist double-lock checkers tailored to the Linux kernel available for both of them. Neither CPPCHECK, CLANG STATIC ANALYZER, nor INFER ship with a double-lock checker, so they could not be used for an independent comparison. SPARSE and CQUAL both require modifications to the analyzed source code. Finally, we excluded SATURN, which we could not build against a recent version of OCAML.

Reproducibility. Evaluation artifacts and detailed instructions are available online.[8] All experiments have been conducted on a virtualized machine with a physical 8-core (16-thread) Intel Xeon E5-2660 v3 CPU, running at 2.6 GHz and with 16 GB of RAM.

5.1   Performance on a Benchmark of Historical Linux Bugs

Setup. We evaluate our tool on a benchmark of 26 known double-lock bugs extracted from historical bug fixes in the Linux kernel. In establishing this benchmark, we first obtained a set of 77 candidates by selecting all commits containing the phrase *"double lock"* in its message.[9] We filtered out 30 cases of false positives (i.e., commits not fixing a double-lock bug), and 18 cases of bugs spanning multiple files. To avoid bias, we removed two commits (3c13ab1 and 1d23d16) that were fixes to bugs found by EBA. However, we kept any bug-fix derived from the other two contenders.

For the 27 remaining commits, we obtained a preprocessed version (under 64-bit x86 *allyes* configuration) of the file where each bug is located. This step excluded one file (commit 553f809) that failed to preprocess. For COCCINELLE,

---

[7] At `scripts/coccinelle/locks/double_lock.cocci`.

[8] https://github.com/iagoabal/2017-vmcai.

[9] Extracted from the Linux kernel's Git repository as of August 3, 2016.

Table 1. Comparison of EBA, SMATCH, and COCCINELLE on 26 historical double-lock bugs in Linux. Times in gray strikeout font indicate that the bug was *not* found by the tool.

bug		TIME (seconds)			bug		TIME (seconds)		
hash ID	depth	E	S	C	hash ID	depth	E	S	C
00dfff7	2	5.0	~~1.5~~	~~0.1~~	1173ff0	0	0.6	1.3	0.1
5c51543	2	2.3	~~1.5~~	~~0.3~~	149a051	0	~~0.7~~	~~0.6~~	~~0.3~~
b383141	2	~~6.1~~	~~2.9~~	~~0.3~~	16da4b1	0	0.4	0.8	0.1
1c81557	1	5.0	~~1.9~~	~~0.6~~	344e3c7	0	0.7	1.3	~~0.1~~
328be39	1	8.9	~~1.7~~	~~0.2~~	2904207	0	5.8	2.0	~~2.8~~
5a276fa	1	~~0.9~~	~~1.2~~	~~0.2~~	59a1264	0	0.2	0.6	0.1
80edb72	1	~~6.3~~	~~2.1~~	~~0.7~~	5ad8b7d	0	0.6	3.4	0.1
872c782	1	1.7	~~2.8~~	~~1.9~~	8860168	0	0.7	1.0	0.1
d7e9711	1	21	~~1.3~~	~~2.7~~	a7eef88	0	0.6	1.2	0.2
023160b	0	1.0	2.6	~~0.1~~	b838396	0	3.3	2.8	1.1
09dc3cf	0	1.2	~~1.4~~	~~0.1~~	ca9fe15	0	0.4	~~0.7~~	1.8
0adb237	0	1.1	1.5	0.2	e1db4ce	0	0.4	1.1	0.2
0e6f989	0	0.4	1.0	0.3	e50fb58	0	0.5	0.9	0.1

we retain the original source file, since it is designed to run on unprocessed C files. We then verified that the alleged bug was indeed present in this particular configuration. Thus, we arrived at a benchmark of 26 double-lock bugs from Linux.

Results. Table 1 shows the results of running EBA, SMATCH, and COCCINELLE on this benchmark. We identify each bug by the commit that fixes it, and we group bugs by *depth*. The depth of a bug corresponds to the number of function calls involved from the first to the second acquisition of the lock, e.g. the bug of Fig. 1 involves one function call and therefore has depth one. For instance, for the first bug in the table, 00dfff7, EBA takes five seconds (5.0) and correctly reports the bug. SMATCH and COCCINELLE take 1.5 and 0.1 seconds respectively, yet are unable to find the bug.

Regarding *effectiveness*, we observe that EBA finds 22 out of the 26 bugs. In comparison, SMATCH and COCCINELLE find 14 and 12 bugs respectively. More specifically, EBA finds six out of the nine interprocedural bugs (depth one or more), whereas SMATCH and COCCINELLE do not manage to find any at all. For the remaining 17 intraprocedural bugs (depth zero), EBA finds all but one (16 out of 17). Remarkably, any bug found by either SMATCH or COCCINELLE, is also intercepted by EBA. Thus, on this benchmark, EBA *is more effective at finding double-lock bugs* than its contenders.

Regarding *false negatives*, we observe that EBA misses five bugs due to limitations in our pointer analysis. This happens, for instance, when the lock object is obtained through the Linux container_of macro (defined in include/linux/kernel.h). For SMATCH, false negatives seem to be due to path-insensitivity and lack of inter-procedural support. COCCINELLE lacks inter-procedural support and, in addition, its double-lock checker does not recognize some common locking functions. All three bug finders make the assumption that the formal parameters of a function do not alias one another—as indeed mostly the case; and thus, all three tools missed bug 149a051.

Regarding *analysis time*, we observe that, for the bugs that all three tools find, EBA is on average about 1.4 times faster than SMATCH, yet COCCINELLE is about five times faster than EBA. Note, however, that SMATCH is checking for more bugs than double locks. Also, EBA and SMATCH analyze a total of 665 KLOC of *preprocessed* C code, whereas COCCINELLE analyzes only 27 KLOC of *unprocessed* C files. In this benchmark, all bugs can be found without including headers, which is an advantage for COCCINELLE. We also observe that variance of execution times is higher for EBA, with six files taking more than five seconds to analyze, and one file taking 21 seconds. These files contain large functions that manipulate multiple locks and, as of now, EBA will check one lock object at a time. We foresee that EBA will speed up considerably with some optimization work, e.g. by performing multiple checks in a single traversal.

5.2   Performance of Analyzing Device Drivers in Linux 4.7

Setup. We use EBA to analyze widely the entire `drivers/` directory of Linux in search of double-lock bugs. EBA was run on the Linux 4.7-rc1 kernel in the 64-bit x86 *allyes* configuration, invoked by Kbuild during a parallel build process with 16 jobs (i.e., `make -j16`). About nine thousand files in `drivers/` were analyzed, and we manually classified each one of the bugs reported, as either a true or a false positive. We repeated this process for SMATCH and COCCINELLE, to confront analysis times and number of false positives. All tools were given 30 seconds to analyze each file.

Results. EBA reported nine bugs in nine different files (i.e., 0.1% of the files analyzed). *Five* of these bug reports have been reported and *confirmed* by the respective Linux maintainers, and *three are now fixed* in Linux 4.9 (see commits 1d23d16, e50525b and bea6403).[10] These bugs affected some TTY, SCSI, USB, Intel IOMMU, and Atheros wireless drivers. The five bugs had depth one or more, and required an inter-procedural analyzer. (SMATCH and COCCINELLE found no bugs, but that is somewhat expected because, presumably, any bugs would have already been reported and fixed.)

EBA analyzes all Linux drivers in *less than half an hour* (23 min) and is only slightly slower than SMATCH which does the same in 16 min (1.4 times faster than EBA). COCCINELLE is significantly faster and completes the analysis in only two minutes, as it scans much smaller unprocessed files.

We classified four of the nine bugs reported by EBA as false positives. Three cases were due to limitations in our pointer analysis, and in one case the reported

---

[10] Bug e50525b was independently found and fixed during beta testing, but that bug-fix was unknown to us.

error trace was not a feasible execution path. One of the false positives reported by EBA still led to a cosmetic fix (see 3e70af8). Both SMATCH and COCCINELLE report more false positives (eight and six, respectively). It is worth noting that, at least in eight of these cases, there was an *unlock* operation being performed through a nested function call—that these tools were not aware of.

6 Conclusion

We have presented a two-step bug-finding technique that uncovers deep resource manipulation bugs in systems-level software. This technique is lightweight and easily scales up to large code bases, such as the Linux kernel. First, a *shape-and-effect* inference system is used to build an abstraction of the program to analyze (Sect. 3). In this abstraction, objects are described by memory *shapes*, and expressions and statements by their operational *effects*. Second, bugs are found by matching temporal bug-patterns against the control-flow graph of this program abstraction (Sect. 4).

We have implemented our technique in a prototype bug finder, EBA, and demonstrated the effectiveness and scalability of our approach (Sect. 5). We have compared the performance of EBA with respect to two bug-finders popular within the Linux community: COCCINELLE and SMATCH. On a benchmark of 26 historical Linux bugs, EBA was able to detect strictly more bugs, and more complex, than the other two tools. EBA is able to analyze nine thousand files of Linux device drivers in less than half an hour, in which time it uncovers five previously unknown bugs. So far, EBA has found *more than a dozen double-lock bugs* in Linux 4.7–4.9 releases, eight of which have already been confirmed, and six are fixed upstream.

References

1. Abal, I.: Shape-region and effect inference for C(IL). Technical report (2016)
2. Abal, I., Brabrand, C., Wasowski, A.: 42 variability bugs in the Linux kernel: A qualitative analysis. In: ASE 2014 (2014)
3. Ball, T., Majumdar, R., Millstein, T., Rajamani, S.K.: Automatic predicate abstraction of C programs. In: PLDI 2001 (2001)
4. Ball, T., Rajamani, S.K.: Bebop: a path-sensitive interprocedural dataflow engine. In: PASTE 2001 (2001)
5. Ball, T., Rajamani, S.K.: The SLAM toolkit. In: CAV 2001 (2001)
6. Banning, J.P.: An efficient way to find the side effects of procedure calls and the aliases of variables. In: POPL 1979 (1979)
7. Berdine, J., Calcagno, C., O'Hearn, P.W.: Smallfoot: Modular automatic assertion checking with separation logic. In: FMCO 2005 (2005)
8. Beyer, D., Henzinger, T.A., Jhala, R., Majumdar, R.: The software model checker BLAST: applications to software engineering. Int. J. Softw. Tools Technol. Transf. 9(5), 505–525 (2007)
9. Birkedal, L., Torp-Smith, N., Reynolds, J.C.: Local reasoning about a copying garbage collector. In: POPL 2004 (2004)

10. Brown, F., Nötzli, A., Engler, D.: How to build static checking systems using orders of magnitude less code. In: ASPLOS 2016 (2016)
11. Brunel, J., Doligez, D., Hansen, R.R., Lawall, J.L., Muller, G.: A foundation for flow-based program matching: using temporal logic and model checking. In: POPL 2009 (2009)
12. Chen, Y., Wu, F., Yu, K., Zhang, L., Chen, Y., Yang, Y., Mao, J.: Instant bug testing service for Linux kernel. In: HPCC/EUC 2013 (2013)
13. Clarke, E., Kroening, D., Lerda, F.: A tool for checking ANSI-C programs (2004)
14. Clarke, E.M., Grumberg, O., Jha, S., Lu, Y., Veith, H.: Counterexample-guided abstraction refinement. In: CAV 2000 (2000)
15. Cooper, K.D., Kennedy, K.: Efficient computation of flow insensitive interprocedural summary information. In: SIGPLAN 1984 (1984)
16. Cooper, K.D., Kennedy, K.: Interprocedural side-effect analysis in linear time. In: PLDI 1988 (1988)
17. Cousot, P., Cousot, R., Feret, J., Mauborgne, L., Miné, A., Rival, X.: Why does Astrée scale up? Form. Methods Syst. Des. **35**(3), 229–264 (2009)
18. Damas, L., Milner, R.: Principal type-schemes for functional programs. In: POPL 1982 (1982)
19. Darwin, I.F.: Checking C Programs with Lint. O'Reilly, Sebastopol (1986)
20. Das, M.: Unification-based pointer analysis with directional assignments. In: PLDI 2000 (2000)
21. Engler, D., Chelf, B., Chou, A., Hallem, S.: Checking system rules using system-specific, programmer-written compiler extensions. In: OSDI 2000 (2000)
22. Foster, J.S., Fähndrich, M., Aiken, A.: Polymorphic versus monomorphic flow-insensitive points-to analysis for C. In: Palsberg, J. (ed.) SAS 2000. LNCS, vol. 1824, pp. 175–198. Springer, Heidelberg (2000). doi:10.1007/978-3-540-45099-3_10
23. Foster, J.S., Johnson, R., Kodumal, J., Aiken, A.: Flow-insensitive type qualifiers. ACM Trans. Program. Lang. Syst. **28**(6), 1035–1087 (2006)
24. Foster, J.S., Terauchi, T., Aiken, A.: Flow-sensitive type qualifiers. In: PLDI 2002 (2002)
25. Hallem, S., Chelf, B., Xie, Y., Engler, D.: A system and language for building system-specific, static analyses. In: PLDI 2002. ACM (2002)
26. Hind, M.: Pointer analysis: Haven't we solved this problem yet? In: PASTE 2001 (2001)
27. Johnson, R., Wagner, D.: Finding user/kernel pointer bugs with type inference. In: Proceedings of the 13th Conference on USENIX Security Symposium, vol. 13, SSYM 2004, pp. 9–9, Berkeley, CA, USA, 2004. USENIX Association (2004)
28. Jouvelot, P., Gifford, D.: Algebraic reconstruction of types and effects. POPL 1991 (1991)
29. Jouvelot, P., Talpin, J.-P.: The type and effect discipline (1993)
30. Kiselyov, O., Shan, C.-C.: Lightweight monadic regions. Haskell (2008)
31. Lawall, J., Laurie, B., Hansen, R.R., Palix, N., Muller, G.: Finding error handling bugs in openssl using coccinelle. In: EDCC 2010 (2010)
32. Leijen, D.: Koka: programming with Row polymorphic Effect Types. In: MSFP 2014 (2014)
33. Livshits, B., Sridharan, M., Smaragdakis, Y., Lhoták, O., Amaral, J.N., Chang, B.-Y.E., Guyer, S.Z., Khedker, U.P., Møller, A., Vardoulakis, D.: In defense of soundiness: a manifesto. Commun. ACM **58**(2), 44–46 (2015)
34. Lucassen, J.M., Types, E.: Towards the integration of functional and imperative programming. Ph.D. thesis (1987)

35. Lucassen, J.M., Gifford, D.K.: Polymorphic effect systems. In: POPL 1988 (1988)
36. Necula, G.C., McPeak, S., Rahul, S.P., Weimer, W.: CIL: intermediate language and tools for analysis and transformation of C programs. In: CC 2002 (2002)
37. Nielson, F., Nielson, H.R.: Type and effect systems. In: Olderog, E.-R., Steffen, B. (eds.) Correct System Design. LNCS, vol. 1710, pp. 114–136. Springer, Heidelberg (1999). doi:10.1007/3-540-48092-7_6
38. Padioleau, Y., Lawall, J.L., Muller, G.: Understanding collateral evolution in Linux device drivers. In: EuroSys 2006 (2006)
39. Palix, N., Thomas, G., Saha, S., Calvès, C., Muller, G., Lawall, J.: Faults in Linux 2.6. ACM Trans. Comput. Syst. 32, 4:1–4:40 (2014)
40. Pratikakis, P., Foster, J.S., Hicks, M.: Locksmith: context-sensitive correlation analysis for race detection. In: PLDI 2006 (2006)
41. Remy, D.: Type inference for records in a natural extension of ML. In: Theoretical Aspects Of Object-Oriented Programming. MIT Press (1993)
42. Reps, T., Horwitz, S., Sagiv, M.: Precise interprocedural dataflow analysis via graph reachability. In: POPL 1995 (1995)
43. Smaragdakis, Y., Balatsouras, G.: Pointer analysis. Found. Trends Program. Lang. 2(1), 1–69 (2015)
44. Steensgaard, B.: Points-to analysis by type inference of programs with structures and unions. In: CC 1996 (1996)
45. Steensgaard, B.: Points-to analysis in almost linear time. In: POPL 1996 (1996)
46. Strom, R.E., Yemini, S.: Typestate: a programming language concept for enhancing software reliability. IEEE Trans. Softw. Eng. 2(1), 157–171 (1986)
47. Talpin, J.-P., Jouvelot, P.: Polymorphic type, region and effect inference. J. Funct. Program. 2, 7 (1992)
48. Tofte, M.: Type inference for polymorphic references. Inf. Comput. 89(1), 1–34 (1990)
49. Tofte, M., Talpin, J.-P.: Implementation of the typed call-by-value λ-calculus using a stack of regions. In: POPL 1994 (1994)
50. Wright, D.A.: A new technique for strictness analysis. In: TAPSOFT 1991 (1991)
51. Xie, Y., Aiken, A.: Scalable error detection using boolean satisfiability. In: POPL 2005 (2005)
52. Yong, S.H., Horwitz, S., Reps, T.: Pointer analysis for programs with structures and casting. In: PLDI 1999 (1999)

Synthesizing Non-Vacuous Systems

Roderick Bloem[1]([⊠]), Hana Chockler[2], Masoud Ebrahimi[1],
and Ofer Strichman[3]([⊠])

[1] Graz University of Technology
[2] King's College London
[3] Information Systems Engineering, IE, Technion
ofers@ie.technion.ac.il

Abstract. Vacuity detection is a common practice accompanying model checking of hardware designs. Roughly speaking, a system satisfies a specification vacuously if it can satisfy a stronger specification obtained by replacing some of its subformulas with stronger expressions. If this happens then part of the specification is immaterial, which typically indicates that there is a problem in the model or the specification itself.

We propose to apply the concept of vacuity to the synthesis problem. In synthesis, there is often a problem that the specifications are incomplete, hence under-specifying the desired behaviour, which may lead to a situation in which the synthesised system is different than the one intended by the designer. To address this problem we suggest an algorithm and a tool for *non-vacuous bounded synthesis*. It combines synthesis for universal and existential properties; the latter stems from the requirement to have at least one interesting witness for each strengthening of the specification. Even when the system satisfies the specification non-vacuously, our tool is capable of improving it by synthesizing a system that has additional interesting witnesses. The user decides when the system reflects their intent.

1 Introduction

Given a temporal specification φ, the goal of *reactive synthesis* [8, 16] is to build a transition system M such that $M \models \varphi$. The motivation of synthesis is clear: rather than building a design and then checking whether it adheres to the specification, focus on the specification alone, and generate automatically a design that satisfies it. In recent years, the theory and especially the tools for synthesis have made significant progress [10].

Along with the greater applicability of synthesis has come significant attention to the quality of the synthesized systems. Often, systems are underspecified, i.e., their specifications do not include certain desirable properties of the system. Hence, we can add an informal element to the definition of the synthesis problem, namely that it is to build a transition system M that in addition to satisfying the specification φ, it also captures the *designer's intent*. Automatically bridging this gap between the formal specification and the designer's intent is the topic of this article. Previous proposals to tackle incomplete specifications include

© Springer International Publishing AG 2017
A. Bouajjani and D. Monniaux (Eds.): VMCAI 2017, LNCS 10145, pp. 55–72, 2017.
DOI: 10.1007/978-3-319-52234-0_4

quantitative specifications to make it easier to specify certain properties [4] and synthesis of systems that are robust against environment errors, even if the way to react to such errors has not been specified explicitly [3,17].

In this paper we suggest a different approach, based on leveraging the notion of *vacuity* [2]. Our conjecture is that if the synthesized system M satisfies φ *non-vacuously*, then M is likely closer to the user's intent, because it satisfies φ in a more "meaningful" way. If our conjecture is right, then this can save some of the effort that is required from the user to complete and refine his/her specification. Consider, for example, the property

$$\varphi = \mathbf{G}\,(req \rightarrow \mathbf{F}\,grant). \tag{1}$$

A system M with one state satisfying $grant$ (regardless of req) satisfies φ, and is indeed a legitimate outcome of synthesising (1). However this system also satisfies stronger properties such as $\mathbf{G}\,\mathbf{F}\,grant$, and indeed it is not likely that M captures the user's intent: the intent is probably that the system also permits a path π in which there are no grants from a point in which there are no requests. When a system satisfies a property regardless of some of its subformulas, as in this example where the behavior of req is immaterial for the satisfaction of φ, we say that the specification is satisfied vacuously (see below a formal definition); in order for a system M to satisfy a property φ non-vacuously we need it to include desired paths like π that are called *interesting witnesses* [2]. These are executions that demonstrate non-vacuous satisfaction of the original property.

There are multiple definitions of vacuity in the literature [1,2,5,6,13,14], but the method that we will describe in this paper is independent of the chosen definition. Most commercially used vacuity-detection tools use the generalised definition by Kupferman and Vardi [13], which is what we will follow here: Let ψ be a subformula in φ. The *strengthening of φ with respect to ψ* is $\varphi[\psi \leftarrow \bot]$.[1] If $M \models \varphi[\psi \leftarrow \bot]$ then ψ is irrelevant for the satisfaction of φ in M, and we say that φ is satisfied in M vacuously with respect to ψ. It follows that M satisfies φ non-vacuously with respect to ψ iff $M \models \mathbf{E}\,\neg\varphi[\psi \leftarrow \bot]$. As shown in [13], it is sufficient to consider strengthenings of φ with respect to atomic propositions (literals, in fact) rather than all subformulas. We note that the definitions of vacuity in the literature, including [13], did not consider the division of the atomic propositions into inputs and outputs, as such division is immaterial in model-checking. As we argue later, in synthesis this division is in fact important.

Our synthesis method requires systems with at least one interesting witness for every possible strengthening of φ. More formally, if φ is a specification in LTL, a model M satisfies φ non vacuously if it satisfies a formula in a simple fragment of CTL* consisting of a conjunction of universal and existential formulas:

$$(M \models \mathbf{A}\,\varphi) \wedge \bigwedge_{\psi \in \mathrm{Lit}(\varphi)} (M \models \mathbf{E}\,\neg\varphi[\psi \leftarrow \bot])\,, \tag{2}$$

---

[1] This means that we swap ψ with **false** if ψ is in positive polarity, and with **true** otherwise. Hence, e.g., if $\varphi \equiv \psi_1 \Rightarrow \Psi_2$, then $\varphi[\psi_1 \leftarrow \bot] \equiv \psi_2$.

where Lit (φ) denotes the literals of φ. One of the contributions of this article is the extension of the *bounded synthesis* [9] algorithm to handle this fragment, based on a new ranking function (the original bounded synthesis algorithm handles only universal formulas).

Even when the system satisfies the specification non-vacuously, our tool is capable of improving it by synthesizing a system that has additional interesting witnesses. The user decides when the system reflects their intent. Thus, we define a partial order stating that system M' is less vacuous than M if it contains all of the interesting witnesses permitted by M and at least one more. This condition can be stated as a formula in the same fragment of CTL* mentioned above. Thus, we generate decreasingly vacuous systems up to *the least vacuous* system for a given number of states. In Sect. 5 we show that if the number of states is unbounded, then for some specifications the chain of less and less vacuous systems is infinite.

We have implemented the non-vacuous bounded synthesis algorithm on top of the PARTY synthesizer [12] which is available for download[2]. Given the informal goal we stated ("capturing the user's intent") naturally it is difficult to prove that our approach works, especially since there are no users in the industry that specify real system for the purpose of synthesis. Our experiments were based, then, on starting from previously published complete specifications, removing parts of them, and activating non-vacuous synthesis. In our experiments, which we describe in Sect. 5, the removed parts of the specification were compensated by our tool. In fact, the generated models not only satisfy the original, complete specifications, but they also realize them less vacuously.

A Motivating Example

We illustrate our ideas with a running example: a specification for an arbiter with two types of requests and two types of grants (i.e., φ_1 and φ_2) and a mutual exclusion between the grants (i.e., φ_3). The specification φ is a conjunction of the following three properties:

$$\varphi_1 = \mathbf{G}\,(r_1 \to \mathbf{F}\,g_1), \quad \varphi_2 = \mathbf{G}\,(r_2 \to \mathbf{F}\,g_2), \quad \varphi_3 = \mathbf{G}\,(\neg(g_1 \wedge g_2)), \quad (3)$$

where r_1 and r_2 are inputs (the 'requests') and g_1 and g_2 are outputs (the 'grants'). The smallest system M_0 satisfying φ, synthesised by our tool, is depicted in Fig. 1a. It consists of two states, s_0 and s_1, where in each state exactly one of the grants is up. It is easy to see that M_0 satisfies φ vacuously. In particular $M_0 \models \varphi_1[r_1 \leftarrow \bot]$ and $M_0 \models \varphi_2[r_2 \leftarrow \bot]$, where the $\bot$ value for r_1 and r_2 is **true** in both φ_1 and φ_2, respectively.

The system generated by our tool in the next step is M_1, depicted in Fig. 1b.[3] This system satisfies φ non-vacuously in all its subformulas. Indeed:

---

[2] www.iaik.tugraz.at/content/research/opensource/non-vacuous_systems.
[3] Note the unusual semantics of LTL on this figure: In the trace $\{g_2, r_1\}, \{g_1, r_1, r_2\}, \{g_2\}^\omega$, the request r_1 on the outgoing edge of s_1 is granted by the label g_1 on the state s_1 itself.

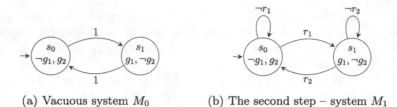

(a) Vacuous system M_0 (b) The second step – system M_1

Fig. 1. Systems of the running example.

1. $M_1 \not\models \varphi_1[r_1 \leftarrow \bot]$, as the path $\pi_1 = s_0^\omega$ corresponds to the output trace $(\neg g_1, g_2)^\omega$, which falsifies $\mathbf{G}\,\mathbf{F}\,g_1$;
2. $M_1 \not\models \varphi_2[r_2 \leftarrow \bot]$, as the path $\pi_1 = s_0, s_1^\omega$ corresponds to the output trace $(\neg g_1, g_2), (g_1, \neg g_2)^\omega$, which falsifies $\mathbf{G}\,\mathbf{F}\,g_2$;
3. the formulas obtained by replacing one of the grants with **false** are unrealisable, i. e., there is no system that can satisfy, for example, $G(\neg r_1)$ because we have no control over the inputs.

In Sect. 4, we discuss ways to improve the synthesised system by increasing the number of its non-vacuous traces. We illustrate these ideas on the results of the next iterations of the tool on our running example.

2 Preliminaries

2.1 Labeled Transition Systems

For the remainder of the paper, let us fix an input alphabet I and a disjoint output alphabet O, and let us define $\mathrm{AP} = I \cup O$, $\varUpsilon = 2^I$, $\varSigma = 2^O$, and $\varGamma = 2^{\mathrm{AP}}$. A *finite, $\varSigma$-labeled $\varUpsilon$-transition system* is a tuple $M = (S, s_0, \tau, o)$, where S is nonempty set of states, $s_0 \in S$ is the initial state, $\tau : S \times \varUpsilon \to S$ is a transition function, and $o : S \to \varSigma$ is a labelling function.

Definition 1 (Path). *A* path *of a transition system M, denoted by π, is an infinite sequence of states $s_0, s_1, \ldots \in S^\omega$ such that for $i > 0$ $\exists v \in \varUpsilon$. $s_i = \tau(s_{i-1}, v)$.*

We denote by $\mathrm{paths}_M(s)$ the set of all paths of M originating at $s \in S$, omitting M when it is clear from the context.

Definition 2 (Trace). *A* trace *corresponding to a path $\pi = s_0, s_1, \ldots$ of a transition system M, denoted $\mathrm{trace}(\pi)$, is an infinite word $v_0 \cup \sigma_0, v_1 \cup \sigma_1, \ldots$ over $\varGamma$, such that for $i \geq 0$, $s_{i+1} = \tau(s_i, v^i)$, and $\sigma^i = o(s_i)$.*

We denote by $\mathrm{traces}(M)$ the set of all traces of M. For an input trace $\pi \in \varUpsilon^\omega$, we denote by $M(\pi)$ the (unique) trace of M whose projection to $\varUpsilon^\omega$ equals π.

2.2   Temporal Logic

Throughout the paper, we denote by φ an LTL formula in negation normal form (NNF), over the set AP of atomic propositions [15]. The semantics of LTL is defined over AP with respect to infinite paths of M in a standard way. In this paper, we synthesise systems that satisfy the following simple fragment of CTL*:

$$\Phi ::= \mathbf{A}\,\varphi \mid \mathbf{E}\,\varphi \mid \Phi \wedge \Phi, \tag{4}$$

where φ is an LTL formula. The semantics of the universal and existential quantifiers over LTL formulas are defined as expected:

Definition 3. *For a state s of a transition system M,*

$$s \models \mathbf{A}\,\varphi \quad iff \quad \forall \pi \in \mathrm{paths}_M(s).\ \pi \models \varphi$$
$$s \models \mathbf{E}\,\varphi \quad iff \quad \exists \pi \in \mathrm{paths}_M(s).\ \pi \models \varphi.$$

A transition system M satisfies a formula ϕ, written $M \models \phi$, if its initial state s_0 does.

2.3   Nondeterministic Büchi Automata

An LTL formula can be represented by a nondeterministic Büchi automata [18]: a tuple $\mathcal{A} = (Q, q_0, \rho, \alpha)$, where Q is a finite set of states, $q_0 \in Q$ is the initial state, $\rho : Q \times \Upsilon \times \Sigma \to \mathcal{P}(Q)$ is the transition relation, and α is the set of accepting states; recall Σ and Υ are defined in Sect. 2.1.

Definition 4 (run). *Given an infinite word $\omega = \upsilon_0 \cup \sigma_0, \upsilon_1 \cup \sigma_1, \ldots$ over $2^{I \cup O}$, a corresponding* run *of an automaton $\mathcal{A}$, denoted by* run (w), *is an infinite path $\pi = q_0, q_1, \cdots \in Q^\omega$ where for all $i \geq 0$, $q_{i+1} \in \rho(q_i, \upsilon^i, \sigma^i)$.*

Definition 5 (accepting run). *An* accepting *run of $\mathcal{A}$ is a run that visits some accepting state infinitely often; a trace is accepted by $\mathcal{A}$ if it has a corresponding accepting run, and the language of $\mathcal{A}$ is the set of all accepted traces.*

From this point forward, we denote by $\mathcal{A}_\varphi$ the nondeterministic Büchi automata that accepts exactly the traces that satisfy φ.

2.4   Vacuity Detection

Informally speaking, a transition system M satisfies a property ψ *vacuously* if not all parts of φ are instrumental for the satisfaction of φ in M (in other words, M satisfies φ in a uninteresting way). As proved in [13], for subformulas that occur in the property only once (or multiple time with the same polarity), this is equivalent to checking the effect of replacing a subformula with $\perp$. Furthermore, if the property is in NNF, it is enough to check the effect of replacing atomic propositions with $\perp$. Hence, we use the following definition of vacuity that allows for efficient detection algorithm:

Definition 6 (Vacuity [2,13]**).** *A transition system* M *satisfies an LTL property* φ *vacuously iff* $M \models \varphi$ *and there exists a literal* ψ *(an atomic proposition or its negation) of* φ *such that* $M \models \varphi[\psi \leftarrow \bot]$, *where* $\varphi[\psi \leftarrow \bot]$ *denotes* φ *with* ψ *replaced by* $\bot$.

The formula $\varphi[\psi \leftarrow \bot]$ is a *strengthening* of φ since $\varphi[\psi \leftarrow \bot] \rightarrow \varphi$ and we call the negation $\varphi_\psi = \neg\varphi[\psi \leftarrow \bot]$ of a strengthening a *witness formula*. An trace π of M that satisfies φ_ψ is called an *interesting witness* for ψ, since it demonstrates that ψ is instrumental to the satisfaction of φ in M; π is an *interesting witness* of M if it is an interesting witness for some subformula ψ of φ.

The concept of witnesses and strengthenings is not restricted to Definition 6, and it lends itself, in theory, to other definitions of vacuity [1,6,7]. The framework proposed in this paper is orthogonal to the particular definition of vacuity, as long as the strengthenings are ω-regular.

2.5   Bounded Synthesis

Bounded synthesis is a method to construct a finite-state labeled transition system that not only satisfies a given temporal specification φ but also fulfills a constraint on its size [9]. The idea is to let an SMT solver synthesize a transition system M (i.e., choose the transitions between and the labeling of the given number of states), such that $M \times \mathcal{A}_{\neg\varphi}$ has an empty language.

The synchronous product $\mathcal{G}$ of a transition system $M = (S, s_0, \tau, o)$ and a Büchi automaton $\mathcal{A}_{\neg\varphi} = (Q, q_0, \rho, \alpha)$ is called the *run graph* of $\mathcal{A}_{\neg\varphi}$ on M.[4] The states of $\mathcal{G}$ are annotated with two functions: a reachability function $\lambda^{\mathbb{B}} : Q \times S \rightarrow \mathbb{B}$ and a ranking function $\lambda^{\#} : Q \times S \rightarrow C \subset \mathbb{N}$, where $C = \{0, \ldots, |Q| \times |S| - 1\}$. Annotations of $\mathcal{G}$ (i.e., $\lambda^{\#}$ and $\lambda^{\mathbb{B}}$ functions) are valid if they satisfy the following constraints. First, the initial state is reachable:

$$\lambda^{\mathbb{B}}(q_0, s_0) . \tag{5}$$

Second, the reachability predicate and the transition system are compatible:

$$\bigwedge_{\substack{q,q'\in Q \\ s,s'\in S \\ v\in \Upsilon}} \lambda^{\mathbb{B}}(q, s) \wedge q' \in \rho(q, o(s), v) \wedge s' \in \tau(s, v) \rightarrow \lambda^{\mathbb{B}}(q', s') . \tag{6}$$

Finally, the ranking function guarantees that the constraint is satisfiable only if the language of the run graph is empty: For *accepting* states, we require that the labelling on the target state is strictly larger than on the source (accepting) state:

$$\bigwedge_{\substack{q\in\alpha,q'\in Q \\ s,s'\in S \\ v\in\Upsilon}} \lambda^{\mathbb{B}}(q, s) \wedge q' \in \rho(q, o(s), v) \wedge s' \in \tau(s, v) \rightarrow \lambda^{\#}(q', s') > \lambda^{\#}(q, s) ; \tag{7}$$

---

[4] Since $\mathcal{G}$ is only used for checking emptiness, the labels are immaterial, and it is customary to use a one-letter automaton (i.e., $|\Sigma| = |\Upsilon| = 1$).

and for *non-accepting* states the labelling on the target states is larger or equal than on the source state:

$$\bigwedge_{\substack{q\in Q\setminus\alpha,q'\in Q \\ s,s'\in S \\ v\in\Upsilon}} \lambda^{\mathbb{B}}(q,s)\wedge q'\in\rho(q,o(s),v)\wedge s'\in\tau(s,v)\to\lambda^{\#}(q',s')\geq\lambda^{\#}(q,s) .$$

(8)

The intuition behind the ranking function is as follows: if the language is not empty, then there is an accepting path (i.e., a lasso-shaped path in the product automaton that includes an accepting state), and then it is impossible to satisfy these constraints over that path. This is because the ranks of states on the cycle cannot be strictly descending. The two automata in Fig. 2 illustrate this point—see caption. Hence, (5)–(8) are satisfiable if and only if the language of the product automaton is empty. The correctness of this construction was proven in [9].

Fig. 2. We can assign a number to each state on the left automaton, that satisfies the inequality constraints, e.g., the 0/1 values labeling the states. Such a labeling is impossible for the automaton on the right, because it has an accepting state in a loop.

Theorem 1 ([9]). *Given a Büchi automaton $\mathcal{A} = (Q, q_0, \rho, \alpha)$ constructed from $\neg\varphi$, transition system $M = (S, s_0, \tau, o)$ satisfies $\mathbf{A}\,\varphi$ iff it corresponds to a solution to the constraints (5)–(8).*

Initially, the LTL specification φ is negated and translated to a Büchi automaton $\mathcal{A}_{\neg\varphi}$. In the next step, (5)–(8) are solved with an SMT solver based on $\mathcal{A}_{\neg\varphi}$. Being unknown, τ, $\lambda^{\mathbb{B}}$, $\lambda^{\#}$ and o (the labeling function) are represented by uninterpreted functions; thus, the quest for finding M is reduced to the problem of satisfiability modulo finite integer arithmetic with uninterpreted functions.

3   Non-vacuous Bounded Synthesis

In this section we describe *non-vacuous bounded synthesis* – a method for constructing a finite-state labeled transition system that fulfils a constraint on its size and satisfies a given temporal specification non-vacuously.

3.1   A Specification for Non-Vacuous Satisfaction

A specification φ is satisfied non-vacuously in M if and only if M contains a witness for each strengthening of φ. In other words, as we stated earlier in (2),

$$M \models \mathbf{A}\,\varphi \wedge \bigwedge_{\psi \in \text{Lit}(\varphi)} \mathbf{E}\,\neg\varphi[\psi \leftarrow \bot]$$

(note that (2) is based on our choice of definition for vacuity). We call $\neg\varphi[\psi \leftarrow \bot]$ the *witness formulas* for non-vacuity of φ.

Note that not all witness formulas add interesting information. For instance, for φ as defined in (3), the witness formula $\neg\varphi_1[g_1 \leftarrow \bot] = \mathbf{F}\,r_1$ is clearly satisfied by a trace of any system, and the same holds for any satisfiable witness formula that contains only input signals.

We continue in the next subsection by showing how existentially-quantified formulas can be synthesized. Then, we can use this technique to synthesise formulas of the form defined in (2).

3.2   Bounded Synthesis for Existential Formulae

Our goal is to synthesize a finite-state labeled transition system with a bound on its size, in which there *exists* an execution path that satisfies a given temporal specification φ. We will define a set of constraints that is different than the case described in Sect. 2.5 to achieve this. Initially, we translate φ to a nondeterministic Büchi automaton $\mathcal{A}_\varphi$ and create the run graph $\mathcal{G}$ of $\mathcal{A}_\varphi$ on M. Then, we use a Boolean marking function $\lambda^* : Q \times S \to \mathbb{B}$ to indicate that a state is on our selected path in $\mathcal{G}$. On that selected path, we impose a ranking function that can only be satisfied if it corresponds to an accepting run.

First, the initial state is marked:

$$\lambda^*(q_0, s_0) \,. \tag{9}$$

Next, if a *non-accepting* state is marked, then at least one of its successors is marked, and the ranking of the destination state is strictly smaller:

$$\bigwedge_{\substack{q \in Q \setminus \alpha \\ s \in S \\ v \in \Upsilon}} \left(\lambda^*(q, s) \to \bigvee_{\substack{q' \in Q \\ s' \in S}} \left(\begin{array}{c} q' \in \rho(q, o(s), v) \wedge s' \in \tau(s, v) \wedge \\ \lambda^*(q', s') \wedge \lambda^\#(q', s') < \lambda^\#(q, s) \end{array} \right) \right) \,. \tag{10}$$

On the other hand if an *accepting state* is marked, then we only require that one of its successors is marked (but in contrast to the previous case, here there is no restriction on the ranking of its successor):

$$\bigwedge_{\substack{q \in \alpha \\ s \in S \\ v \in \Upsilon}} \left(\lambda^*(q, s) \to \bigvee_{\substack{q' \in Q \\ s' \in S}} \left(\begin{array}{c} q' \in \rho(q, o(s), v) \wedge s' \in \tau(s, v) \wedge \\ \lambda^*(q', s') \end{array} \right) \right) \,. \tag{11}$$

Fig. 3. On the left there is no accepting run, and indeed there is no ranking function that can satisfy the constraints. On the right there is an accepting run (the λ^* predicate is marked with '*'), and the fact that there is no constraint on the outgoing edge of the accepting state allows to find a ranking function, namely the numbers 0,1,2,3,4,5 that are marked inside the states.

The two automata in Fig. 3 illustrate our construction—see caption. The following theorem states that these constraints are correct.

Theorem 2. *Given a Büchi automaton $\mathcal{A} = (Q, q_0, \rho, \alpha)$ constructed from a formula φ', a transition system $M = (S, s_0, \tau, o)$ satisfies $\mathbf{E}\,\varphi'$ iff it corresponds to a solution to constraints (9)–(11).*

Proof. ($\Rightarrow$) There is a unique run graph $\mathcal{G} = (G, E)$ for $\mathcal{A}$ on M. Assume M is accepted by $\mathcal{A}$; therefore, $\mathcal{G}$ contains at least one lasso-shaped path $\pi = (q_0, s_0)(q_1, s_1) \ldots [(q_n, s_n) \ldots (q_m, s_m)]^\omega$ such that q_i is accepting for some $i \in [n, m]$. We have to show that in such a case (9)–(11) are satisfiable. Marking all the states on the path clearly satisfies (9), and the λ^* predicate is true along this path as required by constraints (10) and (11). It is left to show that there exists a ranking function that satisfies (10). Indeed the following function, which annotates each state on π by its distance to q_i, is a valid ranking function:

$$\lambda^\#(q_j, s_j) = \begin{cases} i - j & \text{if } j \leq i \\ m - j + i - n + 1 & \text{if } i < j. \end{cases}$$

Indeed, $\lambda^\#(q_j, s_j) > \lambda^\#(q_k, s_k)$ for all $((q_j, s_j)(q_k, s_k)) \in \pi$, unless $j = i$. Recall that only accepting states are bound by constraint (10). The figure below demonstrates this ranking for $n = 3, m = 6$, and $i = 5$.

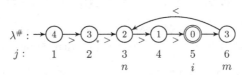

($\Leftarrow$) Assume that (9)–(11) are satisfiable. The set of marked states must include a lasso-shaped path beginning from the initial state, and the fact that (10) is satisfied means that there exists an accepting state in the loop. Hence the run graph must contain an accepting path. □

Finally, synthesising a non-vacuous system—a system that satisfies (2)— amounts to solving the *conjunction* of the constraints that were described in Sect. 2.5 (for the universal part), and the constraints in Sect. 3.2 for each $\psi \in \mathrm{Lit}\,(\varphi)$ (for the existential part). A separate discrete ranking function is required for φ and each of its witness formulas.

Corollary 1. *A finite-state transition system $M = (S, s_0, \tau, o)$ satisfies a temporal specification in the form of the CTL^* fragment defined in (4) iff it corresponds to a solution to constraints (5)–(8) and (9)–(11).*

4 Beyond Vacuity

In the introduction we argued that non-vacuous systems are preferable to vacuous systems because they are more likely to fulfill the designer's intent. This guarantees that for specifications like $\varphi = \mathbf{G}\,(r \rightarrow \mathbf{F}\,g)$, there will be at least one path on which $\mathbf{G}\,\mathbf{F}\,g$ does not hold. Intuitively, this corresponds to the idea that an input r should trigger the output g. However, the definition of vacuity is somewhat too coarse for our purpose. We need a more refined notion, which will enable us to distinguish between systems that are non-vacuous. To that end, in this section we introduce a partial order between such systems. We consider a system *less vacuous* than another if more input traces yield interesting witnesses. For the property above, for example, this corresponds to more witnesses to $\neg \mathbf{G}\,\mathbf{F}\,g$. Intuitively, this approximates the idea of a *trigger*, where g is triggered by r, and should preferably not occur without r.

We show that given a system, we can use a variant of bounded synthesis to synthesize a less vacuous one, which naturally leads to a most interesting system of a given size. If the size is unbounded, however, we show that for some specifications, this order gives rise to infinite chains of ever less vacuous systems.

4.1 A Partial Order on Non-Vacuous Systems

Let M_1 and M_2 be transition systems that satisfy φ. Given a witness formula φ_ψ, we define a relation $M_1 \preccurlyeq_\psi M_2$ to indicate that M_2 has at least the same set of interesting witnesses according to φ_ψ as M_1. Formally, given a specification φ and a witness formula φ_ψ of φ, we define

$$M_1 \preccurlyeq_\psi M_2 \text{ iff } \forall \pi \in \varUpsilon^\omega. \ (M_1(\pi) \models \varphi_\psi) \rightarrow (M_2(\pi) \models \varphi_\psi). \tag{12}$$

We say that M_2 is strictly less vacuous than M_1 if in addition there is at least one input sequence that leads to an interesting witness only in M_2:

$$M_1 \prec_\psi M_2 \text{ iff } M_1 \preccurlyeq_\psi M_2 \text{ and } \exists \pi \in \varUpsilon^\omega. \ (M_1(\pi) \not\models \varphi_\psi) \wedge (M_2(\pi) \models \varphi_\psi). \tag{13}$$

By extending the relation $\prec_\psi$ to the set of all witness formulas, we can compare two transition systems in terms of vacuity. Let $\varPsi$ be the set of all witness formulas for φ. We define the preorder $\preccurlyeq$ as

$$M_1 \preccurlyeq M_2 = \forall \varphi_\psi \in \varPsi. \ M_1 \preccurlyeq_\psi M_2 \,, \tag{14}$$

and the strict partial order $\prec$ as

$$M_1 \prec M_2 = M_1 \preccurlyeq M_2 \text{ and } \exists \varphi_\psi \in \varPsi. \ (M_1 \prec_\psi M_2) \,. \tag{15}$$

In other words, M_2 is at least as non-vacuous as M_1 w.r.t. all possible witnesses and is strictly less vacuous than M_1 w.r.t. at least one witness formula.

Since there is a finite number of transition systems of any size N, for a given LTL formula φ there exists at least one least vacuous system M_N^φ, according to $\prec$. This system may not be unique.

4.2   An Infinite Vacuity Chain

For some formulas, there is an infinite chain of ever less vacuous (and ever larger) systems. As an example, consider the following LTL specification:

$$\varphi = (\mathbf{G}\,r) \to (\mathbf{F}\,g) \, . \tag{16}$$

The only witness formula for φ is

$$\varphi_r = \mathbf{G}\,\neg g \, . \tag{17}$$

Figure 4 depicts an abstract transition system M_k of arbitrary size (i. e., $k + 3$) that realizes specification φ non-vacuously for any k.

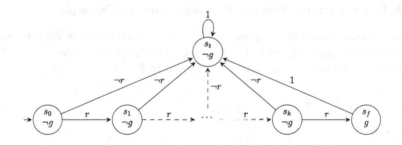

Fig. 4. An example of infinite vacuity chain

Proposition 1. $\forall k.\ M_k \prec_\psi M_{k+1}$.

Proof. We have to show that M_{k+1} is as non-vacuous as M_k and that there exists an input trace that makes M_{k+1} less vacuous w.r.t. φ_r.

First we show $\forall k.\ M_k \preccurlyeq_\psi M_{k+1}$. For each input trace $\pi \in \varUpsilon^\omega$, if $M^k(\pi) \models \mathbf{G}\,\neg g$, then $\pi \models r^j(\neg r)^+(\neg r + r)^\omega$ for some $j \leq k$, so $M_{k+1}(\pi) \models \mathbf{G}\,\neg g$.

To see that $\forall k.\ M_k \prec_\psi M_{k+1}$ holds, note that the input trace $r^{k+1}(\neg r)^\omega$ leads to an intersting trace in M^{k+1} but not in M^k. $\qquad\square$

4.3   Synthesizing a Less Vacuous System

We now discuss how to synthesize a less vacuous system M_2 given a correct system M_1. We do this by expressing the partial order defined above in the simple fragment of CTL* defined in (4).

Given a formula φ or a system M, we use a primed version (φ' or M', respectively) to denote the formula/system obtained by replacing all output literals by primed versions. Given a system M_1 that satisfies φ, we have $M_1 \prec_\psi M_2$ iff

$$M_1' \times M_2 \models \mathbf{A}\,\varphi \wedge \mathbf{A}\,(\varphi_\psi' \rightarrow \varphi_\psi) \wedge \mathbf{E}\,(\neg\varphi_\psi' \wedge \varphi_\psi)\,.$$

Note that φ and φ_ψ consider the outputs of M_2 and φ_ψ' considers the outputs of M_1, while both systems receive the same inputs.

Theorem 3. M_1 *is strictly less vacuous than* M_2 *iff*

$$M_1' \times M_2 \models \mathbf{A}\,(\varphi \wedge \bigwedge_{\varphi_\psi \in \Psi} (\varphi_\psi' \rightarrow \varphi_\psi)) \wedge \mathbf{E}\,(\bigvee_{\varphi_\psi \in \Psi} (\neg\varphi_\psi' \wedge \varphi_\psi))\,. \qquad (18)$$

Note that this equation has the form of (2) and can thus be solved as described in Sect. 3.

If we fix a maximal size for the system, it implies that we can synthesise a maximally non-vacuous one (i.e., least vacuous) by repeated application of this procedure.

4.4   A Least Vacuous System for Our Running Example

Consider once again our running example from the introduction. Figure 5 shows a least vacuous system M_2 with the bound 4 on the number of states (one of the intermediate iterations resulted in M_1 depicted in Fig. 1b).

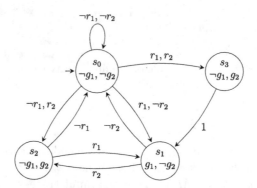

Fig. 5. The final non-vacuous system M_2.

System M_2 is strictly less vacuous than M_1. Recall that the two witness formulas are $\varphi_{r_1} = \mathbf{F}\,\mathbf{G}\,\neg g_1$ and $\varphi_{r_2} = \mathbf{F}\,\mathbf{G}\,\neg g_2$. It is not hard to verify that all interesting paths in M_1 w.r.t. to φ_{r_1} (w.r.t. to φ_{r_2}) are also interesting in w.r.t. to φ_{r_1} (w.r.t. to φ_{r_2}, resp.) in M_2. Also, the trace that results from leaving r_1 and r_2 low all the time is interesting w.r.t. φ_{r_2} in M_2 but not in M_1.

Proposition 2. M_2 *is a least vacuous system with respect to* $\{\varphi_{r_1}, \varphi_{r_2}\}$.

Proof. Let M be an arbitrary system that satisfies φ. For an input sequence $\pi \in \varUpsilon^\omega$, assume that π induces a path in M that satisfies $\varphi_1[r_1 \leftarrow \bot] = \mathbf{F}\,\mathbf{G}\,\neg g_1$. Since this path, in particular, satisfies φ, it also satisfies $\mathbf{F}\,\mathbf{G}\,\neg r_1$ (otherwise there would have been requests that are never granted). Observing Fig. 5, it is easy to see that the same input sequence π would induce a path in M_2 with an infinite suffix $\{s_0, s_2\}^\omega$, hence, in particular, it satisfies $\mathbf{F}\,\mathbf{G}\,\neg g_1$. A similar argument holds for $\varphi_2[r_2 \leftarrow \bot]$. Hence, M is not less vacuous than M_2.

The question whether a given system is a least vacuous one (again, such systems may not be unique) is equivalent to asking whether a less vacuous one exists, which, by (18) can be reduced to CTL* realizability question.

5   Experimental Evaluation

We implemented the described technique in the PARTY synthesizer [12] and conducted the following experiment: first, we synthesized models for three complete and correct specifications; then, we made them incomplete by removing some of the conjuncts in the specification and ran synthesis again; our motivation was to see whether starting with a partial specification, with non-vacuous synthesis we can synthesize a system that satisfies the full specification. Clearly this highly depends on the properties that we choose to remove, but recall that this is not the scenario that we are aiming at anyway. We aim at a scenario in which there is no full specification, and non-vacuous synthesis accelerates the convergence towards the desired system. Since we cannot run such an experiment, the experiments below only give us a certain indication for the power of this technique.

In the three experiments that we conducted, non-vacuous synthesis was able to synthesize a system that satisfies the original, full specification, although we emphasise that this is not guaranteed in general. The synthesized system in all three cases is not identical to the one synthesized according to the full specification, which reflects the fact that many systems can satisfy the same specification. It is up to the user to choose between them.

5.1   A 'Next' Arbiter

The 'next' arbiter of two clients issues a grant for each client in the next step if and only if the client sends a request. The assumption is that clients never send requests simultaneously; thus, issued grants should be mutually exclusive. The complete and incomplete specification of this arbiter for two clients is shown in Fig. 6. The specification should be interpreted as 'every run that satisfies the **assume** predicates should also satisfy the **guarantee** predicates'.

As depicted in Fig. 7a and b, even a slight modification in the specification results in a large gap in the behaviors of the synthesized systems. On the other hand starting from the system depicted in Fig. 7b, three iterations of the non-vacuous synthesis process result in the system shown in Fig. 7c, which satisfies the original, full specification.

Complete Specification	Incomplete Specification
assume	**assume**
$\mathbf{G}\neg(r_1 \wedge r_2)$	$\mathbf{G}\neg(r_1 \wedge r_2)$
guarantee	**guarantee**
$\mathbf{G}(r_1 \longleftrightarrow \mathbf{X}\,g_1) \wedge$	$\mathbf{G}(r_1 \rightarrow \mathbf{X}\,g_1) \wedge$
$\mathbf{G}(r_2 \longleftrightarrow \mathbf{X}\,g_2) \wedge$	$\mathbf{G}(r_2 \rightarrow \mathbf{X}\,g_2) \wedge$
$\mathbf{G}\neg(g_1 \wedge g_2)$	$\mathbf{G}\neg(g_1 \wedge g_2)$

Fig. 6. LTL specification for the 'next' arbiter of two clients. Note that the incomplete specification on the right excludes the right-to-left implications in the guarantee.

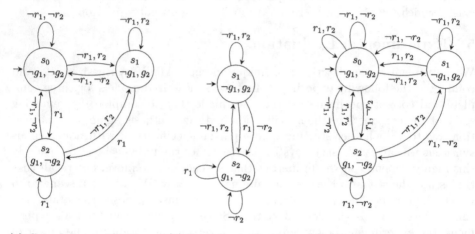

(a) Complete specification   (b) Partial specification   (c) Non-vacuous synthesis from partial specification

Fig. 7. Synthesized arbiters of the complete and incomplete specifications of the 'next' arbiter that appeared in Fig. 6.

5.2 A 'full' Arbiter

A 'full' arbiter of two clients eventually issues a grant for each client if the client sends a request. The complete specification appears in Fig. 8(left), and a partial specification appears in Fig. 8(right). The properties that are removed in the partial specification state that grants are never given *"unnecessarily"*. The transition systems that are synthesized for the full and partial specification appear in Fig. 9a and b respectively. On the other hand, starting from the partial specification, after four iterations the non-vacuous synthesis we get is as shown in Fig. 9c, which again satisfies the full specification.

5.3 A 'Pnueli' Arbiter

A 'Pnueli' arbiter of two clients is a handshake mechanism such that whenever a client sets a request the arbiter will set and keep the corresponding grant high

Complete Specification	Incomplete Specification
guarantee	**guarantee**
$\neg(\neg r_1 \wedge \neg g_1)\, \mathbf{U}(\neg r_1 \wedge g_1) \wedge$	
$\neg(\neg r_1 \wedge \neg g_1)\, \mathbf{U}(\neg r_1 \wedge g_1) \wedge$	
$\neg\mathbf{F}(g_1 \wedge \mathbf{X}(\neg r_1 \wedge \neg g_1) \wedge \mathbf{X}(\neg r_1 \wedge g_1)\,\mathbf{U}(\neg r_1 \wedge g_1)) \wedge$	
$\neg\mathbf{F}(g_2 \wedge \mathbf{X}(\neg r_2 \wedge \neg g_2) \wedge \mathbf{X}(\neg r_2 \wedge g_2)\,\mathbf{U}(\neg r_2 \wedge g_2)) \wedge$	
$\mathbf{G}((\neg r_1 \wedge g_1) \rightarrow \mathbf{F}((r_1 \wedge g_1) \vee \neg g_1)) \wedge$	
$\mathbf{G}((\neg r_2 \wedge g_2) \rightarrow \mathbf{F}((r_2 \wedge g_2) \vee \neg g_2)) \wedge$	
$\mathbf{G}(r_1 \rightarrow \mathbf{F}\,g_1) \wedge$	$\mathbf{G}(r_1 \rightarrow \mathbf{F}\,g_1) \wedge$
$\mathbf{G}(r_2 \rightarrow \mathbf{F}\,g_2) \wedge$	$\mathbf{G}(r_2 \rightarrow \mathbf{F}\,g_2) \wedge$
$\mathbf{G}\,\neg(g_1 \wedge g_2)$	$\mathbf{G}\,\neg(g_1 \wedge g_2)$

Fig. 8. LTL specification for full arbiter of 2 clients.

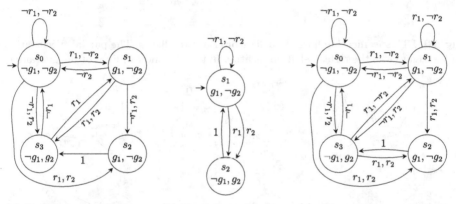

(a) Complete specification (b) Partial specification (c) Non-vacuous synthesis from partial specification

Fig. 9. Synthesized arbiters of complete and incomplete specifications of full arbiter as read in Fig. 8.

as long as the request is high [11]. The complete and incomplete specification of a 'Pnueli' arbiter of two clients is shown in Fig. 10. The incomplete specification allows the arbiter to set a grant and never unset it; therefore, the synthesized system may issue vacuous grants for each client infinitely often unless the other client sends a request—see Fig. 11b. The result of our non-vacuous synthesis from the partial specification again satisfies the full specification, as shown in Fig. 11c, and is synthesised in one step. This system also satisfies the specification in a less vacuous way than the system synthesised from the complete specification. In fact, in this case, if the input to our tool is a *complete* specification, the result is also the system in Fig. 11c.

Complete Specification	Incomplete Specification
assume	**assume**
$\neg r_1 \wedge \neg r_2 \wedge$	$\neg r_1 \wedge \neg r_2 \wedge$
$\mathbf{G}\left((r1 \wedge \neg g1 \to \mathbf{X}\, r_1) \wedge (\neg r_1 \wedge g_1 \to \mathbf{X}\, \neg r1)\right)\wedge$	$\mathbf{G}\left((r1 \wedge \neg g1 \to \mathbf{X}\, r_1) \wedge (\neg r_1 \wedge g_1 \to \mathbf{X}\, \neg r1)\right)\wedge$
$\mathbf{G}\left((r2 \wedge \neg g2 \to \mathbf{X}\, r_2) \wedge (\neg r_2 \wedge g_2 \to \mathbf{X}\, \neg r_2)\right)\wedge$	$\mathbf{G}\left((r2 \wedge \neg g2 \to \mathbf{X}\, r_2) \wedge (\neg r_2 \wedge g_2 \to \mathbf{X}\, \neg r_2)\right)\wedge$
$\mathbf{G}\,\mathbf{F}\,(\neg r_1 \vee \neg g_1)\wedge$	$\mathbf{G}\,\mathbf{F}\,(\neg r_1 \vee \neg g_1)\wedge$
$\mathbf{G}\,\mathbf{F}\,(\neg r_2 \vee \neg g_2)$	$\mathbf{G}\,\mathbf{F}\,(\neg r_2 \vee \neg g_2)$
guarantee	**guarantee**
$\neg g_1 \wedge \neg g_2 \wedge$	$\neg g_1 \wedge \neg g_2 \wedge$
$\mathbf{G}\left(((\neg r_1 \wedge \neg g_1) \to \mathbf{X}\, \neg g_1) \wedge ((r_1 \wedge g_1) \to \mathbf{X}\, g_1)\right)\wedge$	$\mathbf{G}\left(((\neg r_1 \wedge \neg g_1) \to \mathbf{X}\, \neg g_1) \wedge ((r_1 \wedge g_1) \to \mathbf{X}\, g_1)\right)\wedge$
$\mathbf{G}\left(((\neg r_2 \wedge \neg g_2) \to \mathbf{X}\, \neg g_2) \wedge ((r_2 \wedge g_2) \to \mathbf{X}\, g_2)\right)\wedge$	$\mathbf{G}\left(((\neg r_2 \wedge \neg g_2) \to \mathbf{X}\, \neg g_2) \wedge ((r_2 \wedge g_2) \to \mathbf{X}\, g_2)\right)\wedge$
$\mathbf{G}\,\mathbf{F}\,(r_1 \longleftrightarrow g_1)\wedge$	$\mathbf{G}\,\mathbf{F}\,(r_1 \to g_1)\wedge$
$\mathbf{G}\,\mathbf{F}\,(r_2 \longleftrightarrow g_2)\wedge$	$\mathbf{G}\,\mathbf{F}\,(r_2 \to g_2)\wedge$
$\mathbf{G}\,\neg(g_1 \wedge g_2)$	$\mathbf{G}\,\neg(g_1 \wedge g_2)$

Fig. 10. LTL specification for a 'Pnueli' arbiter of two clients. The partial specification on the right lacks the right-to-left implication in the 4th and 5th lines of the guarantee.

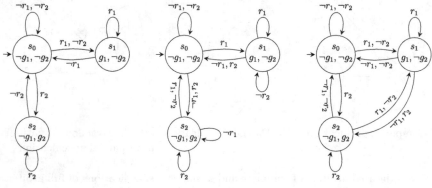

(a) Complete specification   (b) Partial specification   (c) Non-vacuous synthesis from partial specification

Fig. 11. Synthesized arbiters of complete and incomplete specifications of a 'Pnueli' arbiter as read in Fig. 10.

6   Conclusion

In synthesis, it is hard to expect the designer to think of a complete specification. As a result, the large range of possible systems that satisfy the specification permits designs that stand in contrast to the designer's intent. We proposed in this article to apply the concept of vacuity to address this problem. Our method narrows down the range of legitimate synthesised system to those that satisfy the (partial) specification in a *meaningful* way, a well-known concept from using vacuity in model-checking. But as we argued, we do not have to commit to the Boolean nature of the classical definition of vacuity: we showed how a system can be made *less* vacuous, even if it already satisfies the specification non-vacuously. Our experiments showed that our method is capable of synthesising better designs, in the sense that they even satisfy parts of the specification that we deliberately removed and were hence inaccessible to the synthesis algorithm. Perhaps in the future synthesis will be used in the industry, and then our conjecture that this process can save time to the designer will be tested with a user-study.

Our solution is based on a novel bounded synthesis technique that combines universal and existential properties; It paves the way for generalizing our technique to full CTL*. Our tool PARTY is available on the web for others to try and improve.

Acknowledgments. This work was supported by the TU Graz LEAD project "Dependable Internet of Things in Adverse Environments" and the Austrian Science Fund (FWF) under the RiSE National Research Network (S11406). We would like to thank Nir Piterman for his insights on infinite chains of ever less vacuous systems and Ayrat Khalimov for his comments on existential bounded synthesis and his valuable assistance with the implementation.

References

1. Armoni, R., Fix, L., Flaisher, A., Grumberg, O., Piterman, N., Tiemeyer, A., Vardi, M.Y.: Enhanced vacuity detection in linear temporal logic. In: Hunt, W.A., Somenzi, F. (eds.) CAV 2003. LNCS, vol. 2725, pp. 368–380. Springer, Heidelberg (2003). doi:10.1007/978-3-540-45069-6_35
2. Beer, I., Ben-David, S., Eisner, C., Rodeh, Y.: Efficient detection of vacuity in ACTL formulas. Formal Methods Syst. Des. **18**(2), 141–163 (2001)
3. Bloem, R., Chatterjee, K., Greimel, K., Henzinger, T.A., Hofferek, G., Jobstmann, B., Könighofer, B., Könighofer, R.: Synthesizing robust systems. Acta Inf. **51**, 193–220 (2014)
4. Bloem, R., Chatterjee, K., Henzinger, T.A., Jobstmann, B.: Better quality in synthesis through quantitative objectives. In: Bouajjani, A., Maler, O. (eds.) CAV 2009. LNCS, vol. 5643, pp. 140–156. Springer, Berlin (2009). doi:10.1007/978-3-642-02658-4_14
5. Bustan, D., Flaisher, A., Grumberg, O., Kupferman, O., Vardi, M.Y.: Regular vacuity. In: Borrione, D., Paul, W. (eds.) CHARME 2005. LNCS, vol. 3725, pp. 191–206. Springer, Heidelberg (2005). doi:10.1007/11560548_16
6. Gurfinkel, A., Chechik, M.: Extending extended vacuity. In: Hu, A.J., Martin, A.K. (eds.) FMCAD 2004. LNCS, vol. 3312, pp. 306–321. Springer, Heidelberg (2004). doi:10.1007/978-3-540-30494-4_22
7. Chockler, H., Gurfinkel, A., Strichman, O.: Beyond vacuity: towards the strongest passing formula. Formal Methods Syst. Des. **43**(3), 552–571 (2013)
8. Church, A.: Logic, arithmetics, and automata. In: ICM (1963)
9. Finkbeiner, B., Schewe, S.: Bounded synthesis. Int. J. Softw. Tools Technol. Transfer **15**(5), 519–539 (2012)
10. Jacobs, S., Bloem, R., Brenguier, R., Könighofer, R., Pérez, G.A., Raskin, J., Ryzhyk, L., Sankur, O., Seidl, M., Tentrup, L., Walker, A.: The second reactive synthesis competition. In: SYNT (2015)

11. Jobstmann, B., Staber, S., Griesmayer, A., Bloem, R.: Finding and fixing faults. J. Comput. Syst. Sci. **78**(2), 441–460 (2012)
12. Khalimov, A., Jacobs, S., Bloem, R.: PARTY parameterized synthesis of token rings. In: Sharygina, N., Veith, H. (eds.) CAV 2013. LNCS, vol. 8044, pp. 928–933. Springer, Heidelberg (2013). doi:10.1007/978-3-642-39799-8_66
13. Kupferman, O., Vardi, M.: Vacuity detection in temporal model checking. J. Softw. Tools Technol. Transfer **4**(2), 224–233 (2003)
14. Namjoshi, K.S.: An efficiently checkable, proof-based formulation of vacuity in model checking. In: Alur, R., Peled, D.A. (eds.) CAV 2004. LNCS, vol. 3114, pp. 57–69. Springer, Heidelberg (2004). doi:10.1007/978-3-540-27813-9_5
15. Pnueli, A.: The temporal logic of programs. In: FOCS (1977)
16. Pnueli, A., Rosner, R.: On the synthesis of a reactive module. In: POPL (1989)
17. Samanta, R., Deshmukh, J.V., Chaudhuri, S.: Robustness analysis of networked systems. In: Giacobazzi, R., Berdine, J., Mastroeni, I. (eds.) VMCAI 2013. LNCS, vol. 7737, pp. 229–247. Springer, Heidelberg (2013). doi:10.1007/978-3-642-35873-9_15
18. Vardi, M., Wolper, P.: Reasoning about infinite computations. Inf. Comput. **115**(1), 1–37 (1994)

Static Analysis of Communicating Processes Using Symbolic Transducers

Vincent Botbol[1,2][✉], Emmanuel Chailloux[1], and Tristan Le Gall[2]

[1] Sorbonne Universités, UPMC Univ Paris 06, CNRS, LIP6 UMR 7606,
4 Place Jussieu, 75005 Paris, France
vincent.botbol@cea.fr, emmanuel.chailloux@lip6.fr
[2] CEA, LIST, Software Reliability and Security Laboratory,
91191 Gif-sur-Yvette, France
tristan.le_gall@cea.fr

Abstract. We present a general model allowing static analysis based on abstract interpretation for systems of communicating processes. Our technique, inspired by Regular Model Checking, represents set of program states as lattice automata and programs semantics as symbolic transducers. This model can express dynamic creation/destruction of processes and communications. Using the abstract interpretation framework, we are able to provide a sound over-approximation of the reachability set of the system thus allowing us to prove safety properties. We implemented this method in a prototype that targets the MPI library for C programs.

1 Introduction

The static analysis of concurrent programs faces several well-known issues, including how to handle dynamical process creation. This last one is particularly challenging considering that the state space of the concurrent system may not be known nor bounded statically, which depends on the number and the type of variables of the program.

In order to overcome this issue, we combine a symbolic representation based on regular languages (like the one used in Regular Model Checking [1]) with a fixed-point analysis based on abstract interpretation [6]. We define the abstract semantics of a concurrent program by using of a symbolic finite-state transducer [16]. A (classical) finite-state transducer T encodes a set of rules to rewrite words over a finite alphabet. In a concurrent program, if each process only has a finite number of states, then we can represent a set of states of the concurrent program by a language and the transition function by a transducer. However, this assumption does not hold since we consider processes with infinite state space, so we have to represent a set of states of the concurrent program by a lattice automaton [10] and its transition function by a lattice transducer, a new kind of symbolic transducers that we define in this paper. Lattice Automata are able to recognize languages over an infinite alphabet. This infinite alphabet is an abstract domain (intervals, convex polyhedra, etc.) that abstracts process states.

© Springer International Publishing AG 2017
A. Bouajjani and D. Monniaux (Eds.): VMCAI 2017, LNCS 10145, pp. 73–90, 2017.
DOI: 10.1007/978-3-319-52234-0_5

```
1      if (id==0)
2        x := 1
3      else
4        receive(any_id,x);
5
6      create(next);
7      x := x+4;
8      send(next,x)
```

$$l_9 \times (\text{id} \geq 0) \times (x \neq 5 + \text{id} * 4)$$

Fig. 1. Program example   **Fig. 2.** Bad configurations

We show, on Fig. 1 (detailed in Sect. 2), the kind of programs our method is able to analyse. This program generates an unbounded sequence of processes $\{id = 0, x = 5\} \cdot \{id = 1, x = 9\} \cdot \{id = 2, x = 13\} \cdot \ldots$. We want to prove safety properties such as: $x = 5 + \text{id} \times 4$ holds for every process when it reached its final location l_9. The negation of this property is encoded as a lattice automaton *Bad* (Fig. 2) that recognizes the language of all bad configurations. Our verification algorithm is to compute an over-approximation of the reachability set *Reach*, also represented by a lattice automaton, then, by testing the emptiness of the intersection of the languages, we are able to prove this property: $\mathscr{L}(Reach) \cap \mathscr{L}(Bad) = \emptyset$.

Related works. There are many works aiming at the static analysis of concurrent programs. Some of them use the abstract interpretation theory, but either they do not allow dynamic process creation [14] and/or use a different memory model [9] or do not consider numerical properties [8]. In [16], the authors defined symbolic transducers but they did not consider to raise it to the verification of concurrent programs. In [3], there is the same kind of representation that considers infinite state system but can only model finite-state processes. The authors of [5] present a modular static analysis framework targeting POSIX threads. Their model allows dynamic thread creation but lack communications between threads. More practically, [17] is a formal verification tool using a dynamical analysis based on model checking aiming at the detection of deadlocks in Message Passing Interface [15] (MPI) programs but this analysis is not sound and also does not compute the value of the variables.

Contributions. In this article, we define an expressive concurrency language with communication primitives and dynamic process creation. We introduce its concrete semantics in terms of symbolic rewriting rules. Then, we give a way to abstract multi-process program states as a lattice automaton and also abstract our semantics into a new kind of symbolic transducer and specific rules. We also give application algorithms to define a global transition function and prove their soundness. A fixpoint computation is given to obtain the reachability set. Finally, in order to validate the approach, we implemented a prototype as a Frama-C [12] plug-in which targets a subset of MPI using the abstract domain library: Apron [11].

Outline. In Sect. 2, we present the concurrent language and its semantics definition, encoded by rewriting rules and a symbolic transducer. Then, Sect. 3 presents the abstract semantics and the algorithms used to compute the over-approximation of the reachability set of a program. In Sect. 4, we detail the implementation of our prototype targeting a subset of MPI which is mapped by the given semantics and run it on some examples (Sect. 5). We discuss about the potential and the future works of our method in Sect. 6.

2 Programming Language and Its Concrete Semantics

We present a small imperative language augmented with communications primitives such as unicast and multicast communications, and dynamical process creation. These primitives are the core of many parallel programming languages and libraries, such as MPI.

2.1 Language Definition

In our model, memory is distributed: each process executes the same code, with its own set of variables. For the sake of clarity, all variables and expressions have the same type (integer), and we omit the declaration of the variables. Process identifiers are also integers.

$\langle program \rangle ::= \langle instrs \rangle$

$\langle instrs \rangle ::= \langle instr \rangle \text{ ';' } \langle instrs \rangle$

$\langle id \rangle ::= \langle expr \rangle$
    $| \quad \textbf{any\_id}$

$\langle instr \rangle ::= \text{ '\{' } \langle instrs \rangle \text{ '\}'}$
    $| \quad \langle ident \rangle \text{ ':=' } \langle expr \rangle$
    $| \quad \textbf{if} \text{ '(' } \langle expr \rangle \text{ ')' } \langle instr \rangle \textbf{ [else } \langle instr \rangle]$
    $| \quad \textbf{while} \text{ '(' } \langle expr \rangle \text{ ')' } \langle instr \rangle$
    $| \quad \textbf{create} \text{ '(' } \langle ident \rangle \text{ ')'}$
    $| \quad \textbf{send} \text{ '(' } \langle id \rangle \text{ ',' } \langle ident \rangle \text{ ')'}$
    $| \quad \textbf{receive} \text{ '(' } \langle id \rangle \text{ ',' } \langle ident \rangle \text{ ')'}$
    $| \quad \textbf{broadcast} \text{ '(' } \langle expr \rangle \text{ ',' } \langle ident \rangle \text{ ')'}$

$\langle ident \rangle$ and $\langle expr \rangle$ stand for classical identifiers and arithmetic expressions on integers (as defined in the C language)

Communications are *synchronous*: a process with id=orig cannot execute the instruction send(dest, var) unless a process with id=dest is ready to execute the instruction receive(orig, var'); both processes then execute their instruction and the value of var (of process orig) is copied to variable var' (of process dest). We also allow unconditional receptions with all_id meaning that a process with id=orig can receive a variable whenever another process is ready to execute an instruction send(orig,v). broadcast(orig, var) instructions cannot be executed unless all processes reach the same instruction. create(var) dynamically creates a new process that starts its execution at the program entry point. The id of the new process, which is a fresh id, is stored in var, so the current process can communicate with the newly created process. Other instructions are asynchronous. Affectations, conditions and loops keep the same meaning as in the C language.

2.2   Formal Semantics

We model our program using an unbounded set P of processes, ordered by their identifiers ranging from 1 to $|P|$. As usual, the control flow graph (CFG) of the program is a graph where vertices belong to a set L of program points and edges are labelled by a $instr \subseteq L \times Instr \times L$ where $Instr$ are the instructions defined in our language. Finally, V represents the set of variables. Their domain of values is $\mathbb{V} \supseteq \mathbb{N}$. For any expression $expr$ of our language, and any valuation $\rho : V \to \mathbb{V}$, we note $eval(expr, \rho) \in \mathbb{V}$ its value.

Our processes share the same code and have distributed memory: each variable has a local usage in each process. Thus, a *local state* is defined as $\sigma \in \Sigma = Id \times L \times (V \to \mathbb{V})$. It records the identifier of the process, its current location and the value of each local variable.

A *global state* is defined as a *word* of process local states: $\sigma_1 \cdot \sigma_2 \cdot ... \cdot \sigma_n \in \Sigma^*$ where n is the number of running processes and Σ^* is the free monoid on Σ.

The semantics is given as a transition system $\langle \Sigma^*, I, \tau \rangle$, where $I \in \Sigma^*$ is the set of all possible initial program states. As the code is shared, every process starts at the same location l_0 and every variable's value is initialised with 0. Therefore, if there are initially n processes, $I = \{\sigma_1 \cdot ... \cdot \sigma_n\}$ where $\forall i \in n, \sigma_i = \langle i, l_0, (\lambda v \, . \, 0) \rangle$. The transition relation $\tau \subseteq \Sigma^* \times \Sigma^*$ is thoroughly defined in [2]. Here, we directly consider sets $E \in \mathscr{P}(\Sigma^*)$ and Post_τ defined as:

$$\text{Post}_\tau(E) = \{w' \in \Sigma^* \mid \exists w \in E \wedge (w, w') \in \tau\}$$

Post_τ^* is the reflexive and transitive closure of Post_τ. Given an initial set of states $I \in \mathscr{P}(\Sigma^*)$, the *reachability set* $\text{Post}_\tau^*(I)$ contains all states that can be found during an execution of the program. Assuming we want to check whether the program satisfies a safety property (expressed as a *bad configuration*) given by a set of states B that must be avoided, the verification algorithm is simply to test whether $\text{Post}_\tau^*(I) \cap B = \emptyset$; if true, the program is safe.

Therefore, we would like to define Post_τ in a more *operational* way, as a set of rewriting rules that can be applied to I, so we can apply those rules iteratively until we reach the fixpoint $\text{Post}_\tau^*(I)$.

2.3   Symbolic Rewriting Rules

Let us consider a local instruction $(l, a, l') \in instr$; for any set of states E:

$$\text{Post}_{(l,a,l')}(E) = \{\sigma_1 \cdot ... \cdot \langle id, l', \rho' \rangle \cdot ... \cdot \sigma_n) \mid \exists \sigma_1 \cdot ... \cdot \langle id, l, \rho \rangle \cdot ... \cdot \sigma_n) \in E \wedge \rho' = [\![a]\!]\rho\}$$

The effects of $\text{Post}_{(l,al')}$ on E is to rewrite every word of E. Thus, we would like to express it as a rewriting rule G/F where G is a symbolic guard matching a set of words and F a symbolic rewriting function. Since our method uses the framework of abstract interpretation (see Sect. 3), *symbolic* means that we consider elements of some lattice to define the rules. We give the rewriting rule that encodes the execution of a local instruction (l, a, l'):

$$G = \mathsf{T}^* \cdot \langle \_, l, \_ \rangle \cdot \mathsf{T}^* \text{ and } F = \mathsf{Id}^* \cdot f \cdot \mathsf{Id}^* \text{ with } f(X) = \{\langle id, l', [\![a]\!](\rho) \rangle | \langle id, l, \rho \rangle \in X\}$$

The guard matches words composed of any number of processes, then one process with location l, then again any number of processes. The function Id^* means that the processes matched by T^* will be rewritten as the identity and therefore not modified. $\Lambda = \mathscr{P}(\Sigma)$ is the lattice of sets of local states. $f : \Lambda \to \Lambda$ rewrites a set of local states according to the semantics of a. So every word $w \in E$ that matches the guard will be rewritten and we will obtain $\mathrm{Post}_{(l,a,l')}(E)$.

We now give the general definition of those rewriting rules and how to apply them. We remind that the partial order $\sqsubseteq$ can be extended to Λ^* as $u \sqsubseteq v$ if both words have the same length ($|u| = |v|$) and $\forall i < |u|, \bot \neq u_i \sqsubseteq v_i$. Note that we do not allow $\bot$ in words: any word that would contain one or more $\bot$ letters is identified to the smallest element $\bot_{\Lambda^*}$. Therefore, any word $w \in \Lambda^*$ represents a set of words of Σ^*: $\sigma_1 \ldots \sigma_n \in w$ when $\{\sigma_1\} \ldots \{\sigma_n\} \sqsubseteq w$.

Definition 1. *Let Λ be a lattice. A rewriting rule over Λ is given by two sequences $G = (g_0)^* \cdot w_1 \cdot (g_1)^* \cdot w_2 \ldots w_n \cdot (g_n)^*$ and $F = f_0 \cdot h_0 \cdot f_1 \cdot h_1 \cdot \ldots \cdot h_n \cdot f_{n+1}$ such that:*

- *$\forall\, 1 \leq i \leq n, w_i \in \Lambda^*$ and $|w_i| > 0$;*
- *$\forall\, 0 \leq i \leq n, g_i \in \Lambda$;*

  We note $N = |w_1| + |w_2| + \ldots + |w_n|$

- *$\forall\, 0 \leq i \leq n+1, f_i : \Lambda^N \to \Lambda^*$;*
- *$\forall\, 0 \leq i \leq n, h_i : \Lambda^{N+1} \to \Lambda$.*

With this rule, a finite word $w \in \Lambda^*$ is rewritten to $w' \in \Lambda^*$ if:

- *w can be written as a concatenation $w = u_0 \cdot v_1 \cdot u_1 \cdot \ldots \cdot v_n \cdot u_n$ with:*
  - *$\forall\, 0 \leq i \leq n, u_i = \lambda_0 \ldots \lambda_{|u_i|}$ and $\forall\, 0 \leq j \leq |u_i|, \lambda_j \sqsubseteq g_i$,*
  - *$\forall\, 1 \leq i \leq n, v_i \sqsubseteq w_i$;*
- *$w' = v'_0 \cdot u'_0 \cdot v'_1 \cdot u'_1 \cdot \ldots \cdot v'_n \cdot u'_n \cdot v'_{n+1}$ with:*
  - *$\forall\, 0 \leq i \leq n, u'_i = \lambda'_0 \cdot \lambda'_1 \cdot \ldots \cdot \lambda'_{|u_i|}$ and $\forall\, 0 \leq j \leq |u_i|, \lambda'_j = h_i(\lambda_j, v_1, \ldots, v_n)$,*
  - *$\forall\, 0 \leq i \leq n+1, v'_i = f_i(v_1, \ldots, v_n)$.*

For any $N \in \mathbb{N}$, $\mathsf{Id}^* : \Lambda^{N+1} \to \Lambda$ is defined as $\mathsf{Id}^*(x, y_1, \ldots y_N) = x$. Moreover, we denote by $\langle \_, l, \_ \rangle$ the element of $\Lambda = \mathscr{P}(\Sigma)$ defined as $\{\langle id, l, \rho \rangle \mid \forall id, \rho\}$, (the symbol '$\_$' matches anything). With these notations, we can express the transition relation by a set of rewriting rules:

- For every pair of send/receive instructions
  $(l_i, \mathsf{send}(\mathsf{id\_to}, \mathsf{v_i}), l'_i)$ and $(l_j, \mathsf{receive}(\mathsf{id\_from}, \mathsf{v_j}), l'_j)$, we have the rule:

  $$G = \mathsf{T}^* \cdot \langle \_, l_i, \_ \rangle \cdot \mathsf{T}^* \cdot \langle \_, l_j, \_ \rangle \cdot \mathsf{T}^* \text{ and } F = \mathsf{Id}^* \cdot f_1 \cdot \mathsf{Id}^* \cdot f_2 \cdot \mathsf{Id}^* \text{ with}$$

- $f_1(E_1, E_2) = \{\langle id_i, l_i', \rho_i\rangle \mid \langle id_i, l_i, \rho_i\rangle \in E_1 \wedge \langle id_j, l_j, \rho_j\rangle \in E_2 \wedge id_i = \text{eval}(id\_from, \rho_j) \wedge id_j = \text{eval}(id\_to, \rho_i)\}$
- $f_2(E_1, E_2) = \{\langle id_j, l_j', \rho_j[v_j \leftarrow \text{eval}(v_i, \rho_i)]\rangle \mid \langle id_i, l_i, \rho_i\rangle \in E_1 \wedge \langle id_j, l_j, \rho_j\rangle \in E_2 \wedge id_i = \text{eval}(id\_from, \rho_j) \wedge id_j = \text{eval}(id\_to, \rho_i)\}$

and symmetrically when σ_j is located before σ_i in the word of local states. When e.g. $id\_to = \texttt{id\_all}$, the condition $id_j = \text{eval}(id\_to, \rho_i)$ is satisfied for any (id_j, ρ_j).

- for each $\texttt{broadcast}$ instruction $(l, \texttt{broadcast}(\texttt{id\_x}, \texttt{v}), l')$, we have the rule:

$$G = (\langle \_, l, \_\rangle)^* \cdot \langle id\_x, l, \_\rangle \cdot (\langle \_, l, \_\rangle)^* \text{ and } F = F_1^* \cdot f_1 \cdot F_1^* \text{ with}$$

- $F_1^*(E_1, E_2) = \{\langle id_i, l', \rho_i[v \leftarrow \text{eval}(v, \rho_x)]\rangle \mid \langle id_i, l, \rho_i\rangle \in E_1 \wedge \langle id_x, l, \rho_x\rangle \in E_2\}$
- $f_1(E_1) = \{\langle id_x, l', \rho_x\rangle \mid \langle id_x, l, \rho_x\rangle \in E_1\}$

The guard $\langle id\_x, l, \_\rangle$ stands for the set $\{\langle id_i, l_i, \rho_i\rangle \mid l_i = l \wedge id_i = \text{eval}(id\_x, \rho_i)\}$

- finally, for each $\texttt{create}$ instruction $(l, \texttt{create}(\texttt{v}), l')$, we have the rule:

$$G = \top^* \cdot \{\_, l, \_\} \cdot \top^* \text{ and } F = Id^* \cdot f_1 \cdot Id^* \cdot f_2 \text{ with}$$

- $f_1(E_1) = \{\langle id_i, l', \rho_i\rangle \mid \langle id_i, l, \rho_i\rangle \in E_1\}$
- $f_2(E_1) = \{\langle id_n, l_0, (\lambda v \cdot 0)\rangle \mid n = \texttt{fresh\_id}()\}$

where $\texttt{fresh\_id}$ returns a new unique identifier n where $n = |w| + 1$ with w the word of processes.

Example 1. Let us consider consider our running example depicted on Fig. 1. Let us assume we have a set of program states $E = \{\langle id = 0, l_0, x = 0, next = 0\rangle; \langle id = 0, l_9, x = 5, next = 1\rangle.\langle id = 1, l_8, x = 9, next = 2\rangle.\langle id = 2, l_4, x = 0, next = 2\rangle; \langle id = 1, l_8, x = 13, next = 2\rangle.\langle id = 6, l_4, x = 0, next = 0\rangle.\}$, i.e. there is either one process in l_0, or three process in l_9, l_8, l_4 or two processes in l_4, l_8. We consider the symbolic rewriting rule that results from the communication instructions. Its guard is $\top^*.\langle \_, l_8, \_\rangle.\top^*.\langle \_, l_4, \_\rangle.\top^*$ and its rewriting functions $Id^* \cdot f_1 \cdot Id^* \cdot f_2 \cdot Id^*$ with

- $f_1(E_1, E_2) = \{\langle id_i, l_9, \rho_i\rangle \mid \langle id_i, l_8, \rho_i\rangle \in E_1 \wedge \langle id_j, l_4, \rho_j\rangle \in E_2 \wedge id_j = \text{eval}(next, \rho_i)\}$
- $f_2(E_1, E_2) = \{\langle id_j, l_5, \rho_j[x \leftarrow \text{eval}(x, \rho_i)]\rangle \mid \langle id_i, l_8, \rho_i\rangle \in E_1 \wedge \langle id_j, l_4, \rho_j\rangle \in E_2 \wedge id_j = \text{eval}(next, \rho_i)\}$

then $\text{Post}_\tau(E) = \{\langle id = 0, l_9, x = 9, next = 1\rangle.\langle id = 1, l_9, x = 13, next = 2\rangle.\langle id = 2, l_5, x = 13, next = 2\rangle\}$, which is the image of the state with three active processes. There is no possible communication when $\langle id = 1, l_8, x = 13, next = 2\rangle.\langle id = 6, l_4, x = 0, next = 0\rangle$. Even if the locations match the guard, the first process can only send messages to a process with $\texttt{id} = \text{eval}(next, \rho) = 2 \neq 6$.

Transducers. Alternatively, the semantics of local instructions can also be described by a *lattice transducer*. A finite-state transducer is a finite-state automaton but instead of only accepting a language, it also rewrites it. A lattice transducer is similar to a finite-state transducer; however, it is symbolic, i.e. it accepts inputs (and produces outputs) belonging to the lattice Λ, which may be an infinite set.

Definition 2. *A Lattice Transducer is a tuple* $T = \langle \Lambda, Q, Q_0, Q_f, \Delta \rangle$ *where:*

- Λ *is a lattice*
- Q *is a finite set of states*
- $Q_0 \subseteq Q$ *are the initial states set*
- $Q_f \subseteq Q$ *are the final states set*
- $\Delta \subseteq Q \times \Lambda^n \times (\Lambda^n \to \Lambda)^* \times Q$ *with* $n \in \mathbb{N}^0$ *is a finite set of transitions with guards and rewriting functions*

Let $w = \lambda_1 \cdot \ldots \cdot \lambda_n \in \Lambda^n$ and $\{q, G, F, q'\} \in \Delta$ with $G = \gamma_1, ..., \gamma_n$ and $F = f_1, ..., f_m$. We write $q \xrightarrow{w/w'} q'$ when:

$$\begin{cases} \forall i \in [1, n] \ \lambda_i \sqsubseteq \gamma_i \\ w' = f_1(\lambda_1, ..., \lambda_n) \cdot \ldots \cdot f_m(\lambda_1, ..., \lambda_n) \end{cases}$$

For any word $w \in \Lambda^*$, $T(w)$ is the set of words w' such that there exists a sequence $q_0 \xrightarrow{w_1/w'_1} q_1 \xrightarrow{w_2/w'_2} \ldots \xrightarrow{w_n/w'_n} q_f$ with $q_0 \in Q_0$, $q_f \in Q_f$, $w = w_1 \cdot w_2 \ldots w_n$ and $w' = w'_1 . w'_2 \ldots w'_n$. For any language $L \subseteq \Sigma^*$, $T(L) = \cup_{w \in L} T(w)$.

We can express the semantics of the local instructions $\langle l_1, a_1, l'_1 \rangle, \langle l_2, a_2, l'_2 \rangle, \ldots$ by a transducer as shown in Fig. 3.

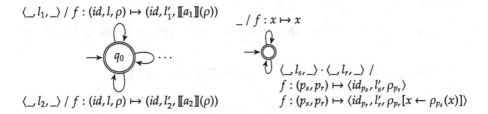

Fig. 3. Local transitions transducer   **Fig. 4.** "Neighbour" communication

For the language we presented, the transducer representation is not fully exploited. Indeed, only single self-looping transitions are present. Yet, in our example program, we notice that communications and dynamic creation are done in their "neighbourhood": processes send their x to their right neighbor, receive from the left and create processes on their right-side. This semantics can be expressed with our transducer representation. We give on Fig. 4 a transducer encoding a "neighbour" version of synchronous communications as send_right and receive_left primitives. In our illustration, we use the locations (l_s, l'_s) and (l_r, l'_r) in order to represent pre and post locations of send_right and receive_left instructions. However, this restriction is not satisfying: we wish to handle point-to-point communications regardless of process locations in words of states. Thus we have to limit the transducer to encode only local transitions.

Therefore, communications are encoded by semantics rules R, and local instructions by a transducer T. We note T_{ext} the transducer extended with semantic rules, i.e. for any language $X \subseteq \Sigma^*$, $T_{ext}(X) = R(X) \cup T(X) = \text{Post}_\tau(X)$. For any initial set of states $I \subseteq \{\mathscr{P}(\Sigma)\}$, we have the reachability set $\text{Post}_\tau^*(I) = T_{ext}^*(I)$. However, $T_{ext}^*(I)$ cannot be computed in general, so we need abstractions.

3   Abstract Semantics

3.1   Lattice Automata as an Abstract Domain

Since Σ may be an infinite set, we must have a way to abstract languages (i.e. subsets of Σ^*) over an infinite alphabet. *Lattice Automata* [10] provide this kind of abstractions. Lattice Automata are similar to finite-state automata, but their transitions are labeled by elements of a lattice. In our case, lattice automata are appropriate because:

- they provide a finite representation of languages over an infinite alphabet;
- we can apply symbolic rewriting rules or a transducer to a lattice automaton (see Sect. 3.2);
- there is a widening operator that ensures the termination of the analysis (see Sect. 3.3).

Definition 3. *A lattice automaton is defined by a tuple* $A = \langle \Lambda, Q, Q_0, Q_f, \delta \rangle$ *where:*

- Λ *is an atomistic lattice[1], the order of which is denoted by* $\sqsubseteq$*;*
- Q *is a finite set of states;*
- $Q_0 \subseteq Q$ *and* $Q_f \subseteq Q$ *are the sets of initial and final states;*
- $\Delta \subseteq Q \times (\Lambda \setminus \{\bot\}) \times Q$ *is a finite transition relation.[2]*

This definition requires Λ to have a set of atoms $\text{Atoms}(\Lambda)$. Abstract lattices like Intervals [6], Octagons [13] and Convex Polyhedra [7] are atomistic, so we can easily find such lattices to do our static analysis. Note that if Λ is atomistic, Λ^N and Λ^* are also atomistic, their atoms belonging to respectively $\text{Atoms}(\Lambda)^N$ and $\text{Atoms}(\Lambda)^*$. Moreover, for any set Σ, the lattice $\mathscr{P}(\Sigma, \subseteq)$ is atomistic and its atoms are the singletons. In the remainder of this paper, we will assume that

---

[1] See [10] or [2].
[2] No transition is labeled by $\bot$.

any lattice we consider is atomistic. Finally, in addition to a widening operator, lattice automata have classic FSA operations ($\cup$, $\cap$, $\subseteq$, etc.).

The language recognized by a lattice automaton A is noted $\mathscr{L}(A)$ and is defined by finite words on the alphabet Atoms(Λ). $w \in \mathscr{L}(A)$ if $w = \lambda_1 \ldots \lambda_n \in$ Atoms(Λ)* and there is a sequence of states and transitions $q_0 \xrightarrow{\lambda_1} q_1 \xrightarrow{\lambda_2} \ldots \xrightarrow{\lambda_n} q_n$ with $q_0 \in Q_0$ and $q_n \in Q_f$.

The reason why we define the language recognized by a lattice automaton as sequence of atoms are discussed in [10]; in a nutshell, this definition implies that two lattice automata that have the same concretisation recognize the same language. Moreover, by introducing a finite partition of the atoms, we can define determinisation and minimisation algorithms similar to the ones for finite-state automata, as well as a canonical form (*normalized* lattice automata).

Abstractions and Concretisations. Assuming there is a Galois connection between $\mathscr{P}(\Sigma)$ and Λ we can extend the concretisation function $\gamma : \Lambda \to \mathscr{P}(\Sigma)$, we can extend it to $\gamma : \Lambda^* \to \mathscr{P}(\Sigma^*)$; if $w = \lambda_1 \ldots \lambda_n \in \Lambda^*$, $\gamma(w) = \{\sigma_1 \ldots \sigma_n | \forall i = 1..n, \sigma_i \in \gamma(\lambda_i)\}$ and for any language L, $\gamma(L) = \cup_{w \in L} \gamma(w)$. Thus, the concretisation of a lattice automaton A is $\gamma(\mathscr{L}(A))$, which can be computed by applying γ to all of A. Lattice automata are not a complete lattice; the abstraction function is defined as: if L is regular (i.e. it can be represented by a lattice automaton with labels in $\mathscr{P}(\Sigma)$) $\alpha(L)$ applies α to each edge; otherwise $\alpha(L) = \top$. The latter case does not happen in practice, since the initial set of states I is regular, and since we only check regular properties. We now present algorithms to apply a symbolic rewriting rule or a lattice transducer to a lattice automaton.

3.2 Algorithms

Application of a Rule. To apply a symbolic rewriting rule to the language recognized by a lattice automaton, we must first identify the subset of words that match the guard $(g_0)^* \cdot w_1 \cdot (g_1)^* \cdot w_2 \ldots w_n \cdot (g_n)^*$. In this guard, it's easier to look first for sequences in the automaton that match $w_1, w_2, \ldots, w_n$. In automaton A a sequence that matches e.g. w_1 begins from state q_b^1 and ends in state q_e^1. Then, we identify the sub-automaton that could match $(g_0)^*$, i.e. all the states that are reachable from an initial state q_0 and correeachable from q_b^1 by considering only transitions labeled by elements λ such that $g_0 \sqcap \lambda \neq \bot$. Once each part is identified, we can apply the rewriting function to each part and then we get a new automaton A'. Since this pattern matching is non deterministic, we have to consider all possible matching sequences. The result of the algorithm is the union of every automaton A' constructed in this way.

We introduce some notations before writing the algorithm. Let $w = \lambda_1 \ldots \lambda_n \in \Lambda^n$ and let A be a lattice automaton. We denote by matches(w, A) the set of matching sequences:

$$\text{matches}(w, A) = \{(q_b, v_1 \ldots v_n, q_e) \mid \exists q_0 \xrightarrow{\lambda'_1} q_1 \xrightarrow{\lambda'_2} \ldots \xrightarrow{\lambda'_n} q_n \in A,$$
$$q_0 = q_b \wedge q_n = q_e \wedge \forall i = 1..n, v_i = \lambda_i \sqcap \lambda'_i \neq \bot\}\}$$

Let (q_b, q_e) be a pair of states of a lattice automaton $A = \langle \Lambda, Q, Q_0, Q_f, \delta \rangle$ and let $\lambda \in \Lambda$. We denote by $A_{q_b \to q_e}$ the sub-automaton $A_{q_b \to q_e} = \langle \Lambda, Q, \{q_b\}, \{q_e\}, \delta \rangle$. For a lattice automaton $A = \langle \Lambda, Q, Q_0, Q_f, \delta \rangle$ and a function $f : \Lambda \to \Lambda$, we denote by $\mathrm{map}(f, A)$ the automaton $\mathrm{map}(f, A) = \langle \Lambda, Q, Q_0, Q_f, f(\delta) \rangle$ where $f(\delta) = \{(q, f(\lambda), q') | (q, \lambda, q') \in \delta \wedge f(\lambda) \neq \bot\}$.

With those notations, we give an algorithm to apply a rewriting rule on a lattice automaton:

```
ApplyRule (G = (g_0)* · w_1 · (g_1)* ... w_n · (g_n)*,  F = f_0 · h_0 · f_1 ... h_n · f_{n+1},  A):
Result := ∅
For all matching sequences
(q_b^1, v^1, q_e^1) ∈ matches(w_1, A),  ...,  (q_b^n, v^n, q_e^n) ∈ matches(w_n, A),
for each initial state q_0 ∈ Q_0^A and each final state q_f ∈ Q_f^A
( Let A_0 = map(x ↦ g_0 ⊓ x, A)_{q_0 → q_b^1},
  A_1 = map(x ↦ g_1 ⊓ x, A)_{q_e^1 → q_b^2},  ...,  A_n = map(x ↦ g_n ⊓ x, A)_{q_e^n → q_f}.
  For i = 0 .. n:
    let A_i' = map(x ↦ h_i(x, v^1, ..., v^n), A_i).
  For i = 0 .. n+1:
    let w_i' = f_i(v^1, ..., v^n).
  Let q_{-1} and q_{n+1} be two fresh states (not in any A_i').
  Let δ^seq = {(q_{-1}, w_0', q_0)(q_b^1, w_1', q_e^1)(q_b^1, w_1', q_e^1) ... (q_b^n, w_n', q_e^n)(q_b^n, w_{n+1}', q_{n+1})}.
  Let A' = ⟨Λ, Q ∪ {q_{-1}, q_{n+1}}, {q_{-1}}, {q_{n+1}}, δ^{A'}⟩ with
  δ^{A'} = δ^seq ∪ δ^{A_0'} ∪ ... ∪ δ^{A_n'}


  Result := Result ∪ A')
return Result
```

This algorithm's complexity is $O(|Q_A|^{n+3} \cdot |\pi|^N \cdot (|Q_A| \cdot n + (n+2) \cdot c(f))$ where $|Q_A|$ is the lattice automaton's size, n is defined as in the algorithm, $|\pi|$ is the lattice automaton's partition (i.e. the number of different locations in the program), N is $|w_1| + |w_2| + \cdots + |w_n|$ and $c(f)$ represents the maximum complexity among the given rewriting functions.

Theorem 1. *Let $R = (g_0)^* \cdot w_1 \cdot (g_1)^* \cdot w_2 \ldots w_n \cdot (g_n)^* / f_0 \cdot h_0 \cdot f_1 \cdot h_1 \cdot \ldots \cdot h_n \cdot f_{n+1}$ be a rewriting rule and A a lattice automaton. If $R(A) = ApplyRule(R, A)$, then we have: $R(\mathscr{L}(A)) \subseteq \mathscr{L}(R(A))$.*

The proof is given in [2]. However, we do not have $R(\mathscr{L}(A)) \supseteq \mathscr{L}(R(A))$ as shown in the following example:

Example 2. Let A the lattice automaton that recognizes the language $L = \{[0, 0], [1, 1]\}$ (i.e. there is only one process, with one integer variable which values is either 0 or 1) and let R be the rewriting rule $\top / f_1.f_2$ where $f_1 : x \mapsto 2x$ and $f_2 : x \mapsto 4x$ then $R(\mathscr{L}(A)) = \{[0, 0].[0, 0], [2, 2].[4, 4]\}$. But $R(A)$ is a lattice automaton that can recognize 4 words:
$\mathscr{L}(R(A)) = \{[0, 0].[0, 0], [2, 2].[4, 4], [0, 0].[4, 4], [2, 2].[0, 0]\}$.

Application of a Transducer. The following algorithm computes the application of a symbolic transducer $T = \langle \Lambda, Q^T, Q_0^T, Q_f^T, \Delta^T \rangle$ to a (language recognized by a) lattice automaton $A = \langle \Lambda, Q^A, Q_0^A, Q_f^A, \Delta^A \rangle$. The idea is to consider the cartesian product $Q^T \times Q^A$ and to create transitions whenever it is allowed by the transducer and the automaton.

ApplyTransducer (T, A):

$\Delta^{T(A)} = \emptyset$
$\forall (p, q) \in Q^T \times Q^A$
$\forall p' \in Q^T, \forall (p, Q, F, p') \in \Delta^T$ with $G \in \Lambda^n$ and $F : \Lambda^n \to \Lambda^*$
$\forall q' \in Q^A$ such that there is a sequence of transitions
$\quad q \xrightarrow{w} q'$ in A with $w \in \Lambda^n$
If $G \sqcap w \neq \bot$ then $\Delta^{T(A)} := \Delta^{T(A)} \cup \{((p, q), F(G \sqcap w), (p', q'))\}$
$\forall (p, q) \in Q_0^{T(A)}$ if $p \in Q_0^T$ and $q \in Q_0^A$
$\forall (p, q) \in Q_f^{T(A)}$ if $p \in Q_f^T$ and $q \in Q_f^A$

Note that $\Delta^{T(A)} = \Delta^{T(A)} \cup \{((p, q), F(G \sqcap w), (p', q'))\}$ means that we add not one but a sequence of transitions (introducing fresh new states). So the set of states of the resulting automata $T(A)$ is the union of $Q^T \times Q^A$ and all the fresh states we added. Figure 5 gives an illustration of an application of a transducer mapping the semantics of the single local instruction of our program $(l_7, [\texttt{x := x + 4}], l_8)$ on single letter program state set (i.e. only one process). Please note that, for the sake of clarity, we use line numbers as locations. l_7 is the location just before the evaluation of the assignment. l_8 is, thus, after the evaluation and l_9 represents the last location symbolising the end of a process execution. Our transducer application algorithm complexity is $O(|Q_A| \cdot |Q_T| \cdot |\Delta_T| \cdot |\pi|^N \cdot c(f))$ where N is the maximum length of all transition guards (here $N - 1$) and $c(f)$ is again the maximum complexity among the given rewriting functions.

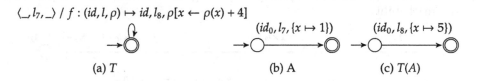

(a) T   (b) A   (c) T(A)

Fig. 5. Transducer application

Theorem 2. *Let T be a symbolic transducer and A a lattice automaton. We have: $T(\mathscr{L}(A)) \subseteq \mathscr{L}(T(A))$.*

The proof is given in [2]. We note $T_{ext}(A) = R(A) \cup T(A)$ the automaton resulting of the union of `ApplyRule(R, A)` and `ApplyTransducer(T, A)`.

3.3   Fixpoint Computation

As we said before, the reachability set is defined as the fixpoint $\text{Post}_\tau^*(I)$; If we can compute $T_{ext}^*(I)$ in the abstract domain of lattice automata, we will get an over-approximation interpretation of this reachability set. However, there are infinitely increasing sequences in this abstract domain, so we need to apply a *widening operator* to ensure the termination of the computation. There exists a widening operator which "lifts" a widening operator ∇_Λ defined for Λ to the abstract domain of lattice automata: $A_1 \nabla A_2$ applies ∇_Λ to each transition of A_1 and A_2 when the two automata have the same "shape"; otherwise, it merges some states of $A_1 \cup A_2$ to obtain an over-approximation (see [10]).

The generic fixpoint algorithm is thus to apply the widening operator ∇ at each step until we reach a post-fixpoint, i.e. we iterate the operator

$$T_\nabla(S) = \begin{cases} S & \text{if } T_{ext}(S) \sqsubseteq S \\ S\nabla(S \cup T_{ext}(S)) & \text{otherwise} \end{cases}$$

This computation gives a post-fixpoint $T^\infty \supseteq T_{ext}(I)$. In practice, this method may yield very imprecise upper bounds. Since Λ contains information about the location of each process, we can improve the precision by applying ∇_Λ only to locations corresponding to an entry point of a loop. It is known [4] that we only need widening to break dependency cycles and [4] gives an extensive study on the choice of widening application locations.

Once we get an over-approximation of the reachability set, we can check any safety property expressed as a set of bad states represented by a lattice automaton B; if $T^\infty \cap B = \emptyset$, then the system is safe. If not, the property may be false, thus we raise an alarm.

On our example (Fig. 1), applying our method using a precise relational numerical abstract domain (e.g. polyhedra) gives us a reachability set. We can prove the safety property given on Fig. 2 by using the following invariant present in the reachability set:

4   Verification of MPI Programs

In order to validate our approach, we applied our method to the Message Passing Interface (MPI). MPI is a specification of a message passing model. Many implementations have been developed and it is widely used in parallel computing for designing distributed programs. Every process has its own memory and *shares a common code*. A notion of *rank* (acting as id) is present in order to differentiate the processes. This paradigm makes a good candidate to map our model onto.

We developed a prototype[3] that targets a MPI subset for the C language. It currently supports *synchronous MPI communications*, integer and floating point values as well as a good subset of the C language. Currently, we do not support dynamic process creation in MPI. This prototype has been implemented as a *Frama-C* plug-in. This plug-in uses a lattice transducer library we developed on top of an existing lattice automata implementation. Our abstract domains are given by the Apron library. This prototype has been written in OCaml. The current size of the plug-in is around 10.000 lines of code and is still a work in progress. Unfortunately, due to licensing issues, its source code is not available yet.

To illustrate our method, we refer, throughout this section, to a small MPI program (Fig. 6). This program runs N processes that each computes $1/2^{(rank+1)}$. Then, the root (i.e. rank = 0) process collects each local result and sums them by a call to the MPI_Reduce primitive.

```
1     int main(int argc, char **argv) {
2        int rank, i;
3        float res, total;
4        MPI_Init(&argc, &argv);
5        MPI_Comm_rank(MPI_COMM_WORLD, &rank);
6        i = 1 << (rank + 1);
7        res = 1. / i;
8        MPI_Reduce(&res, &total, 1, MPI_FLOAT, MPI_SUM, 0, MPI_COMM_WORLD);
9        MPI_Finalize();
10       return 0;
11    }
```

Fig. 6. MPI program computing: $\sum_{i=1}^{n} \frac{1}{2^i}$

4.1 Program State Representation

Each (abstract) local process state is a tuple $\langle l, \lambda \rangle \in L \times \Lambda$, where L is the set of locations and Λ a numerical abstract lattice. In the examples of this section, Λ is the lattice of Intervals. Moreover, we distinguish the value of Id from the other variables.

To illustrate, we give the initial configuration with 2 processes starting at MPI_Init(&argc, &argv) (variable declarations are omitted) and represented as a lattice automaton. At this point, each environment variable is set to $\top$ meaning they are not initialised and can have any possible value.

$\langle Id = [0,0], L = [\text{MPI\_Init}], \rho = \forall \lambda.\top \rangle$ $\langle Id = [1,1], L = [\text{MPI\_Init}], \rho = \forall \lambda.\top \rangle$

$\rightarrow q_0 \longrightarrow q_1 \longrightarrow q_2$

---

[3] The prototype can be found at: https://www-apr.lip6.fr/~botbol/mpai.

4.2   Transducer Automatic Generation

Starting from a MPI/C program, the goal is to automatically generate a lattice transducer that fully encodes the program semantics. To achieve that, we first compute the program's Control Flow Graph (CFG). Then, we translate each CFG transition into a lattice transducer rule yielding the complete transducer encoding the program semantics.

As stated before, we differentiate local instructions that affects only one process at a time from global instructions, such as MPI communications, that modify the global state of the program. The translation of local instructions is straight-forward: we use classical transfer functions that are defined in the Apron library to evaluate the expressions and do the assignments. As shown below, an "if" C statement will be translated into two corresponding rules for both condition cases.

```
1   if (x > 10){
2       ...
3   } else {
4       ...
5   }
6       ...
```

$$\top \times [\texttt{If}] \times \{x \in [11, +\infty]\} \ / \ f : (id, L, \rho) \mapsto id, [L_2], \rho$$

$$\top \times [\texttt{If}] \times \{x \in [-\infty, 10]\} \ / \ f : (id, L, \rho) \mapsto id, [L_4], \rho$$

Below is the transducer generated from all local instructions of the MPI program depicted on Fig. 6. Note that, with this set of local rules, there is no way to evolve from the MPI_Reduce location. As mentioned in the previous section, we dissociate the global rules from the transducer's local rules. Therefore, this transition will be presented in the next section. Finally, in order to model process inactivity, we add a simple rule $\top \ / \ f : x \mapsto x$ meaning that any process at any location might not evolve.

$$\top \times [\texttt{MPI\_Init}] \times \top \ / \ f : (id, l, \rho) \mapsto id, [\texttt{MPI\_Comm\_rank}], \rho$$
$$\top \times [\texttt{MPI\_Comm\_rank}] \times \top \ / \ f : (id, l, \rho) \mapsto id, [\texttt{i = 1 << (rank + 1)}], \rho[rank \leftarrow id]$$
$$\top \times [\texttt{i = 1 << (rank + 1)}] \times \top \ / \ f : (id, l, \rho) \mapsto id, [\texttt{res = 1. / i}], \rho[i \leftarrow 1 << (\rho(rank) + 1)]$$

$$\top \times [\texttt{res = 1. / i}] \times \top \ / \ f : (id, l, \rho) \mapsto id, [\texttt{MPI\_Reduce}], \rho[res \leftarrow 1./\rho(i)]$$
$$\top \times [\texttt{MPI\_Finalize}] \times \top \ / \ f : (id, l, \rho) \mapsto id, [\texttt{return}], \rho$$

4.3   Encoding Communication Primitives

Our prototype currently accepts this subset of MPI primitives : MPI_Send, MPI_Recv, MPI_Bcast, MPI_Comm_rank, MPI_Comm_size and MPI_Reduce. We already described the symbolic rewriting rules in Sect. 3 except for MPI_Comm_rank, MPI_Comm_size, which returns the id of the current process and the total number of processes, and MPI_Reduce. Let us give the semantics of the last one:

```
MPI_Reduce(void* send_data, void* recv_data, int count,
      MPI_Datatype datatype, MPI_Op op, int root, MPI_Comm communicator)
```

This global communication primitive gathers every process' send_data buffer and applies a commutative (the order of reduction is undefined) operator op between every value. The result is then sent to the process of rank root at its recv_data address. count and datatype are respectively the size of these buffers and the type of each value. The communicator defines a group of processes where the communication will occur. We assume a single group.

We cannot represent this global communication in our model with only one rule. Our solution is to break it down into three different ones. The main idea is to spawn a "collector" process that will be in charge of gathering each process' send_data and applying the reduction operation on its accumulator. This collector will move through the program state (i.e. a word of local states) by swapping, at each iteration, with the next process. Before starting to move this collector, we have to ensure that no involved process might evolve. Therefore, we *lock* them using a special location. When the collector reaches the end of the word, it sends its accumulator to the root process through a point-to-point communication, destroys itself and, finally, unlocks the processes. The three skeleton rules used in our prototype are given here:

1. $G_1 = (\top \times [\text{MPI\_Reduce}] \times \top)^*$
   $F_1 = (f : \_ \mapsto -1, [\text{Collector}], \{recv\_data \mapsto e\}) \cdot$
   $(F : ((id, l, \rho), \_) \mapsto id, \text{lock}(l), \rho)$ where e is the neutral element of op

2. $G_2 = (\top \times [\text{MPI\_Reduce}]_{\text{lock}} \times \top)^* \cdot$
   $(\top \times [\text{Collector}] \times \top) \cdot (\top \times [\text{MPI\_Reduce}]_{\text{lock}} \times \top) \cdot$
   $(\top \times [\text{MPI\_Reduce}]_{\text{lock}} \times \top)^*$
   $F_2 = \text{Id}^* \cdot$
   $(f : ((id_{coll}, l_{coll}, \rho_{coll}), (id_{proc}, l_{proc}, \rho_{proc})) \mapsto id_{proc}, l_{proc}, \rho_{proc}) \cdot$
   $(f : ((id_{coll}, l_{coll}, \rho_{coll}), (id_{proc}, l_{proc}, \rho_{proc})) \mapsto$
   $id_{coll}, l_{coll}, \rho_{coll}[\text{recv\_data} \leftarrow \rho_{coll}(\text{recv\_data}) \, [\![op]\!] \, \rho_{proc}(\text{send\_data})]) \cdot$
   Id^*

3. $G_3 = (\top \times [\text{MPI\_Reduce}]_{\text{lock}} \times \top)^* \cdot (\text{root} \times [\text{MPI\_Reduce}]_{\text{lock}} \times \top) \cdot$
   $(\top \times [\text{MPI\_Reduce}]_{\text{lock}} \times \top)^* \cdot (\top \times [\text{Collector}] \times \top)$
   $F_3 = (F : ((id, l, \rho), \_) \mapsto id, [\text{next\_loc}], \rho)$
   $(f : ((id_{root}, l_{root}, \rho_{root}), (id_{coll}, l_{coll}, \rho_{coll})) \mapsto$
   $id_{root}, [\text{next\_loc}], \rho_{proc}[\text{recv\_data} \leftarrow \rho_{coll}(\text{recv\_data})]) \cdot$
   $(F : ((id, l, \rho), \_) \mapsto id, [\text{next\_loc}], \rho)$

For our example program, our prototype automatically instantiates these rules in a set R. In [2], we give an illustration of the iterative applications of R on program state A where both processes have reached the `MPI_Reduce` location by successive application of the transducer T on the initial configuration I. The complete reachability set computed by our prototype on the example program can be found in [2].

5   Experiments

We present in this section some of the analysis results of our prototype. We found several tools that provide a formal verification of MPI programs. One of the most advanced we found is called "In-situ Partial Order" [17] (ISP). It is based on model checking and performs a dynamic analysis in order to detect the presence of *deadlocks*. To the best of our knowledge, our tool is the only one that computes the reachability set. We present some examples where we verify numerical properties and although our prototype focuses on safety properties, it can also detects that program states (i.e. words) in our set are not matched by any rules and therefore detect deadlocks. In these cases, we can raise an alarm (which can be false ones due to our abstractions).

Program	LoC	nb proc.	state space size	nb nodes	nb transitions	exec. time
Deadlock random	23	2	225	4	20	0.5 s
Dining philosophers	42	4	83521	17	112	8 s
Dining philosophers	42	6	24137569	54	447	1232 s
Sum program	11	50	∞	200	601	86 s
pi approximation	26	50	∞	200	751	104 s

We tested our prototype on several examples. We display here the results of significant ones. Our parameters are: the number of processes we start with, the concrete state space size, the number of nodes in the lattice automaton that represents the final reachability set, its number of transitions and the execution time. The concrete state space size is the enumeration of all possible program states; it is infinite when there are integer variables. We prove on these examples two kinds of properties: deadlock detection and numerical safety properties.

First is a potentially deadlocking program "random deadlock" where two processes try to communicates randomly: both test a random condition that leads respectively to a send or a receive call towards the other process. As ISP is dynamic and depends on the MPI execution, it will not always detect this simple deadlock. However, as we compute the reachability set, we easily observe this deadlock and can raise an alarm.

We implemented a MPI version of the dining philosopher problem where philosophers and forks are processes. The forks processes will give permission to "pick them up" and "put them down" modeled by point-to-point communications. Naturally, the program has deadlocks and again the reachability set exhibits them. The growth in computation time is explained by the amount of possible interleavings that our algorithm is currently not capable of filtering and by the precision we wish to attain (thus, no strong abstractions) in order to precisely determine the deadlocks (and not a false alarm).

The next two following examples both implement a floating point value approximation. The first one is our example program used in Fig. 6. The same property is used: total $\in [0, 1]$. The second one is a computation on pi based on the approximation of $\int_0^1 \frac{4}{1+x^2}$ with sums of n intervals dispatched on n processes. Again the property is a framing of the result ($\in [3, 4]$). These two examples display the capacity of our prototype to handle real-life computations. However, we would like to generalize these two examples to any number of processus. We can model an initial configuration with an unbounded number of process and run our analysis on it. Unfortunately, we cannot infer a relation between the process rank or the number of processes with our current numerical domains. Therefore, our *sum program*'s analysis, on an unbounded number of process, can detect that each process computes a local result $\in [0, \frac{1}{2}]$ but the total sum will be abstracted to $[0, +\infty]$.

6   Conclusion

We presented a new way to do static analysis on a model of concurrent programs that allow unicast and multicast communication as well as dynamic process creation. We described the general framework of the method with well-founded abstraction of the semantics and program states. We applied our technique in order to compute reachability sets of MPI concurrent programs with numerical abstract domains. We showed that building such an analysis on a realistic language, such as MPI/C programs, is feasible and yields encouraging results. Moreover, abstract interpretation allows us to verify numerical properties which was not done before on such programs, and the lattice automata allow the analysis to represent (and automatically discover) regular invariants on the whole program states.

Future work includes theoretical and practical improvements of our analyser, especially the application algorithm which is currently not optimized. One way to do that is to run a quick pre-analysis using a simple, non-numerical abstract domain to obtain information (e.g. rewriting rules that are never activated), so that we may simplify the rules before using more costly numerical abstract domains. We also wish to design a specification language allowing us to write regular properties more easily. We will also improve our analyser by taking into account more MPI primitives as well as supporting general C constructs (pointers, functions, etc.) thanks to better interactions with the other Frama-C plugins. Finally, we will deal with asynchronous communications (FIFO queues) and shared variables using non-standard semantics and/or a reduced product with abstract domains that can efficiently abstract these kind of data.

Aknowledgements. We thank the anonymous referees for their careful work and insightful remarks.

References

1. Abdulla, P.A., Jonsson, B., Nilsson, M., Saksena, M.: A survey of regular model checking. In: Gardner, P., Yoshida, N. (eds.) CONCUR 2004. LNCS, vol. 3170, pp. 35–48. Springer, Heidelberg (2004). doi:10.1007/978-3-540-28644-8_3
2. Botbol, V., Chailloux, E., Le Gall, T.: Static analysis of communicating processes using symbolic transducers (extended version). arXiv:abs/1611.07812 (2016)
3. Bouajjani, A., Habermehl, P., Vojnar, T.: Abstract regular model checking. In: Alur, R., Peled, D.A. (eds.) CAV 2004. LNCS, vol. 3114, pp. 372–386. Springer, Heidelberg (2004). doi:10.1007/978-3-540-27813-9_29
4. Bourdoncle, F.: Efficient chaotic iteration strategies with widenings. In: Bjørner, D., Broy, M., Pottosin, I.V. (eds.) Formal Methods in Programming and Their Applications. LNCS, vol. 735, pp. 128–141. Springer, Heidelberg (1993)
5. Carre, J.-L., Hymans, C.: From Single-thread to Multithreaded: An Efficient Static Analysis Algorithm. arXiv:abs/0910.5833 (2009)
6. Cousot, P., Cousot, R.: Abstract interpretation: a unified lattice model for static analysis of programs by construction or approximation of fixpoints. In: Conference Record of POPL 1977: The 4th ACM Symposium on Principles of Programming Languages, pp. 238–252 (1977)
7. Cousot, P., Halbwachs, N.: Automatic discovery of linear restraints among variables of a program. In: Conference Record of POPL 1978: The 5th ACM Symposium on Principles of Programming Languages, pp. 84–96 (1978)
8. Feret, J.: Partitioning the threads of a mobile system. arXiv:0802.0188 (2008)
9. Ferrara, P.: Checkmate: a generic static analyzer of java multithreaded programs. In: 2009 Seventh IEEE International Conference on Software Engineering and Formal Methods, pp. 169–178, November 2009
10. Le Gall, T., Jeannet, B.: Lattice automata: a representation for languages on infinite alphabets, and some applications to verification. In: Nielson, H.R., Filé, G. (eds.) SAS 2007. LNCS, vol. 4634, pp. 52–68. Springer, Berlin, Heidelberg (2007). doi:10.1007/978-3-540-74061-2_4
11. Jeannet, B., Miné, A.: APRON: a library of numerical abstract domains for static analysis. In: Bouajjani, A., Maler, O. (eds.) CAV 2009. LNCS, vol. 5643, pp. 661–667. Springer, Berlin, Heidelberg (2009). doi:10.1007/978-3-642-02658-4_52
12. Kirchner, F., Kosmatov, N., Prevosto, V., Signoles, J., Yakobowski, B.: Frama-C: a software analysis perspective. Formal Aspects Comput. 27(3), 573–609 (2015)
13. Miné, A.: The octagon abstract domain. High. Order Symbol. Comput. 19(1), 31–100 (2006)
14. Miné, A.: Relational thread-modular static value analysis by abstract interpretation. In: McMillan, K.L., Rival, X. (eds.) VMCAI 2014. LNCS, vol. 8318, pp. 39–58. Springer, Heidelberg (2014). doi:10.1007/978-3-642-54013-4_3
15. Snir, M., Otto, S., Huss-Lederman, S., Walker, D., Dongarra, J.: MPI-The Complete Reference: The MPI Core, vol. 1, 2nd edn. MIT Press, Cambridge (1998)
16. Veanes, M., Hoolmeijer, P., Livshits, B., Molnar, D., Bjørner, N.: Symbolic finite state transducers: algorithms and applications. In: Conference Record of POPL 2012: The 39th ACM Symposium on Principles of Programming Languages, pp. 137–150 (2012)
17. Vo, A., Vakkalanka, S., DeLisi, M., Gopalakrishnan, G., Kirby, R.M., Thakur, R.: Formal verification of practical MPI programs. ACM Sigplan Not. 44(4), 261–270 (2009)

Reduction of Workflow Nets for Generalised Soundness Verification

Hadrien Bride, Olga Kouchnarenko, and Fabien Peureux[✉]

Institut FEMTO-ST–UMR CNRS 6174, University of Bourgogne Franche-Comté,
16, Route de Gray, 25030 Besançon, France
{hbride,okouchna,fpeureux}@femto-st.fr

Abstract. This paper proposes a reduction method to verify the generalised soundness of large workflows described as workflow nets–a suited class of Petri nets. The proposed static analysis method is based on the application of six novel *reduction transformations* that transform a workflow net into a smaller one while preserving generalised soundness. The soundness of the method is proved. As practical contributions, this paper presents convincing experimental results obtained using a dedicated tool, developed to validate and demonstrate the effectiveness, efficiency and scalability of this method over a large set of industrial workflow nets.

1 Introduction

Nowadays workflows are extensively used by the economic and scientific communities to model and analyse processes. Indeed, a great diversity of application domains exist today that use workflow management systems on a daily basis in order to control their business processes. These include office automation, healthcare, manufacturing and production, finance and banking, just to name a few. Intuitively, a workflow describes the set of possible runs of a particular system/process by describing the ways in which operations can be carried out to reach its intended goals. With the increasing use of workflows for modelling crucial business processes, analysis and verification of specifications become mandatory to ensure such processes are properly designed and reach the expected level of trust and quality with respect to involving domain and business requirements.

Among proposed workflow modelling languages, workflow Petri nets [1] are well suited for modelling and analysing finite or infinite-state discrete processes exhibiting causalities, concurrencies, and conflicts. Moreover, the development of large and intricate workflow nets can be a difficult task which requires powerful structuring mechanisms [2]. It also forces modellers to follows strict abstraction patterns in order to produce quality workflow nets [3]. For instance, to cope with this challenge, stepwise refinement [4] is often used to ease verification.

Verification of workflow nets is an a posteriori approach: given a workflow net, it checks whether properties (e.g., generalised soundness) hold. Although these properties are usually known to be decidable for workflow nets [5], their verification is a very time consuming task due to the high complexity (EXPSPACE)

© Springer International Publishing AG 2017
A. Bouajjani and D. Monniaux (Eds.): VMCAI 2017, LNCS 10145, pp. 91–111, 2017.
DOI: 10.1007/978-3-319-52234-0_6

with respect to the size of the workflow net under analysis [6]. Unfortunately, most often, the abstraction mechanisms, used by modellers of workflow nets, are not explicitly given or deductible to ease the analysis process.

However, within verification approaches, some generic reduction rules [7] have the ability to reduce workflow nets size while strongly preserving properties of interest (e.g., liveness, boundedness). This allows the analysis of studied properties to be performed on reduced workflow nets, in many cases, greatly decreasing its complexity by alleviating state explosion of their state space, which undermines state exploration methods [8]. More generally, reduction rules are abstraction operations: they reduce the level of details of workflow nets, and aim at capturing the abstraction mechanisms used by modellers of workflow nets. It follows that the inversion of reduction rules (i.e. synthesis rules) are refinement operations. Conceptually, this leads to an analysis paradigm where the analysis of workflow nets is substituted by the analysis of their construction.

Within this paradigm, this paper aims to provide an effective and efficient reduction method based on six novel reduction rules to cope with soundness verification of industrial large-scale models. Soundness is indeed a well-established correctness feature for workflow specification that all workflows should verify [5], since it relies on three major properties: weak termination, proper completion, and quasi-liveness. More precisely, the proposed method makes it possible to automate and improve (in terms of calculation time) the generalised soundness verification of large workflows described as workflow nets. Furthermore, in order to conclusively assess the effectiveness, efficiency and scalability of the proposed reduction method, a dedicated tool has been developed and used to conduct intensive experiments over two benchmarks of 1976 industrial workflow nets, which were previously studied in [9–14] by applying others reduction procedures.

The paper is organized as follows. Section 2 introduces related work about the soundness verification of workflows, and motivates the present work. In Sect. 3 we overview the background of the proposed method, i.e. Petri nets and workflow nets. Section 4 details the proposed method to semi-decide the generalised soundness of arbitrary workflow nets. Section 5 describes the tool, called *Hadara-AdSimul-Red*, developed to support the method, and reports on conclusive experimental results. Finally, Sect. 6 concludes the paper and outlines future work.

2   Related Work

On soundness verification. Many techniques and methods have been investigated in order to verify the soundness of workflow nets [12]. It has been proved that generalised soundness of workflow net is decidable [15,16]. For some subclasses of workflow nets (e.g., well-handled, free choice nets), it has been shown that classical soundness, i.e. (weak) 1-soundness, implies generalised soundness [17]. For these subclasses, generalised soundness can be investigated using model checking techniques. For example, [18] uses the *Woflan* tool to verify soundness of a workflow net through the construction of its reachability graph, whereas [19] uses the well-known *SPIN* model-checker [20]. However, as the state space may be infinite in the general case (even when dealing with particular classes of nets), such approaches cannot be applied without suitable abstractions. Other methods based on structural properties have also been proposed [17,21]. Nonetheless, establishing these characterizations may similarly become intractable.

On reduction rules. To cope with difficulties arising when facing large workflow nets, some works have investigated reduction techniques to transform a workflow net into a smaller one while preserving some properties of interest such as liveness, boundedness and soundness. For example, when using *Woflan* in [18], reduction rules proposed in [7] are used to reduce workflow nets before analysing soundness. For free-choice Petri nets, a complete set of reduction rules preserving well-formedness is proposed in [22]. Reduction rules preserving deadlock and lack of synchronization conflicts of acyclic workflows are given in [23]. Finally, reduction rules preserving liveness and boundedness are proposed for arbitrary workflow nets in [23–27], and for workflow nets extensions in [13,28,29].

The verification method proposed in this paper is based on reduction techniques that are applied to arbitrary workflow nets and that focus on rules preserving generalised soundness. It should be noticed that in contrast with [25] the condition of application of these reduction rules are defined solely structurally and that they extend those previously described in the literature. For instance, all the reduction rules presented in [7] (except the elimination of self-loop place, which cannot be applied to workflow nets) can be seen as special cases of the rules presented in this paper. Further, all abstraction rules (i.e. reduction rules) defined in [24] are also special cases of the rules presented in the present paper.

3   Preliminaries

This section introduces preliminaries on Petri nets [30] and workflow nets [31].

3.1   Petri Nets

Definition 1 (Petri net [30]). *A Petri net is a tuple $\langle P, T, F \rangle$ where P is a finite set of places, T is a finite set of transitions $(P \cap T = \emptyset)$, and $F \subseteq (P \times T) \cup (T \times P)$ is a set of arcs.*

Let $g \in P \cup T$ and $G \subseteq P \cup T$. We use the following notations: $g^{\bullet} = \{g' | (g, g') \in F\}$, $^{\bullet}g = \{g' | (g', g) \in F\}$, $G^{\bullet} = \cup_{g \in G}\ g^{\bullet}$, and $^{\bullet}G = \cup_{g \in G}\ ^{\bullet}g$.

The *marking* of Petri net, representing the number of tokens on each place is a function $M : P \to \mathbb{N}$. It evolves during its execution since transitions change the marking of a Petri net according to the following *firing rules*. A transition t is *enabled* in a marking M if and only if $\forall p \in {}^{\bullet}t, M(p) \geq 1$. When an *enabled* transition t is *fired*, it *consumes* one token from each place of ${}^{\bullet}t$ and *produces* one token in each place of $t^{\bullet}$. Notice that, in the context of *workflow*, specifiers often consider *ordinary* Petri nets [31] (i.e. Petri nets with arcs of weight 1).

Let M_a and M_b be two markings and t a transition of a Petri net N, we denote $M_a \xrightarrow{t} M_b$ the fact that the transition t is *enabled* in marking M_a, and *firing* it results in the marking M_b. The marking M_b is denoted as *directly reachable* from M_a by transition t. Let $M_1, M_2, .., M_n$ be markings and $\sigma = t_1, t_2, .., t_{n-1}$ a sequence of transitions of a Petri net N, we denote $M_1 \xrightarrow{\sigma} M_n$ the fact that $M_1 \xrightarrow{t_1} M_2 \xrightarrow{t_2} .. \xrightarrow{t_{n-1}} M_n$. The marking M_n is then said to be *reachable* from M_1 by the sequence of transitions σ. We denote $\mathcal{R}^N(M)$ the set of markings of N *reachable* from a marking M. Based on these rules, a transition t is *dead* at marking M if it is not *enabled* in any marking M' *reachable* from M. A transition t is *live* if it is not *dead* in any marking *reachable* from the initial marking.

3.2   Workflow Nets

Workflow nets are special cases of Petri nets. They are usually used to model the control-flow dimension of a workflow. They allow the modelling of complex workflow exhibiting concurrencies, conflicts, and causal dependencies of activities. The activities are modelled by transitions, while causal dependencies are modelled by places and arcs. Figure 1 depicts an example of a Petri workflow net. Workflow net, and soundness, k-

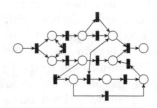

Fig. 1. Example of workflow net

soundness and generalised soundness within workflow nets, are now defined.

Definition 2 (Workflow net [31]). *A Petri net* $N = \langle P, T, F \rangle$ *is a workflow net if and only if:*

– *N has two special places i and o, where $^\bullet i = \emptyset$ and $o^\bullet = \emptyset$, and*
– *for each node $n \in (P \cup T)$ there exists a path from i to o passing through n.*

We denote $M_{i(k)}$ the initial marking (i.e. $M_i(n) = k$ if $n = i$, and 0 otherwise) and $M_{o(k)}$ the final marking (i.e. $M_o(n) = k$ if $n = o$, and 0 otherwise). Intuitively, soundness means that once a workflow has started it should always be able to terminate without leaving tokens in the net. Formally,

Definition 3 (Soundness [5]). *Let* $N = \langle P, T, F \rangle$ *be a workflow net, N is sound if and only if:*

– *$\forall M \in \mathcal{R}^N(M_{i(1)}), M_{o(1)} \in \mathcal{R}^N(M)$ (option to complete),*
– *$\forall M \in \mathcal{R}^N(M_{i(1)}), (M(o) > 0) \Rightarrow (M = M_{o(1)})$ (proper completion), and*
– *$\forall t \in T, \exists M, M' \in \mathcal{R}^N(M_{i(1)}), M \xrightarrow{t} M'$ (no dead transitions).*

The notion of k-soundness in [21] extends the classical soundness to k tokens, while a workflow net is generalised sound if it is k-sound for all $k \in \mathbb{N}$.

Definition 4 (k-soundness [21]). *Let* $N = \langle P, T, F \rangle$ *be a workflow net, and $k \in \mathbb{N}$. N is k-sound if and only if:*

– *$\forall M \in \mathcal{R}^N(M_{i(k)}), M_{o(k)} \in \mathcal{R}(M)$*
– *$\forall t \in T, \exists M, M' \in \mathcal{R}^N(M_{i(1)}), M \xrightarrow{t} M'$*

Definition 5 (Generalised soundness [21]). *Let $N = \langle P, T, F \rangle$ be a workflow net, N is generalised sound if and only if $\forall k \in \mathbb{N}$, N is k-sound.*

4 Verification Method Using Reduction Transformations

This section presents the proposed verification method to check the generalised soundness of arbitrary workflow nets. This method is based on the application of *reduction transformations*. In this way, we define a set of *reduction rules* that allow transforming a workflow net into a smaller one (in terms of the number of nodes) while preserving generalised soundness. We also show that this method is sound: if the successive application of the proposed reduction rules to a workflow net N produces, at the end of this processing (i.e. when no rule can be applied any more), an atomic workflow N_{Atomic}, we can conclude that N is generalised sound. Before describing this method, we first introduce the related basic notions [22].

4.1 Basic Definitions

We define a workflow net transformation rule ϕ as a binary relation on the class of workflow nets. It is fully described by the *conditions of application* under which it can be applied to a *source* workflow net, and the *construction algorithm* that is applied to the *source* workflow net to form a *target* workflow net. Let N, $\tilde{N}$ be two workflow nets and ϕ a transformation rule, the fact that ϕ is *applicable* to N and that applying ϕ to N results in $\tilde{N}$, is denoted $(N, \tilde{N}) \in \phi$. Such a transformation rule ϕ is called a workflow net reduction rule if for all $(N, \tilde{N}) \in \phi$, the number of nodes (i.e. the number of places and transitions) of $\tilde{N}$ is strictly smaller than the number of nodes of N.

Let ψ be a workflow net property, such as generalised soundness (Definition 5), $N \models \psi$ denotes the fact that the workflow net N satisfies ψ. If, for all workflow nets N and $\tilde{N}$, $(N, \tilde{N}) \in \phi$ and $N \models \psi \Rightarrow \tilde{N} \models \psi$, ϕ is said to *preserve* ψ. If the reverse holds as well, i.e. $\tilde{N} \models \psi \Rightarrow N \models \psi$, ϕ is said to *strongly preserve* ψ.

The relation over the class of workflow nets induced by a set of transformation rules is called a kit. Let Φ be the kit induced by the n workflow net transformation rules $\phi_1, .., \phi_n$, Φ defines a binary relation on the class of workflow nets: $(N, \tilde{N}) \in \Phi \Leftrightarrow \exists i \in \{1, .., n\}, (N, \tilde{N}) \in \phi_i$. If a kit is induced by a set of workflow net reduction rules, it is called a reduction kit. We say that Φ (strongly) preserves ψ if and only if $\forall i \in \{1, .., n\}$, ϕ_i (strongly) preserves ψ. Finally, Φ^* denotes the transitive closure of Φ, where $(N_0, N_m) \in \Phi^*$ if and only if there exists a sequence $(\phi_1, N_1), .., (\phi_m, N_m)$ such that $\forall i \in \{1, .., m\}, (N_{i-1}, N_i) \in \phi_i$.

Lemma 1. *Let ψ be a workflow net property, Φ a kit, which strongly preserves ψ, and N, $\tilde{N}$ two workflow nets such that $(N, \tilde{N}) \subset \Phi^*$, then $N \models \psi \Leftrightarrow \tilde{N} \models \psi$.*

Our approach is based on Lemma 1. Indeed, defining a kit Φ of reduction rules, which strongly preserve generalised soundness, enables semi-deciding whether a workflow net N is generalised sound. It holds when $(N, N_{Atomic}) \in \Phi^*$, where $N_{Atomic} = \langle \{i, o\}, \{t\}, \{(i, t), (t, o)\} \rangle$ is a generalised sound workflow net.

4.2   Reduction Kit

This section defines the workflow net reduction rules forming a reduction kit, which strongly preserves generalised soundness as introduced in Definition 5. In what follows, each workflow net reduction rule is defined by giving the *conditions of application* under which it can be applied to a source workflow net $N = \langle P, T, F \rangle$, and the *construction algorithm* to apply to N to produce a target workflow net $\tilde{N} = \langle \tilde{P}, \tilde{T}, \tilde{F} \rangle$. Since the *conditions of application* are defined only structurally, avoiding explicit or symbolic exploration of the state-space of the workflow nets under analysis, the approach does not suffer from state explosion. For clarity, every rule is illustrated by a figure depicting two possible applications of this rule. The first one only considers the plain element of the figure and corresponds to the minimal pattern. The second one considers both the mandatory (plain) and the optional (dashed) elements, and corresponds to a possible extended pattern. Figures are thus not exhaustive but aim to clarify the rules formally described by the related conditions of application and the construction algorithm.

R_1: Remove Place

We define $\phi_{RemoveP}$, a workflow net reduction rule, which strongly preserves generalised soundness and consists in removing a place for which there exists a set of places with the same input transitions as well as the same output transitions. Places removed in such a way are called redundant places as they do not modify the set of correct executions of a workflow net.

Figure 2 illustrates the reduction rule $\phi_{RemoveP}$ formally described as follows.

Conditions on N:	Construction of $\tilde{N}$:
$- \ \exists \ p \in P \setminus \{i, o\}$ $- \ \exists \ G = \{g_1, .., g_n\} \subseteq P \setminus \{i, o, p\}$ $- \ p^\bullet = G^\bullet$ $- \ {}^\bullet p = {}^\bullet G$ $- \ \forall i, j \in \{1, .., n\}, i \neq j \Rightarrow$ $\quad {}^\bullet g_i \cap {}^\bullet g_j = g_i^\bullet \cap g_j^\bullet = \emptyset$	$- \ p^\bullet = \{ot_1, .., ot_n\}$ $- \ outArc := \{p\} \times p^\bullet$ $- \ {}^\bullet p = \{it_1, .., it_m\}$ $- \ inArc := {}^\bullet p \times \{p\}$ $- \ \tilde{P} := P \setminus \{p\}$ $- \ \tilde{T} := T$ $- \ \tilde{F} := F \setminus (inArc \cup outArc)$

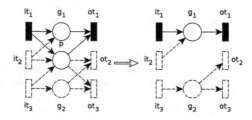

Fig. 2. Reduction rule $\phi_{RemoveP}$ (R_1)

This rule generalises the *Fusion of Parallel Places* rule given in [7] and the *Abstraction of Parallel Places* rule given in [24]. It can also be seen as an adaptation of the rule ϕ_S of [22] (reduction rule proved to be complete with respect to the sub-class of free-choice Petri nets) to the context of ordinary workflow nets.

The inverse of this rule is the only synthesis rule able to add a single place to a workflow net while preserving generalised soundness and is notably used to introduce concurrency. In the context of Petri net, a self-loop place (i.e. a place p such that $^{\bullet}p = p^{\bullet}$) can be added without compromising liveness and boundedness. However, this requires changing the initial marking which is not possible within workflow nets. However, a generalisation of this rule could be applied to an extension of workflow nets modelling resources by marked places.

The soundness of $\phi_{RemoveP}$, with respect to generalised soundness, is given by the following proposition.

Proposition 1 (Soundness of $\phi_{RemoveP}$). $\phi_{RemoveP}$ *is a workflow net reduc-tion rule which strongly preserves generalised soundness.*

Proof. (Sketch). Let $f : (\tilde{P} \to \mathbb{N}) \to (P \to \mathbb{N})$ be a bijective function such that $f(M)(g) = M(g)$ for all $g \in \tilde{P}$ and $f(M)(p) = M(g_1) + .. + M(g_n)$. By conditions on N, every transition that produces (resp. consumes) a token in any of the places of G also produces (resp. consumes) a token in p. Consequently, $\forall k \in \mathbb{N}$ one has: $M \in \mathcal{R}^{\tilde{N}}(M_{i(k)}^{\tilde{N}}), M_o^{\tilde{N}}(k) \in \mathcal{R}^{\tilde{N}}(M) \Leftrightarrow f(M) \in \mathcal{R}^N(M_{i(k)}^N), M_o^N(k) \in \mathcal{R}^N(f(M))$, and transitions $ot_1, .., ot_n, it_1, .., it_m$ of N are not dead if and only if transitions $ot_1, .., ot_n, it_1, .., it_m$ of $\tilde{N}$ are not dead.

R_2: Remove Transition

We define $\phi_{RemoveT}$, a workflow net reduction rule, which strongly preserves generalised soundness and consists in removing a transition for which there exists a set of transitions having the same input and output places. Intuitively, the transitions removed by this rule are transitions whose firing can be simulated by the firing of a set of other transitions.

Figure 3 illustrates the reduction rule $\phi_{RemoveT}$ formally described below.

Let D be a set of places, we define the function $\vartheta : D \to (P \to \mathbb{N})$ such that:

$$\forall\, d \in P,\ \vartheta(D)(d) = \begin{cases} 1, & \text{if } d \in D \\ 0, & \text{otherwise} \end{cases}$$

Let $f_1, f_2, f_3 : P \to \mathbb{N}$ be three functions, we overload the operator $+, -$ and $=$ such that $f_3 = f_1\ \Omega\ f_2 \Leftrightarrow \forall p \in P, f_3(p) = f_1(p)\ \Omega\ f_2(p)$ where $\Omega \in \{+, -\}$. The function ϑ is used to compare inputs and outputs of a set of transitions. Note here that this function does not consider self-loop transitions, a desired property as self-loop transition can be added to places (see rule R_3, introduced in the next subsection).

Conditions on N:	Construction of $\tilde{N}$:
– $\exists\, t \in T$ – $\exists\, G = \{g_1, .., g_n\} \subseteq T \setminus \{t\}$ – $\vartheta_t = \vartheta(t^\bullet) - \vartheta(^\bullet t)$ – $\vartheta_G = \vartheta(g_1^\bullet) + .. + \vartheta(g_n^\bullet) - \vartheta(^\bullet g_1) - .. - \vartheta(^\bullet g_n)$ – $\vartheta_t = \vartheta_G$ – $\forall i, j \in \{1, .., n\}, i \neq j \Rightarrow$ $\quad (^\bullet g_i \cap\, ^\bullet g_j = g_i^\bullet \cap g_j^\bullet = \emptyset)$ – $(\exists\, t_s \in T \setminus (\{t\} \cup G), \forall g \in G, ^\bullet g \subseteq t_s^\bullet) \vee (|G| = 1)$	– $t^\bullet = \{op_1, .., op_{n_1}\}$ – $outArc := \{t\} \times t^\bullet$ – $^\bullet t = \{ip_1, .., ip_{n_2}\}$ – $inArc := ^\bullet t \times \{t\}$ – $\tilde{P} := P$ – $\tilde{T} := T \setminus \{t\}$ – $\tilde{F} := F \setminus (inArc \cup outArc)$

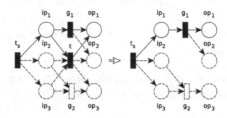

Fig. 3. Reduction rule $\phi_{RemoveT}$ (R_2)

This rule is an original rule generalising the *Fusion of Parallel Transitions* rule of [7] and the *Abstraction of Parallel Transitions* rule of [24]. It is an adaptation of the rule ϕ_S of [22] to the realm of ordinary workflow nets with no restriction on their subclasses. Indeed, outside the scope of free-choice workflow nets, additional constraints are required to ensure that the removed transitions are live. To this end, the liveness of a transition to be removed in such a way is inferred from the liveness of a source transition, a transition that, when fired, enables the transition to be removed. Note that this requirement could be relaxed. Instead of requiring the presence of a source transition, one could require the presence of a sequence of transitions, where each successive transition is enabled by the firing of the previous ones, such that the firing of this sequence of transitions enables the transition to be removed.

The inverse rule of this reduction rule is a synthesis rule able to add a single transition to an arbitrary workflow net based on its structure while preserving generalised soundness and is used to introduce choice.

The soundness of $\phi_{RemoveT}$, with respect to generalised soundness, is given by the following proposition.

Proposition 2. $\phi_{RemoveT}$ *is a workflow net reduction rule which strongly preserves generalised soundness.*

Proof. (Sketch). Let us suppose that $\vartheta_t = \vartheta_G$. By conditions on N, for all k in $\mathbb{N}$, and $\forall M^N$ in $\mathcal{R}^N(M_{i(k)}^N)$, transition t is enabled if and only if transitions $g_1, .., g_n$ are also enabled. Moreover, the firing of t must result in the same marking as the successive firing of transitions $g_1, .., g_n$ in any order. It follows that $\forall k \in \mathbb{N}, M \in \mathcal{R}^N(M_{i(k)}^N), M_o^N(k) \in \mathcal{R}^N(M) \Leftrightarrow M \in \mathcal{R}^{\tilde{N}}(M_{i(k)}^{\tilde{N}}), M_o^{\tilde{N}}(k) \in \mathcal{R}^{\tilde{N}}(M)$. To conclude, suppose $|G| = 1$, then t is not dead in N if and only if g_1 is not dead in $\tilde{N}$. Alternatively, suppose $(\exists\, t_s \in T \setminus (\{t\} \cup G), \forall g \in G, ^\bullet g \subseteq t_s^\bullet)$, then t is not dead in N if and only if t_s is not dead in $\tilde{N}$.

R_3: Remove Self-loop

We define $\phi_{RemoveST}$, a workflow net reduction rule, which strongly preserves generalised soundness and consists in removing a transition whose input places are its output places.

Figure 4 illustrates $\phi_{RemoveST}$ that is formally described below.

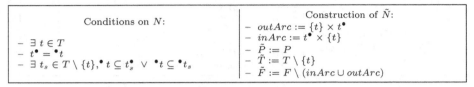

Conditions on N:	Construction of $\tilde{N}$:
$-\ \exists\, t \in T$ $-\ t^\bullet = {}^\bullet t$ $-\ \exists\, t_s \in T \setminus \{t\}, {}^\bullet t \subseteq t_s^\bullet\ \vee\ {}^\bullet t \subseteq {}^\bullet t_s$	$-\ outArc := \{t\} \times t^\bullet$ $-\ inArc := t^\bullet \times \{t\}$ $-\ \tilde{P} := P$ $-\ \tilde{T} := T \setminus \{t\}$ $-\ \tilde{F} := F \setminus (inArc \cup outArc)$

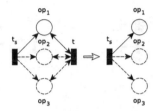

Fig. 4. Reduction rule $\phi_{RemoveST}$ (R_3)

This original rule generalises the *Self-Loop Transition* rule described in [7]. Similarly to rule $\phi_{RemoveT}$, the liveness of a transition removed by this rule also needs to be inferred from the existence of a source transition (alternatively a source sequence of transitions).

The inverse of this reduction rule is a synthesis rule able to add a single transition to an arbitrary workflow net while preserving generalised soundness. It is typically used to introduce choice and repetitive tasks.

The soundness of $\phi_{RemoveST}$, with respect to generalised soundness, is given by the next proposition.

Proposition 3. $\phi_{RemoveST}$ *is a workflow net reduction rule which strongly preserves generalised soundness.*

Proof. (Sketch). By conditions imposed on N, we know that the firing of transition t does not change the markings of N in which it is enabled. It follows that $\forall k \in \mathbb{N}, M \in \mathcal{R}^N(M_{i(k)}^N), M_o^N(k) \in \mathcal{R}^N(M) \Leftrightarrow M \in \mathcal{R}^{\tilde{N}}(M_{i(k)}^{\tilde{N}}), M_o^{\tilde{N}}(k) \in \mathcal{R}^{\tilde{N}}(M)$. Notice that t is not dead in N if and only if t_s is not dead in $\tilde{N}$.

R_4: Remove Transition Place

We define $\phi_{RemoveTP}$, a workflow net reduction rule, which strongly preserves generalised soundness and consists in removing a place and its only input transition. Intuitively, this rule consists in removing a place p and its only input transition t by merging transition t with the output transitions of place p.

The $\phi_{RemoveTP}$ rule is depicted in Fig. 5, and formally described below.

Conditions on N:	Construction of $\tilde{N}$:
$-\ \exists\, p \in P \setminus \{i, o\}$ $-\ ^\bullet p = \{t\}$ $-\ t^\bullet \neq \{p\} \Rightarrow$ $\quad \forall\, ot \in p^\bullet, {}^\bullet ot = \{p\}$ $\quad \wedge\ t^\bullet \cap ot^\bullet = \emptyset$ $-\ t^\bullet = \{p\} \Rightarrow$ $\quad \forall\, ot \in p^\bullet, {}^\bullet t \cap {}^\bullet ot = \emptyset \wedge (\exists\, ot \in$ $\quad p^\bullet,\ {}^\bullet ot = \{p\} \vee \forall\, ip \in$ $\quad {}^\bullet t,\ ip^\bullet = \{t\})$	$-\ t^\bullet \setminus p = \{op_1, .., op_{n_1}\}$ $-\ {}^\bullet t = \{ip_1, .., ip_{n_2}\}$ $-\ p^\bullet = \{ot_1, .., ot_{n_3}\}$ $-\ outT := \{t\} \times t^\bullet \setminus p$ $-\ inT := {}^\bullet t \times \{t\}$ $-\ outP := \{p\} \times p^\bullet$ $-\ inArc := {}^\bullet t \times p^\bullet$ $-\ outArc := p^\bullet \times t^\bullet \setminus p$ $-\ \tilde{P} := P \setminus \{p\},$ $-\ \tilde{T} := T \setminus \{t\}$ $-\ \tilde{F} := (F \cup inArc \cup outArc) \setminus ((t, p) \cup inT \cup outT \cup outP)$

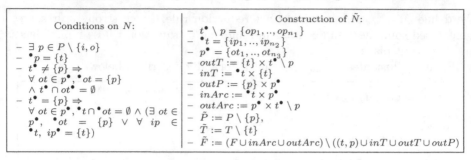

(a) $t^\bullet = \{p\}$ (b) $t^\bullet \neq \{p\}$

Fig. 5. Reduction rule $\phi_{RemoveTP}$ (R_4)

This rule generalises the *Post-Fusion* rule of [25, 29]. Its inverse is a synthesis rule introducing a sequence of tasks (adding a task that has to be accomplished before others) by factoring common input/output places of a set of transitions.

The soundness of $\phi_{RemoveTP}$, with respect to generalised soundness, is given by the following proposition.

Proposition 4. $\phi_{RemoveTP}$ *is a workflow net reduction rule which strongly preserves generalised soundness.*

Proof. (Sketch). In N the transitions $ot_1, .., ot_{n_3}$ have to consume a token in place p. All tokens consumed in place p have to be produced by transition t, which consumes a token in places $ip_1, .., ip_{n_2}$ and produces a token in places $op_1, .., op_{n_1}$ and p. Thus, $ot_1, .., ot_{n_2}$ have to consume a token in $ip_1, .., ip_{n_2}$ and produce a token in $op_1, .., op_{n_1}$. Conversely, the same analysis holds on $\tilde{N}$, we conclude that N is generalised sound if and only if $\tilde{N}$ is generalised sound.

R_5: Remove Place Transition

We define $\phi_{RemovePT}$, a workflow net reduction rule, which strongly preserves generalised soundness and consists in removing a place and its only output transition. Intuitively, this rule consists in removing a place p and its only output transition t by merging transition t with the input transitions of place p.

The $\phi_{RemovePT}$ rule is depicted in Fig. 6, and formally described below.

Conditions on N:

- $\exists \, p \in P \setminus \{i, o\}$
- $p^{\bullet} = \{t\}$
- $^{\bullet}t \neq \{p\} \Rightarrow$
  $\forall \, it \in \, ^{\bullet}p, it^{\bullet} = \{p\}$
  $\wedge \; ^{\bullet}t \cap \, ^{\bullet}it = \emptyset \wedge (\, ^{\bullet}it)^{\bullet} = \{it\}$
- $^{\bullet}t = \{p\} \Rightarrow$
  $\forall \, it \in \, ^{\bullet}p, t^{\bullet} \cap it^{\bullet} = \emptyset$

Construction of $\tilde{N}$:

- $t^{\bullet} = \{op_1, .., op_{n_1}\}$
- $^{\bullet}t \setminus p = \{ip_1, .., ip_{n_2}\}$
- $^{\bullet}p = \{it_1, .., it_{n_3}\}$
- $outT := \{t\} \times t^{\bullet}$
- $inT := \, ^{\bullet}t \setminus p \times \{t\}$
- $inP := \, ^{\bullet}p \times \{p\}$
- $inArc := \, ^{\bullet}t \setminus p \times \, ^{\bullet}p$
- $outArc := \, ^{\bullet}p \times t^{\bullet}$
- $\tilde{P} := P \setminus \{p\}$,
- $\tilde{T} := T \setminus \{t\}$
- $\tilde{F} := (F \cup inArc \cup outArc) \setminus ((p, t) \cup inT \cup outT \cup inP)$

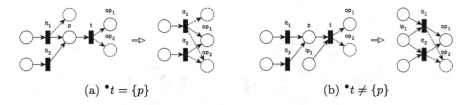

(a) $^{\bullet}t = \{p\}$ (b) $^{\bullet}t \neq \{p\}$

Fig. 6. Reduction rule $\phi_{RemovePT}$ (R_5)

This rule generalises the *Pre-Fusion* rule of [25,29] as well as the reduction rule ϕ_A proposed in [22].

The inverse of this rule is a synthesis rule introducing a sequence of tasks (adding a task that have to be accomplished after others) and able to factor common input/output places of a set of transitions.

The soundness of $\phi_{RemovePT}$, with respect to generalised soundness, is given by the following proposition.

Proposition 5. $\phi_{RemovePT}$ *is a workflow net reduction rule which strongly preserves generalised soundness.*

Proof. (Sketch). In N the transitions $it_1, .., it_{n_3}$ have to produce a token in place p. All tokens produced in place p have to be consumed by transition t, which consumes a token in places $ip_1, .., ip_{n_2}$ and p, and produces a token in places $op_1, .., op_{n_1}$. Thus, $it_1, .., it_{n_3}$ have to consume a token in $ip_1, .., ip_{n_2}$ and produce a token in $op_1, .., op_{n_1}$. Conversely, the same analysis holds on $\tilde{N}$, we conclude that N is generalised sound if and only if $\tilde{N}$ is generalised sound.

R_6: Remove Ring

We define $\phi_{RemoveR}$, a workflow net reduction rule, which strongly preserves generalised soundness, and consists in merging places among a ring. A ring is a set of places strongly connected by transitions with a single input place and a single output place. The transitions forming the ring are also removed. Intuitively, tokens among the places of a ring can freely move from a place of the ring to an other, therefore they might as well be on the same place.

Figure 7 illustrates the rule $\phi_{RemoveR}$ that is formally described below.

Conditions on N:	Construction of $\tilde{N}$:
$- \exists \{p_1,..,p_n\} \subseteq P$ $- \exists \{t_1,..,t_m\} \subseteq T$ $- \forall i \in \{1,..,m\}, |{}^\bullet t_i| = |t_i^\bullet| = 1$ $- \forall i,j \in \{1,..,n\}, {}^\bullet p_i \cap {}^\bullet p_j = p_i^\bullet \cap p_j^\bullet = \emptyset$ $- \forall\ i,j \in \{1,..,m\}, \exists\ \sigma : \{1,..,k\} \rightarrow \{p_1,..,p_n\} \cup \{t_1,..,t_m\}$ a path of length k such that $\sigma(1) = p_i \wedge \sigma(k) = p_j \wedge \forall\ x \in \{1,..,k-1\}, (\sigma(x),\sigma(x+1)) \in F$	$-\ ringArc := (((\{p_1,..,p_n\} \times \{t_1,..,t_m\}) \cup$ $\quad (\{t_1,..,t_m\} \times \{p_1,..,p_n\})) \cap F$ $-\ inT := {}^\bullet p_1 \cup .. \cup {}^\bullet p_n$ $-\ outT := p_1^\bullet \cup .. \cup p_n^\bullet$ $-\ removedA := ((inT \times \{p_1,..,p_n\}) \cup$ $\quad (\{p_1,..,p_n\} \times outT)) \cap F$ $-\ addA := (inT \times p) \cup (p \times outT)$ $-\ \tilde{P} := (P \cup p) \setminus \{p_1,..,p_n\}$ $-\ \tilde{T} := T \setminus \{t_1,..,t_m\}$ $-\ \tilde{F} := (F \cup addA) \setminus removedA$

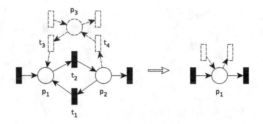

Fig. 7. Reduction rule $\phi_{RemoveR}$ (R_6)

This rule is an original one. Its inverse is a synthesis rule which transforms a place into a ring, distributing its input and output transitions among the places of the created ring.

The soundness of $\phi_{RemoveR}$, with respect to generalised soundness, is given by the following proposition.

Proposition 6 (Soundness of $\phi_{RemoveR}$). $\phi_{RemoveR}$ *is a workflow net reduction rule which strongly preserves generalised soundness.*

Proof. (Sketch). By conditions imposed on N, tokens among the places $p_1,..,p_n$ of a ring can freely move from a place of the ring to an other by firing a sequence of transitions formed with transitions $t_1,..,t_m$. It follows that each token produced (resp. consumed) by an input (resp. output) transition of a place in the ring will eventually be (resp. has been), after (resp. before) the firing of a possibly empty sequence of transitions formed with transitions $t_1,..,t_m$, consumed (resp. produced) by any output (resp. input) transitions of a place of the ring. Likewise, in $\tilde{N}$ each token produced (resp. consumed) by an input (resp. output) transition of p will be (resp. has been) consumed (resp. produced) by an output (resp. input) transition of p. It follows that N is generalised sound if and only if $\tilde{N}$ is generalised sound.

This section defined six reduction rules, which together constitute a generic reduction kit, denoted Φ^*, preserving generalised soundness. These rules generalise the rules previously presented in the literature [7,22–27,29] and thereby extend the range of workflow nets reducible in such a way.

4.3   Verification Algorithm

This section proposes an algorithm, based on the workflow net reduction rules previously described, for semi-deciding the generalised soundness. Our approach is based on Lemma 1. This lemma allows us to infer the generalised soundness a workflow net from its transformed instance as long as the transformation rules applied to obtain it strongly preserve generalised soundness.

The reduction kit Φ^*, composed of the six reduction rules introduced in the previous section, strongly preserves generalised soundness. Therefore, let N and $\tilde{N}$ be two workflow nets such that $(N, \tilde{N}) \in \Phi^*$ then the workflow N is generalised sound if and only if the workflow net $\tilde{N}$ is generalised sound. Furthermore, it is trivial that the workflow net N_{Atomic} (i.e. a workflow net composed of a single transition whose input place is the initial place and output place is the final place) is generalised sound. It follows that if $(N, N_{Atomic}) \in \Phi^*$ then the workflow net N is generalised sound. Since the reduction *kit* Φ^* is not complete with respect to generalized soundness over ordinary workflow nets, this leads to the design of an algorithm to semi-decide whether a workflow net N is generalised sound.

This algorithm proceeds by iteratively trying to apply any of the reduction rules of Φ^* to the input the workflow net N until a fix-point is reached (none of the reduction rules can be applied). If the resulting workflow net equals N_{Atomic}, one can conclude that N is generalised sound. Otherwise, one cannot directly conclude about generalised soundness, but the reduced workflow net is saved to be further analysed using classical techniques such as model-checking.

This procedure is described by Algorithm 1, which is based on: (i) the set of workflow net reduction rules $\Phi = \{R_1, .., R_6\}$, (ii) an auxiliary function $size(N)$, which returns the number of nodes of a workflow net N at each iteration step, (iii) a function $TryApplyRule(\phi, N)$, which returns either $\tilde{N}$ if the rule ϕ can be applied to N to produce $\tilde{N}$, or N otherwise, and (iv) $save(N)$, a function that saves N.

Data: $N = \langle P, T, F \rangle$
Result: Generalised soundness of N
int $sizeN = 0$;
do
  | $sizeN = size(N)$;
  | $N = ApplyReductionRules(N)$;
while $size(N) < sizeN$;
if $N = N_{Atomic}$ then
  | return true;
else
  | $save(N)$;
  | return unknown;
end

Function $ApplyReductionRules(N)$
  forall the $\phi \in \Phi$ **do**
    int $subsizeN = 0$;
    do
      | $subsizeN = size(N)$;
      | $N = TryApplyRule(\phi, N)$;
    while $size(N) < subsizeN$;
  end
  return N;

Algorithm 1. Generalised soundness semi-decision algorithm

Theorem 1. *The procedure described by Algorithm 1 terminates.*

Proof. (Sketch). Every rule applied by Algorithm 1 strictly reduces the number of nodes of N. None of the applied rules can produce a workflow net with less than one node. Thus, it always terminates when no workflow net reduction rules can be applied, providing an atomic sound net or saving a reduced workflow net.

Theorem 2. *The procedure described by Algorithm 1 is sound.*

Proof. (Sketch). The set of workflow net reduction rules strongly preserves generalised soundness. By Theorem 1 the procedure of Algorithm 1 is thus sound.

Before concluding this section, let us remark again that the presented reduction procedure is not complete, and leads to a semi-decision procedure. However, this paper presents generalizations of previously known rules [7,22–27,29]. Consequently, in comparison with the previously cited results, which are also not complete for arbitrary workflow nets, the rules introduced in this paper are able to further reduce workflow nets allowing other analysis approaches (e.g., [16,18]) to be carried out on smaller instances, enabling to increase their scalability. Finally, an extension of the range of reducible workflow nets is a work in progress; to this end, the presented rules would be further generalised or extended to handle generalised Petri nets instead of ordinary ones.

5   Verification Tool and Experimental Results

A dedicated open source tool suite, called *Hadara-AdSimul-Red*[1], has been developed to conduct intensive experiments in order to evaluate the effectiveness, efficiency and scalability of the proposed reduction method. This section presents this tool, as well as convincing experimental results demonstrating its benefits.

5.1   Verification Tool

Figure 8 depicts the global architecture of the verification tool *Hadara-AdSimul-Red*, which has been developed (in C++) to support the proposed method.

This tool takes as input an ordinary workflow net (1), saved as an XML file and conform to an ad-hoc and proprietary standard – a dedicated meta-model –, or to the PNML standard [32] – a generic Petri nets XML format – so that third party editor can be used (e.g., VipTool [33], WoPeD [34],Yasper [35], PIPE [36]).

Hadara-AdSimul-Red (2) then tries to apply any of the six reduction rules presented in Sect. 4.2 to the input workflow net until a fix-point is reached(i.e. none of the reduction rules can be applied) by following the procedure described by Algorithm 1.

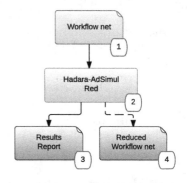

Fig. 8. Tool architecture

Once the computation is completed, the tool provides a result report (3) including the status of the verification regarding the generalised soundness,

---

[1] The tool *Hadara-AdSimul-Red* (including examples and source code) is available in Github: https://github.com/LoW12/Hadara-AdSimul.

and metrics about execution time and size reduction. Whenever the generalised soundness verification is inconclusive (i.e. the workflow net cannot be completely reduced), the resulting reduced workflow net (4) is saved for further analysis.

In order to ease and foster its use, this tool features a Web interface available online[2]. As an example, Fig. 9 shows the Web screenshot displaying the verification results obtained using an industrial workflow net as input. Information and graphical representations of the original and resulting reduced workflow nets are respectively shown at the left and right of the central frame, which displays the spent reduction time, the status of the generalised soundness verification, as well as the reduction factor obtained.

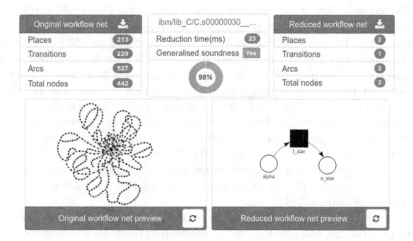

Fig. 9. Screenshot of the *Hadara-AdSimul-Red* verification results

5.2 Experimental Evaluation

This section presents an experimental evaluation of the reduction method proposed in this paper. In a first step, the objectives of this experimentation are stated. In a second step, the experimental protocol, designed to reach the given objectives, is described. Finally, obtained results are presented and discussed.

Objectives – The objectives of this experimental evaluation are to experimentally assess the *effectiveness, efficiency* and *scalability* of the proposed reduction method. Formally, the effectiveness of the proposed reduction method is measured with respect to its ability to reduce the size (number of places and transitions) of the considered workflow nets: given a workflow net of size *OriginalSize*, the effectiveness of the proposed reduction method is given by the ratio *ReducedSize/OriginalSize*, where *ReducedSize* is the size of the workflow net obtained after reduction.

---

[2] http://www.adsimul.com/.

Furthermore, the efficiency of the proposed method is evaluated with respect to the time spent to reduce the considered workflow nets. Finally, it follows that the method is scalable over a considered set of workflow nets of growing size if it is able to effectively and efficiently reduce them.

Experimental Protocol – It considers the benchmark suite of 1976 industrial workflow nets previously studied in [9–12] and more recently in [13,14] where others reduction procedure, also based on reduction rules, have been applied. This benchmark suite is actually composed of two main benchmarks.

The first benchmark, denoted *IBM-bpm*, is a collection of 1386 free choice workflow nets, organized into five libraries (A, B1, B2, B3, and C). All have been derived from industrial business process models provided by IBM®. They have been translated into Petri nets from IBM Web-Sphere Business Modeler[3]'s language (i.e. a language similar to UML activity diagrams [37]) according to [38]. The resulting Petri nets often have multiple sink places and have therefore been completed according to [39] in order to obtain workflow nets. We notably point out that four of the largest workflow nets of this data set are included in the benchmark used by the 2016 Edition of the Model Checking Contest [40]. More information about this data set can be found in the reference paper [12].

The second benchmark, denoted *SAP-ref*, is a collection of 590 workflow nets that have been derived from SAP®'s ERP Software[4] reference models. These 590 industrial workflows have been translated into workflow nets from their original EPCs models [41]. More information about this data set can be found in the reference papers [9–11].

For each workflow net of this benchmark suite, the experimental protocol consists in gathering the obtained reduction factor, the time spent to reach this result, as well as the related generalised soundness verification status.

Results – The experimental results obtained using the dedicated reduction tool described in Sect. 5.1 by applying the experimental protocol introduced previously are now presented. All experimentations have been computed using *Hadara-AdSimul-Red* on a personal laptop featuring an Intel core i7-3740QM @ 2.70 GHz processor (using only a single core). The complete data-sets as well as the obtained experimental results are accessible at https://dx.doi.org/10.6084/m9.figshare.3573756.v5.

Figures 10(a) and (b) respectively present the reduction factors and the sizes of workflow nets of the *IBM-bpm* and *SAP-ref* benchmarks. Table 1 summarizes the overall results of these experiments.

We have analysed 1976 industrial workflow nets and determined that 642 of them are generalised sound (i.e. have been completely reduced). In addition, each workflow has been reduced by an average factor of 82.2%. These experimental results obviously highlight the effectiveness of the proposed reduction method.

---

[3] http://www.ibm.com/software/products/en/modeler-basic.

[4] http://go.sap.com/product/enterprise-management/erp.html.

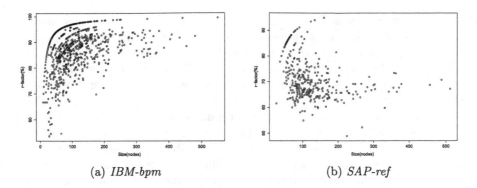

(a) *IBM-bpm*   (b) *SAP-ref*

Fig. 10. Reduction factor with respect to original size

Table 1. Results for the *IBM-bpm* and *SAP-ref* benchmarks

Benchmark	Status	#workflow nets	#Nodes		r-factor(%)		time(ms)	
			avg.	max.	avg.	max.	avg.	max.
IBM-bpm(libA)	Sound	152	61.4	193	93.5	98.4	3.2	44
	unknown	130	99.7	277	86.8	95.1	9.6	51
IBM-bpm(libB1)	Sound	107	38.6	228	86.7	98.7	3.8	67
	unknown	181	98.6	360	82	95.8	7.1	54
IBM-bpm(libB2)	Sound	161	38.9	334	85	99.1	7.3	380
	unknown	202	110.3	404	83	95.8	8.5	60
IBM-bpm(libB3)	Sound	207	47.5	252	87.8	98.8	3.9	56
	unknown	214	125.7	454	85.2	96	8.7	72
IBM-bpm(libC)	Sound	15	127	548	94.4	99.5	7.1	46
	unknown	17	135.6	480	84.7	94.9	5.1	28
IBM-bpm(all)	Sound	642	49	548	**88.4**	99.5	4.6	380
	unknown	744	110.6	480	**84.1**	96	8.3	72
SAP-ref	Sound	0	–	–	–	–	–	–
	unknown	590	97.7	512	**73**	95	9.9	967

With regard to the 1386 free choice workflow nets of *IBM-bpm*, 642 of them were identified as generalised sound by our tool. This results (i.e. the detected soundness) are in agreement with the results obtained during previous experiments applying different analysis techniques to the same data set [12,14] (i.e. the complete subset of generalised sound workflow nets has been identified by our tool). We underline the fact that all 642 sound workflow nets have been identified through structural reduction by our approach whereas only 464 of them have been identified through structural reduction by Woflan [42]. Furthermore, let us point out that workflow nets of this data set have been on average reduced to 13.9% of their original size (i.e. reduced by a factor of 86.1%). This underlines the greater effectiveness of our method compared with the reduction method of [13] where workflow nets of the same data set have only been reduced to about 23% of their original size (i.e. reduced by a factor of about 77%).

Regarding the 590 workflow nets of *SAP-ref*, only three of them are free choice workflow nets. None of those 590 workflow nets has been found to be generalised sound by our method. However, workflow nets of this data set have been on average reduced to 27% of their original size (i.e. reduced by a factor of 73%). These results further highlight the effectiveness of our reduction method over arbitrary workflow nets. Indeed, once more (albeit to a lesser extent), these results show that our reduction method ability exceeds the one of [13] where workflow nets of the same data set have been reduced to about 35% of their original size (i.e. reduced by a factor of about 65%).

Finally, the results of these experiments based on the *IBM-bpm* and *SAP-ref* benchmarks have also illustrated the efficiency of the proposed reduction method. Indeed, workflow nets of these benchmarks whose sizes are ranging from 9 to 548 nodes have been reduced on average in about 8 ms. Such a short analysis time means that this method could be continuously executed by integrated development environment to provide useful feedback and diagnostic information regarding the generalised soundness of in-development workflow nets.

6   Conclusion

This paper presented an effective, efficient and scalable method to semi-decide the generalised soundness of large-scale workflow nets. This method aims to reduce an arbitrary workflow net into a smaller one while preserving generalised soundness. This enable soundness verification to be carried out over smaller instances of workflow nets, thus drastically decreasing the calculation time required for such a verification. To reach this goal, six novel workflow net reduction rules are proposed and proven to be correct with respect to generalised soundness, a well-established correctness notion in the context of workflow specification. These workflow net reduction rules enable the definition of a reliable and efficient algorithm that semi-decides the generalised soundness of workflow nets.

It also presented conclusive experimental results obtained using a dedicated open-source tool suite implementing the method. Indeed, over a benchmark suite of 1976 industrial workflow nets previously studied in [9–14], it demonstrated convincing size reductions benefits. More precisely, these results illustrated the effectiveness, efficiency and scalability of the proposed reduction method to the verification of generalised soundness by providing, for the considered workflow nets, an average size reduction of 82.2%, in an average time of 8 ms, over industrial workflow nets of size up to 548 nodes.

On the basis of these conclusive results and in order to even more increase the effectiveness of this reduction method, we plan as future work to design and experiment more sophisticated strategies to order the workflow net reduction rules application. From a formal point of view, we also would like to extend the range of workflow nets reducible by adding new rules and further generalising the presented rules by considering generalised Petri nets rather than ordinary Petri nets as stated in Sect. 4 of the present paper. Finally, we are investigating the use of the reduction techniques presented in this paper to optimise the verification of workflow net modal specifications [43] in a way similar to [24].

References

1. van der Aalst, W.M.: Three good reasons for using a Petri-net-based workflow management system. J. Inf. Process Integr. Enterprises **428**, 161–182 (1997)
2. Dittrich, G.: Specification with nets. In: Pichler, F., Moreno-Diaz, R. (eds.) EURO-CAST 1989. LNCS, vol. 410, pp. 111–124. Springer, Heidelberg (1990). doi:10.1007/3-540-52215-8_10
3. van der Aalst, W.M.P., Barros, A.P., Hofstede, A.H.M., Kiepuszewski, B.: Advanced workflow patterns. In: Scheuermann, P., Etzion, O. (eds.) CoopIS 2000. LNCS, vol. 1901, pp. 18–29. Springer, Heidelberg (2000). doi:10.1007/10722620_2
4. Suzuki, I., Murata, T.: A method for stepwise refinement and abstraction of Petri nets. J. Comput. Syst. Sci. **27**(1), 51–76 (1983)
5. van der Aalst, W.M., van Hee, K.M., ter Hofstede, A.H., Sidorova, N., Verbeek, H., Voorhoeve, M., Wynn, M.T.: Soundness of workflow nets: classification, decidability, and analysis. J. Formal Aspects Comput. **23**(3), 333–363 (2011)
6. Lipton, R.: The reachability problem requires exponential space. Research report (Yale University. Department of Computer Science). Department of Computer Science, Yale University (1976)
7. Murata, T.: Petri nets: Properties, analysis and applications. IEEE **77**(4), 541–580 (1989)
8. Valmari, A.: The state explosion problem. In: Reisig, W., Rozenberg, G. (eds.) ACPN 1996. LNCS, vol. 1491, pp. 429–528. Springer, Berlin (1998). doi:10.1007/3-540-65306-6_21
9. Mendling, J., Moser, M., Neumann, G., Verbeek, H.M.W., van Dongen, B.F., van der Aalst, W.M.P.: Faulty EPCs in the SAP reference model. In: Dustdar, S., Fiadeiro, J.L., Sheth, A.P. (eds.) BPM 2006. LNCS, vol. 4102, pp. 451–457. Springer, Berlin (2006). doi:10.1007/11841760_38
10. van Dongen, B.F., Jansen-Vullers, M.H., Verbeek, H.M.W., van der Aalst, W.M.: Verification of the SAP reference models using EPC reduction, state-space analysis, and invariants. Comput. Ind. **58**(6), 578–601 (2007)
11. Mendling, J., Verbeek, H.M.W., van Dongen, B.F., van der Aalst, W.M., Neumann, G.: Detection and prediction of errors in EPCs of the SAP reference model. Data Knowl. Eng. **64**(1), 312–329 (2008)
12. Fahland, D., Favre, C., Jobstmann, B., Koehler, J., Lohmann, N., Völzer, H., Wolf, K.: Instantaneous soundness checking of industrial business process models. In: Dayal, U., Eder, J., Koehler, J., Reijers, H.A. (eds.) BPM 2009. LNCS, vol. 5701, pp. 278–293. Springer, Berlin (2009). doi:10.1007/978-3-642-03848-8_19
13. Esparza, J., Hoffmann, P.: Reduction rules for colored workflow nets. In: Stevens, P., Wąsowski, A. (eds.) FASE 2016. LNCS, vol. 9633, pp. 342–358. Springer, Heidelberg (2016). doi:10.1007/978-3-662-49665-7_20
14. Favre, C., Völzer, H., Müller, P.: Diagnostic information for control-flow analysis of workflow graphs (a.k.a. Free-Choice Workflow Nets). In: Chechik, M., Raskin, J.-F. (eds.) TACAS 2016. LNCS, vol. 9636, pp. 463–479. Springer, Berlin (2016). doi:10.1007/978-3-662-49674-9_27

15. Van Hee, K., Sidorova, N., Voorhoeve, M.: Generalised soundness of workflow nets is decidable. In: Cortadella, J., Reisig, W. (eds.) ICATPN 2004. LNCS, vol. 3099, pp. 197–215. Springer, Berlin (2004). doi:10.1007/978-3-540-27793-4_12

16. Hee, K., Oanea, O., Sidorova, N., Voorhoeve, M.: Verifying generalized soundness of workflow nets. In: Virbitskaite, I., Voronkov, A. (eds.) PSI 2006. LNCS, vol. 4378, pp. 235–247. Springer, Berlin (2007). doi:10.1007/978-3-540-70881-0_21

17. Ping, L., Hao, H., Jian, L.: On 1-soundness and soundness of workflow nets. In: Proceedings of the Third Workshop on Modelling of Objects, Components, and Agents Aarhus, Denmark, pp. 21–36 (2004)

18. Verbeek, H.M.W., Basten, T., van der Aalst, W.M.: Diagnosing workflow processes using woflan. Comput. J. **44**(4), 246–279 (2001)

19. Yamaguchi, M., Yamaguchi, S., Tanaka, M.: A model checking method of soundness for workflow nets. IEICE Trans. Fundam. Electron. Commun. Comput. Sci. **92**(11), 2723–2731 (2009)

20. Holzmann, G.J.: The SPIN Model Checker Primer and Reference Manual, vol. 1003. Addison-Wesley, Reading (2004)

21. Barkaoui, K., Ben Ayed, R., Sbai, Z.: Workflow soundness verification based on structure theory of Petri nets. J. Comput. Inf. Sci. **5**(1), 51–61 (2007)

22. Desel, J., Esparza, J.: Free Choice Petri Nets, vol. 40. Cambridge University Press, New York (2005)

23. Lin, H., Zhao, Z., Li, H., Chen, Z.: A novel graph reduction algorithm to identify structural conflicts. In: Proceedings of the 35th Annual Hawaii International Conference on System Sciences HICSS 2002, 10 p. IEEE (2002)

24. Hichami, O.E., Al Achhab, M., Berrada, I., Oucheikh, R., El Mohajir, B.E.: An approach of optimisation and formal verification of workflow Petri nets. J. Theoret. Appl. Inf. Technol. **61**(3), 486–495 (2014)

25. Berthelot, G.: Transformations and decompositions of nets. In: Brauer, W., Reisig, W., Rozenberg, G. (eds.) ACPN 1986. LNCS, vol. 254, pp. 359–376. Springer, Berlin (1987). doi:10.1007/978-3-540-47919-2_13

26. Voorhoeve, M., Van der Aalst, W.: Ad-hoc workflow: problems and solutions. In: 1997 Proceedings of the Eighth International Workshop on Database and Expert Systems Applications, pp. 36–40. IEEE (1997)

27. Sadiq, W., Orlowska, M.E.: Analyzing process models using graph reduction techniques. Inf. Syst. **25**(2), 117–134 (2000)

28. Wynn, M.T., Verbeek, H., van der Aalst, W.M., ter Hofstede, A.H., Edmond, D.: Soundness-preserving reduction rules for reset workflow nets. Inf. Sci. **179**(6), 769–790 (2009)

29. Sloan, R.H., Buy, U.: Reduction rules for time petri nets. Acta Informatica **33**(7), 687–706 (1996)

30. Petri, C.A.: Kommunikation mit Automaten. Ph.D. thesis, Darmstadt University of Technology, Germany (1962)

31. van der Aalst, W.M.: The application of Petri nets to workflow management. J. Circuits Syst. Comput. **8**(1), 21–66 (1998)

32. Weber, M., Kindler, E.: The petri net markup language. In: Ehrig, H., Reisig, W., Rozenberg, G., Weber, H. (eds.) Petri Net Technology for Communication-Based Systems. LNCS, vol. 2472, pp. 124–144. Springer, Berlin (2003). doi:10.1007/978-3-540-40022-6_7

33. Desel, J., Juhás, G., Lorenz, R., Neumair, C.: Modelling and validation with viptool. In: Aalst, W.M.P., Weske, M. (eds.) BPM 2003. LNCS, vol. 2678, pp. 380–389. Springer, Berlin (2003). doi:10.1007/3-540-44895-0_26

34. Freytag, T.: Woped-workflow petri net designer. University of Cooperative Education (2005)
35. Van Hee, K., Oanea, O., Post, R., Somers, L., Van der Werf, J.M.: Yasper: a tool for workflow modeling and analysis. In: 2006 Sixth International Conference on Application of Concurrency to System Design ACSD 2006, pp. 279–282. IEEE (2006)
36. Bonet, P., Lladó, C.M., Puijaner, R., Knottenbelt, W.J.: PIPE v2.5: a Petri net tool for performance modelling. In: Proceedings of the 23rd Latin American Conference on Informatics (CLEI 2007), San Jose, Costa Rica, October 2007
37. Dumas, M., Hofstede, A.H.M.: UML activity diagrams as a workflow specification language. In: Gogolla, M., Kobryn, C. (eds.) UML 2001. LNCS, vol. 2185, pp. 76–90. Springer, Berlin (2001). doi:10.1007/3-540-45441-1_7
38. Fahland, D.: Translating UML2 activity diagrams to Petri nets (2008)
39. Kiepuszewski, B., ter Hofstede, A.H.M., van der Aalst, W.M.: Fundamentals of control flow in workflows. Acta Informatica **39**(3), 143–209 (2003)
40. Kordon, F., Garavel, H., Hillah, L.M., Hulin-Hubard, F., Chiardo, G., Hamez, A., Jezequel, L., Miner, A., Meijer, J., Paviot-Adet, E., Racordon, D., Rodriguez, C., Rohr, C., Srba, J., Thierry-Mieg, Y., Trinh, G., Wolf, K.: Models of the 2016 Edition of the Model Checking Contest, June 2016. http://mcc.lip6.fr/models.php
41. Lohmann, N., Verbeek, E., Dijkman, R.: Petri net transformations for business processes–a survey. In: Jensen, K., Aalst, W.M.P. (eds.) Transactions on Petri Nets and Other Models of Concurrency II. LNCS, vol. 5460, pp. 46–63. Springer, Berlin (2009). doi:10.1007/978-3-642-00899-3_3
42. Verbeek, E., Van Der Aalst, W.M.P.: Woflan 2.0 A petri-net-based workflow diagnosis tool. In: Nielsen, M., Simpson, D. (eds.) ICATPN 2000. LNCS, vol. 1825, pp. 475–484. Springer, Heidelberg (2000). doi:10.1007/3-540-44988-4_28
43. Bride, H., Kouchnarenko, O., Peureux, F.: Verifying modal workflow specifications using constraint solving. In: Albert, E., Sekerinski, E. (eds.) IFM 2014. LNCS, vol. 8739, pp. 171–186. Springer, Heidelberg (2014). doi:10.1007/978-3-319-10181-1_11

Structuring Abstract Interpreters Through State and Value Abstractions

Sandrine Blazy[1], David Bühler[2(✉)], and Boris Yakobowski[2]

[1] IRISA - University of Rennes 1, Rennes, France
sandrine.blazy@irisa.fr
[2] Software Reliability and Security Laboratory, CEA LIST,
P.C. 174, Gif-sur-Yvette 91191, France
{david.buhler,boris.yakobowski}@cea.fr

Abstract. We present a new modular way to structure abstract interpreters. Modular means that new analysis domains may be plugged-
in. These abstract domains can communicate through different means
to achieve maximal precision. First, all abstractions work cooperatively
to emit alarms that exclude the undesirable behaviors of the program.
Second, the state abstract domains may exchange information through
abstractions of the possible value for expressions. Those value abstractions are themselves extensible, should two domains require a novel form
of cooperation. We used this approach to design EVA, an abstract interpreter for C implemented within the FRAMA-C framework. We present
the domains that are available so far within EVA, and show that this
communication mechanism is able to handle them seamlessly.

1   Introduction

Static analysis of C programs by abstract interpretation [9] has known considerable progress in recent years, in terms of both research breakthrough and
industrial-strength implementations. Verifying C programs precisely remains of
paramount importance for at least two reasons. On the one hand, C remains
the choice language for safety-critical programs. Its low-level nature makes the
compilation process simple enough (with non-optimizing compilers) that the
equivalence between the source code and the binary produced can be checked.
This is often a requirement of the qualification process. On the other hand, many
programs routinely used in computers or embedded devices, and thus open to
cyber-attacks, remain written in C (the Linux kernel, bind, openssl, etc.).

Designing sound abstract analyzers that remain precise on large classes of
programs is challenging. Having a sound analyzer generally means that a large
number of false alarms are emitted. To improve precision, the analyzer can be
extended with dedicated analysis *domains*, that will be better suited to handle particular code fragments. However, integrating multiple domains remains
a challenge in itself. First, those domains must remain relatively independent:
adding one domain should not require modifying the existing ones. However,
they must also be able to cooperate, and exchange information.

© Springer International Publishing AG 2017
A. Bouajjani and D. Monniaux (Eds.): VMCAI 2017, LNCS 10145, pp. 112–130, 2017.
DOI: 10.1007/978-3-319-52234-0_7

In abstract interpretation, such communication is usually handled through the use of a *reduced product* [10]. However, such products are hard to define between rich domains. Moreover, reduced products are not modular, and adding a domain requires extensive modifications to existing ones. Thus, abstract analyzers often implement approximations of the reduced product [7]. Furthermore, domains often do not inter-reduce directly, but instead use a communication interface (see e.g. Astrée [11] and Verasco [16]).

The FRAMA-C framework [17] features an abstract interpreter called Value Analysis (abbreviated as VALUE), that has been successfully used to verify safety-critical code [12]. Its main features are an intricate memory abstraction (able to represent efficiently and precisely both low-level concepts such as unions and bitfields, and high-level ones such as arrays), and an instance of a trace partitioning domain [18] (able to unroll loops or to analyze separately the branches of a disjunction). The abstract domain of VALUE is not relational. Aggressive trace partitioning can be used to work around this limitation: the relational information is instead carried out by the disjunction encoded by the multiple states. Nevertheless, relational domains are desirable. Also problematic was the fact that the analyzer has been written around its domain, resulting in a very tight coupling. So far, adding new domains – relational or not – was not possible.

In this work, we go beyond what was done in VALUE and present an abstract interpreter for C, called EVA (for *E*volved *V*alue *A*nalysis). The main novelty of this analyzer —and our contribution— lies in the generic communication language between the abstract domains. This language is based on abstractions of C values, while domains are abstractions of memory states. Both state and value abstractions are extensible, and different domains may communicate through different values. Domains also cooperate to state the *alarms* about the undesirable behaviors that may occur during a program execution. Finally, abstract domains do not need to share the same abstraction for the memory, which facilitates the integration of domains with different granularities in their vision of the program.

The main contributions of our paper are the following:

- A new design for abstract interpreters and the collaboration between domains, relying on a separation between value and state abstractions.
- A semantics and a cooperative emission mechanism for the alarms that report undesirable behaviors.
- An open-source abstract interpreter for C, relying on a modular architecture aimed at easing the introduction of new abstractions.
- An implementation of multiple abstract domains, exercising the various communication mechanisms.

The rest of the paper is organized as follows. The semantics of our language is given in Sect. 2. We propose our new modular architecture in Sect. 3. Value and state abstractions are described in Sects. 4 and 5. The analysis domains we have implemented are presented in Sect. 6. Related and future works are discussed in Sects. 7 and 8.

2   Formalization of Our Language

Abstract interpretation links a very precise, but generally undecidable, concrete semantics to an abstract one – the abstract semantics being a sound approximation of the concrete one. This section defines the syntax of our language, its concrete semantics, and the properties expected from an abstract semantics. The language itself is mostly orthogonal to the rest of the paper. However, it is required to state the soundness properties of abstract transformers.

2.1   Language

Figure 1 introduces the syntax of our language, inspired by that of Miné [20]. Programs operate over a fixed, finite set of variables $x \in \mathcal{X}$, whose types can be **char**, **signed** or **unsigned** integers, floating-point, pointers, arrays of known size or structures. Expressions e are either a scalar constant cst, the application of a n-ary operator $\Diamond$ to n expressions, or the dereference of an address a. A constant is either a rational (for arithmetic values) or the pair (x, i) of a variable x together with a bytes-expressed offset i (for pointers). For readability, we often write $\&x$ for $(x, 0)$. Operators on expressions include arithmetic operations, comparisons and casts between scalar types. Addresses are either a direct expression (interpreted as a pointer), or addresses plus offsets for fields in aggregates and cells in arrays. The dereference $*_\tau a$ of the address a is called a *lvalue*. The direct dereference of a variable $*_\tau(\&x)$ can be written x, as in the C syntax.

$$
\begin{aligned}
arith &::= \textbf{char} \mid (\textbf{signed} \mid \textbf{unsigned}) \; integer \mid float \\
scalar &::= arith \mid type \, \textbf{pointer} \\
\tau \in type &::= scalar \mid \tau\,[n] \mid \{field_i : \tau_i\}_{i \leq n} \\
e \in expr &::= cst \qquad\qquad cst \in \overline{\mathbb{V}} = \mathbb{Q} \cup \{(x,i) \mid x \in \mathcal{X}, \, i \in \mathbb{N}\} \\
&\mid \; \Diamond\,(e^n) \qquad\quad \Diamond \in \{+, \leq, (\tau), \dots\} \\
&\mid \; *_\tau a \\
a \in addr &::= e \mid a.field \mid a[e] \\
stmt &::= *_\tau a := e \mid e{=}{=}0?
\end{aligned}
$$

Fig. 1. Language syntax

Statements are either assignments or tests that halt execution when the condition does not hold. A program P is represented by its control-flow graph, where nodes are integer-numbered program points and edges are labeled by statements. For clarity, we write our examples using a C-like syntax.

2.2   Concrete Semantics

The concrete state of a program is described by an untyped memory $m \in \mathfrak{M}$, mapping *valid* (defined later) byte locations to single-byte characters. The C standard guarantees that a character value fits in one byte. The concrete values

$\overline{\mathbb{V}}_\tau$ of other scalar type τ may be encoded on successive bytes, whose number and meaning depend on the hardware architecture (which we assume known). We assume given the size $\texttt{sizeof}(\tau)$ of each scalar type, as well as a set of bijective functions ϕ_τ, each one interpreting a sequence of n bytes as a value of the scalar type τ of size n (hence of type $\left(\overline{\mathbb{V}}_{\text{char}}\right)^{\texttt{sizeof}(\tau)} \to \overline{\mathbb{V}}_\tau$) and conversely for their inverse. The $\texttt{sizeof}$ function is extended to expressions.

$$\overline{[\![\diamondsuit]\!]} : \overline{\mathbb{V}}^n \to \overline{\mathbb{V}} + \Omega$$

$$\texttt{loc}_\tau(v) \triangleq \begin{cases} (b, i + n)_{0 \leq n < \texttt{sizeof}(\tau)} & \text{if } v = (b, i) \in \mathcal{L}_\tau \\ \Omega & \text{otherwise} \end{cases}$$

$$\mathfrak{m}_\tau[v] \triangleq \phi_\tau\left(\mathfrak{m}\left(\texttt{loc}_\tau(v)\right)\right)$$

$$\overline{[\![\diamondsuit(e^n)]\!]}_\mathfrak{m} \triangleq \overline{[\![\diamondsuit]\!]}\left([\![e]\!]_\mathfrak{m}^n\right) \qquad \overline{[\![*_\tau e]\!]}_\mathfrak{m} \triangleq \mathfrak{m}_\tau[\![[\![e]\!]_\mathfrak{m}]\!]$$

$$\overline{\{\!\!\{*_\tau a := e\}\!\!\}}(\mathfrak{m}) \triangleq \mathfrak{m}\left[\texttt{loc}_\tau\left([\![a]\!]_\mathfrak{m}\right) \mapsto \phi_\tau^{-1}([\![e]\!]_\mathfrak{m})\right]$$

$$\overline{\{\!\!\{e==0?\}\!\!\}}(\mathfrak{m}) \triangleq \begin{cases} \mathfrak{m} & \text{if } \overline{[\![e==0]\!]}_\mathfrak{m} = 1 \\ \bot & \text{otherwise} \end{cases}$$

Fig. 2. Selected rules of the concrete semantics

Concrete values in $\overline{\mathbb{V}}$ are either arithmetic values in $\mathbb{Q}$, or pointer values. A pointer value is either the $\texttt{NULL}$ pointer (interpreted as 0) or a pair of a variable and an offset. A *location* is a pointer value together with a type. A location of type τ is *valid* when its offset plus the size being read (i.e. the size of τ) is smaller than the size of the type of the variable. The set of valid locations of type τ is written $\mathcal{L}_\tau$. Hence, a memory $\mathfrak{m} \in \mathfrak{M}$ has actually type $\mathcal{L}_{\text{char}} \to \overline{\mathbb{V}}_{\text{char}}$.

Figure 2 details some parts of the evaluation $[\![e]\!]_\mathfrak{m}$ of an expression e of scalar type in memory $\mathfrak{m}$. It produces either a value in $\overline{\mathbb{V}}$ or an error Ω, in case of an illegal operation. The evaluation of $\diamondsuit(e^n)$ relies on a semantics $\overline{[\![\diamondsuit]\!]}$ from the values of the arguments to the result, that does not involve $\mathfrak{m}$. It is either defined in the C standard, or implementation-defined. The rules for the evaluation of addresses are not shown. Computing the address of an array cell $e[e']$ shifts the address of e by the evaluation of e', using pointer arithmetic; computing the address of a field is similar. If a pointer expression e evaluates to a valid τ-location l, its dereference $*_\tau e$ interprets the $\texttt{sizeof}(\tau)$ bytes of the memory starting at location n (denoted by $\texttt{loc}_\tau(v)$) as having type τ. Otherwise, the dereference leads to the error value.

The semantics $\{\!\!\{\text{stmt}\}\!\!\}$ of a statement is a transfer function over states, described in the last equations of Fig. 2. An assignment stores in the memory bytes of the lvalue the characters corresponding to the value of the right expression. A test blocks the execution, only allowing states in which the condition holds. The transfer of a statement fails if the evaluation of an expression leads to the error value. An assignment also fails if the written location is not valid.

Our concrete semantics maps each program node n to the set $\mathbb{S}(n)$ of all possible memories at this point. The semantics of the entire program P is then the smallest solution to the following equations:

$$\mathbb{S}(0) \triangleq \mathfrak{M} \qquad \mathbb{S}(j) \triangleq \bigcup_{(i,\text{stmt},j)\in P} \overline{\{\!|\text{stmt}|\!\}}\,(\mathbb{S}(i))$$

2.3 Abstract Semantics

The soundness of an abstract semantics usually relies on a concretization function γ, that connects each abstraction to the sets of concrete elements it models. Then, an abstract semantics $\{\!|\cdot|\!\}^{\#}$ is a sound approximation of a concrete semantics $\{\!|\cdot|\!\}$ if for all abstract values v, $\overline{\{\!|\gamma(v)|\!\}} \subseteq \gamma(\{\!|v|\!\}^{\#})$ (the semantics is implicitly lifted on sets).

$$\gamma : \mathbb{X}^{\#} \to 2^{\overline{\mathbb{X}}} \qquad\qquad x_1 \sqsubseteq x_2 \Rightarrow \gamma(x_1) \subseteq \gamma(x_2)$$
$$\gamma(\top) = 2^{\overline{\mathbb{X}}} \qquad\qquad \gamma(x_1) \cup \gamma(x_2) \subseteq \gamma(x_1 \sqcup x_2)$$
$$\gamma(\bot) = \emptyset \qquad\qquad \gamma(x_1) \cap \gamma(x_2) \subseteq \gamma(x_1 \sqcap x_2)$$

Fig. 3. Soundness requirements for lattices

It is also convenient for the abstractions to have a lattice structure. Figure 3 presents the soundness guarantees required for a lattice $\mathbb{X}^{\#}$, with respect to the concretization. The partial order is consistent with the inclusion of concrete sets. The join $\sqcup$ and the meet $\sqcap$ over-approximate respectively the union and the intersection of sets of concrete values. $\top$ is the greatest value, whose concretization contains all concrete values. The smallest element $\bot$ denotes the abstraction with an empty concretization.

A sound lattice abstraction of concrete memory states defines an over approximation $\{\!|\text{stmt}|\!\}^{\#}$ of its semantics. The following equations define the abstract semantics of a program P: the soundness properties ensure that any solution is a correct approximation of its concrete semantics.

$$\mathbb{S}^{\#}(0) \triangleq \top \qquad \mathbb{S}^{\#}(j) \triangleq \bigsqcup_{(i,\text{stmt},j)\in P} \{\!|\text{stmt}|\!\}^{\#}\left(\mathbb{S}^{\#}(i)\right)$$

3 Architecture of a Modular Abstract Interpreter

In this section, we propose a new architecture to structure an abstract interpreter, introducing the distinction between value and state abstractions. We then describe how this architecture has been implemented in EVA to enable some interactions between abstract domains.

3.1   Hierarchy of Abstractions

We separate the abstractions on which an abstract interpreter relies into both *state* and *value* abstractions. A state abstraction represents the set of concrete states that may occur at a program point during a concrete execution. A value abstraction represents the C values an expression may have in some concrete states. The state abstractions handle the semantics of statements, while the value abstractions operate at the level of expressions. The value abstractions are the communication interface used by the state abstractions to interact with each other. Figure 4 sketches the architecture of a modular analyzer following these principles. The services each layer provides are given on the left, and the syntax fragments on which they operate on the right.

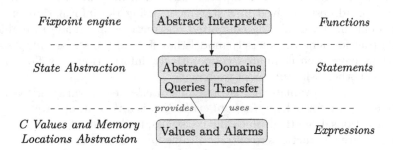

Fig. 4. Overall layers of our architecture

We assume given a fixpoint engine that performs a forward analysis over a control-flow graph. It propagates the state abstractions of an *abstract domain*, inferring properties at each statement. An abstract domain has a join-semilattice structure, fulfilling the properties given in Fig. 3. The join is used when two branches of the graph merge. A widening operator is mandatory, to ensure the convergence of the fixpoint computation. A domain must also provide:

- sound transformers, defining the abstract semantics of the domain. They model the effect of a statement on a state, and must satisfy the properties defined in Sect. 2.3.
- queries, which extract information from abstract states by assigning a *value* to some expressions. They are detailed in Sect. 5.

The communication between abstract domains is achieved through non-relational abstractions of *values* and *locations*. They over-approximate respectively the sets of possible C values for an expression, and the sets of possible memory locations for an address. Values and locations have a meet-semilattice structure, to intersect the values produced by multiple abstract states. They also provide sound approximations of the arithmetic operators on expressions and addresses. As the concrete operators may cause undesirable behavior at execution time, their abstract counterparts also produce *alarms*, which signal the error cases. The alarms are abstractions of the undesirable behaviors (mostly, undefined behaviors [14, Annex J.2]) that the analyzer tracks. Importantly, the alarms are part of the communication interface between abstract domains, along with values and locations. They are all formally defined in Sect. 4, while the interactions between domains are detailed in Sect. 5. In this paper, we do not distinguish values and locations further, as they fulfill the same role and the same requirements.

3.2   Communication Through Value Abstractions

This design has been successfully implemented in EVA, the new modular abstract interpreter of FRAMA-C. EVA features a cooperative evaluation of expressions in a product of abstract states. It computes alarms and value abstractions for each expression or address involved in a statement, using the information provided by each domain. Then, all the computed abstractions are made available for the state transformers, to precisely model the effect of the statement. As these abstractions have been computed cooperatively, information may flow from a domain to another, without direct exchanges.

Within EVA, the evaluator for expressions interleaves forward and backward evaluation steps. Informally, a *forward evaluation* is a bottom-up propagation of value abstractions, from the lvalues and constants, to the root of an expression. It queries the state abstractions to extract a value for variables, and relies otherwise on the value semantics of the C operators. Conversely, a *backward evaluation* is a top-down propagation aiming at reducing the values computed for the subterms of an expression. It relies on the backward counterparts for value operations, which learn information from a result and try to reduce the arguments. Note that all domains may benefit from the reductions achieved by the evaluator.

Importantly, both states and values are extensible, and may be a combination of multiple abstractions. A generic combiner is provided for both of them. For the domain, relational and non-relational abstractions can be composed together. They interact through the shared computation of value abstractions. This may appear to prohibit the communication between abstract domains understanding different value abstractions. However, value abstractions may themselves be combined into a regular reduced product. The inter-reduction between value components indirectly achieves an inter-reduction of abstract domains working on different values, as shown by the example below.

Example 1. We consider two memory domains I and C storing information about the possible values of integer variables. I and C respectively use intervals and congruences as value abstractions. Assume a condition $x > 3$, where I and C provide respectively the interval abstraction $[0..12]$ and the congruence $0[3]$ for x. The two values for x are reduced to $[4..12]$ and $0[3]$ when backward-evaluating the condition. Then, the inter-reduction between values reduces the interval information to $[6..12]$. Finally, I can learn this more precise information for x when it abstracts the effects of the whole condition.

4   Value Abstractions

This section presents the semantics of alarms and value abstractions, that are cooperatively used to approximate the evaluation of expressions.

4.1   Alarms

An abstract interpreter emits an alarm at each program point where it fails to prove the absence of undesirable behaviors. Each alarm may reveal a real bug, or be due to the over-approximations made by some abstractions. As such, alarms are over-approximations of the undesirable behaviors of a program. They stem from illegal operations on expressions. They are produced by the abstract operators on value abstractions, accumulated during expression evaluation, and ultimately raised by the analyzer. By pointing out all the potential run-time errors, alarms are the main result of the analyzer for the end user. In order to produce as few alarms as possible, it is essential that the domains may directly influence the generation of alarms during an evaluation. Thus, in our architecture, alarms are part of the interface between the domains and the analyzer.

Formally, we define alarms as maps from assertions to logical statuses ranging over **true**, **false** or **unknown**. The assertions are guards against the undesirable behaviors. If the status of an assertion is **true**, then its corresponding undesirable behavior never occurs. Otherwise, the undesirable behavior may occur (**unknown** status) or definitely happens if the program point is reachable (**false** status). The alarm maps may be **closed** or **open**: a **closed** map contains all alarms which may occur for the given expression, while an **open** map just gives a status to some of these alarms. **closed** maps are always sound abstractions of all undesirable behaviors of an expression. **open** maps are simpler to assert. They can exclude or guarantee *some* errors but offer no assurance of completeness.

Figure 5 defines the soundness of alarm maps in $\mathbb{A}$. In the concrete semantics, $\mathbb{C}$ operators on expressions may return either a value in $\overline{\mathbb{V}}$ or an error Ω, in case of undesirable behaviors. Given a predicate a, $a\,[e \leftarrow v]$ represents the truth-value of a where expressions e are replaced by concrete values v. We denote by

$$\begin{array}{cc}
\begin{array}{c}
\textbf{unknown} \\
\diagup\quad\diagdown \\
\textbf{true}\quad\textbf{false} \\
\diagdown\quad\diagup \\
\textbf{inconsistency}
\end{array}
&
\begin{array}{c}
\textbf{kind} = \textbf{closed} \mid \textbf{open} \\
\mathbb{A} = (assertion \rightarrow status) \times \textbf{kind}
\end{array}
\end{array}$$

$$e \in expr^n \quad V \subseteq \overline{V}^n \quad A \in \mathbb{A} \quad \overline{[\![\Diamond\,(e^n)]\!]} : \overline{V}^n \rightarrow \overline{V} + \Omega$$

$$\mathbf{A} = (A, kind) \models_{\mathbb{A}} \overline{[\![\Diamond\,(e)]\!]}(V) \Leftrightarrow$$

$$\left\{\begin{array}{llr}
\forall a \in A, \quad \forall v \in \overline{V}^n, \quad \neg a\,[e \leftarrow v] \Leftrightarrow \Diamond\,(v) = \Omega & (1) \\
\forall a \in A, \quad A(a) = \textbf{true} \quad \Rightarrow \forall v \in V, a\,[e \leftarrow v] & (2) \\
\forall a \in A, \quad A(a) = \textbf{false} \quad \Rightarrow \forall v \in V, \neg a\,[e \leftarrow v] & (3) \\
kind = \textbf{closed} \Rightarrow \forall v \in V, \; (\forall a \in A, \; a\,[e \leftarrow v]) \Rightarrow \Diamond\,(v) \neq \Omega & (4)
\end{array}\right.$$

Fig. 5. Semantics of alarms

$\mathbf{A} \models_\mathbb{A} \overline{[\Diamond(e)]}(V)$ the fact that the alarms $\mathbf{A}$ are a sound abstraction of the possible undesirable behaviors of the n-ary operator $\Diamond$ applied to a vector e of expressions whose values are in the concrete set V. This requires that:

- (1) the assertions of $\mathbf{A}$ correspond exactly to undesirable behaviors: for any vector of values v, an assertion in A is not satisfied if and only if $\Diamond(v)$ fails;
- (2 and 3) the precise statuses assigned to assertions in A are correct: the assertions bound to `true` (resp. `false`) in A are satisfied (resp. their negation is satisfied) for all values in V;
- (4) if $\mathbf{A}$ is `closed`, the conjunction of all its assertions ensures the absence of undesirable behavior: if all these assertions are satisfied for values v in V, then the computation of $\Diamond(v)$ succeeds.

This definition extends easily to any expression e and concrete state $\mathfrak{m}$. The evaluation $\overline{[e]}_\mathfrak{m}$ fails if one of its operators fails. A map of alarms A is a sound abstraction of $\overline{[e]}_\mathfrak{m}$ if each assertion of A prevents an undesirable behavior of an operator in e, if the statuses of A are correct in $\mathfrak{m}$, and if the map is `closed`, then the evaluation of e succeeds whenever all the assertions of the map are satisfied. This is denoted by $\mathbf{A} \models_\mathbb{A} \overline{[e]}_\mathfrak{m}$.

The alarms are also equipped with a bounded lattice structure. The join $\sqcup_a$ and meet $\sqcap_a$ are defined pointwise. The domains of the two maps are equalized, by adding in each the assertions present only in the other, with a `true` status for `closed` maps and an `unknown` for `open` ones. Then, the join or meet of the statuses lattice is applied pointwise on the maps. The join with an `open` map returns an `open` map, while the meet with a `closed` map returns a `closed` map. The meet may discover an inconsistency between statuses, which stops the analysis. The bottom of the alarms lattice is the `closed` empty map, denoting an absence of undesirable behavior. Its top is the `open` empty map: any undesirable behavior may happen, and no assertion has a precise status.

4.2 Values

Values in $\mathbb{V}^\#$ are non-relational abstractions of sets of concrete values. They are equipped with a meet-semilattice structure, and provide a forward and a backward abstract counterpart $\mathsf{F}^\#_\Diamond$ and $\mathsf{B}^\#_\Diamond$ for each C operator $\Diamond$ on expressions. We define the soundness of the value abstractions through a concretization function γ_v that connects each value to the set of concrete values it represents. Then, the lattice must have the properties specified in Fig. 3, while the correctness of the abstract semantics is stated in Fig. 6.

Given value abstractions of the arguments, the forward abstract operator $\mathsf{F}^\#_\Diamond$ produces an alarm map and a value: the alarms are a sound abstraction of the undesirable behaviors of the operation, and the value is an over-approximation of the set of possible resulting C values when no undesirable behavior occurs. The forward operators receive the involved expressions needed to return the alarms.

Conversely, the backward operator $\mathsf{B}^\#_\Diamond$ tries to reduce the abstractions for its arguments, according to an abstraction of the result. The reduced abstractions

$$\gamma_v : \mathbb{V}^\# \to 2^{\overline{\mathbb{V}}} \qquad \Bigg| \quad \forall e \in e^n, \, \forall v \in (\mathbb{V}^\#)^n, \, \forall r \in \mathbb{V}^\#,$$

$$F_\Diamond^\# : e^n \to (\mathbb{V}^\#)^n \to \mathbb{V}^\# \times \mathbb{A} \quad \Bigg| \quad \begin{cases} F_\Diamond^\#(e, v) = (r, \mathbf{A}) \Rightarrow \begin{cases} \mathbf{A} \models_\mathbb{A} \overline{[\Diamond(e)]}(\gamma_v(v)) \\ \overline{[\Diamond(e)]}(\gamma_v(v)) \setminus \Omega \subseteq \gamma_v(r) \end{cases} \\ \{x \in \gamma_v(v) \,|\, \overline{[\Diamond(e)]}(x) \in \gamma_v(r)\} \subseteq \gamma_v(B_\Diamond^\#(v, r)) \end{cases}$$

$$B_\Diamond^\# : (\mathbb{V}^\#)^n \times \mathbb{V}^\# \to (\mathbb{V}^\#)^n$$

Fig. 6. Semantics of values

over-approximate all the possible C values for the arguments leading to a value included in the result through the operator. For instance, the backward operator on interval abstractions for the comparison $\top \leq [0..10]$ with result $[1]$ reduces the first argument value to $[-\infty..10]$, and lets the second argument value unchanged.

Values are abstractions of C values of scalar types only. However, in a language such as C, variables may contain addresses. Hence, values must also be abstractions of memory locations, and their abstract transformers encompass all operations involving addresses and lvalues. Such abstractions allow the domains to express properties about memory locations, including pointer aliasing. Thus, the analyzer does not depend on a specific pointer analysis or memory model. Instead, these features are implemented as –potentially dedicated– domains that exchange their results with the others.

5   State Abstraction

Abstract domains carry state abstractions collecting properties about program variables. For an abstract domain $\mathbb{D}$, a concretization γ_d links abstract states S to sets of concrete memories $\mathfrak{m}$. The soundness of an abstract domain is defined according to the concretization.

$$\gamma_d : \mathbb{D} \to \mathcal{P}(\mathfrak{M})$$

An abstract domain supplies the generic evaluator with value abstractions on lvalues, but also on whole expressions. When preparing its answer, it may also request additional information from other domains.

5.1   Domain Queries

A state abstract domain $\mathbb{D}$ must provide two *query* functions, on which the generic evaluator relies. Those functions extract information from an abstract state, translating AST fragments into alarms and value abstractions. Figure 7 shows their signature, as well as their soundness requirements. The explanation of the oracle argument is postponed to the next subsection.

The first query is an abstract semantics $F_{*_\tau}^\#$ for dereferences. It receives the possible memory locations of the dereferenced lvalue, and computes a sound value abstraction of the C values that may be stored in these locations, in all the memories abstracted by a state. It also produces an alarm map that ensures

```
type eval = value * alarms
val F#       : oracle:(exp -> eval) -> state -> location -> eval
   *τ
val F#       : oracle:(exp -> eval) -> state -> exp -> eval
   D
```

$$\forall e \in expr, \; \forall v, l \in \mathbb{V}^{\#}, \; \forall S \in \mathbb{D}, \; \forall \mathbf{A} \in \mathbb{A},$$

$$\begin{cases} \mathrm{F}^{\#}_{*\tau}\,(S, l) = (v, \mathbf{A}) \Rightarrow \forall a \in \gamma_v\,(l)\,, \forall \mathfrak{m} \in \gamma_d\,(S)\,, \begin{cases} \mathbf{A} \models_{\mathbb{A}} \overline{[\![*_{\tau}a]\!]}_{\mathfrak{m}} \\ \mathfrak{m}_{\tau}[a] \in \gamma_v\,(v) \cup \{\Omega\} \end{cases} \\[4mm] \mathrm{F}^{\#}_{\mathrm{D}}\,(S, e) = (v, \mathbf{A}) \Rightarrow \forall \mathfrak{m} \in \gamma_d\,(S)\,, \begin{cases} \mathbf{A} \models_{\mathbb{A}} \overline{[\![e]\!]}_{\mathfrak{m}} \\ [\![e]\!]_{\mathfrak{m}} \in \gamma_v\,(v) \cup \{\Omega\} \end{cases} \end{cases}$$

Fig. 7. Interface and soundness of domains queries

the validity of the location, and that the contents of the read memory slice are proper (i.e. not *indeterminate* in C parlance, and in particular initialized). Using $\mathrm{F}^{\#}_{\Diamond}$ and $\mathrm{F}^{\#}_{*\tau}$, an expression can be fully evaluated by induction on its syntax.

The second query $\mathrm{F}^{\#}_{\mathrm{D}}$ supplies additional information about arbitrary C expressions. It computes sound alarm maps and value abstractions for their evaluations in all the memories abstracted by a state. For instance, a domain tracking inequalities may express that $e_1 - e_2$ is positive when it has inferred $e_1 \geq e_2$. For any query on which the domain has no precise information, the top elements of values and alarms are always a sound over-approximation.

A generic evaluator queries the state domains on each lvalue and expression. If the domain is a combination of domains, all their answers are intersected using the $\sqcap$ operator on alarms and values. Thereby, each domain may easily contribute to reduce the abstract value computed for an expression, or decrease the number of emitted alarms. If the values are themselves a combination of abstractions, each domain may have a precise answer for some value components and return $\top$ for the others. Using this lightweight collaboration mechanism, abstract domains may track a specific undesirable behavior, such as the initialization of variables. Open maps of alarms allow a domain to assert that some alarms cannot happen, without understanding e.g. the contents of variables. They also may collect properties only on a subset of the C language, and rely on the other abstractions to interpret together the whole semantics.

Example 2. Figure 8 illustrates the collaboration between state abstractions, when analyzing the C code at the left, where the value of i ranges between 0 and 4 at the first line. We use intervals as arithmetic value abstractions and maps from memory bases to intervals-expressed byte offsets as pointer value abstractions. Two abstract domains cooperate, an environment mapping integer variables to intervals, and an array domain, able to represent precisely the value of each array cell. A third domain gathering symbolic equalities between expressions will be used later. The state S of the domains at the bullet point is given in the first line of the table, as well as their answers to some queries in the following lines; $[i]$ represents a singleton interval. In this example, each domain has information about some expressions, and returns $\top$ for the others.

		Env	Array	Eq
	State S	$i \mapsto [2]$	$t:$	$tmp = t\,[i] + 1$
		$tmp \mapsto [2..6]$	$[1; 2; 3; 4; 5]$	$i = 2$
	tmp	$[2..6]$	$\top$	$[\![*\,(\&t\,[i]) + 1]\!]^{\#}$
	i	$[2]$	$\top$	$\top$
	$t\,[i]$	$\top$	$[3]$	$\top$
	$t\,[i] + 1$	$\top$	$\top$	$[\![tmp]\!]^{\#}$

```
1   int  t[5] = {1, 2, 3, 4, 5};
2   int  tmp = t[i]+1;
3   if (i == 2)
4     • r = t[i] + 1;
```

$$[\![i]\!]^{\#}(S) = \mathtt{F}^{\#}_{*_{\mathrm{int}}}(S, \&\mathtt{i}) = [2] \sqcap_v \top_v = [2] \tag{1}$$

$$[\![\&t\,[i]]\!]^{\#}(S) = (\&\mathtt{t} \to 0) +^{\#} \mathtt{sizeof\,(int)} \times^{\#} [\![i]\!]^{\#}(S) = \&\mathtt{t} \to 8 \tag{2}$$

$$[\![*\,(\&t\,[i])]\!]^{\#}(S) = \mathtt{F}^{\#}_{*_{\mathrm{int}}}(S, \&\mathtt{t} \to 8) = \top_v \sqcap_v [3] = [3] \tag{3}$$

$$[\![*\,(\&t\,[i]) + 1]\!]^{\#}(S) = [\![*\,(\&t\,[i])]\!]^{\#}(S) +^{\#} [\![1]\!]^{\#}(S) = [4] \tag{4}$$

Fig. 8. Collaboration between domains

We focus on the evaluation of expression $*\,(\&t[i]) + 1$ at line 4. We omit here the calls of the domain queries on non-lvalue expressions, as the domains have no information about them. We also write the abstract value semantics $\mathtt{F}^{\#}_{\Diamond}$ with an infix notation $\Diamond^{\#}$. The equations of Fig. 8 detail the steps of the evaluation, which proceeds bottom-up. First, for the variable i, the environment gives the precise value $[2]$, while the array domain returns $\top_v$. The meet of those two values is $[2]$. Then, the abstract value operator on array subscripts computes an abstraction for the address of $t[i]$, namely $\&\mathtt{t} \to [8]$. Third, using this precise abstraction of the address, the array domain is able to provide a precise value for the dereference of $t[i]$, whichis $[3]$. Last, the abstract addition semantics applied on $t[i]$ and 1 finally leads to $[4]$ as the value being assigned to r.

5.2   Interaction Through the Oracle

To compute precise abstractions for an expression, a domain —and especially a relational one— may need additional information about other expressions. Thus, the domain can request the evaluation of new expressions, through the $\mathtt{oracle}$ argument of the query functions. The oracle triggers the requested evaluation using all available domains, and returns the cooperatively computed abstractions to the initial domain. The oracle has the same specification as the evaluation: in the current state S, it provides an alarm map and a value that are sound approximations of the concrete evaluation of the expression.

$$\mathtt{oracle}\,(S, e) = (v, \mathbf{A}) \Rightarrow \forall \mathrm{m} \in \gamma_d\,(S), \begin{cases} \mathbf{A} \models_{\mathbb{A}} \overline{[\![e]\!]}_\mathrm{m} \\ [\![e]\!]_\mathrm{m} \in \gamma_v\,(v) \cup \{\Omega\} \end{cases}$$

An uncontrolled use of the oracle may lead to (1) a loop in the forward evaluation, or (2) to an infinite chain of evaluations of different expressions. To prevent (1) from happening, the oracle can return $\top$ on re-occurrences of the same expression. The number of recursive uses of the oracle is also limited by a parameter of the analysis, to avoid (2).

```
1  int t[4] = {1, 2, 3, 4};
2  int tmp = t[i]+1;
3  if (i == 2) • r = tmp;
```

$$F^{\#}_{*int}(S, \&tmp) = [2..6] \sqcap_v [\![t[i]+1]\!]^{\#} = [2..6] \sqcap_v [4] = [4]$$

Fig. 9. Using the oracle during evaluation

Thanks to the oracle, the abstract domains share information through value abstractions, without a direct communication between domains. Especially, the oracle allows a relational domain to fully avail the relations it has inferred, and lets the other domains collaborate in leveraging these relations. The following example illustrates this with a simple equality domain.

Example 3. Let us come back to Example 2, but on the variant shown in Fig. 9 and with the equality domain enabled. At line 4, the value of $t[i]+1$ is still assigned to r, but through the intermediate variable tmp. The abstract states shown in Fig. 2 remain valid. Note that the environment domain maps tmp to the interval $[2..6]$, coming from its assignment to $t[i]+1$ at line 2, when i was still imprecisely known; the value for $t[i]$ was then provided by the array domain, and was not reduced by the condition at line 3.

However, the equality domain can use information it has inferred, namely $tmp==t[i]+1$. When the generic evaluator requests a value for tmp, the equality domain queries the value of $t[i]+1$ through the oracle. The main forward evaluation computes the precise interval $[4]$ for $t[i]+1$, as in the initial example. This abstract value is finally returned by the equality domain as a sound value abstraction of tmp. Thanks to the equality domain, we obtain the same precision for the value assigned to r as in the original example.

During the evaluation of $t[i]+1$, the equality domain may request the evaluation of tmp through the oracle. Then, the evaluator detects a loop in the evaluation, and returns the top abstractions without any further computation.

5.3   State Backward Propagation

Within the value abstraction, forward and backward propagators are dual. Likewise, abstract domains must provide the backward counterparts of queries. Figure 10 presents their requirements. When the abstract value $v^{\#}$ stored in a lvalue is reduced, the abstract memory location $l^{\#}$ for the lvalue might be reduced as well (e.g. when some locations of $l^{\#}$ are known not to contain $v^{\#}$). This typically happens on memory accesses through an imprecise pointer. The backward semantics $B^{\#}_{*\tau}$ of dereference serves this purpose: it takes an abstract state, an abstraction of the memory location of a lvalue and its new value abstraction v. It returns a possibly more precise location abstraction, which is an over-approximation of the concrete locations for which the lvalue has a value in $\gamma_v(v)$.

Moreover, the relations known by a relational domain may also induce further interesting reductions. For instance, if $a \leq b$ holds, then any reduction of the infimum of the possible values of a implies the same reduction for b. Hence, when performing a reduction, the generic evaluator notifies the domains through the

```
val B#*τ  :  state -> location -> value -> location
val B#D   :  state -> exp -> value -> (exp * value) list
```

$\forall e \in expr, \forall v, l \in \mathbb{V}^{\#}, \forall S \in \mathbb{D},$

$$\begin{cases} \{a \in \gamma_v(l) \mid \exists \mathfrak{m} \in \gamma_d(S), \mathfrak{m}_\tau[a] \in \gamma_v(v)\} \subseteq \gamma_v(\mathrm{B}^{\#}_{*\tau}(S, l, v)) \\ \forall (e', v') \in \mathrm{B}^{\#}_{\mathbb{D}}(S, e, v), \ \forall \mathfrak{m} \in \gamma_d(S), \ [\![e]\!]_{\mathfrak{m}} \in \gamma_v(v) \Rightarrow [\![e']\!]_{\mathfrak{m}} \in \gamma_v(v') \end{cases}$$

Fig. 10. Backward propagation inside domains

function $\mathrm{B}^{\#}_{\mathbb{D}}$, which returns a list of new reductions to be backward propagated by the evaluator. The new reductions, deduced from the prior one and from the inferences made by the domain, must be correct in the concrete states for which the initial reduction was valid. To avoid diverging, the generic evaluator must limit the number of times this function is used.

5.4 Abstraction of Statement Semantics

The generic transfer function on statements starts by evaluating all involved expressions. For an assignment, the location of the lvalue is also evaluated, and reduced to its valid part. The alarms produced at each step are accumulated, and eventually raised to report all undesirable behaviors that may have occurred at this point. The concrete states satisfying the emitted assertions are ensured to succeed on this statement. Then, the abstract transformers of the domains are applied. They have to be a sound approximation of the program semantics for these safe states. For that purpose, each domain can use the value abstractions that have been cooperatively computed by the evaluator. Thus, an abstract transformer benefits from the properties inferred by all domains.

6 EVA: A Modular Abstract Interpreter for Frama-C

We have implemented the architecture described in this paper in an extensible, modular abstract interpreter named EVA, an open-source plugin of FRAMA-C[1]. EVA handles the subset of C99 commonly used in embedded code, as well as some extensions[2]. It detects the most common undefined behaviors of the C standard [14], including invalid memory accesses, reading uninitialized memory, divisions by zero, integer overflows, undefined bit shifts, writes in const memory, reads of bits of a dangling address, invalid pointer comparisons and subtractions, infinite or NaN floating-point values[3]

---

[1] Directory `src/plugins/value/` of the FRAMA-C source files, available at http://frama-c.com/download.html.

[2] Bitfields, flexible array members and some GNU extensions are supported. Support for dynamic allocation is preliminary. Recursion, `setjmp/longjmp`, `complex` types, `alloca` and variable-length arrays are not supported.

[3] These are not undefined behaviors w.r.t. the ISO C99 or IEEE 754 specifications, but we choose to report them as undesirable errors.

This section presents the value and state abstractions currently available in EVA. In particular, the *Cvalue* domain implements the abstract semantics of VALUE, the former abstract interpreter of FRAMA-C. The five other abstract domains are new. By lack of space, we only give a short overview.

EVA provides several *value abstractions* (and their semantics) establishing an already rich communication interface between abstract domains. These abstractions may be extended to achieve further communication. The current integer abstractions are a reduced product between small sets of discrete integers (whose maximal cardinal is user-configurable), integer intervals and linear congruences. Floating-point abstractions are intervals, excluding infinite and NaNs. Pointer and location abstractions are maps from memory bases (roughly, variables) to byte offsets represented by an integer value. Pointer values may thus express precise alias information between program variables. Such alias information is especially useful for numerical domains that do not include an alias analysis, in particular to process assignments through pointers. Numeric domains may also collaborate to reduce the possible offsets on a variable. The operators for these value abstractions handle all kinds of alarms, and always produce closed maps of alarms. New value abstractions are thus simpler to write: they may limit themselves to a subset of C and focus on a certain kind of alarms (through **open** maps of alarms).

The *Cvalue domain* is the biggest abstract domain of EVA. It is inherited from VALUE, and was retrofitted for EVA. It uses the standard values of EVA. Its state domain is quite involved, and we refer the reader to [3,17] for a more complete explanation. The memory is (roughly) a map from *variable* × *offset* × *width* to abstract values, plus two additional booleans that abstract the possibility that the value may be uninitialized, or a dangling pointer. The memory is untyped, and it is possible to write an abstract value of any type anywhere in the memory. Assignments overlapping existing bindings are automatically handled, and remain precise. Assignments to a very large number of non-contiguous locations are automatically approximated.

The *equality domain* is a symbolic domain tracking Herbrand equalities between C expressions. Our intentions are somewhat similar to those of Miné [21], in particular abstracting over temporary variables resulting from code normalization. The equalities are deduced from equality conditions and from assignments. The (cooperatively computed) information about locations are used to invalidate equalities that may no longer hold after an assignment. This domain uses the oracle and its backward counterpart (Sect. 5.3) to avail its inferred relations. It is thus independent of the chosen value abstraction, and is implemented by a functor from values to state abstractions.

The *symbolic locations domain* tracks accesses to arrays or through pointers in a symbolic way. It intends to precisely analyze codes such as **if**(t[i]<e) v=t[i]. Indeed, when i is imprecise, domains that represent arrays in extenso cannot learn information from the condition (because any cell may be involved). The domain shares some similarities with the *recency* abstraction [1]. Its state is a map from symbolic locations (such as t[i], *p or p−>v) to an abstract value.

Strong reductions are performed on those values when analyzing conditions, to be shared with the other domains when the location is encountered again later.

The *Apron domains*: we have implemented a simple binding to the numerical abstract domains available in APRON [15]. The resulting domains (boxes, octagons, strict or loose convex polyhedra, linear equalities) demonstrate that the relational domains of Apron fit easily within the communication model of EVA. The abstract state is an APRON state. Since those contain no aliasing information, the binding relies instead on the other domains (mostly CVALUE) to evaluate memory locations. A mapping between the APRON dimensions and the variables of the program is used as a correspondence table. The domain answers queries for arithmetic expressions, by translating them into the APRON internal language. Sub-expressions that cannot be handled by APRON are linearized on-the-fly into intervals, using the cooperatively computed value.

The *bitwise domain* aims at adding bitvector-like reasoning to EVA (including on floating-point values and pointers), without resorting to a dedicated implementation. Instead, we reuse the expressivity of the abstraction for sequences of bits in the CVALUE domain. Indeed, this abstraction is already able to extract the possible values of some bits in a memory range. This bitwise domain works on a new kind of value abstractions, namely a sequence of bits of known length. Only the forward and backward abstract semantics for the bitwise C operators, as well as integer casts and multiplication/division by a power of 2, have been implemented. All other operations degenerate to $\top_v$. The reduced product between the standard values and those new bitwise values performs a conversion between the two representations when possible.

The *gauges domain* [22] is a weakly relational domain, able to efficiently infer general linear inequality invariants within loops. Technically, the variables involved in the invariants are all related to *loopcounters*, that model the current number of iterations in each loop. Gauges are especially useful to infer invariants for pointer offsets, as pointer arithmetic introduces +4 or +8 increments (for 32- and 64-bits architecture respectively), that cannot be directly handled by domains such as octagons [19]. The gauge domains communicates integer and pointer values through the standard values of EVA.

We believe the variety of domains presented above validates our design choices on how to structure a collaborative analyzer. Having an implementation of values independent from domains is natural, and avoids code duplication. The cooperative evaluation of value abstractions achieves an exchange of information between abstract domains, without direct interactions. This modularity facilitates the introduction of new abstractions. Furthermore, allowing the relational domains to directly trigger new complete evaluations or backward propagations spares the other domains from processing relational instructions. Finally, having only value and location abstractions as a direct means of communication did not feel limiting, especially since they are extensible.

7   Related Works

Splitting value abstractions from state abstractions was proposed by Cousot [8] to design an abstract interpreter, but was not used to enable a communication between different state abstractions. Cortesi *et al.* [7] survey the use of products (reduced or not) in abstract interpretation. Although most abstract-interpretation-based analysis frameworks use multiple domains internally (e.g. [5]), few explain how the different domains exchange information. In theory, a reduced product considers the equivalence classes of the direct products that have the same concretization, and reduces the result of each abstract operation to the smallest representative of its class. Abstract interpreters usually implement an approximation of the reduced product, but let the domains interact during an operation.

The *open product* [6] achieves the reduction by a set of boolean functions (*queries*) provided by any domain and used by the abstract operators to receive more information from the environment. Our design defines clearly the scope of our queries (through value abstractions), and goes beyond direct queries between domains by sharing all the evaluation engine of expressions to facilitate the interpretation of a statement: abstractions of expressions are automatically computed from properties expressed on subterms (and conversely through backward propagation).

Astrée implements an approximate reduced product through *communication channels* [11]. This mechanism has later been implemented in Clousot and Verasco [13, 16]. Each channel carries an information of a certain kind: interval range, integer congruence, equalities between expressions, etc. New messages can be added if needed, and domains need not to understand all messages. Messages sent on channels play a role similar to our value abstractions, but important differences exist. First, our design allows domains to cooperate at another level, namely by emitting statuses on alarms. Second, maintaining a network of communication channels in parallel of all transfer functions seems more invasive (from an engineering point of view) than using value abstractions. Indeed, the latter are naturally understood by the evaluation functions. Third, our oracle mitigates the need for messages containing relational information, that must be understood and processed by non-relational domains. With the oracle, no new abstract transformer needs to be added. Fourth, the reduced product of value abstractions allows information to flow between domains, even if they understand different values. Thus, domains need not be adapted when a new kind of value is added. Finally, our products are unordered, while communication channels are oriented. This potentially allows for more reduction opportunities in the domains.

Beyer *et al.* [2] propose an extension of *configurable program analysis* (CPA) in which a *precision* information is tracked. This precision is used to dynamically alter the amount of information the abstract domain infers. The composition of two domains is done through a cartesian product, except that the functions related to precision can use information from both domains. This way, it is possible to reduce the precision of a domain when another one is precise enough.

The CodePeer analyzer [4] for Ada uses internally an SSA form on value-numbered expressions to represent its abstract state. A state is a mapping from SSA expressions to an abstract value. (The domains for values include disjunctions of integer intervals and floating-point intervals.) Storing information for entire expressions alleviates the need for relational domains; instead, a value for e.g. $x - y$ is stored. There are some similarities between this state and the partial maps internally used by the EVA evaluator to store the value abstractions of expressions. However, a major difference is that we reset the map after each statement. Keeping such information longer could be useful.

8 Conclusion

EVA is a major development: 13k lines of new or heavily adapted code, out of 53k for EVA, VALUE and all the shared abstractions. It has already replaced VALUE as the default abstract interpreter in the latest version of FRAMA-C. The new domains we have implemented validate our design so far. The separation between value and state abstractions is conceptually useful, and reduce the amount of code that must be written when new state domains are implemented. We plan to mature the domains presented in Sect. 6, and to write new value abstractions (e.g. to represent structs) and state abstractions (e.g. to improve the handling of dynamic allocation).

Regarding collaborative evaluation, two important things remain to be done. First, VALUE uses an automatic summarization mechanism to speed up analyses [23]. It needs to be extended to arbitrary domains, while remaining cost-efficient. Second, in the current implementation of EVA, domains cooperate only to evaluate the C part of the AST. A collaborative evaluation of logical assertions is a worthwhile goal. However, this will probably complexify the abstract values and domains, that will have to understand the fine print of assertions (e.g. real numbers in specifications).

References

1. Balakrishnan, G., Reps, T.: Recency-abstraction for heap-allocated storage. In: Yi, K. (ed.) SAS 2006. LNCS, vol. 4134, pp. 221–239. Springer, Heidelberg (2006). doi:10.1007/11823230_15
2. Beyer, D., Henzinger, T.A., Théoduloz, G.: Program analysis with dynamic precision adjustment. In: ASE, pp. 29–38 (2008)
3. Bonichon, R., Cuoq, P.: A mergeable interval map. Stud. Inform. Univ. 9(1), 5–37 (2011)
4. Boulanger, J.-L. (ed.): Static Analysis of Software: The Abstract Interpretation. Wiley-ISTE, New York (2011)
5. Brat, G., Navas, J.A., Shi, N., Venet, A.: IKOS: A framework for static analysis based on abstract interpretation. In: Giannakopoulou, D., Salaün, G. (eds.) SEFM 2014. LNCS, vol. 8702, pp. 271–277. Springer, Cham (2014). doi:10.1007/978-3-319-10431-7_20

6. Cortesi, A., Le Charlier, B., Van Hentenryck, P.: Combinations of abstract domains for logic programming: open product and generic pattern construction. Sci. Comput. Program. **38**(1–3), 27–71 (2000)
7. Cortesi, A., Costantini, G., Ferrara, P.: A survey on product operators in abstract interpretation. In: Essays Dedicated to D. Schmidt on the Occasion of his 60th Birthday, pp. 325–336 (2013)
8. Cousot, P.: The calculational design of a generic abstract interpreter. In: Calculational System Design. NATO ASI Series F. IOS Press (1999)
9. Cousot, P., Cousot, R.: Abstract interpretation: A unified lattice model for static analysis of programs by construction or approximation of fixpoints. In: Principles of Programming Languages, pp. 238–252 (1977)
10. Cousot, P., Cousot, R.: Systematic design of program analysis frameworks. In: Principles of Programming Languages, pp. 269–282 (1979)
11. Cousot, P., Cousot, R., Feret, J., Mauborgne, L., Miné, A., Monniaux, D., Rival, X.: Combination of abstractions in the ASTRÉE static analyzer. In: Okada, M., Satoh, I. (eds.) ASIAN 2006. LNCS, vol. 4435, pp. 272–300. Springer, Heidelberg (2007). doi:10.1007/978-3-540-77505-8_23
12. Cuoq, P., Hilsenkopf, P., Kirchner, F., Labbé, S., Thuy, N., Yakobowski, B.: Formal verification of software important to safety using the Frama-C tool suite. In: NPIC & HMIT (2012)
13. Fähndrich, M., Logozzo, F.: Static contract checking with abstract interpretation. In: Beckert, B., Marché, C. (eds.) FoVeOOS 2010. LNCS, vol. 6528, pp. 10–30. Springer, Berlin (2011). doi:10.1007/978-3-642-18070-5_2
14. International Organization for Standardization (ISO). International Standard ISO/IEC 9899: 1999 - Programming languages - C. Technical Corrigendum 3 (2007)
15. Jeannet, B., Miné, A.: APRON: A library of numerical abstract domains for static analysis. In: Bouajjani, A., Maler, O. (eds.) CAV 2009. LNCS, vol. 5643, pp. 661–667. Springer, Berlin (2009). doi:10.1007/978-3-642-02658-4_52
16. Jourdan, J.-H., Laporte, V., Blazy, S., Leroy, X., Pichardie, D.: A formally-verified C static analyzer. In: Principles of Programming Language, pp. 247–259 (2015)
17. Kirchner, F., Kosmatov, N., Prevosto, V., Signoles, J., Yakobowski, B.: Frama-C: A software analysis perspective. Formal Asp. Comput. **27**(3), 573–609 (2015)
18. Mauborgne, L., Rival, X.: Trace partitioning in abstract interpretation based static analyzers. In: Sagiv, M. (ed.) ESOP 2005. LNCS, vol. 3444, pp. 5–20. Springer, Berlin (2005). doi:10.1007/978-3-540-31987-0_2
19. Miné, A.: The octagon abstract domain. In: Burd, E., Aiken, P., Koschke, R. (eds.) Proceedings of the Eighth Working Conference on Reverse Engineering, WCRE 2001, Stuttgart, Germany, 2–5 October 2001, p. 310. IEEE Computer Society (2001)
20. Miné, A.: Field-sensitive value analysis of embedded C programs with union types and pointer arithmetics. In: LCTES, pp. 54–63. ACM (2006)
21. Miné, A.: Symbolic methods to enhance the precision of numerical abstract domains. In: Emerson, E.A., Namjoshi, K.S. (eds.) VMCAI 2006. LNCS, vol. 3855, pp. 348–363. Springer, Heidelberg (2005). doi:10.1007/11609773_23
22. Venet, A.J.: The gauge domain: scalable analysis of linear inequality invariants. In: Madhusudan, P., Seshia, S.A. (eds.) CAV 2012. LNCS, vol. 7358, pp. 139–154. Springer, Berlin (2012). doi:10.1007/978-3-642-31424-7_15
23. Yakobowski, B.: Fast whole-program verification using on-the-fly summarization. In: Workshop on Tools for Automatic Program Analysis (2015)

Matching Multiplications in Bit-Vector Formulas

Supratik Chakraborty[1], Ashutosh Gupta[2], and Rahul Jain[2(✉)]

[1] Indian Institute of Technology Bombay, Mumbai, India
[2] Tata Institute of Fundamental Research, Mumbai, India
rahul.jain@tifr.res.in

Abstract. Bit-vector formulas arising from hardware verification problems often contain word-level arithmetic operations. Empirical evidence shows that state-of-the-art SMT solvers are not very efficient at reasoning about bit-vector formulas with multiplication. This is particularly true when multiplication operators are decomposed and represented in alternative ways in the formula. We present a pre-processing heuristic that identifies certain types of decomposed multipliers, and adds special assertions to the input formula that encode the equivalence of sub-terms and word-level multiplication terms. The pre-processed formulas are then solved using an SMT solver. Our experiments with three SMT solvers show that our heuristic allows several formulas to be solved quickly, while the same formulas time out without the pre-processing step.

1 Introduction

In recent years, SMT solving has emerged as a powerful technique for testing, analysis and verification of hardware and software systems. A wide variety of tools today use SMT solvers as part of their core reasoning engines [1–10]. A common approach used in several of these tools is to model the behaviour of a system using formulas in a combination of first-order theories, and reduce the given problem to checking the (un)satisfiability of a formula in the combined theory. SMT solvers play a central role in this approach, since they combine decision procedures of individual first-order theories to check the satisfiability of a formula in the combined theory. Not surprisingly, heuristic techniques to improve the performance of SMT solvers have attracted significant attention over the years (see [11,12] for excellent expositions). In this paper, we add to the repertoire of such heuristics by proposing a pre-processing step that analyzes an input formula, and adds specially constructed assertions to it, without changing the semantics. We focus on formulas in the quantifier-free theory of fixed-width bit-vectors with multiplication, and show by means of experiments that three state-of-the-art SMT solvers benefit significantly from our heuristic when solving many benchmarks with multiplication operators.

The primary motivation for our work comes from word-level bounded model checking (WBMC) [1,4] and word-level symbolic trajectory evaluation (WSTE) [13] of embedded hardware systems. Specifically, we focus on systems that process data, represented as fixed-width bit-vectors, using arithmetic operators. When reasoning about such systems, it is often necessary to check whether

A. Bouajjani and D. Monniaux (Eds.): VMCAI 2017, LNCS 10145, pp. 131–150, 2017.
DOI: 10.1007/978-3-319-52234-0_8

a high-level property, specified using bit-vector arithmetic operators (viz. addition, multiplication, division), is satisfied by a model of the system implementing a data-processing algorithm. For reasons related to performance, power, area, ease of design etc., complex arithmetic operators with large bit-widths are often implemented by composing several smaller, simpler and well-characterized blocks. For example, a 128-bit multiplier may be implemented using one of several multiplication algorithms [14–16] after partitioning its 128-bit operands into narrower blocks. SMT formulas resulting from WBMC/WSTE of such systems are therefore likely to contain terms with higher-level arithmetic operators (viz. 128-bit multiplication) encoding the specification, and terms that encode a lower-level implementation of these operators in the system (viz. a Wallace-tree multiplier). Efficiently reasoning about such formulas requires exploiting the semantic equivalence of these alternative representations of arithmetic operators. Unfortunately, our study, which focuses on systems using the multiplication operator, reveals that three state-of-the-art SMT solvers (Z3 [17], CVC4 [18] and BOOLECTOR [2]) encounter serious performance bottlenecks in identifying these equivalences. Our limited experiments show that these bottlenecks manifest most conspicuously when reasoning about the unsatisfiability of formulas.

A Motivating Example: To illustrate the severity of the problem, we consider the SMT formula arising out of WSTE applied to a pipelined serial multiplier circuit, originally used as a benchmark in [13]. The circuit reads in two 32-bit operands sequentially from a single 32-bit input port, multiplies them and makes the 64-bit result available in an output register.

The property to be checked asserts that if a and b denote the word-level operands that are read in, then after the computation is over, the output register indeed has the product $a *_{[32]} b$, where $*_{[32]}$ denotes 32-bit multiplication. The system implementation, as used in [13], is described in SYSTEMVERILOG (a hardware description language) and makes use of the multiplication operator (i.e., $*$) in SYSTEMVERILOG with 32-bit operands. The Language Reference Manual of SYSTEMVERILOG specifies that this amounts to using a 32-bit multiplication operation directly. The SMT formula resulting from a WSTE run on this example therefore contains terms with only 32-bit multiplication operators, and no terms encoding a lower-level multiplier implementation. This formula is proved unsatisfiable in a fraction of a second by BOOLECTOR, CVC4 and Z3.

We now change the design above to reflect the implementation of 32-bit multiplication by the long-multiplication algorithm [14], where each 32-bit operand is partitioned into 8-bit blocks. The corresponding WSTE run yields an SMT formula that contains terms with 32-bit multiplication operator (derived from the property being checked), and also terms that encode the implementation of a 32-bit multiplier using long-multiplication. Surprisingly, none of BOOLECTOR, CVC4 and Z3 succeeded in deciding the satisfiability of the resulting formula even after 24 h on the same computing platform as in the original experiment. The heuristic strategies in these solvers failed to identify the equivalence of terms encoding alternative representations of 32-bit multiplication, and proceeded to bit-blast the formulas, resulting in this dramatic blowup in run-time.

Problem Formulation: The above example demonstrates that the inability to identify semantic equivalence of alternative representations of arithmetic operators plagues multiple state-of-the-art SMT solvers. This motivates us to ask: *Can we heuristically pre-process an SMT formula containing terms encoding alternative representations of bit-vector arithmetic operators, in a solver-independent manner, so that multiple solvers benefit from it?* We answer this question positively in this paper, for the multiplication operator. The motivating example, that originally timed out after 24 h on three solvers, is shown to be unsatisfiable by Z3 in 0.073 s and by CVC4 in 0.017 s, after applying our heuristic. Although BOOLECTOR does not benefit from our heuristic on this example, it benefits in several other examples, as discussed in Sect. 5.

Term Re-writing vs Adding Tautological Assertions: Prima facie, the above problem can be solved by reverse-engineering a lower-level representation of a bit-vector arithmetic operator, and by re-writing terms encoding this representation with terms using the higher-level bit-vector operator. Indeed, variants of this approach have been used earlier in different contexts [19–23]. In the context of SMT solving, however, more caution is needed. As shown in Example 2 of Sect. 2.2, the same collection of terms (in this case, sums-of-partial-products) can arise from two different word-level multiplication operations. This makes it difficult to decide which of several term re-writes should be used when there are alternatives. Even if the above dilemma doesn't arise, re-writing one term with another is a "peep-hole" transformation that may not always correlate with improved solver performance. For example, one term may enable a re-write rule that helps simplify one sub-formula, while a syntactically distinct but semantically equivalent term may enable another re-write rule that helps simplify another sub-formula. Re-writing one term by another prevents both terms from jointly contributing to simplifications and improving the solver's performance.

In this paper, we propose a heuristic alternative to term re-writing when solving bit-vector formulas with multiplication. Given a bit-vector formula φ containing terms with different representations of multiplication, our heuristic searches for patterns in the terms corresponding to two multiplication algorithms, i.e., long multiplication and Wallace-tree multiplication. Instead of re-writing the matched terms directly with bit-vector multiplication terms, we conjoin φ with assertions that semantically equate a matched term with the corresponding bit-vector multiplication term. Note that each added assertion is a tautology, and hence does not change the semantics of the formula. Since no re-writes are done, we can express multiple semantic equivalences without removing any syntactic term from the formula. This is an important departure from earlier techniques, such as [21], that rely on sophisticated re-writes of the formula. Our experiments show that the added tautological assertions succeed in preventing bit-blasting while solving in several cases, while in other cases, they help in pruning the search space even after bit-blasting. Both effects eventually translate to improved performance of the SMT solver. Furthermore, since our heuristic simply adds assertions to the input formula, it is relatively independent of the internals of any specific solver, and can be used with multiple solvers.

2   Preliminaries

In this section, we present some basics of the theory of quantifier-free fixed-width bit-vector formulas (QF_BV), and discuss two well-known multiplication algorithms of interest.

2.1   QF_BV: A Short Introduction

A bit-vector is a fixed sequence of bits. We denote bit-vectors by x, y, z etc. and often refer to blocks of bits in a bit-vector. For example, we may declare that a bit-vector x is accessed in blocks of width w. Let x_i denote the ith block of bits, with the block containing the least significant bit (LSB) having index 1.

A QF_BV term t and formula F are constructed using the following grammar

$$t ::= t * t \mid t + t \mid x \mid n^w \mid t \bullet t....$$
$$F ::= t = t \mid t \bowtie t \mid \neg F \mid F \vee F \mid F \wedge F \mid F \oplus F \mid ...$$

where x is a bit-vector variable, n^w is a binary constant represented using w bits, $\bowtie$ is a predicate in $\{\leqslant, <, \geqslant, >\}$, and $\bullet$ is a binary operator that concatenates bit-vectors. Note that we have only presented those parts of the QF_BV grammar that are relevant to our discussion. For more details, the reader is referred to [11,24]. We assume that all variables and arithmetic operators are unsigned. Following the SMT-LIB [25] convention, we also assume that arguments and results of an arithmetic operator have the same bit width. Let $len(t)$ denote the bit width of a term t. If $w \geqslant len(t)$, let $zeroExt(t, w)$ be a shorthand for $0^{w-len(t)} \bullet t$.

If an operator op is commutative, when matching patterns, we will not make a distinction between a op b and b op a. We use the notation "$t == s$" to denote that terms t and s are *syntactically identical*. The usual equality predicate, i.e. "$=$", is used to denote *semantic equivalence*. Given bit-vector terms x, y, and t, suppose $w = \max(len(x) + len(y), len(t))$. We use "$[x * y = t]$" to denote the term $x' * y' = t'$, where $x' = zeroExt(x, w)$, $y' = zeroExt(y, w)$, and $t' = zeroExt(t, w)$. Similarly, the notation $[x * y]$ is used to denote $x' * y'$, where $x' = zeroExt(x, len(x) + len(y))$ and $y' = zeroExt(y, len(x) + len(y))$.

State-of-the-art SMT solvers for QF_BV apply several theory-specific simplification and re-write passes to decide the satisfiability of an input QF_BV formula. If the application of these passes does not succeed in solving the problem, the solvers eventually bit-blast the formula, i.e., translate it to an equivalent propositional formula on the constituent bits of the bit-vectors. This reduces the bit-vector satisfiability problem to one of propositional satisfiability (SAT). The bit-blasted problem is then solved using conflict driven clause learning (CDCL) [26,27] based SAT decision procedures. Among the leading SMT solvers for QF_BV available today are Z3 [17], BOOLECTOR [2] and CVC4 [18]; we use these extensively in our experiments to empirically evaluate our heuristic.

In the subsequent discussion, we assume access to a generic QF_BV SMT solver, called SMTSOLVER, with a standard interface. We assume that the interface provides access to two functions: (a) $add(F)$, that adds a formula F to the context of the solver, and (b) *checkSat()*, that checks the satisfiability of the conjunction of all formulas added to the context of the solver. Note that such interfaces are commonly available with state-of-the-art SMT solvers, viz. BOOLECTOR, CVC4 and Z3.

2.2 Multipliers

As discussed in Sect. 1, there are several alternative multiplier implementations that are used in hardware embedded systems. Among the most popular such implementations are long multipliers, Booth multipliers and Wallace-tree multipliers. In this work, we focus only on long multipliers and Wallace-tree multipliers. The study of our heuristic pre-processing step for systems containing Booth multipliers is left as part of future work.

Long Multiplier: Consider bit-vectors x and y that are partitioned into k blocks of width w bits each. Thus the total width of each bit-vector is $k \cdot w$. The long multiplier decomposes the multiplication of two $(k \cdot w)$-bit wide bit-vectors into k^2 multiplications of w-bit wide bit-vectors. The corresponding k^2 products, called *partial products*, are then added with appropriate left-shifts to obtain the final result. The following notation is typically used to illustrate long multiplication.

$$
\begin{array}{rrrr}
 & x_k & & x_1 \\
 & y_k & \cdots & y_1 \quad * \\
\hline
 & x_k * y_1 & \cdots & x_1 * y_1 \\
 & & \vdots & \\
x_k * y_k & \cdots & x_1 * y_k & + \\
\hline
\end{array}
$$

Here, the $x_i * y_j$s are the partial products. The partial product $x_i * y_j$ is left shifted $(i + j - 2) \cdot w$ bits before being added. In the above representation, all partial products that are left-shifted by the same amount are aligned in a single column. After the left shifts, all the partial results are added in some order. Note that the bit-width of each partial product is $2 \cdot w$. Since the syntax of QF_BV requires the bit-widths of the arguments and result of the $*$ operator to be the same, we denote the partial product $x_i * y_j$ as $(0^w \bullet x_i) * (0^w \bullet y_j)$ for our purposes. Note further that the bits of the partial products in neighbouring columns (in the above representation of long multiplication) overlap; hence the sums of the various columns can not be simply concatenated. The long multiplication algorithm does not specify the order of addition of the shifted partial products. Therefore, there are several possible implementations for a given k and w.

Example 1. Consider bit-vectors v_3, v_2, v_1, u_3, u_2, and u_1, each of bit-width 2. Let us apply long multiplication on $v_3 \bullet v_2 \bullet v_1$ and $u_3 \bullet u_2 \bullet u_1$. We obtain the following partial products.

		v_3	v_2	v_1	
		u_3	u_2	u_1	$*$
		$v_3 * u_1$	$v_2 * u_1$	$v_1 * u_1$	
	$v_3 * u_2$	$v_2 * u_2$	$v_1 * u_2$		
$v_3 * u_3$	$v_2 * u_3$	$v_1 * u_3$		$+$	

The following term is one (of several) possible combinations of the partial products using concatenations and summations to obtain the final product.

$$((v_3 * u_3) \bullet (v_3 * u_1) \bullet (v_1 * u_1)) + (0^2 \bullet (v_2 * u_3) \bullet (v_2 * u_1) \bullet 0^2) +$$
$$(0^2 \bullet (v_3 * u_2) \bullet (v_1 * u_2) \bullet 0^2) + (0^4 \bullet (v_2 * u_2) \bullet 0^4) + (0^4 \bullet (v_1 * u_3) \bullet 0^4)$$

Note that we did not concatenate two partial products that appear next to each other in the tabular representation, because their bits can potentially overlap.

Example 2. Consider bit-vectors v_1, v_2, u_1, and u_2, each of bit-width 2. Let us apply long multiplication on $v_2 \bullet 0^2 \bullet v_1$ and $u_2 \bullet v_2 \bullet u_1$. We obtain the following partial products.

		v_2	0^2	v_1	
		u_2	v_2	u_1	$*$
		$v_2 * u_1$	0^4	$v_1 * u_1$	
	$v_2 * v_2$	0^4	$v_1 * v_2$		
$v_2 * u_2$	0^4	$v_1 * u_2$		$+$	

Note that while adding the shifted partial products, if the non-zero bits of a subset of shifted partial products do not overlap, then we can simply concatenate them to obtain their sum. Finally, we can sum the concatenated vectors thus obtained to calculate the overall product. The following is one possible combination of concatenations and summations for the long multiplication in this example.

$$(0^4 \bullet (v_1 * u_2) \bullet (v_1 * u_1)) + ((v_2 * u_2) \bullet (v_2 * u_1) \bullet 0^4) + (0^2 \bullet (v_2 * v_2) \bullet (v_1 * v_2) \bullet 0^2)$$

Example 3. As another interesting example, consider long multiplication applied to $v_2 \bullet 0^2 \bullet v_2$ and $0^2 \bullet v_1 \bullet v_1$, where v_1 and v_2 have bit-width 2. We obtain the following partial products.

		v_2	0^2	v_2	
		0^2	v_1	v_1	$*$
		$v_1 * v_2$	0^4	$v_1 * v_2$	
	$v_1 * v_2$	0^4	$v_1 * v_2$	$+$	

Note that, if we had applied long multiplication to $v_1 \bullet 0^2 \bullet v_1$ and $0^2 \bullet v_2 \bullet v_2$, we would have obtained the same set of shifted partial products. This shows that simply knowing the collections of shifted partial products does not permit uniquely determining the multiplier and multiplicand. Recall that this dilemma was alluded to in Sect. 1, when discussing pattern-matching based re-writing.

Wallace Tree Multiplier [16]: A Wallace tree decomposes the multiplication of two bit-vectors all the way down to single bits. Let us consider bit-vectors x and y that are accessed in blocks of size 1 bit and and are of bit-width k. In a Wallace tree, a partial product $x_i * y_j$ is the multiplication of single bits, and hence is implemented as the conjunction of the bits, i.e., $x_i \wedge y_j$. There is no carry generated due to the multiplication of single bits. The partial product $x_i * y_j$ is aligned with the $(i + j - 2)$th bit of output. Let us consider the oth output bit. All the partial products that are aligned to o are summed using full adders and half adders. Specifically, full adders are used if more than two bits remain to be summed, while half adders are used if only two bits remain to be summed. The carry bits that are generated by adding the partial products for the oth output bit are aligned to the $(o + 1)$th output bit. Finally, these carry bits are added to the partial products generated for $(o + 1)th$ bit using adders, as illustrated in the following figure.

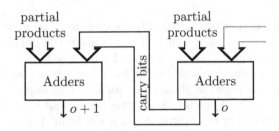

Note that neither a long multiplier nor a Wallace tree multiplier completely specifies an implementation. Therefore, there are several ways to implement a multiplier, and it is non-trivial to verify that an implementation is correct.

3   Pattern Detection

In this section, we present algorithms that attempt to match multiplications that are decomposed using long or Wallace tree multiplication. If we match some subterms of the input formula as instances of multiplication, we add tautologies stating that the terms are equivalent to the product of the matched bit-vectors. Our matching method may find multiple matches for a subterm. We add a tautology for each match to the input and solve using an available solver. Let us first present our method of matching long multiplication.

3.1   Matching Long Multiplication

In Algorithm 1, we present a function MATCHLONG that takes a QF_BV term t and returns a set of matched multiplications. The algorithm and the subsequent algorithms are written such that as soon as it becomes clear that no multiplication can be matched, they return the empty set. At line 1, we match t with a sum of concatenations, and if the match fails then clearly t is not a long multiplication. At line 2, we find a partial product among s_{ij} and extract the block

---

Algorithm 1. MATCHLONG(t)

Require: t : a term in QF_BV
Ensure: M : matched multiplications := $\varnothing$
1: **if** $t == (s_{1k_1} \bullet ... \bullet s_{11}) + ... + (s_{pk_p} \bullet ... \bullet s_{p1})$ **then**
2:    Let w be such that there exists some $s_{ij} == (0^w \bullet a) * (0^w \bullet b)$ and $len(a) =$ $len(b) = w$
3:    $\Lambda := \lambda i.\varnothing$
4:    **for** each s_{ij} **do**
5:      $o := 1 + (\sum_{j' < j} len(s_{ij'}))/w$
6:      **if** $s_{ij} == 0$ **then continue;**
7:      **if** $s_{ij} == (0^w \bullet a) * (0^w \bullet b)$ and $len(a) = len(b) = w$ **then**
8:        $\Lambda_o.insert(a * b)$
9:      **else return** $\varnothing$
10:    **return** GETMULTOPERANDS(Λ,w)
11: **return** $\varnothing$

---

size w used by the long multiplication. The loop at line 4 populates the vector of the set of partial products Λ. Specifically, Λ_i denotes the partial products that are aligned at the ith block. Each s_{ij} must either be 0 or a partial product of the form mentioned in the condition at line 7. Otherwise, t is declared unmatched at line 9. At line 5, we compute the alignment o for s_{ij}. If s_{ij} happens to be a partial product, it is inserted in Λ_o at line 8. At line 10, we call GETMULTOPERANDS to identify the operands of the long multiplication from Λ if t indeed encodes a long multiplication.

3.2   Partial Products to Operands

In Algorithm 2, we present a function GETMULTOPERANDS that takes a vector of multiset of partial products Λ and block width w, and returns a set of matched multiplications. The algorithm proceeds by incrementally choosing a pair of operands with insufficient information and backtracks if the guess is found to be wrong.

At line 1, we compute h and l that establishes the range of the search for the operands. We maintain two candidate operands x and w of bit-width $h.w$. We also maintain a vector of bits $backtrack$ that encodes the possibility of flipping the uncertain decisions. Due to the scheme of the long multiplication, the highest non-empty entry in Λ must be a singleton set. If Λ_h contains a single partial product $a * b$, we assign x_h and y_h the operands of $a * b$ arbitrarily. We assign **ff** to $backtrack_h$, which states that there is no need of backtracking at index h. If Λ_h does not contain a single partial product, we declare the match has failed by returning $\varnothing$. The loop at line 8 iterates over index i from h to 1. In each iteration, it assigns values to x_i, y_i, and $backtrack_i$.

The algorithm may not have enough information at the ith iteration and the chosen value for x_i and y_i may be wrong. Whenever, the algorithm realizes that such a mistake has happened it jumps to line 31. It increases back the value of i

to the latest i' that allows backtracking. It swaps the assigned values of x_i and y_i, and disables future backtracking to i by setting $backtrack_i$ to **ff**.

Let us look at the loop at line 8 again. We also have variables l_x and l_y that contain the least index of the non-zero blocks in x and y, respectively. At line 9, we decrement i and Λ_i is copied to C. At index i, the sum of the aligned partial products is the following.

$$x_h * y_i + \underbrace{x_{h-1} * y_{i+1} + \cdots + x_{i+1} * y_{h-1}}_{\text{operands seen at the earlier iterations}} + x_i * y_h$$

Algorithm 2. GETMULTOPERANDS(Λ, w)

Require: Λ : array of multisets of the partial products
Ensure: M : matched multiplications $:= \varnothing$
1: Let l and h be the smallest and largest i such that $\Lambda_i \neq \varnothing$, respectively.
2: x, y : candidate operands that are accessed in blocks of size w and of size $h.w$
3: **if** $\Lambda_h == \{a * b\}$ **then**
4:    $x_h := a; y_h := b; backtrack_h := $ **ff**;
5: **else**
6:    **return** $\varnothing$
7: $i := h; l_x := h; l_y = h;$
8: **while** $i > 1$ **do**
9:    $i := i - 1; C := \Lambda_i$
10:    **for** $j \in (h-1)..(i+1)$ **do**
11:      **if** $x_j \neq 0$ and $y_{h+i-j} \neq 0$ **then**
12:        **if** $x_j * y_{h+i-j} \notin C$ **then goto** BACKTRACK
13:        $C := C - \{x_j * y_{h+i-j}\}$
14:    **match** C **with**
15:      $\mid \{x_h * b, y_h * d\} \rightarrow x_i := d; y_i := b; backtrack_i := (x_h == y_h);$
16:      $\mid \{x_h * y_h\} \rightarrow x_i := 0; y_i := x_h; backtrack_i := $ **tt**;
17:      $\mid \{x_h * b\} \rightarrow x_i := 0; y_i := b; backtrack_i := (x_h == y_h);$
18:      $\mid \{y_h * b\} \rightarrow x_i := b; y_i := 0; backtrack_i := $ **ff**;
19:      $\mid \{\} \rightarrow x_i := 0; y_i := 0; backtrack_i := $ **ff**;
20:      $\mid \_ \rightarrow$ **goto** BACKTRACK;
21:    **if** $x_i \neq 0$ **then** $l_x := i$
22:    **if** $y_i \neq 0$ **then** $l_y := i$
23:    **if** $l_x + l_y - h < 1$ **then goto** BACKTRACK;
24:    **if** $i == 1$ **then**
25:      **for** $o \in 0..(l-1)$ **do**
26:        $x' := $ Right shift x until o trailing 0 blocks in x
27:        $y' := $ Right shift y until $l - o - 1$ trailing 0 blocks in y
28:        $M := M \cup \{x' * y'\}$
29:    **else**
30:      **continue**;
31:    BACKTRACK:
32:      Choose smallest $i' \in h..(i+1)$ such that $backtrack_{i'} == $ **tt**
33:      **if** no i' found **then return** M
34:      $i := i'$; SWAP(x_i, y_i); $backtrack_i := $ **ff**

We have already chosen the operands of the middle partial products in the previous iterations. Only the partial products at the extreme ends have y_i and x_i that are not assigned yet. In the loop at line 10, we remove the middle partial products. If any of the needed partial product is missing then we may have made a mistake earlier and we jump for backtracking. After the loop, we should be left with at most two partial products in C corresponding to $x_h * y_i$ and $x_i * y_h$. We match C with the five patterns at lines 14–19 and update x_i, y_i, and $backtrack_i$ accordingly. If none of the patterns match, we jump for backtracking at line 20. In some cases we clearly determine the value of x_i and y_i, and we are not certain in the other cases. We set $backtrack_i$ to **tt** in the uncertain cases to indicate that we may return back to index i and swap x_i and y_i. In the following list, we discuss the uncertain cases.

line 15: If C has two elements $x_h * b$ and $y_h * d$, there is an ambiguity in choosing
$\quad$ x_i and y_i if $x_h == y_h$.
line 16: If C has a single element $x_h * y_h$, there are two possibilities.
line 17: If $C = \{x_h * b\}$ and b is not y_h then similar to the first case there is an
$\quad$ ambiguity in choosing x_i and y_i if $x_h == y_h$. Line 18 is similar.
line 19: If C is empty then there is no uncertainty.

At line 21–22, we update l_x and l_y appropriately. The condition at line 23 ensures that the expected least index i such that $\Lambda_i \neq \varnothing$ is greater than 0. At line 24, we check if i is 1, which means a match has been successful. To find the appropriate operands, we need to right shift x and y such that the total number of their trailing zero blocks is $l - 1$. We add the matched $x * y$ to the match store M. And, the algorithm proceeds for backtracking to find if more matchings exist.

3.3   Matching Wallace Tree Multiplication

A Wallace tree has a cascade of adders that take partial products and carry bits as input to produce the output bits. In our matching algorithm, we find the set of inputs to the adders for an output bit and classify them into partial products and carry bits. The half and full adders are defined as follows.

$$sumHalf(a,b) = a \oplus b \qquad sumFull(a,b,c) = a \oplus b \oplus c$$
$$carryHalf(a,b) = a \wedge b \qquad carryFull(a,b,c) = (a \wedge b) \vee (b \wedge c) \vee (c \wedge a)$$

The sum outputs of half/full adders are the results of xor operations of inputs. To find the input to the cascaded adders, we start from an output bit and follow backward until we find the input that is not the result of some xor.

In Algorithm 3, we present a function MATCHWALLACE that takes a QF_BV term t and returns a set of matched multiplications. At line 1, t is matched with a concatenation of single bit terms $t_k,..,t_1$. Similar to Algorithm 1, we maintain the partial product store Λ. For each i, we also maintain the multiset of terms Δ_i that were used as inputs to the adders for the ith bit. In the loop at line 6, we traverse down the subterms until a subterm is not the result of a xor. In the traversal, we also collect the inputs of the visited xors in Δ_i, which will help

Algorithm 3. MatchWallaceTree(t)

Ensure: t : a term in QF_BV
```
 1: if  t == (t_k • ... • t_1)  then
 2:     Λ := λi.∅; Δ : vector of multiset of terms := λi.∅
 3:     for  i ∈ 1..k  do
 4:         if len(t_i) ≠ 1 then return ∅
 5:         S := {t_i}; Δ_i := {t_i}
 6:         while  S ≠ ∅ do
 7:             t ∈ S; S := S − {t}
 8:             if  t == s_1 ⊕ .... ⊕ s_p  then
 9:                 S := S∪{s_1, .., s_p}; Δ_i := Δ_i∪{s_1, .., s_p}
10:             else if  t == carryFull(a, b, c) and a, b, c, a ⊕ b, a ⊕ b ⊕ c ∈ Δ_{i−1} then
11:                 Δ_{i−1} := Δ_{i−1} − {a, b, c, a ⊕ b}
12:             else if  t == carryHalf(a, b) and a, b, a ⊕ b ∈ Δ_{i−1} then
13:                 Δ_{i−1} := Δ_{i−1} − {a, b}
14:             else if  t == a ∧ b then
15:                 Λ_i.insert(a * b);
16:             else return ∅
17:         if Δ_{i−1} ≠ {t_{i−1}} then return ∅
18:         return GetMultOperands(Λ,1)
19: return ∅
```

Algorithm 4. OurSolver(F)

Require: F : a QF_BV formula
Ensure: sat/unsat/undef
```
 1: SMTSolver.add(F)
 2: for  each subterm t in F do
 3:     if  M := MatchLong(t) ∪ MatchWallaceTree(t)  then
 4:         for  each x * y ∈ M do
 5:             SMTSolver.add([x * y = t])
 6: return  SMTSolver.checkSat()
```

us in checking that all the carry inputs in adders for t_{i+1} are generated by the adders for t_i. If the term t is not the result of xors then we have the following possibilities:

line 10–13: If t is the carry bit of a half/full adder, and the inputs, the intermediate result of the sum bit, and the output sum bit of the adder are in Δ_{i-1} then we remove the inputs and intermediate result of the adder from Δ_{i-1}. We do not remove the output sum bit from Δ_{i-1}, since it may be used as input to some other adder.

line 14–15: If t is a partial product, we record it in Λ_i.

line 16: Otherwise, we return $\varnothing$.

At line 17, we check that $\Delta_{i-1} = \{t_{i-1}\}$, i.e., all carry bits from the adders for t_{i-1} are consumed by the adders for t_i exactly once. Again if the check fails, we return $\varnothing$. After the loop at line 3, we have collected the partial products in Λ. At line 18, we call GETMULTOPERANDS$(\Lambda, 1)$ to get all the matching multiplications.

3.4 Our Solver

Using the above pattern matching algorithms, we modify an existing solver, generically called SMTSOLVER, as presented in Algorithm 4. OURSOLVER adds the input formula F in SMTSOLVER. For every subterm of F, we attempt to match with both long multiplication or Wallace tree multiplication. For each discovered matching $x * y$, we add a bit-vector tautology $[x * y = t]$ to the solver, which is obtained after appropriately zero-padding x, y, and t.

4   Correctness

We need to prove that each $[x * y = t]$ added in OURSOLVER is a tautology. First we will prove the correctness of GETMULTOPERANDS. If either of x or y is zero, we assume the term $x * y$ is also simplified to zero.

Theorem 1. *If* $x * y \in$ GETMULTOPERANDS(Λ, w), *then*

$$\Lambda_i = \{x_1 * y_i, ..., x_i * y_1\}$$

where x_k *and* y_k *are the kth block of* x *and* y *of size* w, *respectively.*

Proof. After each iteration of the loop at line 8, if no backtracking triggered, the loop body ensures that the following holds, which one may easily check.

$$\Lambda_i = \{x_h * y_i, x_{h-1} * y_{i+1}, ..., x_i * y_h\} \tag{1}$$

Due to the above equation, if $x_j * y_k \in \Lambda_i$, $i = j + k - h$. If the program enters at line 25, it has a successful match and $i = 1$. Since $l_x + l_y - h \geqslant 1$, $\Lambda_l = \{x_{l_x} * y_{l_y}\}$ and $l = l_x + l_y - h$. We choose $o \leqslant l$, and shift x and y according to lines 26–27. After the shift, we need to write Eq. (1) as follows.

$$\Lambda_i = \{x_{h-(l_x-o-1)} * y_{i-(l_y-l+o)}, ..., x_{i-(l_x-o-1)} * y_{h-(l_y-l+o)}\}. \tag{2}$$

We can easily verify that the sum of the indexes in each of the partial products is $i+1$. Since all x_k is zero for $k > h-(l_x-o)$ and all y_k is zero for $k > h-(l_y-l+o)$, we may rewrite Eq. (2) as follows.

$$\Lambda_i = \{x_1 * y_i, ..., x_i * y_1\}.$$

Theorem 2. *If* $m * n \in$ MATCHLONG(t), $[m * n = t]$ *is a tautology.*

Proof. We collect partial products with appropriate offsets o at line 5. The pattern of t indicates that the net result is the sum of the partial products with the respective offsets. GETMULTOPERANDS(Λ, w) returns the matches that produces the sums. Therefore, $[m * n = t]$ is a tautology.

Theorem 3. *If $m * n \in$ MATCHWALLACETREE(t), $[m * n = t]$ is a tautology.*

Proof. All we need to show is that t sums the partial products stored in Λ. The rest of the proof follows the previous theorem.

Each bit t_i must be the sum of the partial products Λ_i and the carry bits produced by the sum for t_{i-1}. The algorithm identifies the terms that are added to obtain t_i and collects the intermediate results of the sum in Δ_i. We only need to prove that the terms that are not identified as partial products are carry bits of the sum for t_{i-1}. Let us consider such a term t. Let us suppose the algorithm identifies t as an output of the carry bit circuit of a full adder (half adder case is similar) with inputs a, b, and c. The algorithm also checks that a, b, c, $a \oplus b$ and $a \oplus b \oplus c$ are the intermediate results of the sum for t_{i-1}. Therefore, t is one of the carry bits. Since a, b, $a \oplus b$ and c are removed from Δ_{i-1} after the match of the adder, all the identified adders are disjoint. Since we require that all the elements of Δ_{i-1} are eventually removed except t_{i-1}, all carry bits are added to obtain t_i. Therefore, Λ has the expected partial products of a Wallace tree.

5   Experiments

We have implemented[1] our algorithms as a part of the Z3 SMT solver. We evaluate the performance of our algorithms using benchmarks that are derived from hardware verification problems. We compare our tool with Z3, BOOLECTOR and CVC4. Our experiments show that the solvers time out on most of the benchmarks without our heuristic, while a portfolio solver using our heuristic produces results within the set time limit.

Implementation. We have added about 1500 lines of code in the bit vector rewrite module of Z3 because it allows easy access to the abstract syntax tree of the input formula. We call this version of Z3 as instrumented-Z3. An important aspect of the implementation is the ability to exit as early as possible if the match is going to fail. We implemented various preliminary checks including the ones mentioned in Algorithm 1. For example, we ensure that the size of Λ_i is upper bounded appropriately as per the scheme of long multiplication. We exit as soon as the upper bound is violated. We have implemented three versions of OURSOLVER by varying the choice of SMTSOLVER. We used Z3, BOOLECTOR, and CVC4 for the variations.

In each case we stop the instrumented-Z3 solver after running our matching algorithms, print the learned tautologies in a file along with the input formula, and run the solvers in a separate process on the pre-processed formula. The time taken to run our matching algorithms and generate the pre-processed formula is less than one second across all our benchmarks, and hence is not reported. We also experimented by running instrumented-Z3 standalone and found the run times to be similar to that of Z3 running on the pre-processed formula;

---

[1] https://github.com/rahuljain1989/Bit-vector-multiplication-pattern.

hence the run times for instrumented-Z3 are not reported. We use the following versions of the solvers: Z3(4.4.2), BOOLECTOR(2.2.0), CVC4(1.4).

Benchmarks. Our experiments include 20 benchmarks. Initially, we investigated the motivating example described in Sect. 1 involving long multiplication that was not solved by any of the solvers in 24 h. This example inspired our current work and to evaluate it we generated several similar benchmarks. For long multiplication, we generated benchmarks by varying three characteristics, firstly the total bit length of the input bit-vectors, secondly the width of each block, and thirdly assigning specific blocks as equal or setting them to zero. Our benchmarks were written in SYSTEMVERILOG and fed to STEWord [13], a hardware verification tool. STEWord takes a SYSTEMVERILOG design as input and generates an SMT formula in SMT1 format. We convert the SMT1 formula to SMT2 format using BOOLECTOR. In the process, BOOLECTOR extensively simplifies the input formla but retains the overall structure. We have generated benchmarks also for Wallace tree multiplier similar to the long multiplication. For n-bit Wallace tree multiplier, we have written a script that takes n as input and generates all the files needed as input by STEWord. All our benchmarks correspond to the system implementation satisfying the specified property: in other words, the generated SMT formulas were unsatisfiable. For satisfiable formulas the solver was able to find satisfying assignments relatively quickly, both with and without our heuristic. Hence, we do not report results on satisfiable formulas.

Results. We compare our tool with Z3, BOOLECTOR and CVC4. In Tables 1 and 2, we present the results of the experiments. We chose timeout to be 3600 s. In Table 1, we present the timings of the long multiplication and Wallace tree multiplier experiments. The first 13 rows correspond to the long multiplication experiments. The columns under SMTSOLVER are the run times of the solvers to prove the unsatisfiability of the input benchmark. As can be seen from the table, the solvers timed out on most of the benchmarks.

The next three columns present the run times of the three versions of OURSOLVER to prove the satisfiability of the benchmarks. OURSOLVER with CVC4 makes best use of the added tautologies. CVC4 is quickly able to infer that the input formula and the added tautologies are negations of each other justifying the timings. OURSOLVER with BOOLECTOR and Z3 does not make the above inference, leading to more running times. BOOLECTOR and Z3 end up bit-blasting the benchmarks, having not been able to detect the structural similarity. However, the added tautologies help BOOLECTOR and Z3 to reduce the search space, after the SAT solver is invoked on the bit blasted formula.

The last 7 rows correspond to the Wallace tree multiplier experiments. Since the multiplier involves a series of half and full adders, the size of the input formula increases rapidly as the bit vector width increases. Despite the blowup in the formula size, OURSOLVER with Z3 is quickly able to infer that the input formula and the added tautology are negations of each other. However, OURSOLVER with BOOLECTOR and CVC4 do not make the inference, leading to larger run times. This is because of the syntactic structure of the learned tautology from our

Table 1. Multiplication experiments. Times are in seconds. PORTFOLIO column is the least timing among the solvers. Bold entries are the minimum time.

| | SMTSOLVER | | | OURSOLVER | | | |
Benchmark	Z3	BOOLECTOR	CVC4	Z3	BOOLECTOR	CVC4	PORTFOLIO
base	184.3	42.2	16.54	0.53	43.5	**0.01**	0.01
ex1	2.99	0.7	0.36	0.33	0.8	**0.01**	0.01
ex1_sc	t/o	t/o	t/o	1.75	t/o	**0.01**	0.01
ex2	0.78	0.2	0.08	0.44	0.3	**0.01**	0.01
ex2_sc	t/o	1718	2826	3.15	1519	**0.01**	0.01
ex3	1.38	0.3	0.08	0.46	0.7	**0.01**	0.01
ex3_sc	t/o	1068	t/o	3.45	313.2	**0.01**	0.01
ex4	0.46	0.2	0.03	0.82	0.2	**0.01**	0.01
ex4_sc	287.3	62.8	42.36	303.6	12.8	**0.01**	0.01
sv_assy	t/o	t/o	t/o	0.07	t/o	**0.01**	0.01
mot_base	t/o	t/o	t/o	13.03	1005	**0.01**	0.01
mot_ex1	t/o	t/o	t/o	1581	13.8	**0.01**	0.01
mot_ex2	t/o	t/o	t/o	2231	13.7	**0.01**	0.01
wal_4bit	0.09	0.05	**0.02**	0.09	0.1	0.04	0.02
wal_6bit	2.86	0.6	0.85	**0.28**	0.8	14.36	0.28
wal_8bit	209.8	54.6	225.1	**0.59**	30.0	3471	0.59
wal_10bit	t/o	1523	t/o	**1.03**	98.6	t/o	1.03
wal_12bit	t/o	t/o	t/o	**1.55**	182.3	t/o	1.55
wal_14bit	t/o	t/o	t/o	**2.27**	228.5	t/o	2.27
wal_16bit	t/o	t/o	t/o	**2.95**	481.7	t/o	2.95

implementation inside Z3. The input formula has 'and' and 'not' gates as its building blocks, whereas Z3 transforms all 'ands' to 'ors'. Therefore, the added tautology has no 'ands'. The difference in the syntactic structure between the input formula and the added tautology makes it difficult for BOOLECTOR and CVC4 to make the above inference.

We have seen that the solvers fail to apply word level reasoning after adding the tautologies. In such cases, the solvers bit blast the formula and run a SAT solver. In Table 2, we present the number of conflicts and decisions within the SAT solvers. The number of conflicts and decisions on running OURSOLVER with the three solvers are considerably less than their SMTSOLVER counterparts in most of the cases. This demonstrates that the tautologies also help in reducing the search inside the SAT solvers. OURSOLVER with CVC4 has zero conflicts and decisions for all the long multiplication experiments, because the word level reasoning solved the benchmarks. Similarly, OURSOLVER with Z3 has zero conflicts and decisions for all the Wallace tree multiplier experiments.

Table 2. Conflicts and decisions in the experiments. M stands for millions. k stands for thousands.

| Benchmark | SMTSOLVER | | | | | | OURSOLVER | | | | | |
| | Z3 | | BOOLECTOR | | CVC4 | | Z3 | | BOOLECTOR | | CVC4 | |
	Conflicts	Decisions	Conflicts	Decisions	Conflicts	Decisions	Conflicts	Decisions	Conflicts	Decisions	Conflicts	Decisions
base	172 k	203 k	170 k	228 k	127 k	148 k	724	1433	148 k	194 k	0	0
ex1	7444	9065	7320	9892	8396	10 k	474	890	7090	9558	0	0
ex1_sc	t/o —	t/o —	t/o 5.6 M	t/o 7.7 M	t/o 2.1 M	t/o 2.3 M	2564	5803	t/o 5 M	t/o 6.8 M	0	0
ex2	2067	2599	1789	2612	2360	3374	919	1420	1747	2526	0	0
ex2_sc	t/o —	t/o —	3.3 M	4.9 M	1.9 M	2.3 M	5076	8981	2.7 M	4.3 M	0	0
ex3	4109	5402	1682	3166	3374	4754	905	1321	3882	7305	0	0
ex3_sc	t/o —	t/o —	3.8 M	5.9 M	t/o 2.9 M	t/o 3.6 M	4814	9012	805 k	1.4 M	0	0
ex4	647	801	612	715	463	588	630	918	405	519	0	0
ex4_sc	143 k	165 k	130 k	165 k	110 k	130 k	115 k	138 k	67 k	114 k	0	0
sv_assy	t/o —	t/o —	t/o 5.3 M	t/o 9.8 M	t/o 1.8 M	t/o 2.5 M	0	0	t/o 4.7 M	t/o 9.4 M	0	0
mot_base	t/o —	t/o —	t/o 6 M	t/o 10 M	t/o 2.2 M	t/o 2.9 M	12 k	30 k	2.4 M	5.5 M	0	0
mot_ex1	t/o —	t/o —	t/o 4.4 M	t/o 6.1 M	t/o 1.7 M	t/o 2 M	280 k	409 k	30 k	57 k	0	0
mot_ex2	t/o —	t/o —	4.5 M	6.3 M	t/o 1.7 M	t/o 1.9 M	358 k	496 k	30 k	57 k	0	0
wal_4bit	363	435	283	343	396	479	0	0	300	378	442	486
wal_6bit	8077	9831	6887	9544	11 k	12 k	0	0	8523	12 k	68 k	54 k
wal_8bit	180 k	209 k	177 k	249 k	1.2 M	1.1 M	0	0	94 k	174 k	5.9 M	3.8 M
wal_10bit	t/o —	t/o —	2.7 M	3.7 M	t/o 5.4 M	t/o 2.2 M	0	0	249 k	519 k	t/o 2.8 M	t/o 1.2 M
wal_12bit	t/o —	t/o —	t/o 5.2 M	t/o 6 M	t/o 4.1 M	t/o 1.9 M	0	0	416 k	855 k	t/o 2.3 M	t/o 916 k
wal_14bit	t/o —	t/o —	t/o 4.9 M	t/o 6.5 M	t/o 3 M	t/o 907 k	0	0	500 k	999 k	t/o 1.2 M	t/o 412 k
wal_16bit	t/o —	t/o —	t/o 4.8 M	t/o 6.6 M	t/o 1.9 M	t/o 512 k	0	0	941 k	2 M	t/o 672 k	t/o 196 k

Limitations. Although our initial results are promising, our current implementation has several limitations as well. We have only considered a limited space of low-level multiplier representations. Actual representations may include several other optimizations, e.g., multiplying with constants using bit-shifting etc. Multiplier operations may also be applied recursively, e.g., the partial products of a long multiplication may be obtained using Wallace tree multiplier. While we have noticed significant benefits of adding tautological assertions encoding the equivalence of pattern-matched terms with bit-vector multiplication, in general, adding such assertions can hurt solving time as well. This can happen if, for example, the assertions are themselves bit-blasted by the solver, thereby overwhelming the underlying SAT solver. In addition, the added assertions may be re-written by optimization passes of the solver, in which case they may not help in identifying sub-terms representing multiplication in the overall formula. Since the nature of our method is to exploit the potential structure in the input, we must also adapt all parts of the solver to be aware of the sought structure as part of our future work. We are currently working to tag the added assertions such that they are neither simplified in pre-processing nor bit-blasted by the solver. Instead, they should only contribute to the word-level reasoning. Note that our current benchmarks are also limited in the sense that they do not include examples where multiplication is embedded deep in a large formula. We are working to make our implementation robust such that it can reliably work on larger examples, in particular on all the SMT-LIB benchmarks. More results in this direction may be found at [28].

6   Related Work

The quest for heuristic strategies for improving the performance of SMT solvers dates back to the early days of SMT solving. An excellent exposition on several important early strategies can be found in [11]. The importance of orchestrating different heuristics in a problem-specific manner has also been highlighted in [12]. The works that come closest to our work are those developed in the context of verifying hardware implementations of word-level arithmetic operations. There is a long history of heuristics for identifying bit-vector (or word-level) operators from gate-level implementations (see, for example, [19,20,22,23] for a small sampling). The use of canonical representations of arithmetic operations have also been explored in the context of verifying arithmetic circuits like multipliers (see [29,30], among others). However, these representations usually scale poorly with the bit-width of the multiplier. Equivalence checkers determine if two circuits, possibly designed in different ways, implement the same overall functionality. State-of-the-art hardware equivalence checking tools, like Hector [31], make use of sophisticated heuristics like structural similarities between sub-circuits, complex rewrite rules and heuristic sequencing of reasoning engines to detect equivalences between two versions of a circuit. Since these efforts are primarily targeted at establishing the functional equivalence of one circuit with another, replacing one circuit configuration with another often works profitably. However, as argued in Sect. 1, this is not always desirable when checking the satisfiability of a formula obtained from word-level BMC or STE. Hence, our approach differs from the use of rewrites used in hardware equivalence checkers, although there are close parallels between the two.

It is interesting to note that alternative representations of arithmetic operators are internally used in SMT solvers when bit-blasting high- level arithmetic operators. For example, Z3 [17] uses a specific Wallace-tree implementation of multiplication when blasting multiplication operations. Since a wide multiplication operator admits multiple Wallace-tree implementation, this may not match terms encoding the Wallace-tree implementation of the same operator in another part of the formula. Similar heuristics for bit-blasting arithmetic operators are also used in other solvers like BOOLECTOR [2] and CVC4 [18]. However, none of these are intended to help improve the performance of the solver. Instead, they are used to shift the granularity of reasoning from word-level to bit-level for the sake of completeness, but often at the price of performance.

7   Conclusion and Future Work

We have shown how adding tautological assertions that assert the equivalence of different representations of bit-vector multiplication can siginificantly improve the performance of SMT solvers. We are currently extending our procedure to support Booth multiplier and other more complex arithmetic patterns. We are also working to add proof generation support for the added tautological assertions. We could not include proof generation in this work, since the basic infrastructure of proof generation is missing in Z3 bit-vector rewriter module.

References

1. Kroening, D., Clarke, E., Yorav, K.: Behavioral consistency of C and Verilog programs using bounded model checking. In: Proceedings of DAC 2003, pp. 368–371. ACM Press (2003)
2. Brummayer, R., Biere, A.: Boolector: An efficient SMT solver for bit-vectors and arrays. In: Kowalewski, S., Philippou, A. (eds.) TACAS 2009. LNCS, vol. 5505, pp. 174–177. Springer, Berlin (2009). doi:10.1007/978-3-642-00768-2_16
3. EBMC. http://www.cprover.org/ebmc/
4. Clarke, E., Kroening, D., Lerda, F.: A tool for checking ANSI-C programs. In: Jensen, K., Podelski, A. (eds.) TACAS 2004. LNCS, vol. 2988, pp. 168–176. Springer, Berlin (2004). doi:10.1007/978-3-540-24730-2_15
5. Lal, A., Qadeer, S., Lahiri, S.K.: A solver for reachability modulo theories. In: Madhusudan, P., Seshia, S.A. (eds.) CAV 2012. LNCS, vol. 7358, pp. 427–443. Springer, Heidelberg (2012). doi:10.1007/978-3-642-31424-7_32
6. Barnett, M., Chang, B.-Y.E., DeLine, R., Jacobs, B., Leino, K.R.M.: Boogie: A modular reusable verifier for object-oriented programs. In: Boer, F.S., Bonsangue, M.M., Graf, S., Roever, W.-P. (eds.) FMCO 2005. LNCS, vol. 4111, pp. 364–387. Springer, Heidelberg (2006). doi:10.1007/11804192_17

7. Naveh, Y., Emek, R.: Random stimuli generation for functional hardware verification as a CP application. In: Beek, P. (ed.) CP 2005. LNCS, vol. 3709, p. 882. Springer, Heidelberg (2005). doi:10.1007/11564751_120
8. Naveh, Y., Rimon, M., Jaeger, I., Katz, Y., Vinov, M., Marcus, E., Shurek, G.: Constraint-based random stimuli generation for hardware verification. In: Proceedings of AAAI, pp. 1720–1727 (2006)
9. Godefroid, P., Klarlund, N., Sen, K.: DART: directed automated random testing. In: Proceedings of the ACM SIGPLAN 2005 Conference on Programming Language Design and Implementation, Chicago, IL, USA, 12–15 June 2005, pp. 213–223 (2005)
10. Sen, K., Marinov, D., Agha, G.: CUTE: A concolic unit testing engine for C. In: Proceedings of the 10th European Software Engineering Conference held Jointly with 13th ACM SIGSOFT International Symposium on Foundations of Software Engineering, 2005, Lisbon, Portugal, 5–9 September 2005, pp. 263–272 (2005)
11. Barrett, C.W., Sebastiani, R., Seshia, S.A., Tinelli, C.: Satisfiability modulo theories. In: Handbook of Satisfiability, pp. 825–885 (2009)
12. Moura, L., Passmore, G.O.: The strategy challenge in SMT solving. In: Bonacina, M.P., Stickel, M.E. (eds.) Automated Reasoning and Mathematics. LNCS (LNAI), vol. 7788, pp. 15–44. Springer, Berlin (2013). doi:10.1007/978-3-642-36675-8_2
13. Chakraborty, S., Khasidashvili, Z., Seger, C.-J.H., Gajavelly, R., Haldankar, T., Chhatani, D., Mistry, R.: Word-level symbolic trajectory evaluation. In: Kroening, D., Păsăreanu, C.S. (eds.) CAV 2015. LNCS, vol. 9207, pp. 128–143. Springer, Heidelberg (2015). doi:10.1007/978-3-319-21668-3_8
14. Long multiplication. https://en.wikipedia.org/wiki/Multiplication_algorithm#Long_multiplication
15. Booth's multiplication algorithm. https://en.wikipedia.org/wiki/Booth's_multiplication_algorithm
16. Wallace, C.S.: A suggestion for a fast multiplier. IEEE Trans. Electron. Comput. **13**(1), 14–17 (1964)
17. Moura, L., Bjørner, N.: Z3: An efficient SMT solver. In: Ramakrishnan, C.R., Rehof, J. (eds.) TACAS 2008. LNCS, vol. 4963, pp. 337–340. Springer, Heidelberg (2008). doi:10.1007/978-3-540-78800-3_24
18. Barrett, C., Conway, C.L., Deters, M., Hadarean, L., Jovanović, D., King, T., Reynolds, A., Tinelli, C.: CVC4. In: Gopalakrishnan, G., Qadeer, S. (eds.) CAV 2011. LNCS, vol. 6806, pp. 171–177. Springer, Heidelberg (2011). doi:10.1007/978-3-642-22110-1_14
19. Stoffel, D., Kunz, W.: Equivalence checking of arithmetic circuits on the arithmetic bit level. IEEE Trans. CAD Integr. Circuits Syst. **23**(5), 586–597 (2004)
20. Yu, C., Ciesielski, M.J.: Automatic word-level abstraction of datapath. In: IEEE International Symposium on Circuits and Systems, ISCAS 2016, Montréal, QC, Canada, 22–25 May 2016, pp. 1718–1721 (2016)
21. Kölbl, A., Jacoby, R., Jain, H., Pixley, C.: Solver technology for system level to RTL equivalence checking. In: Design, Automation and Test in Europe, DATE 2009, Nice, France, 20–24 April 2009, pp. 196–201 (2009)
22. Subramanyan, P., Tsiskaridze, N., Pasricha, K., Reisman, D., Susnea, A., Malik, S.: Reverse engineering digital circuits using functional analysis. In: Design, Automation and Test in Europe, DATE 13, Grenoble, France, March 18–22, 2013, pp. 1277–1280 (2013)

23. Li, W., Gascón, A., Subramanyan, P., Tan, W.Y., Tiwari, A., Malik, S., Shankar, N., Seshia, S.A.: Wordrev: Finding word-level structures in a sea of bit-level gates. In: 2013 IEEE International Symposium on Hardware-Oriented Security and Trust, HOST 2013, Austin, TX, USA, 2–3 June 2013, pp. 67–74 (2013)

24. Kroening, D., Strichman, O.: Decision Procedures: An Algorithmic Point of View, 1st edn. Springer, Heidelberg (2008)

25. Barrett, C., Fontaine, P., Tinelli, C.: The Satisfiability Modulo Theories Library (SMT-LIB) (2016). www.SMT-LIB.org

26. Marques-Silva, J.P., Sakallah, K.A.: GRASP: A search algorithm for propositional satisfiability. IEEE Trans. Comput. **48**(5), 506–521 (1999)

27. Bayardo, R.J., Jr., Schrag, R.: Using CSP look-back techniques to solve real-world SAT instances. In: Proceedings of the Fourteenth National Conference on Artificial Intelligence and Ninth Innovative Applications of Artificial Intelligence Conference, AAAI 1997, IAAI 1997, 27–31 July 1997, Providence, Rhode Island, pp. 203–208 (1997)

28. Chakraborty, S., Gupta, A., Jain, R.: Matching multiplications in bit-vector formulas. https://arxiv.org/abs/1611.10146

29. Bryant, R.E., Chen, Y.-A.: Verification of arithmetic circuits with binary moment diagrams. In: DAC, pp. 535–541 (1995)

30. Sayed-Ahmed, A., Große, D., Kühne, U., Soeken, M., Drechsler, R.: Formal verification of integer multipliers by combining gröbner basis with logic reduction. In: 2016 Design, Automation & Test in Europe Conference & Exhibition, DATE 2016, Dresden, Germany, 14–18 March 2016, pp. 1048–1053 (2016)

31. HECTOR. http://www.synopsys.com/Tools/Verification/FunctionalVerification/Pages/hector.aspx

Independence Abstractions
and Models of Concurrency

Vijay D'Silva[1], Daniel Kroening[2], and Marcelo Sousa[2](✉)

[1] Google Inc., San Francisco, USA
[2] University of Oxford, Oxford, UK
marcelo.sousa@cs.ox.ac.uk

Abstract. Mathematical representations of concurrent systems rely on two fundamental notions: an atomic unit of behaviour called an event, and a constraint called independence which asserts that the order in which certain events occur does not affect the final configuration of the system. We apply abstract interpretation to study models of concurrency by treating events and independence as abstractions. Events arise as Boolean abstractions of traces. Independence is a parameter to an abstraction that adds certain permutations to a set of sequences of events. Our main result is that several models of concurrent system are a composition of an event abstraction and an independence specification. These models include Mazurkiewicz traces, pomsets, prime event structures, and transition systems with independence. These results establish the first connections between abstraction interpretation and event-based models of concurrency and show that there is a precise sense in which independence is a form of abstraction.

1 Models of Concurrency as Abstractions

Concurrency theory is rich with structures that have been developed for representing and modelling the behaviour of concurrent systems. These include Petri nets [17], process algebra [8], Mazurkiewicz traces [13], partially-ordered multisets (pomsets) [19], various event-based models such as event structures [23], flow event structures [3], and event automata [18], and transition systems augmented with independence information [22]. Research into *comparative concurrency semantics* is concerned with identifying criteria for classifying and comparing these models and constructions that translate between models when possible.

There are several approaches to comparative concurrency semantics. The linear time-branching time spectrum [9] is a classification based on notions of semantic equivalence between processes. The interleaving/non-interleaving classification, is based on whether a model distinguishes between concurrent executions and non-deterministic ones. In an interleaving semantics, the finest representation of a systems execution is a linearly ordered sequence of events and concurrency is understood in terms of the linearizations it induces. Examples of interleaving models include traces, transition systems and synchronization

---

M. Sousa—Supported by a Google PhD Fellowship.

A. Bouajjani and D. Monniaux (Eds.): VMCAI 2017, LNCS 10145, pp. 151–168, 2017.
DOI: 10.1007/978-3-319-52234-0_9

trees [22]. In the non-interleaving view, the behaviour of a system can be viewed as a partial order on transitions or events. Examples of such models are Petri nets, event based models and pomsets.

A third classification is based on the duality of state and observation, also called an automaton-schedule duality [20]. State-based models such as automata represent a system by states and state changes. An event or schedule-oriented model focuses instead on the points of causal interaction between concurrent events. The concurrency cube of [22] combines these three perspectives in classifying and comparing models of concurrency.

Each representation has distinct mathematical properties and leads to different algorithms for analysis of concurrent systems. In particular, partial order reduction [7,11] is based on the theory of Mazurkiewicz traces, which is a linear-time, event-based view, while net unfoldings [6] are based on event structures [23], a branching-time, event based model.

The Abstract Interpretation Perspective. Abstract interpretation is a theory for approximation of semantics. A common, practical application of abstract interpretation is static analysis of programs, but the framework has been applied to compare and contrast semantic models [4]. The abstract interpretation approach to comparative semantics is to start with an expressive semantics that describes all the properties of interest in a system and then derive other semantic representations as abstractions. Certain relationships between semantic models then manifest as relationships between abstractions.

The motivation for this work stems from the development of a program analyzer based on non-interleaving semantics [21]. An analyzer that uses an event-based, non-interleaving representation can succinctly represent concurrent schedules that would require an exponential number of interleavings in an inter-leaving model [6,14]. On the other hand, event-based analyzers do not include data abstraction: at present, distinct states give rise to distinct events, triggering an explosion of events [21]. The research in this paper is a first step towards composing event-based models with abstract domains.

Contribution and Overview. This paper examines different representations of concurrent behaviour as abstractions of a fine-grained semantics of a system. We advance the thesis that the fundamental components of several models of concurrency are parameters to an abstraction functor and the models themselves are abstract domains generated by this functor.

The first component of a concurrency model is an indivisible unit of computation called an event. We define events as Boolean abstractions that satisfy a history condition. The second component of concurrency models is a notion of independence, which dictates when events may fire concurrently. Independence defines an abstraction of a domain of sequences of events. A concurrency model arises as a composition of an event abstraction and an independence specification. We demonstrate that several models of concurrency can be instantiated by our domain functor. This research gives credence to the idea that concurrency itself is a form of abstraction.

2   Order Theory and Abstract Interpretation Primer

Sets and Posets. We denote the subset ordering as $\subseteq$ and strict subset as $\subset$. The *image* of a set $X \subseteq A$ with respect to a relation $R \subseteq A \times C$ is the set $R(X) \triangleq \{y \in C \mid x \in X \text{ and } (x, y) \in R\}$. The *preimage* of $X \subseteq C$ is $R^{-1}(X)$. The composition of $R \subseteq A \times B$ and $S \subseteq B \times C$ is the relation $R \circ S \triangleq \{(a, c) \mid (a, b) \in R \text{ and } (b, c) \in S \text{ for some } b \in B\}$.

We assume the notions of a poset and a lattice. A *bounded lattice* has a least element $\bot$ and a greatest element $\top$, called bottom and top, respectively. A lattice L is *complete* if every subset $S \subseteq L$ has a meet $\sqcap S$ and a join $\sqcup S$. Superscripts and subscripts introduced for disambiguation will always be dropped when they are clear from the context.

Functions. Consider lattices $(L, \sqsubseteq, \sqcap, \sqcup)$ and $(M, \preccurlyeq, \curlywedge, \curlyvee)$. A function $g : L \to M$ is *monotone* if, for all x and y in L, $x \sqsubseteq y$ implies $g(x) \preccurlyeq g(y)$. The function g is a *lattice homomorphism* if it is monotone and satisfies $g(x \sqcap y) = g(x) \curlywedge g(y)$ and $g(x \sqcup y) = g(x) \curlyvee g(y)$ for all x and y. A homomorphism of complete lattices must further commute with arbitrary meets and joins, of Boolean lattices must commute with complements, etc. A homomorphism with respect to some set of lattice operations is one that commutes with those operations. The *De Morgan dual* of a function $f : L \to M$ between Boolean lattices maps x to $\neg f(\neg x)$.

Galois Connections and Closures. Let $(L, \sqsubseteq)$ and $(M, \preccurlyeq)$ be posets. A *Galois connection* $(L, \sqsubseteq) \xleftrightarrow[\alpha]{\gamma} (M, \preccurlyeq)$, is a pair of functions $\alpha : L \to M$ and $\gamma : M \to L$ satisfying that for all $x \in L$ and $y \in M$, $\alpha(x) \preccurlyeq y$ exactly if $x \sqsubseteq \gamma(y)$. When the orders involved are clear, we write $L \xleftrightarrow[\alpha]{\gamma} M$. A Galois connection is a *Galois insertion* if α is surjective. A function in $L \to L$ is called an *operator*. The operator f is *extensive* if $x \sqsubseteq f(x)$, *reductive* if $f(x) \sqsubseteq x$ and *idempotent* if $f(f(x)) = f(x)$. An operator is an *upper closure* if it is monotone, idempotent and extensive and is a *lower closure* if it is monotone, idempotent and reductive. A closure is an upper or a lower closure.

Abstract Domains. A *domain* in the sense of abstract interpretation, is a complete lattice equipped with monotone functions, called *transformers*, and non-monotone operations called widening and narrowing for enforcing the convergence of an analysis. We do not consider widening and narrowing. We use signatures to compare transformers from different domains.

Fix a signature containing a set of symbols *Sig* with an arity function $ar : Sig \to \mathbb{N}$. A domain $\mathcal{A} = (A, O_A)$ is a complete lattice A and a collection of transformers $f^{\mathcal{A}} : A^{ar(f)} \to A$, for each symbol in *Sig*. For notational simplicity, the next definition uses unary transformers. A domain $\mathcal{A} = (A, O_A)$ is an *abstraction* of $\mathcal{C} = (C, O_C)$ if there exists a Galois connection $(C, \leqslant) \xleftrightarrow[\alpha]{\gamma} (A, \sqsubseteq)$ such that for all f in *Sig*, $\alpha \circ f^C \sqsubseteq f^{\mathcal{A}} \circ \alpha$. The *best abstract transformer* corresponding to f^C is the function $\alpha \circ f^C \circ \gamma$, which represents the most precise approximation of a single application of f^C. A *Sig-domain homomorphism* is a complete lattice isomorphism that commutes with transformers of the two domains. A *Sig*-domain *isomorphism* is similarly defined.

Definition 1. *Two abstractions $\mathcal{A} = (A, O_A)$ and $\mathcal{B} = (B, O_B)$, of a concrete domain $\mathcal{C} = (C, O_C)$, specified by Galois connections $(C, \leqslant) \xleftrightarrow[\alpha_A]{\gamma_A} (A, \sqsubseteq_A)$ and $(C, \leqslant) \xleftrightarrow[\alpha_B]{\gamma_B} (B, \sqsubseteq_B)$ are equivalent if there exists a domain isomorphism $h : A \to B$, satisfying that $h(\alpha_A(c)) = \alpha_B(c)$ and $\gamma_A(a) = \gamma_B(h(a))$.*

Process Algebra. We use process algebra only for notational convenience in this paper, and review it informally here. Let *Act* be a set of actions. The terms in a standard process algebra [2] are generated by the grammar below.

$$P ::= a \mid P; Q \mid P + Q \mid P^* \mid P \| Q$$

A process P may be an atomic action a, the sequential composition $P; Q$ of two processes, a choice $P + Q$ between two processes, the iteration P^* of a process, or the parallel composition $P \| Q$ of two processes.

3   Events as Abstractions

The contribution of this section is to show that various notions of an event arise as abstract interpretations. We introduce a new domain of transition sequences, the notion of an event abstraction, and a domain functor for constructing event sequences from an event abstraction.

3.1   The Domain of Transition Sequences

Let *Act* be a set of actions and *State* be a set of states. A labelled relation on *State* is a subset of $Rel \mathrel{\hat{=}} State \times Act \times State$. A *transition* (s, a, t) is an element of a labelled relation in which s is the *source*, t is the *target* and a is the *label*. Moreover, s is the *predecessor* of t and t is the *successor* of s.

The most detailed behaviour we consider for a system is sequences of transitions. Transition sequences are not paths because the endpoints of transitions are duplicated. We refer to $(s_0, a_0, t_0), (s_1, a_1, t_1), \ldots, (s_{n-1}, a_{n-1}, t_{n-1})$ as a *transition sequence* that has length n. The empty sequence ε has length 0. The first and last states in the sequence are s_0 and t_{n-1}, while (s_0, a_0, t_0) and (s_{n-1}, a, t_{n-1}) are the first and last transitions. A transition sequence of length n is *consistent* if adjoining target and source states coincide: $t_i = s_{i+1}$ for all $i < n - 1$. An *inconsistent* transition sequence is not consistent. The concatenation of two transition sequences τ and σ is defined using the standard string concatenation, denoted $\tau \cdot \sigma$, and abbreviated to $\tau\sigma$ when no confusion arises. The sequence τ is the prefix of $\tau\sigma$, denoted $\tau \preccurlyeq \sigma$, where $\preccurlyeq$ is the prefix order.

A *labelled transition system* (LTS) $M = (State, Trans)$ consists of a set of states and a *transition relation* $Trans \subseteq Rel$. A transition (s, a, t) is *enabled* in a state s if (s, a, t) is in *Trans*. A transition sequence is *feasible* if it only contains transitions from *Trans* and is *infeasible* otherwise. A *path* or *history* of length n is a sequence $s_0, a_1, s_1, \ldots, a_{n-1}, s_{n-1}$, which corresponds to a feasible, consistent transition sequence $(s_0, a_1, s_1) \ldots (s_{n-2}, a_{n-1}, s_{n-1})$. Feasibility and consistency are unrelated as there exist transition sequences that infeasible and consistent, and sequences that are feasible and inconsistent.

We recall the main properties of interest for verification, which are reachability of states and the analogous property, firability of transitions. Let $Init_S$ $(Fin_S) \subseteq State$ be a set of initial (final) states. An *initial* transition is one that is enabled in a state in $Init_S$. Some final state is *reachable* if there is a path whose first state is in $Init_S$ and last state is in Fin_S. A history is *firable* if it starts in a state in $Init_S$. A transition is *firable* if it is the last transition of a firable history. An action is firable if it is the label of a firable transition.

We introduce a domain of transition sequences, which consists of all possible sets of transition sequences and transformers for extending such sequences. We write Rel^* for the set of finite sequences of transitions. The *lattice of transition sequences* is $(\mathcal{P}(Rel^*), \subseteq)$. The forward and backwards *enabled* transformers $en_\rightarrow, en_\leftarrow : \mathcal{P}(Rel^*) \rightarrow \mathcal{P}(Rel)$ map from a sequence to the transitions enabled either at the end or before the beginning of the sequence.

$$en_\rightarrow(X) \triangleq \{(s, b, t) \mid \tau(r, a, s) \in X \text{ and } (s, b, t) \in Trans\}$$
$$en_\leftarrow(X) \triangleq \{(r, a, s) \mid (s, b, t)\tau \in X \text{ and } (r, a, s) \in Trans\}$$

The transformers below are defined on $\mathcal{P}(Rel^*) \rightarrow \mathcal{P}(Rel^*)$.

$$st(X) \triangleq \{\sigma(s, a, t) \mid \sigma \in Rel^*, \tau(r, b, t) \in X\}$$
$$tr(X) \triangleq \{\sigma(s, a, t) \mid \sigma \in Rel^*, \tau(s, a, t) \in X\}$$
$$ext_\rightarrow(X) \triangleq \{\tau(s, b, t) \mid \tau \in X, (s, b, t) \in en_\rightarrow(\{\tau\})\}$$
$$ext_\leftarrow(X) \triangleq \{(r, a, s)\tau \mid \tau \in X, (r, a, s) \in en_\leftarrow(\{\tau\})\}$$

The *state closure* transformer *st* extends X with all sequences that have the same terminal state as some sequence in X. The *transition closure* transformer *tr* extends X with all sequences that have the same terminal transition as some sequence in X. These two closures serve two purposes: they allow for states and transitions to be viewed as abstractions of sequences, and they allow for reconstructing a transition system representation of a system from a domain encoding its behaviour. It is easy to reconstruct a transition system from transition sequences, but the task is not as easy in an abstraction.

The *forward extension* transformer $ext_\rightarrow$ extends the end of a sequence with transitions that respect the transition relation and the *backward extension* transformer $ext_\leftarrow$ extends a sequence backwards in a similar manner. The transformers above are existential in that they rely on the existence of a sequence in their argument or in Rel. These transformers have universal variants defined in the standard way by complementation.

$$\widetilde{st} \triangleq \neg \circ st \circ \neg \quad \widetilde{tr} \triangleq \neg \circ tr \circ \neg \quad \widetilde{ext_\rightarrow} \triangleq \neg \circ ext_\rightarrow \circ \neg \quad \widetilde{ext_\leftarrow} \triangleq \neg \circ ext_\leftarrow \circ \neg$$

Proposition 1. *The transformers of the transition sequence domain are monotone and satisfy the following properties.*

1. *There is a Galois connection between* $ext_\to$ *and* $\widetilde{ext}_\leftarrow$.
2. *There is a Galois connection between* $ext_\leftarrow$ *and* $\widetilde{ext}_\to$.
3. *The transformers* st *and* tr *are upper closure operators.*

Let $Init_T$ and Fin_T be sets of initial and final transitions. The standard characterizations of reachability of final states from initial states lifts below to histories as the following fixed point: $\mathsf{lfp}\ x.\ Init_T \cup ext_\to(x)$.

3.2 Events as Abstractions

We illustrate different notions of an event that may arise from a single system.

Example 1. The LTS below represents the operational semantics of the term $((a\|b) \cdot a)^*$. The initial state of this system is r.

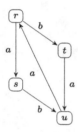

We consider five different notions of an event. An event as a *firable history* corresponds to treating nodes in a computation tree as events. This notion is history and interleaving dependent, so $(r, a, s)(s, b, u)$ and (r, b, t) represent different events. A *prime event*, which we name after the notion used in prime event structures, is history-dependent but *interleaving-independent*. An event respects history but disregards concurrent scheduling differences.

Thus, the sequences $(r, a, s)(s, b, u)$ and (r, b, t) represent the same event because (r, a, s) does not *causally precede* (s, b, u). However, the sequences (r, b, t) and $(r, a, s)(s, b, u)(u, a, r)(r, b, t)$ represent different events because the longer sequence has a history that is not due to concurrent interleaving alone.

Viewing transitions as events leads to a history-independent, interleaving-dependent notion. An *independent transition*, is an equivalence class of transitions that does not distinguish between transitions that arise due to scheduling differences. For example (r, b, t) and (s, b, u) are equivalent, and (r, a, s) and (t, a, u) are equivalent, leading to three events in this example. A *Mazurkiewicz event* is an action, so this system only has two Mazurkiewicz events.   ◁

We formalize events as Boolean abstractions of transition sequences. The prefix condition in Definition 2 is used later to construct event sequences.

Definition 2. *Let* $M = (State, Trans)$ *be a* LTS *with transition sequences* Rel^*. *An event abstraction* Ev, *parameterized by a set* Event, *satisfies these conditions.*

1. *There is a Galois connection* $(\mathcal{P}(Rel^*), \subseteq) \xrightleftharpoons[\alpha_{\mathsf{Ev}}]{\gamma_{\mathsf{Ev}}} (\mathcal{P}(Event), \subseteq)$.
2. *The concretization is a homomorphism with respect to* $\bigcup, \bigcap$ *and complement.*
3. *If* $\alpha_{\mathsf{Ev}}(\{\sigma\}) \neq \emptyset$ *and* $\tau \preccurlyeq \sigma$, *for non-empty* τ, *then* $\alpha_{\mathsf{Ev}}(\{\tau\}) \neq \emptyset$.

The event abstraction is total if $\gamma_{\mathsf{Ev}}(\{e\}) \neq \gamma_{\mathsf{Ev}}(\emptyset)$ *for every event e.*

The first condition above asserts that events are abstractions of sequences of transitions. The second condition ensures that a set of transition sequences of interest can be partitioned into the events they generate and that a concrete transition sequence maps to at most one event. The concretization conditions are weaker than the requirement that γ_{Ev} is a homomorphism of Boolean algebras because the condition $\gamma_{\mathsf{Ev}}(\emptyset) = \emptyset$ is missing. This is because a transition sequence τ may not map to an event. In an event abstraction in which $\alpha_{\mathsf{Ev}}(\{\tau\}) \neq \emptyset$ exactly if τ is a firable history, $\gamma_{\mathsf{Ev}}(\emptyset)$ will contain exactly the infeasible sequences.

Lemma 1. *For every transition sequence* τ, $\alpha_{\mathsf{Ev}}(\{\tau\}) \subseteq \{e\}$ *for some event e.*

We give an alternative characterization of events by equivalence relations, as this formulation is sometimes convenient to use. Recall that a *partial equivalence relation* (PER) on a set S is a symmetric, transitive, binary relation on S. Unlike an equivalence relation, a PER is not reflexive. The quotient $S/\equiv$ contains of equivalence classes of S with respect to $\equiv$ and $[s]_\equiv$ is the equivalence class of s. As $\equiv$ is not reflexive, $[s]_\equiv$ may not be defined.

A PER on transition sequences is *prefix-closed* if whenever $\tau \equiv \sigma$ and there exists τ' such that $\tau' \preccurlyeq \tau$, there exists σ' such that $\tau' \equiv \sigma'$. Note that there is no requirement that σ' be a prefix of σ. A PER $\equiv$ generates a lattice $(\mathcal{P}(Rel^*/\equiv), \subseteq)$ of equivalence classes of sequences. This lattice is an abstraction of transition sequences as given by the functions below.

$$\alpha_\equiv(X) \mathrel{\hat=} \{[s] \mid s \in X, s \equiv s\} \qquad \gamma_\equiv(X) \mathrel{\hat=} \left(\bigcup X\right) \cup \{s \mid s \not\equiv s\}$$

The abstraction replaces sequences by equivalence classes while the concretization is the union the contents of equivalence classes and those sequences on which equivalence is not defined. Lemma 2 shows that prefix-closed PERs and total event abstractions are equivalent ways of defining the same concept.

Lemma 2. *Every total event abstraction is isomorphic to the abstraction generated by a prefix-closed PER.*

Example 2. A PER for the prime event abstraction in Example 1 is the least PER over firable histories satisfying these constraints: $\varepsilon \equiv \varepsilon$, $\tau \equiv \tau$ for all firable histories τ and for all $\tau \equiv \sigma$, $\tau(r, a, s) \equiv \sigma(r, b, t)(t, a, u)$, $\tau(r, b, t) \equiv \sigma(r, a, s)(s, b, u)$. Note that the concatenations above must produce firable histories. ⊲

Since the event abstractions operates over a powerset lattice (of events or equivalence classes of transition sequences), we can relate several event abstractions. In Fig. 1, we illustrate the relationship between the several event abstractions described in Example 1. The *No Events* abstraction simply abstracts any transition sequence to the empty set.

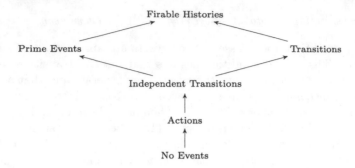

Fig. 1. Relationship between event abstractions.

3.3   The Event Sequence Domain Functor

Events represent an abstract unit of behaviour. The evolution of a system over time has different representations, including as partial orders on events [23] or relations between sets of events [10]. We model behaviour as sequences of events. We introduce a domain functor for generating a domain of event sequences from a domain of events. This domain exploits the prefix-closure condition of Definition 2 to derive event sequences from transition sequences.

Example 3. Consider the sequence $\sigma \,\hat{=}\, (r,a,s)(s,b,u)(u,a,r)(r,b,t)$ from the system in Example 1. When firable histories define events, each prefix of σ of length n represents a unique event e_n. In particular $\alpha_{\mathsf{Ev}}(\{\sigma\}) = \{e_4\}$. The sequence σ can be viewed in terms of the events fired along it: $e_1 e_2 e_3 e_4$.   ◁

The functor $\mathsf{ESeq}(\cdot)$ maps an event abstraction $\mathcal{P}(Rel^*) \xleftrightarrow[\alpha_{\mathsf{Ev}}]{\gamma_{\mathsf{Ev}}} \mathcal{P}(Event)$ to the event sequence abstraction $\mathsf{ESeq}(\mathsf{Ev})$ defined below. When clear from context, we write ESeq for $\mathsf{ESeq}(\mathsf{Ev})$. The lattice of *event sequences* is $(\mathcal{P}(Event^*), \subseteq)$. The abstraction and concretization maps are given below.

$$\alpha_{\mathsf{ESeq}} : \mathcal{P}(Rel^*) \to \mathcal{P}(Event^*)$$

$$\alpha_{\mathsf{ESeq}}(\{\sigma\}) \,\hat{=}\, \begin{cases} \{\varepsilon\} \text{ if } \sigma = \varepsilon \\ \emptyset \text{ if } \alpha_{\mathsf{Ev}}(\{\sigma\}) = \emptyset \\ \{\tau' \cdot e \mid e \in \alpha_{\mathsf{Ev}}(\{\sigma\}), \tau' \in \alpha_{\mathsf{ESeq}}(\{\sigma'\}), \sigma = \sigma'(s,b,t)\}, \text{ o.w.} \end{cases}$$

$$\gamma_{\mathsf{ESeq}} : \mathcal{P}(Event^*) \to \mathcal{P}(Rel^*)$$

$$\gamma_{\mathsf{ESeq}}(\{\sigma\}) \,\hat{=}\, \begin{cases} \{\varepsilon\} \text{ if } \sigma = \varepsilon \\ \{\tau(s,b,t) \mid \tau(s,b,t) \in \gamma_{\mathsf{Ev}}(e), \tau \in \gamma_{\mathsf{ESeq}}(\{\sigma'\}), \sigma = \sigma'c\} \text{ o.w.} \end{cases}$$

$$\alpha_{\mathsf{ESeq}}(X) \,\hat{=}\, \bigcup_{\tau \in X} \alpha_{\mathsf{ESeq}}(\{\tau\}) \qquad \gamma_{\mathsf{ESeq}}(X) \,\hat{=}\, \bigcup_{\sigma \in X} \gamma_{\mathsf{ESeq}}(\{\sigma\})$$

The concretization map goes from a sequence of events to those transition sequences whose prefix closure generates exactly the same event sequence. The enabled event transformers $en_{\rightarrow}^{\mathsf{ESeq}}, en_{\leftarrow}^{\mathsf{ESeq}} : \mathcal{P}(Event^*) \rightarrow \mathcal{P}(Event)$ map an event sequence to events enabled at the beginning or end.

$$en_{\rightarrow}^{\mathsf{ESeq}}(X) \mathrel{\hat{=}} \bigcup \{\alpha_{\mathsf{Ev}}(\{\sigma(s,b,t)\}) \mid (s,b,t) \in en_{\rightarrow}(\{\sigma\}), \sigma \in \gamma_{\mathsf{ESeq}}(X)\}$$

$$en_{\leftarrow}^{\mathsf{ESeq}}(X) \mathrel{\hat{=}} \bigcup \{\alpha_{\mathsf{Ev}}(\{(r,a,s)\}) \mid (r,a,s) \in en_{\leftarrow}(\gamma_{\mathsf{ESeq}}(X))\}$$

Forward enabledness constructs the enabled event by concatenating it with its history, but backwards enabledness is simply the event abstraction of a transition. The extension transformers concatenate a sequence with an enabled event.

$$ext_{\rightarrow}^{\mathsf{ESeq}}(X) \mathrel{\hat{=}} \{\sigma e \mid \sigma \in X, e \in en_{\rightarrow}^{\mathsf{ESeq}}(\{\sigma\})\}$$

$$ext_{\leftarrow}^{\mathsf{ESeq}}(X) \mathrel{\hat{=}} \{e\sigma \mid \sigma \in X, e \in en_{\leftarrow}^{\mathsf{ESeq}}(\{\sigma\})\}$$

We define a few event abstractions below.

Histories. The set of histories *Hist* consists of feasible, consistent transition sequences. The event abstraction Hist maps every history to itself and ignores other sequences. The least fixed point providing firable histories when evaluated on event sequences will concretize to the set of firable histories, representing the *unfoldings* of a transition system.

Transitions. The domain Tr uses transitions in *Rel* as events with maps $\alpha_{\mathsf{Tr}}(X) = \{(r,a,s) \mid \sigma(r,a,s) \in X\}$) and $\gamma_{\mathsf{Tr}}(Y) = \{\sigma(r,a,s) \mid (r,a,s) \in Y\}$. The domain ESeq(Tr) of event sequences is equivalent to the domain of transition sequences. The use of prefixes in α_{ESeq} and γ_{ESeq} is necessary for this equivalence to arise. A simplistic lifting of events to event sequences that ignored prefix information would not lead to this equivalence.

Actions. Consider *Act* to be the set of events and Act as the domain with $\alpha_{\mathsf{Act}}(X) \mathrel{\hat{=}} \{a \mid \sigma(r,a,s) \in X\}$, and $\gamma_{\mathsf{Act}}(Y) \mathrel{\hat{=}} \{\sigma(r,a,s) \in Rel^* \mid a \in Y\}$. The event sequences generated by the domain functor correspond to the language abstraction of the system, where only the sequence of labels is retained and not the underlying states. The least fixed point of firable sequences generates the *Hoare language* for a system [22].

4   Independence as an Abstraction

Independence information is used in a model of concurrency to distinguish the situation in which an event precedes another due to a scheduling choice from that in which the precedence is due to causal dependence. The contribution of this section is a function modelling independence and a functor for generating an abstraction from it.

Example 4. This example shows how concurrent behaviours beyond the scope of Mazurkiewicz traces and prime event structures fit into our framework. We represent which events may fire concurrently by a function *Ind* from event sequences to sets of sets of events.

Consider a system with three events a, b, c in which every two events may occur simultaneously but all three may not. This situation, called a *ternary conflict*, can be modelled by a function $Ind_1(\varepsilon) = \{\{a,b\}, \{a,c\}, \{b,c\}, \{a\}, \{b\}, \{c\}\}$ expressing which events may fire concurrently.

Suppose instead that all three events may fire but only a and c may fire concurrently, we have a *binary conflict* between a and b and between b and c. Further, if a and b can fire concurrently once c has occurred, the conflict is *transient* or is said to be *resolved* by c. To model this situation, consider $Ind_2(\varepsilon) = \{\{a,c\}, \{a\}, \{b\}, \{c\}\}$, encoding the initial conflict, and $Ind(c) = \{\{b,c\}, \{a\}, \{b\}, \{c\}\}$, encoding the situation after c fires. ◁

Definition 3. *An independence function Ind : $Event^* \to \mathcal{P}(\mathcal{P}(Event))$ from event sequences to the set of sets of events that may fire independently after that sequence is one that satisfies the following conditions.*

1. *For all σ and $e \in Event$, $\{e\} \in Ind(\sigma)$.*
2. *For all σ and $X \in Ind(\sigma)$ if $Y \subseteq X$, then $Y \in Ind(\sigma)$ must hold.*
3. *For all σ, $X \in Ind(\sigma)$, $e \in X$, there is $Y \in Ind(\sigma e)$ such that $X \backslash \{e\} \subseteq Y$.*

The first condition expresses that a singleton set of events is an independent set irrespective of the current event sequence. The second condition states that if a set of events can occur concurrently, every subset of those events can also occur concurrently. Thus, we exclude for this paper models based on distributed protocols that require a specific number of participants. The third condition expresses that if a set of events can potentially fire independently, firing some of them will not disable the others. Note that these events may not be enabled at the particular event sequence as the independence function only represents a may fire concurrently relation. Further, these events may still be disabled by an event external to the set. The notion of independence above is a functional representation of the local independence of [12] and generalizes many notions of independence in the literature.

Though independence has syntactic similarities to enabledness, it is fundamentally different. Enabledness is a property of a given system while independence may be viewed either as a property of a system or just of actions. In the context of programs, if atomic statements are treated as events, enabledness dictates which statements of the program may fire but independence dictates which statements of the programming language may execute concurrently. The next definition defines an equivalence on sequences based on independence. Let $perm(S)$ represent all permutations of a finite set S.

Definition 4. *The independence equivalence $\equiv_{Ind}$ generated by Ind : $Event^* \to \mathcal{P}(\mathcal{P}(Event))$ is the least (total) equivalence relation satisfying these conditions.*

1. *For all σ, $X \in Ind(\sigma)$ and $\tau_1, \tau_2 \in perm(X)$, $\sigma\tau_1 \equiv_{Ind} \sigma\tau_2$.*
2. *If $\sigma_1 \equiv_{Ind} \sigma_2$, then for all τ, $\sigma_1\tau \equiv_{Ind} \sigma_2\tau$.*

We introduce an independence domain functor Ind that generates a domain $Ind(Ev, Ind)$ given an event abstraction and an independence function. The lattice of independent sequences $(\mathcal{P}(Event^*/\equiv_{Ind}), \subseteq)$ is the powerset of equivalence classes of independent traces, which abstracts $\mathcal{P}(Event^*)$.

$$\alpha_{Ind}(X) \triangleq \{[\sigma]_{\equiv_{Ind}} \mid \sigma \in X\} \qquad \gamma_{Ind}(X) \triangleq \bigcup X$$

The enabledness transformer on the domain of independent sequences is not a simple lifting because it considers contiguous sequences of independent events that may occur in the future of a sequence and allows for them to fire at the beginning.

Example 5. Suppose a system has three events a, b, c, which are permitted to fire concurrently. Suppose the only trace in the system is abc. As adjoining events are independent, the equivalence class of abc under independence contain all permutations of the events. However, the only event enabled by the concrete system is a, so the only abstract event that would be enabled is $[a]$. To make the concurrently enabled events explicitly visible, we need that $[a]$, $[b]$ and $[c]$ are all enabled in the abstract before any have fired.   ◁

We use a helper function $iext_\to : Event^* \to \mathcal{P}(Event^*)$ which maps a sequence to possible extension consisting only of independent events. The abstract enabledness function $en_\to^{Ind} : \mathcal{P}(Event^*/\equiv_{Ind}) \to \mathcal{P}(Event)$ is also given below.

$$iext_\to(\sigma) \triangleq \mathsf{lfp}X.\, en_\to^{ESeq}(\{\sigma\}) \cup \{\tau e \mid \tau \in X, e \in en_\to^{ESeq}(\{\sigma\tau\}),$$
$$\text{for some } Y \in Ind(\sigma) \text{ and } \theta \in perm(Y), \tau e \preccurlyeq \theta\}$$

$$en_\to^{Ind}(X) \triangleq \{e \mid \text{for some } [\sigma]_{\equiv_{Ind}} \in X, \tau \in iext_\to(\sigma), e\theta \in [\tau]_{\equiv_{Ind}}\}$$

$$ext_\to^{Ind}(X) \triangleq \{[\sigma e]_{\equiv_{Ind}} \mid e \in en_\to^{Ind}(\{[\sigma]_{\equiv_{Ind}}\}), [\sigma]_{\equiv_{Ind}} \in X\}$$

Example 6. Revisit the system in Example 5. $Ind(\varepsilon) = \mathcal{P}(\{a, b, c\})$, with the function on event sequences satisfying the required constraints. The steps in the fixed point computation of $iext_\to(\varepsilon)$ are $\{a\}$, due to the initial enabled event, then $\{a, ab\}$, then $\{a, ab, abc\}$. The set $en_\to^{Ind}(\{\varepsilon\}) = \{a, b, c\}$.   ◁

Binary Independence Relations. Independence in the theory of Mazurkiewicz traces [13], is a irreflexive, symmetric, binary relation on events. The relation need not be transitive. This instance is of particular importance as it arises in several models of concurrency, namely trace theory, prime event structures with binary conflict and transition systems with independence.

A binary independence relation I generates an independence function that maps every sequence to singleton sets and the sets that contain pairwise independent events.

$$Ind_I(\sigma) \triangleq \{Y \subseteq Event \mid |Y| = 1 \text{ or for every } e, e' \in Y.\, e\, I\, e'\}$$

Lemma 3. *Ind_I is an independence function.*

This independence function is *static* as it yields the same independent sets of events irrespectively of the event sequence. Thus, it is clear that a binary independence relation is not sufficient to model ternary or transient conflicts.

Independence Abstraction and Reduction. There is an important distinction between the independence abstraction in this work and the notion of independence already inherent in a semantic model of a concurrent system.

Our independence abstraction extends a transition system so that its behaviour is modelled by a particular model of concurrency with respect to a specified event abstraction and independence function. However, there is a set of valid independence functions associated per model of concurrency. A given LTS has several representations within a model of concurrency, depending on the event abstraction and the associated independence function. We now illustrate how the event abstraction defines a basic independence function. Using such independence functions we obtain complete abstractions in that our abstraction would not add any behaviour.

Example 7. Consider the transition system in the Figure below. The initial state of this system is r.

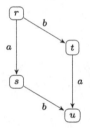

This LTS can be a representation of the term $(a \cdot b) + (b \cdot a)$ or $a \parallel b$. In the former, the event abstraction is represented by a set composed of four events: $\{a_1, a_2, b_1, b_2\}$, where t_i represents the occurrence of the transition t in a path at the i-th position of the path. In this case, the only independence function that yields a complete abstraction is the one that maps any event sequence to singleton sets as two events are never concurrently enabled.

Declaring the events a_1 and b_1 independent will abstract the LTS to the term $(a \parallel b) + (a \cdot b) + (b \cdot a)$. In the case where the LTS is meant to represent the term $a \parallel b$, the event abstraction is represented by a set composed of two events: $\{a, b\}$. In this case, the independence function is constrained to declare the event a independent with the event b. ◁

This observation on completeness is the foundation for algorithmic techniques such as partial order reduction or model checking with representatives [16]. In that view, the equivalence classes generated by an independence function can be used to construct a reduced LTS from the representatives of these equivalent classes. The resulting reduced LTS is complete for certain properties of interest such as deadlock detection. In that case, the independence function is used a reduction. An important question is whether it exists a *largest* independence function, i.e. the valid independence function that generates the smallest number of equivalence classes and if we can devise practical methods to compute it. Our independence abstraction is complete in the following sense:

Let M be a concrete LTS, M_R the reduced LTS generated by some independence function Ind, and N the abstract LTS generated by the same independence function. It is the case that both M and N have the same set of traces.

Example 8. Consider the LTS in Example 5 that only has one trace abc.

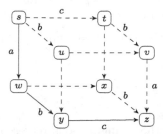

This LTS is depicted in the figure as the solid path from state s to state z. The history preserving event abstraction generates a set with three events $\{a, b, c\}$. The independence abstraction induced by the independence function in Example 5 generates the equivalence classes of traces $\{\{abc, bac, acb\}\}$.

The abstract LTS is the dashed completion of the trace into the cube in the figure. Observe that the initial LTS is a reduction of the cube LTS which is generated by the same independence function and a choice of abc as the representative of the equivalence class.   ◁

5   Instances of Independence Abstractions

The contribution of this section is to demonstrate that models of concurrency arise as compositions of an event abstraction and an independence function. For the remainder of this section, we define independence as a relation between a set of events *Event*.

We now describe the abstraction of this independence function in three models of concurrency: Mazurkiewicz traces, prime event structures and transition systems with independence. The case of asymmetric conflict is analogous as the same independence function is valid for an asymmetric independence relation.

Mazurkiewicz Abstraction and Pomsets. We are immediately in the setting of trace theory if we consider the set of events *Event* as the alphabet and the independence relation as an irreflexive and symmetric relation over events. In this case, the abstraction is simply the Parikh equivalence where equivalent sequences are permutations of words in the language theoretic sense.

Example 9. Consider the event sequence abc and the independence relation as the symmetric closure of the relation $a \; I \; b$ and $b \; I \; c$. The trace abstraction will generate the equivalence classes $\{\{abc, bac, acb\}\}$.   ◁

Unlike the Mazurkiewicz trace abstraction, there is no requirement to abstract actions as events, so multiple events may have the same label. A sequence of events $e_1, \ldots e_n$ represents a linear order $e_1 \leq \cdots \leq e_n$. An equivalence class $[\sigma]_{\equiv_{Ind}}$, represents the partial order generated by the intersection of all linear orders in that class. Since multiple elements of the partial order may have the same label, this representation of the equivalence class is called a *partially ordered multiset* or pomset [19].

Prime Event Structures. A prime event structure (PES) is a tuple $\mathcal{E} \,\hat{=}\,$ $\langle Event, <, \# \rangle$ where $< \subseteq Event \times Event$ is a strict partial order on $Event$, called *causality relation*, and $\# \subseteq Event \times Event$ is a symmetric, irreflexive *conflict relation*, satisfying

- for all $e \in Event$, the *causes* of e, $\lceil e \rceil := \{e' \in Event : e' < e\}$, is a finite set
- for all $e, e', e'' \in Event$, if $e \# e'$ and $e' < e''$, then $e \# e''$

The central concept in a PES is that of a configuration. A *configuration* of $\mathcal{E}$ is any finite set $C \subseteq Event$ satisfying:

- (causally closed) for all $e \in C$ we have $\lceil e \rceil \subseteq C$;
- (conflict free) for all $e, e' \in C$, it holds that $\neg(e \# e')$.

We denote by $Conf(\mathcal{E})$ the set of configurations of $\mathcal{E}$.

We consider the prime event structures where the configurations represent the equivalence classes of the independence abstraction. It is straightforward to see that given an event sequence σ, the independence abstraction will generate an equivalence class composed of permutations of σ and that the intersection of each event sequence in the equivalence class (when seen as a total order) generates a partial order. This partial order is in fact a representation of a Mazurkiewicz trace. Thus, when the conflict relation is generated by the complement of the independence relation, there is a bijection between Mazurkiewicz traces and configurations of a prime event structure.

Example 10. The prime event structure below (on the left) represents the partial semantics of the term $a \cdot ((b \cdot c) + (d \cdot e))$. In the representation of event structures, two events are in conflict if there is a dashed line between them. Also, for the sake of clarity, we only represent immediate conflicts. Two events e, e' are in *immediate conflict*, $e \#^i e'$, iff $e \# e'$ and both $\lceil e \rceil \cup \lceil e' \rceil$ and $\lceil e \rceil \cup \lceil e' \rceil$ are configurations.

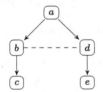   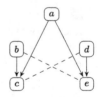

Note that the event b is in conflict with every successor of d, and vice versa. Also, note that if $b\ I\ e$, then the same prime event structure is a representation of the system. For the remainder of this example, we consider that b is not independent with successors of d and vice versa. The independence abstraction that arises by considering $b\ I\ d$ over this prime event structure amounts to removing the conflict between b and d (prime event structure in the center). However, note that the independence abstraction does not simply amount to removing conflicts. In particular, the independence abstraction over the prime event structure in the center that considers $a\ I\ b$ and $a\ I\ d$ removes the causality between those events (prime event structure in the right).   ◁

Transition Systems with Independence. We now study the independence abstraction in transition systems with independence [22]. This model of concurrency has the characteristic of defining events as a derived concept, in particular as equivalence classes of transitions generated by an independence relation on transitions. Thus, this independence relation is used in the event abstraction directly and used in the independence abstraction by lifting the relation over the generated events.

Definition 5. *A labelled transition system with independence (TSI) is a structure* $T = (M_T, I_T)$ *where* M_T *is a labelled transition system and* $I_T \subseteq Rel \times Rel$ *is an* independence relation, *an* irreflexive, symmetric *binary relation such that, using* $\prec$ *to denote the following binary relation on transitions*

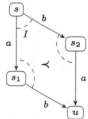

$$(s, a, s_1) \prec (s_2, a, u) \iff$$
$$\exists b \in Act.\ (s, a, s_1)\ I_T\ (s, b, s_2)\ and$$
$$(s, a, s_1)\ I_T\ (s_1, b, u)\ and$$
$$(s, b, s_2)\ I_T\ (s_2, a, u)$$

and $\sim$ *the least* equivalence *relation on transitions which includes* $\prec$, *we have*

T_1. $(s, a, s_1) \prec (s, a, s_2)$ *implies* $s_1 = s_2$;

T_2. $(s, a, s_1)\ I_T\ (s, b, s_2)$ *implies* $\exists u.\ (s, a, s_1)\ I_T\ (s_1, b, u)\ and\ (s, b, s_2)\ I_T\ (s_2, a, u)$;

T_3. $(s, a, s_1)\ I_T\ (s_1, b, u)$ *implies* $\exists s_2.\ (s, a, s_1)\ I_T\ (s, b, s_2)\ and\ (s, b, s_2)\ I_T\ (s_2, a, u)$;

T_4. $(s, a, s_1) \sim (s_2, a, u)\ I_T\ (w, b, w')$ *implies* $(s, a, s_1)\ I_T\ (w, b, w')$.

The event abstraction is generated by the PER $\sim$. Intuitively, an *event* corresponds to a set of transitions associated with the same action. These transitions are equivalent with respect to some property captured by the independence relation. Observe that $\prec$ is not a partial order.

Example 11. Recall the transition system of Example 7 bellow that represents the term $(a \cdot b) + (b \cdot a)$. The initial state of this system is r.

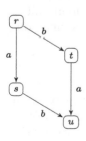

In this initial case, the independence relation is empty as the TSI represents the mutual exclusion between actions a and b. The event abstraction generates one event per transition and the independence relation on events is also the empty relation. Thus, the set of event sequences of this system is $\{\varepsilon, a, b, ab', ba'\}$ where the x' denotes the second transition of label x. If we consider the case where transitions labelled by action a are independent, we obtain the same event and independence abstraction.

Finally, the case where the independence matches to one in Definition 5, the system represents the operational semantics of the term $a \parallel b$. In this case, the event abstraction generates a set with two events a and b, and the independence relation on events considers these events independent.   ◁

Example 12. The independence abstraction for TSI is a completion of the underlying transition system with respect to the concurrency diamonds specified by the independence relation. Consider the following TSIs up to the dashed arrows.

The transition system on the left represents the term $a + b$ while the one on the right represents the term $a \cdot b$. If we consider the transition associated with action a independent with the transition associated with b, these systems are not TSIs as they do not satisfy, respectively, $T2$ and $T3$. The structures $T = (M_T, I_T)$ where M_T is a labelled transition system and $I_T \subseteq Rel \times Rel$ is a *symmetric* binary relation are called pre-transition systems with independence. The independence abstraction extends a pre-transition system with independence into the minimal valid TSI which correspond to extending the pre-TSIs with the dashed arrows. It is clear that these completions are analogous to the ones described in the prime event structure case: the left completion corresponds to removing the conflict between events a and b, and the right completion corresponds to removing the causality between events a and b.   ◁

Beyond Binary Independence. In order to express ternary conflict as in the Example 4, we consider ternary independence relations $\subseteq Event \times \sigma \times Event$. Lifting the independence function defined previously is straightforward.

For more expressive models able to model more refined behaviour such as n-ary conflicts we assume that the independence function *Ind* is provided as input. It is known that models of computation that can represent such behaviours lead to redundancies in the representation when one uses models that are more suited for binary, symmetric independence relations such as prime event structures [10].

6   Related Work

There is a significant body of work devoted to comparing and translating between models for concurrency. For example, see [15] for a uniform approach to compare net classes, [1] for a survey on process algebras, [5] for a comparison and translations between Mazurkiewicz traces and other models, [22] for a categorical study between transition systems with independence and event structures and [10] for *configuration structures*, a general characterization of event models where the notion of state is represented with a set of events, called *configuration*, that respects certain axioms.

The observation that independence is an abstraction is implicit in the original paper [22] that introduces transition systems with independence. In particular, this observation stems from the realization that the state quotient abstraction over a TSI does not necessarily produces a (deterministic) TSI and a completion procedure over a more specialized domain is provided. We have evidence from the lack of methods that combine data abstractions with partial order methods that the phenomenon of counter-intuitive interaction between standard abstractions and independence is important and understudied.

Furthermore, although the idea that events as a derived notion and independence are related, we are not aware of an in-depth study or application of abstraction interpretation theory that precisely formalizes the idea of *independence as abstraction* and provides a systematic separation between these concepts.

7 Conclusion

In this paper, we examined the notions of event and independence, two distinct but related aspects in the representation of concurrent behaviour, as abstractions of a fine-grained semantics of a system. We showed that various notions of systems behaviour arise as abstract interpretations where events are Boolean abstractions of transition sequences. Furthermore, we showed how this event abstraction defines an independent domain functor over the domain of event sequences. Thus, we precisely formalize *independence as an abstraction* and described known models of concurrency such as Mazurkiewicz traces, Winskel prime event structures and transition systems with independence using our framework.

References

1. Baeten, J.C.M.: A brief history of process algebra. Theor. Comput. Sci. **335**(2–3), 131–146 (2005)
2. Bergstra, J.A., Klop, J.W.: Process algebra for synchronous communication. Inf. Control **60**(1–3), 109–137 (1984)
3. Boudol, G.: Flow event structures and flow nets. In: Proceedings of Semantics of Systems of Concurrent Processes, LITP Spring School on Theoretical Computer Science, La Roche Posay, France, 23–27 April 1990, pp. 62–95 (1990)
4. Cousot, P.: Constructive design of a hierarchy of semantics of a transition system by abstract interpretation. Theor. Comput. Sci. **277**(1–2), 47–103 (2002)
5. Diekert, V.: The Book of Traces. World Scientific Publishing Co., Inc., River Edge (1995)
6. Esparza, J., Heljanko, K.: Unfoldings - A Partial-Order Approach to Model Checking. EATCS Monographs in Theoretical Computer Science. Springer, Heidelberg (2008)

7. Flanagan, C., Godefroid, P.: Dynamic partial-order reduction for model checking software. In: Principles of Programming Languages (POPL), pp. 110–121. ACM (2005)
8. Fokkink, W.: Introduction to Process Algebra. Springer, Heidelberg (2000)
9. van Glabbeek, R.: The linear time - branching time spectrum I: the semantics of concrete, sequential processes. In: Bergstra, J., Ponse, A., Smolka, S. (eds.) Handbook of Process Algebra, pp. 3–99. Elsevier, Amsterdam (2001)
10. van Glabbeek, R.J., Plotkin, G.D.: Configuration structures, event structures and petri nets. Theor. Comput. Sci. **410**(41), 4111–4159 (2009)
11. Godefroid, P. (ed.): Partial-Order Methods for the Verification of Concurrent Systems. LNCS, vol. 1032. Springer, Berlin (1996). doi:10.1007/3-540-60761-7
12. Kuske, D., Morin, R.: Pomsets for local trace languages. J. Automata Lang. Comb. **7**(2), 187–224 (2001)
13. Mazurkiewicz, A.: Trace theory. In: Brauer, W., Reisig, W., Rozenberg, G. (eds.) ACPN 1986. LNCS, vol. 255, pp. 278–324. Springer, Berlin, Heidelberg (1987). doi:10.1007/3-540-17906-2_30
14. McMillan, K,L.: Using unfoldings to avoid the state explosion problem in the verification of asynchronous circuits. In: Bochmann, Gregor, Probst, David, Karl (eds.) CAV 1992. LNCS, vol. 663, pp. 164–177. Springer, Berlin, Heidelberg (1993). doi:10.1007/3-540-56496-9_14
15. Padberg, J., Ehrig, H.: Parameterized net classes: a uniform approach to petri net classes. In: Ehrig, H., Padberg, J., Juhás, G., Rozenberg, G. (eds.) Unifying Petri Nets. LNCS, vol. 2128, pp. 173–229. Springer, Berlin, Heidelberg (2001). doi:10. 1007/3-540-45541-8_7
16. Peled, D.: Partial order reduction: model-checking using representatives. In: Penczek, W., Szałas, A. (eds.) MFCS 1996. LNCS, vol. 1113, pp. 93–112. Springer, Berlin, Heidelberg (1996). doi:10.1007/3-540-61550-4_141
17. Petri, C.A.: Fundamentals of a theory of asynchronous information flow. In: IFIP Congress, pp. 386–390 (1962)
18. Pinna, G.M., Poigné, A.: On the nature of events: another perspective in concurrency. Theor. Comput. Sci. **138**(2), 425–454 (1995)
19. Pratt, V.: Modeling concurrency with partial orders. Int. J. Parallel Program. **15**(1), 33–71 (1986)
20. Pratt, V.R.: Event-state duality: the enriched case. In: Proceedings of the 13th International Conference on Concurrency Theory, CONCUR 2002, Brno, Czech Republic, 20–23 August 2002, pp. 41–56 (2002)
21. Rodríguez, C., Sousa, M., Sharma, S., Kroening, D.: Unfolding-based partial order reduction. In: Concurrency Theory (CONCUR). Leibniz International Proceedings in Informatics, vol. 42, pp. 456–469. Dagstuhl Publishing (2015)
22. Sassone, V., Nielsen, M., Winskel, G.: Models for concurrency: towards a classification. Theor. Comput. Sci. **170**(1–2), 297–348 (1996)
23. Winskel, G.: An introduction to event structures. In: School/Workshop on Linear Time, Branching Time and Partial Order in Logics and Models for Concurrency, pp. 364–397 (1988)

Complete Abstractions and Subclassical Modal Logics

Vijay D'Silva[1] and Marcelo Sousa[2]([✉])

[1] Google Inc., San Francisco, USA
[2] University of Oxford, Oxford, UK
marcelo.sousa@cs.ox.ac.uk

Abstract. Forwards-completeness is a concept in abstract interpretation expressing that an abstract and a concrete transformer have the same semantics with respect to an abstraction. When the set of transformers is generated by the signature of a logic, a forwards-complete abstraction of a structure is one that satisfies the same formulae in a given logic. We highlight a connection between models of positive modal logic, which are logics that lack negation and implication, and forwards-completeness. These models, which were discovered independently by researchers in modal logic, model checking, and static analysis of logic programs, correspond to Kripke structures with an order on their states. We show that forwards-completeness provides a new way to synthesize both models for positive modal logics and a notion of simulation for these models. The Kripke structures that can be synthesized using forwards-completeness satisfy a saturation condition which ensures that transition relations behave like best abstract transformers.

1 Logical Semantics from Complete Abstractions

Positive modal logics (PMLs) are those that lack both negation and implication [11]. These logics are of interest for a few reasons. One is that certain problems have a lower complexity when restricted to PMLs; the satisfiability problem for the modal logics K and S4 is PSPACE-complete but is in NP for certain subclassical fragments [26]. PMLs are logical idealizations of query languages for graph databases, so the complexity of model checking PMLs against finite structures is useful in studying disjunctive and conjunctive query complexity [23].

Which structures provide a semantics for PMLs? These logics can be interpreted in standard Kripke structures but due to restrictions of the logic, some meta-logical properties fail. Consider an example (from [3]) of Kripke structures in which every state satisfying $\Box\varphi$ also satisfies $\Box\Box\varphi$, for every formula φ. In a classical modal logic, it is also true that every state of such a structure that satisfies $\Diamond\Diamond\psi$ also satisfies $\Diamond\psi$, for every formula ψ. In a PML, $\Box$ and $\Diamond$ are not related by negation, so deduction systems for PML are incomplete with respect to classical semantics [3,11]. Such issues motivate the need for a semantics in which $\Box$ and $\Diamond$ are unrelated [3].

Supported by a Google Ph.D Fellowship.

A. Bouajjani and D. Monniaux (Eds.): VMCAI 2017, LNCS 10145, pp. 169–186, 2017.
DOI: 10.1007/978-3-319-52234-0_10

In addition to a semantics for a logic, one usually requires a semantic characterization of logical equivalence. For example, first-order structures that satisfy the same formulae in first-order logic are characterized by Ehrenfeucht-Fraïssé games. Similarly, Kripke structures that satisfy the same formulae in classical, infinitary, modal logic, are characterized by bisimulation. In addition, the notion of invariance will also have to apply to the generalizations of Kripke structures in which PMLs are interpreted. Since the semantics considered for PMLs will generalize Kripke structures, the notion of logical equivalence for these structures will have to generalize bisimulation.

Contribution. This paper makes three contributions that highlight a relationship between abstract interpretation and subclassical logics. The first contribution is to demonstrate that abstract interpretation is a tool for deriving semantics for positive modal logics. In particular, the lattice-theoretic semantics of subclassical logics similar to that in [12] can be derived from the constructive characterization of forwards-complete abstractions in [15,17].

The second contribution is to show that there is a duality between structures that have been proposed for increasing the precision of static analysis and those that have been used to prove decidability of model checking infinite state systems. Specifically, abstractions that are complete for disjunction [16], and ideal abstractions [32], are dual to well-quasi ordered systems [1,13]. This duality is an instance of the duality between perfect lattices with operators [12], and representations such as generalized Kripke frames [14], or Chu spaces [27]. Thus, though it is known that completeness is a tool for deriving abstractions, when combined with duality, it may also have applications for proving decidability.

The third second contribution is to derive a new notion of simulation for generalized Kripke structures that characterizes equivalence with respect to PMLs. To derive this simulation, we use the characterization of logical equivalences as forwards-complete abstractions from [10,29].

Overview. Though the structures we present have been derived using abstract interpretation, we present them in reverse order. In Sect. 3, we present *two-sorted Kripke structures* over which PMLs are interpreted. In Sect. 4, we introduce *perfect domains*, which, in abstract interpretation terms, provide the collecting semantics for two-sorted Kripke structures. The relationship between perfect domains and forwards-complete abstractions is in Sect. 5 followed by the two-sorted notion of simulation in Sect. 6.

2   Primer on Lattices

Lattices. Let $\sqsubseteq$ be a partial order and $\sqsubset$ be the corresponding strict order. In a *poset* $(L, \sqsubseteq)$, an element y *covers* an element x if $x \sqsubset y$ holds and every z satisfying $x \sqsubseteq z \sqsubseteq y$ is equal to x or to y. A *lattice* $(L, \sqsubseteq, \sqcap, \sqcup)$ is a poset with a binary, greatest lower bound $\sqcap$, called the *meet*, and a binary, least upper bound $\sqcup$, called the *join*. The meet and join operations extend to *finite* subsets

$S \subseteq L$ and are written $\sqcap S$ and $\sqcup S$. The lattice is written as $(L, \sqsubseteq)$ or L per convenience.

A *bounded* lattice has a least element $\bot$ and a greatest element $\top$, called bottom and top, respectively. A lattice L is *complete* if every subset $S \subseteq L$ has a meet $\sqcap S$ and a join $\bigsqcup S$. Every complete lattice is bounded.

The *distributive law* is the identity $x \sqcap (y \sqcup z) = (x \sqcap y) \sqcup (x \sqcap z)$ (the identity obtained by interchanging meets and joins is equivalent). In a *distributive lattice*, every x, y, and z satisfy the distributive law. A *complement* of an element x in a bounded lattice is an element y satisfying $x \sqcap y = \bot$ and $x \sqcup y = \top$. Complements may not exist and when they do, may not be unique. A unique complement, if it exists, is denoted $\neg x$. A lattice is *complemented* if every element has a complement. A *Boolean lattice* is a complemented, distributive lattice.

The powerset $\mathscr{P}(S)$ consists of all subsets of S. A *downset* is a subset S of a poset $(M, \preccurlyeq)$ satisfying that for all x in S, if there is a y in M with $y \preccurlyeq x$, that y is also in S. The smallest downset containing a set S is denoted $S{\downarrow}$ and the downset of a singleton set $\{x\}$, denoted $x{\downarrow}$, is called *principal*. The poset of downsets of M with the subset order, denoted $(\mathscr{D}(M), \subseteq)$, is a lattice called the *downset lattice*. The notions of up-sets, smallest up-set, denoted $S{\uparrow}$, principal up-set, denoted $x{\uparrow}$, and lattice of up-sets, denoted $\mathscr{U}(S)$, are dually defined.

Perfect Lattices. We recall a family of lattices that provides a semantics for the logics that we consider. A subset S of a poset P is *join-dense* if every x in P is equal to $\bigsqcup Q$ for some subset Q of S. Let L be a bounded lattice. An element $x \neq \bot$ is *completely join-irreducible* if for every subset S of L, $x = \bigsqcup S$ implies that x is in S. As no ambiguity arises in this paper, we abbreviate completely join-irreducible to join-irreducible. In general, join-irreducible elements are not the same as completely join-irreducible elements [9]. The set of join-irreducibles of L is $Irr_\sqcup(L)$. The set of join-irreducibles below x is $Irr_\sqcup(x) \triangleq \{y \in Irr_\sqcup(L) \mid y \sqsubseteq x\}$. Meet-dense sets and completely meet-irreducible elements are dually defined. The set of meet-irreducibles of L is $Irr_\sqcap(L)$ and the set of meet-irreducibles above an element x is $Irr_\sqcap(x)$.

We consider a representation theorem that allows for certain lattices to be reconstructed from a subset of their elements and additional data. This construction also allows for morphisms between lattices to be reconstructed from morphisms between these subsets. The theorem we use is called a *duality theorem* because the morphisms between lattices are in the opposite direction to the morphisms between the subsets, so the category of lattices is not equivalent but is dual to the category of representations.

Definition 1. *A perfect lattice is complete lattice L in which $Irr_\sqcup(L)$ is join-dense and $Irr_\sqcap(L)$ is meet-dense.*

Specifically, it is known that perfect Boolean lattices are exactly the complete, atomic Boolean lattices, and perfect distributive lattices are exactly the doubly algebraic distributive lattices [9]. The lattice of intervals is an example of a non-distributive, perfect lattice.

Functions. Consider lattices $(L, \sqsubseteq, \sqcap, \sqcup)$ and $(M, \preccurlyeq, \curlywedge, \curlyvee)$. A function $g : L \to M$ is *monotone* if, for all x and y in L, $x \sqsubseteq y$ implies $g(x) \preccurlyeq g(y)$. The function g is a *lattice homomorphism* if it is monotone and satisfies $g(x \sqcap y) = g(x) \curlywedge g(y)$ and $g(x \sqcup y) = g(x) \sqcup g(y)$ for all x and y. A homomorphism of complete lattices must further commute with arbitrary meets and joins, of Boolean lattices must commute with complements, etc. The function g is *additive* if every x and y satisfy that $g(x \sqcup y) = g(x) \curlyvee g(y)$, and g is *completely additive* if every set $S \subseteq L$, satisfies $g(\bigsqcup S) = \curlyvee g(S)$. The definitions of *multiplicative* and *completely multiplicative* functions follow by replacing joins with meets.

A function in $L \to L$ is an *operator*. An operator f is *extensive* if $x \sqsubseteq f(x)$, is *reductive* if $f(x) \sqsubseteq x$ and is *idempotent* if $f(f(x)) = f(x)$. An *upper closure operator* is monotone, idempotent, and extensive and a *lower closure operator* is monotone, idempotent, and reductive. A *closure* is an upper or a lower closure.

3   Kripke Structures for Subclassical Modal Logics

This section introduces four different generalizations of Kripke structures parameterized by the modalities that can be interpreted in those structures.

Logical Syntax. We consider a polymodal logic with forward and backward modalities and with infinitary conjunction. Let *Prop* be a countable set of atomic proposition symbols and *Act* be a countable set of action symbols. We use p, q, r for elements of *Prop* and a, b, c for elements of *Act* and Φ for finite set of formulae.

$$\varphi ::= \text{true} \mid \text{false} \mid p \mid [a]_\to \varphi \mid \langle a \rangle_\to \varphi \mid [a]_\leftarrow \varphi \mid \langle a \rangle_\leftarrow \varphi \mid \bigvee \Phi \mid \bigwedge \Phi$$

These formulae will be interpreted in a structure containing states, transitions, and propositions associated with states. Since the logic is polymodal, there are labels associated with transitions. A proposition p expresses that p is true in a state. The formula $\langle a \rangle_\leftarrow \varphi$ expresses that there exists a transition labelled a, which leads to the current state from a state in which φ holds. The formula $[a]_\leftarrow \varphi$ expresses that every transition labelled a, which leads to the current state, is from a state in which φ holds. The formulae $\langle a \rangle_\to \varphi$ and $[a]_\to \varphi$ are the standard, forwards modalities. If the set of actions is a singleton, as in our examples, we abbreviate modalities to $\Box_\to$, $\Diamond_\to$, $\Box_\leftarrow$, and $\Diamond_\leftarrow$. A fragment of the logic over a subset of operators is one closed under only those operators.

Two-Sorted Kripke Structures. Consider a Kripke structure with three states $\{u, v, w\}$, where u is labelled with p and q, v is labelled p, and w is labelled r. The state v satisfies $p \wedge \neg q$, but is not uniquely definable in a logic that lacks negation. The Kripke semantics for intuitionistic modal logics uses an order $u \preccurlyeq v$ to encode that the state u satisfies all formulae satisfied by v. The order allows for representing that u satisfies a formula that v does not but that but there is no intuitionistic formula satisfied only by v.

In a logic containing disjunction, the set of states $\{u, w\}$ is definable by formula $p \vee r$. This set is not definable if conjunction is the only connective in the logic. A structure that provides the semantics for a conjunctive logic needs to express that certain *sets of states* are not distinguishable from each other. A Chu space [27] is one such structure: it contains *objects, attributes*, and a Chu relation between objects and attributes describing which objects satisfy the same *propositional formulae*. In this paper, objects are states, attributes correspond to sets of states called costates, and the Chu relation is restricted to be an order between states and costates as in [12,14].

Definition 2. *A two-sorted poset (twoset)* $M = (L, U, \preccurlyeq)$ *is a poset* $(L \cup U, \preccurlyeq)$ *in which* L *is join-dense and* U *is meet-dense. The Galois relation of the twoset is* $G_M \mathrel{\hat{=}} \{(y, x) \in L \times L \mid$ *for all* z *in* $U, x \preccurlyeq z$ *implies* $y \preccurlyeq z\}$.

Note that the sets L and U need not be disjoint, and that the Galois relation is defined only over the join-irreducible elements. The Galois relation provides a more general notion of indistinguishability than an order and derives its name from the Dedekind-MacNeille completion, as we explain in Sect. 4.2.

The twoset above, like a Chu space, does not provide an interpretation of modalities. A two-sorted Kripke structure is defined over a twoset using the join-irreducibles of the twoset as states and the meet-irreducibles as costates. The transition relation is defined over states but must respect constraints imposed by the Galois relation.

Example 1. We give three examples of two-sorted Kripke structures accompanied with illustrations in Fig. 1. The lattices in the figure are not part of this example. All the examples have three states $\{1, 2, 3\}$ and three costates $\{4, 5, 6\}$. If each state s is viewed a set $\{s\}$, then states represent minimal components of a structure and costates are maximal components. States are labelled with propositions they satisfy. The order in each structure is depicted by a Hasse diagram, with a dashed edge going upwards from s to t if s is less than t. Solid edges with arrowheads represent transitions. We say that a set satisfies a formula if every state in that set satisfies the formula. The signatures below were chosen for illustrating formulae that can be interpreted in a non-Boolean structure but have no other significance.

M_1 shows how a standard Kripke structure is encoded as a two-sorted Kripke structure. The costates represent complements of single states: 4 represents $\{1, 2\}$, 5 represents $\{1, 3\}$ and 6 represents $\{2, 3\}$. The order represents inclusion between a state and costates, which is why a state can be below multiple costates: 2 is below 4 and 6. The states are incomparable in the order because they are distinguishable by backward modalities. The state 1 satisfies $\square_{\leftarrow} \mathsf{false}$ because it has no predecessors, 2 satisfies $p \wedge \Diamond_{\leftarrow} p$ and 3 satisfies q.

M_2 encodes an ordered Kripke structure for interpreting a logic over the operators $\{\Diamond_{\leftarrow}, \Diamond_{\rightarrow}, \square_{\rightarrow}, \vee, \wedge\}$. The order $2 \preccurlyeq_2 1$ indicates that every formula satisfied by 1 is satisfied by 2. Since 2 satisfies $\Diamond_{\leftarrow} p$ but 1 does not, $1 \not\preccurlyeq_2 2$. In fact, 1 is not uniquely definable by a formula in this logic. The costates represent maximal sets of states definable by formulae in this logic: 4 represents $\{1, 2\}$,

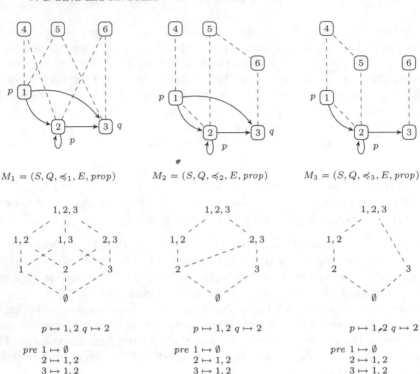

Fig. 1. Three two-sorted Kripke structures and the domains they generate. The structures have states $\{1,2,3\}$ and costates $\{4,5,6\}$. Dashed edges represent order and solid edges are transitions. By the Dedekind-MacNeille, M_1 generates a Boolean lattice, M_2 a distributive lattice and M_3 a non-distributive lattice.

which satisfy p, 5 represents $\{2,3\}$ which satisfy $\Diamond_\leftarrow p$, and 6 represents $\{3\}$, satisfying q. The order is justified by this representation. The set 3 is maximal in that it is not definable by the conjunction of other maximal properties.

M_3 provides an interpretation for a logic over $\{\Diamond_\rightarrow, \wedge\}$. The costate 4 represents $\{1,2\}$, definable by p, 5 represents $\{2\}$, definable by $\Diamond_\rightarrow q$, and 6 represents $\{3\}$. The sets $\{2,3\}$ and $\{1,3\}$ are not definable in this logic.

Definition 3 introduces four kinds of constraints on Kripke structures. Each constraint specifies conditions to be satisfied for a specific modality to be interpreted in that structure. The constraints are named after the transformer used in the lattice-theoretic semantics of the modality. The definitions below use *semi-commutation* conditions of the form $G \circ E_a \subseteq E_a \circ G$. These semi-commutation conditions are based on the form of soundness constraints in abstract interpretation and the constraints on ordered Kripke structures [3].

Definition 3. *A two-sorted Kripke structure* $M = (S, Q, \preccurlyeq, E, prop, act)$, *is a twoset* $(S, Q, \preccurlyeq)$ *with a function* $prop : S \to \mathscr{P}(Prop)$ *labelling states with propositions and a function* $act : E \to \mathscr{P}(Act)$ *labelling edges with actions. Let* E_a *be the set of transitions whose label contains* a *and* G *be the Galois relation of* M. *The Kripke structure* M *is of a type below if it satisfies the conditions shown.*

1. *A pre-Kripke structure satisfies* $G \circ E_a \subseteq E_a \circ G$, *and is saturated if* $G \circ E_a \circ G \subseteq E_a$.
2. *A post-Kripke structure satisfies* $G \circ E_a^{-1} \subseteq E_a^{-1} \circ G$, *and is saturated if* $G \circ E_a^{-1} \circ G \subseteq E_a^{-1}$.
3. *A* $\widetilde{pre}$*-Kripkestructure satisfies* $G^{-1} \circ E_a \subseteq E_a \circ G^{-1}$, *and is saturated if* $G^{-1} \circ E_a \circ G^{-1} \subseteq E_a$.
4. *A* $\widetilde{upost}$*-Kripkestructure satisfies* $G^{-1} \circ E_a^{-1} \subseteq E_a^{-1} \circ G^{-1}$, *and is saturated if* $G^{-1} \circ E_a^{-1} \circ G^{-1} \subseteq E_a^{-1}$.

For simplicity, we drop transition labels in examples and discussion. A standard Kripke structure $M = (S, E, prop)$ defines a two-sorted one $N = (L, U, \subseteq, F, prop)$ with L being singleton sets of states, and U being complements of singleton sets. The transition relation F lifts E to L.

$$ L \mathrel{\hat{=}} \{\{s\} \mid s \in S\} \quad U \mathrel{\hat{=}} \{S \setminus \{s\} \mid s \in S\} \quad F \mathrel{\hat{=}} \{(\{s\}, \{t\}) \mid (s, t) \in E\} $$

The singletons in L are join-irreducibles and join-dense in $L \cup U$ and the sets in U are the meet-irreducibles and are meet-dense. The two-sorted Kripke structure N satisfies the constraints for all four types of non-saturated structures.

An *ordered Kripke structure* $M = (S, \preccurlyeq, E, prop)$ is a poset $(S, \preccurlyeq)$ with a transition relation E that semi-commutes with $\preccurlyeq$. That is, if $r_1 \preccurlyeq r_2$ and (r_2, s_2) is in E, there must exist s_1 such that (r_1, s_1) is in E and $s_1 \preccurlyeq s_2$. An ordered Kripke structure defines the two-sorted one $N = (L, U, \subseteq, F)$ with L being principal downsets of $(S, \preccurlyeq)$, U being complements of principal up-sets and F as before.

$$ L \mathrel{\hat{=}} \{s{\downarrow} \mid s \in S\} \quad U \mathrel{\hat{=}} \{S \setminus s{\uparrow} \mid s \in S\} \quad F \mathrel{\hat{=}} \{(\{s\}, \{t\}) \mid (s, t) \in E\} $$

The singletons in L are join-irreducibles and join-dense in $L \cup U$ and the sets in U are the meet-irreducibles and are meet-dense. Since the transition relation E specifies an order, the relation F will respect the order, and N is a *pre*-Kripke structure but not a *post*-Kripke structure.

Proposition 1 identifies equalities that the structures involved satisfy. In the formulation of completeness in abstract interpretation with closure operators, a transformer f is forward complete with respect to a closure ρ if $\rho \circ f \circ \rho = f \circ \rho$, and is backwards complete if $\rho \circ f \circ \rho = \rho \circ f$. Note the similarity between the equalities on the left below and forwards completeness.

Proposition 1. *Each two-sorted Kripke structure below satisfies the first equality and satisfies the second equality if it is saturated.*

pre	$G \circ E_a \circ G = E_a \circ G$	$G \circ E_a \circ G = E_a$
post	$G \circ E_a^{-1} \circ G = E_a^{-1} \circ G$	$G \circ E_a^{-1} \circ G = E_a^{-1}$
$\widetilde{pre}$	$G^{-1} \circ E_a \circ G^{-1} = E_a \circ G^{-1}$	$G^{-1} \circ E_a \circ G^{-1} = E_a$
$\widetilde{upost}$	$G^{-1} \circ E_a^{-1} \circ G^{-1} = E_a^{-1} \circ G^{-1}$	$G^{-1} \circ E_a^{-1} \circ G^{-1} = E_a^{-1}$

Proof. We prove the statement for the *pre*-case. The relation G is transitive, so $G \circ E \subseteq E \circ G$ implies that $G \circ E \circ G$ is contained in $E \circ G$. The converse direction holds because G is reflexive. The reflexivity of G also entails that E is contained in $G \circ E \circ G$, and the equality for the saturated case follows. The proof for *post*-Kripke structures is identical, with E^{-1} in place of E. The proofs for the universal variants is also identical because G^{-1} is also transitive. $\qquad \square$

Relational Logical Semantics. Let $M = (S, Q, \preccurlyeq, E, prop, act)$ be a two-sorted Kripke structure. The modalities introduced at the beginning of the section have their standard interpretation. The usual notation $M, s \models \varphi$ represents that a state s in M satisfies φ and has the standard inductive definition: $M, s \models p$ if $p \in prop(s)$, $M, s \models \langle a \rangle_\rightarrow \varphi$ if there exists a transition (s, t) such that $a \in act(s, t)$ and t satisfies φ. The semantics of other modalities is similar, and of Boolean operations is standard. The order and costates present in a two-sorted structure do not appear above because those components encode logical indistinguishability and are intended to be invisible to the logic.

4   Domains for Subclassical Modal Logics

We now consider abstract domains for interpreting subclassical modal logics. The domains we consider must satisfy constraints guaranteeing they are the lattice-theoretic duals of two-sorted Kripke structures, which we demonstrate to be the case using the Dedekind-MacNeille completion.

4.1   Perfect Domains

A *signature* is a set of symbols Sig with an arity function $ar : Sig \rightarrow \mathbb{N}$. A *Sig-domain* $\mathcal{A} = (A, O_A)$ is a complete lattice A and a collection of transformers $f^{\mathcal{A}} : A^{ar(f)} \rightarrow A$, for each symbol in Sig. A *Sig homomorphism* $h : (A, O_A) \rightarrow (B, O_B)$ is a complete lattice homomorphism $h : A \rightarrow B$ that also satisfies $h(f^{\mathcal{A}}(a)) = f^{\mathcal{B}}(h(a))$ for every f in Sig and a in A. A *Sig-isomorphism* is *Sig*-homomorphism whose inverse is also a *Sig*-homomorphism. Two *Sig*-domains are isomorphic, denoted $\mathcal{A} \cong \mathcal{B}$, if there exists a *Sig*-isomorphism between them. Perfect domains are perfect lattices with transformers that are either completely additive or completely multiplicative.

Definition 4. *Let Act be a set of actions. A perfect, predecessor domain* $\mathcal{A} = (A, O_A)$ *is a perfect lattice* A *with completely additive transformers* $\{pre_a \mid a \in Act\}$. *Perfect successor domains are similarly defined and use* $post_a$. *Domains for the transformers* $\widetilde{pre}_a$ *and* $\widetilde{upost}_a$ *require them to be completely multiplicative.*

Ideal Abstraction. We give an example of a perfect domain in model checking. The reachability problem for infinite-state systems such as Petri-nets, lossy channel systems, and various types of counter machines is decidable. The decidability proofs show that Kripke structures generated by these systems are well-ordered [1,13]. In lattice-theoretic terms, these decidability proofs compute an ideal abstraction [32] satisfying an ascending or descending chain condition.

An ordered Kripke structure generates a domain $(\mathcal{D}(S, \preccurlyeq), \{pre\})$ where for each downset X, $pre(X) = (E^{-1}(X))\!\downarrow$. The irreducibles of this lattice are below.

$$Irr_{\sqcup}(\mathcal{D}(S, \preccurlyeq)) = \{x\!\downarrow \mid x \in S\} \qquad Irr_{\sqcap}(\mathcal{D}(S, \preccurlyeq)) = \{S \setminus x\!\uparrow \mid x \in S\}$$

Domains satisfying the properties of perfect, distributive domains were identified as candidates for static analysis in which precision was not lost in joins [8], and for disjunctive analysis of logic programs [5,16].

Intervals. We give an example of a perfect domain from abstract interpretation. Consider the set $\mathbb{Z} \cup \{-\infty, \infty\}$ of integers extended with a least element $-\infty$ and a greatest element ∞, with respect to the standard order $\leq$. An interval is either a pair $[a, b]$ satisfying $a \leq b$, or the least element $\bot$ or greatest element $\top$. The lattice of intervals is $(Intv, \sqsubseteq)$, with the order defined as expected.

$$Irr_{\sqcup}(Intv) = \{[a, a] \mid a \in \mathbb{Z}\} \qquad Irr_{\sqcap}(Intv) = \{[-\infty, a], [a, \infty] \mid a \in \mathbb{Z}\}$$

The set of join-irreducibles is the singleton intervals, while the set of meet-irreducibles contains one-way infinite intervals. The set of join-irreducibles is an anti-chain while the set of meet-irreducibles is not. The standard transformer for increment by a constant is one that is completely additive.

4.2   The Dedekind-MacNeille Completion

The relationship between two-sorted Kripke structures systems and perfect domains goes through the Dedekind-MacNeille completion. There is no new material in this subsection and proofs for the claims here are in [9].

Example 2. We illustrate the Dedekind-MacNeille by constructing a non-distributive lattice from the structure M_3 in Fig. 1. The states are $S = \{1, 2, 3\}$ and costates are $Q = \{4, 5, 6\}$. The order defines a function $u : \mathcal{P}(S) \to \mathcal{P}(Q)$ from $X \subseteq S$ to $Y \subseteq Q$ containing supersets of all elements of X. A function $\ell : \mathcal{P}(Q) \to \mathcal{P}(S)$ maps $Y \subseteq Q$ to $X \subseteq S$ containing subsets of all elements of Y. We define these functions below.

$$u \,\hat{=}\, \{\emptyset \mapsto \{4,5,6\}, \{1\} \mapsto \{4\}, \{2\} \mapsto \{4,5\}, \{3\} \mapsto \{6\},$$
$$\{1,2\} \mapsto \{4\}, \{1,3\} \mapsto \emptyset, \{2,3\} \mapsto \emptyset, \{1,2,3\} \mapsto \emptyset\}$$
$$\ell \,\hat{=}\, \{\emptyset \mapsto \{1,2,3\}, \{4\} \mapsto \{1,2\}, \{5\} \mapsto \{2\}, \{6\} \mapsto \{3\},$$
$$\{4,5\} \mapsto \{2\}, \{4,6\} \mapsto \emptyset, \{5,6\} \mapsto \emptyset, \{4,5,6\} \mapsto \emptyset\}$$

The sets satisfying $X = \ell(u(X))$, ordered by subset inclusion, form a lattice, shown below M_3. This domain is not distributive: $(\{2\} \sqcup \{3\}) \sqcap \{1,2\} = \emptyset$, which is not $(\{2\} \sqcap \{1,2\}) \sqcup (\{3\} \sqcap \{1,2\}) = \{2\}$.

The Dedekind-MacNeille completion of a twoset generalizes the powerset of a set and downset of a poset. A set has no structure and its dual representation, generated by the powerset construction, is a Boolean lattice. A poset has enough structure to generate downsets, which together form a distributive lattice. A twoset has even more structure, and its Galois-complete subsets can represent non-distributive lattices. Observe that there is an inversion of complexity in this duality: as a set is equipped with more structure, it generates families of lattices that satisfy fewer axioms.

A twoset $M = (L, U, \preccurlyeq)$ generates the functions $u : \mathscr{P}(L) \to \mathscr{P}(U)$ and $\ell : \mathscr{P}(U) \to \mathscr{P}(L)$, which map a set to its upper- and lower-approximations.

$$u \,\hat{=}\, X \mapsto \{y \in U \mid x \preccurlyeq y \text{ for all } x \in X\} \quad \ell \,\hat{=}\, Y \mapsto \{x \in L \mid x \preccurlyeq y \text{ for all } y \in Y\}$$

The upper and lower approximation functions form a Galois connection. Note that the superset order is used on $\mathscr{P}(U)$.

Proposition 2. *The upper and lower powersets with the approximation functions form a Galois connection* $(\mathscr{P}(L), \subseteq) \xrightleftharpoons[u]{\ell} (\mathscr{P}(U), \supseteq)$.

A subset X of L is *Galois-stable* if $X = \ell(u(X))$. The set of Galois-stable subsets of a twoset M is denoted $\mathscr{G}(M)$. The Galois-stable subsets are closed under arbitrary intersection, though not necessarily under union. The lattice of Galois-stable subsets of an *arbitrary poset*, with L and U being the same, is the *Dedekind-MacNeille completion* of a poset. When applied to twosets, this completion yields a representation of perfect lattices.

Theorem 1. *The Galois stable subsets of a twoset M form a perfect lattice $(\mathscr{G}(M), \subseteq, \sqcap, \sqcup)$ of sets closed under intersection.*

The meet in the theorem is intersection but the join is $\sqcup$ because it may not be union. Consult Sect. 7.30 in [9] for a proof. Theorem 2 shows that perfect lattices have representations as Galois-stable subsets of twosets. For details, see Theorem 7.41 in [9] and Sect. 4 of [12] (where twosets are called perfect posets). The proof given by [9] shows that the map $x \mapsto \ell(u(Irr_{\sqcup}(x)))$ is an isomorphism.

Theorem 2. *[9] A perfect lattice $(L, \sqsubseteq)$ is isomorphic to the lattice of Galois-stable subsets $\mathscr{G}(Irr_{\sqcup}(L), Irr_{\sqcap}(L), \sqsubseteq)$ of join- and meet-irreducibles of L.*

4.3   Domains from Two-Sorted Structures

A two-sorted Kripke structure $M = (L, U, \preccurlyeq, E, prop, act)$ defines a domain $salg(M)$ consisting of the lattice of Galois-closed subsets. The structure defines the transformers below but these transformers may not satisfy the requirements of the domain.

$$\mathcal{G}(M) \doteq \mathcal{G}(L, U, \preccurlyeq)$$
$$p^M \doteq \{s \mid p \text{ is in } prop(s)\}$$
$$pre_a(X) \doteq \{s \mid \text{ for some } t \in X, (s,t) \in E \text{ and } a \in act(s,t)\}$$
$$post_a(X) \doteq \{t \mid \text{ for some } s \in X, (s,t) \in E \text{ and } a \in act(s,t)\}$$
$$\widetilde{upost}_a^M(X) \doteq \{t \mid \text{ for all } s \in S, (s,t) \in E \text{ implies } t \in X, a \in act(s,t)\}$$
$$\widetilde{pre}_a^M(X) \doteq \{s \mid \text{ for all } t \in S, (s,t) \in E \text{ implies } t \in X, a \in act(s,t)\}$$

The definitions of the transformers are identical to the standard definition using the preimage and image of E. A transformer is *Galois-stable* if it maps a Galois-stable set to a Galois-stable set. Before showing that the construction above yields a perfect domain, we need to show that the transformers above are Galois stable. Lemma 1 shows that the semi-commutation conditions are necessary and sufficient for transformers to be Galois-stable. Observe again the connection to completeness. The Galois stable subsets are essentially an abstraction of $\mathscr{P}(L)$, so requiring a transformer to be Galois stable is the same as the completeness condition $\rho \circ f \circ \rho = f \circ \rho$. Thus the constraints proposed on ordered and generalized Kripke structures [3,14] are the transition system analogue of completeness conditions on transformers. The remaining formal claims in this section refer only to predecessor domains for brevity, but the analogous claims apply to all the other kinds of domains and transformers.

Lemma 1. *Consider the transformers generated by M above. M is a pre-Kripke structure exactly if pre_a is Galois stable.*

Proof. Consider a Galois-stable set $X \subseteq S$. For each transformer there are two directions to consider.

(*Predecessors*) The condition is $G \circ E \subseteq E \circ G$.

    (*Semi-commutation to Galois-stability*) Assume the semi-commutation condition. If s is in $pre(X)$, there is a state t in X and a transition (s,t) in E. Semi-commutation implies that for every (s',s) in G, there is a state t' and a transition (s',t') in E with (t',t) in G. The set X is Galois-stable and contains t'. It follows that $pre(X)$ contains s' and is Galois-stable.

    (*Galois-stability to semi-commutation*) Assume that $pre(X)$ is Galois-stable and X is of the form $G^{-1}(t)$, where t is a state. Consider a transition (s,t) in E and a pair (s',s) in G. By definition, $pre(X)$ contains s and, being Galois-stable, contains s'. Moreover, by definition of predecessors, there must be a state t' and transition (s',t') with t' in X. However, X is the preimage of t under G, so t' must be in this preimage. We have shown that $G \circ E \subseteq E \circ G$.

The proofs above for other kinds of transformers are similar. We now consider how to derive a two-sorted Kripke structure from a perfect domain. We extract the join- and meet-irreducibles to form the states and costates of the Kripke structure. A perfect, predecessor domain $\mathcal{A} = (A, O_A)$ with order $\sqsubseteq$ defines a structure $srel(\mathcal{A}) = (L_\mathcal{A}, U_\mathcal{A}, \preccurlyeq_\mathcal{A}, E_\mathcal{A})$ as follows.

$$L_\mathcal{A} \triangleq Irr_\sqcup(A), \qquad U_\mathcal{A} \triangleq Irr_\sqcap(A)$$
$$\preccurlyeq_\mathcal{A} \triangleq (Irr_\sqcup(A) \cup Irr_\sqcap(A))^2 \cap \sqsubseteq$$
$$E_\mathcal{A} \triangleq \{(x, y) \mid x \sqsubseteq pre_a(y) \text{ for some action } a\}$$
$$prop_\mathcal{A}(x) \triangleq \{p \in Prop \mid x \sqsubseteq p^\mathcal{A}\}$$
$$act_\mathcal{A}(x, y) \triangleq \{a \in Act \mid x \sqsubseteq pre_a(y)\}$$

A non-obvious aspect of this construction is that $srel(\mathcal{A})$ is a saturated pre-Kripke structure. So, if we start from a domain, we necessarily obtain a saturated Kripke structure, but if we start from a two-sorted Kripke structure, irrespective of whether it is saturated or not, we obtain a perfect domain.

Lemma 2. *A perfect predecessor domain $\mathcal{A}$ defines a saturated, pre-Kripke structure $srel(\mathcal{A})$.*

Proof. The representation of twosets and perfect lattices already exists, so we only have to show that the transition relation satisfies the semi-commutation conditions. Let G be the Galois relation of $srel(\mathcal{A})$. Consider pairs (x', x) and (y, y') in G and a transition (x, y) in $E_\mathcal{A}$, where all elements are join-irreducibles. The pair (x', y') is in $G \circ E_\mathcal{A} \circ G$ and we have to show that it is in $E_\mathcal{A}$. The element y' being join-irreducible is the greatest element of $\ell(u(y'))$. The element y' being join-irreducible is the greatest element of $\ell(u(y'))$. Since y is in $G^{-1}(y')$, it must be that $y \sqsubseteq y'$. By the same argument, $x' \sqsubseteq x$ holds. By construction, $x \sqsubseteq pre(\ell(u(y)))$ and because pre is monotone, $x' \sqsubseteq pre(\ell(u(y')))$ also holds, showing that (x', y') is in $E_\mathcal{A}$.

The previous statements only showed that we can generate a transition system from a domain and vice-versa. The representation theorem below, shows that we can repeat these constructions without losing information, in the sense that the structures obtained will be isomorphic.

Theorem 3. *A saturated, pre-Kripke structure is isomorphic to the one generated by its domain: $M \cong srel(salg(M))$.*

Proof. Let M be a *pre*-Kripke structure with Galois relation G. The proof of Theorem 2 shows that the map $h : x \mapsto G^{-1}(x)$ is a labelled twoset isomorphism. The condition on transitions has to be verified. If (x, y) is a transition in M, the generated domain satisfies the inequality $\ell(u(x)) \sqsubseteq pre(\ell(u(y)))$ and consequently satisfies that $(\ell(u(x)), \ell(u(y)))$ is a transition in $srel(salg(M))$. We have shown that $(h(x), h(y))$ is a transition. The converse direction is the same.

Theorem 4. *A perfect predecessor domain is isomorphic to the one generated by its Kripke structure: $\mathcal{A} \cong salg(srel(\mathcal{A}))$.*

Proof. The proof of Theorem 2 shows that $h : x \mapsto Irr_\sqcup(x)$ is an isomorphism of perfect lattices. We show that this isomorphism commutes with the predecessor transformer. Consider x and y such that $x \sqsubseteq pre(y)$. The transformer pre is completely additive, so $pre(y) = pre(\bigsqcup Irr_\sqcup(y))$ and the equality $pre(y) = \bigsqcup pre(Irr_\sqcup(y))$ holds. For every element w in $Irr_\sqcup(x)$ there exists an element z in $Irr_\sqcup(y)$ such that $w \sqsubseteq pre(z)$. Thus, there is a transition (w, z) in $srel(\mathcal{A})$ and the generated transformer pre_M satisfies $w \sqsubseteq pre_M(z)$. By taking the join of join-irreducible sets we obtain $h(x) \sqsubseteq pre_M(h(y))$ and, by a similar argument, the converse inequality. Substituting x with $pre(y)$ yields the desired result.

Algebraic Logical Semantics. Positive modal logics can be interpreted in a perfect domain provided it has the transformers corresponding to the required modalities. The *algebraic semantics* of a positive logic $\mathcal{L}$ in a domain $\mathcal{A} = (A, O_A)$ whose operators correspond to those of the logic is given by a function $[\![\cdot]\!] : \mathcal{L} \to A$ defined inductively. $[\![p]\!] \mathrel{\hat{=}} p^{\mathcal{A}}$, $[\![\varphi \wedge \psi]\!] \mathrel{\hat{=}} [\![\varphi]\!] \sqcap [\![\psi]\!]$, $[\![\varphi \vee \psi]\!] \mathrel{\hat{=}} [\![\varphi]\!] \sqcup [\![\psi]\!]$, $[\![\langle a \rangle_\rightarrow \varphi]\!] \mathrel{\hat{=}} pre_a([\![\varphi]\!])$, $[\![[a]_\rightarrow \varphi]\!] \mathrel{\hat{=}} \widetilde{pre}_a([\![\varphi]\!])$, $[\![\langle a \rangle_\leftarrow \varphi]\!] \mathrel{\hat{=}} post_a([\![\varphi]\!])$, $[\![[a]_\leftarrow \varphi]\!] \mathrel{\hat{=}} \widetilde{upost}_a([\![\varphi]\!])$. A formula holds at a *point* in a domain, denoted $\mathcal{A}, a \models \varphi$ if $a \sqsubseteq [\![\varphi]\!]$. The connection between the Kripke semantics provided earlier and algebraic semantics provided here is that a state satisfies a formula precisely if the corresponding lattice element satisfies that formula.

5   Subclassical Modal Domains as Abstractions

We now show that all perfect domains can be viewed as abstractions of powerset lattices with transformers. Since the powerset lattices represent the standard, collecting semantics of Kripke structures, it follows that perfect domains are abstract interpretations of Kripke structures. Moreover, perfect domains over non-distributive lattice also abstract a domain defined over a distributive lattice, meaning that these domains are also abstract interpretations of disjunctive abstractions [8,16] and ideal abstractions [32].

Consider a perfect predecessor domain $\mathcal{C} = (C, O_C)$ with order $\sqsubseteq$. The domain $\mathcal{C}$ defines two predecessor domains $\mathcal{D} = (D, O_D)$ and $\mathcal{B} = (B, O_B)$ which we define below.

$$D \mathrel{\hat{=}} \mathscr{D}(Irr_\sqcup(C), \preccurlyeq) \qquad\qquad B \mathrel{\hat{=}} \mathscr{P}(Irr_\sqcup(C))$$
$$\preccurlyeq \mathrel{\hat{=}} (Irr_\sqcup(C) \times Irr_\sqcup(C)) \cap \sqsubseteq$$
$$pre^{\mathcal{D}} \mathrel{\hat{=}} Y \mapsto Irr_\sqcup(pre^C(\bigsqcup Y)) \qquad pre^{\mathcal{B}} \mathrel{\hat{=}} Y \mapsto Irr_\sqcup(pre^C(\bigsqcup Y))$$

Since the set of join irreducibles below an element is a downset, both $pre^{\mathcal{D}}$ and $pre^{\mathcal{B}}$ above are well defined.

Closure operators have been used to characterize abstract domains [8], so by relating perfect domains using closure operators, we can also show them to be abstractions in the sense of abstract interpretation. We define two closure operators below. The function *b-to-d* generates a distributive abstraction of a Boolean lattice, and the function *d-to-c* generates a non-distributive abstraction of a distributive one.

$$b\text{-}to\text{-}d : B \to B \qquad\qquad d\text{-}to\text{-}c : D \to D$$
$$b\text{-}to\text{-}d \,\hat{=}\, X \mapsto X{\downarrow} \qquad\qquad d\text{-}to\text{-}c \,\hat{=}\, Y \mapsto \ell(u(Y))$$

Theorem 5. *Let $\mathcal{C}$ be a perfect predecessor domain defining the predecessor domains $\mathcal{D}$ and $\mathcal{B}$ as above.*

1. *The function b-to-d is an upper closure and satisfies that $pre^{\mathcal{B}} \circ b\text{-}to\text{-}d = b\text{-}to\text{-}d \circ pre^{\mathcal{D}} \circ b\text{-}to\text{-}d$.*
2. *The function d-to-c is an upper closure and satisfies that $pre^{\mathcal{D}} \circ d\text{-}to\text{-}c = d\text{-}to\text{-}c \circ pre^{\mathcal{C}} \circ d\text{-}to\text{-}c$.*

Recall that forward-completeness when expressed in terms of closure operators asserts the equality $\rho \circ f \circ \rho = f \circ \rho$, See [15,17,29] for more on this characterization. Let us compare the semi-commutation conditions on two-sorted Kripke structures and closure characterizations above.

$$G_M \circ E \subseteq E \circ G_M \qquad\qquad b\text{-}to\text{-}d \circ pre \subseteq pre \circ b\text{-}to\text{-}d$$

The second condition above asserts that the downwards closure of the predecessors of a set of states S should be contained in the predecessors of the downwards closure of S. Downwards closure is an upper closure on the powerset lattice B, so applying it on both sides of the set inequality above, combined with the extensivity of closure operators yields the equality below.

$$pre^{\mathcal{B}} \circ b\text{-}to\text{-}d = b\text{-}to\text{-}d \circ pre^{\mathcal{B}} \circ b\text{-}to\text{-}d$$

Combined with standard substitution arguments yields the equality in Theorem 5. In other words, we can understand perfect domains as forwards-complete abstractions of some powerset domain. In fact, because the powerset domain itself represents a transition system, we can view perfect domains as forwards-complete abstractions of transition systems.

6   Two-Sorted Simulations

In this section, we demonstrate a second application of abstract interpretation to logical semantics of modal logics. A notion of subsumption was presented in [10] as a generalization of simulation to abstract domains. The results of [10] show that this notion enjoys a modal characterization, a fixed point characterization, and many other properties enjoyed by simulation. We use those results to synthesize a notion of simulation for two-sorted Kripke structures.

Definition 5. *Let $\mathcal{A} = (A, O_A)$ and $\mathcal{C} = (C, O_C)$ be perfect predecessor domains. A monotone function $f : C \to A$ is a subsumption if for all c_1, c_2 in C, the inequality $c_1 \sqsubseteq pre^{\mathcal{C}}(c_2)$ implies $f(c_1) \sqsubseteq pre^{\mathcal{A}}(f(c_2))$. An element a subsumes c if $a \sqsubseteq f(c)$.*

Subsumption is similar to homomorphism but with equalities replaced by inequalities, so it shifts emphasis from preserving the structure of a domain to approximating the properties of an element. Subsumption plays the same role for perfect domains that bisimulation plays for Kripke structures and simulation plays for ordered Kripke structures. Those facts follow from the results in [10]. We first define the notion of two-sorted simulation below, with the emphasis that this notion was derived using constructive characterization of abstractions.

Definition 6. *Let $M_1 = (L_1, U_1, \preccurlyeq_1, E_1)$ and $M_2 = (L_2, U_2, \preccurlyeq_2, E_2)$ be two-sorted pre-Kripke structures. A relation $Sim \subseteq L_1 \times L_2$ is a two-sorted simulation if every (r, s) in Sim satisfies: For all states r_1, r_2 of L_1 such that $(r_1, r_2) \in E_1$, if for all q in U_1, the order $r_1 \preccurlyeq q$ implies the order $r_2 \preccurlyeq q$, there exist states s_1, s_2 in L_2 satisfying that (s_1, s_2) is in E_2, for all q in U_2, the order $s_1 \preccurlyeq q$ implies $s_2 \preccurlyeq q$.*

To close the loop, we show how two-sorted simulations in turn generate functions, which are subsumptions. A two-sorted simulation generates a function that maps a Galois stable set to its image with respect to the simulation.

$$salg(Sim) : \mathscr{G}(S_1) \to \mathscr{G}(S_2) \qquad salg(Sim) \ \hat{=} \ \{X \mapsto Sim(X)\}$$

Lemma 3. *The function $f \ \hat{=} \ salg(Sim)$ is a subsumption.*

In the other direction, we can start with a subsumption and synthesize a two-sorted simulation as follows.

$$srel(f) \subseteq Irr_\sqcup(A_1) \times Irr_\sqcup(A_2) \qquad srel(f) \ \hat{=} \ \{(a, b) \mid b \sqsubseteq f(a)\}$$

Lemma 4. *The relation $srel(f)$ is a two-sorted simulation.*

In fact, two-sorted simulations sit in a tight correspondence with additive subsumptions.

Theorem 6. *Let $\mathcal{A}_1$ and $\mathcal{A}_2$ be perfect, predecessor domains, and M_1 and M_2 be pre-Kripke structures.*

1. *Every additive subsumption f from $\mathcal{A}_1$ to $\mathcal{A}_2$ is isomorphic to the subsumption $salg(srel(f))$ from $salg(srel(\mathcal{A}_1))$ to $salg(srel(\mathcal{A}_2))$.*
2. *Every two-sorted simulation Sim from M_1 to M_2 is isomorphic to $srel(salg(Sim))$, a two-sorted simulation from $srel(salg(M_1))$ to $srel(salg(M_2))$.*

We emphasise again that Theorem 6 does not provide a representation for all subsumptions, only additive subsumptions between predecessor domains. The purpose of this case study was to show how one need not invent all the standard notions for the generalization of Kripke structures that we have but that they can be synthesized using abstract interpretation and duality constructions.

7   Related Work and Conclusion

It appears from the literature that a recurring event in both logic and in algorithmic verification is the discovery of lattice-theoretic and relational structures for use towards the same goal. This dichotomy appears to date at least to Boole's conception of logic, which was algebraic and Frege's conception, which was closer to using sets and relations. In the history of modal logic, Lemmon [21, 22] developed a lattice-theoretic semantics for modal logic, while Kripke developed his, by now, well known transition system semantics [20]. While the lattice-theoretic objects required were discovered by Jónsson and Tarski in 1952 [18], they had not observed the connection to modal logic.

The choice of which structure to use leads down different algorithmic paths in program verification. For example, graph- and tableau algorithms were used in the original model checking papers [4, 28], while fixed point algorithms were used in the flow analysis literature [7, 19]. Cousot [6] showed how to go from transition systems to lattices, and such a translation also underlies McMillan's development of symbolic model checking [25].

We are not aware of an in-depth study or application of duality within the verification context. Weaker forms of representation theorems have also been rediscovered in [24] and [29]. Schmidt [30] observed that non-Boolean abstract domains used in static analysis can be viewed as transition systems. His results show how one can derive logics from abstract domains and explore a complementary direction to the one studied in this paper, where we extracted transition systems corresponding to abstract domains.

Topological representations of abstract domains were developed in [31], but this development does not use results from duality theory, hence does not provide a translation between different, existing representations. Topological representations for the domains in this paper can be synthesised using well known topological representations of lattices. We have consciously avoided topological constructions by working with perfect lattices. Our choice is justified by the prevalence of abstract domains based on perfect lattices.

Duality theory has been applied by Abramsky [2] to relate domain theory, modal logic and topological spaces. In a strict mathematical sense, our work overlaps with that of Abramsky but is not subsumed by it and does not generalise it. Our work is simpler because we use discrete duality theory, hence lose the generality provided by topological representations. However, Abramsky considers distributive structures, while we consider non-distributive ones.

Conclusion. Most applications of abstract interpretation focus on its use for approximation of semantics but completeness research has shown that completeness is a prevalent phenomenon as well. In this paper, we demonstrated that completeness constructions have applications to the model theory of subclassical, modal logics. These constructions can be used to synthesize new models from existing ones, and to synthesize a notion of simulation for the these new models. Our work suggests that completeness constructions may also manifest in completions of structures and the study of non-standard models, which are fundamental to model-theoretic analysis of logics, which is a topic for future work.

References

1. Abdulla, P.A., Čeräns, K., Jonsson, B., Tsay, Y.K.: Algorithmic analysis of programs with well quasi-ordered domains. Inf. Comput. **160**(1–2), 109–127 (2000)
2. Abramsky, S.: Domain Theory and the Logic of Observable Properties. Ph.d. thesis, University of London (1987)
3. Celani, S.A., Jansana, R.: A new semantics for positive modal logic. Notre Dame J. Formal Logic **38**(1), 1–18 (1997)
4. Clarke, E.M., Emerson, E.A.: Design and synthesis of synchronization skeletons using branching time temporal logic. In: Grumberg, O., Veith, H. (eds.) 25 Years of Model Checking. LNCS, vol. 5000, pp. 196–215. Springer, Berlin (2008). doi:10.1007/978-3-540-69850-0_12
5. Cousot, P., Cousot, R.: Abstract interpretation and application to logic programs. J. Logic Program. **13**(2–3), 103–179 (1992)
6. Cousot, P.: Semantic foundations of program analysis. In: Muchnick, S., Jones, N. (eds.) Program Flow Analysis: Theory and Applications, pp. 303–342. Prentice-Hall Inc, Englewood Cliffs (1981). Chap. 10
7. Cousot, P., Cousot, R.: Abstract interpretation: a unified lattice model for static analysis of programs by construction or approximation of fixpoints. In: Proceedings of the Principles of Programming Languages, pp. 238–252. ACM, New York (1977)
8. Cousot, P., Cousot, R.: Systematic design of program analysis frameworks. In: Proceedings of the Principles of Programming Languages, pp. 269–282. ACM, New York (1979)
9. Davey, B.A., Priestley, H.A.: Introduction to Lattices and Order. Cambridge University Press, Cambridge (1990)
10. D'Silva, V.: Generalizing simulation to abstract domains. In: D'Argenio, P.R., Melgratti, H. (eds.) CONCUR 2013 – Concurrency Theory. LNCS, vol. 8052. Springer, Heidelberg (2013)
11. Dunn, J.M.: Positive modal logic. Stud. Logica **55**(2), 301–317 (1995)
12. Dunn, J.M., Gehrke, M., Palmigiano, A.: Canonical extensions and relational completeness of some substructural logics. J. Symbolic Logic **70**(3), 713–740 (2005)
13. Finkel, A., Schnoebelen, P.: Well-structured transition systems everywhere!. Theor. Comput. Sci. **256**(1–2), 63–92 (2001)
14. Gehrke, M.: Generalized Kripke frames. Stud. Logica. **84**(2), 241–275 (2006)
15. Giacobazzi, R., Quintarelli, E.: Incompleteness, counterexamples, and refinements in abstract model-checking. In: Cousot, P. (ed.) SAS 2001. LNCS, vol. 2126, pp. 356–373. Springer, Berlin (2001). doi:10.1007/3-540-47764-0_20
16. Giacobazzi, R., Ranzato, F.: Optimal domains for disjunctive abstract interpretation. Sci. Comput. Program. **32**(1–3), 177–210 (1998)
17. Giacobazzi, R., Ranzato, F., Scozzari, F.: Making abstract interpretations complete. J. ACM **47**(2), 361–416 (2000)
18. Jónsson, B., Tarski, A.: Boolean algebras with operators. Am. J. Math. **74**(1), 127–162 (1952)
19. Kildall, G.A.: A unified approach to global program optimization. In: Proceedings of the Principles of Programming Languages, pp. 194–206. ACM, New York (1973)

20. Kripke, S.: A completeness theorem in modal logic. J. Symbolic Logic **24**(1), 1–14 (1959)
21. Lemmon, E.J.: Algebraic semantics for modal logics I. J. Symbolic Logic **31**(1), 46–65 (1966)
22. Lemmon, E.J.: Algebraic semantics for modal logics II. J. Symbolic Logic **31**(2), 191–218 (1966)
23. Libkin, L., Martens, W., Vrgoč, D.: Querying graphs with data. J. ACM **63**(2), 14:1–14:53 (2016)
24. Loiseaux, C., Graf, S., Sifakis, J., Bouajjani, A., Bensalem, S.: Property preserving abstractions for the verification of concurrent systems. Formal Meth. Syst. Des. **6**(1), 11–44 (1995)
25. McMillan, K.L.: Symbolic Model Checking. Kluwer Academic Publishers, Norwell (1993)
26. Nguyen, L.A.: On the complexity of fragments of modal logics. In: Advances in Modal Logic. vol. 5, pp. 249–268. Kings College Publications (2005)
27. Pratt, V.: Chu spaces. Course notes for the School in Category Theory and Applications, July 1999
28. Queille, J.P., Sifakis, J.: Specification and verification of concurrent systems in CESAR. In: Dezani-Ciancaglini, M., Montanari, U. (eds.) Programming 1982. LNCS, vol. 137, pp. 337–351. Springer, Heidelberg (1982). doi:10.1007/3-540-11494-7_22
29. Ranzato, F., Tapparo, F.: Generalized strong preservation by abstract interpretation. J. Logic Comput. **17**(1), 157–197 (2007)
30. Schmidt, D.A.: Internal and external logics of abstract interpretations. In: Logozzo, F., Peled, D.A., Zuck, L.D. (eds.) VMCAI 2008. LNCS, vol. 4905, pp. 263–278. Springer, Berlin (2008). doi:10.1007/978-3-540-78163-9_23
31. Schmidt, D.A.: Inverse-limit and topological aspects of abstract interpretation. Theor. Comput. Sci. **430**, 23–42 (2012)
32. Zufferey, D., Wies, T., Henzinger, T.A.: Ideal abstractions for well-structured transition systems. In: Kuncak, V., Rybalchenko, A. (eds.) VMCAI 2012. LNCS, vol. 7148, pp. 445–460. Springer, Berlin (2012). doi:10.1007/978-3-642-27940-9_29

Using Abstract Interpretation to Correct Synchronization Faults

Pietro Ferrara[1]([✉]), Omer Tripp[2], Peng Liu[3], and Eric Koskinen[4]

[1] Julia Srl, Verona, Italy
pietro.ferrara@juliasoft.com
[2] Google Inc., Menlo Park, USA
trippo@google.com
[3] IBM T.J. Watson Research Center, Yorktown Heights, USA
liup@us.ibm.com
[4] Yale University, New Haven, USA
eric.koskinen@yale.edu

Abstract. We describe a novel use of abstract interpretation in which the abstract domain informs a runtime system to correct synchronization failures. To this end, we first introduce a novel synchronization paradigm, dubbed *corrective synchronization*, that is a generalization of existing approaches to ensuring serializability. Specifically, the correctness of multi-threaded execution need not be enforced by previous methods that either reduce parallelism (pessimistic) or roll back illegal thread interleavings (optimistic); instead inadmissible states can be altered into admissible ones. In this way, the effects of inadmissible interleavings can be compensated for by modifying the program state as a transaction completes, while accounting for the behavior of concurrent transactions. We have proved that corrective synchronization is serializable and give conditions under which progress is ensured. Next, we describe an abstract interpretation that is able to compute these valid serializable post-states w.r.t. a transaction's entry state by computing an under-approximation of the serializable intermediate (or final) states as the fixpoint solution over an inter-procedural control-flow graph. These abstract states inform a runtime system that is able to perform state correction dynamically. We have instantiated this setup to clients of a Java-like Concurrent Map data structure to ensure safe composition of map operations. Finally, we report early encouraging results that the approach competes with or out-performs previous pessimistic or optimistic approaches.

1 Introduction

Concurrency control is a hard problem. While some thread interleavings are admissible (if they involve disjoint memory accesses), there are certain interleaving scenarios that must be inhibited to ensure serializability. The goal is

P. Ferrara and O. Tripp—The research leading to this paper was conducted while the author was at IBM Research.

E. Koskinen—The research was supported by NSF CCF Award #1421126 and conducted partially while the author was at IBM Research.

A. Bouajjani and D. Monniaux (Eds.): VMCAI 2017, LNCS 10145, pp. 187–208, 2017.
DOI: 10.1007/978-3-319-52234-0_11

to automatically detect, with high precision and low overhead, the inadmissible interleavings, and avoid them.

Toward this end, there are currently two main synchronization paradigms:

- *Pessimistic synchronization*: In this approach, illegal interleaving scenarios are avoided conservatively by blocking the execution of one or more of the concurrent threads until the threat of incorrect executions has gone away. Locks, mutexes, semaphores, and some transactional memory (TM) implementations [11,18] are all examples of how to enforce mutual exclusion, or pessimistic synchronization.
- *Optimistic synchronization*: As an alternative to pro-active (pessimistic) synchronization, optimistic synchronization is essentially a reactive approach. The concurrency control system monitors execution, such that when an illegal interleaving scenario arises, it is detected as such and abort-like remediation steps are taken. Many TM implementations operate this way [12], logging memory accesses, aborting transactions, and reversing the effects.

The pessimistic approach is useful if critical sections are short, there is little available concurrency, and the involved memory locations are well known [13]. Optimistic synchronization is most effective when there is a high level of available concurrency. An example is graph algorithms, such as Boruvka, over graphs that are sparse and irregular [16]. In both of these cases, however, the concurrency paradigm is designed to exploit domain-specific windows of opportunity where there is a low amount of conflict. These are, in a sense, low-hanging fruit, and there are many other situations of practical interest where there is unavoidable contention. (We will give a simple example in the next section.) Neither of these existing approaches offer a way to tackle contention head-on.

Corrective Synchronization. In this paper, we take a first step in formulating and exploring a novel synchronization paradigm that generalizes both the pessimistic and optimistic approaches. In our approach, dubbed *corrective synchronization*, conflicting transactions may begin to execute concurrently (unlike pessimism), yet when conflict occurs, the remediation is not simply to abort (unlike optimism). Instead, a thread resolves contention by dynamically *altering* the inadmissible state into an acceptable one, accounting for the behavior of concurrent threads, so as to guarantee serializability.

This paper. Corrective synchronization, as a concept, opens up a vast space of possibilities for concrete synchronization protocols. In this paper, we take a first step in exploring this space with a formalism, proof of serializability, and a novel use of abstract interpretation and dynamic instrumentation. The key idea can be illustrated with our corr t proof rule:

$$\frac{\Gamma, (t, s) \vdash s \rightarrow^* (T, \mu', \sigma, L)}{\Gamma, (t, s) \vdash (T, \mu, \sigma, L) \rightarrow (T, \mu[t \mapsto \mu'(t)], \sigma, L)} \; \text{corr } t$$

As is typical, we model transactions as a transition system where a state configuration s consists of tuples (T, μ, σ, L). Here T is a set of transaction identifiers,

μ is a mapping from transaction id to a thread-local replica of the state, σ is the shared state and, following [15], we use a shared log of events L to track the effects of committed transactions. For our purposes, we include a context Γ which maps each transaction id t to the configuration just before the corresponding transaction began.

The key idea here is thread-local correction, whereby a single thread t can apply a correction by jumping from μ to $\mu[t \mapsto \mu'(t)]$. Thread t is permitted to do so, provided that there was an *alternate execution path* $s \to^* (T, \mu', \sigma, L)$ from the configuration s in which t began to some other (T, μ', σ, L). After a correction, the thread may be able to perform a commit, which (logically) involves replaying the mutation on the shared state. This rule is fairly simple yet has significant consequences and, to the best of our knowledge, nothing like this exists in the literature. One can think of pessimistic synchronization as an almost trivial restriction in which conflicting executions never occur and this rule is never needed. Meanwhile, optimistic synchronization permits only corrections back to thread t's initial configuration. For the purposes of this paper, the alternate path to μ' must be under the same set of concurrent transactions T, though this restriction can be relaxed, which we leave for future work. We have proved that our definition of corrective synchronization is serializable (Sect. 3) and provide conditions under which progress is guaranteed.

Challenges and Contributions. With definitions and serializability established, we move on to two key challenges that pertain to realizing corrective synchronization:

– How do we compute each thread's alternative (serializable) post-states?
– Given an incorrect state, how do we efficiently recover to a correct post-state?

For the sake of concreteness, we focus on concurrent Java-like programs whose shared state is encoded as one or more ConcurrentMap instances. We tackle the above challenges via a novel use of abstract interpretation, equipped with a specialized abstraction for maps, to derive the correct post-states, or "targets", in relation to a given pre-state. Our abstract interpretation computes an under-approximation of the serializable intermediate (or final) states as the fixpoint solution over an inter-procedural control-flow graph. We prove that the computed target states are progress-safe, i.e. the system is not in a stuck state after a correction. We then show how these target states can be used by a runtime system to dynamically correct an execution and jump to a target state.

In summary, this paper makes the following principal contributions. (1) We present an alternative to both the pessimistic and optimistic synchronization paradigms, dubbed *corrective synchronization*, whereby serializability is achieved neither via mutual exclusion nor via rollbacks, but through correction of the post-state according to a relational pre-/post-states specification. (2) We provide a formal description of corrective synchronization. This includes soundness and progress proofs as well as a clear statement of limitations. (3) We have developed an abstract interpretation to derive the prestate/poststates specification for programs that encode the shared state as one or more concurrent maps.

(4) We have developed a runtime system that is able to use pre/post-state specifications to correct behaviors dynamically. (5) We report encouraging preliminary experimental results on a prototype implementation.

2   Technical Overview

We now walk the reader through a high-level overview of corrective synchronization with an example. We describe the conceptual details at a technical level, and then the two main algorithmic steps.

Running Example. As an illustrative example, we refer to the code fragment on Fig. 1, where a shared Map object, (pointed-to by) map, is manipulated by method updateReservation.

Let us assume that different threads invoking this method are all attempting to simultaneously move reservations into the same nslot. Doing so optimistically would lead to multiple rollbacks (even under boosted conflict detection [11], since the operations due to different threads do not commute), and thus poor performance. Pessimistic

```
1  Res updateReservation(Slot oslot, Slot nslot) {
2      Res r = map.remove(oslot);
3      if (r == null)
4          r = new Res();
5      Res dead = map.replace(nslot, r);
6      return dead;
7  }
```

Fig. 1. Example that updates reservation for customers, moving an entry from one date/time slot to another.

mutual exclusion, on the other hand, would block all but one thread until the operation completes, which is far from optimal if new Res() is an expensive operation.

Conceptual Approach. By *corrective synchronization* we mean the ability to transform a concurrent run that, in its present condition, may not be serializable into a run that is serializable. Stated formally, corrective synchronization is a relationship $h \sim h'$ between histories, such that (i) h and h' share the same initial state, and (ii) h and h' share the same log of committed operations (i.e., they agree on the operations on the shared-state). One can think of h' as an alternate parallel reality to h.

The first condition ensures that corrective synchronization yields a feasible outcome. The second is the requirement not to roll back updates to the shared state. These two conditions distinguish corrective synchronization from existing solutions: Unlike pessimistic approaches, bad behaviors may occur under corrective synchronization. That is, they are not avoided, but handled as they manifest. Unlike optimistic solutions, the core handling mechanism is not to retry the transaction (or parts thereof), which implies rolling back (either committed or uncommitted) updates to the shared log, but rather to "warp" to another state. To illustrate our approach, consider the following history:

$$
\begin{aligned}
[\quad & t_1\text{: remove}(10\!:\!00)/\alpha \rightarrow t_2\text{: remove}(13\!:\!00)/\text{null} \\
\hookrightarrow & t_1\text{: if}(\ldots) \qquad\qquad\quad \rightarrow t_2\text{: if}(\ldots)\ \text{new Res}()/\delta \\
\hookrightarrow & \qquad\qquad\qquad\qquad\quad\ \ t_2\text{: replace}(11\!:\!00)/\beta \\
\hookrightarrow & t_1\text{: replace}(11\!:\!00)/\delta \\
\hookrightarrow & t_1\text{: return }\delta \qquad\qquad\quad \rightarrow t_2\text{: return }\beta \qquad\qquad]
\end{aligned}
$$

Each step in this history is labeled with the transaction identifier (t_1 or t_2) and the code that the transaction is executing. With this history, $11:00$ is associated with β in the final state of the map. This history is clearly not serializable. t_2 cannot return β when $11:00$ is associated with β in the final state of the map. However, we can warp to a history that is serializable by applying a correction. In this case, note that there are two possible serializable histories: (i) t_1 goes first and returns β, t_2 goes second and returns α, and in the final state $11:00$ is mapped to δ; (ii) t_2 goes first and returns β, t_1 goes second and returns δ, and in the final state $11:00$ is mapped to α. For the sake of efficiency, we can correct the above execution by chosing serial history (ii) as the target state and the correction is quick and easy: update the map so that $11:00$ is associated with α. Using (i) as a target is also possible, but would have required a correction to the map as well as the return values of t_1 and t_2. Note that the corrective actions above are of a general form, which is not limited to two threads. For any number of threads, the corrected state would have one privileged thread deciding the return value (i.e., the value of dead) for all threads as well as what $11:00$ should be associated with in the map. Also note that the correction does *not* directly modify the shared state; rather, the correction is made to a thread-local replica of the state. After the correction, if the thread is able to commit, then shared-state mutations are applied at commit time.

How does this corrective approach compare to handling of the situation by pessimistic or optimistic approaches? We illustrate the difference between corrective synchronization and classic optimistic and pessimistic synchronization in Fig. 2. We visually represent concurrent execution of two instances of the updateReservation code using pessimistic locks, optimistic TM and corrective synchronization (proceeding horizontally left-to-right). Pessimism serializes execution, and so there is no performance gain whatsoever. As for optimistic and corrective synchronization, we consider the interleaving scenario specified above. Both optimistic and corrective synchronization, allowing the problematic chain of interleavings, reach a nonserializable state. Optimism resolves this by retrying the entire transaction executed by, say, thread t_2. This yields serial execution, similar to the pessimistic run, where t_2 runs after t_1. Corrective synchronization, instead, "fixes" the final state, allowing t_2 to complete without rerunning any or all of its code. Our experiments suggest the corrective actions are—relatively speaking—inexpensive, especially compared to the alternatives of either blocking or aborting/restarting all threads but one.

We refer to corrective synchronization as *sound* if h' is the prefix of a serializable execution of the system. We refer to corrective synchronization as *complete* if for any h, all the h's that satisfy the conditions above are in the relation $\sim$. In the rest of this paper, we describe our method of computing a sound yet

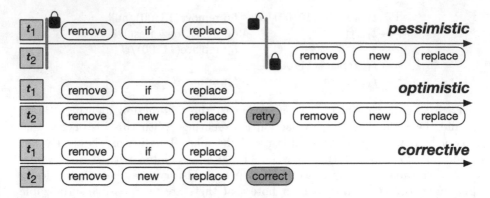

Fig. 2. Interleaved execution of two instances of updateReservation using pessimistic, optimistic, and corrective synchronization.

incomplete set of corrective targets via static analysis of the concurrent library. A solution that is not complete faces the possibility of stuck runs: Given a (potentially) nonserializable execution prefix, the system does not have a corresponding serializable prefix to transition to. In this paper, we do not present a solution to the completeness problem, which we leave as future work. In the meantime, there are two simple strategies to tackle this problem: (i) *manual specification*, whereby the user completes the set of corrective targets to ensure that there are no stuck runs (in our implementation, the targets are computed offline via static analysis, letting the user complete the specification ahead of deployment); and (ii) *complementary techniques*, such as optimism, which the system can default to in the absence of a corrective target.

Computing Corrective Targets. A simpler and more abstract specification to work with, compared to complete execution prefixes, is triplets (s, s', s'') of states, such that there exist prefixes h and h' as above with respective initial and current states (s, s') and (s, s''), respectively. This form of specification is advantageous, because the corresponding runtime instrumentation is minimal compared to tracking traces. At the same time, however, initial and current states are a strict abstraction of complete traces, and so they do not point back to prefixes h and h'.

Mapping back from pairs of states to prefixes requires an oracle. In our work we compute the oracle as a relational abstract interpretation solution over the program that is sound yet incomplete. Specifically, an underapproximation of the serializable intermediate (or final) states is computed as the fixpoint solution over an interprocedural control-flow graph (CFG) of the form: $t_1 \to t_{2...n}^\star \to t_{n+1} \to t_1' \to t_{2...n}'^\star \to t_{n+1}' \to \ldots$, where t, t', etc. denote different transaction types (i.e., transactions executing different code), and n is unbounded, simulating a nondeterministic loop. This representation simulates an unbounded number of instances of transactions that are executed sequentially.

We go into detail about this representation in Sect. 5, but here note that (i) this representation reflects the effects of serial execution of the transactions, and so the corrective targets are guaranteed to be sound; (ii) the nondeterministic loop captures an unbounded number of transactions; and (iii) the first and last transactions of a given type are purposely disambiguated to boost the precision of static analysis over the simulated execution. As an illustration of the third point, in our running example the first transaction t_1 is modeled precisely in inserting the key/value pair into the Map object. Analogously, the last transaction t_{n+1} can be confirmed not to update the key/value mapping.

Runtime Synchronization. The runtime system has two main responsibilities. First, it must track whether an execution has reached a (potentially) bad state. Second, if such a state arises, then the runtime system must map the current state onto a state that shares the same initial state and is known, by the oracle, to have a serializable continuation. We address the first challenge via a coarse conflict-detection algorithm that tracks API-level read/write behaviors (at the level of Map operations). If read/write or write/write conflicts arise, then corrective synchronization is triggered in response. If the oracle was not able to compute a target for the correction (e.g., because of a loss of precision of the static analysis), then our approach can apply optimistic synchronization

We expand on the above challenges in Sect. 5, and provide encouraging experimental results on a simple prototype in Sect. 6. Prior to that, in Sect. 4, we provide a formal statement of corrective synchronization.

3   Semantics of Corrective Synchronization

We now introduce a generic transaction semantics for corrective synchronization. We prove soundness (serializability), and give conditions under which progress is ensured.

Notation. We use the following semantic domains:

$$
\begin{aligned}
c \in \mathcal{C} &:= \text{command} & t \in T \subset \mathcal{T} &:= \text{transaction IDs} \\
\sigma \in \Sigma &:= \text{shared state} & \sigma_t &:= \text{local state of } t \\
L \in \mathcal{L} &:= \text{shared log} & L_t &:= \text{local log of } t \\
s = (T, [t \mapsto (c_t, \sigma_t, L_t)]_{t \in T}, \sigma, L) &\in \mathcal{S} := \text{system state}
\end{aligned}
$$

Following [15], our semantics uses local logs to track local operations, and shared logs to track committed operations. We assume that the set Σ of shared states is closed under composition, denoted $\cdot$. That is, $\forall \sigma, \sigma' \in \Sigma.\ \sigma \cdot \sigma' \in \Sigma$. Hence, we can decompose a given shared state into (disjoint) substates (the standard decomposition being into memory locations), such that we can easily refer to the read/write effects of a given operation. For that, we additionally define two helper functions, $r, w \colon \mathcal{C} \times \mathcal{S} \rightharpoonup \Sigma$, such that r (*resp.* w) computes the portion of the shared state read (*resp.* written) by a given atomic operation. The notation $\rightharpoonup$ denotes that w and r are partial functions. The shared log L consists of pairs $\langle t, o \rangle$, where t is a transaction identifier, o is the operation executed by t, and $w(c) \neq \bot$.

Transition System. Execution of the transition system is represented by five events:

$$\frac{t \notin T}{\text{bgn } t \quad \Gamma \cup (t, (T, \mu, \sigma, L)) \vdash (T, \mu, \sigma, L) \rightarrow (T \cup \{t\}, \mu \cdot [t \mapsto (c, \bot, \epsilon)], \sigma, L)}$$

$$\text{local } t \quad \frac{t \in T, \mathbb{C}[\![c_t, \sigma_t]\!] = (c'_t, \sigma'_t)}{\Gamma \vdash (T, \mu, \sigma, L) \rightarrow (T, \mu[t \mapsto (c'_t, \sigma'_t, L_t)], \sigma, L)}$$

$$\text{cmt } t \quad \frac{t \in T, L_t \neq \epsilon, \text{serpref } L \cdot L_t}{\Gamma \vdash (T, \mu, \sigma, L) \rightarrow (T, \mu[t \mapsto (c_t, \sigma_t, \epsilon)], [\![L_t]\!](\sigma), L \cdot L_t)}$$

$$\text{end } t \quad \frac{t \in T, \mu(t) = (\text{skip}, \_, \epsilon)}{\Gamma \vdash (T, \mu, \sigma, L) \rightarrow (T \setminus \{t\}, \mu \setminus [t \mapsto \mu(t)], \sigma, L)}$$

$$\text{corr } t \quad \frac{t \in T, s \rightsquigarrow (T, \mu', \sigma, L)}{\Gamma, (t, s) \vdash (T, \mu, \sigma, L) \rightarrow (T, \mu[t \mapsto \mu'(t)], \sigma, L)}$$

The bgn event marks the beginning of a transaction. In this and all rules, we work with a context Γ, consisting of pairs (t, s) that correlate transaction identifier t with the state configuration s that immediately preceded t's start, captured in the bgn event. During its execution, a transaction modifies only its local state and local log L_t, as seen in the local event rule. Here t's corresponding local configuration is denoted (c_t, σ_t, L_t) and $\mathbb{C}$ represents the transition relation for local operations. The cmt event fires when a transaction publishes its outstanding log of operations that affect the shared state to the shared state and log. We use helper function serpref: $\mathcal{L} \rightarrow \{\text{true}, \text{false}\}$ to (conservatively) determine whether a given shared log is the prefix of some serializable execution log. The end event marks the termination of a transaction.

Corrective action occurs in the corr event. This event enables a transaction to modify its local state and log, under certain restrictions, as a means to recover from potentially inadmissible thread interleavings. Note that the corr rule only applies changes to t's local configuration. All other transactions retain their original local configurations. The intuition is that corr *corrects* the execution by jumping transaction t to a state that is reachable starting from the entry state through a serialized execution.

Theorem 1 (Soundness). *A terminating execution of the transition system yields a serializable shared log (history).*

Proof Sketch. The cmt event acts as a gatekeeper, demanding that the log prefix $L \cdot L_t$ including the outstanding events about to be committed is serializable. The check executes atomically together with the log update. Hence the system is guaranteed to terminate with a serializable shared log.

Definition 1 (Progress). *We say that the transition system has made progress, transitioning from (global) state s to (global) state s', if the associated event e for $s \xrightarrow{e} s'$ is either a cmt event or an end event.*

Definition 2 (Progress-safe corrective synchronization). *Let* corr *t occur at system state* $s = (T, \mu, \sigma, L)$*, such that state* $s' = (T, \mu[t \mapsto (c_t, \sigma_t, L_t)], \sigma, L)$ *is reached. Assume that there is a reduction* $(\sigma_t, c_t, L_t) \longrightarrow (\sigma'_t, c'_t, L'_t)$*, such that at system state* $s'' = (T, \mu[t \mapsto (\sigma'_t, c'_t, L'_t)], \sigma, L)$ *either (i)* cmt *t is enabled or (ii)* end *t is enabled. Then we refer to* corr *t at* s *with target* (σ_t, c_t, L_t) *as progress safe.*

From the perspective of transaction t, the local states of other transactions are irrelevant to whether a commit (or end) transition is enabled for t. The only cause of a failed commit is if other threads have committed. We can therefore relax the definition above to refer to any system state $s'' = (T', \mu', \sigma, L)$, such that $t \in T'$ and $[t \mapsto (\sigma'_t, c'_t, L'_t)] \in \mu'$.

Given transaction t with local state (σ_t, c_t, L_t), we refer to target (σ'_t, c_t, L'_t) as a *self-corrective target*. After corrective synchronization, the transaction has the same command left to reduce, but its state and outstanding log of operations are modified. A specific instance is $(\sigma_t, \mathsf{skip}, L_t) \rightarrow (\sigma'_t, \mathsf{skip}, L'_t)$. This pattern of corrective synchronization is progress safe if commits are attempted at join points, which enables simulation of alternative control-flow paths (and therefore also logged effects) via corrective synchronization.

Theorem 2 (Progress). *If (i) a* corr *t event only fires when a transaction t reaches a commit point but fails to commit, and (ii) corrective synchronization instances are progress safe, then progress is guaranteed.*

Proof Sketch. Given system state s, if there exists a transaction t that is able to either commit or complete then the proof is done. Otherwise, there is a transaction t that reaches a commit point at some state s' and fails. At this point, corr *t is the only enabled transition for t, and by assumption (ii), the corrective synchronization instance is progress safe. At this point, there are two possibilities. Either t proceeds without other threads modifying the shared state, such that a commit or completion point is reached by t (without corrective synchronization prior to reaching such a point according to assumption (i)), in which case progress has been achieved, or one or more threads interfere with t by committing their effects, in which case too progress has been achieved.*

Definition 3 (Complete corrective synchronization). *We say that the system is complete w.r.t. corrective synchronization if for any state s, if a* corr *t transition is executed in s, then the selected corrective target satisfies progress safety.*

Lemma 1 (Termination). *Assume that the system performs corrective synchronization only on failed commits, and is complete w.r.t. corrective synchronization. Then for any run of the system where finitely many transactions are created, each having only finite serial execution traces, termination is guaranteed.*

Proof Sketch. The first two assumptions guarantee progress, as established above in Theorem 2. Since transactions are finite, each transaction may perform finitely many cmt *transitions before terminating via an* end *transition. This implies that after finitely many transitions, some transaction t will terminate. This argument applies to the resulting system until no transactions are left.*

4   Thread Local Semantics

We now instantiate the theoretical framework introduced in Sect. 3 to a language supporting some standard operations on concurrent shared maps. We define the thread-local concrete semantics of this language instantiating $\mathbb{C}$ of the local rule. Following standard abstract interpretation theory, we then introduce an abstract domain and semantics that computes an approximation of the concrete semantics. This thread-local abstract semantics will be used in Sect. 5 to compute progress-safe corrective "targets".

Language. We focus our formalization on the following language fragment:

$$s ::= \text{m.put}(k, v)\mid v = \text{m.get}(k)\mid \text{m.remove}(k)\mid v = \text{null}$$
$$\mid v = \text{m.putIfAbsent}(k, v)\mid v = \text{new Value}()\mid \text{assert}(b)$$
$$b ::= x == \text{null} \mid x! = \text{null}\mid \text{m.containsK}(k) \mid !\text{m.containsK}(k)$$

The above fragment captures some representative operations from the Java 7 class java.util.concurrent.ConcurrentMap.[1] We represent by m the map shared among all the transactions, and k a shared key. The values inserted or read from the map might be a parameter of the transaction, or created through a new statement. Following the Java library semantics, our language supports (i) $v = \text{m.get}(k)$ that returns the value v related with key k, or null if k is not in the map, (ii) m.remove(k) removes k from the map, (iii) $v = \text{m.putIfAbsent}(k, v)$ relates k to v in m if k is already in m and returns the previous value it was related to, (iv) $v = \text{new Value}(...)$ creates a new value, and (v) $v = \text{null}$ assigns null to variable v. In addition, our language supports a standard assert(b) statement that lets the execution continue iff the given Boolean condition holds. In particular, the language supports checking whether a variable is null, and if the map contains a key. This is necessary to support conditional and loop statements.

Concrete Domain and Semantics. We begin by instantiating the state of a transaction t to the language above. Let Var and Ref be the sets of variables and references, respectively. Keys and values are identified by concrete references, and we assume null is in Ref. We define by Env : Var $\rightarrow$ Ref the environments relating local variables to references. A map is then represented as a function Map : Ref $\rightarrow$ Ref, relating keys to values. The value null represents that the related key is not in the map. A single concrete state is a pair made by an environment and a map. Formally, $\Sigma = \text{Env} \times \text{Map}$. As usual in abstract interpretation, we collect a set of states per program point. Therefore, our concrete domain is made by elements in $\wp(\Sigma)$, and the lattice relies on standard set operators. Formally,

---

[1] http://docs.oracle.com/javase/7/docs/api/java/util/concurrent/ConcurrentMap.html.

$$\mathbb{C}[\![\mathtt{m.put(k, v)}, (e, m)]\!] = (e, m[e(\mathtt{k}) \mapsto e(\mathtt{v})])$$
$$\mathbb{C}[\![\mathtt{v = m.get(k)}, (e, m)]\!] = (e[\mathtt{v} \mapsto m(e(\mathtt{k}))], m)$$
$$\mathbb{C}[\![\mathtt{m.remove(k)}, (e, m)]\!] = (e, m[e(\mathtt{k}) \mapsto \mathtt{null}])$$
$$\mathbb{C}[\![\mathtt{v = m.putIfAbsent(k, v)}, (e, m)]\!] = (e[\mathtt{v} \mapsto m(n)], m') :$$
$$m' = \begin{cases} m[n \mapsto e(\mathtt{v})]) & \text{if } m(e(\mathtt{k})) = \mathtt{null} \\ m & \text{otherwise} \end{cases}$$
$$\mathbb{C}[\![\mathtt{v = new\ Value()}, (e, m)]\!] = (e[\mathtt{v} \mapsto \mathsf{fresh}(\mathtt{t})], m)$$
$$\mathbb{C}[\![\mathtt{v = null}, (e, m)]\!] = (e[\mathtt{v} \mapsto \{\mathtt{null}\}], m)$$
$$\mathbb{C}[\![\mathtt{assert(x == null)}, (e, m)]\!] = (e, m) \text{ if } e(\mathtt{x}) = \mathtt{null}$$
$$\mathbb{C}[\![\mathtt{assert(x! = null)}, (e, m)]\!] = (e, m) \text{ if } e(\mathtt{x}) \neq \mathtt{null}$$
$$\mathbb{C}[\![\mathtt{assert(m.containsK(k))}, (e, m)]\!]$$
$$= (e, m) \text{ if } m(e(\mathtt{k})) \neq \mathtt{null}$$
$$\mathbb{C}[\![\mathtt{assert(!m.containsK(k))}, (e, m)]\!]$$
$$= (e, m) \text{ if } m(e(\mathtt{k})) = \mathtt{null}$$

Fig. 3. Concrete semantics

$\langle \wp(\Sigma), \subseteq, \cup \rangle$. The concrete semantics are given to the right. Figure 3 defines the concrete semantics. For the most part, it formalizes the API specification of the corresponding Java method. Note that $\mathtt{assert}$ is defined only on the states that satisfy the given Boolean conditions. n represents a fresh concrete node in the semantics of $\mathtt{putIfAbsent}$. In this way, the concrete semantics filters out only the states that might execute a branch of an $\mathtt{if}$ or $\mathtt{while}$ statement.

Abstract Domain. Let HeapNode be the set of abstract heap nodes with $\mathtt{null} \in$ HeapNode. Both keys and values are abstracted as heap nodes. As usual with heap abstractions, each heap node might represent one or many concrete references. Therefore, we suppose that a function isSummary : HeapNode $\rightarrow$ {true, false} is provided; isSummary(n) returns true if n might represent many concrete nodes (that is, it is a summary node). We define by Env : Var $\rightarrow$ $\wp$(HeapNode) the set of (abstract) environments relating each variable to the set of heap nodes it might point to. A map is represented as a function Map : HeapNode $\rightarrow$ $\wp$(HeapNode), connecting each key to the set of possible values it might be related to in the map. The value $\mathtt{null}$ represents that the key is not in the map. For instance, $[n_1 \mapsto \{\mathtt{null}, n_2\}]$ represents that the key n_1 might not be in the map, or it is in the map, and it is related to value n_2. An abstract state is a pair made by an abstract environment and an abstract map. We augment this set with a special bottom value $\bot$ to will be used to represent that a statement is unreachable. Formally, $\Sigma = (\text{Env} \times \text{Map}) \cup \{\bot\}$. The lattice structure is obtained by the point-wise application of set operators to elements in the codomain of abstract environments and functions. Therefore, the abstract lattice is defined as $\langle \Sigma, \dot{\subseteq}, \dot{\cup} \rangle$, where $\dot{\subseteq}$ and $\dot{\cup}$ represents the point-wise application of set operators $\subseteq$ and $\cup$, respectively.

Running example. Abstract state $([\mathtt{name} \mapsto \{n_1\}], [n_1 \mapsto \{\mathtt{null}\}])$ represents that key $\mathtt{name}$ is not in the map, while $([\mathtt{name} \mapsto \{n_1\}], [n_1 \mapsto \{n_2\}])$ represents that it is in the map, and it is related to some value n_2. Finally, $([\mathtt{name} \mapsto$

$\{n_1\}], [n_1 \mapsto \{\text{null}, n_2\}])$ represents that **name** (i) might not be in the map, *or* (ii) is in the map related to value n_2.

Concretization Function. We define the concretization function $\gamma_\Sigma : \Sigma \to \wp(\Sigma)$ that, given an abstract state, returns the set of concrete states it represents. First of all, we assume that a function concretizing abstract heap nodes to concrete references is given. Formally, $\gamma_{\text{Ref}} : \text{HeapNode} \to \wp(\text{Ref})$. We assume that this concretization function concretizes **null** into itself ($\gamma_{\text{Ref}}(\text{null}) = \{\text{null}\}$), and that it is coherent w.r.t. the information provided by isSummary ($\neg\text{isSummary}(n) \Leftrightarrow |\gamma_{\text{Ref}}(n)| = 1$).

The concretization of abstract environments relates each variable in the environment to a reference concretized from the node it is in relation with. Similarly, the concretization of abstract maps relates a reference concretized from a heap node representing a key with a reference concretized from a node representing a value. Finally, the concretization of abstract states applies point-wisely the concretization of environments and maps, formalized as:

$$\gamma_{\text{Env}}(e) = \{\lambda x.r : x \in dom(e) \wedge \exists n \in e(x) : r \in \gamma_{\text{Ref}}(n)\} \qquad \gamma_\Sigma(\bot) = \emptyset$$
$$\gamma_{\text{Map}}(m) = \{\lambda r_1.r_2 : \exists n_1 \in dom(m) : r_1 \in \gamma_{\text{Ref}}(n_1) \wedge \exists n_2 \in m(n_1) : r_2 \in \gamma_{\text{Ref}}(n_2)\}$$
$$\gamma_\Sigma(e, m) = \{(e', m') : e' \in \gamma_{\text{Env}}(e) \wedge m' \in \gamma_{\text{Map}}(m)\}$$

Lemma 2 (Soundness of the domain). *The abstract domain is a sound approximation of the concrete domain, that is, they form a Galois connection [3]. Formally,* $\langle \wp(\Sigma), \subseteq, \cup \rangle \xrightleftharpoons[\alpha_\Sigma]{\gamma_\Sigma} \langle \Sigma, \dot\subseteq, \dot\cup \rangle$ *where* $\alpha_\Sigma = \lambda X. \cap \{Y : Y \subseteq \gamma_\Sigma(X)\}$.

Proof Sketch. γ_Σ *is a complete meet-morphism since it produces all possible environments and maps starting from a given reference concretization. Then,* α_Σ *is well-defined since* γ_Σ *is a complete* $\cap$*-morphism. The fact that it forms a Galois connection follows immediately from the definition of* α_Σ *(Proposition 7 of [4]).*

Running example. Consider again abstract state $\sigma = ([\text{name} \mapsto \{n_1\}], [n_1 \mapsto \{\text{null}, n_2\}])$. Suppose γ_{Ref} concretizes n_1 and n_2 into $\{\#1\}$ and $\{\#2\}$, respectively. Then σ is concretized into states $([\text{name} \mapsto \#1], [\#1 \mapsto \text{null}])$ representing that **name** is not in the map and $([\text{name} \mapsto \#1], [\#1 \mapsto \#2])$ representing that **name** is in the map is related to the value pointed-to by reference $\#2$.

Abstract Semantics. Figure 4 is the abstract semantics of statements and Boolean conditions, that, given an abstract state and a statement or Boolean condition of the language introduced above, returns the abstract state resulting from the evaluation of the given statement on the given abstract state. As usual in abstract interpretation-based static analysis [3], this operational abstract semantics is the basis for computing a fixpoint over a CFG representing loops and conditional statements. We focus the formalization on abstract states in Env × Map, since in case of $\bot$ the abstract semantics always returns $\bot$ itself.

(**new**) creates a new heap node through fresh(t) (where t is the identifier of the transaction performing the creation), and assigns it to v. The number of nodes

$$\mathbb{S}[\![\mathbf{v} = \mathbf{new}\ \mathtt{Value()}, (e, m)]\!] = (e[v \mapsto \mathsf{fresh}(\mathtt{t})], m) \tag{new}$$

$$\mathbb{S}[\![\mathbf{v} = \mathtt{null}, (e, m)]\!] = (e[v \mapsto \{\mathtt{null}\}], m) \tag{nlas}$$

$$\mathbb{S}[\![\mathbf{v} = \mathtt{m.get(k)}, (e, m)]\!] = (e[\mathbf{v} \mapsto \bigcup_{n \in e(k)} m(n)], m) \tag{get}$$

$$\mathbb{S}[\![\mathtt{m.put(k, v)}, (e, m)]\!] \tag{put}$$
$$= \begin{cases} (e, m[n \mapsto e(\mathbf{v})]) & \text{if } e(\mathbf{k}) = \{n\} \wedge \neg\mathsf{isSummary}(n) \\ (e, m[n \mapsto m(n) \cup e(\mathbf{v}) : n \in e(\mathbf{k})]) & \text{otherwise} \end{cases}$$

$$\mathbb{S}[\![\mathtt{m.remove(k)}, (e, m)]\!] \tag{rmv}$$
$$= \begin{cases} (e, m[n \mapsto \{\mathtt{null}\}]) & \text{if } e(\mathbf{k}) = \{n\} \wedge \neg\mathsf{isSummary}(n) \\ (e, m[n \mapsto m(n) \cup \{\mathtt{null}\} : n \in e(\mathbf{k})]) & \text{otherwise} \end{cases}$$

$$\mathbb{S}[\![\mathbf{v} = \mathtt{m.putIfAbsent(k, v)}, (e, m)]\!] \tag{pIA}$$
$$= (\pi_1(\mathbb{S}[\![\mathbf{v} = \mathtt{m.get(k)}, (e, m)]\!]), m') :$$
$$m' = \begin{cases} m[n \mapsto e(\mathbf{v})] & \text{if } e(\mathbf{k}) = \{n\} \wedge m(n) = \{\mathtt{null}\} \\ m[n \mapsto m(n) \cup e(\mathbf{v}) : n \in e(\mathbf{k})] & \text{if } \mathtt{null} \in m(n) \wedge |m(n)| > 1 \\ m & \text{otherwise} \end{cases}$$

$$\mathbb{S}[\![\mathtt{assert(x == null)}, (e, m)]\!] \tag{null}$$
$$= \begin{cases} (e[\mathbf{x} \mapsto \{\mathtt{null}\}], m) & \text{if } \mathtt{null} \in e(\mathbf{x}) \\ \bot & \text{otherwise} \end{cases}$$

$$\mathbb{S}[\![\mathtt{assert(x!\, = null)}, (e, m)]\!] \tag{!null}$$
$$= \begin{cases} (e[\mathbf{x} \mapsto e(\mathbf{x}) \setminus \{\mathtt{null}\}], m) & \text{if } \exists n \in \mathsf{HeapNode} : n \neq \mathtt{null} \wedge n \in e(\mathbf{x}) \\ \bot & \text{otherwise} \end{cases}$$

$$\mathbb{S}[\![\mathtt{assert(m.containsK(k))}, (e, m)]\!] \tag{cntK}$$
$$= \begin{cases} \bot & \text{if } \forall n \in e(\mathbf{k}) : m(n) = \{\mathtt{null}\} \\ (e, m[n \mapsto m(n) \setminus \{\mathtt{null}\}]) & \text{if } e(\mathbf{k}) = \{n\} \wedge \neg\mathsf{isSummary}(n) \wedge m(n) \neq \{\mathtt{null}\} \\ (e, m) & \text{otherwise} \end{cases}$$

$$\mathbb{S}[\![\mathtt{assert(!m.containsK(k))}, (e, m)]\!] \tag{!cntK}$$
$$= \begin{cases} \bot & \text{if } \forall n \in e(\mathbf{k}) : \mathtt{null} \notin m(n) \\ (e, m[n \mapsto \{\mathtt{null}\}]) & \text{if } e(\mathbf{k}) = \{n\} \wedge \neg\mathsf{isSummary}(n) \wedge \mathtt{null} \in m(n) \\ (e, m) & \text{otherwise} \end{cases}$$

Fig. 4. Formal definition of the abstract semantics.

is kept bounded by parameterizing the analysis with an upper bound i such that (i) the first i nodes created by a transaction are all concrete nodes, and (ii) all the other nodes are represented by a summary node. Instead, (nlas) relates the given variable to the singleton $\{\mathtt{null}\}$. (get) relates the assigned variable v to all the heap nodes of values that might be related with k in the map. Note that if k is not in the map, then the abstract map m relates it to a null node, and therefore this value is propagated to v then calling get, representing the concrete semantics of this statement. (put) relates k to v in the map. In particular, if k points to a unique non-summary node, it performs a so-called strong update, overwriting previous values related with k. Otherwise, it performs a weak update by adding to the previous values the new ones. Similarly to (put), (rmv) removes k from the map (by relating it to the singleton $\{\mathtt{null}\}$) iff k points to a unique concrete node. Otherwise, it conservatively adds the heap node null to the heap nodes related to all the values pointed by k. (pIA) updates the map like (put) but only if the updated key node might have been absent, that is, when $\mathtt{null} \in m(n)$. The abstract semantics on Boolean conditions produces

$\bot$ statements if the given Boolean condition cannot hold on the given abstract semantics. Therefore, (null) returns $\bot$ if the given variable x cannot be null, or a state relating x to the singleton {null} otherwise. Vice-versa, (!null) returns $\bot$ if x can be only null, or a state relating x to all its previous values except null otherwise. Similarly, (cntK) returns $\bot$ if the given key k is surely not in the map, it refines the possible values of k if it is represented by a concrete node, or it simply returns the entry state otherwise. Vice-versa, (!cntK) returns $\bot$ if k is surely in the map.

Lemma 3 (Soundness of the semantics). *The abstract semantics is a sound approximation of the concrete semantics. Formally, $\forall \text{st}, (e, m) \in \Sigma :$ $\gamma_\Sigma(\mathbb{S}[\![\text{st}, (e, m)]\!]) \supseteq \mathbb{C}[\![\text{st}, \gamma_\Sigma(e, m)]\!]$, where $\mathbb{C}$ represents the pointwise application of the concrete semantics to a set of concrete states.*

Proof Sketch. Follows from case splitting on the statement, and by definition of the concrete and abstract semantics.

Running example. Consider again the code of method getConvertor, and suppose that the Boolean flag **create** is **true**. When we start from the abstract state $([\text{name} \mapsto \{n_1\}], [n_1 \mapsto \{\text{null}\}])$ (representing that **name** is not in the map), we obtain the abstract state $\sigma = ([\text{name} \mapsto \{n_1\}, \text{conv} \mapsto \{\text{null}\}], [n_1 \mapsto \{\text{null}\}])$ after the first statement by rule (get). Then the semantics of the Boolean condition of the **if** statements at line 3 applies rule (null) (that does not modify the abstract state) since conv is null, and we assumed **create** is **true**. Lines 4 and 5 applies rules (new) and (pIA), respectively. Supposing that fresh(t) returns n_2, we obtain $\sigma' = ([\text{name} \mapsto \{n_1\}, \text{conv} \mapsto \{n_2\}], [n_1 \mapsto n_2])$. We then join this state with the one obtained by applying rule (!null) to σ (that is, $\bot$) obtaining σ' itself. The result of this example represents that, when you start the computation passing a key **name** that is not in the map and **true** for the Boolean flag **create**, after executing method getConvertor in isolation you obtain a map relating **name** to the new object instantiated at line 4.

5   Inferring Corrective Targets

We now apply the abstract semantics $\mathbb{S}$ to infer corrective targets. For this paper, we support a restricted transactional model. In particular, we assume that there are n transactions that start the execution together, each transaction commits only once, and all the transactions commit together at the end of the execution. With these assumptions, we can define a system that perform a *global* corrective synchronization at the end of the execution. We leave more expressive inference for future work.

Serialized CFG. We apply the abstract semantics defined in Sect. 4 to compute suitable corrective targets. In particular, we need that these targets are reachable from the same *entry state* through a *serializable execution*. Therefore, we build a CFG that represents certain specific *serialized* executions. In particular, we assume that we have k distinct types of transactions, and we build up a serialized CFG that represents a serialized execution of *at least* 2 instances of each type of transaction.

Let $\{c^1, ..., c^k\}$ be the code of k different transactions. For each transaction type i, we create three static transaction identifiers t_1^i, t_2^i, and t_n^i. t_1^i and t_2^i represent precisely two concrete instances of c^i, while t_n^i is a *summary* abstract instance representing many concrete instances of c^i. We then build a CFG representing a serialized execution of all these abstract transactions. In particular, each transaction type c^i leads to a CFG tc^i that executes (i) first t_1^i, (ii) then t_n^i inside a non-deterministic loop (to over-approximate many instances of c^i), and (iii) finally t_2^i. While the choice of having the two concrete transaction instances before and after the summary instance is arbitrary and other solutions are possible, we found this solution particularly effective in practice as we will show in Sect. 6. The overall serialized CFG tc is then built by concatenating the CFGs of all these transactions.

Let $\mathcal{T}^{\#}$ be the set of abstract transactions, that is $\mathcal{T}^{\#} = \{t_j^i : i \in [1..k], j \in \{1, 2, n\}\}$. Then our semantics on a serialized CFG returns a function in $\Phi : \mathcal{T}^{\#} \to \Sigma$.

Running example. Similarly to other synchronization approaches, such as transactional boosting [11] and foresight [7], applying corrective synchronization at the data-structure level requires a commutativity specification. In the case of concurrent maps, a simple and effective specification is in terms of the accessed key. Hence, for the getConvertor code, we build a serialized CFG where all the transactions share the same key name (to induce potential conflicts). For the sake of presentation, we set create to true. The serialized CFG consists of the sequence of transactions $t_1; t_n^{\star}; t_2$, where $t_n^{\star}$ represents that the code of t_n is inside a loop.

Suppose now we analyze this serialized CFG starting from the abstract state ($[\text{name} \mapsto \{n_1\}], [n_1 \mapsto \{\text{null}\}]$). The abstract semantics computes the following abstract post-state: ($[\text{name} \mapsto \{n_1\}, \text{conv}_1 \mapsto \{n_1^1\}, \text{conv}_n \mapsto \{n_1^1\}, \text{conv}_2 \mapsto \{n_1^1\}], [n_1 \mapsto \{n_1^1\}]$) (where n_b^a represents the a-th node instantiated by transaction t_b, and conv_c represents the local variable conv of transaction t_c). Intuitively, this result means that, if we run a sequence of transactions executing the code of method getConvertor with a map that does not contain key name, then at the end of the execution of all transactions we will obtain a map relating name to the value generated by the first transactions, and all the transactions will return this value.

Extracting Possible Corrective Targets. First notice that, given a transaction t, the corr rule of the transition system introduced in Sect. 3 requires that the state the system corrects to is reachable starting from the state at the beginning of the execution of t (retrieved by $\Gamma(t) = s$ [n.b. abuse of notation]) producing the same shared log (formally, $s \leadsto (T, \mu', \sigma, L)$). Since in our specific instance of the transition system we suppose that all the transactions start together, we assume that there is a unique entry state σ_0 (formally, $\forall t \in T : \Gamma(t) = \sigma_0$). In addition, since all the transactions commit together at the end, we have complete control over the shared log, and when we correct the shared log is always empty, and the shared state is identical to the initial shared state. Therefore, given these restrictions, we only need to compute a μ' such that $\Gamma(t) \rightsquigarrow (T, \mu', \sigma_0, \epsilon)$.

We compute possible corrective targets on the serialized CFG tc using the abstract semantics $\mathbb{S}$. In particular, we need to compute corrective targets that, given an entry state representing a precise observable entry state, are reachable through a serialized execution. However, an abstract state in Σ might represent multiple concrete states. For instance $([\mathtt{k} \mapsto \{n_1\}], [n_1 \mapsto \{\mathtt{null}, n_2\}])$ represents both that $\mathtt{k}$ is (if n_1 is related to n_2 in the abstract map) or is not (when n_1 is related to $\mathtt{null}$). This abstract state therefore might concretize to states belonging, and it cannot be used to define a corrective target. Therefore, we define a predicate $\mathsf{single} : \Sigma \to \{\mathsf{true}, \mathsf{false}\}$ that, given an abstract state, holds iff it represents an exact concrete state. Formally,

$$\mathsf{single}(e, m) \Leftrightarrow \bigwedge \begin{cases} \forall \mathbf{x} \in dom(e) : |e(\mathbf{x})| = 1 \wedge e(\mathbf{x}) = \{n_1\} \wedge \neg\mathsf{isSummary}(n_1) \\ \forall n \in dom(m) : |m(n)| = 1 \wedge m(n) = \{n_2\} \wedge \neg\mathsf{isSummary}(n_2) \end{cases}$$

Note that in general the concretization of an abstract state is not computable. Therefore, we rely on single to check if an abstract state represents one precise concrete state.

Lemma 4. $\forall (e, m) \in \Sigma : \mathsf{single}(e, m) \Rightarrow |\gamma_\Sigma(e, m)| = 1$

Proof Sketch (Proof Sketch). By definition of single, $\neg\mathsf{isSummary}(n)$ *for all the nodes n in e or n. By definition of* $\mathsf{isSummary}$ *we have that* $|\gamma_{\mathsf{Ref}}(n)| = 1$. *Thanks to this result, combined with the definition of* γ_Σ, *we obtain that* $|\gamma_\Sigma(e, m)| = 1$.

The definition of single is extended to states $\phi \in \Phi$ by checking if single holds for all the local states in ϕ. We build up a set of possible entry states $S \subseteq \Phi$ such that $\forall \phi \in S : \mathsf{single}(\phi)$, and we compute the exit states on the serialized CFG tc for all the possible entry states, filtering out only the ones that represents an exact concrete state. Note that since we have a finite number of abstract transactions, and each transaction has a finite number of parameters, we can build up a finite set of entry states representing all the possible concrete situations. Note that, while in general an abstract state rarely represents a precise single concrete state, this is the case for most of the cases we dealt with as shown by our experimental results. This happens since our static analysis targets a specific data structure (maps), and tracks very precise symbolic information on it.

We then use the results of the abstract semantics $\mathbb{S}$ to build up a function $\mathsf{corrTarg}$ that relates each entry state to a set of possible exit states: $\mathsf{corrTarg}(\mathsf{T}, \mathsf{S}) = [\phi \mapsto \{\phi' : \phi' \in \mathbb{S}[\![tc, \phi]\!] \wedge \mathsf{single}(\phi')\} : \phi \in S].$

Running example. Starting from the entry state $([\mathtt{name} \mapsto \{n_1\}], [n_1 \mapsto \{\mathtt{null}\}])$, the exit state computed by the abstract semantics is $([\mathtt{name} \mapsto \{n_1\}, \mathtt{conv}_1 \mapsto \{n_1^1\}, \mathtt{conv}_n \mapsto \{n_1^1\}, \mathtt{conv}_2 \mapsto \{n_1^1\}], [n_1 \mapsto \{n_1^1\}])$. This state satisfies the predicate single since it represents a precise concrete state. Therefore, the relation between this entry and exit state is part of $\mathsf{corrTarg}$.

Dynamic Corrective Synchronization. In our model, when we start the execution we have a finite number of concrete instances of each type of transaction. We denote by $\mathcal{T} = \{s_j^i : j \in [0..m] \land i \in [1..k_j]\}$ the set of identifiers of concrete transactions, where m is the number of different types of transactions, k_j is the number of instances of transaction j, and s_j^i represents the j-th instance of the i-th type of transaction.

We can then bind abstract transaction identifiers to concrete ones. Since the set of abstract transactions is defined as $\mathcal{T}^\# = \{t_j^i : i \in [1..k], j \in \{1, 2, n\}\}$, we bind the first two concrete identifiers to the corresponding abstract identifiers, and all the others to the n abstract instance. We formally define the concretization of transaction identifiers as follows: $\gamma_\mathcal{T}(T) = [t_j^i \mapsto \{s_j^{i'} : (i \in \{1, 2\} \Rightarrow i' = i) \lor 3 \le i' \le k_j\} : t_j^i \in T]$. We can now formalize the concretization of abstract states in Φ by relying on the concretization of local states and transaction identifiers. $\gamma_\Phi(\phi) = \{t \mapsto \sigma : \exists t' \in dom(\phi) : t \in \gamma_\mathcal{T}(t) \land \sigma \in \gamma_\Sigma(\phi(t))\}$.

We now prove that targets computed by corrTarg satisfy the premise of corr.

Theorem 3. *Let $t = $ corrTarg(T, S) be the results computed by our system. Then $\forall \sigma_0 \in \gamma_\Phi(\phi_0), \sigma_n \in \gamma_\Phi(\phi_n) : \phi_0 \in dom(t) \land \phi_n \in t(\phi_0)$ we have that $\sigma_0 \rightsquigarrow \sigma_n$.*

Proof Sketch. By definition of corrTarg, we have that both single(ϕ_0) and single(ϕ_n) hold. Therefore, by Lemma 4 we have that $\gamma_\Sigma(\phi_0) = \{\sigma_0\}$ and $\gamma_\Sigma(\phi_n) = \{\sigma_n\}$. In addition, by definition of corrTarg we have that $\phi_n \in \mathbb{S}[\![tc, \phi_0]\!]$. Then, by Lemma 3 (soundness of the abstract semantics) we have that σ_n is exactly what is computed by the concrete semantics on the given program starting from σ_0, that is, $\sigma_0 \rightsquigarrow \sigma_n$.

Discussion. corrTarg returns a set of possible exit states given an entry state. This means that, given a concrete incorrect post-state, we can choose the exit state produced by corrTarg that requires a *minimal* correction to the incorrect post-state. In this way, we would minimize the runtime overhead of adjusting the concrete state. The target state can be chosen by calculating the number of operations we need to apply to correct the post-state, and select the one with the minimal number. This might be further optimized by hashing the correct post states computed by corrTarg based on similarity. However, we did not investigate this aspect since in our experiments the overhead of correcting the post-state was already almost negligible by choosing a random target. We believe that this is due to our specific setting, that is, concurrent maps. In fact, in this scenario the corrective operations that we have to apply are to put or remove an element, and the corrections always required very few of them. We believe that other data structures (e.g., involving ordering of elements like lists) might require more complicated corrections, and we plan to investigate them as future work.

6   Preliminary Implementation

We now report encouraging results of our preliminary implementation. We have created a Java implementation of our static analysis for composed Map operations (see Sect. 5). Given n types of transactions, our implementation builds a serialized CFG (Sect. 5) and then computes a fixpoint over it relying on the abstract semantics (Sect. 4). We support all the operations listed in Sect. 4. Static analysis running times are negligible compared to the rest of the process, and the analysis converges always in less than a second. Therefore, we do not report the running times of the static analysis.

As explained earlier, the interface with the runtime system is a relational corrective specification mapping pre-states to sets of post-states that are obtainable via serializable execution of the transactions from the pre-state. As a partial example, $[k \mapsto \bot, v \mapsto v] \rightsquigarrow \{[k \mapsto v, v \mapsto v]\}$ denotes that if we started from a pre-state where k was not in the map and the value passed to the function was v, then in the post-state the key k is made to point to the value v pointed-to by the second argument v in the pre-state. The runtime system S is parameterized by the specification, which it loads at the beginning of the concurrent run. As discussed in Sect. 5, in our current prototype all transactions are assumed to start simultaneously. This scenario is useful, for example, in loop parallelization. Each concrete transaction is mapped to its abstract counterpart. The mapping process also binds the concrete arguments of the transaction (i.e., the concrete object references) to their symbolic counterparts (e.g., the k and v symbols above).

During execution, the runtime system monitors commit events. In our prototype, we limit transactions to a single commit point before completion. Corrective synchronization occurs on failed commits, in which case the transaction's shared log, local state and return value are all (potentially) modified according to the corrective specification.

Summary of Subjects and Experiments. We conducted experiments running our implementation on four subjects, all of which are taken from popular open-source code bases and have been used in past studies [23,24]. We considered workload size and concurrency level, ranging from 2 to 23 threads, and summarizing over 10 runs. In each case, we compared against (i) a pessimistic concrete-level variant of STM, as available via version 1.3 of the Deuce STM (the latest version)[2], and (ii) a lock-based synchronization algorithm boosted with Map semantics [11], such that the locks are of the same grain as their corresponding abstract locks in boosted STM. We ran our experiments on two Intel Xeon 2.90 GHz (16 cores) CPUs with 132 GB of RAM.

For lack of space, detailed experimental results, considering factors such as number of threads and size of the workload, are omitted. The table on the right reports the relative gain of STM and corrective synchronization w.r.t. lock-based synchronization. We aggregate performance results, averaging across all workloads and concurrency levels. These results show

	Pessimistic		Corrective	
	wload.	conc.	wload.	conc.
Tomcat	1.5%	3%	29%	30%
dyuproject	18%	24%	30%	29%
Flexive	17%	14%	29%	30%
Gridkit	20%	16%	32%	31%
Average	**14%**	**14%**	**30%**	**30%**

---

[2] https://github.com/DeuceSTM/DeuceSTM.

that, on average, corrective synchronization leads to a gain that is twice the one obtained by STM.

For completeness, we also note the absolute running times, as min/max intervals in seconds, for the lock-based solution for the workload and concurrency configurations respectively: Tomcat – [6,10], [7,12]; dyuproject – [6,9], [7,11]; Flexive – [6,10], [7,11]; and Gridkit – [6,9], [7,11]. The numbers are encouraging, indicating improvement over both locks and STM. More careful engineering, beyond our current prototype implementation, is likely to make the improvement more significant.

7 Related Work

To our knowledge, existing solutions to the problem of correct synchronization assume either the ability to prevent bad interleavings or the ability to roll back execution. We focus our survey of related research on solutions for optimizing the rollback mechanism, and also discuss works on synchronization synthesis backed by static program analysis and on merging state mutations by concurrent threads.

There are two main optimizations to *decrease rollback overhead*: reducing either abort rate or the extent to which a conflicted transaction rolls back. Different solutions have been proposed in each direction [11,17,26]. Others leverage available nondeterminism [25]. None of these approaches perform corrective synchronization. A well-known solution to restrict the extent to which a transaction rolls back is checkpointing [5,14] or nested transactions [1,20]. Elastic transactions [6] avoid wasted work by splitting into multiple pieces. The Push/Pull model [15] also uses local/shared logs, and is flexible enough to express rollback-based transactions but nor corrective synchronization.

In our solution, static analysis is used to identify admissible shared-state configurations to correct to from a given input state. Multiple past works on synchronization synthesis have also *relied on static analysis*, albeit for the extraction of other types of information. Golan-Gueta et al. [8] utilize static analysis to compute a conservative approximation of the possible actions that a transaction may perform in its future from a given intermediate point. This still pessimistic approach enables more granular synchronization compared to the worst-case assumption that the transaction may perform any action in its future. Autolocker [19] applies static analysis to determine a correct locking policy. Hawkins et al. [9] ensure correct synchronization by construction. Prountzos et al. [21] optimize the Galois system [17] via static shape analysis [22].

Finally, we note solutions based on *merging*, or combining, the effects of concurrent threads. Burckhardt and Leijen propose *concurrent revisions* [2], inspirated by version control systems. The idea is to specify a (custom) merge function, based on a revision calculus, such that concurrent state mutations can be reconciled in a deterministic manner. Somewhat similarly, Hendler *et al.* introduce *flat combining* [10]. The idea is to synchronize concurrent accesses to a shared data structure D by having threads post their updates to D into a common list as thead-local records, where a single thread at a time acquires the lock on D, combines and applies the updates, and writes the results back to the threads' request fields. Contrary to these two paradigms, our approach builds on thread-level state correction. This bypasses the need for a coarse-grained lock, as in flat combining, and—unlike concurrent revisions—ensures serializability.

8   Conclusion and Future Work

We have presented an alternative to the lock- and retry-based synchronization methods that we dub *corrective synchronization*. The key insight is to correct a bad execution, rather than aborting/retrying the transaction or conservatively avoiding the bad execution in the first place. We have explored an instantiation of corrective synchronization for composed operations over ConcurrentMaps, where correct states are computed via abstract interpretation. Experimental results with a prototype implementation are encouraging.

There are several directions for future work. First, one may explore other variants of corrective synchronization. For example, one may want to allow multiple threads to decide together corrective target states. One could also improve the abstract domain beyond maps, perhaps using existing domains. Another direction is to integrate corrective synchronization into larger-scale software systems and perform a deep experimental evaluation over the spectrum of synchronization techniques. As part of such an effort, one could develop compositional synchronization methods that integrate corrective synchronization with lock- and STM-based synchronization.

References

1. Beeri, C., Bernstein, P.A., Goodman, N., Lai, M.Y., Shasha, D.E.: A concurrency control theory for nested transactions (preliminary report). In: Proceedings of the 2nd Annual ACM Symposium on Principles of Distributed Computing (PODC 1983), pp. 45–62. ACM Press, New York (1983)
2. Burckhardt, S., Leijen, D.: Semantics of concurrent revisions. In: Barthe, G. (ed.) ESOP 2011. LNCS, vol. 6602, pp. 116–135. Springer, Heidelberg (2011). doi:10.1007/978-3-642-19718-5_7
3. Cousot, P., Cousot, R.: Abstract interpretation: a unified lattice model for static analysis of programs by construction or approximation of fixpoints. In: Proceedings of POPL 1977. ACM Press (1977)
4. Cousot, P., Cousot, R.: Abstract interpretation and application to logic programs. J. Logic Program. **13**, 103–179 (1992)
5. Egwutuoha, I.P., Levy, D., Selic, B., Chen, S.: A survey of fault tolerance mechanisms and checkpoint/restart implementations for high performance computing systems. J. Supercomput. **65**, 1302–1326 (2013)
6. Felber, P., Gramoli, V., Guerraoui, R.: Elastic transactions. In: Keidar, I. (ed.) DISC 2009. LNCS, vol. 5805, pp. 93–107. Springer, Heidelberg (2009). doi:10.1007/978-3-642-04355-0_12
7. Golan-Gueta, G., Ramalingam, G., Sagiv, M., Yahav, E.: Concurrent libraries with foresight. In: Proceedings of the 34th ACM SIGPLAN Conference on Programming Language Design and Implementation, pp. 263–274 (2013)

8. Golan-Gueta, G., Ramalingam, G., Sagiv, M., Yahav, E.: Concurrent libraries with foresight. In: ACM SIGPLAN Conference on Programming Language Design and Implementation, PLDI 2013, Seattle, WA, USA, 16–19 June 2013, pp. 263–274 (2013)
9. Hawkins, P., Aiken, A., Fisher, K., Rinard, M.C., Sagiv, M.: Concurrent data representation synthesis. In: ACM SIGPLAN Conference on Programming Language Design and Implementation, PLDI 2012, Beijing, China, 11–16 June 2012, pp. 417–428 (2012)
10. Hendler, D., Incze, I., Shavit, N., Tzafrir, M.: Flat combining and the synchronization-parallelism tradeoff. In: SPAA 2010: Proceedings of the 22nd Annual ACM Symposium on Parallelism in Algorithms and Architectures, Thira, Santorini, Greece, 13–15 June 2010, pp. 355–364 (2010)
11. Herlihy, M., Koskinen, E.: Transactional boosting: a methodology for highly-concurrent transactional objects. In: Proceedings of the 13th ACM SIGPLAN Symposium on Principles and Practice of Parallel Programming, PPOPP 2008, Salt Lake City, UT, USA, 20–23 February 2008, pp. 207–216 (2008)
12. Herlihy, M., Moss, J.E.B.: Transactional memory: architectural support for lock-free data structures. In: Proceedings of the 20th Annual International Symposium on Computer Architecture, San Diego, CA, pp. 289–300, May 1993
13. Kleen, A.: Scaling existing lock-based applications with lock elision. Commun. ACM **57**(3), 52–56 (2014)
14. Koskinen, E., Herlihy, M.: Checkpoints and continuations instead of nested transactions. In: Meyer auf der Heide, F., Shavit, N. (eds.) SPAA 2008: Proceedings of the 20th Annual ACM Symposium on Parallelism in Algorithms and Architectures, Munich, Germany, 14–16 June 2008, pp. 160–168. ACM (2008)
15. Koskinen, E., Parkinson, M.J.: The push/pull model of transactions. In: Proceedings of the 36th ACM SIGPLAN Conference on Programming Language Design and Implementation, Portland, OR, USA, 15–17 June 2015, pp. 186–195 (2015)
16. Kulkarni, M., Pingali, K., Walter, B., Ramanarayanan, G., Kavita Bala, L., Chew, P.: Optimistic parallelism requires abstractions. In: Proceedings of the 28th ACM SIGPLAN Conference on Programming Language Design and Implementation, PLDI 2007, pp. 211–222. ACM, New York (2007)
17. Kulkarni, M., Pingali, K., Walter, B., Ramanarayanan, G., Kavita Bala, L., Chew, P.: Optimistic parallelism requires abstractions. In: Proceedings of the ACM SIG-PLAN 2007 Conference on Programming Language Design and Implementation, San Diego, California, USA, 10–13 June 2007, pp. 211–222 (2007)
18. Matveev, A., Shavit, N.: Towards a fully pessimistic STM model. In: Proceedings of the Workshop on Transactional Memory (TRANSACT 2012) (2012)
19. McCloskey, B., Zhou, F., Gay, D., Brewer, E.A.: Autolocker: synchronization inference for atomic sections. In: Proceedings of the 33rd ACM SIGPLAN-SIGACT Symposium on Principles of Programming Languages, POPL 2006, Charleston, South Carolina, USA, 11–13 January 2006, pp. 346–358 (2006)
20. Ni, Y., Menon, V.S., Adl-Tabatabai, A.-R., Hosking, A.L., Hudson, R.L., Eliot, J., Moss, B., Saha, B., Shpeisman, T.: Open nesting in software transactional memory. In: Proceedings of the 12th ACM SIGPLAN Symposium on Principles and Practice of Parallel Programming (PPoPP 2007), pp. 68–78. ACM Press, New York (2007)
21. Prountzos, D., Manevich, R., Pingali, K., McKinley, K.S.: A shape analysis for optimizing parallel graph programs. In: Proceedings of the 38th ACM SIGPLAN-SIGACT Symposium on Principles of Programming Languages, POPL 2011, Austin, TX, USA, 26–28 January 2011, pp. 159–172 (2011)

22. Sagiv, S., Reps, T.W., Wilhelm, R.: Parametric shape analysis via 3-valued logic. ACM Trans. Program. Lang. Syst. **24**, 217–298 (2002)
23. Shacham, O., Bronson, N.G., Aiken, A., Sagiv, M., Vechev, M.T., Yahav, E.: Testing atomicity of composed concurrent operations. In Proceedings of the 26th Annual ACM SIGPLAN Conference on Object-Oriented Programming, Systems, Languages, and Applications, OOPSLA 2011, Part of SPLASH 2011, Portland, OR, USA, 22–27 October 2011, pp. 51–64 (2011)
24. Shacham, O., Yahav, E., Golan-Gueta, G., Aiken, A., Bronson, N.G., Sagiv, M., Vechev, M.T.: Verifying atomicity via data independence. In: International Symposium on Software Testing and Analysis, ISSTA 2014, San Jose, CA, USA, 21–26 July 2014, pp. 26–36 (2014)
25. Tripp, O., Koskinen, E., Sagiv, M.: Turning nondeterminism into parallelism. In: Proceedings of the 2013 ACM SIGPLAN International Conference on Object Oriented Programming Systems Languages & Applications, OOPSLA 2013, Part of SPLASH 2013, Indianapolis, IN, USA, 26–31 October 2013, pp. 589–604 (2013)
26. Tripp, O., Yorsh, G., Field, J., Sagiv, M.: Hawkeye: effective discovery of dataflow impediments to parallelization. In: Proceedings of the 2011 ACM International Conference on Object Oriented Programming Systems Languages and Applications, OOPSLA 2011, pp. 207–224. ACM, New York (2011)

Property Directed Reachability for Proving Absence of Concurrent Modification Errors

Asya Frumkin[1]([⊠]), Yotam M.Y. Feldman[1], Ondřej Lhoták[2], Oded Padon[1], Mooly Sagiv[1], and Sharon Shoham[1]

[1] Tel Aviv University, Tel Aviv, Israel
asyafrumkin@mail.tau.ac.il
[2] University of Waterloo, Waterloo, Canada

Abstract. We define and implement an interprocedural analysis for automatically checking safety of recursive programs with an unbounded state space. The main idea is to infer modular universally quantified inductive invariants in the form of procedure summaries that are sufficient to prove the safety property. We assume that the effect of the atomic commands of the program can be modeled via effectively propositional logic. We then propose a variant of the IC3/PDR approach for computing universally quantified inductive procedure summaries that overapproximate the behavior of the program.

We show that Java programs that manipulate collections and iterators can be modeled in effectively propositional logic and that the invariants are often universal. This allows us to apply the new analysis to prove the absence of concurrent modification exceptions in Java programs. In order to check the feasibility of our method, we implemented our analysis on top of Z3, as well as a Java front-end which translates Java programs into effectively propositional formulas.

1 Introduction

Java programs enforce consistency of iterator usage by requiring the absence of concurrent modification exceptions (CME). Intuitively, the idea is to forbid accessing a collection via *stale* iterators. An iterator becomes stale when the collection it iterates is changed not via the iterator itself. The Java standard library imposes this restriction at runtime by throwing a runtime exception when stale iterators are accessed. Note that this can happen both in sequential and concurrent programs. A common example is when adding an element to a collection from inside a loop which iterates it.

In many cases a logical error in the program leads to a CME. Therefore, identifying potential CMEs at compile-time and proving the absence of concurrent modifications can be very useful. Indeed abstract interpretation has been used to prove the absence of CMEs in small to medium size programs [15, 18, 22]. These methods are sound, i.e., whenever the absence of CMEs is proved, the program indeed cannot raise a CME. However, these methods are incomplete, and may result in false alarms due to limitations of the abstraction. Common sources for

© Springer International Publishing AG 2017
A. Bouajjani and D. Monniaux (Eds.): VMCAI 2017, LNCS 10145, pp. 209–227, 2017.
DOI: 10.1007/978-3-319-52234-0_12

imprecision are aliasing of objects in the heap, and complex interaction between various procedures of the program.

1.1 Main Results

Our key insight in this paper is that in many programs the inductive invariants required to prove the absence of CMEs can be expressed as universal first-order formulas and that the problem of checking inductiveness amounts to checking (un)satisfiability in effectively propositional logic. This is surprising since the natural modeling of this problem involves version numbers for iterators. It implies that SAT solvers can be used to check the absence of CMEs for programs annotated with inductive invariants.

In practice it is very hard for programmers to write inductive invariants. Furthermore, Java programs include deep nesting of method calls which makes it practically impossible. Therefore, we implemented a method for automatically inferring universal procedure summaries that applies to recursive programs.

We develop an iterative method for inferring the required procedure summaries for proving absence of CMEs. Technically, we combined the procedure of inferring universally quantified invariants in a property guided way [11] with the techniques of [7,13] for computing procedure summaries.

This paper can be summarized as follows:

- We show that in many cases inductive invariants for proving absence of CMEs are expressible by universally quantifying over all the iterator objects in the program (whose number is unbounded). Specifically, for programs with (potentially recursive) procedures, procedure summaries (Hoare triples) can also be expressed in universal first order logic. This enables to mechanically check the inductiveness in a sound and complete way using EPR solvers [9].
- We develop an iterative method for inferring sufficiently strong universal procedure summaries in order to prove absence of CMEs. The method handles Java programs with recursive procedures and infers procedure summaries, i.e., Hoare triples. Technically this algorithm generalizes [11] and follows the idea of property directed reachability [7,13].
- We implemented the algorithm on top of Ivy [16] and Z3 [4].
- We implemented a front-end for Java using Soot [21] which converts Java programs into EPR and integrates with the above procedure.

2   The Concurrent Modification Problem

The Java Collections Framework (JCF) is an important part of the Java platform as it provides implementations for common collection data structures. An Iterator object is used in order to access the elements in a collection in a sequential manner. Multiple iterators can operate on the same collection. In general, it is an error to modify a collection while an iterator is operating on it and to continue to use the iterator after the modification. Iterators are usually implemented to be fail-fast, meaning that they throw an exception if iteration is resumed after the occurrence of a change in a collection, either directly or via another iterator. The exception, of type ConcurrentModificationException (CME), can be thrown dynamically even in a single-threaded program. All JCF non-concurrent collections provide fail-fast iterators as a safety measure for a very common bug.

In order to prove that a Java program cannot cause a CME to be thrown, a careful examination of the program should be performed. The proof should ensure that all possible execution paths do not cause such an error. Specifically, we call iterators whose collection is modified invalid or stale, and verify that no such iterator is used.

Example 1. Let us consider the code presented in Fig. 1, which contains a class manipulating a list of lists. The method *flatten* transforms a list of lists into a simple list by adding all the items held in the nested lists, to an output list, using the helper method *addList*. Most of the operations in the *main* method are ones that cannot cause a CME. The only location where a collection is modified during iteration is inside the loop in the *addList* method, which is called from *flatten*. The active iterators during this operation, *itr1* and *itr2*, are iterating over the input list *in* while items are being added to the output list *out*. Since in this program *flatten* is called from *main* method with two distinct lists as arguments, none of the iterators becomes invalidated, and the code terminates successfully. However, if the *flatten* method is examined separately from the whole program context, we can conclude that a CME throw is possible due to aliasing. If, for example, the *in* list is equal to the *out* list, both *itr1* and *itr2* would be invalidated inside *addList*'s loop, and the next *itr1.next()* call would throw an exception. Also, if the *out* list is included as one of the lists in the *in* list, *itr2* would be invalidated once *itr1* reaches *out* and the object pointed to by *itr2* is added to *out*. A subsequent *itr2.next()* call would throw an

```
class ListOfLists {
  public static void
        flatten(List in, List out) {
    Iterator itr1 = in.iterator();
    while(itr1.hasNext()) {
      List l = (List) itr1.next();
      addList(out, l);
    }
  }

  public static void
      addList(List lst1, List lst2) {
    Iterator itr2 = lst2.iterator();
    while(itr2.hasNext()) {
      Object o = itr2.next();
      lst1.add(o);
    }
  }
}
```

```
class FlattenTest {
  public static void
        main(String args[]) {
    int length =
        Integer.parseInt(args[0]);
    // create list
    LinkedList ll = new LinkedList();
    LinkedList subl =
        new LinkedList();
    for(int j = 0; j < length; ++j) {
      subl.add(j*j);
    }
    ll.add(subl);
    ll.add(subl);
    List out = new LinkedList();
    ListOfLists.flatten(ll, out);
  }
}
```

Fig. 1. Usage of list of lists implementation that does not cause a CME to be thrown

exception. This example demonstrates that both interprocedural analysis and aliasing information is required in order to prove that a CME does not occur in a program.

Implementation of Iterators in Java. The natural way to implement a check for CMEs in a Java program is by maintaining a version number for every collection. Each iterator of a collection is initialized with the current version number of the collection. Every modification of the collection increments its version number, as well as the version number of the iterator performing it, if such exists. When an iterator is accessing or modifying the underlying collection, the iterator's version number is compared with the collection's version number. A difference between these values implies, that the collection was modified by another iterator, and the operation should not be completed.

This method, implemented as part of the runtime engine in JCF, involves maintaining an integer value for the version number and performing arithmetic operations, such as increment and comparison. However, in spite of the use of integer arithmetic in the implementation, it is possible to analyze CMEs without directly modeling the version numbers. As seen in [18], it suffices that the analysis tracks the Boolean notion of whether an iterator is stale or not. Thus EPR is an appropriate choice for encoding the CME problem.

3 EPR Verification Conditions for CME

In this section we present a description of Java programs that involve direct iterator and collection manipulation. We describe how to encode these programs and their CME verification conditions via EPR formulas.

EPR. The effectively-propositional (EPR) class of logical formulas, also known as Bernays-Schönfinkel-Ramsey class, is a decidable fragment of first-order logic. EPR formulas are of the form $\exists^*\forall^*\phi$ where ϕ is a quantifier-free formula, that contains relation symbols and equality, but no function symbols. The satisfiability of such formulas can be reduced to SAT by substituting the existential variables by Skolem constants and then replacing the universally quantified variables by all possible combinations of constants. The resulting formula is propositional, and is exponentially larger than the original formula. We use an extension of EPR, that allows *stratified* function symbols in the vocabulary, i.e. functions that obey the requirement: if there is a function mapping sort srt_1 to sort srt_2, there cannot be a function mapping srt_2 to srt_1. Extended-EPR formulas maintain the decidability of EPR [16]. In the sequel, we will use the term EPR to refer to the extended EPR fragment.

3.1 Program State

To facilitate CME verification, our model for Java programs partitions Java objects into three distinct types: *container*, *iterator* and *obj*. The container type includes object types that are part of the JCF, meaning classes that implement java.util.Collections or java.util.Map interfaces. The iterator type is used for iterator objects, whose class implements the java.util.Iterator interface. All other Java types, including primitive types, are modeled as obj.

Each iterator object i has a mapping $cnt(i)$ to the container it operates on. A container can hold either objects or containers. The binary relations $member$ and $member\_cnt$ represent an item's presence in a container. For each type X, there is a corresponding unary $used\_X$ relation that holds initialized items. The state of the iterator is kept in the unary relations $stale$ and cme, where the first keeps iterators that are invalid, and the second — iterators on which a CME would be thrown. In addition, for clarity, we use $points\_to$ and $points\_to\_cnt$ as shorthands, defined by $points\_to(i,o) \stackrel{\text{def}}{=} \exists c_0.\ (cnt(i) = c_0) \wedge member(c_0, o)$ and $points\_to\_cnt(i,c) \stackrel{\text{def}}{=} \exists c_0.(cnt(i) = c_0) \wedge member\_cnt(c_0, c)$.

The constructs mentioned above are listed in Table 1 and used as building blocks for implementing a "library" for modeling programs that manipulate collections via iterators. This library supports actions such as add/remove to/from collection, iterator generation, iterator advancement etc. (see Table 2).

In addition to the above mentioned relations we allow program specific binary relations for class fields, where the first argument is an object and the second is the relevant field. We denote the set of all relations used to express the program state as $\mathcal{G}$.

Table 1. Abstraction relations and functions.

Name	Parameters	Description
$cnt(I)$	I: iterator	Function which returns a container, maps iterators to their underlying containers
$member(C, O)$	C: container, O: obj	Object is included in container
$member\_cnt(C_1, C_2)$	C_1: container, C_2: container	Container is included in container
$used\_cnt(C)$	C: container	Container is initialized
$used\_iter(I)$	I: iterator	Iterator is initialized
$used\_obj(O)$	O: obj	Object is initialized
$stale(I)$	I: iterator	Iterator is invalid
$cme(I)$	I: iterator	Concurrent modification occurred

Safety. The safety requirement of the CME problem is that a concurrent modification exception does not occur in any possible execution of the program. In our formulation, the requirement that a program state does not exhibit a CME violation is expressed by the formula $\forall I.\ \neg cme(I)$. Initially, the cme and $stale$ relations are empty.

3.2   Modeling Java Operations in EPR

We provide the interpretation of each Java operation via a two-vocabulary EPR formula, expressing the connection between the pre- and post-states of the operation. The vocabulary $\mathcal{G}$ is used in order to express the pre-state, and $\mathcal{G}' = \{v' \mid v \in \mathcal{G}\}$ is the vocabulary used to express the post-state. Both $\mathcal{G}$ and $\mathcal{G}'$ include only global relations, and the encoding of each primitive operation via an EPR formula is given in Table 2.

Java's Iterator interface defines three methods: *hasNext*, *next* and *remove* (which is optional). An important note is that we do not model the current position of iterators, but only the container they are pointing to, along with the state of the iterator that we represent by the *stale* and *cme* relations. Therefore, the *hasNext* method is not modeled directly. Our collection is unordered and hence, the *next* method is conservatively modeled as a nondeterministic retrieval of any item from the collection, that is, an item from *points_to*. The retrieved item can be either obj or container, depending on the type of the holding container. The operation also checks whether the iterator is in *stale* state and updates *cme* accordingly, simulating a throw of CME. The *remove* method is modeled by updates of the *member* and *member_cnt* relations as the iterator may be traversing either a collection of objects or a collection of collections. This operation also updates the *stale* relation to mark all iterators traversing the current container as stale, except for the current iterator. The *add* method is modeled by inserting the desired object to the *member*/*member_cnt* relations and updating *stale* to hold all iterators for the updated container. Fresh items of type X are created by updating the *used_X* relations of items that were not used yet. New iterators are created with *stale* set to false.[1] We note, that in addition to the abstraction involved in making collections unordered, we also do not model arithmetic operations and specific data properties, and conservatively overapproximate them via nondeterminism.

3.3   Modeling Programs Using EPR

From the formulas encoding the primitive operations, we derive a modular symbolic representation of programs by representing each procedure separately, based on the functional approach to interprocedural analysis [20]. For simplicity of the presentation, we consider only procedures without loops; if needed, loops can be transformed into recursive procedures.

Our definitions are inspired by [13]. A program $\mathcal{A}$ is a pair $\langle \Pi, \mathcal{G} \rangle$, where Π is a non-empty set of procedures with a designated procedure $\mathcal{M}$ (*main*) serving as the entry point. $\mathcal{G}$ is a set of predicate symbols representing the program's global state. For simplicity, we assume there are no global program variables. A procedure $\mathcal{P}$ is a tuple $\langle i_{\mathcal{P}}, o_{\mathcal{P}}, \Sigma_{\mathcal{P}}, \beta_{\mathcal{P}} \rangle$, where $i_{\mathcal{P}}$ and $o_{\mathcal{P}}$ are lists of constant symbols denoting the formal parameters and formal output variables, respectively, with the assumption that $i_{\mathcal{P}} \cap o_{\mathcal{P}} = \emptyset$.

---

[1] The translation also incorporates the fact that once a CME occurs, the normal control-flow of the program is interrupted by the exception.

Table 2. Java statements and their EPR interpretation. c denotes a container, i an iterator, and o an obj.

Java statement	Interpretation
$i.hasNext()$	–
$o = i.next()$	$points\_to(i, o) \land (\forall I.\ cme'(I) \iff cme(I) \lor$ $(I = i \land stale(i)))$
$c = i.next()$	$points\_to\_cnt(i, c) \land (\forall I.\ cme'(I) \iff cme(I) \lor$ $(I = i \land stale(i)))$
$c.add(o)$	$\forall C, O, I.\ (member'(C, O) \iff member(C, O) \lor$ $(C = c \land O = o)) \land (stale'(I) \iff stale(I) \lor$ $(cnt(I) = c \land used\_itr(I)))$
$c_1.add(c_2)$	$\forall C_1, C_2, I.\ (member\_cnt'(C_1, C_2) \iff$ $member\_cnt(C_1, C_2) \lor (C_1 = c_1 \land C_2 = c_2)) \land$ $(stale'(I) \iff stale(I) \lor (cnt(I) = c_1 \land used\_itr(I)))$
$i.remove()$	$\exists o, c.\ \forall C, C', O, I.$ $((used\_obj(o) \land (member'(C, O) \iff$ $member(C, O) \land (C \neq cnt(i) \lor O \neq o)))$ $\lor (used\_cnt(c) \land (member\_cnt'(C, C') \iff$ $member\_cnt(C, C') \land (C \neq cnt(i) \lor C' \neq c))))$ $\land (stale'(I) \iff stale(I) \lor (cnt(I) = cnt(i) \land I \neq i$ $\land used\_itr(I)))$
$c = new\ Collection()$	$\neg used\_cnt(c) \land (\forall I.\ used\_itr(I) \Rightarrow (cnt(I) \neq c)) \land$ $(\forall O.\ \neg member(c, O)) \land (\forall C.\ \neg member\_cnt(c, C) \land$ $\neg member\_cnt(C, c)) \land (\forall C.\ used\_cnt'(C) \iff$ $used\_cnt(C) \lor C = c)$
$i = c.iterator()$	$\neg used\_itr(i) \land (cnt(i) = c) \land (\forall I.\ stale'(I) \iff$ $stale(I) \land I \neq i) \land (\forall I.\ used\_itr'(I) \iff$ $used\_itr(I) \lor I = i)$
$o = new\ Object()$	$\neg used\_obj(o) \land (\forall C.\ \neg member(C, o)) \land$ $(\forall O.\ used\_obj'(O) \iff used\_obj(O) \lor O = o)$

$\Sigma_\mathcal{P}$ is a second-order predicate of arity $|i_\mathcal{P} \cup o_\mathcal{P} \cup \mathcal{G} \cup \mathcal{G}'|$ that represents the behavior of $\mathcal{P}$ when reasoning about the behavior of procedures that call $\mathcal{P}$. It is used as a placeholder for a description of the behavior of $\mathcal{P}$.

The method body $\beta_\mathcal{P}$ expresses the behavior of the procedure body of $\mathcal{P}$ w.r.t. the behavior of callee procedures by referring to the second-order predicates $\Sigma_\mathcal{Q}$ for every procedure $\mathcal{Q}$ called from $\mathcal{P}$.

$\beta_\mathcal{P}$ is an EPR formula defined over a vocabulary that consists of the following:

- $\mathcal{G}, \mathcal{G}'$ which are used to represent the global state before and after the execution of procedure $\mathcal{P}$.
- Pairs of vocabularies $\mathcal{G}_{cs}, \mathcal{G}'_{cs}$ for every call site cs in $\mathcal{P}$, and the second-order predicate symbol Σ_Q for every procedure $\mathcal{Q}$ called by $\mathcal{P}$. In case of consecutive call sites cs_1, cs_2, the vocabularies $\mathcal{G}'_{cs_1}$ and $\mathcal{G}_{cs_2}$ will coincide.
- $i_\mathcal{P}$ which represents the formal parameters of $\mathcal{P}$, and $o_\mathcal{P}$ which represents the formal returns of $\mathcal{P}$.

The second-order predicates in $\beta_\mathcal{P}$ appear only positively and in the following form: let cs be a call-site in $\mathcal{P}$ that invokes $\mathcal{Q}$. In $\beta_\mathcal{P}$ this is expressed by $\Sigma_Q(i_{cs}, o_{cs}, \mathcal{G}_{cs}, \mathcal{G}'_{cs})$, where i_{cs} are the actual parameters of the call and o_{cs} are its actual returns, which are either constants $(i_\mathcal{P}, o_\mathcal{P})$ or quantified variables (typically existentially quantified which represent local variables of $\mathcal{P}$).

Recall that the body of $\mathcal{P}$ consists of sequential code. Hence, such a formulation is derived in a straightforward way.

```
main() {
        R(a) = true;
        S(b) = false;
        f(a, b);
        f(b, a);
}
```

Fig. 2. A small program with procedure calls

Example 2. Let us consider the example in Fig. 2. The program has two unary global relations R, S and an entry procedure *main*, that includes two local variables a and b. Procedure f, whose code is omitted, has two formal parameters and no formal returns. *main* procedure calls f twice, once with a serving as first argument and b as second, and then with b as first argument and a as second. The body of procedure *main* is given by the formula:

$$\beta_\mathcal{M} = \exists a, b.\ R'(a) \wedge \neg S'(b) \wedge \Sigma_f(\langle a, b \rangle, \emptyset, \langle R', S' \rangle, \langle R'', S'' \rangle) \wedge$$
$$\Sigma_f(\langle b, a \rangle, \emptyset, \langle R'', S'' \rangle, \langle R''', S''' \rangle)$$

Note, that $\beta_\mathcal{M}$ includes 4 lists of global variables: $\langle R, S \rangle$, $\langle R', S' \rangle$, $\langle R'', S'' \rangle$, $\langle R''', S''' \rangle$ (R, S are not constrained by this formula).

3.4   Verification Conditions

The accurate semantics of $\beta_\mathcal{P}$ has a least-fixed-point characterization as described in [13]. We omit the semantics definition and provide only the verification conditions for safety properties.

In order to allow verification of interprocedural programs we will use *procedure summaries*.

Procedure Summaries. The summary $\mathcal{S}_{\mathcal{P}}$ of a procedure $\mathcal{P}$ overapproximates the input/output relation of the procedure. In our setting, it is provided by a universal first-order formula over a vocabulary that consists of two copies of the global relations $\mathcal{G}$, $\mathcal{G}'$: one for the pre-state and one for the post-state, the formal arguments $i_{\mathcal{P}}$ and the formal returns $o_{\mathcal{P}}$.

Given the set of procedure summaries of a program $\mathcal{S}_{\Pi}$ we can now describe the behavior of procedure $\mathcal{P}$ w.r.t. the summaries $\mathcal{S}_{\Pi}$. Formally, let $\mathcal{S}_{\Pi}$ be a function mapping every procedure $\mathcal{Q}$ to a summary. When $\mathcal{S}_{\Pi}$ is clear from the context, we use $\mathcal{S}_{\mathcal{Q}}$ as a shorthand for $\mathcal{S}_{\Pi}(\mathcal{Q})$. Let $\mathcal{CS}$ be the set of all $(cs, \mathcal{Q})$ where cs is call-site in $\mathcal{P}$ that invokes $\mathcal{Q}$. Note that if $\mathcal{P}$ is recursive then $\mathcal{Q}$ might be $\mathcal{P}$ itself.

The behavior of $\mathcal{P}$ w.r.t. the summaries $\mathcal{S}_{\Pi}$ is obtained by replacing every predicate symbol $\Sigma_{\mathcal{Q}}$ in $\beta_{\mathcal{P}}$ with $\mathcal{S}_{\mathcal{Q}}$, applied over the vocabulary determined by the call-site. Formally, it is captured by the formula $\beta_{\mathcal{P}}(\mathcal{S}_{\Pi})$, defined as follows:

$$\beta_{\mathcal{P}}(\mathcal{S}_{\Pi}) = \beta_{\mathcal{P}}\Big[\mathcal{S}_{\mathcal{Q}}\big[(i_{cs}, o_{cs}, \mathcal{G}\ _{cs}, \mathcal{G}'_{cs})/(i_{\mathcal{Q}}, o_{\mathcal{Q}}, \mathcal{G}, \mathcal{G}')\big]$$

$$/\Sigma_{\mathcal{Q}}(i_{cs}, o_{cs}, \mathcal{G}\ _{cs}, \mathcal{G}'_{cs}) \mid (cs, \mathcal{Q}) \in \mathcal{CS}\Big]$$

Every satisfying model of $\beta_{\mathcal{P}}(\mathcal{S}_{\Pi})$ describes a pair of feasible input-output states of $\mathcal{P}$ when assuming that the semantics of every called procedure is its summary. It also describes the intermediate input-output states of every call-site. Formally, this is captured by the notion of a $\mathcal{P}$-*trace*, defined below.

$\mathcal{P}$-*Traces and* $\mathcal{P}$-*Transitions.* For a procedure $\mathcal{P}$, a $\mathcal{P}$-trace $\sigma_{\mathcal{P}}$ is a model over the signature of $\beta_{\mathcal{P}}$, excluding the second-order predicates. Note that $\sigma_{\mathcal{P}}$ includes interpretations to all the copies of the global relations in $\beta_{\mathcal{P}}$.

In contrast, a $\mathcal{P}$-*transition* is a structure over the vocabulary $i_{\mathcal{P}}, \mathcal{G}, o_{\mathcal{P}}, \mathcal{G}'$ that describes a pair of input-output states of $\mathcal{P}$. During the algorithm we extract transitions from traces in the following ways:

- Given a $\mathcal{P}$-trace $\sigma_{\mathcal{P}}$, we denote by $\sigma_{\mathcal{P}}(\mathcal{P})$ the $\mathcal{P}$-transition that is obtained from $\sigma_{\mathcal{P}}$ by dropping the interpretation of the call-site copies of $\mathcal{G}$.
- Given a $\mathcal{P}$-trace $\sigma_{\mathcal{P}}$, for every call-site $(cs, \mathcal{Q}) \in \mathcal{CS}$ of $\mathcal{P}$ we denote by $\sigma_{\mathcal{P}}(cs)$ the $\mathcal{Q}$-transition that is extracted from $\sigma_{\mathcal{P}}$ in the following way. $\sigma_{\mathcal{P}}(cs)$ is defined over the same domain as $\sigma_{\mathcal{P}}$ and it provides interpretation for $\mathcal{G}, \mathcal{G}'$ in the same way $\mathcal{G}\ _{cs}, \mathcal{G}'_{cs}$ are interpreted in $\sigma_{\mathcal{P}}$, and provides interpretation to $i_{\mathcal{Q}}, o_{\mathcal{Q}}$ as the interpretation of the actual parameters and returns of the call-site i_{cs}, o_{cs} in $\sigma_{\mathcal{P}}$. Intuitively this is a decomposition of the trace within $\mathcal{P}$ to a list of transitions, where each transition corresponds to a procedure call within the trace.

Verification Conditions. A safety property is provided by a $\forall^*\exists^*$-formula $Safe$ over $i_{\mathcal{M}}, \mathcal{G}, o_{\mathcal{M}}, \mathcal{G}'$ that specifies a requirement on the input-output relation of the *main* procedure (where $i_{\mathcal{M}}$ and $o_{\mathcal{M}}$ denote the input and output parameters of the *main* procedure, respectively). Note that for the CME problem, it suffices to require safety of *main* since code that is unreachable from *main* cannot cause an exception in run-time, and *cme* becoming true in some procedure manifests itself in the *main* procedure as well in our translation. Further, once *cme* becomes true, it remains true.

The verification conditions for safety properties are provided by the following lemma.

Lemma 1 (Verification conditions). *Let $\mathcal{A}$ be a program with a set of procedures Π and a main procedure $\mathcal{M}$, and let Safe be the safety property of $\mathcal{M}$. Let $\mathcal{S}_\Pi$ be a function mapping each procedure in Π to a summary. If it holds that $\forall \mathcal{P} \in \Pi.\ \beta_\mathcal{P}(\mathcal{S}_\Pi) \Rightarrow \mathcal{S}_\mathcal{P}$ and $\beta_\mathcal{M}(\mathcal{S}_\Pi) \Rightarrow$ Safe then the program is safe.*

The first condition in the lemma guarantees that the $\mathcal{S}_\Pi$ summaries are overapproximations of all the reachable behaviors of each procedure. The second condition establishes that *main* is safe w.r.t the summaries in $\mathcal{S}_\Pi$. Hence, the program is safe according to our definition of program safety.

Note that given that bodies $\beta_\mathcal{P}$ are EPR formulas and the safety property *Safe* is a $\forall^*\exists^*$ formula, then if the summaries $\mathcal{S}_\mathcal{P}$ are provided as universally quantified formulas, the verification conditions are EPR formulas. Namely, checking them amounts to checking unsatisfiability of EPR formulas and is hence decidable.

3.5   Illustrative Example

We illustrate the modeling and the use of procedure summaries for the flatten example from Fig. 1. We wish to prove that executing the *main* procedure does not lead to a CME. As explained, we do this in a modular way by constructing procedure summaries for the procedures transitively called from *main*, namely the *flatten* and *addList* procedures.

We start by discussing the *addList* procedure. This procedure does not lead to a CME as long as lst1 and lst2 are different lists. This can be expressed in the procedure summary by the following formula:

$$\forall I. \neg cme(I) \wedge lst1 \neq lst2 \rightarrow \neg cme'(I)$$

As for the *flatten* procedure, as discussed in Sect. 2, it does not lead to a CME as long as in and out point to different lists, and out is not a member of the in list. This can be expressed in the procedure summary by the following formula:

$$\forall I.\ cme(I) \wedge in \neq out \wedge \neg member\_cnt(in, out) \rightarrow \neg cme'(I)$$

Using additional formulas, it is possible to construct summaries for this example that satisfy the conditions of Lemma 1, and thus prove that the program is safe. The algorithm presented in Sect. 4 constructs such summaries.

4   Inference of Universally Quantified Procedure Summaries

In the previous section we defined the verification conditions using EPR formulas, based on procedure summaries sufficient to imply the safety property. In this section we tackle the problem of inferring such procedure summaries for a given program and safety property. To this end we develop a property-directed reachability algorithm that infers universally quantified procedure summaries in an interprocedural fashion.

The algorithm is based on UPDR [11] and interprocedural PDR algorithms [7,13]. Upon termination the algorithm returns either universal summaries of the procedures that are sufficient to prove the safety of the program, or a counterexample. Similarly to UPDR, a counterexample discovered by the algorithm is an *abstract* counterexample. This may correspond to a real, concrete counterexample, but it is also possible that the program is in fact safe. In the latter case the abstract counterexample is a proof that the safety of the program *cannot* be proved by universal procedure summaries, i.e. there is no approximation of each procedure's semantics by universal summaries that is accurate enough to establish the safety property. In our tool we attempt to distinguish between the cases using *bounded-model checking* in order to find a concrete counterexample that matches the abstract one. Note that termination of the algorithm is not guaranteed.

4.1   Definitions

We begin by defining the required notations to describe the algorithm. For the remainder of this section we fix a specific program $\langle \Pi, \mathcal{G} \rangle$ whose designated entry point is $\mathcal{M} \in \Pi$.

The algorithm maintains a sequence of frames $\mathcal{F}_0, \mathcal{F}_1, \ldots, \mathcal{F}_n$. Intuitively a frame $\mathcal{F}_i$ provides procedure summaries that constitute an overapproximation of the possible input-output relations of the procedures when the call-stack depth is bounded by i. The sequence is gradually modified and extended throughout the algorithm's run.

Technically, a *frame* $\mathcal{F}_i$ maps every procedure in Π to a summary of the procedure. Summaries themselves consist of a conjunction of universally quantified clauses, also referred to as *lemmas*. The following properties of the frame sequence are maintained by the algorithm: for all $0 \leq i < n$,

1. $\mathcal{F}_i(\mathcal{M}) \rightarrow Safe$
2. $\forall \mathcal{P} \in \Pi.\ \mathcal{F}_i(\mathcal{P}) \Rightarrow \mathcal{F}_{i+1}(\mathcal{P})$
3. $\forall \mathcal{P} \in \Pi.\ \beta_{\mathcal{P}}(\mathcal{F}_i) \Rightarrow \mathcal{F}_{i+1}(\mathcal{P})$

Intuitively, the first property means that $\mathcal{F}_i$ is sufficient to prove the safety property when the stack depth is bounded to i (for every frame except the last one, which the algorithm refines). The second property means that frames are monotonic (since increasing the allowed stack depth does not remove possible behaviors), and the third property means that the summary of a procedure in frame $\mathcal{F}_{i+1}$ encompasses at least the possible behaviors of the procedure when its callees behave according to the summaries in frame $\mathcal{F}_i$. These properties ensure that the summaries of every $\mathcal{F}_i$ indeed overapproximate the behavior when the stack depth is bounded to i. Note that if for some $i < n$ the implication of property 2 holds in the opposite direction as well, then $\mathcal{F}_i$ satisfies the requirements of Lemma 1 and hence the program is safe.

Generalization by Diagrams. The essence of UPDR and the key to obtaining universally quantified invariants is the way the algorithm generates more lemmas for strengthening the frames. This is based on the notion of a *diagram* [11], which provides a structural abstraction of transitions by an existential formulae.

Let $s = (\sigma_{in}, \sigma_{out})$ be a finite $\mathcal{P}$-transition. A diagram $\mathcal{D}(s)$ is an existential formula defined over the same vocabulary that describes the set of models that contain $(\sigma_{in}, \sigma_{out})$ as a substructure. Let $U = \{e_1, \ldots, , e_{|U|}\}$ be the universe of s. The diagram is defined [11] as

$$\mathcal{D}(\sigma_{in}, \sigma_{out}) = \exists x_{e_1}, \ldots, x_{e_{|U|}} . \varphi_{dist} \wedge \varphi_{const} \wedge \varphi_{rel}$$

where

- $x_{e_1}, \ldots, x_{e_{|U|}}$ are fresh variables,
- φ_{dist} is a conjunction of the inequalities $x_{e_i} \neq x_{e_j}$ for every $e_i \neq e_j \in U$,
- φ_{const} is a conjunction of the equalities $c = x_e$ for every constant symbol $c \in i_\mathcal{P} \cup o_\mathcal{P}$ and $e \in U$ whose interpretation in s is c,
- φ_{rel} is conjunction of atomic formulas $p(x_{e_{i_1}}, \ldots, x_{e_{i_a}})$ for every predicate symbol of arity a and elements $\bar{e} = e_{i_1}, \ldots, e_{i_a} \in U$ such that the interpretation of $p(\bar{e})$ in s is true, and $\neg p(x_{e_{i_1}}, \ldots, x_{e_{i_a}})$ if it is false.

The existentially quantified $x_{e_1}, \ldots, x_{e_{|U|}}$ represent elements that constitute a substructure isomorphic to s when x_{e_i} takes the role of e_i.

It should be noted that all the satisfiability checks performed by the algorithm are of EPR formulas, and since EPR enjoys the finite-model property [17], the structures used by the algorithm are indeed all finite.

4.2   Interprocedural UPDR

Algorithm 1 presents the algorithm as set of rules, following [7,13]. In addition to the frame sequence $\mathcal{F}_0, \mathcal{F}_1, \ldots, \mathcal{F}_n$, where n is the current frame index, the algorithm also maintains a queue of reachability queries $\mathcal{L}$. A reachability query c is a tuple $\langle i, \mathcal{P}, s \rangle$, where i is a frame index, $\mathcal{P}$ a procedure symbol, and s is a $\mathcal{P}$-transition. In addition, the algorithm holds a set $\mathcal{R}$ of queries that were found to be reachable. Initially, $\mathcal{L}$ and $\mathcal{R}$ are empty and $n = 0$. The first frame $\mathcal{F}_0$ is initialized to $\lambda \mathcal{Q}$. *false*, which expresses the idea that a stack depth of 0 does not allow any transition from pre-state to post-state to be made by $\mathcal{P}$.

The rules are applied, possibly in a non-deterministic order, until either the algorithm terminates with a proof of safety when the frame sequence converges, or the algorithm encounters a reachable bad transition of main and terminates with an abstract counterexample. In the latter case, bounded-model checking is performed as an attempt find a concrete counterexample matching the abstract one. As in UPDR, an abstract counterexample may rely on transitions to a sub-structure, here on a structure that describes a procedure's transition. Assuming that the abstract counterexample was found in frame i, the algorithm traverses the program call-graph until depth i and generates a formula that describes all the possible bounded executions that match the abstract counterexample call-tree. It then uses this formula to check whether a possible execution violates the safety property by performing a satisfiability check. If a concrete counterexample is found, it is reported. Otherwise, the abstract counterexample serves as a proof that no universal summary exists for this program although the program may still be safe.

Unfold opens a new frame with permissive procedure summaries, to be refined until the summaries of the frame are strong enough to exclude all the bad behaviors (although the summaries may not yet be inductive). While a bad transition is allowed by the summaries the algorithm attempts to strengthen the frame sequence to exclude that bad transition (**Candidate**), in a way that maintains the frame sequence invariants. This is done by placing the bad transition in the reachability query queue for further processing.

The next rules process reachability queries in the queue. **Strengthen** applies when the summaries of the previous frame are restrictive enough to exclude the possibility of a transition in question in the successive frame. In this case we intuitively learned that the transition is impossible for the bounded behavior of the procedure, and we strengthen the summaries of the procedure in the frame sequence with a new lemma that reflects it. To obtain a universal strengthening of the frames we try to exclude not just the concrete transition itself, but all the transitions in the diagram. This makes the strengthening process more powerful since it excludes more transitions, which must be excluded if universal summaries are to be used. To achieve convergence we further generalize the strengthening lemma by interpolation (using unsat cores).

Decide applies when the procedure summaries of the previous frame are insufficient to exclude the transition in question. In this case we attempt to (recursively) refine procedure summaries of the called procedures. This is done by analyzing a specific trace of the procedure that matches the query, and trying to exclude at least one of the transitions made by called procedures along this trace. To this end, the transitions of all the called procedures are added to the queue of reachability queries. Note that in this sense, the reachability queries unfold into a tree where each node represents a procedure call and a transition associated with it. Note further that if at least one of these transitions will turn out to be unreachable (in the corresponding frame) by **Strengthen**, then its frame will be refined, causing the trace of the caller to be unreachable as well. **Reachable-Base** and **Reachable-Ind** handle the case that none of the called procedures' transitions can be excluded, since they are all reachable and hence the transition of the caller is marked reachable.

Algorithm 1. Interprocedural UPDR algorithm

Input: Program $\langle \Pi, \mathcal{G} \rangle$ with main procedure $\mathcal{M} \in \Pi$ and safety property $Safe$
Output: $Safe$, $Not\ Safe$ (+ concrete counterexample) or
$\qquad\qquad No\ Universal\ Summaries$
Data:
  1. Current frame index $n \in \mathbb{N}$
  2. Sequence of frames $\mathcal{F}_0, \mathcal{F}_1, \ldots, \mathcal{F}_n$
  3. Reachability query queue $\mathcal{L} = \langle c_1, \ldots, c_k \rangle$, where $c_j = \langle i, \mathcal{P}, s \rangle$ is a
     reachability query with $i \leq n$, $\mathcal{P} \in \Pi$ and s a transition.
  4. Set of reachable transitions $\mathcal{R}$, which holds tuples of the form $\langle i, \mathcal{P}, s \rangle$ where
     $i \leq n$, $\mathcal{P} \in \Pi$ and s is a transition: a structure over $i_\mathcal{P}, \mathcal{G}, o_\mathcal{P}, \mathcal{G}'$.

Init: $n = 0$, $\mathcal{F}_0 = \lambda \mathcal{P}.\ false$, $\mathcal{L} = \emptyset$, $\mathcal{R} = \emptyset$.
while $true$ **do**

  Unreachable: If there exists an $i < n$ s.t. $\forall \mathcal{P} \in \Pi.\ \mathcal{F}_{i+1}(\mathcal{P}) \Rightarrow \mathcal{F}_i(\mathcal{P})$
  $\qquad\qquad\qquad$ return $Safe$.
  Reachable: If there exists a query $c = \langle n, \mathcal{M}, s \rangle \in \mathcal{L}$ s.t. $c \in \mathcal{R}$, perform
  $\qquad\qquad\qquad$ bounded model checking to find a concrete counterexample. If
  $\qquad\qquad\qquad$ found, return $Not\ Safe$. Else, return $No\ Universal\ Summaries$.
  Unfold: If $\beta_\mathcal{M}(\mathcal{F}_n) \Rightarrow Safe$ then set $\mathcal{F}_{n+1} := \lambda \mathcal{P}.\ true$, increment n to
  $\qquad\qquad n + 1$, and set $\mathcal{L} := \emptyset$.
  Candidate: If exists a $\mathcal{M}$-trace $\sigma_\mathcal{M}$ s.t. $\sigma_\mathcal{M} \models \beta_\mathcal{M}(\mathcal{F}_n) \wedge \neg Safe$, add
  $\qquad\qquad\qquad \langle n, \mathcal{M}, \sigma_\mathcal{M}(\mathcal{M}) \rangle$ to $\mathcal{L}$.
  Decide: If there exists a query $c = \langle i, \mathcal{P}, s \rangle \in \mathcal{L}$ with $i > 0$ and a $\mathcal{P}$-trace
  $\qquad\qquad \sigma_\mathcal{P}$ s.t. $\sigma_\mathcal{P} \models \beta_\mathcal{P}(\mathcal{F}_{i-1}) \wedge \mathcal{D}(s)$, add $\langle i - 1, \mathcal{Q}, \sigma_\mathcal{P}(cs) \rangle$ to $\mathcal{L}$ for
  $\qquad\qquad$ every $(cs, \mathcal{Q}) \in \mathcal{CS}$.
  Reachable-Base: If there exists a query $c = \langle 1, \mathcal{P}, s \rangle \in \mathcal{L}$ and a $\mathcal{P}$-trace $\sigma_\mathcal{P}$
  $\qquad\qquad\qquad\qquad$ such that $\sigma_\mathcal{P} \models \beta_\mathcal{P}(\mathcal{F}_0) \wedge \mathcal{D}(s)$, add c to $\mathcal{R}$.
  Reachable-Ind: If there exists a query $c = \langle i, \mathcal{P}, s \rangle \in \mathcal{L}$ with $i > 1$ and a
  $\qquad\qquad\qquad\quad \mathcal{P}$-trace $\sigma_\mathcal{P}$ s.t. $\sigma_\mathcal{P} \models \beta_\mathcal{P}(\mathcal{F}_{i-1}) \wedge \mathcal{D}(s)$, and
  $\qquad\qquad\qquad\quad \langle i - 1, \mathcal{Q}, \sigma_\mathcal{P}(cs) \rangle \in \mathcal{R}$ for every $(cs, \mathcal{Q}) \in \mathcal{CS}$, then add c
  $\qquad\qquad\qquad\quad$ to $\mathcal{R}$.
  Strengthen: If there exists a query $c = \langle i, \mathcal{P}, s \rangle \in \mathcal{L}$ with $i > 0$ s.t.
  $\qquad\qquad\qquad \beta_\mathcal{P}(\mathcal{F}_{i-1}) \Rightarrow \neg \mathcal{D}(s)$, then compute
  $\qquad\qquad\qquad \varphi = \text{UNSAT-CORE}(\beta_\mathcal{P}(\mathcal{F}_{i-1}), \mathcal{D}(s))$. Set
  $\qquad\qquad\qquad \mathcal{F}_j(\mathcal{P}) := \mathcal{F}_j(\mathcal{P}) \wedge \varphi$ for all $0 \leq j \leq i$.
  Push: If φ is a conjunct of $\mathcal{F}_{i-1}(\mathcal{P})$ and $\beta_\mathcal{P}(\mathcal{F}_{i-1}) \Rightarrow \varphi$ then set
  $\qquad\qquad \mathcal{F}_i(\mathcal{P}) := \mathcal{F}_i(\mathcal{P}) \wedge \varphi$.
  Reachability-Cache: If $\langle i, \mathcal{P}, s \rangle \in \mathcal{L}$ and $\langle j, \mathcal{P}, s_0 \rangle \in \mathcal{R}$ with $j \leq i$ and
  $\qquad\qquad\qquad\qquad\quad s \models \mathcal{D}(s_0)$, then add $\langle i, \mathcal{P}, s \rangle$ to $\mathcal{R}$.

end

The rest of the rules provide optimizations over the basic algorithm. **Push** attempts to push learned summary lemmas to the next frames when possible, in an attempt to achieve two equivalent frames as quickly as possible. **Reachability-Cache** attempts to avoid the need to go back in the frame sequence in order to understand that a transition is in fact reachable by reusing known reachable transitions. Note that since we are working with relaxed reachability it is sufficient to find a reachable transition in the diagram of the transition in question.

Lemma 2 (Correctness). *If the algorithm terminates with the result* Safe *then the safety property holds for the program. If the algorithm terminates with the result* Not Safe *then there is an execution of the program that violates the property. If the algorithm terminates with the result* No Universal Summaries *then there is no function S_P that maps every procedure to a universally quantified summary which satisfies the verification conditions of Lemma 1.*

5   Implementation and Experiments

We have implemented an interprocedural version of UPDR on top of the Ivy framework [16]. The framework is implemented in Python (2.7), and uses Z3 (4.4.2 32 bit) for satisfiability checking. We also implemented a front-end in Java, based on the Soot framework [21], that translates Java programs to Ivy's relational modeling language (RML). The experiments reported here were run on a machine with a 3.4 GHz Intel Core i7-4770 8-core, 32 GB of RAM, running Ubuntu 14.04.

The Soot-based front-end transforms Java programs to an intermediate language based on Ivy's RML. It splits every Java method to its basic blocks, and each basic block is transformed to a procedure that requires a summary, and can include calls to other procedures, including itself. For uniformity of implementation loops are effectively translated to tail recursions. A by-product of this is that the interprocedural analysis sees many procedures for every Java method, i.e., one for each basic block. In addition, due to our abstraction of the non-CME related operations, some of these procedures contain just a `skip` instruction, and their summary is trivial.

We evaluated our implementation on several Java programs that manipulate collections via iterators and are known to be safe. The test programs were inspired by code examples taken from [18] (*worklist, map_test*), an example (*flatten*) and a false alarm example (*sm*) taken from the tool in [15], and our own implementation (*div, c*). The *worklist* example contains a class that manipulates a list class field. The *div* example includes a method that divides a list recursively and inserts some of its items to an output list. The *map_test* example performs basic checks on a sorted map structure. The *c* test includes two iterators operating on the same collection when one is an alias to the other. The *flatten* example includes a class that performs a flattening of a list of lists structure.

For all programs, the analysis was able to prove the absence of CMEs. The results are summarized in Table 3. In addition, we intentionally inserted bugs to the code of *c* and *worklist* and our tool succeeded in detecting them.

To examine the effect of different code properties on our algorithm, we applied our tool on a few slightly different versions of a simple safe program. The *simple_loop* example has a single main method that iterates over a collection and

Table 3. Experimental results.

Program	#Lines	#Meth.	Time	#Sum. (#Tot)	Max F.	#Z3	Max sum.	D.	W.	N.
simple_loop	11	1	66	4(15)	7	706	7	0	1	1
call_outside_loop	17	2	89	8(20)	7	1507	12	0	1	1
call_in_loop	17	2	91	8(20)	13	1816	10	0	1	1
update_call_in_loop	18	2	142	8(20)	13	2726	17	1	1	1
call_depth2_in_loop	22	3	177	11(22)	15	3433	17	2	1	1
call_depth2	22	3	97	5(22)	14	1712	1	2	1	1
sm	53	6	514	8(27)	11	5263	14	1	2	1
div	27	2	291	7(22)	11	2767	15	rec	2	rec
worklist	26	5	577	8(26)	17	7475	41	3	2	1
map_test	40	3	306	10(24)	14	4753	16	1	1	1
c	18	3	33	8(18)	6	791	8	2	2	0
flatten	45	3	800	14(27)	18	10412	39	2	1	2
c_error	18	3	35	—	5	662	—	2	2	0
flatten_error	45	3	790	—	15	8746	—	2	1	2

#Lines denotes the number of code lines and **#Meth.** is the number of methods. **Time** is measured in seconds. **#Sum** is the number of non-trivial computed summaries, i.e. summaries that are not equivalent to true, while **#Tot** is the overall number of summaries. **Max F.** denotes the highest frame reached by the algorithm. **#Z3** represents the number of calls to Z3. **Max sum.** denotes the number of clauses in the largest obtained summary. **D.** denotes the maximal depth of the call-graph, where a collection update occurs (*main* method is treated as 0 depth). **W.** is the maximal number of calls to functions that update collections from a single method. **N.** is the maximal number of nested loops that contain updates. **rec** represents a recursive program.

updates it. The *call_outside_loop* and *call_in_loop* programs are similar, but also contain a method that has no effect on the collection, and is called outside of the iteration loop (*call_outside_loop*) or from within the loop (*call_in_loop*). The *update_call_in_loop* example calls a method that updates a collection from the loop body. *call_depth2_in_loop*, *call_depth2* perform the same updates as before, but wraps the update inside another method. The properties we checked in this test are the depth of collection updates (add/remove) in the call-graph and the loop nesting depth of the updates. The results show that both properties have a major effect on the running times, frame number and number of Z3 calls.

The results indicate that the main factor affecting the run-time of the analysis is not the code length, but rather the location of collection updates in the call-graph. When the call-graph is deeper, the generated summaries are usually larger, more calls to Z3 are preformed, and run-time grows. Methods that do not manipulate collections do not appear to affect the size of the summaries. Thus, we expect that our method can be applied to large programs, with reasonably shallow update depth, width and nesting. We also expect that an additional engineering effort can significantly reduce the run-time of the analysis, as we regard our implementation as a proof-of-concept rather than an optimized implementation.

6   Related Work

Property Directed Reachabilty. The IC3/PDR algorithm [2,5] has led to many successful applications both in software and in hardware verification. More recently, UPDR (Universal PDR) [11] introduced the idea of using diagrams as a way to lift PDR to infinite state systems. Our work builds on these works, and can be seen as an application of UPDR to infer universally quantified procedure summaries rather then loop invariants.

Interprocedural Analysis. Interprocedural analysis [19,20] is an important theme for verification and program analysis. Following the introduction of the IC3/PDR algorithm, [7,12,13] developed a way to apply it to interprocedural analysis. The main idea, which we also apply in this work, is to infer procedure summaries in the same way PDR infers loop invariants. While this line of works has been applied in the context of various array theories and arithmetic, our work is the first to apply it using EPR, inferring universal summaries by using diagrams.

Modeling with Decidable Logics. While any logic that fully describes computer programs is undecidable, there have been many attempts to identify decidable logic fragments that are still useful for analyzing programs. Decidability has the potential to make program verification tools more predictable and useful. The array property fragment [3] and its variants are often used to analyze programs that use arrays and perform simple arithmetic. Logics such as Mona [6], Strand [14] and EPR [8,9] have been used to model heap manipulating programs. In this context, our work is using the EPR logic, and identifies a new problem domain for which it can be useful: proving the absence of concurrent modification errors in Java programs. Extending the range of applicability of decidable logics is an ongoing research effort, and our work can be seen as another step in this process.

Concurrent Modification Errors and Analyzing Java Programs. Several static analyses have been developed to detect possible Concurrent Modification Exceptions in Java programs, as well as violations of other typestate properties involving multiple objects. [1] presented a flow-sensitive typestate analysis based on an intraprocedural must-alias analysis that can rule out CME violations if the collection is created, iterated over, and modified only within a single procedure. [15] evaluated an interprocedural context-sensitive analysis of aliasing and multi-object typestate that can rule out CME violations, but does not reason precisely about objects that escape to the heap and are no longer directly referenced by any local variable. [10] presented a specification language for describing properties such as CME violations and a pragmatic static verifier that is neither sound nor complete, but effective in practice.

Acknowledgments. We would like to thank Nikolaj Bjørner, Roman Manevich and Eran Yahav for their helpful discussions, and the Programming Languages team in TAU for their support and feedback on the paper. The research leading to these results has received funding from the European Research Council under the European Union's Seventh Framework Programme (FP7/2007-2013)/ERC grant agreement no [321174].

References

1. Bodden, E., Lam, P., Hendren, L.J.: Finding programming errors earlier by evaluating runtime monitors ahead-of-time. In: Proceedings of the 16th ACM SIGSOFT International Symposium on Foundations of Software Engineering, Atlanta, Georgia, USA, 9–14 November 2008, pp. 36–47 (2008)
2. Bradley, A.R.: SAT-based model checking without unrolling. In: Jhala, R., Schmidt, D. (eds.) VMCAI 2011. LNCS, vol. 6538, pp. 70–87. Springer, Berlin (2011). doi:10.1007/978-3-642-18275-4_7
3. Bradley, A.R., Manna, Z., Sipma, H.B.: What's decidable about arrays? In: Emerson, E.A., Namjoshi, K.S. (eds.) VMCAI 2006. LNCS, vol. 3855, pp. 427–442. Springer, Berlin (2005). doi:10.1007/11609773_28
4. de Moura, L., Bjørner, N.: Z3: an efficient SMT solver. In: Ramakrishnan, C.R., Rehof, J. (eds.) TACAS 2008. LNCS, vol. 4963, pp. 337–340. Springer, Berlin, Heidelberg (2008). doi:10.1007/978-3-540-78800-3_24
5. Eén, N., Mishchenko, A., Brayton, R.K.: Efficient implementation of property directed reachability. In: Bjesse, P., Slobodová, A. (eds.) International Conference on Formal Methods in Computer-Aided Design, FMCAD 2011, Austin, TX, USA, 30 October–02 November 2011, pp. 125–134. FMCAD Inc. (2011)
6. Henriksen, J.G., Jensen, J., Jørgensen, M., Klarlund, N., Paige, R., Rauhe, T., Sandholm, A.: Mona: Monadic second-order logic in practice. In: Brinksma, E., Cleaveland, W.R., Larsen, K.G., Margaria, T., Steffen, B. (eds.) TACAS 1995. LNCS, vol. 1019, pp. 89–110. Springer, Heidelberg (1995). doi:10.1007/3-540-60630-0_5
7. Hoder, K., Bjørner, N.: Generalized property directed reachability. In: Cimatti, A., Sebastiani, R. (eds.) SAT 2012. LNCS, vol. 7317, pp. 157–171. Springer, Berlin (2012). doi:10.1007/978-3-642-31612-8_13
8. Itzhaky, S., Banerjee, A., Immerman, N., Lahav, O., Nanevski, A., Sagiv, M.: Modular reasoning about heap paths via effectively propositional formulas. In: Proceedings of the 41st Annual ACM SIGPLAN-SIGACT Symposium on Principles of Programming Languages, POPL, pp. 385–396 (2014)
9. Itzhaky, S., Banerjee, A., Immerman, N., Nanevski, A., Sagiv, M.: Effectively propositional reasoning about reachability in linked data structures. In: Sharygina, N., Veith, H. (eds.) CAV 2013. LNCS, vol. 8044, pp. 756–772. Springer, Heidelberg (2013). doi:10.1007/978-3-642-39799-8_53
10. Jaspan, C., Aldrich, J.: Checking framework interactions with relationships. In: Drossopoulou, S. (ed.) ECOOP 2009. LNCS, vol. 5653, pp. 27–51. Springer, Heidelberg (2009). doi:10.1007/978-3-642-03013-0_3

11. Karbyshev, A., Bjørner, N., Itzhaky, S., Rinetzky, N., Shoham, S.: Property-directed inference of universal invariants or proving their absence. In: Kroening, D., Păsăreanu, C.S. (eds.) CAV 2015. LNCS, vol. 9206, pp. 583–602. Springer, Heidelberg (2015). doi:10.1007/978-3-319-21690-4_40

12. Komuravelli, A., Bjørner, N., Gurfinkel, A., McMillan, K.L.: Compositional verification of procedural programs using horn clauses over integers and arrays. In: Kaivola, R., Wahl, T. (eds.) Formal Methods in Computer-Aided Design, FMCAD 2015, Austin, Texas, USA, 27–30 September 2015, pp. 89–96. IEEE (2015)

13. Komuravelli, A., Gurfinkel, A., Chaki, S.: SMT-based model checking for recursive programs. Formal Methods Syst. Des. **48**(3), 175–205 (2016)

14. Madhusudan, P., Qiu, X.: Efficient decision procedures for heaps using STRAND. In: Yahav, E. (ed.) SAS 2011. LNCS, vol. 6887, pp. 43–59. Springer, Heidelberg (2011). doi:10.1007/978-3-642-23702-7_8

15. Naeem, N.A., Lhoták, O.: Typestate-like analysis of multiple interacting objects. In: Proceedings of the 23rd Annual ACM SIGPLAN Conference on Object-Oriented Programming, Systems, Languages, and Applications, OOPSLA 2008, Nashville, TN, USA, 19–23 October 2008, pp. 347–366 (2008)

16. Padon, O., McMillan, K.L., Panda, A., Sagiv, M., Shoham, S.: Ivy: safety verification by interactive generalization. In: Proceedings of the 37th ACM SIGPLAN Conference on Programming Language Design and Implementation, PLDI 2016, Santa Barbara, CA, USA, 13–17 June 2016, pp. 614–630 (2016)

17. Piskac, R., de Moura, L.M., Bjørner, N.: Deciding effectively propositional logic using DPLL and substitution sets. J. Autom. Reasoning **44**(4), 401–424 (2010)

18. Ramalingam, G., Warshavsky, A., Field, J., Goyal, D., Sagiv, M.: Deriving specialized program analyses for certifying component-client conformance. In: Proceedings of the 2002 ACM SIGPLAN Conference on Programming Language Design and Implementation (PLDI), Berlin, Germany, 17–19 June 2002, pp. 83–94 (2002)

19. Reps, T.W., Horwitz, S., Sagiv, M.: Precise interprocedural dataflow analysis via graph reachability. In: Cytron, R.K., Lee, P. (eds.) Conference Record of POPL 1995: 22nd ACM SIGPLAN-SIGACT Symposium on Principles of Programming Languages, San Francisco, California, USA, 23–25 January 1995, pp. 49–61. ACM Press (1995)

20. Sharir, M., Pnueli, A.: Two approaches to interprocedural data flow analysis, In: Program Flow Analysis: Theory and Applications, pp. 189–234. Prentice-Hall, Englewood Cliffs (1981). Chap. 7

21. Vallée-Rai, R., Co, P., Gagnon, E., Hendren, L.J., Lam, P., Sundaresan, V.: Soot - a java bytecode optimization framework. In: Proceedings of the 1999 Conference of the Centre for Advanced Studies on Collaborative Research, Mississauga, Ontario, Canada, 8–11 November 1999, p. 13 (1999)

22. Yahav, E., Ramalingam, G.: Verifying safety properties using separation and heterogeneous abstractions. In: Proceedings of the ACM SIGPLAN 2004 Conference on Programming Language Design and Implementation 2004, Washington, DC, USA, 9–11 June 2004, pp. 25–34 (2004)

Stabilizing Floating-Point Programs Using Provenance Analysis

Yijia Gu$^{(\boxtimes)}$ and Thomas Wahl

College of Computer and Information Science, Boston, USA
{guyijia,wahl}@ccs.neu.edu

Abstract. Floating-point arithmetic is a loosely standardized approximation of real arithmetic available on many computers today. Architectural and compiler differences can lead to diverse calculations across platforms, for the same input. If left untreated, platform dependence, called *volatility* in this paper, seriously interferes with result reproducibility and, ultimately, program portability. We present an approach to *stabilizing* floating-point programs against volatility. Our approach, dubbed *provenance analysis*, traces volatility observed in a given intermediate expression E back to volatility in preceding statements, and quantifies individual contributions to the volatility in E. Statements contributing the most are then stabilized, by disambiguating the arithmetic using expression rewriting and control pragmas. The benefit of *local* (as opposed to program-wide) stabilization is that compilers are free to engage performance- or precision-enhancing optimizations across program fragments that do not destabilize E. We have implemented our technique in a dynamic analysis tool that reports both volatility and provenance information. We demonstrate that local program stabilization often suffices to reduce platform dependence to an acceptable level.

1 Introduction

Floating-point arithmetic (FPA) is a loosely standardized approximation of real arithmetic available on many computers today. The use of approximation incurs commonly underestimated risks for the reliability of embedded software. One root cause for these risks is the relatively large degree of freedom maintained in the most widely adopted FPA standardization, IEEE 754 [1]: the freedom for hardware vendors to offer specialized instructions for operations with increased precision (such as *fused multiply-add* [FMA]), and the freedom for compilers to reorder complex calculations more or less at will.

The price we pay for these freedoms is reduced reproducibility of results, especially for software that is run on diverse, possibly heterogeneous hardware. For example, distributing a computation across nodes in a cluster may rearrange the code in ways that produce results very different from what was observed in the comfort of the office PC environment. This platform dependence of results,

---

Work supported by US National Science Foundation grant no. CCF-1253331.

A. Bouajjani and D. Monniaux (Eds.): VMCAI 2017, LNCS 10145, pp. 228–245, 2017.
DOI: 10.1007/978-3-319-52234-0_13

called *volatility* in this paper, translates de facto into non-portability and, ultimately, inferior reliability. Examples of *discrete* program behaviors that may be affected, for certain inputs, when moving from one platform to another include the program's control flow, and invariants that hold on some platforms but not others [8,14,16]. Problems of this nature are hard to detect using traditional testing, as most developers cannot afford to run their programs on a multitude of platforms and compare the results.

In this paper we present an approach to identifying such problems *without* the need to run the given program on diverse platforms. Our approach employs a dynamic analysis that executes the program on inputs of interest, such as from a given test suite. For each input I and each intermediate program expression E, we compute a (tight) interval, called the *volatile bound*, such that the value of E on input I is guaranteed to be contained in that interval, *no matter how the program is compiled* on the path to E, subject only to IEEE 754 compliance of the platform. The volatile bound interval is computed via an abstract domain that takes any possible expression evaluation order into account, as well as the possibility of FMA contraction, for every expression on the path to E (not only for E itself). Our analysis technique issues a warning when the observed volatility becomes critical, for example when E is of the form c < 0 and 0 is inside the volatile bound for c: this means the comparison is *unstable* for the given input—the subsequent control flow depends on the execution platform.

Our technique then goes a significant step further and proposes ways to fix this instability. A naive way is to "determinize" the compilation of the entire program, using compiler flags that enforce "strict evaluation", such as /fp:strict for Visual Studio C++. This unfortunately destroys optimizations that compilers can apply to harmless (stable) fragments of the code; it may thus needlessly reduce a program's precision and efficiency [5]. We propose a more fine-grained approach that aims to stabilize only *some* evaluation aspects, of *some* statements S that contribute *most* to the instability in the target expression E. We call the information of what these statements are the *provenance* of E's instability. Provenance information also includes what kinds of ambiguities in S's evaluation are responsible for E's instability, i.e. evaluation order or the potential for FMA application. This allows very fine-grained, local code stabilization, after which the user can repeat the analysis, to determine whether the critical instability in E has disappeared.

We have implemented our technique in a library called ifloat. Given a program and a test suite, the goal of the library is to stabilize the program against expression volatility, for all inputs, using provenance analysis. It is immaterial on what platform the analysis itself is executed. We conclude the paper with experiments that illustrate on a number of benchmarks how the volatility of critical expressions diminishes as local stabilization measures are applied. We demonstrate the high precision of our (necessarily approximate) analysis compared to an idealistic but unrealistic one that compiles and runs the program twice—with and without stabilization measures.

2   A Motivating Example

We use the C program fragment shown in Listing 1.1 as an example to illustrate our approach. The code is used in *Ray Tracing* applications[1] in computational geometry. Consider the input

$$
\begin{aligned}
&\texttt{r} = \{-10.4194345474, -15, -14\}, \quad \texttt{radiusSq} = 0.015625 \\
&\texttt{s} = \{-10.998046875, -16, -15\} \, .
\end{aligned}
\tag{1}
$$

to function raySphere. On this input, the program takes different execution paths on an Nvidia GPU and on an Intel CPU. The cause for this unwelcome divergence is a difference in the calculations that propagate to the conditional if (D > 0): the value computed for D in the GPU is −0.11892647 (the branch is skipped), while on the CPU it is 0.14415550 (the branch is taken). Depending on what happens in the branch, the behavioral differences of this program on the two platforms can now have unlimited consequences.

```
float dot3(float *a, float *b) {
  return a[0]*b[0] + a[1]*b[1] +
    a[2]*b[2]; }

int raySphere(float *r, float *s,
    float radiusSq) {
  float A, B, C, D;
  A = dot3(r,r);
  B = -2.0 * dot3(s,r);
  C = dot3(s,s) - radiusSq;
  D = B*B - 4*A*C;
  if (D > 0)
    ...; }
```

Listing 1.1. Ray Tracing

```
ifloat dot3(ifloat *a, ifloat *b) {
  return a[0]*b[0] + a[1]*b[1] +
    a[2]*b[2]; }

int raySphere(ifloat *r, ifloat *s,
    ifloat radiusSq) {
  ifloat A, B, C, D;
  A = dot3(r,r);                 // 11
  B = -2.0 * dot3(s,r);          // 12
  C = dot3(s,s) - radiusSq;      // 13
  D = B*B - 4*A*C;               // 14
  if (D > 0)
    ...; }
```

Listing 1.2. Ray Tracing with ifloat

The numeric instability eventually leading to the decision divergence is due to the presence (GPU) or absence (CPU) of FMA hardware instructions on the two processors. FMA is a contraction of floating-point multiplication and addition in expressions of the form a * b + c, so that the multiplication is in effect performed without intermediate rounding. Such expressions come up in Listing 1.1 in function dot3 and in the expression defining D.

To analyze and debug the Ray Tracing program for instability issues using our library, we first change all float types in the program to ifloat. To enable our tool to identify the root cause of the divergence, we add comment labels to each statement in the raySphere function that we wish to include in the analysis. The program after these transformations is shown in Listing 1.2.

Compiling and running the transformed program outputs a *volatile bound* of [−0.252806664, 0.156753913] for D. This interval overapproximates the set of

---

[1] http://www.cc.gatech.edu/~phlosoft/photon/.

values any IEEE 754-compliant compiler/hardware combination can possibly produce, for input (1). Due to the size of this interval, and the looming D > 0 branch, our `ifloat` library generates a warning to tell users that the code may have instability (platform dependency) problems.

To fix the instability problem, one could now simply "determinize" the floating-point compilation of the program. This can be achieved using strict-evaluation compiler flags, such as `/fp:strict` in Visual Studio C++, which typically disable FMA and force a specific evaluation order for chained operations. However, there is of course a trade-off between reproducibility on the one hand, and platform-specific precision and performance on the other: program-wide code determinization prevents optimizations that compilers could otherwise apply to harmless (stable) fragments of the code; they may thus needlessly reduce a program's precision and efficiency [5]. Instead, we propose a more fine-grained approach that only fixes *some* evaluation aspects of *select* statements, namely those that affect the comparison, or any other user-provided critical expression. At the end of this section we show, using the Ray Tracing program, how to achieve statement-level fixation in C++.

But how do we determine which statements to stabilize? Identifying those merely based on the volatile bounds of the expressions computed in them is insufficient. To see this, we list in Table 1 the volatile bounds of the intermediate variables on the path to the computation of D. The size of D's volatile bound clearly dominates that for the other variables, suggesting that we should fix the evaluation of the expression for D itself. However, turning off FMA and forcing left-to-right evaluation for the assignment to D results in a volatile bound of $[-0.250000000, 0.125000000]$, nearly unchanged from the bound before stabilization. The new bound clearly still permits diverging control flows.

Table 1. Volatile bounds of intermediate variables

Variable	Volatile bound		Strict value
A	(601.957031250,	601.957031250)	601.957031250
B	(−1129.186889648,	−1129.186767578)	−1129.186889648
C	(529.548950195,	529.549011230)	529.548950195
D	(−0.252806664,	0.156753913)	0.125000000

Instead, our analysis of the transformed program produces information on the *provenance* of the instability of D's value, i.e., for each preceding statement, a measure of how much its instability contributes to that of D. In addition, we output the reason of the instability in each statement, to guide the programmer as to what aspect of the evaluation to fix. This output is shown in Table 2.

Consider a pair of the form (L, U) in the "Provenance for D" column in the row for label `li`. The left component L ("lower") specifies by how much the left boundary of the volatile bound interval for D shifts, due to the numeric instability in the computation at li (analogously for U ["upper"]). That is, a negative value for L indicates that the volatile bound interval expands (to the left). We see that statement 12 contributes most to the expansion of D's volatile bound to the left.

Table 2. Provenance information for D and reason for instability contribution

Stmt. label	Provenance for D	Reason
11	(0.000000000, 0.000000000)	null
12	(−0.275680393, 0.000000000)	FMA
13	(−0.146962166, 0.000000000)	order
14	(−0.002806664, 0.031753913)	FMA+order

The instability in 12 is due to use or non-use of FMA; ordering uncertainty has no effect at all, for input (1). After disabling FMA *only* for the statement labeled 12 (details of how to do this at the end of this section), our analysis results in a new volatile bound for D of $[-0.002806663, 0.156753913]$; the corresponding provenance information is shown in Table 3.

Table 3. Provenance information for the calculation of D after partial stabilization

Stmt. label	Provenance for D	Reason
11	(0.000000000, 0.000000000)	null
12	(0.000000000, 0.000000000)	null
13	(−0.146962166, 0.000000000)	order
14	(−0.002806664, 0.031753913)	FMA+order

From this bound we conclude that the comparison D > 0 still suffers from instability (which is now, however, less likely to materialize in practice). To further increase the lower bound of D, we force left-to-right evaluation order for 13. The volatile bound for D becomes $[0.125000000, 0.156753913]$, making the comparison stable and consistent with strict evaluation. The stabilized version of the Ray Tracing program is shown in Listing 1.3 (differences in red).

```
float dot3(float *a, float *b) {
  return a[0]*b[0] + a[1]*b[1] + a[2]*b[2]; }

int raySphere(float *r, float *s, float radiusSq) {
  float A, B, C, D;
  A = dot3(r,r);
  {
    #pragma STDC FP_CONTRACT off
    B = -2.0 * (s[0] * r[0] + s[1] * r[1] + s[2] * r[2]);
  }
  C =((s[0]*s[0] + s[1]*s[1]) + s[2]*s[2]) - radiusSq;
  D = B*B - 4*A*C;
  if (D > 0)
    ...; }
```

Listing 1.3. Stable version of Ray Tracing, obtained using compiler pragmas and parentheses (dot3 partially inlined)

In practice, little is gained by stabilizing a numeric computation for a single input. Instead, in our experiments we determine provenance information embedded into a dynamic analysis tool on a test suite that comes with the given program. Given a critical target expression E, our tool determines which preceding statement causes the greatest expansion of E's volatile bound, maximized across all inputs. The identified cause of volatility for that statement is then lifted. The analysis repeats until an acceptable level of stability is achieved. In the technical part of this paper (Sects. 4, 5, 6 and 7) we describe details of our provenance analysis for a given input. The application of this analysis across a test suite is discussed in Sect. 8.

3   Background: Volatility in Floating-Point Arithmetic

We use standard symbols like $+$ and $*$ for real-arithmetic operators, and circled symbols like $\oplus$ and $\otimes$ for floating-point operators. The latter are defined by the IEEE 754 standard [1, "the Standard" in this paper], for instance floating-point addition as $x \oplus y = rd(x + y)$, where rd is the rounding function (often refered to as *rounding mode*). The Standard postulates five such functions, all of which satisfy the following **monotonicity property**:

$$\forall x, y \in \mathbb{R}: \ x \leq y \implies rd(x) \leq rd(y) \ . \tag{2}$$

Unlike binary operations, floating-point *expressions*, which feature chains of operations as in $x \oplus y \oplus z$, do not come with a guarantee of reproducibility: compilers have the freedom to evaluate such expressions in any order. It is well known that $(x \oplus y) \oplus z$ and $x \oplus (y \oplus z)$ can return different results, e.g. due to an effect known as *absorption* when x is much larger than y and z. As a result, floating-point addition lacks associativity, as does multiplication.

Other sources of non-reproducibility are differences in the available floating-point hardware. The most prominent example is the *fused multiply-add* (FMA) operation, defined by $fma(a, b, c) = (a * b) \oplus c$. That is, the two operations are performed as if the intermediate multiplication result was not rounded at all. Not all architectures provide this operation; if they do, there is no mandate for the compiler to compute $a \otimes b \oplus c$ via FMA. Worse, expressions like $a \otimes b \oplus c \otimes d$ permit multiple ways of applying FMA.

Definitions and notation. Expressions that suffer from ambiguities due to reordering of $\oplus$ and $\otimes$ expressions and due to (non-)use of FMA are called *volatile* in this paper [14]. Formally, these are parenthesis-free expressions of the form

$$x_{11} \otimes x_{12} \ldots \otimes x_{1n} \oplus \ldots \oplus x_{m1} \otimes x_{m2} \ldots \otimes x_{mn} \ ,$$

which includes chains of addition, chains of multiplication, and dot products.

"Platform parameters" refers to compiler and hardware parameters, namely the availability of FMA, and collectively the decisions made by the compiler about expression evaluation. We refer to an instantiation of such parameters as an *expression evaluation model* M. We denote by $\Psi(I, M)$ the value of (volatile) expression Ψ on input I and expression evaluation model M. A volatile expression Ψ is *stable on input* I if, for all evaluation models M_1, M_2, we have $\Psi(I, M_1) = \Psi(I, M_2)$.

Relevant for the goal of stabilization in this paper is the *strict* expression evaluation model M_{str}, defined as the model that disables FMA support and evaluates sums and products from left to right. Enforcing this model is supported on many compiler platforms, such as using the /fp:strict flag in Visual Studio C++. Finally, as this paper is about numeric reproducibility, we treat the occurrence of special floating-point data like NaN or $\pm\infty$ as a failure and abort.

4   Provenance of Volatility: Overview

A volatile expression Ψ can be evaluated under a number of different evaluation models M. In general, this in turn can give rise to as many different results, for a fixed input I. One way to capture these results $\Psi(I, M)$ is using an interval:

Definition 1. *Given volatile expression Ψ and input I, the **volatile bound** $[\downarrow\Psi(I), \uparrow\Psi(I)]$ is the interval defined by*

$$\downarrow\Psi(I) = \min_M \Psi(I, M) , \quad \uparrow\Psi(I) = \max_M \Psi(I, M) . \tag{3}$$

The size of the volatile bound characterizes the volatility of Ψ for input I: the larger the bound, the more volatile Ψ. We extend the above definition to input intervals $\mathbb{I}$ over floating-point numbers: $[\downarrow\Psi(\mathbb{I}), \uparrow\Psi(\mathbb{I})]$ is the interval defined by

$$\downarrow\Psi(\mathbb{I}) = \min_{I\in\mathbb{I}} \min_M \Psi(I, M) , \quad \uparrow\Psi(\mathbb{I}) = \max_{I\in\mathbb{I}} \max_M \Psi(I, M) . \tag{4}$$

However, with this definition the size of the bound no longer characterizes the volatility of the expression. For example, given assignment statement $r = x \oplus y$, if the input intervals for x and y are large, the resulting bound for r will also be large, but only due to the uncertainty in inputs, not different evaluation models.

To be able to distinguish input uncertainty from evaluation uncertainty, we introduce the concept of *volatile error*, which measures the difference between an arbitrary evaluation model and the *strict* evaluation model M_{str} (Sect. 3):

Definition 2. *The **volatile error** of Ψ on input I is the pair $(\underline{e}, \bar{e})$ with*

$$\underline{e} = \min_M \Psi(I, M) - \Psi(I, M_{str}) , \quad \bar{e} = \max_M \Psi(I, M) - \Psi(I, M_{str}) . \tag{5}$$

Values $\underline{e}$ and $\bar{e}$ represent the "drift" of Ψ on input I, relative to $\Psi(I, M_{str})$, to the left and right due to different evaluations: we have $\underline{e} \leq 0 \leq \bar{e}$; an expression's value is platform-independent iff $\underline{e} = \bar{e} = 0$.

Definition 2 lends itself to being extended to the case of input intervals $\mathbb{I}$: in this case, the volatile error of Ψ is the pair $(\underline{e}, \bar{e})$ with

$$\begin{aligned} \underline{e} &= \min_{I\in\mathbb{I}} \min_M \Psi(I, M) - \min_{I\in\mathbb{I}} \Psi(I, M_{str}) , \\ \bar{e} &= \max_{I\in\mathbb{I}} \max_M \Psi(I, M) - \max_{I\in\mathbb{I}} \Psi(I, M_{str}) \end{aligned} \tag{6}$$

The pair $(\underline{e}, \bar{e})$ represents the enlargement of the volatile bound purely due to evaluation uncertainties. For instance, for $\Psi := x \oplus y$, we indeed have $\underline{e} = \bar{e} = 0$.

As we have seen in Sect. 2, knowing the volatile error for a single expression is not enough. We are also interested in the provenance (origin) of volatility in some variable v at some program point: it denotes the expansion of the volatile bound for v due to the volatility in some preceding source expression S. It is thus a measure of the amount of "blame" to be assigned to S. Formally:

Definition 3. *Let v be a variable at some program point, and S be an expression. Let $[l, r]$ be v's volatile bound at that point, and $[\bar{l}, \bar{r}]$ be v's volatile bound at the same point but in a modified program where expression S has been stabilized to be computed under the strict evaluation model M_{str}. The* **provenance pair** *(Δ_l, Δ_r) for v and S is given by $\Delta_l = l - \bar{l}$, $\Delta_r = r - \bar{r}$.*

For example, when $\Delta_l < 0$, then the volatility in S causes v's left volatile bound to shift to the left—the bound interval expands. Likewise, when $\Delta_r > 0$, the volatility in S causes v's right volatile bound to shift to the right—the bound again expands. When $(\Delta_l, \Delta_r) = (0, 0)$, the volatility in S has no influence on v. This can be the case for example because S is not volatile, or is stable for the given input, or is not on any control path that reaches v's program point.

Precisely computing the provenance pair for a target variable v and a source expression S is expensive: applying Definition 3 would require the computation of volatile bounds from scratch as many times as we have volatile source expressions S. Since our goal is to employ our analysis at runtime (where small overhead is paramount), our method instead computes the necessary information in a linear sweep over the program. The price we pay is that we only compute an approximation (Δ'_l, Δ'_r), as described in the rest of this paper. The approximation has properties similar to those of (Δ_l, Δ_r): larger values $|\Delta'_l|$ and Δ'_r indicate heavier influence of S's volatility on v and hence suggest which source expression to stabilize first.

If the source expressions S_i on the path to the program point of v share program variables, stabilizing one of them generally affects the volatility contribution of the others. Our technique therefore proceeds in rounds, as illustrated in Sect. 2: after stabilizing one source expression, we recompute the (approximate) provenance pairs for v and all S_i from scratch, and repeat the ranking and statement stabilization process. For target variables v that are used in branches, assertions or other *decisions*, a natural point to stop is when the decision has become stable, i.e. platform independent, for all inputs. For other target variables, e.g. in branch-free programs, more heuristic stoppage criteria can be used; we discuss these further in our experiments in Sect. 8.

5   An Abstract Domain for Tracking Volatility

Similar in spirit to earlier work that tracks precision loss in a floating-point program relative to a real-arithmetic calculation [11,15], we use *affine arithmetic* to abstractly represent floating-point values under platform uncertainty. The abstract values are affine-linear combinations of real numbers tagged with symbolic variables that label these real numbers as various "error contributions". Formally, the *provenance form* is a term

$$p = d + \sum_{l \in \mathcal{L}} e_l \cdot \eta_l + e_* \cdot \eta_* \tag{7}$$

where d, e_l, and e_* are real numbers, $\mathcal{L}$ is the set of program statement labels, and η_l and η_* are symbolic variables indicating reordering errors contributed by the statement at label l and *higher-order* error (combinations of different error terms after propagation), respectively. Value d represents the value of p under strict evaluation and incorporates rounding errors but not reordering uncertainty. We also define the real-valued *projection* of provenance form p as $\pi(p) = d + \sum_{l \in \mathcal{L}} e_l + e_*$. The abstract values form a lattice via the provenance ordering defined as $p^i < p^j \Leftrightarrow \pi(p^i) < \pi(p^j)$. Binary arithmetic operations on forms p^i, p^j are defined as

$$p^i \pm p^j = (d^i \pm d^j) + \sum_{l \in \mathcal{L}} (e_l^i \pm e_l^j) \cdot \eta_l + (e_*^i \pm e_*^j) \cdot \eta_* \tag{8}$$

$$p^i * p^j = (d^i * d^j) + \sum_{l \in \mathcal{L}} (e_l^i * d^j + e_l^j * d^i) \cdot \eta_l + \left(\sum_{l_1, l_2 \in \mathcal{L} \cup \{*\}} e_{l_1}^i * e_{l_2}^j \right) \cdot \eta_* \tag{9}$$

The multiplication rule in (9) is a simplification of the term obtained by multiplying out the sums for p^i and p^j: the higher-order terms have been merged into one, which would otherwise complicate the analysis significantly, with little benefit.

We use a pair $(L(v), U(v))$ of two provenance forms to abstractly representation the boundary points of volatile bound of some variable v. For $l \in \mathcal{L}$, denote by $(\underline{e}_l, \bar{e}_l)$ the contribution of volatile errors of the statement at label l; then

$$L(v) = \underline{d} + \sum_{l \in \mathcal{L}} \underline{e}_l \cdot \eta_l + \underline{e}_* \cdot \eta_*, \qquad U(v) = \bar{d} + \sum_{l \in \mathcal{L}} \bar{e}_l \cdot \eta_l + \bar{e}_* \cdot \eta_*.$$

Forms $L(v)$ and $U(v)$ tell us which expressions affect v's volatile bound, in which direction (up or down), and by how much:

Example 1. *For the program shown in Sect. 2, the initial provenance forms for* `radiusSq` *are* $(0.015625, 0.015625)$. *All values* e_l *and* e_* *are 0, since there is no volatility in the input. Suppose after executing the statement in* l2, *we have* $(L(B), U(B)) = (-1129.18688965, -1129.186767578 + 0.00012207 \cdot \eta_{l2})$. *This means that the volatile error at* l2 *increases the upper bound of B by* 0.00012207 *and has no effect on its lower bound.*

Our method is an instance of concretization-based abstract interpretation [6]. The collecting semantics for an abstract program state $(L(v), U(v))$ after assigning to variable v is the set of possible values of v under all evaluation models;

the concretization function thus is $\gamma((L(v), U(v))) = [\pi(L(v)), \pi(U(v))]$. With the concrete transfer function F for the program, our goal is an abstract transfer function G that maintains the following relationship:

$$F \circ \gamma \subseteq \gamma \circ G .$$

We construct G separately for volatile and non-volatile expressions (Sects. 6 and 7).

6   Abstract Transfer Functions for Volatile Expressions

If the assignment statement at label l contains the volatile expression $v = x_{11} \otimes x_{12} \ldots \otimes x_{1n} \oplus \ldots \oplus x_{m1} \otimes x_{m2} \ldots \otimes x_{mn}$, we need to propagate the volatile errors existing in x_{ij} (Sect. 6.1), but also calculate the new volatile error introduced at l in v by reordering and FMA (Sect. 6.2).

6.1   Propagating Existing Volatile Error

The propagation follows the spirit of interval analysis, but uses the operations for provenance forms from Sect. 5 and assumes strict evaluation in the current expression (new reordering error ignored). Given two (L, U) pairs x_i, x_j, we have

$$x_i + x_j = (L(x_i) + L(x_j) + \underline{d}'_{ij}, U(x_i) + U(x_j) + \bar{d}'_{ij})$$
$$x_i - x_j = (L(x_i) - U(x_j) + \underline{d}'_{ij}, U(x_i) - L(x_j) + \bar{d}'_{ij})$$
$$x_i * x_j =$$
$$(\min(L(x_i) * L(x_j), L(x_i) * U(x_j), U(x_i) * L(x_j), U(x_i) * U(x_j)) + \underline{d}'_{ij},$$
$$\max(L(x_i) * L(x_j), L(x_i) * U(x_j), U(x_i) * L(x_j), U(x_i) * U(x_j)) + \bar{d}'_{ij})$$

The min/max functions use the order relation defined in Sect. 5. Values $\underline{d}'_{ij}/\bar{d}'_{ij}$ account for rounding errors of $\oplus, \ominus, \otimes$ and are defined as $d' = rd(\pi(p)) - \pi(p)$. Rounding error d' is added to p via $p + d' = (d + d') + \sum_{l \in \mathfrak{L}} e_l \cdot \eta_l + e_* \cdot \eta_*$. For example, in $L(x_i) + L(x_j) + \underline{d}'_{ij}$, $\underline{d}'_{ij}$ is defined as $\underline{d}'_{ij} = rd(\pi(L(x_i) + L(x_j))) - \pi(L(x_i) + L(x_j))$.

As in interval analysis, we ignore the relation between x_i and x_j; thus the resulting provenance form overapproximates possible values of v with M_{str}.

Theorem 4. *Let $(L'(v), U'(v))$ be the resulting provenance forms for v. Then:*

$$[\min_{I \in \mathbb{I}} v(I, M_{str}), \max_{I \in \mathbb{I}} v(I, M_{str})] \subseteq [\pi(L'(v)), \pi(U'(v))] ,$$

where $\mathbb{I} = [\pi(L(x_{11})), \pi(U(x_{11}))] \times \ldots \times [\pi(L(x_{mn})), \pi(U(x_{mn}))]$.

The theorem follows easily from the properties of interval analysis.

6.2   Calculating Fresh Volatile Error

By Formula (6) in Definition 2 of the volatile error, to calculate the volatile error introduced at l we need two bounds: the bound of v under M_{str}, which is approximated by $[\pi(L'(v)), \pi(U'(v))]$ (calculated in the previous step), and the volatile bound of v. In this section we show how to obtain a sound approximation for the latter. We only show this for the lower bound; the upper bound calculation is analogous.

Our approach consists of two steps. First we transform each sub-monomial $x_{i1} \otimes x_{i2} \ldots \otimes x_{in}$ into two-const form $c_i^{\dashv} \otimes c_i^{\vdash}$, done in Algorithm 6.1. The reason for choosing this form is that we need to consider possible ways of applying FMA between adjacent sub-monomials.

Algorithm 6.1. Compute the two-const form for monomial m

Input: $m := u_1 \otimes \ldots \otimes u_n$, where u_i can be a constant or a variable,
    $\downarrow u_i = \pi(L(u_i))$ and $\uparrow u_i = \pi(U(u_i))$

1 $\downarrow m = +\infty$;
2 **for** $(c_1, \ldots, c_n) \in \{\downarrow u_1, \uparrow u_1\} \times \ldots \times \{\downarrow u_n, \uparrow u_n\}$ **do**
3 $\quad (t^{\dashv}, t^{\vdash}) = getMin_{mul}(c_1, \ldots, c_n)$;
4 $\quad$ **if** $\downarrow m > t^{\dashv} * t^{\vdash}$ **then**
5 $\quad\quad \downarrow m = t^{\dashv} * t^{\vdash}$;
6 $\quad\quad c^{\dashv} = t^{\dashv}$;
7 $\quad\quad c^{\vdash} = t^{\vdash}$;
8 $\quad$ **end**
9 **end**
10 **return** $(c^{\dashv}, c^{\vdash})$;

Function $getMin_{mul}$ in Algorithm 6.1 is defined as

$$getMin_{mul}(c_1, \ldots, c_n) = (N[1, L[1, n]], N[L[1, n] + 1, n])$$

where $N[i, i] = c_i$, $N[i, j] = N[i, L[i, j]] \otimes N[L[i, j] + 1, j]$ for $i < j$, and

$$L[i, j] = \begin{cases} \underset{k : i \leq k < j}{\operatorname{argmin}} |N[i, k] * N[k + 1, j]| & \text{if } sign(m) = + \\ \underset{k : i \leq k < j}{\operatorname{argmax}} |N[i, k] * N[k + 1, j]| & \text{if } sign(m) = - \end{cases}.$$

Function $sign(m)$ returns the sign of the multiplication result of the monomial. Note that we use real multiplication in the definition of $L[i, j]$ instead of $\otimes$ as in the definition for $N[i, j]$: the multiplication in FMA is done in real. We can prove that $(N[1, L[1, n]], N[L[1, n] + 1, n])$ is the pair such that its multiplication $N[1, L[1, n]] \otimes N[L[1, n] + 1, n]$ is the minimum value of the monomial.

After transformation, the whole polynomial expression is transformed into standard dot product: $c_1^{\dashv} \otimes c_1^{\vdash} \oplus \ldots \oplus c_n^{\dashv} \otimes c_n^{\vdash}$. In the second sub-step we obtain the lower bound of the dot product, $\downarrow v$, using a method presented in previous work [14, Sect. 2.4], which accounts for all possible evaluation models for the dot product expression. It can be shown that $[\downarrow v, \uparrow v]$ is an over-approximation of the volatile bound of v. Together with $(L'(v), U'(v))$, we can now get the volatile error e_l for v of

$$\underline{e}_l = \downarrow v - \pi(L'(v)), \quad \bar{e}_l = \uparrow v - \pi(U'(v)) .$$

The final provenance form for v is $(L'(v) + \underline{e}_l \cdot \eta_l, U'(v) + \bar{e}_l \cdot \eta_l)$. It follows:

Theorem 5. *Let* $(L'(v) + \underline{e}_l \cdot \eta_l, U'(v) + \bar{e}_l \cdot \eta_l)$ *be the resulting provenance forms for* v, *and* $\mathbb{I} = [\pi(L(x_{11})), \pi(U(x_{11}))] \times \ldots \times [\pi(L(x_{mn})), \pi(U(x_{mn}))]$. *Then*

$$[\min_{I \in \mathbb{I}} \min_M v(I, M), \max_{I \in \mathbb{I}} \max_M v(I, M)] \subseteq [\pi(L'(v) + \underline{e}_l \cdot \eta_l), \pi(U'(v) + \bar{e}_l \cdot \eta_l)] .$$

6.3 Identifying the Cause of Volatility

To help the user fix reproducibility problems, we *classify* the cause of the volatility into three categories: *FMA*, *Order* and *FMA+Order*, which respectively indicates that the volatility is due to the use/non-use of FMA, reordering of the computation, or both. The definitions of the three categories are shown in Table 4. Here the $[\downarrow v_{nofma}, \uparrow v_{nofma}]$ represents the volatile

Table 4. Categories of volatility

Category	Definition
Stable	$\downarrow v = \uparrow v$
FMA	$\downarrow v \neq \uparrow v$ $\wedge \downarrow v_{nofma} = \uparrow v_{nofma}$
Order	$\downarrow v \neq \uparrow v$ $\wedge \downarrow v_{nofma} = \downarrow v$ $\wedge \uparrow v_{nofma} = \uparrow v$
FMA+Order	otherwise

bound of v without considering FMA contraction. It can be obtained by modifying the return value in Algorithm 6.1. Instead of returning the tuple $(c^\dashv, c^\vdash)$, we simply return the floating-point value $c^\dashv \otimes c^\vdash$. Then the whole volatile expression is transformed to $v = c_1 \otimes 1 \oplus \ldots \oplus c_n \otimes 1$, where $c_i = c_i^\dashv \otimes c_i^\vdash$. The second sub-step is the same as in Sect. 6.2.

7 Transfer Functions for Non-volatile Expressions

Numerical programs generally contain expressions other than polynomials, such as involving division and *sqrt* operations. We assume that such expressions behave the same on all platforms and hence do not introduce new volatile error. We still need to propagate existing volatile error through them, which is the topic of this section. Our approach applies to any uni-variate function that is *monotone and twice continuously differentiable* in its domain.

Let $\vec{\eta} = (\eta_i)$ be an $|\mathfrak{L}|$-dimensional vector. The provenance form $p = d + \sum_{l \in \mathfrak{L}} e_l \cdot \eta_l + e_* \cdot \eta_*$ can be viewed as a function f of $|\mathfrak{L}| + 1$ variables, namely all η_i and η_*, defined over the line segment $\overline{AB}$ from point $A = (\vec{0}, 0)$ to point $B = (\vec{1}, 1)$: note that $f(\vec{1}, 1) = \pi(p)$. Let g be a uni-variate function such that $\varphi = g \circ f$ is twice continuously differentiable in $\overline{AB}$. By the Taylor expansion theory [17], there exists a point C in the interior of $\overline{AB}$ such that

$$\varphi(B) = \varphi(A) + \sum_{l \in \mathfrak{L} \cup \{*\}} \frac{\partial \varphi}{\partial \eta_l}(A) \cdot 1 + \frac{1}{2} \sum_{l_1, l_2 \in \mathfrak{L} \cup \{*\}} \frac{\partial^2 \varphi}{\partial \eta_{l_1} \partial \eta_{l_2}}(C) \cdot 1 \cdot 1. \tag{10}$$

Now our plan is to transfer Formula (10) back to provenance form. Recall that, in our definition of provenance form, e_l reflects the shift of the volatile bound (lower or upper) due to the statement at l. Thus, by the definition of derivative, $\frac{\partial \varphi}{\partial \eta_l}(A)$ approximates the change of the volatile bound of g because of e_l. We also need to handle the formula's final term, $\frac{1}{2}\sum_{l_1,l_2 \in \mathcal{L} \cup \{*\}} \frac{\partial^2 f}{\partial \eta_{l_1} \partial \eta_{l_2}}(C)$, which contains the unknown parameter C. Here we apply interval analysis on the values along $\overline{AB}$ that C can take, to get an interval e''. This interval overapproximates the change of the bound of g due to higher-order error terms according to the definition of second derivative. Based on the above discussion, we get the following "quasi-provenance form" for g for the given input p.

$$g(p) = \varphi(A) + \sum_{l \in \mathcal{L}} \frac{\partial \varphi}{\partial \eta_l}(A) \cdot \eta_l + (\frac{\partial \varphi}{\partial \eta_*}(A) + e'') \cdot \eta_* \tag{11}$$

The only difference to the provenance form is that the coefficient of η_* is an interval instead of a constant. We also define $[\downarrow g(p), \uparrow g(p)]$ as

$$\downarrow g(p) = \varphi(A) + \sum_{l \in \mathcal{L}} \frac{\partial \varphi}{\partial \eta_l}(A) \cdot \eta_l + \downarrow(\frac{\partial \varphi}{\partial \eta_*}(A) + e'') \cdot \eta_*$$

$$\uparrow g(p) = \varphi(A) + \sum_{l \in \mathcal{L}} \frac{\partial \varphi}{\partial \eta_l}(A) \cdot \eta_l + \uparrow(\frac{\partial \varphi}{\partial \eta_*}(A) + e'') \cdot \eta_*$$

Using the quasi-provenance form, we can design the volatile error propagation for g as the follows. If g is monotonously increasing in interval $[\pi(L(v)), \pi(U(v))]$, we have $g((L(v), U(v))) = (\downarrow g(L(v)), \uparrow g(U(v)))$. If g is monotonously decreasing, we have $g((L(v), U(v))) = (\downarrow g(U(v)), \uparrow g(L(v)))$.

Theorem 6. *Let g be a uni-variate, monotone, and twice continuously differentiable function. Given abstract input $(L(v), U(v))$, let $(L'(v), U'(v))$ be the abstract result (obtained via the abstract transfer function of g). Then*

$$[g(\pi(L(v)), g(\pi(U(v)))] \subseteq [\pi(L'(v)), \pi(U'(v))] .$$

The above discussion assumes that g can be calculated in infinite precision. In floating-point reality we need to consider rounding errors for g. This can be accommodated by attaching correction terms to the resulting provenance forms: $(L'(v) + \underline{d}, U'(v) + \bar{d})$, where $\underline{d} = \widetilde{g}(\pi(L(v))) - \pi(L'(v))$, $\bar{d} = \widetilde{g}(\pi(U(v))) - \pi(U'(v))$, and $\widetilde{g}$ is the floating-point version of g.

8   Implementation and Evaluation

We have implemented the above techniques in a runtime library. The core of the library is a customized datatype called `ifloat`, which keeps track of the volatile errors during execution, for each variable. Our library can be applied to programs that do not use mixed floating-point types or mixed rounding modes. In our experiments we use single-precision float as the numeric data type, and *round-to-nearest-ties-to even* as the rounding mode (as in most programs). Polynomial expressions containing parentheses have "partial volatility"; we treat them by moving the parenthesized part outside the expression, via a temporary variable.

The calculations of provenance forms are defined in $\mathbb{R}$, as shown in Sect. 5. In our implementation we use the `mpq_class` type in the GMP library [13] as an approximation. We have overloaded the following operators in our `ifloat` datatype: $+ - * /$ sqrt. Note that the result of `sqrt` may be irrational, in which case Formula (10) may not be representable by `mpq_class`. To solve this problem, we use a double precision float together with outward rounding modes to get an interval that contains the true value of `sqrt`. As a result, we get an *interval linear form* [18] of Formula (11),

$$\sqrt{p} = [\sqrt{d}] + \sum_{l \in \mathcal{L}} \frac{e_l}{2[\sqrt{d}]} \cdot \eta_l + (\frac{e_*}{2[\sqrt{d}]} + e'') \cdot \eta_*,$$

where $[\sqrt{d}] = [RD(\sqrt{d}), RU(\sqrt{d})]$ (rounding down and up, resp.). Consequently,

$$\downarrow\sqrt{p} = \downarrow[\sqrt{d}] + \sum_{l \in \mathcal{L}} \downarrow\frac{e_l}{2[\sqrt{d}]} \cdot \eta_l + \downarrow(\frac{e_*}{2[\sqrt{d}]} + e'') \cdot \eta_*$$

$$\uparrow\sqrt{p} = \uparrow[\sqrt{d}] + \sum_{l \in \mathcal{L}} \uparrow\frac{e_l}{2[\sqrt{d}]} \cdot \eta_l + \uparrow(\frac{e_*}{2[\sqrt{d}]} + e'') \cdot \eta_*.$$

It can be shown that Theorem 6 still holds.

Library usage. Our library can be used in the classical test-evaluation-fix iterative fashion. Users replace all native float types with `ifloat` and label all assignment statements that contain volatile expressions. Currently we make these changes manually; they can easily be automated. Our library outputs the provenance forms for user-selected variables. From the two forms the user can locate which statement makes the most significant contribution to the target variable's volatility, and how to stabilize it. After (partial) stabilization, we re-run the analysis. If the resulting bound is within a user-specified threshold, we can guarantee that the actual volatility will not exceed the same threshold, since our volatile bound is a conservative approximation.

Benchmarks. We have tested our approach on a number of numeric programs. Benchmarks *fft* (Fast Fourier Transform) and *sor* (Jacobi Successive Over-relaxation) are from SciMark 2.0 [19]; *nbody* [9] models the orbits of Jovian planets. The remaining programs are from a numerical analysis book [4]: *triple* is the Gaussian triple integral algorithm; *adam* is the adams-forth order predictor-corrector algorithm; *crout* is the crout reduction for tri-diagonal linear systems; *choleski* and *ldl* are standard algorithms that factor a positive-definite matrix. The benchmarks can be found at http://github.com/yijiagu/ifloat.

Experiments. We have tested our benchmarks with 10 random generated inputs (except *nbody*, which comes with its own test inputs). All experiments are run on Ubuntu 15.10 with 8 GB memory; Table 5 shows the results. Column **Input** specifies the input matrix size; * means that the benchmark requires scalar inputs. Columns **Volatile Bound** and v_{str} show the volatile bound of the final result for each benchmark and the corresponding value under strict evaluation. These volatile bounds are sound based on the theorems in Sect. 6 and 7. If the output is a matrix as well, we define its volatility to be that of the cell with the largest volatile bound in the matrix, maximized over all test cases; that cell is shown under **Variable**.

Table 5. Volatility for the benchmarks

Program	Input	Variable	Volatile bound		v_{str}
sor	[100 × 100]	G[67][55]	(0.720786273,	0.720786631)	0.720786452
fft	[16 × 2]	X[14]	(0.123653859,	0.123654306)	0.123654097
nbody	*	energy	(−0.169289380,	−0.169289351)	−0.169289351
triple	*	AJ	(−40.967014313,	−40.966991425)	−40.967002869
adam	*	W0	(−0.728196859,	−0.728196740)	−0.728196859
crout	[10 × 10]	A[0]	(1.282013535,	1.282219410)	1.282117963
choleski	[15 × 15]	A[11][11]	(4.187705517,	4.187705994)	4.187705994
ldl	[15 × 15]	A[11][10]	(0.102230683,	0.102230750)	0.102230720

Table 6 shows the provenance information for the selected variable. We only list the labels whose statements contribute the most to the target variable's lower (Column 2) and upper bound (Column 4). Table 6 also compares the contribution calculated by our approach (Columns 2+4) to the precise shift, according to Definition 3 (Column 3+5). In most cases, these two sets of values are very close.[2] It shows that the provenance outputs from our library are indeed a good approximation of statements' volatility contribution to the final result. Noted that in some cases the actual value is larger than the predicted value. However, this does not violate our claim that the volatile bound is sound. In all experiments, our approach accurately pinpoints the statements that contribute the most to the volatility of the final result. Thus, instead of naively recompiling and rerunning the analysis for each target variable and source expression, library users execute the program with our library *once*. From the output provenance forms they can identify the most-to-blame statements and to what extent they may improve the situation by stabilizing these statements. To assist in this process, Columns 2+4 also list the cause of statements' volatility.

---

[2] An exception is $A[11][11]$ for *choleski*: inspection shows that this anomaly is due to the rounding error. In fact, its left bound 4.187705517 and right bound 4.187705994 are two adjacent floating-point numbers.

Table 6. Provenance information for the benchmarks

Variable	Predicted e_{max}	Actual e_{max}	Predicted $\bar{e}_{max}$	Actual $\bar{e}_{max}$
G[67][55]	L1: −0.000000132 (Reorder)	−0.000000179	L1: 0.000000178 (Reorder)	0.000000179
X[14]	L2: −0.000000158 (FMA+Reorder)	−0.000000179	L2: 0.000000079 (FMA+Reorder)	0.000000060
energy	L7: −0.000000018 (FMA+Reorder)	−0.000000029	L9: 0.000000014 (FMA+Reorder)	0.000000000
AJ	L2: −0.000004037 (FMA)	−0.000003815	L8: 0.000005997 (FMA)	0.000007629
W0	L3: −0.000000014 (FMA+Reorder)	0.000000000	L2: 0.000000016 (FMA+Reorder)	0.000000060
A[0]	L1: −0.000098395 (FMA)	−0.000100494	L1: 0.000098380 (FMA)	0.000101450
A[11][11]	L1: −0.000000007 (FMA+Reorder)	−0.000000477	L2: 0.000000027 (FMA+Reorder)	0.000000000
A[11][10]	L2: −0.000000040 (FMA+Reorder)	−0.000000037	L2: 0.000000035 (FMA+Reorder)	0.000000030

The code linked against our library is currently up to 3 orders of magnitude slower than the original code with single precision. This is due to the extra information tracked by our library, and also the extensive use of rational arithmetic in the process. We point out that the performance of the library is not our main concern: we view it as a unit testing tool for examining a program's numerically intensive parts. Our solution is effective in that it eases the testing workload by avoiding multiple recompilations and reruns on different platforms. The runtime in our experiments is acceptable; each test input takes less than a few seconds. In the future, we plan to replace rational arithmetic in the analysis by floating-point calculations, to enable application to larger examples.

9   Related Work

Analyzing the behavior of numerical programs across computing environments has become an important research topic, due to an increased awareness of reproducibility issues on heterogeneous (CPU/GPU/FPGA) platforms. The research presented here was inspired by our own work in [14], where we designed an efficient technique to compute the volatile bound of an expression, for a fixed input. In the present work, we embed this technique in a dynamic analysis framework, and go a significant step further: tracing volatility errors back to relevant source statements and specific causes (FMA/reordering), and stabilizing the program, by partially fixing the evaluation of these source statements.

[2] presents a formally verified C compiler that guarantees IEEE-compliant floating-point machine code, which is achieved by enforcing "a single way to

compile" [2], akin to strict semantics. This ensures code stability, but does not address the question of whether there is any significant instability in the program in the first place, nor how much stability is "healthy" for the program. Work in [3, 21] proves a maximum rounding error *under platform variations*. The approach is deductive and not suitable for identifying inputs that cause platform dependence. Since our error representation (the provenance form) allows us to isolate errors due to volatility, we are able to trace sources of platform sensitivity, and can offer ways to repair it; a question that has not been addressed in any previous work, to the best of our knowledge.

The methodology used in our work is in part inspired by research on tracing the rounding error propagation for numerical programs. Fluctuat [10–12] is a static analysis tool based on abstract interpretation that locates the sources of rounding errors in the program. [7] designs a runtime library that provides a guaranteed upper bound of rounding errors for programs written in Scala. All these works use affine arithmetic [20] as the underlying algebraic structure to keep track of the rounding error. In this paper, we adopt a similar data structure, manifest in the provenance form, to instead trace the volatile error.

10   Conclusions and Future Work

In this paper we have established that platform and compiler dependencies of numeric code can be traced back to their sources dynamically, incurring a performance penalty that is acceptable for software test runs. The slow-down is currently too large to permit running the analysis as monitors in deployed code. Future work includes decreasing this performance hit, for example by conservatively using floating-point calculations during the analysis, rather than expensive but more precise rational arithmetic.

References

1. IEEE Standards Association. IEEE standard for floating-point arithmetic (2008). http://grouper.ieee.org/groups/754/
2. Boldo, S., Jourdan, J.-H., Leroy, X., Melquiond, G.: A formally-verified C compiler supporting floating-point arithmetic. In: 21st IEEE Symposium on Computer Arithmetic (ARITH), pp. 107–115. IEEE (2013)
3. Boldo, S., Nguyen, T.M.T.: Hardware-independent proofs of numerical programs. In: Muñoz, C. (ed.) Second NASA Formal Methods Symposium (NFM 2010), vol. NASA/CP-2010-216215, pp. 14–23. NASA, Washington D.C., April 2010
4. Burden, R.L., Faires, J.D.: Numerical analysis. Cengage Learning (2010)
5. Corden, M.J., Kreitzer, D.: Consistency of floating-point results using the Intel® compiler or why doesn't my application always give the same answer? (2010). http://software.intel.com/sites/default/files/article/164389/fp-consistency-102511.pdf
6. Cousot, P., Cousot, R.: Systematic design of program analysis frameworks. In: Proceedings of the 6th ACM SIGACT-SIGPLAN Symposium on Principles of Programming Languages, POPL 1979, pp. 269–282. ACM, New York (1979)

7. Darulova, E., Kuncak, V.: Trustworthy numerical computation in Scala. ACM Sigplan Not. **46**, 325–344 (2011). ACM
8. de Dinechin, F.: Computing with floating point. http://lyoncalcul.univ-lyon1.fr/IMG/pdf/FloatingPoint.pdf
9. Fulgham, B., Gouy, I.: The Computer Language Benchmarks Game (2010). http://shootout.alioth.debian.org
10. Putot, S., Goubault, E., Martel, M.: Static analysis-based validation of floating-point computations. In: Alt, R., Frommer, A., Kearfott, R.B., Luther, W. (eds.) Num. Software with Result Verification. LNCS, vol. 2991, pp. 306–313. Springer, Berlin (2004). doi:10.1007/978-3-540-24738-8_18
11. Goubault, E.: Static analyses of the precision of floating-point operations. In: Cousot, P. (ed.) SAS 2001. LNCS, vol. 2126, pp. 234–259. Springer, Berlin (2001). doi:10.1007/3-540-47764-0_14
12. Goubault, E., Putot, S.: Static analysis of finite precision computations. In: Jhala, R., Schmidt, D. (eds.) VMCAI 2011. LNCS, vol. 6538, pp. 232–247. Springer, Berlin (2011). doi:10.1007/978-3-642-18275-4_17
13. Granlund, T., and the GMP development team: GNU MP: The GNU Multiple Precision Arithmetic Library, 6.1.1 edn. (2016). http://gmplib.org/
14. Gu, Y., Wahl, T., Bayati, M., Leeser, M.: Behavioral non-portability in scientific numeric computing. In: Träff, J.L., Hunold, S., Versaci, F. (eds.) Euro-Par 2015. LNCS, vol. 9233, pp. 558–569. Springer, Berlin (2015). doi:10.1007/978-3-662-48096-0_43
15. Martel, M., Cea Recherche Technologique: Semantics of roundoff error propagation in finite precision computations. J. High. Order Symbolic Comput. **19**, 7–30 (2006)
16. Meng, Q., Humphrey, A., Schmidt, J., Berzins, M.: Preliminary experiences with the Uintah framework on Intel Xeon Phi and stampede. In: Proceedings of the Conference on Extreme Science and Engineering Discovery Environment: Gateway to Discovery, p. 48. ACM (2013)
17. Mikusinski, P., Taylor, M.: An Introduction to Multivariable Analysis from Vector to Manifold. Springer Science & Business Media, New York (2012)
18. Miné, A.: The octagon abstract domain. High. Order Symbol. Comput. **19**(1), 31–100 (2006)
19. Pozo, R., Miller, B.: SciMark 2.0, December 2002. http://math.nist.gov/scimark2/
20. Stolfi, J., De Figueiredo, L.H.: An introduction to affine arithmetic. Trends Appl. Comput. Math. **4**(3), 297–312 (2003)
21. Tuyen, N.T.M., Marché, C.: Proving floating-point numerical programs by analysis of their assembly code. Research Report RR-7655, INRIA, June 2011

Dynamic Reductions for Model Checking Concurrent Software

Henning Günther[1], Alfons Laarman[1(✉)], Ana Sokolova[2], and Georg Weissenbacher[1]

[1] TU Wien, Vienna, Austria
alfons@laarman.com
[2] University of Salzburg, Salzburg, Austria

Abstract. Symbolic model checking of parallel programs stands and falls with effective methods of dealing with the explosion of interleavings. We propose a dynamic reduction technique to avoid unnecessary interleavings. By extending Lipton's original work with a notion of bisimilarity, we accommodate dynamic transactions, and thereby reduce dependence on the accuracy of static analysis, which is a severe bottleneck in other reduction techniques.

The combination of symbolic model checking and dynamic reduction techniques has proven to be challenging in the past. Our generic reduction theorem nonetheless enables us to derive an efficient symbolic encoding, which we implemented for IC3 and BMC. The experiments demonstrate the power of dynamic reduction on several case studies and a large set of SVCOMP benchmarks.

1 Introduction

The rise of multi-threaded software—a consequence of a necessary technological shift from ever higher frequencies to multi-core architectures—exacerbates the challenge of verifying programs automatically. While automated software verification has made impressive advances recently thanks to novel symbolic model checking techniques, such as lazy abstraction [5,26], interpolation [33], and IC3 [8] for software [6,9], multi-threaded programs still pose a formidable challenge.

The effectiveness of model checking in the presence of concurrency is severely limited by the state explosion caused through thread interleavings. Consequently, techniques that avoid thread interleavings, such as partial order reduction (POR) [19,38,41] or Lipton's reduction [32], are crucial to the scalability of model checking, while also benefitting other verification approaches [11,14,17].

These reduction techniques, however, rely heavily on the identification of statements that are either independent or commute with the statements of all other threads, i.e. those that are *globally independent*. For instance, the single-action rule [31]—a primitive precursor of Lipton reduction—states that a sequential block of statements can be considered an atomic transaction if all but one of

This work is supported by the Austrian National Research Network S11403-N23 (RiSE) of the Austrian Science Fund (FWF) and by the Vienna Science and Technology Fund (WWTF) through grant VRG11-005.

A. Bouajjani and D. Monniaux (Eds.): VMCAI 2017, LNCS 10145, pp. 246–265, 2017.
DOI: 10.1007/978-3-319-52234-0_14

the statements are globally independent. Inside an atomic block, all interleavings of other threads can be discarded, thus yielding the reduction.

Identifying these globally independent statements requires non-local *static analyses*. In the presence of pointers, arrays, and complicated branching structures, however, the results of an up-front static analysis are typically extremely conservative, thus a severe bottleneck for good reduction.

Figure 1 shows an example with two threads (T1 and T2). Let's assume static analysis can establish that pointers p and q never point to the same memory throughout the program's (parallel) execution. This means that statements involving the pointers are globally independent, hence they globally commute, e.g. an interleaving *p++; *q = 1 always yields the same result as *q = 1; *p++;. Assuming that *p++; is also independent of the other statements from T2 (b = 2 and c = 3), we can reorder any trace of the parallel program to a trace where *p++ and *q = 2 occur subsequently without affecting the resulting state. The figure shows one example. Therefore, a syntactic transformation from *p++; *q = 2 to atomic{*p++; *q = 2} is a valid static reduction.

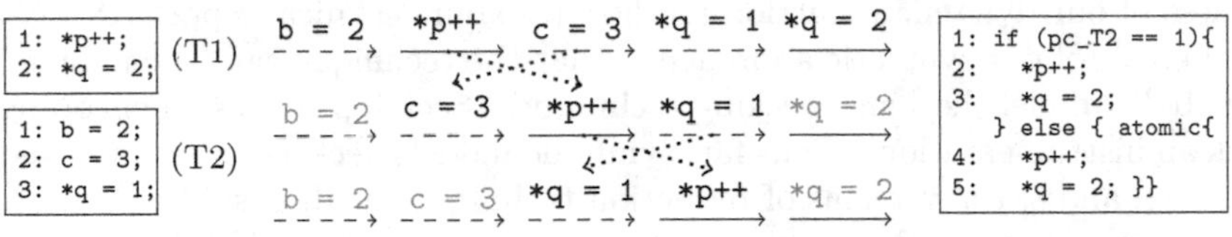

Fig. 1. *(Left) C code for threads T1 and T2. (Middle) Reordering (dotted lines) a multi-threaded execution trace (T1's actions are represented with straight arrows and T2's with 'dashed' arrows). (Right) The instrumented code for T1.*

Still, it is often hard to prove that pointers do not overlap throughout a program's execution. Moreover, in many cases, pointers might temporarily overlap at some point in the execution. For instance, assume that initially p points to the variable b. This means that statements b = 2 and *p++ no longer commute, because b = 2; b++ yields a different result than b++; b = 2. Nevertheless, if b = 2 already happened, then we can still swap instructions and achieve the reduction as shown in Fig. 1. Traditional, static reduction methods cannot distinguish whether b = 2 already happened and yield no reduction. Sect. 2 provides various other real-world examples of hard cases for static analysis.

In Sect. 4.2, we propose a dynamic reduction method that is still based on a similar syntactic transformation. Instead of merely making sequences of statements atomic, it introduces branches as shown in Fig. 1 (T1'). A dynamic commutativity condition determines whether the branch with or without reduction is taken. In our example, the condition checks whether the program counter of T2 (pc_T2) still points to the statement b = 2 (pc_T2 == 1). In that case, no reduction is performed, otherwise the branch with reduction is taken. In addition to conditions on the program counters, we provide other heuristics comparing pointer and array values dynamically.

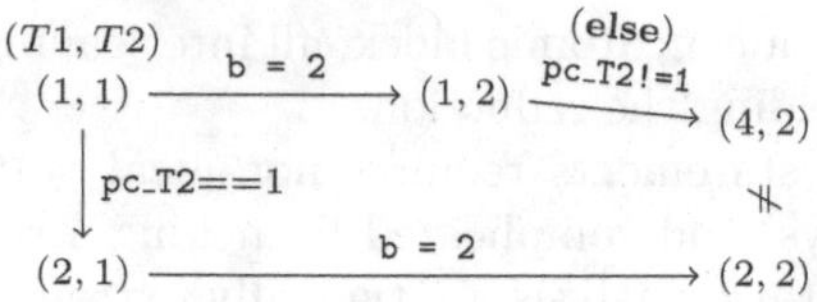

$(T1, T2)$ (else)

$(1, 1) \xrightarrow{\text{b = 2}} (1, 2) \xrightarrow{\text{pc\_T2!=1}} (4, 2)$

$\downarrow$ pc_T2==1 $\nleftrightarrow$

$(2, 1) \xrightarrow{\text{b = 2}} (2, 2)$

$4 \xrightarrow{\text{*p++}} 5$

$\mathbb{R} \qquad\qquad \mathbb{R}$

$2 \xrightarrow{\text{*p++}} 3$

Fig. 2. *Loss of commutativity* 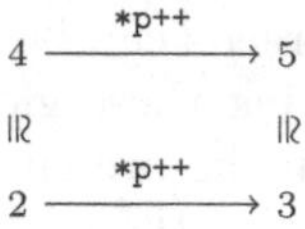   **Fig. 3.** *Bisimulation (T1)*

The instrumented code (T1') however poses one problem: the branching condition no longer commutes with the statement that enables it. In this case, the execution of b = 2 disables the condition, thus before executing b = 2, T1' ends up at Line 2, whereas after b = 2 it ends up at Line 4 (see Fig. 2). To remedy this, we require in Sect. 4.3 that the instrumentation guarantees bisimilarity of target states. Figure 3 shows that locations 2 and 4 of T1' are bimilar, written $2 \cong 4$, which implies that any statement executable from the one is also executable from the other, ending again in a bisimilar location, e.g. $3 \cong 5$. As bisimularity is preserved under parallel composition, e.g. $(4, 2) \cong (2, 2)$, we can prove the correctness of our dynamic reduction method (see our technical report [18]).

The benefit of our syntactic approach is that the technique can be combined with symbolic model checking checking techniques (Sect. 5 provides an encoding for our lean instrumentation). Thus far, symbolic model checkers only supported more limited and static versions of reduction techniques as discussed in Sect. 7.

We implemented the dynamic reduction and encoding for LLVM bitcode, mainly to enable support for C/C++ programs without dealing with their intricate semantics (the increased instruction count of LLVM bitcode is mitigated by the reduction). The encoded transition relation is then passed to the Vienna Verification Tool (VVT) [24], which implements both BMC and IC3 algorithms extended with abstractions [6]. Experimental evaluation shows that (Sect. 6) dynamic reduction can yield several orders of magnitude gains in verification times.

2 Motivating Examples

Lazy Initialization. We illustrate our method with the code in Fig. 4. The main function starts two threads executing the worker_thread function, which processes the contents of data in the for loop at the end of the function. Using a common pattern, a worker thread lazily delays the initialization of the global data pointer until it is needed. It does this by reading some content from disc and set-

```
int *data = NULL;
void worker_thread(int tid) {
c:    if (data == NULL) {
d:        int *tmp = read_from_disk(1024);
W:        if (!CAS(&data, NULL, tmp)) free(tmp);
      }
      for (int i = 0; i < 512; i++)
R:        process(data[i + tid * 512]);
      }
int main () {
a:    pthread_create(worker_thread, 0); // T1
b:    pthread_create(worker_thread, 1); // T2
      }
```

Fig. 4. *Lazy initialization*

ting the pointer atomically via a compare-and-swap operation (CAS) at label W (whose semantics here is an atomic C-statement: if (data==NULL) { data = tmp; return 1; } else return 0;). If it fails (returns 0), the locally allocated data is freed as the other thread has won the race.

The subsequent read access at label R is only reachable once data has been initialized. Consequently, the write access at W cannot possibly interfere with the read accesses at R, and the many interleavings caused by both threads executing the for loop can safely be ignored by the model checker. This typical pattern is however too complex for static analysis to efficiently identify, causing the model checker to conservatively assume conflicting accesses, preventing any reduction.

Hash Table. The code in Fig. 5 implements a lockless hash table (from [30]) inserting a value v by scanning the bucket array T starting from hash, the hash value calculated from v. If an empty bucket is found (T[index]==E), then v is atomically inserted using the CAS operation. If the bucket is not empty, the operation checks whether the value was already inserted in the bucket (T[index] == v). If that is not the case, then it probes the next bucket of T until either v is found to be already in the table, or it is inserted in an empty slot, or the table is full. This basic bucket search order is called a linear *probe sequence*.

A thread performing find-or-put(25), for instance, merely reads buckets T[2] to T[5]. However, other threads might write an empty bucket, thus causing interference. To show that these reads are independent, the static analysis would have to demonstrate that the writes happen to different buckets. Normally this is done via alias analysis that tries to identify the buckets that are written to (by the CAS operation). However, because of the hashing and the probe sequence, such an analysis can only conclude that all buckets may be written. So all operations involving T, including the reads, will be classified as non-commuting. However if we look at the state of individual buckets, it turns out that a common pattern is followed using the CAS operation: A bucket is only written when it is empty, thereafter it doesn't change. In other words,

```
int T[10] = {E,E,22,35,46,25,E,E,91,E};

int find-or-put(int v) {
    int hash = v / 10;
    for (int i = 0; i < 10; i++) {
        int index = (i + hash) % 10;
        if (CAS(&T[index], E, v)) {
            return INSERTED;
        } else if (T[index] == v)
            return FOUND;
    }
    return TABLE_FULL;
}
int main() {
    pthread_create(find-or-put, 25);
    pthread_create(find-or-put, 42);
    pthread_create(find-or-put, 78);
}
```

```
int x = 0, y = 0;
int *p1, *p2;

void worker(int *p) {
    while (*p < 1024)
        *p++;
}
int main(){
a:  if (*)
b:      { p1 = &x; p2 = &y; }
    else
c:      { p1 = &y; p2 = &x; }
    pthread_create(worker, p1); // T1
    pthread_create(worker, p2); // T2
    pthread_join(t1);
    pthread_join(t2);
    return x+y;
}
```

Fig. 5. Lockless hash table.   Fig. 6. Load balancing.

when a bucket T[i] does not contain E, then any operation on it is a read and consequently is independent.

Load Balancing. Figure 6 shows a simplified example of a common pattern in multi-threaded software; load balancing. The work to be done (counting to 2048) is split up between two threads (each of which counts to 1024). The work assignment is represented by pointers p1 and p2, and a dynamic hand-off to one of the two threads is simulated using non-determinism (the first if branch). Static analysis cannot establish the fact that the partitions are independent, because they are assigned dynamically. But because the pointer is unmodified after assignment, its dereference commutes with that in other worker threads.

Section 4 shows how our examples can be reduced with dynamic commutativity.

3   Preliminaries

A concurrent program consists of a finite number of sequential procedures, one for each thread i. We model the syntax of each thread i by a control flow graph (CFG) $G_i = (V_i, \delta_i)$ with $\delta_i \subseteq V_i \times A \times V_i$ and A being the set of actions, i.e., statements. V_i is a finite set of locations, and $(l, \alpha, l') \in \delta_i$ are (CFG) edges. We abbreviate the actions for a thread i with $\Delta_i = \{\alpha \mid \exists l, l' \colon (l, \alpha, l') \in \delta_i)\}$.

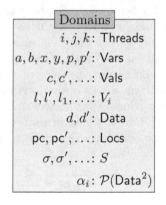

Domains
$i, j, k \colon$ Threads
$a, b, x, y, p, p' \colon$ Vars
$c, c', \ldots \colon$ Vals
$l, l', l_1, \ldots \colon V_i$
$d, d' \colon$ Data
$\mathsf{pc}, \mathsf{pc}', \ldots \colon$ Locs
$\sigma, \sigma', \ldots \colon S$
$\alpha_i \colon \mathcal{P}(\mathsf{Data}^2)$

A state of the concurrent system is composed of (1) a location for each thread, i.e., a a tuple of thread locations (the set Locs contains all such tuples), and (2) a data valuation, i.e., a mapping from variables (Vars) to data values (Vals). We take Data to be the set of all data valuations. Hence, a state is a pair, $\sigma = (\mathsf{pc}, d)$ where $\mathsf{pc} \in \prod_i V_i$ and $d \in$ Data. The locations in each CFG actually correspond to the values of the thread-local program counters for each thread. In particular, the global locations correspond to the global program counter pc being a tuple with $\mathsf{pc}_i \in V_i$ the thread-local program counter for thread i. We use $\mathsf{pc}[i := l]$ to denote $\mathsf{pc}[i := l]_i = l$ and $\mathsf{pc}[i := l]_j = \mathsf{pc}_j$ for all $j \neq i$.

Each possible action α semantically corresponds to a binary relation $\alpha \subseteq$ Data $\times$ Data representing the evolution of the data part of a state under the transition labelled by α. We call α the transition relation of the statement α, referring to both simply as α. We also use several simple statements from programming languages, such as C, as actions.

The semantics of a concurrent program consisting of a finite number of threads, each with CFG $G_i = (V_i, \delta_i)$, is a transition system with data (TS) $C = (S, \rightarrow)$ with $S =$ Locs $\times$ Data, Locs $= \prod_i V_i$ and $\rightarrow = \bigcup_i \rightarrow_i$ where $\rightarrow_i$ is given by $(\mathsf{pc}, d) \rightarrow_i (\mathsf{pc}', d')$ for $\exists \alpha \colon \mathsf{pc}_i = l \wedge (l, \alpha, l') \in \delta_i \wedge (d, d') \in \alpha \wedge \mathsf{pc}' = \mathsf{pc}[i := l']$. We also write $(\mathsf{pc}, d) \xrightarrow{\alpha}_i (\mathsf{pc}', d')$ for $\mathsf{pc}_i = l \wedge (l, \alpha, l') \in \delta_i \wedge (d, d') \in$

$\alpha \wedge \mathsf{pc}' = \mathsf{pc}[i := l']$. Hence, the concurrent program is an asynchronous execution of the parallel composition of all its threads. Each step (transition) is a local step of one of the threads. Each thread i has a unique initial location $\mathsf{pc}_{0,i}$, and hence the TS has one initial location pc_0. Moreover, there is an initial data valuation d_0 as well. Hence, the initial state of a TS is $\sigma_0 \triangleq (\mathsf{pc}_0, d_0)$.

Since we focus on preserving simple safety properties (e.g. assertions) in our reduction, w.l.o.g., we require one sink location per thread l_{sink} to represent errors (it has no outgoing edges, no selfloop). Correspondingly, error states of a TS are those in which at least one thread is in the error location.

In the following, we introduce additional notation for states and relations. Let $R \subseteq S \times S$ and $X \subseteq S$. Then left restriction of R to X is $X /\!/ R \triangleq R \cap (X \times S)$ and right restriction is $R \backslash\!\backslash X \triangleq R \cap (S \times X)$. The complement of X is denoted $\overline{X} \triangleq S \backslash X$ (the universe of all states remains implicit in this notation). Finally, R does not enable X if $\overline{X} /\!/ R \backslash\!\backslash X = \emptyset$, and R does not disable X if $X /\!/ R \backslash\!\backslash \overline{X} = \emptyset$.

Commutativity. We let $R \circ Q$ denote the *sequential composition* of two binary relations R and Q, defined as: $\{(x, z) \mid \exists y \colon (x, y) \in R \wedge (y, z) \in Q\}$. Moreover, let:

$$R \bowtie Q \triangleq R \circ Q = Q \circ R \qquad \text{(both-commute)}$$

$$R \overrightarrow{\bowtie} Q \triangleq R \circ Q \subseteq Q \circ R \quad (R \text{ right commutes with } Q)$$

$$R \overleftarrow{\bowtie} Q \triangleq R \circ Q \supseteq Q \circ R \quad (R \text{ left commutes with } Q)$$

Illustrated graphically for transition relations, $\rightarrow_i$ right commutes with $\rightarrow_j$ iff

$$\forall \sigma, \sigma', \sigma'' \colon \quad \begin{matrix} \sigma \\ \downarrow_i \\ \sigma' \ \rightarrow_j \ \sigma'' \end{matrix} \quad \Rightarrow \exists \sigma''' \colon \begin{matrix} \sigma \ \rightarrow_j \ \sigma''' \\ \downarrow_i \qquad \downarrow_i \\ \sigma' \ \rightarrow_j \ \sigma'' \end{matrix} \qquad (1)$$

Conversely, $\rightarrow_j$ *left commutes* with $\rightarrow_i$. The typical example of (both) commuting operations $\xrightarrow{\alpha}_i$ and $\xrightarrow{\beta}_i$ is when α and β access a disjoint set of variables. Two operations may commute even if both access the same variables, e.g., if both only read or both (atomically) increment/decrement the same variable.

Lipton Reduction. Lipton [32] devised a method that merges multiple sequential statements into one atomic operation, thereby radically reducing the number of states reachable from the initial state as Fig. 7 shows for a transition system composed of two (independent, thus commuting) threads.

Lipton called a transition $\xrightarrow{\alpha}_i$ a right/left mover if and only if it satisfies:

$$\xrightarrow{\alpha}_i \overrightarrow{\bowtie} \bigcup_{j \neq i} \rightarrow_j \text{ (right mover)} \qquad \xrightarrow{\alpha}_i \overleftarrow{\bowtie} \bigcup_{j \neq i} \rightarrow_j \text{ (left mover)}$$

Both-movers are transitions that are both left and right movers, whereas *non-movers* are neither. The sequential composition of two movers is also a corresponding mover, and vice versa. Moreover, one may always safely classify an action as a non-mover, although having more movers yields better reductions.

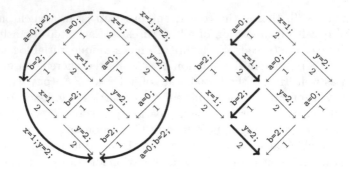

Fig. 7. Example transition system composed of two independent threads (twice). Thick lines show a Lipton reduced system (left) and a partial-order reduction (right).

Lipton reduction only preserves halting. We present Lamport's [31] version, which preserves safety properties such as $\Box\varphi$: Any sequence $\xrightarrow{\alpha_1}_i \circ \xrightarrow{\alpha_2}_i \circ \cdots \circ \xrightarrow{\alpha_{n-1}}_i \circ \xrightarrow{\alpha_n}_i$ can be *reduced* to a single *transaction* $\xrightarrow{\alpha}_i$ where $\alpha = \alpha_1; \ldots; \alpha_n$ (i.e. a compound statement with the same local behavior), if for some $1 \le k < n$:

L1. statements before α_k are right movers, i.e.: $\xrightarrow{\alpha_1}_i \circ \cdots \circ \xrightarrow{\alpha_{k-1}}_i \overrightarrow{\bowtie} \bigcup_{j\neq i} \rightarrow_j$,

L2. statements after α_k are left movers, i.e.: $\xrightarrow{\alpha_{k+1}}_i \circ \cdots \circ \xrightarrow{\alpha_n}_i \overleftarrow{\bowtie} \bigcup_{j\neq i} \rightarrow_j$,

L3. statements after α_1 do not block, i.e.: $\forall\sigma \exists\sigma': \sigma \xrightarrow{\alpha_1}_i \circ \cdots \circ \xrightarrow{\alpha_n}_i \sigma'$, and

L4. φ is not disabled by $\xrightarrow{\alpha_1}_i \circ \cdots \circ \xrightarrow{\alpha_{k-1}}_i$, nor enabled by $\xrightarrow{\alpha_{k+1}}_i \circ \cdots \circ \xrightarrow{\alpha_n}_i$.

The action α_k might interact with other threads and therefore is called the *commit* in the database terminology [36]. Actions preceding it are called *pre-commit* actions and gather resources, such as locks. The remaining actions are *post-commit* actions that (should) release these resources. We refer to pre(/post)-commit transitions including source and target states as the *pre(/post) phase*.

4   Dynamic Reduction

The reduction outlined above depends on the identification of movers. And to determine whether a statement is a mover, the analysis has to consider <u>all</u> other statements in <u>all</u> other threads. Why is the definition of movers so strong? The answer is that 'movability' has to be preserved in all future computations for the reduction not to miss any relevant behavior.

For instance, consider the system composed of x=0; y=2 and y=1; x=y with initial state $\sigma_0 = (\mathsf{pc}_0, d_0)$, $d_0 = (x = 0, y = 0)$ and $\mathsf{pc}_0 = (1,1)$ using line numbers as program counters. Figure 8 shows the TS of this system, from which we can

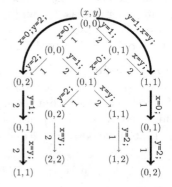

Fig. 8. Transition system of $\xrightarrow{x:=0}_1 \xrightarrow{y:=2}_1 \parallel \xrightarrow{y:=1}_2 \xrightarrow{x:=y}_2$. Thick lines show an incorrect reduction, missing $(2,2)$ and $(1,2)$.

derive that x:=0 and y:=1 do not commute except in the initial state (see the diamond structure of the top 3 and the middle state). Now assume, we have a dynamic version of Lipton reduction that allows us to apply the reduction atomic{x=0; y=2;} and atomic{y=1; x=y;}, but only in the initial state where both x=0 and y=1 commute. The resulting reduced system, as shown with bold arrows, now discards various states. Clearly, a safety property such as $\Box\neg(x = 1 \wedge y = 2)$ is not preserved anymore by such a reduction, even though x=0 and y=1 never disable the property (L4 in Sect. 3 holds).

The mover definition comparing all behaviors of all other threads is thus merely a way to (over)estimate the computational future. But we can do better, without precisely calculating the future computations (which would indulge in a task that the reduction is trying to avoid in the first place). For example, unreachable code should not negatively impact movability of statements in the entire program. By the same line of reasoning, we can conclude that lazy initialization procedures (e.g. Fig. 4) should not eliminate movers in the remainder of the program. Intuitively, one can run the program until after initialization, then remove the initialization procedure and restart the verification using that state as the new initial state. Similarly, reading unchanging buckets in the hash table of Fig. 5 should not cause interference. And the dynamically assigned, yet disjoint, pointers of Fig. 6 never overlap, so their dereferences can also become movers *after* their assignment. The current section provides dynamic notion of movability and a generalized reduction theorem that can use this new notion. Proofs of all lemmas and theorems can be found in our technical report [18].

4.1   Dynamic Movers

Recall from the example of Fig. 1 that we introduce branches in order to guide the dynamic reductions. This section formalizes the concept of a dynamic both-moving condition, guarding these branches. We only consider both movers for ease of explanation. Nonetheless, our report [18] considers left and right movers.

Definition 1 (Dynamic both-moving conditions).
A state predicate (a subset of states) c_α is a dynamic both-moving condition for a CFG edge $(l, \alpha, l') \in \delta_i$, if for all $j \neq i$ and $\beta \in \Delta_j$: $(c_\alpha /\!\!/ \xrightarrow{\alpha}_i) \bowtie (c_\alpha /\!\!/ \xrightarrow{\beta}_j)$ and both $\xrightarrow{\alpha}_i$, $\xrightarrow{\beta}_j$ do not disable c_α, i.e. $c_\alpha /\!\!/ \xrightarrow{\beta}_j \backslash\!\!\backslash \overline{c_\alpha} = c_\alpha /\!\!/ \xrightarrow{\alpha}_i \backslash\!\!\backslash \overline{c_\alpha} = \emptyset$.

One key property of a dynamic both-moving condition for $\alpha \in \Delta_i$ is its monotonicity: In the transition system, the condition c_α can be enabled by remote threads ($j \neq i$), but never disabled. While the definition allows us to define many practical heuristics, we have identified the following both-moving conditions as useful. Although our heuristics still rely on static analysis, the required information is easier to establish (e.g. with basic control-flow analysis and the identification of CAS instructions) than for the global mover condition. When static analysis still fails to derive enough information for establishing one of these heuristics, $c_\alpha :=$ false can safely be taken, destining α as a non-mover statically.

Reachability. As in Fig. 4, interfering actions, such as the write at label W, may become unreachable once a certain program location has been reached. The dynamic condition for the read $\alpha \triangleq$ process(data[i + tid * 512])$_i$ therefore becomes: $c_\alpha := \bigwedge_{j\neq i} \bigwedge_{l \in L(j)}$ pc$_j \neq l$, where $L(j)$ is the set of all locations in V_j that can reach the location with label W in V_j. For example, for thread T1 we obtain $c_\alpha :=$ pc_T2 != a,b,c,d,W (abbreviated). Deriving this condition merely requires a simple reachability check on the CFG.

Static pointer dereference. If pointers are not modified in the future, then their dereferences commute if they point to different memory locations. For thread T1 in the pointer example in Fig. 6, we obtain $c_\alpha :=$ p1 != p2 && pc_T2 != a,b,c (here *p++ is the pointer dereference with p = p1).

Monotonic atomic. A CAS instruction CAS(p, a, b) is monotonic, if its expected value a is never equal to the value b that it tries to write. Assuming that no other instructions write to the location where p refers to, this means that once it is set to b, it never changes again. In the hash table example in Fig. 5, there is only a CAS instruction writing to the array T. The dynamic moving condition is: $c_\alpha :=$ T[index] != E.

Lemma 1. *The above conditions are dynamic both-moving conditions.*

4.2 Instrumentation

Figure 1 demonstrated how our instrumentation adds branches to dynamically implement the basic single-action rule. Lipton reduction is more complicated. Here, we provide an instrumentation that satisfies the constraints on these phases (see L1–L4 in Sect. 3). Roughly, we transform each CFG $G_i = (V_i, \delta_i)$ into an instrumented $G'_i \triangleq (V'_i, \delta'_i)$ as follows:

1. Replicate all $l_a \in V_i$ to new locations in $V'_i = \left\{ l^N_a, l^R_a, l^L_a, l^{R'}_a, l^{L'}_a \mid l_a \in V_i \right\}$: Respectively, there are external , pre- , and post- locations, plus two auxiliary pre- and post- locations for along branches.
2. Add edges/branches with dynamic moving conditions according to Table 1.

The rules in Table 1 precisely describe the instrumented edges in G'_i: for each graph part in the original G_i (middle column), the resulting parts of G'_i are shown (right column). As no non-movers are allowed in the post phase, R4 only checks the dynamic moving condition for all outgoing transitions of a post-location l^L_a. If it fails, the branch goes to an external location l^N_a from where the actual action can be executed (R1). If it succeeds, then the action commutes and can safely be executed while remaining in the post phase (R5). We do this from an intermediary post location $l^{L'}_a$. Since transitions α thus need to be split up into two steps in the post phase, dummy steps need to be introduced in the

Table 1. The CFG instrumentation

$G_i \triangleq (V_i, \delta_i)$	V_i', δ' in G_i' (pictured)
R1 $\forall (l_a, \alpha, l_b) \in \delta_i:$	l_a^N $\xrightarrow{c_\alpha \,/\!/\, \alpha} l_b^R$ $\xrightarrow{\neg c_\alpha \,/\!/\, \alpha} l_b^L$
R2 $\forall (l_a, \alpha, l_b) \in \delta_i:$	$l_a^{R'}$ $\xrightarrow{c_\alpha \,/\!/\, \alpha} l_b^R$ $\xrightarrow{\neg c_\alpha \,/\!/\, \alpha} l_b^L$
R3 $\forall l_a \in V_i:$	$l_a^R \xrightarrow{\;\;true\;\;} l_a^{R'}$
R4 $\forall l_a \in V_i \setminus LFS_i:$	l_a^L $\xrightarrow{c(l_a)} l_a^{L'}$ $\xrightarrow{\neg c(l_a)} l_a^N$ with $c(l_a) \triangleq$ $\bigwedge_{(l_a,\alpha,l_b)\in\delta_i} c_\alpha$
R5 $\forall (l_a, \alpha, l_b) \in \delta_i, l_a \in V_i \setminus LFS_i:$	$l_a^{L'} \xrightarrow{\;\;\alpha\;\;} l_b^L$
R6 $\forall l_a \in LFS_i:$	$l_a^L \xrightarrow{\;\;true\;\;} l_a^N$

pre phase (R1 and R2) to match this (R3), otherwise we lose bisimilarity (see subsequent subsection). As an intermediary pre location, we use $l_a^{R'}$.

All new paths in the instrumented G_i' adhere to the pattern:
$l_1^N \xrightarrow{\alpha_1} l_2^R \dots l_k^R \xrightarrow{\alpha_k} l_{k+1}^L \dots l_n^L \xrightarrow{\alpha_n} l_{n+1}^N$. Moreover, using the notion of *location feedback sets* (LFS) defined in Definition 2, R4 and R6 ensure that all cycles in the post phase contain an external state. This is because our reduction theorem (introduced later) allows non-terminating transactions as long as they remain in the pre-commit phase (it thus generalizes L3). Figure 9 shows a simple example CFG with its instrumentation. The subsequent reduction will completely hide the internal states, avoiding exponential blowup in the TS (see Sect. 4.3).

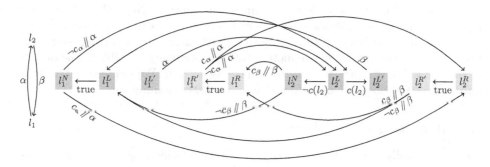

Fig. 9. Instrumentation (right) of a 2-location CFG (left) with $LFS = \{l_1\}$.

Definition 2 (LFS). *A location feedback set (LFS) for thread i is a subset $LFS_i \subseteq V_i$ such that for each cycle $C = l_1, .., l_n, l_1$ in G_i it holds that $LFS_i \cap C \neq \emptyset$. The corresponding (state) feedback set (FS) is: $C_i \triangleq \{(pc, d) \mid pc_i \in LFS_i\}$.*

Corollary 1 ([29]). $\bigcup_i C_i$ *is a feedback set in the TS.*

The instrumentation yields the following 3/4-partition of states for all threads i:

$$\mathcal{E}_i \triangleq \{(pc, d) \mid pc_i \in \{l_{sink}^N, l_{sink}^R, l_{sink}^L\}\} \qquad \text{(Error)} \qquad (2)$$

$$\mathcal{R}_i \triangleq \{(pc, d) \mid pc_i \in \{l^R, l^{R'}\}\} \setminus \mathcal{E}_i \qquad \text{(Pre-commit)} \qquad (3)$$

$$\mathcal{L}_i \triangleq \{(pc, d) \mid pc_i \in \{l^L, l^{L'}\}\} \setminus \mathcal{E}_i \qquad \text{(Post-commit)} \qquad (4)$$

$$\mathcal{F}_i \triangleq \{(pc, d) \mid pc_i \in \{l^N\}\} \setminus \mathcal{E}_i \qquad \text{(Ext./non-error)} \qquad (5)$$

$$\mathcal{N}_i \triangleq \mathcal{F}_i \uplus \mathcal{E}_i \qquad \text{(External)} \qquad (6)$$

The new initial state is (pc_0', d_0), with $\forall i \colon pc_{0,i}' = l_{0,i}^N$. Let $\text{Locs}' \triangleq \prod_i V_i'$ and $C' \triangleq (\text{Locs}' \times \text{Data}, \to')$ be the transition system of the instrumented CFG. The instrumentation preserves the behavior of the original system:

Lemma 2. *An error state is $\to$-reachable in the original system iff an error state is $\to'$-reachable in the instrumented system.*

Recall the situation illustrated in Fig. 3 within the example in Fig. 1. Rules R1, R2, and R4 of our instrumentation in Table 1 give rise to a similar problem as illustrated in the following.

Hence, our instrumentation introduces non-movers. Nevertheless, we can prove that the target states are bisimilar. This enables us to introduce a weaker notion of commutativity up to bisimilarity which effectively will enable a reduction along one branch (where reduction was not originally possible). The details of the reduction are presented in the following section. We emphasize that our implementation does not introduce any unnecessary non-movers.

4.3   Reduction

We now formally define the notion of thread bisimulation required for the reduction, as well as commutativity up to bisimilarity.

Definition 3 (thread bisimulation). *An equivalence relation R on the states of a TS $(S, \to)$ is a thread bisimulation iff*

$$\forall \sigma, \sigma', \sigma_1, i: \quad \begin{array}{c} \sigma \;\;\to_i\;\; \sigma_1 \\ \Big|{\scriptstyle \mathcal{R}} \\ \sigma' \end{array} \quad \Rightarrow \exists \sigma_1': \quad \begin{array}{ccc} \sigma \;\;\to_i\;\; \sigma_1 \\ \Big|{\scriptstyle \mathcal{R}} \quad\quad \Big|{\scriptstyle \mathcal{R}} \\ \sigma' \;\;\to_i\;\; \sigma_1' \end{array}$$

Standard bisimulation [34,37] is an equivalence relation R which satisfies the property from Definition 3 when the indexes i of the transitions are removed. Hence, in a thread bisimulation, in contrast to standard bisimulation, the transitions performed by thread i will be matched by transitions performed by the same thread i. As we only make use of thread bisimulations, we will often refer to them simply as bisimulations.

Definition 4 (commutativity up to bisimulation). *Let R be a thread bisimulation on a TS $(S, \to)$. The right and left commutativity up to R of the transition relation $\to_i$ with $\to_j$, notation $\to_i \overrightarrow{\bowtie}_R \to_j$ / $\to_i \overleftarrow{\bowtie}_R \to_j$ are defined as follows.*

$$\to_i \overrightarrow{\bowtie}_R \to_j \iff \qquad\qquad \to_i \overleftarrow{\bowtie}_R \to_j \iff$$

$$\begin{array}{ccc} \sigma_1 & & \sigma_1 \xrightarrow{} _j \sigma_4 \\ \Big\downarrow & \Rightarrow \exists \sigma_3', \sigma_4: \Big\downarrow & \quad\searrow \\ \sigma_2 \to_j \sigma_3 & \sigma_2 \to_j \sigma_3 & \sigma_3' \\ & & (\sigma_3, \sigma_3') \in R \end{array} \qquad \begin{array}{ccc} \sigma_1 \to_i \sigma_2 & & \sigma_1 \to_i \sigma_2 \\ \searrow & \Rightarrow \exists \sigma_3', \sigma_4: \searrow & \\ \sigma_3 & \sigma_4 \to_i \sigma_3' & \searrow \sigma_3 \\ & & (\sigma_3, \sigma_3') \in R \end{array}$$

Our reduction works on parallel transaction systems (PT), a specialized TS. While its definition (Definition 5) looks complicated, most rules are concerned with ensuring that all paths in the underlying TS form transactions, i.e. that they conform to the pattern $\sigma_1 \xrightarrow{\alpha_1} \sigma_2 \cdots \sigma_k \xrightarrow{\alpha_k} \sigma_{k+1} \cdots \sigma_n \xrightarrow{\alpha_n} \sigma_{n+1}$, where α_k is the non-mover, etc. We have from the perspective of thread i that: σ_1 and σ_{n+1} are *external* , $\forall 1 < x \le k\colon \sigma_x$ *pre-commit* , and $\forall k < x \le n\colon \sigma_x$ *post-commit* states. The rest of the conditions ensure bisimilarity and constrain error locations.

The reduction theorem, Theorem 1, then tells us that reachability of error states is preserved (and reflected) if we consider only PT-paths between globally external states $\mathcal{N}$. The reduction thus removes all internal states $\mathcal{I}$ where $\mathcal{I} \triangleq \bigcup_i \mathcal{I}_i$ and $\mathcal{I}_i \triangleq \mathcal{L}_i \cup \mathcal{R}_i$ (at least one internal phase).

Definition 5 (transaction system). *A parallel transaction system PT is a transition system $TS = (S, \to)$ whose states are partitioned in three sets of phases and error states in one of the phases, for each thread i. For each thread i, there exists a thread bisimulation relation $\cong_i$. Additionally, the following properties hold (for all i, all $j \ne i$):*

1. $S = \mathcal{R}_i \uplus \mathcal{L}_i \uplus \mathcal{N}_i$ and $\mathcal{N}_i = \mathcal{E}_i \uplus \mathcal{F}_i$ *(the 3/4-partition)*
2. $\forall \sigma \in \mathcal{L}_i\colon \exists \sigma' \in \mathcal{N}_i\colon \sigma \to_i^+ \sigma'$ *(post phases terminate)*
3. $\to_i \subseteq \mathcal{L}_j^2 \cup \mathcal{R}_j^2 \cup \mathcal{E}_j^2 \cup \mathcal{F}_j^2$ *(i preserves $j's$ phase)*

4. $\mathcal{E}_i /\!/\!\!\rightarrow_i \backslash\!\backslash \overline{\mathcal{E}_i} = \emptyset$ *(local transitions preserve errors)*
5. $\mathcal{L}_i /\!/\!\!\rightarrow_i \backslash\!\backslash \mathcal{R}_i = \emptyset$ *((locally) post does not reach pre)*
6. $\cong_i \subseteq \mathcal{E}_i^2 \cup \overline{\mathcal{E}_i}^2$ *(bisimulation preserves (non)errors)*
7. $\cong_i \subseteq \mathcal{L}_j^2 \cup \mathcal{R}_j^2 \cup \mathcal{E}_j^2 \cup \mathcal{F}_j^2$ *($\cong_i$ entails j-phase-equality)*
8. $(\rightarrow_i \backslash\!\backslash \mathcal{R}_i) \overrightarrow{\bowtie}_{\{j\}} \rightarrow_j$ *(i to pre right commutes up to $\cong_j$ with j)*
9. $(\mathcal{L}_i /\!/\!\!\rightarrow_i) \overleftarrow{\bowtie}_{\{i,j\}} \rightarrow_j$ *(i from post left commutes up to $\cong_{\{i,j\}}$ with j)*

In item 8 and item 9, $\overrightarrow{\bowtie}_Z$ and $\overleftarrow{\bowtie}_Z$ (for a set of threads Z) are short notations for $\overrightarrow{\bowtie}_{\cong_Z}$ and $\overleftarrow{\bowtie}_{\cong_Z}$, respectively, with $\cong_Z$ being the transitive closure of the union of all $\cong_i$ for $i \in Z$.

Theorem 1. *The block-reduced transition relation $\rightsquigarrow$ of a parallel transaction system $PT = (S, \rightarrow)$ is defined in two steps:*

$$\hookrightarrow_i \triangleq \mathcal{N}_{j \neq i} /\!/\!\!\rightarrow_i \qquad \text{(i only transits when all j are in external)}$$

$$\rightsquigarrow_i \triangleq \mathcal{N}_i /\!/ (\hookrightarrow_i \backslash\!\backslash \overline{\mathcal{N}_i})^* \hookrightarrow_i \backslash\!\backslash \mathcal{N}_i \qquad \text{(block steps skip internal states } \overline{\mathcal{N}_i})$$

Let $\rightsquigarrow \triangleq \bigcup_i \rightsquigarrow_i$, $\mathcal{N} \triangleq \bigcap_i \mathcal{N}_i$ and $\mathcal{E} \triangleq \bigcup_i \mathcal{E}_i$. We have $p \rightarrow^* q$ for $p \in \mathcal{N}$ and $q \in \mathcal{E}$ if and only if $p \rightsquigarrow^* q'$ for $q' \in \mathcal{E}$.

Our instrumentation from Table 1 in Sect. 4.2 indeed gives rise to a *PT* (Lemma 3) with the state partitioning from (Eqs. 2–6). The following equivalence relation $\sim_i$ over locations becomes the needed bisimulation $\cong_i$ when lifted to states. (The locations in the rightmost column of Table 1 are intentionally positioned such that vertically aligned locations are bisimilar.)

$$\sim_i \triangleq \left\{ (l^X, l^Y) \mid l \in V_i \wedge X, Y \in \{L, R\} \right\} \cup \left\{ (l^X, l^Y) \mid l \in V_i \wedge X, Y \in \{N, R', L'\} \right\}$$

$$\cong_i \triangleq \left\{ ((\mathsf{pc}, d), (\mathsf{pc}', d')) \mid d = d' \wedge \mathsf{pc}_i \sim_i \mathsf{pc}'_i \wedge \forall j \neq i : \mathsf{pc}_j = \mathsf{pc}'_j \right\}$$

The dynamic both-moving condition in Definition 1 is sufficient to prove (item 8–9). The LFS notion in Definition 2 is sufficient to prove post-phase termination (item 2).

Lemma 3. *The instrumented TS $C' = (\mathsf{Locs}' \times \mathsf{Data}, \rightarrow')$ is a PT.*

All of the apparent exponential blowup of the added phases ($5^{|\mathsf{Threads}|}$) is hidden by the reduction as $\rightsquigarrow$ only reveals external states $\mathcal{N} \triangleq \bigcap_i \mathcal{N}_i$ (note that $S = \mathcal{I} \uplus \mathcal{N}$) and there is only one instrumented external location (replicated sinks can be eliminated easily with a more verbose instrumentation).

5   Block Encoding of Transition Relations

We implement the reduction by encoding a transition relation for symbolic model checking. Transitions encoded as SMT formulas may not contain cycles. Although our instrumentation conservatively eliminates cycles in the post-commit phase of transactions with external states, cycles (without external locations) can still occur in the pre-phase. To break these remaining cycles, we use a refined location feedback set LFS'_i of the instrumented CFG without external locations $G'_i \setminus \{l^N \in V'_i\}$ (this also removes edges incident to external locations).

Now, we can construct a new block-reduced relation $\twoheadrightarrow$. It resembles the definition of $\rightsquigarrow$ in Theorem 1, except for the fact that the execution of thread i can be interrupted in an internal state C'_i (LFS'_i lifted to states) in order to break the remaining cycles.

$$\twoheadrightarrow \triangleq \bigcup_i \twoheadrightarrow_i , \text{ where } \twoheadrightarrow_i \triangleq \mathcal{X}_i /\!\!/ (\hookrightarrow_i \setminus \overline{\mathcal{X}_i})^* \hookrightarrow_i \setminus \mathcal{X}_i \text{ with } \mathcal{X}_i \triangleq \mathcal{N}_i \cup C'_i$$

Here, the use of $\hookrightarrow_i$ (from Theorem 1) warrants that only thread i can transit from the newly exposed internal states $C'_i \subseteq \mathcal{N}_{j \neq i}$. Therefore, by carefully selecting the exposed locations of C'_i, e.g. only l^R_a, the overhead is limited to a factor two.

To encode $\twoheadrightarrow$, we identify blocks of paths that start and end in external or LFS locations, but do not traverse external or LFS locations and encode them using large blocks [4]. This automatically takes care of disallowing intermediate states, except for the states C'_i exposed by the breaking of cycles. At the corresponding locations, we thus add constraints to the scheduler encoding to only allow the current thread to execute. To support pthreads constructs, such as locks and thread management, we use similar scheduling mechanisms.

6 Experiments

We implemented the encoding with dynamic reduction in the Vienna Verification Tool (VVT) [23,24]. VVT implements CTIGAR [6], an IC3 [8] algorithm with predicate-abstraction, and bounded model checking (BMC) [25]. VVT came fourth in the concurrency category of SVComp 2016 [3] the first year it participated, only surpassed by tools based on BMC or symbolic simulation.

We evaluated our dynamic reductions on the running examples and compared the running time of the following configurations:

– BMC with all dynamic reductions (*BMC-dyn* in the graphs);
– BMC with only static reductions and phase variables from [16] (*BMC-phase*);
– IC3 with all dynamic reductions (*IC3-dyn*); and
– IC3 with only static reductions and phase variables from [16] (*IC3-phase*).

We used a one-hour time limit for each run and ran each instance four times. Variation over the four runs was insignificant, so we omit plotting it. Missing values in the graphs indicate a timeout. The whole process, including heuristic derivation, instrumentation and encoding, is automated.

Lazy Initialization. We implemented a version of the program in Fig. 4 where the function process counts array elements. As verification condition, we used the correct total count. As no other heuristic applies, only the reachability heuristic can contribute. Figure 10a shows that both BMC and IC3 benefit enormously from the obtained dynamic reductions: With static reductions, IC3 can only verify the program for one thread and BMC for three, while with dynamic reduction, both BMC and IC3 scale to seven threads.

Hashtable. The lockless hash table of Fig. 5 is used in the following three experiments. In each, we expected benefits from the monotonic atomic heuristic.

1. Every thread attempts to insert an already-present element into the table. The verification condition is that every *find-or-put* operation returns FOUND. Since a successful lookup operation doesn't change the hash table, the dynamic reduction takes full effect: While the static reduction can only verify two threads for BMC and four for IC3, the dynamic reduction can handle six threads for BMC and more than seven for IC3.
2. Each thread inserts one element into an empty hash table. The verification condition is that all inserted elements are present in the hash table after all threads have finished executing. We now see in Fig. 10c that the dynamic reduction benefits neither BMC nor IC3. This is because every thread changes the hash table thus forcing an exploration of all interleavings.

   The overhead of using dynamic reductions, while significant in the BMC case, seems to be non-existent in IC3.
3. Since both of the previous cases can be considered corner-cases (the hash table being either empty or full), this configuration has half of the threads inserting values already present while the other half insert new values.

   While the difference between static and dynamic reductions is not as extreme as before, we can still see that we profit from dynamic reductions, being able to verify two more threads in the IC3 case.

Load Balancing. We used the load-balancing example (Fig. 6), expecting the static pointer heuristic to improve the dynamic reductions. We verified that the computed sum of the counters is indeed the expected result. Our experiment revealed that dynamic reductions reduce the runtime from 15 minutes to 97 s for two threads already.

Dynamic Locking. In addition to the earlier examples of Sect. 2, we also study the effect of lock pointer analysis. To this end, we created a parallel program in which multiple threads use a common lock to access two global variables. To simulate locks in complex object structures (that are common, but impossible to track for static analysis), the single lock these threads use is randomly picked, similar to how the work load is assigned in Fig. 6. We extended our static pointer dereference heuristic to also determine whether other critical sections with the same conflicting operations are protected by the same lock, potentially allowing the critical section to become a single transaction. In the critical section we again count. The total is used as verification condition. Fig. 10e shows that the dynamic reduction indeed kicks in and benefits both IC3 and BMC.

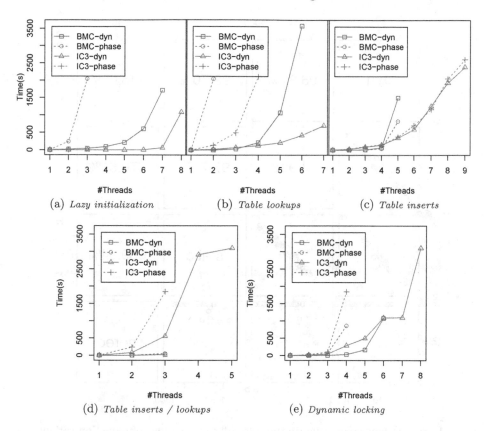

(a) *Lazy initialization* (b) *Table lookups* (c) *Table inserts*

(d) *Table inserts / lookups* (e) *Dynamic locking*

Fig. 10. Hash table and dynamic locking benchmark results

SVComp. We also ran our IC3 implementation on the `pthread-ext` and `pthread-atomic` categories of the *software verification competition* (SVComp) benchmarks [2,3]. In instances with an unbounded number of threads, we introduced a limit of three threads. To check the effect of different reduction-strategies on the verification time, we tested the following reductions:

dyn: Dynamic with all heuristics from Sect. 4.1.
phase: Dynamic phases only (equal to [16]).
static: Static (as in Sect. 3).
nored: No reduction, all interleavings considered.

Figure 11 shows that static Lipton reduction yields an average six-fold decrease in runtime when compared to no reduction. Enabling the various dynamic improvements (*dyn, phase*) does not show improvement over the static case (*static*), since most of the benchmarks are either too small or do not have opportunities for reductions, but also not much overhead (up to 7%). Comparing the *nored* case with the other cases shows the benefit of removing intermediate states.

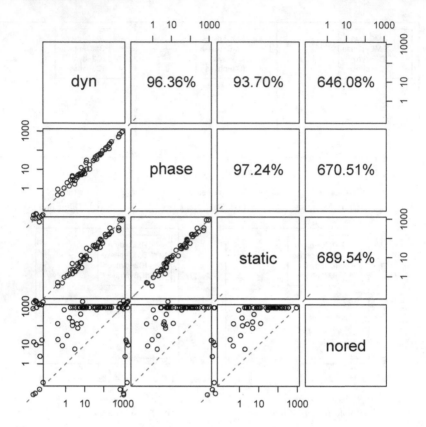

Fig. 11. Scatterplots comparing runtimes for all combinations of reduction variants on SVComp benchmarks. The upper half shows relative accumulated runtimes for these combinations.

7   Related Work

Lipton's reduction was refined multiple times [10,12,20,31,40]. It has recently been applied in the context of compositional verification [39]. Qadeer and Flanagan [16] introduce dynamic phase variables to identify internal and external states. They also provided a dynamic solution for determining locked regions. Their approach, however, does not solve the examples featured in the current paper. Moreover, in [16], the phases of target locations of non-deterministic transitions are required to agree. This restriction is not present in our encoding.

Grumberg et al. [21] present underapproximation-widening, which iteratively refines an under-approximated encoding of the system. In their implementation, interleavings are constrained to achieve the under-approximation. Because refinement is done based on verification proofs, irrelevant interleavings will never be considered. The technique currently only supports BMC and the implementation is not available, so we did not compare against it.

Kahlon et al. [27] extend the dynamic solution of [16], by supporting a strictly more general set of lock patterns. They incorporate the transactions into the stubborn set POR method [42] and encode these in the transition relation in similar fashion as in Alur et al. [1]. Unlike ours, their technique does not support other constructs than locks.

While in fact it is sufficient for item 2 of Definition 5 to pinpoint a single state in each bottom SCC of the CFG, we use feedback sets because the encoding in Sect. 5 also requires them. Moreover, we take a syntactical definition for ease of explanation. Semantic heuristics for better feedback sets can be found in [29] and can easily be supported via state predicates. (Further optimizations are possible [29].) Obtaining the smallest (vertex) LFS is an NP-complete problem well known in graph theory [7]. As CFGs are simple graphs, estimations via basic DFS suffice. (In POR, similar approaches are used for *the ignoring problem* [35, 42].)

Elmas et al. [14] propose dynamic reductions for type systems, where the invariant is used to weaken the mover definition. The over-approximations performed in IC3, however, decrease the effectiveness of such approaches.

In POR, similar techniques have been employed in [13] and the earlier-mentioned *necessary enabling sets* of [19, 41]. Completely dynamic approaches exist [15], but symbolic versions remain highly static [1]. Notable exceptions are peephole and monotonic POR by Wang et al. [28, 43]. Like sleep sets [19], however, these only reduce the number of transitions—not states—which is crucial in e.g. IC3 to cut counterexamples to induction [8]. Cartesian POR [22] is a dynamic form of Lipton reduction for explicit-state model checking.

8 Conclusions

Our work provides a novel dynamic reduction for symbolic software model checking. To accomplish this, we presented a reduction theorem generalized with bisimulation, facilitating various dynamic instrumentations as our heuristics show. We demonstrated its effectiveness with an encoding used by the BMC and IC3 algorithms in the model checker VVT.

References

1. Alur, R., Brayton, R.K., Henzinger, T.A., Qadeer, S., Rajamani, S.K.: Partial-order reduction in symbolic state space exploration. In: Grumberg, O. (ed.) CAV 1997. LNCS, vol. 1254, pp. 340–351. Springer, Heidelberg (1997). doi:10.1007/3-540-63166-6_34
2. Beyer, D.: The software verification competition website. http://sv-comp.sosy-lab.org/2016/
3. Beyer, D.: Reliable and reproducible competition results with benchexec and witnesses (Report on SV-COMP 2016). In: Chechik, M., Raskin, J.-F. (eds.) TACAS 2016. LNCS, vol. 9636, pp. 887–904. Springer, Heidelberg (2016). doi:10.1007/978-3-662-49674-9_55
4. Beyer, D., Cimatti, A., Griggio, A., Erkan Keremoglu, M., Sebastiani, R.: Software model checking via large-block encoding. In: FMCAD, pp. 25–32. IEEE (2009)

5. Beyer, D., Henzinger, T.A., Théoduloz, G.: Configurable software verification: concretizing the convergence of model checking and program analysis. In: Damm, W., Hermanns, H. (eds.) CAV 2007. LNCS, vol. 4590, pp. 504–518. Springer, Heidelberg (2007). doi:10.1007/978-3-540-73368-3_51

6. Birgmeier, Johannes, Bradley, Aaron, R., Weissenbacher, Georg: Counterexample to induction-guided abstraction-refinement (CTIGAR). In: Biere, Armin, Bloem, Roderick (eds.) CAV 2014. LNCS, vol. 8559, pp. 831–848. Springer, Cham (2014). doi:10.1007/978-3-319-08867-9_55

7. Bondy, J.A., Murty, U.S.R.: Graph Theory with Applications, vol. 290. Macmillan, London (1976)

8. Bradley, A.R.: SAT-based model checking without unrolling. In: Jhala, R., Schmidt, D. (eds.) VMCAI 2011. LNCS, vol. 6538, pp. 70–87. Springer, Heidelberg (2011). doi:10.1007/978-3-642-18275-4_7

9. Cimatti, A., Griggio, A., Mover, S., Tonetta, S.: IC3 modulo theories via implicit predicate abstraction. In: Ábrahám, E., Havelund, K. (eds.) TACAS 2014. LNCS, vol. 8413, pp. 46–61. Springer, Heidelberg (2014). doi:10.1007/978-3-642-54862-8_4

10. Cohen, E., Lamport, L.: Reduction in TLA. In: Sangiorgi, D., Simone, R. (eds.) CONCUR 1998. LNCS, vol. 1466, pp. 317–331. Springer, Heidelberg (1998). doi:10.1007/BFb0055631

11. Dimitrov, D., et al.: Commutativity race detection. ACM SIGPLAN Not. **49**(6), 305–315 (2014)

12. Doeppner Jr., T.W.: Parallel program correctness through refinement. In: POPL, pp. 155–169. ACM (1977)

13. Dwyer, M.B., Robby, J.H., Ranganath, V.P.: Exploiting object escape, locking information in partial-order reductions for concurrent object-oriented programs. FMSD **25**(2–3), 199–240 (2004)

14. Elmas, T., Qadeer, S., Tasiran, S.: A calculus of atomic actions. In: POPL, pp. 2–15. ACM (2009)

15. Flanagan, C., Godefroid, P.: Dynamic partial-order reduction for model checking software. In: POPL, vol. 40, no. 1, pp. 110–121. ACM (2005)

16. Flanagan, C., Qadeer, S.: Transactions for software model checking. ENTCS **89**(3), 518–539 (2003). Software Model Checking

17. Flanagan, C., Qadeer, S.: A type and effect system for atomicity. In: PLDI, pp. 338–349. ACM (2003)

18. Günther, H., Laarman, A., Sokolova, A., Weissenbacher, G.: Dynamic reductions for model checking concurrent software (2016). https://arxiv.org/abs/1611.09318

19. Godefroid, P. (ed.): Partial-Order Methods for the Verification of Concurrent Systems. LNCS, vol. 1032. Springer, Heidelberg (1996)

20. Gribomont, E.P.: Atomicity refinement and trace reduction theorems. In: Alur, R., Henzinger, T.A. (eds.) CAV 1996. LNCS, vol. 1102, pp. 311–322. Springer, Heidelberg (1996). doi:10.1007/3-540-61474-5_79

21. Grumberg, O., Lerda, F., Strichman, O., Theobald, M.: Proof-guided under approximation-widening for multi-process systems. In: POPL, pp. 122–131. ACM (2005)

22. Gueta, G., Flanagan, C., Yahav, E., Sagiv, M.: Cartesian partial-order reduction. In: Bošnački, D., Edelkamp, S. (eds.) SPIN 2007. LNCS, vol. 4595, pp. 95–112. Springer, Heidelberg (2007). doi:10.1007/978-3-540-73370-6_8

23. Günther, H.: The Vienna verification tool website. http://vvt.forsyte.at/. Accessed 21 Nov 2016

24. Günther, H., Laarman, A., Weissenbacher, G.: Vienna verification tool: IC3 for parallel software. In: Chechik, M., Raskin, J.-F. (eds.) TACAS 2016. LNCS, vol. 9636, pp. 954–957. Springer, Heidelberg (2016). doi:10.1007/978-3-662-49674-9_69

25. Günther, H., Weissenbacher, G.: Incremental bounded software model checking. In: SPIN, pp. 40–47. ACM (2014)
26. Henzinger, T.A., Jhala, R., Majumdar, R., Sutre, G.: Lazy abstraction. In: POPL, pp. 58–70. ACM (2002)
27. Kahlon, V., Gupta, A., Sinha, N.: Symbolic model checking of concurrent programs using partial orders and on-the-fly transactions. In: Ball, T., Jones, R.B. (eds.) CAV 2006. LNCS, vol. 4144, pp. 286–299. Springer, Heidelberg (2006). doi:10.1007/11817963_28
28. Kahlon, V., Wang, C., Gupta, A.: Monotonic partial order reduction: an optimal symbolic partial order reduction technique. In: Bouajjani, A., Maler, O. (eds.) CAV 2009. LNCS, vol. 5643, pp. 398–413. Springer, Heidelberg (2009). doi:10.1007/978-3-642-02658-4_31
29. Kurshan, R., Levin, V., Minea, M., Peled, D., Yenigün, H.: Static partial order reduction. In: Steffen, B. (ed.) TACAS 1998. LNCS, vol. 1384, pp. 345–357. Springer, Heidelberg (1998). doi:10.1007/BFb0054182
30. Laarman, A.W., van de Pol, J.C., Weber, M.: Boosting multi-core reachability performance with shared hash tables. In: FMCAD, pp. 247–255. IEEE-CS (2010)
31. Lamport, L., Schneider, F.B.: Pretending atomicity. Technical report, Cornell University (1989)
32. Lipton, R.J.: Reduction: a method of proving properties of parallel programs. Commun. ACM 18(12), 717–721 (1975)
33. McMillan, K.L.: Lazy abstraction with interpolants. In: Ball, T., Jones, R.B. (eds.) CAV 2006. LNCS, vol. 4144, pp. 123–136. Springer, Heidelberg (2006). doi:10.1007/11817963_14
34. Milner, R.: Communication and Concurrency. Prentice Hall, New York (1989)
35. Nalumasu, R., Gopalakrishnan, G.: An efficient partial order reduction algorithm with an alternative proviso implementation. FMSD 20(3), 231–247 (2002)
36. Papadimitriou, C.: The Theory of Database Concurrency Control. Principles of Computer Science Series. Computer Science Press, San Jose (1986)
37. Park, D.: Concurrency and automata on infinite sequences. In: Deussen, P. (ed.) GI-TCS 1981. LNCS, vol. 104, pp. 167–183. Springer, Berlin, Heidelberg (1981). doi:10.1007/BFb0017309
38. Peled, D.: All from one, one for all: on model checking using representatives. In: Courcoubetis, C. (ed.) CAV 1993. LNCS, vol. 697, pp. 409–423. Springer, Heidelberg (1993). doi:10.1007/3-540-56922-7_34
39. Popeea, C., Rybalchenko, A., Wilhelm, A.: Reduction for compositional verification of multi-threaded programs. In: FMCAD, pp. 187–194. IEEE (2014)
40. Stoller, S.D., Cohen, E.: Optimistic synchronization-based state-space reduction. In: Garavel, H., Hatcliff, J. (eds.) TACAS 2003. LNCS, vol. 2619, pp. 489–504. Springer, Heidelberg (2003). doi:10.1007/3-540-36577-X_36
41. Valmari, A.: Eliminating redundant interleavings during concurrent program verification. In: Odijk, E., Rem, M., Syre, J.-C. (eds.) PARLE 1989. LNCS, vol. 366, pp. 89–103. Springer, Heidelberg (1989). doi:10.1007/3-540-51285-3_35
42. Valmari, A.: Stubborn sets for reduced state space generation. In: Rozenberg, G. (ed.) ICATPN 1989. LNCS, vol. 483, pp. 491–515. Springer, Heidelberg (1991). doi:10.1007/3-540-53863-1_36
43. Wang, C., Yang, Z., Kahlon, V., Gupta, A.: Peephole partial order reduction. In: Ramakrishnan, C.R., Rehof, J. (eds.) TACAS 2008. LNCS, vol. 4963, pp. 382–396. Springer, Heidelberg (2008). doi:10.1007/978-3-540-78800-3_29

Synthesising Strategy Improvement and Recursive Algorithms for Solving 2.5 Player Parity Games

Ernst Moritz Hahn[1], Sven Schewe[2(✉)], Andrea Turrini[1], and Lijun Zhang[1]

[1] State Key Laboratory of Computer Science,
Institute of Software, CAS, Beijing, China
[2] University of Liverpool, Liverpool, UK
sven.schewe@liverpool.ac.uk

Abstract. 2.5 player parity games combine the challenges posed by 2.5 player reachability games and the qualitative analysis of parity games. These two types of problems are best approached with different types of algorithms: strategy improvement algorithms for 2.5 player reachability games and recursive algorithms for the qualitative analysis of parity games. We present a method that—in contrast to existing techniques— tackles both aspects with the best suited approach and works exclusively on the 2.5 player game itself. The resulting technique is powerful enough to handle games with several million states.

1 Introduction

Parity games are non-terminating zero sum games between two players, Player 0 and Player 1. The players move a token along the edges of a finite graph without sinks. The vertices are *coloured*, i.e. labelled with a priority taken from the set of natural numbers. The infinite sequence of vertices visited by the token is called the run of a graph, and each run is coloured according to the minimum priority that appears infinitely often on the run. A run is winning for a player if the parity of its colour agrees with the parity of the player.

Parity games come in two flavours: games with random moves, also called 2.5 player games, and games without random moves, called 2 player games. For 2 player games, the adversarial objectives of the two players are to ensure that the lowest priority that occurs infinitely often is even (for Player 0) and odd (for Player 1), respectively. For 2.5 player games, the adversarial objectives of the two players are to maximise the likelihood that the lowest priority that occurs infinitely often is even resp. odd.

Solving parity games is the central and most expensive step in many model checking [1,16,20,34,48], satisfiability checking [34,43,46,48], and synthesis [39, 44] methods. As a result, efficient algorithms for 2 player parity games have been studied intensively [3–5,19,21,22,31,32,34,36–38,40–42,45,47,49].

Parity games with 2.5 players have recently attracted attention [6–10,17, 18,26,50]. This attention, however, does not mean that results are similarly

© Springer International Publishing AG 2017
A. Bouajjani and D. Monniaux (Eds.): VMCAI 2017, LNCS 10145, pp. 266–287, 2017.
DOI: 10.1007/978-3-319-52234-0_15

rich or similarly diverse as for 2 player games. Results on the existence of pure strategies and on approximation algorithms [17,50] are decades younger than similar results for 2 player games, while algorithmic solutions [7,9] focus on strategy improvement techniques only.

The qualitative counterpart of 2.5 player games, where one of the players has the goal to win almost surely while the other one wants to win with a non-zero chance, can be reduced to 2 player parity games, cf. [12] or attacked directly on the 2.5 player game with recursive algorithm [30]. The more interesting quantitative analysis can be approached through a reduction to 2.5 player reachability games [2], which can then be attacked with strategy improvement algorithms [14,22,36,40,45]. Alternatively, entangled strategy improvement algorithms can also run concurrently the 2.5 player parity game directly (for the quantitative aspects) and on a reduction to 2 player parity games (for the qualitative aspects) [7,9]. (Or, likewise, run on the larger game with an ordered quality measure that gives preference to the likelihood to win and uses the progress measure from [4] or [47] as a tie-breaker.)

This raises the question if strategy improvement techniques can be directly applied on 2.5 player parity games, especially as such games are memoryless determined and therefore satisfy a main prerequisite for the use of strategy improvement algorithms. The short answer is that strategy algorithms for 2.5 player parity games simply do not work. Classical strategy improvement algorithms follow a joint pattern. They start with an arbitrary strategy f for one of the players (say Player 0). This strategy f maps each vertex of Player 0 to a successor, and thus resolves all moves of Player 0. This strategy is then *improved* by changing the strategy f at positions, where it is *profitable* to do so. The following steps are applied repeatedly until there is no improvement in Step 2.

1. Evaluate the simpler game resulting from fixing f.
2. Identify all changes to f that, when applied once[1], lead to an improvement.
3. Obtain a new strategy f' from f by selecting some subset of these changes.

So where does this approach go wrong? The first step works fine. After fixing a strategy for Player 0, we obtain a 1.5 player parity game, which can be solved efficiently with standard techniques [15].

It is also not problematic to identify the profitable switches in the second step. The winning probability for the respective successor vertex provides a natural measure for the profitability of a switch. We will show in Sect. 5 that, as usual for strategy improvement, any combination of such profitable switches will lead to an improvement.

The problem arises with the optimality guarantees. Strategy improvement algorithms guarantee that a strategy that cannot be improved is optimal. In the next paragraph, we will see an example, where this is not the case. Moreover, we will see that it can be necessary to change several decisions in a strategy f in order to obtain an improvement, something which is against the principles of strategy improvement.

---

[1] In classic strategy improvement algorithms, the restriction to implementing a change once is made to keep it easy to identify the improvements. Such changes will also lead to an improvement when applied repeatedly.

1.1   An Illustrating Example

Consider the example 2.5 player parity game $\mathcal{P}_e$ depicted in Fig. 1. Square vertices are controlled by Player 0, while triangular ones are controlled by Player 1. In circular vertices, a random successor vertex is chosen with the given probability. In v_w, Player 0 wins with certainty (and therefore in particular almost surely), while she loses with certainty in v_l. In $v_{0.55}$ (or $v_{0.95}$), Player 0 wins with probability 0.55 (or 0.95). For the nodes v_0 and v_1, we can see that the mutually *optimal strategy* for Player 0 and Player 1 are to play $e_{0,2}$ and $e_{1,1}$, respectively. Player 0 therefore wins with probability 0.95 when the game starts in v_0 and both players play optimally.

1.2   Naive Strategy Iteration

Strategy iteration algorithms start with an arbitrary strategy, and use an *update rule* to get profitable switches. These are edges, where the new target vertex has a higher probability of reaching the winning region (when applied once) compared to the current vertex. As usual with strategy improvement, any combination of profitable switches leads to a strictly better strategy for Player 0. We illustrate that, if done naively, it may lead to values that are only locally maximal. Assume that initially Player 0 chooses the edge $e_{0,1}$ from v_0, then the best counter strategy of Player 1 is to choose $e_{1,2}$ from v_1. The winning probability for Player 0 under these strategies is 0.55.

In strategy iteration, an update rule allows a player to switch actions only if the switching offers some *improvement*. Since by switching to the edge $e_{0,2}$ Player 0 would obtain the same winning probability, no strategy iteration can be applied, and the algorithm terminates with a sub-optimal solution.

Let us try to get some insights from this problem. Observe that Player 1 can entrap the play in the left vertices v_0 and v_1 when Player 0 chooses the edge $e_{0,2}$, such that the almost sure winning region of Player 0 cannot be reached. However, this comes to the cost of losing almost surely for Player 1, as the dominating colour on the resulting run is 0. Broadly speaking, Player 0 must find a strategy that maximises her chance of reaching her almost sure winning regions, but only

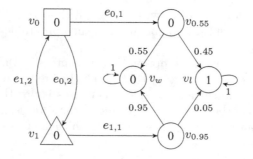

Fig. 1. A probabilistic parity game $\mathcal{P}_e$.

under the constraint that the counter strategy of Player 1 does not introduce new almost sure winning regions for Player 0.

1.3 Solutions from the Literature

In the literature, two different solutions to this problem have been discussed. Neither of these solutions works fully on the game graph of the 2.5 player parity game. Instead, one of them uses a reduction to reachability games through a simple gadget construction [2], while the other uses strategy improvement on two levels, for the qualitative update described above, and for an update within subgames of states that have the same value [7,9]; this requires to keep a pair of entangled strategies.

Gadget Construction for a Reduction to Reachability Games. In [2], it is shown that 2.5 player parity games can be solved by reducing them to 2.5 player reachability games and solving them, e.g. by using a strategy improvement approach. For this reduction, one can use the simple gadgets shown in Fig. 2a. There, when a vertex is passed by, the token goes to an accepting sink with probability wprob and to a losing sink with probability lprob, both depending on the priority of the node (and continues otherwise as in the parity game). For accordingly chosen wprob, lprob, any optimal strategy for this game is an optimal strategy for the parity game. To get this guarantee, however, the termination probabilities have to be very small indeed. In [2], they are constructed from the expression $(n!^2 2^{2n+3} M^{2n^2})^{-1}$ where n is the number of vertices and M is an integer depending on the probabilities occurring in the model. Unfortunately, these small probabilities render this approach very inefficient and introduce numerical instability.

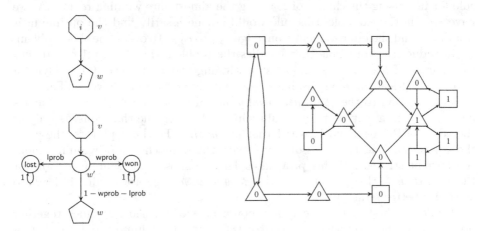

Fig. 2. Left: the gadget construction from [12] (a). Right: The qualitative game resulting from the game from Fig. 1 when using the gadget construction from [12] (b).

Classic Strategy Improvement for 2.5 Player Parity Games. In [7,9], the concept of strategy improvement algorithms has been extended to 2.5 player parity games. To overcome the problem that the natural quality measure—the likelihood of winning—is not fine enough, this approach constructs classical 2 player games played on translations of the value classes (the set of vertices with the same likelihood of winning). These subgames are translated using a gadget construction similar to the one used for qualitative solutions for 2.5 player to a solution to 2 player games from [12] (Fig. 2a). This results in the 2 player game shown in the right part of Fig. 2b.

The strategy improvement algorithm keeps track of 'witnesses $\omega = (\pi, \overline{\pi}_Q)$', which consists of a strategy π on the 2.5 player parity game, and a strategy $\overline{\pi}_Q$ defined on the 2 player game Q obtained from this 2.5 player game using the gadget construction from [12]. The strategies are entangled in that π is the translation[2] of $\overline{\pi}_Q$. That is, the strategies have to concur on the nodes of Player 0 from the 2.5 player game, and each update on π (resp. $\overline{\pi}_Q$) on the decisions from these vertices will translate to an update on the strategy of $\overline{\pi}_Q$ (resp. π) on the same vertices.

The valuation of one of these vertices is an ordered pair, consisting of the chance of obtaining the parity objective as the primary measure, and the value obtained in the quantitative game restricted to the individual value classes (vertices with the same chance of obtaining the parity objective) as a secondary measure [7,9].

1.4   Novel Strategy Iteration Algorithm

We show that we can apply strategy improvement techniques with two different update rules directly on the 2.5 player game. The first rule is a standard update rule for increasing the chance of reaching the almost sure winning region. As we have seen in the example, this rule would not necessarily find the optimum: it would not find the improvement from edge $e_{0,1}$ to $e_{0,2}$. To overcome this problem, we introduce a second rule that handles the problem that Player 1 can reduce the chances of reaching the almost sure winning region of Player 0 by playing a strategy that leads to a larger almost sure winning region for Player 0. This step uses a reduction to the *qualitative* evaluation of these games. Player 0 changes her strategy in a way that she would win on the subgame that consists only of the edges of Player 0 and Player 1 that are *neutral*. For both players, these are the edges that lead to successor states with the same chance of winning under the current strategy. If this provides a larger almost sure winning region for Player 0 than f, then update f in this *new winning region* accordingly leads to a strictly better strategy f'.

While the first rule alone is not powerful enough, the two rules together provide the guarantee that a strategy that cannot be improved by either of them is optimal.

---

[2] In the notation of [7,9], $\pi = \mathsf{Tr}_{\mathrm{almost}}(\overline{\pi}_Q)$.

Note that the second rule is a non-standard rule for strategy improvement. Not only does it not rely on an improvement that is obtained when a change is applied once, it also requires to apply a fixed set of changes (in the new region) in one step for correctness. This is quite unusual for strategy improvement algorithms, where the combination of updates selected is irrelevant for correctness.

A further significant difference to the method from [7,9] is that we do not have to revert to solving transformed games. Instead, we use the new generalisation of McNaughton's algorithm to the qualitative solution of 2.5 player parity games [30]. This method seems to maintain the good practical performance known for classic recursive techniques, which have proven to be much faster than strategy improvement for the qualitative analysis of parity games [25]. A consequence of this choice is that we solve the qualitative games completely when there is no progress through the naive update step, which reduces the number of times that qualitative updates have to be considered.

This way, we use strategy improvement for the quantitative part of the analysis, where it has its strengths, while leaning on a variation [30] of McNaughton's algorithm [21,37,49] for the qualitative part of the analysis, where prior research suggests that recursive algorithms outperform strategy improvement [25].

Note that our quality measure strategy improvement is the same as the primary measure used in classical strategy improvement for 2.5 player parity games [7,9]. Different from that approach, we do not need to resort to gadget constructions for progressing within value classes, but can overcome the lack of progress w.r.t. the primary measure through invoking a performant algorithm for solving 2.5 player games quantitatively [30].

1.5   Organisation of the Paper

We first introduce the standard terms and concepts in Sect. 2. We then recall the strategy improvement algorithms in Sect. 3, describe our algorithm in Sect. 4, show its correctness in Sect. 5, and offer an experimental evaluation in Sect. 6.

2   Terms and Concepts

A *probability distribution* over a finite set A is a function $\mu \colon A \to [0,1] \cap \mathbb{Q}$ with $\sum_{a \in A} \mu(a) = 1$. We denote by $Distr(A)$ the set of probability distributions over A.

Definition 1. *An arena is a tuple* $\mathfrak{A} = (V_0, V_1, V_r, E, \mathsf{prob})$, *where*

- V_0, V_1, *and* V_r *are three finite disjoint sets of* vertices *owned by the three players: Player 0, Player 1, and Player random, respectively. Let* $V \stackrel{def}{=} V_0 \cup V_1 \cup V_r$;
- $E \subseteq V \times V$ *is a set of* edges *such that* (V, E) *is a* sinkless *directed graph, i.e. for each* $v \in V$ *there exists* $v' \in V$ *such that* $(v, v') \in E$; *for* $\sigma \in \{0, 1, r\}$ *we let* $E_\sigma \stackrel{def}{=} E \cap (V_\sigma \times V)$.

– prob: $V_r \rightarrow Distr(V)$ *is the* successor distribution function. *We require that for each* $v \in V_r$ *and each* $v' \in V$, $\mathsf{prob}(v)(v') > 0$ *if and only if* $(v, v') \in E$.

If $V_0 = \emptyset$ or $V_1 = \emptyset$, we call $\mathfrak{A}$ a *Markov decision process* (MDP) or 1.5 player game. If both $V_0 = V_1 = \emptyset$, we call $\mathfrak{A}$ a *Markov chain* (MC). Given an arena $\mathfrak{A} = (V_0, V_1, V_r, E, \mathsf{prob})$, we define the following concepts.

– A *play* is an infinite sequence $\pi = v_0 v_1 v_2 v_3 \ldots$ such that $(v_i, v_{i+1}) \in E$ for all $i \in \mathbb{N}$. We define $\pi(i) \overset{\text{def}}{=} v_i$. We denote by $\mathsf{Play}(\mathfrak{A})$ the set of all plays of $\mathfrak{A}$.
– For $\sigma \in \{0, 1\}$, a *(pure memoryless) strategy* f_σ of Player σ is a mapping $f_\sigma \colon V_\sigma \rightarrow V$ from the vertices V_σ of Player σ to their successor states, i.e. for each $v \in V_\sigma$, $(v, f_\sigma(v)) \in E$. We denote the set of Player 0 and 1 strategies by Strats_0 and Strats_1, respectively.
– Given a strategy f_0 for Player 0, we define the *induced MDP* as $\mathfrak{A}_{f_0} = (\emptyset, V_1, V_r \cup V_0, E_{f_0}, \mathsf{prob}_{f_0})$ with $E_{f_0} \overset{\text{def}}{=} (E \setminus V_0 \times V) \cup \{ (v, f_0(v)) \mid v \in V_0 \}$ and

$$\mathsf{prob}_{f_0}(v)(v') \overset{\text{def}}{=} \begin{cases} \mathsf{prob}(v)(v') & \text{if } v \in V_r, \\ 1 & \text{if } v \in V_0 \text{ and } v' = f_0(v), \\ 0 & \text{otherwise,} \end{cases}$$

and similarly for Player 1.
– Given strategies f_0, f_1 for Player 0 and Player 1, respectively, we denote by $\mathfrak{A}_{f_0, f_1} \overset{\text{def}}{=} (\mathfrak{A}_{f_0})_{f_1}$ the *induced MC* of the strategies.
– If $\mathfrak{A}$ is a MC, we denote by $\mathbf{P}^{\mathfrak{A}}(v) \colon \Sigma^{\mathfrak{A}} \rightarrow [0, 1]$ the uniquely induced [33] probability measure on $\Sigma^{\mathfrak{A}}$, the σ-algebra on the *cylinder sets* of the plays of $\mathfrak{A}$, under the condition that the initial node is v, where, for a finite prefix $\pi' = v_0 v_1 \ldots v_n$ of a play π, the probability of the cylinder set $C_{\pi'}$ of π' is defined as $\mathbf{P}^{\mathfrak{A}}(v)(C_{\pi'}) = \prod_{i=0}^{n-1} \mathsf{prob}(v_i)(v_{i+1})$ if $v_0 = v$, 0 otherwise. For a generic arena $\mathfrak{A}$ and strategies f_0 and f_1 of Player 0 and Player 1, respectively, we let $\mathbf{P}^{\mathfrak{A}}_{f_0, f_1}(v) \overset{\text{def}}{=} \mathbf{P}^{\mathfrak{A}_{f_0, f_1}}(v)$.

Definition 2. *A* 2.5 player game, *also referred to as* Markov game *(MG), is a tuple* $\mathcal{P} = (V_0, V_1, V_r, E, \mathsf{prob}, \mathsf{win})$, *where* $\mathfrak{A} = (V_0, V_1, V_r, E, \mathsf{prob})$ *is an arena and* $\mathsf{win} \subseteq \mathsf{Play}(\mathfrak{A})$ *is the* winning condition *for Player 0, the set of plays for which Player 0 wins.*

The notions of plays, strategies, induced 1.5 player games, etc. extend to 2.5 player games by considering their underlying arena.

We consider two types of winning conditions, reachability and parity objectives.

Definition 3. *A 2.5 player* reachability game *is a 2.5 player game* $\mathcal{P}$ *in which the winning condition* win *is defined by a* target set $\mathsf{R} \subseteq V$. *Then, we have* $\mathsf{win} = \{ \pi \in \mathsf{Play}(\mathcal{P}) \mid \exists i \geq 0 : \pi(i) \in \mathsf{R} \}$. *For 2.5 player reachability games, we also use the notation* $\mathcal{P} = (V_0, V_1, V_r, E, \mathsf{prob}, \mathsf{R})$.

Definition 4. *A 2.5 player parity game (MPG) is a 2.5 player game $\mathcal{P}$ in which the winning condition* win *is defined by the* priority function pri$: V \to \mathbb{N}$ *mapping each vertex to a natural number. We call the image of* pri *the set of* priorities *(or: colours), denoted by $\mathcal{C}$. Note that, since V is finite, $\mathcal{C}$ is finite as well. We extend* pri *to plays, using* pri$: \pi \mapsto \liminf_{i \to \infty} \text{pri}(\pi(i))$. *Then, we have* win $= \{ \pi \in$ Play$(\mathcal{P}) \mid \}$pri(π) *is even. For 2.5 player parity games, we also use the notation $\mathcal{P} = (V_0, V_1, V_r, E, \text{prob}, \text{pri})$. We denote with $|\mathcal{P}|$ the size of a 2.5 player parity game, referring to the space its overall representation takes.*

Note that in the above discussion we have defined strategies as mappings from vertices of the respective player to successor vertices. More general definitions of strategies exist that e.g. use randomised choices (imposing a probability distributions over the edges chosen) or take the complete history of the game so far into account. However, it is known that, for finite 2.5 player parity and reachability games, the simple pure memoryless strategies we have introduced above suffice to obtain mutually optimal infima and suprema [12].

We also use the common intersection and subtraction operations on directed graphs for arenas and games: given an MG $\mathcal{P}$ with arena $\mathfrak{A} = (V_0, V_1, V_r, E, \text{prob})$,

- $\mathcal{P} \cap V'$ denotes the MG $\mathcal{P}'$ we obtain when we restrict the arena $\mathfrak{A}$ to $\mathfrak{A} \cap V' \overset{\text{def}}{=}$ $(V_0 \cap V', V_1 \cap V', V_r \cap V', E \cap (V' \times V'), \text{prob}\restriction_{V' \cap V_r})$,
- for $E' \supseteq E_r$, we denote by $\mathcal{P} \cap E'$ the MG $\mathcal{P}'$ we obtain when restricting arena $\mathfrak{A}$ to $\mathfrak{A} \cap E' \overset{\text{def}}{=} (V_0, V_1, V_r, E \cap E', \text{prob})$.

Note that the result of such an intersection may or may not be substochastic or contain sinks. While we use these operations freely in intermediate constructions, we make sure that, whenever they are treated as games, they have no sinks and are not substochastic.

Definition 5. *Let $\mathcal{P} = (V_0, V_1, V_r, E, \text{prob}, \text{win})$ be a 2.5 player game, and let f_0 and f_1 be two strategies for player 0 and 1, respectively. The value $\text{val}^{\mathcal{P}}_{f_0, f_1}: V \to [0, 1]$ is defined as*

$$\text{val}^{\mathcal{P}}_{f_0, f_1}(v) \overset{def}{=} \mathbf{P}^{\mathcal{P}}_{f_0, f_1}(v)(\{ \pi \in \text{Play}(\mathcal{P}) \mid \pi \in \text{win} \}).$$

We also define

$$\text{val}^{\mathcal{P}}_{f_0}(v) \overset{def}{=} \inf_{f_1' \in \text{Strats}_1} \text{val}^{\mathcal{P}}_{f_0, f_1'}(v),$$

$$\text{val}^{\mathcal{P}}_{f_1}(v) \overset{def}{=} \sup_{f_0' \in \text{Strats}_0} \text{val}^{\mathcal{P}}_{f_0', f_1}(v),$$

$$\text{val}^{\mathcal{P}}(v) \overset{def}{=} \sup_{f_0' \in \text{Strats}_0} \inf_{f_1' \in \text{Strats}_1} \text{val}^{\mathcal{P}}_{f_0', f_1'}(v).$$

We write $\text{val}^{\mathcal{P}}_{f'} \geq \text{val}^{\mathcal{P}}_{f}$ if, for all $v \in V$, $\text{val}^{\mathcal{P}}_{f'}(v) \geq \text{val}^{\mathcal{P}}_{f}(v)$ holds, and $\text{val}^{\mathcal{P}}_{f'} > \text{val}^{\mathcal{P}}_{f}$ if $\text{val}^{\mathcal{P}}_{f'} \geq \text{val}^{\mathcal{P}}_{f}$ and $\text{val}^{\mathcal{P}}_{f'} \neq \text{val}^{\mathcal{P}}_{f}$ hold.

Definition 6. *Given a vertex $v \in V$, a strategy f_σ for Player σ is called v-winning if, starting from v, Player σ wins almost surely in the MDP defined by f_σ (that is, $\text{val}^P_{f_\sigma}(v) = 1 - \sigma$). For $\sigma \in \{0,1\}$, a vertex v in V is v-winning for Player σ if Player σ has a v-winning strategy f_σ. We call the set of v-winning vertices for Player σ the* winning region *of Player σ, denoted W_σ. Note for $v \in W_0$, $\text{val}^P(v) = 1$, whereas for $v \in W_1$ we have $\text{val}^P(v) = 0$.*

3   Strategy Improvement

A strategy improvement algorithm takes a memoryless strategy f of one player, in our case of Player 0, and either infers that the strategy is optimal, or offers a family $\mathcal{I}_f$ of strategies, such that, for all strategies $f' \in \mathcal{I}_f$, $\text{val}^P_{f'} > \text{val}^P_f$ holds.

The family $\mathcal{I}_f$ is usually given through *profitable switches*. In such a case, $\mathcal{I}_f$ is defined as follows.

Definition 7. *Given a 2.5 player game $P = (V_0, V_1, V_r, E, \text{prob}, \text{win})$ and a strategy f for Player 0, the* profitable switches, *denoted $\text{profit}(P, f)$, for Player 0 are the edges that offer a strictly higher chance of succeeding (under the given strategy). That is, $\text{profit}(P, f) = \{ (v, v') \in E_0 \mid \text{val}^P_f(v') > \text{val}^P_f(v) \}$. We also define the* unprofitable switches *accordingly as $\text{loss}(P, f) = \{ (v, v') \in E_0 \mid \text{val}^P_f(v') < \text{val}^P_f(v) \}$.*

$\mathcal{I}_f$ is the set of strategies that can be obtained from f by applying one or more profitable switches to f: $\mathcal{I}_f = \{ f' \in \text{Strats}_0 \mid f' \neq f \text{ and } \forall v \in V_0 : f'(v) = f(v) \text{ or } (v, f'(v)) \in \text{profit}(P, f) \}$.

Strategy improvement methods can usually start with an arbitrary strategy f_0, which is then updated by selecting some $f_{i+1} \in \mathcal{I}_{f_i}$ until $\mathcal{I}_{f_i}$ is eventually empty. This f_i is then guaranteed to be optimal. The update policy with which the profitable switch or switches are selected is not relevant for the correctness of the method, although it does impact on the performance and complexity of the algorithms. In our implementation, we use a 'greedy switch all' update policy, that is we perform any switch we can perform and change the strategy to the locally optimal switch.

For 2.5 player reachability games, strategy improvement algorithms provide optimal strategies.

Theorem 1 (cf. [14]). *For a 2.5 player reachability game P, a strategy improvement algorithm with the profitable switches/improved strategies as defined in Definition 7 terminates with an optimal strategy for Player 0.*

In the strategy improvement step, for all $v \in V$ and all $f' \in \mathcal{I}_f$, it holds that $\text{val}^P_{f'}(v) = \text{val}^P_{f'}(f'(v)) \geq \text{val}^P_f(f(v)) = \text{val}^P_f(v)$. Moreover, strict inequality is obtained at some vertex in V. As we have seen in the introduction, this is not the case for 2.5 player parity games: in the example from Fig. 1, for a strategy f with $f(v_0) = v_{0.55}$, the switch from edge $e_{0,1}$ to $e_{0,2}$ is not profitable. Note, however, that it is not unprofitable either.

4   Algorithm

We observe that situations where the naive strategy improvement algorithm described in the previous section gets stuck are *tableaux*: no profitable switches are available. However, switches that are *neutral* in that applying them once would neither lead to an increased nor to a decreased likelihood of winning can still lead to an improvement, and can even happen that combinations of such neutral switches are required to obtain an improvement. As usual with strategy improvement algorithms, neutral switches cannot generally be added to the profitable switches: not only would one lose the guarantee to improve, one can also reduce the likelihood of winning when applying such changes.

Overcoming this problem is the main reason why strategy improvement techniques for MPG would currently have to use a reduction to 2.5 player reachability games (or other reductions), with the disadvantages discussed in the introduction. We treat these tableaux directly and avoid reductions. We first make formal what neutral edges are.

Definition 8. *Given a 2.5 player game* $\mathcal{P} = (V_0, V_1, V_r, E, \mathsf{prob}, \mathsf{win})$ *and a strategy f for Player* 0, *we define the set of* neutral edge $\mathsf{neutral}(\mathcal{P}, f)$ *as follows:*

$$\mathsf{neutral}(\mathcal{P}, f) \stackrel{def}{=} E_r \cup \{\, (v, v') \in E_0 \cup E_1 \mid \mathsf{val}_f^{\mathcal{P}}(v') = \mathsf{val}_f^{\mathcal{P}}(v) \,\}.$$

Based on these neutral edges, we define an update policy on the subgame played only on the neutral edges. The underlying idea is that, when Player 0 can win in case the game only uses neutral edges, then Player 1 will have to try to break out. He can only do this by changing his decision from one of his states in a way that is profitable for Player 0.

Definition 9. *Given a 2.5 player game* $\mathcal{P} = (V_0, V_1, V_r, E, \mathsf{prob}, \mathsf{win})$ *and a strategy f for Player* 0, *we define the* neutral subgame of $\mathcal{P}$ for f as $\mathcal{P}' = \mathcal{P} \cap \mathsf{neutral}(\mathcal{P}, f)$. *Based on* $\mathcal{P}'$ *we define the set* $\mathcal{I}'_f$ *of additional strategy improvements as follows.*

Let W_0 *and* W'_0 *be the winning regions of Player* 0 *on* $\mathcal{P}$ *and* $\mathcal{P}'$, *respectively. If* $W_0 = W'_0$, *then* $\mathcal{I}'_f = \emptyset$. *Otherwise, let* $\mathcal{W}$ *be the set of strategies that are* v-*winning for Player* 0 *on* $\mathcal{P}'$ *for all vertices* $v \in W'_0$. *Then we set*

$$\mathcal{I}''_f = \left\{ f_0 \in \mathsf{Strats}_0 \;\middle|\; \begin{array}{l} \exists f_w \in \mathcal{W} : \forall v \in W'_0 : f_0(v) = f_w(v) \\ \text{and } \forall v \notin W'_0 : f_0(v) = f(v) \end{array} \right\},$$

$$\mathcal{I}'_f = \{\, f' \in \mathcal{I}''_f \mid \forall v \in W_0 : f'(v) = f(v) \,\}.$$

We remark that $W_0 \subseteq W'_0$ always holds. Intuitively, we apply a qualitative analysis on the neutral subgame, and if the winning region of Player 0 on the neutral subgame is larger than her winning region on the full game, then we use the new winning strategy on the new part of the winning region. Intuitively, this forces Player 1 to leave this area eventually (or to lose almost surely). As he cannot do this through neutral edges, the new strategy for Player 0 is superior over the old one.

Example 1. Consider again the example MPG $\mathcal{P}_e$ from Fig. 1 and the strategy such that $f_0(v_0) = v_{0.55}$. Under this strategy, $\mathsf{neutral}(\mathcal{P}_e, f_0) = E_r \cup \{(v_0, v_{0.55}), (v_0, v_1), (v_1, v_0)\}$; the resulting neutral subgame $\mathcal{P}'_e$ is the same as $\mathcal{P}_e$ except for the edge $e_{1,1}$. In $\mathcal{P}'_e$, the winning region W'_0 is $W'_0 = \{v_0, v_1, v_w\}$, while the original region was $W_0 = \{v_w\}$. The two sets $\mathcal{I}'_{f_0}$ and $\mathcal{I}''_{f_0}$ contain only the strategy f'_0 such that $f'_0(v_0) = v_1$. In order to avoid to lose almost surely in W'_0, Player 1 has to change his strategy from $f_1(v_1) = v_0$ to $f'_1(v_1) = v_{0.95}$ in $\mathcal{P}_e$. Consequently, strategy f'_0 is superior to f_0: the resulting winning probability is not 0.55 but 0.95 for v_0 and v_1.

Note that using $\mathcal{I}'_f$ or $\mathcal{I}''_f$ in the strategy iteration has the same effect. Once a run has reached W_0 in the neutral subgame, it cannot leave it. Thus, changing the strategy f_0 from $\mathcal{I}''_f$ to a strategy f' with $f'(v) = f(v)$ for $v \in W_0$ and $f'(v) = f_0(v)$ for $v \notin W_0$ will not change the chance of winning: $\mathsf{val}^{\mathcal{P}'}_{f_0} = \mathsf{val}^{\mathcal{P}'}_{f'}$ and $\mathsf{val}^{\mathcal{P}}_{f_0} = \mathsf{val}^{\mathcal{P}}_{f'}$. This also implies $\mathcal{I}''_f \neq \emptyset \Rightarrow \mathcal{I}'_f \neq \emptyset$, since $\mathcal{I}'_f$ contains all strategies that belong to $\mathcal{I}''_f$ and that agree with f only on the original winning region W_0. Using $\mathcal{I}'_f$ simplifies the proof of Lemma 1, but it also emphasises that one does not need to re-calculate the strategy on a region that is already winning.

Our extended strategy improvement algorithm applies updates from either of these constructions until no further improvement is possible. That is, we can start with an arbitrary Player 0 strategy f_0 and then apply $f_{i+1} \in \mathcal{I}_{f_i} \cup \mathcal{I}'_{f_i}$ until $\mathcal{I}_{f_i} = \mathcal{I}'_{f_i} = \emptyset$. We will show that therefore f_i is an optimal Player 0 strategy.

For the algorithm, we need to calculate $\mathcal{I}_{f_i}$ and $\mathcal{I}'_{f_i}$. Calculating $\mathcal{I}_{f_i}$ requires only to solve 1.5 player parity games [15], and we use ISCASMC [27,28] to do so. Calculating $\mathcal{I}'_{f_i}$ requires only qualitative solutions of neutral subgame $\mathcal{P}'$. For this, we apply the algorithm from [30].

A more algorithmic representation of our algorithm with a number of minor design decisions is provided in the arXiv version [29] of this paper. The main design decision is to favour improvements from $\mathcal{I}_{f_i}$ over those from $\mathcal{I}'_{f_i}$. This allows for calculating $\mathcal{I}'_{f_i}$ only if $\mathcal{I}_{f_i}$ is empty. Starting with calculating $\mathcal{I}_{f_i}$ first is a design decision, which is slightly arbitrary. We have made it because solving 1.5 player games quantitatively is cheaper than solving 2.5 player games qualitatively and we believe that the guidance for the search is, in practice, better in case of quantitative results. Likewise, we have implemented a 'greedy switch all' improvement strategy, simply because this is believed to behave well in practice. We have, however, not collected evidence for either decision and acknowledge that finding a good update policy is an interesting future research.

5   Correctness

5.1   Correctness Proof in a Nutshell

The correctness proof combines two arguments: the correctness of *all* basic strategy improvement algorithms for reachability games and a reduction from 2.5

player parity games to 2.5 player reachability games with arbitrarily close winning probabilities for similar strategy pairs. In a nutshell, if we approximate close enough, then three properties hold for a game $\mathcal{P}$ and a strategy f of Player 0:

1. all 'normal' strategy improvements of the parity game correspond to strategy improvements in the reachability game (Corollary 2);
2. if Player 0 has a larger winning region W_0' in the neutral subgame (cf. Definition 9) for $P \cap \mathsf{neutral}(\mathcal{P}, f)$ than for $\mathcal{P}_f$, then replacing f by a winning strategy in $\mathcal{I}_f'$ leads to an improved strategy in the reachability game (Lemma 1); and
3. if neither of these two types of strategy improvements are left, then a strategy improvement step on the related 2.5 player reachability game will not lead to a change in the winning probability on the 2.5 player parity game (Lemma 2).

5.2   Two Game Transformations

In this subsection we discuss two game transformations that change the likelihood of winning only marginally and preserve the probability of winning, respectively. The first transformation turns 2.5 player parity games into 2.5 player reachability games such that a strategy that is an optimal strategy for the reachability game is also optimal for the parity game (cf. [2]).

Definition 10. *Let $\mathcal{P} = (V_0, V_1, V_r, E, \mathsf{prob}, \mathsf{pri})$, $\varepsilon \in (0, 1)$, and $n \in \mathbb{N}$. We define the 2.5 player reachability game $\mathcal{P}_{\varepsilon,n} = (V_0, V_1, V_r'', E'', \mathsf{prob}', \{\mathsf{won}\})$ with*

- $V_r'' = V_r \cup V' \cup \{\mathsf{won}, \mathsf{lost}\}$, *where (i) V' contains primed copies of the vertices; for ease of notation, the copy of a vertex v is referred to as v' in this construction; (ii) won and lost are fresh vertices; they are a winning and a losing sink, respectively;*
- $E' = \{(v, w') \mid (v, w) \in E\} \cup \{(\mathsf{won}, \mathsf{won}), (\mathsf{lost}, \mathsf{lost})\}$;
- $E'' = E' \cup \{(v', v) \mid v \in V\} \cup \{(v', \mathsf{won}) \mid v \in V\} \cup \{(v', \mathsf{lost}) \mid v \in V\}$;
- $\mathsf{prob}'(v)(w') = \mathsf{prob}(v)(w)$ *for all $v \in V_r$ and $(v, w) \in E$;*
- $\mathsf{prob}'(v')(\mathsf{won}) = \mathsf{wprob}(\varepsilon, n, \mathsf{pri}(v))$,
- $\mathsf{prob}'(v')(\mathsf{lost}) = \mathsf{lprob}(\varepsilon, n, \mathsf{pri}(v))$,
- $\mathsf{prob}'(v')(v) = 1 - \mathsf{wprob}(\varepsilon, n, \mathsf{pri}(v)) - \mathsf{lprob}(\varepsilon, n, \mathsf{pri}(v))$ *for all $v \in V$, and*
- $\mathsf{prob}'(\mathsf{won})(\mathsf{won}) = \mathsf{prob}'(\mathsf{lost})(\mathsf{lost}) = 1$.

where $\mathsf{lprob}, \mathsf{wprob}: (0, 1) \times \mathbb{N} \times \mathbb{N} \to [0, 1]$ are two functions with $\mathsf{lprob}(\varepsilon, n, c) + \mathsf{wprob}(\varepsilon, n, c) \leq 1$ for all $\varepsilon \in (0, 1)$ and $n, c \in \mathbb{N}$.

Intuitively, this translation replaces all the vertices by the gadgets from Fig. 2a.

Note that $\mathcal{P}_{\varepsilon,n}$ and $\mathcal{P}$ have similar memoryless strategies. By a slight abuse of the term, we say that a strategy f_σ of Player σ on $\mathcal{P}_{\varepsilon,n}$ is *similar* to her strategy f_σ' on $\mathcal{P}$ if $f_\sigma': v \mapsto f_\sigma(v)'$ holds, i.e. when v is mapped to w by f_σ, then v is mapped to w' by f_σ'.

Theorem 2 (cf. [2]). *Let* $\mathcal{P} = (V_0, V_1, V_r, E, \text{prob}, \text{pri})$ *be a 2.5 player parity game. Then, there exist* $\varepsilon \in (0,1)$ *and* $n \geq |\mathcal{P}|$ *such that we can construct* $\mathcal{P}_{\varepsilon,n}$ *and the following holds: for all strategies* $f_0 \in \text{Strats}_0$, $f_1 \in \text{Strats}_1$, *and all vertices* $v \in V$, *it holds that* $\left|\text{val}^{\mathcal{P}}_{f_0,f_1}(v) - \text{val}^{\mathcal{P}_{\varepsilon,n}}_{f_0',f_1'}(v)\right| < \varepsilon$, $\left|\text{val}^{\mathcal{P}}_{f_0,f_1}(v) - \text{val}^{\mathcal{P}_{\varepsilon,n}}_{f_0',f_1'}(v')\right| < \varepsilon$, $\left|\text{val}^{\mathcal{P}}_{f_0}(v) - \text{val}^{\mathcal{P}_{\varepsilon,n}}_{f_0'}(v)\right| < \varepsilon$, $\left|\text{val}^{\mathcal{P}}_{f_0}(v) - \text{val}^{\mathcal{P}_{\varepsilon,n}}_{f_0'}(v')\right| < \varepsilon$, $\left|\text{val}^{\mathcal{P}}_{f_1}(v) - \text{val}^{\mathcal{P}_{\varepsilon,n}}_{f_1'}(v)\right| < \varepsilon$, *and* $\left|\text{val}^{\mathcal{P}}_{f_1}(v) - \text{val}^{\mathcal{P}_{\varepsilon,n}}_{f_1'}(v')\right| < \varepsilon$, *where* f_0' *resp.* f_1' *are similar to* f_0 *resp.* f_1.

The results of [2] are stronger in that they show that the probabilities grow sufficiently slow for the reduction to be polynomial, but we use this construction only for correctness proofs and do not apply it in our algorithms. For this reason, existence is enough for our purpose. As [2] does not contain a theorem that directly makes the statement above, we have included a simple construction (without tractability claim) with a correctness proof in the arXiv version [29] of this paper.

We will now introduce a second transformation that allows us to consider changes in the strategies in many vertices at the same time.

Definition 11. *Let* $\mathcal{P} = (V_0, V_1, V_r, E, \text{prob}, \text{win})$ *and a region* $R \subseteq V$. *Let* $\mathcal{F}_R = \{f : R \cap V_0 \to V \mid \forall v \in R : (v, f(v)) \in E\}$ *denote the set of memoryless strategies for Player 0 restricted to* R. *The transformation results in a parity game* $\mathcal{P}^R = (V_0', V_1', V_r', E', \text{prob}', \text{pri}')$ *such that*

- $V_0'' = V_0 \cup R$, $V_0''' = (V_0 \cap R) \times \mathcal{F}_R$, *and* $V_0' = V_0'' \cup V_0'''$;
- $V_1'' = V_1 \setminus R$, $V_1''' = (V_1 \cap R) \times \mathcal{F}_R$, *and* $V_1' = V_1'' \cup V_1'''$;
- $V_r'' = V_r \setminus R$, $V_r''' = (V_r \cap R) \times \mathcal{F}_R$, *and* $V_r' = V_r'' \cup V_r'''$;
- $E' = \{(v,w) \in E \mid v \in V \setminus R\} \cup \{(v,(v,f)) \mid v \in R \text{ and } f \in \mathcal{F}_R\} \cup \{((v,f),(w,f)) \mid v, w \in R, (v,w) \in E \text{ and either } v \notin V_0 \text{ or } f(v) = w\} \cup \{((v,f),w) \mid v \in R, w \notin R, (v,w) \in E \text{ and either } v \notin V_0 \text{ or } f(v) = w\}$;
- $\text{prob}'(v)(w) = \text{prob}(v)(w)$, $\text{prob}'((v,f))(w) = \text{prob}(v)(w)$, *and* $\text{prob}'((v,f))((w,f)) = \text{prob}(v)(w)$; *and*
- $\text{pri}'(v) = \text{pri}(v)$ *for all* $v \in V$ *and* $\text{pri}'((v,f)) = \text{pri}(v)$ *otherwise.*

Intuitively, the transformation changes the game so that, every time R is entered, Player 0 has to fix her memoryless strategy in the game. The fact that in the resulting game the strategy f for Player 0 is fixed entering R is due to the jump from the original vertex v to (v, f) whenever $v \in R$. Once in R, either the part v of (v, f) is under the control of Player 1 or Player random, i.e. $v \notin V_0$, so it behaves as in $\mathcal{P}$, or the next state w (or (w, f) if $w \in R$) is the outcome of f, i.e. $w = f(v)$.

It is quite obvious that this transformation does not impact on the likelihood of winning. In fact, Player 0 can simulate every memoryless strategy $f : V_0 \to V$ by playing a strategy $f_R : V_0' \to V'$ that copies f outside of R (i.e. for each $v \in V_0 \setminus R$, $f_R(v) = f(v)$) and moves to the $f \restriction_R$ (i.e. f with a preimage restricted to R) copy from states in R (i.e. for each $v \in V_0 \cap R$, $f_R(v) = (v, f \restriction_R)$): there is a one-to-one correspondence between playing in $\mathcal{P}$ with strategy f and playing in $\mathcal{P}^R$ with strategy f_R when starting in V.

Theorem 3. *For all $v \in V$, all $R \subseteq V$, and all memoryless Player 0 strategies f, $\mathsf{val}_f^{\mathcal{P}}(v) = \mathsf{val}_{f_R}^{\mathcal{P}^R}((v, f \restriction_R))$, $\mathsf{val}^{\mathcal{P}}(v) = \sup\limits_{f \in \mathsf{Strats}_0(\mathcal{P})} \mathsf{val}^{\mathcal{P}^R}((v, f \restriction_R))$, and $\mathsf{val}^{\mathcal{P}}(v) = \mathsf{val}^{\mathcal{P}^R}(v)$ hold.*

5.3   Correctness Proof

For a given game $\mathcal{P}$, we call an $\varepsilon \in (0,1)$ *small* if it is at most $\frac{1}{5}$ of the smallest difference between all probabilities of winning that can occur on any strategy pair for any state in any game $\mathcal{P}^R$ for any $R \subseteq V$. For every small ε, we get the following corollary from Theorem 2.

Corollary 1 (preservation of profitable and unprofitable switches). *Let $n \geq |\mathcal{P}|$, f be a Player 0 strategy for $\mathcal{P}$, f' be the corresponding strategy for $\mathcal{P}_{\varepsilon,n}$, $\varepsilon \in (0,1)$ be small, $v \in V$, $w = f(v)$, and $(v,u) \in E$. Then $\mathsf{val}_f^{\mathcal{P}}(u) > \mathsf{val}_f^{\mathcal{P}}(w)$ implies $\mathsf{val}_{f'}^{\mathcal{P}_{\varepsilon,n}}(u) > \mathsf{val}_{f'}^{\mathcal{P}_{\varepsilon,n}}(w')$, and $\mathsf{val}_f^{\mathcal{P}}(u) < \mathsf{val}_f^{\mathcal{P}}(w)$ implies $\mathsf{val}_{f'}^{\mathcal{P}_{\varepsilon,n}}(u) < \mathsf{val}_{f'}^{\mathcal{P}_{\varepsilon,n}}(w')$.*

It immediately follows that all combinations of profitable switches can be applied, and will lead to an improved strategy: for small ε, a profitable switch for f_i from $f_i(v) = w$ to $f_{i+1}(v) = u$ implies $\mathsf{val}_{f_i}^{\mathcal{P}}(u) \geq \mathsf{val}_{f_i}^{\mathcal{P}}(w) + 5\varepsilon$ since by definition, we have that $\mathsf{val}_{f_i}^{\mathcal{P}}(u) > \mathsf{val}_{f_i}^{\mathcal{P}}(w)$ (as the switch is profitable); in particular, $\mathsf{val}_{f_i}^{\mathcal{P}}(u) = \mathsf{val}_{f_i}^{\mathcal{P}}(w) + \delta$ with $\delta \in \mathbb{R}^{>0}$; since $\varepsilon \leq \frac{1}{5}\delta$, we have that $\mathsf{val}_{f_i}^{\mathcal{P}}(u) \geq \mathsf{val}_{f_i}^{\mathcal{P}}(w) + 5\varepsilon$. The triangular inequalities provided by Theorem 2 imply that $\mathsf{val}_{f_i'}^{\mathcal{P}_{\varepsilon,n}}(u') \geq \mathsf{val}_{f_i'}^{\mathcal{P}_{\varepsilon,n}}(w') + 3\varepsilon$, since $\left| \mathsf{val}_{f_i}^{\mathcal{P}} - \mathsf{val}_{f_i'}^{\mathcal{P}_{\varepsilon,n}} \right| < \varepsilon$. Consequently, since under f_{i+1}' we have that $\mathsf{val}_{f_{i+1}'}^{\mathcal{P}_{\varepsilon,n}}(v') = \mathsf{val}_{f_i'}^{\mathcal{P}_{\varepsilon,n}}(u')$, it follows that $\mathsf{val}_{f_{i+1}'}^{\mathcal{P}_{\varepsilon,n}}(v) \geq \mathsf{val}_{f_i'}^{\mathcal{P}_{\varepsilon,n}}(v) + 3\varepsilon$, and, using triangulation again, we get $\mathsf{val}_{f_{i+1}}^{\mathcal{P}}(v) \geq \mathsf{val}_{f_i}^{\mathcal{P}}(v) + \varepsilon$. Thus, we have the following corollary:

Corollary 2. *Let $\mathcal{P}$ be a given 2.5 player parity game, and f_i be a strategy with profitable switches ($\mathsf{profit}(\mathcal{P}, f_i) \neq \emptyset$). Then, $\mathcal{I}_{f_i} \neq \emptyset$, and for all $f_{i+1} \in \mathcal{I}_{f_i}$, $\mathsf{val}_{f_{i+1}}^{\mathcal{P}} > \mathsf{val}_{f_i}^{\mathcal{P}}$.*

We now turn to the case that there are no profitable switches for f in the game $\mathcal{P}$. Corollary 1 shows that, for the corresponding strategy f' in $\mathcal{P}_{\varepsilon,n}$, all profitable switches lie within the neutral edges for f in $\mathcal{P}$, provided f has no profitable switches.

We expand the game by fixing the strategy of Player 0 for the vertices in $R \cap V_0$ for a region $R \subseteq V$. The region we are interested in is the winning region of Player 0 in the neutral subgame $\mathcal{P} \cap \mathsf{neutral}(P, f)$. The game is played as follows.

For every strategy $f_R \colon R \cap V_0 \to V$ such that $(r, f_R(r)) \in E$ holds for all $r \in R$, the game has a copy of the original game intersected with R, where the choices of Player 0 on the vertices in R are fixed to the single choice defined by the respective strategy f_R. We define $\|\mathcal{P}\| = \max\{ |\mathcal{P}^R| \mid R \subseteq V \}$.

We consider the case where the almost sure winning region of Player 0 in the neutral subgame $\mathcal{P}' = \mathcal{P} \cap \mathsf{neutral}(\mathcal{P}, f_i)$ is strictly larger than her winning region in $\mathcal{P}_{f_i}$.

Lemma 1. *Let $\mathcal{P}$ be a given 2.5 player parity game, and f_i be a strategy such that the winning region W_0' for Player 0 in the neutral subgame $\mathcal{P}' = \mathcal{P} \cap \mathsf{neutral}(\mathcal{P}, f_i)$ is strictly larger than her winning region W_0 in $\mathcal{P}_{f_i}$. Then $\mathcal{I}_{f_i}' \neq \emptyset$ and, $\forall f_{i+1} \in \mathcal{I}_{f_i}'$, $\mathsf{val}_{f_{i+1}}^{\mathcal{P}} > \mathsf{val}_{f_i}^{\mathcal{P}}$.*

Proof. The argument is an extension of the common argument for strategy improvement made for the modified reachability game. We first recall that the strategies in $\mathcal{I}_{f_i}'$ differ from f_i only on the winning region W_0' of Player 0 in the neutral subgame $\mathcal{P}'$. Assume that we apply the change *once*: the first time W_0' is entered, we play the new strategy, and after it is left, we play the old strategy. If the reaction of Player 1 is to stay in W_0', Player 0 will win almost surely in $\mathcal{P}$. If he leaves it, the value is improved due to the fact that Player 1 has to take a disadvantageous edge to leave it.

Consider the game $\mathcal{P}^{W_0'}$ and fix $f_{i+1} \in \mathcal{I}_{f_i}'$. Using Theorem 3, this implies that, when first in a state $v \in W_0'$, Player 0 moves to (v, f_{i+1}) for some $f_{i+1} \in \mathcal{I}_{f_i}'$, then the likelihood of winning is either improved or 1 for any counter strategy of Player 1. For all $v \in W_0' \setminus W_0$, this implies a strict improvement. For an $n \geq \|\mathcal{P}\|$ and a small ε, we can now follow the same arguments as for the Corollaries 1 and 2 on $\mathcal{P}^{W_0'}$ to establish that $\mathsf{val}_{(f_{i+1})_{W_0'}}^{\mathcal{P}^{W_0'}} > \mathsf{val}_{(f_i)_{W_0'}}^{\mathcal{P}^{W_0'}}$ holds, where the inequality is obtained through the same steps: $\mathsf{val}_{(f_i)_{W_0'}}^{\mathcal{P}^{W_0'}} \big((v, f_{i+1}|_{W_0}) \big) > \mathsf{val}_{(f_i)_{W_0'}}^{\mathcal{P}^{W_0'}} (v)$ implies $\mathsf{val}_{(f_i)_{W_0'}}^{\mathcal{P}^{W_0'}} \big((v, f_{i+1}|_{W_0}) \big) \geq \mathsf{val}_{(f_i)_{W_0'}}^{\mathcal{P}^{W_0'}} (v) + 5\varepsilon$; this implies $\mathsf{val}_{(f_i)_{W_0'}}^{\mathcal{P}_{\varepsilon,n}^{W_0'}} \big((v, f_{i+1}|_{W_0})' \big) \geq \mathsf{val}_{(f_i)_{W_0'}}^{\mathcal{P}_{\varepsilon,n}^{W_0'}} (v) + 3\varepsilon$; and this implies $\mathsf{val}_{(f_{i+1})_{W_0'}}^{\mathcal{P}_{\varepsilon,n}^{W_0'}} (v) = \mathsf{val}_{(f_{i+1})_{W_0'}}^{\mathcal{P}_{\varepsilon,n}^{W_0'}} \big((v, f_{i+1}|_{W_0})' \big) \geq \mathsf{val}_{(f_i)_{W_0'}}^{\mathcal{P}_{\varepsilon,n}^{W_0'}} (v) + 3\varepsilon$ and we finally get $\mathsf{val}_{(f_{i+1})_{W_0'}}^{\mathcal{P}^{W_0'}} (v) = \mathsf{val}_{(f_{i+1})_{W_0'}}^{\mathcal{P}^{W_0'}} \big((v, f_{i+1}|_{W_0}) \big) > \mathsf{val}_{(f_i)_{W_0'}}^{\mathcal{P}^{W_0'}} (v)$.

With Theorem 3, we obtain that $\mathsf{val}_{f_{i+1}}^{\mathcal{P}} > \mathsf{val}_{f_i}^{\mathcal{P}}$ holds.   □

Let us finally consider the case where there are no profitable switches for Player 0 in $\mathcal{P}_{f_i}$ and her winning region on the neutral subgame $\mathcal{P} \cap \mathsf{neutral}(\mathcal{P}, f_i)$ coincides with her winning region in $\mathcal{P}_{f_i}$.

Lemma 2. *Let $\mathcal{P}$ be an MPG and f_i be a strategy such that the set of profitable switches is empty and the neutral subgame $\mathcal{P} \cap \mathsf{neutral}(\mathcal{P}, f_i)$ has the same winning region for Player 0 as her winning region in $\mathcal{P}_{f_i}$ ($\mathcal{I}_{f_i} = \mathcal{I}_{f_i}' = \emptyset$). Then, every individual profitable switch in the reachability game $\mathcal{P}_{\varepsilon,n}$ from f_i to f_{i+1} implies $\mathsf{val}_{f_{i+1}}^{\mathcal{P}} = \mathsf{val}_{f_i}^{\mathcal{P}}$ and $\mathsf{neutral}(\mathcal{P}, f_{i+1}) = \mathsf{neutral}(\mathcal{P}, f_i)$.*

Proof. When there are no profitable switches in the parity game $\mathcal{P}$ for f_i, then all profitable switches in the reachability game $\mathcal{P}_{\varepsilon,n}$ for f_i (if any) must be within the set of neutral edges neutral$(\mathcal{P}, f_i)$ in the parity game $\mathcal{P}$. We apply one of these profitable switches at a time. By our definitions, this profitable switch is neutral in the 2.5 player parity game.

Taking this profitable (in the reachability game $\mathcal{P}_{\varepsilon,n}$ for a small ε and some $n \geq \|\mathcal{P}\|$) switch will improve the likelihood of winning for Player 0 in the reachability game. By our definition of ε, this implies that the likelihood of winning cannot be decreased on any position in the parity game.

To see that the quality of the resulting strategy cannot be higher for Player 0 in the 2.5 player parity game, recall that Player 1 can simply follow his optimal strategy on the neutral subgame. The likelihood of winning for Player 0 is the likelihood of reaching her winning region, and this winning region has not changed. Moreover, consider the evaluation of the likelihood of reaching this winning region: since by fixing the strategy for Player 1 the resulting game is an MDP, such an evaluation can be obtained by solving a linear programming problem (cf. the arXiv version [29] for more details). The old minimal non-negative solution to the resulting linear programming problem is a solution to the new linear programming problem, as it satisfies all constraints.

Putting these arguments together, likelihood of winning in the parity game is not altered in any vertex by this change. Hence, the set of neutral edges is not altered.   □

This lemma implies that *none* of the subsequently applied improvement steps applied on the 2.5 player reachability game has any effect on the quality of the resulting strategy on the 2.5 player parity game. Together, the above lemmas and corollaries therefore provide the correctness argument.

Theorem 4. *The algorithm is correct.*

Proof. Lemma 2 shows that, when $\mathcal{I}_{f_i}$ and $\mathcal{I}'_{f_i}$ are empty (i.e. when the algorithm terminates), then the updates in the related 2.5 player reachability game will henceforth (and thus until termination) not change the valuation for the 2.5 player parity game. With Theorems 1 and 2 and our selection of small ε, it follows that f_i is an optimal strategy. The earlier lemmas and corollaries in this subsection show that every strategy $f_{i+1} \in \mathcal{I}_{f_i} \cup \mathcal{I}'_{f_i}$ satisfies $\mathsf{val}^{\mathcal{P}}_{f_{i+1}} > \mathsf{val}^{\mathcal{P}}_{f_i}$. Thus, the algorithm produces strategies with strictly increasing quality in each step until it terminates. As the game is finite, then also the set of strategies is finite, thus the algorithm will terminate after finitely many improvement steps with an optimal strategy.   □

As usual with strategy improvement algorithms, we cannot provide good bounds on the number of iterations. As reachability games are a special case of 2.5 player games, all selection rules considered by Friedmann [23, 24] will have exponential lower bounds.

6   Implementation and Experimental Results

We have written a prototypical implementation for the approach of this paper, which accepts as input models in the same format as the probabilistic model checker PRISM-GAMES [13], an extension of PRISM [35] to stochastic Markov games. As case study, we consider an extension of the robot battlefield presented in [30], consisting of $n \times n$ square tiles, surrounded by a solid wall; four marked zones $zone_1, \ldots, zone_4$ at the corners, each of size 3×3; and two robots, R_0 and R_1, acting in strict alternation. Each tile can be occupied by at most one robot at a time. When it is the turn of a robot, this robot can move as follows: decide a direction and move one tile forward; decide a direction and attempt to move two tiles forward. In the latter case, the robot moves two tiles forward with 50% probability, but only one tile forward with 50% probability. If the robot would run into a wall or into the other robot, it stops at the tile before the obstacle. Robot R_1 can also shoot R_0 instead of moving, which is destroyed with probability p_{destr}^d where p_{destr} is the probability of destroying the robot and d is the Euclidean distance between the two robots. Once destroyed, R_0 cannot move any more. We assume that we are in control of R_0 but cannot control the behaviour of R_1. Our goal is to maximise, under any possible behaviour of R_1, the probability of fulfilling a certain objective depending on the zones, such as repeatedly visiting all zones infinitely often, visiting the zones in a specific order, performing such visits without entering other zones in the meanwhile, and so on. As an example, we can specify that the robot eventually reaches each zone by means of the probabilistic LTL (PLTL) formula $\langle\langle R_0 \rangle\rangle \mathcal{P}_{\max=?}[\bigwedge_{i=1,\ldots,4} \mathbf{F}\,zone_i]$ requiring to maximise the probability of satisfying $\bigwedge_{i=1,\ldots,4} \mathbf{F}\,zone_i$ by controlling R_0 only.

The machine we used for the experiments is a 3.6 GHz Intel Core i7-4790 with 16 GB 1600 MHz DDR3 RAM of which 12 GB assigned to the tool; the timeout has been set to 30 min. We have applied our tool on a number of properties that require the robot R_0 to visit the different zones in a certain order. In Table 1 we report the performance measurements for these properties. Column "property" shows the PLTL formula we consider, column "n" the width of the battlefield instance, and column "b" the number of bullets R_1 can shoot. For the "MPG" part, we present the number of "vertices" of the resulting MPG and the number of "colours". In the remaining columns, for each value of "p_{destr}", we report the achieved maximum probability "$p_{\max}$" and the time "t_{sol}" in seconds needed to solve the game. Note that we cannot compare to PRISM-GAMES because it does not support general PLTL formulas, and we are not aware of other tools to compare with.

As we can see, the algorithm performs quite well on MPGs with few million states. It is worth mentioning that a large share of the time spent is due to the evaluation of the 1.5 player parity games in the construction of the profitable switches. For instance, such an evaluation required 137 s out of 172 for the case $n = 9$, $b = 5$, and $p_{destr} = 0.1$. Since a large part of these 1.5 player games are similar, we are investigating how to avoid the repeated evaluation of similar parts to reduce the running time. Generally, all improvements in the quantitative solution of 1.5 player parity games and the qualitative solution of 2.5 player parity games will reduce the running time of our algorithm.

Table 1. Robots analysis: different reachability properties

Property	n	b	MPG Vertices	Colours	$p_{destr} = 0.1$ p_{max}	t_{sol}	$p_{destr} = 0.3$ p_{max}	t_{sol}	$p_{destr} = 0.5$ p_{max}	t_{sol}	$p_{destr} = 0.7$ p_{max}	t_{sol}	$p_{destr} = 0.9$ p_{max}	t_{sol}
Reachability $\langle\!\langle R_0 \rangle\!\rangle \mathcal{P}_{max=?}$ $[\mathbf{F}zone_1 \wedge \mathbf{F}zone_2 \wedge \mathbf{F}zone_3 \wedge \mathbf{F}zone_4]$	7	1	663 409	2	0.9614711	33	0.8178044	22	0.6247858	22	0.3961410	21	0.1384328	23
	7	2	1 090 537	2	0.9244309	56	0.6742610	66	0.4017138	57	0.1708971	58	0.0230085	52
	7	3	1 517 665	2	0.8926820	89	0.5793073	87	0.2995397	77	0.0953904	86	0.0060025	68
	7	4	1 944 793	2	0.8667039	112	0.5385632	109	0.2409219	96	0.0649772	107	0.0026513	85
	7	5	2 371 921	2	0.8571299	147	0.5062357	144	0.2167625	127	0.0506530	140	0.0019157	112
Ordered reachability $\langle\!\langle R_0 \rangle\!\rangle \mathcal{P}_{max=?}$ $[\mathbf{F}(zone_1 \wedge \mathbf{F}zone_2)]$	8	1	528 168	2	0.9613511	23	0.8176058	19	0.6246643	21	0.3962011	20	0.1384974	19
	8	2	868 986	2	0.9243652	35	0.6999023	44	0.4522051	35	0.2083732	42	0.0320509	40
	8	3	1 209 804	2	0.9091132	62	0.6538475	71	0.3643938	56	0.1352710	60	0.0131408	58
	8	4	1 550 622	2	0.9013742	91	0.6200998	91	0.3316778	72	0.1168758	74	0.0097312	71
	8	5	1 891 440	2	0.8977303	113	0.6031945	108	0.3207408	90	0.1138603	88	0.0093679	83
Reach-avoid $\langle\!\langle R_0 \rangle\!\rangle \mathcal{P}_{max=?}$ $[\neg zone_1 \mathbf{U} zone_2 \wedge \neg zone_4 \mathbf{U} zone_2 \wedge \mathbf{F}zone_3]$	9	1	833 245	4	0.9447793	46	0.8005413	31	0.6125397	35	0.3914531	25	0.1372075	24
	9	2	1 370 827	4	0.9095579	81	0.6824329	52	0.4411181	61	0.2089446	49	0.0302023	45
	9	3	1 908 409	4	0.8972146	108	0.6375883	68	0.3792906	84	0.1444959	71	0.0106721	66
	9	4	2 445 991	4	0.8936231	148	0.6221536	93	0.3478172	117	0.1158094	103	0.0051508	89
	9	5	2 983 573	4	0.8918034	172	0.6162166	109	0.3366050	136	0.1010400	120	0.0035468	105
Reachability $\langle\!\langle R_0 \rangle\!\rangle \mathcal{P}_{max=?}$ $[\mathbf{F}zone_1 \wedge \mathbf{F}zone_2 \wedge \mathbf{F}zone_3 \wedge \mathbf{F}zone_4]$	10	1	3 307 249	2	0.9614711	186	0.8178044	141	0.6247858	142	0.3961410	142	0.1384328	141
	10	2	5 440 429	2	0.9244267	296	0.6755372	414	0.4017718	374	0.1665626	732	0.0207851	615
	10	3	7 573 609	2	0.8931881	570	0.5742127	572	0.2864117	509	0.0847474	1019	0.0043153	861
	10	4	9 706 789	2	0.8676441	530	0.5239018	794	0.2248369	735	0.0479367	1396	0.0009959	1610
	10	5	11 839 969	2	0.8503684	968	0.4885654	980	0.1866995	971	0.0305890	1708	—TO—	

7   Discussion

We have combined a recursive algorithm for the quantitative solution of 2.5 player parity games with a strategy improvement algorithm, which lifts these results to the qualitative solution of 2.5 player parity games. This shift is motivated by the significant acceleration in the qualitative solution of 2.5 player parity games: while [11] scaled to a few thousand vertices, [30] scales to tens of millions of states. This changes the playing field and makes qualitative synthesis a realistic target. It also raises the question if this technique can be incorporated smoothly into a quantitative solver.

Previous approaches [7,9] have focused on developing a progress measure that allows for joining the two objective. This has been achieved in studying strategy improvement techniques that give preference to the likelihood of winning, and overcome stalling by performing strategy improvement on the larger qualitative game from [12] on the value classes.

This approach was reasonable at the time, where the updates benefited from memorising the recently successful strategies on the qualitative game. Moreover, focussing on value classes keeps the part of the qualitative game under consideration small, which is a reasonable approach when the cost of qualitative strategy improvement is considered significant. Building on a fast solver for the qualitative analysis, we can afford to progress in larger steps.

The main advancement, however, is as simple as it is effective. We use strategy improvement where it has a simple direct meaning (the likelihood to win), and we do not use it where the progress measure is indirect (progress measure within a value class). This has allowed us to transfer the recent performance gains from qualitative solutions of 2.5 player parity games [30] to their quantitative solution.

The difference in performance also explains the difference in the approach regarding complexity. Just as the deterministic subexponential complexity of solving 2.5 player games qualitatively is not very relevant in [30] (as this approach would be very slow in practice), the expected subexponential complexity in [9] is bought by exploiting a random facet method, which implies that only one edge is updated in every step. From a theoretical angle, these complexity considerations are interesting. From a practical angle, however, strategy improvement algorithms that use multiple switches in every step are usually faster and therefore preferable.

Acknowledgement. This work is supported by the National Natural Science Foundation of China (Grants Nos. 61472473, 61532019, 61550110249, 61550110506), by the National 973 Program (No. 2014CB340701), the CDZ project CAP (GZ 1023), the CAS Fellowship for International Young Scientists, the CAS/SAFEA International Partnership Program for Creative Research Teams, and the EPSRC grant EP/M027287/1.

References

1. Alur, R., Henzinger, T.A., Kupferman, O.: Alternating-time temporal logic. JACM **49**(5), 672–713 (2002)
2. Andersson, D., Miltersen, P.B.: The complexity of solving stochastic games on graphs. In: Dong, Y., Du, D.-Z., Ibarra, O. (eds.) ISAAC 2009. LNCS, vol. 5878, pp. 112–121. Springer, Heidelberg (2009). doi:10.1007/978-3-642-10631-6_13
3. Berwanger, D., Dawar, A., Hunter, P., Kreutzer, S.: DAG-width and parity games. In: Durand, B., Thomas, W. (eds.) STACS 2006. LNCS, vol. 3884, pp. 524–536. Springer, Heidelberg (2006). doi:10.1007/11672142_43
4. Björklund, H., Vorobyov, S.: A combinatorial strongly subexponential strategy improvement algorithm for mean payoff games. DAM **155**(2), 210–229 (2007)
5. Browne, A., Clarke, E.M., Jha, S., Long, D.E., Marrero, W.R.: An improved algorithm for the evaluation of fixpoint expressions. TCS **178**(1–2), 237–255 (1997)
6. Chatterjee, K.: The complexity of stochastic müller games. Inf. Comput. **211**, 29–48 (2012)
7. Chatterjee, K., de Alfaro, L., Henzinger, T.A.: The complexity of quantitative concurrent parity games. In: SODA, pp. 678–687. SIAM (2006)
8. Chatterjee, K., de Alfaro, L., Henzinger, T.A.: Strategy improvement for concurrent reachability and turn-based stochastic safety games. J. Comput. Syst. Sci. **79**(5), 640–657 (2013)
9. Chatterjee, K., Henzinger, T.A.: Strategy improvement and randomized subexponential algorithms for stochastic parity games. In: Durand, B., Thomas, W. (eds.) STACS 2006. LNCS, vol. 3884, pp. 512–523. Springer, Heidelberg (2006). doi:10.1007/11672142_42
10. Chatterjee, K., Henzinger, T.A.: Strategy improvement for stochastic rabin and streett games. In: Baier, C., Hermanns, H. (eds.) CONCUR 2006. LNCS, vol. 4137, pp. 375–389. Springer, Heidelberg (2006). doi:10.1007/11817949_25
11. Chatterjee, K., Henzinger, T.A., Jobstmann, B., Radhakrishna, A.: GIST: a solver for probabilistic games. In: Touili, T., Cook, B., Jackson, P. (eds.) CAV 2010. LNCS, vol. 6174, pp. 665–669. Springer, Heidelberg (2010). doi:10.1007/978-3-642-14295-6_57
12. Chatterjee, K., Jurdziński, M., Henzinger, T.A.: Quantitative stochastic parity games. In: SODA 2004, pp. 121–130 (2004)
13. Chen, T., Forejt, V., Kwiatkowska, M., Parker, D., Simaitis, A.: PRISM-games: a model checker for stochastic multi-player games. In: Piterman, N., Smolka, S.A. (eds.) TACAS 2013. LNCS, vol. 7795, pp. 185–191. Springer, Heidelberg (2013). doi:10.1007/978-3-642-36742-7_13
14. Condon, A.: On algorithms for simple stochastic games. Adv. Comput. Complex. Theory **13**, 51–73 (1993)
15. Courcoubetis, C., Yannakakis, M.: The complexity of probabilistic verification. J. ACM **42**(4), 857–907 (1995)
16. de Alfaro, L., Henzinger, T.A., Majumdar, R.: From verification to control: dynamic programs for omega-regular objectives. In: LICS, pp. 279–290 (2001)
17. de Alfaro, L., Majumdar, R.: Quantitative solution of omega-regular games. In: Vitter, J.S., Spirakis, P.G., Yannakakis, M. (eds.) Proceedings on 33rd Annual ACM Symposium on Theory of Computing, 6–8 July 2001, Heraklion, Crete, Greece, pp. 675–683. ACM (2001)
18. de Alfaro, L., Majumdar, R.: Quantitative solution of omega-regular games. J. Comput. Syst. Sci. **68**(2), 374–397 (2004)

19. Emerson, E.A., Jutla, C.S.: Tree automata, μ-calculus and determinacy. In: FOCS, pp. 368–377 (1991)
20. Emerson, E.A., Jutla, C.S., Sistla, A.P.: On model-checking for fragments of μ-calculus. In: Courcoubetis, C. (ed.) CAV 1993. LNCS, vol. 697, pp. 385–396. Springer, Heidelberg (1993). doi:10.1007/3-540-56922-7_32
21. Emerson, E.A., Lei, C.-L.: Efficient model checking in fragments of the propositional μ-calculus. In: LICS, pp. 267–278 (1986)
22. Fearnley, J.: Non-oblivious strategy improvement. In: LPAR, pp. 212–230 (2010)
23. Friedmann, O.: An exponential lower bound for the parity game strategy improvement algorithm as we know it. In: LICS, pp. 145–156 (2009)
24. Friedmann, O., Hansen, T.D., Zwick, U.: A subexponential lower bound for the random facet algorithm for parity games. In: SODA, pp. 202–216 (2011)
25. Friedmann, O., Lange, M.: Solving parity games in practice. In: Liu, Z., Ravn, A.P. (eds.) ATVA 2009. LNCS, vol. 5799, pp. 182–196. Springer, Heidelberg (2009). doi:10.1007/978-3-642-04761-9_15
26. Gimbert, H., Horn, F.: Solving simple stochastic games with few random vertices. LMCS 5(2:9), 1–17 (2009)
27. Hahn, E.M. Li, G., Schewe, S., Turrini, A., Zhang, L.: Lazy probabilistic model checking without determinisation. In: CONCUR. LIPIcs, vol. 42, pp. 354–367 (2015)
28. Hahn, E.M., Li, Y., Schewe, S., Turrini, A., Zhang, L.: ISCASMC: a web-based probabilistic model checker. In: Jones, C., Pihlajasaari, P., Sun, J. (eds.) FM 2014. LNCS, vol. 8442, pp. 312–317. Springer, Heidelberg (2014). doi:10.1007/978-3-319-06410-9_22
29. Hahn, E.M., Schewe, S., Turrini, A., Zhang, L.: Synthesising strategy improvement, recursive algorithms for solving 2.5 player parity games. arXiv:1607.01474
30. Hahn, E.M., Schewe, S., Turrini, A., Zhang, L.: A simple algorithm for solving qualitative probabilistic parity games. In: Chaudhuri, S., Farzan, A. (eds.) CAV 2016. LNCS, vol. 9780, pp. 291–311. Springer, Heidelberg (2016). doi:10.1007/978-3-319-41540-6_16
31. Jurdziński, M.: Small progress measures for solving parity games. In: Reichel, H., Tison, S. (eds.) STACS 2000. LNCS, vol. 1770, pp. 290–301. Springer, Heidelberg (2000). doi:10.1007/3-540-46541-3_24
32. Jurdziński, M., Paterson, M., Zwick, U.: A deterministic subexponential algorithm for solving parity games. SIAM J. Comput. 38(4), 1519–1532 (2008)
33. Kemeny, J.G., Snell, J.L., Knapp, A.W.: Denumerable Markov Chains. D. Van Nostrand Company, Princeton (1966)
34. Kozen, D.: Results on the propositional μ-calculus. TCS 27, 333–354 (1983)
35. Kwiatkowska, M., Norman, G., Parker, D.: PRISM 4.0: verification of probabilistic real-time systems. In: Gopalakrishnan, G., Qadeer, S. (eds.) CAV 2011. LNCS, vol. 6806, pp. 585–591. Springer, Heidelberg (2011). doi:10.1007/978-3-642-22110-1_47
36. Ludwig, W.: A subexponential randomized algorithm for the simple stochastic game problem. Inf. Comput. 117(1), 151–155 (1995)
37. McNaughton, R.: Infinite games played on finite graphs. Ann. Pure Appl. Logic 65(2), 149–184 (1993)
38. Obdržálek, J.: Fast mu-calculus model checking when tree-width is bounded. In: Hunt, W.A., Somenzi, F. (eds.) CAV 2003. LNCS, vol. 2725, pp. 80–92. Springer, Heidelberg (2003). doi:10.1007/978-3-540-45069-6_7
39. Piterman, N.: From nondeterministic Büchi, Streett automata to deterministic parity automata. J. Log. Methods Comput. Sci. 3(3:5), 1–21 (2007)

40. Puri, A.: Theory of hybrid systems and discrete event systems. Ph.D. thesis, Computer Science Department, University of California, Berkeley (1995)
41. Schewe, S.: An optimal strategy improvement algorithm for solving parity and payoff games. In: Kaminski, M., Martini, S. (eds.) CSL 2008. LNCS, vol. 5213, pp. 369–384. Springer, Heidelberg (2008). doi:10.1007/978-3-540-87531-4_27
42. Schewe, S.: Solving parity games in big steps. J. Comput. Syst. Sci. **84**, 243–262 (2017)
43. Schewe, S., Finkbeiner, B.: Satisfiability and finite model property for the alternating-time μ-calculus. In: Ésik, Z. (ed.) CSL 2006. LNCS, vol. 4207, pp. 591–605. Springer, Heidelberg (2006). doi:10.1007/11874683_39
44. Schewe, S., Finkbeiner, B.: Synthesis of asynchronous systems. In: Puebla, G. (ed.) LOPSTR 2006. LNCS, vol. 4407, pp. 127–142. Springer, Heidelberg (2007). doi:10.1007/978-3-540-71410-1_10
45. Schewe, S., Trivedi, A., Varghese, T.: Symmetric strategy improvement. In: Halldórsson, M.M., Iwama, K., Kobayashi, N., Speckmann, B. (eds.) ICALP 2015. LNCS, vol. 9135, pp. 388–400. Springer, Heidelberg (2015). doi:10.1007/978-3-662-47666-6_31
46. Vardi, M.Y.: Reasoning about the past with two-way automata. In: Larsen, K.G., Skyum, S., Winskel, G. (eds.) ICALP 1998. LNCS, vol. 1443, pp. 628–641. Springer, Heidelberg (1998). doi:10.1007/BFb0055090
47. Vöge, J., Jurdziński, M.: A discrete strategy improvement algorithm for solving parity games (Extended abstract). In: Emerson, E.A., Sistla, A.P. (eds.) CAV 2000. LNCS, vol. 1855, pp. 202–215. Springer, Heidelberg (2000). doi:10.1007/10722167_18
48. Wilke, T.: Alternating tree automata, parity games, and modal μ-calculus. Bull. Soc. Math. Belg. **8**(2), 359 (2001)
49. Zielonka, W.: Infinite games on finitely coloured graphs with applications to automata on infinite trees. TCS **200**(1–2), 135–183 (1998)
50. Zielonka, W.: Perfect-information stochastic parity games. In: Walukiewicz, I. (ed.) FoSSaCS 2004. LNCS, vol. 2987, pp. 499–513. Springer, Heidelberg (2004). doi:10.1007/978-3-540-24727-2_35

Counterexample Validation and Interpolation-Based Refinement for Forest Automata

Lukáš Holík, Martin Hruška, Ondřej Lengál[✉], Adam Rogalewicz, and Tomáš Vojnar

FIT, Brno University of Technology, IT4Innovations Centre of Excellence, Czech Republic
lengal@fit.vutbr.cz

Abstract. In the context of shape analysis, counterexample valida-tion and abstraction refinement are complex and so far not sufficiently resolved problems. We provide a novel solution to both of these problems in the context of fully-automated and rather general shape analysis based on forest automata. Our approach is based on backward symbolic exe-cution on forest automata, allowing one to derive automata-based inter-polants and refine the automata abstraction used. The approach allows one to distinguish true and spurious counterexamples and guarantees progress of the abstraction refinement. We have implemented the app-roach in the FORESTER tool and present promising experimental results.

1 Introduction

In [14,17], *forest automata* (FAs) were proposed as a formalism for representing sets of heap graphs within a fully-automated and scalable *shape analysis* of pro-grams with complex *dynamic linked data structures*. FAs were implemented in the FORESTER tool and successfully used to verify programs over a wide range of data structures, such as different kinds of lists (singly- and doubly-linked, circu-lar, nested, and/or having various additional pointers), different kinds of trees, as well as skip lists. FAs have the form of tuples of *tree automata* (TAs), allowing abstract transformers corresponding to heap operations to have a *local impact* (i.e., to change just a few component TAs instead of the entire heap represen-tation), leading to scalability. To handle complex nested data structures, FAs may be *hierarchically nested*, i.e., lower-level FAs can be used as (automatically derived) alphabet symbols of higher-level FAs.

Despite FORESTER managed to verify a number of programs, it suffered from two important deficiencies. Namely, due to using abstraction and the lack of

Supported by the Czech Science Foundation (projects 14-11384S and 16-24707Y) and the IT4IXS: IT4Innovations Excellence in Science project (LQ1602). M. Hruška is a holder of the Brno Ph.D. Talent Scholarship, funded by the Brno City Municipality.

A. Bouajjani and D. Monniaux (Eds.): VMCAI 2017, LNCS 10145, pp. 288–309, 2017.
DOI: 10.1007/978-3-319-52234-0_16

mechanisms for checking validity of possible counterexamples, it could report *spurious errors*, and, moreover, it was unable to refine the abstraction using the spurious counterexample. Interestingly, as discussed in the related work section, this problem is common for many other approaches to shape analysis, which may perhaps be attributed to the complexity of heap abstractions. In this paper, we tackle the above problem by providing a novel method for *validation of possible counterexample traces* as well as a *counterexample guided abstraction refinement* (CEGAR) loop for shape analysis based on FAs.

Our counterexample validation is based on *backward symbolic execution* of a candidate counterexample trace on the level of FAs (with no abstraction on the FAs) while checking *non-emptiness of its intersection* with the forward symbolic execution (which was abstracting the FAs). For that, we have to revert not only abstract transformers corresponding to program statements but also various meta-operations that are used in the forward symbolic execution and that significantly influence the way sets of heap configurations are represented by FAs. In particular, this concerns *folding* and *unfolding* of nested FAs (which we call *boxes*) as well as *splitting*, *merging*, and *reordering* of component TAs, which is used in the forward run for the following two reasons: to prevent the number of component TAs from growing and to obtain a canonic FA representation.

If the above meta-operations were not reverted, we would not only have problems in reverting some program statements but also in intersecting FAs obtained from the forward and backward run. Indeed, the general problem of checking emptiness of intersection of FAs that may use different boxes and different component TAs (i.e., intuitively, different decompositions of the represented heap graphs) is open. When we carefully revert the mentioned operations, it, however, turns out that the FAs obtained in the forward and backward run use *compatible* decomposition and hierarchical structuring of heap graphs, and so checking emptiness of their intersection is possible. Even then, however, the intersection is not trivial as the boxes obtained in the backward run may represent smaller sets of sub-heaps, and hence we cannot use boxes as symbols and instead have to perform the intersection *recursively* on the boxes as well.

Our abstraction on FAs is a modification of the so-called *predicate language abstraction* [10]. This particular abstraction collapses those states of component TAs that have non-empty intersection with the same predicate languages, which are obtained from the backward execution. We show that, in case the intersection of the set of configurations of the above described forward and backward symbolic runs is empty, we can derive from it an *automata interpolant* allowing us to get more predicate languages and to refine the abstraction such that progress of the CEGAR loop is guaranteed (in the sense that we do not repeat the same abstract forward run).

We have implemented the proposed approach in FORESTER and tested it on a number of small but challenging programs. Despite there is, of course, a lot of space for further optimisations, the experimental results are very encouraging. FORESTER can now not only verify correct programs with complex dynamic data structures but also reliably report errors in such programs. For some classes of dynamic data structures (notably skip lists), FORESTER is, to the best of our knowledge, the only tool that can provide both sound verification as well as reliable error reporting in a fully automated analysis (i.e., no manually provided heap predicates, no invariants, etc.). Moreover, for some classes of programs (e.g., various kinds of doubly-linked lists, trees, and nested lists), the only other tool that we are aware to be able to provide such functionality is our older automata-based tool [7], which is, however, far less scalable due to the use of a monolithic heap encoding based on a single TA. Finally, the refinement mechanism we introduced allowed us to verify some programs that were before out of reach of FORESTER due to handling finite domain data stored in the heap (which can be used by the programs themselves or introduced by tagging selected elements in dynamic data structures when checking properties such as sortedness, reordering, etc.).

2   Related Work

Many different approaches to shape analysis have been proposed, using various underlying formalisms, such as logics [9,18,21,24,25,27], automata [7,8, 12,14,17], graphs [11,13], or graph grammars [15]. Apart from the underlying formalisms, the approaches differ in their degree of automation, in the heap structures they can handle, and in their scalability. The shape analysis based on forest automata proposed in [17] that we build on in this paper belongs among the most general, fully automated approaches, still having decent scalability.

As noted also in the recent work [2], a common weakness of the current approaches to shape analysis is a lack of proper support for checking spuriousness of counterexample traces, possibly followed by automated refinement of the employed abstraction. This is exactly the problem that we tackle in this paper. Below, we characterize previous attempts on the problem and compare our approach with them.

The work [4] adds a CEGAR loop on top of the TVLA analyzer [25], which is based on *3-valued predicate logic with transitive closure*. The refinement is, however, restricted to adding more pointer variables and/or data fields of allocated memory cells to be tracked only (together with combining the analysis with classic predicate analysis on data values). The analysis assumes the other necessary heap predicates (i.e., the so-called core and instrumentation relations in terms of [25]) to be fixed in advance and not refined. The work [20] also builds on TVLA but goes further by learning more complex instrumentation relations using inductive logic programming. The core relations are still fixed in advance though. Compared with both of these works, we do not assume any predefined fixed predicates. Moreover, the approach of [20] is not CEGAR-based—it refines the abstraction whenever it hits a possible counterexample in which some loss of precision happened, regardless of whether the counterexample is real or not.

In [23], a CEGAR-based approach was proposed for automated refinement of the so-called *Boolean heap abstraction* using disjunctions of universally quantified Boolean combinations of first-order predicates with free variables and transitive closure. Unlike our work, the approach assumes the analyzed programs to be annotated by procedure contracts and representation invariants of data structures. New predicates are inferred using finite-trace weakest preconditions on the annotations, and hence new predicates with reachability constraints can only be inferred via additional heuristic widening on the inferred predicates. Moreover, the approach is not appropriate for handling nested data structures, such as lists of lists, requiring nested reachability predicates.

In the context of approaches based on *separation logic*, several attempts to provide counterexample validation and automated abstraction refinement have appeared. In [3], the SLAYER analyzer was extended by a method to check spuriousness of counterexample traces via bounded model checking and SMT. Unlike our work, the approach may, however, fail in recognising that a given trace represents a real counterexample. Moreover, the associated refinement can only add more predicates to be tracked from a pre-defined set of such predicates. In [2], another counterexample analysis for the context of separation logic was proposed within a computation loop based on the Impact algorithm [19]. The approach uses bounded backwards abduction to derive so-called spatial interpolants and to distinguish between real and spurious counterexample traces. It allows for refinement of the predicates used but only by extending them by data-related properties. The basic predicates describing heap shapes are provided in advance and fixed. Another work based on backwards abduction is [5]. The work assumes working with a parametrized family of predicates, and the refinement is based on refining the parameter. Three concrete families of this kind are provided, namely, singly-linked lists in which one can remember bigger and bigger multisets of chosen data values, remember nodes with certain addresses, or track ordering properties. The basic heap predicates are again fixed. The approach does not guarantee recognition of spurious and real counterexamples nor progress of the refinement.

Unlike our approach, none of the so-far presented works is based on automata, and all of the works require some fixed set of shape predicates to be provided in advance. Among *automata-based approaches*, counterexample analysis and refinement was used in [7] (and also in some related, less general approaches like [6]). In that case, however, a single tree automaton was used to encode sets of memory configurations, which allowed standard abstraction refinement from abstract regular (tree) model checking [10] to be used. On the other hand, due to using a single automaton, the approach did not scale well and had problems with some heap transformations.

The basic formalism of forest automata using fixed abstraction and user-provided database of boxes was introduced in [14]. We later extended the basic framework with automatic learning of boxes in [17]. The work [1] added ordering relations into forest automata to allow verification of programs whose safety depends on relations among data values from an unbounded domain. In [14, 17], we conjectured that counterexample validation and abstraction refinement should be possible in the context of forest automata too. However, only now, do we show that this is indeed the case, but also that much more involved methods than those of [10] are needed.

3   Forest Automata and Heaps

We consider sequential non-recursive C programs, operating on a set of pointer variables and the heap, using standard statements and control flow constructs. Heap cells contain zero or several pointer or data fields.

Configurations of the considered programs consist of memory-allocated data and an assignment of variables. *Heap memory* can be viewed as a (directed) graph whose nodes correspond to allocated memory cells. Every node contains a set of named pointer and data fields. Each pointer field points to another node (we model the NULL and undefined locations as special memory nodes pointed by variables NULL and undef, respectively), and the same holds for pointer variables of the program. Data fields of memory nodes hold a data value. We use the term *selector* to talk both about pointer and data fields. For simplification, we model data variables as pointer variables pointing to allocated nodes that contain a single data field with the value of the variable, and therefore consider only pointer variables hereafter.

We represent heap memory by partitioning it into a tuple of trees, the so-called *forest*. The leaves of the trees contain information about roots of which trees they should be merged with to recover the original heap. Our *forest automata* symbolic representations of sets of heaps is based on representing sets of forests using tuples of tree automata.

Let us now formalize these ideas. In the following, we use $f : A \rightharpoonup B$ to denote a partial function from A to B (also viewed as a total function $f : A \rightarrow (B \cup \{\top\})$, assuming that $\top \notin B$). We also assume a bounded data domain $\mathbb{D}$.

Graphs and Heaps. Let Γ be a finite set of *selectors* and Ω be a finite set of *references* s.t. $\Omega \cap \mathbb{D} = \emptyset$. A *graph* g over $\langle \Gamma, \Omega \rangle$ is a tuple $\langle V_g, next_g \rangle$ where V_g is a finite set of *nodes* and $next_g : \Gamma \rightarrow (V_g \rightharpoonup (V_g \cup \Omega \cup \mathbb{D}))$ maps each selector $a \in \Gamma$ to a partial mapping $next_g(a)$ from nodes to nodes, references, or data values. References and data values are treated as special terminal nodes that are not in the set of regular nodes, i.e., $V_g \cap (\Omega \cup \mathbb{D}) = \emptyset$. For a graph g, we use V_g to denote the nodes of g, and for a selector $a \in \Gamma$, we use a_g to denote the mapping $next_g(a)$. Given a finite set of variables $\mathbb{X}$, a *heap* h over $\langle \Gamma, \mathbb{X} \rangle$ is a tuple $\langle V_h, next_h, \sigma_h \rangle$ where $\langle V_h, next_h \rangle$ is a graph over $\langle \Gamma, \emptyset \rangle$ and $\sigma_h : \mathbb{X} \rightarrow V_h$ is a (total) map of variables to nodes.

Forest Representation of Heaps. A graph t is a *tree* if its nodes and pointers (i.e., not references nor data fields) form a tree with a unique root node, denoted $root(t)$. A *forest* over $\langle \Gamma, \mathbb{X} \rangle$ is a pair $\langle t_1 \cdots t_n, \sigma_f \rangle$ where $t_1 \cdots t_n$ is a sequence of trees over $\langle \Gamma, \{\overline{1}, \ldots, \overline{n}\} \rangle$ and σ_f is a (total) mapping $\sigma_f : \mathbb{X} \rightarrow \{\overline{1}, \ldots, \overline{n}\}$. The elements in $\{\overline{1}, \ldots, \overline{n}\}$ are called *root references* (note that n must be the number of trees in the forest). A forest $\langle t_1 \cdots t_n, \sigma_f \rangle$ over $\langle \Gamma, \mathbb{X} \rangle$ represents a heap over $\langle \Gamma, \mathbb{X} \rangle$, denoted $\otimes \langle t_1 \cdots t_n, \sigma_f \rangle$, obtained by taking the union of the trees of $t_1 \cdots t_n$ (assuming w.l.o.g. that the sets of nodes of the trees are disjoint), connecting root references with the corresponding roots, and mapping every defined variable x to the root of the tree indexed by x. Formally, $\otimes \langle t_1 \cdots t_n, \sigma_f \rangle$

is the heap $h = \langle V_h, next_h, \sigma_h \rangle$ defined by (i) $V_h = \bigcup_{i=1}^{n} V_{t_i}$, and (ii) for $a \in \Gamma$ and $v \in V_{t_k}$, if $a_{t_k}(v) \in \{\overline{1}, \ldots, \overline{n}\}$ then $a_h(v) = root(t_{a_{t_k}(v)})$ else $a_h(v) = a_{t_k}(v)$, and finally (iii) for every $x \in \mathbb{X}$, $\sigma_h(x) = root(t_{\sigma_f(x)})$.

3.1 Forest Automata

A forest automaton is essentially a tuple of tree automata accepting a set of tuples of trees that represents a set of graphs via their forest decomposition, associated with a mapping of variables to root references.

Tree Automata. A (finite, non-deterministic) *tree automaton* (TA) over $\langle \Gamma, \Omega \rangle$ is a triple $A = (Q, q_0, \Delta)$ where Q is a finite set of *states* (we assume $Q \cap (\mathbb{D} \cup \Omega) = \emptyset$), $q_0 \in Q$ is the *root state* (or initial state), denoted $root(A)$, and Δ is a set of *transitions*. Each transition is of the form $q \to \overline{a}(q_1, \ldots, q_m)$ where $m \geq 0$, $q \in Q$, $q_1, \ldots, q_m \in (Q \cup \Omega \cup \mathbb{D})^1$, and $\overline{a} = a^1 \cdots a^m$ is a sequence of different symbols from Γ.

Let t be a tree over $\langle \Gamma, \Omega \rangle$, and let $A = (Q, q_0, \Delta)$ be a TA over $\langle \Gamma, \Omega \rangle$. A *run* of A over t is a total map $\rho : V_t \to Q$ where $\rho(root(t)) = q_0$ and for each node $v \in V_t$ there is a transition $q \to \overline{a}(q_1, \ldots, q_m)$ in Δ with $\overline{a} = a^1 \cdots a^m$ such that $\rho(v) = q$ and for all $1 \leq i \leq m$, we have (i) if $q_i \in Q$, then $a_t^i(v) \in V_t$ and $\rho(a_t^i(v)) = q_i$, and (ii) if $q_i \in \Omega \cup \mathbb{D}$, then $a_t^i(v) = q_i$. We define the *language* of A as $L(A) = \{t \mid \text{there is a run of } A \text{ over } t\}$, and the language of a state $q \in Q$ as $L(A, q) = L((Q, q, \Delta))$.

Forest Automata. A *forest automaton* (FA) over $\langle \Gamma, \mathbb{X} \rangle$ is a tuple of the form $F = \langle A_1 \cdots A_n, \sigma \rangle$ where $A_1 \cdots A_n$, with $n \geq 0$, is a sequence of TAs over $\langle \Gamma, \{\overline{1}, \ldots, \overline{n}\} \rangle$ whose sets of states $Q_1, \ldots, Q_n$ are mutually disjoint, and $\sigma : \mathbb{X} \to \{\overline{1}, \ldots, \overline{n}\}$ is a mapping of variables to root references. A forest $\langle t_1 \cdots t_n, \sigma_f \rangle$ over $\langle \Gamma, \mathbb{X} \rangle$ is *accepted* by F iff $\sigma_f = \sigma$ and there are runs $\rho_1, \ldots, \rho_n$ such that for all $1 \leq i \leq n$, ρ_i is a run of A_i over t_i. The *language* of F, denoted as $L(F)$, is the set of heaps over $\langle \Gamma, \mathbb{X} \rangle$ obtained by applying $\otimes$ on forests accepted by F.

Cut-Points and the Dense Form. A *cut-point* of a heap h is its node that is either pointed by some variable or is a target of more than one selector edge. The roots of forests that are not cut-points in the represented heaps are called *false roots*. A forest automaton is *dense* if its accepted forests do not have false roots. Each forest automaton can be transformed into a set of dense forest automata that together have the same language as the original. This property is a part of canonicity, which can be achieved by normalization, introduced in [14] for the purpose of checking entailment of forest automata. A transformation to the dense form is essential in the symbolic execution of a program.

---

[1] For simplicity, data values and references are used as special leaf states accepting the data values and references they represent, instead of having additional leaf transitions to accept them.

3.2   Boxes

Forest automata, as defined in Sect. 3.1, can represent heaps with cut-points of an unbounded in-degree as, e.g., in singly-linked lists (SLLs) with head/tail pointers (indeed there can be any number of references from leaf nodes to a certain root). The basic definition of FAs cannot, however, deal with heaps with an unbounded number of cut-points since this would require an unbounded number of TAs within FAs. An example of such a set of heaps is the set of all doubly-linked lists (DLLs) of an arbitrary length, where each internal node is a cut-point. The solution provided in [14] is to allow FAs to use other nested FAs, called *boxes*, as symbols to "hide" recurring subheaps and in this way eliminate cut-points. The alphabet of a box itself may also include boxes, these boxes are, however, required to form a finite hierarchy—they cannot be recursively nested. The language of a box is a set of heaps over two special variables, in and out, which correspond to the input and the output port of the box. For simplicity of presentation, we give only a simplified version of boxes; see [14] for a more general definition that allows boxes with an arbitrary number of output ports.

A *nested forest automaton* over $\langle \Gamma, \mathbb{X} \rangle$ is an FA over $\langle \Gamma \cup \mathcal{B}, \mathbb{X} \rangle$ where $\mathcal{B}$ is a finite set of *boxes*. A *box* B over Γ is a nested FA $\langle A_1 \cdots A_n, \sigma_\square \rangle$ over $\langle \Gamma, \{\text{in}, \text{out}\} \rangle$ such that $\sigma_\square(\text{in}) \neq \sigma_\square(\text{out})$ and $A_1 \cdots A_n$ do not contain an occurrence of B (even a nested one). Unless stated otherwise, the FAs in the rest of the paper are nested.

In the case of a nested FA F, we need to distinguish between its language $L(F)$, which is a set of heaps over $\langle \Gamma \cup \mathcal{B}, \mathbb{X} \rangle$, and its *semantics* $[\![F]\!]$, which is a set of heaps over $\langle \Gamma, \mathbb{X} \rangle$ that emerges when all boxes in the heaps of the language are recursively *unfolded* in all possible ways. Formally, given heaps h and h', the heap h' is an *unfolding* of h if there is an edge $(B, u, v) \in next_h$ with a box $B = \langle A_1 \cdots A_n, \sigma_\square \rangle$ in h, such that h' can be constructed from h by substituting (B, u, v) with some $h_B \in [\![B]\!]$ such that $\sigma_\square(\text{in}) = u$ and $\sigma_\square(\text{out}) = v$. The substitution is done by removing (B, u, v) from h and uniting the heap-graph of h with that of h_B. We then write $h \rightsquigarrow_{(B,u,v)/h_B} h'$, or only $h \rightsquigarrow h'$ if the precise edge (B, u, v) and heap h_B are not relevant. We use $\rightsquigarrow^*$ to denote the reflexive transitive closure of $\rightsquigarrow$. The *semantics* of F, written as $[\![F]\!]$, is the set of all heaps h' over $\langle \Gamma, \mathbb{X} \rangle$ for which there is a heap h in $L(F)$ such that $h \rightsquigarrow^* h'$.

4   Program Semantics

The dynamic behaviour of a program is defined by its control flow graph, a mapping $p : \mathbb{T} \rightarrow (\mathbb{L} \times \mathbb{L})$ where $\mathbb{T}$ is a set of program statements, and $\mathbb{L}$ is a set of program locations. Statements are partial functions $\tau : \mathbb{H} \rightharpoonup \mathbb{H}$ where $\mathbb{H}$ is the set of heaps over the selectors Γ and variables $\mathbb{X}$ occurring in the program, which are used as representations of program configurations. The initial configuration is $h_{\text{init}} = \langle \emptyset, \emptyset, \emptyset \rangle$. We assume that statements are indexed by their line of code, so that no two statements of a program are equal. If $p(\tau) = (\ell, \ell')$, then the program p can move from ℓ to ℓ' while modifying the heap h at location ℓ

into $\tau(h)$. We assume that $\mathbb{X}$ contains a special variable pc that always evaluates to a location from $\mathbb{L}$, and that every statement updates its value according to the target location. Note that a single program location can have multiple succeeding program locations (which corresponds, e.g., to conditional statements), or no successor (which corresponds to exit points of a program). We use $src(\tau)$ to denote ℓ and $tgt(\tau)$ to denote ℓ' in the pair above. Every program p has a designated location ℓ_{init} called its *entry point* and $\ell_{err} \in \mathbb{L}$ called the error location[2].

A *program path* π in p is a sequence of statements $\pi = \tau_1 \cdots \tau_n \in \mathbb{T}^*$ such that $src(\tau_1) = \ell_{init}$, and, for all $1 < i \leq n$, it holds that $src(\tau_i) = tgt(\tau_{i-1})$. We say that π is *feasible* iff $\tau_n \circ \cdots \circ \tau_1(h_{init})$ is defined. The program p is safe if it contains no feasible program path with $tgt(\tau_n) = \ell_{err}$. In the following, we fix a program p with locations $\mathbb{L}$, variables $\mathbb{X}$, and selectors Γ.

5 Symbolic Execution with Forest Automata

Safety of the program p is verified using symbolic execution in the domain $\mathbb{F}$ of forest automata over $\langle \Gamma, \mathbb{X} \rangle$. The program is executed symbolically by iterating abstract execution of program statements and a generalization step. These high-level operations are implemented as sequences of atomic operations and splitting. Atomic operations are functions of the type $o : \mathbb{F} \rightharpoonup \mathbb{F}$. Splitting splits a forest automaton F into a set $\mathcal{S}$ of forest automata such that $[\![F]\!] = \bigcup_{F' \in \mathcal{S}} [\![F']\!]$. Splitting is necessary for some operations since forest automata are not closed under union, i.e., some sets of heaps expressible by a finite union of forest automata are not expressible by a single forest automaton.

To show an example of sets of heaps not expressible using a single FA, assume that the statement x = y->sel is executed on a forest automaton that encodes cyclic singly linked lists of an arbitrary length where y points to the head of the list. If the list is of length 1, then x will, after execution of the statement, point to the same location as y. If the list is longer, x and y will point to different locations. In the former case, the configuration has a single tree component, with both variables pointing to it. In the latter case, the two variables point to two different components. These two configurations cannot be represented using a single forest automaton.

The symbolic execution explores the program's *abstract reachability tree* (ART). Elements of the tree are forest automata corresponding to sets of reachable configurations at particular program locations. The tree is rooted by the forest automaton F_{init} s.t. $[\![F_{init}]\!] = \{h_{init}\}$. Every other node is a result of an application of an atomic operation or a split on its parent, and the applied operation is recorded on the tree edge between the two. The atomic operation corresponds to one of the following: symbolic execution of an effect of a program

---

[2] For simplification, we assume checking the error line (un-)reachability property only, which is, anyway, sufficient in most practical cases. For detection of garbage (which is not directly expressible as line reachability), we can extend the formalism and check for garbage after every command, and if a garbage is found, we jump to ℓ_{err}.

statement, generalization, or an auxiliary meta-operation that modifies the FAs while keeping its semantics (e.g., connects or cuts its components). Splitting appears in the tree as a node with several children connected via edges labelled by a special operation *split*. The said operations are described in more detail in Sect. 7.

The tree is expanded starting from the root as follows: First, a symbolic configuration in the parent node is generalized by iterating the following three operations: (i) transformation to the dense form, (ii) application of regular abstraction over-approximating sets of sub-graphs between cut-points of the represented heaps, (iii) folding boxes to decrease the number of cut-points in the represented heaps, until fixpoint. The transformation into the dense form is performed in order to obtain the most general abstraction in the subsequent step. A configuration where one more loop of the transformation-abstraction-folding sequence has no further effect is called *stable*. Operations implementing effects of statements are then applied on stable configurations. Exploration of a branch is terminated if its last configuration is entailed by a symbolic configuration with the same program location reached previously elsewhere in the tree.

A *symbolic path* is a path between a node and one of its descendants in the ART, i.e., a sequence of FAs and operations $\omega = F_0 o_1 F_1 \ldots o_n F_n$ such that $F_i = o_i(F_{i-1})$. A *forward run* is a symbolic path where $F_0 = F_{\text{init}}$. We write ωi to denote the prefix of ω ending by F_i and ωi to denote its suffix from F_i. A forward run that reaches ℓ_{err} is called an *abstract counterexample*. We associate every operation o with its *exact semantics* $\hat{o}$, defined as $\hat{o}(H) = \bigcup_{h \in H} \{\tau(h)\}$ if o implements the program statement τ, and as the identity for all other operations (operations implementing generalization, splitting, etc.), for a set of heaps H. The *exact execution* of ω is a sequence $h_0 \cdots h_n$ such that $h_0 \in [\![F_0]\!]$ and $h_i \in \hat{o}(\{h_{i-1}\}) \cap [\![F_i]\!]$ for $0 < i \leq n$. We say that ω is *feasible* if it has an exact execution, otherwise it is *infeasible/spurious*. The atomic operations are either semantically precise, or over-approximate their exact semantics, i.e., it always holds that $\hat{o}([\![F]\!]) \subseteq [\![o(F)]\!]$. Therefore, if the exploration of the program's ART finds no abstract counterexample, there is no exact counterexample, and the program is safe.

The regular abstraction mentioned above is based on over-approximating sets of reachable configurations using some of the methods described later in Sect. 9. The analysis starts with some initial abstraction function, which may, however, be too rough and introduce spurious counterexamples. The main contribution of the present paper is that we are able to analyse abstract counterexamples for spuriousness using the so-called *backward run* (cf. Sect. 8), and if the counterexamples are indeed spurious, we can *refine* the abstraction used to avoid the given spurious error symbolic path, and continue with the analysis, potentially further repeating the analyse-refine steps. We will describe the backward run and abstraction refinement shortly in the following section and give a more thorough description in Sects. 8 and 9.

5.1   Counterexample Analysis and Abstraction Refinement

Assume that the forward run $\omega = F_0 o_1 F_1 \cdots o_n F_n$ is spurious. Then there must be an index $i > 0$ such that the symbolic path ωi is feasible but $\omega i - 1$ is not. This means that the operation o_i over-approximated the semantics of ω and introduced into $[\![F_i]\!]$ some heaps that are not in $\hat{o}_i([\![F_{i-1}]\!])$ and that are *bad* in the sense that they make ωi feasible. An *interpolant for* ω is then a forest automaton I_i representing the bad heaps of $[\![F_i]\!]$ that were introduced into $[\![F_i]\!]$ by the over-approximation in o_i and are disjoint from $\hat{o}_i([\![F_{i-1}]\!])$. Formally,

1. $[\![I_i]\!] \cap \hat{o}_i([\![F_{i-1}]\!]) = \emptyset$ and
2. ω_i is infeasible from all $h \in [\![F_i]\!] \setminus [\![I_i]\!]$.

In the following, we describe how to use backward run, which reverts operations of the forward run on the semantic level, to check spuriousness of an abstract counterexample. Moreover, we show how to derive interpolants from backward runs reporting spurious counterexamples, and how to use those interpolants to refine the operation of abstraction so that it will not introduce the bad configurations in the same way again. A *backward run* for ω is the sequence $\overline{\omega} = \overline{F}_0 \cdots \overline{F}_n$ such that

1. $\overline{F}_n = F_n$ and
2. $[\![\overline{F}_{i-1}]\!] = \hat{o}_i^{-1}([\![\overline{F}_i]\!]) \cap [\![F_{i-1}]\!]$, that is, $\overline{F}_{i-1}$ represents the *weakest precondition* of $[\![\overline{F}_i]\!]$ w.r.t. $\hat{o}_i$ that is *localized* to $[\![F_{i-1}]\!]$.

If there is an $\overline{F}_i$ such that $[\![\overline{F}_i]\!] = \emptyset$ (and, consequently, $[\![\overline{F}_0]\!] = \emptyset, \ldots, [\![\overline{F}_{i-1}]\!] = \emptyset$), the forward run is spurious. In such a case, an interpolant I_i for ω can be obtained as $\overline{F}_{i+1}$ where $i + 1$ is the smallest index such that $[\![\overline{F}_{i+1}]\!] \neq \emptyset$. We elaborate on the implementation of the backward run in Sect. 8.

We note that our use of interpolants differs from that of McMillan [22] in two aspects. First, due to the nature of our backward run, we compute an interpolant over-approximating the source of the suffix of a spurious run, not the effect of its prefix. Second, for simplicity of implementation in our prototype, we do not compute a sequence of localized interpolants but use solely the interpolant obtained from the beginning of the longest feasible suffix of the counterexample for a global refinement. It would also, however, be possible to use the sequence $\overline{F}_i, \ldots, \overline{F}_n$ as localized interpolants.

In Sect. 9, we show that using the interpolant I_i, it is possible to refine regular abstraction o_i (the only over-approximating operation) to exclude the spurious run. The *progress guarantees* for the next iterations of the CEGAR loop are then the following:

1. for any FA F such that $[\![F]\!] \subseteq [\![F_{i-1}]\!]$ that is compatible with F_{i-1} (as defined in Sect. 6) it holds that $[\![o_i(F)]\!] \cap [\![I_i]\!] = \emptyset$,
2. forward runs $\omega' = F_0' o_1 F_1' \cdots o_n F_n'$ such that for all $1 \leq j \leq n$, $[\![F_i']\!] \subseteq [\![F_i]\!]$ and F_i' is compatible with F_i are excluded from the ART.

The compatibility intuitively means that boxes are folding the same sub-heaps of represented heaps and that the TA components are partitioning them in the same way.

6 Intersection of Forest Automata

The previous section used intersection of semantics of forest automata to detect spuriousness of a counterexample. In this section, we give an algorithm that computes an under-approximation of the intersection of semantics of a pair of FAs, and later give conditions (which are, in fact, met by the pairs of FAs in our backward run analysis) on the intersected FAs to guarantee that the computed intersection is precise.

A simple way to compute the intersection of semantics of two FAs, denoted as $\cap$, is component-wise, that is, for two FAs $F = \langle A_1 \cdots A_n, \sigma \rangle$ and $F' = \langle A'_1 \cdots A'_n, \sigma \rangle$, we compute the FA $F \cap F' = \langle (A_1 \cap A'_1) \cdots (A_n \cap A'_n), \sigma \rangle$—note that the assignments need to be equal. The tree automata product construction for our special kind of tree automata synchronizes on data values and on references. That is, a pair (a, b) that would be computed by a classical product construction where a or b is a reference or a data value is replaced by a if $a = b$, and removed otherwise.

The above algorithm is, however, incomplete, i.e., it only guarantees $[\![F \cap F']\!] \subseteq [\![F]\!] \cap [\![F']\!]$. To increase the precision, we take into account the semantics of the boxes in the product construction, yielding a construction denoted using $\sqcap$. When synchronising two rules in the TA product, we recursively call intersection of forest automata. That is, we compute the FA $F \sqcap F'$ in a similar way as $\cap$, but replace the tree automata product $A \cap A'$ by its variant $A \sqcap A'$. For $A = (Q, q_0, \Delta)$ and $A' = (Q', q'_0, \Delta')$, it computes the TA $A \sqcap A' = (Q \times Q', (q_0, q'_0), \Delta \sqcap \Delta')$ where $\Delta \sqcap \Delta'$ is built as follows:

$$
\begin{aligned}
\Delta \sqcap \Delta' = \{ (q, q') \to \bar{a} \sqcap \bar{a}'((q_1, q'_1), \ldots, (q_m, q'_m)) \mid q \to \bar{a}(q_1, \ldots, q_m) \in \Delta, \\
q' \to \bar{a}'(q'_1, \ldots, q'_m) \in \Delta' \}.
\end{aligned}
$$

Suppose $\bar{a} = a_1 \cdots a_m$, $\bar{a}' = a'_1 \cdots a'_m$, and that there is an index $0 \le i \le m$ such that if $j \le i$, a_j and a'_j are not boxes, and if $i < j$, a_j and a'_j are boxes. The vector of symbols $\bar{a} \sqcap \bar{a}'$ is created as $(a_1 \sqcap a'_1) \cdots (a_m \sqcap a'_m)$ if $a_i \sqcap a'_i$ is defined for all i's, otherwise the transition is not created. The symbol $a_i \sqcap a'_i$ is defined as follows:

1. for $j \le i$, $a_j \sqcap a'_j$ is defined as a_j if $a_j = a'_j$ and is undefined otherwise,
2. for $j > i$, $a_j \sqcap a'_j$ is the intersection of FAs (both a_j and a'_j are boxes, i.e., FAs).

Compatibility of Forest Automata. For a forest automaton $F = \langle A_1 \cdots A_n, \sigma \rangle$, its version with marked components is the FA $F^D = \langle A_1 \cdots A_n, \sigma \cup \sigma_{\mathsf{root}} \rangle$ where σ_{root} is the mapping $\{\mathsf{root}_1 \mapsto 1, \ldots, \mathsf{root}_n \mapsto n\}$. The *root variables* root_i are fresh variables that point to the roots of the tree components in $L(F)$. $[\![F^D]\!]$ then contains the same heaps as $[\![F]\!]$, but the roots of the components from $L(F)$ remain visible as they are explicitly marked by the root variables. In other words, the root variables track how the forest decomposition of heaps in $L(F)$

partitions the heaps from $[\![F]\!]$. By removing the root variables of $h^D \in [\![F^D]\!]$, we get the original heap $h \in [\![F]\!]$. We call h^D the *component decomposition of* h *by* F.

Using the notion of component decomposition, we further introduce a notion of the *representation* of a heap by an FA. Namely, the *representation* of a box-free heap h by an FA F with $h \in [\![F]\!]$ records how F represents h, i.e., (i) how F decomposes h into components, and (ii) how its sub-graphs enclosed in boxes are represented by the boxes. Formally, the representation of h by F is a pair $repre = (h^D, \{repre_1, \ldots, repre_n\})$ such that h^D is the component decomposition of h by F, and $repre_1, \ldots, repre_n$ are obtained from the sequence of unfoldings

$$h_0 \rightsquigarrow_{(B_1, u_1, v_1)/g_1} h_1 \rightsquigarrow_{(B_2, u_2, v_2)/g_2} \cdots \rightsquigarrow_{(B_n, u_n, v_n)/g_n} h_n$$

with $h_0 = h^D$ and $h_n \in L(F^D)$, such that for each $1 \leq i \leq n$, $repre_i$ is (recursively) the representation of g_i in B_i.

We write $[\![repre]\!]$ to denote $\{h\}$, and, for a set of representations R, we let $[\![R]\!] = \bigcup_{repre \in R} [\![repre]\!]$. The set of *representations accepted by a forest automaton* F is the set $Repre(F)$ of all representations of heaps from $[\![F]\!]$ by F. We say that a pair of FAs F and F' is *(representation) compatible* iff $[\![F]\!] \cap [\![F']\!] = [\![Repre(F) \cap Repre(F')]\!]$. The compatibility of a pair of FAs intuitively means that for every heap from the semantic intersection of the two FAs, at least one of its representations is shared by them.

Lemma 1. *For a pair F and F' of compatible FAs, it holds that $[\![F \sqcap F']\!] = [\![F]\!] \cap [\![F']\!]$.*

To illustrate the reason why compatibility is necessary in the backward run (cf. Sect. 5.1), consider a forward run that reaches an error line after passing through an FA F_k with the language consisting of a single configuration with one edge $n_1 \xrightarrow{DLL} n_2$. The box encloses a DLL segment, i.e., its output port is the *next*-successor of the input port, and the input is the *prev*-successor of the output port. Assume that the backward run then arrives with an FA $o_{k+1}^{-1}(F_{k+1})$ with the same language as F_k up to using the edge $n_2 \xrightarrow{revDLL} n_1$ with a reversed DLL-segment, where the output is the *prev*-successor of the input. Despite F_k and $o_{k+1}^{-1}(F_{k+1})$ have the same semantics, their languages are different and incompatible: In $L(F_k)$, n_1 has a successor and n_2 does not, while it is the other way round in $L(o_{k+1}^{-1}(F_{k+1}))$. The intersection computed using $\sqcap$ will be empty. Under-approximating the intersection this way can lead to wrong spuriousness detection and ineffective abstraction refinement. Enforcing compatibility rules out such situations and guarantees that the intersection computed using $\sqcap$ is precise.

7 Implementation of the Forward Run

This section describes the operations that are used to implement the forward symbolic execution over FAs. To be able to implement the backward run, we will need to maintain compatibility between the forward run and the so-far constructed part of the backward run. Therefore, we will present the operations used in the forward run mainly from the point of view of their effect on the representation of heaps (in the sense of Sect. 6). Then, in Sect. 8, we will show how this effect is inverted in the backward run such that, when starting from compatible configurations, the inverted operations preserve compatibility of the configurations in the backward run with their forward run counterparts.

We omit most details of the way the operations are implemented on the level of manipulations with rules and states of FAs. We refer the reader to [14, 26] for the details. We note that when we talk about removing a component or inserting a component in an FA, this also includes renaming references and updating assignments of variables. When a component is inserted at position i, all references to $\overline{j}$ with $j > i$ are replaced by $\overline{i+1}$, including the assignment σ of variables. When a component is removed from position i, all references to $\overline{j}$ with $j > i$ are replaced by references to $\overline{j-1}$.

Splitting. Splitting has already been discussed in Sect. 5. It splits the symbolic execution into several branches such that the union of the FAs after the split is semantically equal to the original FA. The split is usually performed when transforming an FA into several FAs that have only one variant of a root rule of some of their components. From the point of view of a single branch of the ART, splitting is an operation, denoted further as *split*, that transforms an FA F into an FA F' s.t. $[\![F']\!] \subseteq [\![F]\!]$ and $Repre(F') \subseteq Repre(F)$. Therefore, F is compatible with F'.

Operations Modifying Component Decomposition. This class of operations is used to implement transformation of FAs to the dense form and as pre-processing steps before the operations of folding, unfolding, and symbolic implementation of program statements. They do not modify the semantics of forest automata, but change the component decomposition of the represented heaps.

- *Connecting of components.* When the j-th component A_j of a forest automaton F accepts trees with false roots, then A_j can be connected to the component that refers to it. Indeed, as such roots are not cut-points, a reference $\overline{j}$ to them can appear only in a single component, say A_k, and at most once in every tree from its language (because a false root can have at most one incoming edge). For simplicity, assume that A_j has only one root state q that does not appear on the right-hand sides of rules. The connection is done by adding the states and rules of A_j to A_k, replacing the reference $\overline{j}$ in the rules of A_k by q. The j-th component is then removed from F. The previous sequence of actions is denoted as the operation *connect*$[j, k, q]$ below.
- *Cutting of a component.* Cutting divides a component with an index j into two. The part of the j-th component containing the root will accept tree prefixes of the original trees, and the new k-th component will accept their remaining sub-trees. The cutting is done at a state q of A_j, which appears exactly once in each run (the FA is first transformed to satisfy this). Occurrences of q at the

right-hand sides of rules are replaced by the reference $\overline{k}$ to the new component, and q becomes the root state of the new component. We denote this operation by $cut[j, k, q]$.

- *Swapping of components.* The operation $swap[j, k]$ swaps the j-th and the k-th component (and renames references and assignments accordingly).

Folding of Boxes. The folding operation assumes that the concerned FA is first transformed into the form $F = \langle A_{\text{in}} A_2 \cdots A_{n-1} A_{\text{out}} A'_1 \cdots A'_m, \sigma \rangle$ by a sequence of splitting, cutting, and swapping. The tuple of TAs $A_{\text{in}} A_2 \cdots A_{n-1} A_{\text{out}}$ will then be folded into a new box B with A_{in} as its input component and A_{out} as its output. Moreover, the operation is given sets of selectors $S_{\text{in}}, S_{\text{out}}$ of roots of components in A_{in} and A_{out} that are to be folded into B. The box $B = \langle A_{\text{in}}^B A_2 \cdots A_{n-1} A_{\text{out}}^B, \{\text{in} \mapsto 1, \text{out} \mapsto n\} \rangle$ arises from F by taking $A_{\text{in}} A_2 \cdots A_{n-1} A_{\text{out}}$ and by removing selectors that are not in S_{in} and S_{out} from root rules of A_{in} and A_{out} to obtain A_{in}^B and A_{out}^B respectively.

Folding returns the forest automaton $F' = \langle A'_{\text{in}} A'_{\text{out}} A'_1 \cdots A'_m, \sigma' \rangle$ that arises from F as follows. All successors of the roots accepted in A_{in} and A_{out} reachable over selectors from S_{in} and S_{out} are removed in A'_{in} and A'_{out} respectively (since they are enclosed in B). The root of the trees of A'_{in} gets an additional edge labelled by B, leading to the reference $\overline{n}$ (the output port), and the components $A_2 \cdots A_{n-1}$ are removed (since they are also enclosed in B). This operation is denoted as $fold[n, S_{\text{in}}, S_{\text{out}}, B]$.

Unfolding of Boxes. Unfolding is called as a preprocessing step before operations that implement program statements in order to expose the selectors accessed by the statement. It is called after a sequence of cutting, splitting, and swapping that changes the forest automaton into the form $F' = \langle A'_{\text{in}} A'_{\text{out}} A'_1 \cdots A'_m, o' \rangle$ where trees of A'_{in} have a reference $\overline{2}$ to A'_{out} accessible by an edge going from the root and labelled by the box B that is to be unfolded. Furthermore, assume that the box B is of the form $\langle A_{\text{in}}^B A_2 \cdots A_{n-1} A_{\text{out}}^B, \{\text{in} \mapsto 1, \text{out} \mapsto n\} \rangle$ and the input and the output ports have outgoing selectors from the sets S_{in} and S_{out} respectively. The operation returns the forest automaton F that arises from F' by inserting components $A_{\text{in}}^B A_2 \cdots A_{n-1} A_{\text{out}}^B$ in between A'_{in} and A'_{out}, removing the B successor of the root in A'_{in}, merging A_{in}^B with A'_{in}, and A_{out}^B with A'_{out}. The merging on the TA level consists of merging root transitions of the TAs. We denote this operation as $unfold[n, S_{\text{in}}, S_{\text{out}}, B]$.

Symbolic Execution of Program Statements. We will now discuss our symbolic implementation of the most essential statements of a C-like programming language. We assume that the operations are applied on an FA $F = \langle A_1 \cdots A_n, \sigma \rangle$.

- x := malloc(): A new $(n + 1)$-th component A_{new} is appended to F s.t. it contains one state and one transition with all selector values set to $\sigma(\text{undef})$. The assignment $\sigma(\text{x})$ is set to $\overline{n+1}$.
- x := y->sel and y->sel := x: If $\sigma(\text{y}) = \sigma(\text{undef})$, the operation moves to the error location. Otherwise, by splitting, cutting, and unfolding, F is transformed into the form where $A_{\sigma(\text{y})}$ has only one root rule and the rule has

a `sel`-successor that is a root reference $\overline{j}$. The statement `x := y->sel` then changes $\sigma(\mathtt{x})$ to $\overline{j}$, and `y->sel := x` changes the reference $\overline{j}$ in $A_{\sigma(\mathtt{y})}$ to $\sigma(\mathtt{x})$.

- `assume(x ~ y)` where $\sim\, \in \{==, !=\}$: This statement tests the equality of $\sigma(\mathtt{x})$ and $\sigma(\mathtt{y})$ and stops the current branch of the forward run if the result does not match $\sim$.

- `assume(x->data ~ y->data)` where $\sim$ is some data comparison: We start by unfolding and splitting F into the form where $A_{\sigma(\mathtt{x})}$ and $A_{\sigma(\mathtt{y})}$ have only one root rule with exposed `data` selector. The data values at the `data` selectors are then compared and the current branch of the forward run is stopped if they do not satisfy $\sim$. The operation moves to the error locations if $\sigma(\mathtt{x})$ or $\sigma(\mathtt{x})$ are equal to $\sigma(\mathtt{undef})$.

- `free(x)`: The component $A_{\sigma(\mathtt{x})}$ is removed, and all references to $\sigma(\mathtt{x})$ are replaced by $\sigma(\mathtt{undef})$.

The updates are followed by checking that all components are reachable from program variables in order to detect garbage. If some component is not reachable, the execution either moves to the error location, or—if the analysis is set to ignore memory leaks—removes the unreachable component and continues with the execution.

Regular Abstraction. Regular abstraction is described in Sect. 9. It is preceded by a transformation to the dense form by connecting and splitting the FA.

8   Inverting Operations in the Backward Run

We now present how we compute the weakest localized preconditions (*inversions* for short) of the operations from Sect. 7 in the backward run. As mentioned in Sect. 7, it is crucial that compatibility with the forward run is preserved. Let $F_i = o(F_{i-1})$ appear in the forward run and $\overline{F}_i$ be an already computed configuration in the backward run s.t. F_i and $\overline{F}_i$ are compatible. We will describe how to compute $\overline{F}_{i-1}$ such that it is also compatible with F_{i-1}.

Inverting most operations is straightforward. The operation $cut[j, k, q]$ is inverted by $connect[k, j, q_k]$ where q_k is the root state of A_k, $swap[j, k]$ is inverted by $swap[k, j]$, and *split* is not inverted, i.e., $\overline{F}_{i-1} = \overline{F}_i$.

One of the more difficult cases is $connect[j, k, q]$. Assume for simplicity that k is the index of the last component of F_{i-1}. Connecting can be inverted by cutting, but prior to that, we need to find *where* the k-th component of $\overline{F}_i$ should be cut. To find the right place for the cut, we will use the fact that the places of connection are marked by the state q in the FA F_i from the forward run. We use the tree automata product $\sqcap$ from Sect. 6, which propagates the information about occurrences of q to $\overline{F}_i$, to compute the product of the k-th component of F_i and the k-th component of $\overline{F}_i$. We replace the k-th component of $\overline{F}_i$ by the product, which results in an intermediate FA $\overline{F}_i'$. The product states with the first component q now mark the places where the forward run connected the components (they were leaves referring to the k-th component). This is where the backward run will cut the components to revert the connecting. Before that, though, we replace the mentioned product states with q by a new state q'. This replacement does not change the language because q was appearing exactly once in every run (because in the forward run, it is the root state of the connected component that does not appear on the right-hand sides of rules), therefore, a product state with q can appear at most once in every run of the product too. Finally, we compute $\overline{F}_{i-1}$ as $cut[k,j,q'](\overline{F}'_i)$.

Folding is inverted by unfolding and vice versa. Namely, $fold[n, S_{\text{in}}, S_{\text{out}}, B]$ is inverted by $unfold[n, S_{\text{in}}, S_{\text{out}}, B']$ and $unfold[n, S_{\text{in}}, S_{\text{out}}, B]$ by $fold[n, S_{\text{in}}, S_{\text{out}}, B']$ where the box B' (un-)folded in the backward run might be semantically smaller than B (since the backward run is returning with a subset of configurations of the forward run).

Regular abstraction is inverted using the intersection construction from Sect. 6. That is, if o_i is a regular abstraction, then $\overline{F}_{i-1} = \overline{F}_i \sqcap F_{i-1}$.

Finally, inversions of abstract statements compute the FA $\overline{F}_{i-1} = \langle \overline{A}'_1 \cdots \overline{A}'_n, \overline{\sigma}' \rangle$ from $\overline{F}_i = \langle \overline{A}_1 \cdots \overline{A}_m, \overline{\sigma} \rangle$ and $F_{i-1} = \langle A_1 \cdots A_n, \sigma \rangle$ as follows:

- $\mathtt{x = malloc()}$: We obtain $\overline{F}_{i-1}$ from $\overline{F}_i$ by removing the j-th TA, for $\overline{\sigma}(\mathtt{x}) = \overline{j}$. The value of $\overline{\sigma}'(\mathtt{x})$ is set to $\sigma(\mathtt{x})$.
- $\mathtt{x := y\text{->}sel}$: Inversion is done by setting $\overline{\sigma}'(\mathtt{x})$ to the value of $\sigma(\mathtt{x})$ from F_{i-1}.
- $\mathtt{y\text{->}sel := x}$: The target of the $\mathtt{sel}$-labelled edge from the root of $A_{\overline{\sigma}'(\mathtt{y})}$ is set to its target in $A_{\sigma(\mathtt{y})}$.
- $\mathtt{assume(...)}$: Tests do not modify FAs and as we are returning with a subset of configurations from the forward run, they do not need to be inverted, i.e., $\overline{F}_{i-1} = \overline{F}_i$.
- $\mathtt{free(x)}$: First, the component of F_{i-1} at the index $\sigma(\mathtt{x})$, which was removed in the forward run, is inserted at the same position in $\overline{F}_i$, and $\overline{\sigma}'(\mathtt{x})$ is set to that position. Then we must invert the rewriting of root references pointing to $\sigma(\mathtt{x})$ to $\sigma(\mathtt{undef})$ done by the forward run. For this, we compute the $\sqcap$ forest automata product from Sect. 6 with F_{i-1}, but modified so that instead of discarding reached pairs $(\sigma(\mathtt{undef}), \sigma(\mathtt{x}))$, it replaces them by $\sigma(\mathtt{x})$. Intuitively, the references to $\mathtt{x}$ are still present at F_{i-1}, so their occurrences in the product mark the occurrences of references to $\mathtt{undef}$ that were changed to point to $\mathtt{undef}$ by $\mathtt{free(x)}$. The modified product therefore redirects the marked root references to $\mathtt{undef}$ back to $\mathtt{x}$.

The Role of Compatibility in the Backward Run. Inversions of regular abstraction, component connection, and $\mathtt{free(x)}$, use the TA product construction $\sqcap$ from Sect. 6. The precision of all intersection and product computations in the backward run depends on the compatibility of the backward and forward run. Inverting the program statements also depends on the compatibility of the backward and forward run. Particularly, inversions of $\mathtt{x := y\text{->}sel}$ and $\mathtt{y\text{->}sel := x}$ use indices of components from F_{i-1}. They therefore depend on the property that heaps from $\overline{F}_i$ are decomposed into components in the same way. The compatibility is achieved by inverting every step of folding and unfolding, and every operation of connecting, cutting, and swapping of components.

9   Regular Abstractions over Forest Automata

Our abstraction over FAs is based on automata abstraction from the framework of *abstract regular tree model checking* (ARTMC) [10]. This framework comes with two abstractions for tree automata, *finite height abstraction* and *predicate abstraction*. Both of them are based on merging states of a tree automaton that are equivalent according to a given equivalence relation. Formally, given a tree automaton $A = (Q, q_0, \Delta)$, its abstraction is the TA $\alpha(A) = (Q/_\sim, [q_0]_\sim, \Delta_\sim)$ where $\sim$ is an equivalence relation on Q, $Q/_\sim$ is the set of $\sim$'s equivalence classes, $[q_0]_\sim$ denotes the equivalence class of q_0, and $\Delta_\sim$ arises from Δ by replacing occurrences of states in transitions by their equivalence classes. It holds that $|Q/_\sim| \leq |Q|$ and $L(A) \subseteq L(\alpha(A))$.

Finite height abstraction is a function α_h that merges states with languages equivalent up to a given tree height h. Formally, it merges states of A according to the equivalence relation $\sim^h$ defined as follows: $q_1 \sim^h q_2 \Leftrightarrow L^{\leq h}(A, q_1) = L^{\leq h}(A, q_2)$ where $L^{\leq h}(A, q)$ is the language of tree prefixes of trees from of $L(A, q)$ up to the height h. *Predicate language abstraction* is a function $\alpha_{[\mathcal{P}]}$ parameterized by a set of predicate languages $\mathcal{P} = \{P_1, \ldots, P_n\}$ represented by tree automata. States are merged according to the equivalence $q \sim_{\mathcal{P}} q'$, which holds for the two states if their languages $L(A, q)$ and $L(A, q')$ intersect with the same subset of predicate languages from $\mathcal{P}$.

Abstraction on Forest Automata. We extend the abstractions from ARTMC to FAs by applying the abstraction over TAs to the components of the FAs. Formally, let α be a tree automata abstraction. For an FA $F = \langle A_1 \cdots A_n, \sigma \rangle$, we define $\alpha(F) = \langle \alpha(A_1) \cdots \alpha(A_n), \sigma \rangle$. Additionally, in the case of predicate abstraction, which uses automata intersection to annotate states by predicate languages, we use the intersection operator $\sqcap$ from Sect. 6, which descends recursively into boxes and is thus more precise from the point of view of the semantics of FAs. Since the abstraction only over-approximates languages of the individual components, it holds that $[\![F]\!] \subseteq [\![\alpha(F)]\!]$ and $Repre(F) \subseteq Repre(\alpha(F))$—and so F and $\alpha(F)$ are compatible.

Abstraction Refinement. The finite height abstraction may be refined by simply increasing the height h. Advantages of finite height abstraction are its relative simplicity and the fact that the refinement does not require counterexample analysis. A disadvantage is that the refinement done by increasing the height is quite rough. Moreover, the cost of computing in the abstract domain rises quickly with increasing the height of the abstraction as exponentially more concrete configurations may be explored before the abstraction closes the analysis of a particular branch. The finite height abstraction was used—in a specifically fine-tuned version—in the first versions of FORESTER [14,17], which successfully verified a number of benchmarks, but the refinement was not sufficiently flexible to prove some more challenging examples.

Predicate abstraction, upon which we build in this paper, offers the needed additional flexibility. It can be refined by adding new predicates to $\mathcal{P}$ and gives strong guarantees about excluding counterexamples. In ARTMC, interpolants in the form of tree automata I_i are extracted from spurious counterexamples in the way described in Sect. 5.1. The interpolant is then used to refine the abstraction so that the spurious run is excluded from the program's ART.

The guarantees shown to hold in [10] on the level of TAs are the following. Let A and $I = (Q, q_0, \Delta)$ be two TAs and let $\mathcal{P}(I) = \{L(I, q) \mid q \in Q\}$ denote the set of languages of states of I. Then, if $L(A) \cap L(I) = \emptyset$, it is guaranteed that $L(\alpha_{[\mathcal{P}(I)]}(A)) \cap L(I) = \emptyset$. That is, when the abstraction is refined with languages of all states of I, it will exclude $L(I)$—unless applied on a TA whose language is already intersecting $L(I)$.

We can generalize the result of [10] to forest automata in the following way, implying the progress guarantees of CEGAR described in Sect. 5.1. For a forest automaton $F = \langle A_1 \cdots A_n, \sigma \rangle$, let $\mathcal{P}(F) = \bigcup_{i=1}^{n} \mathcal{P}(A_i)$.

Lemma 2. *Let F and I be FAs s.t. I is compatible with $\alpha_{[\mathcal{P}]}(F)$ and $[\![F]\!] \cap [\![I]\!] = \emptyset$. Then $[\![\alpha_{[\mathcal{P} \cup \mathcal{P}(I)]}(F)]\!] \cap [\![I]\!] = \emptyset$.*

We note that the lemma still holds if $\mathcal{P}(I)$ is replaced by $\mathcal{P}(A_i)$ only where A_i is the i-th component of I and $L(A_i \sqcap A_i') = \emptyset$ for the i-th component A_i' of $\alpha_{[\mathcal{P}]}(F)$.

10   Experiments

We have implemented our counterexample analysis and abstraction refinement as an extension of FORESTER and evaluated it on a set of C programs manipulating singly- and doubly-linked list, trees, skip-lists, and their combinations. We were able to analyse all of them fully automatically without any need to supply manually crafted predicates nor any other manual aid. The test cases are described in detail in [16].

We present our experimental results in Table 1. The table gives for each test case its name, information whether the program is safe or contains an error, the number of lines of code, the time needed for the analysis, the number of refinements, and, finally, the number of predicates learnt during the abstraction refinement. The experiments were performed on a computer with Intel Core i5 @2.50 GHz CPU and 8 GiB of memory running the Debian Sid OS with the Linux kernel.

Some of the test cases consider dynamic data structures without any data stored in them, some of them data structures storing finite-domain data. Such data can be a part of the data structure itself, as, e.g., in red-black trees, they can arise from some finite data abstraction, or they are also sometimes used to mark some selected nodes of the data structure when checking the way the data structure is changed by a given algorithm (e.g., one can check whether an arbitrarily chosen successive pair of nodes of a list marked red and green is swapped when the list is reversed—see e.g. [10]).

As the results show, some of our test cases do not need refinement. This is because the predicate abstraction is *a priori* restricted in order to preserve the

Table 1. Results of experiments.

Program	Status	LoC	Time [s]	Refnm	Preds	Program	Status	LoC	Time [s]	Refnm	Preds
SLL (delete)	safe	33	0.02	0	0	DLL (rev)	safe	39	0.70	0	0
SLL (bubblesort)	safe	42	0.02	0	0	CDLL	safe	32	0.02	0	0
SLL (insersort)	safe	36	0.04	0	0	DLL (insersort)	safe	42	0.56	0	0
SLLOfCSLL	safe	47	0.02	0	0	DLLOfCDLL	safe	54	1.76	0	0
SLL01	safe	70	1.20	1	1	**DLL01**	safe	73	0.65	2	2
CircularSLL	safe	49	3.57	3	3	**CircularDLL**	safe	52	37.22	18	24
OptPtrSLL	safe	59	1.90	3	3	**OptPtrDLL**	safe	62	1.87	5	5
QueueSLL	safe	71	11.32	10	10	**QueueDLL**	safe	74	44.68	14	14
GBSLL	safe	64	0.84	3	3	**GBDLL**	safe	71	1.89	4	4
GBSLLSent	safe	68	0.85	3	3	**GBDLLSent**	safe	75	2.19	4	4
RGSLL	safe	72	14.41	22	38	**RGDLL**	safe	76	78.76	26	26
WBSLL	safe	62	0.84	5	5	**WBDLL**	safe	71	1.37	7	7
SortedSLL	safe	76	227.12	15	15	**SortedDLL**	safe	82	36.67	11	11
EndSLL	safe	45	0.07	2	2	**EndDLL**	safe	49	0.10	3	3
TreeRB	error	130	0.08	0	0	**TreeWB**	error	125	0.05	0	0
TreeCnstr	safe	52	0.31	0	0	**TreeCnstr**	error	52	0.03	0	0
TreeOfCSLL	safe	109	0.57	0	0	**TreeOfCSLL**	error	109	0.56	1	3
TreeStack	safe	58	0.20	0	0	**TreeStack**	error	58	0.01	0	0
TreeDsw	safe	72	1.87	0	0	**TreeDsw**	error	72	0.02	0	0
TreeRootPtr	safe	62	1.43	0	0	**TreeRootPtr**	error	62	0.17	2	6
SkipList	safe	84	3.36	0	0	**SkipList**	error	84	0.08	1	1

forest automata "interconnection graph" [17], which roughly corresponds to the reachability relation among variables and cut-points in the heaps represented by a forest automaton (an approach used already with the finite height abstraction in former versions of FORESTER).

Table 1 also provides a comparison with the version of FORESTER from [17]. In particular, the highlighted cases are not manageable by that versions of FORESTER. These cases can be split into two classes. In the first class there are safe programs where the initial abstraction is too coarse and introduces spurious counterexamples, and the abstraction thus needs to be refined. The other class consists of programs containing a real error (which could not be confirmed without the backward run). The times needed for analysis are comparable in both versions of FORESTER.

To illustrate a typical learnt predicate, let us consider the test case *GBSLL*. This program manipulates a list with nodes storing two data values, green and blue, for which it holds that a green node is always followed by a blue one. The program also contains a tester code to test this property. FORESTER first learns two predicates describing particular violations of the property: (1) a green node is at the end of the list and (2) there are two green nodes in a row. After that, FORESTER derives a general predicate representing all lists with the needed invariant, i.e., a green node is followed by a blue one. The program is then successfully verified.

Another example comes from the analysis of the program *TreeCSLL*, which creates and deletes a tree where every tree node is also the head of a circular list. It contains an undefined pointer dereference error in the deletion of the circular lists. FORESTER first finds a spurious error (an undefined pointer dereference too) in the code that creates the circular lists. In particular, the abstraction introduces a case in which a tree node that is also the head of a list needs not be allocated, and an attempt of accessing its next selector causes an undefined pointer dereference error. This situation is excluded by the first refinement, after which the error within the list deletion is correctly reported. Notice that, in this case, the refinement learns a property of the shape, not a property over the stored data values. The ability to learn shape as well as data properties (as well as properties relating shape with data) using a uniform mechanism is one the features of our method which distinguishes it from most of the related work.

11   Discussion and Future Work

Both the described forward and backward symbolic execution are quite fast. We believe that the efficiency of the backward run (despite the need of computing expensive automata products) is to a large degree because it inverts unfolding (by folding). Backward run is therefore carried out with configurations encoded in a compact folded form.

FORESTER was not able to terminate on a few tree benchmarks. For a program manipulating a red-black tree using the rebalancing procedures, the initial forward run did not terminate. For another tree-based implementation of a set that includes a tester code checking full functional correctness, the CEGAR did not learn the right predicates despite many refinements. The non-termination of the forward run is probably related to the initial restrictions of the predicate abstraction. Restricting the abstraction seems to be harmful especially in the case of tree structures. If the abstraction remembers unnecessary fine information about tree branches, the analysis will explore exponentially many variants of tree structures with different branches satisfying different properties. The scenario where CEGAR seems to be unable to generalize is related to the splitting of the symbolic execution. The symbolic runs are then too specialised and CEGAR learns a large number of too specialised predicates from them (which are sometimes irrelevant to the "real" cause of the error).

A closer examination and resolution of these issues is a part of our future work. Allowing the abstraction more freedom is mostly an implementation issue, although nontrivial to achieve in the current implementation of FORESTER. Resolving the issue of splitting requires to cope with the domain of forest automata not being closed under union. This is possible, e.g., by modifying the definition of the FA language, which currently uses the Cartesian product of sets of trees, so that it would connect tree components based on reachability relation between them (instead of taking all elements of the Cartesian product). Another possibility would be to use sets of forest automata instead of individual ones as the symbolic representation of sets of heaps.

References

1. Abdulla, P.A., Holík, L., Jonsson, B., Lengál, O., Trinh, C.Q., Vojnar, T.: Verification of heap manipulating programs with ordered data by extended forest automata. Acta Informatica **53**(4), 357–385 (2016). http://dx.doi.org/10.1007/s00236-015-0235-0
2. Albargouthi, A., Berdine, J., Cook, B., Kincaid, Z.: Spatial interpolants. In: Vitek, J. (ed.) ESOP 2015. LNCS, vol. 9032, pp. 634–660. Springer, Heidelberg (2015). doi:10.1007/978-3-662-46669-8_26
3. Berdine, J., Cox, A., Ishtiaq, S., Wintersteiger, C.M.: Diagnosing abstraction failure for separation logic–based analyses. In: Madhusudan, P., Seshia, S.A. (eds.) CAV 2012. LNCS, vol. 7358, pp. 155–173. Springer, Heidelberg (2012). doi:10.1007/978-3-642-31424-7_16
4. Beyer, D., Henzinger, T.A., Théoduloz, G.: Lazy shape analysis. In: Ball, T., Jones, R.B. (eds.) CAV 2006. LNCS, vol. 4144, pp. 532–546. Springer, Heidelberg (2006). doi:10.1007/11817963_48
5. Botinčan, M., Dodds, M., Magill, S.: Refining existential properties in separation logic analyses. Technical report (2015). arXiv:1504.08309
6. Bouajjani, A., Habermehl, P., Moro, P., Vojnar, T.: Verifying programs with dynamic 1-selector-linked structures in regular model checking. In: Halbwachs, N., Zuck, L.D. (eds.) TACAS 2005. LNCS, vol. 3440, pp. 13–29. Springer, Heidelberg (2005). doi:10.1007/978-3-540-31980-1_2
7. Bouajjani, A., Habermehl, P., Rogalewicz, A., Vojnar, T.: Abstract regular tree model checking of complex dynamic data structures. In: Yi, K. (ed.) SAS 2006. LNCS, vol. 4134, pp. 52–70. Springer, Heidelberg (2006). doi:10.1007/11823230_5
8. Bouajjani, A., Bozga, M., Habermehl, P., Iosif, R., Moro, P., Vojnar, T.: Programs with lists are counter automata. Form. Methods Syst. Des. **38**(2), 158–192 (2011)
9. Bouajjani, A., Drăgoi, C., Enea, C., Sighireanu, M.: Accurate invariant checking for programs manipulating lists and arrays with infinite data. In: Chakraborty, S., Mukund, M. (eds.) ATVA 2012. LNCS, vol. 7561, pp. 167–182. Springer, Heidelberg (2012). doi:10.1007/978-3-642-33386-6_14
10. Bouajjani, A., Habermehl, P., Rogalewicz, A., Vojnar, T.: Abstract regular (tree) model checking. Int. J. Softw. Tools Technol. Transf. **14**(2), 167–191 (2012)
11. Chang, B.-Y.E., Rival, X., Necula, G.C.: Shape analysis with structural invariant checkers. In: Nielson, H.R., Filé, G. (eds.) SAS 2007. LNCS, vol. 4634, pp. 384–401. Springer, Heidelberg (2007). doi:10.1007/978-3-540-74061-2_24
12. Deshmukh, J.V., Emerson, E.A., Gupta, P.: Automatic verification of parameterized data structures. In: Hermanns, H., Palsberg, J. (eds.) TACAS 2006. LNCS, vol. 3920, pp. 27–41. Springer, Heidelberg (2006). doi:10.1007/11691372_2
13. Dudka, K., Peringer, P., Vojnar, T.: Byte-precise verification of low-level list manipulation. In: Logozzo, F., Fähndrich, M. (eds.) SAS 2013. LNCS, vol. 7935, pp. 215–237. Springer, Heidelberg (2013). doi:10.1007/978-3-642-38856-9_13
14. Habermehl, P., Holík, L., Rogalewicz, A., Šimáček, J., Vojnar, T.: Forest automata for verification of heap manipulation. Form. Methods Syst. Des. **41**(1), 83–106 (2012)
15. Heinen, J., Noll, T., Rieger, S.: Juggrnaut: graph grammar abstraction for unbounded heap structures. In: Proceedings of 3rd International Workshop on Harnessing Theories for Tool Support in Software–TTSS 2009. ENTCS, vol. 266, pp. 93–107. Elsevier (2010)

16. Holík, L., Hruška, M., Lengál, O., Rogalewicz, A., Vojnar, T.: Counterexample validation and interpolation-based refinement for forest automata. Technical report FIT-TR-2016-03 (2016). http://www.fit.vutbr.cz/~lengal/pub/FIT-TR-2016-03.pdf

17. Holík, L., Lengál, O., Rogalewicz, A., Šimáček, J., Vojnar, T.: Fully automated shape analysis based on forest automata. In: Sharygina, N., Veith, H. (eds.) CAV 2013. LNCS, vol. 8044, pp. 740–755. Springer, Heidelberg (2013). doi:10.1007/978-3-642-39799-8_52

18. Jensen, J.L., Jørgensen, M.E., Schwartzbach, M.I., Klarlund, N.: Automatic verification of pointer programs using monadic second-order logic. In: Proceedings of 1997 ACM SIGPLAN Conference on Programming Language Design and Implementation–PLDI 1997, pp. 226–234. ACM (1997)

19. McMillan, K.L.: Lazy abstraction with interpolants. In: Ball, T., Jones, R.B. (eds.) CAV 2006. LNCS, vol. 4144, pp. 123–136. Springer, Heidelberg (2006). doi:10.1007/11817963_14

20. Loginov, A., Reps, T., Sagiv, M.: Abstraction refinement via inductive learning. In: Etessami, K., Rajamani, S.K. (eds.) CAV 2005. LNCS, vol. 3576, pp. 519–533. Springer, Heidelberg (2005). doi:10.1007/11513988_50

21. Magill, S., Tsai, M.H., Lee, P., Tsay, Y.K.: Automatic numeric abstractions for heap-manipulating programs. In: Proceedings of 37th Annual SIGPLAN-SIGACT Symposium on Principles of Programming Languages–POPL 2010, pp. 211–222. ACM (2010)

22. McMillan, K.L.: Interpolation and SAT-based model checking. In: Hunt, W.A., Somenzi, F. (eds.) CAV 2003. LNCS, vol. 2725, pp. 1–13. Springer, Heidelberg (2003). doi:10.1007/978-3-540-45069-6_1

23. Podelski, A., Wies, T.: Counterexample-guided focus. In: Proceedings of 37th Annual SIGPLAN-SIGACT Symposium on Principles of Programming Languages–POPL 2010, pp. 249–260. ACM (2010)

24. Qin, S., He, G., Luo, C., Chin, W.N., Chen, X.: Loop invariant synthesis in a combined abstract domain. J. Symbol. Comput. 50, 386–408 (2013)

25. Sagiv, M., Reps, T., Wilhelm, R.: Parametric shape analysis via 3-valued logic. ACM Trans. Program. Lang. Syst. 24(3), 217–298 (2002)

26. Šimáček, J.: Harnessing forest automata for verification of heap manipulating programs. Ph.D. thesis, Grenoble Alpes University, France (2012). https://tel.archives-ouvertes.fr/tel-00805794

27. Yang, H., Lee, O., Berdine, J., Calcagno, C., Cook, B., Distefano, D., O'Hearn, P.: Scalable shape analysis for systems code. In: Gupta, A., Malik, S. (eds.) CAV 2008. LNCS, vol. 5123, pp. 385–398. Springer, Heidelberg (2008). doi:10.1007/978-3-540-70545-1_36

Block-Wise Abstract Interpretation
by Combining Abstract Domains with SMT

Jiahong Jiang[1], Liqian Chen[1(✉)], Xueguang Wu[1], and Ji Wang[1,2]

[1] School of Computer Science, National University of Defense Technology,
Changsha, China
{jhjiang,lqchen,xueguangwu,wj}@nudt.edu.cn
[2] State Key Laboratory of High Performance Computing, Changsha, China

Abstract. Statement-wise abstract interpretation that calculates the abstract semantics of a program statement by statement, is scalable but may cause precision loss due to limited local information attached to each statement. While Satisfiability Modulo Theories (SMT) can be used to characterize precisely the semantics of a loop-free program fragment, it is challenging to analyze loops efficiently using plainly SMT formula. In this paper, we propose a block-wise abstract interpretation framework to analyze a program block by block via combining abstract domains with SMT. We first partition a program into blocks, encode the transfer semantics of a block through SMT formula, and at the exit of a block we abstract the SMT formula that encodes the post-state of a block w.r.t. a given pre-state into an abstract element in a chosen abstract domain. We leverage the widening operator of abstract domains to deal with loops. Then, we design a disjunctive lifting functor on top of abstract domains to represent and transmit useful disjunctive information between blocks. Furthermore, we consider sparsity inside a large block to improve efficiency of the analysis. We develop a prototype based on block-wise abstract interpretation. We have conducted experiments on the benchmarks from SV-COMP 2015. Experimental results show that block-wise analysis can check about 1x more properties than statement-wise analysis does.

Keywords: Abstract interpretation · SMT · Abstract domains · Block encoding · Sparsity

1 Introduction

Static analysis based on abstract interpretation (AI) often considers each statement as an individual transfer function, and computes fix-point based on "iteration+widening" strategy [12]. However, the statement-by-statement analysis may cause precision loss due to the limited local information in each statement. It is often the case that the composition of the optimal transformers of individual statements in a sequence does not result in the optimal transformer for the whole sequence [26].

© Springer International Publishing AG 2017
A. Bouajjani and D. Monniaux (Eds.): VMCAI 2017, LNCS 10145, pp. 310–329, 2017.
DOI: 10.1007/978-3-319-52234-0_17

On the other hand, most numerical abstract domains have limitations in expressing disjunctive information, and thus may cause precision loss when dealing with control-flow joins. Satisfiability Modulo Theories (SMT) is expressive for describing constraints, and could represent disjunctions and quantifiers that are common in program semantics. Recently, much attention has been paid on describing semantics of a program through SMT [2,5,24,27,34]. Nevertheless, loops in programs are challenging to cope with in analysis based on purely SMT formulas.

To exploit both advantages of abstract domains and SMT, we propose a framework of block-wise abstract interpretation (BWAI) that extends statement-by-statement analysis to block-by-block analysis by combining SMT and abstract domains. The main idea is following: we first partition a program into several blocks, and then encode a "SMT-expressible" block (e.g., a block without loops) into a SMT formula; we translate the abstract domain representation of the pre-state to a SMT formula at the entry of the block and translate the post-state in SMT formula back to abstract domain representation; in the whole, we compute the fixpoint based on "iteration+widening" strategy block by block and use widening operators at widening points. The strategy of block partitioning is the basis of the BWAI, and two extreme partitioning strategies are to minimize the size of a block and to maximize the size of a block. One extreme strategy to minimize the size of a block considers each statement as a block, in which case the BWAI is degenerated to statement-wise abstract interpretation (SWAI).

Under the BWAI framework, at the exit of a block, we will abstract soundly a SMT formula to the usually less precise abstract element in an abstract domain. Such abstraction may cause precision loss and lead to false positives. Hence, we design a lifting functor on top of base abstract domains to represent and transmit between blocks the useful information that is out of the expressiveness of the base abstract domain but may be helpful for precision of successive analysis. Furthermore, the SMT formula for a block of large size may be so complicated that abstracting it into an abstract element in an abstract domain may be too costly or even run out of memory. To alleviate this problem, we leverage the sparsity inside a large block to improve the efficiency and scalability of BWAI. Finally, we develop a prototype based on BWAI, and have conducted experiments on benchmarks from SV-COMP 2015 [1]. The experimental results show that our BWAI analysis can prove around 66% of the properties in the benchmarks while analysis based on SWAI can prove only around 34% of the properties.

The rest of this paper is organized as follows. Section 2 presents a motivating example of block-wise abstract interpretation (BWAI). In Sect. 3, we present the BWAI framework. Section 4 presents the lifting functor on top of abstract domains to fit for BWAI. In Sect. 5, we leverage the block-wise sparsity in a large block to improve the efficiency of analysis. Section 6 describes our implementation together with preliminary experimental results. Section 7 discusses related work. Finally, conclusions as well as future work are given in Sect. 8.

2   A Motivating Example

In this section, we give a motivating example shown in Fig. 1(a), which is extracted from $pc\_sfifo.c$ in the directory "systemc" of SV-COMP 2015. Program $pc\_sfifo.c$ simulates reading and writing operations on buffers in operating system. Figure 1(a) shows a fragment of $pc\_sfifo.c$. For this example, using SWAI with the octagon abstract domain, we fail to prove the unreachability of the error at line 24. In the following, we illustrate how our BWAI approach works for this example.

```
int q_free, p_dw_st, c_dr_st;
int c_num_read, p_num_write;
...
1  if(brandom()){
2    p_dw_st = 0;
3    c_dr_st = 0;
4    q_free = 1;
5    p_num_write = 0;
6    c_num_read = 0;
7  }else{
8    p_dw_st = 2;
9    c_dr_st = 0;
10   q_free = 0;
11   p_num_write = 1;
12   c_num_read = 0;
13 }
14 while(brandom()){
15   if(p_dw_st == 0){
16     p_dw_st = 1;
17     do_write_p();
18   }
19   if(c_dr_st == 0){
20     c_dr_st = 1;
21     do_read_c();
22   }
23 }
24 if(p_num_write < c_num_read){/ * error() * /}
25 ...
```

```
void do_write_p(void){
  if(q_free == 1){
    q_free = 0;
    c_dr_st = 0;
    p_num_write+ = 1;
  }
  p_dw_st = 2;
}

void do_read_c(void){
  if(q_free == 0){
    q_free = 1;
    p_dw_st = 0;
    c_num_read+ = 1;
  }
  c_dr_st = 2;
}
```

(a)   (b)

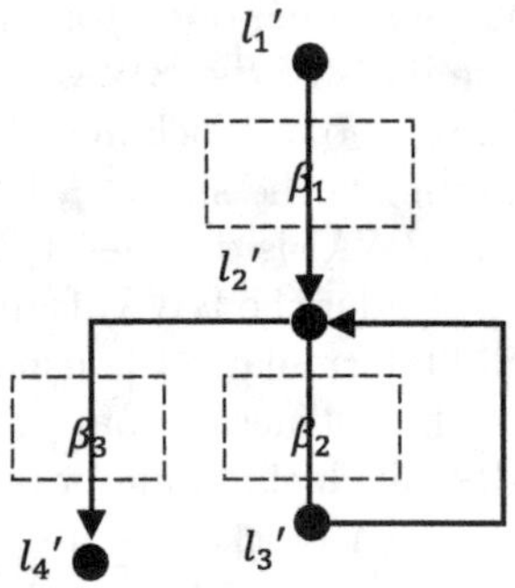

Fig. 1. A motivating example extracted from SV-COMP 2015

To perform BWAI, we first partition the program and get the block-wise control flow graph (CFG) as shown in Fig. 1(b), where β_1 contains the code fragment from location ℓ_1 to ℓ_{14} in Fig. 1(a) (where ℓ_i represents the program point at the beginning of the i-th line throughout this paper), β_2 contains the code fragment from location ℓ_{14} to ℓ_{23} in Fig. 1(a) (i.e., the loop body), β_3 contains the code fragment outside the loop including locations ℓ_{14}, ℓ_{24} and ℓ_{25}

in Fig. 1(a) when $brandom()==$**false**. Note that the code in line 14 (i.e., the head of the **while** loop) turns to an $assume$ statement in blocks β_2 and β_3. Hence, program points ℓ'_1, ℓ'_2, ℓ'_3 and ℓ'_4 in Fig. 1(b) are respectively corresponding to locations ℓ_1, ℓ_{14}, ℓ_{23} and ℓ_{25} in Fig. 1(a). And the location ℓ'_2 is the widening point in Fig. 1(b).

When analyzing the block-wise CFG, we characterize the transfer semantics of a block using a SMT formula. E.g., the transfer semantic of block β_1 can be encoded into SMT formula "$\varphi_1^{trans} \triangleq ite(brandom1 ==$ **true**, $(p\_dw\_st = 0) \wedge (c\_dr\_st = 0) \wedge (q\_free = 1) \wedge (p\_num\_read = 0) \wedge (c\_num\_read = 0), (p\_dw\_st = 2) \wedge (c\_dr\_st = 0) \wedge (q\_free = 0) \wedge (p\_num\_read = 1) \wedge (c\_num\_read = 0)$". Then, we compute the post-state of block β_1 based on the SMT formula given a pre-state, and get an abstract element in an abstract domain at location ℓ'_2. However, converting a SMT formula into a specific abstract domain representation may cause precision loss. E.g., when analyzing block β_1 given a pre-state $\top$, we get the abstract Octagon representation at location ℓ'_2 as "$(-1 \le p\_dw\_st - q\_free \le 2) \wedge ... \wedge (0 \le p\_dw\_st \le 2 \wedge 0 \le q\_free \le 1)$", which causes precision loss (e.g., we in fact know "$((p\_dw\_st = 0) \wedge (c\_dr\_st = 0)) \vee ((p\_dw\_st = 2) \wedge (c\_dr\_st = 0))$" according to the SMT formula φ_1^{trans} that encodes precisely the concrete transfer semantics of β_1). And eventually this precision loss leads to the failure of proving the unreachability of the error at line 24 in Fig. 1(a).

To prove the property, we need more expressive information at location ℓ'_2. In this paper, we choose a predicate set for each block and partition the post state at the exit location of the block according to the value of the predicates. E.g., the predicate sets we choose for block β_1 and β_2 are $\mathbb{P}_1 = \mathbb{P}_2 = \{p_0, p_1, p_2, p_3, p_4\}$, where $p_0 \triangleq (p\_dw\_st == 0)$, $p_1 \triangleq (c\_dr\_st == 0)$, $p_2 \triangleq (q\_free == 0)$, $p_3 \triangleq (q\_free == 1)$ and $p_4 \triangleq (p\_num\_write - c\_num\_read < 0)$. Assume the base abstract domain is Octagon. With the predicate set $\mathbb{P}_1$, we partition the post-state of β_1 at location ℓ'_2 and transmit the disjunctive information to analysis of block β_2. Finally, after the fixpoint iteration converges, we could get at location ℓ'_2 the invariant "$0 \le p\_num\_write - c\_num\_read \le 1$" which proves unreachability of the error at line 24 in Fig. 1(a).

3   Block-Wise Abstract Interpretation Framework

3.1   Block Partitioning and Block Encoding

We first present a cutpoint-based approach [19] to partition a program into blocks. The main idea is to select cutpoints from program points, and take the program fragment between two adjacent cutpoints as a block. Let the tuple $\langle \mathcal{L}, \mathcal{E}, \ell_0, \mathcal{L}_e \rangle$ denote the CFG of a program $\mathcal{P}$, where $\mathcal{L}$ is the set of nodes denoting program points, $\mathcal{E}$ is the set of transfer edges, $\ell_0 \in \mathcal{L}$ is the entry node of $\mathcal{P}$, which has no incoming edges, and $\mathcal{L}_e \subseteq \mathcal{L}$ is the set of exit nodes, which have no outcoming edges.

We use **SubGraph**$(\ell_i, \ell_j) \triangleq \langle \mathcal{L}_{(i,j)}, \mathcal{E}_{(i,j)}, \ell_i, \ell_j \rangle$ to represent the subgraph determined by the node ℓ_i and ℓ_j (with a unique entry node ℓ_i and a unique exit node ℓ_j), where $\mathcal{L}_{(i,j)}$ is the set of nodes in all paths from ℓ_i to ℓ_j and

$\mathcal{E}_{(i,j)}$ is the set of the corresponding edges. We call $\mathbf{SubGraph}(\ell_i, \ell_j)$ is $\mathcal{L}'$-free if $\mathcal{L}_{(i,j)} \cap \mathcal{L}' = \emptyset$, where $\mathcal{L}' \subseteq \mathcal{L}$ is a subset of program points. Assume $\mathcal{T}$ (e.g., Linear Real Arithmetic, **LRA**) is one theory of SMT. We call an expression is $\mathcal{T}$-Encodable, if it can be encoded by theory $\mathcal{T}$. E.g., expressions that only involve linear computations on program variables of real number type are **LRA**-Encodable expressions. We call $\mathbf{SubGraph}(\ell_i, \ell_j)$ is $\mathcal{T}$-Encodable if all expressions appearing in $\mathcal{E}_{(i,j)}$ are $\mathcal{T}$-Encodable. Here, we provide the syntactic description of a $\mathcal{T}$-Encodable block β:

$$\tau ::= \mathbf{skip} | x := \mathbf{exp}, \qquad \beta ::= \tau | \mathbf{if}(\mathbf{b})\{\beta_1\}\mathbf{else}\{\beta_2\} | \beta_1; \beta_2$$

where **exp** is a $\mathcal{T}$-Encodable expression, τ is a **skip** or assignment statement, **b** is a $\mathcal{T}$-Encodable condition expression and β_1, β_2 are $\mathcal{T}$-Encodable blocks. From the syntactic description, we know that $\mathcal{T}$-Encodable block β is loop-free and we assume that β has a unique entry point ℓ_β^{en} and a unique exit point ℓ_β^{ex}.

We say a subset of program points $\mathcal{L}_c \subseteq \mathcal{L}$ is a set of cutpoints w.r.t. the theory $\mathcal{T}$, if $\mathcal{L}_c$ satisfies the following conditions: (1) $\ell_0 \in \mathcal{L}_c$ and $\mathcal{L}_e \subseteq \mathcal{L}_c$; (2) all program points at the head of loops are in $\mathcal{L}_c$; (3) program points before and after statements that are not $\mathcal{T}$-Encodable in SMT are in $\mathcal{L}_c$; (4) $\forall \ell_i \in \mathcal{L}_c \setminus (\{\ell_0\} \cup \mathcal{L}_e)$, $\exists \ell_j \in \mathcal{L}_c$, s.t. ℓ_i and ℓ_j determine a subgraph (i.e. $\mathbf{SubGraph}(\ell_i, \ell_j)$) and $\mathbf{SubGraph}(\ell_i, \ell_j)$ is $\mathcal{L}_c \setminus (\{\ell_i\} \cup \{\ell_j\})$-free. An extreme set of cutpoints is $\mathcal{L}$ itself, in which case we consider each individual statement as a block. Based on a set of chosen cutpoints, a program can be partitioned into blocks and we get a **CFG with blocks**, denoted as a tuple $\langle \mathcal{L}, \mathcal{L}_c, \mathcal{E}, \mathcal{B}, \ell_0, \mathcal{L}_e \rangle$, where $\mathcal{B}$ is a set of blocks. If a block involves **skip** statements only, we consider this block as an empty block and do not show in the CFG with blocks. Now we present our strategy to choose the set of cutpoints and the corresponding partitioning strategy based on cutpoints.

To make the analysis as precise as possible, we try to partition a program into blocks such that the code size of each block is as large as possible. Hence, we propose a greedy block partitioning strategy (GBP), that is, we only take as cutpoints the loop heads and program points before and after the statement that is not $\mathcal{T}$-Encodable in SMT.

Now we present how to encode the transfer semantics of $\mathcal{T}$-Encodable block β via a SMT formula φ. First, we assume the block β is in a SSA (Static Single Assignment) form [15] such that: (1) in all paths from ℓ_β^{en} to ℓ_β^{ex}, each variable is assigned at most once; (2) the index of each variable in the **then**-branch and **else**-branch is unified at each join point. We use the standard SSA algorithm [15] to translate a program fragment into this format. Let $\xi \colon \mathcal{B} \to \mathcal{F}$ denote the map from a set of blocks $\mathcal{B}$ to a set of SMT formulas $\mathcal{F}$. We define $\xi(\mathbf{skip}) \triangleq$ **true**; $\xi(x := \mathbf{exp}) \triangleq (x = \theta(\mathbf{exp}))$, where $\theta(\mathbf{exp})$ is the SMT encoding for the expression **exp**; $\xi(\mathbf{if}(\mathbf{b})\{\beta_1\}\mathbf{else}\{\beta_2\}) \triangleq ite(\theta(\mathbf{b}), \xi(\beta_1), \xi(\beta_2))$, where $\theta(\mathbf{b})$ is the SMT encoding for condition expression **b**; $\xi(\beta_1; \beta_2) \triangleq \xi(\beta_1) \wedge \xi(\beta_2)$. We use function ξ to encode the whole $\mathcal{T}$-Encodable block as a SMT formula.

3.2 Block-Wise Iteration Strategy Combining SMT and Abstract Domains

In BWAI, the transfer semantics of a block is encoded as a SMT formula, while at cutpoints we maintain abstract domain representation. Hence, before and after cutpoints, we need conversion operators to convert abstract domain representation into a SMT formula and also to convert a SMT formula into abstract domain representation.

Let $[\![\beta_j]\!]^\sharp : \mathcal{S}^\sharp \to \mathcal{S}^\sharp$ characterize the abstract semantics of block β_j, where $\mathcal{S}^\sharp$ denotes the set of abstract states. Assume that the entry point and exit point of β_j are ℓ'_j and ℓ'_{j+1} respectively in the CFG with blocks. If the abstract value at cutpoint ℓ'_j is a_j, then the abstract value at cutpoint ℓ'_{j+1} will be $a_{j+1} \triangleq [\![\beta_j]\!]^\sharp(a_j)$. In the following, we will show how to calculate $[\![\beta_j]\!]^\sharp$.

Let $\nu: \mathcal{A} \to \mathcal{F}$ be the map from a set of abstract values in an abstract domain to a set of SMT formulas, and $\nu(a) = \varphi$ where a is an abstract value and φ is a SMT formula. It is often exact to translate abstract value a to the corresponding SMT formula φ, because constraints in most numerical abstract domains could be encoded as SMT formulas directly. E.g., the constraint "$x \in [m_i, m_s]$" in the Box domain could be encoded as a SMT formula "$x \geq m_i \wedge x \leq m_s$".

Let $\zeta : \mathcal{F} \to \mathcal{A}$ be the map from a set of SMT formulas $\mathcal{F}$ to a set of abstract values in an abstract domain $\mathcal{A}$. It is worthy noting that a SMT formula φ is often out of the expressiveness of numerical abstract domains, e.g., when φ involves disjunctions. Computing the function ζ is essentially a problem of symbolic abstraction that aims to calculate the consequence of φ in the abstract domain $\mathcal{A}$. To guarantee the soundness of static analysis, we need a sound conversion operator ζ. Let $\mathbf{Sol}(\varphi)$ denote the solution set of the constraints corresponding to SMT formula φ. We call abstract value a a *sound* abstraction of φ in domain $\mathcal{A}$ if $\mathbf{Sol}(\varphi) \subseteq \mathbf{Sol}(\nu(a))$. We call abstract value a the *best* abstraction in domain $\mathcal{A}$ of SMT formula φ if (1) $\mathbf{Sol}(\varphi) \subseteq \mathbf{Sol}(\nu(a))$ and (2) for all $a' \in \mathcal{A}$, s.t. $\mathbf{Sol}(\varphi) \subseteq \mathbf{Sol}(\nu(a'))$, we have $a \sqsubseteq^\sharp a'$ where $\sqsubseteq^\sharp$ is the inclusion operator in the abstract domain $\mathcal{A}$.

We compute the function ζ via optimization techniques based on SMT (namely, SMT-opt). The SMT-opt problem is to solve "$\max e \; s.t. \; \varphi$", where φ is a SMT formula and e is an objective function in SMT format [7,24]. In this paper, we only consider using of abstract domains based on templates which include a large subset of commonly used abstract domains, such as boxes, octagons [25], TCMs [32], etc. The templates determine objective functions and the given SMT formula encoding the post-state determines the constraint space in the SMT-opt problem. We then get the corresponding template abstract domain representation by computing the maximum and minimum value of objective function under the SMT constraint space. It is worthy noting that based on SMT-opt, we get the sound abstraction of a SMT formula in a template abstract domain. Let e_i ($1 \leq i \leq n$, where n is the number of templates) be a template, we get c_i by solving the SMT-opt problem "$\max e_i \; s.t. \; \varphi$", and thus get $e_i \leq c_i$ as a constraint in the template abstract domain representation. Overall, $\bigwedge_{i=1}^{n} e_i \leq c_i$

gives the resulting constraint representation in the template abstract domain. Obviously, $\mathbf{Sol}(\varphi) \subseteq \mathbf{Sol}(e_i \leq c_i)$. We have $\mathbf{Sol}(\varphi) \subseteq \mathbf{Sol}(\bigwedge_{i=1}^{n} e_i \leq c_i)$, which guarantees soundness of ζ via SMT-opt. In fact, we get the best abstraction of a SMT formula in a template abstract domain based on SMT-opt. E.g., to get the best abstract representation of Octagon domain for φ, we solve a series of SMT-opt problems like "$\mathbf{max}\ (\pm x \pm y)\ s.t.\ \varphi$", which would give the best abstraction of formula φ in the Octagon domain.

Overall, to compute the post abstract value of the transfer semantic of a block represented by a SMT formula φ_j^{trans}, we first transform the abstract value a_j at the entry of the block to SMT format φ_j^{pre} such that $\varphi_j^{pre} = \nu(a_j)$, then abstract the SMT formula "$\varphi_j^{pre} \wedge \varphi_j^{trans}$" to an abstract value a_{j+1}, such that $a_{j+1} = [\![\beta_j]\!]^{\sharp}(a_j) \triangleq \zeta(\varphi_j^{pre} \wedge \varphi_j^{trans})$.

Now, we briefly describe the iteration strategy on CFG with blocks in the framework of BWAI, to compute the abstract fix-point of a program. In the whole, we still solve the fix-point based on "iteration+widening" strategy. We deal with the statements which are not encoded by SMT based on abstract domains (e.g., the statements which are not $\mathcal{T}$-expressible), the same as in SWAI. When analyzing the block β which is encoded by SMT, we transform the abstract domain representation at the entry point ℓ_{β}^{en} to a SMT formula, and abstract the post-state in SMT format to an abstract value in an abstract domain at the exit point ℓ_{β}^{ex} based on the ζ operator. At the widening points $\mathcal{L}_w$, we still use the widening operator of the abstract domain. Overall, our iteration strategy in the framework of BWAI is extended from the one of SWAI, but combines SMT and abstract domains.

4   Abstract Domain Lifting Functor for BWAI

In the framework of BWAI, inside a block we take the advantage of SMT to encode the semantics of the block and use abstract domain representation to transfer information between blocks. Hence, when the block involves behaviors which are beyond the expressiveness of the chosen abstract domain but could be encoded precisely by SMT formula (e.g., disjunctive behaviors), the analysis of BWAI is often more precise than that of SWAI for this block. However, under BWAI, we have to convert the SMT-format representation to specific abstract domain representation at the exit point of a block, which may cause precision loss. E.g., in the motivating example shown in Sect. 2, at the exit point of block β_1, if we use convex abstract domain to abstract the SMT formula that involves disjunction, it would cause precision loss and eventually leads to the failure of proving the unreachability of the error. To express and pass the disjunctive information between blocks, we seek to use abstract domains that could characterize disjunctions. In this section, we present a lifting functor for abstract domains to express disjunctions in order to fit for BWAI for the sake of precision.

The main idea of the lifting functor is to generate a predicate set $\mathbb{P}_i$ for each block β_i through a pre-analysis, and the predicates are all $\mathcal{T}$-Encodable.

After analyzing block β_i, we partition the post-state at the exit point $\ell^{ex}_{\beta_i}$ according to different evaluation results of predicates in the set $\mathbb{P}_i$. Note that several approaches are available to utilize predicates to partition the state [8,16,18]. In this paper, we take the advantage of binary decision tree (BDT) [8] to implement the partitioning of a state with respect to predicates. A branch node in the BDT stores a predicate, and each leaf stores abstract value in the base domain under specific evaluation results of predicates. We denote the binary decision tree in parenthesized form

$$[\![p_1 : [\![p_2 : (a_1), (a_2)]\!], [\![p_2 : (a_3), (a_4)]\!]]\!]$$

where p_1, p_2 are predicates in $\mathbb{P}_i$, and $a_j (1 \leq j \leq 4)$ is an abstract value in an abstract domain. It encodes that if p_1 and p_2 are true then a_1 holds, if p_1 is true and p_2 is false then a_2 holds, if p_1 is false and p_2 is true then a_3 holds, or if p_1 and p_2 are false then a_4 holds. Note that the above abstract domain representation precisely encodes the same information as the following SMT formula $(p_1 \wedge p_2 \wedge \nu(a_1)) \vee (p_1 \wedge \neg p_2 \wedge \nu(a_2)) \vee (\neg p_1 \wedge p_2 \wedge \nu(a_3)) \vee (\neg p_1 \wedge \neg p_2 \wedge \nu(a_4))$.

4.1   Predicate Selection

In this subsection, we introduce our strategy to determine the predicate set. The criterion of choosing the predicate set for the current block is to improve the precision of successive analysis through transmitting necessary disjunctive information. Hence, we mainly select predicates for current block from branch conditions in successive blocks. Note that in this paper an **assert**(b) statement is transformed into a branch test statement (as in the benchmarks of SV-COMP 2015) and thus the properties to be checked in successive blocks are in fact also added into the predicate set.

We call block β_j is the **direct syntactic successor** of block β_i, if in the CFG with blocks, there exists one path from β_i to β_j without passing through other blocks. Let **DirSynSucc**(β_i) denote the set of direct syntactic successors of block β_i and $\beta_j \in$ **DirSynSucc**(β_i). To transmit information of β_i to block β_j at the location $\ell^{ex}_{\beta_i}$, we need to choose a predicate set for β_i to partition the abstract state at the location $\ell^{ex}_{\beta_i}$. Our strategy is to pick the branch conditions in block β_j. Let $\eta : \mathcal{B} \rightarrow 2^C$ denote the map from a set of block $\mathcal{B}$ to the powerset of branch conditions appearing in $\mathcal{B}$. We define $\eta(\textbf{skip}) \triangleq \emptyset$, $\eta(x := \textbf{exp}) \triangleq \emptyset$, $\eta(\textbf{if}(b)\{\beta_1\}\textbf{else}\{\beta_2\}) \triangleq \{b\} \cup \eta(\beta_1) \cup \eta(\beta_2)$, and $\eta(\beta_1; \beta_2) \triangleq \eta(\beta_1) \cup \eta(\beta_2)$. In fact, $\eta(\beta_i)$ collects the branch conditions from the block β_i. E.g., for Fig. 1(b), we have $\eta(\beta_2) = \{p\_dw\_st == 0, c\_dr\_st == 0, q\_free == 0, q\_free == 1\}$ and $\eta(\beta_3) = \{p\_num\_write - c\_num\_read < 0\}$. Since both β_2 and β_3 are syntactic successors of β_1. Hence, for block β_1 we choose the predicate set as $\eta(\beta_2) \cup \eta(\beta_3)$, i.e., $\mathbb{P}_1 = \{p\_dw\_st == 0, c\_dr\_st == 0, q\_free == 0, q\_free == 1, p\_num\_write - c\_num\_read < 0\}$. In general, the predicate set we choose for block β_i is $\mathbb{P}_i \triangleq \bigcup \{\eta(\beta_k) | \beta_k \in$ **DirSynSucc**$(\beta_i)\}$.

The complexity of the analysis based on the lifting functor for BWAI is exponential to the height of the BDT which is equal to the number of predicates in $\mathbb{P}$.

If $\mathbb{P}$ contains n predicates, the height of BDT is n, and the abstract state at the exit point ℓ_β^{ex} is a disjunction with 2^n individuals. In practice, we must balance between precision and efficiency through adjusting the size of predicate set. The predicate set is tightly coupled with each individual block, so the complexity is determined by the size of predicate set for each block locally. In practice, we set a threshold N_{β_i} for each block to restrict the maximum size of predicate set.

4.2   Abstract Domain Lifting Functor Based on BDT

Let $\mathcal{FUNC} : \mathcal{PS} \times \mathcal{D} \to \mathcal{BDT}$, where $\mathcal{PS}$ is a set of predicate sets, $\mathcal{D}$ is a set of base abstract domains, and $\mathcal{BDT}$ is a set of BDT domains on top of base abstract domains. $\mathcal{FUNC}$ defines a lifting functor of base abstract domains in the BWAI framework. Given a predicate set $\mathbb{P}$ and a base abstract domain $\mathcal{A}$, $\mathcal{FUNC}(\mathbb{P}, \mathcal{A})$ gives a domain in BDT format, denoted by $\mathcal{PA}$. The predicates in $\mathbb{P}$ determine the elements on the branch nodes of BDT, $\mathcal{A}$ determines the base abstract domain representation on the leaves of BDT, and each element in the $\mathcal{PA}$ is of BDT format.

The concretization function of $\mathcal{PA}$, denoted by $\gamma_{\mathcal{PA}}$, and abstraction function, denoted by $\alpha_{\mathcal{PA}}$, can be extended easily from $\gamma_{\mathcal{A}}$ and $\alpha_{\mathcal{A}}$ in the base domain $\mathcal{A}$. The concretization function of domain $\mathcal{PA}$ is defined as $\gamma_{\mathcal{PA}}(pa) \triangleq \gamma_{\mathcal{A}}(\bigvee_0^{2^k-1} a_i)$, where pa is the element in the domain $\mathcal{PA}$, k is the size of the predicate set, a_i $(0 \leq i \leq 2^k - 1)$ is the abstract value in the base abstract domain on the i-th leaf. The abstraction function $\alpha_{\mathcal{PA}}$ is computed by calling the abstraction function $\alpha_{\mathcal{A}}$ in the base domain $\mathcal{A}$ multiple times. For example, assume $\bigwedge_{i=1}^m \sum_{j=1}^n A_{ij} \times x_j \leq c_i$ denotes the constraint system of a template polyhedron, where A_{ij} is the fixed coefficient, m is the number of constraints, n is the dimension of variables. According to different evaluations of predicates in $\mathcal{P}$, we call the SMT-based optimization $\mathbf{max}(\sum_{j=1}^n A_{ij} \times x_j)$ s.t. $(\psi_p \wedge \varphi)$ for each linear template $(\sum_{j=1}^n A_{ij} \times x_j)$, where ψ_p is the conjunction of the constraints corresponding to the predicates on the top-down path in the BDT, φ is the SMT formula characterizing the current state. Then we get a base abstract domain representation on a leaf of the BDT. Other domain operators for $\mathcal{PA}$ derived by the lifting functor can be implemented on top of the domain operators of the base domain $\mathcal{A}$, similarly as in [8].

Example 1. Assume the base domain we use is Octagon. For the example in Fig. 1(a), if we use SMT inside blocks but only use the base domain at cutpoints, we will fail to prove the unreachability of the error in line 24 in Fig. 1. However, if we use the lifting functor over the Octagon domain, we first get $\mathbb{P}_1 = \mathbb{P}_2 = \{p_0, p_1, p_2, p_3, p_4\}$ and $\mathbb{P}_3 = \emptyset$, where $p_0 \triangleq (p\_dw\_st == 0)$, $p_1 \triangleq (c\_dr\_st == 0)$, $p_2 \triangleq (q\_free == 0)$, $p_3 \triangleq (q\_free == 1)$ and $p_4 \triangleq (p\_num\_write - c\_num\_read < 0)$. At exit point of a block, we use the respective predicate set to partition the post-state and get the abstract domain representation in BDT format. E.g., in Fig. 1(b), after the fixpoint iteration converges, at ℓ_2', we get the abstract value in BDT format on top of octagons as $[\![p_0 : [\![p_1 : (oct_1), (oct_2)]\!], [\![p_1 : (oct_3), (oct_4)]\!]]\!]$ (note that the BDT is reduced because different values of p_2, p_3, p_4 do not change the abstract value at leaves), where $oct_1 = (p\_num\_write - c\_num\_read = 0) \wedge ... \wedge (p\_num\_write = 0) \wedge (c\_num\_read = 0)$, $oct_2 = (p\_num\_write - c\_num\_read = 0) \wedge ... \wedge (1 \leq p\_num\_write \leq +\infty) \wedge (1 \leq c\_num\_read \leq +\infty)$, $oct_3 = (p\_num\_write - c\_num\_read = 1) \wedge ... \wedge (p\_num\_write = 1) \wedge (c\_num\_read = 0)$ and $oct_4 = \bot$. Eventually, at location ℓ'_2 in Fig. 1(b) we get the invariant "$0 \leqslant p\_num\_write - c\_num\_read \leqslant 1$" which implies the unreachability of the error in line 24 in Fig. 1(a).

5   BWAI Considering Sparsity in a Large Block

BWAI based on the greedy block partitioning (GBP) strategy described in Sect. 3.1 could get the most precise analysis inside a block. Nevertheless, when the number of branch conditions in a block is too large, the size of the predicate set for the previous block becomes large, which will result in a large BDT representation and degrade the efficiency of analysis. Especially, sometimes the SMT formula for a block of large size may be too complicated to be solved as a SMT-opt problem. In this paper, we say a block is a *large* block, if the number of assignment statements in this block is greater than the threshold N_{assign} or the number of branch conditions in this block is greater than the threshold N_{branch}, where the two thresholds N_{assign} and N_{branch} are set by users. To improve the scalability of analysis, we divide a large block into several small ones by exploiting sparsity [30] inside this block.

5.1   Dividing a Large Block Based on Variable Clustering

In this paper, we divide a large block into a series of small blocks based on the concept of variable clustering [22]. We use **Cluster** : $\mathcal{B} \rightarrow 2^{\mathcal{VAR}}$ to denote the map from a set of blocks $\mathcal{B}$ to a powerset of variables appearing in $\mathcal{B}$. Given a block β, **Cluster**(β) satisfies that (1) for any $s \in$ **Cluster**(β), we have $s \neq \emptyset$; (2) for any $s1$, $s2 \in$ **Cluster**(β), we have $s1 \cap s2 = \emptyset$ and $\bigcup$ **Cluster**$(\beta) =$ **Vars**(β), where **Vars**(β) is the set of variables appearing in β. **Cluster**(β) defines a partitioning of the variable set of block β. In this paper, we use **Cluster**(β) to denote the variable clustering for block β. To be more clear, we compute variable clusters based on data dependencies among variables. First, we get the data dependency graph among variables in the block, and generate a cluster for each isolated subgraph. Based on variable clustering, we partition a large block into small blocks such that each block involves variables from the same cluster. To do that, we put a sub-cutpoint between two statements if these two statements involve variables from different variable clusters. The statements between two adjacent sub-cutpoints (cutpoints) define a small block.

5.2   Analysis Considering Block-Wise Sparsity

Based on variable clustering, we divide a large block into several small ones such that each small block involves only its own variable cluster. Thus, we only need to consider relations among variables appearing within the same small block. Hence, the dimension of considered variables in abstract values is largely reduced. Furthermore, the semantic dependencies between small blocks may become sparse and thus we only need to propagate the abstract value from the current block to those blocks that have data flow dependency on the current block. Hence, we decompose the semantics of a large block into semantics based on small blocks, and consider both spatial and temporal sparsity inside the large block.

Considering Block-Wise Spatial Sparsity. We project out those variables which are not used in the current block from the abstract state at the entry of the block, which could reduce the dimension and also the size of the corresponding SMT formula when analyzing the block.

Considering Block-Wise Temporal Sparsity. The block-wise temporal sparsity is based on the following observation: the syntactic successor block of the current block may have no data flow dependency on the current block. We call a block β_j is a **direct semantic successor** of β_i, if (1) β_i and β_j belong to the same "large block", and β_j shares the same variable cluster with β_i; (2) β_j is reachable from β_i; (3) there is no other block β_k between β_i and β_j satisfying (1) and (2). We use **DirSemSucc**(β_i) to denote the set of direct semantic successors of β_i.

Considering the block-wise temporal sparsity, we propagate abstract values from a block to its direct semantic successor blocks instead of direct syntactic successor blocks, which could avoid unnecessary propagations along the transition edges in CFG with blocks. In addition, we choose the predicate set for a block by extracting branch conditions from its direct semantic successor blocks, instead of its direct syntactic successor blocks. The size of predicate set chosen based on direct semantic successor of a small block is usually much smaller than that chosen by considering the large block as a whole.

Example 2. We take an example extracted from *test_lock.c* in the directory "locks" of SV-COMP 2015. As shown in Fig. 2(a), we consider the loop body as a large block β and get the variable clustering $\{\{lk1, p1\}, \{lk2, p2\}\}$. Based on the variable clusters, we repartition the block β at locations ℓ_4, ℓ_6, ℓ_8 (recall that ℓ_i represents the program point at the beginning of the i-th line) and get the CFG with blocks as shown in Fig. 2(b), i.e., $\beta_1 = \mathbf{SubGraph}(\ell_1, \ell_4)$, $\beta_2 = \mathbf{SubGraph}(\ell_4, \ell_6)$, $\beta_3 = \mathbf{SubGraph}(\ell_6, \ell_8)$ and $\beta_4 = \mathbf{SubGraph}(\ell_8, \ell_{10})$. When we analyze the block β_1, which only involves variables $p1$ and $lk1$, we project out unrelated variables (e.g., $p2$ and $lk2$) based on block-wise spatial sparsity and consider the abstract value over only the variable set $\{p1, lk1\}$. In Fig. 2(b), $\beta_3 \in \mathbf{DirSemSucc}(\beta_1)$ and $\beta_4 \in \mathbf{DirSemSucc}(\beta_2)$, as shown by the dashed lines. Analysis considering block-wise temporal sparsity propagates the abstract value from β_1 to β_3 instead of β_2. Moreover, the predicate set $\mathbb{P}_1$ for block β_1 is $\{(p1! = 0 \ \&\& \ lk1! = 1)\}$ which is generated according to the branch conditions in its semantic successor block β_3. Note that, without considering

```
1 while(brandom()){
2   if(p1 ! = 0)
3     lk1 = 1;
4   if(p2 ! = 0)
5     lk2 = 1;
6   if(p1 ! = 0 && lk1 ! = 1)
7     //error()
8   if(p2 ! = 0 && lk2 ! = 1)
9     //error()
10 }
```

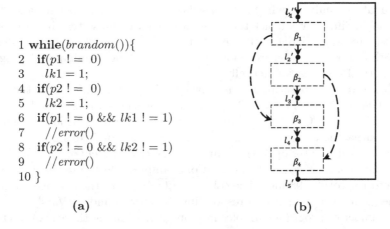

(a)   (b)

Fig. 2. A illustrating example extracted from SV-COMP 2015

block-wise temporal sparsity, we would get a much larger predicate set $\{p1 ! = 0, p2 ! = 0, (p1 ! = 0 \&\& lk1 ! = 1), (p2 ! = 0 \&\& lk2 ! = 1)\}$ for the large block (i.e., **SubGraph**(ℓ_1, ℓ_{10})). For the example shown in Fig. 2(a), analysis considering both block-wise spatial and temporal sparsity can also successfully prove the unreachability of the errors in line 7 and 9. The example in Fig. 2 shows a typical patten of programs in the "locks" directory in SV-COMP 2015. During experiments (in Sect. 6), we find the analysis considering block-wise sparsity is much more efficient than the one without considering block-wise sparsity.

6   Implementation and Experiments

We have implemented the framework of BWAI as a tool prototype named BWCAI, based on the frontend CIL [29], numerical abstract domain library Apron [23], and SMT optimizer νZ [7]. We have conducted experiments on benchmarks from directories in the C branch of SV-COMP 2015 [1], including directories "loop-lit", "locks", "systemc", "termination-crafted", "termination-crafted-lit" and "termination-restricted-15".

Most benchmarks in the directories "loop-lit", "locks", "systemc" are to simulate the behaviors in operating system. Error locations are inserted manually in each benchmark in these three directories, which are classified as "true-unreachable" and "false-unreachable". "true-unreachable" indicates the error in the example is indeed unreachable, while "false-unreachable" indicates the error in the example is reachable actually. Because abstract interpretation guarantees soundness of the analysis, if we analyze benchmarks with tag "false-unreachable", we find that the errors are all reachable. Hence, we pick the examples with tag "true-unreachable" as the experimental benchmarks and set the unreachability of "false error locations" as the property to check. Examples in the "termination-crafted", "termination-crafted-lit" and "termination-restricted-15" are programs for termination analysis, which are classified to "true-termination" and "false-termination". Similarly, we pick the examples with tag "false-termination" which contain no recurring calls as the experimental benchmarks (since under the framework of abstract interpretation, analysis on "true-termination" programs returns normal termination actually).

Table 1 gives the description information of the benchmarks in the experiments. The column "SV-COMP directories" provides the source location of benchmarks in SV-COMP 2015. We select several examples which are with tag "true-unreachable" as well as "false-termination" and omit examples that contain complicated pointer operations, array accesses and recurring calls. The column "Number of files" gives the number of examples selected in the corresponding directories, totally 98 files. The column "$\overline{\text{LOCs}}$" gives the average number of code lines of programs in the corresponding directories and "$\overline{\#\text{Vars}}$" means the average number of program variables in a program. Among these six directories, the average code size of examples in the directory "systemc" is the largest, and the largest single program has 1973 lines of code.

Table 1. Discription of benchmarks from SV-COMP 2015

SV-COMP directories	Number of files	$\overline{\text{LOCs}}$	$\overline{\#\text{Vars}}$
locks	11	163	20
loop-lit	14	21	3
systemc	20	996	65
termination-crafted	16	10	2
termination-crafted-lit	12	11	3
termination-restricted-15	25	21	2

Table 2 summarizes the analysis results on these examples based on the Box and Octagon domain in the framework of SWAI, as well as BWAI with and without using the lifting functor. Column "#Y" presents the number of properties successfully proved, which is the number of error locations proved unreached. Column "t(s)" gives the average analysis time (including the time for block partitioning, block encoding and selecting predicates) in seconds in the corresponding directory when the analysis runs on a double core of 4.0 GHz Intel Core i5 on Ubuntu 14.04. In Table 2, we use the GBP strategy by default to partition the program. For the Octagon domain, we use the same variable package [13] manually for SWAI and BWAI, to reduce the cost.

From the analysis result, we find that if we use the same abstract domain, analysis based on BWAI (even without using lifting functor) is always more precise than that based on SWAI, especially for benchmarks in the directory "locks". Programs in the directory "locks" are used to simulate the lock and unlock operations in operating system, which often contain one large loop that involves intensive disjunctive behaviors (e.g., disequalities and branches) and the

Table 2. Experimental results on benchmarks from SV-COMP 2015

SV-COMP direc-tories (Number of files)	SWAI				BWAI				BWAI + lifting functor			
	Box		Oct		Box		Oct		Box		Oct	
	#Y	t(s)	#Y	t(s)	#Y	t(s)	#Y	t(s)	#Y	t(s)	#Y	t(s)
locks(11)	0	0.28	0	6.40	11	0.81	11	23.30	11	9.13	11	435.14
loop-lit(14)	1	0.09	2	0.12	1	0.17	3	0.43	3	0.95	7	6.77
systemc(20)	0	24.77	0	89.74	0	63.46	0	343.66	1	846.35	5	4733.16
termination-crafted(16)	13	0.08	13	0.09	13	0.12	16	0.14	14	0.35	16	5.22
termination crafted-lit(12)	10	0.08	10	0.09	10	0.13	10	0.19	10	0.44	10	2.13
termination-restricted-15(25)	6	0.09	8	0.09	9	0.14	14	0.20	10	3.05	16	16.75

error location is inside the loop body. When using the GBP strategy, analysis based on BWAI could check the property in the loop body based on SMT with no need of converting to abstract domain representation. From the row "locks(11)", we see that analysis based on Box domain under the framework of BWAI could check all properties in all the 11 benchmarks, while the analysis based on Octagon domain in the framework of SWAI could check none.

Moreover, from the analysis result, we can see that BWAI analysis with lifting functor is more precise than that without lifting functor under the framework of BWAI. From the row "loop-lit(14)", we see that analysis based on the BDT domain on top of Octagon domain could check 7 examples out of 14, while using only the base Octagon domain could check 3 examples. Most programs in the directory "loop-lit" contain multiple-phases loops which involve disjunctive behaviors, but the property to check is outside the loop. BWAI analysis without lifting functor could not check the property, because the SMT formula needs to be abstracted as base abstract domain representation (such as boxes, octagons, etc.) at the end of loop body. However, when using lifting functor based on BDT, the BWAI could maintain and pass the disjunctive information to the successive analysis. Based on the Box domain, BWAI without lifting functor could prove 44 out of 98 benchmarks, and BWAI with lifting functor could prove 5 more ones; based on the Octagon domain, BWAI without lifting functor could prove 54 out of 98 benchmarks while BWAI with lifting functor could check 11 more ones. Overall, our BWAI with lifting functor could prove around 66% benchmarks (65 out of 98 ones), around one times more than SWAI, which could only check about 34% properties (33 out of 98 ones).

We have also conducted comparison experiments using BWAI with and without considering sparsity. We find that without considering sparsity, the analysis time on each program in "locks" is too long (>5 h). This is because all programs in "locks" contain at least 11 branches inside a large loop. Hence, when using lifting functor without considering sparsity, the predicate set for the loop body has at least 11 predicates, which results in a very large BDT. Nevertheless, when considering block-wise sparsity, we partition the large loop body into small blocks, and the average size of predicate set for a small block is 2. The analysis time "9.13 s" and "435.14 s" for the directory "locks" shown in Table 2, is the result when considering block-wise sparsity.

Moreover, we have also conducted the comparison experiments with UFO, which also combines SMT-opt and abstract domains [3, 24]. The comparison results between UFO (the version of [24]) and BWCAI (BWAI using BDT on top of Octagon domain) is shown in Table 3. Column "$\#Y_{com}$" presents the number of properties which could be proved by both tools. Column "$\#Y_{UFO}$" presents the number of properties which could be proved by UFO only, while Column "$\#Y_{BWCAI}$" presents the number of properties which could be proved by BWCAI only. Column "$\#N_{com}$" presents the number of properties which could be proved by none of them. From Table 3, we can find that UFO could prove more programs than BWCAI in directories "loop-lit" and "systemc", while BWCAI could prove more programs than UFO in directories "termination-crafted", "termination-crafted-lit" and "termination-restricted-15", which shows that the sets of properties proved by the two tools are complementary.

Table 3. Experimental comparison results between BWCAI and UFO

SV-COMP directories (Number of files)	UFO		BWCAI		$\#Y_{com}$	$\#Y_{UFO}$	$\#Y_{BWCAI}$	$\#N_{com}$
	$\#Y_t$	t(s)	$\#Y_t$	t(s)				
locks(11)	11	0.91	11	435.14	11	0	0	0
loop-lit(14)	10	38.98	7	28.42	7	3	0	4
systemc(20)	18	1278.16	5	4733.16	5	13	0	2
termination-crafted(16)	8	0.22	16	5.22	8	0	8	0
termination-crafted-lit(12)	8	0.16	10	2.13	8	0	2	2
termination-restricted-15(25)	11	2.85	16	16.75	10	1	6	8

Properties in serval examples could not be checked by BWCAI because they need templates whose expressiveness is beyond octagons, while UFO could check them by using interpolants which are less limited to specific templates. E.g., UFO proves the property in "*jm2006_variant_true-unreachable-call*.c" (from the directory "loop-lit"), while BWCAI fails to prove it. However, if adding the template "$x - y + z - i + j$" (that is out of the expressiveness of the Octagon domain), BWCAI could also prove it. On the other hand, UFO *guesses* (typically using interpolants) an inductive invariant by generalizing it from finite paths through the CFG of the program. Hence when the behaviors of the loop in the program are not inductive and the depth of the loop is large, UFO often does not perform well. E.g., *"AlternDiv_false-termination.c"* (from the directory "termination-restricted-15") involves two phases in one loop, and its concrete execution is switching between these two phases back and forth. UFO fails to check the property of it, while BWCAI could prove this property by using BDT on top of the Box domain as well as the Octagon domain. For analysis time, UFO usually costs less time than BWCAI for these programs in Table 3. However, we notice that UFO often costs much more time for the programs that involve multiple-phases loops than other programs. When we manually enlarge the loop bound in those programs, the analysis time based on UFO increases dramatically. E.g., if we manually modify the loop bound from 100 to 10000 in program *"gj2007_true-unreach-call.c"* (from the directory "loop-lit"), the analysis time based on UFO turns into ">1 h" from 143 s, while the analysis time based on BWAI almost does not change.

7 Related Work

The use of block encoding via SMT in software verification has gained much attention recently, especially in software model checking (SMC). Beyer et al. propose large block encoding [5] and adjustable block encoding [6] techniques for SMC based on abstract reachability tree (ART) with CEGAR-based refinement. Their main goal is to improve the efficiency of ART-based software model checking by reducing the number of program paths to explore through large (adjustable) block encoding. Our idea of block encoding is inspired from their work, but our main goal in this paper is to improve the precision of statement-by-statement abstract interpretation through block encoding. Moreover, they use boolean predicate abstraction to represent the abstract successor state in SMC, while we use numerical abstractions to over-approximate the abstract successor state in AI.

Combining decision procedures and abstract interpretation has received increasing attentions recently. Cousot et al. [14] propose to combine abstract interpretation and decision procedures through reduced product or its approximation, e.g., to perform iterated reduction between numerical and SMT-based logic abstract domains. Henry et al. propose a path-sensitive analysis which combines abstract interpretation and SMT-solving, and implement a tool named PAGAI [20]. PAGAI performs fix-point iteration by first focusing temporarily on a certain subset of paths inside the CFG and use "path focusing" [27] technique based on SMT-solving to obtain a new path [21] that needs to enumerate. In this paper we consider a block as a whole, encode all paths in the block as a single SMT formula, and then transform the problem of computing successor abstract value w.r.t a SMT formula into SMT-opt problems.

The recent work by Li et al. [24] on using SMT-based symbolic optimization to implement the best abstract transformer, is the closest related work to our work. They propose an efficient SMT-based optimization algorithm namely SYMBA, and use SYMBA to calculate the best abstract transformer for numerical abstract domains in UFO [2,24]. In this paper, we also use SMT-based optimization technique to compute the abstract value given a SMT formula. In our implementation, we use νZ [7] which is a SMT-based optimizer, but we could also use SYMBA. However, the abstract value we use SMT-based optimization to compute is in a lifting domain of base numerical domains extended with BDT. Besides, we use only abstract interpretation while UFO combines abstraction based over-approximation and interpolation based under-approximation. The experimental comparison results of our approach and UFO [3] using SYMBA in Sect. 6 show that the sets of properties proved by the two approaches are complementary.

The problem of computing the best symbolic abstract transformers is first considered by Reps et al. in [31] and has gained much attention recently. Reps et al. have done a series of work on constructing abstract transformers relying on decidable logics [33,34]. The main idea is to use a least and a greatest fix-point computation to maintain an over-approximation and an under-approximation of the desired result. In general, their approach fits for arbitrary numerical abstract domains, but the iteration process may not terminate and thus needs a threshold to stop the iteration, which gives over- and under- approximations for the best abstract transformer. In this paper, we use SMT-based optimizer to compute the best abstract transformer but only for template based abstract domains. Monniaux et al. propose a method for computing optimal abstract transformers over template linear constraint domains but their approach is based on quantifier elimination [26,28], while we use SMT-based optimization.

Recently, to deal with disjunctive properties, a variety of abstract domains have been designed to allow describing disjunctive information inside the domain representation. Examples include abstract domains supporting *max* operation [4], abstract value function [9,11], interval linear constraints [10], set minus [17], decision diagrams [18], etc. More recently, Chen et al. propose a binary decision tree (BDT) abstract domain functor which provides a new prospective on partitioning the trace semantics of programs as well as separating properties in leaves [8]. In this paper, we use an abstract domain lifting functor based on BDT, but we further propose a specific selection strategy for predicate set as the branch nodes in BDT to fit for BWAI. We choose for the current block the predicate set that is determined locally by its direct syntactic/semantical successor blocks, while [8] determines the branch nodes in BDT based on a branch condition path abstraction that abstracts the history of the control flow to the current program point.

8   Conclusion and Future Work

We extend statement-by-statement abstract interpretation to block-by-block abstract interpretation, and propose block-wise abstract interpretation (BWAI) by combining abstract domains with SMT. In the framework of BWAI, we use a SMT formula to encode precisely the transfer semantics of a block and then analyze the block as a whole, which usually gives more precise results than using abstract domains to analyze the block statement by statement. Moreover, in order to transmit useful disjunctive information between blocks which is obtained by SMT-based analysis inside a block, we propose a lifting functor on top of abstract domains to fit for BWAI. The lifting functor is implemented based on binary decision trees, wherein the branch nodes are determined by a selection of predicates according to the direct successor relationship between blocks. Furthermore, to improve the efficiency of BWAI, we consider block-wise sparsity in a large block by dividing a large block further into a set of small blocks. Experimental results on a set of benchmarks from SV-COMP 2015 show that our BWAI approach could prove around one times more benchmarks than SWAI (our BWAI approach could prove 66% ones, while SWAI approach could only prove 34% ones).

For the future work, we will consider more flexible block partitioning strategies to balance between precision and efficiency. Also, we plan to develop more powerful SMT-based optimization solvers to support more SMT theories (such as the array theory).

Acknowledgments. We thank Arie Gurfinkel for the help on using UFO. This work is supported by the 973 Program under Grant No. 2014CB340703, the NSFC under Grant Nos. 61120106006, 91318301, 61532007, 61690203, and the Open Project of Shanghai Key Laboratory of Trustworthy Computing under Grant No. 07dz22304201504.

References

1. http://sv-comp.sosy-lab.org/2015/
2. Albarghouthi, A., Gurfinkel, A., Chechik, M.: From under-approximations to over-approximations and back. In: Flanagan, C., König, B. (eds.) TACAS 2012. LNCS, vol. 7214, pp. 157–172. Springer, Heidelberg (2012). doi:10.1007/978-3-642-28756-5_12
3. Albarghouthi, A., Li, Y., Gurfinkel, A., Chechik, M.: UFO: a framework for abstraction- and interpolation-based software verification. In: Madhusudan, P., Seshia, S.A. (eds.) CAV 2012. LNCS, vol. 7358, pp. 672–678. Springer, Heidelberg (2012). doi:10.1007/978-3-642-31424-7_48
4. Allamigeon, X., Gaubert, S., Goubault, É.: Inferring min and max invariants using max-plus polyhedra. In: Alpuente, M., Vidal, G. (eds.) SAS 2008. LNCS, vol. 5079, pp. 189–204. Springer, Heidelberg (2008). doi:10.1007/978-3-540-69166-2_13
5. Beyer, D., Cimatti, A., Griggio, A., Keremoglu, M.E., Sebastiani, R.: Software model checking via large-block encoding. In: FMCAD 2009, pp. 25–32. IEEE (2009)
6. Beyer, D., Keremoglu, M.E., Wendler, P.: Predicate abstraction with adjustable-block encoding. In: FMCAD 2010, pp. 189–198. IEEE (2010)
7. Bjørner, N., Phan, A.-D., Fleckenstein, L.: νZ - an optimizing SMT solver. In: Baier, C., Tinelli, C. (eds.) TACAS 2015. LNCS, vol. 9035, pp. 194–199. Springer, Heidelberg (2015). doi:10.1007/978-3-662-46681-0_14
8. Chen, J., Cousot, P.: A binary decision tree abstract domain functor. In: Blazy, S., Jensen, T. (eds.) SAS 2015. LNCS, vol. 9291, pp. 36–53. Springer, Heidelberg (2015). doi:10.1007/978-3-662-48288-9_3

9. Chen, L., Liu, J., Miné, A., Kapur, D., Wang, J.: An abstract domain to infer octagonal constraints with absolute value. In: Müller-Olm, M., Seidl, H. (eds.) SAS 2014. LNCS, vol. 8723, pp. 101–117. Springer, Heidelberg (2014). doi:10.1007/978-3-319-10936-7_7

10. Chen, L., Miné, A., Wang, J., Cousot, P.: Interval polyhedra: an abstract domain to infer interval linear relationships. In: Palsberg, J., Su, Z. (eds.) SAS 2009. LNCS, vol. 5673, pp. 309–325. Springer, Heidelberg (2009). doi:10.1007/978-3-642-03237-0_21

11. Chen, L., Miné, A., Wang, J., Cousot, P.: Linear absolute value relation analysis. In: Barthe, G. (ed.) ESOP 2011. LNCS, vol. 6602, pp. 156–175. Springer, Heidelberg (2011). doi:10.1007/978-3-642-19718-5_9

12. Cousot, P., Cousot, R.: Abstract interpretation: a unified lattice model for static analysis of programs by construction or approximation of fixpoints. In: POPL 1977, pp. 238–252. ACM (1977)

13. Cousot, P., Cousot, R., Feret, J., Mauborgne, L., Miné, A., Rival, X.: Why does astrée scale up? Formal Methods Syst. Des. **35**(3), 229–264 (2009)

14. Cousot, P., Cousot, R., Mauborgne, L.: The reduced product of abstract domains and the combination of decision procedures. In: Hofmann, M. (ed.) FoSSaCS 2011. LNCS, vol. 6604, pp. 456–472. Springer, Heidelberg (2011). doi:10.1007/978-3-642-19805-2_31

15. Cytron, R., Ferrante, J., Rosen, B.K., Wegman, M.N., Zadeck, F.K.: Efficiently computing static single assignment form and the control dependence graph. ACM Trans. Program. Lang. Syst. **13**(4), 451–490 (1991)

16. Fischer, J., Jhala, R., Majumdar, R.: Joining dataflow with predicates. In: ESEC-FSE 2005, pp. 227–236. ACM (2005)

17. Ghorbal, K., Ivančić, F., Balakrishnan, G., Maeda, N., Gupta, A.: Donut domains: efficient non-convex domains for abstract interpretation. In: Kuncak, V., Rybalchenko, A. (eds.) VMCAI 2012. LNCS, vol. 7148, pp. 235–250. Springer, Heidelberg (2012). doi:10.1007/978-3-642-27940-9_16

18. Gurfinkel, A., Chaki, S.: BOXES: a symbolic abstract domain of boxes. In: Cousot, R., Martel, M. (eds.) SAS 2010. LNCS, vol. 6337, pp. 287–303. Springer, Heidelberg (2010). doi:10.1007/978-3-642-15769-1_18

19. Gurfinkel, A., Chaki, S., Sapra, S.: Efficient predicate abstraction of program summaries. In: Bobaru, M., Havelund, K., Holzmann, G.J., Joshi, R. (eds.) NFM 2011. LNCS, vol. 6617, pp. 131–145. Springer, Heidelberg (2011). doi:10.1007/978-3-642-20398-5_11

20. Henry, J., Monniaux, D., Moy, M.: PAGAI: a path sensitive static analyser. Electron. Notes Theor. Comput. Sci. **289**, 15–25 (2012)

21. Henry, J., Monniaux, D., Moy, M.: Succinct representations for abstract interpretation. In: Miné, A., Schmidt, D. (eds.) SAS 2012. LNCS, vol. 7460, pp. 283–299. Springer, Heidelberg (2012). doi:10.1007/978-3-642-33125-1_20

22. Heo, K., Oh, H., Yang, H.: Learning a variable-clustering strategy for octagon from labeled data generated by a static analysis. In: Rival, X. (ed.) SAS 2016. LNCS, vol. 9837, pp. 237–256. Springer, Heidelberg (2016). doi:10.1007/978-3-662-53413-7_12

23. Jeannet, B., Miné, A.: APRON: a library of numerical abstract domains for static analysis. In: Bouajjani, A., Maler, O. (eds.) CAV 2009. LNCS, vol. 5643, pp. 661–667. Springer, Heidelberg (2009). doi:10.1007/978-3-642-02658-4_52

24. Li, Y., Albarghouthi, A., Kincaid, Z., Gurfinkel, A., Chechik, M.: Symbolic optimization with SMT solvers. In: POPL 2014, vol. 49, pp. 607–618. ACM (2014)

25. Miné, A.: The octagon abstract domain. High. Order Symb. Comput. **19**(1), 31–100 (2006)

26. Monniaux, D.: Automatic modular abstractions for template numerical constraints. Log. Methods Comput. Sci. **6**(3), 501–516 (2010)

27. Monniaux, D., Gonnord, L.: Using bounded model checking to focus fixpoint iterations. In: Yahav, E. (ed.) SAS 2011. LNCS, vol. 6887, pp. 369–385. Springer, Heidelberg (2011). doi:10.1007/978-3-642-23702-7_27

28. Monniaux, D.P.: Automatic modular abstractions for linear constraints. In: POPL 2009, vol. 44, pp. 140–151. ACM (2009)

29. Necula, G.C., McPeak, S., Rahul, S.P., Weimer, W.: CIL: intermediate language and tools for analysis and transformation of C programs. In: Horspool, R.N. (ed.) CC 2002. LNCS, vol. 2304, pp. 213–228. Springer, Heidelberg (2002). doi:10.1007/3-540-45937-5_16

30. Hakjoo, O., Heo, K., Lee, W., Lee, W., Park, D., Kang, J., Yi, K.: Global sparse analysis framework. ACM Trans. Program. Lang. Syst. **36**(3), 1–44 (2014)

31. Reps, T., Sagiv, M., Yorsh, G.: Symbolic implementation of the best transformer. In: Steffen, B., Levi, G. (eds.) VMCAI 2004. LNCS, vol. 2937, pp. 252–266. Springer, Heidelberg (2004). doi:10.1007/978-3-540-24622-0_21

32. Sankaranarayanan, S., Sipma, H.B., Manna, Z.: Scalable analysis of linear systems using mathematical programming. In: Cousot, R. (ed.) VMCAI 2005. LNCS, vol. 3385, pp. 25–41. Springer, Heidelberg (2005). doi:10.1007/978-3-540-30579-8_2

33. Thakur, A., Elder, M., Reps, T.: Bilateral algorithms for symbolic abstraction. In: Miné, A., Schmidt, D. (eds.) SAS 2012. LNCS, vol. 7460, pp. 111–128. Springer, Heidelberg (2012). doi:10.1007/978-3-642-33125-1_10

34. Thakur, A., Reps, T.: A method for symbolic computation of abstract operations. In: Madhusudan, P., Seshia, S.A. (eds.) CAV 2012. LNCS, vol. 7358, pp. 174–192. Springer, Heidelberg (2012). doi:10.1007/978-3-642-31424-7_17

Solving Nonlinear Integer Arithmetic
with MCSAT

Dejan Jovanović[(✉)]

SRI International, Menlo Park, USA
dejan.jovanovic@sri.com

Abstract. We present a new method for solving nonlinear integer arithmetic constraints. The method relies on the MCSat approach to solving nonlinear constraints, while using branch and bound in a conflict-directed manner. We report encouraging experimental results where the new procedure outperforms state-of-the-art SMT solvers based on bit-blasting.

1 Introduction

Integer arithmetic is a natural language to describe problems in many areas of computing. In fields such as operations research, constraint programming, and software verification, integers are the core domain of interest. Automation of reasoning about integers has traditionally focused on linear problems (e.g. [10, 15, 21]). There, powerful methods based on the simplex method and branch-and-bound perform peculiarly well in practice, even though the underlying problem is NP-complete [27]. The branch-and-bound methods use a solver for the reals to find a solution to the problem. If a solution is found in the reals, with a variable x assigned to a non-integer value v, then the solver performs a "split" by introducing a lemma $(x \leq \lfloor v \rfloor) \vee (x \geq \lceil v \rceil)$. Although more powerful methods are available (e.g., cutting planes [14,20]), branch and bound is still the most prominent method for solving integer problems due to its simplicity and practical effectiveness.

In the case of *nonlinear* integer arithmetic the hurdles stand much higher. The celebrated result of Matiyasevich [25] resolved Hilbert's 10th problem in the negative by showing that satisfiability in the nonlinear case is undecidable. This is in contrast to arithmetic over the reals, where the full theory is decidable [29], and can be solved by effective decision procedures such as virtual term substitution (VTS) [30], cylindrical algebraic decomposition (CAD) [5], and NLSat [19]. In this paper, we focus on the quantifier-free theory of nonlinear integer arithmetic in the usual setting of satisfiability modulo theories (SMT). We are interested in developing a satisfiability procedure that is effective on problems arising in practical applications and can be used in a combination framework to

The research presented in this paper has been supported by NSF grant 1528153, NASA Cooperative Agreements NNX14AI05A and NNA10DE73C, and by DARPA under agreement number FA8750-16-C-0043.

A. Bouajjani and D. Monniaux (Eds.): VMCAI 2017, LNCS 10145, pp. 330–346, 2017.
DOI: 10.1007/978-3-319-52234-0_18

decide problems that involve combinations of theories (e.g., mixed integer-real arithmetic with uninterpreted functions).

Most of the current SMT solvers that support nonlinear integer arithmetic (CVC4 [2], Z3 [7], and SMT-RAT [6], APROVE [13]) rely on the *bit-blasting* approach described in [12]. In the bit-blasting approach, an integer satisfiability problem is reduced to a SAT problem by first bounding the integer variables, and then encoding the problem bit-by-bit into a pure SAT problem. The resulting SAT problem can then be discharged with an off-the-shelf SAT solver. Although this approach is limited in its deductive power, it is an effective model finder for practical problems with small solutions. The bit-blasting approach can not detect unsatisfiability unless the problem is bounded. But, since in practical applications many problems are mostly linear, some solvers (e.g. Z3 and CVC4) additionally apply linear and interval reasoning to detect some cases of unsatisfiability. Notably, a recent approach relying on branch-and-bound has been explored in the context of CAD and VTS [22]. Although interesting, the approach provides limited improvements and is only used to supplement the existing techniques.

This paper presents a new method for solving nonlinear integer problems that is based on the MCSat (model-constructing satisfiability) approach to SMT [8,18], where the application of branch-and-bound has more appeal. The new method reasons directly in the integers, and takes advantage of the MCSat-based solver for nonlinear real arithmetic [17,19]. Due to the model-constructing nature of MCSat, the new method is able to perform the branch-and-bound "splits" in a *conflict-driven* manner. The conflict-driven branching strategy allows the solver to focus on the relevant areas of the search space and forget the splits that are not useful anymore. This is in contrast to the standard branch-and-bound approaches in SMT where the splitting strategy is delegated to the whims of the underlying SAT solver and is therefore hard to control. The new method can be used in combination with other theories and can also be used to decide mixed real-integer problems where the bit-blasting approach does not apply.

We start by introducing the relevant background and concepts in Sect. 2. We then present relevant elements of MCSat and the main algorithm in Sect. 3. We have implemented the new method in the YICES2 [9] solver and we present an empirical evaluation in Sect. 4 showing that the new method is highly effective.[1]

2   Background

We assume that the reader is familiar with the usual notions and terminology of first-order logic and model theory (for an introduction see e.g. [4]).

As usual, we denote the ring of integers with $\mathbb{Z}$ and the field of real numbers with $\mathbb{R}$. Given a vector of variables x we denote the set of polynomials with integer coefficients and variables x as $\mathbb{Z}[x]$. A polynomial $f \in \mathbb{Z}[y, x]$ is of the form

---

[1] YICES2 won the nonlinear categories of the 2016 SMT competition http://smtcomp. sourceforge.net/2016/.

$$f(\boldsymbol{y}, x) = a_m \cdot x^{d_m} + a_{m-1} \cdot x^{d_{m-1}} + \cdots + a_1 \cdot x^{d_1} + a_0,$$

where $0 < d_1 < \cdots < d_m$, and the coefficients a_i are polynomials in $\mathbb{Z}[\boldsymbol{y}]$ with $a_m \neq 0$. We call x the *top variable* and the highest power d_m is the *degree* of the polynomial f. We denote the set of variables appearing in a polynomial f as vars(f) and call the polynomial *univariate* if vars$(f) = \{x\}$ for some variable x. Otherwise the polynomial is *multivariate*, or a constant polynomial (if it contains no variables). A number $\alpha \in \mathbb{R}$ is a *root of the polynomial* $f \in \mathbb{Z}[x]$ iff $f(\alpha) = 0$. We denote the set of real roots of a univariate polynomial f as roots(f).

A *polynomial constraint* C is a constraint of the form $f \nabla 0$ where f is a polynomial and $\nabla \in \{<, \leq, =, \neq, \geq, >\}$. If a constraint C is over a univariate polynomial $f(x)$ we also call it univariate. The solution set of a univariate constraint C in $\mathbb{R}$ is a set of intervals with endpoints in roots$(f) \cup \{-\infty, \infty\}$ that we denote by feasible(C). Given a set of univariate constraints $\mathcal{C} = \{C_1, \ldots, C_n\}$, we denote the solution set of $\mathcal{C}$ by feasible$(\mathcal{C}) = \cap_i$ feasible(C_i).

An atom is either a polynomial constraint or a Boolean variable, and formulas are defined inductively with the usual Boolean connectives $(\wedge, \vee, \neg)$. Given a formula $F(\boldsymbol{x})$ we say that a type-consistent variable assignment $\boldsymbol{x} \mapsto \boldsymbol{a}$ satisfies F if the formula F evaluates to $\top$ in the standard semantics of Booleans and integers. If there is such a variable assignment, we say that $\mathcal{F}$ is *satisfiable*, otherwise it is *unsatisfiable*.

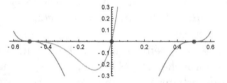

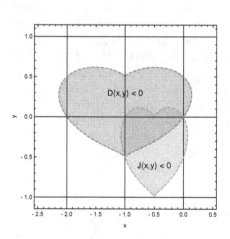

Fig. 2. Roots of $D(-1, y)$ and $J(-1, y)$ from Example 1, with real solutions of $(D < 0) \wedge (J < 0)$ marked in green. (Color figure online)

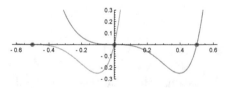

Fig. 1. Solution space of constraints from Example 1.

Fig. 3. Roots of $D(0, y)$ and $J(0, y)$ from Example 1, with no solution for $(D < 0) \wedge (J < 0)$.

Example 1. Consider the "heart" polynomial $H(x,y) = (x^2 + y^2 - 1)^3 - x^2 y^3$, and its two instances $D(x,y) = H(x+1, 2y)$, and $J(x,y) = H(2x+1, 2y-1)$. From D and J we can construct two polynomial constraints

$$D(x,y) < 0, \qquad\qquad\qquad J(x,y) < 0. \qquad\qquad (1)$$

The solution space of (1) in $\mathbb{R}^2$ is presented in Fig. 1. Considering the real geometry of Fig. 1, integer solutions might only exist for $x = -1$ and $x = 0$. Substituting the values -1 and 0 in the constraints gives univariate polynomial constraints

$$\mathcal{C} = \{\, D(-1,y) < 0,\ J(-1,y) < 0\,\}, \quad \mathcal{D} = \{\, D(0,y) < 0,\ J(0,y) < 0\,\}.$$

With symbolic root isolation[2] for univariate polynomials, we can compute the real solutions of these sets of constraints as

$$\mathsf{feasible}(\mathcal{C}) = (-0.5, 0) \cap (-0.5, 0.5) = (-0.5, 0),$$
$$\mathsf{feasible}(\mathcal{D}) = (-0.5, 0) \cap (0, 0.5) = \emptyset.$$

Depiction of the roots and feasible intervals of $\mathcal{C}$ and $\mathcal{D}$ is presented in Figs. 2 and 3, respectively.

Since in both cases the solution sets do not include any integer points, we can conclude that (1) does not have integer solutions and is therefore unsatisfiable.

3   Algorithm

As Example 1 illustrates, one way to solve integer problems is to understand the real geometry of the underlying problem, and use it to enumerate the potential integer solutions. The new method we present here explores the real geometry through the NLSat solver within the MCSat approach to SMT. We start by introducing the relevant parts of the MCSat framework. The purpose of the MCSat exposition is to make the paper self-contained and to simplify and generalize the concepts already presented in [8,18]. A reader familiar with MCSat can skip directly to the integer-specific Sect. 3.4.

The MCSat architecture consists of the core solver that manages the relevant terms, the solver trail, and the reasoning plugins. The core solver drives the solving process, and is responsible for dispatching notifications and handling requests from the plugins, while the plugins reason about the content of the trail with respect to the set of currently relevant terms. In the case of purely integer problems, the only relevant plugins are the arithmetic plugin and the Boolean plugin. The most important duty of the core is to perform conflict analysis when the reasoning plugins detect a conflict state. In order to check satisfiability of a formula F, the core solver notifies active plugins about the formula. The plugins analyze the formula and report all the relevant terms of F back to the core.

---

[2] Root isolation for univariate polynomials with integer coefficients can be done efficiently with algorithms based on Strum sequences or Descartes' rule of signs [1].

Once the relevant terms are collected, the core adds the assertion $(F \rightsquigarrow \top)$ to the trail, and the search starts as described in Sect. 3.5.

In this paper we focus on the details of the base calculus and the needed integer reasoning capabilities. For more information on other plugins and combination of theories, we refer the interested reader to [18].

3.1 The Trail

The central data structure in the MCSat framework is the solver trail. It is a generalized version of the trail found in modern SAT solvers and is a representation of the partial (and potentially inconsistent) model being constructed by the solver. The purpose of the trail is to maintain the assignment of relevant terms so that, if the satisfiability algorithm terminates with a positive answer, the satisfying assignment can simply be read off the trail.

Relevant terms are variables and Boolean terms, excluding negation. Intuitively, when invoking theory-specific semantics to evaluate a compound Boolean term t or its negation $\neg t$, the relevant terms are the term t itself and the closest sub-terms of t that are needed to compute its value.

Example 2. Consider the terms $t_1 \equiv (x + y^2 < z)$ and $t_2 \equiv (\neg b_1 \wedge (b_2 \vee b_3))$. In order to compute the value of t_1 or $\neg t_1$ under integer semantics, we need to know the values of terms x, y, and z. For evaluation of t_2 or $\neg t_2$, we need to know the values of terms b_1 and $(b_2 \vee b_3)$. The set of relevant terms therefore must include the terms $\{x, y, z, (x + y^2 < z), b_1, b_2, b_3, (b_2 \vee b_3), (\neg b_1 \wedge (b_2 \vee b_3))\}$.

A *trail* is a sequence of trail elements, where each element is either a *decision*, or a *propagation*. A decision is an assignment of a value v to a relevant term t, denoted as $t \mapsto v$. A propagation is an implied assignment of a value v to a relevant term t, and E is an explanation of the implication, denoted as $t \xrightarrow{E} v$. In both cases, we say that t *is assigned* in M.[3] In order to properly define an explanation, we first explain how the trail can be used to evaluate terms.

A trail can be seen as a partial model under construction and we can use the trail to evaluate compound terms based on the values of their sub-terms. A term t (and $\neg t$, if Boolean) *can be evaluated* in the trail M if t itself is assigned in M, or if all closest relevant sub-terms of t needed for evaluation are assigned in M (and its value can therefore be computed). Note that some terms can be evaluated in two different ways (by direct assignment, or by evaluation of sub-terms), potentially resulting in two different values. In order to account for this ambiguity, we define an evaluation predicate $\mathsf{evaluates}[M](t, v)$ that returns **true** if the term t can evaluate to the value v in trace M. In addition, we define $\mathsf{reasons}[M](t, v)$ to be the set of relevant sub-terms of t that were used in evaluating t to v.

Definition 1 (Evaluation Consistency). *A trail M is* evaluation-consistent *if there is no term that evaluates to two different values in M.*

---

[3] For simplicity, we denote formulas asserted to the solver as propagations with no explanation.

Example 3. In the trail $M = [\![(x < 0) \mapsto \top, x \mapsto 0]\!]$ the following hold.

- Terms $(x < 0)$ and x are assigned and can be evaluated to $\top$ and 0, respectively, with reasons$[M](x < 0, \top) = \{x < 0\}$ and reasons$[M](x, 0) = \{x\}$.
- Term $(x < 0)$ can also be evaluated to $\bot$, since its closest relevant sub-term x is assigned, with reasons$[M](x < 0, \bot) = \{x\}$.
- The term $(x^2 = 0)$ can be evaluated to $\top$ since the only closest relevant sub-term x is assigned, with reasons$[M](x^2 = 0, \top) = \{x\}$.
- The term $(x^2 = 0) \vee \neg(x < 0)$ *can not* be evaluated, since its closest relevant sub-terms are $(x^2 = 0)$ and $(x < 0)$, but $(x^2 = 0)$ is not assigned.
- The trail M is *not evaluation consistent* because the term $(x < 0)$ can evaluate to two different values.

The following lemma shows that evaluation consistency is a fundamental property of a trail in model-constructing satisfiability methods.

Lemma 1. *Given a formula F, if an evaluation-consistent trail M assigns all relevant sub-terms of F, and* evaluates$[M](F, \top)$, *then the model induced by M satisfies F.*

In the MCSat setting, we require the reasoning plugins to ensure evaluation-consistency for the terms they are responsible for. Usually, a plugin is responsible for terms relevant to a theory, i.e., constraints of the theory and values for terms of the theory's principle types. The plugin must detect evaluation inconsistencies in the trail for the constraints they are responsible for, and not introduce any new ones when making assignment decisions.

Explanations. We now define the explanations appearing in the trail propagations. An *explanation* E describes a valid substitution of a term with another term, under given assumptions, and is of the form

$$[A_1, \ldots, A_n] \implies \{t \mapsto s\}.$$

A propagation is only allowed to appear in the trail if the accompanying explanation is valid. In a trail $[\![M, t \overset{E}{\rightsquigarrow} v, \ldots]\!]$, the explanation E is a *valid explanation* for the marked propagation if

1. the formula $A_1 \wedge \ldots \wedge A_n \implies t = s$ is valid;
2. each assumption A_i can evaluate to $\top$ in M; and
3. the substitution term s can evaluate to v in M.

The three examples below illustrate the three typical propagation types.

Example 4 (Boolean Propagation). Consider the trail

$$[\![(x \vee y \vee z) \rightsquigarrow \top, x \mapsto \bot, y \mapsto \bot]\!].$$

Boolean propagation over clauses is the core deduction mechanism in a SAT solver. When all but one literals of a clause are assigned to $\bot$ in the trail, we can propagate that the unassigned literal must have the value $\top$. In the example above, we can propagate $z \overset{E}{\rightsquigarrow} \top$, where the explanation E is

$$[(x \vee y \vee z), \neg x, \neg y] \implies \{z \mapsto \top\}.$$

Example 5 (Evaluation Propagation). Consider the trail $[\![\; x \mapsto 0, y \mapsto 1 \;]\!]$ and the atom $(x + y < 0)$. Since all the variables of the atom are assigned in the trail, we can propagate its value as $(x + y < 0) \overset{E}{\rightsquigarrow} \bot$. The explanation E of this propagation can be $[\neg(x + y < 0)] \implies \{(x + y < 0) \mapsto \bot\}$.

Example 6 (Value Propagation). Consider the trail

$$[\![\; (x \leq z) \rightsquigarrow \top, (z \leq y) \rightsquigarrow \top, x \mapsto 0, y \mapsto 0 \;]\!].$$

Since $0 \leq z \leq 0$, we can propagate $z \overset{E}{\rightsquigarrow} 0$. In order to explain this propagation we can use the following valid explanation E

$$[x \leq z, z \leq y, x = y] \implies \{z \mapsto x\}.$$

Note that the explanation E introduces a new term in the set of assumptions.

3.2   Unit Reasoning

As Lemma 1 states, by maintaining evaluation consistency, we can guarantee that the model induced by the trail is a consistent assignment. In order to make the checking of evaluation consistency more operational, we use evaluation watch lists and the concept of unit consistency.

Let t_0 be a relevant compound term and its closest relevant sub-terms be $t_1, \ldots, t_n$. We call $w = (\text{eval } t_0 \; t_1 \; \ldots \; t_n)$ an *evaluation watch-list*. Given a trail M, if all but one elements of w are assigned in M, with t_i being the one unassigned element, we say that w has become *unit* in M with respect to t_i. For a given a set of relevant terms $\mathcal{R}$, and a term $t \in \mathcal{R}$, we denote by $\text{units}(\mathcal{R}, t)$ the set of evaluation watch lists for the terms in $\mathcal{R}$ that are unit in M with respect to the term t.

Example 7 (Boolean unit constraints). Consider the clause $(x \vee y)$. This clause, with its sub-terms x and y, corresponds to the evaluation watch list

$$w = (\text{eval } (x \vee y) \; x \; y).$$

Now consider the trails

$$M_1 = [\![\; (x \vee y) \rightsquigarrow \top, x \mapsto \bot \;]\!], \qquad M_2 = [\![\; x \mapsto \bot, y \mapsto \bot \;]\!].$$

- In trail M_1, variable y is unassigned making w unit with respect to y. Through Boolean reasoning, we can deduce that variable y has to be assigned to $\top$.
- In trail M_2, on the other hand, w is unit with respect to term $(x \vee y)$. Through Boolean reasoning, we can deduce that term $(x \vee y)$ must be assigned to $\bot$.

Example 8 (Arithmetic unit constraints). Consider the constraint $(x \leq y^2)$. This constraint with its relevant sub-terms x and y corresponds to the evaluation watch list

$$w = (\text{eval } (x \leq y^2) \; x \; y).$$

Now consider the trails

$$M_1 = [\![(x \leq y^2) \rightsquigarrow \bot, x \mapsto 2]\!], \qquad M_2 = [\![x \mapsto 2, y \mapsto 2]\!].$$

- In trail M_1, variable y is unassigned making w unit with respect to y. Through arithmetic reasoning, we can deduce that y can only be assigned to a value in $(-\sqrt{2}, \sqrt{2})$.
- In trail M_2, on the other hand, w is unit with respect to $(x \leq y^2)$. Through arithmetic reasoning, we can deduce that the term $(x \leq y^2)$ must be assigned to $\top$.

Evaluation watch lists are enough to capture clauses that become unit during Boolean constraint propagation (BCP) process in modern SAT solvers. But, as the examples above show, they can be used to reason about arbitrary Boolean and non-Boolean terms.

Definition 2 (Unit Consistency). *Assume a set of relevant terms $\mathcal{R}$ and a trail M. We call $\mathcal{R}$ unit consistent in M if, for each term $t \in \mathcal{R}$ that is not yet assigned in M, there exists a value v such that the assignment $t \mapsto v$ is evaluation-consistent with M.*

In a unit inconsistent trail, there is a term that can not be correctly assigned to a value. This is a sign that the trail is in conflict and we need to revise it. On the other hand, in a unit consistent trail, for every unassigned term there is a value that the term can be assigned to without breaking evaluation consistency.

From an implementation standpoint, evaluation watch lists provide an efficient mechanism for detecting unit inconsistencies due to the following.

1. Unit watch lists can be detected efficiently by watching 2 terms in every evaluation watch lists (generalization of the two-watched-literals approach from [26]).
2. Once a watch-list becomes unit, reasoning about the underlying constraint is simplified by the fact that the constraint involves only one variable (e.g., BCP on unit clauses, or finding solutions of univariate arithmetic constraints).

3.3 Conflict Analysis

We call a clause $C \equiv (L_1 \vee \ldots \vee L_n)$ a *conflict clause* in a trail M, if each literal L_i can be evaluated to $\bot$ in M. If the trail M is unit-inconsistent or evaluation-inconsistent, it is the responsibility of the reasoning plugin that detected the inconsistency to produce a *valid* conflict clause.

Example 9 (Boolean conflicts). Consider the trail

$$M = [\![\,(x \wedge y) \mapsto \top, y \overset{E}{\leadsto} \bot\,]\!].$$

Trail M is not evaluation consistent since the term $(x \wedge y)$ can evaluate to both $\top$ and $\bot$ is M. The Boolean reasoning plugin can respond to this inconsistency by returning a clause $(\neg(x \wedge y) \vee y)$. This clause is a conflict clause since all literals evaluate to $\bot$ in M, and is also a valid statement of Boolean logic.

Example 10 (Arithmetic Conflicts). Consider the set of relevant terms $\mathcal{R} = \{x, y, (y < z), (z < x)\}$ and the trail

$$M = [\![\,(y < z) \mapsto \top, (z < x) \mapsto \top, y \mapsto 0, x \mapsto 0\,]\!].$$

Using the watch list mechanism, the arithmetic reasoning plugin can detect that we have two unit constraints with respect to z. These unit constraints on z imply that $z > 0$ and $z < 0$, making the trail M unit inconsistent. The plugin can respond to this inconsistency by reporting a conflict clause

$$(y < z) \wedge (z < x) \Rightarrow (y < z) \equiv \neg(y < z) \vee \neg(z < x) \vee (y < z).$$

This clause is a conflict clause since all of its literals evaluate to $\bot$ in M, and it is also a valid statement of arithmetic.

Explanations of Propagations. During the conflict-analysis process, we resolve any propagated terms out of the conflict clause. We do so by using the substitution provided by the explanation. Since the conflicts are always represented by single clauses, the substitutions appearing in explanations will only be applied to clauses. Moreover, they will not indiscriminately substitute all occurrences of the target term. Instead, they will rely on a given trail M to select which occurrences to replace. We denote this *evaluation-based substitution* of term t with term s in a clause C as $C\{t \mapsto s\}_M$, and define it as follows.

$$(L_1 \vee \ldots \vee L_n)\{t \mapsto s\}_M = (L_1\{t \mapsto s\}_M \vee \ldots \vee L_n\{t \mapsto s\}_M)$$

$$L\{t \mapsto s\}_M = \begin{cases} L\{t \mapsto s\} & \text{if } s \in \mathsf{reasons}[M](L, \bot), \\ L & \text{otherwise.} \end{cases}$$

Intuitively, the substitution of t by s in the conflict clause C should only replace the occurrences of t that were needed to evaluate the clause to $\bot$.

Using substitution as the basis of our explanations allows us to fully extend the mechanics of a modern SAT solver to first-order reasoning. In Boolean satisfiability, the main rule of inference is Boolean resolution. Since we are working with more general theories, we generalize the resolution to a variant of ground paramodulation [28] we call *conflict-directed paramodulation*. The paramodulation rule relies on substitution as a core operation. Both resolution and paramodulation rules are shown side-by-side in Fig. 4. We denote by $\mathsf{resolve}[M](E, C)$ the result of applying the paramodulation rule, with evaluation-based substitution,

$$\frac{A \vee x \qquad \neg x \vee B}{A \vee B} \qquad\qquad \frac{A \vee (t = s) \qquad B}{A \vee B\{t \mapsto s\}}$$

Fig. 4. Boolean resolution and ground paramodulation rules. The Boolean rule can be seen as an instance of ground paramodulation with the substitution $\{x \mapsto \top\}$.

to the explanation E and clause C. More precisely, if $E = [A_1, \ldots, A_n] \implies \{s \mapsto t\}$ then

$$\mathsf{resolve}[M](E, C) = (\neg A_1 \vee \ldots \vee \neg A_n \vee C\{t \mapsto s\}_M).$$

Example 11 (Resolution). Consider the trail

$$M = [\![\, (y = x + 1) \rightsquigarrow \top, (y \leq z) \rightsquigarrow \top, (z \leq x) \rightsquigarrow \top, x \mapsto 0, y \overset{E}{\rightsquigarrow} 1 \,]\!].$$

The first three entries in the trail are assertions that we are checking for satisfiability, followed by a decision that assigns x to 0. As x is assigned to 0, the constraint $y = x + 1$ becomes unit in y and implies that $y = 1$. The explanation of the propagation is

$$E : [y = x + 1] \implies \{y \mapsto x + 1\}.$$

The constraints $(y \leq z)$ and $(z \leq x)$ are unit in variable z and assigned to $\top$. These two constraint simplify to $1 \leq z \leq 0$ in M and therefore imply an inconsistency on variable z. This inconsistency can be explained by a conflict clause

$$(y \leq z) \wedge (z \leq x) \rightarrow (y \leq x) = \neg(y \leq z) \vee \neg(z \leq x) \vee (y \leq x) \equiv C_0.$$

The clause C_0 is a valid starting point for conflict analysis because it is a valid statement and can be evaluated to $\bot$ in M.

In order to resolve the conflict, we can go back in the trail and resolve the trail elements from the conflict clause one by one. The top propagation to resolve is $y \overset{E}{\rightsquigarrow} 1$, and we can use conflict-directed paramodulation to obtain

$$\begin{aligned} C_1 \equiv \mathsf{resolve}[M](E, C_0) &\equiv \neg(y = x + 1) \vee C_0\{y \mapsto x + 1\}_M \\ &\equiv \neg(y = x + 1) \vee \neg(y \leq z) \vee \neg(z \leq x) \vee (x + 1 \leq x) \\ &\equiv \neg(y = x + 1) \vee \neg(y \leq z) \vee \neg(z \leq x). \end{aligned}$$

Note that we apply the substitution only to the last literal in C_0 since that is the only literal where y was used to evaluate it to $\bot$, i.e. $y \in \mathsf{reasons}[M](y \leq x, \bot)$. The new clause C_1 is still in conflict (all literals evaluate to $\bot$), and we can resolve the remaining literals as usual to obtain an empty clause and conclude that the assertions are unsatisfiable.

It is worth noting that the MCSat presentation from [8,18] did *not allow* ropagation of non-Boolean values. This was precisely because the underlying resolution process was based on Boolean resolution.

3.4   Integer Reasoning

The nonlinear integer reasoning we describe bellow assumes an existing MCSat plugin for reasoning about nonlinear real arithmetic. We use the existing NLSat plugin [17,19] to provide this functionality and, in order to extend it to integer reasoning, we extend the plugin to detect unit inconsistencies over integer constraints, and explain those inconsistencies with appropriate conflict clauses.

Given a trail M and a variable y, the procedure $\mathsf{explain}_{\mathbb{R}}(M, y)$ explains the unit inconsistencies in the reals, and the procedure $\mathsf{explain}_{\mathbb{Z}}(M, y)$ explains the unit inconsistencies in the integers. Both procedures return a valid conflict clause, where the $\mathsf{explain}_{\mathbb{R}}(M, y)$ procedure is inherited from NLSat.

For each arithmetic variable y, we maintain the set of nonlinear constraints $\mathcal{C} = \{C_1, \ldots, C_n\}$ that are unit with respect to y. This means that these constraints are asserted in the trail, and that all variables other than y from $\mathcal{C}$ are also assigned in the trail. We can therefore simplify each constraint in $\mathcal{C}$ by substituting the values of assigned variables and obtain a set of nonlinear constraints $\mathcal{C}_u$ that is *univariate* in y. From there, by isolating the roots of the polynomials involved, we can compute the set $\mathsf{feasible}(\mathcal{C}_u)$ of values that y can take in the context of the current trail. If $\mathsf{feasible}(\mathcal{C}_u)$ contains an integer point, then the trail is feasible with respect to the variable y, otherwise the trail is infeasible and we need to report a conflict.

If $\mathsf{feasible}(\mathcal{C}_u)$ is an empty set, then there is no possible value for y and we are in a *conflict over* $\mathbb{R}$, so we can employ $\mathsf{explain}_{\mathbb{R}}(M, y)$ to explain the conflict and produce a valid conflict clause. Otherwise, the solution set for y is a set of intervals

$$\mathsf{feasible}(\mathcal{C}_u) = (l_1, u_1) \cup (l_2, u_2) \cup \cdots \cup (l_n, u_n),$$

with real endpoints, where no interval contains an integer point. Here, again, we will reduce conflict explanation to $\mathsf{explain}_{\mathbb{R}}$, but by explaining several conflicts. Consider the (non-integer) point $m = (l_1 + u_1)/2$ and the following two trails

$$M_1 = [\![M, (y \leq \lfloor m \rfloor) \mapsto \top]\!], \qquad M_2 = [\![M, (y \geq \lceil m \rceil) \mapsto \top]\!].$$

These two trails are the branches of M around the point m.

The trail M_1 is unit inconsistent in $\mathbb{R}$ with respect to y and we can therefore apply $\mathsf{explain}_{\mathbb{R}}$ to obtain a conflict clause. Since the inconsistency was initiated by adding the constraint $(y \leq \lfloor m \rfloor)$, the conflict clause must include this constraint and is therefore of the form

$$\mathsf{explain}_{\mathbb{R}}(M_1, y) \equiv \neg(y \leq \lfloor m \rfloor) \vee D_1.$$

Moreover, we know that all literals in the clause D_1 evaluate to $\bot$ in the original trail M.

In trail M_2, the added constraint eliminates the first interval of possible values for y and we can call the integer conflict explanation $\mathsf{explain}_{\mathbb{Z}}$ on M_2.[4] Again,

---

[4] By reducing the number of intervals we guarantee termination.

since the added assertion $(y \geq \lceil m \rceil)$ is necessary for explaining the inconsistency in M_2, the explanation clause for M_2 will be of the form

$$\mathsf{explain}_{\mathbb{Z}}(M_2, y) \equiv \neg(y \geq \lceil m \rceil) \vee D_2 \equiv (y \leq \lfloor m \rfloor) \vee D_2.$$

Again, we know that all literals in the clause D_2 evaluate to $\bot$ in the original trail M.

In both cases above the explanation clauses are valid in the integers. We can therefore resolve the common literal with Boolean resolution and obtain a valid clause that we use as the final explanation

$$\mathsf{explain}_{\mathbb{Z}}(M, y) \equiv D_1 \vee D_2.$$

Since literals of both D_1 and D_2 evaluate to $\bot$, the explanation clause is indeed a valid conflict clause for M being inconsistent with respect to y.

3.5 Main Algorithm

The core algorithm behind MCSat is based on the search-and-resolve loop common in modern SAT solvers (e.g. [11]). The main loop of the solver performs a direct search for a satisfying assignment and terminates either by finding an assignment that satisfies the original problem, or deduces that the problem is unsatisfiable. The main check() method is presented in Algorithm 1.

Algorithm 1. MCSAT::CHECK()

Data: solver trail M, relevant variables/terms to assign in *queue*

```
1  while true do
2  |    propagate()
3  |    if a plugin detected conflict and the conflict clause is C then
4  |    |    R ← analyzeConflict(M, C)
5  |    |    if R = ⊥ then return unsat
6  |    |    backtrackWith(M, R)
7  |    else
8  |    |    if queue.empty() then return sat
9  |    |    x ← queue.pop()
10 |    |    ownerOf(x).decideValue(x)
```

The search process goes forward, making continuous progress, either through propagation, conflict analysis, or by making a decision. The propagate() procedure invokes the (unit) propagation procedures provided by the enabled plugins. Each plugin is allowed to propagate new information to the top of the trail. If a plugin detects an inconsistency, it communicates the conflict to the solver by producing a conflict clause. This allows the solver to analyze the conflict using the analyzeConflict() procedure. If conflict analysis learns the empty clause ⊥, the problem is proved unsatisfiable. Otherwise the learned clause is used to backtrack the search, new relevant terms are collected from the learned clause R, and the search continues.

If the plugins have performed propagation to exhaustion, and no conflict was detected, the procedure makes progress by deciding a value for an unassigned variable. The solver picks an unassigned variable x to be assigned, and relegates the choice of the value to the plugin responsible for assigning x. A choice of value for the selected unassigned variable should exist, as otherwise some plugin should have detected the unit inconsistency. MCSat uses a uniform heuristic to select the next variable, regardless of its type. The heuristic is based on how often a variable is used in conflict resolution, and is popularly used in CDCL-style SAT solvers [26]. If all the relevant variables and terms are assigned to a value, then the trail is evaluation consistent and represents the satisfying assignment for the original problem.

4 Experiments

We have implemented the new method on top of NLSat in the MCSat framework within the YICES2 SMT solver [9].[5] For representation and advanced operations on polynomials, such as root isolation and explanation of conflicts through CAD projection, we rely on the LibPoly library.[6]

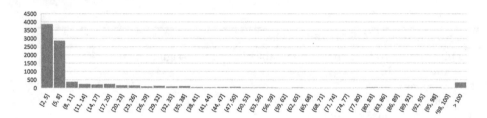

Fig. 5. Distribution of problems with respect to the number of integer variables involved (number of variables on the x axis, and number of problems with this number of variables on the y axis)

We have evaluated the new procedure on nonlinear integer benchmarks from the SMT-LIB library [3] (denoted as QF_NIA in the library). Most of the benchmarks in the library come from practical applications and are grouped into the following problem sets. The AProVE problems encode program termination conditions [13] and have between 2 and 985 integer variables. The calypto problem set contains problems relevant in hardware equivalence checking, with problems having between 3 and 50 integer variables. The LassoRanker problems encode termination conditions of lasso-shaped programs and have between 15 and 35

---

[5] Available at http://yices.csl.sri.com/.
[6] Available at http://sri-csl.github.io/libpoly/.

problem set	YICES2			APROVE			SMT-RAT			z3		
	solved	unsat	time (s)	solved	unsat	time (s)	solved	unsat	time (s)	solved	unsat	time (s)
AProVE (8829)	**8727**	**765**	**10197**	8028	0	7713	8251	223	9080	8310	285	22705
calypto (177)	**176**	**97**	**370**	77	0	1650	168	89	659	175	96	2517
LassoRanker (120)	101	97	664	3	0	5	24	21	9	**107**	**103**	**8065**
LCTES (2)	0	0	0	0	0	0	0	0	0	0	0	0
leipzig (167)	95	1	3541	162	0	3101	161	0	5075	**162**	**0**	**1080**
mcm (186)	12	0	5394	0	0	0	22	0	3622	**47**	**19**	**29368**
UltimateAutomizer (7)	**7**	**7**	**0**	0	0	0	1	1	2	**7**	**7**	**0**
UltimateLassoRanker (32)	**32**	**26**	**6**	6	0	16	30	24	118	32	26	20
	9150	**993**	**20172**	8276	0	12485	8657	358	18565	8840	536	63755

Fig. 6. Experimental evaluation. Each row corresponds to a different problem set. Each column corresponds to a different solver. Each table entry shows the number of problems solved, the number of unsatisfiable problems solved, and the total time it took for the solved instances.

integer variables. The set LCTES contains problems that involve integer division, with 673 integer variables each. The leipzig problems encode termination conditions for rewriting systems and have between 24 and 2606 integer variables. The mcm problems encode the MCM problem from [24], and have between 6 and 201 integer variables. The UltimateAutomizer set contains software verification queries from [16], with problems having between 4 and 144 integer variables. The UltimateLassoRanker problems encode non-termination of lasso-shaped programs [23], and have between 38 and 272 integer variables. To give an idea of the kinds of problems involved, Fig. 5 presents distribution of number of problems by number of integer variables. The largest problems are in the leipzig set, with 10 problems with over 1000 integer variables and the largest problem having 2606 variables.[7]

To put the results in context, we compare YICES2 with other state-of-the-art solvers that support nonlinear integer arithmetic, namely, APROVE [13], SMT-RAT [6], and z3 [7]. The results are presented in Fig. 6. Each solver was run with a timeout of 40 min. Each column of the table corresponds to a different solver, and each row corresponds to a different problem set. For each problem set and solver combination we report the number of problems that the tool has solved, how many of the solved problems were unsatisfiable, and the total time (in seconds) that the tool took to solve those problems. For a more detailed comparison a scatter-plot of the performance of YICES2 and other solvers is presented in Fig. 7.[8]

As can be seen from these results, YICES2 is very efficient overall and solves the most problems from the SMT-LIB benchmarks. But, the new method truly excels on unsatisfiable problems, where it outperforms the other solvers by a significant margin. The real advantage of the new methods becomes apparent

---

[7] All benchmarks are available at http://smtlib.cs.uiowa.edu/.

[8] For convenience, we've made the detailed results is available at https://docs.google. com/spreadsheets/d/1Gu9PZMvgJ6dCjwXnTdggKRUP1uI6kz6lpI2dpWEsWVU.

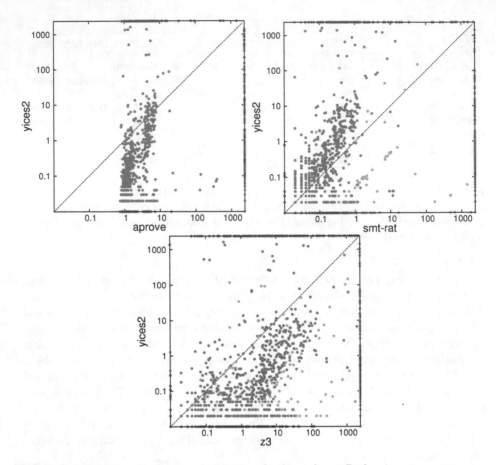

Fig. 7. Scatter-plot comparison of YICES2 and other solvers. Red points represent satisfiable problems, and green points represent unsatisfiable problems. Each axis (log scale) corresponds to the amount of time (in seconds) that each solver spent on the problem. Points below the $y = x$ line are the problems where YICES2 performs faster, and points on the top and right edges are problems where one of the solver ran out of time or terminated for other reasons. (Color figure online)

when solving problems (such as Example 1) where no combination of linear reasoning, interval reasoning, or bit-blasting can deduce unsatisfiablity (while other solvers fail on the problem, Example 1 is trivial for YICES2). The problems that YICES2 managed to show unsatisfiable contained as many as 468 integer variables, which is very encouraging considering the complexity of the underlying decision problem.

5   Conclusion

We have presented a new method for solving nonlinear integer problems based on the model-constructing approach to SMT and branch and bound. As opposed to existing methods that mostly rely on bit-blasting, the new method reasons directly in the integers and performs the branch-and-bound "splits" in a *conflict-driven* manner. The new method has been implemented in the YICES2 SMT solver and we have presented an extensive empirical evaluation where the new method is highly effective, and excels on unsatisfiable problems that can not be solved by other methods.

References

1. Albrecht, R., Buchberger, B., Collins, G.E., Loos, R.: Computer Algebra: Symbolic and Algebraic Computation, vol. 4. Springer, Vienna (2012)
2. Barrett, C., Conway, C.L., Deters, M., Hadarean, L., Jovanović, D., King, T., Reynolds, A., Tinelli, C.: CVC4. In: Gopalakrishnan, G., Qadeer, S. (eds.) CAV 2011. LNCS, vol. 6806, pp. 171–177. Springer, Heidelberg (2011). doi:10.1007/978-3-642-22110-1_14
3. Barrett, C., Stump, A., Tinelli, C.: The satisfiability modulo theories library (SMT-LIB), vol. 15, pp. 18–52 (2010). www.SMT-LIB.org
4. Barrett, C.W., Sebastiani, R., Seshia, S.A., Tinelli, C.: Satisfiability modulo theories. Handb. Satisf. **185**, 825–885 (2009)
5. Collins, G.E.: Quantifier elimination for real closed fields by cylindrical algebraic decomposition. In: Automata Theory and Formal Languages 2nd GI Conference Kaiserslautern, 20–23 May, pp. 134–183 (1975)
6. Corzilius, F., Kremer, G., Junges, S., Schupp, S., Ábrahám, E.: SMT-RAT: an open source C++ toolbox for strategic and parallel SMT solving. In: Heule, M., Weaver, S. (eds.) SAT 2015. LNCS, vol. 9340, pp. 360–368. Springer, Heidelberg (2015). doi:10.1007/978-3-319-24318-4_26
7. de Moura, L., Bjørner, N.: Z3: an efficient SMT solver. In: Ramakrishnan, C.R., Rehof, J. (eds.) TACAS 2008. LNCS, vol. 4963, pp. 337–340. Springer, Heidelberg (2008). doi:10.1007/978-3-540-78800-3_24
8. Moura, L., Jovanović, D.: A model-constructing satisfiability calculus. In: Giacobazzi, R., Berdine, J., Mastroeni, I. (eds.) VMCAI 2013. LNCS, vol. 7737, pp. 1–12. Springer, Heidelberg (2013). doi:10.1007/978-3-642-35873-9_1
9. Dutertre, B.: Yices 2.2. In: Biere, A., Bloem, R. (eds.) CAV 2014. LNCS, vol. 8559, pp. 737–744. Springer, Heidelberg (2014). doi:10.1007/978-3-319-08867-9_49
10. Dutertre, B., Moura, L.: A fast linear-arithmetic solver for DPLL(T). In: Ball, T., Jones, R.B. (eds.) CAV 2006. LNCS, vol. 4144, pp. 81–94. Springer, Heidelberg (2006). doi:10.1007/11817963_11
11. Eén, N., Sörensson, N.: An extensible SAT-solver. In: Giunchiglia, E., Tacchella, A. (eds.) SAT 2003. LNCS, vol. 2919, pp. 502–518. Springer, Heidelberg (2004). doi:10.1007/978-3-540-24605-3_37
12. Fuhs, C., Giesl, J., Middeldorp, A., Schneider-Kamp, P., Thiemann, R., Zankl, H.: SAT solving for termination analysis with polynomial interpretations. In: Marques-Silva, J., Sakallah, K.A. (eds.) SAT 2007. LNCS, vol. 4501, pp. 340–354. Springer, Heidelberg (2007). doi:10.1007/978-3-540-72788-0_33
13. Giesl, J., et al.: Proving termination of programs automatically with AProVE. In: Demri, S., Kapur, D., Weidenbach, C. (eds.) IJCAR 2014. LNCS (LNAI), vol. 8562, pp. 184–191. Springer, Heidelberg (2014). doi:10.1007/978-3-319-08587-6_13
14. Gomory, R.E.: Outline of an algorithm for integer solutions to linear programs. Bull. Am. Math. Soc. **64**(5), 275–278 (1958)

15. Griggio, A.: A practical approach to satisfiability modulo linear integer arithmetic. J. Satisf. Boolean Model. Comput. **8**, 1–27 (2012)
16. Heizmann, M., Hoenicke, J., Podelski, A.: Software model checking for people who love automata. In: Sharygina, N., Veith, H. (eds.) CAV 2013. LNCS, vol. 8044, pp. 36–52. Springer, Heidelberg (2013). doi:10.1007/978-3-642-39799-8_2
17. Jovanović, D.: SMT beyond DPLL(T): a new approach to theory solvers and theory combination. Ph.D. thesis, Courant Institute of Mathematical Sciences, New York (2012)
18. Jovanović, D., Barrett, C., De Moura, L.: The design and implementation of the model constructing satisfiability calculus. In: Formal Methods in Computer-Aided Design (FMCAD), pp. 173–180 (2013)
19. Jovanović, D., De Moura, L.: Solving non-linear arithmetic. In: International Joint Conference on Automated Reasoning, pp. 339–354 (2012)
20. Jovanović, D., De Moura, L.: Cutting to the chase: solving linear integer arithmetic. J. Autom. Reason. **51**(1), 79–108 (2013)
21. King, T.: Effective algorithms for the satisfiability of quantifier-free formulas over linear real and integer arithmetic. Ph.D. thesis, Courant Institute of Mathematical Sciences, New York (2014)
22. Kremer, G., Corzilius, F., Ábrahám, E.: A generalised branch-and-bound approach and its application in SAT modulo nonlinear integer arithmetic. In: Gerdt, V.P., Koepf, W., Seiler, W.M., Vorozhtsov, E.V. (eds.) CASC 2016. LNCS, vol. 9890, pp. 315–335. Springer, Heidelberg (2016). doi:10.1007/978-3-319-45641-6_21
23. Leike, J., Heizmann, M.: Geometric series as nontermination arguments for linear lasso programs. In: 14th International Workshop on Termination, p. 55 (2014)
24. Lopes, N.P., Aksoy, L., Manquinho, V., Monteiro, J.: Optimally solving the MCM problem using pseudo-boolean satisfiability (2011)
25. Matiyasevich, Y.V.: Hilbert's Tenth Problem. The MIT Press, Cambridge (1993)
26. Moskewicz, M.W., Madigan, C.F., Zhao, Y., Zhang, L., Malik, S.: Chaff: engineering an efficient SAT solver. In: Proceedings of the 38th Annual Design Automation Conference, pp. 530–535 (2001)
27. Papadimitriou, C.H.: On the complexity of integer programming. J. ACM **28**(4), 765–768 (1981)
28. Robinson, G., Wos, L.: Paramodulation and theorem-proving in first-order theories with equality. Mach. Intell. **4**, 135–150 (1969)
29. Tarski, A.: A decision method for elementary algebra and geometry. Technical report R-109, Rand Corporation (1951)
30. Weispfenning, V.: Quantifier elimination for real algebra - the quadratic case and beyond. Appl. Algebra Eng. Commun. Comput. **8**(2), 85–101 (1997)

Accuracy of Message Counting Abstraction in Fault-Tolerant Distributed Algorithms

Igor Konnov[1(✉)], Josef Widder[1], Francesco Spegni[2], and Luca Spalazzi[2]

[1] TU Wien (Vienna University of Technology), Vienna, Austria
konnov@forsyte.at
[2] UnivPM, Ancona, Italy

Abstract. Fault-tolerant distributed algorithms are a vital part of mission-critical distributed systems. In principle, automatic verification can be used to ensure the absence of bugs in such algorithms. In practice however, model checking tools will only establish the correctness of distributed algorithms if message passing is encoded efficiently. In this paper, we consider abstractions suitable for many fault-tolerant distributed algorithms that count messages for comparison against thresholds, e.g., the size of a majority of processes. Our experience shows that storing only the numbers of sent and received messages in the global state is more efficient than explicitly modeling message buffers or sets of messages. Storing only the numbers is called message-counting abstraction. Intuitively, this abstraction should maintain all necessary information. In this paper, we confirm this intuition for asynchronous systems by showing that the abstract system is bisimilar to the concrete system. Surprisingly, if there are real-time constraints on message delivery (as assumed in fault-tolerant clock synchronization algorithms), then there exist neither timed bisimulation, nor time-abstracting bisimulation. Still, we prove this abstraction useful for model checking: it preserves ATCTL properties, as the abstract and the concrete models simulate each other.

1 Introduction

The following algorithmic idea is pervasive in fault-tolerant distributed computing [13, 21, 30, 33, 36, 39]: each correct process counts messages received from distinct peers. Then, given the total number of processes n and the maximum number of faulty processes t, a process performs certain actions only if the message counter reaches a threshold such as $n - t$ (this number ensures that faulty processes alone cannot prevent progress in the computation). A list of benchmark algorithms that use such thresholds can be found in [27]. On the left of Fig. 1, we give an example pseudo code [36]. This algorithm works in a timed environment [35] (with a time bound τ^+ on message delays) in the presence of Byzantine faults ($n > 3t$) and provides safety and liveness guarantees such as:

Supported by: the Austrian Science Fund (FWF) through the National Research Network RiSE (S11403 and S11405), and project PRAVDA (P27722); and by the Vienna Science and Technology Fund (WWTF) through project APALACHE (ICT15-103).

© Springer International Publishing AG 2017
A. Bouajjani and D. Monniaux (Eds.): VMCAI 2017, LNCS 10145, pp. 347–366, 2017.
DOI: 10.1007/978-3-319-52234-0_19

```
 1  local myval_i ∈ {0,1}                    21  local myval_i ∈ {0,1}
 2                                           22  global nsntEcho ∈ N_0 initially 0
 3                                           23  local hasSent ∈ B initially F
 4                                           24  local rcvdEcho ∈ N_0 initially 0
 5                                           25
 6  do atomically                           26  do atomically
 7    -- messages are received implicitly   27    if (*) -- choose non-deterministically
 8    if myval_i = 1                        28      and rcvdEcho < nsntEcho + f
 9      and not sent ECHO before            29    then rcvdEcho++;
10    then send ECHO to all                 30
11                                          31    if myval_i = 1 and hasSent = F
12    if received ECHO                      32    then { nsntEcho++; hasSent = T; }
13        from at least t + 1 distinct processes  33
14      and not sent ECHO before            34
15    then send ECHO to all                 35    if rcvdEcho ≥ t + 1 and hasSent = F
16                                          36    then { nsntEcho++; hasSent = T; }
17    if received ECHO                      37
18        from at least n − t distinct processes  38    if rcvdEcho ≥ n − t
19    then accept                           39    then accept
20  od                                      40  od
```

Fig. 1. Pseudocode of a broadcast primitive to simulate authenticated broadcast [36] (left), and pseudocode of its message-counting abstraction (right)

(a) If a correct process accepts (that is, executes Line 19) at time T, then all correct processes accept by time $T + 2\tau^+$.

(b) If all correct processes start with $myval_i = 0$, then no correct process ever *accepts*.

(c) If all correct processes start with $myval_i = 1$, then at least one correct process eventually accepts.

As is typical for the distributed algorithms literature, the pseudo code from Fig. 1 omits "unnecessary book-keeping" details of message passing. That is, neither the local data structures that store the received messages nor the message buffers are explicitly described. Hence, if we want to automatically verify such an algorithm design, it is up to a verification expert to find adequate modeling and proper abstractions of message passing.

The authors of [23] suggested to model message passing using message counters instead of keeping track of individual messages. This modeling was shown experimentally to be efficient for fixed size systems, and later a series of parameterized model checking techniques was based upon it [22,23,25–27]. The encoding on the right of Fig. 1 is obtained by adding a global integer variable nsntEcho. Incrementing this variable (Line 36) encodes that a correct process executes Line 15 of the original pseudo code. The ith process keeps the number of received messages in a local integer variable rcvdEcho$_i$ that can be increased, as long as the invariant rcvdEcho$_i \leq$ nsntEcho $+ f$ is preserved, where f is the actual number of Byzantine faulty processes in the run. (This models that correct processes can receive up to f messages sent by faulty processes.) In fact, this modeling can be seen as a *message-counting abstraction* of a distributed system that uses message buffers.

The broadcast primitive in Fig. 1 is also used in the seminal clock synchronization algorithm from [35]. For clock synchronization, the precision of the clocks depends on the timing behavior[1] of the message system that the processes use to re-synchronize; e.g., in [35] it is required that each message sent at an instant T by a correct process must be delivered by a correct recipient process in the time interval $[T + \tau^-, T + \tau^+]$ for some bounds τ^- and τ^+ fixed in each run.

The standard theory of timed automata [7] does not account for message passing directly. To incorporate messages, one specifies a message passing system as a network of timed automata, i.e., a collection of timed automata that are scheduled with respect to interleaving semantics and interact via rendezvous, synchronous broadcast, or shared variables [12]. In this case, there are two typical ways to encode message passing: (i) for each pair of processes, introduce a separate timed automaton that models a channel between the processes, or (ii) introduce a single timed automaton that stores messages from timed automata (modeling the processes) and delivers the messages later by respecting the timing constraints. The same applies to Timed I/O automata [24]. Both solutions maintain much more details than required for automated verification of distributed algorithms such as [35]: First, processes do not compare process identifiers when making transitions, and thus are symmetric. Second, processes do not compare identifiers in the received messages, but only count messages.

For automated verification purposes, it appears natural to model such algorithms with timed automata that use a message-counting abstraction. However, the central question for practical verification is: *how precise is the message-counting abstraction?* In other words, given an algorithm A, what is the strongest equivalence between the model $M_S(A)$ using message sets and the model $M_C(A)$ using message counting. If the message counting abstraction is too coarse, then this may lead to spurious counterexamples, which may result in many refinement steps [17], or even may make the verification procedure incomplete.

Contributions. We introduce timed and untimed models suitable for the verification of threshold-based distributed algorithms, and establish relations between these models. An overview of the following contributions is depicted in Fig. 2:

– We define a model of processes that count messages. We then compose them into asynchronous systems (interleaving semantics). We give two variants: message passing, where the messages are stored in sets, and message counting, where only the number of sent messages is stored in shared variables.
– We then show that in the asynchronous case, the message passing and the message counting variants are bisimilar. This proves the intuition that underlies the verification results from [22, 23, 25, 27]. It explains why no spurious counterexamples due to message-counting abstraction were experienced in the experimental evaluation of the verification techniques from [22].

---

[1] As we deal with distributed algorithms and timed automata, the notion of a *clock* appears in two different contexts in this paper, which should not be confused: The problem of clock synchronization is to compute adjustment for the hardware clocks (oscillators). In the context of timed automata, clocks are special variables used to model the timing behavior of a system.

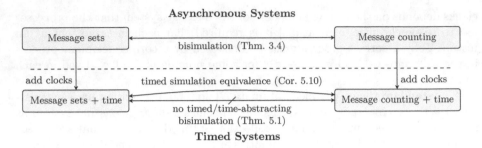

Fig. 2. Relationship between different modeling choices.

- We obtain timed models by adding timing constraints on message delays that restrict the message reception time depending on the sending times.
- We prove the surprising result that, in general, there is neither timed bisimulation nor time-abstracting bisimulation between the message passing and the message counting variants.
- Finally, we prove that there is timed simulation equivalence between the message passing and the message counting variants. This paves a way for abstraction-based model checking of timed distributed algorithms [35].

In the following section, we briefly recall the classic definitions of transition systems, timed automata, and simulations [7,16]. However, the timed automata defined there do not provide standard means to express processes that communicate via asynchronous message passing, as required for distributed algorithms. As we are interested in timed automata that capture this structure, we first define asynchronous message passing in Sect. 3 and then add timing constraints in Sect. 4 via message sets and message counting.

2   Preliminaries

We recall the classic definitions to the extent necessary for our work, and add two non-standard notions: First, our definition of a timed automaton assumes partitioning of the set of clocks into two disjoint sets: the message clocks (used to express the timing constraints of the message system underlying the distributed algorithm) and the specification clocks (used to express the specifications). Second, we assume that clocks are "not ticking" before they are started (more precisely, they are initialized to $-\infty$).

We will use the following sets: the set of Boolean values $\mathbb{B} = \{\mathsf{F}, \mathsf{T}\}$, the set of natural numbers $\mathbb{N} = \{1, 2, \dots\}$, the set $\mathbb{N}_0 = \mathbb{N} \cup \{0\}$, the set of non-negative reals $\mathbb{R}_{\geq 0}$, and the set of time instants $\mathbb{T} := \mathbb{R}_{\geq 0} \cup \{-\infty\}$.

Transition Systems. Given a finite set AP of atomic propositions, a *transition system* is a tuple $TS = (S, S^0, R, L)$ where S is a set of states, $S^0 \subseteq S$ are the initial states, $R \subseteq S \times S$ is a transition relation, and $L : S \to 2^{\mathsf{AP}}$ is a labeling function.

Clocks. A clock is a variable that ranges over the set $\mathbb{T}$. We call a clock that has the value $-\infty$ *uninitialized*. For a set X of clocks, a *clock valuation* is a function $\nu : X \to \mathbb{T}$. Given a clock valuation ν and a $\delta \in \mathbb{R}_{\geq 0}$, we define $\nu + \delta$ to be the valuation ν' such that $\nu'(c) = \nu(c) + \delta$ for $c \in X$ (Note that $-\infty + \delta = -\infty$). For a set $Y \subseteq X$ and a clock valuation $\nu : X \to \mathbb{T}$, we denote by $\nu[Y := 0]$ the valuation ν' such that $\nu'(c) = 0$ for $c \in Y \cap X$ and $\nu'(c) = \nu(c)$ for $c \in X \setminus Y$. Given a set of clocks Z, the set of *clock constraints* $\Psi(Z)$ is defined to contain all expressions generated by the following grammar:

$$\zeta := c \leq a \mid c \geq a \mid c < a \mid c > a \mid \zeta \wedge \zeta \qquad \text{for } c \in Z, a \in \mathbb{N}_0$$

Timed Automata. Given a set of atomic propositions AP and a finite transition system (S, S^0, R, L) over AP, which models discrete control of a system, we model the system's real-time behavior with a *timed automaton*, i.e., a tuple $TA = (S, S^0, R, L, X \cup U, I, E)$ with the following properties:

- The set $X \cup U$ is the disjoint union of the sets of *message clocks* X and *specification clocks* U.
- The function $I : S \to \Psi(X \cup U)$ is a *state invariant*, which assigns to each discrete state a clock constraint over $X \cup U$, which must hold in that state. We denote by $\mu, \nu \models I(s)$ that the clock valuations μ and ν satisfy the constraints of $I(s)$.
- $E : R \to \Psi(X \cup U) \times 2^{(X \cup U)}$ is a *state switch relation* that assigns to each transition a guard on clock values and a (possibly empty) set of clocks that must be reset to zero, when the transition takes place.

We assume that AP is disjoint from $\Psi(X \cup U)$. Thus, the discrete behavior does not interfere with propositions on time. The semantics of a timed automaton $TA = (S, S^0, R, L, X \cup U, I, E)$ is an infinite transition system $TS(TA) = (Q, Q^0, \Delta, \lambda)$ over propositions $\mathsf{AP} \cup \Psi(U)$ with the following properties [6]:

1. The set Q of states consists of triples (s, μ, ν), where $s \in S$ is the discrete component of the state, whereas $\mu : X \to \mathbb{T}$ and $\nu : U \to \mathbb{T}$ are valuations of the message and specification clocks respectively such that $\mu, \nu \models I(s)$.
2. The set $Q^0 \subseteq Q$ of initial states comprises triples (s_0, μ_0, ν_0) with $s_0 \in S_0$, and clocks are set to $-\infty$, i.e., $\forall c \in X.\ \mu_0(c) = -\infty$ and $\forall c \in U.\ \nu_0(c) = -\infty$.
3. The transition relation Δ contains pairs $((s, \mu, \nu), (s', \mu', \nu'))$ of two kinds of transitions:
   (a) A time step: $s' = s$ and $\mu' = \mu + \delta$, $\nu' = \nu + \delta$, for $\delta > 0$, provided that for all $\delta' : 0 < \delta' \leq \delta$ the invariant is preserved, i.e., $\mu + \delta', \nu + \delta' \models I(s)$.
   (b) A discrete step: there is a transition $(s, s') \in R$ with $(\varphi, Y) = E((s, s'))$ whose guard φ is enabled, i.e., $\mu, \nu \models \varphi$, and the clocks from Y are reset, i.e., $\mu' = \mu[Y \cap X := 0]$, $\nu' = \nu[Y \cap U := 0]$, provided that $\mu', \nu' \models I(s)$.
   Given a transition $(q, q') \in \Delta$, we write $q \xrightarrow{\delta}_\Delta q'$ for a time step with delay $\delta \in \mathbb{R}_{\geq 0}$, or $q \to_\Delta q'$ for a discrete step.
4. The labeling function $\lambda : Q \to 2^{\mathsf{AP} \cup \Psi(U)}$ is defined as follows. For any state $q = (s, \mu, \nu)$, the labeling $\lambda(q) = L(s) \cup \{\varphi \in \Psi(U) : \mu, \nu \models \varphi\}$.

Comparing System Behaviors. For transition systems $TS_i = (S_i, S_i^0, R_i, L_i)$ for $i \in \{1,2\}$, a relation $H \subseteq S_1 \times S_2$ is a *simulation*, if (i) for each $(s_1, s_2) \in H$ the labels coincide $L_1(s_1) = L_2(s_2)$, and (ii) for each transition $(s_1, t_1) \in R_1$, there is a transition $(s_2, t_2) \in R_2$ such that $(t_1, t_2) \in H$. If, in addition, the set $H^{-1} = \{(s_2, s_1) \colon (s_1, s_2) \in H\}$ is also a simulation, then H is called *bisimulation*.

Further, if TA_1 and TA_2 are timed automata with $TS(TA_i) = (Q_i, Q_i^0, \Delta_i, \lambda_i)$ for $i \in \{1,2\}$, then a simulation $H \subseteq Q_1 \times Q_2$ is called *timed simulation* [29], and a bisimulation $B \subseteq Q_1 \times Q_2$ is called *timed bisimulation* [15].

For transition systems $TS_i = (S_i, S_i^0, R_i, L_i)$ for $i \in \{1,2\}$, we say that a simulation $H \subseteq S_1 \times S_2$ is *initial*, if $\forall s \in S_1^0 \; \exists t \in S_2^0. \; (s, t) \in H$. A bisimulation $B \subseteq S_1 \times S_2$ is initial, if the simulations B and B^{-1} are initial. The same applies to timed (bi-)simulations. Then, for $i \in \{1,2\}$, we recall the standard preorders and equivalences on a pair of transition systems $TS_i = (S_i, S_i^0, R_i, L_i)$, and on a pair of timed automata TA_i, where $TS(TA_i) = (Q_i, Q_i^0, \Delta_i, \lambda_i)$:

1. $TS_1 \approx TS_2$ (*bisimilar*), if there is an initial bisimulation $B \subseteq S_1 \times S_2$.
2. $TA_1 \preceq^t TA_2$ (TA_2 *time-simulates* TA_1), if there is an initial timed simulation $H \subseteq Q_1 \times Q_2$.
3. $TA_1 \approx^t TA_2$ (*time-bisimilar*), if there is an initial timed bisimulation $B \subseteq Q_1 \times Q_2$.
4. $TA_1 \simeq^t TA_2$ (*time-simulation equivalent*), if $TA_1 \preceq^t TA_2$ and $TA_2 \preceq^t TA_1$.

Timed bisimulation forces time steps to advance clocks by the same amount of time. A coarser relation — called time-abstracting bisimulation [37] — allows two transition systems to advance clocks at "different speeds". Given two timed automata TA_i, for $i \in \{1,2\}$ and the respective transition systems $TS(TA_i) = (Q_i, Q_i^0, \Delta_i, \lambda_i)$, a binary relation $B \subseteq Q_1 \times Q_2$ is a *time-abstracting bisimulation* [37], if the following holds for every pair $(q_1, q_2) \in B$:

1. The labels coincide: $\lambda_1(q_1) = \lambda_2(q_2)$;
2. For all j and k such that $\{j, k\} = \{1, 2\}$, and each discrete step $q_j \rightarrow_{\Delta_j} r_j$, there is a discrete step $q_k \rightarrow_{\Delta_k} r_k$ and $(r_j, r_k) \in B$;
3. For all j and k such that $\{j, k\} = \{1, 2\}$, a delay $\delta \in \mathbb{R}_{\geq 0}$, and a time step $q_j \xrightarrow{\delta}_{\Delta_j} r_j$, there is a delay $\delta' \in \mathbb{R}_{\geq 0}$ and a time step $q_k \xrightarrow{\delta'}_{\Delta_k} r_k$ such that $(r_j, r_k) \in B$.

By substituting δ' with δ, one obtains the definition of timed bisimulation.

3   Asynchronous Message Passing Systems

Timed automata as defined above neither capture processes nor communication via messages, as would be required to model distributed algorithms. Hence we now introduce these notions and then construct an asynchronous system using processes and message passing (or message counting). We assume that at every step a process receives and sends at most one message [19]. In Sect. 4, we add time to this modeling in order to obtain a timed automaton.

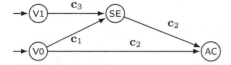

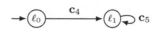

Fig. 3. A graphical representation of a process discussed in Example 3.1

Fig. 4. A simple two-state process (used later for Theorem 5.1)

Single Correct Process. We assume a (possibly infinite) set of control states $\mathcal{L}$ and a subset $\mathcal{L}_0 \subseteq \mathcal{L}$ of initial control states. We fix a finite set MT of message types. We assume that the control states in $\mathcal{L}$ keep track of the messages sent by a process. Thus, $\mathcal{L}$ comes with a predicate is_sent: $\mathcal{L} \times$ MT $\to \mathbb{B}$, where is_sent(ℓ, m) evaluates to true if and only if a message of type m has been sent according to the control state ℓ. Finally, we introduce a set Π of parameters and store the parameter values in a vector $\mathbf{p} \in \mathbb{N}_0{}^{|\Pi|}$. As noted in [22], parameter values are typically restricted with a resilience condition such as $n > 3t$ (less than a third of the processes are faulty), so we will assume that there is a set of all admissible combinations of parameter values $\mathbf{P}_{RC} \subseteq \mathbb{N}_0{}^{|\Pi|}$.

The behavior of a single process is defined as a *process transition relation* $\mathcal{T} \subseteq \mathcal{L} \times \mathbb{N}_0{}^{|\Pi|} \times \mathbb{N}_0{}^{|MT|} \times \mathcal{L}$ encoding transitions guarded by conditions on message counters that range over $\mathbb{N}_0{}^{|MT|}$: when $(\ell, \mathbf{p}, \mathbf{c}, \ell') \in \mathcal{T}$, a process can make a transition from the control state ℓ to the control state ℓ', provided that, for every $m \in$ MT, the number of received messages of type m is greater than or equal to $\mathbf{c}(m)$ in a configuration with parameter values $\mathbf{p}$.

Example 3.1. The process shown in Fig. 1 can be written in our definitions as follows. The algorithm is using only one message type, and thus MT = {ECHO}. We assume a set of control states $\mathcal{L} = \{V0, V1, SE, AC\}$: V0 and V1 encode the initial states where $myval = 0$ and $myval = 1$ respectively, pc = SE encodes the status "ECHO sent before", and pc = AC encodes the status "accept". The initial control states are: $\mathcal{L}_0 = \{V0, V1\}$. The transition relation contains four types of transitions: $t_1^P = (V0, \mathbf{p}, \mathbf{c}_1, SE)$, $t_2^P = (V0, \mathbf{p}, \mathbf{c}_2, AC)$, $t_3^P = (V1, \mathbf{p}, \mathbf{c}_3, SE)$, and $t_4^P = (SE, \mathbf{p}, \mathbf{c}_2, AC)$, for any $\mathbf{p} \in \mathbb{N}_0{}^{|\Pi|}$ and $\mathbf{c}_1, \mathbf{c}_2, \mathbf{c}_3$ satisfying the following: $\mathbf{c}_1(ECHO) \geq \mathbf{p}(t) + 1$, $\mathbf{c}_2(ECHO) \geq \mathbf{p}(n) - \mathbf{p}(t)$, and $\mathbf{c}_3(ECHO) \geq 0$. Finally, is_sent$(\ell, ECHO)$ iff $\ell \in \{SE, AC\}$. A concise graphical representation of the transition relation is given in Fig. 3. There, each edge represents multiple transitions of the same type. Let us observe that while the action of sending a message can be inferred by simply checking all the transitions going from a state s to a state t such that $\neg$is_sent(s) and is_sent(t), the action of receiving an individual message is not part of the process description at this level. However, if a guarded transition is taken, this implies that a threshold has been reached, e.g., in case of $\mathbf{c}_1$, at least $t + 1$ messages were received. ◁

Table 1. The message-passing and message-counting interpretations

Message passing (MP)	Message counting (MC):
$Msg_{MP} \triangleq MT \times Proc$	$Msg_{MC} \triangleq MT \times \{C, F\}$
$MsgSets_{MP} \triangleq 2^{MT \times Proc}$	$MsgSets_{MC} \triangleq \{0, \dots, |Corr|\}^{|MT|} \times \{0, \dots, |Byz|\}^{|MT|}$
Initial messages, $init \in MsgSets$	
$init_{MP} \triangleq \emptyset$	$init_{MC} \triangleq ((0, \dots, 0), (0, \dots, 0))$
Count messages, $card : MT \times MsgSets \to \mathbb{N}_0$	
$card_{MP}(m, M) \triangleq |\{p \in Proc: (m, p) \in M\}|$	$card_{MC}(m, (c_C, c_F)) \triangleq c_C(m) + c_F(m)$
Add a message, $add : Msg \times MsgSets \to MsgSets$	
$add_{MP}(\langle m, p \rangle, M) \triangleq M \cup \{\langle m, p \rangle\}$	$add_{MC}((m, tag), (c_C, c_F)) \triangleq (c'_C, c'_F)$ such that
	$c'_C(m) = c_C(m) + 1$ and $c'_F(m) = c_F(m)$, if $tag = C$
	$c'_F(m) = c_F(m) + 1$ and $c'_C(m) = c_C(m)$, if $tag = F$
	and $c'(m') = c(m)$ for $m' \in MT, m' \neq m$
Is there a message to deliver? $inTransit : Msg \times MsgSets \times MsgSets \to \mathbb{B}$	
$inTransit_{MP}(\langle m, p \rangle, M, M') \triangleq$	$inTransit_{MC}((m, tag), (c_C, c_F), (c'_C, c'_F)) \triangleq$
$(p \in Corr \wedge \langle m, p \rangle \in M' \setminus M) \vee (p \in Byz \wedge \langle m, p \rangle \notin M)$	$(tag = C \wedge c'_C > c_C) \vee (tag = F \wedge c_F < |Byz|)$

We make two assumptions typical for distributed algorithms [19,35]:

A1 Processes do not forget that they have sent messages: If $(\ell, \mathbf{p}, \mathbf{c}, \ell') \in \mathcal{T}$, then is_sent$(\ell, m) \to$ is_sent(ℓ', m) for every $m \in MT$.

A2 At each step a process sends at most one message to all: If $(\ell, \mathbf{p}, \mathbf{c}, \ell') \in \mathcal{T}$ and $\neg$is_sent$(\ell, m) \wedge$ is_sent$(\ell', m) \wedge \neg$is_sent$(\ell, m') \wedge$ is_sent(ℓ', m') then $m = m'$.

Then, we call $(MT, \mathcal{L}, \mathcal{L}_0, \mathcal{T})$ a process template.

Asynchronous Message Passing and Counting in Presence of Byzantine Faults. In this section we introduce two ways of modeling message passing: by storing messages in sets, and by counting messages. As in [23], we do not explicitly model Byzantine processes [32], but capture their effect on the correct processes in the form of spurious messages. Although we do not discuss other kinds of faults (e.g., crashes, symmetric faults, omission faults), it is not hard to model other faults by following the modeling in [23].

We fix a set of processes Proc, which is typically defined as $\{1, \dots, n\}$ for $n \geq 1$. Further, assume that there are two disjoint sets: the set Corr $\subseteq$ Proc of correct processes, and Byz $\subseteq$ Proc of Byzantine processes (possibly empty), with Byz $\cup$ Corr = Proc. Given a process template $(MT, \mathcal{L}, \mathcal{L}_0, \mathcal{T})$, we refer to $(MT, \mathcal{L}, \mathcal{L}_0, \mathcal{T}, Corr, Byz)$ as a *design*. Note that a design does not capture how processes interact with messages. To do so, in Table 1, we define message passing (MP) and message counting (MC) models as interpretations of the signature $(Msg, MsgSets, init, card, add, inTransit)$, with the following informal meaning:

- Msg: the set of all messages that can be exchanged by the processes,
- $MsgSets$: collections of messages,
- $init$: the empty collection of messages,
- $card$: a function that counts messages of the given type,
- add: a function that adds a message to a collection of messages,

- *inTransit*: a function that checks whether a message is in transit and thus can be received.

Transition Systems. Fix interpretations $(Msg_I, MsgSets_I, init_I, card_I, add_I, inTransit_I)$ for $I \in \{MP, MC\}$. Then, we define a transition system $TS^I = (S^I, S_0^I, R^I, L^I)$ of processes from Proc that communicate with respect to interpretation I. We call *message-passing system* the transition system obtained using the interpretation MP, and *message-counting system* the transition system obtained using the interpretation MC.

The set S^I contains configurations, i.e., tuples $(\mathbf{p}, \mathsf{pc}, \mathsf{rcvd}, \mathsf{sent})$ having the following properties: (a) $\mathbf{p} \in \mathbb{N}_0^{|\Pi|}$, (b) $\mathsf{pc} : \mathsf{Corr} \to \mathcal{L}$, (c) $\mathsf{rcvd} : \mathsf{Corr} \to MsgSets_I$, and (d) $\mathsf{sent} \in MsgSets_I$. In a configuration, for every process $p \in \mathsf{Corr}$, the values $\mathsf{pc}(p)$ and $\mathsf{rcvd}(p)$ comprise the *local view* of the process p, while the components sent and $\mathbf{p}$ comprise the *shared state* of the distributed system. A configuration $\sigma \in S^I$ belongs to the set S_0^I of initial configurations, if for each process $p \in \mathsf{Corr}$, it holds that: (a) $\sigma.\mathsf{pc}(p) \in \mathcal{L}_0$, (b) $\sigma.\mathsf{rcvd}(p) = init_I$, (c) $\sigma.\mathsf{sent} = init_I$, and (d) $\sigma.\mathbf{p} \in \mathbf{P}_{RC}$.

Definition 3.2. *The transition relation R^I contains a pair of configurations $(\sigma, \sigma') \in S^I \times S^I$, if there is a correct process $p \in \mathsf{Corr}$ that satisfies:*

1. *There exists a local transition $(\ell, \mathbf{p}, \mathbf{c}, \ell') \in \mathcal{T}$ satisfying $\sigma.\mathsf{pc}(p) = \ell$ and $\sigma'.\mathsf{pc}(p) = \ell'$ and for all m in MT, $\mathbf{c}(m) = card_I(m, \sigma'.\mathsf{rcvd}(p))$. Also, it is required that $\sigma.\mathbf{p} = \sigma'.\mathbf{p} = \mathbf{p}$.*
2. *Messages are received and sent according to the signature:*
   (a) *Process p receives no message: $\sigma'.\mathsf{rcvd}(p) = \sigma.\mathsf{rcvd}(p)$, or there is a message in transit in σ that is received in σ', i.e., there is a message $msg \in Msg_I$ satisfying:*
       $inTransit_I(msg, \sigma.\mathsf{rcvd}(p), \sigma.\mathsf{sent}) \wedge \sigma'.\mathsf{rcvd}(p) = add_I(msg, \sigma.\mathsf{rcvd}(p)).$
   (b) *The shared variable sent is changed iff process p sends a message, that is, $\sigma'.\mathsf{sent} = add_I(msg, \sigma.\mathsf{sent})$, if and only if $\neg\mathsf{is\_sent}(\sigma.\mathsf{pc}(p), m)$ and $\mathsf{is\_sent}(\sigma'.\mathsf{pc}(p), m)$, for every $m \in$ MT and $msg \in Msg_I$ of type m.*
3. *The processes different from p do not change their local states:*
   $\sigma'.\mathsf{pc}(q) = \sigma.\mathsf{pc}(q)$ and $\sigma'.\mathsf{rcvd}(q) = \sigma.\mathsf{rcvd}(q)$ for $q \in \mathsf{Corr} \setminus \{p\}$.

The labeling function $L^I : S^I \to \mathcal{L}^{|\mathsf{Corr}|} \times \left(\mathbb{N}_0^{|\mathsf{MT}|}\right)^{|\mathsf{Corr}|}$ labels each configuration $\sigma \in S^I$ with the vector of control states and message counters, i.e., $L^I(\sigma) = ((\ell_1, \ldots, \ell_{|\mathsf{Corr}|}), (\mathbf{c}_1, \ldots, \mathbf{c}_{|\mathsf{Corr}|}))$ such that $\ell_p = \sigma.\mathsf{pc}(p)$ and $\mathbf{c}_p(m) = card_I(m, \sigma.\mathsf{rcvd}(p))$ for $p \in \mathsf{Corr}$, $m \in \mathsf{MT}$. (For simplicity we use the convention that $\mathsf{Corr} = \{1, \ldots j\}$, for some $j \in \mathbb{N}$.) Note that L^I labels a configuration with the process control states and the number of messages received by each process.

The message-passing transition systems have the following features. The messages sent by *correct* processes are stored in the shared set sent. In this modeling, the messages from Byzantine processes are not stored in sent explicitly, but can be received at any step. Each correct process $p \in \mathsf{Corr}$ stores received messages in its local set rcvd(p), whose elements originate from the messages stored in the set sent or from Byzantine processes.

The message-counting transition systems have the following features. Messages are not stored explicitly, but are only counted. We maintain two vectors of counters: (i) representing the number of messages that originate from correct processes (these messages have the tag C), and (ii) representing the number of messages that originate from faulty processes (these messages have the tag F). Each correct process $p \in$ Corr keeps two such vectors of counters $\mathbf{c_C}$ and $\mathbf{c_F}$ in its local variable rcvd(p). In the following, we refer to $\mathbf{c_C}$ and $\mathbf{c_F}$ using the notation $[\text{rcvd}(p)]_C$ and $[\text{rcvd}(p)]_F$. The number of sent messages is also stored as a pair of vectors $[\text{sent}]_C$ and $[\text{sent}]_F$. By the definition of the transition relation R^{MC}, the vector $[\text{sent}]_F$ is always equal to the zero vector, whereas the correct process p can increment its counter $[\text{rcvd}(p)]_F$, if $[\text{rcvd}(p)]_F(m) < |\text{Byz}|$, for every $m \in \text{MT}$.

To prove bisimulation between a message-passing system and a message-counting system — built from the same design — we introduce the following relation on the configurations of both systems:

Definition 3.3. *Let $H^{\#} \subseteq S^{MP} \times S^{MC}$ such that $(\sigma, \sigma^{\#}) \in H^{\#}$ if for all processes $p \in$ Corr and message types $m \in$ MT:*

1. $\sigma^{\#}.\text{pc}(p) = \sigma.\text{pc}(p)$
2. $\sigma^{\#}.[\text{rcvd}(p)]_C(m) = |\{q \in \text{Corr}: \langle m, q \rangle \in \sigma.\text{rcvd}(p)\}|$
3. $\sigma^{\#}.[\text{rcvd}(p)]_F(m) = |\{q \in \text{Byz}: \langle m, q \rangle \in \sigma.\text{rcvd}(p)\}|$
4. $\sigma^{\#}.[\text{sent}]_C(m) = |\{q \in \text{Corr}: \langle m, q \rangle \in \sigma.\text{sent}\}|$
5. $\sigma^{\#}.[\text{sent}]_F(m) = 0$
6. $\{q \in \text{Proc}: \langle m, q \rangle \in \sigma.\text{sent}\} \subseteq \text{Corr}$
7. $\sigma.\text{rcvd}(p) \subseteq \sigma.\text{sent} \cup \{\langle m, q \rangle : m \in \text{MT}, q \in \text{Byz}\}$
8. $\text{is\_sent}(\sigma.\text{pc}(p), m) \leftrightarrow \langle m, p \rangle \in \sigma.\text{sent}$

Theorem 3.4. *For a message-passing system TS^{MP} and a message-counting system TS^{MC} defined over the same design, $H^{\#}$ is a bisimulation.*

The key argument to prove the Theorem 3.4 is that given a message counting state $\sigma^{\#}$, if a step increases a counter rcvd(p), in the message passing system this transition can be mirrored by receiving an arbitrary message in transit. In fact, in both systems, once a message is sent it can be received at any future step. We will see that in the timed version this argument does not work anymore, due to the restricted time interval in which a message must be received.

4   Messages with Time Constraints

We now add time constraints to both, message-passing systems and message-counting systems. Following the definitions from distributed algorithms [35,40], we assume that every message is delivered within a predefined time bound, that is, not earlier than τ^- time units and not later than τ^+ times units since the instant it was sent, with $0 \leq \tau^- \leq \tau^+$. We use naturals for τ^- and τ^+ for consistency with the literature on timed automata.

As can be seen from Sect. 2, to define a timed automaton, one has to provide an invariant and a switch relation. In the following, we fix the invariants and switch relations with respect to the timing constraints τ^- and τ^+ on messages. However, the specifications of distributed algorithms may refer to time, e.g., "If a correct process accepts the message *(round k)* at time t, then every correct process does so by time $t + t_{\text{del}}$" [35]. Therefore, we assume that a *specification invariant* (or *user invariant*) $I_U : 2^{\text{AP}} \to \Psi(U)$ and a *specification switch relation* (or *user switch relation*) $E_U : 2^{\text{AP}} \times 2^{\text{AP}} \to \Psi(U) \times 2^U$ are given as input. Then, we will refer to the tuple $(\mathcal{L}, \mathcal{L}_0, \mathcal{T}, \text{Proc}, I_U, E_U)$ as a *timed design* and we will assume that a timed design is fixed in the following.

Using a timed design, we will use message-passing and message-counting systems to derive two timed automata. For a message of type m sent by a correct process p, the message-passing system uses a clock $c \langle m, p \rangle$ to store *the delay since the message $\langle m, p \rangle$ was sent*. The message-counting system stores *the delay since the ith message of type m was sent*, for all i and m. Both timed automata specify an invariant to constrain the time required to deliver a message.

Definition 4.1 (Message-passing timed automaton). *Given a message-passing system $TS^{MP} = (S^{MP}, S_0^{MP}, R^{MP}, L^{MP})$ defined over a timed system design $(\mathcal{L}, \mathcal{L}_0, \mathcal{T}, \text{Proc}, I_U, E_U)$, we say that a timed automaton $TA^{MP} = (S^{MP}, S_0^{MP}, R^{MP}, L^{MP}, U \cup X^{MP}, I^{MP}, E^{MP})$ is a* message-passing timed automaton, *if it has the following properties:*

1. *There is one clock per message that can be sent by a correct process: $X^{MP} = \{c \langle m, p \rangle : m \in \text{MT}, p \in \text{Corr}\}$.*
2. *For each discrete transition $(\sigma, \sigma') \in R^{MP}$, the state switch relation $E^{MP}(\sigma, \sigma')$ ensures the specification invariant and resets the given specification clocks and the clocks corresponding to the message sent in transition (σ, σ'). That is, if (φ_U, Y_U) is the guard, and specification clocks are in $E_U(L^{MP}(\sigma), L^{MP}(\sigma'))$, then $E^{MP}(\sigma, \sigma') = (\varphi_U, Y_U \cup \{c \langle m, p \rangle : \langle m, p \rangle \in \sigma'.\text{sent} \setminus \sigma.\text{sent}\})$.*
3. *Each state $\sigma \in S^{MP}$ has the invariant $I^{MP}(\sigma) = I_U(L^{MP}(\sigma)) \wedge \varphi_{MP}^- \wedge \varphi_{MP}^+$ composed of:*
   (a) the specification invariant $I_U(L^{MP}(\sigma))$;
   (b) the lower bound on the age of received messages:
   $\varphi_{MP}^- = \bigwedge_{\langle m, p \rangle \in M} c \langle m, p \rangle \geq \tau^-$ *for $M = \{\langle m, p \rangle \in \text{MT} \times \text{Corr} : \exists q \in \text{Corr}. \langle m, p \rangle \in \sigma.\text{rcvd}(q)\}$; and*
   (c) the upper bound on the age of messages that are in transit: $\varphi_{MP}^+ = \bigwedge_{\langle m, p \rangle \in M} 0 \leq c \langle m, p \rangle \leq \tau^+$ for $M = \{\langle m, p \rangle \in \text{MT} \times \text{Corr} : \langle m, p \rangle \in \sigma.\text{sent} \setminus \bigcap_{q \in \text{Corr}} \sigma.\text{rcvd}(q)\}$.

Definition 4.2 (Message-counting timed automaton). *Given a message-counting system $TS_{MC} = (S^{MC}, S_0^{MC}, R^{MC}, L^{MC})$ defined over a timed design $(\mathcal{L}, \mathcal{L}_0, \mathcal{T}, \text{Proc}, I_U, E_U)$, we say that a timed automaton $TA_{MC} = (S^{MC}, S_0^{MC}, R^{MC}, L^{MC}, U \cup X^{MC}, I^{MC}, E^{MC})$ is a* message-counting timed automaton, *if it has the following properties:*

1. *There is one clock per message type and number of messages sent. That is, $X^{MC} = \{c \langle m, i \rangle : m \in \text{MT}, 1 \leq i \leq |\text{Corr}|\}$.*

2. For each discrete transition $(\sigma, \sigma') \in R^{MC}$, the state switch relation $E^{MC}(\sigma, \sigma')$ ensures the specification invariant and resets the given specification clocks and the clocks corresponding to message counters updated by (σ, σ'). That is, if $(\varphi_U, Y_U) = E_U(L^{MC}(\sigma), L^{MC}(\sigma'))$, then the switch relation $E^{MC}(\sigma, \sigma')$ is $(\varphi_U, Y_U \cup \{c \langle m, k \rangle : m \in \mathsf{MT}, k = \sigma'.\mathsf{sent}(m) = \sigma.\mathsf{sent}(m) + 1\})$.
3. Each state $\sigma \in S^{MC}$ has the invariant $I^{MC}(\sigma) = I_U(L^{MC}(\sigma)) \wedge \varphi_{MC}^- \wedge \varphi_{MC}^+$ composed of:
   (a) the specification invariant $I_U(L^{MC}(\sigma))$;
   (b) $\varphi_{MC}^- = \bigwedge_{m \in \mathsf{MT}} a(m) > 0 \rightarrow c \langle m, a(m) \rangle \geq \tau^-$ for the numbers $a(m) = \max_{p \in \mathsf{Corr}} [\sigma.\mathsf{rcvd}(p)(m)]_{\mathsf{c}}$. If a correct process has received $a(m)$ messages of type m from correct processes, then the $a(m)$-th message of type m, for every $m \in \mathsf{MT}$, was sent at least τ^- time units earlier.
   (c) $\varphi_{MC}^+ = \bigwedge_{m \in \mathsf{MT}} \bigwedge_{b(m) < j \leq \sigma.\mathsf{sent}(m)} 0 \leq c \langle m, j \rangle \leq \tau^+$ for the numbers $b(m) = \min_{p \in \mathsf{Corr}} [\sigma.\mathsf{rcvd}(p)(m)]_{\mathsf{c}}$. If there is a correct process that has received $b(m)$ messages of type m from correct processes, then for every number of messages $j > b(m)$, the respective clock is bounded by τ^+.

While the number of employed clocks is the same, the latter model is "more abstract": by forgetting the identity of the sender, indeed, several configurations of the message-passing timed automaton can be mapped on the same configuration of the message-counting timed automaton.

5   Precision of Message Counting with Time Constraints

While Theorem 3.4 establishes a strong equivalence — that is, a bisimulation relation — between message-passing transition systems, we will show in Theorem 5.1 that message-passing timed automata and message-counting timed automata are not necessarily equivalent in the sense of timed bisimulation. Remarkably, such automata are also not necessarily equivalent in the sense of time-abstracting bisimulation. These results show an upper bound on the degree of precision achievable by model checking of timed properties of FTDAs by counting messages. Nevertheless, we show that such automata simulate each other, and thus they satisfy the same ATCTL formulas (Corollarys 5.10 and 6.2).

Theorem 5.1. *There exists a timed design whose message-passing timed automaton* TA^{MP} *and message-counting timed automaton* TA^{MC} *satisfy:*

1. *There is no initial timed bisimulation between* TA^{MP} *and* TA^{MC}.
2. *There is no initial time-abstracting bisimulation between* TA^{MP} *and* TA^{MC}.

Proof (sketch). We give an example of a timed design proving Point 2. Since timed bisimulation is a special case of time-abstracting bisimulation, this example also proves Point 1.

We use the process template shown in Fig. 4 on page 7. Formally, this template is defined as follows: there is one parameter, i.e., $\Pi = \{n\}$, one message type, i.e., $\mathsf{MT} = \{M\}$, and two control states, i.e., $\mathcal{L} = \{\ell_0, \ell_1\}$. There are two

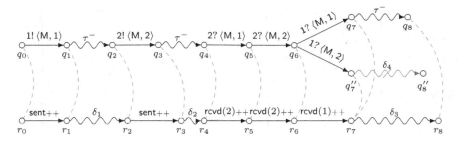

Fig. 5. Two runs of TA^{MP} (above) and one run of TA^{MC} (below) that violate time-abstracting bisimulation when $\tau^+ = 2\tau^-$. Circles and edges illustrate states and transitions. Edge labels are as follows: τ^- or δ_i designate a time step with the respective delay; i! $\langle M, j \rangle$ and i? $\langle M, j \rangle$ designate send and receive of a message $\langle M, j \rangle$ by process i in the message-passing system; sent++ and rcvd(i)++ designate send and receive of a message M by some process and process i respectively.

types of transitions: $t_1^P = (\ell_0, \mathbf{p}, \mathbf{c}_4, \ell_1)$ and $t_2^P = (\ell_1, \mathbf{p}, \mathbf{c}_5, \ell_1)$. The conditions $\mathbf{c}_4$ and $\mathbf{c}_5$ require that $\mathbf{c}_4(M) = 0$ and $\mathbf{c}_5(M) \geq 0$ respectively. Every process sends a message of type M when going from ℓ_0 to ℓ_1, i.e., is_sent$(\ell, M) = \mathsf{T}$ iff $\ell = \ell_1$. Then the processes self-loop in the control state ℓ_1 (by doing so, they can receive messages from the other processes).

Consider the system of two correct processes and no Byzantine processes, that is, Corr $= \{1, 2\}$ and Byz $= \emptyset$. We fix the upper bound on message delays to be $\tau^+ = 2\tau^- > 0$. For the sake of this proof, we set $U = \emptyset$, and thus I_U and E_U are defined trivially. Together, these constraints define a timed design.

Figure 5 illustrates two runs of a TA^{MP} and a run of TA^{MC} that should be matched by a time-abstracting bisimulation, if one exists. We show by contradiction that no such relation exists. Note that the message $\langle M, 1 \rangle$ has been received by all processes at the timed state q_7 and has not been received by the first process at the timed state q_7''. Thus the timed state q_7 admits a time step, while the timed state q_7'' does not. Indeed, on one hand, the timed automaton TA^{MP} can advance the clocks by at most $\tau^+ - \tau^- = \tau^-$ time units in q_7 before the clock attached to the message $\langle M, 2 \rangle$ expires; on the other hand, in q_7'', the timed automaton TA^{MP} cannot advance the clocks before the clock attached to the message $\langle M, 1 \rangle$ expires. However, both states must be time-abstract related to the state r_7 of TA^{MC}, because they both received the same number of messages of type M and thus their labels coincide, from which we derive the required contradiction. Hence, proving that there is no time-abstracting bisimulation. □

From Theorem 5.1, it follows that message counting abstraction is not precise enough to preserve an equivalence relation as strong as bisimulation. However, for abstraction-based model checking a coarser relation, namely, timed-simulation equivalence, would be sufficient. In one direction, timed-simulation is easy: a discrete configuration of a message-passing timed automaton can be mapped to the configuration of the message-counting timed automaton by just counting

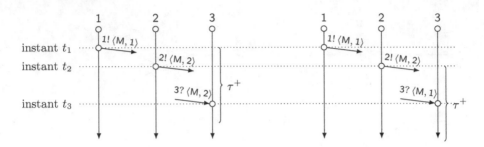

Fig. 6. Receiving messages in order relaxes constraints of delay transitions

the messages for each message type, while the clocks assignments are kept the same. The other direction is harder: A first approach would be to map a configuration of a message-counting timed automaton to all the configurations of the message-passing timed automaton, where the message counters are equal to the cardinalities of the sets of received messages. This mapping is problematic because of the interplay of message re-ordering and timing constraints:

Example 5.2 Figure 6 exemplifies a problematic behavior that originates from the interplay of message re-ordering and timing constraints on message delays. In the figure we see the space-time diagram of two timed message passing runs, where first process 1 sends $\langle M, 1 \rangle$ at instant t_1, and then process 2 sends $\langle M, 2 \rangle$ at a later time $t_2 > t_1$. In the run on the left, process 3 receives $\langle M, 2 \rangle$ at instant t_3 and has not received $\langle M, 1 \rangle$ before. In the run on the right process 3 receives $\langle M, 1 \rangle$ at instant t_3. Hence, at t_3 on the left $\langle M, 1 \rangle$ is in transit, while on the right $\langle M, 2 \rangle$ is in transit, which has been sent after $\langle M, 1 \rangle$. As indicated by the τ^+ intervals, due to the invariants from Definition 4.1[3c], the left run is more restricted: On the left within one time step the clocks can be advanced by $\tau^+ - (t_3 - t_1)$ while on the right the clocks can advance further, namely, by $\tau^+ - (t_3 - t_2) > \tau^+ - (t_3 - t_1)$. Message counting timed automata abstract away the origin of the messages, and intuitively, relate the sending of the ith message to the reception of i messages, which correspond to runs where messages are received "in order", like in the run on the right. We shall formalize this below.   ◁

In the following, we exclude from the simulation relation those states where an in-transit message has been sent before a received one, and only consider so-called well-formed states where the messages are received in the *chronological* order of the sending (according to the clocks of timed automata). Indeed, we use the fact that the timing constraints of well-formed states in the message-passing system match the timing constraints in the message-counting system.

Definition 5.3 (Well-formed state). *For a message-passing timed automaton* TA^{MP} *with* $TS(TA^{MP}) = (Q, Q_0, \Delta, \lambda)$, *a state* $(s, \mu, \nu) \in Q$ *is* well-formed, *if for* *each message type* $m \in$ MT, *each process* $p \in$ Corr *that has received a message* $\langle m, p' \rangle$ *has also received all messages of type* m *sent earlier than* $\langle m, p' \rangle$:

$$\langle m, p' \rangle \in s.\text{rcvd}(p) \wedge \mu(c \langle m, p'' \rangle) > \mu(c \langle m, p' \rangle) \tag{1}$$
$$\rightarrow \langle m, p'' \rangle \in s.\text{rcvd}(p) \; for \; p', p'' \in \text{Corr}$$

Observe that because messages can be sent at precisely the same time, there can be different well-formed states s and s' with $s.\text{rcvd}(p) \neq s'.\text{rcvd}(p)$. Also, considering only well-formed states does not imply that the messages are received according to the sending order in a run (which would correspond to FIFO).

We will use a mapping WF to abstract arbitrary states of any message passing timed automaton to sets of well-formed states in the same automaton.

Definition 5.4 *Given a message-passing timed automaton* TA^{MP} *with the transition system* $TS(TA^{MP}) = (Q, Q_0, \Delta, \lambda)$, *we define a mapping* WF $: Q \rightarrow 2^Q$ *that maps an automaton state* $(s, \mu, \nu) \in Q$ *into a set of well-formed states with each* $(s', \mu', \nu') \in$ WF$((s, \mu, \nu))$ *having the following properties:*

1. $\mu' = \mu$, $\nu' = \nu$, $s'.\text{sent} = s.\text{sent}$, *and* $s.\text{pc}(p) = s'.\text{pc}(p)$ *for* $p \in$ Corr, *and*
2. $|\{q : \langle m, q \rangle \in s'.\text{rcvd}(p)\}| = |\{q : \langle m, q \rangle \in s.\text{rcvd}(p)\}|$ *for* $m \in$ MT, $p \in$ Corr.

One can show that every timed state $q \in Q$ has at least one state in WF(q):

Proposition 5.5. *Let* TA^{MP} *be a message-passing timed automaton, and* $TS(TA^{MP}) = (Q, Q_0, \Delta, \lambda)$. *For every state* $q \in Q$, *the set* WF(q) *is not empty.*

Using Proposition 5.5, one can show that the well-defined states simulate all the timed states of a message-passing timed automaton:

Theorem 5.6. *If* TA^{MP} *is a message-passing timed automaton, and if* $TS(TA^{MP}) = (Q, Q_0, \Delta, \lambda)$, *then* $\{(q, r) : q \in Q, r \in$ WF$(q)\}$ *is an initial timed simulation.*

Theorem 5.6 suggests that timed automata restricted to well-formed states might help us in avoiding the negative result of Theorem 5.1. To this end, we introduce a *well-formed message-passing timed automaton*. Before that, we note that Eq. (1) of Definition 5.3 can be transformed to a state invariant. We denote such a state invariant as I^{WF}.

Definition 5.7 (Well-formed MPTA). *Given a message-passing timed automaton* $TA^{MP} = (S, S_0, R, L, U \cup X, I, F)$, *its well-formed restriction* TA^{MP}_{WF} *is the timed automaton* $(S, S_0, R, L, U \cup X, I \wedge I^{WF}, E)$.

Since the well-formed states are included in the set of timed states, and the well-formed states simulate timed states (Theorem 5.6), we obtain the following:

Corollary 5.8. *Let* TA^{MP} *be a message-passing timed automaton and* TA^{MP}_{WF} *be its well-formed restriction. These timed automata are timed-simulation equivalent:* $TA^{MP} \simeq^t TA^{MP}_{WF}$.

states of a message-passing automaton   states of a message-counting automaton

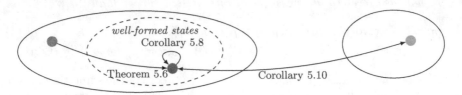

Fig. 7. Simulations constructed in Theorems 5.6–5.10. Small circles depict states of the transition systems. An arrow from a state s to a state t illustrates that the pair (s, t) belongs to a timed simulation

As a consequence of Theorems 3.4, 5.6, and Corollary 5.8, one obtains that there is a timed bisimulation equivalence between a well-formed message-passing timed automaton and the corresponding message-counting timed automaton, which is obtained by forgetting the sender of the messages and just counting the sent and delivered messages.

Theorem 5.9. *Let TA^{MP} be a message-passing timed automaton and TA^{MC} be a message-counting timed automaton defined over the same timed system design. Further, let TA_{WF}^{MP} be the well-formed restriction of TA^{MP}. There exists an initial timed bisimulation: $TA_{WF}^{MP} \approx^t TA^{MC}$.*

By collecting Theorem 5.9 and Corollary 5.8 we conclude that there is a timed simulation equivalence between MPTA and MCTA:

Corollary 5.10. *Let TA^{MP} be a message-passing timed automaton and TA^{MC} be a message-counting timed automaton defined over the same timed system design. TA^{MP} and TA^{MC} are timed-simulation equivalent: $TA^{MP} \simeq^t TA^{MC}$.*

Figure 7 uses arrows to depict the timed simulations presented in this work.

6   Conclusions

Asynchronous Systems. For systems considered in Sect. 3, we conclude from Theorem 3.4 that message-counting systems are detailed enough for model checking of properties written in CTL*:

Corollary 6.1. *For a CTL* formula φ, a message-passing system TS^{MP} and a message-counting system TS^{MC} defined over the same design, $TS^{MP} \models \varphi$ if and only if $TS^{MC} \models \varphi$.*

The corollary implies that the message counting abstraction does not introduce spurious behavior. In contrast, data and counter abstractions introduced in [22] may lead to spurious behavior as only simulation relations have been shown for these abstractions.

Timed Systems. For systems considered in Sect. 4, we consider specifications in the temporal logic ATCTL [14], which restricts TCTL [6] as follows: first, negations only appear next to propositions $p \in \mathsf{AP} \cup \Psi(U)$, and second, the temporal operators are restricted to $\mathsf{AF}_{\sim c}$, $\mathsf{AG}_{\sim c}$, and $\mathsf{AU}_{\sim c}$.

To derive that message-counting timed automata are sufficiently precise for model checking of ATCTL formulas (in the following corollary), we combine the following results: (i) Simulation-equivalent systems satisfy the same formulas of ACTL, e.g. see [11, Theorem 7.76]; (ii) Reduction of TCTL model checking to CTL model checking by clock embedding [11, p. 706]; (iii) Corollary 5.10.

Corollary 6.2. *For a message-passing timed automaton TA^{MP} and a message-counting timed automaton TA^{MC} defined over the same timed design and an ATCTL-formula φ, the following holds: $TA^{MP} \models \varphi$ if and only if $TA^{MC} \models \varphi$.*

Future Work. Most of the timed specifications of interest for FTDAs (e.g., fault-tolerant clock synchronization algorithms [35,39,40]) are examples of time-bounded specifications, thus belonging to the class of timed safety specifications. These algorithms can be encoded as message-passing timed automata (Definition 4.1). In this paper, we have shown that model checking of these algorithms can also be done at the level of message-counting timed automata (Definition 4.2). Based on this it appears natural to apply the abstraction-based parameterized model checking technique from [22]. However, we are still facing the challenge of having a parameterized number of clocks in Definition 4.2. We are currently working on another abstraction that addresses this issue. This will eventually allow us to do parameterized model checking of timed fault-tolerant distributed algorithms using UPPAAL [12] as back-end model checker.

Related Work. As discussed in [23], while modeling message passing is natural for fault-tolerant distributed algorithms (FTDAs), message counting scales better for asynchronous systems, and also builds a basis for efficient parameterized model checking techniques [22,28]. We are interested in corresponding results for timed systems, that is, our long-term research goal is to build a framework for the automatic verification of timed properties of FTDAs. Such kind of properties are particularly relevant for the analysis of distributed clock synchronization protocols [35,39,40]. This investigation combines two research areas: (i) verification of FTDAs and (ii) parameterized model checking (PMC) of timed systems.

To the best of our knowledge, most of the existing literature on (i) can model only the discrete behaviors of the algorithms themselves [4,5,18,20,22,28,38]. Consequently they can neither reason about nor verify their timed properties. This motivated us to extend existing techniques for modeling and abstracting FTDAs, such as message passing and message counting systems together with the message counting abstraction, to timed systems.

Most of the results about PMC of timed systems [1–3,8–10,31,34] are restricted to systems whose interprocess communication primitives have other systems in mind than FTDAs. For instance, the local state space is fixed and finite and independent of the parameters, while message counting in FTDAs requires that the local state space depends on the parameters. This motivated us to introduce the notions of *message passing timed automata* and *message counting timed automata*. Besides, the literature typically focuses on decidability, e.g., [1,3,9,34] analyze decidability for different variants of the parameterized model checking problem (e.g., integer vs. continuous time, safety vs. liveness, presence vs. absence of controller). Our work focuses on establishing relations between different timed models, with the goal of using these relations for abstraction-based model checking.

References

1. Abdulla, P.A., Deneux, J., Mahata, P.: Multi-clock timed networks. In: LICS, pp. 345–354 (2004)
2. Abdulla, P.A., Haziza, F., Holík, L.: All for the price of few. In: Giacobazzi, R., Berdine, J., Mastroeni, I. (eds.) VMCAI 2013. LNCS, vol. 7737, pp. 476–495. Springer, Heidelberg (2013). doi:10.1007/978-3-642-35873-9_28
3. Abdulla, P.A., Jonsson, B.: Model checking of systems with many identical timed processes. Theor. Comput. Sci. **290**(1), 241–264 (2003)
4. Alberti, F., Ghilardi, S., Orsini, A., Pagani, E.: Counter abstractions in model checking of distributed broadcast algorithms: some case studies. In: CILC, pp. 102–117 (2016)
5. Alberti, F., Ghilardi, S., Pagani, E.: Counting constraints in flat array fragments. In: Olivetti, N., Tiwari, A. (eds.) IJCAR 2016. LNCS (LNAI), vol. 9706, pp. 65–81. Springer, Heidelberg (2016). doi:10.1007/978-3-319-40229-1_6
6. Alur, R., Courcoubetis, C., Dill, D.: Model-checking for real-time systems. In: LICS, pp. 414–425 (1990)
7. Alur, R., Dill, D.L.: A theory of timed automata. Theor. Comput. Sci. **126**(2), 183–235 (1994)
8. Aminof, B., Kotek, T., Rubin, S., Spegni, F., Veith, H.: Parameterized model checking of rendezvous systems. In: Baldan, P., Gorla, D. (eds.) CONCUR 2014. LNCS, vol. 8704, pp. 109–124. Springer, Heidelberg (2014). doi:10.1007/978-3-662-44584-6_9
9. Aminof, B., Rubin, S., Zuleger, F., Spegni, F.: Liveness of parameterized timed networks. In: Halldórsson, M.M., Iwama, K., Kobayashi, N., Speckmann, B. (eds.) ICALP 2015. LNCS, vol. 9135, pp. 375–387. Springer, Heidelberg (2015). doi:10.1007/978-3-662-47666-6_30
10. Außerlechner, S., Jacobs, S., Khalimov, A.: Tight cutoffs for guarded protocols with fairness. In: Jobstmann, B., Leino, K.R.M. (eds.) VMCAI 2016. LNCS, vol. 9583, pp. 476–494. Springer, Heidelberg (2016). doi:10.1007/978-3-662-49122-5_23
11. Baier, C., Katoen, J.-P.: Principles of Model Checking. MIT Press, Massachusetts (2008)
12. Behrmann, G., David, A., Larsen, K.G., Håkansson, J., Pettersson, P., Yi, W., Hendriks, M.: UPPAAL 4.0. In: QEST, pp. 125–126 (2006)
13. Bracha, G., Toueg, S.: Asynchronous consensus and broadcast protocols. J. ACM **32**(4), 824–840 (1985)
14. Bulychev, P., Chatain, T., David, A., Larsen, K.G.: Efficient on-the-fly algorithm for checking alternating timed simulation. In: Ouaknine, J., Vaandrager, F.W. (eds.) FORMATS 2009. LNCS, vol. 5813, pp. 73–87. Springer, Heidelberg (2009). doi:10.1007/978-3-642-04368-0_8

15. Čerāns, K.: Decidability of bisimulation equivalences for parallel timer processes. In: Bochmann, G., Probst, D.K. (eds.) CAV 1992. LNCS, vol. 663, pp. 302–315. Springer, Heidelberg (1993). doi:10.1007/3-540-56496-9_24

16. Clarke, E., Grumberg, O., Peled, D.: Model Checking. MIT Press, Massachusetts (1999)

17. Clarke, E., Grumberg, O., Jha, S., Lu, Y., Veith, H.: Counterexample-guided abstraction refinement for symbolic model checking. J. ACM **50**(5), 752–794 (2003)

18. Drăgoi, C., Henzinger, T.A., Veith, H., Widder, J., Zufferey, D.: A logic-based framework for verifying consensus algorithms. In: McMillan, K.L., Rival, X. (eds.) VMCAI 2014. LNCS, vol. 8318, pp. 161–181. Springer, Heidelberg (2014). doi:10.1007/978-3-642-54013-4_10

19. Fischer, M.J., Lynch, N.A., Paterson, M.S.: Impossibility of distributed consensus with one faulty process. J. ACM **32**(2), 374–382 (1985)

20. Fisman, D., Kupferman, O., Lustig, Y.: On verifying fault tolerance of distributed protocols. In: Ramakrishnan, C.R., Rehof, J. (eds.) TACAS 2008. LNCS, vol. 4963, pp. 315–331. Springer, Heidelberg (2008). doi:10.1007/978-3-540-78800-3_22

21. Függer, M., Schmid, U.: Reconciling fault-tolerant distributed computing and systems-on-chip. Distrib. Comput. **24**(6), 323–355 (2012)

22. John, A., Konnov, I., Schmid, U., Veith, H., Widder, J.: Parameterized model checking of fault-tolerant distributed algorithms by abstraction. In: FMCAD, pp. 201–209 (2013)

23. John, A., Konnov, I., Schmid, U., Veith, H., Widder, J.: Towards modeling and model checking fault-tolerant distributed algorithms. In: Bartocci, E., Ramakrishnan, C.R. (eds.) SPIN 2013. LNCS, vol. 7976, pp. 209–226. Springer, Heidelberg (2013). doi:10.1007/978-3-642-39176-7_14

24. Kaynar, D.K., Lynch, N.A., Segala, R., Vaandrager, F.W.: The Theory of Timed I/O Automata. Morgan & Claypool Publishers, San Rafael (2006)

25. Konnov, I., Lazić, M., Veith, H., Widder, J.: A short counterexample property for safety and liveness verification of fault-tolerant distributed algorithms. In: POPL 2017. (to appear, preliminary version at arXiv:1608.05327)

26. Konnov, I., Veith, H., Widder, J.: On the completeness of bounded model checking for threshold-based distributed algorithms: reachability. In: Baldan, P., Gorla, D. (eds.) CONCUR 2014. LNCS, vol. 8704, pp. 125–140. Springer, Heidelberg (2014). doi:10.1007/978-3-662-44584-6_10

27. Konnov, I., Veith, H., Widder, J.: SMT and POR beat counter abstraction: parameterized model checking of threshold-based distributed algorithms. In: Kroening, D., Păsăreanu, C.S. (eds.) CAV 2015. LNCS, vol. 9206, pp. 85–102. Springer, Heidelberg (2015). doi:10.1007/978-3-319-21690-4_6

28. Konnov, I., Veith, H., Widder, J.: What you always wanted to know about model checking of fault-tolerant distributed algorithms. In: Mazzara, M., Voronkov, A. (eds.) PSI 2015. LNCS, vol. 9609, pp. 6–21. Springer, Heidelberg (2010). doi:10.1007/978-3-319-41579-6_2

29. Lynch, N., Vaandrager, F.: Forward and backward simulations for timing-based systems. In: Bakker, J.W., Huizing, C., Roever, W.P., Rozenberg, G. (eds.) REX 1991. LNCS, vol. 600, pp. 397–446. Springer, Heidelberg (1992). doi:10.1007/BFb0032002

30. Mostéfaoui, A., Mourgaya, E., Parvédy, P.R., Raynal, M.: Evaluating the condition-based approach to solve consensus. In: DSN, pp. 541–550 (2003)

31. Namjoshi, K.S., Trefler, R.J.: Uncovering symmetries in irregular process networks. In: Giacobazzi, R., Berdine, J., Mastroeni, I. (eds.) VMCAI 2013. LNCS, vol. 7737, pp. 496–514. Springer, Heidelberg (2013). doi:10.1007/978-3-642-35873-9_29

32. Pease, M., Shostak, R., Lamport, L.: Reaching agreement in the presence of faults. J. ACM **27**(2), 228–234 (1980)

33. Song, Y.J., Renesse, R.: Bosco: one-step byzantine asynchronous consensus. In: Taubenfeld, G. (ed.) DISC 2008. LNCS, vol. 5218, pp. 438–450. Springer, Heidelberg (2008). doi:10.1007/978-3-540-87779-0_30

34. Spalazzi, L., Spegni, F.: Parameterized model-checking of timed systems with conjunctive guards. In: Giannakopoulou, D., Kroening, D. (eds.) VSTTE 2014. LNCS, vol. 8471, pp. 235–251. Springer, Heidelberg (2014). doi:10.1007/978-3-319-12154-3_15

35. Srikanth, T.K., Toueg, S.: Optimal clock synchronization. J. ACM **34**(3), 626–645 (1987)

36. Srikanth, T.K., Toueg, S.: Simulating authenticated broadcasts to derive simple fault-tolerant algorithms. Distrib. Comput. **2**, 80–94 (1987)

37. Tripakis, S., Yovine, S.: Analysis of timed systems using time-abstracting bisimulations. FMSD **18**, 25–68 (2001)

38. Tsuchiya, T., Schiper, A.: Verification of consensus algorithms using satisfiability solving. Distrib. Comput. **23**(5–6), 341–358 (2011)

39. Widder, J., Schmid, U.: Booting clock synchronization in partially synchronous systems with hybrid process and link failures. Distrib. Comput. **20**(2), 115–140 (2007)

40. Widder, J., Schmid, U.: The theta-model: achieving synchrony without clocks. Distrib. Comput. **22**(1), 29–47 (2009)

Efficient Elimination of Redundancies
in Polyhedra by Raytracing

Alexandre Maréchal$^{(\boxtimes)}$ and Michaël Périn

Université Grenoble-Alpes, VERIMAG, 38000 Grenoble, France
{alex.marechal,michael.perin}@imag.fr

Abstract. A polyhedron can be represented as constraints, generators or both in the double description framework. Whatever the representation, most polyhedral operators spend a significant amount of time to maintain minimal representations. To minimize a polyhedron in constraints-only representation, the redundancy of each constraint must be checked with respect to others by solving a linear programming (LP) problem. We present an algorithm that replaces most LP problem resolutions by distance computations. It consists in launching rays starting from a point within the polyhedron and orthogonal to its bounding hyperplanes. A face first encountered by one of these rays is an irredundant constraint of the polyhedron. Since this procedure is incomplete, LP problem resolutions are required for the remaining undetermined constraints. Experiments show that our algorithm drastically reduces the number of calls to the simplex, resulting in a considerable speed improvement. To follow the geometric interpretation, the algorithm is explained in terms of constraints but it can also be used to minimize generators.

1 Redundancy in Polyhedra

Convex polyhedra are used in static analysis [2] and automatic parallelization [6] to capture linear inequalities of the form $\sum_{i=1}^{n} a_i x_i \leq b$ relating the program variables $x_1, \ldots, x_n$.[1] A polyhedron $\mathscr{P}$ can be defined as the set of points $\boldsymbol{x} = (x_1, \ldots, x_n)$ that satisfy a system of inequalities $\boldsymbol{Ax} \leq \boldsymbol{b}$. The ℓth row of the augmented matrix $[\boldsymbol{A}| - \boldsymbol{b}]$ is a vector $\boldsymbol{C_\ell} = (a_{\ell 1}, \ldots, a_{\ell n}, -b_\ell)$ which encodes the constraint $\sum_{i=1}^{n} a_{\ell i} x_i \leq b_\ell$. A constraint $\boldsymbol{C_\ell}$ defines the bounding hyperplane normal to $(a_{\ell 1}, \ldots, a_{\ell n})$ and shifted by b_ℓ (see Fig. 1). Alternatively the same set of points can be defined as the convex combination of generators (vertices and rays), *i.e.* $\{\boldsymbol{x} \mid \boldsymbol{x} = \sum_{i=1}^{v} \beta_i \boldsymbol{v_i} + \sum_{i=1}^{r} \lambda_i \boldsymbol{R_i}, \ \beta_i, \lambda_i \geq 0, \ \sum \beta_i = 1\}$ where $\boldsymbol{R_i}$'s and $\boldsymbol{v_i}$'s denote respectively rays and vertices. Figure 1 shows two polyhedra $\mathscr{P}_a$ and $\mathscr{P}_b$ defined in double description as the set of constraints $\{C_1 : x_2 - x_1 \leq 1, \ C_2 : x_2 - x_1 \geq -2, \ C_3 : x_1 \geq 1, \ C_4 : x_1 + x_2 \geq 2\}$ and the set of

---

This work was partially supported by the European Research Council under the European Union's Seventh Framework Programme (FP/2007-2013)/ERC Grant Agreement nr. 306595 "STATOR".

[1] We only deal with convex polyhedra. For readability, we will omit the adjective *convex* in the following.

© Springer International Publishing AG 2017
A. Bouajjani and D. Monniaux (Eds.): VMCAI 2017, LNCS 10145, pp. 367–385, 2017.
DOI: 10.1007/978-3-319-52234-0_20

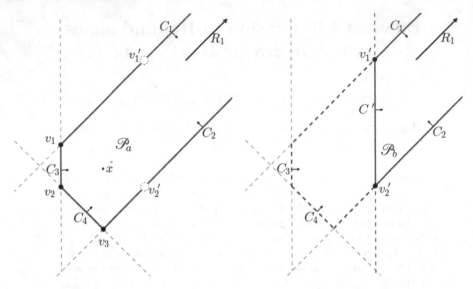

Fig. 1. Emergence of redundant constraints and generators in polyhedra.

generators $\{\boldsymbol{v_1}:(1,2),\ \boldsymbol{v_2}:(1,1),\ \boldsymbol{v_3}:(2,0),\ \boldsymbol{R_1}:(1,1)\}$ for $\mathscr{P}_a$; respectively as $\{\boldsymbol{C_1},\boldsymbol{C_2},\boldsymbol{C'}:x_1\geq 3\}$ and $\{\boldsymbol{v_1'}:(3,4),\ \boldsymbol{v_2'}:(3,1),\ \boldsymbol{R_1}\}$ for $\mathscr{P}_b$.

The addition of new constraints or generators introduces redundancies which must be removed to reduce memory consumption and avoid useless computations in subsequent operations. In constraints-only representation, redundant constraints tend to grow exponentially during the computation of a projection by Fourier-Motzkin elimination [18]. For a description by generators the same pitfall occurs when a polyhedron is sliced with a constraint [8]. The emergence of redundancies is illustrated by Fig. 1: when constraint $\boldsymbol{C'}$ is added into $\mathscr{P}_a$ to form $\mathscr{P}_b$, constraints $\boldsymbol{C_3}$ and $\boldsymbol{C_4}$ become redundant. Conversely, the addition of points $\boldsymbol{v_1},\boldsymbol{v_2},\boldsymbol{v_3}$ into $\mathscr{P}_b$ generates $\mathscr{P}_a$ and makes $\boldsymbol{v_1'}$ and $\boldsymbol{v_2'}$ redundant.

Characterization of Redundancy. A ray $\boldsymbol{R_k}$ is redundant if it is a nonnegative combination of the other rays and a point $\boldsymbol{v_k}$ is redundant if it is a convex combination of the other generators, *i.e.* $\boldsymbol{v_k} = \sum_i \beta_i \boldsymbol{v_i} + \sum_i \lambda_i \boldsymbol{R_i}$ for some $\beta_i, \lambda_i \geq 0$ with $\sum \beta_i = 1$ and $\beta_k = 0$. Back to our running example, the equations $\boldsymbol{v_1'} = 1 \times \boldsymbol{v_1} + 2 \times \boldsymbol{R_1}$ and $\boldsymbol{v_2'} = 1 \times \boldsymbol{v_3} + 1 \times \boldsymbol{R_1}$ prove the redundancy of $\boldsymbol{v_1'}$ and $\boldsymbol{v_2'}$ in $\mathscr{P}_a$. Therefore, these equations account for *certificates of redundancy*.

Intuitively, a constraint is redundant if it is useless, in the sense that adding it does not change the geometrical space delimited by the polyhedron. Formally, a constraint $\boldsymbol{C_k}$ is redundant if it is a nonnegative combination of other constraints. As we did for generators, we can find equations that prove the redundancy of $\boldsymbol{C_3}$ and $\boldsymbol{C_4}$ in $\mathscr{P}_b$, but we need to consider the tautological constraint $\boldsymbol{C_0}:1 \geq 0$ as being part of the system in order to exactly fit the constant b of the redundant constraint.

Example 1. The equations $C_3 = 1 \times C' \oplus 2 \times C_0$ and $C_4 = 2 \times C' \oplus 1 \times C_2 \oplus 2 \times C_0$ are called *the Farkas decomposition* of C_3 and C_4. They act as certificates of redundancy. Indeed, $C_3 : x_1 \geq 1 \equiv (x_1 \geq 3) \oplus 2 \times (1 \geq 0)$ and $C_4 : x_1 + x_2 \geq 2 \equiv 2 \times (x_1 \geq 3) \oplus (x_2 - x_1 \geq -2) \oplus 2 \times (1 \geq 0)$ where $(l \geq r) \oplus (l' \geq r') \overset{def}{=} l + l' \geq r + r'$.

If only one representation is available – as generators or as constraints – discovering redundancy requires solving linear programming (LP) problems of the form "does there exist nonnegative scalars satisfying some linear equations?":

$$\exists \lambda_0, \ldots, \lambda_p \geq 0, \ C_k = \sum_{i=0, i \neq k}^{p} \lambda_i C_i \qquad \text{(1) for constraints}$$

$$\exists \lambda_1, \ldots, \lambda_r \geq 0, \ R_k = \sum_{i=1, i \neq k}^{r} \lambda_i R_i \qquad \text{(2) for rays}$$

$$\exists \beta_1, \ldots, \beta_v, \lambda_1, \ldots, \lambda_r \geq 0, \ v_k = \sum_{i=1, i \neq k}^{v} \beta_i v_i + \sum_{i=1}^{r} \lambda_i R_i \quad \text{(3) for vertices}$$

$$\wedge \sum_{i=1, i \neq k}^{v} \beta_i = 1$$

Polyhedral Cones. The way to reconcile the two definitions of redundancy is to switch to *polyhedral cones* to get a homogeneous system of constraints and only rays as generators. The trick for changing a polyhedron $\mathscr{P}$ into a cone is to associate an extra variable η to the constant term b as follows [19]: $Ax \leq b \equiv$

$$\eta(Ax) \leq \eta b \equiv A(\eta x) - \eta b \leq 0 \equiv [A| - b] \begin{pmatrix} \eta x \\ \eta \end{pmatrix} \leq 0 \text{ for any } \eta > 0. \text{ It can be}$$

proved [9] that $x \in \mathbb{Q}^n$ belongs to $\mathscr{P}$ if and only if $\begin{pmatrix} x \\ 1 \end{pmatrix} \in \mathbb{Q}^{n+1}$ belongs to the cone $\{ x' \in \mathbb{Q}^{n+1} \mid A'x' \leq 0 \}$ where $A' = [A| - b]$. Using this transformation, operators on polyhedra can be implemented as computations on their associated cones producing a cone that, once intersected with the hyperplane $\eta = 1$, is the expected polyhedron. We switch back to polyhedra in illustrations as they are easier to draw. Considering cones simplifies the presentation: the constant term of constraints and the vertices disappear from definitions. Then, we end up with the same definition of redundancy for constraints (1) and for generators (2): a vector is redundant if it is a nonnegative combination of the others vectors.

Deciding Redundancy. The redundant/irredundant status of a constraint or a ray depends on the satisfiability of an existential problem *(1, 2)* involving linear equations but also inequalities ($\bigwedge_i \lambda_i \geq 0$). Thus, such a problem does not fall within the realm of linear algebra but in that of LP for which the simplex algorithm is a standard solver [5]. In practice, the simplex performs much better than its theoretical exponential complexity – but still remains a costly algorithm. So, much research has been devoted to identifying many cases where the simplex can be avoided. Wilde [19] and Lassez *et al.* [13] suggest several *fast redundancy-detection criteria* before switching to the general LP problem:

- **The quasi-syntactic redundancy test** considers pairs of constraints and looks for single constraint redundancies of the form $C' = \lambda C$ with $\lambda > 0$, e.g. $C' : 4x_1 - 6x_2 \geq 2$ is redundant with respect to $C : x_1 - 3x_2 \geq 1$ since $C' = 2 \times C$.
- **The bound shifting test** exploits the implication $\sum_{i=1}^{n} a_i x_i \leq b \implies \sum_{i=1}^{n} a_i x_i \leq b'$ if $b \leq b'$. Hence, when the coefficients of two constraints C and C' only differ on b and b' with $b \leq b'$ then C' is redundant and the certificate is $C' = C \oplus (b' - b) \times C_0$ where C_0 is the tautology $0 \leq 1$.
- **The combination of single variable inequalities** such as $x_1 \leq b_1$ and $x_2 \leq b_2$ entails for instance the redundancy of $C : 2x_1 + 3x_2 \leq b$ with $2b_1 + 3b_2 < b$. The corresponding certificate is $C = 2 \times (x_1 \leq b_1) \oplus 3 \times (x_2 \leq b_2) \oplus (2b_1 + 3b_2 - b) \times (0 \leq 1)$.

While these criteria can detect certain redundancies at low-cost, in this paper we investigate the other side of redundancy: we provide a *fast criterion to detect irredundant constraints*. The combination of the two approaches limits the usage of the simplex to constraints that are neither decided by our criteria nor by those of Wilde and Lassez *et al.*

Contributions. We present an algorithm that replaces most LP problem resolutions by distance computations. It is detailed in Sect. 4, after introducing useful notations in Sect. 2. The geometric intuition of our irredundancy criterion is simple: consider ray traces starting from a point within the polyhedron and orthogonal to its bounding hyperplanes. The hyperplane first encountered by one of these rays is an actual face of the polyhedron. It is therefore an irredundant constraint. Since this procedure is incomplete, LP problem resolutions are required for the remaining undetermined constraints. Experiments of Sect. 5 show that our algorithm drastically reduces the number of calls to the simplex, resulting in a considerable speed improvement. In addition, our algorithm generates certificates of correctness, precision and minimality which make it usable in a certified static analyzer. Certificates are presented in Sect. 3. To follow the geometric interpretation, the algorithm is explained below in terms of constraints but it can similarly be used to minimize generators. We conclude in Sect. 6 by a discussion of the potential benefit of integrating our algorithm in the double description framework.

2   Notations

Vectors and matrices are written in boldface to be distinguished from scalars, e.g. $\mathbf{0}$ is a vector of 0. For clarity and without loss of generality the rest of the paper will focus on *polyhedral cones over rationals*. A polyhedral cone $\mathcal{P}$ of p constraints on n variables $(x_1, \ldots, x_n)$ is a conjunction (written as a set) of homogeneous linear constraints $\{C_1, \ldots, C_p\}$ of the form $C_\ell : \sum_{i=1}^{n} a_{\ell i} x_i \leq 0$ where $C_\ell = (a_{\ell 1}, \ldots, a_{\ell n})$. The inner product of vectors offers a convenient notation $\langle C_\ell, x \rangle \leq 0$ for that inequality. Then, the cone $\mathcal{P}$ corresponds to a matrix inequality $Ax \leq 0$ where the rows of A are the vectors $C_1, \ldots, C_p$.

Finally, $\{C_1, \ldots, C_p\}$, $\bigwedge_{\ell=1}^{p} \langle C_\ell, x \rangle \leq 0$ or $Ax \leq 0$ are three equivalent ways of denoting a polyhedral cone $\mathcal{P}$. We use $[\![\mathcal{P}]\!]$ to specifically refer to the set of points defined by $\mathcal{P}$. Given a cone $\mathcal{P} : Ax \leq 0$, the same system with a strict inequality defines $\overset{\circ}{\mathcal{P}}$, *the interior of* $\mathcal{P}$, and $\overset{\circ}{x}$ denotes a point of $[\![\overset{\circ}{\mathcal{P}}]\!] \overset{def}{=} \{x \mid Ax < 0\}$.

3   Certifying a Minimization of Polyhedra

Our minimization algorithm is part of the Verimag Polyhedra Library (VPL) which operates on rational polyhedra in constraints-only representation. It was originally designed by Fouilhé *et al.* [7] as an abstract domain for the VERASCO certified static analyzer whose soundness is proved in COQ [12]. VERASCO can collaborate with an external library in OCAML such as the VPL, provided that it produces certificates of correctness, allowing a COQ-checker to verify the results computed in OCAML. In this section we recall the algorithm used in the original VPL for minimizing a *polyhedral cone represented as a set of constraints*. It is the standard algorithm but extended to produce on-the-fly *certificates of correctness, precision and minimality*. We recall the *fundamental theorem of linear inequalities* due to Farkas (1894) which ensures the existence of such certificates. Revisiting this theorem with a geometrical interpretation reveals an efficient way to determine irredundant constraints, which will be the key of our algorithm (Sect. 4).

Minimizing a cone $\mathcal{P}$ consists in removing all redundant constraints such that the result, $\mathcal{P}_M$, represents the same geometrical space, *i.e.* $[\![\mathcal{P}]\!] = [\![\mathcal{P}_M]\!]$. Two certificates are needed to prove that equality: (1) one for the inclusion $[\![\mathcal{P}]\!] \subseteq [\![\mathcal{P}_M]\!]$ which guarantees *the correctness of the minimization* and (2) another one for $[\![\mathcal{P}_M]\!] \subseteq [\![\mathcal{P}]\!]$ which justifies its *precision*. A third certificate (3) ensures *the minimality of the result* showing that all constraints of $\mathcal{P}_M$ are irredundant.

Certificate (1) must prove that each point of $[\![\mathcal{P}]\!]$ belongs to $[\![\mathcal{P}_M]\!]$. In the particular case of minimization, inclusion (1) is trivial because $\mathcal{P}_M$ is obtained by only removing constraints from $\mathcal{P}$, which necessarily leads to a larger set of points. By contrast, the existence of certificates (2) and (3) is not straightforward but the consequence of the following theorem, which we rephrased in our constraint terminology to ease its interpretation.

Theorem 1 (Fundamental theorem of linear inequalities [17, 7.1 p. 85]**).** *Let* $C_1, \ldots, C_p$ *and* C' *be vectors in a n-dimensional space. Then,*

(I) either C' *is redundant and there exists a Farkas decomposition of* C' *that is a nonnegative linear combination of linearly independent vectors from* $C_1, \ldots, C_p$, *i.e.* $C' = \lambda_1 C_1 + \ldots + \lambda_p C_p$ *for some scalars* $\lambda_1, \ldots, \lambda_p \geq 0$.
(II) or C' *is irredundant and there exists a n-dimensional vector* w *such that* $\langle C', w \rangle > 0$ *and* $\langle C_1, w \rangle, \ldots, \langle C_p, w \rangle \leq 0$.

The standard algorithm (Algorithm 1) exploits the redundancy criterion (I) of the theorem which was already illustrated in Sect. 1 Example 1. The existence of a *Farkas decomposition* of C' is decided by solving a LP problem. If the simplex algorithm returns a solution $\boldsymbol{\lambda}$ then the pair $(\boldsymbol{C'}, \boldsymbol{\lambda})$ is recorded as a *certificate of precision* (2) which proves that the removed constraint was indeed redundant. To get rid of all the redundancies, Algorithm 1 needs one execution of the simplex algorithm for each constraint.

Given an existential LP problem, the simplex can return either a solution or an explanation of the lack of solution. The proof of Theorem 1 and the simplex algorithm have strong connections which result in an interesting feature of the VPL simplex: calling $\mathsf{simplex}(\exists \lambda_i \geq 0,\ \boldsymbol{C'} = \sum_i \lambda_i \boldsymbol{C_i})$ returns either SUCCESS$(\boldsymbol{\lambda})$ or FAILURE$(\boldsymbol{w})$ such that $\langle \boldsymbol{C'}, \boldsymbol{w} \rangle > 0 \bigwedge_i \langle \boldsymbol{C_i}, \boldsymbol{w} \rangle \leq 0$.[2] This feature is a consequence of Theorem 1 and requires no additional computation.

When the simplex returns FAILURE$(\boldsymbol{w})$, the irredundancy criterion (II) of the theorem tells that $\boldsymbol{C'}$ is irredundant and must be kept in the set of constraints. Algorithm 1 builds the *certificate of minimality* (3) by associating a *witness point* to each constraint of the minimized polyhedron $\mathcal{P}_M$.

While the standard algorithm focuses on criterion (I), we revisit the theorem paying attention to the geometrical interpretation of criterion (II): when a constraint $\boldsymbol{C'}$ is irredundant, its associated bounding hyperplane is *a frontier* of the polyhedron separating the inside from the outside. Part (II) of the theorem ensures that we can exhibit a witness point $\boldsymbol{w}$, outside of $[\![\mathcal{P}]\!]$, satisfying all constraints of $\mathcal{P}$ except $\boldsymbol{C'}$. The rest of the paper is dedicated to an algorithm that efficiently discovers such witness points.

Algorithm 1. The standard minimization algorithm (used in VPL 1.0)

Input   : A set of constraints $\{C_1, \ldots, C_p\}$.
Output: $\mathcal{P}_M$ = the irredundant constraints of $\{C_1, \ldots, C_p\}$
          (R, I) = the redundancy and irredundancy certificates

$\mathcal{P}_M \leftarrow \{C_1, \ldots, C_p\}$
for C' *in* $\{C_1, \ldots, C_p\}$ **do**

  switch $\mathsf{simplex}\left(\exists \lambda_i \geq 0,\ C' = \displaystyle\sum_{C_i \in \mathcal{P}_M \backslash C'} \lambda_i C_i\right)$ **do**

    case SUCCESS $(\boldsymbol{\lambda})$: $R \leftarrow R \cup \{(C', \boldsymbol{\lambda})\}$; $\mathcal{P}_M \leftarrow \mathcal{P}_M \backslash C'$
    case FAILURE $(\boldsymbol{w})$: $I \leftarrow I \cup \{(C', \boldsymbol{w})\}$

return $(\mathcal{P}_M, R, I)$

---

4   An Efficient Minimization Algorithm

Building up on the geometric interpretation of Theorem 1, we present a new minimization algorithm for polyhedral cones that brings two major improvements: it reduces the number of calls to the simplex algorithm and limits the constraints they involve. The key idea of the algorithm is to trace rays starting from a point

---

[2] Conversely, $\mathsf{simplex}(\exists \boldsymbol{w}, \langle \boldsymbol{C'}, \boldsymbol{w} \rangle > 0 \bigwedge_i \langle \boldsymbol{C_i}, \boldsymbol{w} \rangle \leq 0)$ returns either SUCCESS$(\boldsymbol{w})$ or FAILURE$(\boldsymbol{\lambda})$ such that $\boldsymbol{C'} = \sum_i \lambda_i \boldsymbol{C_i}$.

in the interior of the cone. The first hyperplane encountered by a ray is a frontier of the polyhedron, thus an irredundant constraint. Unfortunately, with a limited number of rays, some frontiers can be missed depending on the cone and the position of the interior point. This *raytracing procedure* is thus incomplete and LP problem resolutions are still required for the remaining undetermined constraints.

While the simplex algorithm is used in the standard minimization to discover Farkas decompositions, we rather use it to get closer to a witness point, and only when all previous rays failed to prove the irredundancy of a constraint. Of course, if the constraint is redundant, the simplex algorithm returns no point at all but an explanation of its failure which is nothing else than a Farkas decomposition proving the redundancy.

4.1 The Frontier Detection Criterion

We now detail the process of finding witness points by raytracing. We consider a cone $\mathcal{P}$ with a nonempty interior. Then, there exists a point $\mathring{x}$ in $\mathring{\mathcal{P}}$. The basic operation of our algorithm consists in sorting the constraints of $\mathcal{P}$ with respect to the order in which they are hit by a *ray*, *i.e.* a half-line starting at the interior point $\mathring{x}$ and extending along a given direction d.

Consider the constraint $\langle C, x \rangle \leq 0$. The hyperplane of the constraint is $\{x \mid \langle C, x \rangle = 0\}$, *i.e.* the set of points orthogonal to vector C. The ray starting at $\mathring{x}$ and extending in direction d is the set of points $\{x(t) \mid x(t) = \mathring{x} + t \times d, \ t \geq 0\}$. Let us assume that the ray hits the C-hyperplane at point x_c. Then, there exists $t_c \geq 0$ such that $x_c = \mathring{x} + t_c \times d$ and so, $x_c - \mathring{x} = t_c \times d$. Therefore, the distance $\|\mathring{x} - x_c\|$ is just a scaling by $|t_c|$ of the norm $\|d\|$ which does not depend on C. Hence, *by computing $|t_c|$ for each constraint we will be able to know in which order the constraints are hit by the ray.* Prior to computing t_c we check if the ray can hit the constraint, *i.e.* $\langle C, d \rangle \neq 0$. Then, we use the fact that $x_c \in \{x \mid \langle C, x \rangle = 0\}$ to get $t_c = -\frac{\langle C, \mathring{x} \rangle}{\langle C, d \rangle}$. Indeed,

$$0 = \langle C, x_c \rangle = \langle C, \mathring{x} + t_c \times d \rangle = \langle C, \mathring{x} \rangle + t_c \times \langle C, d \rangle.$$

Hence, the basic operation of our raytracing algorithm consists in two evaluations of each constraint C of $\mathcal{P}$ at $\mathring{x}$ and d in order to compute the scalar t_c. Let us explain how we exploit this information to discover actual frontiers of $\mathcal{P}$.

Note that any direction could be used to sort the constraints with respect to the order of intersection by a ray. We choose successively for d the opposite direction of the normal vector of each bounding hyperplane of $\mathcal{P}$. This heuristic ensures that each hyperplane will be hit by at least one ray. As illustrated by Fig. 2, a direction $d \overset{def}{=} -C$ necessarily intersects the C-hyperplane and may potentially cross many other constraints for some values of t. Considering a direction $d_i = -C_i$, we sort the intersected hyperplanes with respect to the increasing order of the scalar t, which is proportional to the distance between the interior point $\mathring{x}$ and the intersection point $x(t)$ of an hyperplane and the ray RAY$(\mathring{x}, d_i)$. We obtain a sorted *intersection list* of pairs (t, S_t) where S_t is the

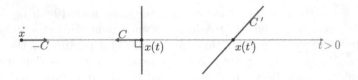

Fig. 2. The ray starting at the interior point $\mathring{x}$ and orthogonal to a constraint C meets C and possibly others constraints.

set of the (possibly many) constraints vanishing at $x(t)$. If a constraint C is not hit by the ray (because $\langle C, d_i \rangle = 0$), then C is not added to the intersection list. The head pair provides the constraints which are encountered first by the ray. At the heart of our algorithm is the following proposition: "If the head of an intersection list is a pair $(t, \{C\})$ with *a single constraint*, then C is a frontier of $\mathcal{P}$; otherwise we cannot conclude from this list." This will be proved in Sect. 4.2 (Proposition 1) when we will come to the generation of witness points.

Example 2. Here are the sorted intersection lists obtained for the 6-constraints polyhedron of Fig. 3. The list I_i records the constraints met along $\mathrm{RAY}(\mathring{x}, -C_i)$ from $\mathring{x}$ orthogonally to the hyperplane of C_i. It satisfies $t_i < t'_i < t''_i < t'''_i$.

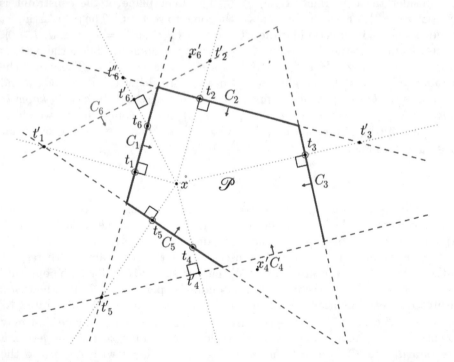

Fig. 3. Detection of some frontiers of a polyhedron by looking at their intersections with rays starting from an interior point $\mathring{x}$ and orthogonal to a constraint. The thick lines are the discovered frontiers, confirmed by the doubly-circled intersection points.

$$I_1 = [\ (t_1, \{C_1\});\ (t'_1, \{C_5, C_6\});\ (t''_1, \{C_2\})\ ]$$
$$I_2 = [\ (t_2, \{C_2\});\ (t'_2, \{C_6\});\ (t''_2, \{C_3\});\ (t'''_2, \{C_1\})\ ]$$
$$I_3 = [\ (t_3, \{C_3\});\ (t'_3, \{C_2\});\ (t''_3, \{C_4\})\ ]\quad I_4 = [\ (t_4, \{C_5\});\ (t'_4, \{C_4\});\ (t''_4, \{C_3\})\ ]$$
$$I_5 = [\ (t_5, \{C_5\});\ (t'_5, \{C_1, C_4\})\ ]\qquad\qquad I_6 = [\ (t_6, \{C_1\});\ (t'_6, \{C_6\});\ (t''_6, \{C_2\})\ ]$$

These lists reveal that C_1, C_2, C_3 and C_5 are frontiers of $\mathcal{P}$; C_1 and C_5 are even confirmed twice. Our criterion fails to decide the status of C_4 and C_6 because, in any of the considered directions, they are never encountered first. This situation is legitimate for the redundant constraint C_6 but also happens for C_4 even if it is a frontier of $\mathcal{P}$.

At this point (line 10 of Algorithm 2), we run the simplex to determine the irredundancy of the remaining constraints. In order to keep LP problems as small as possible, we build them incrementally as follows. Consider an unde-termined constraint C_i and let I_i be the intersection list resulting from the direction $d_i = -C_i$. We pose a LP problem to find a point x'_i satisfying $\langle C_i, x'_i \rangle > 0 \wedge \langle C', x'_i \rangle \leq 0$, where C' is the single constraint that appears at the head of I_i. As said earlier, C' is a frontier because it is the first hyper-plane encountered by the ray. We illustrate the algorithm on the case of a single head constraint as it is the most frequent one. If the head set contains several constraints we cannot know which one is a frontier, thus we add all of them in the LP problem (lines 13-14 of Algorithm 2). We distinguish two cases depending on the satisfiability of the existential LP problem: If the problem of line 15 is unsatisfiable, the simplex returns FAILURE(λ), C_i is redundant with respect to C' and the Farkas decomposition of C_i is $\lambda \times C'$. Otherwise, the simplex exhibits a point x'_i which satisfies $\langle C_i, x'_i \rangle > 0 \wedge \langle C', x'_i \rangle \leq 0$. Here, we cannot conclude on C_i's redundancy since x'_i is a witness showing that C_i is irredundant with respect to C' alone, but C_i could still be redundant with respect to the other constraints.

To check the irredundancy of C_i, we launch a new ray RAY($\mathring{x}, x'_i - \mathring{x}$) from $\mathring{x}$ to x'_i in direction $d = x'_i - \mathring{x}$. As before, we compute the intersection list of this ray with all the constraints but this time we know for sure that C_i will precede C' in the list.[3] Then, we analyze the head of the list: if C_i is the *single* first element, then it is a frontier. Otherwise the first element, say C'', is added to the LP problem, which is now asked for a point x''_i such that $\langle C_i, x''_i \rangle > 0 \wedge \langle C', x''_i \rangle \leq 0 \wedge \langle C'', x''_i \rangle \leq 0$ resulting in a new RAY($\mathring{x}, x''_i - \mathring{x}$). The way we choose rays guarantees that the previous constraints $C', C'', \ldots$ will always be hit after C_i by the next ray. Therefore, ultimately the constraint C_i will be hit first by a ray, or it will be proved redundant. Termination is guaranteed because the first constraint struck by the new ray is either C_i and we are done, or a not already considered constraint and there is a finite number of constraints in $\mathcal{P}$. Observe that this algorithm builds incremental LP problems which contain only frontiers that were between $\mathring{x}$ and the hyperplane of C_i at some step.

---

[3] As this property is a pure technicality it is not given here but is available in [15].

Example 2 (continued). In the above example, we found out that C_1, C_2, C_3 and C_5 were frontiers. To determine the status of C_4, we solve the LP problem $\exists x'_4$, $\langle C_4, x'_4 \rangle > 0 \wedge \langle C_5, x'_4 \rangle \leq 0$ because C_5 is the head of I_4. The simplex finds such a point x'_4 and the next step is to compute the intersection list corresponding to $\mathrm{RAY}(\mathring{x}, x'_4 - \mathring{x})$. This list will reveal C_4 as an actual frontier.

Similarly, the intersection list I_6 of the example suggests to solve the LP problem $\exists x'_6$, $\langle C_6, x'_6 \rangle > 0 \wedge \langle C_1, x'_6 \rangle \leq 0$ to launch a new ray toward C_6. This problem is satisfiable and the simplex returns $\mathrm{SUCCESS}(x'_6)$. Then, we compute the intersection list corresponding to $\mathrm{RAY}(\mathring{x}, x'_6 - \mathring{x})$ and this time the head of the list is C_2. We thus add C_2 to the previous LP problem and call the simplex on $\exists x''_6$, $\langle C_6, x''_6 \rangle > 0 \wedge \langle C_1, x''_6 \rangle \leq 0 \wedge \langle C_2, x''_6 \rangle \leq 0$. This problem has no solution: the simplex returns $\mathrm{FAILURE}(\boldsymbol{\lambda} = (1,1))$ showing that C_6 is redundant and its Farkas decomposition is $C_6 = 1 \times C_1 + 1 \times C_2$.

Algorithm 2. Raytracing algorithm

Input   : A set of constraints $\mathcal{P} = \{C_1, \ldots, C_p\}$; a point $\mathring{x} \in \mathring{\mathcal{P}}$
Output : $\mathcal{P}_M$: minimized version of $\mathcal{P}$
Data   : $LP[i]$: LP problem associated to C_i ; $I[i]$: intersection list of C_i
Function: $\mathtt{intersectionList}(d, \{C_1, \ldots, C_q\})$ returns the intersection list
              obtained by intersecting $\{C_1, \ldots, C_q\}$ with ray d

1 **Function** $\mathtt{updateFrontiers}$ $(I[i],\ \mathcal{P}_M,\ \mathcal{P})$
2 | **if** head $(I[i]) = (t_F, \{F\})$ **then**
3 | | $\mathcal{P}_M \leftarrow \mathcal{P}_M \cup \{F\}$
4 | | $\mathcal{P} \leftarrow \mathcal{P} \setminus F$
5 | **return** $(\mathcal{P}_M,\ \mathcal{P})$

6 $\mathcal{P}_M \leftarrow \emptyset$; $LP \leftarrow \mathtt{arrayOfSize}(p)$; $I \leftarrow \mathtt{arrayOfSize}(p)$

7 **for** C_i *in* $\mathcal{P}$ **do**   /* First step of raytracing with orthogonal rays */
8 | $I[i] \leftarrow \mathtt{intersectionList}\,(\mathrm{RAY}(\mathring{x}, -C_i), \mathcal{P})$
9 | $(\mathcal{P}_M,\ \mathcal{P}) \leftarrow \mathtt{updateFrontiers}\,(I[i], \mathcal{P}_M, \mathcal{P})$

10 **while** $\mathcal{P} \neq \emptyset$ **do**
11 | **for** C_i *in* $\mathcal{P}$ **do**
12 | | $(t, S) \leftarrow \mathtt{head}(I[i])$
13 | | **for** C *in* S **do**
14 | | | $LP[i] \leftarrow LP[i] \wedge \langle C, x'_i \rangle \leq 0$
15 | | **switch** simplex $(\exists x'_i,\ \langle C_i, x'_i \rangle > 0 \wedge LP[i])$ **do**
16 | | | **case** $\mathrm{SUCCESS}$ (x'_i):
17 | | | | $I[i] \leftarrow \mathtt{intersectionList}\,(\mathrm{RAY}(\mathring{x}, x'_i - \mathring{x}), \mathcal{P} \cup \mathcal{P}_M)$
18 | | | | $(\mathcal{P}_M,\ \mathcal{P}) \leftarrow \mathtt{updateFrontiers}\,(I[i], \mathcal{P}_M, \mathcal{P})$
19 | | | **case** $\mathrm{FAILURE}$ $(\boldsymbol{\lambda})$: $\mathcal{P} \leftarrow \mathcal{P} \setminus C_i$ /* C_i is redundant */
20 | | |

21 **return** $\mathcal{P}_M$

4.2   Irredundancy Certificates

Let us explain how we compute witness points from the intersection lists defined in the previous section. From now on, we will denote a constraint by $\boldsymbol{F}$ if it is a frontier and by $\boldsymbol{C}$ when we do not know if it is a redundant constraint or an actual frontier. Let us come back to the list of the intersections of constraints of $\mathcal{P}$ with a ray $\{\boldsymbol{x}(t) \mid \boldsymbol{x}(t) = \mathring{\boldsymbol{x}} + t \times \boldsymbol{d},\ t \geq 0\}$ for a direction $\boldsymbol{d}$.

Proposition 1. *If the head of an intersection list contains a single constraint $\boldsymbol{F}$, then we can build a* witness *point satisfying the irredundancy criterion of Theorem 1 which proves that $\boldsymbol{F}$ is a frontier:*

(a) *For a list $[(t_F, \{\boldsymbol{F}\})]$, we take the witness $\boldsymbol{w}_a = \mathring{\boldsymbol{x}} + (t_F + 1) \times \boldsymbol{d}$*
(b) *For a list $[(t_F, \{\boldsymbol{F}\}); (t', S'); \ldots]$ with at least two pairs, we define the witness $\boldsymbol{w}_b = \mathring{\boldsymbol{x}} + \frac{t_F + t'}{2} \times \boldsymbol{d}$.*

Proof. Let us prove that these witness points attest that $\boldsymbol{F}$ is an irredundant constraint. According to Theorem 1, it amounts to proving that $\bigwedge_{C \in \mathcal{P} \backslash F} \langle \boldsymbol{C}, \boldsymbol{w} \rangle \leq 0$ $\wedge \langle \boldsymbol{F}, \boldsymbol{w} \rangle > 0$ for $\boldsymbol{w}_a$ (resp. $\boldsymbol{w}_b$).

Let us first study the sign of $\langle \boldsymbol{F}, \boldsymbol{x}(t) \rangle$ at point $\boldsymbol{x}(t) = \mathring{\boldsymbol{x}} + t \times \boldsymbol{d}$. Note that $\langle \boldsymbol{F}, \boldsymbol{x}(t) \rangle = \langle \boldsymbol{F}, \mathring{\boldsymbol{x}} + t \times \boldsymbol{d} \rangle \overset{(\dagger)}{=} \langle \boldsymbol{F}, \mathring{\boldsymbol{x}} \rangle + t \times \langle \boldsymbol{F}, \boldsymbol{d} \rangle$. By construction, $\langle \boldsymbol{F}, \boldsymbol{x}(t_F) \rangle = 0$ then, by equation $(\dagger)$, $-\langle \boldsymbol{F}, \mathring{\boldsymbol{x}} \rangle = t_F \times \langle \boldsymbol{F}, \boldsymbol{d} \rangle$. Recall that $t_F \geq 0$, $\langle \boldsymbol{F}, \boldsymbol{d} \rangle \neq 0$ since the ray hits $\boldsymbol{F}$ and $\langle \boldsymbol{F}, \mathring{\boldsymbol{x}} \rangle < 0$ because $\mathring{\boldsymbol{x}} \in \mathcal{P}$. Thus, $\langle \boldsymbol{F}, \boldsymbol{d} \rangle$ and t_F are necessarily positive. Consequently, for a frontier $\boldsymbol{F}$ found in a direction $\boldsymbol{d}$, $\langle \boldsymbol{F}, \boldsymbol{x}(t) \rangle = \langle \boldsymbol{F}, \mathring{\boldsymbol{x}} \rangle + t \times \langle \boldsymbol{F}, \boldsymbol{d} \rangle$ is positive for any $t > t_F$. Hence, in case (a) $\langle \boldsymbol{F}, \boldsymbol{w}_a \rangle \overset{def}{=} \langle \boldsymbol{F}, \boldsymbol{x}(t_F + 1) \rangle > 0$ and in case (b) $\langle \boldsymbol{F}, \boldsymbol{w}_b \rangle \overset{def}{=} \langle \boldsymbol{F}, \boldsymbol{x}(\frac{t_F + t'}{2}) \rangle > 0$ since $t_F < \frac{t_F + t'}{2} < t'$.

Let us now study the sign of $\langle \boldsymbol{C}, \boldsymbol{x}(t) \rangle$ for constraints other than $\boldsymbol{F}$:

(a) Consider the list $[(t_F, \{\boldsymbol{F}\})]$. By construction, it means that no other constraint $\boldsymbol{C}$ of $\mathcal{P}$ is struck by the RAY$(\mathring{\boldsymbol{x}}, \boldsymbol{d})$, *i.e.* whatever the value $t \geq 0$, the sign of $\langle \boldsymbol{C}, \boldsymbol{x}(t) \rangle = \langle \boldsymbol{C}, \mathring{\boldsymbol{x}} \rangle + t \times \langle \boldsymbol{C}, \boldsymbol{d} \rangle$ does not change. As $\langle \boldsymbol{C}, \boldsymbol{x}(t=0) \rangle = \langle \boldsymbol{C}, \mathring{\boldsymbol{x}} \rangle < 0$ because $\mathring{\boldsymbol{x}} \in \mathcal{P}$, we can conclude that $\forall t \geq 0$, $\langle \boldsymbol{C}, \boldsymbol{x}(t) \rangle < 0$. Thus, in particular, $\langle \boldsymbol{C}, \boldsymbol{w}_a \rangle \overset{def}{=} \langle \boldsymbol{C}, \boldsymbol{x}(t_F + 1) \rangle < 0$ for any $\boldsymbol{C} \in \mathcal{P} \backslash \boldsymbol{F}$.
(b) Consider now the list $[(t_F, \{\boldsymbol{F}\}); (t', S'); \ldots]$. A constraint $\boldsymbol{C}$ that appears in the set S' vanishes at point $\boldsymbol{x}(t')$ with $t' > t_F \geq 0$. The previous reasoning $(\dagger)$ (on $\boldsymbol{F}$) based on equation $\langle \boldsymbol{C}, \boldsymbol{x}(t) \rangle = \langle \boldsymbol{C}, \mathring{\boldsymbol{x}} \rangle + t \times \langle \boldsymbol{C}, \boldsymbol{d} \rangle$ is valid for $\boldsymbol{C}$, hence proving $\langle \boldsymbol{C}, \boldsymbol{d} \rangle > 0$. Thus, $\langle \boldsymbol{C}, \boldsymbol{x}(t) \rangle$ is negative for $t < t'$ (zero for $t = t'$ and positive for $t' < t$). Finally, $\langle \boldsymbol{C}, \boldsymbol{w}_b \rangle \overset{def}{=} \langle \boldsymbol{C}, \boldsymbol{x}(\frac{t_F + t'}{2}) \rangle < 0$ since $\frac{t_F + t'}{2} < t'$. The same reasoning applies to any other pair (t, S_t) in the tail of the list.

Figure 4($\mathcal{P}_b$) shows the irredundancy witness points w_1, w_2, w_1', w_2' of constraints $\boldsymbol{C_1}, \boldsymbol{C_2}$ and $\boldsymbol{C}'$. The irredundancy of $\boldsymbol{C}'$ is confirmed three times by different rays respectively orthogonal to $\boldsymbol{C}', \boldsymbol{C_3}$ and $\boldsymbol{C_4}$, leading to witnesses w_1' (twice) and w_2'.

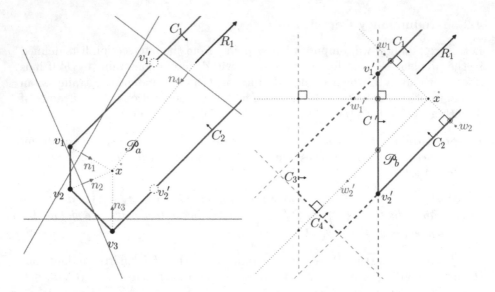

Fig. 4. Irredundancy witnesses for generators of $\mathscr{P}_a$ and constraints of $\mathscr{P}_b$.

4.3 Minimizing Generators

So far, to ease the understanding, we presented the raytracing for constraints-only polyhedra, but it works as well for generators. Indeed, we manipulated constraints as vectors and all our explanations and proofs are based on inner product. Moreover, Theorem 1 is not limited to constraints, it holds for any vector space and can be rephrased for generators. This time the irredundancy certificate for a generator g' is a vector n such that $\langle g_1, n \rangle, \ldots, \langle g_p, n \rangle \leq 0$ and $\langle g', n \rangle > 0$. Such a vector defines a hyperplane orthogonal to n, i.e. $\{x \mid \langle n, x \rangle = 0\}$. It is called a *separating hyperplane* because it isolates generator g' from the other ones. Figure 4($\mathscr{P}_a$) shows the separating hyperplanes defined by n_1, n_2, n_3 and n_4. They respectively justify the irredundancy of v_1, v_2, v_3 and R_1 in $\mathscr{P}_a$.

4.4 Using Floating Points in Raytracing

It is possible to make raytracing even more efficient by using floating points instead of rationals. Thereby, we experimented floating points in both LP problem resolutions and distance computations. The rational coefficients of constraints are translated into floating points. It introduces a loss in precision which does not jeopardize the result because the certificate checking controls the minimization process. However, we must pay attention to the generation of *exact* (*i.e.* rational) certificates from floating point computations. The solution we propose differs depending on the kind of certificate.

Witness Points. Checking a certificate of irredundancy consists in evaluating the sign of $\langle C_i, w \rangle$ for all constraints C_i of $\mathcal{P}$ with the provided witness point w.

A witness point w must then be given with rational coefficients to avoid sign errors if $\langle C_i, w \rangle$ is too close to 0. Thus, the witness point $w^{\mathbb{F}}$ obtained with floating point computations is translated into a rational one $w^{\mathbb{Q}}$, without loss of precision (each floating point $0.d_1...d_m 10^e$ is changed into a rational $\frac{d_1...d_m \cdot 10^e}{10^m}$). Then we check the irredundancy certificate with $w^{\mathbb{Q}}$ and the rational version of the constraints. If the verification passes, then $w^{\mathbb{Q}}$ is indeed a witness point. In the rare case of failure, using the exact simplex of the VPL on the LP problem will fix the approximation error by providing a rational witness point.

Farkas Decompositions. To prove a redundancy we need to exhibit the Farkas decomposition of the redundant constraint. To obtain an exact decomposition from the floating LP solution, we record which constraint is actually part of the decomposition.[4] Then, we run the exact simplex on a LP problem involving only those constraints to retrieve the exact Farkas decomposition.

5 Experiments

This section is devoted to the comparison of three minimization algorithms:

- **The Standard Minimization Algorithm** (SMA). The standard Algorithm 1 of Sect. 3 is available in the VPL since version 1.0. It works on rationals and can generate certificates of precision, minimality and correctness.
- **The Rational Raytracing Algorithm** (RRA). RRA and SMA use the same LP solver, thus comparing their running time is relevant to estimate the efficiency of raytracing with respect to the standard algorithm.
- **The Floating point Raytracing Algorithm** (FRA). FRA implements raytracing with floating points as explained in Sect. 4.4. LP problems are solved by the GNU LP Kit which provides a simplex algorithm on floating points.

These three algorithms are all implemented in the current version (2.0) of the VPL.[5] For computing the exact Farkas decomposition that proves a constraint's irredundancy, the three algorithms ultimately rely on the VPL simplex in rational. They use the same datastructures (e.g. for constraints), allowing more reliable timing comparisons between them. Moreover, they share the same preprocessing step of finding a point within the polyhedron interior. This point is obtained by solving a LP problem checking the emptiness of the polyhedron with strict inequalities. The time measurements given below include this step but not the reconstruction of exact certificates from floating point ones.

---

[4] What is needed from the floating point solution is the set of basic variables and an ordering of the nonnull λ_i coefficients to speed up the search in exact simplex.

[5] https://github.com/VERIMAG-Polyhedra.

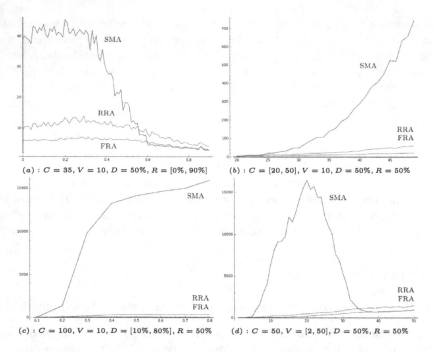

(a) : $C = 35, V = 10, D = 50\%, R = [0\%, 90\%]$

(b) : $C = [20, 50], V = 10, D = 50\%, R = 50\%$

(c) : $C = 100, V = 10, D = [10\%, 80\%], R = 50\%$

(d) : $C = 50, V = [2, 50], D = 50\%, R = 50\%$

Fig. 5. Execution time in milliseconds of SMA (blue), RRA (red) and FRA (green) depending on respectively (a) redundancy, (b) number of constraints, (c) density and (d) number of variables. (Color figure online)

Benchmarks. Throughout the paper, we focused on cones to simplify both notations and explanations. However, our algorithm works for general convex polyhedra and we build our experiments as follows. To compare the three algorithms, we asked them to minimize polyhedra that were generated randomly from four parameters that will be detailed further: the number of variables ($V \in [2, 50]$), the number  of constraints ($C \in [2, 50]$), the redundancy rate ($R \in [0\%, 90\%]$) and the density rate ($D \in [10\%, 80\%]$). Each constraint is created by giving a random integer between -100 and 100 to the coefficient of each variable, within the density rate. All constraints are attached the same constant bound ≤ 20. Such polyhedra have a convex potatoid shape, shown on the right hand side. We do not directly control the number of generators but we count them using the APRON interface [11] to polyhedral libraries in double description. Among all our measurements, the number of generators ranged from 10 to 6400 and this number grows polynomially in the number of constraints. This covers a wide variety of polyhedra and our experiments show that raytracing is always more efficient.

Redundancy Rate. The effect of redundancy on execution time is displayed on Fig. 5(a). These measures come from the minimization of polyhedra with 10

variables and 35 constraints, and a redundancy rate ranging from 0% to 90% of
the number of constraints. To generate a redundant constraint, we randomly pick
two constraints and produce a nonnegative combination of them. We took care
of avoiding redundancies that can be discarded by the fast detection criteria of
Sect. 1. The graph clearly shows that raytracing has a big advantage on polyhedra
with few redundancies. This phenomenon was expected: raytracing is good at
detecting irredundancy at low-cost. SMA becomes similar to raytracing when the
redundancy rate is high. This is explained by the implementation details given in
previous paragraphs: when a redundant constraint is found, it is removed from
the LP problem. Thus, if the redundancy rate reaches a very high level, the LP
problem becomes smaller and smaller at each iteration, lowering the impact of
using floating points. Moreover, the heuristic used by our algorithm never hits if
almost all constraints are redundant, which makes the raytracing computations
useless. To be fair between raytracing and the standard algorithm, we set the
redundancy rate at 50% in the other experiments.

Number of Constraints. Figure 5(b) measures the minimization time depending
on the number of constraints for polyhedra with 10 variables. FRA and RRA scale
better with respect to the number of constraints than SMA: experiments show
that when C ranges from 20 to 50 constraints, SMA has a quadratic evolution
compared to raytracing algorithms.

Density Rate. The density of a polyhedron is the (average) rate of nonnull
coefficients within a constraint. For instance, a density of 60% with 10 variables
means that on average, constraints have 6 nonnull coefficients. Figure 5(c) shows
the execution time for 10-dimensional polyhedra with 100 constraints, where
the density rate D goes from 10% to 80%. The raytracing algorithms are almost
insensitive to density, whereas the execution time of the standard algorithm
blows up with density. Actually, having a lot of nonnull coefficients in constraints
tends to create huge numerators and denominators because a pivot in the simplex
performs many combinations of constraints. The blow up does not happen in RRA
because LP problems are much smaller in the raytracing algorithms.

Number of Variables. The effect of the dimension on execution time is shown on
Fig. 5(d). Whereas raytracing seems linearly impacted by the dimension, SMA has
a behaviour that may look a bit strange. After a dramatic increase of execution
time, the curve falls down when the dimension reaches about half the number of
constraints. It finally joins and sticks to FRA curve. This phenomenon may be
explained by the number of pivots needed to solve the LP problem. The closer
the dimension is to the number of constraints, the fewer pivots are needed, thus
making SMA competitive even with more LP problems to solve.

Table 1 shows results for several values of dimension and number of constraints. Again, each cell of this table gives the average values resulting from
the minimization of 50 convex potatoids, with a density and a redundancy both
fixed at 50%. For each pair (number of variables × number of constraints), Table 1
gives the number of LP problems that were solved and their size (*i.e.* the number

Table 1. Time measures of the three minimization algorithms SMA, RRA and FRA for different values of variables and constraints.

Var		5 constraints			10 constraints			25 constraints			50 constraints			100 constraints		
		SMA	RRA	FRA	SMA	RRA	FRA	SMA	RRA	FRA	SMA	RRA	FRA	SMA	RRA	FRA
2	# lp	2	0	0	3	1	1	6	2	2	9	5	5	15	11	11
	lp size	3	3	3	4	3	4	6	3	4	8	3	4	12	3	5
	time (ms)	0.05	0.03	0.02	0.04	0.05	0.09	0.10	0.14	0.14	0.27	0.30	0.34	0.83	**0.71**	0.80
	speed up	-	1.8	1.9	-	0.77	0.48	-	0.74	0.73	-	0.90	0.79	-	**1.2**	1.0
5	# lp	5	2	2	10	6	6	24	16	16	46	34	34	90	72	73
	lp size	5	3	4	9	3	5	20	4	7	36	5	8	65	5	9
	time (ms)	0.09	0.15	0.18	0.29	0.45	0.50	3.8	**2.0**	1.8	29.8	**7.1**	5.4	178	**26.0**	18.8
	speed up	-	0.61	0.51	-	0.65	0.59	-	1.9	2.1	-	4.2	5.5	-	**6.8**	9.5
10	# lp	5	2	2	10	5	5	25	13	13	50	28	28	100	58	58
	lp size	5	3	4	9	4	5	22	7	7	44	10	8	87	13	11
	time (ms)	0.18	0.30	0.32	0.60	1.1	0.86	17.6	**10.8**	6.0	811	**65.9**	23.5	14936	**336**	64.0
	speed up	-	0.59	0.55	-	0.57	0.70	-	1.6	2.9	-	12.3	34.5	-	**44.5**	233

of constraints they involve) on average. It contains also the computation time of the minimization in milliseconds and the speed up of raytracing compared to SMA. Results of Table 1 show that for small polyhedra, either in dimension or in number constraints, raytracing does not help. Indeed, for such small LP problems, the overhead of our algorithm is unnecessary and leads to time losses. Raytracing becomes interesting for larger polyhedra, where the speed improvement is significant. For instance, FRA is 44.5 times faster with 10 variables and 100 constraints than SMA. The gain can be explained by the number of LP problems solved and their average size, noticeably smaller in raytracing than in SMA. As expected, raytracing is faster with floating points.

We also compare through APRON with libraries in double description, the results are available in [15]. Not surprisingly the minimization time is significantly larger than that of SMA, FRA and RRA, as it must first compute all generators using Chernikova's algorithm.

6   Conclusion and Future Work

In this paper, we present a new algorithm to minimize the representation of a polyhedron, available in the VPL. It is based on raytracing and provides an efficient irredundancy check in which LP executions are replaced by distance computations. The *raytracing procedure* is incomplete and LP problem resolutions are still required for deciding the redundancy of the remaining constraints. However, our algorithm reduces not only the number of LP problems solved along the minimization, but also their size by an incremental approach. Moreover, it is usable for polyhedra in single representation, as constraints or as generators. It can be used either with rational or floating coefficients. In both cases, it can produce certificates of correctness, precision and minimality.

Parallelizing. Our raytracing algorithm is well-suited to parallelization: computing the intersection lists could be done by as many threads as rays. These computations boil down to matrix multiplications for which there exist efficient libraries, e.g. the LAPACK library [1]. Actually, to fully benefit from parallelism, the algorithm should be implemented in C because OCAML does not support native concurrency yet. Exploiting multi-cores, the number of ray traces could be greatly increased, and applying the raytracing principle from several interior points would allow us to discover frontiers even more easily.

Redundancy in the Double Description Framework (DDF). Our algorithm has been designed to minimize polyhedra in single representation, but the principle of raytracing can be reused in the double description framework, where it could *quickly detect irredundant constraints.* Redundancy is easier to detect when the two representations of a polyhedron are available. Let the pair $(\mathscr{C}, \mathscr{G})$ denote the set of constraints and the set of generators of a polyhedron in $\mathbb{Q}^n$ and $(\mathscr{C}_M, \mathscr{G}_M)$ be its minimal version. A constraint $C \in \mathscr{C}$ is irredundant if it is saturated by at least n irredundant generators, *i.e.* $\exists g_1, \ldots, g_n \in \mathscr{G}_M, \langle C, g_i \rangle = 0$. Similarly, a generator $g \in \mathscr{G}$ is irredundant if it is the intersection of at least n irredundant constraints *i.e.* $\exists C_1, \ldots, C_n \in \mathscr{C}_M, \langle C_i, g \rangle = 0$. Think for instance of a line in 2D being defined by two points and a point being the intersection of at least two lines. The principle of the minimization algorithm is the following [10]: build the *boolean saturation matrix* S of size $|\mathscr{C}| \times |\mathscr{G}|$ defined by $S[C][g] := (\langle C, g \rangle = 0)$, then iteratively remove constraints (and the corresponding rows of S) which are insufficiently saturated and do the same for generators (and columns of S) until reaching a stable matrix. The remaining constraints and generators form the minimal version $(\mathscr{C}_M, \mathscr{G}_M)$ which mutually justify the irredundancy of each other. This algorithm is appealing compared to its counterpart in single representation but the number of evaluation of $\langle C, g \rangle$ is huge when each variable x_i ranges in an interval $[l_i, u_i]$. Such a product of intervals can be represented by $2n$ constraints (two inequalities $l_i \leq x_i \land x_i \leq u_i$ per variable)which corresponds to 2^n vertices [3].[6] Therefore, the size of S is $n2^{n+1}$. To limit the computations, the saturation matrix is not fully constructed. Let us summarize the improved algorithm [19]: (1) Some constraints are removed by the *fast redundancy detection* recalled in Sect. 1. (2) The irredundant generators of $\mathscr{G}_M$ are constructed from the remaining constraints using Chernikova's algorithm [4] with some optimized adjacency criteria [8,14,20]. The adjacency criterion ensures that the construction cannot produce redundant generators [16]. (3) Finally, the saturation matrix is built to remove the constraint redundancies but a row is only completed if the constraint never finds enough saturating generators, otherwise the computation of the row is interrupted.

We believe that our orthogonal raytracing phase can be used at Step (3) to *quickly discover irredundant constraints*, which therefore do not have to be confirmed by the saturation matrix. The cost of this initial raytracing is reasonable:

---

[6] The opposite phenomena ($2n$ vertices corresponding to 2^n constraints) also exists but hardly ever occurs in practice [3].

$\mathscr{C}$ rays and $2 \times |\mathscr{C}|$ evaluations per ray resulting in $2 \times |\mathscr{C}|^2$ computations of inner products. It could therefore benefit to minimization in the DDF especially when $|\mathscr{C}| \ll |\mathscr{G}|$ as in hypercubes.

References

1. Anderson, E., Bai, Z., Bischof, C., Blackford, S., Demmel, J., Dongarra, J., Croz, J., Greenbaum, A., Hammarling, S., McKenney, A., Sorensen, D.: LAPACK Users' Guide, 3rd edn. Society for Industrial and Applied Mathematics, Philadelphia (1999)
2. Bagnara, R., Hill, P.M., Zaffanella, E.: Applications of polyhedral computations to the analysis and verification of hardware and software systems. Theoret. Comput. Sci. **410**(46), 4672–4691 (2009)
3. Benoy, F., King, A., Mesnard, F.: Computing convex hulls with a linear solver. TPLP: Theory Pract. Log. Program. **5**(1–2), 259–271 (2005)
4. Chernikova, N.V.: Algorithm for discovering the set of all the solutions of a linear programming problem. USSR Comput. Math. Math. Phys. **8**, 282–293 (1968)
5. Chvatal, V.: Linear Programming. Series of Books in the Mathematical Sciences. W. H. Freeman, New York (1983)
6. Feautrier, P., Lengauer, C.: Polyhedron model. In: Padua, D. (ed.) Encyclopedia of Parallel Computing, vol. 1, pp. 1581–1592. Springer, Berlin (2011)
7. Fouilhé, A., Monniaux, D., Périn, M.: Efficient certificate generation for the abstract domain of polyhedra. In: Static Analysis Symposium (2013)
8. Fukuda, K., Prodon, A.: Double description method revisited. In: Deza, M., Euler, R., Manoussakis, I. (eds.) CCS 1995. LNCS, vol. 1120, pp. 91–111. Springer, Heidelberg (1996). doi:10.1007/3-540-61576-8_77
9. Goldman, A.J., Tucker, A.W.: Polyhedral convex cones. In: Kuhn, H.W., Tucker, A.W. (eds.) Linear Inequalities and Related Systems. Annals of Mathematics Studies, vol. 38, pp. 19–40. Princeton University Press, Princeton (1956)
10. Halbwachs, N.: Détermination automatique de relations linéaires vérifiées par les variables d'un programme. Ph.D. thesis, Université scientifique et médicale de Grenoble, (in French) (1979)
11. Jeannet, B., Miné, A.: APRON: a library of numerical abstract domains for static analysis. In: Bouajjani, A., Maler, O. (eds.) CAV 2009. LNCS, vol. 5643, pp. 661–667. Springer, Heidelberg (2009). doi:10.1007/978-3-642-02658-4_52
12. Jourdan, J.-H., Laporte, V., Blazy, S., Leroy, X., Pichardie, D.: A formally-verified C static analyzer. In: ACM Principles of Programming Languages (POPL), pp. 247–259. ACM Press, January 2015
13. Lassez, J.-L., Huynh, T., McAloon, K.: Simplification and elimination of redundant linear arithmetic constraints. In: Constraint Logic Programming, pp. 73–87. MIT Press, Cambridge (1993)
14. Le Verge, H.: A note on Chernikova's algorithm. Research report RR-1662, INRIA (1992)
15. Maréchal, A., Périn, M.: Efficient elimination of redundancies in polyhedra using raytracing. Technical report TR-2016-6, Verimag, Université Grenoble-Alpes, October 2016
16. Motzkin, T.S., Raiffa, H., Thompson, G.L., Thrall, R.M.: The double description method. In: Contributions to the Theory of Games. Annals of Mathematics Studies, vol. 2, pp. 51–73. Princeton University Press, Princeton (1953)

17. Schrijver, A.: Theory of Linear and Integer Programming. Wiley-Interscience Series in Discrete Mathematics and Optimization. Wiley, Hoboken (1999)
18. Simon, A., King, A.: Exploiting sparsity in polyhedral analysis. In: Hankin, C., Siveroni, I. (eds.) SAS 2005. LNCS, vol. 3672, pp. 336–351. Springer, Heidelberg (2005). doi:10.1007/11547662_23
19. Wilde, D.K.: A library for NG polyhedral operations. Master's thesis, Oregon State University, Corvallis, Oregon, December 1993. Also Published as IRISA Technical report PI 785, Rennes, France (1993)
20. Zolotykh, N.Y.: New modification of the double description method for constructing the skeleton of a polyhedral cone. Comput. Math. Math. Phys. **52**(1), 146–156 (2012)

Precise Thread-Modular Abstract Interpretation of Concurrent Programs Using Relational Interference Abstractions

Raphaël Monat[1,2] and Antoine Miné[3]([⊠])

[1] École Normale Supérieure de Lyon, Lyon, France
raphael.monat@ens-lyon.org
[2] École Normale Supérieure, Paris, France
[3] Sorbonnes Universités, UPMC Univ. Paris 6,
Laboratoire d'informatique de Paris 6 (LIP6), 4, Pl. Jussieu, 75005 Paris, France
antoine.mine@lip6.fr

Abstract. We present a static analysis by abstract interpretation of numeric properties in multi-threaded programs. The analysis is sound (assuming a sequentially consistent memory), parameterized by a choice of abstract domains and, in order to scale up, it is modular, in that it iterates over each thread individually (possibly several times) instead of iterating over their product. We build on previous work that formalized rely-guarantee verification methods as a concrete, fixpoint-based semantics, and then apply classic numeric abstractions to abstract independently thread states and thread interference. This results in a flexible algorithm allowing a wide range of precision versus cost trade-offs, and able to infer even flow-sensitive and relational thread interference. We implemented our method in an analyzer prototype for a simple language and experimented it on several classic mutual exclusion algorithms for two or more threads. Our prototype is instantiated with the polyhedra domain and employs simple control partitioning to distinguish critical sections from surrounding code. It relates the variables of all threads using polyhedra, which limits its scalability in the number of variables. Nevertheless, preliminary experiments and comparison with ConcurInterproc show that modularity enables scaling to a large number of thread instances, provided that the total number of variables stays small.

Keywords: Program verification · Concurrent programs · Abstract interpretation · Thread-modular analyses · Rely-guarantee methods · Numeric invariant generation

1 Introduction

In order to exploit the full potential of multi-core processors, it is necessary to turn to parallel programming, a trend also followed in critical application domains, such as avionics and automotive. Unfortunately, concurrent programs are difficult to design correctly, and difficult to verify. In particular, the large

© Springer International Publishing AG 2017
A. Bouajjani and D. Monniaux (Eds.): VMCAI 2017, LNCS 10145, pp. 386–404, 2017.
DOI: 10.1007/978-3-319-52234-0_21

space of possible executions makes it impractical for tests to achieve a good coverage. Likewise, formal methods that do not cover the whole range of possible executions (e.g. context bounded methods [30]) can miss errors. In this article, we study sound static analysis methods based on abstract interpretation [7] that consider a superset of all possible executions, and are thus suitable for the certification of concurrent critical software. The concurrency model we consider is that of multi-thread software, with arbitrary preemption and a global, shared memory. This model is challenging to analyze as thread instructions that can actually execute concurrently are not apparent at the syntactic level, and every access to a global variable can actually be a communication between threads.

In the last few years, sound static analysis methods based on abstract interpretation [7] have established themselves as successful techniques to verify non-functional correctness properties (e.g. the absence of run-time error) on *sequential* programs with a large *data space* and complex numeric computations. Our aim is to extend these sound methods to multi-threaded concurrent programs by tackling the large *control space* inherent to these programs. We focus in particular on scaling in the number of threads. This is achieved by combining precise, relational abstractions with thread-modular analysis methods. More precisely, we base our work on the thread-modular concrete semantics introduced in [27], but our abstractions differ as we employ polyhedral abstractions [9] and control partitioning [8] to represent fully-relational flow-sensitive thread-local invariants and thread interference relations, aiming at a higher precision.

Thread-Modular Analysis. A classic view of abstract interpretation consists in propagating an abstract representation of a set of memory states (e.g., a box or polyhedron) along the control-flow graph, using loop acceleration such as widening until a stable abstract element is found [4]. While this technique can be extended easily to concurrent programs by constructing a product control-flow graph of threads, it does not scale up for a large number of threads due to the combinatorial explosion of the control space. Another view consists in a more literal interpretation, defined as usual by induction on the program syntax, but using abstract representations of collected program states. This flavor of abstract interpretation is much more efficient in memory (it does not store an abstract element for each control location) and has been exploited for the efficient analysis of large sequential programs [2]. The extension to concurrent programs is more difficult than for control-flow graphs as the set of interleavings of thread executions cannot be defined conveniently by induction on the syntax. In this article, we consider thread-modular analysis methods, which decompose the analysis of a multi-threaded program into the analysis of its individual threads. They combine two benefits: the complexity of analyzing a program is closer to that of analyzing the sum of its threads than their products, and existing efficient analysis methods for sequential programs (such as abstract interpretation by induction on the syntax) can be reused without much effort on concurrent ones.

The main difficulty in designing a thread-modular analysis is to soundly and precisely account, during the analysis of one thread, for the effect of the other threads. One solution would be to specify a range of possible values for each

Thread 1	Thread 2
1 : **while random do**	a : **while random do**
2 : **if** $X < Y$ **then**	b : **if** $Y < 10$ **then**
3 : $X \leftarrow X + 1$	c : $Y \leftarrow Y + 1$
4 : **fi**	d : $X \leftarrow (X + Y)/2$
od	e : **fi**
	od

Fig. 1. An example of concurrent program.

shared variable, but this puts a large burden on the programmer. Moreover, as shown in the following paragraph, range information is not always sufficient. We solve both problems by providing a method capable of *automatically* inferring *relations* over the shared variables, whose shape is completely specified by the choice of an abstract domain.

Simple Interference. Consider, as motivating example, the program in Fig. 1. Thread 1 repeatedly increments X while it is less than Y. Thread 2 repeatedly increments Y until 10 and computes into X the average of X and Y. Initially, $X \leftarrow 0$ and $Y \leftarrow 1$. Although this example is artificial for the sake of presentation, experimental evidence (Sect. 4) shows that the precision brought by our analysis is also required when analyzing real-world algorithms, such as Lamport's Bakery algorithm and Peterson's mutual exclusion algorithm. In the following, we assume a sequentially consistent execution model [22].

Existing thread-modular analyses [5,11,12,15,21,27] first analyze each thread in isolation, then gather interference from this first, unsound analysis, and perform a second analysis of each thread in the context of this interference; these analyses uncover more behaviors of threads, hence more interference, so that other rounds of analyses with increasing sets of interference will be performed, until the interference set reaches a fixpoint (possibly with the help of a widening), at which point the analysis accounts for all the possible behaviors of the concurrent program. In [5,25], the interference corresponds to the set of values that each thread can store into each variable, possibly further abstracted (e.g., as intervals). A thread reading a variable may either read back the last value it stored into it, or one of the values from the interference set of other threads. These analyses are similar to rely-guarantee reasoning [20], a proof method which is precise (it is relatively complete), but relies on the user to provide interference as well as program invariants. However, we consider here automated analyses, which are necessarily incomplete, but parameterized by a choice of abstractions.

In the example, using interval abstractions, the first analysis round uncovers the interference $X \leftarrow [0, 1], Y \leftarrow [1, 1]$ from Thread 1, and $X \leftarrow [0, 5], Y \leftarrow [1, 10]$ from Thread 2. A second round uncovers $X \leftarrow [1, 10]$, at which point the set of interference is stable. When running a final time every thread analysis using these interference, we get that X and Y are bounded by $[0, 10]$. However, the relation $X \leq Y$ that additionally holds cannot be found with the method of [5,25]. The reason is that interference is handled in a non-relational way: the analysis cannot express (and so, infer) that, when $X \leq Y$ is established by a thread, the relation is left invariant by the interference of the other thread.

Relational Interference. In the present article, we enrich the notion of interference to allow such relational information to be inferred and exploited during the analysis. More precisely, following [27], we see interference generated by an instruction of a thread as a relation linking the variable values before the execution of the instruction (denoted x, y) and the variable values after its execution (denoted as x', y'). Our contribution is then to use relational domains to represent both relations between variables (such as $x \leq y \wedge x' \leq y'$ when $X \leq Y$ remains invariant) and input-output relations (such as $x' = x+1$ for $X \leftarrow X+1$). Furthermore, we distinguish interference generated at different control states, in our case, a pair (l, l') of control locations of Thread 1 and Thread 2, to enable flow-sensitive interference. In the example of Fig. 1, we have a piece of interference from Thread 1 being $(l, l') = (3, 4)$; $x < y$; $x' = x+1$; $y = y'$. For Thread 2, the interference from program point d to e is: $y \leq 10$; $x \leq y$; $y = y'$; $2x' = x+y$. We note that the global invariant $X \leq Y$ is preserved. To achieve an effective analysis, the states and relations manipulated by the semantics are actually abstracted, using classic numeric abstract domains (such as polyhedra [9]), as well as partitioning of control locations. The analysis is thus parametric, and allows a large choice of trade-offs between cost, precision, and expressiveness. Our prototype implementation uses the Apron [19] and BddApron [17] libraries. The correctness of the analysis is proved in the thread-modular abstract interpretation framework introduced in [27]. Yet, we stress on the fact that the abstract analysis subsequently derived in [27] is not able to precisely analyze the example from Fig. 1, as it does not exploit the capabilities of relational numeric domains to represent interference as relations, while we do.

Contribution. To sum up, we build on previous theoretical work [27] to develop a thread-modular static analysis by abstract interpretation of a simple numeric language, which goes beyond the state of the art [5,11,12,15,21,27] by being fully relational and flow-sensitive. In [27], a small degree of flow-sensitivity and relationality was added to an existing scalable analysis in the form of specialized abstract domains designed to remove specific false alarms, following the design by refinement methodology of Astrée [3]. Here, starting from the same thread-modular semantics, we build a different abstract analysis targeting small but intricate algorithms that require a higher level of precision than [27]. Merging our analysis with [27] in order to achieve a higher precision only for programs parts that require it while retaining overall scalability remains a future work.

We present examples and experimental results to demonstrate that the analysis is sufficiently precise to prove the correctness of small but non-trivial mutual exclusion algorithms, and that it scales well, allowing the analysis of a few hundreds (albeit small) threads in a matter of minutes. An experimental comparison with ConcurInterproc [18] shows that our approach is several orders of magnitude more scalable, with a comparable level of precision.

Limitations. We assume a sequentially consistent execution model [22], i.e., the execution of a concurrent program is an interleaving of executions of its threads. We ignore the additional difficulty caused by weakly consistent memories [1]; indeed, we believe that an extension to weakly consistent memories is possible, but orthogonal to our work. Our analysis is nevertheless useful with respect to a model obeying the "data-race freedom guarantee" as it can be easily extended to detect data races (a race is simply a read or write instruction at a control-point where some interference can occur). An additional limitation is that we consider a fixed number of threads. Our method can be extended to consider several instances of threads, possibly an unbounded number, while keeping a fixed, finite number of variables in the abstract. We would employ a uniform abstraction: firstly, thread variables are replaced with summary abstract variables that account for all the possible instances of that variable; secondly, we add interference from a thread to itself, to account for the effect of one instance of a thread on another instance of the same thread. This would achieve a sound, but uniform analysis (unlike [12]). More importantly, our implementation is only a limited prototype. We analyze small programs written in a basic language with no functions and only numeric variables. Yet, these programs are inspired from actual algorithms and challenging parts of real programs. We focus on scalability in the number of threads, and did not include in our prototype state-of-the-art abstractions necessary to handle full languages and achieve scalability for large data space (as done in [27]). Indeed, our prototype employs a polyhedron domain to relate all the variables of all the threads, without any form of packing. The extension to realistic languages and experimentation on larger programs is thus left as future work. Finally, the control partitioning we currently use relies on user annotations (Sect. 3.5), although it could easily be automated (e.g., using heuristics to detect which program parts are likely to be critical sections).

Outline. The rest of the article is organized as follows: Sect. 2 introduces a simple numeric multi-threaded language and its thread-modular concrete semantics; Sect. 3 presents our abstract, computable semantics, parameterized by a classic numeric abstraction; Sect. 4 presents our prototype implementation and our experimental results; Sect. 5 discusses related work and Sect. 6 concludes.

2   Concrete Semantics of the Analysis

2.1   Programs

We focus on a simple language presented in Fig. 2. A program is a set of threads, defined over a set of global variables. There are no local variables in our language: they are transformed into global variables. The construction $[k_1, k_2]$ is the syntax for a random number chosen between k_1 and k_2. It expresses non-determinism, useful to model, for instance, program inputs.

We assume we have a fixed number of threads $\mathcal{T}$: in particular, there is no dynamic creation of threads. $\mathcal{L}$ is the set of program points, and $\mathcal{V}$ is the set of

⟨arithmetic expressions⟩ ::= $k \in \mathbb{Z}$ | $[k_1, k_2]$ | $X \in \mathcal{V}$ | $a_1 \dagger a_2$, $\dagger \in \{+, -, \times, /, \%\}$

⟨boolean expressions⟩ ::= $b_1 \bullet b_2$ | not b_1 | $a_1 \square a_2$

$\bullet \in \{\vee, \wedge\}$, $\square \in \{<, >, \leq, \geq, =, \neq\}$

⟨threads⟩ ::= c_1 ; c_2 | ^{l_1} if b then $^{l_2}c_1$ else $^{l_3}c_2$ fi ^{l_4}
| while ^{l_1}b do ^{l_2} c od ^{l_3} | $^{l_1}X \leftarrow e^{l_2}$

⟨program⟩ ::= thread 1 || thread 2 || ... || thread n

Fig. 2. Simple language to analyze.

variables. A control state associates a current control point to each thread. It is defined as $\mathcal{C} = \mathcal{T} \to \mathcal{L}$. A memory state maps each variable to a value; the domain of memory states is $\mathcal{M} = \mathcal{V} \to \mathbb{Z}$ and the domain of program states is $\mathcal{S} = \mathcal{C} \times \mathcal{M}$. An interference is created by a thread when it assigns a value to a variable. It can be seen as a transition between two program states. The interference domain is denoted as $\mathcal{I} = \mathcal{T} \times (\mathcal{S} \times \mathcal{S})$. An interference $(t, (c_1, \rho_1), (c_2, \rho_2))$ means that, when the memory state is $\rho_1 \in \mathcal{M}$ and the control points are defined on every thread using $c_1 \in \mathcal{C}$, the execution of thread t changes the memory state into ρ_2, and the control points are now defined using c_2. Moreover, an interference generated by a threat t changes only the control point of t, so: $\forall t' \in \mathcal{T} \setminus \{t\}, c_1(t') = c_2(t')$.

2.2 Thread-Modular Concrete Semantics

We present in Fig. 3 a concrete semantics of programs with interference, using an accumulating semantics. By accumulating semantics, we mean that $(R, I) \subseteq \mathbb{S}[\![stat]\!]_t(R, I)$: the analysis adds new reachable states to R and interference to I, keeping already accumulated states and interference intact. It is important to gather the set of all interference accumulated during all possible executions of each thread, to inject into the analysis of other threads, and we also accumulate states to keep a consistent semantic flavor. Such a semantics is also the natural result of specializing the thread-modular reachability semantics of [27] to the transition systems generated by our language (left implicit here for space reasons). $\mathbb{E}[\![expr]\!]\rho$ is the usual evaluation of an arithmetic or a boolean expression $expr$ given a memory state ρ. Its signature is $\mathbb{E}[\![expr]\!] : \mathcal{M} \to \mathcal{P}(\mathbb{Z})$, due to the non-determinism of $[k_1, k_2]$.

Intuitively, the analysis is the iteration of two steps:

1. For each thread t, analyze t and take into account any number of "valid" interference created by other threads.
2. For each thread t, collect the interference created by this thread t.

In Eq. (1), we express the fact that $\mathbb{S}[\![stat]\!]_t$ needs a statement $stat$ of a thread t, a global program state, and a set of interference, in order to compute a resulting program state and a new set of interference. The interference given in input is used to compute the effect of the other threads on thread t. The set of all interference, including those collected during this analysis, is given in the

$$\mathbb{S}[\![stat]\!]_t, \mathbb{B}[\![bexpr]\!]_t : \mathcal{P}(\mathcal{S}) \times \mathcal{P}(\mathcal{I}) \to \mathcal{P}(\mathcal{S}) \times \mathcal{P}(\mathcal{I}) \tag{1}$$

$$\mathbb{S}[\![^{l_1}X \leftarrow e^{l_2}]\!]_t(R, I) = \tag{2}$$

let $I_1 = \{(t, (c, \rho), (c[t \mapsto l_2], \rho[X \mapsto v])) \mid (c, \rho) \in R, v \in \mathbb{E}[\![e]\!]\rho, c(t) = l_1\}$ in

let $R_1 = \{(c', \rho') \mid \exists (c, \rho), (t, (c, \rho), (c', \rho')) \in I_1\}$ in

let $R_2 = lfp\ \lambda S.\ itf(S, t, I, R_1)$ in $R \cup R_2, I \cup I_1$

$$\mathbb{B}[\![^{l_1}b^{l_2}]\!]_t(R, I) = \tag{3}$$

let $I_1 = \{(t, (c, \rho), (c[t \mapsto l_2], \rho)) \mid (c, \rho) \in R, true \in \mathbb{E}[\![e]\!]\rho, c(t) = l_1\}$ in

let $R_1 = \{(c', \rho') \mid \exists (c, \rho), (t, (c, \rho), (c', \rho')) \in I_1\}$ in

let $R_2 = lfp\ \lambda S.\ itf(S, t, I, R_1)$ in $R \cup R_2, I \cup I_1$

$$itf : (S, t, I, R) \mapsto R \cup \{(c', \rho') \mid \exists t' \in \mathcal{T} \setminus \{t\}, (c, \rho) \in S, (t', (c, \rho), (c', \rho')) \in I\}$$

$$\mathbb{S}[\![stat_1 \ ; \ stat_2]\!]_t = \mathbb{S}[\![stat_2]\!]_t \circ \mathbb{S}[\![stat_1]\!]_t$$

$$\mathbb{S}[\![^{l_1}if\ b\ then\ ^{l_2}tt\ else\ ^{l_3}ff\ fi\ ^{l_4}]\!]_t X = \tag{4}$$

let $T = \mathbb{S}[\![^{l_2}tt^{l_4}]\!]_t(\mathbb{B}[\![^{l_1}b^{l_2}]\!]_t X)$ in

let $F = \mathbb{S}[\![^{l_3}ff^{l_4}]\!]_t(\mathbb{B}[\![^{l_1}\neg b^{l_3}]\!]_t X)$ in

$X \mathbin{\dot\cup} T \mathbin{\dot\cup} F$ $\qquad\qquad$ where $\dot\cup$ is the element-wise union on pairs

$$\mathbb{S}[\![while\ ^{l_1}b\ do\ ^{l_2}c\ od^{l_3}]\!]_t X = \tag{5}$$

$X \mathbin{\dot\cup} \mathbb{B}[\![^{l_1}\neg b^{l_3}]\!]_t(lfp\ \lambda Y.(X \mathbin{\dot\cup} \mathbb{S}[\![^{l_2}c^{l_1}]\!]_t(\mathbb{B}[\![^{l_1}b^{l_2}]\!]_t Y)))$

(a) Thread-modular concrete semantics.

$$f : \begin{cases} \mathcal{P}(\mathcal{S}) \times \mathcal{P}(\mathcal{I}) \longrightarrow \mathcal{P}(\mathcal{S}) \times \mathcal{P}(\mathcal{I}) \\ (R, I) \longmapsto \dot\bigcup_{t \in \mathcal{T}} \mathbb{S}[\![stats_t]\!]_t(R \cup S_0, I) \end{cases}$$

(b) Definition of the thread-modular analysis operator f.

Fig. 3. Definition of the concrete analysis.

output. Similarly, we can filter a domain with a boolean expression using $\mathbb{B}[\![b]\!]_t$. In that case, the new interference only reflects the change in control point.

We now detail the concrete semantics, presented in Fig. 3a. In Eq. (2), I_1 is the interference created by the new assignment $X \leftarrow e$: it is a transition from the state before the assignment to the state after the assignment. R_1 is the set of program states before any interference is applied (only the assignment is applied). In R_2, the function itf applies one interference to the set of states S, i.e., a transition that can be performed by another thread $t' \neq t$ according to the interference set I. As an arbitrary number of transitions from other threads can be executed between two transitions of the current thread, we actually apply the reflexive transitive closure of this interference relation, which can be expressed as the least fixpoint (lfp) of itf. This fixpoint is computed on $(\mathcal{P}(\mathcal{S}), \subseteq)$; it exists as $\lambda S.\ itf(S, t, I, R)$ is monotonic. We note that the computation of I_1 is very similar to the transfer function for the assignment in the usual sequential case $(\mathbb{S}[\![^{l_1}X \leftarrow e^{l_2}]\!](R) = \{(c[t \mapsto l_2], \rho[X \mapsto v]) \mid (c, \rho) \in R, v \in \mathbb{E}[\![e]\!]\rho\})$; our thread-modular semantics applies such an operation, followed by interference-related computations. We will use this remark in the next section to design an abstract thread-modular semantics on top of well-known abstract operators for sequential programs. This will allow us to reuse existing abstract domains and know-how in our concurrent analysis. Equation (3) is quite similar: we create a new instance of interference, that can change the control points from l_1 to l_2 if b is satisfied. This way, R_1 is the set of program states obtained just after the boolean filtering has been applied. Then, we collect the reachable states found when applying interference caused by the other threads. The computation of R_2 is the same in Eqs. (2) and (3), and relies on the fixpoint computation of itf.

The rules for the other statements (sequences, conditionals, loops) are similar to the usual semantics for sequential programs. These rules can be reduced to the rules of assignment and boolean filtering by induction over the syntax.

Let $stats_t$ be the statement body of thread t, and S_0 be the set of initial program states. The thread-modular concrete semantics is defined as computing $lfp\ f$, where f is defined in Fig. 3b. This fixpoint is computed over the lifting of powersets; it exists as f is increasing. When f is called, it analyzes each thread once and returns two sets: the accumulated program states and the accumulated interference. During the first few iterations, some pieces of interference are not discovered yet, so the analysis may not be sound yet. When the set of interference is stable, however, the analysis is sound: all execution cases are taken into account. This is why we compute a *fixpoint* of f, and not only the first iterations.

The soundness and completeness (for state properties) of this semantics was proved in [26,27] on an arbitrary transition system. This semantics is naturally too concrete to be computable. We will abstract it in the next section.

3   Abstract Semantics

Compared to the semantics of a sequential program, the semantics of the previous section embeds a rich and precise control information due to the possible thread preemption, which makes it difficult to analyze efficiently. In order to be able to reuse classic state abstraction techniques, we first reduce the complexity of the control information by abstraction in Sect. 3.1. Then, we simplify our analysis by abstracting the memory states and the interference into numeric domains.

3.1   Abstractions of States and Interference

We suppose we are given a partition of control locations $\mathcal{L}$ into a set $\mathcal{L}^\#$ of abstract control locations, through some abstraction $\alpha_{\mathcal{L}} : \mathcal{L} \rightarrow \mathcal{L}^\#$, which is extended pointwise to control states as $\alpha_{\mathcal{L}} : (\mathcal{T} \rightarrow \mathcal{L}) \rightarrow (\mathcal{T} \rightarrow \mathcal{L}^\#)$. In our implementation, control locations are manually specified using a program annotation, and the automatic determination of a good partitioning is left as future work. This function is used to abstract interference information, as shown by the function α_C in Eq. (7). In contrast, for program states, our control abstraction

$$\alpha_{\mathcal{M}}(t) : \begin{cases} \mathcal{P}(\mathcal{S}) \longrightarrow \mathcal{L} \to \mathcal{P}(\mathcal{M}) \\ X \longmapsto \lambda L.\{e \mid (c,e) \in X \ \wedge c(t) = L\} \end{cases} \tag{6}$$

$$\alpha_{\mathcal{C}} : \begin{cases} \mathcal{P}(\mathcal{I}) \longrightarrow \mathcal{T} \to \mathcal{P}(((\mathcal{T} \to \mathcal{L}^{\#}) \times \mathcal{M})^2) \\ X \longmapsto \lambda t.\{((\alpha_{\mathcal{L}}(c_b), b), (\alpha_{\mathcal{L}}(c_e), e)) \mid (c_b, c_e) \in \mathcal{C}^2, (t, (c_b, b), (c_e, e)) \in X\} \end{cases} \tag{7}$$

$$\gamma_{\mathcal{D}^{\#}} : (\mathcal{L} \to \mathcal{D}^{\#}) \longrightarrow (\mathcal{L} \to \mathcal{P}(\mathcal{M})) \tag{8}$$

$$\gamma_{\mathcal{I}^{\#}} : (\mathcal{T} \to \mathcal{I}^{\#}) \longrightarrow (\mathcal{T} \to \mathcal{P}(((\mathcal{T} \to \mathcal{L}^{\#}) \times \mathcal{M})^2)) \tag{9}$$

Fig. 4. Abstractions and concretizations of states and interference.

$\alpha_{\mathcal{M}}(t)$ in Eq. (6) keeps the control information $c(t) \in \mathcal{L}$ intact for the current thread and abstracts away the control information $c(t')$ of other threads $t' \neq t$, hence the shift from control in $\mathcal{C} = \mathcal{T} \to \mathcal{L}$ to control in $\mathcal{L}$, which makes the analysis of a thread rather similar to a flow-sensitive sequential analysis. The abstract semantics presented in the next section will have its precision and computational cost strongly dependent upon the choice of $\mathcal{L}^{\#}$.

3.2 Thread-Modular Abstract Semantics

We assume we are given an arbitrary numeric domain $\mathcal{D}^{\#}$ to abstract the contents of the program states, and denote by $\gamma_{\mathcal{D}^{\#}}$ the associated concretization function. Likewise, we assume that an arbitrary numeric domain $\mathcal{I}^{\#}$ is provided to abstract interference, and denote by $\gamma_{\mathcal{I}^{\#}}$ its concretization. The signatures of these concretizations are given in Eqs. (8) and (9). Our concrete states feature control point information as well as numeric variables. This is translated in the abstract domains $\mathcal{D}^{\#}, \mathcal{I}^{\#}$ by two types of variables: original numeric variables, and auxiliary control point variables, called aux_t for $t \in \mathcal{T}$. We thus consider here that numbers are used as control points $\mathcal{L}$ in order to stay within the realm of numeric domains. Moreover, interference abstraction is partitioned by thread.

As the sets of interference are abstracted into a relational numeric domain, we can represent a transition using an initial, non-primed variable, and a final, primed variable. For example, to express that x can change from 1 to 2, we write $x = 1 \wedge x' = 2$. Similarly, an interference increasing a variable x, can be written as $x' \geq x + 1$. We show how we can use existing numeric abstract domains used in the analysis of sequential programs to abstract our concrete thread-modular analysis. We assume given abstract operations, such as simultaneously assigning a set of arithmetic expressions $\mathcal{A}$ to a set of variables, adding uninitialized variables, renaming and deleting variables. The signature of these functions is presented in Fig. 5. We also suppose we have a join and a meet (abstracting respectively the union and the intersection), and a widening operator, respectively denoted $\cup^{\#}$, $\cap^{\#}$, and ∇. These are standard operations, implemented in abstract domain libraries, such as Apron [19] and BddApron [17].

We now define a function *apply*, applying an instance of interference to a numeric domain. In a sense, *apply* gives the image of an abstract domain under an

$$assign : \mathcal{X}^{\#} \times \mathcal{P}(\mathcal{V} \times \mathcal{A}) \rightarrow \mathcal{X}^{\#} \qquad add : \mathcal{X}^{\#} \times \mathcal{P}(\mathcal{V}) \rightarrow \mathcal{X}^{\#}$$

$$rename : \mathcal{X}^{\#} \times \mathcal{P}(\mathcal{V}^2) \rightarrow \mathcal{X}^{\#} \qquad delete : \mathcal{X}^{\#} \times \mathcal{P}(\mathcal{V}) \rightarrow \mathcal{X}^{\#}$$

Fig. 5. Signatures of usual abstract operators with $\mathcal{X}^{\#} \in \{\mathcal{D}^{\#}, \mathcal{I}^{\#}\}$.

$$extend : \begin{cases} \mathcal{D}^{\#} \longrightarrow \mathcal{I}^{\#} \\ R^{\#} \longmapsto add(R^{\#}, \{x' \mid x \in \mathrm{Var}(R^{\#})\}) \end{cases}$$

$$img : \begin{cases} \mathcal{I}^{\#} \longrightarrow \mathcal{D}^{\#} \\ I^{\#} \longmapsto \text{let } X = \{x \in \mathrm{Var}(I^{\#}) \mid x' \in \mathrm{Var}(I^{\#})\} \text{ in} \\ \qquad \text{let } R_1^{\#} = delete(I^{\#}, X) \text{ in} \\ \qquad rename(R_2^{\#}, \{(x', x) \mid x \in X\}) \end{cases}$$

$$apply : \begin{cases} \mathcal{D}^{\#} \times \mathcal{I}^{\#} \longrightarrow \mathcal{D}^{\#} \\ R^{\#}, I^{\#} \longmapsto \text{let } R_1^{\#} = extend(R^{\#}) \text{ in} \\ \qquad \text{let } R_2^{\#} = R_1^{\#} \cap^{\#} I^{\#} \text{ in} \\ \qquad img(R_2^{\#}) \end{cases}$$

Fig. 6. Definition of *extend*, *img* and *apply*.

abstract interference relation. We first implement two auxiliary functions, called *extend* and *img*, defined in Fig. 6. We introduce a new function Var associating to each abstract domain its variables. The function *extend* creates a copy of every variable in the abstract domain, thus creating an interference relation. On the other hand, *img* returns the image set of an interference relation. With these two functions, we can now give a procedure computing the result of applying a piece of interference, given an initial abstract memory domain: we first add primed copies of the variables of the abstract memory domain. We can then intersect the resulting abstract memory domain $R_1^{\#}$ with the interference. Then, we have to get the image of the relation, which is the part where the variables are primed. The obtained abstract domain is restricted to the states reachable after an instance of interference is applied to the abstract initial domain.

The abstract semantics is presented in Fig. 7a. We abstract the concrete semantics of Eq. (2) and Eq. (3) in Eq. (11) and Eq. (12). The transition from the concrete to the abstract semantics is straightforward, by composition of *apply*, *assign*, *extend*, and *img*. We only briefly comment on the definition of Eq. (11), as Eq. (12) is similar. $I_{l''}^{\#}$ represents any interference starting from the abstract state $R^{\#}(l_1)$ (by definition of *extend*). Then, we constrain this interference so that $I_l^{\#}$ represents interference from $R^{\#}(l_1)$ to the state of the program just after the assignment is done. $I_l^{\#}$ is by construction the abstract version of I_1 from Eq. (2). Recall that aux_t are auxiliary variables representing control locations, and that $\alpha_{\mathcal{L}}$ returns a numeric abstract control point. By construction of *img*, $R_1^{\#}$ is the abstract version of R_1, representing the image of the interference $I_l^{\#}$. $R_2^{\#}$ represents all reachable states after any possible interference has been applied to $R_1^{\#}$. This concludes the case of assignments. The if and while statements are

$$\mathbb{S}^{\#}[\![stat]\!]_t : (\mathcal{L} \to \mathcal{D}^{\#}) \times (\mathcal{T} \to \mathcal{I}^{\#}) \longrightarrow (\mathcal{L} \to \mathcal{D}^{\#}) \times (\mathcal{T} \to \mathcal{I}^{\#}) \tag{10}$$

$$\mathbb{S}^{\#}[\![^{l_1}X \leftarrow e^{l_2}]\!]_t(R^{\#}, I^{\#}) = \tag{11}$$

$\quad$ let $I_{l''}^{\#} = extend(R^{\#}(l_1))$ in

$\quad$ let $I_{l'}^{\#} = assign(I_{l''}^{\#}, \{(X', e)\} \cup \{(Y', Y) \mid Y \in Var(R^{\#}) \setminus \{X, \mathtt{aux\_t}\}\})$ in

$\quad$ let $I_l^{\#} = assign(I_{l'}^{\#}, \{(\mathtt{aux\_t}, \alpha_{\mathcal{L}}(l_1)), (\mathtt{aux\_t'}, \alpha_{\mathcal{L}}(l_2))\})$ in

$\quad$ let $R_1^{\#} = img(I_l^{\#})$ in

$\quad$ let $R_2^{\#} = \lim \lambda Y^{\#}. \; Y^{\#} \triangledown itf^{\#}(Y^{\#}, t, I^{\#}, R_1^{\#})$ in

$\quad R^{\#}[l_2 \mapsto R^{\#}(l_2) \cup^{\#} R_2^{\#}], I^{\#}[t \mapsto I^{\#}(t) \cup^{\#} I_l^{\#}]$

$$\mathbb{B}^{\#}[\![^{l_1}b^{l_2}]\!]_t(R^{\#}, I^{\#}) = \tag{12}$$

$\quad$ let $I_{l''}^{\#} = extend(\mathbb{F}^{\#}[\![b]\!](R^{\#}(l_1)))$ in

$\quad$ let $I_{l'}^{\#} = assign(I_{l''}^{\#}, \{(Y', Y) \mid Y \in Var(R^{\#}) \setminus \{\mathtt{aux\_t}\}\})$ in

$\quad$ let $I_l^{\#} = assign(I_{l'}^{\#}, \{(\mathtt{aux\_t}, \alpha_{\mathcal{L}}(l_1)), (\mathtt{aux\_t'}, \alpha_{\mathcal{L}}(l_2))\})$ in

$\quad$ let $R_1^{\#} = img(I_l^{\#})$ in

$\quad$ let $R_2^{\#} = \lim \lambda Y^{\#}. \; Y^{\#} \triangledown itf^{\#}(Y^{\#}, t, I^{\#}, R_1^{\#})$ in

$\quad R^{\#}[l_2 \mapsto R^{\#}(l_2) \cup^{\#} R_2^{\#}], I^{\#}[t \mapsto I^{\#}(t) \cup^{\#} I_l^{\#}]$

$$itf^{\#} : (S^{\#}, t, I^{\#}, R^{\#}) \mapsto R^{\#} \cup^{\#} \bigcup_{t' \in \mathcal{T} \setminus \{t\}}^{\#} apply(S^{\#}, I^{\#}(t'))$$

$\mathbb{S}^{\#}[\![^{l_1}\text{if } b \text{ then } {}^{l_2}tt \text{ else } {}^{l_3}ff \text{ fi } {}^{l_4}]\!]_t X^{\#} =$

$\quad$ let $T = \mathbb{S}^{\#}[\![^{l_2}tt^{l_4}]\!]_t \circ \mathbb{B}^{\#}[\![^{l_1}b^{l_2}]\!]_t X^{\#}$ in

$\quad$ let $F = \mathbb{S}^{\#}[\![^{l_3}ff^{l_4}]\!]_t \circ \mathbb{B}^{\#}[\![^{l_1}\neg b^{l_3}]\!]_t X^{\#}$ in

$\quad X^{\#} \dot{\cup}^{\#} T \dot{\cup}^{\#} F$

$\mathbb{S}^{\#}[\![\text{while } {}^{l_1}b \text{ do } {}^{l_2}c \text{ od}^{l_3}]\!]_t X =$

$\quad X^{\#} \dot{\cup}^{\#} \mathbb{B}^{\#}[\![^{l_1}\neg b^{l_3}]\!]_t (\lim \lambda Y. Y \; \dot{\triangledown} \; (X^{\#} \dot{\cup}^{\#} \mathbb{S}^{\#}[\![^{l_2}c^{l_1}]\!]_t \circ \mathbb{B}^{\#}[\![^{l_1}b^{l_2}]\!]_t Y))$

(a) Definition of the abstract semantics.

$$f^{\#} : \begin{cases} (\mathcal{T} \to (\mathcal{L} \to \mathcal{D}^{\#})) \times (\mathcal{T} \to \mathcal{I}^{\#}) \longrightarrow (\mathcal{T} \to (\mathcal{L} \to \mathcal{D}^{\#})) \times (\mathcal{T} \to \mathcal{I}^{\#}) \\ \quad (R^{\#}, I^{\#}) \quad\quad\quad\quad \longmapsto \lambda t. R_t'^{\#}, \dot{\cup}_{t \in \mathcal{T}}^{\#} I_t'^{\#} \end{cases}$$

$$\text{with } R_t'^{\#}, I_t'^{\#} = \mathbb{S}^{\#}[\![stats_t]\!]_t(R^{\#}(t) \cup^{\#} S_0^{\#}, I^{\#})$$

(b) Definition of the analysis operator $f^{\#}$.

$$\gamma : \begin{cases} (\mathcal{T} \to (\mathcal{L} \to \mathcal{D}^{\#})) \times (\mathcal{T} \to \mathcal{I}^{\#}) \longrightarrow \mathcal{P}(\mathcal{S}) \times \mathcal{P}(\mathcal{I}) \\ \quad (r, i) \quad\quad\quad\quad\quad \longmapsto \bigcup_{t \in \mathcal{T}} \gamma_{\mathcal{M}}(t) \circ \gamma_{\mathcal{D}^{\#}}(r(t)), \gamma_{\mathcal{C}} \circ \gamma_{\mathcal{I}^{\#}}(i) \end{cases}$$

(c) Definition of the main concretization.

Fig. 7. Definitions of our abstract analysis.

abstracted in a classic way, by induction on the syntax. As usual [7], we changed the *lfp* operators into limits of an iteration with widening, so that convergence is ensured. $\mathbb{F}^{\#}[\![b]\!]$ is the usual abstract boolean filtering operator.

The abstract version $f^{\#}$ of the analysis operator f from Fig. 3b is defined in Fig. 7b. $S_0^{\#}$ represents the abstracted initial program states, abstracting S_0.

3.3   Soundness of the Analysis

We first define a concretization operator going from our abstract states to our concrete ones, before stating the soundness result. Figure 7c presents the global concretization, where $\gamma_{\mathcal{M}}(t)$ and $\gamma_{\mathcal{C}}$ are the adjoints associated to the abstractions $\alpha_{\mathcal{M}}(t)$ and $\alpha_{\mathcal{C}}$ presented in Fig. 4. The analysis presented is sound, i.e.:

$$\textit{lfp } f \subseteq \gamma(\lim \lambda Y.Y \mathrel{\dot{\nabla}} f^{\#}(Y))$$

3.4   Retrieving Flow-Insensitive Interference Analysis

The analysis presented in Sect. 3.2 can by very costly, depending on the choice of $\mathcal{L}^{\#}$. For many analyses, choosing $\mathcal{L}^{\#}$ to be a singleton is sufficient to be precise enough and having an easily computable analysis. In that case, the set of interference becomes flow-insensitive, and the analysis is an extension of existing analyses. For example, the thread-modular analysis presented in [28] is non-relational and can be retrieved by choosing a non-relational domain for $\mathcal{I}^{\#}$ and $\mathcal{L}^{\#}$ to be a singleton. On the contrary, when choosing $\mathcal{L}^{\#}$ to be $\mathcal{L}$, the analysis would be roughly equivalent to analyzing the product of the control flow graphs (the main difference being that the control information would be stored in auxiliary variables, and possibly subject to numeric abstraction).

3.5   On the Way to Proving Mutual Exclusion: Growing $\mathcal{L}^{\#}$

When $\mathcal{L}^{\#}$ is a singleton, the interference set is too coarse, and some properties are impossible to prove. For example, to verify mutual exclusion properties, we need to use a separate abstract control point at the beginning of the critical section to partition the abstract state. This is what we call control partitioning. In order to partition the abstract state, we need a richer $\mathcal{L}^{\#}$.

Let us consider Peterson's mutual exclusion algorithm as described in ConcurInterproc [18], and presented in Fig. 8. We suppose that b0, b1, and turn are boolean variables, and that at the beginning, $\neg b0 \land \neg b1$ holds. If there is no control point separation between lines 1–3 and 4–5, then, the following execution order is possible: we first execute lines 1–2 of each thread. We suppose that then, turn is true (the other case is symmetric). At that point, the condition in the while loop of Thread 1 is satisfied, and, in Thread 2, the interference $b1' = \neg b1$ (created at line 5 in Thread 1) can be applied, enabling the two threads to access simultaneously the mutual exclusion section, here embodied by the skip statements. If a label separation is created, instead, this spurious execution is not possible anymore, and mutual exclusion is actually inferred.

	Thread 1	Thread 2
1	b1 ← true	b2 ← true
2	turn ← false	turn ← true
3	while(b2 ∧ ¬turn) do skip od	while(b1 ∧ turn) do skip od
4	skip	skip
5	b1 ← false	b2 ← false

Fig. 8. Peterson's mutual exclusion algorithm.

Indeed, let us set $\mathcal{L}^{\#} = \{[1,3];[4,5]\}$ for both threads. This time, when the variable **turn** holds, the control state is $(1,2) \mapsto (3,4)$, and we cannot apply the interference $b1' = \neg b1$ of Thread 1: we are at label 3, and $3 \notin [4,5]$. In all the cases we observed in practice (discussed in the following section), splitting the control locations at the beginning of the critical section provides a sufficient gain in precision to infer mutual exclusion.

4   Implementation and Experimental Results

4.1   Implementation

We implemented an analyzer prototype, called Batman, in order to assess the precision and scalability of our analysis. It consists of roughly 1700 lines of OCaml code, and can use either the Apron [19] or BddApron [17] libraries to manipulate abstract domains. We implemented a simple widening with thresholds, as well as increasing and decreasing iterations. The analyzer uses functors, so that switching from one relational domain to another is easy. In order to show the benefit of thread-modular analyses, we compare our results with those obtained by ConcurInterproc [18], another academic analyzer for numeric properties of multi-threaded programs, which is relational but not thread-modular. We use a similar type of language: it supports a fixed number of integer and boolean variables, if and while statements, assignments, and a fixed number of threads. Our analyzer does not support procedures, unlike ConcurInterproc.

4.2   Precision of the Analysis

Batman is able to automatically infer the relational invariants described previously. We present the results we obtained on some examples.

Relational Analysis. Using our fully relational analysis, we are able to prove more properties on the example provided in Fig. 1 than what was presented in [27], because the assignment $x \leftarrow (x+y)/2$ is keeping the invariant $x \leq y$. This cannot be expressed using the analysis provided in [27]. Moreover, invariants are simpler to express using the polyhedron-based interference: $x+1 \leq x'$ means that when this interference is applied, it increases x. We experimented on several simple examples proposed in recent work [27]. The results are presented in Fig. 9b. The flow-sensitivity column describes whether the abstraction of interference was flow-sensitive (i.e., $\mathcal{L}^{\#}$ is not a singleton) or flow-insensitive.

Mutual Exclusion Algorithms. We are also able to analyze classic mutual exclusion algorithms such as Peterson's algorithm [29], presented in Fig. 8, and Lamport's Bakery algorithm [23]. To infer the mutual exclusion property automatically, we need to give the analyzer a partition of the control points, and we use a simple annotation system for this. Splitting the control locations at the beginning of the critical section was sufficient for all our tests. We also need the interference abstraction to be relational to infer mutual exclusion. Partitioning heuristics could be developed to improve the automation of the analysis. These heuristics were not in the prototype used for our experiments due to lack of time, and their development is left for future work.

4.3 Scalability of the Analysis

We also studied the scalability of the analysis as a function of the number of threads. We thus considered algorithms able to synchronize an arbitrary number of threads. Note that the polyhedral domain does not scale up with the number of variables; hence, there is no hope to scale up in the number of threads for algorithms that require additional variables for each thread. We performed some experiments with both the polyhedron and the more scalable octagon domain.

Ideal Case. In order to study the scalability limit of the thread-modular analysis independently from the scalability of the numeric domain, we can consider the ideal case of programs where the number of global variables is fixed, whatever the number of threads. As example, we present, in Fig. 9a, a simple mutual exclusion algorithm based on token passing, with only two variables, and show that our method scales up to hundreds of threads, while ConcurInterproc does not. In this example, we used the polyhedral domain. As the numeric domain is a parameter of our analysis, we can consider the scalability in the number of variables to be an orthogonal problem to that of the scalability in the number of threads, and this article addresses the later rather than the former.

Lamport's Bakery Algorithm. We tested the scalability of Lamport's Bakery algorithm, ensuring mutual exclusion for an arbitrary number n of threads. However, the number of variables for the global program is linear in n, and the size of the whole program is quadratic in n (this is a consequence of our encoding of arrays into scalar variables). This setting does not really promise to be scalable, but we are still able to analyze up to 7 threads, and the mutual exclusion is inferred each time. As mentioned above, to infer the mutual exclusion property within the critical section, both the flow-sensitive and relational properties of the interference are required. For each thread, we have two different elements of $\mathcal{L}^\#$, one before the critical section and one after. This is sufficient to infer the mutual exclusion property. The results are presented in Fig. 9b. ConcurInterproc seems to be unable to infer the mutual exclusion, and is less scalable here: it takes 90 s to analyze 3 threads, and 22 h to analyze 4 threads.

Thread 1	Thread 2	Thread 3
while true do	while true do	while true do
while f != 1 do	while f != 2 do	while f != 3 do
skip	skip	skip
od	od	od
$X \leftarrow 1$	$X \leftarrow 2$	$X \leftarrow 3$
$f \leftarrow [1,3]$	$f \leftarrow [1,3]$	$f \leftarrow [1,3]$
od	od	od

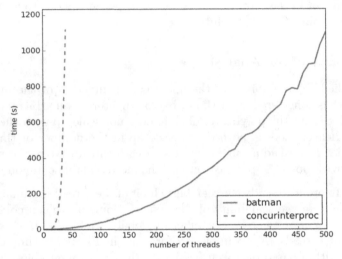

(a) Analysis of a token-passing mutual exclusion algorithm.

Reference (in [27])	Flow-sensitivity	Results	Time, polyhedron
Fig. 1	✗	$0 \leq X \leq Y$	0.30s
Fig. 4	✗	$0 \leq T \leq L \leq C \leq H \leq 10^4$	0.26s
Fig. 5 (a)	✗	$0 \leq X$	0.44s
Fig. 5 (a)	✓	$0 \leq X \leq 100$	0.35s
Fig. 5 (b)	✗	thread 1: $X \leq Y \leq 100$ thread 2: $0 \leq Y \leq X$	0.78s
Fig. 5 (b)	✓	$0 \leq X = Y \leq 100$	0.44s

Algorithm name	Number of threads	Flow-sensitivity	Mutual exclusion	Time, polyhedron	Time, octagons
Peterson	2	✓	✓	0.67s	0.72s
Lamport	3	✓	✓	6.5s	27s
Lamport	4	✓	✓	49s	6m 33s
Lamport	5	✓	✓	5m 10s	49m 45s
Lamport	6	✓	✓	−	151m 8s
Lamport	7	✓	✓	−	12h

(b) Analysis result.

Fig. 9. Experimental evaluation of our approach.

5   Related Work

Many articles have been devoted to the analysis of multi-threaded programs. We cite only the most relevant. Our article can be seen as an extension of the first thread-modular abstract interpreters [5,25] that were non-relational and flow-insensitive. We achieve higher levels of precision, when parameterized with relational domains. We build on a theoretical framework for complete concrete thread-modular semantics [27]. However, while [27] then explores the end of the spectrum concerned with scalable but not very precise analyses (using relationality only in a few selected points), we explore the other end in order to prove properties of small but intricate programs not precisely analyzed by [27]. We also study the scalability of fully-relational analyses for large numbers of threads. ConcurInterproc [18] is a static analyzer for concurrent programs. It is not thread-modular and, as shown in our benchmarks, does not scale as well as our approach, even though both use the same polyhedral numeric abstraction. Kusano and Wang [21] extend the flow-insensitive abstract interpretation of [5,25] by maintaining flow-sensitive information about interference using constraints, while not maintaining numeric information on them; hence, their method is complementary to ours. Farzan and Kincaid [12] also model interference in a thread-modular abstract interpreter using constraints, but focus instead on parameterized programs with an unbounded number of thread instances.

Modular verification techniques for concurrent programs also include flow analyses. Dwyer [11] proposed a flow method to check properties expressed with finite automata. Grunwald and Srinivasan [15] consider the reaching definition problem for explicitly parallel programs. These works focus on monotone dataflow equations, which is not the general case for abstract interpretation.

Model-checking of concurrent programs is a very well developed field. To prevent the state explosion problem in the specific case of concurrent programs, partial order reduction methods have been introduced by Godefroid [13]. Our method differs in that we do not have to consider explicit interleavings, and that we employ abstractions, allowing a loss of precision to achieve a faster analysis. A more recent method to reduce the cost of model-checking consists in only analyzing a program up to a fixed number of interleavings [30]. Our approach differs as we retain the soundness of the analysis. Counter-example guided abstract refinement methods have also been adapted to concurrent programs; one such example is [10]. As in the case of analyzing sequential programs, these methods are based on a sequence of analyses with increasingly more expressive finite abstract domains of predicates, which may not terminate. By contrast, our method is based on abstract interpretation, and so iterates in (possibly infinite) abstract domains employing widenings to ensure termination. Thread-modular model-checking has also been advocated, as in [6], which helps with the scalability issue. However, the method uses BDDs, and is thus limited to finite data-spaces. By contrast, we employ abstract interpretation techniques in order to use infinite-state abstract domains (such as polyhedra). [14] proposes a general framework to express and synthesize a large variety of static analyses from sets of rules, based on Horn clauses, which includes rely-guarantee analyses for multi-threaded programs; while [16] proposes a related approach based on constraints. Following predicate abstraction and CEGAR methods, the memory abstraction in these works is often limited by the inherent Cartesian abstraction [24], which cannot thus infer relations between variables from different threads.

6   Conclusion

We have proposed a general analysis by abstract interpretation for numeric properties of concurrent programs that is thread-modular, takes soundly into account all the thread interleavings, and is parameterized by a choice of numeric and control abstractions. The novelty of our approach is its ability to precisely control trade-offs between cost and precision when analyzing thread interference, from a coarse, flow-insensitive and non-relational abstraction (corresponding to the state-of-the-art) to fully flow-sensitive and relational abstractions. We showed on a few simple example analyses with our prototype that relational interference allows proving properties that could only be handled by non-modular analyses before, while we also benefit from the scalability of thread-modular methods. We believe that this opens the door to the design of scalable and precise analyses of realistic concurrent programs, provided that adequate abstractions are designed.

Future work will include designing such abstractions, and in particular designing heterogeneous abstractions able to restrict the flow-sensitivity and relationality to program parts requiring more precision. We would also like to remove the current limitation that every variable is considered to be global and appears in all thread-local and interference abstractions, which limits the scalability of our analysis. It would also be interesting to have a more comprehensive experimental evaluation, as well comparisons with other approaches. Fine-grained control of which variables are taken into account in each abstraction should be possible using packing techniques or weakly relational domains [2,3]. Likewise, the control abstraction used in the interference is currently set manually, but we believe that automation is possible using heuristics (such as guessing plausible locations of critical sections). We consider integrating this method into [27] in order to gain more precision when necessary while retaining the overall scalability. Other future work includes handling weakly consistent memories, and the non-uniform analysis of unbounded numbers of threads, which requires integrating other forms of abstractions into our analysis.

References

1. Atig, M.F., Bouajjani, A., Burckhardt, S., Musuvathi, M.: On the verification problem for weak memory models. In: POPL 2010, pp. 7–18. ACM, January 2010
2. Bertrane, J., Cousot, P., Cousot, R., Feret, J., Mauborgne, L., Miné, A., Rival, X.: Static analysis and verification of aerospace software by abstract interpretation. In: Infotech@Aerospace. AIAA, vol. 2010-3385, pp. 1–38. AIAA, April 2010
3. Blanchet, B., Cousot, P., Cousot, R., Feret, J., Mauborgne, L., Miné, A., Monniaux, D., Rival, X.: A static analyzer for large safety-critical software. In: PLDI 2003, pp. 196–207. ACM, June 2003

4. Bourdoncle, F.: Efficient chaotic iteration strategies with widenings. In: BjØrner, D., Broy, M., Pottosin, I.V. (eds.) Formal Methods in Programming and Their Applications, FMPA 1993. LNCS, vol. 735, pp. 128–141. Springer, Heidelberg (1993)
5. Carré, J.L., Hymans, C.: From single-thread to multithreaded: an efficient static analysis algorithm. Technical report. arXiv:0910.5833v1, EADS October 2009
6. Cohen, A., Namjoshi, K.S.: Local proofs for global safety properties. Formal Methods Syst. Des. **34**(2), 104–125 (2008)
7. Cousot, P., Cousot, R.: Abstract interpretation: a unified lattice model for static analysis of programs by construction or approximation of fixpoints. In: POPL 1977, pp. 238–252. ACM, January 1977
8. Cousot, P., Cousot, R.: Invariance proof methods and analysis techniques for parallel programs. In: Automatic Program Construction Techniques, Chap. 12, pp. 243–271. Macmillan, New York (1984)
9. Cousot, P., Halbwachs, N.: Automatic discovery of linear restraints among variables of a program. In: POPL 1978, pp. 84–97. ACM (1978)
10. Donaldson, A., Kaiser, A., Kroening, D., Tautschnig, M., Wahl, T.: Counterexample-guided abstraction refinement for symmetric concurrent programs. Formal Methods Syst. Des. **41**(1), 25–44 (2012)
11. Dwyer, M.B.: Modular flow analysis for concurrent software. In: ASE 1997, pp. 264–273. IEEE Computer Society (1997)
12. Farzan, A., Kincaid, Z.: DUET: static analysis for unbounded parallelism. In: Sharygina, N., Veith, H. (eds.) CAV 2013. LNCS, vol. 8044, pp. 191–196. Springer, Heidelberg (2013). doi:10.1007/978-3-642-39799-8_12
13. Godefroid, P.: Partial-order methods for the verification of concurrent systems - an approach to the state-explosion problem. Ph.D. thesis, University of Liege, Computer Science Department (1994)
14. Grebenshchikov, S., Lopes, N.P., Popeea, C., Rybalchenko, A.: Synthesizing software verifiers from proof rules. In: PLDI 2012, pp. 405–416. ACM (2012)
15. Grunwald, D., Srinivasan, H.: Data flow equations for explicitly parallel programs. In: PPOPP 1993, pp. 159–168. ACM (1993)
16. Gupta, A., Popeea, C., Rybalchenko, A.: Threader: a constraint-based verifier for multi-threaded programs. In: Gopalakrishnan, G., Qadeer, S. (eds.) CAV 2011. LNCS, vol. 6806, pp. 412–417. Springer, Heidelberg (2011). doi:10.1007/978-3-642-22110-1_32
17. Jeannet, B.: BddApron. http://pop-art.inrialpes.fr/~bjeannet/bjeannet-forge/bddapron/bddapron.pdf
18. Jeannet, B.: Relational interprocedural verification of concurrent programs. Softw. Syst. Model. **12**(2), 285–306 (2013)
19. Jeannet, B., Miné, A.: APRON: a library of numerical abstract domains for static analysis. In: Bouajjani, A., Maler, O. (eds.) CAV 2009. LNCS, vol. 5643, pp. 661–667. Springer, Heidelberg (2009). doi:10.1007/978-3-642-02658-4_52
20. Jones, C.B.: Development methods for computer programs including a notion of interference. Ph.D. thesis, Oxford University, June 1981
21. Kusano, M., Wang, C.: Flow-sensitive composition of thread-modular abstract interpretation. In: FSE 2016, pp. 799–809. ACM (2016)
22. Lamport, L.: How to make a multiprocessor computer that correctly executes multiprocess programs. IEEE Trans. Comput. **28**, 690–691 (1979). IEEE Computer Society
23. Lamport, L.: A new solution of Dijkstra's concurrent programming problem. Commun. ACM **17**(8), 453–455 (1974)

24. Malkis, A., Podelski, A., Rybalchenko, A.: Thread-modular verification is cartesian abstract interpretation. In: Barkaoui, K., Cavalcanti, A., Cerone, A. (eds.) ICTAC 2006. LNCS, vol. 4281, pp. 183–197. Springer, Heidelberg (2006). doi:10.1007/11921240_13
25. Miné, A.: Static analysis of run-time errors in embedded critical parallel C programs. In: Barthe, G. (ed.) ESOP 2011. LNCS, vol. 6602, pp. 398–418. Springer, Heidelberg (2011). doi:10.1007/978-3-642-19718-5_21
26. Miné, A.: Static analysis by abstract interpretation of sequential and multi-thread programs. In: Proceedings of the 10th School of Modelling and Verifying Parallel Processes (MOVEP 2012), pp. 35–48, 3–7 December 2012
27. Miné, A.: Relational thread-modular static value analysis by abstract interpretation. In: McMillan, K.L., Rival, X. (eds.) VMCAI 2014. LNCS, vol. 8318, pp. 39–58. Springer, Heidelberg (2014). doi:10.1007/978-3-642-54013-4_3
28. Miné, A.: Static analysis of run-time errors in embedded real-time parallel C programs. Logical Methods Comput. Sci. (LMCS) 8(26), 63 (2012)
29. Peterson, G.L.: Myths about the mutual exclusion problem. Inf. Process. Lett. 12(3), 115–116 (1981)
30. Qadeer, S., Rehof, J.: Context-bounded model checking of concurrent software. In: Halbwachs, N., Zuck, L.D. (eds.) TACAS 2005. LNCS, vol. 3440, pp. 93–107. Springer, Heidelberg (2005). doi:10.1007/978-3-540-31980-1_7

Detecting All High-Level Dataraces in an RTOS Kernel

Suvam Mukherjee[✉], Arun Kumar, and Deepak D'Souza

Indian Institute of Science, Bangalore, India
{suvam,deepakd}@csa.iisc.ernet.in, aruns.siva@gmail.com

Abstract. A high-level race occurs when an execution interleaves instructions corresponding to user-annotated critical accesses to shared memory structures. Such races are good indicators of atomicity violations. We propose a technique for detecting *all* high-level dataraces in a system library like the kernel API of a real-time operating system (RTOS) that relies on flag-based scheduling and synchronization. Our methodology is based on model-checking, but relies on a meta-argument to bound the number of task processes needed to orchestrate a race. We describe our approach in the context of FreeRTOS, a popular RTOS in the embedded domain.

1 Introduction

Atomicity violations [13] precisely characterize the bugs in a method library that arise due to *concurrent* use of the methods in the library. An execution of an application program that uses the library is said to exhibit an atomicity violation if its behaviour cannot be matched by any "serialized" version of the execution, where none of the method calls interleave with each other. As one may expect, such bugs can be pernicious and difficult to detect.

A necessary condition for an atomicity violation to occur in a library L is that two method invocations should be able to "race" (or interleave) in an execution of an application that uses L. In fact it is often necessary for two "critical" access paths in the source code of the methods (more precisely the instructions corresponding to them) to interleave in an execution, to produce an atomicity violation. With this in mind, we could imagine that a user (or the developer herself) annotates blocks of code in each method as critical accesses to a particular unit of memory structures. We can now say that an execution exhibits a "high-level" race (with respect to this annotation) if it interleaves two critical accesses to the same memory structure.

Suppose we now had a way of finding the precise set R of pairs of critical accesses that could race with each other, across *all* executions in *all* applications programs that use L. We call this the problem of finding all high-level races in L. The user can now focus on the set R, which is hopefully a small fraction of the set of all possible pairs, and investigate each of them to see whether they could lead to atomicity violations. We note that the user can *soundly* disregard the

© Springer International Publishing AG 2017
A. Bouajjani and D. Monniaux (Eds.): VMCAI 2017, LNCS 10145, pp. 405–423, 2017.
DOI: 10.1007/978-3-319-52234-0_22

pairs outside R as they can never race to begin with, and hence can never be the cause of any atomicity violation.

In this paper we are interested in the problem of finding all high-level races in a library like the Application Programmer Interface (API) of a real-time kernel. The particular system we are interested in is a real-time operating system (RTOS) called FreeRTOS [23]. FreeRTOS is one of the most popular operating systems in the embedded industry, and is widely used in real-time embedded applications that run on microcontrollers with small memory. FreeRTOS is essentially a library of API functions written in C and Assembly, that an application programmer invokes to create and manage tasks. Despite running on a *single* processor or core, the execution of tasks (and hence the kernel API functions) can interleave due to interrupts and context-switches, leading to potential races on the kernel data-structures.

The kind of control-flow and synchronization mechanisms that kernels like FreeRTOS use are non-standard from a traditional programming point of view. To begin with, the control-flow *between* threads is very non-standard. In a typical concurrent program, control could potentially switch between threads at *any* time. However in FreeRTOS, control switching is restricted and depends on whether interrupts have been disabled, the value of certain flag variables like `SchedulerSuspended`, and whether the task is running as part of an interrupt service routine (ISR). Secondly, FreeRTOS does not use standard synchronization mechanisms like locks, but relies instead on mechanisms like disabling interrupts and flag-based synchronization. This makes it difficult to use or adapt some of the existing approaches to high-level race detection like [3,28] or classical datarace detection like [9,29], which are based on standard control-flow and lock-based synchronization.

An approach based on model-checking could potentially address some of the hurdles above: one could model the control-flow and synchronization mechanism in each API function faithfully, create a "generic" task process that non-deterministically calls each API function, create a model (say M_n) that runs n of these processes in parallel, and finally model-check it for data-races. But this approach has some basic roadblocks: certain races need a minimum number of processes running to orchestrate it—how does one determine a sufficient number of processes n that is guaranteed to generate *all* races? Secondly, even with a small number of processes, the size of the state-space to be explored by the model-checker could be prohibitively large.

The approach we propose and carry out in this paper is based on the model-checking approach above, but finds a way around the hurdles mentioned. The key idea is to create a set of *reduced* models, say $\mathcal{M}_{red}$, in which each model essentially runs only three API functions at a time. We then argue that a race that shows up in M_n, for *any* n, must also be a race in one of the reduced models in $\mathcal{M}_{red}$. Model-checking each of these reduced models is easy, and gives us a way of finding *all* data-races that may ever arise due to use of the FreeRTOS API. We note that the number of API functions to run in each reduced model (three in this case), and the argument of sufficiency, is specific to FreeRTOS. In general, this will depend on the library under consideration.

On applying this technique to FreeRTOS (with our own annotation of critical accesses) we found a total of 48 pairs of critical accesses that could race. Of these 10 were found to be false positives (i.e. they could not happen in an actual execution of a FreeRTOS application). Of the remaining, 16 were classified as harmful, in that they could be seen to lead to atomicity violations. The bottom-line is that the user was able to disregard 99.8% of an estimated 41,000 potential high-level races.

In the next couple of sections we describe how FreeRTOS works and our notion of high-level races in its context. In Sect. 4 we describe how we model the API functions and control-flow in Spin, and give our reduction argument in Sect. 5. We describe our experimental results in Sect. 6 and related work in Sect. 7.

2 Overview of FreeRTOS

FreeRTOS [23] is a real-time kernel meant for use in embedded applications that run on microcontrollers with small to mid-sized memory.

It allows an application to organise itself into multiple independent tasks (or threads) that will be executed according to a priority-based preemptive scheduling policy. It is implemented as a library of functions (or an API) written mostly in C, that an application programmer can include with their code and invoke as functions. The API provides the programmer ways to create and schedule tasks, communicate between tasks (via message queues, semaphores, etc.), and carry out time-constrained blocking of tasks.

Figure 1 shows a simple FreeRTOS application. In main the application first creates a queue with the capacity to hold a single message of type int. It then creates two tasks called "Prod" and "Cons" of priority 2 and 1 respectively using the TaskCreate API function which adds these two tasks to the "Ready" list. The FreeRTOS scheduler is then started by the call to StartScheduler. The scheduler schedules the Prod task first, being the highest priority ready task. Prod sends a message to the queue, and then asks to be delayed for two time units. This results in Prod being put into the "Delayed" list. The next available task,

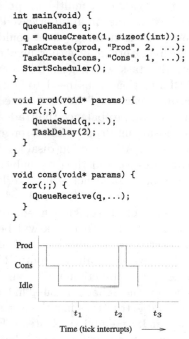

```
int main(void) {
  QueueHandle q;
  q = QueueCreate(1, sizeof(int));
  TaskCreate(prod, "Prod", 2, ...);
  TaskCreate(cons, "Cons", 1, ...);
  StartScheduler();
}

void prod(void* params) {
  for(;;) {
    QueueSend(q,...);
    TaskDelay(2);
  }
}

void cons(void* params) {
  for(;;) {
    QueueReceive(q,...);
  }
}
```

Fig. 1. An example FreeRTOS application and its execution

Cons, is run next. It dequeues the message from the queue, but is blocked when it tries to dequeue again. The scheduler now makes the Idle task run. A timer interrupt now occurs, causing an ISR called IncrementTick to be run. This routine increments the current tick count, and checks the delayed list to see if any tasks need to be woken up. There are none, so the Idle task resumes execution. However when the second tick interrupt occurs, the ISR finds that the Prod task needs to be woken up, and moves it to the ready list. As Prod is now the highest priority ready task, it executes next. This cycle repeats, ad infinitum.

The FreeRTOS kernel maintains a bunch of data-structures, variables and flags, some of which are depicted in Fig. 2. Tasks that are ready to run are kept in the ReadyTasksList, an array which maintains—for each priority—a pointer to a linked list of tasks of that priority that are ready to run. When a running task delays itself, it is moved from the ReadyTasksList to the DelayedTaskList, with an appropriate time-to-awake value. User-defined queues, like q in the example application, are maintained by the kernel as a chunk of memory to store the data (shown as QueueData in the figure), along with an integer variable MessagesWaiting that records the number of messages in the queue, and two associated lists WaitingToSend and WaitingToReceive that respectively contain the tasks that are blocked on sending to and receiving from the queue.

Even though FreeRTOS applications typically run on a *single* processor (or a *single core* of a multi-core processor), the kernel API functions can interact with each other in an interleaved manner. While a function invoked by the current task is running, there could be an interrupt due to which an ISR runs, which in turn may either invoke another API function, or unblock a higher priority task which goes on to execute another API function. The FreeRTOS API functions thus need to use some kind of synchronization mechanism to ensure "exclusive" access to the kernel data-structures. They do so in a variety of ways, to balance the trade-off between securing fully exclusive access and not losing interrupts. The strongest exclusion is achieved in a "critical section," where an API function disables interrupts to the processor, completes its critical accesses, and then re-enables interrupts. During such a critical section no preemption (and hence no interleaving) is possible. The second kind of exclusion is achieved by "suspending" the scheduler. This is done by setting the kernel flag SchedulerSuspended to 1. While the scheduler is suspended (i.e. this flag is set), no other task will be scheduled to run; however, unlike in a critical section, *interrupts* can still occur and an ISR can execute some designated API functions (called "fromISR" functions which are distinguished from the other "task" functions). The implicit protocol is that these functions will check whether the SchedulerSuspended flag is set, and if so they will not access certain data-structures like the ReadyTasksList, but move tasks when required to the PendingReadyList instead. Figure 2 shows some of the structures protected by the SchedulerSuspended flag.

The final synchronization mechanism used in FreeRTOS is a pair of per-user-queue "locks" (actually *flags* which also serve as *counters*) called RxLock and

TxLock, that protect the `WaitingToReceive` and `WaitingToSend` lists associated with the queue. When a task executes an API function that accesses a user-queue, the function sets these locks (increments them from their initial value of −1 to 0). Any fromISR function that now runs will now avoid accessing the waiting lists associated with this queue, and instead increment the corresponding lock associated with the queue to record the fact that data has been added or removed from the queue. When the interrupted function resumes, it will move a task from the waiting list back to the ready list, for each increment of a lock done by an ISR. These locks and the lists they protect are also depicted in Fig. 2.

Figure 3 shows parts of the implementation of two FreeRTOS APIs. The `QueueSend` function is used by a task to enqueue an item in a user-defined queue `pxQ`. Lines 3–9 are done with interrupts disabled, and corresponds to the case when there is place in the queue: the item is enqueued, a task at the head of `WaitingToReceive` is moved to the `ReadyTasksList`, and the function returns successfully. In lines 14–26, which corresponds to the case when the queue is full, the function enables interrupts, checks again that the queue is still full (since after enabling interrupts, an ISR could have removed something from the queue), and goes on to move itself from the Ready queue to the `WaitingToSend` list of `pxQ`. This whole part is done by first suspending the scheduler and locking `pxQ`, and finally unlocking the queue and resuming the scheduler. The call to `LockQueue` in line 16

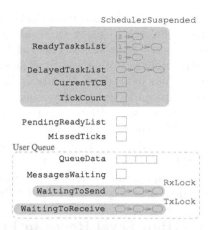

Fig. 2. Kernel data-structures and protecting flags in FreeRTOS

```
int QueueSend(QHandle pxQ, void *ItemToQueue) {
1   // Repeat till successful send
2   DISABLE_INTERRUPTS();
3   if(!QueueFull(pxQ)) { // Queue is not full
4     // Copy data to queue
5     CopyDataToQueue(pxQ, ItemToQueue);
6     if(!empty(pxQ->WaitingToReceive)) {
7       ... // Move task from WaitingToReceive
8       ... // to ReadyTasksList
9     }
10    ENABLE_INTERRUPTS();
11    return PASS;
12  }
13  // Reach here when queue is full
14  ENABLE_INTERRUPTS();
15  ++SchedulerSuspended; // Suspend scheduler
16  LockQueue(pxQ);//Inc Tx(Rx)Lock with ints disabled
17  if(QueueFull(pxQ)) { // Check if queue still full
18    ... // Move current task from ReadyTasksList
19    ... // to WaitingToSend
20  }
21  UnlockQueue(pxQ);//Move tasks from waiting lists
22    // and unlock, with ints disabled
23  --SchedulerSuspended; // Resume scheduler
24  if (...) { // higher priority task woken
25    YIELD();
26  }
}
```

```
void IncrementTick() {
1   if(SchedulerSuspended == 0) {
2     ++TickCount;
3     if(TickCount == 0) {
4       ... // swap delayed lists
5       DelayedTaskList = OverflowDelayedTaskList;
6     }
7     ... // Move tasks whose time-to-awake is now,
8     ... // from DelayedTaskList to ReadyTasksList.
9   }
10  else {
11    ++MissedTicks;
12  }
}
```

Fig. 3. Excerpts from FreeRTOS functions

increments both `RxLock` and `TxLock`. The call to `UnlockQueue` in line 21 decrements `RxLock` as many times as its value exceeds 0, each time moving a task (if present) from `WaitingToSend` to Ready. It does a similar sequence of steps with `TxLock`. Both these functions first disable interrupts and re-enable them once their job is done. Finally, in lines 24–26, the function checks to see if it has unblocked a higher priority task, and if so "yields" control to the scheduler.

The second API function in Fig. 3 is the `IncrementTick` function that is called by the timer interrupt, and which we consider to be in the fromISR category of API functions. If the scheduler is *not* suspended, it increments the `TickCount` counter, and moves tasks in the `DelayedTaskList` whose time-to-awake equals the current tick count, to the Ready list. If the scheduler *is* suspended, it simply increments the `MissedTicks` counter.

3   High-Level Races in FreeRTOS

In this section we describe our notion of a high-level race in a system library like FreeRTOS. Essentially a race occurs when two "critical" access paths in two API functions interleave. We make this notion more precise below.

Consider a system library L. Our notion of a race in L is parameterized by a set S of shared memory structures maintained by the library, and a set C of "critical accesses" of structures in S. The set of structures in S is largely determined by the developer's design for thread-safe access. We can imagine that the developer has in mind a partition of the shared memory structures into "units" which can be independently accessed: thus, it is safe for two threads to simultaneously access two *distinct* units, while it is potentially unsafe for two threads to access the *same* unit simultaneously. For instance, in FreeRTOS, the set S could contain shared variables like `SchedulerSuspended`, or shared data-structures like `ReadyTasksList`, or an entire user-queue. The set of critical accesses C would comprise contiguous blocks of code in the API functions of L, each of which corresponds to an access of one of these units in S. The accesses are "critical" in that they are *not* meant to interleave with other accesses to the same unit of structures. Each critical access comes with a classification of being a *write* or *read* access to a particular shared structure v in S. For example, we could have the block of code in lines 17–20 of the `QueueSend` function in Fig. 3, as a critical write to the user-queue structure, in C. Finally, we say that a pair of accesses in C are *conflicting* if they both access the same structure v in S and at least one is a write access.

An execution of an application program A that uses L—an L-execution for short—is an interleaving of the execution of the tasks (or threads) it creates. An execution of a task in turn is a (feasible) sequence of instructions that follows the control-flow graph of its compiled version. Since these tasks may periodically invoke the functions in L, portions of their execution will correspond to the critical paths in these functions. We say that an L-execution exhibits an (S, C) *high-level race* (or just (S, C)-*race* for short) on a structure v in S, if it *interleaves* the execution paths corresponding to two conflicting critical accesses to v (i.e. the second critical access begins before the first ends).

When do we say an $(\mathcal{S}, \mathcal{C})$-race is "harmful"? We can use the notion of atomicity violation from [13] (see also [10]) to capture this notion. Consider an L-execution ρ. Each task in the application may invoke functions in L along ρ, and some of these invocations may overlap (or interleave) with invocations of functions of L in other tasks. A *linearized* version of ρ follows the same sequence of invocations of the functions in L along ρ, except that *overlapping* invocations are re-ordered so that they no longer overlap. We refer the reader to [17] for a more formal definition of linearizability. We can now say that an L-execution ρ exhibits an *atomicity violation* if there is *no* linearized version of the execution that leaves the shared memory structures in the same state as ρ. This definition differs slightly from [13] in that we prefer to use the notion of linearizability rather than serializability.

For a given $(\mathcal{S}, \mathcal{C})$, we say that an $(\mathcal{S}, \mathcal{C})$-race is *harmful* if there is an L-execution that contains this race, exhibits an atomicity violation, and this race plays a role (possibly along with other threads) in producing this atomicity violation. Otherwise we say the race is *benign*. Finally, we say that a given $(\mathcal{S}, \mathcal{C})$ pair is *safe* for L, if every L-execution that exhibits an atomicity violation also exhibits an $(\mathcal{S}, \mathcal{C})$-race. We note that we can always obtain a safe $(\mathcal{S}, \mathcal{C})$ by putting all memory structures into a single unit in $\mathcal{S}$ and entire method bodies into $\mathcal{C}$. However this would lead to lots of false positives, and it is thus preferable to have as finely-granular an $(\mathcal{S}, \mathcal{C})$ as possible.

We now proceed to describe our choice of what we believe to be safe choice of $\mathcal{S}$ and $\mathcal{C}$ for FreeRTOS. Some natural candidates for units in $\mathcal{S}$ are the various task lists like ReadyTasksList and DelayedTaskList. For a user-defined queue, one could treat the entire queue—comprising QueueData, MessagesWaiting, and the WaitingToSend and WaitingToReceive lists—as a single unit. However, this view would go against the fact that, by design, a task could be accessing the WaitingToSend component, while an ISR accesses the QueueData component. Hence, we keep each component of a user-defined queue as a separate unit in $\mathcal{S}$. Finally, we include all shared flags like SchedulerSuspended, pointer variables like CurrentTCB, and counters and locks like TickCount and xRxLock, in $\mathcal{S}$. Corresponding to this choice of units in $\mathcal{S}$, we classify, for example, the following blocks of code as critical accesses in $\mathcal{C}$: line 3 of the QueueSend function as a read access of MessagesWaiting, line 5 as a write to QueueData, line 6 as a read of WaitingToSend, and lines 7–8 as a write to both WaitingToReceive and ReadyTasksList.

We now give a couple of examples of races with respect to the set of structures $\mathcal{S}$ and accesses $\mathcal{C}$ described above. Assume for the sake of illustration, that the QueueSend function did *not* disable interrupts in line 2. Consider an execution of the example application in Fig. 1, in which the Prod task calls the QueueSend function, and begins the critical write to ReadyTasksList. At this point a timer interrupt comes and causes the IncrementTick ISR to run and execute the critical write to ReadyTasksList in lines 7–8. This execution would constitute a race on ReadyTasksList.

As a second example, consider the write access to `SchedulerSuspended` in the equivalent of line 15 of the `QueueReceive` function, and the read access of the same variable in line 1 of `IncrementTick`. Then an execution of the example application of Fig. 1 in which `Cons` calls the `QueueReceive` function when the queue is empty and executes the equivalent of line 15 to suspend the scheduler, during which it is interrupted by the `IncrementTick` ISR which goes on to execute line 1. This execution constitutes a race between the `QueueReceive` and `IncrementTick` API functions on the `SchedulerSuspended` variable.

The race on `ReadyTasksList` above is an example of a harmful race since it could lead to the linked list being in an inconsistent state that cannot be produced by any linearization of the execution. The race on `SchedulerSuspended` turns out to be benign, essentially due to the variable being declared to be *volatile* (so reads/writes to it are done directly from memory), and fact that an ISR runs to *completion* before we can switch back to `QueueReceive`.

4 Modelling FreeRTOS in Spin

In this section we describe how we model the FreeRTOS API and check for $(\mathcal{S}, \mathcal{C})$-races using the model-checking tool Spin. Spin's modelling language Promela can be used to model finite-state concurrent systems with standard communication and synchronization mechanisms (like message channels, semaphores, and locks). One can then model-check the system model to see if it satisfies a given state assertion or LTL property. For more details on Spin we refer the reader to [18].

Our first aim is to generate a Promela model M_n which captures the possible interleavings of critical accesses in any FreeRTOS application with at most n tasks. To make this more precise, consider a FreeRTOS application that—along any execution—creates at most n tasks. We denote such an application by A_n. We now define a Promela model M_n that has the following property (**P**):

For every execution of A_n, which exercises the critical accesses within the FreeRTOS API functions in a certain interleaved manner, there is a corresponding execution in M_n with a similar manner of interleaving.

For a given n, the Promela model M_n is built as follows. We introduce four semaphores called `task`, `sch`, `isr`, and `schsus` to model the possible control switches between processes. Recall that a (binary) semaphore has two possible states 0 and 1, and blocking operations `up` and `down` which respectively change the state from 0 to 1 and 1 to 0. Initially all the semaphores are down (i.e. 0) except `sch` which is 1 to begin with. The semaphores are used to indicate when a particular API function is enabled. For example when the `sch` semaphore is up, the scheduler process—which first tries to down the `sch` semaphore—is enabled. Similarly, the `task` semaphore controls when a task function is enabled, and the `isr` semaphore controls when a fromISR function is enabled. The `schsus` semaphore is used to ensure that whenever a task function is interrupted while the scheduler is *suspended*, control returns to the interrupted task function only.

```
inline QueueSend() {                        inline interrupt() {
  // do in a loop                             if
  interrupt();                                :: SchedulerSuspended==0 ->
  // atomically, so no interrupts                up(isr); down(task)
  _MessagesWaiting++;                         :: SchedulerSuspended==1 ->
  _MessagesWaiting--;                            up(isr); down(schsus)
  if                                          :: skip;
  :: skip ->                                  fi}
      // Copy data to queue
      _queueData += 2; _queueData -= 2;     inline LockQueue() {
      // Check if WaitingToReceive is non-empty //Inc Tx(Rx)Lock with ints disabled
      _WaitingToReceive++; _WaitingToReceive--; _TxLock +=2; TxLock++;
      // Move task from WaitingToReceive to Ready _TxLock -= 2;
      _WaitingToReceive += 2; _WaitingToReceive -= 2; _RxLock +=2; RxLock++;
      _ReadyTasksList += 2; _ReadyTasksList -= 2; _RxLock -= 2;}
  :: skip;
  fi                                        inline UnlockQueue() {
  // end of atomic, so interrupts enabled     // atomically
  interrupt();                                do
  if                                          :: TxLock > 0 -> ... --TxLock;
  :: ++SchedulerSuspended; interrupt();         //Move tasks from
     LockQueue(); interrupt();                  //WaitingToReceive to Ready
     // Move current task from Ready to WaitingToSend :: TxLock = 0 -> break;
     _ReadyTasksList += 2;interrupt();_ReadyTasksList -= 2; od
     _WaitingToSend += 2;interrupt();_WaitingToSend -= 2; TxLock = -1; // unlock queue
     UnlockQueue(); interrupt();                //end atomic
     --SchedulerSuspended;  // Resume scheduler interrupt();
     if                                         ... // Similarly for RxLock}
     :: up(sch); down(task); // Yield
     :: skip;
     fi
  :: skip;
  fi
}
```

Fig. 4. Promela model of the `QueueSend` API function

Each API function is modelled as a Promela function with the same name. We model variables of FreeRTOS that are critical to maintaining mutual exclusion, like `SchedulerSuspended`, `RxLock` and `TxLock`. We capture conditionals involving these variables and updates to these variables faithfully, and abstract the remaining conditionals conservatively to allow control-flow (non-deterministically) through both true and false branches of the conditional.

For each structure $v \in S$, we introduce a numeric variable called "$\_v$", which is initialized to 0. For each critical write access to a structure v in an API function F, we add a statement $\_v\ +=\ 2$ (short for $\_v\ =\ \_v\ +\ 2$) at the beginning of the block, and the statement $\_v\ -=\ 2$ at the end of the block, in the Promela version of F. Similarly, for a read access of v we add the statements $\_v++$ and $\_v--$ at appropriate points in the function. The possible context-switches due to an interrupt or yield to the scheduler are captured by uping the isr or sch semaphore. In particular, at any point in a function where an interrupt can occur (i.e. whenever interrupts are *not* disabled or an ISR itself is running), we add a call to `interrupt()` which essentially up's the isr semaphore and waits till a down is enabled on the task semaphore. The Promela function corresponding to the `QueueSend` function is shown in Fig. 4.

Each task in A_n is abstracted and conservatively modelled by a single process called `taskproc` in M_n, which repeatedly chooses a task API function

```
proctype scheduler() {
  do
  :: down(sch);
     if
     :: SchedulerSuspended==0 -> up(task)
     :: SchedulerSuspended==1 -> up(schsus)
     :: up(isr)
     fi
  od
}

proctype taskproc() {
  do
  :: down(task); QueueSend(); up(sch);
  :: ...
  :: down(task); TaskDelay(); up(sch);
  od
}

proctype isrproc() {
  do
  :: down(isr); IncrementTick(); up(sch);
  :: ...
  :: down(isr); QueueSendFromISR(); up(sch);
  od
}

init {
  run scheduler();
  // start n task and 1 ISR process
  run taskproc(); ...; run taskproc();
  run isrproc();
}
```

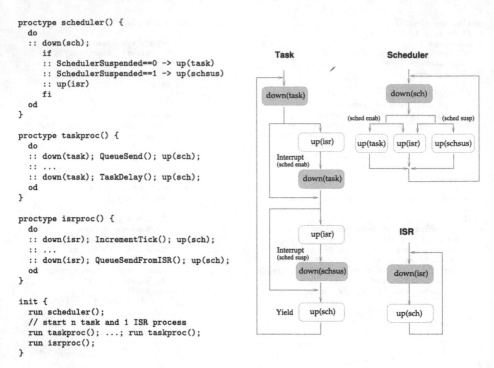

Fig. 5. (a) Promela model M_n and (b) Control flow and switching in M_1

non-deterministically and calls it. In a similar way, we model the fromISR API functions, and the `isrproc` process repeatedly invokes one of these non-deterministically. The Promela code of model M_n is depicted in Fig. 5(a). Thus M_n runs one `scheduler` process, one `isrproc` process, and n `taskproc` processes. Figure 5(b) illustrates the way the semaphores are used to model the control-switches.

Let us define what we consider to be a race in M_n. Let the statements in M_n be $s_1, \ldots, s_m$. If statement s_i is part of the definition of API F we write $\Gamma(s_i) = F$. An execution of M_n is a sequence of these statements that follows the control-flow of the model, and is *feasible* in that each statement is *enabled* in the state in which it is executed. We say an execution ρ of M_n exhibits a datarace on a structure v, involving statements s_i and s_j if (a) s_i and s_j are both increments of _v, (b) at least one increments _v by 2, and (c) ρ is of the form $\pi_1 \cdot s_i \cdot \pi_2 \cdot s_j$ with the segment π_2 not containing the decrement of _v corresponding to s_i. Note that the value of _v along ρ will exceed 2 after s_j.

It is not difficult to see that M_n satisfies the property (**P**) above. Consequently, any race on a structure v $\in \mathcal{S}$ in application A_n will have a corresponding execution in M_n which exhibits a datarace on _v. Thus, it follows that by model-checking M_n for the invariant

```
((_ReadyTasksList < 3) && (_DelayedTaskList < 3) && ...)
```

we will find all races that may arise in an n-task application A_n. We note that there may be some false positives, due to conservative modelling of conditionals in the API functions, or because of 3 consecutive read accesses.

There are now two hurdles in our path. The first is that we need to model-check M_n for *each* n, as it is possible that some races manifest only for certain values of n. Secondly, model-checking even a single M_n may be prohibitively time-consuming due to the large state-space of these models. In fact, as we report in Sect. 6, Spin times out even on M_2, after running for several hours. We propose a way out of this problem, by first proving a meta-claim that any race between API functions F and G in M_n, will also manifest in a *reduced* model, $M_{F,G,I}$, in which we have a process that runs *only* F, one that runs *only* G, another that runs a fromISR function I, along with the scheduler process, and an ISR process that runs only the IncrementTick function. We denote this set of reduced models by $\mathcal{M}_{red}$. We then go on to model-check each of these reduced models for dataraces. Though there are now thousands of models to check, each one model-checks in a few seconds, leading to tractable overall running time.

In the next section we justify our meta-claim.

5   Reduction to $\mathcal{M}_{red}$

Before we proceed with our reduction claim, we note that this claim may not hold for a general library. Consider for example the library L with three API functions F, G, and H shown in Fig. 6. Suppose the variable x belongs to the set of structures $\mathcal{S}$ and the lines 2 and 6 constitute a critical read and write access, respectively, to x. Then the $(\mathcal{S}, \mathcal{C})$-race on x involving lines these

```
F() {            G() {            H() {
1 ...            4 ...            7 ...
2 read(x);       5 if (flag)      8 flag := true;
3 ...            6   write(x);    9 ...
}                }                }
```

Fig. 6. Example library where $\mathcal{M}_{red}$ does not suffice.

accesses will never show up in any reduced model in $\mathcal{M}_{red}$, since we need all three functions to execute in order to produce this race. Thus, as we do for FreeRTOS below, any choice regarding the structure of models in $\mathcal{M}_{red}$ and the argument for its sufficiency, must be tailored for a given library and the way it has been modelled.

We now describe our reduction claim for our FreeRTOS model:

Theorem 1. *Let* $n \geq 1$, *and let* ρ *be an execution of* M_n *exhibiting a race involving statements* s_i *and* s_j *of* M_n. *Then there exists a model* $M \in \mathcal{M}_{red}$, *and an execution* ρ_{red} *of* M, *which also exhibits a race on* s_i *and* s_j.

We justify this claim in the rest of this section. By the construction of M_n, the execution ρ must be of the form

$$\pi_1 \cdot \mathtt{down(task)} \cdot \pi_2 \cdot s_i \cdot \mathtt{up(isr)} \cdot \pi_3 \cdot s_k$$

where s_i is a statement in API function F, and $\mathtt{down(task)} \cdot \pi_2 \cdot s_i \cdot \mathtt{up(isr)}$ is the portion of ρ corresponding to the racy invocation of F. We note that s_i must be part of a task function, while s_k could be part of either a task or fromISR function.

We consider two cases corresponding to whether the `SchedulerSuspended` flag is 1 or 0 after the statement s_i in ρ. Let us consider the first case where `SchedulerSuspended` is 1 after s_i. In this case, the statement s_k must belong to a fromISR function, say I. This is because the scheduler remains suspended after s_i in ρ (only F can resume it, and F never executes after $s_i \cdot$ `up(isr)` in ρ), and hence no task API function can run in this suffix of ρ. Further, since interrupts run to completion, the path π_3 must be of the form $\pi_3' \cdot \pi_4 \cdot s_k$, where π_3' comprises a sequence of fromISR functions, and $\pi_4 \cdot s_k$ is an initial path in I, beginning with a `down(isr)`.

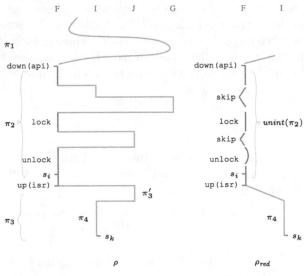

Consider the path π_2 that begins in F, contains some interrupting paths that visit other task or fromISR functions, and ends at s_i in F. We define an "uninterrupted" version of π_2, denoted $unint(\pi_2)$, to be the path that replaces each interrupt path by a `skip` statement (note that this non-deterministic branch exists in each interrupt call). In addition, the portion of π_2 that goes through an `UnlockQueue` call may have to change, since the path through an

Fig. 7. The execution ρ and its reduction ρ_{red}

`UnlockQueue` depends on the values of `RxLock` and `TxLock` and these values may have changed by eliding the interrupt paths from π_2. Nevertheless, there is a path through `UnlockQueue` enabled for these new values, and we use these paths to obtain a feasible path $unint(\pi_2)$ through F.

We can now define the reduced path ρ_{red} we need as follows (see Fig. 7):
$\rho_{red} =$ `down(sch)` $\cdot$ `up(task)` $\cdot$ `down(task)` $\cdot unint(\pi_2) \cdot s_i \cdot$ `up(isr)` $\cdot \pi_4 \cdot s_k$.

We need to argue that ρ_{red} is a valid execution of $M_{F,*,I}$ (here "*" stands for an arbitrary task function). We have already argued that

$$\text{down(sch)} \cdot \text{up(task)} \cdot \text{down(task)} \cdot unint(\pi_2) \cdot s_i \cdot \text{up(isr)}$$

is a valid execution of the model. Let the resulting state after this path be u'. It remains to be shown that the path $\pi_4 \cdot s_k$ is a feasible initial path in I, beginning in state u'.

Let us call two states v and w *equivalent* if they satisfy the following conditions: (a) the value of the control semaphores are the same (i.e. $v(\text{isr}) = w(\text{isr})$, etc.), (b) the value of `SchedulerSuspended` is the same, (c) $v(\text{RxLock}) = -1$ iff $w(\text{RxLock}) = -1$ and $v(\text{RxLock}) \geq 0$ iff $w(\text{RxLock}) \geq 0$, and (d) similarly for `TxLock`. By inspection of the conditionals in any fromISR function J in the model, we observe that the set of feasible initial paths through J, beginning from *equivalent* states is exactly the same. Let u be the resulting state after the prefix $\delta = \pi_1 \cdot \text{down(task)} \cdot \pi_2 \cdot s_i \cdot \text{up(isr)}$ of ρ, and let v be the resulting state after $\delta \cdot \pi_3' \cdot \text{up(isr)}$. To argue that $\pi_4 \cdot s_k$ is a feasible initial path in I beginning from state u', it is thus sufficient to argue that the states u' and v are equivalent.

To do this we argue that (a) u' and u are equivalent, and (b) that u and v are equivalent. To see (a), clearly the value of the control semaphores are identical in u and u'. Further, the value of `SchedulerSuspended` continues to be 1 in u' as well, as we are only excising paths from π_2 that are "balanced" in terms of setting and unsetting this flag. Finally, if the value of `RxLock` was -1 in u, it continues to be -1 in u' as well, since an `UnlockQueue` always resets the flag to -1. If the value of `RxLock` was 0 or more in u, then we must be between a `LockQueue` and its corresponding `UnlockQueue`. In this case the value of `RxLock` would have been set to 0 in u'. A similar argument holds for `TxLock` as well, and we are done. To see that the claim (b) holds, we note that only fromISR functions can execute between u and v, and they always either leave the value of `RxLock` and `TxLock` intact, or increment them if their value was already ≥ 0.

Thus, ρ_{red} is a valid execution of $M_{F,*,I}$, and it clearly contains a race on s_i and s_k. This completes the proof of the first case we were considering. The second case where `SchedulerSuspended` is 0 after δ is handled in a similar way. The detailed proof is available in [21].

6 Experimental Results

Of the 69 API functions in FreeRTOS v6.1.1, we model 17 task and 8 fromISR functions. These 25 library functions form the "core" of the FreeRTOS API. The remaining 44 functions are either defined in terms of these core functions, or they simply invoke the core functions with specific arguments, or are synchronization constructs. For example, the functions `xQueuePeek` and `xSemaphoreTake` are listed as library functions. However, they are defined in terms of the core function `xQueueGenericReceive`, which we do model. Thus, modelling these additional functions would be redundant: the races would still be in the core library functions which they invoke.

Our tool-chain is as follows: the user provides a Promela file which models each library function, as well as a template for the reduced models. Next, a Java program creates the "reduced" models (2023 of them in this case) from this Promela template. We then verify these reduced models using Spin. The output of the verification phase is a set of error trails, one corresponding to each interleaving which results in the violation of an assertion. The trails are not in a human readable format, so we need to perform a *simulation* run in Spin using these trails. The output of the simulation run is a set of human readable error traces. However, the number of such traces can be large (around 70,870 were generated during our experiments) and it is infeasible to manually parse them to find the list of races. Instead, we have yet another Java program which scans through these traces and reports the list of unique racing pairs. By a racing pair, we mean statements (s_i, s_k) constituting the race, along with the data-structure v involved (we also indicate a trace exhibiting the race).

While the model and the reduction argument need to be tailor-made for different kernel APIs, the software component of the tool-chain is fairly straightforward to reuse. Given a Promela model of some kernel API other than FreeR-TOS, where the modelling follows the rules outlined in Sect. 4 (and the model is shown to be reducible), the tool-chain can be used to detect races with minimal changes.

An important point to consider here is the guarantees provided by the Spin tool itself. Spin does *not* exhaustively search for *all* possible violations of an assertion [18]. Instead, it is guaranteed to report *at least* one counter-example if the property is not satisfied. Hence, we make use of an iterative strategy. After each iteration, we change the assertion statement to suppress reporting the detected races again. We continue this process until no further assertion violations are detected by Spin. Thus, by the final iteration, we are *guaranteed* to have flagged every high-level datarace.

All our experiments were performed on a quad-core Intel Core i7 machine with 32 GB RAM, running Ubuntu 14.04. We use Spin version 6.4.5 for our experiments.

Evaluating M_2. The verification of M_2 on our machine took up memory in excess of 32 GB. As a result, we had to kill the verification run prematurely. Even on on a more powerful machine with 4 quad-Xeon processors (16 cores), 128 GB of RAM, running Ubuntu 14.04, the verification run took 39 GB of RAM, while executing for more than 3 hours, before timing out. The total number of tracked states was 4.43×10^8. Using rough calculations, we estimated that the total amount of memory needed to store the full state space of this model (assuming that the size of a single state is 100 bytes) is around 1 TB. On the contrary, while model-checking the 2023 reduced models, the RAM usage never exceeded 9 GB.

Evaluating $\mathcal{M}_{red}$. Recall that each $M_{F,G,I} \in \mathcal{M}_{red}$ comprises 5 processes: the first process runs the task function F, the second runs the task function G, and the third runs the ISR I (excluding the tick interrupt), the fourth runs the tick interrupt in a loop, while the fifth process runs the scheduler. Since there are 17 task functions and 7 fromISR functions (excluding the tick), we generate $17 \times 17 \times 7 = 2023$ models. We model check these reduced models in iterations, suppressing reported races to ensure they are not flagged again in subsequent iterations. In particular, we suppress reporting races on the SchedulerSuspended flag, which by design are aplenty. We have manually verified (along with discussion with the FreeRTOS developers) that these races are benign.

In the first iteration, the verification of $\mathcal{M}_{red}$ generated 38 assertion violations. Of these, 10 were false positives, owing to three consecutive read accesses or the conservative modeling of the conditionals. Among the rest, 16 can be definitely classified as harmful. In the second iteration, the tool reported 10 assertion violations, all of them being potentially benign races involving the variable pxCurrentTCB.

The cause was an unprotected read of the variable in the function vTaskResume. As there were several races involving this statement (it would race with every access, protected or otherwise, of

Iteration	#Violations	F.P.	Harmful	Benign?	Time
1	38	10	16	12	1.5 hr
2	10	-	-	10	2.4 hr
3	-	-	-	-	1.84 hr

Fig. 8. Experimental evaluation of $\mathcal{M}_{red}$

pxCurrentTCB in almost all other functions), we supressed races involving this statement. With this change, we performed a third iteration of the verification process, which resulted in no further assertion violations.

The FreeRTOS API is quite carefully written. Despite the complexity of the possible task interactions, there are not many harmful races. Among the 16 harmful races detected after the first iteration, most involved the function vQueueDelete, which deletes the queue passed to it as argument. Several operations are involved as part of the deletion (removal of the queue from the registry, deallocating the memory assigned to the queue, etc.). Surprisingly, the set of operations, which forms a critical access path for the queue data-structure, is devoid of any synchronization. This causes critical access paths of the queue in other functions, for example xQueueReceiveFromISR (which reads the contents of the queue), to interleave with the path in vQueueDelete. The race is harmful because functions can potentially observe an inconsistent (partially deleted) state of the queue, which it would not otherwise observe along any linearized execution. We reported this bug to the FreeRTOS developers, and they argue that this is not serious since queue delete operations are rare and are usually performed at the end of the application's lifetime.

The other harmful races involve the QueueRegistry data-structure (which is essentially an array), where addition and deletion of items in the QueueRegistry can interleave, thereby causing a function to observe an inconsistent state of the registry. Some of the sample races are given in Table. 1.

Table 1. Some sample detected races. "H" indicates harmful races and "PB" indicates possibly benign.

Structure	Library functions involved	Scenario	H/PB
xQueueRegistry	P1: vQueueAddToRegistry P2: vQueueUnregisterQueue	While P1 reads the registry, P2 modifies it Read-write race	H
userQueue	P1: vQueueDelete P2:xQueueSend	P2 sends data to a queue while it is being deleted by P1. Write-write race	H
uxPriority	P1: xTaskCreate P2: vTaskPrioritySet	P1 checks the value of uxPriority while it is being set by P2. The result is never an inconsistent state	PB

A summary of the various statistics of the experiments is given in Fig. 8. The running times are reported in hours. All artifacts of this work are available online at https://bitbucket.org/suvam/freertos.

7   Related Work

Along with work on detecting high-level races and atomicity violations, we also consider work on detecting classical (location-based) races as some of these techniques could be adapted for high-level races as well. We group the work into three categories below and discuss them in relation to our work. The table alongside summarizes the applicability of earlier approaches to our problem setting.

Dynamic Analysis Based Approaches. Artho et al. [3] coined the term "high-level datarace" and gave an informal definition of it in terms of accessing a set of shared variables (what we call a unit in S) "atomically." They define a notion of a thread's "view" of the set of shared variables, and flag potential races whenever two threads have inconsistent views. They then provide a lockset based algorithm, for detecting view inconsistencies dynamically along an execution. Among the techniques for detecting atomicity violations, Atomizer [11] uses the notion of left/right moving actions, SVD [31] uses atomic regions as subgraphs of the dynamic PDG, AVIO [20] uses interleaving accesses, and [30] uses a notion of trace-equivalence; to check if a given execution exhibits an atomicity violation. Techniques for dynamically detecting classical dataraces use locksets computed along an execution (for example [5,24]), or use the happens-before ordering (for example [7,12]), to detect races. None of these techniques apply directly to the kind of concurrency and synchronization model of FreeRTOS (there are no explicit locks, and no immediate analogue of the happens-before relation). Most importantly, by design these techniques explore only a part of the execution space and hence cannot detect *all* races.

Static Analysis Based Approaches. von Praun and Gross [28] and Pessanha et al. [6] extend the view-based approach of [3] to carry out a static analysis to detect high-level races. The notion of views could be used to obtain an annotation of critical accesses (an S and C in our setting) for methods in a library. However definition of views are lock-based and it is not clear what is the corresponding notion in our setting, and whether it would correspond intuitively to what we need.

Flannegan and Qadeer [13] give a type system based static analysis for proving atomicity of methods (i.e. the method's actions can be serialized with respect to interleavings with actions of another thread). The actions of a method are typed as left/right-movers and the analysis soundly infers methods to be atomic. Wang and Stoller [30] extend this type system for lock-free synchronization. In our setting, the notion of left/right-movers is not immediate, and such an approach will likely have a large number of false positives. Static approaches for classical race detection (e.g. [9,27,29]) are typically based on a lockset-based data-flow analysis, where the analysis keeps track of the set of locks that are "must" held at each access to a location and reports a race if two conflicting accesses hold disjoint locks. In [1] the locksets are built into a type system which associates a lock with each field declaration. All the approches above can handle libraries and can detect all races in principle, but in practice are too imprecise (lots of false positives) and often use unsound filters (for example [6,29]) that improve precision at the expense of missing real races.

Schwarz et al. [25,26] provide a precise data-flow analysis for checking races in FreeRTOS-like applications that handles flag-based synchronization and interrupt-driven scheduling. The technique is capable of detecting all races, but is applicable only to a given application rather than a library.

Model-Checking Approaches. In [2] Alur et al. study the problem of deciding whether a finite-state model satisfies properties like serializability and linearizability. This approach is attractive as in principle it could be used to verify freedom from atomicity violations. However, the number of threads need to be bounded (hence they cannot handle libraries) and the running time is prohibitive (exponential in number of transitions for serializability, and doubly-exponential in number of threads for linearizability). Farzan and Madhusudan [10] consider a stronger notion of serializability called "conflict serializability" and give a monitoring algorithm to detect whether a given execution is conflict-serializable or not. This also leads to a model-checking algorithm for conflict-serializability based atomicity violations. Again, this is applicable only to applications rather than libraries.

Several researchers have used model-checking tools like Slam, Blast, and Spin to precisely model various kinds of control-flow and synchronization mechanisms and detect errors exhaustively [8,14–16,32]. All these approaches are for specific application programs rather than libraries. Chandrasekharan et al. [4] follow a similar approach to ours for verifying thread-safety of a multicore version of FreeRTOS. However, the library there uses explicit locks and a standard notion of control-flow between threads. Further, they use a model which is the equivalent of M_2, which does not scale in our setting Fig. 9.

Earlier Work	FreeRTOS-like Concurrency	Handles Libraries	Can Detect all races
[3], [11], [31], [20], [30], [22], [5], [24], [7], [12], [32]	No	No	No
[27], [9], [29], [28], [6], [13], [30], [1], [4]	No	Yes	Yes
[2], [10], [16], [19]	No	No	Yes
[26], [25]	Yes	No	Yes

Fig. 9. Applicability of earlier work to our setting.

8   Conclusion

We have considered the problem of detecting all high-level races in a concurrent library, as an aid to zeroing-in on atomicity-related bugs in the library. We propose a solution to this problem for the FreeRTOS kernel which is representative of small embedded real-time kernels. The approach is based on model-checking but crucially uses a meta-level argument to bound the size of the model.

References

1. Abadi, M., Flanagan, C., Freund, S.N.: Types for safe locking: static race detection for Java. ACM Trans. Program. Lang. Syst. (TOPLAS) **28**(2), 207–255 (2006)
2. Alur, R., McMillan, K.L., Peled, D.A.: Model-checking of correctness conditions for concurrent objects. Inf. Comput. **160**(1–2), 167–188 (2000)
3. Artho, C., Havelund, K., Biere, A.: High-level data races. Software Test., Verification & Reliab. **13**, 207–227 (2003)
4. Chandrasekaran, P., Kumar, K.B.S., Minz, R.L., D'Souza, D., Meshram, L.: A multi-core version of FreeRTOS verified for datarace and deadlock freedom. In: Proceedings of ACM/IEEE Formal Methods and Models for Codesign (MEM-OCODE), pp. 62–71 (2014)
5. Choi, J.-D., Lee, K., Loginov, A., O'Callahan, R., Sarkar, V., Sridharan, M.: Efficient and precise datarace detection for multithreaded object-oriented programs. In: Proceedings of ACM SIGPLAN Programming Languages Design and Implementation (PLDI), pp. 258–269. ACM, New York (2002)
6. Dias, R.J., Pessanha, V., Lourenço, J.M.: Precise detection of atomicity violations. In: Biere, A., Nahir, A., Vos, T. (eds.) HVC 2012. LNCS, vol. 7857, pp. 8–23. Springer, Heidelberg (2013). doi:10.1007/978-3-642-39611-3_8
7. Dinning, A., Schonberg, E.: Detecting access anomalies in programs with critical sections. In: Proceedings of ACM/ONR Workshop on Parallel and Distributed Debugging (PADD), pp. 85–96. ACM, New York (1991)
8. Elmas, T., Qadeer, S., Tasiran, S.: Precise race detection and efficient model checking using locksets. Technical Report MSR-TR–118, Microsoft Research (2005)
9. Engler, D., Ashcraft, K.: Racerx: effective, static detection of race conditions and deadlocks. SIGOPS Oper. Syst. Rev. **37**(5), 237–252 (2003)
10. Farzan, A., Madhusudan, P.: Monitoring atomicity in concurrent programs. In: Gupta, A., Malik, S. (eds.) CAV 2008. LNCS, vol. 5123, pp. 52–65. Springer, Heidelberg (2008). doi:10.1007/978-3-540-70545-1_8
11. Flanagan, C., Freund, S.N.: Atomizer: a dynamic atomicity checker for multi-threaded programs. Sci. Comput. Program. **71**(2), 89–109 (2008)
12. Flanagan, C., Freund, S.N.: Fasttrack: Efficient and precise dynamic race detection. In: Proceedings of ACM SIGPLAN PLDI, pp. 121–133. ACM, New York (2009)
13. Flanagan, C., Qadeer, S.: A type and effect system for atomicity. In: Proceedings of ACM SIGPLAN Programming Language Design and Implementation (PLDI), pp. 338–349 (2003)
14. Havelund, K., Lowry, M.R., Penix, J.: Formal analysis of a space-craft controller using SPIN. IEEE Trans. Softw. Eng. **27**(8), 749–765 (2001)
15. Havelund, K., Skakkebæk, J.U.: Applying model checking in Java verification. In: Dams, D., Gerth, R., Leue, S., Massink, M. (eds.) SPIN 1999. LNCS, vol. 1680, pp. 216–231. Springer, Heidelberg (1999). doi:10.1007/3-540-48234-2_17

16. Henzinger, T.A., Jhala, R., Majumdar, R.: Race checking by context inference. In: Proceedings of ACM SIGPLAN Programming Language Design and Implementation (PLDI), pp. 1–13 (2004)
17. Herlihy, M., Wing, J.M.: Linearizability: a correctness condition for concurrent objects. ACM Trans. Program. Lang. Syst. **12**(3), 463–492 (1990)
18. Holzmann, G.J.: The model checker spin. IEEE Trans. Softw. Eng. **23**, 279–295 (1997)
19. Kahlon, V., Sinha, N., Kruus, E., Zhang, Y.: Static data race detection for concurrent programs with asynchronous calls. In: ACM SIGSOFT FSE, pp. 13–22. ACM, New York (2009)
20. Lu, S., Tucek, J., Qin, F., Zhou, Y.: AVIO: detecting atomicity violations via access interleaving invariants. In: Proceedings of Architectural Support for Programming Languages and Operating Systems (ASPLOS), pp. 37–48 (2006)
21. Mukherjee, S., Arunkumar, S., D'Souza, D.: Proving an RTOS kernel free of dataraces. Technical Report CSA-TR-2016-1, Department of Computer Science and Automation, IISc (2016)
22. Qadeer, S., Wu, D.: KISS: keep it simple and sequential. In: Proceedings of ACM SIG-PLAN Programming Languages Design and Implementaion (PLDI), pp. 14–24 (2004)
23. Real Time Engineers Ltd., The FreeRTOS Real Time Operating System (2014)
24. Savage, S., Burrows, M., Nelson, G., Sobalvarro, P., Anderson, T.: Eraser: a dynamic data race detector for multithreaded programs. ACM Trans. Comput. Syst. (TOCS) **15**(4), 391–411 (1997)
25. Schwarz, M.D., Seidl, H., Vojdani, V., Apinis, K.: Precise analysis of value-dependent synchronization in priority scheduled programs. In: McMillan, K.L., Rival, X. (eds.) VMCAI 2014. LNCS, vol. 8318, pp. 21–38. Springer, Heidelberg (2014). doi:10.1007/978-3-642-54013-4_2
26. Schwarz, M.D., Seidl, H., Vojdani, V., Lammich, P., Müller-Olm, M.: Static analysis of interrupt-driven programs synchronized via the priority ceiling protocol. In: Proceedings ACM SIGPLAN-SIGACT Principles of Programming Languages (POPL), pp. 93–104 (2011)
27. Sterling, N.: WARLOCK - a static data race analysis tool. In: Proceedings of Usenix Winter Technical Conference, pp. 97–106 (1993)
28. von Praun, C., Gross, T.R.: Static detection of atomicity violations in object-oriented programs. J. Object Technol. **3**(6), 103–122 (2004)
29. Voung, J. W., Jhala, R., Lerner, S.: RELAY: static race detection on millions of lines of code. In: Proceedings of ESEC/SIGSOFT Foundation of Software Engineering (FSE), pp. 205–214 (2007)
30. Wang, L., Stoller, S.D.: Runtime analysis of atomicity for multithreaded programs. IEEE Trans. Softw. Eng. **32**(2), 93–110 (2006)
31. Xu, M., Bodík, R., Hill, M.D.: A serializability violation detector for shared-memory server programs. In: Proceedings of ACM SIGPLAN Programming Language Design and Implementation (PLDI), pp. 1–14 (2005)
32. Zeng, R., Sun, Z., Liu, S., He, X.: McPatom: a predictive analysis tool for atomicity violation using model checking. In: Donaldson, A., Parker, D. (eds.) SPIN 2012. LNCS, vol. 7385, pp. 191–207. Springer, Heidelberg (2012). doi:10.1007/978-3-642-31759-0_14

Reachability for Dynamic Parametric Processes

Anca Muscholl[1,2(✉)], Helmut Seidl[3], and Igor Walukiewicz[4]

[1] LaBRI, University of Bordeaux, Bordeaux, France
[2] TUM-IAS, Munich, Germany
anca.muscholl@gmail.com
[3] Fakultät für Informatik, TU München, Munich, Germany
[4] LaBRI, CNRS, University of Bordeaux, Bordeaux, France

Abstract. In a dynamic parametric process every subprocess may spawn arbitrarily many, identical child processes, that may communicate either over global variables, or over local variables that are shared with their parent. We show that reachability for dynamic parametric processes is decidable under mild assumptions. These assumptions are e.g. met if individual processes are realized by pushdown systems, or even higher-order pushdown systems. We also provide algorithms for subclasses of pushdown dynamic parametric processes, with complexity ranging between NP and DEXPTIME.

1 Introduction

Programming languages such as Java, Erlang, Scala offer the possibility to generate recursively new threads (or processes, actors,...). Threads may exchange data through globally accessible data structures, e.g. via static attributes of classes like in Java, Scala. In addition, newly created threads may locally communicate with their parent threads, in Java, e.g., via the corresponding thread objects, or via messages like in Erlang.

Various attempts have been made to analyze systems with recursion and dynamic creation of threads that may or may not exchange data. A single thread executing a possibly recursive program operating on finitely many local data, can conveniently be modeled by a *pushdown system*. Intuitively, the pushdown formalizes the call stack of the program while the finite set of states allows to formalize the current program state together with the current values of the local variables. For such systems reachability of a bad state or a regular set of bad configurations is decidable [1,17]. The situation becomes more intricate if multiple threads are allowed. Already for two pushdown threads reachability is undecidable if communication via a 2-bit global is allowed. In absence of global variables, reachability becomes undecidable already for two pushdown threads if a rendezvous primitive is available [16]. A similar result holds if finitely many locks are

---

Work supported by the Technische Universität München - Institute for Advanced Study, funded by the German Excellence Initiative and the EU Seventh Framework under grant agreement nr. 291763.

A. Bouajjani and D. Monniaux (Eds.): VMCAI 2017, LNCS 10145, pp. 424–441, 2017.
DOI: 10.1007/978-3-319-52234-0_23

allowed [10]. Interestingly, decidability is retained if locking is performed in a disciplined way. This is, e.g., the case for nested [10] and contextual locking [3]. These decidability results have been extended to dynamic pushdown networks as introduced by Bouajjani et al. [2]. This model combines pushdown threads with dynamic thread creation by means of a spawn operation, while it ignores any exchange of data between threads. Indeed, reachability of dedicated states or even regular sets of configurations stays decidable in this model, if finitely many global locks together with nested locking [12,14] or contextual locking [13] are allowed. Such regular sets allow, e.g., to describe undesirable situations such as concurrent execution of conflicting operations.

Here, we follow another line of research where models of multi-threading are sought which allow exchange of data via shared variables while still being decidable. The general idea goes back to Kahlon, who observed that various verification problems become decidable for multi-pushdown systems that are *parametric* [9], i.e., systems consisting of an arbitrary number of indistinguishable pushdown threads. Later, Hague extended this result by showing that an extra designated leader thread can be added without sacrificing decidability [7]. All threads communicate here over a shared, bounded register *without* locking. It is crucial for decidability that only one thread has an identity, and that the operations on the shared variable do not allow to elect a second leader. Later, Esparza et al. clarified the complexity of deciding reachability in that model [5]. La Torre et al. generalized these results to hierarchically nested models [11]. Still, the question whether reachability is decidable for *dynamically evolving* parametric pushdown processes, remained open.

We show that reachability is decidable for a very general class of dynamic processes with parametric spawn. We require some very basic properties from the class of transitions systems that underlies the model, like e.g. effective non-emptiness check. In our model every sub-process can maintain e.g. a pushdown store, or even a higher-order pushdown store, and can communicate over global variables, as well as via local variables with its sub-processes and with its parent. As in [5,7,11], all variables have bounded domains and no locks are allowed.

Since the algorithm is rather expensive, we also present meaningful instances where reachability can be decided by simpler means. As one such instance we consider the situation where communication between sub-processes is through global variables only. We show that reachability for this model can effectively be reduced to reachability in the model of Hague [5,7], giving us a precise characterization of the complexity for pushdown threads as PSPACE. As another instance, we consider a parametric variant of *generalized futures* where spawned sub-processes may not only return a single result but create a stream of answers. For that model, we obtain complexities between NP and DEXPTIME. This opens the venue to apply e.g. SAT-solving to check safety properties of such programs.

Overview. Section 2 provides basic definitions, and the semantics of our model. In Sect. 3 we show a simpler semantics, that is equivalent w.r.t. reachability. Section 4 introduces some prerequisites for Sect. 5, which is the core of the proof. Section 6 considers some special instances of dynamic parametric pushdown processes. The full version of the paper is available at http://arxiv.org/abs/1609.05385.

2   Basic Definitions

In this section we introduce our model of dynamic parametric processes. We refrain from using some particular program syntax; instead we use potentially infinite state transition systems with actions on transitions. Actions may manipulate local or global variables, or spawn *parametrically* some sub-processes: this means that an unspecified number of sub-processes is created — all with the same designated initial state. Making the spawn operation parametric is the main abstraction step that allows us to obtain decidability results.

Before giving formal definitions we present two examples in order to give an intuitive understanding of the kind of processes we are interested in.

Example 1. A dynamic parametric process can, e.g., be defined by an explicitly given finite transition system:

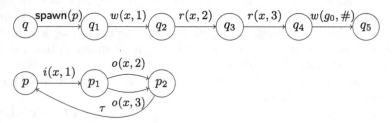

In this example, the root starts in state q by spawning a number of sub-processes, each starting in state p. Then the root writes the value 1 into the local variable x, and waits for some child to change the value of x first to 2, and subsequently to 3. Only then, the root will write value $\#$ into the global variable g_0. Every child on the other hand, when starting execution at state p, waits for value 1 in the variable x of the parent and then chooses either to write 2 or 3 into x, then returns to the initial state. The read/write operations of the children are denoted as input/output operations $i(x, v)$, $o(x, v)$, because they act on the parent's local. Note that at least two children are required to write $\#$.

More interesting examples require more program states. Here, it is convenient to adopt a programming-like notation as in the next example.

Example 2. Consider the program from Fig. 1. The conditional if($*$) denotes non-deterministic choice. There is a single global variable which is written to by the call `write(#)`, and a single local variable x per sub-process, with initial value 0. The corresponding local of the parent is accessed via the keyword `parent`.

The states of the dynamic parametric process correspond to the lines in the listing, the transitions represent the control flow, they are labeled with atomic statements of the program.

```
1 root() {
      spawn(p);
      switch (x) {
4     case 2:    write(#);
      }
  }
7
  p() {
      switch (parent.x) {
10    case 0 :   spawn(p);
                 if (*) parent.x = 1
                 else switch (x) {
13               case 1 : parent.x = 1; break;
                 case 2 : break;
                 }; break;
16    case 1 :   spawn(p);
                 if (*) parent.x = 0
                 else switch (x) {
19               case 1: parent.x = 2; break;
                 case 2: parent.x = 2; break;
                 };
22    }
  }
```

Fig. 1. A program defining a dynamic parametric process.

The question is whether the root can eventually write #? This would be the case if the value of the root's local variable becomes 2. This in turn may occur once the variable x of some descendant is set to 1. In order to achieve this, cooperation of several sub-processes is needed. Here is one possible execution.

1. The root spawns two sub-processes in state p, say T_1 and T_2.
2. T_1 changes the value of the local variable of the root to 1 (line 11).
3. T_2 then can take the case 1 branch and first spawn T_3.
4. T_3 takes the case 0 branch, spawns a new process and changes the value of parent.x to 1.
5. As the variable parent.x of T_3 is the local variable of T_2, the latter can now take the second branch of the nondeterministic choice and change parent.x to 2 (line 19) — which is the local variable of the root.

In the following sections we present a formal definition of our parametric model, state the reachability problem, and the main results.

2.1 Transition Systems

A *dynamic parametric process* S is a transition system over a dedicated set of action names. One can think of it as a control flow graph of a program. In this transition system the action names are uninterpreted. In Sect. 2.2 we will define their semantics. The transition system is specified by a tuple $\mathcal{S} = \langle Q, G, X, V, \Delta, q_{\text{init}}, v_{\text{init}} \rangle$ consisting of:

- a (possibly infinite) set Q of states,
- finite sets G and X of global and local variables, respectively, and a finite set V of values for variables; these are used to define the set of labels,
- an initial state $q_{\text{init}} \in Q$, and an initial value $v_{\text{init}} \in V$ for variables,
- a set of rules Δ of the form $q \xrightarrow{a} q'$, where the label a is one of the following:
  - τ, that will be later interpreted as a silent action,
  - $r(x, v)$, $w(x, v)$, will be interpreted as a read or a write of value $v \in V$ from or to a local or global variable $x \in X \cup G$ of the process,
  - $i(x, v)$, $o(x, v)$, will be interpreted as a read or a write of value $v \in V$ to or from a local variable $x \in X$ of the parent process,
  - $\mathsf{spawn}(q)$, will be interpreted as a spawn of an arbitrary number (possibly zero) of new sub-processes, all starting in state $q \in Q$. We assume that the number of different $\mathsf{spawn}(q)$ operations appearing in Δ is finite.

Observe that the above definition ensures that the set of labels of transitions is finite.

We are particularly interested in classes of systems when Q is not finite. This is the case when, for example, individual sub-processes execute recursive procedures. For that purpose, the transition system $\mathcal{S}$ may be chosen as a configuration graph of a *pushdown system*. In this case the set Q of states is $Q_l \cdot \Gamma^*$ where Q_l is a finite set of control states, and Γ is a finite set of pushdown symbols. The (infinite) transition relation Δ between states is specified by a finite set of rewriting rules of the form $qv \xrightarrow{a} q'w$ for suitable $q, q' \in Q_l, v \in \Gamma^*, w \in \Gamma^*$.

Instead of plain recursive programs, we could also allow *higher-order* recursive procedures, realized by higher-order pushdown systems or even collapsible pushdown systems as considered, e.g., in [8, 15]. Here, procedures may take other procedures as arguments.

2.2   Multiset Semantics

In this section we provide the operational semantics of dynamic parametric processes, where we interpret the operations on variables as expected, and the spawns as creation of sub-processes. The latter operation will not create one sub-process, but rather an arbitrary number of sub-processes. There will be also a set of global variables to which every sub-process has access by means of reads and writes.

As a dynamic parametric process executes, sub-processes may change the values of local and global variables and spawn new children. The global state of the entire process can be thus represented as a tree of sub-processes with the initial process at the root. Nodes at depth 1 are the sub-processes spawned by the root; these children can also spawn sub-processes that become nodes at depth 2, etc., see e.g., Fig. 3(a). Every sub-process has a set of local variables, that can be read and written by itself, as well as by its children.

A global state of a dynamic parametric process S has the form of a *multiset configuration tree*, or *m-tree* for short. An m-tree is defined recursively by

$$t ::= (q, \lambda, M)$$

where $q \in Q$ is a sub-process state, $\lambda : X \to V$ is a valuation of (local) variables, and M is a *finite multiset* of m-trees. We consider only m-trees of finite depth. Another way to say this is to define m-trees of depth at most k, for every $k \in \mathbb{N}$

$$M\text{-}trees_0 = Q \times (X \to V) \times []$$
$$M\text{-}trees_k = Q \times (X \to V) \times \mathcal{M}(M\text{-}trees_{k-1}) \qquad \text{for } k > 0$$

where for any U, $\mathcal{M}(U)$ is the set of all finite multisubsets of U. Then the set of all m-trees is given by $\bigcup_{k \in \mathbb{N}} M\text{-}trees_k$.

We use standard notation for multisets. A multiset M over a universe U is a mapping $M : U \to \mathbb{N}_0$. It is finite if $\sum_{t \in U} M(t) < \infty$. A finite multiset M may also be represented by $M = [n_1 \cdot t_1, \ldots, n_k \cdot t_k]$ if $M(t_i) = n_i$ for $i = 1, \ldots, k$ and $M(t) = 0$ otherwise. In particular, the empty multiset is denoted by $[]$. For convenience we may omit multiplicities $n_i = 1$. We say that $t \in M$ whenever $M(t) \geq 1$, and $M \subseteq M'$ whenever $M(t) \leq M'(t)$ for all $t \in M'$. Finally, $M + M'$ is the mapping with $(M + M')(t) = M(t) + M'(t)$ for all $t \in U$. For convenience, we also allow the short-cut $[n_1 \cdot t_1, \ldots, n_k \cdot t_k]$ for $[n_1 \cdot t_1] + \ldots + [n_k \cdot t_k]$, i.e., we allow also multiple occurrences of the same tree in the list. Thus, e.g., $[3 \cdot t_1, 5 \cdot t_2, 1 \cdot t_1] = [4 \cdot t_1, 5 \cdot t_2]$.

The *semantics* of a dynamic parametric process S is a transition system denoted $[\![S]\!]$. The states of $[\![S]\!]$ are m-trees, and the set of possible edge labels is:

$$\Sigma = \{\tau\} \cup \{\text{spawn}\} \times Q \cup$$
$$\{i(x,v), o(x,v), r(y,v), w(y,v), \bar{r}(y,v), \bar{w}(y,v) : x \in X, y \in X \cup G, v \in V\}.$$

Notice that we have two new kinds of labels $\bar{r}(y,v)$ and $\bar{w}(y,v)$. These represent the actions of child sub-processes on global variables $y \in G$, or on the local variables $x \in X$ shared with the parent.

Throughout the paper we will use the notation

$$\Sigma_{ext} = \{i(x,v), o(x,v), r(g,v), w(g,v) : x \in X, g \in G, v \in V\}$$

for the set of so-called *external actions*. They are called external because they concern the *external variables*: these are either the global variables, or the local variables of the parent of the sub-process. Words in Σ_{ext}^* will describe the *external behaviors* of a sub-process, i.e., the interactions via external variables: these are either the global variables, or the local variables of the parent of the sub-process. Words in Σ_{ext}^* will describe the *external behaviors* of a sub-process, i.e., the interactions via external variables.

The initial state is given by $t_{\text{init}} = (q_{\text{init}}, \lambda_{\text{init}}, [])$, where λ_{init} maps all locals to the initial value v_{init}. A transition between two states of $[\![S]\!]$ (m-trees) $t_1 \overset{a}{\Longrightarrow}_S t_2$ is defined by induction on the depth of m-trees. We will omit the subscript S for better readability. The definition is given in Fig. 2.

External transitions:

$$(q_1, \lambda, M) \overset{a}{\Longrightarrow} \quad (q_2, \lambda, M) \quad \text{if } q_1 \overset{a}{\longrightarrow} q_2 \qquad \text{for } a \in \Sigma_{ext}$$

$$(q, \lambda, M_1) \overset{\bar{r}(g,v)}{\Longrightarrow} (q, \lambda, M_2) \quad \text{if } M_1 \overset{r(g,v)}{\Longrightarrow} M_2 \text{ for } g \in G$$

$$(q, \lambda, M_1) \overset{\bar{w}(g,v)}{\Longrightarrow} (q, \lambda, M_2) \quad \text{if } M_1 \overset{w(g,v)}{\Longrightarrow} M_2 \text{ for } g \in G$$

Internal transitions:

$$(q_1, \lambda, M) \overset{\tau}{\Longrightarrow} \quad (q_2, \lambda, M) \quad \text{if } q_1 \overset{\tau}{\longrightarrow} q_2$$

$$(q_1, \lambda, M_1) \overset{\mathsf{spawn}(p)}{\Longrightarrow} (q_2, \lambda, M_2) \text{ if } q_1 \overset{\mathsf{spawn}(p)}{\longrightarrow} q_2 \text{ and } M_2 = M_1 + [n \cdot (p, \lambda_{\mathsf{init}}, [])] \text{ for some } n \geq 0$$

$$(q_1, \lambda, M) \overset{w(x,v)}{\Longrightarrow} (q_2, \lambda', M) \quad \text{if } q_1 \overset{w(x,v)}{\longrightarrow} q_2 \text{ and } \lambda' = \lambda[v/x]$$

$$(q_1, \lambda, M) \overset{r(x,v)}{\Longrightarrow} (q_2, \lambda, M) \quad \text{if } q_1 \overset{r(x,v)}{\longrightarrow} q_2 \text{ and } v = \lambda(x)$$

$$(q, \lambda, M_1) \overset{\bar{r}(x,v)}{\Longrightarrow} (q, \lambda, M_2) \quad \text{if } M_1 \overset{i(x,v)}{\Longrightarrow} M_2 \text{ and } v = \lambda(x)$$

$$(q, \lambda, M_1) \overset{\bar{w}(x,v)}{\Longrightarrow} (q, \lambda', M_2) \quad \text{if } M_1 \overset{o(x,v)}{\Longrightarrow} M_2 \text{ and } \lambda' = \lambda[v/x]$$

Here, we say that
$$M_1 \overset{a}{\Longrightarrow} M_2 \quad \text{for } a \in \Sigma_{ext}$$
if there is a multi-subset $M_1 = M' + [n_1 \cdot t_1, \ldots, n_r \cdot t_r]$ (where the t_i need not necessarily be distinct) and executions $t_i \overset{\alpha_i a}{\Longrightarrow} t_i'$ for $i = 1, \ldots, r$ for sequences $\alpha_i \in (\Sigma \setminus \Sigma_{ext})^*$ and $M_2 = M' + [n_1 \cdot t_1', \ldots, n_r \cdot t_r']$.

Fig. 2. Multiset semantics of dynamic parametric processes.

External transitions describe operations on external variables, be they global or not. For globals, these operations may come from the child sub-processes. In this case we relabel them as $\bar{r}, \bar{w}$ actions. This helps later to identify the rule that has been used for the transition (see Proposition 2). Note that the values of global variables are not part of the program state. Accordingly, these operations therefore can be considered as unconstrained input/output actions.

Internal transitions may silently change the current state, spawn new sub-processes or update or read the topmost local variables of the process. The expression $\lambda[v/x]$ denotes the function $\lambda' : X \to V$ defined by $\lambda'(x') = \lambda(x')$ for $x' \neq x$ and $\lambda'(x) = v$. In the case of spawn, the initial state of the new sub-processes is given by the argument, while the fresh local variables are initialized with the default value. In the last two cases (cf. Fig. 2) the external actions $i(x, v)$, $o(x, v)$ of the child sub-processes get relabeled as the corresponding internal actions $\bar{r}(x, v)$, $\bar{w}(x, v)$ on the local variables of the parent.

We write $t_1 \overset{\alpha}{\Longrightarrow} t_2$ for a sequence of transitions complying with the sequence α of action labels. Note that we allow several child sub-processes to move in one step (see definition of $M_1 \overset{\alpha}{\Longrightarrow} M_2$ in Fig. 2). While this makes the definition slightly more complicated, it simplifies some arguments later. Observe also that the semantics makes the actions (labels) at the top level explicit, while the actions of child sub-processes are explicit only if they refer to globals or affect the local variables of the parent.

2.3   Problem Statement and Main Result

In this section we define the reachability problem and state our main result in Theorem 1: it says that the reachability problem is decidable for dynamic parametric processes built upon an *admissible* class of systems. The notion of admissible class will be introduced later in this section. Before we do so, we introduce a *consistency* requirement for runs of parametric processes. Recall that our semantics does not constrain the operations on global variables. Their values are not stored in the overall state. At some moment, though, we must require that sequences of read/write actions on some global variable $y \in G$ can indeed be realized via reading from and writing to y.

Definition 1 (Consistency). *Let $y \in G$ be a global variable. A sequence $\alpha \in \Sigma^*$ is y-consistent if in the projection of α on operations on y, every read action $r(y, v)$ or $\bar{r}(y, v)$ which is not the first operation on y in α is immediately preceded either by $r(y, v), \bar{r}(y, v)$ or by $w(y, v)$ or $\bar{w}(y, v)$. The first operation on y in α can be either $r(y, v_{\mathsf{init}}), \bar{r}(y, v_{\mathsf{init}})$ or $w(y, v), \bar{w}(y, v)$ for some v.*

A sequence α is consistent *if it is y-consistent for every variable $y \in G$. Let Consistent be the set of all consistent sequences. As we assume both G and V to be finite, this is a regular language.*

Our goal is to decide reachability for dynamic parametric processes.

Definition 2 (Consistent run, reachability). *A* run *of a dynamic parametric process S is a path in $[\![S]\!]$ starting in the initial state, i.e., a sequence α such that $t_{\mathsf{init}} \stackrel{\alpha}{\Longrightarrow}_S t$ holds. If α is consistent, it is called a* consistent run.

The reachability problem *is to decide if for a given S, there is a consistent run of $[\![S]\!]$ containing an external write or an output action of some distinguished value #.*

Our definition of reachability talks about a particular value of some variable, and not about a particular state of the process. This choice is common, e.g., reaching a bad state may be simulated by writing a particular value, that is only possible from bad states. The definition admits not only external writes but also output actions because we will also consider processes without external writes.

We cannot expect the reachability problem to be decidable without any restriction on S. Instead of considering a particular class of dynamic parametric processes, like those build upon pushdown systems, we will formulate mild conditions on a class of such systems that turn out to be sufficient for deciding the reachability problem. These conditions will be satisfied by the class of pushdown systems, that is our primary motivation. Still we prefer this more abstract approach for two reasons. First, it simplifies notations. Second, it makes our results applicable to other cases as, for example, configuration graphs of higher-order pushdown systems with collapse.

In order to formulate our conditions, we require the notion of *automata*, with possibly infinitely many states. An *automaton* is a tuple:

$$\mathcal{A} = \langle Q, \Sigma, \Delta \subseteq Q \times \Sigma \times Q, F \subseteq Q \rangle$$

where Q is a set of states, Σ is a finite alphabet, Δ is a transition relation, and F is a set of accepting states. Observe that we do not single out an initial state. Apart from the alphabet, all other components may be infinite sets.

We now define what it means for a class of automata to have sufficiently good decidability and closure properties.

Definition 3 (Admissible class of automata). *We call a class C of automata* admissible *if it has the following properties:*

1. Constructively decidable emptiness check: For every automaton A from C and every state q of A, it is decidable if A has some path from q to an accepting state, and if the answer is positive then the sequence of labels of one such path can be computed.
2. Alphabet extension: There is an effective construction that given an automaton A from C, and an alphabet Γ disjoint from the alphabet of A, produces the automaton $A \circlearrowleft \Gamma$ that is obtained from A by adding a self-loop on every state of A on every letter from Γ. Moreover, $A \circlearrowleft \Gamma$ also belongs to C.
3. Synchronized product with finite-state systems: There is an algorithm that from a given automaton A from C and a finite-state automaton A' over the same alphabet, constructs the *synchronous product* $A \times A'$, that belongs to C, too. The states of the product are pairs of states of A and A'; there is a transition on some letter from such a pair if there is one from both states in the pair. A pair of states (q, q') is accepting in the synchronous product iff q is an accepting state of A and q' is an accepting state of A'.

There are many examples of admissible classes of automata. The simplest is the class of finite automata. Other examples are (configuration graphs of) pushdown automata, higher-order pushdown automata with collapse, VASS with action labels, lossy channel systems, etc. The closure under alphabet extensions required by Definition 3 is only added for convenience, e.g. for building synchronized products of automata over the same alphabets of actions.

From a dynamic parametric process S we obtain an automaton A_S by declaring all states final. That is, given the transition system $S = \langle Q, G, X, V, \Delta, q_{\text{init}}, v_{\text{init}} \rangle$ we set $A_S = \langle Q, \Sigma_{G,X,V}, \Delta, Q \rangle$, where $\Sigma_{G,X,V}$ is the alphabet of actions appearing in Δ. The automaton A_S is called the *associated automaton* of S.

Theorem 1. *Let C be an admissible class of automata. The reachability problem for dynamic parametric processes with associated automata in C, is decidable.*

As a corollary of the above theorem, we obtain that the reachability problem is decidable for *pushdown dynamic parametric processes*, that is where each subprocess is a pushdown automaton. Indeed, in this case C is the class of pushdown automata. Similarly, we get decidability for dynamic parametric processes with subprocesses being higher-order pushdown automata with collapse, and the other classes listed above.

3   Set Semantics

The first step towards deciding reachability for dynamic parametric processes is to simplify the semantics. The idea of using a set semantics instead of a multiset semantics already appeared in [4,5,9,11]. It reflects the idea that in the context of parametrization, the semantics can be chosen as accumulative, in the sense that we are only interested in sets of reachable configurations, rather then counting their multiplicities. We adapt the set semantics to our model, and show that it is equivalent to the multiset semantics — at least as far as the reachability problem is concerned.

Set configuration trees or *s-trees* for short, are of the form

$$s ::= (q, \lambda, S)$$

where $q \in Q$, $\lambda : X \to V$, and S is a finite set of s-trees. As in the case of m-trees, we consider only *finite* s-trees. In particular, this means that s-trees necessarily have finite depth. Configuration trees of depth 0 are those where S is empty. The set *S-trees$_k$* of s-trees of depth $k \geq 0$ is defined in a similar way as the set *M-trees$_k$* of multiset configuration trees of depth k.

With a given dynamic parametric process $\mathcal{S}$, the set semantics associates a transition system $[\![\mathcal{S}]\!]_s$ with s-trees as states. Its transitions have the same labels as in the case of multiset semantics. Moreover, we will use the same notation as for multiset transitions. It should be clear which semantics we are referring to, as we use t for m-trees and s for s-trees.

As expected, the initial s-tree is $s_{\text{init}} = (q_{\text{init}}, \lambda_{\text{init}}, \emptyset)$. The transitions are defined as in the multiset case but for multiset actions that become set actions:

$$S \overset{\text{spawn}(p)}{\Longrightarrow} S \cup \{(p, \lambda_{\text{init}}, \emptyset)\} \qquad \text{and} \qquad S_1 \overset{a}{\Longrightarrow} S_2 \quad \text{if } a \in \Sigma_{ext}$$

for $S_2 = S_1 \cup B$ where for each $s_2 \in B$ there is some $s_1 \in S_1$ so that $s_1 \overset{\alpha a}{\Longrightarrow} s_2$ for some sequence $\alpha \in (\Sigma \setminus \Sigma_{ext})^*$.

The reachability problem for dynamic parametric processes under the set semantics asks, like in the multiset case, whether there is some consistent run of $[\![\mathcal{S}]\!]_s$ that contains an external write or an output of a special value $\#$.

Proposition 1. *The reachability problems of dynamic parametric processes under the multiset and the set semantics, respectively, are equivalent.*

4   External Sequences and Signatures

In this section we introduce the objects that will be useful for summarizing the behaviors of sub-processes. Since our constructions and proofs will proceed by induction on the depth of s-trees, we will be particularly interested in sequences of external actions of subtrees of processes, and in signatures of such sequences, as defined below. Recall the definition of the alphabet of external actions Σ_{ext} (see page 6). Other actions of interest are the spawns occurring in $\mathcal{S}$:

$$\Sigma_{sp} = \{\text{spawn}(p) : \text{spawn}(p) \text{ is a label of a transition in } \mathcal{S}\}$$

Recall that according to our definitions, Σ_{sp} is finite.

For a sequence of actions α, let $ext(\alpha)$ be the subsequence of external actions in α, with additional renaming of $\bar{w}$, and $\bar{r}$ actions to actions without a bar, if they refer to global variables $g \in G$:

$$ext(a) = \begin{cases} r(g,v) & \text{if } a = r(g,v) \text{ or } a = \bar{r}(g,v) \\ w(g,v) & \text{if } a = w(g,v) \text{ or } a = \bar{w}(g,v) \\ a & \text{if } a = i(x,v) \text{ or } a = o(x,v) \\ \epsilon & \text{otherwise} \end{cases}$$

Let $\xRightarrow{\alpha}_k$ stand for the restriction of $\xRightarrow{\alpha}$ to s-trees of depth at most k (the trees of depth 0 have only the root). This allows to define a family of languages of *external behaviors* of trees of processes of height k. This family will be the main object of our study.

$$Ext_k = \{\text{spawn}(p)\, ext(\alpha) : (p, \lambda_{\text{init}}, \emptyset) \xRightarrow{\alpha}_k s \text{ for some } s, \text{spawn}(p) \in \Sigma_{sp}\}$$

The following definitions introduce abstraction and concretization operations on (sets of) sequences of external actions. The abstraction operation extracts from a sequence its *signature*, that is, the subsequence of first occurrences of external actions:

Definition 4 (Signature, canonical decomposition). *The signature of a word $\alpha \in \Sigma_{ext}^*$, denoted $\text{sig}(\alpha)$, is the subsequence of first appearances of actions in α.*

For a word α with signature $\text{sig}(\alpha) = b_0 b_1 \cdots b_k$, the (canonical) decomposition is $\alpha = b_0 \alpha_1 b_1 \alpha_2 b_2 \cdots \alpha_k b_k \alpha_{k+1}$, where b_i does not appear in $\alpha_1 \cdots \alpha_i$, for all i.

For words $\beta \in \Sigma_{sp} \cdot \Sigma_{ext}^*$ the signature is defined by $\text{sig}(\text{spawn}(p)\alpha) = \text{spawn}(p) \cdot \text{sig}(\alpha)$.

The above definition implies that α_1 consists solely of repetitions of b_0. In Example 2 the signatures of the executions at level 1 are $\text{spawn}(p)i(x,0)o(x,1)$, $\text{spawn}(p)i(x,1)o(x,2)$, and $\text{spawn}(p)i(x,1)o(x,0)$. Observe that all signatures at level 1 in this example are prefixes of the above signatures.

While the signature operation removes actions from a sequence, the concretization operation lift inserts them in all possible ways.

Definition 5 (lift). *Let $\alpha \in \Sigma_{ext}^*$ be a word with signature $b_0, \ldots, b_n$ and canonical decomposition $\alpha = b_0 \alpha_1 b_1 \alpha_2 b_2 \cdots \alpha_k b_k \alpha_{k+1}$. A lift of α is any word $\beta = b_0 \beta_1 b_1 \beta_2 b_2 \cdots \beta_k b_k \beta_{k+1}$, where β_i is obtained from α_i by inserting some number of actions $b_0, \ldots, b_{i-1}$, for $i = 1, \ldots, k+1$. We write $\text{lift}(\alpha)$ for the set of all such words β. For a set $L \subseteq \Sigma_{ext}^*$ we define*

$$\text{lift}(L) = \bigcup \{\text{lift}(\alpha) : \alpha \in L\}$$

We also define $\text{lift}(\text{spawn}(p) \cdot \alpha)$ as the set $\text{spawn}(p) \cdot \text{lift}(\alpha)$, and similarly $\text{lift}(L)$ for $L \subseteq \Sigma_{sp} \cdot \Sigma_{ext}^*$.

Observe that $\alpha \in \text{lift}(\text{sig}(\alpha))$. Another useful property is that if $\beta \in \text{lift}(\alpha)$ then α, β agree in their signatures.

5   Systems Under Hypothesis

This section presents the proof of our main result, namely, Theorem 1 stating that the reachability problem for dynamic parametric processes is decidable for an admissible class of systems. Our algorithm will analyze a process tree level by level. The main tool is an abstraction (summarization) of child sub-processes by their external behaviors. We call it *systems under hypothesis*.

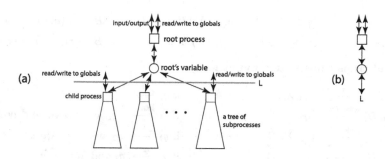

Fig. 3. Reduction to a system under hypothesis.

Let us briefly outline this idea. A configuration of a dynamic parametric process is a tree of sub-processes, Fig. 3(a). The root performs (1) input/output external operations, (2) read/writes to global variables, and (3) internal operations in form of reads/writes to its local variables, that are also accessible to the child sub-processes. We are now interested in possible sequences of operations on the global variables and the local variables of the root, that can be done by the child sub-processes. If somebody provided us with the set L_p of all such possible sequences, for child sub-processes starting at state p, for all p, we could simplify our system as illustrated in Fig. 3(b). We would replace the set of all sub-trees of the root by (a subset of) $L = \{\mathsf{spawn}(p)\beta : \beta \in \mathsf{pref}(L_p), \mathsf{spawn}(p) \in \Sigma_{sp}\}$ summarizing the possible behaviors of child sub-processes.

A set $L \subseteq \Sigma_{sp} \cdot \Sigma_{ext}^*$ is called a *hypothesis*, as it represents a guess about the possible behaviors of child sub-processes.

Let us now formalize the notion of *execution of the system under hypothesis*. For that, we define a system $\mathcal{S}_L$ that cannot spawn child sub-processes, but instead may use the hypothesis L. We will show that if L correctly describes the behavior of child sub-processes then the set of runs of $\mathcal{S}_L$ equals the set of runs of $\mathcal{S}$ with child sub-processes. This approach provides a way to compute the set of possible external behaviors of the original process tree level-wise: first for systems restricted to s-trees of height at most 1, then 2, ..., until a fixpoint is reached.

The configurations of $\mathcal{S}_L$ are of the form (q, λ, B), where λ is as before a valuation of local variables, and $B \subseteq \mathsf{pref}(L)$ is a set of sequences of external actions for sets of sub-processes.

The initial state is $r_{init} = (q_{init}, \lambda_{init}, \emptyset)$. We will use r to range over configurations of $\mathcal{S}_L$. Transitions between two states $r_1 \dashrightarrow_L r_2$ are listed in Fig. 4. Notice that transitions on actions of child sub-processes are modified so that now L is used to test if an action of a simulated child sub-process is possible.

External transitions under hypothesis:

$(q_1, \lambda, B) \xdashrightarrow{a}_L (q_2, \lambda, B)$ if $q_1 \xrightarrow{a} q_2$ if $a \in \Sigma_{ext}$

$(q, \lambda, B) \xdashrightarrow{\overline{w}(g,v)}_L (q, \lambda, B \cup B' \cdot \{w(g,v)\})$ if $\emptyset \neq B' \subseteq B$, $B' \cdot \{w(g,v)\} \subseteq \mathsf{pref}(L)$

$(q, \lambda, B) \xdashrightarrow{\overline{r}(g,v)}_L (q, \lambda, B \cup B' \cdot \{r(g,v)\})$ if $\emptyset \neq B' \subseteq B$, $B' \cdot \{r(g,v)\} \subseteq \mathsf{pref}(L)$

Internal transitions under hypothesis:

$(q_1, \lambda, B) \xdashrightarrow{\tau}_L (q_2, \lambda, B)$ if $q_1 \xrightarrow{\tau} q_2$

$(q_1, \lambda, B) \xdashrightarrow{\mathsf{spawn}(p)}_L (q_2, \lambda, B \cup \{\mathsf{spawn}(p)\})$ if $q_1 \xrightarrow{\mathsf{spawn}(p)} q_2$ and $\mathsf{spawn}(p) \in \mathsf{pref}(L)$

$(q_1, \lambda, B) \xdashrightarrow{w(x,v)}_L (q_2, \lambda', B)$ if $q_1 \xrightarrow{w(x,v)} q_2$ and $\lambda' = \lambda[v/x]$

$(q_1, \lambda, B) \xdashrightarrow{r(x,v)}_L (q_2, \lambda, B)$ if $q_1 \xrightarrow{r(x,v)} q_2$ and $\lambda(x) = v$

$(q, \lambda, B) \xdashrightarrow{\overline{w}(x,v)}_L (q, \lambda', B \cup B' \cdot \{o(x,v)\})$ if $\emptyset \neq B' \subseteq B$, $B' \cdot \{o(x,v)\} \subseteq \mathsf{pref}(L)$
                                    $\lambda' = \lambda[v/x]$

$(q, \lambda, B) \xdashrightarrow{\overline{r}(x,v)}_L (q, \lambda, B \cup B' \cdot \{i(x,v)\})$ if $\emptyset \neq B' \subseteq B$, $B' \cdot \{i(x,v)\} \subseteq \mathsf{pref}(L)$,
                                    $\lambda(x) = v$

Fig. 4. Transitions under hypothesis ($g \in G$, $x \in X$).

We list below two properties of $\dashrightarrow_L$. In order to state them in a convenient way, we introduce a *filtering* operation filter on sequences. The point is that external actions of child sub-processes are changed to $\overline{r}$ and $\overline{w}$, when they are exposed at the root of a configuration tree. In the definition below we rename them back; additionally, we remove irrelevant actions. So $\mathsf{filter}(\alpha)$ is obtained by the following renaming of α:

$$\mathsf{filter} : \quad \begin{aligned} \overline{r}(x,v) &\to i(x,v), & \overline{r}(g,v) &\to r(g,v), \\ \overline{w}(x,v) &\to o(x,v), & \overline{w}(g,v) &\to w(g,v), \\ a &\to a & &\text{if } a \in \Sigma_{sp}, \\ a &\to \epsilon & &\text{otherwise} \end{aligned}$$

The next two lemmas follow directly from the definition of $\dashrightarrow_L$.

Lemma 1. *If* $(q, \lambda, \emptyset) \xdashrightarrow{\alpha}_L (q', \lambda', B)$ *then* $B \subseteq \mathsf{pref}(L)$, *and every* $\beta \in B$ *is a scattered subword of* $\mathsf{filter}(\alpha)$.

Lemma 2. *If* $L_1 \subseteq L_2$ *and* $(p, \lambda, \emptyset) \xdashrightarrow{\alpha}_{L_1} r$ *then* $(p, \lambda, \emptyset) \xdashrightarrow{\alpha}_{L_2} r$.

The next lemma states a basic property of the relation $\overset{\alpha}{\dashrightarrow}_L$. If we take for L the set of all possible behaviors of child sub-processes with s-trees of height at most k, then $\overset{\alpha}{\dashrightarrow}_L$ gives us all possible behaviors of a system with s-trees of height at most $k + 1$. This corresponds exactly to the situation depicted in Fig. 3. The proof of the lemma is rather technical.

Lemma 3. *Suppose* $L = Ext_k$. *For every* p, q, λ, *and* α *we have:* $(p, \lambda_{\mathsf{init}}, \emptyset) \overset{\alpha}{\dashrightarrow}_L (q, \lambda, B)$ *for some* B *iff* $(p, \lambda_{\mathsf{init}}, \emptyset) \overset{\alpha}{\Longrightarrow}_{k+1} (q, \lambda, S)$ *for some* S.

The question we will pursue now is whether in the lemma above, we may replace Ext_k with some simpler set and still get all computations of the system of height $k + 1$. The key observation here here is that the lift operation (cf. Definition 5) does not add new behaviours:

Lemma 4. *Assume that* $L \subseteq \Sigma_{sp} \cdot \Sigma_{ext}^*$ *and* $L' = \mathsf{lift}(L)$. *Then* $(p, \lambda_{\mathsf{init}}, \emptyset) \overset{\alpha}{\dashrightarrow}_L (q, \lambda, B)$ *for some* $B \subseteq \mathsf{pref}(L)$ *iff* $(p, \lambda_{\mathsf{init}}, \emptyset) \overset{\alpha}{\dashrightarrow}_{L'} (q, \lambda, B')$ *for some* $B' \subseteq \mathsf{pref}(L')$.

So Lemma 3 says that child sub-processes can be abstracted by their external behaviors. Lemmas 2 and 4 allow to abstract a set L of external behaviors by a subset $L_1 \subseteq L$, as long as $L \subseteq \mathsf{lift}(L_1)$ holds. This property suggests to use a *well-quasi-order* to characterize a smallest such subset, which we call *core*:

Definition 6 (Order, core). *We define an order on* Σ_{ext}^* *by* $\alpha \preccurlyeq \beta$ *if* $\beta \in \mathsf{lift}(\alpha)$. *This extends to an order on* $\Sigma_{sp} \cdot \Sigma_{ext}^*$: $\mathsf{spawn}(p)\alpha \preccurlyeq \mathsf{spawn}(q)\beta$ *if* $p = q$ *and* $\alpha \preccurlyeq \beta$. *For a set* $L \subseteq \Sigma_{sp} \cdot \Sigma_{ext}^*$, *we define* $\mathsf{core}(L)$ *as the set of* minimal *words in* L *with respect to the relation* $\preccurlyeq$.

The following lemma is easy to see:

Lemma 5. *The relation* $\preccurlyeq$ *is a well-quasi-order on words with equal signature. Since the number of signatures is finite, the set* $\mathsf{core}(L)$ *is finite for every set* $L \subseteq \Sigma_{sp} \cdot \Sigma_{ext}^*$.

Consider, e.g., the set $L = Ext_1$ of all external behaviors of depth 1 in Example 1. Then $\mathsf{core}(L)$ consists of the sequences:

$\mathsf{spawn}(q)\, w(g_0, \#)$, $\mathsf{spawn}(p)\, i(x, 1)o(x, 2)o(x, 3)$, $\mathsf{spawn}(p)\, i(x, 1)o(x, 3)o(x, 2)$

together with all their prefixes (recall that k in Ext_k refers to s-trees of depth *at most* k).

The development till now can be summarized by the following:

Corollary 1. *For a set* $L \subseteq \Sigma_{sp} \cdot \Sigma_{ext}^*$ *and its core* $L' = \mathsf{core}(L)$: $(p, \lambda_{\mathsf{init}}, \emptyset) \overset{\alpha}{\dashrightarrow}_L (q, \lambda, B)$ *for some* $B \subseteq L$ *iff* $(p, \lambda_{\mathsf{init}}, \emptyset) \overset{\alpha}{\dashrightarrow}_{L'} (q, \lambda, B')$ *for some* $B' \subseteq L'$.

Proof. Since $\mathsf{core}(L) \subseteq L$, the right-to-left implication follows by monotonicity. For the other direction we observe that $L \subseteq \mathsf{lift}(\mathsf{core}(L))$, so we can use Lemma 4 and monotonicity. □

Now we turn to the question of computing the relation $\overset{\alpha}{\dashrightarrow}_L$ for a *finite* set L. For this we need our admissibility assumptions from page 9.

Proposition 2. *Let C be an admissible class of automata, and let S be a transition system whose associated automaton is in C. Suppose we have two sets $L, L' \subseteq \Sigma_{sp} \cdot \Sigma_{ext}^*$ with $L \subseteq L' \subseteq \mathsf{lift}(L)$. Consider the set*

$$K = \{\mathsf{spawn}(p)\,ext(\alpha) : \mathsf{spawn}(p) \in \Sigma_{sp} \text{ and } (p, \lambda_{\mathsf{init}}, \emptyset)\overset{\alpha}{\dashrightarrow}_{L'}r', \text{for some} r'\}$$

determined by S and L'. If L is finite then we can compute the sets

$$core(K) \quad and \quad core(\{\alpha \in K : \alpha consistent\}).$$

The proof of the above proposition works by augmenting the transition system S by a finite-state component taking care of the valuation of local variables and of prefixes of L that were used in the hypothesis. For this we use the last two conditions of Definition 3. The admissibility of C (constructively decidable emptiness) is then used to compute the core of the language of the automaton thus obtained.

Corollary 2. *The sets $core(Ext_0)$ and $core(Ext_0 \cap Consistent)$ are computable.*

Corollary 3. *Under the hypothesis of Proposition 2: for every $k \geq 0$, we can compute $core(Ext_k)$ and $core(Ext_k \cap Consistent)$.*

Proof. We start with $L_0 = core(Ext_0)$ that we can compute by Corollary 2. Now assume that $L_i = core(Ext_i)$ has already been computed. By Lemma 3, L_{i+1} equals the core of $\{\mathsf{spawn}(p)\,ext(\alpha) : (p, \lambda_{\mathsf{init}}, \emptyset)\overset{\alpha}{\dashrightarrow}_{L_i}r, \text{ some} r\}$ which, by Proposition 2, is effectively computable.   □

Now we have all ingredients to prove Theorem 1.

Proof (of Theorem 1). Take a process S as in the statement of the theorem. The external behaviors of S are described by the language

$$L = \bigcup_{k \in \mathbb{N}} \{\mathsf{spawn}(p)\,ext(\alpha) : (p, \lambda_{\mathsf{init}}, \emptyset)\overset{\alpha}{\dashrightarrow}_{Ext_k}r, \text{ for some } r\}$$

If we denote $L_k = core(Ext_k)$ then by Corollary 1, the language L is equal to

$$L' = \bigcup_{k \in \mathbb{N}} \{\mathsf{spawn}(p)\,ext(\alpha) : (p, \lambda_{\mathsf{init}}, \emptyset)\overset{\alpha}{\dashrightarrow}_{L_k}r, \text{ for some } r\}$$

By definition, $Ext_0 \subseteq Ext_1 \subseteq \cdots$ is an increasing sequence of sets. By Lemma 5, this means that there is some m so that $core(Ext_m) = core(Ext_{m+i})$, for all i. Therefore, L' is equal to

$$\{\mathsf{spawn}(p)\,ext(\alpha) : (p, \lambda_{\mathsf{init}}, \emptyset)\overset{\alpha}{\dashrightarrow}_{L_m}r, \text{ for some } r\}$$

By Corollary 3, the set $L_m = core(Ext_m)$ is computable and so is $core(L' \cap Consistent)$. Finally, we check if in this latter set there is a sequence starting with $\mathsf{spawn}(q_{\mathsf{init}})$ and an external write or an output of $\#$.   □

6   Simpler Cases

In this section we consider pushdown dynamic parametric processes, i.e., the case where each sub-process can have its own stack. We show several restrictions of the model yielding rather reasonable complexity for deciding reachability. Proofs are omitted in this section, they can be found in the full version of the paper http://arxiv.org/abs/1609.05385.

We start with the case where sub-processes cannot write to their own variables, but only to the variables of the parent. This corresponds to the situation when after a parent has created child sub-processes, these child sub-processes may communicate computed results to the parent, and to other sub-processes created by the parent, but the parent cannot communicate to child sub-processes. We call such a situation *systems with generalized futures*. We have seen an example of such a system in Fig. 1. Technically, systems with generalized futures are obtained by disallowing $w(x, v)$ actions in our general definition. We need two more restrictions: first, we rule out global variables altogether; second, we require that the initial value v_{init} of a register can be neither read nor written. The first of the two restrictions follows the intuition that a parent should not communicate with child sub-processes; the reason behind the second restriction is that we want to avoid tracking when an initial value has been overwritten.

The reachability problem here is defined by the occurrence of an output action $o(x, \#)$ of some special value $\#$.

For systems with generalized futures, reachability can be decided by a cheaper approach, based on signatures instead of cores.

Theorem 2. *The reachability problem for pushdown dynamic parametric processes with generalized futures is decidable in* DEXPTIME *(exponential in* $|V|$, $|X|$, *and polynomial in the size of the pushdown automaton defining* $\mathcal{S}$.*)*

A further simplification is to disallow $i(x, v)$ actions. This means that child sub-processes cannot read the value of the variable of their parents. Accordingly, they still can report results, but no longer communicate between themselves. We call this class *systems with simple futures*.

Theorem 3. *The reachability problem is* NP-*complete for pushdown dynamic parametric processes with simple futures, provided the number of variables is fixed. The complexity becomes* PTIME *if the number of values is also fixed.*

The two restrictions above disallowed global variables. The final restriction we consider is to disallow local variables and to admit global variables instead. It turns out that such systems can be *flattened* — implying that nesting of sub-process creation does no longer add to expressivity. Accordingly, the complexity is the same as for the parametrized model of [5, 7]:

Theorem 4. *The reachability problem for pushdown dynamic parametric processes without local variables is* PSPACE-*complete, assuming that the number of variables is fixed.*

7   Conclusions

We have studied systems with parametric process creation where sub-processes may communicate via both global and local shared variables. This kind of communication can model e.g. communication with message queues of capacity one. We have shown that under mild conditions, the reachability problem for this model is decidable. The algorithm relies on abstracting the behavior of the created child sub-processes by means of finitely many minimal behaviors. This set of minimal behaviors is obtained by a fixpoint computation whose termination relies on well-quasi-orderings. This bottom-up approach is different from the ones used before [5,7,11]. In particular, the presented approach avoids computing downward closures, showing that effectively computable downward closure is not needed in the general decidability results on flat systems from [11]. In particular, note that lossy channel systems form an admissible class of systems, whereas their downward closures are not effective.

We have also considered special cases for pushdown dynamic parametric processes where we obtained solutions of a relatively low complexity. In absence of local variables we have shown that reachability can be reduced to reachability for systems without dynamic sub-process creation, implying that reachability is PSPACE-complete. For the (incomparable) case where communication is restricted to child sub-processes reporting their results to siblings and their parents, we have also provided a dedicated method with DExptime complexity. We conjecture that this bound is tight. Finally, when sub-processes can report results only to their parents, the problem becomes just NP-complete.

An interesting problem for further research is to study the reachability of a particular *set* of configurations as considered, e.g., for dynamic pushdown networks [2]. One such set could, e.g., specify that all children of a given sub-process have terminated. For dynamic pushdown networks with nested or contextual locking, such kinds of barriers have been considered in [6,13]. It remains as an intriguing question whether or not similar concepts can be handled also for dynamic parametric processes.

References

1. Bouajjani, A., Esparza, J., Maler, O.: Reachability analysis of pushdown automata: application to model-checking. In: Mazurkiewicz, A., Winkowski, J. (eds.) CONCUR 1997. LNCS, vol. 1243, pp. 135–150. Springer, Heidelberg (1997). doi:10.1007/3-540-63141-0_10
2. Bouajjani, A., Müller-Olm, M., Touili, T.: Regular symbolic analysis of dynamic networks of pushdown systems. In: Abadi, M., Alfaro, L. (eds.) CONCUR 2005. LNCS, vol. 3653, pp. 473–487. Springer, Heidelberg (2005). doi:10.1007/11539452_36
3. Chadha, R., Madhusudan, P., Viswanathan, M.: Reachability under contextual locking. In: Flanagan, C., König, B. (eds.) TACAS 2012. LNCS, vol. 7214, pp. 437–450. Springer, Heidelberg (2012). doi:10.1007/978-3-642-28756-5_30

4. Durand-Gasselin, A., Esparza, J., Ganty, P., Majumdar, R.: Model checking parameterized asynchronous shared-memory systems. In: Kroening, D., Păsăreanu, C.S. (eds.) CAV 2015. LNCS, vol. 9206, pp. 67–84. Springer, Heidelberg (2015). doi:10. 1007/978-3-319-21690-4_5
5. Esparza, J., Ganty, P., Majumdar, R.: Parameterized verification of asynchronous shared-memory systems. J. ACM **63**(1), 10 (2016)
6. Gawlitza, T.M., Lammich, P., Müller-Olm, M., Seidl, H., Wenner, A.: Join-lock-sensitive forward reachability analysis for concurrent programs with dynamic process creation. In: Jhala, R., Schmidt, D. (eds.) VMCAI 2011. LNCS, vol. 6538, pp. 199–213. Springer, Heidelberg (2011). doi:10.1007/978-3-642-18275-4_15
7. Hague, M.: Parameterised pushdown systems with non-atomic writes. In: Chakraborty, S., Kumar, A. (eds.) IARCS Annual Conference on Foundations of Software Technology and Theoretical Computer Science, FSTTCS 2011, 12–14 December 2011, Mumbai, India, vol. 13, LIPIcs, pp. 457–468. Schloss Dagstuhl - Leibniz-Zentrum für Informatik (2011)
8. Hague, M., Murawski, A.S., Ong, C.-H.L., Serre, O.: Collapsible pushdown automata and recursion schemes. In: LICS 2008, pp. 452–461. IEEE Computer Society (2008)
9. Kahlon, V.: Parameterization as abstraction: a tractable approach to the dataflow analysis of concurrent programs. In: Proceedings of the Twenty-Third Annual IEEE Symposium on Logic in Computer Science, LICS 2008, 24–27 June 2008, Pittsburgh, PA, USA, pp. 181–192. IEEE Computer Society (2008)
10. Kahlon, V., Ivančić, F., Gupta, A.: Reasoning about threads communicating via locks. In: Etessami, K., Rajamani, S.K. (eds.) CAV 2005. LNCS, vol. 3576, pp. 505–518. Springer, Heidelberg (2005). doi:10.1007/11513988_49
11. La Torre, S., Muscholl, A., Walukiewicz, I.: Safety of parametrized asynchronous shared-memory systems is almost always decidable. In: Aceto, L., de Frutos-Escrig, D. (eds.) 26th International Conference on Concurrency Theory, CONCUR, Madrid, Spain, September 1.4, vol. 42, LIPIcs, pp. 72–84. Schloss Dagstuhl - Leibniz-Zentrum für Informatik (2015)
12. Lammich, P., Müller-Olm, M.: Conflict analysis of programs with procedures, dynamic thread creation, and monitors. In: Alpuente, M., Vidal, G. (eds.) SAS 2008. LNCS, vol. 5079, pp. 205–220. Springer, Heidelberg (2008). doi:10.1007/978-3-540-69166-2_14
13. Lammich, P., Müller-Olm, M., Seidl, H., Wenner, A.: Contextual locking for dynamic pushdown networks. In: Logozzo, F., Fähndrich, M. (eds.) SAS 2013. LNCS, vol. 7935, pp. 477–498. Springer, Heidelberg (2013). doi:10.1007/978-3-642-38856-9_25
14. Lammich, P., Müller-Olm, M., Wenner, A.: Predecessor sets of dynamic pushdown networks with tree-regular constraints. In: Bouajjani, A., Maler, O. (eds.) CAV 2009. LNCS, vol. 5643, pp. 525–539. Springer, Heidelberg (2009). doi:10.1007/978-3-642-02658-4_39
15. Ong, C.-H.L.: On model-checking trees generated by higher-order recursion schemes. In: LICS 2006, pp. 81–90 (2006)
16. Ramalingam, G.: Context-sensitive synchronization-sensitive analysis is undecidable. ACM Trans. Program. Lang. Syst. **22**(2), 416–430 (2000)
17. Walukiewicz, I.: Pushdown processes: games and model checking. In: Alur, R., Henzinger, T.A. (eds.) CAV 1996. LNCS, vol. 1102, pp. 62–74. Springer, Heidelberg (1996). doi:10.1007/3-540-61474-5_58

Conjunctive Abstract Interpretation Using Paramodulation

Or Ozeri$^{(\boxtimes)}$, Oded Padon, Noam Rinetzky, and Mooly Sagiv

School of Computer Science, Tel Aviv University, Tel Aviv, Israel
orozery@post.tau.ac.il

Abstract. Scaling static analysis is one of the main challenges for program verification in general and for abstract interpretation in particular. One way to compactly represent a set of states is using a formula in *conjunctive normal form* (*CNF*). This can sometimes save exponential factors. Therefore, CNF formulae are commonly used in manual program verification and symbolic reasoning. However, it is not used in abstract interpretation, due to the complexity of reasoning about the effect of program statements when the states are represented this way.

We present algorithms for performing abstract interpretation on CNF formulae recording equality and inequalities of ground terms. Here, terms correspond to the values of variables and of addresses and contents of dynamically allocated memory locations, and thus, a formula can represent pointer equalities and inequalities. The main idea is the use of the rules of paramodulation as a basis for an algorithm that computes logical consequences of CNF formulae, and the application of the algorithm to perform joins and transformers.

The algorithm was implemented and used for reasoning about low level programs. We also show that our technique can be used to implement best transformers for a variant of *Connection Analysis* via a non-standard interpretation of equality.

1 Introduction

Arguably, the greatest challenge in abstract interpretation [6] is managing the trade-off between the cost and the precision of the abstraction. This trade-off appears in an especially stark light in the handling of disjunction. An abstract domain that is closed under logical disjunction allows the analysis to enumerate cases, greatly enhancing its precision. However, this can quickly lead to an explosion of cases and intractability. An alternative is to use a Cartesian/conjunctive abstract domain. In this case, we are limited to logical conjunctions of facts drawn from rather simple abstract domains. This approach has the disadvantage that it cannot capture correlations between the components of the abstraction, thus quickly loses precision.

In this paper, we consider points between these two extremes. Our abstract domain will consist of logical formulae in *conjunctive normal form* (*CNF*).

This work is supported by EU FP7 ERC grant agreement n^o [321174].

A. Bouajjani and D. Monniaux (Eds.): VMCAI 2017, LNCS 10145, pp. 442–461, 2017.
DOI: 10.1007/978-3-319-52234-0_24

For atomic formulae, we support pointer equalities where ground terms correspond to pointer expressions. This approach is consistent with the way in which manually constructed program invariants are written. That is, they tend to consist of a large conjunction of relatively simple formulae containing a few disjunctions. Note that in contrast to standard may- and must- points-to analysis (see, e.g., [19]), CNF formulae permit conditional information. For example, consider the following code fragment:

$$\text{if } (\mathsf{x} \neq 0) \text{ then } \mathsf{y} := [\mathsf{x}]; \text{ if } (\mathsf{y} \neq 0) \text{ then } \mathsf{t} := [\mathsf{y}]$$

which loads into y the contents of the memory location pointed to by x, provided the value of the latter is not *null* (0), and then, if the value assigned to y is not null, loads into t the contents of the memory location that y now points to. The conjunction of the following clauses, where $a \implies b$ is used as syntactic sugar for $\neg a \lor b$, records the conditional aliasing generated by the above code fragment:

$$x \neq 0 \implies y = [x] \text{ and } y \neq 0 \implies t = [y] \, .$$

A key advantage of using CNF formulae is that they can be exponentially more succinct then DNF formulae used, e.g., in predicate abstraction. For example, to express the information recorded by the above clauses, we need four disjuncts:

$$x = 0 \land y = 0 \quad , \quad x \neq 0 \land y = [x] \land y = 0,$$
$$x = 0 \land y \neq 0 \land t = [y] \, , \text{ or } x \neq 0 \land y = [x] \land y \neq 0 \land t = [y] \, .$$

The greatest challenge in our domain is reasoning about the effect of program statements and program joins. The reason is that even a simple statement, e.g., variable copy, can have a complicated effect on a CNF formula. Moreover, it may require rather complicated reasoning about the interactions between different clauses. For example, computing the effect of the statement y := NULL on the set of states described by the above CNF formula requires considering both conjuncts to observe that the set of post-states can be described by the following conjuncts:

$$y = 0 \text{ and } x \neq 0 \land [x] \neq 0 \implies t = [[x]].$$

This is in contrast to disjunctive domains where the effect of transformers is computed distributively by applying them to each disjunct. Indeed, disjunctive domains are incremental in nature.

We solve the last challenge by adapting a technique from theorem proving called *paramodulation* (see, e.g., [15]). Paramodulation is a refinement of the *resolution* [16] procedure for reasoning about equalities. The main idea is to implicitly represent equalities avoiding the costs of transitive inferences. However, utilizing paramodulation in abstract interpretation is not a panacea. First, paramodulation is usually applied in a context of checking validity, and we need to compute logical consequences. Second, in the context of abstract interpretation, the transformers are repeatedly computed many times, which can be expensive. Third, it is not clear how to ensure that the reasoning does not lead to plethora of terms leading to non-scalability and divergence of the static analysis.

Main Results. The main results of this paper can be summarized as follows:

1. We develop a parametric abstract domain comprised of CNF formulae. Particular abstract domains can be instantiated by setting different bounds on the sizes of clauses and terms. This allows to modify the precision/performance tradeoff in our analyses simply by varying these bounds (Section 3).
2. We describe a technique for computing join operators (Sect. 3) and applying abstract transformers (Sect. 4) based on a novel algorithm for performing semantic reduction [6] (Sect. 5). The algorithm is based on finding the logical consequences of CNF formulae. In general, consequence finding is a hard problem and requires many calls to expensive SAT solver. However, for reasoning about equalities, the problem is somewhat easier since we can compactly represent equivalence classes and leverage the properties of equivalence relations and of function congruence [14][1] to detect important consequences using paramodulation [15].
3. We apply our technique to the problem of *Connection Analysis* [9] (Sect. 6). Connection analysis treats the program's heap (dynamically allocated memory) as an undirected graph, and infers whether two pointer variables may never point to the same weakly connected heap-component. We obtain a new abstract interpretation algorithm for connection analysis using heap-connectivity as a non-standard interpretation of equality, and adapting the abstract meaning of statements accordingly. Furthermore, we prove that the resulting transformers are the *best* (most precise conservative) *abstract transformers* [6], and demonstrate that our analysis can infer properties that existing connection analyses [3,9] cannot.
4. We implemented our analysis algorithms in a proof-of-concept analyzer. We report on an initial empirical evaluation using a few small benchmarks, and discuss certain heuristics, based on *ordered paramodulation* (see, e.g., [15]) that can improve the performance of the analysis but may, in principal, hurt its precision. (Section 7).

2   Programming Language and Running Example

We formalize our results using a simple imperative programming language for sequential procedure-less programs. We assume the reader is familiar with the notion of *control-flow graphs* (see, e.g., [1]), and only define the necessary terminology.

Syntax. A program $P = (V, E, v_{entry}, v_{exit}, c)$ is a *control-flow graph (CFG)*: Nodes $v \in V$ correspond to *program points* and edges $e \in E$ indicate possible transfer of control. Every edge e is associated with a primitive command $c(e)$. In this paper, with the exception of Sect. 6, we use the primitive commands listed in Fig. 1, which are typical for pointer-manipulating programs. They include

---

[1] Function congruence means that if x and y are equal then, for any function $f(\cdot)$, so are $f(x)$ and $f(y)$. Congruence naturally generalizes to functions with multiple arguments.

the ubiquitous `skip` command, conditionals involving variables, assignments to variables, dynamic memory allocation, (possibly destructive) accesses to memory locations via pointers, and assignment commands $v: = \mathtt{f}(v_1, \ldots, v_k)$ involving any function (operator) $\mathtt{f}$ coming from an arbitrary set F of *pure* functions over values ($\mathtt{f}$ is a pure function if its evaluation does not change the state. For example, in the running example, $F = \{+\}$, where $+$ is the arithmetic addition operator). Our technique is independent of the choice of the functions included in F, as, unless stated otherwise, our analysis treats them as uninterpreted functions.

Formally, our language allows for only two forms of conditionals: $v = v'$ and $v \neq v'$. However, we can encode arbitrary conditionals by using a function which returns, e.g., 1 if the condition holds and 0 otherwise. For example, We can encode the *less-than* relation $v < v'$ as a function $\mathtt{f}_<(v, v') = $ if $v < v'$ then 1 else 0.

command	Comment
`skip`	skip.
`assume`($v \bowtie v'$)	Acts as `skip` if $v \bowtie v'$ holds, and blocks the execution otherwise.
$v := c$	Assigns the constant value c to a local variable v.
$v := v'$	Copies the value of v' to v. We require that v is different from v'.
$v := \mathtt{malloc}(v')$	Dynamically allocates a block of memory comprised of v' locations.
$v := [v']$	Loads the value stored in (the dynamically allocated) memory location v' to a local variable v. We require that v is different from v'.
$[v] := v'$	Stores the value of v' at (the dynamically allocated) memory location v.
$v := \mathtt{f}(v_1, \ldots, v_k)$	Assigns the result of applying a pure function (operator) $\mathtt{f}$ to v. We require that v is different from $v_1, \ldots, v_k$ and expect $\mathtt{f}$ not to be $[\,\cdot\,]$.

Fig. 1. Primitive commands. We assume the programing language allows to apply an arbitrary, but finite, set of pure functions $\mathtt{f} \in F$. We leave the set F unspecified. $\bowtie$ is either $=$ or $\neq$.

Operational Semantics. Let $Val \supseteq \mathbb{N}$ be the semantic domains of *values*. A concrete state $\sigma = \langle \rho, h \rangle \in \Sigma$ is comprised of an *environment* $\rho : \mathrm{Var} \to Val$ mapping a fixed, but arbitrary, finite set of variable names to their values, and a *heap* $h : \mathbb{N}^+ \rightharpoonup \mathsf{Val}$ mapping allocated memory locations (addresses), represented as non zero natural numbers, to values. The semantics of programs is defined using a *concrete transition relation* $T \subseteq \Sigma \times \Sigma$. For simplicity, we assume that accessing an unallocated address blocks the execution.[2] With the exception of this, the semantics is standard.

Running Example. Figure 2 shows `find_last`, a program which we use as our running example. For clarity, the figure also provides an implementation of the

---

[2] Our analysis does not prove memory safety. Thus, our results can be adapted to the case where such an operation leads to an error state in the following way: The properties we infer hold unless the program performs a memory error, e.g., dereferencing a null-valued pointer or accessing an unallocated memory address.

program in C. find_last gets as an input a pointer s to a nil-terminated string, i.e., a '\0'-terminated array of characters, and a character c. It returns a pointer to the last occurrence of c in s, or NULL if c does not appear in s. Our analysis successfully verifies that the find_last either returns NULL or a pointer to a memory location containing the same value as c.

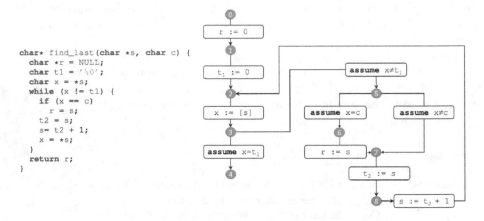

```c
char* find_last(char *s, char c) {
    char *r = NULL;
    char t1 = '\0';
    char x = *s;
    while (x != t1) {
        if (x == c)
            r = s;
        t2 = s;
        s= t2 + 1;
        x = *s;
    }
    return r;
}
```

Fig. 2. The running example. Program points are depicted as solid numbered circles. Edges are decorated with rectangles labeled with primitive commands.

3   Equality-Based Parametric Abstract Domain

We define a parametric family of abstract domains $(\Phi_{\mathcal{F}}^{k,d}, \sqsubseteq)$ comprised of ground quantifier-free logical formulae in first order logic (FOL) in conjunctive-normal form (CNF).[3] The only allowed predicate symbol is equality, applied to terms constructed using function and constant symbols coming from a fixed, but arbitrary, finite vocabulary $\mathcal{F}$. Technically, we represent formulae as sets of *clauses*, where each clause C is a set of *literals*. A literal L is either an *atom* or its negation. An atom $s \simeq t$ is an instance of the equality predicate $\simeq$ applied to two terms, s and t. The abstract domain is parameterized by the vocabulary $\mathcal{F}$, and by two natural numbers: k (dubbed *max-clause*) is the maximal number of literals in a clause, and d (dubbed *rank*) is the maximal number of nested function applications that may be used to construct a term.

Figure 3 defines the abstract states in $\Phi_{\mathcal{F}}^{k,d}$ for arbitrary $\mathcal{F}$, k, and d. We denote the set of well-formed terms over vocabulary $\mathcal{F}$ by $\mathcal{T}_{\mathcal{F}}$ and the *rank* of a term by rank(t). For example, the ranks of the terms 0, a + 1, and f(a) + 1, are zero, one, and two, respectively.[4] We denote the subset of $\mathcal{T}_{\mathcal{F}}$, containing all terms with rank d or less by

---

[3] A ground formula is a formula which does not contain free variables.

[4] We assume the reader is familiar with the notions of well-formedness, ranking and meaning of terms in FOL, and do not formalize them here. For a formal definition, see, e.g., [15, Chap. 7].

$$\mathcal{T}_{\mathcal{F}}^d \stackrel{\text{def}}{=} \{t \in \mathcal{T}_{\mathcal{F}} \mid \text{rank}(t) \leq d\} \ .$$

In the following, we often refer to an abstract state $\varphi \in \Phi_{\mathcal{F}}^{k,d}$ as a *formula*. Also, for clarity, we write atoms and literals as $s \simeq t$ and $s \not\simeq t$ instead of $\{s, t\}$ and $\neg\{s, t\}$, respectively. Note that, e.g., $s \simeq t$ and $t \simeq s$ denote the same atom. Also note that our restrictions ensure that $\Phi_{\mathcal{F}}^{k,d}$ is finite for any allowed choice of $\mathcal{F}$, k, and d. We denote the set of CNF formulae over vocabulary $\mathcal{F}$ involving terms of rank d or less by $\Phi_{\mathcal{F}}^d$ and the set of all CNF formulae over vocabulary $\mathcal{F}$ by $\Phi_{\mathcal{F}}$:

$$\Phi_{\mathcal{F}}^d = \bigcup_{0 \leq k} \Phi_{\mathcal{F}}^{k,d} \qquad\qquad \Phi_{\mathcal{F}} = \bigcup_{0 \leq d} \Phi_{\mathcal{F}}^d \ .$$

$$\varphi \in \Phi_{\mathcal{F}}^{k,d} \stackrel{\text{def}}{=} \mathcal{P}\left(\mathcal{C}_{\mathcal{F}}^{k,d}\right) \quad \textbf{Formulae} \qquad L \in \mathcal{L}_{\mathcal{F}}^d \stackrel{\text{def}}{=} \{A, \neg A \mid A \in \mathcal{A}_{\mathcal{F}}^d\} \ \textbf{Literals}$$
$$C \in \mathcal{C}_{\mathcal{F}}^{k,d} \stackrel{\text{def}}{=} \{C \subseteq \mathcal{L}_{\mathcal{F}}^d \mid |C| \leq k\} \ \textbf{Clauses} \qquad A \in \mathcal{A}_{\mathcal{F}}^d \stackrel{\text{def}}{=} \{\{s, t\} \mid s, t \in \mathcal{T}_{\mathcal{F}}^d\} \ \textbf{Atoms}$$

Fig. 3. Abstract states (formulae). k and d are arbitrary natural numbers.

The Least-Upper Bound (Join) Operator. The abstract domain is ordered by subsumption.

$$\varphi_1 \sqsubseteq \varphi_2 \iff \forall C_2 \in \varphi_2. \exists C_1 \in \varphi_1. C_1 \subseteq C_2 \ .$$

The least upper bound operator in $\Phi_{\mathcal{F}}^{k,d}$, denoted by $\cdot \sqcup^k \cdot$, is defined as follows:

$$\varphi_1 \sqcup^k \varphi_2 = \{C_1 \cup C_2 \mid C_1 \in \varphi_1 \ , \ C_2 \in \varphi_2\} \cap \mathcal{C}_{\mathcal{F}}^{k,d} \ .$$

It easy to see that under the subsumption order $\sqsubseteq$, the set $\emptyset$ is the top element $\top$ of the domain and that $\{\emptyset\}$ is its bottom element $\bot$.

Concretization Function. A concrete state $\sigma \in \Sigma$ models a formula φ if it satisfies all of its clauses, where a clause C is satisfied if at least of one its literals, which is either an equality or inequality holds. Figure 4 defines the forcing semantics $\sigma \models \varphi$ which determines whether a state $\sigma \in \Sigma$ satisfies a formula $\varphi \in \Phi_{\mathcal{F}}$. The interpretation of a term $t \in \mathcal{T}_{\mathcal{F}}$ in a state σ, denoted by $\sigma(t)$, is defined inductively in a standard way (See footnote 4). A formula (abstract state) represents the set of concrete states which satisfies it:

$$\gamma : \Phi_{\mathcal{F}}^{k,d} \to \mathcal{P}\left(\Sigma\right) \stackrel{\text{def}}{=} \gamma(\varphi) = \{\sigma \in \Sigma \mid \sigma \models \varphi\}.$$

Note that $\gamma(\emptyset) = \Sigma$ and $\gamma(\{\emptyset\}) = \emptyset$.

Example 1. We use the function symbol $[\cdot]$ to represent the contents of the heap. For example, let $\sigma = \langle \rho, h \rangle$, where $\rho = [x \mapsto 1, y \mapsto 2]$ and $h = [1 \mapsto 2, 2 \mapsto 3]$, then

$$\sigma \models x \simeq 1, \quad \sigma \models [x] \simeq 2, \quad \text{and} \quad \sigma \models [[x]] \simeq 3.$$

Example 2. In our running example, our analysis proves that the formula resulting at program point 4, where find_last terminates, contains the clause $\{r \simeq 0, [r] \simeq c\}$. The models of this clause are all the states where r, the return value of find_last, is either NULL or points to a memory location containing the same value as c.

$$\sigma \models \varphi \iff \forall C \in \varphi . \sigma \models C \qquad \sigma \models s \simeq t \iff \sigma(s) = \sigma(t)$$
$$\sigma \models C \iff \exists L \in C . \sigma \models L \qquad \sigma \models s \not\simeq t \iff \sigma \not\models s \simeq t$$

Fig. 4. Forcing semantics

We say that a formula φ_1 is a *semantic consequence* of a formula φ_2, denoted by $\varphi_1 \models \varphi_2$, if for any concrete state $\sigma \in \Sigma$ such that $\sigma \models \varphi_1$, it holds that $\sigma \models \varphi_2$. The subsumption order is an under-approximation of the *implication order*, i.e., for any concrete state σ and any formulae φ_1, φ_2, if $\varphi_1 \sqsubseteq \varphi_2$ then $\varphi_1 \models \varphi_2$. The other direction is not true. Thus, as it is often the case in logical domains (see, e.g., [8]), our domain does not have an abstraction function which maps every set of concrete state to its most precise representation in the abstract domain. For example, $\varphi_a = \{\{x \simeq y, y \not\simeq z\}, \{y \simeq z\}\}$ and $\varphi_b = \{\{x \simeq z\}, \{y \simeq z\}\}$ represent the same set of concrete states but neither $\varphi_a \not\sqsubseteq \varphi_b$ nor $\varphi_b \not\sqsubseteq \varphi_a$. Furthermore, there might be formulae such that $\varphi_1 \sqsubseteq \varphi_2$ and yet $\varphi_2 \models \varphi_1$. For example, let $\varphi_c = \{\{x \simeq y\}, \{y \simeq z\}\}$. It is easy to see that $\varphi_c \sqsubseteq \varphi_a$ and that $\varphi_2 \models \varphi_1$. This suggests, that analyses in our domain can benefit from applying *semantic reduction*, as we discuss below.

3.1 Semantic Reduction

A *semantic reduction operator* SR over an abstraction domain $(A, \sqsubseteq)$ with respect to a given concretization function $\gamma : A \to \Sigma$ is an idempotent total function $SR : A \to A$ which allows to find a possibly more precise representation of the set of concrete states S represented by an abstract state $a \in A$. Technically, SR should have the following properties: $SR(a) \sqsubseteq a$, $SR(SR(a)) = SR(a)$, and, most importantly, $\gamma(SR(a)) = \gamma(a)$ [6]. Semantic reduction operators can help improve the precision of an abstract interpretation algorithm because both the abstract transformers and the join operator are monotonic. Thus, applying a semantic reduction operator before, e.g., applying the join operator, may result in an abstract state which represents less concrete states than the abstract state resulting form a naive join, i.e.,

$$\forall a_1, a_2 \in A . \gamma(SR(a_1) \sqcup SR(a_2)) \subseteq \gamma(a_1 \sqcup a_2).$$

It is sound to use SR in this way because for any $a \in A$, it holds that $\gamma(SR(a)) = \gamma(a)$.

We leverage the fact that our domain tracks equality between terms to define a semantic reduction operator $SR^{k,d}$ which finds semantic consequences stemming from the reflexivity, symmetry and transitivity properties of the equality predicate and the insensitivity of functions to substitutions of equal arguments (i.e., if x and y are equal then $f(x) = f(y)$ for any function f), that can be expressed in the abstract domain $\Phi_{\mathcal{F}}^{k,d}$.

We improve the precision of the analysis by employing two semantic reduction steps before applying the join operator.

$$\varphi_1 \hat{\sqcup}^{k,d} \varphi_2 = SR^{k,d}(\varphi_1) \sqcup^k SR^{k,d}(\varphi_2).$$

Before formally defining $SR^{k,d}(\cdot)$, we show it can indeed improve the analysis precision.

Example 3. Let $\varphi_1 = \{\{x \simeq z\}\}$ and $\varphi_2 = \{\{x \simeq y\}, \{y \simeq z\}\}$. Note that $\varphi_1, \varphi_2 \in \Phi_{\{x,y,z\}}^{1,0}$, and that $\varphi_1 \sqcup^1 \varphi_2 = \emptyset = \top$. However, by leveraging the transitivity of $\simeq$, we have $\gamma(\varphi_2) = \gamma(\varphi_3)$, for $\varphi_3 = \varphi_2 \cup \{\{x \simeq z\}\}$. Note that $\varphi_1 \sqcup^1 \varphi_3 = \{\{x \simeq z\}\} \sqsubset \top$.

Example 4. Consider the formulae $\varphi_1 = \{\{r \simeq s\}, \{x \simeq c\}, \{x \simeq [s]\}\}$, which contains clauses which appear in the formula propagated to program point 7 of our running example from the true branch, and $\varphi_2 = \{\{r \simeq 0, c \simeq [r]\}\}$, which is a loop invariant, and propagated to program point 7 from the false-branch. If max-clause is two and max-rank is one, we get $\varphi_1 \sqcup^1 \varphi_2 = \emptyset = \top$, whereas $SR^{2,1}(\varphi_1) \sqsubseteq \{\{c \simeq [r]\}\}$, $\varphi_1 \hat{\sqcup}^{2,1} \varphi_2 = \varphi_2$, which helps establish that φ_2 is indeed a loop invariant.

Saturation-Based Semantic Reduction. Algorithm 1 shows a saturation-based implementation of our semantic reduction operator. The procedure invokes a function $\mathsf{PMStep}(C_1, C_2)$ which, given two clauses $C_1, C_2 \in \mathcal{C}_{\mathcal{F}}^{k,d}$, returns a set of clauses $S \subseteq \mathcal{C}_{\mathcal{F}}^{2k-1,2d}$ which are semantic consequences of the two, i.e., $\{C_1, C_2\} \models S$. Technically, $\mathsf{PMStep}(C_1, C_2)$ is implemented using paramodulation, which, intuitively, computes logical consequences that can be inferred from the aforementioned properties of the equality predicate $\simeq$ by *directly* applying the paramodulation rules to C_1 and C_2. We provide a short technical overview of paramodulation in Sect. 5, and here consider it as a black box.

Algorithm 1. Semantic reduction procedure based on saturation.

---

1 Procedure: $SR^{k,d}$

2 Input: $\varphi \in \Phi_{\mathcal{F}}^{k,d}$

3 Output: $\varphi' \in \Phi_{\mathcal{F}}^{k,d}$ such that $\varphi \subseteq \varphi'$ and $\gamma(\varphi) = \gamma(\varphi')$

4 $\varphi' \leftarrow \varphi$

5 **while** $\exists C_1, C_2 \in \varphi'.\ \mathsf{PMStep}(C_1, C_2) \cap \mathcal{C}_{\mathcal{F}}^{k,d} \not\subseteq \varphi'$ **do**

6 $\quad$ take $C_1, C_2 \in \varphi'$ s.t. $\mathsf{PMStep}(C_1, C_2) \cap \mathcal{C}_{\mathcal{F}}^{k,d} \not\subseteq \varphi'$

7 $\quad$ $\varphi' \leftarrow \varphi' \cup \left(\mathsf{PMStep}(C_1, C_2) \cap \mathcal{C}_{\mathcal{F}}^{k,d} \right)$

Algorithm 1 operates by saturating the initial set of clauses φ with respect to the consequence finding procedure PMStep. This is obtained by iteratively applying PMStep to clauses in φ', and to the resulting clauses, and so forth, until reaching a fixpoint, where we say the set of clauses φ' is saturated. Note that for any $C \in \varphi'$, we also apply $PMStep(C, C)$. In practice, the saturation procedure is implemented by keeping a worklist of new clauses to which PMStep should be applied. Algorithm 1 is guaranteed to terminate because $\mathcal{C}_{\mathcal{F}}^{k,d}$ is finite for any fixed $\mathcal{F}$, k, and d.

4   Abstract Transformers

Figure 5, defines the abstract semantics $[\![c]\!]^{\sharp} : \Phi_{\mathcal{F}}^{k,d} \rightarrow \Phi_{\mathcal{F}}^{k,d}$ over our equality-based abstract domain for arbitrary $\mathcal{F}$, k, and d. The transformers use the auxiliary function $remSym(\varphi, s) = \varphi \cap \Phi_{\mathcal{F}\backslash\{s\}}^{k,d}$. The function takes as input a formula φ and a symbol s, which may be either a variable name or a function symbol, and returns a formula $\varphi' \subseteq \varphi$ which is comprised of all the clauses in φ that do not include symbol s. Intuitively, $remSym(\varphi, s)$ acts as a *havoc(·)* operator [2] which forgets any information regarding s. For example, for $\varphi = \{\{r \simeq v\}, \{[u] \simeq [w]\}, \{[r] \not\simeq v, u \simeq w\}\}$,

$$remSym(\varphi, r) = \{\{[u] \simeq [w]\}\} \quad \text{and} \quad remSym(\varphi, []) = \{\{r \simeq v\}\}.$$

Our programming language has, essentially, two types of primitive statements: assignments and assume commands. Thus, the transformers follow two different patterns:

$$SR^{2,1}(\varphi) = \varphi \cup \{\{c \not\simeq t_1\}, \{[s] \not\simeq t_1\}, \{[s] \simeq c\}\}$$
$$[\![v := c]\!]^{\sharp}(\varphi) \stackrel{\text{def}}{=} remSym(SR^{k,d}(\varphi), v) \cup \{\{v \simeq c\}\}$$
$$[\![v := v']\!]^{\sharp}(\varphi) \stackrel{\text{def}}{=} remSym(SR^{k,d}(\varphi), v) \cup \{\{v \simeq v'\}\}$$
$$[\![v := f(v_1, \ldots, v_k)]\!]^{\sharp}(\varphi) \stackrel{\text{def}}{=} remSym(SR^{k,d}(\varphi), v) \cup \{\{v \simeq f(v_1, \ldots, v_k)\}\}$$
$$[\![v := [v']]\!]^{\sharp}(\varphi) \stackrel{\text{def}}{=} remSym(SR^{k,d}(\varphi), v) \cup \{\{v \simeq [v']\}\}$$
$$[\![[v] := v']\!]^{\sharp}(\varphi) \stackrel{\text{def}}{=} remSym(SR^{k,d}(\varphi), []) \cup \{\{[v] \simeq v'\}\}$$
$$[\![v := \mathtt{malloc}(v')]\!]^{\sharp}(\varphi) \stackrel{\text{def}}{=} remSym(SR^{k,d}(\varphi), v)$$
$$[\![\mathtt{assume}(v = v')]\!]^{\sharp}(\varphi) \stackrel{\text{def}}{=} \varphi \cup \{\{v \simeq v'\}\}$$
$$[\![\mathtt{assume}(v \neq v')]\!]^{\sharp}(\varphi) \stackrel{\text{def}}{=} \varphi \cup \{\{v \not\simeq v'\}\}$$

Fig. 5. Abstract transformers.

The transformers for assignments of the form $v := e$ (where v is a variable and e is an expression) take an abstract state φ and first performs a semantic reduction, then remove from the resulting formula any clause which contains v, and, finally, add a clause which records the equality of v and e. This mimics the overwriting (destructive) nature of assignments. For example, the set of concrete states that arises at program point 6 in our running example, can be represented by the abstract state

$$\varphi = \{\{r \simeq 0, [r] \simeq c\}, \{x \simeq [s]\}, \{x \not\simeq t_1\}, \{x \simeq c\}\}$$

Applying the transformer for the instruction $r:=s$ to φ, we first apply a semantic reduction on φ, yielding:

$$SR^{2,1}(\varphi) = \varphi \cup \{\{c \not\simeq t_1\}, \{[s] \not\simeq t_1\}, \{[s] \simeq c\}\}$$

Next, we apply remSym to forget all facts that mention the old value of r:

$$\mathrm{remSym}(SR^{2,1}(\varphi), r) = SR^{2,1}(\varphi) \setminus \{\{r \simeq 0, [r] \simeq c\}\}$$

And finally, we add an equality indicating the new value of r equals the value of s. Thus,

$$[\![r:=s]\!]^\sharp(\varphi) = \{\{x \simeq [s]\}, \{x \not\simeq t_1\}, \{x \simeq c\}, \{c \not\simeq t_1\}, \{[s] \not\simeq t_1\}, \{[s] \simeq c\}, \{r \simeq s\}\}.$$

The transformers for $\mathtt{assume}(\ )$ commands, leverage our restriction that the only allowed conditions are equalities and inequalities, which can be readily translated into the domain. In fact, our restrictions ensure that $[\![\mathtt{assume}(\ )]\!]^\sharp$ is the *best abstract transformer* [6]. For example, consider the abstract state $\varphi = \{\{r \simeq 0, [r] \simeq c\}, \{x \simeq [s]\}, \{t_1 \simeq 0\}\}$ which represents all the states that can arise at program point 3 of our running example. Applying the transformer of $\mathtt{assume}(x = t_1)$, we get:

$$[\![\mathtt{assume}(x{=}t_1)]\!]^\sharp(\varphi) = \{\{r \simeq 0, [r] \simeq c\}, \{x \simeq [s]\}, \{t_1 \simeq 0\}, \{x \simeq t_1\}\},$$

which indicates that when the program terminates at program point 4, the value of variable x is (unsurprisingly) zero.

We note that in our analysis, we only apply $\mathrm{remSym}(\varphi, s)$ where s is either a variable or to the function $[\cdot]$. Also note that the interpretation of destructive updates (assignment to heap locations) in our analysis is, by design, extremely conservative: It leads to a loss of all the information we had regarding the contents of the heap in the abstract state prior to the assignment due to possible aliasing.

5 Consequence Finding by Paramodulation

In Sect. 3, we presented a semantic reduction operator which utilizes a function $\mathrm{PMStep}(C_1, C_2)$ that finds all the *direct* consequences that can be inferred from two clauses C_1, C_2 based on properties of the equality relation. In this section, we explain how to implement PMStep using *paramodulation* [15]. In Sect. 7, we describe an over-approximation of PMStep so it becomes more efficient, but less precise. In our experiment, we use the more efficient operator.

5.1 A Bird's-Eye View of Paramodulation

Paramodulation is a reasoning technique which is used for automated theorem proving. It is a semi algorithm for determining the unsatisfiability of a formula φ in first order logic with equality. It is refutation-complete: given an unsatisfiable formula, it is guaranteed to terminate. Technically, it is a specialization of *reso-lution*-based reasoning [16] to first-order logic with equality. In the following, we provide an informal overview of paramodulation. For a formal description, see, e.g., [15].

Roughly speaking, paramodulation is based on the use of special inference rules which leverage the reflexivity, symmetry, and transitivity of the equality relation, as well as *function congruence* [14] (See footnote 1), i.e., the insensitiv-ity of functions valuation with respect to substitution of equal arguments. More technically, paramodulation works by inferring logical consequences in an itera-tive manner: It keeps generating consequences, i.e. new clauses which are logically derived from the clauses of the input formula or from previously derived ones by applying the *paramodulation rules*. The rules are sound: any logical consequence $\{C_1, C_2\} \vdash C$ is also a semantic consequence $\{C_1, C_2\} \models C$. When used for sat-isfiability checking, paramodulation is often coupled with a search strategy, e.g., ordered paramodulation [15], which limits the applications of the rules while main-taining refutation completeness. In our setting, we do not aim to refute the satis-fiability of a formula, but rather use the rules of paramodulation to infer logical consequences. Thus, we avoid discussing the search strategies often used together with paramodulation, and focus on describing the underlying rules.

$$\frac{C_1 \cup \{l \simeq r\} \quad C_2 \cup \{s \simeq t\}}{C_1 \cup C_2 \cup \{s[r]_p \simeq t\}} \; s|_p = l \quad \begin{matrix} \text{\small SUPERPOSITION} \\ \text{\small RIGHT} \end{matrix} \qquad \frac{C \cup \{s \not\simeq s\}}{C} \quad \begin{matrix} \text{\small EQUALITY} \\ \text{\small RESOLUTION} \end{matrix}$$

$$\frac{C_1 \cup \{l \simeq r\} \quad C_2 \cup \{s \not\simeq t\}}{C_1 \cup C_2 \cup \{s[r]_p \not\simeq t\}} \; s|_p = l \quad \begin{matrix} \text{\small SUPERPOSITION} \\ \text{\small LEFT} \end{matrix} \qquad \frac{C \cup \{s \simeq t\} \cup \{s \simeq t'\}}{C \cup \{t \not\simeq t'\} \cup \{s \simeq t'\}} \quad \begin{matrix} \text{\small EQUALITY} \\ \text{\small FACTORING} \end{matrix}$$

Fig. 6. Ground rules of paramodulation.

Paramodulation uses four inference rules, dubbed the *paramodulation rules* [15]. These rules, simplified to the case where only ground clauses are considered, are shown in Fig. 6. The *superposition right* rule is applied to a pair of clauses. One clause contains the literal $l \simeq r$, for some arbitrary terms l and r, and the other clause contains the literal $s \simeq t$, for some arbitrary terms s and t, such that l is a *sub-term* of s. Technically, l is a sub-term of s if either l is (syn-tacticly) equal to s, or s is of the form $f(s_1, \ldots, s_k)$, for some function symbol f, and l is a sub-term of s_i, for some $i = 1..k$. Figure 6 records this requirement as a side condition to the rule using the notation $s|_p = l$. The latter holds if l is a sub-term of s in a specific *position* p. Note that l can occur as a sub-term of l multiple times. For example, the term a appears twice in the term $f(g(a), a)$. Following [15], we use the notation $s|_p$ to identify a particular sub-term of s and the notation $s[r]_p$ to denote the term obtained by substituting the sub-term of s at position p with r. For example, if p_1 and p_2 identify, respectively, the first and second occurrences of a in $f(g(a), a)$ then $f(g(a), a)[b]_{p_1} = f(g(b), a)$ and $f(g(a), a)[b]_{p_2} = f(g(a), b)$. For brevity, we avoid formalizing the rather standard notions of sub-terms, positions, and substitutions, (see, e.g., [15]), and rely on the reader intuitive understanding, instead.

Algorithm 2. PMStep: A procedure for computing direct logical consequences.

---

1 Procedure: PMStep
2 Input: $C_1, C_2 \in \mathcal{C}_{\mathcal{F}}^{k,d}$
3 Output: $\varphi \in \Phi_{\mathcal{F}}^{2k-1,2d}$ such that $\{C_1, C_2\} \models \varphi$
4 **if** $C_1 \neq C_2$ **then**
5 $\quad\big|\quad \varphi \leftarrow \texttt{SuperpositionRight}(C_1, C_2) \cup \texttt{SuperpositionRight}(C_2, C_1) \cup$
6 $\quad\big|\qquad \texttt{SuperpositionLeft}(C_1, C_2) \cup \texttt{SuperpositionLeft}(C_2, C_1)$
7 **else**
8 $\quad\big|\quad \varphi \leftarrow \texttt{EqualityResolution}(C_1) \cup \texttt{EqualityFactoring}(C_1)$

Example 5. We demonstrate the use of the superposition rules using clauses $C_1 = \{u + v \not\simeq 0, v \simeq u\}$ and $C_2 = \{[v] \simeq 0, v \not\simeq u\}$. The only relevant choice for term l in either of the rules is to be v. Using superposition-right and setting s to be $[v]$, we can infer the clause $\{u + v \not\simeq 0, v \not\simeq u, [u] \simeq 0\}$. Using superposition-left and setting s to be v, we infer the clause $\{u + v \not\simeq 0, [v] \simeq 0, u \not\simeq u\}$.

The *equality resolution* rule applies to a single clause containing a literal of the form $s \not\simeq s$. Such a literal is always false due to reflexivity of $\simeq$. The rule thus allows to remove the literal from the clause that contains it.

Example 6. Applying the equality-resolution rule to the clause $\{u + v \not\simeq 0, [v] \simeq 0, u \not\simeq u\}$ allows to infer the clause $\{u + v \not\simeq 0, [v] \simeq 0\}$.

The *equality factoring* rule can be applied to a clause containing two literals of the form $s \simeq t$ and $s \simeq t'$. The rule allows replacing one of the equalities by an inequality between t and t'.

Example 7. Let $C = \{[u] \simeq [v], [u] \simeq 0\}$. There are two possible inferences by the equality factoring rule: by taking s to be $[u]$ and t' to be 0 we get $\{[v] \not\simeq 0, [u] \simeq 0\}$, and by taking s to be $[u]$ and t' to be $[v]$ we get $\{0 \not\simeq [v], [u] \simeq [v]\}$.

Note that superposition rules operate on two clauses, while the equality rules operate on a single clause. Also note that it may be possible to apply the superposition rules to a single clause and itself (i.e., $C_1 = C_2$). However, this will yield a clause which is subsumed by the input clause, and we thus avoid it.

5.2 Direct Consequence Finding

Algorithm 2 presents an implementation of the PMStep procedure which was used as a key ingredient of our semantic reduction algorithm (see Sect. 3). By abuse of notation, we refer to each of the paramodulation rules shown Fig. 6 as a function which returns the set of clauses that rule can infer.

PMStep uses the superposition rules when invoked with two different clauses, and the equality resolution and equality factoring rules when it is given two identical clauses as input. For example, let $C = \{s \not\approx s, t \not\approx t\}$, then $\mathsf{PMStep}(C, C) = \texttt{EqualityResolution}(C) = \{\{s \not\approx s\}, \{t \not\approx t\}\}$. Note that $\mathsf{PMStep}(C, C)$ does not return the empty clause, although it is a consequence of C, because it is not a direct consequence: Obtaining it, requires applying the equality resolution rule twice. Since the paramodulation rules are sound, it follows that the returned set of clauses (formula) φ satisfies the requirement that $\{C_1, C_2\} \models \varphi$.

When applying a paramodulation rule to clauses in $\Phi_{\mathcal{F}}^{k,d}$, the maximal clause size of any inferred clause is $2k - 1$ (the so-called *resolved literals* do not appear in the result clause). Under the same conditions, the maximal rank of any inferred clause is $2d$, as the only way the rules create new terms is via substitution. Thus, the formula φ returned by PMStep is in $\Phi_{\mathcal{F}}^{2k-1,2d}$. Termination of the PMStep procedure is self-evident.

We note that although the paramodulation rules are refutation complete, they are incomplete when used, as in our case, for consequence finding. That is to say that they may not be able to produce all semantic consequences, not even up to subsumption. For example, applying the paramodulation rules to the formula $\varphi = \{\{f(a) \not\approx f(b)\}\}$ yields no consequences, as none of the rules can be applied. However, the clause $\{a \not\approx b\}$ is a semantic consequence of φ. An unfortunate by product of this incompleteness is that the abstract transformers, defined in Sect. 4, are incomplete, even if we place no bound on the maximal size or rank of clauses. For example, let $\varphi = \{\{f(a, v) \not\approx f(b, v)\}\}$. Applying our transformers, we get that $[\![v := c]\!]^{\sharp}(\varphi) = \{\{v \simeq c\}\}$, while the best abstract transformer must also infer the clause $\{a \not\approx b\}$. In spite of this incompleteness, our initial experiments (see Sect. 7) show that the paramodulation rules can be used to prove interesting properties of programs.

6   Connection Analysis

In the previous section, we developed an analysis which tracks equalities and inequalities between variables and memory locations, and supports limited disjunction via CNF. The atomic literals represented equalities and inequalities, and the analysis benefited from the fact that equality is an equivalence relation (i.e. it is reflexive, transitive, and symmetric) to employ paramodulation. In this section, we present an additional application of the techniques presented so far, that uses a different domain, where the atomic literals represent an equivalence relation other than equality, namely *heap connectivity*. The key idea is to reinterpret $s \simeq t$ to denote the fact that s is *heap-connected* to t. Because this relation is an equivalence relation, and because our domain here will not include any function symbols, the paramodulation rules can be used to obtain sound abstract transformers. As we shall see, the obtained transformers are the best abstract transformers [6] for this domain.

Static analysis of heap connectivity is known as *connection analysis* [9]. Connection analysis arose from the need to automatically parallelize sequential programs. It is a kind of pointer analysis that aims to prove that two pointer variables can never point to the same (undirected) *heap component*: We say that two heap objects are *heap-connected* in a state σ when it is possible to reach from one object to the other, following paths in the heap of σ, ignoring pointer direction. Two variables are *heap-connected* when they point to connected heap objects. Connection analysis soundly determines whether variables are *not* heap-connected. Despite its conceptual simplicity, connection analysis is flow-sensitive, and the effect of program statements is non-distributive.

```
(node*, node*) build_lists() {
    node *x = (node*) malloc(sizeof(node)), *y = (node*) malloc(sizeof(node));
    while (*) {
        node *z = (node*) malloc(sizeof(node)); z->next = null;
        if (*) { z->next = x; x = z
        } else { z->next = y; y = z;  } }
    return (x, y); }
```

Fig. 7. Program `build_lists()`. `node` is a record with a single field of type `node*` named `next`.

Example 8. Program `build_lists`, shown in Fig. 7, constructs two disjoint singly-linked lists. For clarity, the program is written in a C-like language. The program first allocates the tails of the lists, and then, iteratively, prepends a newly allocated object to one of the lists. The program returns pointers to the heads of the two lists it created. Our analysis proves that the two lists are disjoint, by proving the loop invariant $x \not\equiv y$. We note that existing connection analyses [3,9] cannot prove this property.

Concrete Semantics. In the context of this section, a concrete state $\sigma = \langle \rho, h \rangle \in \Sigma$ is comprised of an environment ρ and a heap h. The heap $h = \langle V, F \rangle$ is a finite labeled graph, where V is a finite set of objects and $E \subseteq V \times \mathsf{Fields} \times V$ is set of labeled edges that represent pointer fields of objects. The environment $\rho :$ Var $\rightharpoonup V$ maps some of the variables to objects in the heap. Variables not mapped by ρ, or fields of an object for which no outgoing edge exists, are said to be equal to *null*. The heap-connected relation in state $\sigma = \langle \rho, h \rangle$ is determined by ρ and by the weakly connected components of h. The programming language allows read and write operations to both variables and object fields, and operations to allocate new objects. Its operational semantics, described by a transition relation $\mathrm{TR}_c \subseteq \Sigma \times \Sigma$ for every command c, is standard, and omitted.

Abstract Semantics. The abstract domain of existing connection analyses [3,9] is based on a partitioning of the program variables into disjoint sets. Two variables are in the same set, often referred to as a *connection set*, when the two *may* be heap-connected. Note that at the loop header, it is possible that x and z are heap-connected and that y and z are heap-connected. However, it is never the case that all three variables are heap-connected. Existing connection analyses maintain a single partitioning of the variables, and hence have to conservatively determine that x and y might be heap-connected.

In a way, the abstract domains of [3,9] maintain a conjunction of clauses of the form $x \not\equiv y$, which record that x and y are definitely not heap-connected

(In [9], clauses of the form $x \not\simeq null$ which records that variable x is definitely not equal to *null* are also tracked). In contrast, our analysis allows to track more complicated correlations between variables using clauses that contain more than one literal. More specifically, our analysis also uses clauses that record whether the value of a variable is definitely null or whether two variables are *connected*, where a variable x is *connected* to variable y in σ if they are heap-connected in σ or if the value of x and y is *null* in σ. We record the connected-relation utilizing a non standard interpretation of the equality predicate $\cdot \simeq \cdot$:

$$\sigma \models s \simeq t \iff s \text{ is connected to } t \text{ in } \sigma \qquad \sigma \models s \simeq null \iff \text{the value of } s \text{ in } \sigma \text{ is } null$$
$$\sigma \models s \not\simeq t \iff \sigma \not\models s \simeq t \qquad\qquad\qquad \sigma \models s \not\simeq null \iff \sigma \not\models s \simeq null$$

Note that $\cdot \simeq \cdot$ is an equivalence relation: It is reflexive, symmetric, and transitive.

$$\tau^{TR}_{v:=0} \stackrel{def}{=} \mathsf{frame}(v) \cup \{\{v' \simeq 0'\}\}$$
$$\tau^{TR}_{v:=u} \stackrel{def}{=} \mathsf{frame}(v) \cup \{\{v' \simeq u'\}\}$$
$$\tau^{TR}_{v:=\mathtt{malloc}} \stackrel{def}{=} \mathsf{frame}(v) \cup \{\{v' \not\simeq 0'\}\} \cup \{\{v' \not\simeq u'\} \mid u \in \mathsf{Var} \setminus \{v\}\}$$
$$\tau^{TR}_{v:=u\text{->}f} \stackrel{def}{=} \mathsf{frame}(v) \cup \{\{v' \simeq u', v' \simeq 0'\}, \{u \not\simeq 0\}\}$$
$$\tau^{TR}_{v\text{->}f:=0} \stackrel{def}{=} \{\{v \not\simeq 0\}\} \cup \{\{x \not\simeq y \implies x' \not\simeq y'\} \mid x,y \in \mathsf{Var} \cup \{0\}\} \cup$$
$$\qquad\qquad \{\{x \simeq y \land x \not\simeq v \implies x' \simeq y'\} \mid x,y \in \mathsf{Var} \cup \{0\}\} \cup$$
$$\qquad\qquad \{\{x \simeq y \land x \simeq v \implies (x' \simeq v' \lor y' \simeq v' \lor x' \simeq y')\} \mid x,y \in \mathsf{Var}\}$$
$$\tau^{TR}_{v\text{->}f:=u} \stackrel{def}{=} \{\{v \not\simeq 0\}, \{u \not\simeq 0\}, \{u' \simeq v'\}\} \cup \{\{x \simeq y \implies x' \simeq y'\} \mid x,y \in \mathsf{Var} \cup \{0\}\} \cup$$
$$\qquad\qquad \{\{x \not\simeq y \land x \not\simeq v \land x \not\simeq u \implies x' \not\simeq y'\} \mid x,y \in \mathsf{Var} \cup \{0\}\}$$

$$\mathsf{frame}(v) \stackrel{def}{=} \{\{x \simeq y \implies x' \simeq y'\}, \{x \not\simeq y \implies x' \not\simeq y'\} \mid x,y \in \mathsf{Var} \setminus \{v\} \cup \{0\}\}$$

Fig. 8. The abstract transition relation of commands in the connection analysis.

Abstract Domain. As connection analysis concerns only connection between variables, we restrict the vocabulary $\mathcal{F}$ to include only the constants representing the local variables, and thus have no function symbols. This means that by construction, all terms would be constants, having max-rank of zero. In this setting, the number of terms is finite, and hence the clause size is also bounded; there can be at most $O(|\mathsf{Var}|^2)$ literals (Var is the set of variables in the program.) Our analysis uses a domain $\Phi^{k,0}_{\mathsf{Var}}$ with k large enough to ensure that neither the semantic reduction operator nor the join operator filters out clauses due to their size. In this setting the join operator is additive. For these reasons, we do not use semantic reduction in the join.

Best Abstract Transformers. We define the abstract transformers in a uniform way using *two-vocabulary* formulae which describe the abstract transition relation of every command: Given a command c, we define a formula τ^{TR}_c over the vocabulary $\mathcal{F}_2 = \mathcal{F} \cup \mathcal{F}'$ comprised of constants $v \in \mathcal{F}$ pertaining to program variables at the pre-state and primed constants $v' \in \mathcal{F}' = \{v' \mid v \in \mathcal{F}\}$ pertaining to program variables at the post-state (For technical reasons, we also include a primed version of *null*). We note that the finiteness of our abstract domain allows us to encode any transformer in this way. The abstract transformer for c is defined as follows:

$$[\![c]\!]^{\sharp}(\varphi) \overset{\text{def}}{=} \text{remSym}(SR(\varphi \cup \tau_c^{\text{TR}}), \mathcal{F})[v/v' \mid v \in \mathcal{F}].$$

$[\![c]\!]^{\sharp}$ conservatively determines the effect of c on the set of states that φ represents in four stages: Firstly, it conjoins φ with τ_c^{TR}, thus effectively restricting the abstract transition relation to consider only pre-states represented by φ. Secondly, it applies our semantic reduction operator to find possible semantic consequence. This helps to propagate information encoded in φ regarding the pre-state into conjuncts containing only constants coming from $\mathcal{F}'$ describing the post-state. Thirdly, the transformer removes any conjuncts which mention variables coming from the pre-state.[5] Finally, the transformer replaces every primed constant with the corresponding unprimed constant, thus obtaining again a formula representing the set of post-states which is expressible in our domain. Note that, in particular, if $\emptyset \in SR(\varphi)$ then $\emptyset \in abs[\![c]\!](\varphi)$.

Figure 8 shows the formulae encoding the abstract transition relation of primitive commands. Assigning *null* to a variable v records the fact that the connection relation between all other variables in the post state needs to be as in the pre-state (this is captures by the auxiliary formula frame(v)) and that v is connected to *null*. Copying the value of a variable u into v has a similar effect, except that v is connected in the post state to u. Assigning v the address of a freshly allocated memory means that v cannot be connected to any other variable, and cannot be connected to *null* as well. Successfully loading a value from the heap y := x → f implies that x is not null (recall that our semantics blocks before dereferencing a null-valued pointer) and that either y becomes connected to x or it is nullified, in case this is the value of the f-field of u. Without loss of generality, we assume that every destructive update command x → f := y in the program is replaced by a command x → f := null; if (y ≠ null) x → f := y which nullifies the f-field of x and updates it later only to a non-*null* value. Thus, applying the last transformer in Fig. 8 is guaranteed to merge together the two heap components of x and y. The most complicated transition relation pertains to the command x → f := null which conservatively records that only the heap-component x can be affected. More specifically, the component can be split into two subcomponents, which, in turn, may split the set of variables connected to x into two arbitrary partitions.

Soundness. It is easy to see that the abstract transition relation indeed overapproximates the concrete one. Interestingly, it is still sound to use the paramodulation rules as means to perform semantic reduction because any logical consequence they derive is also a semantic consequence under the non-standard interpretation of $\simeq$.

Precision. We say that a pair of states σ_1, σ_2 satisfies a two-vocabulary formulae $\tau \in \Phi_{\mathcal{F}_2}$, denoted by $\langle \sigma_1, \sigma_2 \rangle \models \tau$, if $\sigma_1 \models \tau \cap \Phi_{\mathcal{F}}$ and $\sigma_2 \models \tau \cap \Phi_{\mathcal{F}'}$, i.e.,

---

[5] remSym($SR(\cdot, \mathcal{F})$ is the obvious extension of the symbol elimination function remSym($\cdot, v$), described in Sect. 4, from a single symbol v to the removal of all symbols coming from $\mathcal{F}$.

σ_1 and σ_2 satisfy all the clauses of the formulae containing terms built using symbols coming $\mathcal{F}$ and $\mathcal{F}'$, respectively. The following theorem ensures that the abstract transition relation described by the formulae in Fig. 8 is the most precise conservative transition relation.

Theorem 1. *Let c be a command. The following holds:*
(soundness) $\forall \sigma, \sigma' \in \Sigma. \langle \sigma, \sigma' \rangle \in \mathrm{TR}_c \implies \langle \sigma, \sigma' \rangle \models \tau_c^{\mathrm{TR}}$, *and*
(precision) $\forall \varphi, \varphi' \in \Phi_{\mathcal{F}}. (\forall \sigma, \sigma' \in \Sigma. \sigma \models \varphi \wedge \langle \sigma, \sigma' \rangle \in \mathrm{TR}_c \implies \sigma' \models \varphi') \implies$
$$(\forall \sigma, \sigma' \in \Sigma. \langle \sigma, \sigma' \rangle \models \varphi \wedge \tau_c^{\mathrm{TR}} \implies \sigma' \models \varphi').$$

The key reason for the transformers we obtain to be the best abstract transformers, is that restricting our domain to contain only terms corresponding to program variables (i.e., constant symbols) ensures that $\mathrm{remSym}(SR(\varphi), v)$ yields a *strongest* formula that is implied from φ and does not contain the symbol v.

Theorem 2. *Let $\varphi \in \Phi_{\mathcal{F}}$ be a ground CNF formula, where $\mathcal{F}$ contains only constant symbols. Let $C \in \Phi_{\mathcal{F}}$ be a clause such that $\varphi \models C$, and that v does not appear in C. It holds that $\mathrm{remSym}(SR(\varphi), v) \models C$.*

We can now prove that our abstract transformers are the *best* (most precise conservative) abstract transformers [6] in our domain. The proof goes in two stages. Firstly, we show in Theorem 1 that the abstract transition relation described by the formulae given in Fig. 8 is the most precise conservative transition relation. Secondly, we use Theorem 2 to conclude that there cannot be a more precise formula in our abstract domain that can represent the possible post-states describe by $\varphi \cup \tau_c^{\mathrm{TR}}$.

Theorem 3. *The abstract transformers shown in Fig. 8 are the best transformers.*

7   Implementation and Experimental Results

We implemented our analyses and applied them to analyze a few low-level pointer-manipulating programs. We noticed that most of the running time was spent in applying the paramodulation rules. Often, this happens right before a function symbol is eliminated. To improve the performance of our tool, we modified the implementation of the semantic reduction step in our transformers to use *ordered paramodulation* [15]. In a nutshell, ordered paramodulation is given an order over the function symbols $\mathcal{F}$, which it then extends to an order over terms, literals, and clauses in a standard way. Ordered paramodulation ensures that the rules are applied to literals according to their order. Nevertheless, ordered paramodulation is refutation complete. We leveraged the ordered execution of rules by setting the function symbol which is to about be eliminated to be the highest symbol in the order. Additionally, we forbid the use of a paramodulation rule in the case where none of the input clauses contain the symbol which is to be eliminated. These modifications greatly improve the performance of our tool. Theoretically, this modification reduces the precision of our transformers. However, in our experiments

they did not. Another simple optimization we made, is to apply the equality resolution rule to every consequence clause that we generate by the paramodulation
rules, as well as discarding any generated clause containing a trivially satisfiable
literal of the form $s \simeq s$. This can help reduce the size of the clause and prevents
the semantic reduction operator from filtering it out.

| Benchmark | C code | | LLVM code | | k | d | Running time | | Inv. Size | |
	# of lines	# of vars	# of lines	# of vars			Unord	Ord	CL	LI
find_last	10	6	37	14	2	1	30.49s	13.81s	6	9
find_last					2	2	85.92s	30.04s	7	10
find_last					2	3	191.43s	58.02s	7	10
resource_manager	34	14	74	17	2	∞	208.84s	40.32s	126	247
cve_2014_7841	40	11	68	21	2	∞	3.54s	0.94s	N/A	
build_lists	15	4	43	14	∞	0	—	11.12s	182	562

Fig. 9. Benchmarks characteristics and Experimental results. k is max-clause an d is
max-rank. Unord and Ord stand for unordered and ordered paramodulation, respectively. A timeout of one hour was set for each test. CL and LI stand for the number of
clauses and literals, respectively, in the loop invariant.

Experimental Evaluation. Our analysis handles low level pointer programs,
Thus, we implemented it to analyze Intel x86 binary code, and experimented
with code generated by compiling C programs. Our tool, written in Python 2.7,
compiles C programs using GCC Version 4.8.4 with all optimizations disabled,
and then disassembles the generated code using python package *distorm3* version 3.3.4. The tests were done using a single thread on a Windows 7 machine
equipped with Intel Core i5-5300U and 8 GB of RAM.

Figure 9 summarizes the characteristics of the analyzed procedures and the
running time of the analysis, with different max-clause (k) and max-rank (d)
parameters.

- find_last is our running example. We were able to prove that it either returns
  NULL or a pointer to a memory location containing the same value as c.
- resource_manager is a simulation of a controller for a microphone and a
  camera. It runs a state-machine which executes an infinite loop, where it
  receives commands from the user, such as start/end video call and start/end
  audio call. Our analysis proves that it always holds that if the camera is turned
  on, then so is the microphone.
- CVE_2014_7841 is a simplification of a published null pointer dereference vulnerability in the SCTP protocol implementation of the linux kernel [20]. Our
  analysis proves the suggested fix prevents the relevant null dereference errors.
- build_lists is the example shown Fig. 7. Our connection analysis proved that
  the generated lists are disjoint. We note that existing analyses cannot prove
  this property because they maintain a single partitioning of the variables in
  every program point. In contrast, our analysis was able to prove for the end
  state the formula $x \not\simeq y$.

8 Related Work, Discussion, Conclusions, and Future Work

Abstract Interpretation [5] algorithms cope with a persistent tension between the precision of an analysis, specifically its ability to maintain relational and disjunctive information, and the cost of the analysis. The *reduced product* [6] and *reduced cardinal power* [6] operations are two examples of operations that increase the precision of an abstract domain, while making the analysis more expensive. The *reduced relative power* operation [10] is another such operation, which allows to keep implication correlations between two abstract domains. Applying this operation to an abstract domain and itself is known as *autodependency*. Such implication correlations can be viewed as CNF formulae where each clause contains exactly two literals. In the context of abstract interpretation of logic programs CNF have been considered from the lattice and logical perspective [4,11,13,17]. In this context, the key contribution of our work is the use of paramodulation to implement both the abstract join and the abstract transformers.

Resolution, superposition, and *paramodulation* have been the subject of vast study in the theorem proving community (see, e.g., [15] for an introduction with extensive bibliography). While their most common use has been satisfiability checking, it has also been explored as a technique for *consequence finding* [12]. A technique called *kernel resolution* [7,18] has been explored to obtain completeness for consequence finding. In this context, our work presents a new application for consequence finding in program analysis, as a basis for constructing abstract join and abstract transformers. In this work we explore the use of paramodulation for consequence finding, which was sufficient for our applications. More elaborate consequence finding techniques can be used to obtain more precise transformers and join operations, and this presents an interesting direction for future study.

References

1. Aho, A.V., Sethi, R., Ullman, J.D.: Compilers: Principles, Techniques and Tools. Addison-Wesley, Reading (1988)
2. Barnett, M., Chang, B.-Y.E., DeLine, R., Jacobs, B., Leino, K.R.M.: Boogie: a modular reusable verifier for object-oriented programs. In: Boer, F.S., Bonsangue, M.M., Graf, S., Roever, W.-P. (eds.) FMCO 2005. LNCS, vol. 4111, pp. 364–387. Springer, Heidelberg (2006). doi:10.1007/11804192_17
3. Castelnuovo, G., Naik, M., Rinetzky, N., Sagiv, M., Yang, H.: Modularity in lattices: a case study on the correspondence between top-down and bottom-up analysis. In: Blazy, S., Jensen, T. (eds.) SAS 2015. LNCS, vol. 9291, pp. 252–274. Springer, Heidelberg (2015). doi:10.1007/978-3-662-48288-9_15
4. Codish, M., Demoen, B.: Analyzing logic programs using "PROP"-ositional logic programs and a magic wand. J. Log. Program. **25**(3), 249–274 (1995)

5. Cousot, P., Cousot, R.: Abstract interpretation: a unified lattice model for static analysis of programs by construction of approximation of fixed points. In: ACM SIGPLAN-SIGACT Symposium on Principles of Programming Languages, pp. 238–252 (1977)
6. Cousot, P., Cousot, R.: Systematic design of program analysis frameworks. In: ACM SIGPLAN-SIGACT Symposium on Principles of Programming Languages, pp. 269–282. ACM Press, New York (1979)
7. del Val, A.: A new method for consequence finding and compilation in restricted languages. In: Hendler, J., Subramanian, D. (eds.) Proceedings of 16th National Conference on Artificial Intelligence and 11th Conference on Innovative Applications of Artificial Intelligence, 18–22 July 1999, Orlando, Florida, USA, pp. 259–264. AAAI Press/The MIT Press (1999)
8. Distefano, D., O'Hearn, P.W., Yang, H.: A local shape analysis based on separation logic. In: Hermanns, H., Palsberg, J. (eds.) TACAS 2006. LNCS, vol. 3920, pp. 287–302. Springer, Heidelberg (2006). doi:10.1007/11691372_19
9. Ghiya, R., Hendren, L.J.: Connection analysis: a practical interprocedural heap analysis for C. In: Huang, C.-H., Sadayappan, P., Banerjee, U., Gelernter, D., Nicolau, A., Padua, D. (eds.) LCPC 1995. LNCS, vol. 1033, pp. 515–533. Springer, Heidelberg (1996). doi:10.1007/BFb0014221
10. Giacobazzi, R., Ranzato, F.: The reduced relative power operation on abstract domains. Theoret. Comput. Sci. **216**(1–2), 159–211 (1999)
11. Giacobazzi, R., Scozzari, F.: A logical model for relational abstract domains. ACM Trans. Program. Lang. Syst. **20**(5), 1067–1109 (1998)
12. Inoue, K.: Consequence-finding based on ordered linear resolution. In: Mylopoulos, J., Reiter, R. (eds.) Proceedings of 12th International Joint Conference on Artificial Intelligence, 24–30 August 1991, Sydney, Australia, pp. 158–164. Morgan Kaufmann (1991)
13. Marriott, K., Søndergaard, H.: Precise and efficient groundness analysis for logic programs. LOPLAS **2**(1–4), 181–196 (1993)
14. Nelson, G., Oppen, D.C.: Fast decision procedures based on congruence closure. J. ACM **27**(2), 356–364 (1980)
15. Robinson, A., Voronkov, A. (eds.): Handbook of Automated Reasoning, vol. 1. Elsevier Science Publishers B. V., Amsterdam (2001)
16. Robinson, J.A.: A machine-oriented logic based on the resolution principle. J. ACM **12**(1), 23–41 (1965)
17. Scozzari, F.: Logical optimality of groundness analysis. Theoret. Comput. Sci. **277**(1–2), 149–184 (2002)
18. Simon, L., del Val, A.: Efficient consequence finding. In: Nebel, B. (ed.) Proceedings of 17th International Joint Conference on Artificial Intelligence, IJCAI 2001, 4–10 August 2001, Seattle, Washington, USA, pp. 359–370. Morgan Kaufmann (2001)
19. Smaragdakis, Y., Balatsouras, G.: Pointer analysis. Found. Trends Program. Lang. **2**(1), 1–69 (2015)
20. US-CERT/NIST: Vulnerability summary for cve-2014-7841, April 2014. https://web.nvd.nist.gov/view/vuln/detail?vulnId=CVE-2014-7841

Reasoning in the Bernays-Schönfinkel-Ramsey Fragment of Separation Logic

Andrew Reynolds[1], Radu Iosif[2(✉)], and Cristina Serban[2]

[1] The University of Iowa, Iowa City, USA
[2] Verimag/CNRS/Université de Grenoble Alpes, Grenoble, France
iosif@imag.fr

Abstract. Separation Logic (SL) is a well-known assertion language used in Hoare-style modular proof systems for programs with dynamically allocated data structures. In this paper we investigate the fragment of first-order SL restricted to the Bernays-Schönfinkel-Ramsey quantifier prefix $\exists^*\forall^*$, where the quantified variables range over the set of memory locations. When this set is uninterpreted (has no associated theory) the fragment is PSPACE-complete, which matches the complexity of the quantifier-free fragment [7]. However, SL becomes undecidable when the quantifier prefix belongs to $\exists^*\forall^*\exists^*$ instead, or when the memory locations are interpreted as integers with linear arithmetic constraints, thus setting a sharp boundary for decidability within SL. We have implemented a decision procedure for the decidable fragment of $\exists^*\forall^*$ SL as a specialized solver inside a DPLL(T) architecture, within the CVC4 SMT solver. The evaluation of our implementation was carried out using two sets of verification conditions, produced by (i) unfolding inductive predicates, and (ii) a weakest precondition-based verification condition generator. Experimental data shows that automated quantifier instantiation has little overhead, compared to manual model-based instantiation.

1 Introduction

Separation Logic (SL) is a popular logical framework for program verification, used by a large number of methods, ranging from static analysis [6,10,28] to Hoare-style proofs [19] and property-guided abstraction refinement [1]. The salient features that make SL particularly attractive for program verification are the ability of defining (i) recursive data structures using small and natural inductive definitions, (ii) weakest pre- and post-condition calculi that capture the semantics of programs with pointers, and (iii) compositional verification methods, based on the principle of local reasoning (analyzing separately pieces of program working on disjoint heaps).

Consider, for instance, the following inductive definitions, describing an acyclic and a possibly cyclic list segment, respectively:

$$\widehat{\mathsf{ls}}(\mathsf{x},\mathsf{y}) \equiv \mathsf{emp} \wedge \mathsf{x} = \mathsf{y} \ \vee \ \mathsf{x} \neq \mathsf{y} \wedge \exists \mathsf{z} \,.\, \mathsf{x} \mapsto \mathsf{z} * \widehat{\mathsf{ls}}(\mathsf{z},\mathsf{y}) \quad \text{acyclic list segment from } \mathsf{x} \text{ to } \mathsf{y}$$
$$\mathsf{ls}(\mathsf{x},\mathsf{y}) \equiv \mathsf{emp} \wedge \mathsf{x} = \mathsf{y} \ \vee \ \exists \mathsf{u} \,.\, \mathsf{x} \mapsto \mathsf{u} * \mathsf{ls}(\mathsf{u},\mathsf{y}) \qquad\qquad \text{list segment from } \mathsf{x} \text{ to } \mathsf{y}$$

© Springer International Publishing AG 2017
A. Bouajjani and D. Monniaux (Eds.): VMCAI 2017, LNCS 10145, pp. 462–482, 2017.
DOI: 10.1007/978-3-319-52234-0_25

Intuitively, an acyclic list segment is either empty, in which case the head and the tail coincide (emp $\wedge$ x $=$ y), or it contains at least one element which is disjoint from the rest of the list segment. We denote by x $\mapsto$ z the fact that x is an allocated memory location, which points to z, and by x $\mapsto$ z $*$ $\widehat{\mathsf{ls}}$(z, y) the fact that x $\mapsto$ z and $\widehat{\mathsf{ls}}$(z, y) hold over disjoint parts of the heap. The constraint x $\neq$ y, in the inductive definition of $\widehat{\mathsf{ls}}$, captures the fact that the tail of the list segment is distinct from every allocated cell in the list segment, which ensures the acyclicity condition. Since this constraint is omitted from the definition of the second (possibly cyclic) list segment ls(x, y), its tail y is allowed to point inside the set of allocated cells.

Automated reasoning is the key enabler of push-button program verification. Any procedure that checks the validity of a logical entailment between inductive predicates requires checking the satisfiability of formulae from the base (non-inductive) assertion language, as shown by the example below. Consider a fragment of the inductive proof showing that any acyclic list segment is also a list segment, given below:

$$
\frac{\dfrac{\widehat{\mathsf{ls}}(z,y) \vdash \mathsf{ls}(z,y)}{x \neq y \wedge x \mapsto z * \widehat{\mathsf{ls}}(z,y) \vdash \exists u \,.\, x \mapsto u * \mathsf{ls}(u,y)} \quad \begin{array}{l} x \neq y \wedge x \mapsto z \models \exists u \,.\, x \mapsto u \\ \text{by instantiation } u \leftarrow z \end{array}}{\widehat{\mathsf{ls}}(x,y) \vdash \mathsf{ls}(x,y)}
$$

The first (bottom) inference in the proof corresponds to one of the two cases produced by unfolding both the antecedent and consequent of the entailment (the second case emp $\wedge$ x $=$ y $\vdash$ emp $\wedge$ x $=$ y is trivial and omitted for clarity). The second inference is a simplification of the sequent obtained by unfolding, to a sequent matching the initial one (by renaming z to x), and allows to conclude this branch of the proof by an inductive argument, based on the principle of infinite descent [5].

The simplification applied by the second inference above relies on the validity of the entailment x $\neq$ y $\wedge$ x $\mapsto$ z $\models$ $\exists$u $.$ x $\mapsto$ u, which reduces to the (un)satisfiability of the formula x $\neq$ y $\wedge$ x $\mapsto$ z $\wedge$ $\forall$u $.$ $\neg$x $\mapsto$ u. The latter falls into the Bernays-Schönfinkel-Ramsey fragment, defined by the $\exists^*\forall^*$ quantifier prefix, and can be proved unsatisfiable using the instantiation of the universally quantified variable u with the existentially quantified variable z (or a corresponding Skolem constant). In other words, this formula is unsatisfiable because the universal quantified subformula asks that no memory location is pointed to by x, which is contradicted by x $\mapsto$ z. The instantiation of u that violates the universal condition is u $\leftarrow$ z, which is carried over in the rest of the proof.

The goal of this paper is mechanizing satisfiability of the Bernays-Schönfinkel-Ramsey fragment of SL, without inductively defined predicates[1]. This fragment is defined by the quantifier prefix of the formulae in prenex normal form. We consider formulae $\exists x_1 \ldots \exists x_m \forall y_1 \ldots \forall y_n \,.\, \phi(x_1, \ldots, x_m, y_1, \ldots, y_n)$,

---

[1] Strictly speaking, the Bernays-Schönfinkel-Ramsey class refers to the $\exists^*\forall^*$ fragment of first-order logic with equality and predicate symbols, but no function symbols [17].

where ϕ is any quantifier-free formula of SL, consisting of pure formulae from given base theory T, and points-to atomic propositions relating terms of T, combined with unrestricted Boolean and separation connectives, and the quantified variables range essentially over the set of memory locations. In a nutshell, the contributions of the paper are two-fold:

1. We draw a sharp boundary between decidability and undecidability, proving essentially that the satisfiability problem for the Bernays-Schönfinkel-Ramsey fragment of SL is PSPACE-complete, if the domain of memory locations is an uninterpreted set, whereas interpreting memory locations as integers with linear arithmetic constraints, leads to undecidability. Moreover, undecidability occurs even for uninterpreted memory locations, if we extend the quantifier prefix to $\exists^*\forall^*\exists^*$.
2. We have implemented an effective decision procedure for quantifier instantiation, based on counterexample-driven learning of conflict lemmas, integrated within the DPLL(T) architecture [12] of the CVC4 SMT solver [2]. Experimental evaluation of our implementation shows that the overhead of the push-button quantifier instantiation is negligible, compared to the time required to solve a quantifier-free instance of the problem, obtained manually, by model inspection.

Related Work. The first theoretical results on the decidability and computational complexity of SL (without inductive definitions) were found by Calcagno, Yang and O'Hearn [7]. They showed that the satisfiability problem for SL is undecidable, in the presence of quantifiers, assuming that each memory location can point to two other locations, i.e. using atomic propositions of the form $x \mapsto (y, z)$. Decidability can be recovered by considering the quantifier-free fragment, proved to be PSPACE-complete, by a small model argument [7]. Refinements of these results consider decidable fragments of SL with one record field (atomic points-to propositions $x \mapsto y$), and one or two quantified variables. In a nutshell, SL with one record field and separating conjunction only is decidable with non-elementary time complexity, whereas adding the magic wand adjoint leads to undecidability [4]. Decidability, in the presence of the magic wand operator, is recovered by restricting the number of quantifiers to one, in which case the logic becomes PSPACE-complete [9]. This bound is sharp, because allowing two quantified variables leads to undecidability, and decidability with non-elementary time complexity if the magic wand is removed [8].

SMT techniques were applied to deciding the satisfiability of SL in the work of Piskac, Wies and Zufferey [21,22]. They considered quantifier-free fragments of SL with separating conjunction in positive form (not occurring under negation) and without magic wand, and allowed for hardcoded inductive predicates (list and tree segments). In a similar spirit, we previously defined a translation to multi-sorted second-order logic combined with counterexample-driven instantiation for set quantifiers to define a decision procedure for the quantifier-free fragment of SL [25]. In a different vein, a tableau-based semi-decision procedure is given by Méry and Galmiche [11]. Termination of this procedure is guaranteed for the (decidable) quantifier-free fragment of SL, yet no implementation is available for comparison.

A number of automated theorem provers have efficient and complete approaches for the Bernays-Schönfinkel-Ramsey fragment of first-order-logic, also known as effectively propositional logic (EPR) [3,16]. A dedicated approach for EPR in the SMT solver Z3 was developed in [20]. An approach based on finite model finding is implemented in CVC4 [26], which is model-complete for EPR. Our approach is based on counterexample-guided quantifier instantiation, which has been used in the context of SMT solving in previous works [13,23].

2   Preliminaries

We consider formulae in multi-sorted first-order logic. A *signature* Σ consists of a set Σ^s of sort symbols and a set Σ^f of (sorted) *function symbols* $f^{\sigma_1 \cdots \sigma_n \sigma}$, where $n \geq 0$ and $\sigma_1, \ldots, \sigma_n, \sigma \in \Sigma^s$. If $n = 0$, we call f^{σ} a *constant symbol*. In this paper, we consider signatures Σ containing the Boolean sort, and write $\top$ and $\bot$ for the Boolean constants *true* and *false*. For this reason, we do not consider predicate symbols as part of a signature, as predicates are viewed as Boolean functions. Additionally, we assume for any finite sequence of sorts $\sigma_1, \ldots, \sigma_n \in \Sigma^s$, the *tuple* sort $\sigma_1 \times \ldots \times \sigma_n$ also belongs to Σ^s, and that Σ^f includes the ith tuple projection function for each $i = 1, \ldots, n$. For each $k > 0$, let σ^k denote the k-tuple sort $\sigma \times \ldots \times \sigma$.

Let Vars be a countable set of first-order variables, each $x^{\sigma} \in$ Vars having an associated sort σ. First-order terms and formulae over the signature Σ (called Σ-terms and Σ-formulae) are defined as usual. For a Σ-formula φ, we denote by $\mathrm{Fvc}(\varphi)$ the set of free variables and constant symbols in φ, and by writing $\varphi(x)$ we mean that $x \in \mathrm{Fvc}(\phi)$. Whenever $\mathrm{Fvc}(\phi) \cap$ Vars $= \emptyset$, we say that ϕ is a *sentence*, i.e. ϕ has no free variables. A Σ-*interpretation* $\mathcal{I}$ maps:(1) each sort symbol $\sigma \in \Sigma$ to a non-empty set $\sigma^{\mathcal{I}}$, (2) each function symbol $f^{\sigma_1, \ldots, \sigma_n, \sigma} \in \Sigma$ to a total function $f^{\mathcal{I}} : \sigma_1^{\mathcal{I}} \times \ldots \times \sigma_n^{\mathcal{I}} \to \sigma^{\mathcal{I}}$ where $n > 0$, and to an element of $\sigma^{\mathcal{I}}$ when $n = 0$, and (3) each variable $x^{\sigma} \in$ Vars to an element of $\sigma^{\mathcal{I}}$. For an interpretation $\mathcal{I}$ a sort symbol σ and a variable x, we denote by $\mathcal{I}[\sigma \leftarrow S]$ and, respectively $\mathcal{I}[x \leftarrow v]$, the interpretation associating the set S to σ, respectively the value v to x, and which behaves like $\mathcal{I}$ in all other cases[2]. For a Σ-term t, we write $t^{\mathcal{I}}$ to denote the interpretation of t in $\mathcal{I}$, defined inductively, as usual. A satisfiability relation between Σ-interpretations and Σ-formulas, written $\mathcal{I} \models \varphi$, is also defined inductively, as usual. We say that $\mathcal{I}$ is *a model of* φ if $\mathcal{I}$ satisfies φ.

A (multi-sorted first-order) *theory* is a pair $T = (\Sigma, \mathbf{I})$ where Σ is a signature and $\mathbf{I}$ is a non-empty set of Σ-interpretations, the *models* of T. We assume that Σ always contains the equality predicate, which we denote by $\approx$, as well as projection functions for each tuple sort. A Σ-formula φ is T-*satisfiable* if it is satisfied by some interpretation in $\mathbf{I}$. We write E to denote the empty theory (with equality), whose signature consists of a sort U with no additional

---

[2] By writing $\mathcal{I}[\sigma \leftarrow S]$ we ensure that all variables of sort σ are mapped by $\mathcal{I}$ to elements of S.

function symbols, and LIA to denote the theory of linear integer arithmetic, whose signature consists of the sort Int, the binary predicate symbol $\geq$, function $+$ denoting addition, and the constants $0, 1$ of sort Int, interpreted as usual. In particular, there are no uninterpreted function symbols in LIA. By ELIA we denote the theory obtained by extending the signature of LIA with the sort U of E and the equality over U.

Let $T = (\Sigma, \mathbf{I})$ be a theory and let Loc and Data be two sorts from Σ, with no restriction other than the fact that Loc is always interpreted as a countable set. Also, we consider that Σ has a designated constant symbol $\mathsf{nil}^{\mathsf{Loc}}$. The *Separation Logic* fragment $\mathsf{SL}(T)_{\mathsf{Loc},\mathsf{Data}}$ is the set of formulae generated by the following syntax:

$$\varphi := \phi \mid \mathsf{emp} \mid \mathsf{t} \mapsto \mathsf{u} \mid \varphi_1 * \varphi_2 \mid \varphi_1 -\!\!* \varphi_2 \mid \neg \varphi_1 \mid \varphi_1 \wedge \varphi_2 \mid \exists x^\sigma . \varphi_1(x)$$

where ϕ is a Σ-formula, and t, u are Σ-terms of sorts Loc and Data, respectively. As usual, we write $\forall x^\sigma . \varphi(x)$ for $\neg \exists x^\sigma . \neg \varphi(x)$. We omit specifying the sorts of variables and constants when they are clear from the context.

Given an interpretation $\mathcal{I}$, a *heap* is a finite partial mapping $h : \mathsf{Loc}^{\mathcal{I}} \rightharpoonup_{\mathsf{fin}} \mathsf{Data}^{\mathcal{I}}$. For a heap h, we denote by $\mathrm{dom}(h)$ its domain. For two heaps h_1 and h_2, we write $h_1 \# h_2$ for $\mathrm{dom}(h_1) \cap \mathrm{dom}(h_2) = \emptyset$ and $h = h_1 \uplus h_2$ for $h_1 \# h_2$ and $h = h_1 \cup h_2$. We define the *satisfaction relation* $\mathcal{I}, h \models_{\mathsf{SL}} \phi$ inductively, as follows:

$$
\begin{aligned}
\mathcal{I}, h &\models_{\mathsf{SL}} \phi & &\Longleftrightarrow \mathcal{I} \models \phi \text{ if } \phi \text{ is a } \Sigma\text{-formula} \\
\mathcal{I}, h &\models_{\mathsf{SL}} \mathsf{emp} & &\Longleftrightarrow h = \emptyset \\
\mathcal{I}, h &\models_{\mathsf{SL}} \mathsf{t} \mapsto \mathsf{u} & &\Longleftrightarrow h = \{(\mathsf{t}^{\mathcal{I}}, \mathsf{u}^{\mathcal{I}})\} \text{ and } \mathsf{t}^{\mathcal{I}} \not\approx \mathsf{nil}^{\mathcal{I}} \\
\mathcal{I}, h &\models_{\mathsf{SL}} \phi_1 * \phi_2 & &\Longleftrightarrow \text{there exist heaps } h_1, h_2 \text{ s.t. } h = h_1 \uplus h_2 \text{ and } \mathcal{I}, h_i \models_{\mathsf{SL}} \phi_i, i = 1, 2 \\
\mathcal{I}, h &\models_{\mathsf{SL}} \phi_1 -\!\!* \phi_2 & &\Longleftrightarrow \text{for all heaps } h' \text{ if } h' \# h \text{ and } \mathcal{I}, h' \models_{\mathsf{SL}} \phi_1 \text{ then } \mathcal{I}, h' \uplus h \models_{\mathsf{SL}} \phi_2 \\
\mathcal{I}, h &\models_{\mathsf{SL}} \exists x^S . \varphi(x) & &\Longleftrightarrow \mathcal{I}[x \leftarrow s], h \models_{\mathsf{SL}} \varphi(x), \text{ for some } s \in S^{\mathcal{I}}
\end{aligned}
$$

The satisfaction relation for Σ-formulae, Boolean connectives $\wedge$, $\neg$, and linear arithmetic atoms, are the classical ones from first-order logic. Notice that the range of a quantified variable x^S is the interpretation of its associated sort $S^{\mathcal{I}}$.

A formula φ is said to be *satisfiable* if there exists an interpretation $\mathcal{I}$ and a heap h such that $\mathcal{I}, h \models_{\mathsf{SL}} \varphi$. The (SL, T)-*satisfiability problem* asks, given an SL formula φ, whether there exists an interpretation $\mathcal{I}$ of T and a heap h such that $\mathcal{I}, h \models_{\mathsf{SL}} \varphi$. We write $\varphi \models_{\mathsf{SL}} \psi$ if for every interpretation $\mathcal{I}$ and heap h, if $\mathcal{I}, h \models_{\mathsf{SL}} \varphi$ then $\mathcal{I}, h \models_{\mathsf{SL}} \psi$, and we say that φ *entails* ψ in this case.

The Bernays-Schönfinkel-Ramsey Fragment of SL. In this paper we address the satisfiability problem for the class of sentences $\phi \equiv \exists x_1 \ldots \exists x_m \forall y_1 \ldots \forall y_n . \varphi(x_1, \ldots, x_m, y_1, \ldots, y_n)$, where φ is a quantifier-free formula of $\mathsf{SL}(T)_{\mathsf{Loc},\mathsf{Data}}$. We shall denote this fragment by $\exists^* \forall^* \mathsf{SL}(T)_{\mathsf{Loc},\mathsf{Data}}$. It is easy to see that any sentence ϕ, as above, is satisfiable if and only if the sentence $\forall y_1 \ldots \forall y_n . \varphi[c_1/x_1, \ldots, c_m/x_m]$ is satisfiable, where $c_1, \ldots, c_m$ are fresh (Skolem) constant symbols. The latter is called the *functional form* of ϕ.

As previously mentioned, SL is used mainly specify properties of a program's heap. If the program under consideration uses pointer arithmetic, as in C or C++, it is useful to consider LIA for the theory of memory addresses. Otherwise, if the program only compares the values of the pointers for equality, as in

Java, one can use E for this purpose. This distinction led us to considering the satisfiability problem for $\exists^*\forall^*\mathsf{SL}(T)_{\mathsf{Loc},\mathsf{Data}}$ in the following cases:

1. Loc is interpreted as the sort U of E and Data as U^k, for some $k \geq 1$. The satisfiability problem for the fragment $\exists^*\forall^*\mathsf{SL}(\mathsf{E})_{U,U^k}$ is PSPACE-complete, and the proof follows a small model property argument.
2. as above, with the further constraint that U is interpreted as an infinite countable set, i.e. of cardinality $\aleph_0$. In this case, we prove a cut-off property stating that all locations not in the domain of the heap and not used in the interpretation of constants, are equivalent from the point of view of an SL formula. This satisfiability problem is reduced to the unconstrained one above, and also found to be PSPACE-complete.
3. both Loc and Data are interpreted as Int, equipped with addition and total order, in which case $\exists^*\forall^*\mathsf{SL}(\mathsf{LIA})_{\mathsf{Int},\mathsf{Int}}$ is undecidable.
4. Loc is interpreted as the sort U of E, and Data as $U \times \mathsf{Int}$. Then $\exists^*\forall^*\mathsf{SL}(\mathsf{ELIA})_{U,U\times\mathsf{Int}}$ is undecidable.

Additionally, we prove that the fragment $\exists^*\forall^*\exists^*\mathsf{SL}(\mathsf{E})_{U,U^k}$, with two quantifier alternations, is undecidable, if $k \geq 2$. The question whether the fragment $\exists^*\forall^*\mathsf{SL}(\mathsf{ELIA})_{U,\mathsf{Int}}$ is decidable is currently open, and considered for future work. For space reasons, all missing proofs are given in [24].

3   Decidability and Complexity Results

This section defines the decidable cases of the Bernays-Schönfinkel-Ramsey fragment of SL, with matching undecidable extensions. The decidable fragment $\exists^*\forall^*\mathsf{SL}(\mathsf{E})_{U,U^k}$ relies on a small model property given in Sect. 3.1. Undecidability of $\exists^*\forall^*\mathsf{SL}(\mathsf{LIA})_{\mathsf{Int},\mathsf{Int}}$ is obtained by a refinement of the undecidability proof for Presburger arithmetic with one monadic predicate [14], in Sect. 3.4.

3.1   Small Model Property

The decidability proof for the quantifier-free fragment of SL [7,30] relies on a small model property. Intuitively, no quantifier-free SL formula can distinguish between heaps in which the number of invisible locations, not in the range of the set of free variables, exceeds a certain threshold, linear in the size of the formula. Then a formula is satisfiable iff it has a heap model of size linear in the size of the input formula.

For reasons of self-containment, we recall a number of definitions and results from [30]. Some of them are slightly modified for our purposes, but these changes have no effect on the validity of the original proofs for the Lemmas 1 and 2 below. In the rest of this section, we consider formulae of $\mathsf{SL}(\mathsf{E})_{U,U^k}$, meaning that (i) Loc $= U$, and (ii) there exists an integer $k > 0$ such that Data $= U^k$, where U is the (uninterpreted) sort of E. We fix k for the rest of this section.

Definition 1 *[30, Definition 90]. Given a set of locations S, the equivalence relation $=_S$ between k-tuples of locations is defined as $\langle v_1, \ldots, v_k \rangle =_S \langle v'_1, \ldots, v'_k \rangle$ if and only if*

- *if $v_i \in S$ then $v_i = v'_i$, and*
- *if $v_i \notin S$ then $v'_i \notin S$,*

for all $i = 1, \ldots, k$.

Intuitively, $=_S$ restricts the equality to the elements in S. Observe that $=_S$ is an equivalence relation and that $S \subseteq T$ implies $=_T\, \subseteq\, =_S$. For a set S, we write $\|S\|$ for its cardinality, in the following.

Definition 2 *[30, Definition 91]. Given an interpretation $\mathcal{I}$, an integer $n > 0$, a set of variables $X \subseteq \mathsf{Vars}$ and a set of locations $S \subseteq U^{\mathcal{I}}$, for any two heaps $h, h' : U^{\mathcal{I}} \rightharpoonup_{\mathrm{fin}} (U^{\mathcal{I}})^k$, we define $h \sim^{\mathcal{I}}_{n,X,S} h'$ if and only if*

1. $\mathcal{I}(X) \cap \mathrm{dom}(h) = \mathcal{I}(X) \cap \mathrm{dom}(h')$,
2. *for all $\ell \in \mathcal{I}(X) \cap \mathrm{dom}(h)$, we have $h(\ell) =_{\mathcal{I}(X) \cup S} h'(\ell)$,*
3. *if $\|\mathrm{dom}(h) \backslash \mathcal{I}(X)\| < n$ then $\|\mathrm{dom}(h) \backslash \mathcal{I}(X)\| = \|\mathrm{dom}(h') \backslash \mathcal{I}(X)\|$,*
4. *if $\|\mathrm{dom}(h) \backslash \mathcal{I}(X)\| \geq n$ then $\|\mathrm{dom}(h') \backslash \mathcal{I}(X)\| \geq n$.*

Observe that, for any $n \leq m$ and $S \subseteq T$ we have $\sim^{\mathcal{I}}_{m,X,T}\, \subseteq\, \sim^{\mathcal{I}}_{n,X,S}$. In addition, for any integer $k > 0$, subset $S \subseteq U^{\mathcal{I}}$ and location $\ell \in U^{\mathcal{I}}$, we consider the function $prun^{\ell}_{k,S}(\ell_1, \ldots, \ell_k)$, which replaces each value $\ell_i \notin S$ in its argument list by ℓ.

Lemma 1 *[30, Lemma 94]. Given an interpretation $\mathcal{I}$ and a heap $h : U^{\mathcal{I}} \rightharpoonup_{\mathrm{fin}} (U^{\mathcal{I}})^k$, for each integer $n > 0$, each set of variables $X \subseteq \mathsf{Vars}$, each set of locations $L \subseteq U^{\mathcal{I}}$ such that $L \cap \mathcal{I}(X) = \emptyset$ and $\|L\| = n$, and each location $v \in U^{\mathcal{I}} \backslash (\mathcal{I}(X) \cup \{\mathrm{nil}^{\mathcal{I}}\} \cup L)$, there exists a heap $h' : U^{\mathcal{I}} \rightharpoonup_{\mathrm{fin}} (U^{\mathcal{I}})^k$, with the following properties:*

1. $h \sim^{\mathcal{I}}_{n,X,L} h'$,
2. $\mathrm{dom}(h') \backslash \mathcal{I}(X) \subseteq L$,
3. *for all $\ell \in \mathrm{dom}(h')$, we have $h'(\ell) = prun^v_{k, \mathcal{I}(X) \cup L}(h(\ell))$.*

Next, we define the following measure on quantifier-free SL formulae:

$$|\phi * \psi| = |\phi| + |\psi| \qquad |\phi \mathbin{-\!\!*} \psi| = |\psi| \qquad |\phi \wedge \psi| = \max(|\phi|, |\psi|) \qquad |\neg\phi| = |\phi|$$
$$|t \mapsto u| = 1 \qquad\quad |\mathrm{emp}| = 1 \qquad |\phi| = 0 \text{ if } \phi \text{ is a } \Sigma\text{-formula}$$

Intuitively, $|\varphi|$ is the maximum number of invisible locations, that are not in $\mathcal{I}(\mathrm{Fvc}(\varphi))$, and which can be distinguished by the quantifier-free $\mathsf{SL(E)}_{U,U^k}$ formula φ. The crux of the PSPACE-completeness proof for quantifier-free $\mathsf{SL(E)}_{U,U^k}$ is that two heaps equivalent up to $|\varphi|$ invisible locations are also equivalent from the point of view of satisfiability of φ, which provides a small model property for this fragment [7, 30].

Lemma 2 *[30, Proposition 95]. Given a quantifier-free $\mathsf{SL(E)}_{U,U^k}$ formula φ, an interpretation $\mathcal{I}$, and two heaps h and h', if $h \sim^{\mathcal{I}}_{|\varphi|,\mathrm{Fvc}(\varphi),\emptyset} h'$ and $\mathcal{I}, h \models_{\mathsf{SL}} \varphi$ then $\mathcal{I}, h' \models_{\mathsf{SL}} \varphi$.*

Our aim is to extend this result to $\exists^*\forall^*\mathsf{SL(E)}_{U,U^k}$, in the first place. This new small model property is given by the next lemma.

Lemma 3. *Let $\varphi(x_1^U, \ldots, x_n^U)$ be a quantifier-free $\mathsf{SL(E)}_{U,U^k}$-formula, and $\varphi^\forall \equiv \forall x_1^U \ldots \forall x_n^U \, . \, \varphi(x_1^U, \ldots, x_n^U)$ be its universal closure. Then $\varphi^\forall$ has a model if and only if there exists an interpretation $\mathcal{I}$ and a heap $h : U^{\mathcal{I}} \rightharpoonup_{\mathrm{fin}} (U^{\mathcal{I}})^k$ such that $\mathcal{I}, h \models_{\mathsf{SL}} \varphi^\forall$ and:*

1. *$\|U^{\mathcal{I}}\| \leq |\varphi| + \|\mathrm{Fvc}(\varphi^\forall)\| + n$,*
2. *$\mathrm{dom}(h) \subseteq L \cup \mathcal{I}(\mathrm{Fvc}(\varphi^\forall))$,*
3. *for all $\ell \in \mathrm{dom}(h)$, we have $h(\ell) \in (\mathcal{I}(\mathrm{Fvc}(\varphi^\forall)) \cup \{\mathsf{nil}^{\mathcal{I}}\} \cup L \cup \{v\})^k$,*

where $L \subseteq U^{\mathcal{I}} \backslash \mathcal{I}(\mathrm{Fvc}(\varphi^\forall))$ is a set of locations such that $\|L\| = |\varphi| + n$ and $v \in U^{\mathcal{I}} \backslash (\mathcal{I}(\mathrm{Fvc}(\varphi^\forall)) \cup \{\mathsf{nil}^{\mathcal{I}}\} \cup L)$ is an arbitrary location.

We are ready to prove two decidability results, based on the above small model property, concerning the cases where (i) Loc is interpreted as a countable set with equality, and (ii) Loc is interpreted as an infinite countable set with no other operators than equality.

3.2   Uninterpreted Locations Without Cardinality Constraints

In this section, we consider the satisfiability problem for the fragment $\exists^*\forall^*\mathsf{SL(E)}_{U,U^k}$, where the location sort U can be interpreted by any (possibly finite) countable set, with no other operations than the equality, and the data sort consists of k-tuples of locations.

Theorem 1. *The satisfiability problem for $\exists^*\forall^*\mathsf{SL(E)}_{U,U^k}$ is PSPACE-complete.*

Proof. PSPACE-hardness follows from the fact that satisfiability is PSPACE-complete for quantifier-free $\mathsf{SL(E)}_{U,U^k}$ [7]. To prove membership in PSPACE, consider the formula $\phi \equiv \exists x_1 \ldots \exists x_m \forall y_1 \ldots \forall y_n \, . \, \varphi(\mathbf{x}, \mathbf{y})$, where φ is a quantifier-free $\mathsf{SL(E)}_{U,U^k}$ formula. Let $\mathbf{c} = \langle c_1, \ldots, c_m \rangle$ be a tuple of constant symbols, and $\widetilde{\phi} \equiv \forall y_1 \ldots \forall y_n \, . \, \varphi(\mathbf{c}, \mathbf{y})$ be the functional form of ϕ, obtained by replacing x_i with c_i, for all $i = 1, \ldots, m$. By Lemma 3, $\widetilde{\phi}$ has a model if and only if it has a model $\mathcal{I}, h$ such that:

- $\|U^{\mathcal{I}}\| \leq |\varphi| + n + m$,
- $\mathrm{dom}(h) \subseteq L \cup \mathbf{c}^{\mathcal{I}}$,
- $\forall \ell \in \mathrm{dom}(h) \, . \, h(\ell) \in (\mathcal{I}(\mathbf{c}) \cup \{\mathsf{nil}^{\mathcal{I}}\} \cup L \cup \{v\})^k$,

where $L \subseteq U^{\mathcal{I}} \backslash \mathcal{I}(\mathbf{c})$, $\|L\| = |\varphi| + m$ and $v \in U^{\mathcal{I}} \backslash (\mathcal{I}(\mathbf{c}) \cup \{\mathsf{nil}^{\mathcal{I}}\} \cup L)$. We describe below a nondeterministic polynomial space algorithm that decides satisfiability of $\widetilde{\phi}$. First, nondeterministically chose a model $\mathcal{I}, h$ that meets the above requirements. Then we check, for each tuple $\langle u_1, \ldots, u_n \rangle \in (U^{\mathcal{I}})^n$ that $\mathcal{I}[y_1 \leftarrow u_1] \ldots [y_n \leftarrow u_n], h \models_{\mathsf{SL}} \varphi$. In order to enumerate all tuples from $(U^{\mathcal{I}})^n$ we need $n \cdot \lceil \log_2(|\varphi| + n + m) \rceil$ extra bits, and the check for each such tuple can be done in PSPACE, according to [7, Sect. 5]. □

This result is somewhat surprising, because the classical Bernays-Schönfinkel fragment of first-order formulae with predicate symbols (but no function symbols) and quantifier prefix $\exists^* \forall^*$ is known to be NEXPTIME-complete [17, Sect. 7]. The explanation lies in the fact that the interpretation of an arbitrary predicate symbol $P(x_1, \ldots, x_n)$ cannot be captured using only points-to atomic propositions, e.g. $x_1 \mapsto (x_2, \ldots, x_n)$, between locations and tuples of locations, due to the interpretation of points-to's as heaps[3] (finite partial functions).

The following lemma sets a first decidability boundary for $\mathsf{SL(E)}_{U,U^k}$, by showing how extending the quantifier prefix to $\exists^* \forall^* \exists^*$ leads to undecidability.

Lemma 4. *The satisfiability problem for $\exists^* \forall^* \exists^* \mathsf{SL(E)}_{U,U^k}$ is undecidable, if $k \geq 2$.*

Observe that the result of Lemma 4 sets a fairly tight boundary between the decidable and undecidable fragments of SL. On the one hand, simplifying the quantifier prefix to $\exists^* \forall^*$ yields a decidable fragment (Theorem 1), whereas $\mathsf{SL(E)}_{U,U}$ ($k = 1$) without the magic wand ($-\!\!*$) is decidable with non-elementary time complexity, even when considering an unrestricted quantifier prefix [4].

3.3   Uninterpreted Locations with Cardinality $\aleph_0$

We consider the stronger version of the satisfiability problem for $\exists^* \forall^* \mathsf{SL(E)}_{U,U^k}$, where U is interpreted as an infinite countable set (of cardinality $\aleph_0$) with no function symbols, other than equality. Instances of this problem occur when, for instance, the location sort is taken to be Int, but no operations are used on integers, except for testing equality.

Observe that this restriction changes the satisfiability status of certain formulae. For instance, $\exists x \forall y . \mathsf{y} \not\approx \mathsf{nil} \Rightarrow (\mathsf{y} \mapsto \mathsf{x} * \top)$ is satisfiable if U is interpreted as a finite set, but becomes unsatisfiable when U is infinite. The reason is that this formula requires every location from $U^{\mathcal{I}}$ apart from nil to be part of the domain of the heap, which is impossible due the fact that only finite heaps are considered by the semantics of SL.

In the following proof, we use the formula $\mathsf{alloc}(\mathsf{x}) \equiv \mathsf{x} \mapsto (\mathsf{x}, \ldots, \mathsf{x}) -\!\!* \bot$, expressing the fact that a location variable x is *allocated*, i.e. its interpretation is part of the heap's domain [4]. Intuitively, we reduce any instance of the $\exists^* \forall^* \mathsf{SL(E)}_{U,U^k}$ satisfiability problem, with U of cardinality $\aleph_0$, to an instance of the same problem without this restriction, by the following cut-off argument:

---

[3] If $x_1 \mapsto (x_2, \ldots, x_n)$ and $x_1 \mapsto (x_2', \ldots, x_n')$ hold, this forces $x_i = x_i'$, for all $i = 2, \ldots, n$.

if a free variable is interpreted as a location which is neither part of the heap's domain, nor equal to the interpretation of some constant, then it is not important which particular location is chosen for that interpretation.

Theorem 2. *The satisfiability problem for $\exists^*\forall^* \mathsf{SL(E)}_{U,U^k}$ is PSPACE-complete if U is required to have cardinality $\aleph_0$.*

Proof. PSPACE-hardness follows from the PSPACE-completeness of the satisfiability problem for quantifier-free SL, with uninterpreted locations [7, Sect. 5.2]. Since the reduction from [7, Sect. 5.2] involves no universally quantified variables, the $\aleph_0$ cardinality constraint has no impact on this result.

Let $\exists x_1 \ldots \exists x_m \forall y_1 \ldots \forall y_n . \varphi(\mathbf{x}, \mathbf{y})$ be a formula, and $\forall y_1 \ldots \forall y_n . \varphi(\mathbf{c}, \mathbf{y})$ be its functional form, obtained by replacing each x_i with c_i, for $i = 1, \ldots, m$. We consider the following formulae, parameterized by y_i, for $i = 1, \ldots, n$:

$$\psi_0(y_i) \equiv \mathsf{alloc}(y_i)$$
$$\psi_1(y_i) \equiv \bigvee_{j=1}^m y_i = c_j$$
$$\psi_2(y_i) \equiv y_i = d_i$$
$$\mathsf{external} \equiv \bigwedge_{i=1}^n (\neg\mathsf{alloc}(d_i) \wedge \bigwedge_{j=1}^m d_i \neq c_j)$$

where $\{d_i \mid i = 1, \ldots, n\}$ is a set of fresh constant symbols. We show the following fact:

Fact 1. *There exists an interpretation $\mathcal{I}$ and a heap h such that $\|U^{\mathcal{I}}\| = \aleph_0$ and $\mathcal{I}, h \models_{\mathsf{SL}} \forall y_1 \ldots \forall y_n . \varphi(\mathbf{c}, \mathbf{y})$ iff there exists an interpretation $\mathcal{I}'$, not constraining the cardinality of $U^{\mathcal{I}'}$, and a heap h' such that:*

$$\mathcal{I}', h' \models_{\mathsf{SL}} \mathsf{external} \wedge \forall y_1 \ldots \forall y_n \bigwedge_{\langle t_1, \ldots, t_n \rangle \in \{0,1,2\}^n} \underbrace{\bigwedge_{i=1}^n (\psi_{t_i}(y_i) \Rightarrow \varphi(\mathbf{c}, \mathbf{y}))}_{\Psi_{\langle t_1, \ldots, t_n \rangle}}$$

To show membership in PSPACE, consider a nondeterministic algorithm that choses $\mathcal{I}'$ and h' and uses $2n$ extra bits to check that $\mathcal{I}', h' \models_{\mathsf{SL}} \mathsf{extern} \wedge \forall y_1 \ldots \forall y_n . \Psi_{\langle t_1, \ldots, t_n \rangle}$ separately, for each $\langle t_1, \ldots, t_n \rangle \in \{0, 1, 2\}^n$. By Lemma 3, the sizes of $\mathcal{I}'$ and h' are bounded by a polynomial in the size of $\Psi_{\langle t_1, \ldots, t_n \rangle}$, which is polynomial in the size of φ, and by Theorem 1, each of these checks can be done in polynomial space. $\square$

3.4   Integer Locations with Linear Arithmetic

In the rest of this section we show that the Bernays-Schönfinkel-Ramsey fragment of SL becomes undecidable as soon as we use integers to represent the set of locations and combine SL with linear integer arithmetic (LIA). The proof relies on an undecidability argument for a fragment of Presburger arithmetic with one monadic predicate symbol, interpreted over finite sets. Formally, we denote by $(\exists^*\forall^* \cap \forall^*\exists^*) - \mathsf{LIA}$ the set of formulae consisting of a conjunction between two linear arithmetic formulae, one with quantifier prefix in the language $\exists^*\forall^*$, and another with quantifier prefix $\forall^*\exists^*$.

Theorem 3. *The satisfiability problem is undecidable for the fragment* $(\exists^*\forall^* \cap \forall^*\exists^*) - \text{LIA}$, *with one monadic predicate symbol, interpreted over finite sets of integers.*

Proof. We reduce from the following variant of *Hilbert's 10th Problem*: given a multivariate Diophantine polynomial $R(x_1,\ldots,x_n)$, the problem "does $R(x_1,\ldots,x_n) = 0$ have a solution in $\mathbb{N}^n$?" is undecidable [18].

By introducing sufficiently many free variables, we encode $R(x_1,\ldots,x_n) = 0$ as an equisatisfiable Diophantine system of degree at most two, containing only equations of the form $x = yz$ (resp. $x = y^2$) and linear equations $\sum_{i=1}^{k} a_i x_i = b$, where $a_1,\ldots,a_k, b \in \mathbb{Z}$. Next, we replace each equation of the form $x = yz$, with y and z distinct variables, with the quadratic system $2x + t_y + t_z = t_{y+z} \wedge t_y = y^2 \wedge t_z = z^2 \wedge t_{y+z} = (y+z)^2$, where t_y, t_z and t_{y+z} are fresh (free) variables. In this way, we replace all multiplications between distinct variables by occurrences of the squaring function. Let $\Psi_{R(x_1,\ldots,x_n)=0}$ be the conjunction of the above equations. It is manifest that $R(x_1,\ldots,x_n) = 0$ has a solution in $\mathbb{N}^n$ iff $\Psi_{R(x_1,\ldots,x_n)=0}$ is satisfiable, with all free variables ranging over $\mathbb{N}$.

Now we introduce a monadic predicate symbol P, which is intended to denote a (possibly finite) set of consecutive perfect squares, starting with 0. To capture this definition, we require the following:

$$P(0) \wedge P(1) \wedge \forall x \forall y \forall z \, . \, P(x) \wedge P(y) \wedge P(z) \wedge x < y < z \wedge$$
$$(\forall u \, . \, x < u < y \vee y < u < z \Rightarrow \neg P(u)) \Rightarrow z - y = y - x + 2 \qquad \text{(sqr)}$$

Observe that this formula is a weakening of the definition of the infinite set of perfect squares given by Halpern [14], from which the conjunct $\forall x \exists y \, . \, y > x \wedge P(y)$, requiring that P is an infinite set of natural numbers, has been dropped. Moreover, notice that sqr has quantifier prefix $\forall^3\exists$, due to the fact that $\forall u$ occurs implicitly under negation, on the left-hand side of an implication. If P is interpreted as a finite set $P^{\mathcal{I}} = \{p_0, p_1, \ldots, p_N\}$ such that (w.l.o.g.) $p_0 < p_1 < \ldots < p_N$, it is easy to show, by induction on $N > 0$, that $p_i = i^2$, for all $i = 0, 1, \ldots, N$.

The next step is encoding the squaring function using the monadic predicate P. This is done by replacing each atomic proposition $x = y^2$ in $\Psi_{R(x_1,\ldots,x_n)=0}$ by the formula $\theta_{x=y^2} \equiv P(x) \wedge P(x + 2y + 1) \wedge \forall z \, . \, x < z < x + 2y + 1 \Rightarrow \neg P(z)$.

Fact 2. *For each interpretation $\mathcal{I}$ mapping x and y into $\mathbb{N}$, $\mathcal{I} \models x = y^2$ iff $\mathcal{I}$ can be extended to an interpretation of P as a finite set of consecutive perfect squares such that $\mathcal{I} \models \theta_{x=y^2}$.*

Let $\Phi_{R(x_1,\ldots,x_n)=0}$ be the conjunction of sqr with the formula obtained by replacing each atomic proposition $x = y^2$ with $\theta_{x=y^2}$ in $\Psi_{R(x_1,\ldots,x_n)=0}$. Observe that each universally quantified variable in $\Phi_{R(x_1,\ldots,x_n)=0}$ occurs either in sqr or in some $\theta_{x=y^2}$, and moreover, each $\theta_{x=y^2}$ belongs to the $\exists^*\forall^*$ fragment of LIA. $\Phi_{R(x_1,\ldots,x_n)=0}$ belongs thus to the $\exists^*\forall^* \cap \forall^*\exists^*$ fragment of LIA, with P being the only monadic predicate symbol. Finally, we prove that $R(x_1,\ldots,x_n) = 0$ has a solution in $\mathbb{N}^n$ iff $\Phi_{R(x_1,\ldots,x_n)=0}$ is satisfiable.

"$\Rightarrow$" Let $\mathcal{I}$ be a valuation mapping $x_1, \ldots, x_n$ into $\mathbb{N}$, such that $\mathcal{I} \models R(x_1, \ldots, x_n) = 0$. Obviously, $\mathcal{I}$ can be extended to a model of $\Psi_{R(x_1,\ldots,x_n)=0}$ by assigning $t_x^{\mathcal{I}} = (x^{\mathcal{I}})^2$ for all auxiliary variables t_x occurring in $\Psi_{R(x_1,\ldots,x_n)=0}$. We extend $\mathcal{I}$ to a model of $\Phi_{R(x_1,\ldots,x_n)=0}$ by assigning $P^{\mathcal{I}} = \{n^2 \mid 0 \le n \le \sqrt{m}\}$, where $m = \max\{(x^{\mathcal{I}} + 1)^2 \mid x \in \mathrm{Fvc}(\Psi_{R(x_1,\ldots,x_n)=0})\}$. Clearly $P^{\mathcal{I}}$ meets the requirements of sqr. By Fact 2, we obtain that $\mathcal{I} \models \theta_{x=y^2}$ for each subformula $\theta_{x=y^2}$ of $\Phi_{R(x_1,\ldots,x_n)=0}$, thus $\mathcal{I} \models \Phi_{R(x_1,\ldots,x_n)=0}$.

"$\Leftarrow$" If $\mathcal{I} \models \Psi_{R(x_1,\ldots,x_n)=0}$ then, by sqr, $P^{\mathcal{I}}$ is a set of consecutive perfect squares, and, by Fact 2, $\mathcal{I} \models x = y^2$ for each subformula $\theta_{x=y^2}$ of $\Phi_{R(x_1,\ldots,x_n)=0}$. Then $\mathcal{I} \models \Psi_{R(x_1,\ldots,x_n)=0}$ and consequently $\mathcal{I} \models R(x_1, \ldots, x_n) = 0$. $\square$

We consider now the satisfiability problem for the fragment $\exists^*\forall^*\mathsf{SL}(\mathsf{LIA})_{\mathsf{Int},\mathsf{Int}}$ where both Loc and Data are taken to be the Int sort, equipped with addition and total order. Observe that, in this case, the heap consists of a set of lists, possibly with aliases and circularities. Without losing generality, we consider that Int is interpreted as the set of positive integers[4].

The above theorem cannot be directly used for the undecidability of $\exists^*\forall^*\mathsf{SL}(\mathsf{LIA})_{\mathsf{Int},\mathsf{Int}}$, by interpreting the (unique) monadic predicate as the (finite) domain of the heap. The problem is with the sqr formula, that defines the interpretation of the monadic predicate as a set of consecutive perfect squares $0, 1, \ldots, n^2$, and whose quantifier prefix lies in the $\forall^*\exists^*$ fragment. We overcome this problem by replacing the sqr formula above with a definition of such sets in $\exists^*\forall^*\mathsf{SL}(\mathsf{LIA})_{\mathsf{Int},\mathsf{Int}}$. Let us first consider the following properties expressed in SL [4]:

$$\sharp x \ge 1 \equiv \exists u \,.\, u \mapsto x * \top$$
$$\sharp x \le 1 \equiv \forall u \forall t \,.\, \neg(u \mapsto x * t \mapsto x * \top)$$

Intuitively, $\sharp x \ge 1$ states that x has at least one predecessor in the heap, whereas $\sharp x \le 1$ states that x has at most one predecessor. We use $\sharp x = 0$ and $\sharp x = 1$ as shorthands for $\neg(\sharp x \ge 1)$ and $\sharp x \ge 1 \wedge \sharp x \le 1$, respectively. The formula below states that the heap can be decomposed into a list segment starting with x and ending in y, and several disjoint cyclic lists:

$$x \xrightarrow{\circlearrowright +} y \equiv \sharp x = 0 \wedge \mathsf{alloc}(x) \wedge \sharp y = 1 \wedge \neg\mathsf{alloc}(y) \wedge$$
$$\forall z \,.\, z \not\approx y \Rightarrow (\sharp z = 1 \Rightarrow \mathsf{alloc}(z)) \wedge \forall z \,.\, \sharp z \le 1$$

We forbid the existence of circular lists by adding the following arithmetic constraint:

$$\forall u \forall t \,.\, u \mapsto t * \top \Rightarrow u < t \qquad\qquad\qquad\text{(nocyc)}$$

We ask, moreover, that the elements of the list segment starting in x are consecutive perfect squares:

$$\mathsf{consqr}(x) \equiv x = 0 \wedge x \mapsto 1 * \top \wedge \forall z \forall u \forall t \,.\, z \mapsto u * u \mapsto t * \top \Rightarrow t - u = u - z + 2$$
$$\text{(consqr)}$$

---

[4] Extending the interpretation of Loc to include negative integers does not make any difference for the undecidability result.

Observe that the formula $\exists x \exists y \ . \ x \xrightarrow{\circlearrowleft}{}^{+} y \wedge \mathsf{nocyc} \wedge \mathsf{consqr}(x)$ belongs to $\exists^*\forall^*\mathsf{SL(LIA)}_{\mathsf{Int,Int}}$.

Theorem 4. *The satisfiability problem for* $\exists^*\forall^*\mathsf{SL(LIA)}_{\mathsf{Int,Int}}$ *is undecidable.*

Proof. We use the same reduction as in the proof of Theorem 3, with two differences:

- we replace sqr by $\exists x \exists y \ . \ x \xrightarrow{\circlearrowleft}{}^{+} y \wedge \mathsf{nocyc} \wedge \mathsf{consqr}(x)$, and
- define $\theta_{x=y^2} \equiv \mathsf{alloc}(x) \wedge \mathsf{alloc}(x+2y+1) \wedge \forall z \ . \ x < z < x+2y+1 \Rightarrow \neg\mathsf{alloc}(z)$.
  $\qquad\qquad\qquad\qquad\qquad\qquad\qquad\qquad\qquad\qquad\qquad\qquad\qquad\qquad\quad\square$

It is tempting, at this point to ask whether interpreting locations as integers and considering subsets of LIA instead may help recover the decidability. For instance, it has been found that the Bernays-Schönfinkel-Ramsey class is decidable in presence of integers with difference bounds arithmetic [29], and the same type of question can be asked about the fragment of $\exists^*\forall^*\mathsf{SL(LIA)}_{\mathsf{Int,Int}}$, with difference bounds constraints only.

Finally, we consider a variant of the previous undecidability result, in which locations are the (uninterpreted) sort U of E and the data consists of tuples of sort $U \times \mathsf{Int}$. This fragment of SL can be used to reason about lists with integer data. The undecidability of this fragment can be proved along the same lines as Theorem 4.

Theorem 5. *The satisfiability problem for* $\exists^*\forall^*\mathsf{SL(ELIA)}_{U,U \times \mathsf{Int}}$ *is undecidable.*

4   A Procedure for $\exists^*\forall^*$ Separation Logic in an SMT Solver

This section presents a procedure for the satisfiability of $\exists^*\forall^*\mathsf{SL(E)}_{U,U^k}$ inputs[5]. Our procedure builds upon our previous work [25], which gave a decision procedure for quantifier-free $\mathsf{SL}(T)_{\mathsf{Loc,Data}}$ inputs for theories T where the satisfiability problem for quantifier-free T-constraints is decidable. Like existing approaches for quantified formulas in SMT [13,23], our approach is based on incremental quantifier instantiation based on a stream of candidate models returned by a solver for quantifier-free inputs. Our approach for this fragment exploits the small model property given in Lemma 3 to restrict the set of quantifier instantiations it considers to a finite set.

Figure 1 gives a counterexample-guided approach for establishing the satisfiability of input $\exists \mathbf{x} \forall \mathbf{y} \, \varphi(\mathbf{x}, \mathbf{y})$. We first introduce tuples of fresh constants $\mathbf{k}$ and $\mathbf{e}$ of the same type as $\mathbf{x}$ and $\mathbf{y}$ respectively. Our procedure will be based on finding a set of instantiations of $\forall \mathbf{y} \, \varphi(\mathbf{k}, \mathbf{y})$ that are either collectively unsatisfiable or are satisfiable and entail our input. Then, we construct a set L which

---

[5] The procedure is incorporated into the master branch of the SMT solver CVC4 (https://github.com/CVC4), and can be enabled by command line parameter
`--quant-epr`.

---

solve($\exists \mathbf{x} \forall \mathbf{y}\, \varphi(\mathbf{x}, \mathbf{y})$) where $\mathbf{x} = (x_1, \ldots, x_m)$ and $\mathbf{y} = (y_1, \ldots, y_n)$:

Let $\mathbf{k} = (k_1, \ldots, k_m)$ and $\mathbf{e} = (e_1, \ldots, e_n)$ be fresh constants of the same type as $\mathbf{x}$ and $\mathbf{y}$.
Let $L = L' \cup \{k_1, \ldots, k_m\}$ where L' is a set of fresh constants s.t. $|L'| = |\varphi(\mathbf{x}, \mathbf{y})| + n$.
Return **solve_rec**($\exists \mathbf{x} \forall \mathbf{y}\, \varphi(\mathbf{x}, \mathbf{y}), \emptyset, L$).

solve_rec($\exists \mathbf{x} \forall \mathbf{y}\, \varphi(\mathbf{x}, \mathbf{y}), \Gamma, L$):

1. If Γ is $(\mathsf{SL}, \mathsf{E})$-unsat, return "unsat".
2. Assume $\exists \mathbf{x} \forall \mathbf{y}\, \varphi(\mathbf{x}, \mathbf{y})$ is equivalent to $\exists \mathbf{x} \forall \mathbf{y}\, \varphi_1(\mathbf{x}, \mathbf{y}) \wedge \ldots \wedge \forall \mathbf{y}\, \varphi_p(\mathbf{x}, \mathbf{y})$.

   If $\Gamma_j' = \Gamma \cup \{\neg \varphi_j(\mathbf{k}, \mathbf{e}) \wedge \bigwedge\limits_{i=1}^{n} \bigvee\limits_{t \in L} e_i \approx t\}$ is $(\mathsf{SL}, \mathsf{E})$-unsat for all $j = 1, \ldots, p$, return "sat".
3. Otherwise, let $\mathcal{I}, h \models_{\mathsf{SL}} \Gamma_j'$ for some $j \in \{1, \ldots, p\}$.

   Let $\mathbf{t} = (t_1, \ldots, t_n)$ be such that $e_i^{\mathcal{I}} = t_i^{\mathcal{I}}$ and $t_i \in L$ for each $i = 1, \ldots, n$.
   Return **solve_rec**($\exists \mathbf{x} \forall \mathbf{y}\, \varphi(\mathbf{x}, \mathbf{y}), \Gamma \cup \{\varphi_j(\mathbf{k}, \mathbf{t})\}, L$).

Fig. 1. A counterexample-guided procedure for $\exists^* \forall^* \mathsf{SL}(\mathsf{E})_{U, U^k}$ formulas $\exists \mathbf{x} \forall \mathbf{y}\, \varphi(\mathbf{x}, \mathbf{y})$, where U is an uninterpreted sort in the signature of E.

is the union of constants $\mathbf{k}$ and a set L' of fresh constants whose cardinality is equal to $|\varphi(\mathbf{x}, \mathbf{y})|$ (see Sect. 3.1) plus the number of universal variables n in our input. Conceptually, L is a finite set of terms from which the instantiations of $\mathbf{y}$ in $\forall \mathbf{y}\, \varphi(\mathbf{k}, \mathbf{y})$ can be built.

After constructing L, we call the recursive subprocedure solve_rec on Γ (initially empty) and L. This procedure incrementally adds instances of $\forall \mathbf{y}\, \varphi(\mathbf{k}, \mathbf{y})$ to Γ. In step 1, we first check if Γ is (SL, T)-unsatisfiable using the procedure from [25]. If so, our input is (SL, T)-unsatisfiable. Otherwise, in step 2 we consider the *miniscoped* form of our input $\exists \mathbf{x} \forall \mathbf{y}\, \varphi_1(\mathbf{x}, \mathbf{y}) \wedge \ldots \wedge \forall \mathbf{y}\, \varphi_p(\mathbf{x}, \mathbf{y})$, that is, where quantification over $\mathbf{x}$ is distributed over conjunctions. In the following, we may omit quantification on conjunctions φ_j that do not contain variables from $\mathbf{y}$. Given this formula, for each $j = 1, \ldots, p$, we check the (SL, T)-satisfiability of set Γ_j' containing Γ, the negation of $\forall \mathbf{y}\, \varphi_j(\mathbf{k}, \mathbf{y})$ where $\mathbf{y}$ is replaced by fresh constants $\mathbf{e}$, and a conjunction of constraints that says each e_i must be equal to at least one term in L for $i = 1, \ldots, n$. If Γ_j' is (SL, T)-unsatisfiable for each $j = 1, \ldots, p$, our input is (SL, T)-satisfiable. Otherwise in step 3, given an interpretation $\mathcal{I}$ and heap h satisfying Γ_j', we construct a tuple of terms $\mathbf{t} = (t_1, \ldots, t_n)$ used for instantiating $\forall \mathbf{y}\, \varphi_j(\mathbf{k}, \mathbf{y})$. For each $i = 1, \ldots, n$, we choose t_i to be a term from L whose interpretation is the same as e_i. The existence of such a t_i is guaranteed by the fact that $\mathcal{I}$ satisfies the constraint from Γ_j' that tells us e_i is equal to at least one such term. This selection ensures that instantiations on each iteration are chosen from a finite set of possibilities and are unique. In practice, the procedure terminates, both for unsatisfiable and satisfiable inputs, before considering all $\mathbf{t}$ from L^n for each $\forall \mathbf{y}\, \varphi_j(\mathbf{x}, \mathbf{y})$.

Theorem 6. *Let U be an uninterpreted sort belonging to the signature of* E. *For all $\exists^*\forall^*\mathsf{SL}(\mathsf{E})_{U,U^k}$ formulae ψ of the form $\exists \mathbf{x}\, \forall \mathbf{y}\, \varphi(\mathbf{x}, \mathbf{y})$, $\mathsf{solve}(\psi)$:*

1. *Answers "unsat" only if ψ is* $(\mathsf{SL}, \mathsf{E})$*-unsatisfiable.*
2. *Answers "sat" only if ψ is* $(\mathsf{SL}, \mathsf{E})$*-satisfiable.*
3. *Terminates.*

We discuss a few important details regarding our implementation of the procedure.

Matching Heuristics. When constructing the terms $\mathbf{t}$ for instantiation, it may be the case that $e_i^{\mathcal{I}} = u^{\mathcal{I}}$ for multiple $u \in L$ for some $i \in \{1, \ldots, n\}$. In such cases, the procedure will choose one such u for instantiation. To increase the likelihood of the instantiation being relevant to the satisfiability of our input, we use heuristics for selecting the best possible u among those whose interpretation is equal to e_i in $\mathcal{I}$. In particular, if $e_i^{\mathcal{I}} = u_1^{\mathcal{I}} = u_2^{\mathcal{I}}$, and Γ' contains predicates of the form $e_i \mapsto v$ and $u_1 \mapsto v_1$ for some v, v_1 where $v^{\mathcal{I}} = v_1^{\mathcal{I}}$ but no predicate of the form $u_2 \mapsto v_2$ for some v_2 where $v^{\mathcal{I}} = v_2^{\mathcal{I}}$, then we strictly prefer term u_1 over term u_2 when choosing term t_i for e_i.

Finding Minimal Models. Previous work [26] developed efficient techniques for finding small models for uninterpreted sorts in CVC4. We have found these techniques to be beneficial to the performance of the procedure in Fig. 1. In particular, we use these techniques to find Σ-interpretations $\mathcal{I}$ in $\mathsf{solve\_rec}$ that interpret U as a finite set of minimal size. When combined with the aforementioned matching heuristics, these techniques lead to finding useful instantiations more quickly, since more terms are constrained to be equal to e_i for $i = 1, \ldots, n$ in interpretations $\mathcal{I}$.

Symmetry Breaking. The procedure in Fig. 1 introduces a set of fresh constants L, which in turn introduce the possibility of discovering Σ-interpretations $\mathcal{I}$ that are isomorphic, that is, identical up to renaming of constants in L'. Our procedure adds additional constraints to Γ that do not affect its satisfiability, but reduce the number of isomorphic models. In particular, we consider an ordering $\prec$ on the constants from L', and add constraints that ensure that all models $(\mathcal{I}, h)$ of Γ are such that if $\ell_1^{\mathcal{I}} \notin \mathrm{dom}(h)$, then $\ell_2^{\mathcal{I}} \notin \mathrm{dom}(h)$ for all ℓ_2 such that $\ell_1 \prec \ell_2$.

Example 1. Say we wish to show the validity of the entailment $\mathsf{x} \neq \mathsf{y} \wedge \mathsf{x} \mapsto \mathsf{z} \models_{\mathsf{SL}} \exists \mathsf{u} . \mathsf{x} \mapsto \mathsf{u}$, from the introductory example (Sect. 1), where $\mathsf{x}, \mathsf{y}, \mathsf{z}, \mathsf{u}$ are of sort U of E. This entailment is valid iff the $\exists^*\forall^*\mathsf{SL}(\mathsf{E})_{U,U^k}$ formula $\exists \mathsf{x} \exists \mathsf{y} \exists \mathsf{z} \forall \mathsf{u} . \mathsf{x} \not\approx \mathsf{y} \wedge \mathsf{x} \mapsto \mathsf{z} \wedge \neg \mathsf{x} \mapsto \mathsf{u}$ is $(\mathsf{SL}, \mathsf{E})$-unsatisfiable. A run of the procedure in Fig. 1 on this input constructs tuples $\mathbf{k} = (k_x, k_y, k_z)$ and $\mathbf{e} = (e_u)$, and set $L = \{k_x, k_y, k_z, \ell_1, \ell_2\}$, noting that $|\mathsf{x} \not\approx \mathsf{y} \wedge \mathsf{x} \mapsto \mathsf{z} \wedge \neg \mathsf{x} \mapsto \mathsf{u}| = 1$. We then call $\mathsf{solve\_rec}$ where Γ is initially empty. By miniscoping, our input is equivalent to $\exists \mathsf{x} \exists \mathsf{y} \exists \mathsf{z} . \mathsf{x} \not\approx \mathsf{y} \wedge \mathsf{x} \mapsto \mathsf{z} \wedge \forall \mathsf{u} . \neg \mathsf{x} \mapsto \mathsf{u}$. On the first two recursive calls to $\mathsf{solve\_rec}$, we may add $k_x \not\approx k_y$ and $k_x \mapsto k_z$ to Γ by trivial instantiation of the first two conjuncts. On the third recursive call, Γ is $(\mathsf{SL}, \mathsf{E})$-satisfiable, and we check the satisfiability of:

$$\Gamma' = \{k_x \neq k_y, k_x \mapsto k_z, k_x \mapsto e_u \wedge (e_u \approx k_x \vee e_u \approx k_y \vee e_u \approx k_z \vee e_u \approx \ell_1 \vee e_u \approx \ell_2)\}$$

Since $k_x \mapsto k_z$ and $k_x \mapsto e_u$ are in Γ', all Σ-interpretations $\mathcal{I}$ and heaps h such that $\mathcal{I}, h \models_{\mathsf{SL}} \Gamma'$ are such that $e_u^{\mathcal{I}} = k_z^{\mathcal{I}}$. Since $k_z \in L$, we may choose to add the instantiation $\neg k_x \mapsto k_z$ to Γ, after which Γ is $(\mathsf{SL}, \mathsf{E})$-unsatisfiable on the next recursive call to solve_rec. Thus, our input is $(\mathsf{SL}, \mathsf{E})$-unsatisfiable and the entailment is valid.   ∎

A modified version of the procedure in Fig. 1 can be used for $\exists^*\forall^*\mathsf{SL}(T)_{\mathsf{Loc},\mathsf{Data}}$-satisfiability for theories T beyond equality, and where Loc and Data are not restricted to uninterpreted sorts. Notice that in such cases, we cannot restrict Σ-interpretations $\mathcal{I}$ in solve_rec to interpret each e_i as a member of finite set L, and hence we modify solve_rec to omit the constraint restricting variables in **e** to be equal to a term from L in the check in Step 2. This modification results in a procedure that is sound both for "unsat" and "sat", but is no longer terminating in general. Nevertheless, it may be used as a heuristic for determining $\exists^*\forall^*\mathsf{SL}(T)_{\mathsf{Loc},\mathsf{Data}}$-(un)satisfiability.

5   Experimental Evaluation

We implemented the solve procedure from Fig. 1 within the CVC4 SMT solver[6] (version 1.5 prerelease). This implementation was tested on two kinds of benchmarks: (i) finite unfoldings of inductive predicates, mostly inspired by benchmarks used in the SL-COMP'14 solver competition [27], and (ii) verification conditions automatically generated by applying the weakest precondition calculus of [15] to the program loops in Fig. 2. All experiments were run on a 2.80 GHz Intel(R) Core(TM) i7 CPU machine with 8 MB of cache[7].

```
1: while w ≠ nil do              1: while u ≠ nil do
2:     assert(w.data = c₀)        2:     assert(u.data = c₀)
3:     v := w;                     3:     w := u.next;
4:     w := w.next;                4:     u.next := v;
5:     dispose(v);                 5:     v := u;
6:     do                         6:     u := w;
                                   7:     do
```

$$\textbf{(z)disp}$$
$$\mathsf{list}^0(x) \triangleq \mathsf{emp} \wedge x = \mathsf{nil}$$
$$\mathsf{list}^n(x) \triangleq \exists y . x \mapsto y * \mathsf{list}^{n-1}(y)$$

$$\textbf{(z)rev}$$
$$\mathsf{zlist}^0(x) \triangleq \mathsf{emp} \wedge x = \mathsf{nil}$$
$$\mathsf{zlist}^n(x) \triangleq \exists y . x \mapsto (c_0, y) * \mathsf{zlist}^{n-1}(y)$$

Fig. 2. Program loops

We compared our implementation with the results of applying the CVC4 decision procedure for the quantifier-free fragment of SL [25] to a variant of the

[6] Available at http://cvc4.cs.nyu.edu/web/.

[7] The CVC4 binary and examples used in these experiments are available at http:// cs.uiowa.edu/~ajreynol/VMCAI2017-seplog-epr.

benchmarks, obtained by manual quantifier instantiation, as follows. Consider checking the validity of the entailment $\exists \mathbf{x} \cdot \phi(\mathbf{x}) \models_{\mathsf{SL}} \exists \mathbf{y} \cdot \psi(\mathbf{y})$, which is equivalent to the unsatisfiability of the formula $\exists \mathbf{x} \forall \mathbf{y} \cdot \phi(\mathbf{x}) \wedge \neg \psi(\mathbf{y})$. We first check the satisfiability of ϕ. If ϕ is not satisfiable, the entailment holds trivially, so let us assume that ϕ has a model. Second, we check the satisfiability of $\phi \wedge \psi$. Again, if this is unsatisfiable, the entailment cannot hold, because there exists a model of ϕ which is not a model of ψ. Else, if $\phi \wedge \psi$ has a model, we add an equality $x = y$ for each pair of variables $(x, y) \in \mathbf{x} \times \mathbf{y}$ that are mapped to the same term in this model, the result being a conjunction $E(\mathbf{x}, \mathbf{y})$ of equalities. Finally, we check the satisfiability of the formula $\phi \wedge \neg \psi \wedge E$. If this formula is unsatisfiable, the entailment is valid, otherwise, the check is inconclusive. The times in Table 1 correspond to checking satisfiability of $\exists \mathbf{x} \forall \mathbf{y} \cdot \phi(\mathbf{x}) \wedge \neg \psi(\mathbf{y})$ using the solve procedure (Fig. 1), compared to checking satisfiability of $\phi \wedge \neg \psi \wedge E$, where E is manually generated.

In the first set of experiments (Table 1) we have considered inductive predicates commonly used as verification benchmarks [27]. Here we check the validity of the entailment between lhs and rhs, where both predicates are unfolded $n = 1, 2, 3, 4, 8$ times. The entailment between pos_2^1 and neg_4^1 is skipped because it is not valid (since the negated formula is satisfiable, we cannot generate the manual instantiation).

The second set of experiments considers the verification conditions of the forms $\varphi \Rightarrow \mathsf{wp}(\mathsf{l}, \phi)$ and $\varphi \Rightarrow \mathsf{wp}^n(\mathsf{l}, \phi)$, where $\mathsf{wp}(\mathsf{l}, \phi)$ denotes the weakest precondition of the SL formula ϕ with respect to the sequence of statements l, and $\mathsf{wp}^n(\mathsf{l}, \phi) = \mathsf{wp}(\mathsf{l}, \ldots \mathsf{wp}(\mathsf{l}, \mathsf{wp}(\mathsf{l}, \phi)) \ldots)$ denotes the iterative application of the weakest precondition n times in a row. We consider the loops depicted in Fig. 2, where, for each loop l, we consider the variant zl as well, which tests that the data values contained within the memory cells are equal to a constant c_0 of sort Loc, by the assertions on line 2. The postconditions are specified by finite unfoldings of the inductive predicates list and zlist.

We observed that, compared to checking the manual instantiation, the fully automated solver was less than $0.5\,\mathrm{s}$ slower on 72% of the test cases, and less than $1\,\mathrm{s}$ slower on 79% of the test cases. The automated solver experienced 3 timeouts, where the manual instantiation succeeds (for $\widehat{\mathsf{tree}}$ vs. tree with $n = 8$, $\widehat{\mathsf{ts}}$ vs. ts with $n = 3$, and $\mathsf{list}^n(u) * \mathsf{list}^0(v)$ vs. $\mathsf{wp}^n(\mathbf{rev}, u = \mathsf{nil} \wedge \mathsf{list}^n(v))$ with $n = 8$). These timeouts are caused by the first call to the quantifier-free SL decision procedure, which fails to produce a model in less than $300\,\mathrm{s}$ (time not accounted for in the manually produced instance of the problem).

6   Conclusions and Future Work

We present theoretical and practical results for the existence of effective decision procedures for the fragment of Separation Logic obtained by restriction of formulae to quantifier prefixes in the set $\exists^* \forall^*$. The theoretical results range from undecidability, when the set of memory locations is taken to be the set of integers and linear arithmetic constraints are allowed, to PSPACE-completeness, when

Table 1. Experimental results

lhs	rhs		$n=1$	$n=2$	$n=3$	$n=4$	$n=8$
Unfoldings of inductive predicates							
$\widehat{\mathsf{ls}}(x,y)\triangleq\mathsf{emp}\wedge x=y\vee$ $\exists z . x\neq y\wedge x\mapsto z*\widehat{\mathsf{ls}}(z,y)$	$\mathsf{ls}(x,y)\triangleq\mathsf{emp}\wedge x=y\vee$ $\exists z . x\mapsto z*\mathsf{ls}(z,y)$	solve	<0.01 s	0.02 s	0.03 s	0.05 s	0.21 s
		manual	<0.01 s	<0.01 s	<0.01 s	<0.01 s	<0.01 s
$\widetilde{\mathsf{tree}}(x)\triangleq\mathsf{emp}\wedge x=\mathsf{nil}\vee$ $\exists l\exists r . l\neq r\wedge x\mapsto(l,r)*\mathsf{tree}(l)*$ $\mathsf{tree}(r)$	$\mathsf{tree}(x)\triangleq\mathsf{emp}\wedge x=\mathsf{nil}\vee$ $\exists l\exists r . x\mapsto(l,r)*\mathsf{tree}(l)*\mathsf{tree}(r)$	solve	<0.01 s	0.04 s	1.43 s	23.42 s	>300 s
		manual	<0.01 s	<0.01 s	<0.01 s	<0.01 s	0.09 s
$\widetilde{\mathsf{ts}}(x,a)\triangleq\mathsf{emp}\wedge x=\mathsf{nil}\vee$ $\exists l\exists r . x\neq y\wedge x\mapsto$ $(l,r)*\widetilde{\mathsf{ts}}(l,y)*\mathsf{tree}(r)\vee$ $\exists l\exists r . x\neq y\wedge x\mapsto$ $(l,r)*\mathsf{tree}(l)*\widetilde{\mathsf{ts}}(r,y)$	$\mathsf{ts}(x,a)\triangleq\mathsf{emp}\wedge x=\mathsf{nil}\vee$ $\exists l\exists r . \wedge x\mapsto(l,r)*\mathsf{ts}(l,y)*$ $\mathsf{tree}(r)\vee$ $\exists l\exists r . \wedge x\mapsto(l,r)*\mathsf{tree}(l)*$ $\mathsf{ts}(r,y)$	solve	<0.01 s	0.81 s	>300 s	>300 s	>300 s
		manual	<0.01 s	0.03 s	103.89 s	>300 s	>300 s
$\mathsf{pos}_1(x,a)\triangleq x\mapsto a\vee\exists y\exists b .$ $x\mapsto a*\mathsf{pos}_1(y,b)$	$\mathsf{neg}_1(x,a)\triangleq\neg x\mapsto a\vee\exists y\exists b .$ $x\mapsto a*\mathsf{neg}_1(y,b)$	solve	0.34 s	0.01 s	0.31 s	0.76 s	21.19 s
		manual	0.04 s	0.05 s	0.08 s	0.12 s	0.53 s
$\mathsf{pos}_1(x,a)\triangleq x\mapsto a\vee\exists y\exists b .$ $x\mapsto a*\mathsf{pos}_1(y,b)$	$\mathsf{neg}_2(x,a)\triangleq x\mapsto a\vee\exists y\exists b .$ $\neg x\mapsto a*\mathsf{neg}_2(y,b)$	solve	0.03 s	0.12 s	0.23 s	0.46 s	3.60 s
		manual	0.05 s	0.08 s	0.08 s	0.12 s	0.54 s
$\mathsf{pos}_2(x,a)\triangleq x\mapsto a\vee\exists y .$ $x\mapsto a*\mathsf{pos}_2(a,y)$	$\mathsf{neg}_3(x,a)\triangleq\neg x\mapsto a\vee\exists y .$ $x\mapsto a*\mathsf{neg}_3(a,y)$	solve	0.04 s	0.13 s	0.28 s	0.48 s	4.20 s
		manual	0.01 s	0.03 s	0.05 s	0.09 s	0.45 s
$\mathsf{pos}_2(x,a)\triangleq x\mapsto a\vee\exists y .$ $x\mapsto a*\mathsf{pos}_2(a,y)$	$\mathsf{neg}_4(x,a)\triangleq x\mapsto a\vee\exists y .$ $\neg x\mapsto a*\mathsf{neg}_4(a,y)$	solve	—	0.08 s	0.15 s	0.26 s	1.33 s
		manual	—	0.03 s	0.06 s	0.09 s	0.46 s
Verification conditions							
$\mathsf{list}^n(w)$	$\mathsf{wp}(\mathbf{disp},\mathsf{list}^{n-1}(w))$	solve	0.01 s	0.03 s	0.08 s	0.19 s	1.47 s
		manual	<0.01 s	0.01 s	0.02 s	0.05 s	0.26 s
$\mathsf{list}^n(w)$	$\mathsf{wp}^n(\mathbf{disp},\mathsf{emp}\wedge w=\mathsf{nil})$	solve	0.01 s	0.06 s	0.17 s	0.53 s	7.08 s
		manual	<0.01 s	0.02 s	0.08 s	0.14 s	2.26 s
$\mathsf{zlist}^n(w)$	$\mathsf{wp}(\mathbf{zdisp},\mathsf{zlist}^{n-1}(w))$	solve	0.04 s	0.05 s	0.09 s	0.19 s	1.25 s
		manual	<0.01 s	0.01 s	0.02 s	0.04 s	0.29 s
$\mathsf{zlist}^n(w)$	$\mathsf{wp}^n(\mathbf{zdisp},\mathsf{emp}\wedge w=\mathsf{nil})$	solve	0.01 s	0.10 s	0.32 s	0.87 s	11.88 s
		manual	0.01 s	0.02 s	0.07 s	0.15 s	2.20 s
$\mathsf{list}^n(u)*\mathsf{list}^0(v)$	$\mathsf{wp}(\mathbf{rev},\mathsf{list}^{n-1}(u)*\mathsf{list}^1(v))$	solve	0.38 s	0.06 s	0.11 s	0.16 s	0.56 s
		manual	0.07 s	0.03 s	0.07 s	0.11 s	0.43 s
$\mathsf{list}^n(u)*\mathsf{list}^0(v)$	$\mathsf{wp}^n(\mathbf{rev},u=\mathsf{nil}\wedge\mathsf{list}^n(v))$	solve	0.38 s	0.07 s	0.30 s	68.68 s	>300 s
		manual	0.08 s	0.06 s	0.11 s	0.23 s	1.79 s
$\mathsf{zlist}^n(u)*\mathsf{zlist}^0(v)$	$\mathsf{wp}(\mathbf{zrev},\mathsf{zlist}^{n-1}(u)*$ $\mathsf{zlist}^1(v))$	solve	0.22 s	0.07 s	0.15 s	0.21 s	0.75 s
		manual	0.04 s	0.02 s	0.04 s	0.06 s	0.31 s
$\mathsf{zlist}^n(u)*\mathsf{zlist}^0(v)$	$\mathsf{wp}^n(\mathbf{zrev},u=\mathsf{nil}\wedge\mathsf{zlist}^n(v))$	solve	0.23 s	0.09 s	0.17 s	0.30 s	2.06 s
		manual	0.04 s	0.02 s	0.05 s	0.09 s	0.48 s

locations and data in the cells belong to an uninterpreted sort, equipped with equality only. We have implemented a decision procedure for the latter case in the CVC4 SMT solver, using an effective counterexample-driven instantiation of the universal quantifiers. The procedure is shown to be sound, complete and termination is guaranteed when the input belongs to a decidable fragment of SL.

As future work, we aim at refining the decidability chart for $\exists^*\forall^*\mathsf{SL}(T)_{\mathsf{Loc},\mathsf{Data}}$, by considering the case where the locations are interpreted as integers, with weaker arithmetics, such as sets of difference bounds, or octagonal constraints. These results are likely to extend the application range of our tool, to e.g. solvers working on SL with inductive definitions and data constraints. The current implementation should also benefit from improvements of the underlying quantifier-free SL and set theory solvers.

References

1. Albargouthi, A., Berdine, J., Cook, B., Kincaid, Z.: Spatial interpolants. In: Vitek, J. (ed.) ESOP 2015. LNCS, vol. 9032, pp. 634–660. Springer, Heidelberg (2015). doi:10.1007/978-3-662-46669-8_26
2. Barrett, C., Conway, C.L., Deters, M., Hadarean, L., Jovanović, D., King, T., Reynolds, A., Tinelli, C.: CVC4. In: Gopalakrishnan, G., Qadeer, S. (eds.) CAV 2011. LNCS, vol. 6806, pp. 171–177. Springer, Heidelberg (2011). doi:10.1007/978-3-642-22110-1_14
3. Baumgartner, P., Fuchs, A., Tinelli, C.: Implementing the model evolution calculus. Int. J. Artif. Intell. Tools **15**(1), 21–52 (2006)
4. Brochenin, R., Demri, S., Lozes, E.: On the almighty wand. Inf. Comput. **211**, 106–137 (2012)
5. Brotherston, J., Simpson, A.: Sequent calculi for induction and infinite descent. J. Logic Comput. **21**(6), 1177–1216 (2011)
6. Calcagno, C., Distefano, D.: Infer: an automatic program verifier for memory safety of C programs. In: Bobaru, M., Havelund, K., Holzmann, G.J., Joshi, R. (eds.) NFM 2011. LNCS, vol. 6617, pp. 459–465. Springer, Heidelberg (2011). doi:10.1007/978-3-642-20398-5_33
7. Calcagno, C., Yang, H., O'Hearn, P.W.: Computability and complexity results for a spatial assertion language for data structures. In: Hariharan, R., Vinay, V., Mukund, M. (eds.) FSTTCS 2001. LNCS, vol. 2245, pp. 108–119. Springer, Heidelberg (2001). doi:10.1007/3-540-45294-X_10
8. Demri, S., Deters, M.: Two-variable separation logic and its inner circle. ACM Trans. Comput. Logic **16**(2) (2015). Article no. 15
9. Demri, S., Galmiche, D., Larchey-Wendling, D., Méry, D.: Separation logic with one quantified variable. In: Hirsch, E.A., Kuznetsov, S.O., Pin, J.É., Vereshchagin, N.K. (eds.) CSR 2014. LNCS, vol. 8476, pp. 125–138. Springer, Heidelberg (2014). doi:10.1007/978-3-319-06686-8_10
10. Dudka, K., Peringer, P., Vojnar, T.: Predator: a practical tool for checking manipulation of dynamic data structures using separation logic. In: Gopalakrishnan, G., Qadeer, S. (eds.) CAV 2011. LNCS, vol. 6806, pp. 372–378. Springer, Heidelberg (2011). doi:10.1007/978-3-642-22110-1_29

11. Galmiche, D., Méry, D.: Tableaux and resource graphs for separation logic. J. Logic Comput. **20**(1), 189–231 (2010)
12. Ganzinger, H., Hagen, G., Nieuwenhuis, R., Oliveras, A., Tinelli, C.: DPLL(T): fast decision procedures. In: Alur, R., Peled, D.A. (eds.) CAV 2004. LNCS, vol. 3114, pp. 175–188. Springer, Berlin (2004). doi:10.1007/978-3-540-27813-9_14
13. Ge, Y., Moura, L.: Complete instantiation for quantified formulas in satisfiabiliby modulo theories. In: Bouajjani, A., Maler, O. (eds.) CAV 2009. LNCS, vol. 5643, pp. 306–320. Springer, Heidelberg (2009). doi:10.1007/978-3-642-02658-4_25
14. Halpern, J.Y.: Presburger arithmetic with unary predicates is π_1^1 complete. J. Symbolic Logic **56**(2), 637–642 (1991)
15. Ishtiaq, S.S., O'Hearn, P.W.: Bi as an assertion language for mutable data structures. ACM SIGPLAN Not. **36**, 14–26 (2001)
16. Korovin, K.: iProver - an instantiation-based theorem prover for first-order logic (system description). In: Proceedings of 4th International Joint Conference on Automated Reasoning, IJCAR 2008, Sydney, Australia, 12–15 August 2008, pp. 292–298 (2008)
17. Lewis, H.R.: Complexity results for classes of quantificational formulas. J. Comput. Syst. Sci. **21**(3), 317–353 (1980)
18. Matiyasevich, Y.: Enumerable sets are diophantine. J. Sovietic Math. **11**, 354–358 (1970)
19. Nguyen, H.H., Chin, W.-N.: Enhancing program verification with lemmas. In: Gupta, A., Malik, S. (eds.) CAV 2008. LNCS, vol. 5123, pp. 355–369. Springer, Heidelberg (2008). doi:10.1007/978-3-540-70545-1_34
20. Piskac, R., de Moura, L.M., Bjørner, N.: Deciding effectively propositional logic using DPLL and substitution sets. J. Autom. Reasoning **44**(4), 401–424 (2010)
21. Piskac, R., Wies, T., Zufferey, D.: Automating separation logic using SMT. In: Sharygina, N., Veith, H. (eds.) CAV 2013. LNCS, vol. 8044, pp. 773–789. Springer, Heidelberg (2013). doi:10.1007/978-3-642-39799-8_54
22. Piskac, R., Wies, T., Zufferey, D.: Automating Separation Logic with Trees and Data. In: Biere, A., Bloem, R. (eds.) CAV 2014. LNCS, vol. 8559, pp. 711–728. Springer, Heidelberg (2014). doi:10.1007/978-3-319-08867-9_47
23. Reynolds, A., Deters, M., Kuncak, V., Tinelli, C., Barrett, C.W.: Counter example-guided quantifier instantiation for synthesis in SMT. In: Proceedings of Computer Aided Verification - 27th International Conference, CAV 2015, San Francisco, CA, USA, 18–24 July 2015, Part II, pp. 198–216 (2015)
24. Reynolds, A., Iosif, R., Serban, C.: Reasoning in the Bernays-Schoenfinkel-Ramsey fragment of separation logic. CoRR abs/1610.04707 (2016). http://arxiv.org/abs/1610.04707
25. Reynolds, A., Iosif, R., Serban, C., King, T.: A decision procedure for separation logic in SMT. In: Proceedings of 14th International Symposium on Automated Technology for Verification and Analysis, ATVA 2016, Chiba, Japan, 17–20 October 2016, pp. 244–261 (2016)
26. Reynolds, A., Tinelli, C., Goel, A., Krstić, S.: Finite model finding in SMT. In: Sharygina, N., Veith, H. (eds.) CAV 2013. LNCS, vol. 8044, pp. 640–655. Springer, Heidelberg (2013). doi:10.1007/978-3-642-39799-8_42
27. Sighireanu, M., Cok, D.: Report on SL-COMP 2014. J. Satisfiability Boolean Model. Comput. **1** (2014)

28. Toubhans, A., Chang, B.-Y.E., Rival, X.: An abstract domain combinator for separately conjoining memory abstractions. In: Müller-Olm, M., Seidl, H. (eds.) SAS 2014. LNCS, vol. 8723, pp. 285–301. Springer, Heidelberg (2014). doi:10.1007/978-3-319-10936-7_18
29. Voigt, M., Weidenbach, C.: Bernays-Schönfinkel-Ramsey with simple bounds is nexptime-complete. CoRR abs/1501.07209 (2015)
30. Yang, H.: Local reasoning for stateful programs. Ph.D. thesis, University of Illinois at Urbana-Champaign (2001)

Finding Relevant Templates via the Principal Component Analysis

Yassamine Seladji[(✉)]

STIC Laboratory, University of Tlemcen, Tlemcen, Algeria
yassamine.seladji@gmail.com

Abstract. The polyhedral model is widely used for the static analysis of programs, thanks to its expressiveness but it is also time consuming. To cope with this problem, weak-polyhedral analysis have been developed which offer a good trade off between expressiveness and efficiency. Some of these analysis are based on templates which fixed the form of the program's invariant. These templates are defined statically at the beginning of the analysis, without taking into account the dynamic of programs. Finding good templates is a difficult problem. In this article, we present a method that uses the Principal Component analysis to compute an interesting template. We demonstrate the relevancy of the obtained templates on several benchmarks.

1 Introduction

Static analysis is used to verify some safety properties on programs, like for example the absence of runtime errors. Static analysis uses the (concrete) program semantic function F to define a program invariant X, such that $F(X) = X$. This represents the set of reachable program states, but is however not computable. To deal with that, an over-approximation is introduced using abstract interpretation [6,8]. The main idea is to define a new (abstract) semantic function $F^{\sharp}$ that computes an abstract program invariant that includes the concrete one. This inclusion guarantees the safety of the result but not its accuracy: the larger the over-approximation is, the higher the probability to add false alarms. This over-approximation is due to the type of elements manipulated by $F^{\sharp}$; the most common and expressive abstraction is to represent the reachable states of numerical programs as convex polyhedra [7], that represent the linear relations existing between program variables. This is known as the polyhedra abstract domain [7]. The applicability of this analysis is faced with the compromise between precision and complexity: the standard Kleene algorithms (union, intersection) for computing with polyhedra are as precise as possible, but are mainly exponential in the number of program variables. To deal with that, a lot of effort have been done by the researchers in the field to reduce this complexity and find a good trade-off between expressiveness and efficiency. A lot of domains have been developed, known as the weakly relational abstract domains [11,14,16,20,21], as for example octagons [16], templates [20] and zonotopes [11] abstract domains. These domains allow to express only a certain kind of linear relations between

© Springer International Publishing AG 2017
A. Bouajjani and D. Monniaux (Eds.): VMCAI 2017, LNCS 10145, pp. 483–499, 2017.
DOI: 10.1007/978-3-319-52234-0_26

variables: for example, the octagon abstract domain encodes relations of the kind $\pm x \pm y \leq c$ for $c \in \mathbb{R}$. Other domains [20,21] use templates to express relations between variables. In general, these templates are fixed by users at the beginning of the analysis. This technique does not take into account the dynamic of programs. The template polyhedral domain presented in [19,20] is defined using templates. These templates are arbitrary fixed and they represent linear expressions on the left hand sides of polyhedra constraints. The goal of the program analysis is to determine constants on the right hand sides of the corresponding constraints. So that forms a fixed point under the program's semantics. Indeed, the entire constraints form program invariants. This analysis has been improved in [5] by using parametrized templates. In these specific templates, the left hand side is a fixed linear expression where the right one is a parametrized linear expression. The corresponding parametrized constraint is of the form $x_1 - x_2 \leq ax_3 + bx_4 + c$ wherein $x_1, \ldots, x_4$ are program variables and a, b, c are unknown parameters. These parameters will be computed by the analysis. This technique partially addresses the problem of how to define dynamically relevant templates to improve the polyhedral analysis.

In [21], authors define an abstract domain based on support functions. The corresponding analysis uses templates, which represent a set of directions uniformly distributed on the unit sphere. The analysis can be done in a linear time and its results can be very close to the one obtained using the polyhedral analysis, in the case where the templates are well chosen. Indeed, the analysis in [21] computes the templates abstraction of the least fixed point obtained using the polyhedral analysis. Which means that the accuracy of this analysis depends strongly on the chosen templates.

Finding good templates in a dynamic way is certainly difficult and still an open problem. In this paper, we propose a novel idea to help the definition of relevant templates by taking into account the dynamics of programs. For that, we use statistical tools, known as *Principal Component Analysis* (or PCA [13]). The PCA are also used to approximate the reachable sets for hybrid systems. In [4], authors use PCA to compute the constraints of the polytopes that overapproximate the reachable sets. And in [23], the PCA are used to find the orientations of the rectangular approximations.

For this work, we were inspired from the work of Amato et al [2], where PCA are used to refine the box abstract domain by changing the axis in which boxes are defined.

The interesting idea in using the PCA is that the principal components computed by the PCA can be seen as an interesting choice of templates, in which the variances of the used data is taken into account. In our case, the definition of these data is very important. They should help us to guess the shape of the analysis result. This is discussed later.

In this paper, we combine our technique with the analysis presented in [21], to show how our method can improve such analysis.

This article is organized as follows. First of all, to give an intuition of the idea, we apply it on a simple example in Sect. 2. Section 3 introduces the important backgrounds. In Sect. 4, we present our main contribution, while in Sect. 5 we show some experimental results.

2   Idea by Example

Considering the linear filter given in Fig. 1. To apply the PCA, we make the choice to use as data the vertices of the polyhedron obtained using the polyhedral analysis on this filter. We take the polyhedron obtained in the 5th Kleene iteration. We make this choice because our relevant templates should take into account the shape of the polyhedron and not the shape of the whole execution traces. Now, we apply the PCA on the obtained set of points. Intuitively The PCA gives a mean direction to the considered set of points (here the vertices of our polyhedron). The result is given in Fig. 2, where the blue points are the vertices of the polyhedron obtained in the 5th Kleene iteration. The principal component is represented by the bold direction where the dashed one represents its perpendicular one. These directions are added to the set of template, noted Δ_{PCA}. This is not enough to build a relevant Δ_{PCA} set. Therefore, the PCA is able to sort out the points of the most influential to the least influential in the PCA computation. We use this specification to remove $n \in \mathbb{N}$ points that mostly influence the computation of the previous principal components. Then, we apply the PCA again on the new set of points, and add the obtained principal components to Δ_{PCA}. This technique is iterated $t \in \mathbb{N}$ times. To obtain Δ_{PCA} with a big cardinality.

In Fig. 3, we show the directions obtained in the different iterations, such that in each sub-figure we present the principal components obtained using a reduced set of points. Note that, in each step we obtain two principal components, which represent the 2 axes of the 2-dimensional space.

```
double input() {
        double u = 10.0;
        double l = 0.0;
        return ( rand()/(double)RAND_MAX ) * (u-l) + l;
}
int main() {
        double xn, yn, ynm1, ynm2;
        xn=xnm1=xnm2=yn=ynm1=ynm2=0;
        while (true) {
          yn = xn + 0.5*ynm1 - 0.45*ynm2;
          ynm2=ynm1,
          ynm1=yn;
          xn = input();
        }
        return 0;
}
```

Fig. 1. The body of the linear filter uses as an example.

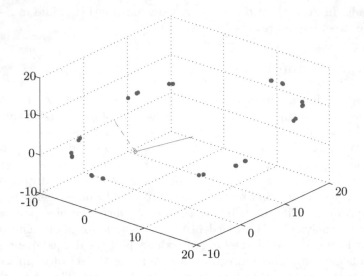

Fig. 2. The result obtained using the vertices set of points. (Color figure online)

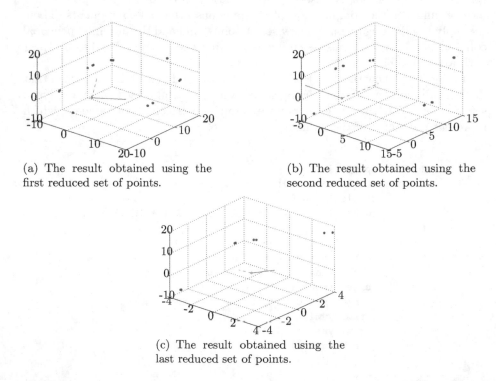

(a) The result obtained using the first reduced set of points.

(b) The result obtained using the second reduced set of points.

(c) The result obtained using the last reduced set of points.

Fig. 3. The principal components obtained using different subsets of the set of points generated for the introductory example. These results are computed using PCA.

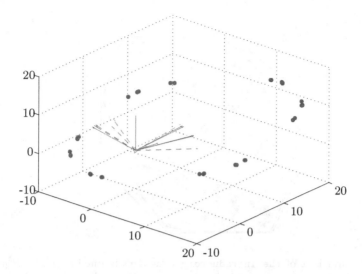

Fig. 4. The directions generated using PCA on the introductory example.

In this example, we choose to take 20 directions generated using PCA, which are given in Fig. 4. In this direction set, we also added the orthonormal directions i.e. $\pm X$ for each variable X, and for each direction d given by the PCA, we added $-d$ to have a better coverage of the space. Thus, we use Δ_{PCA} to analyze the program of Fig. 1 using the analysis in [21], noted $\mathbb{P}^{\sharp}_{\Delta}$. The analysis terminates after 2.784 s. The obtained invariant is given in Fig. 5. The polyhedron obtained with the $\mathbb{P}^{\sharp}_{\Delta}$ analysis using PCA templates is closer to the result of the polyhedral analysis than the one obtained with the $\mathbb{P}^{\sharp}_{\Delta}$ analysis using only orthogonal directions.

3 Background

In this article, we are interested in computing a relevant template that allows to improve the corresponding analysis. This template fixes the linear relations between the program's variables. So, it influences the quality of the program's invariants. We denote this template by Δ. In this section, we start by presenting the abstract domain based on support function, noted by $\mathbb{P}^{\sharp}_{\Delta}$. The $\mathbb{P}^{\sharp}_{\Delta}$ will be combined with Δ to show its relevancy. Then, we present the theoretical framework of the PCA (Principal Component Analysis) The tool used to compute the template Δ

3.1 Weak-Polyhedral Analysis Based on Support Function

The Weak-polyhedra abstract domain presented in [21] is based on support function [12]. This domain is an abstraction of convex polyhedra over $\mathbb{R}^n$, where n is the number of variables of the program being analyzed. We denote by $\mathbb{P}^{\sharp}_{\Delta}$ the

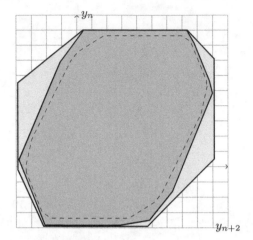

Fig. 5. The invariant of **the introductory example** obtained with the $\mathbb{P}_\Delta^\sharp$ analysis using PCA directions is given with the dark polyhedron, the light polyhedron is the one obtained with the $\mathbb{P}_\Delta^\sharp$ analysis using orthogonal directions and the dashed one is the 200th Kleene iterates obtained using polyhedra abstract domain.

abstract domain of convex polyhedra over $\mathbb{R}^n$. The lattice definition is closed to the lattice of the Template abstract domain [20]. $\mathbb{P}_\Delta^\sharp$ is parametrized by a finite set of directions $\Delta = \{d_1, \dots, d_l\}$. Where directions in Δ are uniformly distributed on the unit sphere, noted B^n. The definition of $\mathbb{P}_\Delta^\sharp$ is given in Definition 1.

Definition 1. *Let $\Delta \subseteq B^n$ be the set of directions. We define $\mathbb{P}_\Delta^\sharp$ as the set of all functions from Δ to $\mathbb{R}_\infty$, i.e. $\mathbb{P}_\Delta^\sharp = \Delta \to \mathbb{R}_\infty$. We denote $\perp_\Delta$ (resp. $\top_\Delta$) the function such that $\forall d \in \Delta, \perp_\Delta(d) = -\infty$ (resp. $\top_\Delta(d) = +\infty$).*

For each $\Omega \in \mathbb{P}_\Delta^\sharp$, we write $\Omega(d)$ the value of Ω in direction $d \in \Delta$. Intuitively, Ω is a support function with finite domain.

The abstraction and concretization functions of $\mathbb{P}_\Delta^\sharp$ are defined in Definition 2.

Definition 2. *Let $\Delta \subseteq B^n$ be the set of directions.*
We define the concretization function $\gamma_\Delta : \mathbb{P}_\Delta^\sharp \to \mathbb{P}$ by:

$$\forall \Omega \in \mathbb{P}_\Delta^\sharp, \ \gamma_\Delta(\Omega) = \bigcap_{d \in \Delta} \{x \in \mathbb{R}^n, <x, d> \leq \Omega(d)\} .$$

where, $<x, d>$ is the scalar product of x by the direction d.
The abstraction function $\alpha_\Delta : \mathbb{P} \to \mathbb{P}_\Delta^\sharp$ is defined by:

$$\forall P \in \mathbb{P}, \alpha_\Delta(P) = \begin{cases} \perp & \text{if } P = \emptyset \\ \top & \text{if } P = \mathbb{R}^n \\ \lambda d. \ \delta_P(d) & \text{otherwise} \end{cases} .$$

where, $\delta_P(d)$ is the support function of the polyhedron P *in the direction d, and* $\mathbb{P}$ *represents the polyhedra abstract domain.*

Note that, the concretization of an abstract element of $\mathbb{P}_\Delta^\sharp$ is a polyhedron defined by the intersection of half-spaces, where each one is characterized by its normal vector $d \in \Delta$ and the coefficient $\Omega(d)$. The abstraction function on the other side is the restriction of the support function of the polyhedron on the set of directions Δ. The order structure of $\mathbb{P}_\Delta^\sharp$ is defined using properties of support functions [12].

The static analysis of a program consists in computing the least fixed point of a monotone map. To do so, the most used method is Kleene Algorithm. We combine Kleene algorithm and the $\mathbb{P}_\Delta^\sharp$ abstract domain to perform the analysis. For that, We consider loops of the form:

```
while(C)
  X=AX+b;
```

We suppose that A is a real matrix, b may be a set of real values, given as a polyhedra P_b, and C is a guard. Such loops include for example linear filters in which P_b represents the possible values of the new input at each loop iteration. We assume that the program variables belong initially to the polyhedron P_0. Using properties of support function in the case of loops without guard, we can define the abstract element obtained in the ith Kleene iteration as follows:

$$\forall d \in \Delta,\, \Omega_i(d) = \max\Big(\delta_{P_0}(d),\, \max_{j\in[1,i]}\big(\delta_{P_0}(A^{Tj}d) + \sum_{k=1}^{j} \delta_{P_b}(A^{T(k-1)}d)\big)\Big) \qquad (1)$$

This formulas allows us to define a special version of Kleene algorithm. The obtained algorithm has a polynomial complexity in the number of iterations and linear in the number of directions in Δ. In addition, its result is as accurate as possible: at each iteration, we have that $\Omega_i = \alpha_\Delta(P_i)$, such that Ω_i (resp. P_i) is the result of the ith Kleene iteration using the $\mathbb{P}_\Delta^\sharp$ (respectively the polyhedra abstract domain). So $\Omega_\infty = \alpha_\Delta(P_\infty)$, with Ω_∞ is the fixed point obtained in the $\mathbb{P}_\Delta^\sharp$ analysis and P_∞ is the one obtained using polyhedra domain. This new version of Kleene algorithm is also generalized to the case of loops with guard and non-linear loops [21].

3.2   The Principal Component Analysis (PCA)

The Principal Component Analysis (PCA) [17,22,24] is a statistical tool. It is widely used to extract relevant informations from a complex data set by reducing its dimensionality.

For example, PCA is commonly used for analyzing data, which are constructed by considering multiple measurements (age, salary, children, ...) from a sample of population. The number of measurement types is the dimension of data. Let $n \in \mathbb{N}$ be the number of the considered measurement types, they can be represented as a set of points in an n-dimensional space using the orthonormal basis. PCA computes a new orthogonal coordinate system that better expresses

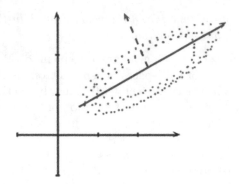

Fig. 6. Te principal component (blue axis) for a given set of points (red points) (Color figure online)

these points. *What does best express the points mean?* It means that the axis where the points (variables) are most spread out when projected onto it, i.e. the new axis maximize the variance of the projection of the initial points. This is illustrated in Fig. 6, where the axis in blue represent the principal components of the red set of points.

The PCA uses the notion of covariance, which is useful to find out how much the dimensions vary from the mean with respect to each other. The covariance is always measured between 2 dimensions. Its definition is given in Definition 3.

Definition 3. *Let X and Y be two measurements and $\forall i \in \mathbb{N}$ let x_i and y_i be, respectively, the corresponding data. The covariance formulas between X and Y, noted $cov(X, Y)$, is given as follow:*

$$cov(X, Y) = \frac{\sum_{i=1}^{n}(x_i - \bar{X})(y_i - \bar{Y})}{(n - 1)}$$

with, $\bar{X}$ and $\bar{Y}$ represent, respectively, the mean of X and Y.

In the case where we have more than two dimensions, we need to compute the covariance between each pair of measurements (dimensions). In fact, for an n-dimensional data set, we should calculate $\frac{n!}{(n-2)!-2}$ different covariance values. These values are putted in a covariance matrix, noted C. C is an $n \times n$ matrix, where n is the dimensions of the data set, such that, $\forall i, j \in \mathbb{N}$, $C_{ij} = cov(X, Y)$ with X is the dimension of the ith row and Y is the dimension of the jth column. To illustrate this idea, let us take an example of covariance matrix for an imaginary 3 dimensional data set X, Y and Z. The corresponding covariance matrix is calculated as follow:

$$C = \begin{pmatrix} cov(X, X) & cov(X, Y) & cov(X, Z) \\ cov(Y, X) & cov(Y, Y) & cov(Y, Z) \\ cov(Z, X) & cov(Z, Y) & cov(Z, Z) \end{pmatrix}$$

We note that, below the main diagonal, the covariance value is between one of the dimensions and itself, which represents the variance of this dimension. We have also that $cov(X, Y) = cov(Y, X)$, so the matrix is symmetrical about the main diagonal.

In the next step, we need to compute the eigenvectors and eigenvalues of the obtained covariance matrix. Note that the covariance matrix is square, so their eigenvectors and eigenvalues exist and can be computed by using for example the Singular Value Decomposition (SVD) [15]. These are rather important, as they tell us useful information about our data set. The obtained eigenvectors allow us to extract lines that characterise data. So, the eigenvector with the highest eigenvalue is the **principle component** of the data set. It represents the most significant relationship between the data dimensions. So, using the eigenvalues, the eigenvectors can be ordered from highest to lowest, which represents the components in order of significant. Note that, the lengths of the eigenvectors should be 1. In the set of the obtained eigenvectors, we have for each eigenvector its perpendicular (orthogonal) one. In Fig. 6, the blue axe represents the principal component obtained by applying PCA on the red points, where the dashed blue axis is its perpendicular.

The PCA is represented by the set of all the obtained eigenvectors. Afterwards, data can be transformed using these new patterns (axis), where the patterns are the axis that most closely describe the relationships between data. This is helpful because we have now classified our data points as a combination of the contribution from each of those axis.

4   PCA Templates

In this section, we harness the strength of the PCA to define a relevant template. That by taking into account characteristics of the program that we want to analyze. In the $\mathbb{P}_\Delta^\sharp$ analysis [21] the used template represents a set of directions. Let Δ be the set of directions and X the vector of the program variables. $\forall d \in \Delta$, $\langle d, X \rangle = d_1 x_1 + \cdots + d_n x_n$, this scalar product represents the left hand side of the program invariant. Its right hand side is computed by the analysis using support functions. To be close to the accuracy of the polyhedral analysis, the used directions should represent the coefficients of the left hand side of the invariants obtained using the polyhedral analysis. For that, we should be able to guess the shape of the final polyhedron at the beginning of the analysis, which is a hard problem. Thanks to the PCA we can explore the dynamic of the program behavior to extract information that helps us to guess some interesting directions. The most important step is the computation of a relevant set of points on which the PCA should be applied. We call this step the **PCA points collection**. Afterwards, the PCA is applied on the obtained set of points to compute the corresponding templates.

4.1   PCA Point Collection

The PCA is applied to a set of data. In our method, we represent this set of data by a set of points, noted D_{PCA}, computed in a pre-analysis. The relevant choice of this set is very important, because the spread of these points is taken into account in the PCA computation. So, to obtain a relevant set of directions, the chosen set D_{PCA} should give us informations on the evolution of the polyhedra in the polyhedral analysis. The intuitive idea is to execute the polyhedral analysis for a fixed $n \in \mathbb{N}$ Kleene iterations. Then, we take the vertices of the obtained polyhedron as the set D_{PCA}. This method is, specially, interesting in the case of linear filters, for which the general shape of their invariants can be guessed quickly with vertices of polyhedra obtained in the first Kleene iterations. But generally, for a large numbers of programs, it is not the case and the PCA analysis may need a large amount of Kleene iterations, that can be time consuming. Let us emphasize that we do not choose to use the partial traces of programs, because in the $\mathbb{P}^{\sharp}_{\Delta}$ analysis the relevant set of directions should consider the shape of the polyhedron.

A more sophisticated idea consists of performing a pre-analysis using the $\mathbb{P}^{\sharp}_{\Delta}$ analysis, with as template a set of random directions uniformly distributed on the unit sphere. That what we call the standard $\mathbb{P}^{\sharp}_{\Delta}$ analysis. The obtained fixed point is used, afterwards, to generate the set D_{PCA}. We recall that the execution time of the $\mathbb{P}^{\sharp}_{\Delta}$ analysis is linear in the number of directions in Δ. So, we perform this pre-analysis with a large number of directions in Δ. In [21], the authors show that the $\mathbb{P}^{\sharp}_{\Delta}$ analysis is close to the accuracy of to the polyhedral analysis. The bottleneck is that the $\mathbb{P}^{\sharp}_{\Delta}$ analysis with a big Δ generates a polyhedron with a large number of constraints. Which means that the computation of their vertices can be time consuming.

To construct the set D_{PCA}, we propose to generate points on the border of the polyhedron instead of computing their vertices.

Let P be the polyhedron obtained with this pre-analysis. P can be defined as the intersection of $m \in \mathbb{N}$ half-spaces (m is the cardinality of Δ) *i.e.* $\mathsf{P} = \bigcap_{i=1}^{m} H_i$ where $H_i = \{x \in \mathbb{R}^n : \langle x, d_i \rangle \le \delta_{\mathsf{P}}(d_i)\}$ with $\langle x, d_i \rangle$ is the scalar product of x by the direction d_i and $\delta_{\mathsf{P}}(d_i)$ is the result of the support function of P in the direction d_i. We recall that $\delta_{\mathsf{P}}(d_i)$ is the result of the $\mathbb{P}^{\sharp}_{\Delta}$ pre-analysis.

The idea is to compute one point p_i per half-space H_i, then the obtained p_i is added to D_{PCA}. The computation of these points is known as a convex optimization problem and to solve it, we may solve m LP (Linear Programming) problems given as follows:

$$\min \langle x, d \rangle - \delta_{\mathsf{P}}(d)$$

$$s.t. : \forall d' \in \Delta, \langle x, d' \rangle \le \delta_{\mathsf{P}}(d')$$

Even, if we use the sophisticated LP solvers as for example the simplex [9] or the interior point algorithm [18], this method cab be time consuming.

To deal with that, we propose an alternative way to compute D_{PCA} called the **center projection method**. First of all, we compute the Chebyshev center [3] of P which is the center of the largest ball contained in P, noted $\mathbb{B}^n$, where $\mathbb{B}^n$ is unique, this is given in Definition 4.

Definition 4. *Let P be a polyhedron, such that $\mathsf{P} = \bigcap_{i=1}^{m} H_i$ where $H_i = \{x \in \mathbb{R}^n : \langle x, d_i \rangle \le \delta_{\mathsf{P}}(d_i)\}$ with d_i is a direction in $\mathbb{R}^n$ and $\delta_{\mathsf{P}}(d_i)$ is the result of the* *support function of* P *in this direction. Let* $\mathbb{B}^n$ *be the largest ball contained in* P, *such that:* $\mathbb{B}^n = \{x_c + u : \|u\| \leq r\}$ *where* x_c *is the center of* $\mathbb{B}^n$ *and* r *its radius.* x_c *represents the Chebyshev center of* P.

Using Definition 4, the Chebyshev center of P, noted x_c and the corresponding radius r can be obtained by solving the following LP problem:

$$\max r$$

$$s.t. : \langle x_c, d_i \rangle + r\|d_i\|_2 \leq \delta_{\mathsf{P}}(d_i)$$

Afterwards, The obtained center x_c should be projected to all planes that support faces of P. That is what we call the **center projection method**. The set of obtained points represents the set D_{PCA}. The center projection method is given in Definition 5.

Definition 5. *Let* $\forall i \in [1, m]$, L_i *be the plane that support the half-space* H_i, *such that:*

$$L_i = \{x \in \mathbb{R}^n : \langle x, d_i \rangle = \delta_{\mathsf{P}}(d_i)\}.$$

Let $proj(x_c, L_i)$ *be the center projection method of* x_c *on* L_i, *which is defined as follows:*

$$proj(x_c, L_i) = x_c + \left(\frac{\delta_{\mathsf{P}}(d_i) - \langle x_c, d_i \rangle}{\|d_i\|^2} \right) d_i.$$

Using Definition 5, the center projection method should be applied to all faces of P. Here, we emphasize that the point obtained using the center projection method may belong to P, in other terms, if $x_i = proj(x_c, L_i)$ then x_i may belong to the face of P supported by the plane L_i. If it is the case, we add x_i to the set D_{PCA}. Otherwise, we move x_c in $\mathbb{B}^n$ in a random way and we apply the center projection method until we find the point that belongs to the corresponding face of P. We execute this method for a fixed number of iterations, if the corresponding projected point could not be found then we ignore the corresponding face in the D_{PCA} computation. This does not affect a lot the efficiency of our method, because D_{PCA} should contain an amount number of points on the surface of P and not necessary one point per P face. Notice that, this restriction guarantees the termination of the corresponding algorithm given in Algorithm 1. In this algorithm, we apply LP solver only one time to compute x_c, which makes it efficient and not time consuming.

4.2   The PCA Computation

Once the set of points defined, we used it to compute the set of directions, noted Δ_{PCA}. The set Δ_{PCA} will be used afterwards as a relevant set of directions to performed the $\mathbb{P}^{\sharp}_{\Delta}$ analysis. Using the set D_{PCA}, the construction of the set Δ_{PCA} is done as follows:

Algorithm 1. The PCA point collection

Require: P, n
  $x_c = LPsolver(\text{P})$
  for $i = 0$ to $m - 1$ **do**
    $j = 0$
    $x = proj(x_c, L_i)$
    while $x \not\subseteq \text{P}$ or $j \leq n - 1$ **do**
      $x = proj(move(x_c, \mathbb{B}^n), L_i)$
      $j = j + 1$
    end while
    if $x \subseteq \text{P}$ **then**
      $D_{PCA}[i] = x$
    end if
  end for
  return D_{PCA}

---

1 The obtained set of points D_{PCA} is considered as the initial set of data, on which the PCA is performed. The PCA is applied to the whole set of points. It computes $n \in \mathbb{N}$ principal components, where n represents the dimension of the space (the number of program variables). Note that, these n components represents the principal components and their orthogonal ones. The obtained principal components are considered as a relevant directions, because, as presented in Sect. 3.2, they represent the most significant relationship between the points in D_{PCA}. We can choose to take all the obtained principal components or just a sub-set of the most significant ones. Then, the chosen components and their orthogonal ones are considered as relevant directions and added to the set Δ_{PCA}. We added also for each component its opposite. Note that, at this step, the cardinality of Δ_{PCA} does not exceed $2n$ (the number of the obtained principal components). In the $\mathbb{P}_\Delta^\sharp$ analysis, the bigger the cardinality of Δ_{PCA} is, the more accurate the result is. So, it can be interesting to compute more principal components.

2 The PCA gives techniques to sort the initial data set from the most to the less influenced data in the computation of the previous principal components, this is known as *the contribution of the observation (data) to a component* [1]. Therefore, the importance of data for a component can be obtained by computing the ratio of the squared factor score of these data by the eigenvalue associated to that component. The factor score of data represents the value of the projection of this data onto the principal component. The definition of the data contribution is stated in Definition 6.

Definition 6. *Let C be a component obtained using the PCA. The contribution of the ith data to the component C, denoted by $contr_{i,C}$, is defined as follows:*

$$contr_{i,C} = \frac{f_{i,C}^2}{\theta_C}$$

such that, θ_C is the eigenvalue associated to the C component. And $f_i \in \mathbb{R}$ is the factor score of the ith data.

Using Definition 6, we can find the n points that mostly contribute to the computation of the first component, where $n \le m$ with m is the cardinality of Δ_{PCA}. Note that, n is chosen statically at the beginning of the analysis. Afterwards, these points are removed from the initial set Δ_{PCA}. Then the PCA is applied again to the new set of points to computed new axis, that are not orthogonal to the first ones, and that best represent the reduced set of points.

3 To compute more directions Δ_{PCA}, this method can be iterated t times, where t can be defined statically by the user.

This method is given in Algorithm 2, where the function $PCA(D_{PCA}, K)$ returns the K first principal components obtained by applying the PCA on Δ_{PCA}, and $MaxContrib(D_{PCA}, n, C)$ is the function that determines the set of n points, which mostly contribute to the computation of the principal component C obtained in the previous iteration.

Algorithm 2. The PCA Direction Generation

Require: D_{PCA}, t, k, n
   $\Delta_{PCA} = Comp = \{\}$
   for $i = 0$ to $t - 1$ **do**
      $Comp = PCA(D_{PCA}, K)$
      $\Delta_{PCA} = \Delta_{PCA} \cup Comp$
      $C = Comp[0]$
      $D_{PCA} = D_{PCA}/MaxContrib(D_{PCA}, n, C)$
   end for
   return Δ_{PCA}

Using Algorithm 2, we compute a set of directions that contain many information on how the points are distributed in the space. Afterwards, the obtained set Δ_{PCA} is used as template to perform the $\mathbb{P}_{\Delta}^{\sharp}$ analysis.

5   Experimentations

To show the efficiency of our method, we combine it with the $\mathbb{P}_{\Delta}^{\sharp}$ analysis and apply it to analyze several programs. The experimentations are done on 2.4 GHz Intel Core2 Duo laptop, with 8 Gb of RAM. The used benchmarks contain a number of stable linear systems and digital filters, known to be hard to analyze using the polyhedral analysis. Table 1 shows the execution time obtained using the $\mathbb{P}_{\Delta}^{\sharp}$ analysis with Δ and Δ_{PCA}, such that: Δ is a set of directions uniformly distributed on a surface of the n-dimensional sphere, and Δ_{PCA} is the one obtained using the PCA method. The cardinality of the both of them are noted, respectively, $|\Delta|$ and $|\Delta_{PCA}|$. In this experimentation, we choose to take

Table 1. Table of results obtained using our analysis and the polyhedral one.

| Program | | $\mathbb{P}^{\sharp}_{\Delta}$ with PCA | | | $\mathbb{P}^{\sharp}_{\Delta}$ | |
Name	$|V|$	$|\Delta_{PCA}|$	$t(s)$		$|\Delta|$	$t(s)$
filter2	4	332	1.154		332	0.11
lead_leg_controller	5	350	164		350	93.356
Linear_quadratic_gaussian_regulator	7	398	23.648		398	13.11
Observer_based_controller	10	500	7.171		500	2.33
Butterworth_low_pass_filter	9	542	6.029		542	1.67
Dampened_oscillator	6	332	2.814		332	1.06
Harmonic_oscillator	6	332	1.017		332	0.08
lp_iir_9600_2	6	372	0.968		372	0.023
lp_iir_9600_4	10	500	2.197		500	0.186
lp_iir_9600_4_elliptic	10	500	3.253		500	0.471
lp_iir_9600_6_elliptic	14	692	10.781		692	3.636
bs_iir_9600_12000_10_chebyshev	22	1268	98.012		1268	53.986

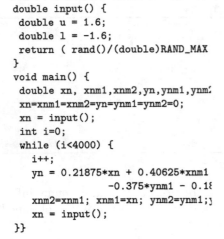

```
double input() {
  double u = 1.6;
  double l = -1.6;
  return ( rand()/(double)RAND_MAX
}
void main() {
  double xn, xnm1,xnm2,yn,ynm1,ynm2
  xn=xnm1=xnm2=yn=ynm1=ynm2=0;
  xn = input();
  int i=0;
  while (i<4000) {
    i++;
    yn = 0.21875*xn + 0.40625*xnm1
                -0.375*ynm1 - 0.18
    xnm2=xnm1; xnm1=xn; ynm2=ynm1;
    xn = input();
}}
```

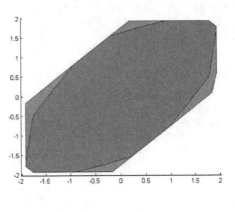

Fig. 7. (Left) The body of the program called lp_iir_9600_40_2. (Right) The red poly-hedron is the post fixed point obtained using Δ_{PCA} direction set. The blue polyhedron is the one obtained using Δ set. (Color figure online)

300 directions plus the orthogonal directions, and that for the both sets Δ and Δ_{PCA}. We have also that $|V|$ is the number of programs variables, and the column labeled t is the execution time (in seconds). Note that, the execution time of the $\mathbb{P}^{\sharp}_{\Delta}$ analysis with PCA contains the execution time of the pre-analysis used in our method to compute the set of initial points D_{PCA} and the direction set Δ_{PCA}, plus the $\mathbb{P}^{\sharp}_{\Delta}$ analysis execution time.

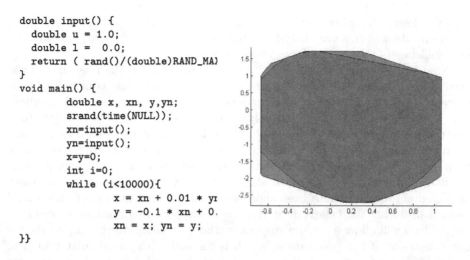

```
double input() {
  double u = 1.0;
  double l =  0.0;
  return ( rand()/(double)RAND_MA)
}
void main() {
      double x, xn, y,yn;
      srand(time(NULL));
      xn=input();
      yn=input();
      x=y=0;
      int i=0;
      while (i<10000){
          x = xn + 0.01 * yr
          y = -0.1 * xn + 0.
          xn = x; yn = y;
}}
```

Fig. 8. (Left) The body of the program called *Dampened_oscillator*. (right) The red polyhedron is the post fixed point obtained using Δ_{PCA} direction set. The blue polyhedron is the one obtained using Δ set. (Color figure online)

We emphasize that for most of these programs the polyhedral analysis with widening did not terminate before the time-out (more than 10 min). This table thus shows the efficiency of our method with several programs. Remember that the computed fixed point is also precise: it is the abstraction, in $\mathbb{P}^{\sharp}_{\Delta}$, of the least fixed point obtained with the polyhedra abstract domain. To illustrate this precision, we display on Figs. 7 and 8 the results of the $\mathbb{P}^{\sharp}_{\Delta}$ analysis using the PCA directions Δ_{PCA}, given by the red polyhedra, and the one obtained using the uniformed distributed directions Δ, given by the blue polyhedra. Note that the red polyhedra are contained into the blue polyhedra, this shows the quality of the invariant we compute. The $\mathbb{P}^{\sharp}_{\Delta}$ analysis with PCA is a little bit slower than the standard $\mathbb{P}^{\sharp}_{\Delta}$ analysis, but its result is more accurate. So, we obtain a good trade off between execution time and precision.

6   Conclusion

We recall that the sub-polyhedral analysis based support function, noted $\mathbb{P}^{\sharp}_{\Delta}$, uses a finite set of direction to perform the analysis. This initial set is statically chosen by the user at the beginning of the analysis. In this article, we present a method that allows us to define a relevant set of direction with taking into account the dynamic of the analyzed program. For that, we use a statistical tool called PCA (Principal Component Analysis). The presented method needs a pre-analysis step, in this step we compute a set of points on which the PCA is applied. The obtained principal components are considered as an interesting directions, because they take into account the spreads of the points in the space. So, the definition of the set of points is important. The PCA is applied iteratively on several set of points, to define set with several relevant directions. Afterwards, the resulted set of this pre-analysis is used to perform the $\mathbb{P}^\sharp_\Delta$ analysis. We show the efficiency of this methods on several benchmarks.

Note that, the precision of the $\mathbb{P}^\sharp_\Delta$ analysis depends on the relevancy of the used direction set. This analysis, in most cases, is not time consuming, even if we use a large number n of directions generated using the PCA method. The problem is that the resulted polyhedron contains a lot of constraints (one constraint per direction), and is thus hard to be, eventually, re-used as an entry of another analysis. We plan to develop a minimization method, that allows us to keep only $K \leq N$ relevant directions. For that, we are looking at apply pruning methods developed in [10], which allow to keep K linear functions from a set of N templates in order to best approximate the value function of an optimal control problem. We believe that the use of support functions to represent a polyhedron will allow us to use efficient methods to compute the importance of one constraint of the polyhedron, which is an apriori to the algorithm of [10]. These ideas are the subject of our ongoing works. As future work, we are also interested in adapting the techniques of parametrized templates used in [5] to define the set of directions we use. In this way, we believe we could change it during the analysis and thus gain in precision.

Acknowledgement. We want to thank A. Chapoutot, M. Martel and O. Bouissou for their helpful suggestions and precious advices. The authors are also thankful to the anonymous reviewers for their helpful comments.

References

1. Abdi, H., Williams, L.J.: Principal component analysis (2010)
2. Amato, G., Parton, M., Scozzari, F.: Discovering invariants via simple component analysis. J. Symb. Comput. **47**(12), 1533–1560 (2012)
3. Boyd, S., Vandenberghe, L.: Convex Optimization. Cambridge University Press, New York (2004)
4. Chen, X., Ábrahám, E.: Choice of directions for the approximation of reachable sets for hybrid systems. In: Computer Aided Systems Theory - EUROCAST 2011–13th International Conference, Las Palmas de Gran Canaria, Spain (2011)
5. Colón, M.A., Sankaranarayanan, S.: Generalizing the template polyhedral domain. In: Barthe, G. (ed.) ESOP 2011. LNCS, vol. 6602, pp. 176–195. Springer, Heidelberg (2011). doi:10.1007/978-3-642-19718-5_10
6. Cousot, P., Cousot, R.: Comparing the Galois connection and widening/narrowing approaches to abstract interpretation. In: Bruynooghe, M., Wirsing, M. (eds.) PLILP 1992. LNCS, vol. 631, pp. 269–295. Springer, Heidelberg (1992). doi:10.1007/3-540-55844-6_142
7. Cousot, P., Halbwachs, N.: Automatic discovery of linear restraints among variables of a program. In: POPL, pp. 84–97. ACM Press (1978)
8. Cousot, P., Cousot, R.: Abstract interpretation: a unified lattice model for static analysis of programs by construction or approximation of fixpoints. In: POPL, pp. 238–252. ACM Press (1977)
9. Gale, D.: Linear programming and the simplex method. Notices AMS **54**(3), 364–369 (2007). Spanoudakis, G., Kloukinas, C., Mahbub, K.

10. Gaubert, S., McEneaney, W.M., Qu, Z.: Curse of dimensionality reduction in max-plus based approximation methods: theoretical estimates and improved pruning algorithms. In: CDC-ECE. IEEE (2011)
11. Goubault, E., Putot, S., Védrine, F.: Modular static analysis with zonotopes. In: Proceedings of Static Analysis - 19th International Symposium, SAS 2012, Deauville, France (2012)
12. Hiriart-Urrut, J.B., Lemaréchal, C.: Fundamentals of Convex Analysis. Springer, Berlin (2004)
13. Jolliffe, I.: Principal Component Analysis. Springer, New York (1986)
14. Laviron, V., Logozzo, F.: Subpolyhedra: a family of numerical abstract domains for the (more) scalable inference of linear inequalities. In: STTT (2011)
15. Lieven De Lathauwer, B.D.M., Vandewalle, J.: A multilinear singular value decomposition. SIAM. J. Matrix Anal. Appl. 21(4), 1253–1278 (2000)
16. Miné, A.: The octagon abstract domain. Higher-Order Symbolic Comput. 19(1), 31–100 (2006)
17. Moore, B.: Principal component analysis in linear systems: controllability, observability, and model reduction. IEEE Trans. Autom. Control 26(1), 17–32 (1981)
18. Nesterov, Y., Nemirovskiĭ, A.: Interior-point polynomial algorithms in convex programming. SIAM studies in applied mathematics, Society for Industrial and Applied Mathematics (1994). http://opac.inria.fr/record=b1084763
19. Sankaranarayanan, S., Colón, M.A., Sipma, H., Manna, Z.: Efficient strongly relational polyhedral analysis. In: Emerson, E.A., Namjoshi, K.S. (eds.) VMCAI 2006. LNCS, vol. 3855, pp. 111–125. Springer, Heidelberg (2005). doi:10.1007/11609773_8
20. Sankaranarayanan, S., Sipma, H.B., Manna, Z.: Scalable analysis of linear systems using mathematical programming. In: Cousot, R. (ed.) VMCAI 2005. LNCS, vol. 3385, pp. 25–41. Springer, Heidelberg (2005). doi:10.1007/978-3-540-30579-8_2
21. Seladji, Y., Bouissou, O.: Numerical abstract domain using support functions. In: Proceedings of NASA Formal Methods, 5th International Symposium, NFM 2013, Moffett Field, CA, USA, pp. 155–169 (2013)
22. Shlens, J.: A tutorial on principal component analysis. CoRR (2014)
23. Stursberg, O., Krogh, B.H.: Efficient representation and computation of reachable sets for hybrid systems. In: Maler, O., Pnueli, A. (eds.) HSCC 2003. LNCS, vol. 2623, pp. 482–497. Springer, Heidelberg (2003). doi:10.1007/3-540-36580-X_35
24. Tipping, M.E.: Bishop: probabilistic principal component analysis. J. Royal Stat. Soc. Ser B (Statistical Methodology) 61(3), 611–622 (1999)

Sound Bit-Precise Numerical Domains

Tushar Sharma[1]([⊠]) and Thomas Reps[1,2]

[1] University of Wisconsin, Madison, WI, USA
tsharma@cs.wisc.edu
[2] GrammaTech, Inc., Ithaca, NY, USA

Abstract. This paper tackles the challenge of creating a numerical abstract domain that can identify affine-inequality invariants while handling overflow in arithmetic operations over bit-vector data-types. The paper describes the design and implementation of a class of new abstract domains, called the *Bit-Vector-Sound, Finite-Disjunctive* (*BVSFD*) domains. We introduce a framework that takes an abstract domain $\mathcal{A}$ that is sound with respect to mathematical integers and creates an abstract domain $BVS(\mathcal{A})$ whose operations and abstract transformers are sound with respect to machine integers. We also describe how to create abstract transformers for $BVS(\mathcal{A})$ that are sound with respect to machine arithmetic. The abstract transformers make use of an operation $WRAP(av, v)$—where $av \in \mathcal{A}$ and v is a set of program variables—which performs wraparound in av for the variables in v.

To reduce the loss of precision from $WRAP$, we use finite disjunctions of $BVS(\mathcal{A})$ values. The constructor of finite-disjunctive domains, $FD_k(\cdot)$, is parameterized by k, the maximum number of disjunctions allowed.

We instantiate the $BVS(FD_k)$ framework using the abstract domain of *polyhedra* and *octagons*. Our experiments show that the analysis can prove 25% of the assertions in the SVCOMP loop benchmarks with $k = 6$, and 88% of the array-bounds checks in the SVCOMP array benchmarks with $k = 4$.

1 Introduction

This paper tackles the challenges of implementing a bit-precise relational domain capable of expressing program invariants. The paper describes the design and implementation of a new framework for abstract domains, called the *Bit-Vector-Sound Finite-Disjunctive* (*BVSFD*) domains, which are capable of capturing useful program invariants such as inequalities over bit-vector-valued variables.

Supported, in part, by a gift from Rajiv and Ritu Batra; by DARPA under cooperative agreement HR0011-12-2-0012; by NSF under grant CCF-0904371; DARPA MUSE award FA8750-14-2-0270 and DARPA STAC award FA8750-15-C-0082; and by the UW-Madison Office of the Vice Chancellor for Research and Graduate Education with funding from the Wisconsin Alumni Research Foundation. Any opinions, findings, and conclusions or recommendations expressed in this publication are those of the authors, and do not necessarily reflect the views of the sponsoring agencies. T. Reps has an ownership interest in GrammaTech, Inc., which has licensed elements of the technology discussed in this publication.

© Springer International Publishing AG 2017
A. Bouajjani and D. Monniaux (Eds.): VMCAI 2017, LNCS 10145, pp. 500–520, 2017.
DOI: 10.1007/978-3-319-52234-0_27

The need for bit-vector invariants. The polyhedral domain [10] (denoted as *POLY*) is capable of expressing relational affine inequalities over rational (or real) variables. Previous research [21, 26, 27, 29, 37, 42] has also provided weaker forms of polyhedral domains that are capable of expressing some affine inequalities. For instance, the octagon abstract domain [26] (denoted as *OCT*) can express only relational inequalities involving at most two variables where the coefficients on the variables are only allowed to be plus or minus one. However, the native machine-integer data-types used in programs (e.g., int, unsigned int, long, etc.) perform bit-vector arithmetic, and arithmetic operations wrap around on overflow. Thus, the underlying point space used in the aforementioned abstract domains does not faithfully model bit-vector arithmetic, and consequently the conclusions drawn from an analysis based on these domains are, in general, unsound, unless special steps are taken [8, 41].

Example 1. The following C-program fragment incorrectly computes the average of two int-valued variables [5]:

```
int low, high, mid;
assume(0 <= low <= high);
mid = (low + high)/2;
assert(0<=low<=mid<=high);
```

A static analysis based on polyhedra or octagons would draw the wrong conclusion that the assertion always holds. In particular, assuming 32-bit ints, when the sum of low and high is greater than $2^{31} - 1$, the sum overflows, and the resulting value of mid is smaller than low. Consequently, there exist runs in which the assertion fails. These runs are overlooked when the polyhedral domain is used for static analysis because the domain fails to take into account the bit-vector semantics of program variables.   □

The problem that we wish to solve is not one of merely *detecting* overflow—e.g., to restrain an analyzer from having to explore what happens after an overflow occurs. On the contrary, our goal is to be able to track soundly the effects of arithmetic operations, including wrap-around effects of operations that overflow. This ability is useful, for instance, when analyzing code generated by production code generators, such as dSPACE TargetLink [12], which use the "compute-through-overflow" technique [14]. Furthermore, clever idioms for bit-twiddling operations, such as the ones explained in [43], sometimes rely on overflow [11].

Challenges in dealing with bit-vectors. Some of the ideas used in designing an inequality domain for reals do not carry over to ones designed for bit-vectors. First, in bit-vector arithmetic, additive constants cannot be cancelled on both sides of an inequality, as illustrated in the following example.

Example 2. Let x and y be 4-bit unsigned integers. Figures 1a and b depict the solutions in bit-vector arithmetic of the inequalities $x + y + 4 \leq 7$ and $x + y \leq 3$, respectively. Although $x + y + 4 \leq 7$ and $x + y \leq 3$ are syntactically quite similar, their solution spaces are quite different. In particular, because of wrap-around of

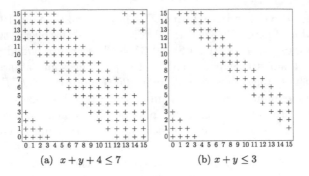

Fig. 1. Each + represents a solution of the indicated inequality in 4-bit unsigned bit-vector arithmetic.

values computed on the left-hand sides using bit-vector arithmetic, one cannot just subtract 4 from both sides to convert the inequality $x + y + 4 \leq 7$ into $x + y \leq 3$. □

Second, in bit-vector arithmetic, positive constant factors cannot be cancelled on both sides of an inequality; for example, if x and y are 4-bit bit-vectors, then $(4, 4)$ is in the solution set of $2x + 2y \leq 4$, but not of $x + y \leq 2$.

While some simple domains do exist that are capable of representing certain kinds of inequalities over bit-vectors (e.g., intervals with a congruence constraint, sometimes called "strided-intervals" [3,28,34,38]), such domains are non-relational; that is, they are not capable of expressing relations among several variables. On the other hand, there exist relational bit-precise domains [6,30], but they cannot express inequalities. The abstract domain in [40] can handle certain kind of bit-vector inequalities, but it needs the client to provide a template for inequalities. Moreover, the domain is incapable of expressing simple inequalities of form $x \leq y$, because they have variables on both side of the inequality.

Simon et al. [41] introduced sound wrap-around to ensure that the polyhedral domain is sound over bit-vectors. The wrap-around operation is called selectively on the abstract-domain elements while calculating the fixpoint. The operation is called selectively to preserve precision while not compromising on soundness with respect to the concrete semantics. The Verasco static analyzer [17] provides a bit-precise parametrized framework for abstract domains using the wrap-around operation. This approach has two disadvantages:

- The wrap around operation almost always loses information due to calls on join: the convex hull of the elements that did not overflow with those that did usually does not satisfy many inequality constraints.
- They do not show how to create abstract transformers automatically.

We introduce a class of abstract domains, called $BVS(\mathcal{A})$, that is sound with respect to bitvectors whenever $\mathcal{A}$ is sound with respect to mathematical integers. The $\mathcal{A}$ domain can be any numerical abstract domain. For example, it can be the polyhedral domain, which can represent useful program invariants as inequalities. We also describe how to create abstract transformers for $BVS(\mathcal{A})$ that are sound with respect to bitvectors. For $v \subseteq Var$ and $av \in \mathcal{A}$, we denote the result by $WRAP_v(av)$; the operation performs wraparound on av for variables in v. We give an algorithm for $WRAP_v(av)$ that works for any relational abstract domain (see Sect. 4.1). We use a finite number of disjunction of $\mathcal{A}$ elements—captured in the domain $FD_k(\mathcal{A})$—to help retain precision. The finite disjunctive domain is parametrized by the maximum number of disjunctions allowed in the domain (referred to as k). Note that $k=1$ is the same as convex polyhedra with wrap-around [41].

Example 3. Consider the following C-program fragment, which correctly computes the average of two `int`-valued variables [5]:

```
low  = (x<=y)? x:y;
high = (x<=y)? y:x;
mid  = low+(high-low)/2;
assert((x<=mid<=y)||(y<=mid<=x));
```

In this example, the domain of convex polyhedra with wrap-around is insufficient to prove the assertion. The reason is that the assertion is a disjunction of two polyhedral invariants. However, $BVS(FD_k(POLY))$ for $k = 2$ is able to prove the assertion.   □

Problem statement. These challenges lead to the following problem statement:

Given a relational numeric domain over integers, capable of expressing inequalities, (i) provide an automatic method to create a relational abstract domain that can capture inequalities over bit-vector-valued variables; (ii) create sound bit-precise abstract transformers; and (iii) use them to identify inequality invariants over a set of program variables.

Related work and contributions. Our work incorporates a number of ideas known from the literature, including

- the use of relational abstract domains [10,21,25,27,33,42] that are sound over mathematical integers and capable of expressing inequalities.
- the use of a wrap-around operation [2,7,41] to ensure that the abstraction is sound with respect to the concrete semantics of the bitvector operations.
- the use of finite disjunctions [1,15,36] over abstract domains to obtain more precision.
- the use of instruction reinterpretation [13,16,22,24,31,32] to obtain an abstract transformer automatically for an edge from a basic block to its successor.

Our contribution is that we put all of these to work together in a parametrized framework, along with a mechanism to increase precision by performing wrap-around on abstract values lazily.

- We propose a framework for abstract domains, called $BVSFD_k(\mathcal{A})$, to express bit-precise relational invariants by performing wrap-around over abstract domain $\mathcal{A}$ and using disjunctions to retain precision. This abstract domain is parametrized by a positive value k, which provides the maximum number of disjunctions that the abstract domain can make use of.
- We provide a generic technique via reinterpretation to create the abstract transformer for the path through a basic block to a given successor, such that the transformer incorporates lazy wrap-around.
- We present experiments to show how the performance and precision of $BVSFD_k$ analysis changes with the tunable parameter k.

Section 2 introduces the terminology and notation used in the rest of the paper. Section 3 demonstrates our framework with the help of an example. Section 4 introduces the $BVSFD_k$ abstract-domain framework, and formalizes abstract-transformer generation for the framework. Section 5 presents experimental results. Section 6 concludes.

2   Terminology

Abstract domains and vocabularies. Let abstract domain $\mathcal{A}$ and concrete domain $\mathcal{C}$ be related by a Galois connection $\mathcal{G} = \mathcal{C} \xrightarrow[\alpha]{\gamma} \mathcal{A}$. Often $\mathcal{A}$ is really a family of abstract domains, in which case $\mathcal{A}[V]$ denotes the specific instance of $\mathcal{A}$ that is defined over vocabulary V, where V is a tuple of variables $(v_1, v_2, ..., v_n)$. Each variable v_i also has an associated size in bits, denoted by $s(v_i)$. The domain $\mathcal{C}$ is the powerset of the set of concrete states.

2.1   Concretization

Given an abstract value $A \in \mathcal{A}[V]$, where V consists of n variables $(v_1, v_2, ..., v_n)$, the concretization of A, denoted by $\gamma_{\mathcal{A}[V]}(A)$, is the set of concrete states covered by A.

A concrete state σ is a mapping from variables to their concrete values, $\sigma : V \to \Pi_{v \in V} BV^{s(v)}$, where $s(v)$ is the size of variable v in bits and BV^b is a bitvector with b bits.

$$\gamma_{\mathcal{A}[V]}(A) = \bigcup_{(a_1, a_2, ..., a_n) \in A} \mu_V(bv_1, bv_2, ..., bv_n), \textbf{where } bv_i = a_i \% 2^{s(v_i)} \textbf{ for } i \in 0..n$$

$\mu_V(bv_1, bv_2, ..., bv_n)$ takes a tuple of bitvectors corresponding to vocabulary V and returns all concrete stores where each variable v_i in V has the value bv_i.

2.2   Wrap-Around Operation

The wrap-around operation, denoted by $WRAP^{ty}_{V'}(A)$, takes an abstract-domain value $A \in \mathcal{A}[V]$, a subset V' of the vocabulary V, and the desired type ty for vocabulary V'. It returns an abstract value A' such that the wrap-around behavior of the points in A is soundly captured. This operation is performed by

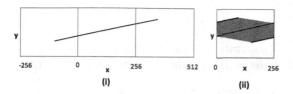

Fig. 2. Wrap-around on variable x, treated as an unsigned char.

displacing the concrete values in $\gamma_{\mathcal{A}[V]}(A)$ that are outside the bitvector range for ty in vocabulary V' to the correct bitvector range by appropriate linear transformations.

For example, in Fig. 2, the result of calling wrap-around on the line in (i) for variable x leads to an abstract value that is the abstraction of the points in the three line segments in (ii). For the abstract domain of polyhedra, that abstraction is the shaded area in (ii).

2.3   Soundness

An abstract value $A \in \mathcal{A}[V]$ is sound with respect to a set of concrete values $C \in \mathcal{C}$, if $\gamma_{\mathcal{A}[V]} \supseteq C$.

2.4 $\mathcal{L}(ELang)$: A Concrete Language Featuring Finite Integer Arithmetic

We borrow the simple language featuring finite-integer arithmetic from Sect. 2.1 of [41] (with minor syntactic changes). An ELang program is a sequence of basic blocks with execution starting from the first block. Each basic block consists of a sequence of statements and a list of control-flow instructions.

$$
\begin{array}{rcl}
\langle ELang \rangle & :: & (Block)* \\
\langle Block \rangle & :: & l : (\langle Stmt \rangle \;;)^* \; \langle Next \rangle \\
\langle Next \rangle & :: & \textbf{jump } l; \\
& | & \textbf{if } v \; \langle Op \rangle_{\langle Type \rangle} \; \langle Expr \rangle \textbf{ then jump } l \; ; \; \langle Next \rangle \\
\langle Op \rangle & :: & < \; | \leq \; | = \; | \neq \; | \geq \; | > \\
\langle Expr \rangle & :: & n \; | \; n * v + \langle Expr \rangle \\
\langle Stmt \rangle & :: & v = \langle Expr \rangle \\
& | & v{:}\langle Type \rangle = v{:}\langle Type \rangle \\
\langle Type \rangle & :: & (\textbf{uint} \; | \; \textbf{int}) \; \langle Size \rangle \\
\langle Size \rangle & :: & \textbf{1} \; | \; \textbf{2} \; | \; \textbf{4} \; | \; \textbf{8}
\end{array}
$$

The statements are restricted to an assignment of a linear expression or a cast operation. The control-flow instruction consists of either a jump statement, or a conditional that is followed by more control-flow instructions. The assignment and condition instructions expect the variable and the expression involved to have the same type.

3   Overview

In this section, we motivate and illustrate the design of our analysis using the *BVSFD* domain. The two important steps in abstract interpretation (AI) are:

1. Abstraction: The abstraction of the program is constructed using the abstract domain and abstract semantics.
2. Fixpoint analysis: Fixpoint iteration is performed on the abstraction of the program to provide invariants.

In the typical setup of AI, the set of states that can arise at each program point in the program is safely represented by the abstract-domain element found as the fixed point. This setup can be used to prove assertions. When the abstract-domain elements are themselves abstract transformers, the results provide function summaries or loop summaries [9,39]. In principle, summaries can be computed offline for large libraries of code so that client static analyses can use them to provide verification results efficiently.

A static analyzer needs a way to construct abstract transformers for the concrete operations in the programs. Reinterpretation [13,16,22,24,31,32] provides an automatic way to construct abstract transformers. For an analysis that provides function summaries or loop summaries, the fixpoint analysis is performed using equality, join ($\sqcup$), and abstract-composition ($\circ$) operations on abstract transformers.

Example 4. This example illustrates a function f that takes two 32-bit integers x and y at different rates, and resets their values to zero in case y is negative or overflows to a negative value. The function summary that we would like to obtain states that the relationship $x' \leq y'$ holds. Here, the unprimed and primed variables denote the pre-state vocabulary variables and the post-state vocabulary variables, respectively.

```
L0:  f(int x, int y) {
L1:     assume(x<=y)
L2:     while(*) {
L3:        if(*)
L4:           x=x+1, y=y+1
L5:        y=y+1
L6:        if (y<=0)
L7:           x=0, y=0
L8:     }
END: }
```

This example illustrates that merely detecting overflow would not be useful to assert the $x <= y$ relationship at the end of the function.   □

3.1   Creation of Abstract Transformers

Consider the analysis for Example 4 with the abstract domain $BVSFD_2(OCT)$. The first step involves constructing the abstraction of the concrete operations in the program as abstract transformers.

For instance, the abstract transformer for the concrete operations starting from node $L0$ and ending at node $L2$, denoted by $\tau^{\#}_{L0 \to L2}$, is defined as

$$\{m \leq x, y \leq M \wedge x' = x \wedge y' = y \wedge x' \leq y'\},$$

where m and M represent the minimum and maximum values for a signed 32-bit integer, respectively. The constraints $\{m \leq x, y \leq M\}$ are the bounding constraints on the pre-state vocabulary that are added because $L0$ is the entry point of the function, and the function expects three 32-bit signed values x and y as input. The equality constraints $\{x' = x, y' = y\}$ specify that the variables x and y are unchanged. Finally, the constraint $\{x' \leq y'\}$ is added as a consequence of the *assume* call.

Now consider other concrete transformations, such as $L4 \to L5$ and $L5 \to L6$. For the transformation $L4 \to L5$, the values for x' and y' might overflow because of the increment operations at $L4$. Consequently, the value of the incoming variable y in the transformation $L5 \to L6$ might have overflowed as well. There are two ways to design the abstract transformer to deal with these kind of scenarios: (1) a naive eager approach, (2) a lazy approach.

Eager Abstract Transformers. In the naive eager approach, the abstract transformers are created such that the pre-state vocabulary is always bounded as per the type requirements. For this example, that would mean that the pre-state vocabulary variables x and y are bounded in the range $[m, M]$. Consequently, the abstract transformers for $L4 \to L5$ and $L5 \to L6$ are:

- $\tau^{\#E}_{L4 \to L5} = \{m \leq x, y \leq M \wedge x' = x + 1 \wedge y' = y + 1\}$
- $\tau^{\#E}_{L5 \to L6} = \{m \leq x, y \leq M \wedge x' = x \wedge y' = y + 1\}$.

Because the eager approach expects the pre-state vocabulary to be bounded, an abstract-composition operation $a_1 \circ a_2$, where a_1 and a_2 are abstract transformers, needs to call the *WRAP* operation (Sect. 2.2) for the entire post-state vocabulary of a_2, for correctness. For instance, let $a_1 = \{m \leq u \leq M \wedge u' = u\}$ and $a_2 = \{m \leq u \leq M \wedge u' = M + 1\}$. The abstract transformer a_1 preserves u and a_2 changes the value of u' to $M + 1$. The composition of these operations matches the pre-state vocabulary of a_1 with the post-state vocabulary of a_2, by renaming them to the same temporary variables and performing a meet. For this particular example, it will perform $\{m \leq u'' \leq M \wedge u' = u''\} \sqcap WRAP_{u''}(\{m \leq u \leq M \wedge u'' = M + 1\})$, where it has matched the pre-state vocabulary variable u of a_1 with the post-state vocabulary variable u' of a_2, by renaming them both to a temporary variable u''. Note that in the absence of the *WRAP* operation on the post-state vocabulary of a_2, the meet operation above will return the empty element $\bot$. This result would be unsound because the value of u' in a_2 should have overflowed to m.

Now consider the composition $\tau^{\#E}_{L5 \to L6} \circ \tau^{\#E}_{L4 \to L5}$. After matching, composition will perform the meet of:

- $\{m \leq x'', y'' \leq M \wedge x' = x'' \wedge y' = y'' + 1\}$
- $WRAP_{\{x'',y''\}}\{m \leq x, y \leq M \wedge x'' = x + 1 \wedge y'' = y + 1\}$

The result of *WRAP* will be a join of four values. The four values are the combinations of cases where x'' and y'' might or might not overflow. As a result, the final composition will give an abstract transformer that overapproximate those four values. For $BVSFD_2(OCT)$, it will result in a loss of precision because it cannot express the disjunction of these four values precisely.

Lazy Abstract Transformers. The eager approach to creating abstract transformers forces a call to *WRAP* at each compose operation. The lazy approach can avoid unneccessary calls to *WRAP* by not adding any bounding constraints to the pre-state vocabulary. The abstract transformer $\tau_{L4 \to L5}^{\#L}$ is defined as $\{x' = x + 1 \wedge y' = y + 1\}$ and $\tau_{L5 \to L6}^{\#L}$ is defined as $\{x' = x \wedge y' = y + 1\}$. The abstract transformer $\tau_{L4 \to L5}^{\#L}$ is sound, because the concretization of the abstract transformer, denoted by $\gamma(\tau_{L4 \to L5}^{\#L})$, overapproximates the collecting concrete semantics for $L4 \to L5$ (see proposition 1 in [41]). A similar argument can be made for the abstract transformer $\tau_{L5 \to L6}^{\#L}$. The composition $\tau_{L5 \to L6}^{\#L} \circ \tau_{L4 \to L5}^{\#L}$ gives $\{x' = x + 1 \wedge y' = y + 2\}$. Thus, the lazy abstract transformer can retain precision by avoiding unnecessary calls to *WRAP*. However, one cannot avoid calling *WRAP* for every kind of abstract transformer and still maintain soundness. Consider the abstract transformer $\tau_{L5 \to L7}^{\#L}$, which is similar to $\tau_{L5 \to L6}^{\#L}$, but must additionally handle the branch condition for $L6 \to L7$. Defining it in a similar vein as $L4 \to L5$ will result in $\{x' = x \wedge y' = y + 1 \wedge y' \leq 0\}$. While the first three constraints are sound, the fourth constraint representing the branch condition, is unsound with respect to the concrete semantics. The reason is that y' might overflow to a negative value, in which case the condition evaluates to true and the branch to $L7$ is taken. However, the abstract transformer does not capture that behavior and is, therefore, unsound with respect to the concrete semantics. To achieve soundness in the presence of a branch condition, the following steps are performed for each variable v' involved in a branch condition:

- A backward dependency analysis is performed to find the subset V_b of the pre-state vocabulary on which v' depends. For the edge $L5 \to L6$, only y' is involved in a branch condition. The backward-dependency analysis yields $V_b = \{y\}$, because the only pre-state vocabulary variable that y' depends on is y.
- The bounding constraints for the vocabulary V_b are added to the abstract transformer. For example, after adding bounding constraints, $\tau_{L5 \to L6}^{\#L}$ becomes $\{m \leq y \leq M \wedge x' = x \wedge y' = y + 1 \wedge y' \leq 0\}$.
- The wrap operation is called on the abstract transformer for the variable v'. For the edge $L5 \to L6$, this step will soundly set the abstract transformer to the disjunction of
  - $\{m \leq y \leq M - 1 \wedge x' = x \wedge y' = y + 1 \wedge y' \leq 0\}$
  - $\{y = M - 1 \wedge x' = x \wedge y' = m\}$

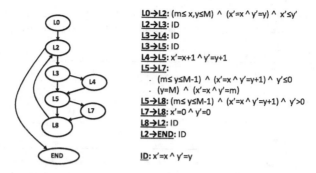

$$L0{\rightarrow}L2: (m{\leq} x,y{\leq}M) \wedge (x'{=}x \wedge y'{=}y) \wedge x'{\leq}y'$$
$$L2{\rightarrow}L3: \text{ID}$$
$$L3{\rightarrow}L4: \text{ID}$$
$$L3{\rightarrow}L5: \text{ID}$$
$$L4{\rightarrow}L5: x'{=}x{+}1 \wedge y'{=}y{+}1$$
$$L5{\rightarrow}L7:$$
$$\cdot\ (m{\leq} y{\leq}M{-}1) \wedge (x'{=}x \wedge y'{=}y{+}1) \wedge y'{\leq}0$$
$$\cdot\ (y{=}M) \wedge (x'{=}x \wedge y'{=}m)$$
$$L5{\rightarrow}L8: (m{\leq} y{\leq}M{-}1) \wedge (x'{=}x \wedge y'{=}y{+}1) \wedge y'{>}0$$
$$L7{\rightarrow}L8: x'{=}0 \wedge y'{=}0$$
$$L8{\rightarrow}L2: \text{ID}$$
$$L2{\rightarrow}END: \text{ID}$$

$$\underline{ID}: x'{=}x \wedge y'{=}y$$

Fig. 3. Lazy abstract transformers with the $BVSFD_2(POLY)$ domain for Example 4. ID refers to the identity transformation.

Note that the abstract domain $BVSFD_2(OCT)$ can precisely express the above disjunction because the number of disjunctions is ≤ 2.

Our analysis uses the lazy approach to create abstract transformers, because it can provide more precise function summaries. Figure 3 illustrates the lazy abstract transformers generated for Example 4.

3.2 Fixed-Point Computation

To obtain function summaries, an iterative fixed-point computation needs to be performed. Table 1 provides some snapshots of the fixpoint analysis with the $BVSFD_2(OCT)$ domain for Example 4.

To simplify the discussion, we focus only on three program points: $L2$, $L5$, and $L7$. Each row in the table shows the intermediate value of path summaries from $L0$ to each of the three program points. Quiescence is discovered during the fifth iteration. The abstract value in row (i) and column $L2$ shows the intermediate path summary for $L2$ calculated after one iteration of the analysis. It states that the pre-state vocabulary variables x and y are bounded and neither of them has been modified, because at this iteration the analysis has not considered the paths that go through the loop. At row (i) and column $L5$, the domain precisely captures the disjunction of two paths arising at the conditional at $L3$. The abstract value at row (i), column $L7$ is obtained as the composition of the abstract transformer $L5 \rightarrow L7$ with the path summary at $L5$ in row (i). The abstract-composition operations for abstract values with disjunctions performs abstract composition for all pairs of abstract transformers in the arguments, and then does a join on that set of values. To obtain the abstract transformer for $L7$ in row (i), it computes the join of the following values:

1. $B_x \wedge (m \leq y \leq M - 1) \wedge (x' = x) \wedge (y' = y + 1) \wedge (y' \leq 0)$
2. $B_x \wedge (m \leq y \leq M - 2) \wedge (x' = x + 1) \wedge (y' = y + 2) \wedge (y' \leq 0)$
3. $B_x \wedge (y = M) \wedge (x' = x) \wedge (y' = m)$
4. $B_x \wedge (M \leq y \leq M - 1) \wedge (x' = x) \wedge (m \leq y' \leq m + 1)$

Table 1. Snapshots in the fixed-point analysis for Example 4 using the $BVSFD_2(OCT)$ domain. $B_{v_1,v_2,..,v_n}$ are the bounding constraints for the variables $v_1,v_2,..v_n$.

Node	L2	L5	L7
(i)	• $B_{x,y} \wedge (x' = x) \wedge$ $(y' = y)$	• $B_{x,y} \wedge (x' = x) \wedge$ $(y' = y)$ • $B_{x,y} \wedge (x' = x + 1) \wedge$ $(y' = y + 1)$	• $B_{x,y} \wedge (m \leq y' \leq 0) \wedge$ $(x \leq x' \leq x + 1) \wedge$ $(y \leq y' \leq y + 2) \wedge$ $(x' \leq y')$ • $B_{x,y} \wedge (m \leq y' \leq m + 1)$ $\wedge (x \leq x' \leq x + 1)$
(ii)	• $B_{x,y,y'} \wedge$ $(x \leq x' \leq x + 1) \wedge$ $(y \leq y' \leq y + 2) \wedge$ $(x' \leq y')$ • $B_{x,y} \wedge (x' = 0) \wedge$ $(y' = 0)$	• $B_{x,y} \wedge (x \leq x' \leq x + 2) \wedge$ $(y \leq y' \leq y + 3) \wedge$ $(x' \leq y')$ • $B_{x,y} \wedge (0 \leq x' \leq 1) \wedge$ $(y' = x')$	• $B_{x,y} \wedge (m \leq y' \leq 0) \wedge$ $(x \leq x' \leq x + 2) \wedge$ $(y \leq y' \leq y + 4) \wedge$ $(x' \leq y')$ • $B_{x,y} \wedge (m \leq y' \leq m + 3)$ $\wedge (x \leq x' \leq x + 2)$
(iii)	• $B_{x,y,y'} \wedge$ $(x \leq x' \leq x + 2) \wedge$ $(y \leq y' \leq y + 4) \wedge$ $(x' \leq y')$ • $B_{x,y} \wedge (0 \leq x' \leq 1) \wedge$ $(0 \leq y' \leq 2) \wedge$ $(x' \leq y')$	• $B_{x,y} \wedge (x \leq x' \leq x + 3) \wedge$ $(y \leq y' \leq y + 5) \wedge$ $(x' \leq y')$ • $B_{x,y} \wedge (0 \leq x' \leq 2) \wedge$ $(0 \leq y' \leq 4) \wedge (x' \leq y')$	• $B_{x,y} \wedge (m \leq y' \leq 0) \wedge$ $(x \leq x' \leq x + 3) \wedge$ $(y \leq y' \leq y + 6) \wedge$ $(x' \leq y')$ • $B_{x,y} \wedge (m \leq y' \leq m + 5)$ $\wedge (x \leq x' \leq x + 3)$
(iv)	• $B_{x,y,y'} \wedge (x \leq x') \wedge$ $(y \leq y') \wedge (x' \leq y')$ • $B_{x,y,y'} \wedge (0 \leq x') \wedge$ $(x' \leq y')$	• $B_{x,y} \wedge (x \leq x') \wedge$ $(y \leq y') \wedge (x' \leq y')$ • $B_{x,y} \wedge (0 \leq x') \wedge$ $(x' \leq y')$	• $B_{x,y} \wedge (m \leq y' \leq 0) \wedge$ $(x \leq x') \wedge (y \leq y') \wedge$ $(x' \leq y')$ • $B_{x,y,y'} \wedge (m \leq y' \leq 0)$

Our abstract-domain framework uses a distance heuristic (see Sect. 4.1) to merge abstract values that are closest to each other. For this particular case, the abstract transformers (1) and (2) describe the scenarios where y' does not overflow, and are merged to give the first disjunct of row (i), column $L7$. Similarly, the abstract transformers (3) and (4) describe the scenarios where y' overflows, and are merged to give the second disjunct of row (i), column $L7$.

In the second iteration, shown in row (ii), the first disjunct for $L2$ is the join of the effect of first iteration of the loop, where x and y are incremented, with the old value, where x and y are unchanged. Additionally, the second disjunct in row (ii), column $L2$ captures the case where both x and y are set to 0 at program point $L7$. Iteration (iii) proceeds in a similar manner, and finally the value at $L2$ saturates due to widening. The value of $L2$ at iteration (iv) is propagated to the end of the function to give the following function summary:

• $B_{x,y,y'} \wedge (x \leq x') \wedge (y \leq y') \wedge (x' \leq y')$
• $B_{x,y,y'} \wedge (0 \leq x') \wedge (x' \leq y')$

Thus, the function summary enables us to establish that $x' \leq y'$ is true at the end of the function.

Algorithm 1 Wrap for a single variable

1: **function** WRAP(a, v, ty)
2:     **if** a is $\bot$ **then**
3:         **return** $\bot$
4:     $(m, M) \leftarrow Range(ty)$
5:     $s \leftarrow (M - m) + 1$
6:     $[l, u] \leftarrow GetBounds(a, v)$
7:     **if** $l \neq -\infty \wedge u \neq \infty$ **then**
8:         $\langle q_l, q_u \rangle \leftarrow \langle \lfloor (l - m)/s \rfloor, \lfloor (u - m)/s \rfloor \rangle$
9:         $b \leftarrow \mathcal{C}(m \le v) \sqcap \mathcal{C}(v \le M)$
10:        **if** $l = -\infty \vee u = \infty \vee (q_u - q_l) > t$ **then**
11:           **return** $RM_{\{v\}}(a) \sqcap b$
12:     **else**
13:         **return** $\bigcup_{q \in [q_l, q_u]} ((a \triangleright v := v - qs) \sqcap b)$

Type	Operation	Description
$\mathcal{A}$	$\top$	top element
$\mathcal{A}$	$\bot$	bottom element
bool	$(a_1 == a_2)$	equality
$\mathcal{A}$	$(a_1 \sqcap a_2)$	meet
$\mathcal{A}$	$(a_1 \sqcup a_2)$	join
$\mathcal{A}$	$(a_1 \nabla a_2)$	widen
$\mathcal{A}$	$\pi_W(a)$	project on vocabulary W
$\mathcal{A}$	$RM_W(a)$	remove vocabulary W
$\mathcal{A}$	$\rho(a_1, v_1, v_2)$	rename variable v_1 to v_2
$\mathcal{A}$	$\mathcal{C}(le_1 \; op \; le_2)$	construct abstract value
set[$\mathcal{A}$]	$WRAP_W^{ty}(a_1)$	wrap vocabulary W
D	$\mathcal{D}(a_1, a_2)$	distance

Fig. 4. Abstract-domain interface for $\mathcal{A}$.

4 The *BVSFD* Abstract-Domain Framework

In this section, we present the intuition and formalism behind the design and implementation of the *BVSFD* abstract-domain framework.

4.1 Abstract-Domain Constructors

BVSFD uses of the following abstract-domain constructors:

- Bit-Vector-Sound Constructor: This constructor, denoted by $BVS[\mathcal{A}]$, takes an arbitrary abstract domain and constructs a bit-precise version of the domain that is sound with respect to the concrete semantics. It needs the base domain $\mathcal{A}$ to provide a *WRAP* operator.
- Finite-Disjunctive Constructor: This constructor, denoted by $FD_k[\mathcal{A}]$, takes an abstract domain $\mathcal{A}$ and a parameter k, and constructs a finite-disjunctive version of the domain, where the number of disjunctions in any abstract value should not exceed k. This constructor uses a distance measure, denoted by $\mathcal{D}$, to determine which disjuncts are combined when the number of disjunctions exceeds k.

The $BVSFD_k[\mathcal{A}]$ domain is constructed as $BVS[FD_k[\mathcal{A}]]$. Figure 4 shows the interface that the base abstract domain $\mathcal{A}$ needs to provide to instantiate the $BVSFD_k[\mathcal{A}]$ framework.

The first seven operations are standard abstract-domain operations. The remove-vocabulary operation $RM_W(\mathcal{A})$, can be implemented as $\pi_{V-W}(\mathcal{A})$, where V is the full vocabulary. The rename operation $\rho(\mathcal{A}, v_1, v_2)$ can be easily implemented in most abstract-domain implementations through simple variable renaming and/or variable-order permutation. The construct operation, denoted by $\mathcal{C}$, constructs an abstract value from the linear constraint $le_1 = le_2$, where le_1 and le_2 are linear expressions, and operation op $\in \{=, \le, \ge\}$. This operation is available for any numeric abstract domain that can capture linear constraints.

If the domain cannot express a specific type of linear constraint (for instance, the octagon domain cannot express linear constraints with more than two variables), it can safely return $\top$. The $WRAP$ operation is similar to the wrap operation in [41], except that it returns a set of abstract-domain values, whose disjunction correctly captures the wrap-around behavior. The $WRAP$ operation from [41] is modified to return a set of abstract-domain values by placing values in a set instead of calling join. Algorithm 1 shows how wrap is performed for a single variable. It takes the abstract value a and perform wrap-around on variable v, treated as type ty. Line 4 obtains the range for a type, and line 5 calculates the size of that range. Line 6 obtains the range of v in abstract value a. This operation can be implemented by projecting a on v and reading the resultant interval. Lines 7–8 calculate the range of the quadrants for the variable v. Line 9 computes the bounding constraints on v, treated as type ty. Line 10 compares the number of quadrants to a threshold t. If the number of quadrants exceeds t, the result is computed by removing constraints on v in a using the RM operation, and adding the bounding constraints to the final result. Otherwise, for each quadrant, the appropriate value is computed by displacing the quadrants to the correct range. The displacing of the abstract value a for the quadrant q, denoted by $a \rhd v := v - qs$, is implemented as $RM_{\{u\}}(\rho(a, v, u) \sqcap \mathcal{C}(v = u - qs))$. We used $t = 16$ in the experiments reported in Sect. 5.

We implement $\mathcal{D}(a_1, a_2)$ by converting a_1 and a_2 into the strongest boxes b_1 and b_2 that overapproximate a_1 and a_2, and computing the distance between b_1 and b_2. A box is essentially a conjunction of intervals on each variable in the vocabulary. We measure the distance between two boxes as a tuple (d_1, d_2), where d_1 is the number of incompatible intervals, and d_2 is the sum of the distances between $compatible$ intervals. Two intervals are considered to be $incompatible$ if one is unbounded in a direction that the other one is not. For example, intervals $[0, \infty]$ and $[-7, \infty]$ are compatible, but $[0, 17]$ and $[-7, \infty]$, and $[-\infty, 12]$ and $[-7, \infty]$ are not. The $distance$ between two compatible intervals is 0 if their intersection is non-empty; otherwise, it is the difference of the lower bound of the higher interval and the upper bound of the lower interval. For example, the distance between $[0, 11]$ and $[17, 21]$ is $(17 - 11) = 6$. Given two distances $d = (d_1, d_2)$ and $d' = (d'_1, d'_2)$, $d > d'$ iff either (i) $d_1 > d'_1$, or (ii) $d_1 = d'_1 \wedge d_2 > d'_2$. If the number of disjunctions in an abstract value exceeds parameter k, the abstract-domain constructor $FD_k[\mathcal{A}]$ merges (using join) the pair of abstract-domain elements that are closest as measured by the distance measure.

4.2   Abstract Transformers

In this section, we describe how the abstract transformers are generated using reinterpretation [16,22,24,31,32]. The reinterpretation consists of a domain of abstract transformers $BVSFD_k[\mathcal{A}[V; V']]$, a domain of abstract integers $BVSFD_k^{\mathrm{INT}}[\mathcal{A}[t; V]]$, and operations to lookup a variable's value in the post-state of an abstract transformer and to create an updated version of a given abstract transformer [13]. Here, V denotes the pre-state vocabulary variables, V' denotes the post-state vocabulary variables, and t denotes a temporary variable not in V

or V'. Given blocks $B : [l : s_1; ...s_n; nxt]$ and $B' : [l' : t'; ...t_n; nxt]$ in an $ELang$ program (see Sect. 2.4), where B' is a successor of B, reinterpretation of B can provide an abstract transformer for the transformation that starts from the first instruction in B and ends in the first instruction in B', denoted by $B \rightarrow B'$.

Rule 1 in Fig. 5 specifies how abstract-transformer evaluation for basic-block pairs feeds into abstract-transformer evaluation on a sequence of statements. The evaluation on a sequence of statements starts with the identity abstract transformer, denoted by id. Rule 2 states that the abstract transformer for a sequence of instruction can be broken down into an abstract transformer for a smaller sequence of instruction, by recursively performing statement-level abstract interpretation $[\![.]\!]^\sharp_{Stmt}$ on the first instruction in the sequence. In this rule and subsequent $[\![.]\!]^\sharp_{Next}$ and $[\![.]\!]^\sharp_{Stmt}$ rules, "a" denotes the intermediate abstract transformer value. It starts as id at the beginning of the instruction sequence, and gets updated or accessed by assignment and control-flow statements in the sequence.

Rules 3, 4, and 5 handle control-flow statements. Rule 3 delegates the responsibility of executing the last instruction in the statement sequence to $[\![.]\!]^\sharp_{Next}$. Rule 4 deals with unconditional-jump instructions. The label is checked against a goal label and either $\bot$ or the current transformer a is returned accordingly. Rule 5 handles conditional branching. It conjoins the input transformer with p in the true case and n in the false case. p and n are calculated by performing abstract versions of op and $!op$, respectively, on the sound abstract integers corresponding to v_{Int} and v_{exp}. Here, $!op$ denotes the negation of the op symbol. For example, negation of $\leq$ is $>$. The sound version of an abstract integer is created by calling $LazyWrap^{type}$ (see rule 20). This function is the key component behind lazy abstract-transformer generation (see Sect. 3.1). In our implementation, we compute $DependentVoc_t(i)$ by looking at the constraints in i and returning the vocabulary subset $d \subseteq V$ that depend on t. B_d refers to the bounding constraints on the variables in vocabulary d.

Rules 6 and 7 handle assignment statements. Assignment to a linear expression merely performs a post-state-vocabulary update on the current abstract transformer "a." Note that this rule does not call $WRAP$ even though the result of computing exp can go out of bounds. Rule 7 handles the cast operation. $s(t_1)$ and $s(t_2)$ gets the size for the types t_1 and t_2, respectively. For a downcast operation, it performs simple update. In the case of upcast, $LazyWrap^{type}$ is called to preserve soundness (see Sect. 6 of [41]).

Rules 8, 9, 10, and 11 handle reinterpretation of expressions. Rules 8, 10, and 11 delegate computation to the corresponding abstract-integer operations. Rule 9 performs a variable lookup in the current value of abstract transformer "a."

Rules 12 to 20 deal with the operations on abstract integers in $BVSFD_k^{INT}[\mathcal{A}[t; V]]$. Rule 12 constructs an abstract integer from a constant. Rule 13 finds out if a variable is a constant. This operation is used by abstract multiplication (Rule 14) to determine if the multiplication of two abstract integers is linear or not. Rules 14–18 use vocabulary-removal(RM) and variable-rename operations (ρ) to ensure that the vocabulary of the output is $\{t\} \cup V$.

Basic Block:

$$[\![B \to B']\!]^{\sharp}_{Block} = [\![s_1; ...; s_n; nxt]\!]^{\sharp}_{Seq}(id, l') \tag{1}$$

$$[\![s_1; ...; s_n; nxt]\!]^{\sharp}_{Seq}(a, l') = [\![s_2; ...; s_n; nxt]\!]^{\sharp}_{Seq}(([\![s_1]\!]^{\sharp}_{Stmt}a), l') \tag{2}$$

Control Flow:

$$[\![nxt]\!]^{\sharp}_{Seq}(a, l') = [\![nxt]\!]^{\sharp}_{Next}(a, l') \tag{3}$$

$$[\![\text{jump } l'']\!]^{\sharp}_{Next}(a, l') = \text{ if } l'' \text{ is } l' \text{ then } a \text{ else } \bot \tag{4}$$

$$[\![\text{if } v \ op_{type} \ exp \text{ then jump } l''; nxt]\!]^{\sharp}_{Next}(a, l') = \tag{5}$$

$$\text{if } l'' \text{ is } l' \text{ then } a \sqcap p \text{ else } a \sqcap n, \text{where}$$

$$p = v_{Int} \ op_{type} \ exp_{Int}, \ n = v_{Int} \ !op \ exp_{Int},$$

$$v_{Int} = LazyWrap^{type}([\![v]\!]^{\sharp}_{Expr}a), \ exp_{Int} = LazyWrap^{type}([\![exp]\!]^{\sharp}_{Expr}a)$$

Assignments:

$$[\![v = exp]\!]^{\sharp}_{Stmt}a = update(a, v', [\![exp]\!]^{\sharp}_{Expr}a) \tag{6}$$

$$[\![v_1 : t_1 = v_2 : t_2]\!]^{\sharp}_{Stmt}a = \text{if } s(t_1) \leq s(t_2) \tag{7}$$

$$\text{then } update(a, v'_1, [\![v_2]\!]^{\sharp}_{Expr}a)$$

$$\text{else } update(a, v'_1, LazyWrap^{t_1}([\![v_2]\!]^{\sharp}_{Expr}a))$$

Expressions:

$$[\![n]\!]^{\sharp}_{Expr}a = const\_int(n) \tag{8}$$

$$[\![v]\!]^{\sharp}_{Expr}a = lookup(v', a) \tag{9}$$

$$[\![exp_1 * exp_2]\!]^{\sharp}_{Expr}a = mult([\![exp_1]\!]^{\sharp}_{Expr}a, [\![exp_2]\!]^{\sharp}_{Expr}a) \tag{10}$$

$$[\![exp_1 + exp_2]\!]^{\sharp}_{Expr}a = add([\![exp_1]\!]^{\sharp}_{Expr}a, [\![exp_2]\!]^{\sharp}_{Expr}a) \tag{11}$$

Abstract Integers:

$$const\_int(n) = C(t = n) \tag{12}$$

$$get\_const(i) = \text{if } \pi_{\{t\}}(i) \text{ is } \{t = n\} \text{ then } (true, n) \text{ else } (false, 0), \tag{13}$$

$$mult(i_i, i_2) = \text{let } (b, n) = get\_const(i_i) \text{ in} \tag{14}$$

$$(\text{if } b \text{ then } RM_{\{t'\}}(\rho(i_1, t, t') \sqcap C(t = n * t')) \text{ else } \top)$$

$$add(i_i, i_2) = RM_{\{t', t''\}}(\rho(i_1, t, t') \sqcap \rho(i_2, t, t'') \sqcap C(t = t' + t'')) \tag{15}$$

$$i_i \ op \ i_2 = RM_{\{t', t''\}}(\rho(i_1, t, t') \sqcap \rho(i_2, t, t'') \sqcap C(t' \ op \ t'')), \tag{16}$$

$$\text{where } op \in \{=, \leq, \geq\}$$

$$i_i > i_2 = RM_{\{t', t''\}}(\rho(i_1, t, t') \sqcap \rho(i_2, t, t'') \sqcap C(t' \geq t'' + 1)) \tag{17}$$

$$i_i < i_2 = RM_{\{t', t''\}}(\rho(i_1, t, t') \sqcap \rho(i_2, t, t'') \sqcap C(t' \leq t'' - 1)) \tag{18}$$

$$i_i \neq i_2 = (i_i < i_2) \sqcup (i_1 > i_2) \tag{19}$$

$$LazyWrap^{type}(i) = WRAP^{type}_{\{t\}}(i \sqcap C(B_d)), \text{where } d = DependentVoc_t(i) \tag{20}$$

Variable lookup and update:

$$lookup(a, v') = \pi_{V \cup \{t\}}(a \sqcap \{t = v'\}) \tag{21}$$

$$update(a, v', i) = RM_{\{v'\}}(a) \sqcap RM_{\{t\}}(i \sqcap \{v' = t\}) \tag{22}$$

Fig. 5. Reinterpretation semantics for $\mathcal{L}(ELANG)$.

Rules 21 and 22 are variable lookup and update operations. Lookup takes an abstract transformer $a \in BVSFD_k$ and a variable $v' \in V'$, and returns the abstract integer $i \in BVSFD_k^{\mathrm{INT}}$ such that the relationship of t with V in i is the same as the relationship of v' with V in a. The variable-update operation works in the opposite direction. Update takes an abstract transformer $a \in BVSFD_k$, a variable $v' \in V'$, and $i \in BVSFD_k^{\mathrm{INT}}$, and returns $a' \in BVSFD_k$ such that the relationship of v' with V in a' is the same as the relationship of t with V in i, and all the other relationships that do not involve v' remain the same.

5   Experimental Evaluation

In this section, we compare the performance and precision of the bit-precise disjunctive-inequality domain $BVSFD_k$ for different values of k. We perform this comparison for the base domains of octagons and polyhedra. The abstract transformers for the $BVSFD$ domain were automatically synthesized for each path through a basic block to one of its successor by using reinterpretation (see Sect. 4.2). We also perform array-out-of-bounds checking to quantify the usefulness of the precision gain for different values of k. The experiments were designed to shed light on the following questions:

1. How much does the performance of the analysis degrade as k is increased?
2. How much does the precision of the analysis increase as k is increased?
3. What is the value of k beyond which no further precision is gained?
4. What is the effect of adding sound bit-precise handling of variables on performance and precision?

5.1   Experimental Setup

Given a C file, we first create the corresponding LLVM bitcode [20,23]. We then feed the bitcode to our solver, which uses the WALi [18] system to create a Weighted Pushdown System (WPDS) corresponding to the LLVM CFG. The transitions in the WPDS correspond to CFG edges from a basic block to one of its successors. The semiring weights on the edges are abstract transformers in the $BVSFD_k$ abstract domain. We then perform interprocedural analysis by performing post[*] followed by the path-summary operation [35] to obtain overapproximating function summaries and an overapproximation of the reachable states at all branch points. We used EWPDS merge functions [19] to preserve local variables across call sites. We used the *Pointset_Powerset* [1] framework in the Parma Polyhedra Library [2,33] to implement the $FD_k[\mathcal{A}]$ constructor. For each example used in the experiments, we use a timeout of 200 seconds.

5.2   Assertion Checking

For this set of experiments, we picked the subset of the SVCOMP [4] loop benchmarks for which all assertions hold. Because our analyzer is sound, we are interested in the percentage of true assertions that it can verify. Table 2 provides

Table 2. Information about the loop benchmarks containing true assertions, a subset of the SVCOMP benchmarks.

Benchmark	Examples	Instructions	Assertions
Loop-invgen	18	2373	90
Loop-lit	15	1173	16
Loops	34	3974	32
Loop-acceleration	19	1001	19
Total	86	8521	158

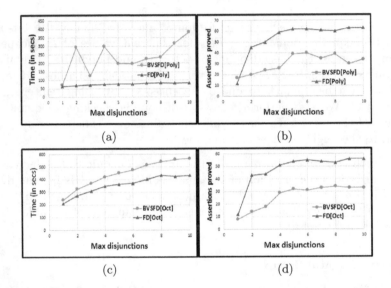

(a)   (b)

(c)   (d)

Fig. 6. Precision and performance numbers for SV-COMP loop benchmarks.

information about the benchmarks that we used. We performed the analysis on these examples and performed assertion checking by checking whether the program points corresponding to assertion failures had the bottom abstract state.

Figure 6a and b show the performance and precision numbers, respectively, for the loop SVCOMP benchmarks, with *POLY* as the base domain. The results answer the experimental questions as follows:

1. With two exceptions, at $k = 2$ and $k = 4$, the performance steadily decreases as the number of maximum allowed disjunctions k is increased. The analysis times for $k = 2$ and $k = 4$ do not fit the trend because one example times out for $k = 2$ or $k = 4$, but does not time out for $k = 3$ or $k = 5$. This behavior can be attributed to the non-monotonic behaviors of the finite-disjunctive join and widening operations.
2. The precision, measured as the number of proved assertions, increases from $k = 1$ to $k = 6$. From $k = 7$ onwards the change in precision is haphazard.

3. The analysis achieves the best precision at $k = 6$, where it proves 40 out of 157 assertions.
4. The sound analysis using $BVSFD_k[POLY]$ is 1.1–4.6 times slower than the unsound analysis using $FD_k[POLY]$, and is able to prove 44–142% of the assertions obtained with $FD_k[POLY]$.

Figure 6c and d show the performance and precision numbers, respectively, for the loop SVCOMP benchmarks, with OCT as the base domain. The results answer the experimental questions as follows:

1. The performance steadily decreases with increase in k.
2. The precision, measured as the number of proved assertions, increases from $k = 1$ to $k = 5$. From $k = 5$ onwards the precision is essentially unchanged.
3. The analysis achieves the best precision at $k = 8$, where it proves 34 out of 157 assertions.
4. The sound analysis using $BVSFD_k[OCT]$ is 1.1–1.3 times slower than the unsound analysis using $FD_k[OCT]$, and is able to prove 33–67% of the assertions obtained with $FD_k[OCT]$.

In our experiments, we found the $BVSFD_k[OCT]$-based analysis to be 1–3.3x slower than $BVSFD_k[POLY]$. This slowdown occurs because the maximum vocabulary size in abstract transformers is ≤ 12, and abstract operations for octagons are slower than that of polyhedra for such a small vocabulary size.

5.3   Array-Bounds Checking

We perform array-bound checking using invariants from the $BVSFD_k$ analysis. For each array access and update we create an error state that is reached when an array bound is violated. These array-bounds checks are verified by checking if the path summaries at the error states are $\perp$. There are 88 examples in the benchmark, with a total of 14,742 instructions and 598 array-bounds checks. Figure 7 lists the number of array-bound checks proven for each application, for different values of k, for the SVCOMP array benchmarks.

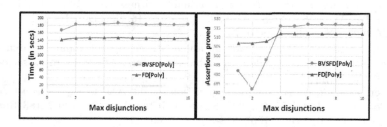

Fig. 7. Precision and performance numbers for SV-COMP array benchmarks with $POLY$ as the base domain.

The results answer the experimental questions as follows:

1. The performance of the analysis increases by 9% from $k = 1$ to $k = 2$. After $k = 2$, the performance stabilizes.
2. With one exception at $k = 2$, the precision—measured as the number of array-bounds checks proven—increases from $k = 1$ to $k = 4$. From $k = 4$ onwards the precision is essentially unchanged.
3. The analysis achieves the best precision at $k = 4$, where it proves 515 out of the 598 array-bounds checks.
4. The sound analysis using $BVSFD_k[POLY]$ is 1.18–1.26 times slower than the unsound analysis using $FD_k[POLY]$, and is able to prove 95–101% of the array-bound checks obtained with $FD_k[POLY]$.

6   Conclusion

The key contribution of the paper is to provide a framework for abstract domains that not only expresses bit-precise relational invariants, but enables improved precision by using a finite number of disjunctions. The maximum number of allowed disjunctions k in the analysis can be customized by the user. This framework, denoted by $BVSFD_k$, can be instantiated for any numerical abstract domain that can handle simple inequalities. We also provide a generic approach to create sound abstract transformers for $BVSFD_k$. Our experimental results with *polyhedra* and *octagons* illustrate the practical benefits of the approach.

References

1. Bagnara, R., Hill, P., Zaffanella, E.: Widening operators for powerset domains. STTT **8**(4/5), 449–466 (2006)
2. Bagnara, R., Hill, P.M., Zaffanella, E.: The parma polyhedra library: toward a complete set of numerical abstractions for the analysis and verification of hardware and software systems. Sci. Comput. Program. **72**(1–2), 3–21 (2008)
3. Balakrishnan, G., Reps, T.: WYSINWYX: what you see is not what you execute. TOPLAS **32**(6), 202–213 (2010)
4. Beyer, D.: Software verification and verifiable witnesses. In: Baier, C., Tinelli, C. (eds.) TACAS 2015. LNCS, vol. 9035, pp. 401–416. Springer, Heidelberg (2015). doi:10.1007/978-3-662-46681-0_31
5. Bloch, J.: Extra, extra - read all about it: nearly all binary searches and mergesorts are broken. googleresearch.blogspot.com/2006/06/extra-extra-read-all-about-it-nearly.html
6. Brauer, J., King, A.: Automatic abstraction for intervals using boolean formulae. In: Cousot, R., Martel, M. (eds.) SAS 2010. LNCS, vol. 6337, pp. 167–183. Springer, Heidelberg (2010). doi:10.1007/978-3-642-15769-1_11
7. Brauer, J., King, A.: Transfer function synthesis without quantifier elimination. LMCS **8**(3), 63 (2012)
8. Bygde, S., Lisper, B., Holsti, N.: Fully bounded polyhedral analysis of integers with wrapping. In: International Workshop on Numerical and Symbolic Abstract Domains (2011)

9. Cousot, P., Cousot, R.: Static determination of dynamic properties of programs. In: Proceedings of 2nd International Symposium on Programming, Paris, April 1976

10. Cousot, P., Halbwachs, N.: Automatic discovery of linear constraints among variables of a program. In: POPL (1978)

11. Dietz, W., Li, P., Regehr, J., Adve, V.: Understanding integer overflow in C/C++. In: ICSE (2012)

12. dSPACE TargetLink. www.dspace.com/en/pub/home/products/sw/pcgs/targetli. cfm

13. Elder, M., Lim, J., Sharma, T., Andersen, T., Reps, T.: Abstract domains of affine relations. TOPLAS **36**(4), 1–13 (2014)

14. Garner, H.L.: Theory of computer addition and overflow. IEEE Trans. Comput. **27**(4), 297–301 (1978)

15. Ghorbal, K., Ivančić, F., Balakrishnan, G., Maeda, N., Gupta, A.: Donut domains: efficient non-convex domains for abstract interpretation. In: VMCAI (2012)

16. Jones, N., Mycroft, A.: Data flow analysis of applicative programs using minimal function graphs. In: POPL, pp. 296–306 (1986)

17. Jourdan, J.-H., Laporte, V., Blazy, S., Leroy, X., Pichardie, D.: A formally-verified C static analyzer. In: POPL (2015)

18. Kidd, N., Lal, A., Reps, T.: WALi: the weighted automaton library (2007). www. cs.wisc.edu/wpis/wpds/download.php

19. Lal, A., Reps, T., Balakrishnan, G.: Extended weighted pushdown systems. In: Etessami, K., Rajamani, S.K. (eds.) CAV 2005. LNCS, vol. 3576, pp. 434–448. Springer, Heidelberg (2005). doi:10.1007/11513988_44

20. Lattner, C., Adve, V.: LLVM: a compilation framework for lifelong program analysis & transformation. In: International Symposium on Code Generation and Optimization (2004)

21. Laviron, V., Logozzo, F.: Subpolyhedra: a (more) scalable approach to infer linear inequalities. In: VMCAI (2009)

22. Lim, J.: Transformer specification language: a system for generating analyzers and its applications. Ph.D. thesis, Computer Science Department, University of Wisconsin, Madison, WI, Technical report 1689, May 2011

23. LLVM: Low level virtual machine. llvm.org

24. Malmkjær, K.: Abstract interpretation of partial-evaluation algorithms. Ph.D. thesis, Department of Computer and Information Science, Kansas State University, Manhattan, Kansas (1993)

25. Miné, A.: The octagon abstract domain. Higher-Order Symbolic Comput. **19**(1), 31–100 (1006)

26. Miné, A.: The octagon abstract domain. In: WCRE (2001)

27. Miné, A.: A few graph-based relational numerical abstract domains. In: Hermenegildo, M.V., Puebla, G. (eds.) SAS 2002. LNCS, vol. 2477, pp. 117–132. Springer, Heidelberg (2002). doi:10.1007/3-540-45789-5_11

28. Miné, A.: Abstract domains for bit-level machine integer and floating-point operations. In: IJCAR, pp. 55–70 (2012)

29. Monniaux, D.: Automatic modular abstractions for template numerical constraints. LMCS **6**(3), 4 (2010)

30. Müller-Olm, M., Seidl, H.: Analysis of modular arithmetic. TOPLAS **29**(5), 29:1–29:27 (2007)

31. Mycroft, A., Jones, N.: A relational framework for abstract interpretation. In: Programs as Data Objects (1985)

32. Nielson, F.: Two-level semantics and abstract interpretation. Theor. Comp. Sci. **69**, 117–242 (1989)
33. PPL: The Parma polyhedra library. www.cs.unipr.it/ppl/
34. Reps, T., Balakrishnan, G., Lim, J.: Intermediate-representation recovery from low-level code. In: PEPM (2006)
35. Reps, T., Schwoon, S., Jha, S., Melski, D.: Weighted pushdown systems and their application to interprocedural dataflow analysis. SCP **58**(1–2), 206–263 (2005)
36. Sankaranarayanan, S., Ivančić, F., Shlyakhter, I., Gupta, A.: Static analysis in disjunctive numerical domains. In: Yi, K. (ed.) SAS 2006. LNCS, vol. 4134, pp. 3–17. Springer, Berlin (2006). doi:10.1007/11823230_2
37. Sankaranarayanan, S., Sipma, H.B., Manna, Z.: Scalable analysis of linear systems using mathematical programming. In: Cousot, R. (ed.) VMCAI 2005. LNCS, vol. 3385, pp. 25–41. Springer, Berlin (2005). doi:10.1007/978-3-540-30579-8_2
38. Sen, R., Srikant, Y.: Executable analysis using abstract interpretation with circular linear progressions. In: MEMOCODE (2007)
39. Sharir, M., Pnueli, A.: Two approaches to interprocedural data flow analysis. In: Program Flow Analysis: Theory and Applications. Prentice-Hall (1981)
40. Sharma, T., Thakur, A., Reps, T.: An abstract domain for bit-vector inequalities. TR-1789, Computer Science Department, University of Wisconsin, Madison, WI (2013)
41. Simon, A., King, A.: Taming the wrapping of integer arithmetic. In: Nielson, H.R., Filé, G. (eds.) SAS 2007. LNCS, vol. 4634, pp. 121–136. Springer, Heidelberg (2007). doi:10.1007/978-3-540-74061-2_8
42. Simon, A., King, A., Howe, J.: Two variables per linear inequality as an abstract domain. In: International Workshop on Logic Based Program Development and Transformation, pp. 71–89 (2002)
43. Warren Jr., H.: Hacker's Delight. Addison-Wesley, Boston (2003)

IC3 - Flipping the E in ICE

Yakir Vizel[1(✉)], Arie Gurfinkel[2], Sharon Shoham[3], and Sharad Malik[1]

[1] Princeton University, Princeton, USA
yvizel@princeton.edu
[2] University of Waterloo, Waterloo, Canada
[3] Tel-Aviv University, Tel-Aviv, Israel

Abstract. Induction is a key element of state-of-the-art verification techniques. Automatically synthesizing and verifying inductive invariants is at the heart of *Model Checking* of safety properties. In this paper, we study the relationship between two popular approaches to synthesizing inductive invariants: SAT-based Model Checking (SAT-MC) and Machine Learning-based Invariant Synthesis (MLIS). Our goal is to identify and formulate the theoretical similarities and differences between the two frameworks. We focus on two flagship algorithms: IC3 (an instance of SAT-MC) and ICE (an instance of MLIS). We show that the two frameworks are very similar yet distinct. For a meaningful comparison, we introduce *RICE*, an extension of ICE with *relative induction* and show how IC3 can be implemented as an instance of RICE. We believe this work contributes to the understanding of inductive invariant synthesis and will serve as a foundation for further improvements to both SAT-MC and MLIS algorithms.

1 Introduction

State-of-the-art verification techniques [1–3,5,7,9] use *induction* to verify a system with respect to a safety specification. Typically, this is a two phase process. In the first phase, a candidate inductive invariant *Inv* is chosen (the details of this choice depend on each particular technique). The second phase checks that *Inv* is really an inductive invariant and is usually done by a variety of techniques including symbolic execution, simulation, SAT- and SMT-solving. In this paper, we are focusing on *invariant inference* techniques that automate both phases.

An inductive invariant *Inv* represents a set of states closed under forward reachability: *Inv* includes all the initial states, and all states reachable from states in *Inv*. Thus, an inductive invariant over-approximates the set of all reachable states. The invariant is called *safe* when it satisfies the specification (i.e., it does not include any states that reach a *bad* state). It is possible for an invariant to be non-inductive (i.e., not closed under reachability) or non-safe (include a *bad* state). In the context of safety verification, invariant inference is restricted to discovering safe inductive invariants. While there are many such approaches, in this paper, we study the relationship between *SAT-based model checking (SAT-MC)* [1], *Machine Learning-based Invariant Synthesis (MLIS)* [3,4,6,8].

© Springer International Publishing AG 2017
A. Bouajjani and D. Monniaux (Eds.): VMCAI 2017, LNCS 10145, pp. 521–538, 2017.
DOI: 10.1007/978-3-319-52234-0_28

SAT-based model checking algorithms, such as IC3/PDR [1,2], Interpolation [7] and others [5,9], are based on safe inductive invariant inference. These algorithms iteratively conjecture safe candidate invariants until either a candidate is proven inductive or a counterexample is found. While these algorithms differ in the details of candidate discovery, they all rely on a close interaction between the main algorithm and the decision procedure used. MLIS algorithms, such as ICE [3], have been recently proposed as a Machine Learning-based alternatives for invariant inference. MLIS algorithms have two main components: a *Learner* and a *Teacher*. In each iteration of the algorithm, a learner generates a candidate invariant, and the teacher validates the conjecture and, if necessary, generates feedback in a form of a positive or negative example. The learner uses the example to improve its conjecture. The process continues until the teacher determines that the candidate is a safe inductive invariant. While, to our knowledge, ICE does not produce counterexamples, we ignore this distinction in this paper.

The goal of this paper is to study and formulate the theoretical similarities and differences between SAT-MC and MLIS approaches by focusing on the two flagship algorithms: IC3 and ICE. We concede that the comparison is somewhat complicated by the fact that ICE is a generic framework (with many potential instances), while IC3 (and algorithms that derive from it) are specific instances of SAT-based MC. At a high-level of abstraction, IC3 and ICE exhibit many similarities. It is quite natural to view the SAT-solver in IC3 as a *Teacher* and the rest of the algorithm as a *Learner* with satisfying assignments playing the role of examples. However, instead of a single candidate, IC3 maintains a collection of candidates (called a *trace* of *frames*). It reacts to the examples given by the SAT-solver by strengthening and weakening these candidates, until one of the candidates is determined to be safe and inductive. The goal of this paper is to formalize this correspondence.

When all the low-level details are taken into account, IC3 does not fit into the ICE framework. In particular, the main query used by IC3 is not whether a candidate is inductive, but whether it is inductive *relative* to a given formula. Thus, we extend the ICE framework with relative induction, calling the result *RICE*. We then show that, with the exception of several details, IC3 is as an instance of RICE and that decoupling IC3 into a Learner and a Teacher enables various different behaviors, which depend on both how the Learner reacts to examples given by the Teacher, and to how the Teacher generates the examples. This leads to many interesting observations.

As an example, IC3 only makes use of positive examples that are part of the *initial states*. Yet, positive examples in RICE may be any reachable state. Due to that, fitting IC3 into RICE requires care when encountering reachable states. We show that when reachable states are taken into account, the results is a variant of IC3, namely Quip [5].

2   Preliminaries

In this section, we briefly present two algorithms for safety verification: IC3/PDR and ICE. To simplify the presentation, we describe the algorithms in the finite-state case, where the transition system to be verified is encoded using propositional formulas.

2.1 Safety Verification

A symbolic transition system T is a tuple $(\mathcal{V}, Init, Tr, Bad)$, where $\mathcal{V}$ is a set of Boolean variables. A state of the system is a complete valuation to all variables in $\mathcal{V}$ (i.e., the set of states is $\{0,1\}^{\mathcal{V}}$). We write $\mathcal{V}'$ ($= \{v' \mid v \in \mathcal{V}\}$) for the set of *primed* variables, used to represent the next state. *Init* and *Bad* are formulas over $\mathcal{V}$ denoting the set of initial states and bad states, respectively, and Tr is a formula over $\mathcal{V} \cup \mathcal{V}'$, denoting the transition relation. With abuse of notation, we use formulas and the sets of states (or transitions) that they represent interchangeably. In addition, we sometimes use a state s to denote the formula (cube) that characterizes it. For a formula φ over $\mathcal{V}$, we use $\varphi(\mathcal{V}')$, or φ' in short, to denote the formula in which every occurrence of $v \in V$ is replaced by $v' \in \mathcal{V}'$.

For a set of states S and a transition relation Tr, the forward image, $post^i_{Tr}(S)$, is the set of states reachable from S in i steps or less of the Tr. Formally, it is defined as follows:

$$\begin{cases} post^0_{Tr}(S) = S \\ post^i_{Tr}(S) = post^{i-1}_{Tr}(S) \cup \{t \mid s \in S \wedge (s,t) \in Tr\} \end{cases} \tag{1}$$

Similarly, the backward image $pre^i_{Tr}(S)$, is the set of all states that can reach S in i steps or less. Formally, it is defined as follows:

$$\begin{cases} prc^0_{Tr}(S) = S \\ pre^i_{Tr}(S) = pre^{i-1}_{Tr}(S) \cup \{t \mid s \in S \wedge (t,s) \in Tr\} \end{cases} \tag{2}$$

We often omit the transition relation Tr when it is clear from the context, writing $post^i(S)$ and $pre^i(S)$. We denote transitive closure of *post* and *pre* as $post^*$ and pre^*, respectively.

We say that a state s in T is reachable if $s \in post^*(Init)$, and a state s is *bad* when $s \in pre^*(Bad)$. A transition system T is UNSAFE when the intersection of $post^*(Init)$ and $pre^*(Bad)$ is non-empty. That is, T has a bad reachable state. T is SAFE when $post^*(Init)$ and $pre^*(Bad)$ are disjoint. It is well known that T is SAFE iff there exists a formula *Inv*, called a *safe inductive invariant*, that satisfies:

$$Init(\mathcal{V}) \Rightarrow Inv(\mathcal{V}) \quad Inv(\mathcal{V}) \wedge Tr(\mathcal{V}, \mathcal{V}') \Rightarrow Inv(\mathcal{V}') \quad Inv(\mathcal{V}) \Rightarrow \neg Bad(\mathcal{V}) \tag{3}$$

2.2 IC3/PDR

IC3 [1,2] is a SAT-based MC algorithm for safety verification. It maintains a growing sequence of candidate invariants, referred to as an *inductive trace*.

An *inductive trace*, or simply a trace, is a sequence of CNF formulas $\boldsymbol{F} = [F_0, \ldots, F_N]$ that satisfy:

$$Init \Rightarrow F_0 \qquad \forall 0 \le i < N \cdot F_i(\mathcal{V}) \wedge Tr(\mathcal{V}, \mathcal{V}') \rightarrow F_{i+1}(\mathcal{V}') \qquad (4)$$

The *size* of $\boldsymbol{F} = [F_0, \ldots, F_N]$ is N. For a $k \le N$, $\boldsymbol{F}^k = [F_0, \ldots, F_k]$ is a k-prefix of $\boldsymbol{F}$. Each element F_i of the trace is called a *frame*, and each conjunct of F_i is called a *lemma*. With abuse of notation, we sometimes view a frame as a set of lemmas.

A trace is *safe* if each F_i is safe: $\forall i \cdot F_i \Rightarrow \neg Bad$; it is *monotone* if $\forall 0 \le i < N \cdot F_i \Rightarrow F_{i+1}$. It is easy to see that the definition of a monotone inductive trace ensures that F_i overapproximates $post^i_{Tr}(S)$.

Given a monotone safe trace $[F_0, \ldots, F_N]$, if there exists i s.t. $i < N$ and $F_{i+1} \Rightarrow F_i$, then F_i is a safe inductive invariant.

A high-level description of IC3 is given in Algorithm 1. Our presentation of IC3 is rather non-standard, but we find it useful for the rest of the presentation. Many details are omitted and simplified. For a more standard and complete presentation, we refer the reader to [1,2]. In addition to a monotone (and safe up to F_{N-1}) trace, IC3 maintains a queue Q of *Counterexamples To Induction (CTIs)*, such that $Q \subseteq pre^*(Bad)$. The function MinBad returns the minimal frame in $\boldsymbol{F}$ that includes a state $s \in Q$. If no such frame is found, a new frame is initialized to *true*, and MinBad returns a state $s \notin Bad$ from the new frame (s is also added to Q). The function Strengthen (line 4) tries to strengthen the frame returned by MinBad by blocking the bad state s at the corresponding frame. While doing so, it iteratively adds more bad states from $pre^*(Bad)$ to Q. If an initial state is added to Q, IC3 terminates and returns a counterexample (line 5). Otherwise, it uses the fact that a state $s \in pre^*(Bad)$ is unreachable in a given number of steps to add a lemma that strengthens the proper candidate invariants. The function Push (line 7) "pushes" lemmas from one frame to a subsequent frame. A lemma ℓ in F_j indicates that some states (i.e., $\neg \ell$) are unreachable in up to j steps. If a lemma is pushed to F_{j+1}, it indicates those states are unreachable in up to $j + 1$ steps. In case all lemmas from F_j were pushed to F_{j+1}, the candidate F_j is a safe inductive invariant and IC3 terminates (line 7).

IC3 is incremental both in the way it computes the candidates (via iterative strengthening), and the way it uses previously learned lemmas during its execution.

Importantly, the discovery of bad states, generation of lemmas and pushing, are preformed using *relative induction* queries. A formula *RelInv* is inductive relative to a formula G if it satisfies:

$$Init(\mathcal{V}) \Rightarrow RelInv(\mathcal{V}) \qquad (RelInv(\mathcal{V}) \wedge G(\mathcal{V})) \wedge Tr(\mathcal{V}, \mathcal{V}') \Rightarrow RelInv(\mathcal{V}') \qquad (5)$$

For example, given a trace $\boldsymbol{F} = [F_0, \ldots, F_N]$, assume that IC3 tries to block a bad state $s \in F_i$, where $0 < i \le N$. s is unreachable in i steps when both $Init \wedge s$ and $(F_{i-1} \wedge \neg s) \wedge Tr \wedge s'$ are unsatisfiable, i.e. if $\neg s$ is inductive relative to F_{i-1}. In this case, s can be removed from F_i by adding some lemma c, such

Input: A transition system $T = (\mathcal{V}, \mathit{Init}, \mathit{Tr}, \mathit{Bad})$
1   $F_0 \leftarrow \mathit{Init}$; $\boldsymbol{F} = [F_0, \mathit{true}]$; $Q \leftarrow \emptyset$;
2   **repeat**
3      $(s, k) \leftarrow \text{MINBAD}(\boldsymbol{F}, Q)$;
4      $r \leftarrow \text{STRENGTHEN}(s, k, Q)$;
5   **if** $r = \mathit{cex}$ **then return** UNSAFE;
6   **if** $r = \mathit{blocked}$ **then**
7   **if** $\text{PUSH}(\boldsymbol{F})$ **then return** SAFE;
8   **until** ∞;

Algorithm 1. IC3/PDR: Main loop.

that $\mathit{Init} \Rightarrow c$ and $c \Rightarrow \neg s$, to F_i. The lemma c is found by repeatedly executing relative induction queries starting with $\neg s$ and greedily dropping literals. The details are irrelevant for our purposes, but are available in [1,2].

2.3 ICE

ICE [3] is an ML-based framework for synthesizing safe inductive invariants. A high level description of ICE is shown in Algorithm 2. Following the ML paradigm of active learning, ICE consists of two components: a *Teacher* and a *Learner*. The Teacher and the Learner communicate in the following manner: The Learner synthesizes a candidate invariant J (line 11) and sends it to the Teacher (line 12) that either confirms J is a safe inductive invariant (line 13) or finds an (counter-)example that rules J out (line 14). In the latter case, the Learner uses the examples returned by the Teacher to synthesize a different candidate. Note that Q accumulates all examples returned by the Teacher. The newly synthesized candidate must conform with all of the examples the Teacher has reported.

Definition 1 (ICE Examples). *Let S be a set of states. An ICE state is a triple (E, C, I), where $E \subseteq S$ is a set of E-Examples, $C \subseteq S$ is a set of C-Examples, and $I \subseteq S \times S$ is a set of I-Examples.*

Definition 2. *Let S be a set of states. A set $J \subseteq S$ is* consistent *with an ICE state (E, C, I) if (a) $E \subseteq J$, (b) $J \cap C = \emptyset$ and (c) for every $(s, t) \in I$, if $s \in J$, then $t \in J$.*

In the context of learning inductive invariants, S is the set of states in a transition system T. Each E-example is a reachable state of T (i.e., $E \subseteq post^*(\mathit{Init})$), each C-example is a state that reaches a bad state (i.e., $C \subseteq pre^*(\mathit{Bad})$), and each I-example is a pair of states $(s, t) \in \mathit{Tr}$.

The Teacher in the ICE framework must return one of the ICE-Examples as a reason showing why J is not a safe inductive invariant, according to the following rules:

Input: A transition system $T = (\mathcal{V}, \mathit{Init}, \mathit{Tr}, \mathit{Bad})$

9 $Q \leftarrow \emptyset$; LEARNER() ; TEACHER(T);
10 **repeat**
11 $\quad J \leftarrow$ LEARNER.SYNCANDIDATE(Q);
12 $\quad \varepsilon \leftarrow$ TEACHER.ISIND(J);
13 $\quad$ **if** $\varepsilon = \bot$ **then return** SAFE;
14 $\quad Q \leftarrow Q \cup \{\varepsilon\}$;
15 **until** ∞;

Algorithm 2. ICE: Main loop.

- I-example: $\exists (s,t) \in \mathit{Tr} \cdot s \in J \wedge t \notin J$
- C-example: $\exists s \in \mathrm{pre}^*(\mathit{Bad}) \cdot s \in J$
- E-example: $\exists s \in \mathrm{post}^*(\mathit{Init}) \cdot s \notin J$

If multiple choices are possible, the Teacher is free to chose an example to return, but it must return an example if one exists.

If J is not a safe inductive invariant, the Learner needs to modify it in order to be consistent with the new example provided by the Teacher. The required modification depends on the kind of an example the Teacher returns. Given a C-example, J must be strengthened to exclude the bad state, while for an E-example, J must be weakened to include the reachable state. In the case of an I-example (s,t), both options are possible. More precisely, either s is removed from J or t is included in J. The ICE framework leaves the details of how the candidate is improved to an underlying learning algorithm. The only requirement is that each new candidate must be consistent with the current ICE state. In particular, the new candidate might be incomparable to the previous one: it does not have to be the result of pure strengthening or weakening.

3   The RICE Framework for Invariant Synthesis

In this section, we present our MLIS framework *RICE* that extends ICE with relative induction. In an MLIS framework such as ICE, the Learner can only control the Teacher indirectly through the query interface. On the other hand, MC-SAT algorithms such as IC3 rely on a tight integration with a SAT-solver. In Sect. 4, we show that allowing for relatively inductive queries provides the Learner sufficient power to control the Teacher.

As in ICE, a RICE state is a triple (E, C, I) (see Definition 1). Recall that F is inductive relative to G when $F \wedge G \wedge \mathit{Tr} \Rightarrow F'$. A pair (F, G) is consistent with a RICE state (E, C, I), if F is consistent (as in ICE) with E and C, and F is consistent with all pairs $\{(s,t) \in I \mid s \in G\}$. Formally,

Definition 3. *Let S be a set of states in a transition system T. A set $F \subseteq S$ is* consistent *with a RICE state (E, C, I) relative to a set $G \subseteq S$, if $E \subseteq F$, $F \cap C = \emptyset$ and for every $(s,t) \in I$, if $s \in F \cap G$, $t \in F$ as well.*

Input: A transition system $T = (\mathcal{V}, \mathit{Init}, \mathit{Tr}, \mathit{Bad})$

16 $Q \leftarrow \emptyset \,;\, H \leftarrow \mathit{false}$;
17 LEARNER() ; TEACHER(T);
18 **repeat**
19 $\quad$ $(F, G) \leftarrow$ LEARNER.SYNCANDANDBASE(Q);
20 $\quad$ $\varepsilon \leftarrow$ TEACHER.ISRELIND(F, G);
21 $\quad$ **if** $\varepsilon = \bot \wedge G = \mathit{true}$ **then return** SAFE;
22 $\quad$ $Q \leftarrow Q \cup \{\varepsilon\}$;
23 **until** ∞;

Algorithm 3. RICE.

That is, the *base* set G can be used to communicate to the Teacher which I-examples the Learner is interested in.

Accordingly, the Teacher in a RICE framework must adhere to the following rules. Given a formula F (called a *candidate*) and a formula G (called a *base*), then if any one of the following holds:

- $\exists (s, t) \in \mathit{Tr} \cdot s \in (F \wedge G) \wedge t \notin F$ (I-example)
- $\exists s \in \mathrm{pre}^*(\mathit{Bad}) \cdot s \in F$ (C-example)
- $\exists s \in \mathrm{post}^*(\mathit{Init}) \cdot s \notin F$ (E-example)

the Teacher returns a corresponding ICE-example, and, otherwise, it returns $\bot$ to indicate that no ICE-example exists. We refer to such a Teacher as a RICE-Teacher.

The RICE framework is shown in Algorithm 3. There are a few major differences compared to ICE. First, the Learner returns a pair (F, G) as a candidate and asks the Teacher if F is inductive relative to G (lines 19–20). If an ICE-example exists, it is added to Q and the Learner must synthesize a new pair (F, G) that is consistent with Q (Definition 3). Second, when no ICE example exists the behavior depends on the value of G. Whenever G is *true* the Learner asks if F is a safe inductive invariant (similar to ICE). Thus, only when $G = \mathit{true}$ and no ICE-examples exists, RICE terminates declaring F a safe inductive invariant (line 21).

Note that termination of the RICE framework depends on the Learner setting G to *true* occasionally. It is easy to see that RICE simulates ICE whenever the learner sets G to *true* infinitely often: When G is set to *true*, the set F in the pair (F, G) is in fact an ICE-candidate (it is consistent with the ICE-state). Therefore, the sequence of steps between two subsequent candidates with $G = \mathit{true}$ can be viewed as an active variant of the ICE Learner: instead of computing a candidate F in isolation, it communicates with the Teacher. In this sense, RICE is a generalization of ICE, in which the Learner is an active learning algorithm.

Lemma 1. *RICE terminates if $G = \mathit{true}$ infinitely often.*

4   IC3 as an Instance of (R)ICE

RICE and ICE are generic MLIS frameworks. In this section, we show that IC3 is an instance of RICE by suggesting an IC3-specific implementations for both the Learner and the Teacher.

Re-factoring IC3 into a Teacher and a Learner. In an MLIS framework, the Learner does not have a direct access to the transition system T. It learns information about it only through the interaction with the Teacher. Thus, when re-factoring IC3 for an MLIS framework, we delegate the role traditionally taken by the SAT-solver to the Teacher and keep the rest for the Learner.

Challenges in Simulating the IC3 Queries. While RICE supports relative induction queries, these do not immediately correspond to the queries performed by IC3. There are two reasons for that. First, the requirement of the Learner to be consistent with the current RICE state, and second, the requirement of the Teacher to return an ICE-example when it exists. Namely, if neither I-example nor E-example exist, F is inductive relative to G. Yet, the converse does not necessarily hold – relative induction only requires $Init \Rightarrow F$, hence, E-examples might exist even when F is inductive relative to G. Moreover, if F contains a bad state, the Teacher will return a C-example even when F is inductive relative to G. This highlights the complexity in simulating relative induction queries of IC3 using the Teacher-Learner paradigm.

4.1   The IC3-Learner

Contrary to the "white-box" implementation of IC3, in the MLIS framework the Learner has no control over the "type" of answers the Teacher returns (e.g., the Teacher is free to choose between C- and I-examples when both are available). Therefore, the Learner must be robust such that soundness and completeness are maintained even when the Teacher is adversarial.

Similarly to the original IC3, the IC3-Learner maintains a monotone inductive trace $\boldsymbol{F}$. In addition, it maintains the RICE state, $Q = (I, C, E)$, containing the ICE-examples returned by the Teacher (which can be viewed as a generalization of the set of CTIs maintained by IC3). However, the IC3-Learner maintains the I-examples *explicitly*. These are only maintained implicitly by IC3 – they are captured by the lemmas that were not pushed.

Detailed Description of the IC3-Learner. The IC3-Learner is shown in Algorithm 4. It maintains an inductive trace $\boldsymbol{F}$ and the RICE state, $Q = (I, C, E)$, containing the ICE-examples returned by the Teacher, where $C(Q)$, $E(Q)$ and $I(Q)$ denote all C-examples, E-examples and I-examples in Q, respectively. Intuitively, from the learning perspective, each element of the trace is a candidate to be a safe inductive invariant. The Learner refines those candidates incrementally based on answers returned by the Teacher. Each iteration of the loop either discovers a new C-example that is added to Q or removes a C-example from a given candidate F_k (line 27). In the latter case, other candidates are refined as well based on the refinement of F_k (line 30).

Input: initial states *Init* and a RICE-Teacher TEACHER

```
24  F₀ ← Init ; F = [F₀, true] ; Q ← ∅;
25  repeat
26  |   (s, k) ← MINBAD(F, Q) ;                        // s is a C-example
27  |   r ← STRENGTHEN(s, k, Q);
28  |   if r = cex then return UNSAFE;
29  |   if r = blocked then
30  |   |   if PUSH(F, Q, k − 1) then return SAFE;
31  until ∞;
```

Algorithm 4. IC3-Learner.

Input: a trace F and a set of ICE-examples Q

```
32  N ← F.size() ; k ← min({N + 1} ∪ {j | C(Q) ∩ Fⱼ ≠ ∅});
33  if k < N + 1 then s ← a state from C(Q) ∩ Fₖ;
34  else
35  |   ε ← TEACHER.ISRELIND(F_N ∧ ¬C(Q), true) ;
36  |   if ε ≠ ⊥ then Q ← Q ∪ {ε};
37  |   if ε is a C-example then
38  |   |   s ← ε ; k ← min{j | C(Q) ∩ Fⱼ ≠ ∅}
39  |   else
40  |   |   F.addFrame(true);
41  |   |   s ← a state from C(Q) ; k ← N + 1;
42  return (s, k);
```

Algorithm 5. IC3-Learner: implementation of MINBAD.

The candidate F_k and the C-example to be removed are set by calling MINBAD (line 26). MINBAD (shown in Algorithm 5) returns the minimal element of F that contains a C-example from Q. In particular, if no C-example from $C(Q)$ exists in any element of F, MINBAD calls the Teacher. If the Teacher returns a C-example, then it necessarily belongs to one of the existing frames. Hence, it is added to Q and the minimal frame, F_k, in which it resides is returned. Otherwise, a new frame is initialized to *true*. The new frame necessarily contains one of the existing C-examples from $C(Q)$, and is therefore returned. Since MINBAD returns the minimal k, we have that $\forall 0 \leq i < k \cdot F_i \Rightarrow \neg C(Q)$. We refer to such a prefix F^{k-1} as Q-safe:

Definition 4. *Let* $F = [F_0, \ldots, F_N]$ *be an inductive trace,* Q *a RICE state and* $0 \leq j \leq N$. *If* $\forall 0 < i \leq j \cdot F_i \Rightarrow \neg C(Q)$, *then* F^j *is* Q *safe.*

Removing C-examples by Strengthening. The IC3-Learner's function STRENGTHEN is shown in Algorithm 6. It is used to remove a C-example s from frame F_k. If $k = 0$, i.e., the C-example is in F_0 then no safe inductive invariant exists and, thus, STRENGTHEN concludes a counterexample exists. Otherwise, it asks the Teacher if $\neg s \wedge \neg C(Q)$ is inductive relative to F_{k-1}. Note that this is in contrast to the original IC3 that checks if $\neg s$ is inductive relative to F_{k-1}. The

Input: a state s, index k, set of ICE-examples Q

43 **if** $k = 0$ **then return** cex;

44 $\varepsilon \leftarrow$ TEACHER.ISRELIND$(\neg s \wedge \neg C(Q), F_{k-1})$;

45 **if** ε *is an E-example* **then return** cex;

46 **if** $\varepsilon = \perp$ **then**

47 | $\quad c \leftarrow$ GENERALIZE$(\neg s, F_{k-1}, F_k, Q)$;

48 | $\quad \forall 0 \leq j \leq k \cdot F_j \leftarrow F_j \wedge c$;

49 | $\quad$ **return** blocked;

50 $Q \leftarrow Q \cup \{\varepsilon\}$;

51 **return** not_blocked;

Algorithm 6. IC3-Learner: implementation of STRENGTHEN.

conjunct $\neg C(Q)$ is added to the query in order to conform with the requirement of providing a candidate that is consistent with the RICE state. In particular, it prevents the Teacher from returning a C-example that already exists in Q. Moreover, using this query is sound since the property that $F_{k-1} \Rightarrow \neg C(Q)$ ($\boldsymbol{F}^{k-1}$ is Q-safe) ensures that relative inductiveness of $\neg s \wedge \neg C(Q)$ w.r.t. F_{k-1} implies relative inductiveness of $\neg s$ as well.

If an E-example e is returned, then a counterexample to the property must exist (line 45) since the reachable state e is either s or some other state in $C(Q)$. On the other hand, if either an I-example or a C-example is returned, STRENGTHEN treats it as a new C-example that is added to Q (line 50). The justification for treating I-examples as C-examples is that in this case an I-example represents a predecessor to a bad state (either s, or another state in $C(Q)$), and is, therefore, also a C-example.

In case no ICE-example is returned, $\neg s \wedge \neg C(Q)$ is relatively inductive (and, hence, also $\neg s$), and a new lemma that blocks s is added to F_k and to all previous frames (lines 47–49).

Finding a New Lemma by Generalization. Whenever a C-example s is blocked, the fact that $\boldsymbol{F}^{k-1}$ is Q-safe implies that

$$F_0 \Rightarrow \neg s \qquad (F_{k-1} \wedge \neg s)(\mathcal{V}) \wedge Tr(\mathcal{V}, \mathcal{V}') \Rightarrow \neg s(\mathcal{V}') \qquad (6)$$

holds. Generalization relies on the above and tries to find a lemma c such that $c \Rightarrow \neg s$, $F_0 \Rightarrow c$ and

$$(F_{k-1} \wedge c)(\mathcal{V}) \wedge Tr(\mathcal{V}, \mathcal{V}') \Rightarrow c(\mathcal{V}') \qquad (7)$$

The generalization procedure is shown in Algorithm 7. The invariant of the main loop is that c is inductive relative to F_i. The loop starts by looking for a new stronger lemma d s.t. $d \Rightarrow c$. If d is not consistent with the current I- and E-examples, a new d is tried. Note that $\neg s$ itself is consistent with the I- and E-examples (this is ensured by STRENGTHEN), hence a d that is consistent with the I- and E-examples always exists. Otherwise, a relative induction query is sent to the Teacher (line 57). If an ICE-example is found, it is added to Q. Otherwise,

Input: a lemma $\neg s$, frames F_i and F_{i+1}, and a set of ICE-examples Q

52 $c \leftarrow \neg s$;
53 **repeat**
54 $\quad$ choose d s.t. $d \Rightarrow c$;
55 $\quad$ **if** $d \equiv c$ **then break**;
56 $\quad$ **if** $\neg$IE-CONSISTENT(d, F_i, Q) **then continue**;
57 $\quad$ $\varepsilon \leftarrow$ TEACHER.ISRELIND$(d \wedge \neg C(Q) \wedge F_{i+1}, F_i)$;
58 $\quad$ **if** $\varepsilon = \perp$ **then** $c \leftarrow d$;
59 $\quad$ **else** $Q \leftarrow Q \cup \{\varepsilon\}$;
60 **until** ∞;
61 **return** c

Algorithm 7. IC3-Learner: implementation of GENERALIZE.

Input: a lemma l, a frame F_i, and a set of ICE-examples Q

62 **if** $\exists (s, t) \in I(Q) \cdot s \in (F_i \wedge l) \wedge t \notin l$ **then return** *false*;
63 **if** $\exists s \in E(Q) \cdot s \notin l$ **then return** *false*;
64 **return** *true*

Algorithm 8. IC3-Learner: implementation of IE-CONSISTENT.

$d \wedge \neg C(Q) \wedge F_{i+1}$ is inductive relative to F_i, and therefore c is updated. The loop terminates, and the corresponding lemma is returned, when c does not change.

It is important to note that while GENERALIZE tries to find a lemma d that is inductive relative to F_i, it asks the Teacher if $d \wedge \neg C(Q) \wedge F_{i+1}$ is inductive relative to F_i. The addition of $\neg C(Q)$ to the query is similar in reason and justification to STRENGTHEN. As for the addition of F_{i+1}, the following properties:

$$\begin{cases} F_i(\mathcal{V}) \Rightarrow F_{i+1}(\mathcal{V}), \text{ and} \\ F_i(\mathcal{V}) \wedge Tr(\mathcal{V}, \mathcal{V}') \Rightarrow F_{i+1}(\mathcal{V}') \end{cases} \tag{8}$$

imply that the query is equivalent to asking if $d \wedge \neg C(Q)$ is inductive relative to F_i. Adding F_{i+1} to the candidate is meant to prevent the Teacher from returning C-examples (bad states) that are already known to be blocked by F_{i+1}.

Making Conjectures by Pushing. Similarly to the original IC3, the IC3-Learner also tries to push lemmas (line 30). PUSH is shown in Algorithm 9. PUSH takes a trace F, a RICE state Q, and an index k such that F^k is Q-safe. Given a lemma $c \in F_i$ for $i \leq k$, the Learner first checks if pushing is prevented by any of the known I-examples or E-examples (line 68). If not, the Learner asks if $c \wedge \neg C(Q) \wedge F_{i+1}$ is inductive relative to F_i. Again, we emphasize that this is sufficient to show that c is inductive relative to F_i. Therefore, if no ICE-example is returned, c is added to F_{i+1} (line 70).

In addition, any I-example that is returned by the Teacher is either an indication that c is not inductive relative to F_i or that a C-example exists. This is justified by the following lemma:

Lemma 2. *Let Q be a RICE state, and $\boldsymbol{F}$ be an inductive trace such that $\boldsymbol{F}^k$ is Q-safe. For $0 \leq i \leq k$ and $c \in F_i$, if $(s,t) \in Tr$ has the property that $s \in F_i \wedge c \wedge \neg C(Q) \wedge F_{i+1}$ and $t \notin c \wedge \neg C(Q) \wedge F_{i+1}$, then $s \in F_i \wedge c$ and in addition either (i) $t \notin c$ or (ii) $i = k$ and s is a bad state in F_k.*

Proof. The fact that $s \in F_i \wedge c$ is trivial. As for the second part, consider first the case where $i < k$. Note that in this case $(c \wedge \neg C(Q) \wedge F_{i+1}) \equiv c \wedge F_{i+1}$ (due to $\boldsymbol{F}^k$ being Q-safe). Thus, $t \notin c \wedge F_{i+1}$, or equivalently, $t \in \neg c \vee \neg F_{i+1}$. Let us assume $t \in \neg F_{i+1}$, this contradicts $s \in F_i$ and $F_i \wedge Tr \Rightarrow F'_{i+1}$. By that, $t \in \neg c$, equivalently, $t \notin c$. Now consider the case where $i = k$. In this case F_{k+1} may include a C-example. Still, $t \in \neg F_{k+1}$ does not hold (due to the same argument as in the $i < k$ case). Hence $t \in \neg c \vee C(Q)$. Thus, either $t \in \neg c$ or $t \in C(Q)$. In the former case, $t \notin c$. Otherwise, s is a bad state (a predecessor of a C-example). $\qquad\square$

Therefore, in case an I-example is returned by the Teacher, it is added to Q and c is not pushed since it is not inductive relative to F_i. If the post-state of the I-example is in c, the I-example is treated as a C-example (this can only happen when $i = k$).

However, there are additional possibilities. Since $c \wedge \neg C(Q) \wedge F_{i+1}$ may include a bad state, or exclude a reachable state, a C-example or an E-example are possible. Recall that we assume a Teacher that returns ICE-examples when those exist, therefore, if a C- or E-example exists it is returned even if $c \wedge \neg C(Q) \wedge F_{i+1}$ is inductive relative to F_i.

Whenever a C-example is returned by the Teacher, PUSH terminates (line 73) and the IC3-Learner goes back to the main loop to process a new candidate and a new C-example. In case of an E-example, it is added to Q and c is skipped.

Remark 1. The use of IE-CONSISTENT in lines 56 and 68 prevents the need to approach the Teacher in cases where a previous answer that is recorded in the RICE state Q already provides the desired information (e.g., whether a lemma is relative inductive). In this sense, the IC3-Learner can be understood as an optimized version of IC3 which uses memoization.

Safe Inductive Invariant. In case all lemmas in F_i are pushed to F_{i+1}, then F_i is an inductive invariant. If F_i is also safe, i.e. $F_i \Rightarrow \neg Bad$, then the IC3-Learner terminates and reports that a safe inductive invariant is found. Recall that the IC3-Learner maintains an inductive trace, and, therefore, checking for safety is done by asking the Teacher if F_i is inductive relative to *true* (line 75). Since we know that it is indeed an inductive invariant, if F_i is not safe, the Teacher returns a new C-example, and the IC3-Learner goes back to the main loop.

Lemma 3. *If the IC3-Learner returns UNSAFE, a counterexample exists.*

Proof. A counterexample is detected in Algorithm 6. There are two cases: either a C-example s is also an initial state and, therefore, $Init \cap pre^*(Bad) \neq \emptyset$, or a C-example is found to be an E-example and, therefore, $post^*(Init) \cap pre^*(Bad) \neq \emptyset$.

Input: a trace F, a set of ICE-examples Q, a number k
65 **foreach** $i \leftarrow 1$ **to** k **do**
66     $r \leftarrow true$;
67   **foreach** $c \in F_i$ **do**
68   **if** $\neg\text{IE-CONSISTENT}(c, F_i, Q)$ **then** $(r \leftarrow false$; **continue**);
69        $\varepsilon \leftarrow \text{TEACHER.ISRELIND}(c \wedge \neg C(Q) \wedge F_{i+1}, F_i)$;
70   **if** $\varepsilon = \bot$ **then** $F_{i+1} \leftarrow F_{i+1} \wedge c$;
71   **else**
72           $r \leftarrow false$; $Q \leftarrow Q \cup \{\varepsilon\}$;
73   **if** $\text{TYPE}(\varepsilon) = C$-*example* **then return** *false*;
74   **if** r **then**
75        $\varepsilon \leftarrow \text{TEACHER.ISRELIND}(F_i, true)$;
76   **if** $\varepsilon = \bot$ **then return** *true*;
77        $Q \leftarrow Q \cup \{\varepsilon\}$;
78 **return** *false*;

Algorithm 9. IC3-Learner: implementation of PUSH.

We conclude this section with a few formal claims on soundness and completeness of IC3-Learner.

Lemma 4. *If the IC3-Learner returns SAFE, a safe inductive invariant exists.*

Lemma 5. *For a finite-state system T, the IC3-Learner terminates.*

Shortcomings of the IC3-Learner. Since the Teacher must produce an ICE-example whenever it exists, relative induction queries will fail as long as there is a potential E- or C-example. Since both generalization and pushing are done via relative induction queries, this means that the IC3-Learner is limited to generating frames F_i that are between reachable ($post^*(Init) \Rightarrow F_i$) and safe ($F_i \Rightarrow \neg pre^*(Bad)$) regions. Note, however, that multiple frames might still be constructed because the frames must be closed under the transitions of the system. The search for such a frame might construct several candidates (i.e., frames). Another consequence of the Teacher's specification is that a frame will never be added before all the previous frames become safe. Therefore, MINBAD will always return a state from the last frame. In the next section, we address these limitations by placing additional restrictions on the Teacher.

4.2 An IC3-Teacher

In the previous section, we described an IC3-style Learner that assumes a generic Teacher. The behavior of the IC3-Learner is highly dependent on the answers returned by the Teacher. In order for the IC3 MLIS framework to behave like IC3, some additional restrictions must be imposed on the Teacher.

Requiring the Teacher to always produce E- and C-examples when they exists is unrealistic. Such a Teacher is required to look arbitrary far into the future

Input: A candidate F, a base G, numbers m and n

79 **if** $\exists s \in pre^m(Bad) \cdot s \in F$ **then return** C-example s;
80 **if** $\exists (s, t) \in Tr \cdot s \in (F \wedge G) \wedge t \notin F$ **then return** I-example (s, t);
81 **if** $\exists s \in post^n(Init) \cdot s \notin F$ **then return** E-example s;
82 **return** $\perp$;

Algorithm 10. IC3-Teacher: implementation of IsRelInd.

(for E-examples) or past (for C-examples). In most IC3 implementations there are two implicit assumptions. First, $Init$ is known a-priori and E-examples are restricted to $post^0(Init)$ (which is simply $Init$). Second, in every query to the Teacher, C-examples (i.e., bad states) are restricted to $pre^m(Bad)$ for some fixed m (which is determined by the algorithm and changes between queries). These two assumptions relate to the fact that IC3 maintains a safe inductive trace. Therefore, F_i over-approximates $post^i(Init)$, and is disjoint from $pre^{N-i}(Bad)$. Note that these requirements are easier to achieve, than over-approximating $post^*(Init)$, and being disjoint from $pre^*(Bad)$, respectively.

We use these observations to suggest an IC3-Teacher shown in Algorithm 10. Using IC3-Teacher, the IC3-Learner can restrict the E- and C-examples returned by setting specific bounds on them. By using this IC3-Teacher, the resulting algorithm is closer to IC3 than the one that uses the unrestricted RICE-Teacher.

Considering the IC3-Teacher from Algorithm 10, we write IsRelInd$(\psi, F_i, \infty, \infty)$ for the non-restrictive calls (i.e., parameters m and n are unlimited).

Lemma 6. *If every call of the form* IsRelInd$(\psi, F_i, \infty, \infty)$ *in IC3-Learner is replaced by* IsRelInd$(\psi, F_i, N - i - 1, 0)$, *then the combination of the IC3-Learner (Algorithm 4) and IC3-Teacher (Algorithm 10) simulates IC3. In particular, every generalization and pushing step of IC3 is also feasible in the MLIS implementation.*

Note that one could consider the restricted IC3-Teacher as an abstraction of the unrestricted IC3-Teacher. The abstraction is with respect to the answers the Teacher returns. More precisely, the IC3-Teacher can indicate that a candidate is relative inductive more often, since it can ignore C- and E-examples when a bound is applied. The key element in both the IC3-Teacher and RICE-Teacher, is to never miss an I-example. In fact, restricting the IC3-Teacher to return C- and E-examples from $pre^0(Bad)$ and $post^0(Init)$ respectively (i.e. using IsRelInd$(\psi, F_i, 0, 0)$) will also allow to simulate IC3, and will also be simulated by IC3, making the two simulation-equivalent.

5 IC3 Variants

The behavior of RICE is determined by how the Learner reacts to ICE-examples, and how the Teacher generates them. In this section, we analyze how different instances for both the IC3-Learner and IC3-Teacher affect the result.

Recall that in (R)ICE, the Learner suggests a candidate invariant, and the Teacher either confirms the candidate or gives an ICE-example that rules out the candidate. In the case of an E- and C-example s, the Learner must either include (E-example) or exclude (C-example) s from the candidate. In the case of an I-example (s,t), the Learner can either exclude s or include t. This gives some freedom to the Learner. In this section, we show how the IC3 Learner can handle I-examples, and show that different implementations result in different variants of IC3.

5.1   IC3 and Quip

IC3-Learner in Sect. 4.1 reacts to all ICE-examples. This is in contrast to a classical IC3 that is built around blocking C-examples, while E-examples are only treated implicitly by considering *Init*, and I-examples are implicitly present in generalization and pushing. In all cases, IC3 *weakens* the candidate with which the I-example is associated.

A variant of IC3 called QUIP [5] is different. It is based on the following observation: given a lemma $c \in F_i$, if c cannot be pushed to F_{i+1}, then either F_i is too weak to support c, or c cannot be pushed because it excludes a reachable state. In the context of RICE, if an I-example (s,t) is returned when trying to push c, either s can be removed from F_i, or an E-example exists that shows that c can never be part of an inductive invariant. Note that the IC3-Learner described previously uses this observation implicitly when checking whether a lemma c is consistent with all E-examples.

The pushing phase of an alternative IC3-Learner that explicitly exploits the above observation is shown in Algorithm 11. The main differences compared to the previously described PUSH (Algorithm 9) are in line 88 and line 94. Note that the function FINDREACHORSTRENGTHEN (called in line 94) is similar to how IC3 handles C-examples. It receives a state s, and either blocks it (by strengthening F) or proves s is reachable. Using FINDREACHORSTRENGTHEN and allowing the Teacher to find E-examples that are not restricted to *Init* only reflect the changes to how the IC3-Learner reacts to I- and E-examples during pushing. We describe these differences in more detail below:

E-examples: QUIP uses E-examples that are not restricted to *Init* (line 88). If a lemma excludes a reachable state it is marked to never be pushed again. Note that this already exists in the IC3-Learner to ensure that a candidate is always consistent with the current RICE state. Yet, in general, this is not present in the classical IC3. Furthermore, QUIP forces the Teacher to discover reachable states from I-examples using FINDREACHORSTRENGTHEN. FINDREACHORSTRENGTHEN is similar to how IC3 handles C-examples but discovers reachable states that are added as E-examples.

I-examples: In IC3, when a lemma $c \in F_i$ cannot be pushed due to an I-example, it is skipped and not added to F_{i+1}. Hence, F_{i+1} is weaker than F_i. In contrast, QUIP tries to strengthen F_i. For example, let (s,t) be an

Input: a trace F, a set of all ICE examples Q, a number k

83 **foreach** $i \leftarrow 1$ **to** k **do**
84 | $r \leftarrow$ true;
85 | **foreach** $c \in F_i$ **do**
86 | | **if** $\neg$IE-CONSISTENT(c, F_i, Q) **then** $(r \leftarrow$ false ; **continue**);
87 | | **repeat**
88 | | | $\varepsilon \leftarrow$ TEACHER.ISRELIND$(c \wedge \neg C(Q), F_i, N - i - 1, i + 1)$;
89 | | | **if** $\varepsilon = \bot$ **then** $(F_{i+1} \leftarrow F_{i+1} \wedge c$; **break**);
90 | | | **else**
91 | | | | $Q \leftarrow Q \cup \{\varepsilon\}$;
92 | | | | **if** ε *is a C-example* **then return** false;
93 | | | | **else if** ε *is an I-example* (s, t) **then**
94 | | | | | **if** FINDREACHORSTRENGTHEN$(c, F, Q, i - 1) = reach$
| | | | | **then**
95 | | | | | | Add t to Q as an E-example;
96 | | | | | | $r \leftarrow$ false;
97 | | | | | | **break**;
98 | | **until** ∞;
99 | | **if** r **then**
100 | | | $\varepsilon \leftarrow$ TEACHER.ISRELIND$(F_i, true)$;
101 | | | **if** $\varepsilon = \bot$ **then return** true;
102 | | | $Q \leftarrow Q \cup \{\varepsilon\}$;
103 **return** false

Algorithm 11. QUIPPUSH.

I-example. QUIP treats s as a bad state and tries to remove it from F_i by calling FINDREACHORSTRENGTHEN (line 94). If it succeeds it can try and push c again. Otherwise, QUIP discovers that s is reachable in i steps and, therefore, t is reachable in $i + 1$ steps. In this case, t is an E-example.

Note that if the Teacher happens to prioritize E-examples over I-examples, then the QUIP-Learner does not extract reachable states from I-examples, but does still force pushing by strengthening.

The above description is not confined to pushing only. I- and E-examples can also be used during generalization. Note that currently the function GENERALIZE calls IE-CONSISTENT and thus takes into account every E-example in Q.

In addition, *weakening* can be applied differently. Currently, if a given lemma $c \in F_i$ is non-pushable, instead of giving up on that lemma and weakening by not adding it to F_{i+1}, the IC3-Learner can choose to weaken the lemma itself such that it becomes pushable.

6   Conclusions

In this paper, we introduced the RICE framework for Machine Learning-based Invariant Synthesis (MLIS). RICE is an extension of the ICE MLIS framework [3,4]. It extends the MLIS-Teacher to support relative-induction queries. This improves the communication between the MLIS-Teacher and the MLIS-Learner. In particular, it allows the Learner to be statefull (i.e., *active* in Machine Learning terminology) and better guide the Teacher to desired responses.

We showed that a well-known SAT-based Model Checking (SAT-MC) algorithm IC3 [1] can be formulated as an instance of RICE. We do so, by designing a specific IC3-Learner and a corresponding IC3-Teacher in the MLIS framework. We showed how ICE-examples are handled by the IC3-Learner, and explicated sufficient requirements on the IC3-Teacher for the combination to simulate the IC3 algorithm. Furthermore, we showed that different variants of IC3 correspond to different instances of the IC3-Teacher. In particular, we show that a recent SAT-MC algorithm QUIP [5] is an instance of the RICE MLIS framework in which the Teacher does not restrict E-examples to the set of initial states *Init*, and the Learner guides the Teacher to discover useful E-examples.

Our work opens many avenues for future exploration in similarities and differences between MLIS and SAT-MC frameworks for invariant synthesis. From the MLIS perspective, an interesting question is how to include other active learning algorithms effectively into the framework and how to make the Learner incremental. From the SAT-MC perspective, an interesting question is how to incorporate new forms of weakening other than "pushing". For example, individual lemmas can be weakened by adding literals to make the frames consistent with all (implicit) ICE-examples generated by the run of a SAT-MC algorithm so far. We hope to explore these fruitful directions in the future.

Acknowledgments. The research leading to these results has received funding from the European Research Council under the European Union's Seventh Framework Programme (FP7/2007–2013)/ERC grant agreement No. [321174].

References

1. Bradley, A.R.: SAT-based model checking without unrolling. In: Jhala, R., Schmidt, D. (eds.) VMCAI 2011. LNCS, vol. 6538, pp. 70–87. Springer, Berlin (2011). doi:10.1007/978-3-642-18275-4_7
2. Eén, N., Mishchenko, A., Brayton, R.K.: Efficient implementation of property directed reachability. In: International Conference on Formal Methods in Computer-Aided Design, FMCAD 2011, Austin, TX, USA, 30 October–02 November 2011, pp. 125–134 (2011)
3. Garg, P., Löding, C., Madhusudan, P., Neider, D.: ICE: a robust framework for learning invariants. In: Biere, A., Bloem, R. (eds.) CAV 2014. LNCS, vol. 8559, pp. 69–87. Springer, Cham (2014). doi:10.1007/978-3-319-08867-9_5
4. Garg, P., Neider, D., Madhusudan, P., Roth, D.: Learning invariants using decision trees and implication counterexamples. In: Proceedings of the 43rd Annual ACM SIGPLAN-SIGACT Symposium on Principles of Programming Languages, POpPL, St. Petersburg, FL, USA, 20–22 January 2016, pp. 499–512 (2016)
5. Gurfinkel, A., Ivrii, A.: Pushing to the top. In: Formal Methods in Computer-Aided Design, FMCAD, Austin, Texas, USA, 27–30 September 2015, pp. 65–72 (2015)

6. Löding, C., Madhusudan, P., Neider, D.: Abstract learning frameworks for synthesis. In: Chechik, M., Raskin, J.-F. (eds.) TACAS 2016. LNCS, vol. 9636, pp. 167–185. Springer, Heidelberg (2016). doi:10.1007/978-3-662-49674-9_10
7. McMillan, K.L.: Interpolation and SAT-based model checking. In: Hunt, W.A., Somenzi, F. (eds.) CAV 2003. LNCS, vol. 2725, pp. 1–13. Springer, Heidelberg (2003). doi:10.1007/978-3-540-45069-6_1
8. Sharma, R., Gupta, S., Hariharan, B., Aiken, A., Liang, P., Nori, A.V.: A data driven approach for algebraic loop invariants. In: Felleisen, M., Gardner, P. (eds.) ESOP 2013. LNCS, vol. 7792, pp. 574–592. Springer, Heidelberg (2013). doi:10.1007/978-3-642-37036-6_31
9. Vizel, Y., Gurfinkel, A.: Interpolating property directed reachability. In: Biere, A., Bloem, R. (eds.) CAV 2014. LNCS, vol. 8559, pp. 260–276. Springer, Heidelberg (2014). doi:10.1007/978-3-319-08867-9_17

Partitioned Memory Models for Program Analysis

Wei Wang[1]($\boxtimes$), Clark Barrett[2], and Thomas Wies[1]

[1] New York University, New York City, USA
wwang1109@cims.nyu.edu
[2] Stanford University, Stanford, USA

Abstract. Scalability is a key challenge in static analysis. For imperative languages like C, the approach taken for modeling memory can play a significant role in scalability. In this paper, we explore a family of memory models called *partitioned memory models* which divide memory up based on the results of a points-to analysis. We review Steensgaard's original and field-sensitive points-to analyses as well as Data Structure Analysis (DSA), and introduce a new *cell-based* points-to analysis which more precisely handles heap data structures and type-unsafe operations like pointer arithmetic and pointer casting. We give experimental results on benchmarks from the software verification competition using the program verification framework in Cascade. We show that a partitioned memory model using our cell-based points-to analysis outperforms models using other analyses.

1 Introduction

Solvers for Satisfiability Modulo Theories (SMT) are widely used as back ends for program analysis and verification tools. In a typical application, portions of a program's source code together with one or more desired properties are translated into formulas which are then checked for satisfiability by an SMT solver. A key challenge in many of these applications is scalability: for larger programs, the solver often fails to report an answer within a reasonable amount of time because the generated formula is too complex. Thus, one key objective in program analysis and verification research is finding ways to reduce the complexity of SMT formulas arising from program analysis.

For imperative languages like C, the modeling of memory can play a significant role in formula complexity. For example, a *flat model* of memory represents all of memory as a single array of bytes. This model is simple and precise and can soundly and accurately represent type-unsafe constructs and operations like unions, pointer arithmetic, and casts. On the other hand, the flat model implicitly assumes that any two symbolic memory locations could alias or overlap, even when it is known statically that such aliasing is impossible. Introducing *disjointness* constraints for every pair of non-overlapping locations leads to a quadratic blow-up in formula size, quickly becoming a bottleneck for scalability.

© Springer International Publishing AG 2017
A. Bouajjani and D. Monniaux (Eds.): VMCAI 2017, LNCS 10145, pp. 539–558, 2017.
DOI: 10.1007/978-3-319-52234-0_29

The *Burstall model* [6] is a well-known alternative that addresses this by having a separate array for each distinct type in the language. It is based on the assumption that pointers with different types never alias, eliminating the need for disjointness constraints between such pointers. However, it cannot model many type-unsafe operations, making it unsuitable for languages like C.

This paper discusses a family of memory models, which we call *partitioned memory models*, whose goal is to provide much of the efficiency of the Burstall model without losing the accuracy of the flat model. These models rely on a points-to analysis to determine a conservative approximation of which areas of memory may alias or overlap. The memory is then partitioned into distinct arrays for each of these areas.

When deciding which points-to analysis performs best in this context, there are two key attributes to consider: (1) the precision of the analysis (i.e. how many alias groups are generated); and (2) the ability to track the access size of objects in the alias group. The first is important because more alias groups means more partitions and fewer disjointness constraints. The second is important because if we know that all objects in the group are of a certain access size, then we can model the corresponding partition as an array whose elements are that size. After a review of existing field-sensitive points-to analyses (including Steensgaard's original analysis [27], Steensgaard's field-sensitive analysis [26], and Data Structure Analysis (DSA) [18]), we introduce a new *cell-based* points-to analysis and show that it improves on both of these attributes when compared to existing analyses. This is supported by experiments using the Cascade verification platform [29].

2   Memory Models for C Program Analysis

Consider the C code in Fig. 1. We will look at how to model the code using the flat memory model, the Burstall memory model, and the partitioned memory models.

```
int a;

void foo() {
    int *b = &a;
    *b = 0xFFF;
    char *c = (char *) b;
    *c = 0x0;
    assert(a != 0xFFF);
}
```

Fig. 1. Code with unsafe pointer cast.

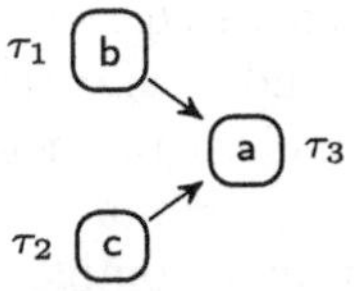

Fig. 2. The points-to graph of foo. Each τ_i represents a distinct alias group.

Flat Model. In the flat model, a single array of bytes is used to track all memory operations, and each program variable is modeled as the content of some address in memory. Suppose M is the memory array, a is the *location* in M which stores the value of the variable a, and b is the *location* in M which stores the value of the variable b. We could then model the first two lines of foo in Fig. 1 (following SMT-LIB syntax [3]) as follows:

```
(assert (= M1 (store M b a))                       ; M[b] := a
(assert (= M2 (store M1 (select M1 b) #xfff)) ; M[M[b]] := 0xfff
```

This is typical of the flat model: each program statement layers another store on top of the current model of memory. As a result, the depth of nested stores can get very large. Also, note that C guarantees that the memory regions of any two variables are non-overlapping. But the flat model must explicitly model this using an assumption on each pair of variables. This can be done with the following disjointness predicate, where p and q denote locations of variables, and $size(p)$ is the size of the memory region starting at location p:

$$disjoint(p, q) \equiv p + size(p) \leq q \vee q + size(q) \leq p.$$

For the code in Fig. 1, the required assumption is: $disjoint(a, b) \wedge disjoint(a, c) \wedge disjoint(c, b)$. Deeply nested stores and the need for such disjointness assertions severely limit the scalability of the flat model.

Burstall Model. In the Burstall model, memory is split into several arrays based on the *type* of the data being stored. In Fig. 1, there are four different types of data, so the model would use four arrays: M_{int}, M_{char}, M_{int*} and M_{char*}. In this model, a is a location in M_{int}, b is a location in M_{int*}, and c is a location in M_{char*}. Disjointness is guaranteed implicitly by the distinctness of the arrays. The depth of nested stores is also limited to the number of stores to locations having the same type rather than to the number of total stores to memory. Both of these features greatly improve performance. However, the model fails to prove the assertion in Fig. 1. The reason is that the assumption that pointers to different types never alias is incorrect for type-unsafe languages like C.

Partitioned Models. In the partitioned memory model, memory is divided into regions based on information acquired by running a points-to analysis.[1] The result of a standard points-to analysis is a points-to graph whose vertices are sets of program locations called alias groups. An edge from an alias group τ_1 to an alias group τ_2 indicates that dereferencing a location in τ_1 gives a location in τ_2. As an example, the points-to graph for the code in Fig. 1 is shown in Fig. 2. There are three alias groups identified: one for each of the variables a, b, and c. We can thus store the values for these variables in three different memory arrays (making their disjointness trivial). Note that according to the points-to graph, a dereference of either b or c must be modeled using the array containing the location of a, meaning that the model is sufficiently precise to prove the assertion. Like the Burstall model, the partitioned model divides memory into multiple arrays, reducing the burden on the solver. However, it does this in a way that is sound with respect to type-unsafe behavior.

---

[1] A formal presentation of the semantics of the partitioned memory model is presented in [28].

The points-to analysis employed by the partitioned memory model must derive points-to relations that are also functions. That is, each node must have only a single successor in the points-to graph. This is because the successor determines the array to use when modeling a pointer dereference. The unification-based analyses proposed by Steensgaard [27] naturally guarantee this property. However, inclusion-based analyses proposed by Andersen [1] and others violate it. For this reason, we focus on Steensgaard's method and its variants.

Partitioned memory models that rely on unification-based points-to analyses are already used in a number of verification tools. For example, SMACK [24] leverages data structure analysis (DSA) [18], a field-sensitive and context-sensitive points-to analysis, to divide the memory. SeaHorn [13] uses a simpler context-insensitive variant of DSA. CBMC [7] and ESBMC [20] also use may-points-to information to refine their memory models. These tools illustrate the practical value of partitioned memory models. Note that in each case, the efficiency of the memory model depends heavily on the precision of the underlying points-to analysis. The more precise the analysis, the more partitions there are, which means fewer disjointness constraints and shallower array terms, both of which reduce the size and difficulty of the resulting SMT formulas.

3   Field-Sensitive Points-to Analyses

Field-sensitivity is one dimension that measures the precision of points-to analyses. We say a pointer analysis is field-sensitive if it tracks individual record fields with a set of unique locations. That is, a store to one field does not affect other fields. In this sense, a field-sensitive analysis is much more precise than a field-insensitive one. Unfortunately, field-sensitivity is complicated by the weak type system of the C language. With the presence of union types, pointer casts, and pointer arithmetic, fields may not be guaranteed to be disjoint. The original Steensgaard's points-to analysis treats fields as a single alias group, while his field-sensitive analysis [26] improves the precision by separating fields into distinct alias groups only if the fields do not participate in any type-unsafe operations. Yong et al. [30] also propose to collapse fields upon detecting a field access through a pointer whose type does not match the declared type of the field. However, none of these analyses are able to distinguish fields on heap data structures (dynamic memory allocations).

Lattner et al. [18] present a data structure based points-to analysis (DSA), a unification-based, field-sensitive, and context-sensitive analysis. DSA explicitly tracks the type information and data layout of heap data structures and performs a conservative but safe field-sensitive analysis. The other key feature of DSA is that two objects allocated at the same location in a function called from different call sites are distinguished. It is in this sense that the analysis is context-sensitive. This feature, however, is orthogonal to our focus in this paper.

DSA computes a Data Structure Graph (DS graph) to explicitly model the heap. A DS graph consists of a set of nodes (DS nodes) representing memory objects and a set of points-to edges. Each DS node tracks the type information and data layout of the represented objects. If two DS nodes or their inner fields may be pointed to by the same pointer, they are merged together. When two DS nodes are merged, their type information and data layouts are also merged if *compatible*; otherwise, both nodes are *collapsed*, meaning that all fields are combined into a single alias group. To illustrate the DS node merging and collapsing process, we use the code in Fig. 3 as a running example (for simplicity, we assume pointers are 32 bits in this example).

```
typedef struct list {
  struct list *prev, *next;
  int32 data;
} list;

void bar(int32 undef, list **p) {
  list *k = malloc(sizeof(list));
  k->data = 1;
  p = undef < 0 ?
      &k->prev : &k->next;
}
```

```
void foo(int32 undef, list **p) {
  list *k1 = malloc(sizeof(list));
  list *k2 = malloc(sizeof(list));
  k1->data = 1; k2->data = 2;
  p = undef < 0 ?
      &k1->next : &k2->prev;
}
```

Fig. 3. Code for running example.

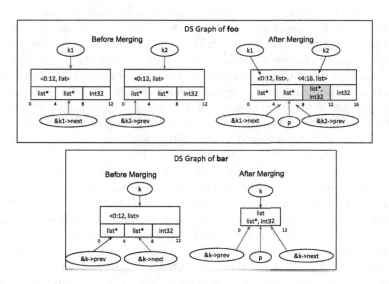

Fig. 4. DS Graph for function foo and bar (see [18]). Note that the numbers under each DS node are the offsets of its inner fields in bytes.

In function foo, an alias relationship between k1−>next and k2−>prev is introduced via a conditional assignment. The aliasing of the two fields, as mentioned above, causes the merging of their containing DS nodes. The merging process is shown in Fig. 4. Before being merged, the DS nodes pointed to by k1 and k2 are disjoint, and each holds the type information of structure list , including the field layout. During the process of merging, the DS node pointed by k2 is shifted by 4 bytes to align the aliased fields and is then merged with the node pointed to by k1. In the resulting graph, we can see that the aliased fields k1−>next and k2−>prev are placed together, but the subsequent fields k1−>data and k2−>next are also placed in the same cell (colored gray), even though they are not aliased.

In function bar, the conditional assignment introduces an alias relationship between two fields in the same DS node pointed to by k. In this case, as shown in Fig. 4, the whole DS node is collapsed and all the fields are merged into a single alias group. The reason for this is that in DSA, if a DS node is merged with itself with shifting, this is considered an *incompatible* merge. In other words, DSA does not support field sensitivity for records with inner field aliasing.

As shown above, while DSA does support field-sensitive points-to analysis on heap data structures, the computed alias information is still rather conservative. By performing the merging process at the object level (DS nodes) rather than at the field level, invalid alias relationships are introduced. Partly to address these issues, we developed a novel *cell-based* field-sensitive (CFS) points-to analysis.

4   Cell-Based Points-to Analysis

A *cell*[2] is a generalization of an alias group. Initially, each program expression that corresponds to a memory location at runtime (i.e. an l-value) is associated with a unique cell whose *size* is a positive integer denoting the size (in bytes) of the values that expression can have. In addition, each cell has a type, which is *scalar* unless its associated program expression is of structure or union type (in which case the cell type is *record*). Under certain conditions, the analysis may merge cells. If two cells of two different sizes are merged, then the result is a cell whose size is $\top$. The analysis maintains an invariant that the locations associated with any two isolated scalar cells are *always disjoint*, which makes the memory partitioning using the analysis possible.

Our analysis creates a points-to graph whose vertices are cells. The graph has two kinds of edges. A *points-to* edge plays the same role here as in the points-to graphs mentioned in the previous section: $\alpha \rightharpoonup \beta$ denotes that dereferencing some expression associated with cell α yields an address that must be in one of the locations associated with cell β. A key contribution of our approach which improves precision is that unlike other field-sensitive analyses (e.g. [18,26]), inner cells (fields) may be nested in *more than one* outer cell (record). Thus, we use additional graph edges to represent containment relations. A *contains edge* $\alpha \hookrightarrow_{i,j} \beta$ denotes that cell α is of record type and that β is associated with a field of the record whose location is at an offset of i from the record start and whose size in

---

[2] We borrow this term from Miné [19], but use it in a different context. Miné aimed to build a cell-based abstract domain for value analysis, while we target a cell-based points-to analysis.

bytes is $j - i$. Each cell may have multiple outgoing contains edges to its inner cells and multiple incoming contains edges from its outer cells.

Fig. 5. Concrete memory state and its graph representation.

Figure 5 shows a simple example. On the left is the memory layout of a singly-linked list with one element. The element is a record with two fields, a data value and a *next* pointer (which points back to the element in this case). The graph, shown on the right, contains three cells. The square cell is associated with the entire record element and the round cells with the inner fields (here and in the other points-to graphs below, we follow the convention that square cells are of record type and round cells are of scalar type). The solid edge is a points-to edge from the next field to the record cell, and the dashed edges are contains edges from the record cell to the field cells. These contains edges are labeled with their corresponding starting and ending offsets within the record. The following properties hold for contains edges:

- reflexivity: $\alpha \hookrightarrow_{0,s} \alpha$, if α is a cell with a numeric size s;
- transitivity: if $\alpha_1 \hookrightarrow_{i_1,j_1} \alpha_2$ and $\alpha_2 \hookrightarrow_{i_2,j_2} \alpha_3$, then $\alpha_1 \hookrightarrow_{i_1+i_2,i_1+j_2} \alpha_3$;
- linearity: if $\alpha_1 \hookrightarrow_{i_1,j_1} \alpha_2$ and $\alpha_1 \hookrightarrow_{i_2,j_2} \alpha_3$, then $\alpha_2 \hookrightarrow_{i_2-i_1,j_2-i_1} \alpha_3$ if $i_1 \leq i_2 < j_2 \leq j_1$.

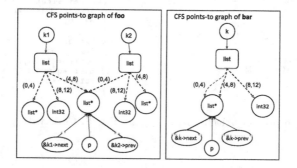

Fig. 6. CFS points-to graph for function foo and bar.

Let us revisit the running example from Fig. 3. The points-to graphs computed by our cell-based points-to analysis are shown in Fig. 6. In these graphs, record fields are separated out into individual cells. When field aliasing is detected, the individual field cells are merged (rather than their containing record cells), and any associated contains edges are kept unchanged. As shown in the graph on the left, in function foo, fields k1->next and k2->prev are merged into a single cell with contains edges from the record cells pointed to by k1 and k2, while other unaliased fields are kept separate. In function bar, as shown in the graph on the right, fields k->prev and k->next share the same cell with two incoming contains edges from the record cell pointed to by k, each labeled with different offsets. The record cell itself is not collapsed. Note that for these examples (and unlike DSA), our analysis introduces no extraneous alias relationship. Below, we explain our analysis in more detail by illustrating how it behaves in the presence of various type-unsafe operations.

Union types declare fields that share the same memory region. In a union, all fields with scalar types (e.g. float or int) are aliased. If there are nested records in a union, then two nested fields are aliased only if their offset ranges overlap. Both cases can be captured naturally in our analysis using contains edges.

Pointer arithmetic is particularly problematic for points-to analyses as it can (in principle) be used to access any location in the memory. We follow the standard approach of assuming that pointer arithmetic will not move a pointer outside of the memory object it is pointing to [30]. This assumption, coupled with the appropriate checks in the verification tool, is still sound in the sense that if it is possible to access invalid memory, the tool will detect it [10]. In our algorithm, any cell pointed to by operands of a pointer arithmetic expression is collapsed, meaning all of its outer record and inner field cells are merged into a single scalar cell. Consider function buz in Fig. 7. The call to foo(undef, p) induces the same graph for foo as in Fig. 6. However, the expression *(p + undef) results in this graph being collapsed into a single cell (colored in gray), as shown on the left of Fig. 9.

```
list** buz(int32 undef) {
   list **p;
   foo(undef, p);
   *(p + undef) = 0;
   return p;
}
```

Fig. 7. Code with pointer arithmetic.

```
typedef struct dlist {
   struct dlist *prev, *next;
} dlist;

dlist qux(int32 undef) {
   list **p;
   foo(undef, p);
   dist *q = (dist *) p;
   return *q;
}
```

Fig. 8. Code with pointer casting.

Pointer casting creates an alternative view of a memory region. To model this, a fresh cell is added to the points-to graph representing the new view. To illustrate, consider function qux in Fig. 8. Again, the function call foo(undef, p) induces the same graph for foo as in Fig. 6. After the call, pointer p is cast to the type dlist *. A new record cell (colored in gray) is added to the graph as shown in the middle of Fig. 9. The newly added cell is essentially a copy of the cell pointed to by p except that the offset intervals are enlarged in order to match the size of dlist . The casting introduces an alias between k1−>data and k2−>next, as both may alias with q−>next. By applying the properties of contains edges, the graph can be simplified into the one on the right of Fig. 9, which precisely captures the alias introduced by casting.

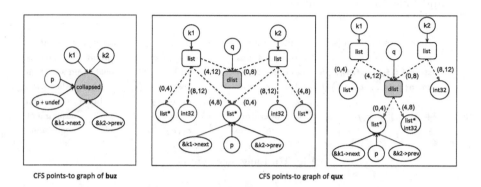

CFS points-to graph of **buz**   CFS points-to graph of **qux**

Fig. 9. CFS point-to graphs of function buz and qux.

Another contribution of our analysis is that we track the *size* of each alias group (either a numeric value or $\top$). The size enables further improvements in the memory model: the memory array for an alias group whose size is $\top$ is modeled as an array of bytes, while the memory array for a group whose size is some numeric value n can be modeled as an array of n-byte elements. For these latter arrays, it then becomes possible to read or write n bytes with a single array operation (whereas with an array of bytes, n operations are needed). Not having to decompose array accesses into byte-level operations reduces the size and complexity of the resulting SMT formulas.

5   Constraint-Based Analysis

In this section, we formalize the cell-based field-sensitive points-to analysis described above using a constraint framework. Our constraint-based program analysis is divided into two phases: constraint generation and constraint resolution. The constraint generation phase produces constraints from the program source code in a syntax-directed manner. The constraint resolution phase then computes a solution of the constraints in the form of a cell-based field-sensitive points-to graph. The resulting graph describes a safe partitioning of the memory for all reachable states of the program.

5.1   Language and Constraints

For the formal treatment of our analysis, we consider the idealized C-like language shown in Fig. 10. To simplify the presentation, complex assignments are broken down to simpler assignments between expressions of scalar types, static arrays are represented as pointers to dynamically allocated regions, and a single type ptr is used to represent all pointer types. Function definitions, function calls, and function pointers are omitted.[3]

$t ::=$	uint8 | int8 | ... | int64	integer types	e	$::=$	$n \mid x$	constants, variables
	ptr	pointer types			$*e \mid \&e$	pointer operations
	struct $\{ t_1 f_1; \ldots t_n f_n; \}$ S	structure types			$(t*)\,e \mid e.f$	cast, field selection
	union $\{ t_1 f_1; \ldots t_n f_n; \}$ U	union types			$(t*)\,\mathrm{malloc}(e)$	heap allocation
					$e_1 \odot e_2$	binary operation
$\odot ::=$	$+ \mid - \mid * \mid /$	operators			$e_1 = e_2$	assignment
					e_1, e_2	sequencing

Fig. 10. Language syntax

Let $\mathbb{C}$ be an infinite set of *cell variables* (denoted τ or τ_i). We will use cell variables to assign program expressions to cells in the resulting points-to graph. To do so, we assume that each subexpression e' of an expression e is labeled with a *unique* cell variable τ, with the exception that program variables x are always assigned the same cell variable, τ_x. Cell variables associated with program variables and heap allocations are called *source* variables. To avoid notational clutter, we do not make cell variables explicit in our grammar. Instead, we write $e : \tau$ to indicate that the expression e is labeled by τ.

Constraints. The syntax of our constraint language is defined as follows:

$$\eta \quad ::= \quad i \mid \top \mid \mathsf{size}(\tau) \qquad i \in \mathbb{N}$$
$$\phi \quad ::= \quad i < \eta \mid \eta_1 = \eta_2 \mid \tau_1 = \tau_2 \mid \tau_1 \rightharpoonup \tau_2 \mid \tau_1 \hookrightarrow_{i,j} \tau_2 \mid \tau_1 \trianglelefteq \tau_2$$
$$\mid \quad \mathsf{source}(\tau) \mid \mathsf{scalar}(\tau) \mid \mathsf{cast}(i, \tau_1, \tau_2) \mid \mathsf{collapsed}(\tau) \mid \phi_1 \wedge \phi_2 \mid \phi_1 \vee \phi_2$$

Here, a term η denotes a *cell size*. The constant $\top$ indicates an unknown cell size. A constraint ϕ is a positive Boolean combination of cell size constraints, equalities on cell variables, points-to edges $\tau_1 \rightharpoonup \tau_2$, contains edges $\tau_1 \hookrightarrow_{i,j} \tau_2$ and special predicates whose semantics we describe in detail below. We additionally introduce syntactic shorthands for certain constraints. Namely, we write $i \sqsubseteq \eta$ to stand for the constraint $i = \eta \vee \eta = \top$, $i \leq \eta$ to stand for $i < \eta \vee i = \eta$, and $i \preceq \eta$ to stand for $i \leq \eta \vee \eta = \top$.

Constraints are interpreted in cell-based field-sensitive points-to graphs (CFPGs). A CFPG is a tuple $G = (C, cell, size, source, scalar, contains, ptsto)$ where

---

[3] They can be handled using a straightforward adaptation of Steensgaard's approach.

- C is a finite set of cells,
- $cell : \mathbb{C} \to C$ is an assignment from cell variables to cells,
- $size : C \to \mathbb{N} \cup \{\top\}$ is an assignment from cells to cell sizes,
- $source \subseteq C$ is a set of *source cells*,
- $scalar \subseteq C$ is a set of *scalar cells*,
- $contains \subseteq C \times \mathbb{N} \times \mathbb{N} \times C$ is a *containment relation* on cells, and
- $ptsto : C \to C$ is a *points-to map* on cells.

For $c_1, c_2 \in C$, and $i, j \in \mathbb{N}$, we write $c_1 \overset{G}{\hookrightarrow}_{i,j} c_2$ as notational sugar for $(c_1, i, j, c_2) \in contains$, and similarly $c_1 \overset{G}{\to} c_2$ for $ptsto(c_1) = c_2$. Let $contains'$ be the projection of $contains$ onto $C \times C$: $contains'(c_1, c_2) \equiv \exists i, j. \; contains(c_1, i, j, c_2)$.

The functions and relations of G must satisfy the following consistency properties. These properties formalize the intuition of the containment relation and the roles played by source and scalar cells:

- the $contains'$ relation is reflexive (for cells of known size), transitive, and anti-symmetric. More specifically,

$$\forall c \in C. \; size(c) \neq \top \implies c \overset{G}{\hookrightarrow}_{0, size(c)} c \tag{1}$$

$$\forall \begin{pmatrix} c_1, c_2, c_3 \in C, \\ i_1, i_2, j_1, j_2 \in \mathbb{N} \end{pmatrix} . \, c_1 \overset{G}{\hookrightarrow}_{i_1, j_1} c_2 \wedge c_2 \overset{G}{\hookrightarrow}_{i_2, j_2} c_3 \implies c_1 \overset{G}{\hookrightarrow}_{i_1 + i_2, i_1 + j_2} c_3 \tag{2}$$

$$\forall \begin{pmatrix} c_1, c_2 \in C, \\ i_1, i_2, j_1, j_2 \in \mathbb{N} \end{pmatrix} . \, c_1 \overset{G}{\hookrightarrow}_{i_1, j_1} c_2 \wedge c_2 \overset{G}{\hookrightarrow}_{i_2, j_2} c_1 \implies c_1 = c_2 \tag{3}$$

- cells that are of unknown size or that point to other cells must be scalar:

$$\forall c \in C. \; size(c) = \top \implies c \in scalar \tag{4}$$

$$\forall c, c' \in C. \; c \overset{G}{\to} c' \implies c \in scalar \tag{5}$$

- the $contains$ relation must satisfy the following linearity property:

$$\forall \begin{pmatrix} c_1, c_2, c_3 \in C, \\ i_1, i_2, j_1, j_2 \in \mathbb{N} \end{pmatrix} . \begin{pmatrix} i_1 \leq i_2 < j_2 \leq j_1 \; \wedge \\ c_1 \overset{G}{\hookrightarrow}_{i_1, j_1} c_2 \; \wedge \\ c_1 \overset{G}{\hookrightarrow}_{i_2, j_2} c_3 \end{pmatrix} \implies c_2 \overset{G}{\hookrightarrow}_{i_2 - i_1, j_2 - i_1} c_3 \tag{6}$$

- scalar cells do not contain other cells:

$$\forall c, c' \in C, i, j \in \mathbb{N}. \; c \in scalar \wedge c \overset{G}{\hookrightarrow}_{i,j} c' \implies c = c' \tag{7}$$

- overlapping scalar cells are equivalent. The notion of overlap is formally expressed as

$$overlap^G(c_1, c_2) \equiv \exists \begin{pmatrix} c \in C, \\ i_1, i_2, j_1, j_2 \in \mathbb{N} \end{pmatrix} . \begin{pmatrix} c \overset{G}{\hookrightarrow}_{i_1, j_1} c_1 \; \wedge \\ c \overset{G}{\hookrightarrow}_{i_2, j_2} c_2 \end{pmatrix} \wedge \begin{pmatrix} i_1 \leq i_2 < j_1 \; \vee \\ i_2 \leq i_1 < j_2 \end{pmatrix}$$

$$\forall c, c' \in C. \; c \in scalar \wedge c' \in scalar \wedge overlap^G(c, c') \implies c = c' \tag{8}$$

– cell sizes must be consistent with the *contains* relation:

$$\forall \begin{pmatrix} c_1, c_2 \in C, \\ i, j \in \mathbb{N} \end{pmatrix}. c_1 \overset{G}{\hookrightarrow}_{i,j} c_2 \implies \begin{pmatrix} 0 \leq i < j \wedge \\ j \preceq size(c_1) \wedge j - i \sqsubseteq size(c_2) \end{pmatrix} \quad (9)$$

Semantics of Constraints. Let G be a CFPG with components as above. For a cell variable $\tau \in \mathbb{C}$, we define $\tau^G = cell(\tau)$ and for a size term η we define $\eta^G = size(\tau^G)$ if $\eta = size(\tau)$ and $\eta^G = \eta$ otherwise. The semantics of a constraint ϕ is given by a satisfaction relation $G \models \phi$, which is defined recursively on the structure of ϕ in the expected way. Size and equality constraints are interpreted in the obvious way using the term interpretation defined above. Though, note that we define $G \not\models i < \top$ and $G \not\models i = \top$. Points-to constraints $\tau_1 \rightharpoonup \tau_2$ are interpreted by the points-to map $\tau_1^G \overset{G}{\rightharpoonup} \tau_2^G$; contains constraints $\tau_1 \hookrightarrow_{i,j} \tau_2$ are interpreted by the containment relation $\tau_1^G \overset{G}{\hookrightarrow}_{i,j} \tau_2^G$; and source and scalar are similarly interpreted by *source* and *scalar*.

Intuitively, a cast predicate $\mathsf{cast}(k, \tau_1, \tau_2)$ states that cell τ_2 is of size k and is obtained by a pointer cast from cell τ_1. Thus, any source cell that contains τ_1 at offset i must also contain τ_2 at that offset. That is, $G \models \mathsf{cast}(k, \tau_1, \tau_2)$ iff:

$$\forall c \in C, i, j \in \mathbb{N}. \ c \in source \wedge c \overset{G}{\hookrightarrow}_{i,j} \tau_1^G \implies c \overset{G}{\hookrightarrow}_{i,i+k} \tau_2^G.$$

The predicate $\mathsf{collapsed}(\tau)$ indicates that τ points to a cell c that may be accessed in a type-unsafe manner, e.g., due to pointer arithmetic. Then, $G \models \mathsf{collapsed}(\tau)$ iff

$$\forall c, c' \in C, i, j \in \mathbb{N}. \ \tau^G \overset{G}{\rightharpoonup} c \wedge c' \overset{G}{\hookrightarrow}_{i,j} c \implies c' = c.$$

The predicate $\tau_1 \unlhd \tau_2$ (taken from [26]) is used to state the equivalence of the points-to content of τ_1 and τ_2. Formally, $G \models \tau_1 \unlhd \tau_2$ iff

$$\forall c \in C. \ \tau_1^G \overset{G}{\rightharpoonup} c \implies \tau_2^G \overset{G}{\rightharpoonup} c.$$

5.2   Constraint Generation

The first phase of our analysis generates constraints from the target program in a syntax-directed bottom-up fashion. The constraint generation is described by the inference rules in Fig. 11. Recall that each program expression e is labeled with a cell variable τ. The judgment form $e : \tau | \phi$ means that for the expression e labeled by the cell variable τ, we infer the constraint ϕ over the cell variables of e (including τ). A box with annotated ϕ in the premise of an inference rule is used to indicate that ϕ is the conjunction of the formulas contained in the box. Thus, the formula in the box is the constraint inferred in the conclusion of that rule.

For simplicity, we assume the target program is well-typed. Our analysis relies on the type system to infer the byte sizes of expressions and the field layout within records (e.g. structures or unions). To this end, we assume a type environment $\mathcal{T}$ that assigns C types to program variables. Moreover, we assume the following functions: $typeof(\mathcal{T}, e)$ infers the type of an expression following the standard type inference rules in the C language; $|t|$ returns the byte size of the type t; and $offset(t, f)$ returns the offset of a field f from the beginning of its enclosing record type t. Finally, $isScalar(t)$ returns true iff the type t is an integer or pointer type.

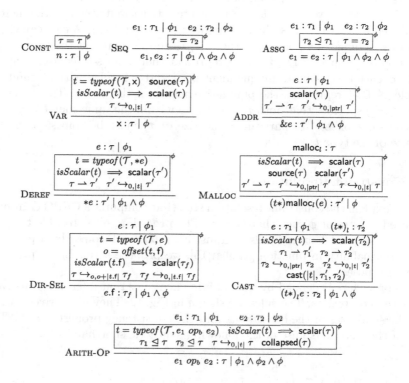

Fig. 11. Constraint generation rules.

The inference rules are inspired by the formulation of Steensgaard's field-insensitive analysis due to Forster and Aiken [12]. We adapt them to our cell-based field-sensitive analysis. Note that implications of the form $isScalar(t) \implies scalar(\tau)$, which we use in some of the rules, are directly resolved during the rule application and do not yield disjunctions in the generated constraints.

We only discuss some of the rules in detail. The rule MALLOC generates the constraints for a malloc operation. We assume that each occurrence of malloc in the program is tagged with a unique identifier l and labeled with a unique cell variable τ representing the memory allocated by that malloc. The return value of malloc is a pointer with associated cell variable τ'. Thus, τ' points to τ.

The rules DIR-SEL, ARITH-OP, and CAST are critical for the field-sensitive analysis. In particular, DIR-SEL generates constraints for field selections. A field f within a record expression e is associated with a cell variable τ_f. The rule states there must be a contains-edge from the cell variable τ associated with e to τ_f with appropriate offsets. Rule ARITH-OP is for operations that may involve pointer arithmetic. The cell variables τ_1, τ_2 and τ are associated with e_1, e_2, and $e_1 \odot e_2$, respectively. Any cells pointed to by τ_1 and τ_2 must be equal, which is expressed by the constraints $\tau_1 \trianglelefteq \tau$ and $\tau_2 \trianglelefteq \tau$. Moreover, if τ points to another cell τ', then pointer arithmetic collapses all relevant cells containing τ', since we can no longer guarantee structured access to the memory represented by τ'. Rule CAST handles pointer cast operations. A cast can change the points-to range of a pointer. In the rule, τ_1 and τ_2 represent the operand and result pointer, respectively. τ_1' and τ_2' represent their points-to contents. Similar to malloc, each cast $t*$ has a unique identifier l and is labeled with a unique cell variable τ_2' that represents the points-to content of the result. The constraint $\mathsf{cast}(s, \tau_1', \tau_2')$ specifies that both τ_1' and τ_2' are within the same source containers with the same offsets. In particular, the size of τ_2' must be consistent with $|t|$ (the size of the type t).

5.3   Constraint Resolution

We next explain the constraint resolution step that computes a CFPG G from the generated constraint ϕ such that $G \models \phi$. The procedure must be able to reason about containment between cells, a transitive relation. Inspired by a procedure for the reachability in function graphs [15], we propose a rule-based procedure for this purpose.

The procedure is defined by a set of inference rules that infer new constraints from given constraints. The rules are shown in Fig. 12. They are derived directly from the semantics of the constraints and the consistency properties of CFPGs. Some of the rules make use of the following syntactic shorthand:

$$\mathsf{overlap}(\tau, \tau_1, i_1, j_1, \tau_2, i_2, j_2) \equiv \tau \hookrightarrow_{i_1,j_1} \tau_1 \wedge \tau \hookrightarrow_{i_2,j_2} \tau_2 \wedge i_1 \leq i_2 \wedge i_2 < j_1$$

We omit the rules for reasoning about equality and inequality constraints, as they are straightforward. We also omit the rules for detecting conflicts. The only possible conflicts are inconsistent equality constraints such as $i = \top$ and inconsistent inequality constraints such as $i < \top$.

Our procedure maintains a *context* of constraints currently asserted to be true. The initial context is the set of constraints collected in the first phase. At each step, the rewrite rules are applied on the current context. For each rule, if the antecedent formulas are matched with formulas in the context, the consequent formula is added back to the context. The rules are applied until a conflict-free saturated context is obtained. The rule SPLIT branches on disjunctions. Note that the rules do not generate new disjunctions. All disjunctions come from the constraints of the form $i \preceq \eta$ and $i \sqsubseteq \eta$ in the initial context. Each disjunction in the initial context has at least one satisfiable branch. Our procedure uses a greedy heuristic that first chooses for each disjunction the branch

$$\text{SIZE1}\ \frac{\tau_1 \hookrightarrow_{i,j} \tau_2 \quad size(\tau_1)=k}{j \le k} \qquad \text{SIZE2}\ \frac{\tau_1 \hookrightarrow_{i,j} \tau_2 \quad size(\tau_2)=k}{j - i = k} \qquad \text{REFL}\ \frac{size(\tau) = i}{\tau \hookrightarrow_{0,i} \tau}$$

$$\text{TRANS}\ \frac{\tau_1 \hookrightarrow_{i_1,j_1} \tau_2 \quad \tau_2 \hookrightarrow_{i_2,j_2} \tau_3}{\tau_1 \hookrightarrow_{i_1+i_2,i_1+j_2} \tau_3} \qquad \text{ANTISYM}\ \frac{\tau_1 \hookrightarrow_{i_1,j_1} \tau_2 \quad \tau_2 \hookrightarrow_{i_2,j_2} \tau_1}{\tau_1 = \tau_2}$$

$$\text{COLLAPSE1}\ \frac{\tau_1 \hookrightarrow_{i,j} \tau_2 \quad scalar(\tau_1)}{\tau_1 = \tau_2} \qquad \text{LINEAR}\ \frac{\tau \hookrightarrow_{i_1,j_1} \tau_1 \quad \tau \hookrightarrow_{i_2,j_2} \tau_2 \quad i_1 \le i_2 < j_2 \le j_1}{\tau_1 \hookrightarrow_{i_2-i_1,j_2-i_1} \tau_2}$$

$$\text{COLLAPSE2}\ \frac{collapsed(\tau) \quad \tau \rightharpoonup \tau_1 \quad \tau' \hookrightarrow_{i,j} \tau_1}{\tau' = \tau_1} \qquad \text{CAST}\ \frac{cast(k,\tau_1,\tau_2) \quad source(\tau) \quad \tau \hookrightarrow_{i,j} \tau_1}{\tau \hookrightarrow_{i,i+k} \tau_2}$$

$$\text{SCALAR}\ \frac{size(\tau) = \top}{scalar(\tau)} \qquad \text{OVERLAP}\ \frac{scalar(\tau_1) \quad scalar(\tau_2) \quad overlap(\tau,\tau_1,i_1,j_1,\tau_2,i_2,j_2)}{\tau_1 = \tau_2}$$

$$\text{POINTS}\ \frac{\tau \rightharpoonup \tau_1 \quad \tau \rightharpoonup \tau_2}{\tau_1 = \tau_2} \qquad \text{PTREQ}\ \frac{\tau_1 \trianglelefteq \tau_2 \quad \tau_1 \rightharpoonup \tau}{\tau_2 \rightharpoonup \tau} \qquad \text{SPLIT}\ \frac{\phi_1 \vee \phi_2}{\phi_1 \quad \phi_2}$$

Fig. 12. Constraint resolution rules

that preserves more information and then backtracks on a conflict to choose the other branch. For example, for a disjunct $i \sqsubseteq \eta$, we first try $i = \eta$ before we choose $\eta = \top$. Once a conflict-free saturated context has been derived, we construct the CFPG using the equivalence classes of cell variables induced by the derived equality constraints as cells of the graph. The other components can be constructed directly from the constraints.

Termination. To see that the procedure terminates, note that none of the rules introduce new cell variables τ. Moreover, the only rules that can increase the offsets i, j in containment constraints $\tau_1 \hookrightarrow_{i,j} \tau_2$ are CAST and TRANS. The application of these rules can be restricted in such a way that the offsets in the generated constraints do not exceed the maximal byte size of any of the types in the input program. With this restriction, the rules will only generated a bounded number of containment constraints.

Soundness. The soundness proof of the analysis is split into three steps. First, we prove that the CFPG resulting from the constraint resolution indeed satisfies the original constraints that are generated from the program. The proof shows that the inference rules are all consequences of the semantics of the constraints and the consistency properties of CFPGs. The second step defines an abstract semantics of programs in terms of abstract stores. These abstract stores only keep track of the partition of the byte level memory into alias groups according to the computed CFPG. We then prove that the computed CFPG is a safe inductive invariant of the abstract semantics. The safety of the abstract semantics is defined in such a way that it guarantees that the computed CFPG describes a valid partition of the reachable program states into alias groups. Finally, we prove that the abstract semantics simulates the concrete byte-level semantics of programs. The details of the soundness proof are omitted due to space restrictions.

6 Experiments

To assess the impact of different memory models in a verification setting, we implemented both the flat memory model and the partitioned memory model in the Cascade verification framework [29], a competitive[4] C verification tool that uses bounded model checking and SMT solving. For the partitioned memory model, a points-to analysis is run as a preprocessing step, and the resulting points-to graph is used to: (i) determine the element size of the memory arrays; (ii) select which memory array to use for each read or write (as well as for each memory safety check); and (iii) add disjointness assumptions where needed (for distinct locations assigned to the same memory array). We implemented several points-to analyses, including Steensgaard's original and field-sensitive analyses, the data structure analysis (DSA), and our cell-based points-to analysis.

Benchmarks. For our experiments, we used a subset of the SVCOMP'16 benchmarks [4], specifically the Heap Data Structures category (consisting of two subcategories HeapReach and HeapMemSafety) as these contained many programs with heap-allocated data structures. For HeapReach, we checked for reachability of the ERROR label in the code. For HeapMemSafety, we checked for invalid memory dereferences, invalid memory frees, and memory leaks.

Configuration. Like other bounded model checkers, Cascade relies on function inlining and loop unrolling. It takes as parameters a function-inline depth d and a loop-unroll bound b. It then repeatedly runs its analysis, inlining all functions up to depth d, and using a set of successively larger unrolls until the bound b is reached. There are four possible results: *unknown* indicates that no result could be determined (for our experiments this happens only when the depth of function calls exceeds d); *unsafe* indicates that a violation was discovered; *safe* indicates that no violations exist *within the given loop unroll bound*; and *timeout* indicates the analysis could not be completed within the time limit provided. For the reachability benchmarks, we set $d = 6$ and $b = 1024$; for the memory safety benchmarks, we set $d = 8$ and $b = 200$ (these values were empirically determined to work well for SV-COMP). Note that Cascade may report *safe* even if a bug exists, if this bug requires executing a loop more times than is permitted by the unroll limit (the same is true of other tools relying on bounded model checking, like CBMC and LLBMC). For other undiscovered bugs, it reports *unknown* or *timeout*.

Table 1 reports results for the flat model (Flat) and partitioned models using the original (field-insensitive) Steensgaard analysis (St-fi), the field-sensitive Steensgaard analysis (St-fs), the context-insensitive DSA (DSA-local),[5] and our cell-based field-sensitive points-to analysis (CFS). More detail is shown in the scatter plots in Fig. 13. These results show that the baseline partitioned model

---

[4] Cascade placed 3rd in the Heap Data Structures category of SV-COMP 2016 [4].

[5] We used a context-insensitive version of DSA to make a fair comparison because the other analyses are also context-insensitive. Context sensitivity could be added to any of them, improving the results.

Table 1. Comparison of various memory models in l. Experiments were performed on an Intel Core i7 (3.7 GHz) with 8 GB RAM. The timeout was 850 s. "#solved" is the number of benchmarks correctly solved within the given limits. In the columns labeled "False", a benchmark is solved if Cascade found a bug that violates the specified property. In the columns labeled "True", a benchmark is solved if Cascade completed its analysis up to the maximum unroll and inlining limits without finding a bug. "time" is the average time spent on the benchmarks (solved and unsolved) in each category. "ptsTo" is the average time spent on the points-to analysis in each category.

| | HeapReach(81) | | | | | | HeapMemSafety(190) | | | | | |
| | False(25) | | | True(56) | | | False(83) | | | True(107) | | |
	#solved	time(s)	ptsTo(s)	#solved	time(s)	ptsTo(s)	#solved	time(s)	ptsTo(s)	#solved	time(s)	ptsTo(s)
Flat	19	112.8	-	29	228.7	-	50	357.3	-	38	567.5	-
St-fi	19	96.4	0.06	33	168.3	0.08	54	306.2	0.04	39	548.0	0.03
St-fs	19	92.8	0.14	33	168.5	0.17	58	274.8	0.05	42	527.4	0.05
DSA-local	19	94.6	0.09	33	168.1	0.11	54	305.2	0.07	39	550.4	0.07
CFS	19	**69.4**	0.11	33	168.3	0.14	**66**	**182**	0.05	**50**	**461.8**	0.05

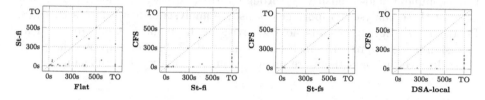

Fig. 13. Scatter plots showing a benchmark-by-benchmark comparison of various memory models over all the 271 benchmarks. The timeout (TO) was set to 850 s.

(St-fi) already improves significantly over the flat model. Of the partitioned models, the cell-based model (CFS) is nearly uniformly superior to the others.

To compare the precision of the different points-to analyses, we also computed the number of alias groups computed by each algorithm. Over the 190 benchmarks in HeapMemSafety, CFS always computes more or the same number of alias groups than the other analyses (it is better than DSA-local on 10 benchmarks, St-fs on 67 benchmarks, and St-fi on 165 benchmarks). The same is true of the 81 benchmarks in HeapReach, (better than DSA-local on 2 benchmarks, St-fs on 28 benchmarks and St-fi on 52 benchmarks). The precision advantage of CFS over DSA-local is somewhat limited because field aliasing does not occur too frequently in these programs.

The other advantage of CFS is that it tracks the access size of objects in each alias group. The only other analysis that does this is St-fs, and as a result, St-fs solves more benchmarks than DSA-local, even though the alias information computed by DSA-local is much more precise. This shows the advantage of tracking size information for memory modeling applications.

7   Related Work

Several memory models have been proposed as alternatives to the flat model. Cohen *et al.* [8] simulate a typed memory model over untyped C memory by adding additional disjointness axioms. Their approach introduces quantified axioms which can sometimes be challenging for SMT solvers. Böhme *et al.* [5] propose a variant of Cohen's memory model. CCured [21] separates pointers by their usage (not alias information) and skips bounds checking for "safe" pointers. Quantified disjointness axioms are also introduced. Rakamarić *et al.* [25] propose a variant of the Burstall model that employs type unification to cope with type-unsafe behaviors. However, in the presence of type casting, the model can easily degrade into the flat model. Havoc [9,16] refines the Burstall model with field-sensitivity that is only applicable to field-safe code fragments. Lal *et al.* [17] split memory in order to reason about the bitvector operations and integer operations separately. Frama-C [11] develops various models at different abstraction levels. However, no attempt is made to further partition the memory.

For points-to analyses in general, we refer the reader to the survey by Hind [14]. Yong *et al.* [30] propose a framework for a spectrum of analyses from complete field-insensitivity through various levels of field-sensitivity, but none of these analyses support field-sensitive analysis of heap data structures. Pearce *et al.* [22,23] extends field-sensivity on heap data structures with an inclusion-based approach, and Balatsouras *et al.* [2] further improve the precision. However, none of them are precise enough to analyze field-aliasing.

8   Conclusion

In this paper, we introduced partitioned memory models and showed how to use various points-to analyses to generate coarser or finer partitions. A key contribution was a new cell-based points-to analysis algorithm, which improves on earlier field-sensitive points-to analyses, more precisely modeling heap data structures and type-unsafe operations in the C language.

In SV-COMP 2016, Cascade won the bronze medal in the Heap Data Structures category using the cell-based partitioned memory model. We conclude that the cell-based partitioned memory model is a promising approach for obtaining both scalability and precision when modeling memory.

References

1. Andersen, L.O.: Program analysis and specialization for the C programming language. Ph.D. thesis, University of Copenhagen, May 1994
2. Balatsouras, G., Smaragdakis, Y.: Structure-sensitive points-to analysis for C and C++. In: Static Analysis Symposium (SAS) (2016)
3. Barrett, C., Stump, A., Tinelli, C.: The SMT-LIB standard - version 2.0. In: Proceedings of the 8th International Workshop on Satisfiability Modulo Theories (SMT) (2010)
4. Beyer, D.: Reliable and reproducible competition results with benchexec and witnesses (reported on SV-COMP 2016). In: Tools and Algorithms for the Construction and Analysis of Systems (TACAS) (2016)
5. Böhme, S., Moskal, M.: Heaps, data structures: a challenge for automated provers. In: Conference on Automated Deduction (CADE) (2011)

6. Burstall, R.M.: Some techniques for proving correctness of programs which alter data structures. Mach. Intell. **7**, 23–50 (1972)
7. Clarke, E., Kroening, D., Lerda, F.: A tool for checking ANSI-C programs. In: Tools and Algorithms for the Construction and Analysis of Systems (TACAS) (2004)
8. Cohen, E., Moskal, M., Tobies, S., Schulte, W.: A precise yet efficient memory model for C. Electron. Notes Theor. Comput. Sci. (ENTCS) **254**, 85–103 (2009)
9. Condit, J., Hackett, B., Lahiri, S.K., Qadeer, S.: Unifying type checking and property checking for low-level code. In: Principles of Programming Languages (POPL) (2009)
10. Conway, C.L., Dams, D., Namjoshi, K.S., Barrett, C.: Pointer analysis, conditional soundness, and proving the absence of errors. In: Static Analysis Symposium (SAS) (2008)
11. Cuoq, P., Kirchner, F., Kosmatov, N., Prevosto, V., Signoles, J., Yakobowski, B.: Frama-C a software analysis perspective. In: Software Engineering and Formal Methods (SEFM) (2012)
12. Foster, J.S., Fähndrich, M., Aiken, A.: Flow-insensitive points-to analysis with term and set constraints. Technical report CSD-97-964, University of California, Berkeley (1997)
13. Gurfinkel, A., Kahsai, T., Komuravelli, A., Navas, J.A.: The SeaHorn verification framework. In: Computer Aided Verification (CAV) (2015)
14. Hind, M.: Pointer analysis: haven't we solved this problem yet? In: Program Analysis for Software Tools and Engineering (PASTE) (2001)
15. Lahiri, S.K., Qadeer, S.: Back to the future: revisiting precise program verification using SMT solvers. In: Principles of Programming Languages (POPL) (2008)
16. Lahiri, S.K., Qadeer, S., Rakamarić, Z.: Static and precise detection of concurrency errors in systems code using SMT solvers. In: Computer Aided Verification (CAV) (2009)
17. Lal, A., Qadeer, S.: Powering the static driver verifier using Corral. In: Foundations of Software Engineering (FSE) (2014)
18. Lattner, C., Lenharth, A., Adve, V.: Making context-sensitive points-to analysis with heap cloning practical for the real world. In: Programming Language Design and Implementation (PLDI) (2007)
19. Miné, A.: Field-sensitive value analysis of embedded C programs with union types and pointer arithmetics. In: Language, Compilers, and Tool Support for Embedded Systems (LCTES) (2006)
20. Morse, J., Ramalho, M., Cordeiro, L., Nicole, D., Fischer, B.: ESBMC 1.22 (competition contribution). In: Tools and Algorithms for the Construction and Analysis of Systems (TACAS) (2014)
21. Necula, G.C., McPeak, S., Weimer, W.: CCured: type-safe retrofitting of legacy code. In: Principles of Programming Languages (POPL) (2002)
22. Pearce, D.J., Kelly, P.H.J., Hankin, C.: Efficient field-sensitive pointer analysis for C. In: Program Analysis for Software Tools and Engineering (PASTE) (2004)
23. Pearce, D.J., Kelly, P.H.J., Hankin, C.: Efficient field-sensitive pointer analysis of C. ACM Trans. Program. Lang. Syst. **30**(1), 4 (2007)
24. Rakamarić, Z., Emmi, M.: SMACK: decoupling source language details from verifier implementations. In: Computer Aided Verification (CAV) (2015)
25. Rakamarić, Z., Hu, A.J.: A scalable memory model for low-level code. In: Verification, Model Checking, and Abstract Interpretation (VMCAI) (2009)
26. Steensgaard, B.: Points-to analysis by type inference of programs with structures and unions. In: Compiler Construction (CC) (1996)

27. Steensgaard, B.: Points-to analysis in almost linear time. In: Principles of Programming Languages (POPL) (1996)
28. Wang, W.: Partition memory models for program analysis. Ph.D. thesis, New York University, May 2016
29. Wang, W., Barrett, C., Wies, T.: Cascade 2.0. In: Verification, Model Checking, and Abstract Interpretation (VMCAI) (2014)
30. Yong, S.H., Horwitz, S., Reps, T.: Pointer analysis for programs with structures and casting. In: Programming Language Design and Implementation (PLDI) (1999)

Author Index

Printed in the United States
By Bookmasters